MW01554503

BMW X3

(E83)

Service Manual
2.5i, 3.0i, 3.0si, xDrive 30i
2004, 2005, 2006, 2007, 2008, 2009, 2010

B BentleyPublishers®
.com

BENTLEY PUBLISHERS® | Automotive Reference™

Bentley Publishers, a division of Robert Bentley, Inc.
1734 Massachusetts Avenue
Cambridge, MA 02138 USA
800-423-4595 / 617-547-4170

Information that makes
the difference®

BentleyPublishers®
.com

Technical contact information
We welcome your feedback. Please submit corrections and additions to our BMW technical discussion forum at:

http://www.BentleyPublishers.com

Updates and corrections
We will evaluate submissions and post appropriate editorial changes online as updates or tech discussion. Appropriate updates and corrections will be added to the book in future printings. Check for updates and corrections for this book before beginning work on your vehicle. See the following web address for additional information:

http://www.BentleyPublishers.com/updates/

WARNING—Important Safety Notice

Do not use this manual for repairs unless you are familiar with automotive repair procedures and safe workshop practices. This manual illustrates the workshop procedures for some maintenance and service work. It is not a substitute for full and up-to-date information from the vehicle manufacturer or for proper training as an automotive technician. Note that it is not possible for us to anticipate all of the ways or conditions under which vehicles may be serviced or to provide cautions as to all of the possible hazards that may result.

We have endeavored to ensure the accuracy of the information in this manual. Please note, however, that considering the vast quantity and the complexity of the service information involved, we cannot warrant the accuracy or completeness of the information contained in this manual.

FOR THESE REASONS, NEITHER THE PUBLISHER NOR THE AUTHOR MAKES ANY WARRANTIES, EXPRESS OR IMPLIED, THAT THE INFORMATION IN THIS MANUAL IS FREE OF ERRORS OR OMISSIONS, AND WE EXPRESSLY DISCLAIM THE IMPLIED WARRANTIES OF MERCHANTABILITY AND OF FITNESS FOR A PARTICULAR PURPOSE, EVEN IF THE PUBLISHER OR AUTHOR HAVE BEEN ADVISED OF A PARTICULAR PURPOSE, AND EVEN IF A PARTICULAR PURPOSE IS INDICATED IN THE MANUAL. THE PUBLISHER AND AUTHOR ALSO DISCLAIM ALL LIABILITY FOR DIRECT, INDIRECT, INCIDENTAL OR CONSEQUENTIAL DAMAGES THAT RESULT FROM ANY USE OF THE EXAMPLES, INSTRUCTIONS OR OTHER INFORMATION IN THIS MANUAL. IN NO EVENT SHALL OUR LIABILITY, WHETHER IN TORT, CONTRACT OR OTHERWISE, EXCEED THE COST OF THIS MANUAL.

Before attempting any work on your BMW, read 001 Warnings and Cautions and any WARNING or CAUTION that accompanies a procedure in the manual. Review the WARNINGS and CAUTIONS each time you prepare to work on your BMW.

Your common sense and good judgment are crucial to safe and successful service work. Read procedures through before starting them. Think about whether the condition of your car, your level of mechanical skill or your level of reading comprehension might result in or contribute in some way to an occurrence which might cause you injury, damage your car or result in an unsafe repair. If you have doubts for these or other reasons about your ability to perform safe repair work on your car, have the work done at an authorized BMW dealer or other qualified shop.

Part numbers listed in this manual are for identification purposes only, not for ordering. Always check with your authorized BMW dealer to verify part numbers and availability before beginning service work that may require new parts.

Special tools required to perform certain service operations are identified in the manual and are recommended for use. Use of improper tools may be detrimental to the car's safe operation as well as the safety of the person servicing the car.

The vehicle manufacturer will continue to issue service information updates and parts retrofits after the editorial closing of this manual. Some of these updates and retrofits will apply to procedures and specifications in this manual. We regret that we cannot supply updates to purchasers of this manual.

ISBN 978-0-8376-1731-2   editorial closing 10/ 2014   Job code: BX30-03

Library of Congress Cataloging-in-Publication Data

BMW X3 (E83) service manual : 2.5i, 3.0i, 3.0si 2004, 2005, 2006, 2007, 2008, 2009, 2010.
    pages cm
  Includes index.
  ISBN 978-0-8376-1731-2 (alk. paper)
  1. BMW X3 sport utility vehicle--Maintenance and repair--Handbooks, manuals, etc. I.
Robert Bentley, inc.
  TL230.5.B68B68 2014
  629.224--dc23
              2014030887

0 General Data and Maintenance

001	Warnings and Cautions	010	Product Familiarization
002	Vehicle Identification and VIN Decoder	020	Maintenance

1 Engine

100	Engine–General	120	Ignition System
110	Engine Removal and Installation	121	Battery, Starter, Alternator
113	Cylinder Head Removal and Installation	130	Fuel Injection (M54 engine)
		131	Fuel Injection (N52 engine)
117	Camshaft Timing Chain	160	Fuel Tank and Fuel Pump
119	Lubrication System	170	Radiator and Cooling System
		180	Exhaust System

2 Transmission

200	Transmission–General	250	Gearshift Linkage
210	Clutch	260	Driveshafts
230	Manual Transmission	270	Transfer Case
240	Automatic Transmission		

3 Suspension, Steering and Brakes

300	Suspension, Steering and Brakes–General	320	Steering and Wheel Alignment
		330	Rear Suspension
310	Front Suspension	331	Rear Axle Differential
311	Front Axle Differential	340	Brakes

4 Body

400	Body–General	411	Doors
410	Fenders, Engine Hood	412	Trunk Lid, Tailgate

5 Body Equipment

510	Exterior Trim, Bumpers	515	Central Locking and Anti-theft
512	Door Windows	520	Seats
513	Interior Trim	540	Sunroof

6 Electrical System

600	Electrical System–General	630	Lights
611	Wipers and Washers	640	Heating and Air-conditioning
612	Switches	650	Radio
620	Instruments		

7 Equipment and Accessories

720	Seat Belts
721	Airbag System

ECL
ELE
OBD

ECL	Electrical Component Locations
ELE	Electrical Wiring Diagrams
OBD	On-Board Diagnostics

Foreword

For the BMW owner with basic mechanical skills and for independent auto service professionals, this manual includes many of the specifications and procedures that were available in an authorized BMW dealer service department as this manual went to press. The BMW owner with no intention of working on his or her car will find that owning and referring to this manual will make it possible to be better informed and to more knowledgeably discuss repairs with a professional automotive technician.

For those intending to do maintenance and repair on their BMW, it is essential that safety equipment be used and safety precautions observed when working on the vehicle. A minimum safety equipment list includes hand protection, eye protection and a fire extinguisher. A selection of good quality hand tools is also needed. This includes a torque wrench to ensure that fasteners are tightened in accordance with specifications. In some cases, the text refers to special tools that are recommended or required to accomplish adjustments or repairs. These tools are often identified by their BMW special tool number and illustrated.

Disclaimer

We have endeavored to ensure the accuracy of the information in this manual. When the vast array of data presented in the manual is taken into account, however, no claim to infallibility can be made. We therefore cannot be responsible for the result of any errors that may have crept into the text. Please also read the **WARNING— Important Safety Notice** on the copyright page at the beginning of this book.

Prior to starting a repair procedure, read the procedure, **001 Warnings and Cautions** and the warnings and cautions that accompany the procedure. Reading a procedure before beginning work helps you determine in advance the need for specific skills, identify hazards, prepare for appropriate capture and handling of hazardous materials, and the need for particular tools and replacement parts such as gaskets.

Bentley Publishers encourages comments from the readers of this manual with regard to errors, and suggestions for improvement of our product. These communications have been and will be carefully considered in the preparation of this and other manuals. If you identify inconsistencies in the manual, you may have found an error. Please contact the publisher and we will endeavor to post applicable corrections on our website. Posted updates and corrections should be reviewed before beginning work. Please see the following web address:

http://www.BentleyPublishers.com/updates/

BMW will continue to issue service information and parts retrofits after the editorial closing of this manual. Some of this updated information may apply to procedures and specifications in this manual. For the latest information, please see the following web address:

http://www.bmwtechinfo.com/

BMW offers extensive warranties, especially on components of the fuel delivery and emission control systems. Therefore, before deciding to repair a BMW that may be covered wholly or in part by any warranties issued by BMW of North America, LLC, consult your authorized BMW dealer. You may find that the dealer can make the repair either free or at minimum cost. Regardless of its age, or whether it is under warranty, your BMW is both an easy car to service and an easy car to get serviced. So if at any time a repair is needed that you feel is too difficult to do yourself, a trained BMW technician is ready to do the job for you.

Bentley Publishers

001 Warnings and Cautions

PLEASE READ THESE WARNINGS AND CAUTIONS BEFORE PROCEEDING WITH MAINTENANCE AND REPAIR WORK.

WARNINGS—
See also CAUTIONS

- Read the important safety notice on the copyright page at the beginning of the book.

- Some repairs may be beyond your capability. If you lack the skills, tools and equipment or a suitable workplace for any procedure described in this manual, we suggest you leave such repairs to an authorized BMW dealer service department or other qualified shop.

- Thoroughly read each procedure and the **WARNINGS** and **CAUTIONS** that accompany the procedure. Also review posted corrections at **www.BentleyPublishers.com/updates/** before beginning work.

- If any procedure, tightening torque, wear limit, specification or data presented in this manual does not appear to be appropriate for a specific application, contact the publisher or the vehicle manufacturer for clarification before using the information in question.

- Do not reuse any fasteners that are worn or deformed. Many fasteners are designed to be used only once and become unreliable and may fail when used a second time. This includes, but is not limited to, nuts, bolts, washers, self-locking nuts or bolts, circlips and cotter pins. Replace these fasteners with new parts.

- Do not work under a lifted car unless it is solidly supported on stands designed for the purpose. Do not support a car on cinder blocks, hollow tiles or other props that may crumble under continuous load. Do not work under a car that is supported solely by a jack. Do not work under the car while the engine is running.

- If you are going to work under a car on the ground, make sure that the ground is level. Block the wheels to keep the car from rolling. Disconnect the battery negative (–) terminal to prevent others from starting the car while you are under it.

- Do not run the engine unless the work area is well ventilated. Carbon monoxide kills.

- Remove rings, bracelets and other jewelry so that they cannot cause electrical shorts, get caught in running machinery, or be crushed by heavy parts.

- Tie long hair behind your head. Do not wear a necktie, a scarf, loose clothing, or a necklace when you work near machine tools or running engines. If your hair, clothing, or jewelry were to get caught in the machinery, severe injury could result.

- Do not attempt to work on your car if you do not feel well. You increase the danger of injury to yourself and others if you are tired, upset or have taken medication or any other substance that may keep you from being fully alert.

- Illuminate your work area adequately but safely. Use a portable safety light for working inside or under the car. Make sure the bulb is enclosed by a wire cage. The hot filament of an accidentally broken bulb can ignite spilled fuel, vapors or oil.

- Catch draining fuel, oil, or brake fluid in suitable containers. Do not use food or beverage containers that might mislead someone into drinking from them. Store flammable fluids away from fire hazards. Wipe up spills at once, but do not store the oily rags, which can ignite and burn spontaneously.

- Observe good workshop practices. Wear goggles when you operate machine tools or work with battery acid. Wear gloves or other protective clothing whenever the job requires working with harmful substances.

- Greases, lubricants and other automotive chemicals contain toxic substances, many of which are absorbed directly through the skin. Read the manufacturer's instructions and warnings carefully. Use hand and eye protection. Avoid direct skin contact.

- Disconnect the battery negative (–) terminal whenever you work on the fuel system or the electrical system. Do not smoke or work near heaters or other fire hazards. Keep an approved fire extinguisher handy.

- Friction materials (such as brake pads and shoes or clutch discs) contain asbestos fibers or other friction materials. Do not create dust by grinding, sanding, or by cleaning with compressed air. Avoid breathing dust. Breathing any friction material dust can lead to serious diseases and may result in death.

- Batteries give off explosive hydrogen gas during charging. Keep sparks, lighted matches and open flame away from the top of the battery. If hydrogen gas escaping from the cap vents is ignited, it may ignite gas trapped in the cells and cause the battery to explode.

- The air-conditioning system is filled with chemical refrigerant, which is hazardous. Make sure the system is serviced only by a trained technician using approved refrigerant recovery/recycling equipment, trained in related safety precautions, and familiar with regulations governing the discharge and disposal of automotive chemical refrigerants.

Continued on next page

WARNINGS (continued)

- Do not expose any part of the A/C system to high temperatures such as open flame. Excessive heat increases system pressure and may cause the system to burst.

- Some aerosol tire inflators are highly flammable. Be extremely cautious when repairing a tire that may have been inflated using an aerosol tire inflator. Keep sparks, open flame or other sources of ignition away from the tire repair area. Inflate and deflate the tire at least four times before breaking the bead from the rim. Completely remove the tire from the rim before attempting any repair.

- Cars covered by this manual are equipped with a multiple restraint system (MRS) that automatically deploys airbags and pyrotechnic seat belt tensioners in case of a frontal or side impact. These are explosive devices. Handled improperly or without adequate safeguards, they can be accidently activated and cause serious injury.

- The ignition system produces high voltages that can be fatal. Avoid contact with exposed terminals and use extreme care when working on a car with the engine running or the ignition switched ON.

- Place jack stands only at locations specified by the manufacturer. The vehicle lifting jack supplied with the vehicle is intended for tire changes only. Use a heavy duty floor jack to lift vehicle before installing jack stands. See **020 Maintenance**.

- Battery acid (electrolyte) can cause severe burns. Flush contact area with water, then seek medical attention.

- Aerosol cleaners and solvents may contain hazardous or deadly vapors and are highly flammable. Use only in a well ventilated area. Do not use on hot surfaces (engines, brakes, etc.).

- Due to risk of personal injury, be sure the engine is cold before beginning work on the cooling system.

CAUTIONS—
See also WARNINGS

- If you lack the skills, tools and equipment, or a suitable workshop for any procedure described in this manual, leave such repairs to an authorized BMW dealer or other qualified shop.

- BMW is constantly improving its cars and sometimes these changes, both in parts and specifications, are made applicable to earlier models. Any part numbers listed in this manual are for reference only. Check with your authorized BMW dealer parts department for the latest information.

- Before starting a job, make certain that you have the necessary tools and parts on hand. Read all the instructions thoroughly, and do not attempt shortcuts. Use tools appropriate to the work and use only replacement parts meeting BMW specifications.

- Use pneumatic and electric tools only to loosen threaded parts and fasteners. Do not use these tools to tighten fasteners, especially on light alloy parts. Use a torque wrench to tighten fasteners to the tightening torque specification listed.

- Be mindful of the environment and ecology. Before you drain the crankcase, find out the proper way to dispose of the oil. Do not pour oil onto the ground, down a drain, or into a stream, pond or lake. Dispose of waste in accordance with federal, state and local laws.

- The control module for the anti-lock brake system (ABS) cannot withstand temperatures from a paint-drying booth or a heat lamp in excess of 203°F (95°C). Do not subject to temperatures in excess of 185°F (85°C) for more than two hours.

- Before doing any electrical welding on cars equipped with ABS, disconnect the battery negative (–) terminal (ground strap) and the ABS control module connector.

- Make sure ignition is switched OFF before disconnecting battery.

- Label battery cables before disconnecting. On some models, battery cables are not color coded.

- Disconnecting the battery may erase fault code(s) stored in control module memory. Using special BMW diagnostic equipment, check for fault codes prior to disconnecting the battery cables. If the malfunction indicator light (MIL) is illuminated, see **OBD On-Board Diagnostics** at the back of this manual. (This light may be identified as the Check Engine light or the Service Engine Soon light.) If any other system faults are detected (indicated by an illuminated warning light), see an authorized BMW dealer.

- If a normal or rapid charger is used to charge battery, disconnect the battery remove it from the vehicle in order to avoid damaging the vehicle.

- Do not quick-charge the battery (for boost starting) for longer than one minute. Wait at least one minute before boosting the battery a second time.

- Connect and disconnect a battery charger only with the battery charger switched OFF.

- Sealed or "maintenance free" batteries should be slow-charged only, at an amperage rate that is approximately 10% of the battery's ampere-hour (Ah) rating.

- Do not allow battery charging voltage to exceed 16.5 volts. If the battery begins producing gas or boiling violently, reduce the charging rate. Boosting a sulfated battery at a high charging rate can cause an explosion.

- Do not use steel fasteners on engine components made of aluminum-magnesium alloy. Use aluminum fasteners only. Test fasteners for aluminum composition with magnet.

- Replace aluminum bolts each time they are loosened. Follow torque instructions, including angle of rotation specifications, when installing aluminum fasteners.

002 Vehicle Identification and VIN Decoder

Some of the information in this manual applies only to cars of a particular model year or range of years. For example, 2004 refers to the 2004 model year but does not necessarily match the calendar year in which the car was manufactured or sold. To be sure of the model year of a particular car, check the vehicle identification number (VIN) on the car.

The VIN is a unique sequence of 17 characters assigned by BMW to identify each individual car. When decoded, the VIN tells the country and year of manufacture; make, model and serial number; assembly plant and even some equipment specifications.

The BMW VIN plate is mounted on the top of the dashboard, on the driver's side where the number can be seen through the windshield. The 10th character is the model year code: 4 for 2004, 5 for 2005, 6 for 2006, 7 for 2007, 8 for 2008, 9 for 2009, A for 2010. The table below explains the codes in the VIN for 2004 through 2010 BMW E83 X3 Series cars.

Sample VIN: WBX PA73 4 X 4 A 9 9 9 9 9 9

position   1 2 3   4 5 6 7   8 9 10 11   12-17

VIN position	Description	Decoding information	
1 - 3	Country of manufacture	WBX	BMW, Graz Austria, X3
4 - 5	Line	PA PC	2004 - 2006 passenger vehicle 2007 - 2010 (LCI) passenger vehicle
6	Engine type	7 9	2.5 liter 6-cylinder 3.0 liter 6-cylinder
7	Vehicle type	3 C	Passenger vehicle (2004 - 2009) Passenger vehicle (2010)
8	Restraint system	4	Multiple restraint system
9	Check digit	0 - 9 or X, calculated by NHTSA	
10	Model year	4 5 6 7 8 9 A	2004 2005 2006 2007 2008 2009 2010
11	Assembly plant	W	Graz, Austria
12-17	Serial number	Sequential production number for specific vehicle	

010 Product Familiarization

GENERAL

The information included in this section is based on introductory information for 2004 through 2010 BMW X3 vehicles sold in the USA and Canada. The content provided here is intended to serve as a product familiarization guide. Note that the information presented is subject to change and should be used as a general reference only.

WARNING—
- *Always check the BMW factory repair information or the publisher's website at www.bentleypublishers.com for information that may supersede any information included in this section.*

PRODUCT OVERVIEW

The BMW X3 was introduced in model year 2004. Conceived and engineered by BMW, the X3 was an addition to the X family of SAV's. Based on the 3 Series sportwagon, its size, weight and capabilities more closer match those of the BMW X5.

The chassis and many parts were taken either directly or in modified form from the E46 3 Series or the X5. Approximately 35% of the parts were designed exclusively for the X3.

The X3 was delivered initially in one of two versions; the 2.5i (referring to a 2.5 liter inline six-cylinder engine) and the 3.0i (referring to a 3.0 liter inline six-cylinder engine). In addition to the more powerful engine, the 3.0 also received additional luxury features.

A six speed manual transmission was standard on all X3's with a 5-speed automatic optional.

Later models saw the introduction of new 3.0 liter Valvetronic motor as of model year 2007, which also corresponded to a mid-life facelift (called life cycle impulse, or LCI).

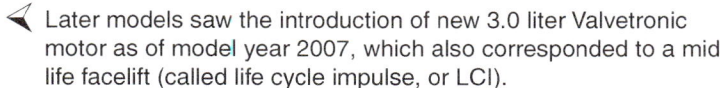

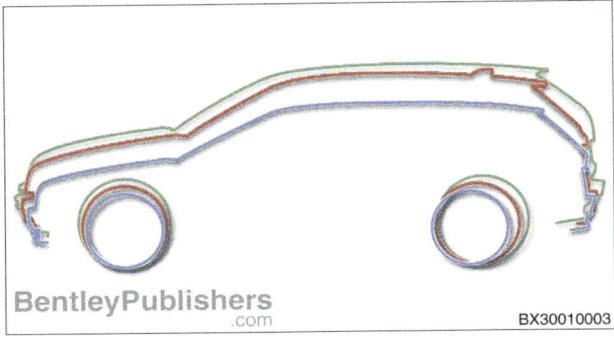

BentleyPublishers.com

BX30010003

◁ The X3 (red outline) was significantly larger than the 3 Series sportwagon (blue outline), but only slightly smaller than the X5 (green outline).

BMW X3 size comparison			
	E46 sportwagon	E83 X3 3.0i	E53 X5 3.0i
Length in mm (in)	4478 (176.3)	4563 (179.6)	4667 (183.7)
Width in mm (in)	1739 (68.5)	1848 (72.8)	1872 (73.7)
Height in mm (in)	1429 (56.3)	1631 (64.2)	1715 (67.5)
Empty weight in kg (lbs)	1670 (3682)	1730 (3814)	2056 (4533)
Payload in kg (in)	425 (937)	500 (1102)	544 (1200)
Luggage compartment capacity in liters (ft^3)	435 - 1345 (15.4 - 47.5)	480 - 1560 (17.0 - 55.1)	465 - 1550 (16.4 - 54.7)

The X3 incorporated the following features:

- New four-wheel drive system with variable power distribution (xDrive).

- Multifunctional panorama glass sunroof.

- Best-in-class ratio of power output and fuel efficiency.

- Four wheel independent suspension with all road vehicle (ON/OFF road capabilities) and high ground clearance.

- Unitized body and chassis provides car like ride and handling.

Panorama sunroof

BX30010011

M•MT 4584

BentleyPublishers.com

BX30101010

Technical Data

BMW X3 specifications (2004)

Engine	M54B25	M54B30
Cylinders / valves per cylinder	6/4	6/4
Capacity (cc)	2494	2979
Stroke / bore (mm)	75 / 84	89.6 / 84
Output (hp)	184@6000	225@6000
Maximum torque (ft-lb)	175@3500	214@3500
Compression	10.5:1	10.2:1
Motor electronics	MS45	MS45 MS45.1 w/auto
Fuel requirement	Premium unleaded (91 pump octane)	Premium unleaded (91 pump octane)
Maximum Engine Speed (RPM)	6500	6500
Manual Transmission	ZF GS6X37BZ	ZF GS6X37BZ
Automatic Transmission	GM GA5R390R	GM GA5R390R
Empty Weight in kg (lb)	1707 (3763)	1730 (3814)
Maximum Load in kg (lb)	500 (1102)	500 (1102)
Wheels	7J17 Cast Alum. ET39 (styling 110)	8J17 Cast Alum. ET46 (styling 112)
Tires	215/60R17 96H M+S	235/55R17 99H M+S

BX30010001

BX30010004

BODY

The X3 is derived from the E46 3 Series sharing many identical parts, but it is a unique design.

Various reinforcement measures were necessary to guarantee the required level of rigidity. As an example, the front axle crossmember is bolted to the body at 6 points, the front end is stabilized with a front strut cross-brace (load factor higher than the M3), seat crossmembers and reinforcement plates in the B-pillars provide additional protection in the event of a side impact and the rear engine brackets are made of light high-tensile steel.

The hood has a side support to prevent it from moving in the event of a crash. This prevents the hood from jumping out of its anchoring into the windshield.

Body Shell

◁ The body shell panels are stamped and assembled at the Magna Steyr plant in Graz, Austria.

To reduce weight, the front radiator support of is made of a hybrid steel injection-molded with plastic. The air ducts are cast in. In the case of an accident this radiator support must be replaced and not repaired.

DRIVETRAIN

The transfer case, driveshafts, differentials and drive axles make up the drivetrain. The rear driveshaft is a two piece unit using a center bearing, while the front drive shaft is a single piece.

The right front drive axle extends through the oil sump, resulting in a low center of gravity for enhanced driving dynamics and additional ground clearance.

xDrive

The X3 features an advanced AWD system called xDrive. Housed in the transfer case behind the transmission, xDrive operates as follows:

• Driving torque is always transmitted to the rear wheels, and under most conditions to all four wheels.

• Torque transmitted to the front wheels is controlled by a multi-disc clutch that can be fully open, fully engaged or at any level of partial engagement in between.

• Engagement pressure on multi-disc clutch is applied by a servo motor, which in turn is directed by an electronic control system with inputs via sensors for:
-Rotational speed of each wheel
-Steering angle
-Brake light switch
-Vehicle yaw and lateral acceleration

xDrive clutch assembly

BX30010013

X3 Drivetrain

Front differential

Front driveshaft

xDrive transfer case

Rear driveshaft

Rear differential

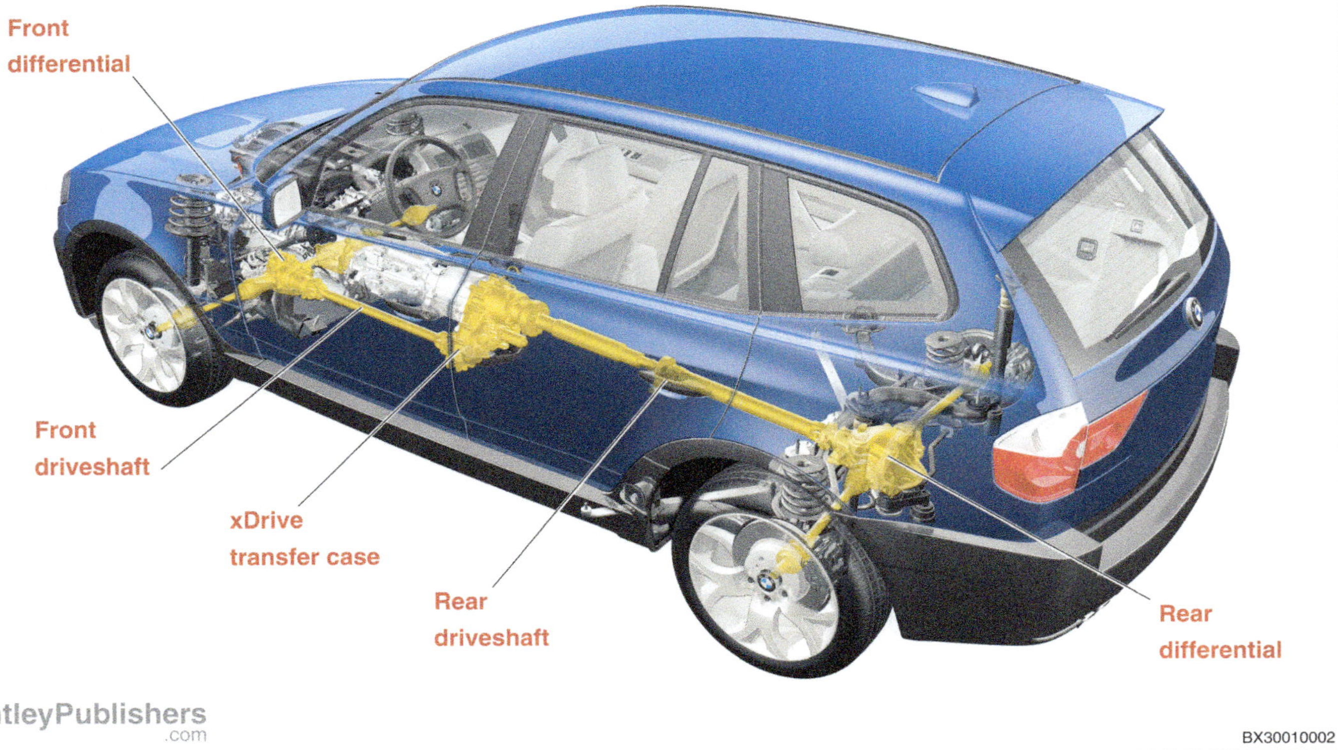

BX30010002

SUSPENSION, STEERING, BRAKES

The design criteria for the X3 was to develop a vehicle with superb handling and sporty driving characteristics, yet produce an all wheel drive vehicle that could also be used off-road.

The front suspension utilizes a double pivot spring strut axle with MacPherson struts. The double-pivot concept features two lower arms (hence the designation double-pivot) that work in concert with the spring / shock-absorber strut.

The rear axle design is based on the E46 3 Series sportwagon, with barrel springs and separate twin tube gas-shock absorbers. The rear subframe is mounted to the body using four vibration absorbing rubber mounts. Aluminum is used extensively in the rear suspension for weight saving.

The brake system is a hydraulic dual-circuit brake system with front/rear split vacuum boost power assist.

Tire deflation warning (RDW) is a standard feature on the 2004 - 2006 E83. 2007 and later E83 vehicles are equipped with the tire pressure monitoring system RDC which was introduced in March 2006.

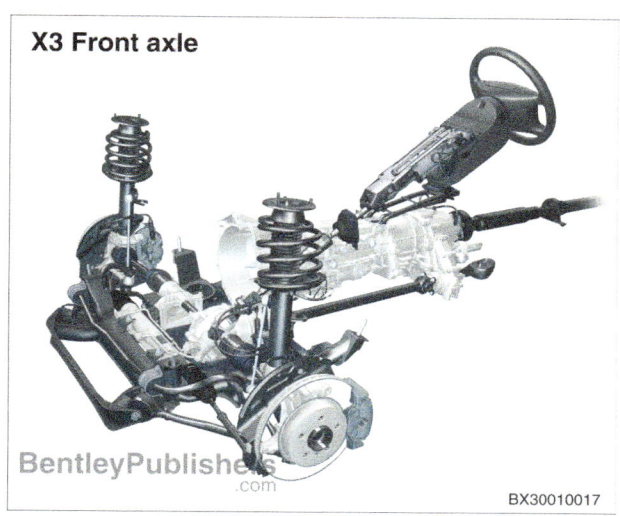

X3 Front axle

BX30010017

X3 Suspension and steering systems

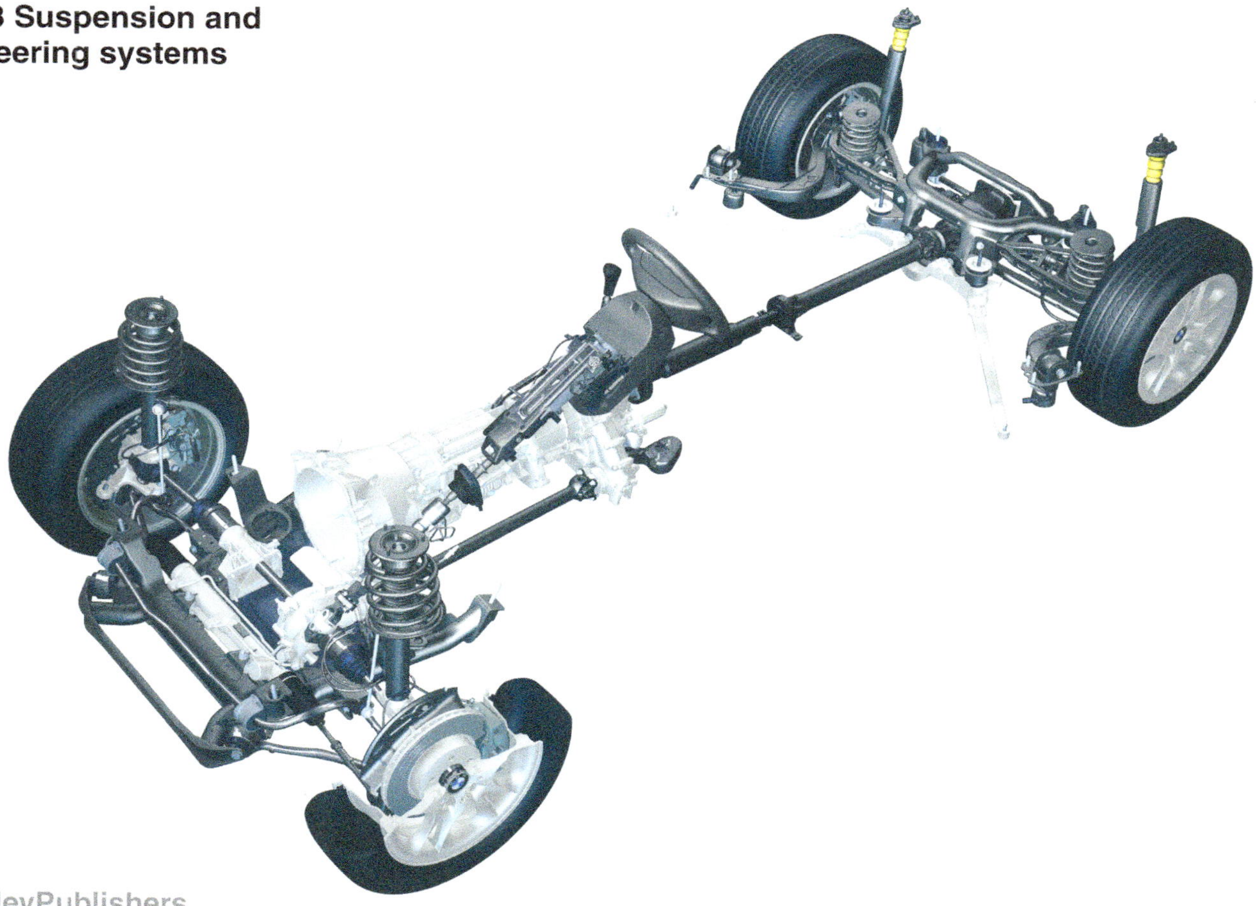

BentleyPublishers.com

BX30010015

2004 X3

BX30010014

MODEL YEAR CHANGES

◁ The X3 was introduced to the North American market in late 2003 as a 2004 model. This model remained virtually unchanged until the 2007 model year release.

2007 X3

BX30010008a

As of model year 2007, the E83 received a redesign known as the LCI (Life Cycle Impulse). The LCI facelift included many visual exterior and interior upgrades, the introduction of a new engine, as well as a series of improvements in interior trim and fittings.

◁ The identifiable LCI redesign with 3-peice painted bumper and a double kidney grill with light titanium colored bars that extends further down.

2005 (pre-LCI) X3

BentleyPublishers
.com

BX30010009

2004 - 2006 models

BMW offered its initial entry in the mid-size sport-utility segment in two configurations: The more affordable X3 2.5i, and the more powerful 3.0i.

NOTE—

• *For model year 2006, the 2.5 liter engine was discontinued.*

Both models were fitted with a six-speed manual transmission as standard, and BMW's xDrive electronically controlled all-wheel drive driveline.

◄ A 5-speed (GM5) automatic transmission featuring Steptronic was offered for both models.

The 2.5i base model was trimmed with standard features, including power-assisted/memory functions; a four-way adjustable steering wheel; six-way manually adjustable front seats; a 10-speaker audio system; imitation leather upholstery; and an automatic climate control system.

An optional BMW onboard navigation system with a large, easy-to-read color monitor in 16 : 9 format (ratio between width and height) was also available.

The 3.0i model added rain-sensing windshield wipers; cruise control; a leather-wrapped steering wheel with integrated cruise and audio controls; six-way power-adjustable front seats; and an on-board computer. Options included 18-inch wheels and high performance tires.

The sports package included a sports suspension, 18-inch wheels, and a special exterior, interior, steering wheel and seats.

M54 double-VANOS engine

2004 through 2006 models are fitted with the M54 engine. This aluminium-block engine features overhead camshafts, four valves per cylinder, hydraulic valve adjustment elements, and BMW's double-VANOS system (variable valve timing) to optimize torque, power and emission control.

◄ The double-VANOS system is a combined hydraulic and mechanical camshaft control device controlled by a Siemens engine management system. The VANOS system uses camshaft adjusters to continuously modify intake and exhaust camshaft timing as a function of accelerator pedal position and engine speed.

Double-VANOS significantly enhances emission management, increases output and torque, and offers better idling quality and fuel economy.

M54 engine performance data	
2.5i 0 - 60 mph	8.6 (w / man. trans.) 9.3 sec (w / auto. trans.)
3.0i 0 - 60 mph	7.6 (w / man. trans.) 7.9 sec (w / auto. trans.)

N52 3.0 liter Valvetronic engine

B309010030

2007 -2010 models

Updates for the 2007 - 2009 models included:

• New generation 3.0 liter N52 Valvetronic engine. The N52 featured many innovations, including the composite magnesium/aluminum crankcase, Valvetronic system and the 3-stage DISA intake manifold. The oil level dipstick was eliminated.

• 6-speed (GM6) automatic transmission with exceptional shift dynamics and improved efficiency; dynamic driving control DSC (dynamic stability control) with additional functions including increased braking readiness, fading compensation, dry brake function, and revised hill descent control (HDC).

• Life cycle impulse (LCI) - interior and exterior-design freshening.

pre-LCI

LCI

BX30010018

◁ Redesigned rear taillights and modified headlight assemblies.

The front and rear bumpers were also redesigned and painted in body color.

The front bumper, which was previously a two-piece design, is three pieces on the LCI vehicles. A top section painted in body color and a bottom cover that is also painted are clipped to the black carrier.

The rear bumper on the E83 LCI is made up of four main parts (previously one-piece on non-LCI vehicles). Two black side panels and one exhaust finisher also in black are fitted on a carrier painted in the car color. The panel at the lower edge of the rear hatch is also painted in body color, giving the LCI X3 an overall higher grade impression.

Another identifiable LCI feature is the double kidney grill that extends further downward.

LCI interior redesign

BX30010019

◁ The LCI also included a wide-ranging redesign of the interior, including the instrument panel, steering wheel, center console, seats, door upholstery, storage compartments and roof liner.

020 Maintenance

GENERAL

The information given in this repair group includes the routine checks and maintenance steps that are both required by BMW under the terms of the vehicle warranty protection and recommended by BMW to ensure long and reliable vehicle operation.

Service interval indicator (SIA IV)

 The BMW service interval indicator (SIA IV) appears in the instrument cluster display. The indicator is shown for five seconds with the key (terminal R) switched on. The actual mileage remaining until the next service is displayed. The text "OIL SERVICE" or "INSPECTION" will also illuminate to show which service is coming due.

Based on fuel consumption and distance traveled, the SIA processor calculates the distance remaining to the next service. When the preset total fuel consumption is reached, the instrument cluster indicates that service is required. A flashing message and a negative (–) symbol in front of the number indicate that the service interval has been exceeded. After the service is performed the SIA can be reset to zero.

NOTE—

An OIL SERVICE interval will always be followed by an INSPECTION interval, which will then be followed by an OIL SERVICE interval, and so on.

Inspection I, Inspection II

There are two inspection requirements, alternating throughout a vehicle's maintenance history. If the last inspection interval was Inspection I, the next inspection interval (following an oil service) will be Inspection II, the next after that will be Inspection I, and so on.

Oil change service tasks are listed in **Table d** at the rear of this section. Inspection I tasks are listed in **Table e**. Inspection II tasks are in **Table f**.

NOTE—

* *For reference, Inspection I is normally due at intervals with a maximum of 30,000 miles or 24 months. Inspection II is normally due at intervals with a maximum of 60,000 miles or 48 months.*

020

Service interval indicator (SIA), resetting

The SIA signals the need for basic routine maintenance including:

- Engine oil and oil filter change.
- BMW-recommended additional maintenance (Inspection I and Inspection II).

When the specified maintenance (as listed in **Table a** through **Table c**) has been carried out, the SIA memory should be reset. The SIA is reset with the trip odometer reset button in the instrument cluster:

— Begin with ignition key in the OFF position.

◁ Press and hold trip odometer button (**arrow**) in instrument cluster, then turn ignition key to ACCESSORY position.

— Keep button pressed for 5 seconds until one of the following words appear: OIL SERVICE, or INSPECTION, with the word reset.

— Release button and press and hold it again until reset begins to flash.

— While display is flashing, press button (**arrow**) briefly to reset service interval.

— After display has shown the new interval, the following will appear: END SIA.

NOTE—

- *The system can only be reset again after 10 liters (2.5gal) of fuel have been consumed.*

BASIC SERVICE INFORMATION

Diagnostic trouble codes (DTCs), accessing

Diagnostic trouble codes (DTCs) that are stored in the engine control module (ECM) or other electronic modules may be accessed as follows:

— Place transmission selector lever in PARK or NEUTRAL. Engage parking brake. Make sure ignition is OFF.

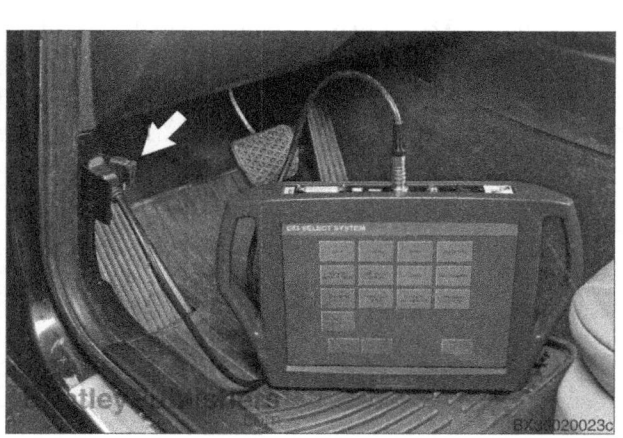

◁ Connect diagnostic scan tool to OBD II plug (**arrow**) in left footwell.

— Start engine and let idle.

— Follow scan tool instructions as they appear.

— For additional information, see **OBD On-Board Diagnostics**.

Non-reusable fasteners

Many fasteners must be replaced with new ones once removed. These include but are not limited to: aluminum or stretch bolts, nuts (self-locking, nylock, etc.), roll pins, clips and washers. On models with the N52 engines, aluminum fasteners are used extensively on the engine. Aluminum fasteners must always be replaced once loosened. Use genuine BMW replacement parts for this purpose.

> **WARNING—**
> • *Failure to replace fasteners designed for single use could cause personal injury or vehicle damage. See an authorized BMW dealer for applications and ordering information.*

Tightening fasteners

It is good practice to tighten fasteners on a component gradually and evenly to avoid misalignment or over-stressing any one portion of the component. For components sealed with gaskets, this method helps to ensure that the gasket seals correctly.

 Where there are several fasteners, tighten them in a sequence alternating between opposite sides of the component. Repeat the sequence until all the fasteners are evenly tightened to the proper specification.

For some repairs a specific tightening sequence is necessary, or particular order of assembly is required. Such special conditions are noted in the text, and the necessary sequence is described or illustrated. Where no specific torque is listed, use **Table a** as a general guide for tightening fasteners.

NOTE—
• *Metric bolt classes or grades are marked on the bolt head.*
• *Do not confuse wrench size with bolt diameter.*
• *Values in* **Table a** *are for reference only.*

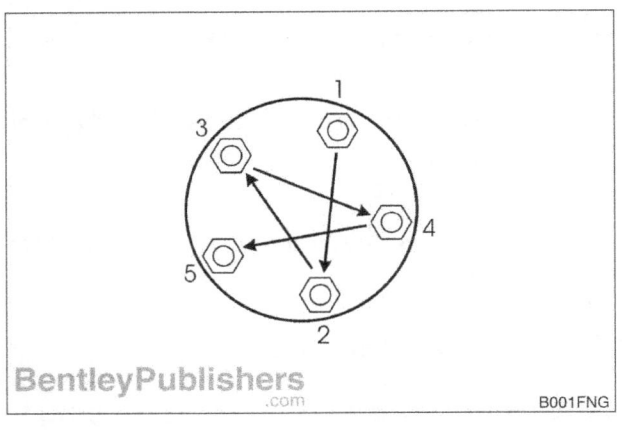

BentleyPublishers
.com

B001FNG

Table a. General bolt tightening torques in Nm (max. permissible)						
	Bolt Class (according to DIN 267)					
Bolt diameter	**5.6**	**5.8**	**6.8**	**8.8**	**10.9**	**12.9**
M5	2.5	3.5	4.5	6	8	10
M6	4.5	6	7.5	10	14	17
M8	11	15	18	24	34	40
M10	23	30	36	47	66	79
M12	39	52	62	82	115	140
M14	62	82	98	130	180	220
M16	94	126	150	200	280	340
M18	130	174	210	280	390	470

020

Buying parts

Many of the maintenance and repair tasks in this manual call for the installation of new parts, or the use of new gaskets and other materials when reinstalling parts. Most often, the parts that are needed should be on hand before beginning the job. Read the introductory text and the complete procedure to determine which parts are needed.

For some bigger jobs, partial disassembly and inspection is required to determine a complete parts list. Read the procedure carefully and, if necessary, make other arrangements to get the necessary parts while your vehicle is disassembled.

Genuine BMW parts

Genuine BMW replacement parts from an authorized BMW dealer are designed and manufactured to the same high standards as the original parts. They will be the correct material, manufactured to the same specifications, and guaranteed to fit and work as intended. Most genuine BMW parts carry a limited warranty.

Many independent repair shops make a point of using genuine BMW parts, even though they may at times be more expensive than parts from other sources. They know the value of doing the job right with the right parts. Parts from other sources may be as good as BMW parts, particularly if manufactured by one of BMW's original equipment suppliers, but it is often difficult to know.

BMW is constantly updating and improving their vehicles, often making improvements during a given model year. BMW may recommend a newer, improved part as a replacement, and your authorized dealer's parts department will know about it and provide it. The BMW parts organization is best equipped to deal with your BMW parts needs.

Non-returnable parts

Some parts cannot be returned. The best example is electrical parts, which are almost universally considered non-returnable. Buy electrical parts carefully, and be as sure as possible that a replacement is needed, especially for expensive parts such as electronic control modules. It may be wise to let an authorized BMW dealer or other qualified shop confirm your diagnosis before replacing an expensive non-returnable part.

Model and model year

When ordering parts it is important that you know the correct model and engine designation for your vehicle. This E83 manual covers X3 models with 6-cylinder engines. For information on engine codes and engine applications, see **100 Engine–General**.

Model year is not necessarily the same as date of manufacture or date of sale. A 2004 model may have been manufactured in late 2003, and perhaps not sold until early 2005. It is still a 2004 model. Model years covered by this manual are 2004 to 2010.

Service

BMW dealers are uniquely qualified to provide service for BMW vehicles. Their authorized relationship with the large BMW service organization means that they have access to special tools and equipment, together with the latest and most accurate repair information.

The BMW dealer's service technicians are highly trained and very capable. Authorized BMW dealers are committed to supporting the BMW product. On the other hand, there are many independent shops that provide quality repair work. Checking with other BMW owners for recommendations on service facilities is good way to learn of reputable BMW shops in your area.

Tools

Most maintenance can be accomplished with a small selection of tools. Tools range in quality from inexpensive junk, which may break at first use, to very expensive and well-made tools for the professional. The best tools for most do-it-yourself BMW owners lie somewhere in between.

Many reputable tool manufacturers offer good quality, moderately priced tools with a lifetime guarantee. These are your best buy. They cost a little more, but they are good quality tools that will do what is expected of them. Sears' Craftsman® line is one such source of good quality tools.

Some of the repairs covered in this manual require the use of special tools, such as a custom puller or specialized electrical test equipment. These special tools are called out in the text and can be purchased through an authorized BMW dealer. As an alternative, some specialty tools, including scan tools, may be purchased from the following tool manufacturers or distributors:

Specialty tool suppliers

Assenmacher Specialty
Tools, Inc.
800-525-2943
www.asttool.com

Samstag Sales
615-735-3388
www.samstagsales.com

Autologic Diagnostics (UK)
877-945-6442
http://www.autologic.us/

ZDMAK Tools
(877) 938-6657
www.zdmak.com

Baum Tools Unlimited, Inc.
800-848-6657
www.baumtools.com

Zelenda Automotive, Inc.
888-892-8348
www.zelenda.com

Identification plates and labels

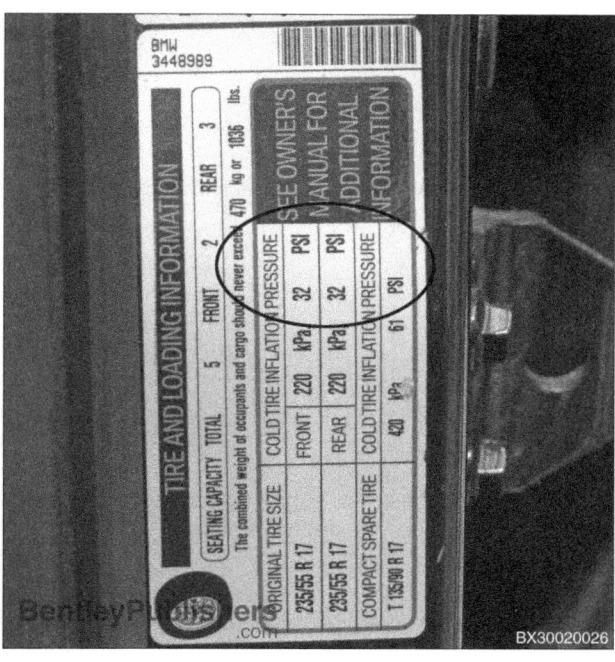

◄ **Vehicle identification number (VIN).** This is a combination of letters and numbers that identify the particular vehicle. The VIN appears on the state registration document, and on the vehicle itself. One location is on the right front strut tower (**arrow**), another in the lower left corner of the windshield. See **002 Vehicle Identification and VIN Decoder**.

◄ **Tire Pressures.** Recommended tire pressures as well as wheel size, tire size, gross vehicle weight, and carrying capacity are listed on a sticker on the driver door jam below the door latch.

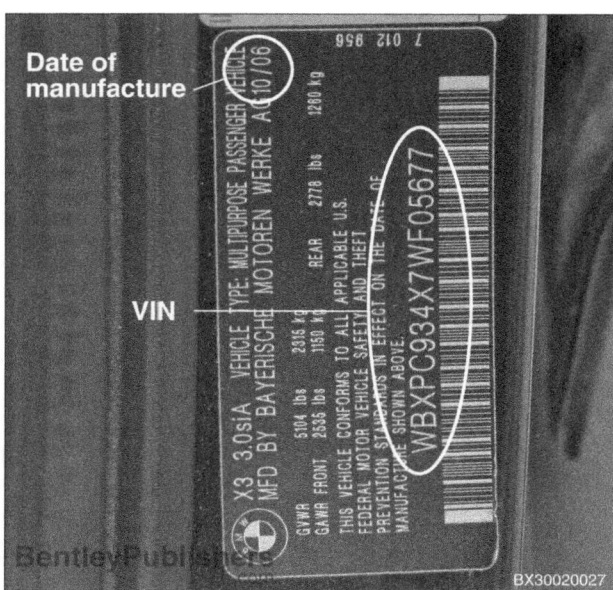

◄ **Date of manufacture and VIN.** This information is necessary when ordering replacement parts or determining if any of the warranty recalls are applicable to your vehicle. The VIN sticker on the driver door jam below the door latch specifies the month and year that the vehicle was built.

Engine code. X3 vehicles covered in this manual are powered by 6-cylinder engines. For information on engine codes and engine applications, see **100 Engine–General**.

Transmission code. The transmission type with its identifying code may be important when buying parts such as seals or gaskets. For information on transmission codes and applications, see **200 Transmission–General**.

RAISING VEHICLE

Raising vehicle safely using vehicle jack

◄ Prior to raising vehicle, check that there is a hard rubber jack pad (**arrow**) in the jacking position on the vehicle.

> **WARNING—**
> • It is not a safe practice to lift the vehicle if the jack pad is missing. Replace missing jacking pad at the earliest opportunity.

◄ For safety and to avoid damaging vehicle, use jack supplied with vehicle only at four jacking points (**arrows**) just behind front wheels or just in front of rear wheels. There must a visible hard rubber jacking pad at each point.

> **NOTE—**
> • BMW X5 model shown in photo.

— Park vehicle on flat, level surface.

— If changing a tire, loosen lug bolts before raising vehicle. See **Changing a tire** in this repair group.

— Use wheel chock to block wheel that is opposite and farthest from jack to prevent vehicle from unexpectedly rolling.

> **WARNING—**
> • Do not rely on the transmission or the parking brake to keep the vehicle from rolling.

◄ Place jack into position, making sure base of jack is resting on flat, solid surface. Position jack so that jack is positioned squarely under jacking pad.

> **WARNING—**
> • If the jacking pad is missing from the body, it is not safe to raise the car using the supplied jack. The jack can slip out of position if the pad is missing.

— Raise vehicle slowly while constantly checking position of jack and vehicle.

> **WARNING—**
> • Watch the jack closely. Make sure it stays stable and does not shift or tilt.

Working under vehicle safely

> **WARNING —**
> - *A jack is a temporary lifting device. Do not use a jack alone to support the vehicle while you are under it.*
> - *Do not work under a lifted vehicle unless it is solidly supported on jack stands that are intended for that purpose.*
> - *Do not use wood, concrete blocks or bricks to support a vehicle. Wood may split. Blocks and bricks, while strong, are not designed for that kind of load and may break or collapse.*
> - *Use care when removing major (heavy) components from one end of the vehicle. The sudden change in weight and balance can cause vehicle to tip off the lift or jack stands.*
> - *Do not support vehicle at engine oil pan, transmission, fuel tank, or on front or rear axle. Serious damage may result.*

— Disconnect negative (-) cable from battery so that vehicle cannot be started. Let others know what you are doing.

> **CAUTION—**
> - *Prior to disconnecting the battery, read the battery disconnection cautions given in* **001 Warnings and Cautions**.

— Raise vehicle slowly. If necessary, see **Raising vehicle safely using vehicle jack** in this repair group.

> **WARNING —**
> - *When raising vehicle using a floor jack or hydraulic lift, carefully position jack on jack pad to prevent damaging vehicle body.*

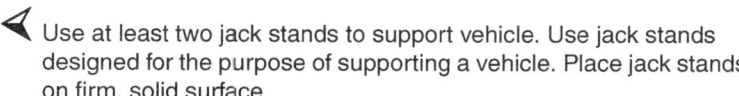 Use at least two jack stands to support vehicle. Use jack stands designed for the purpose of supporting a vehicle. Place jack stands on firm, solid surface.

— Lower vehicle slowly until its weight is fully supported by jack stands. Watch to make sure that the jack stands do not tip or lean as the vehicle settles on them.

— Observe jacking precautions again when raising vehicle to remove jack stands.

Jack stands

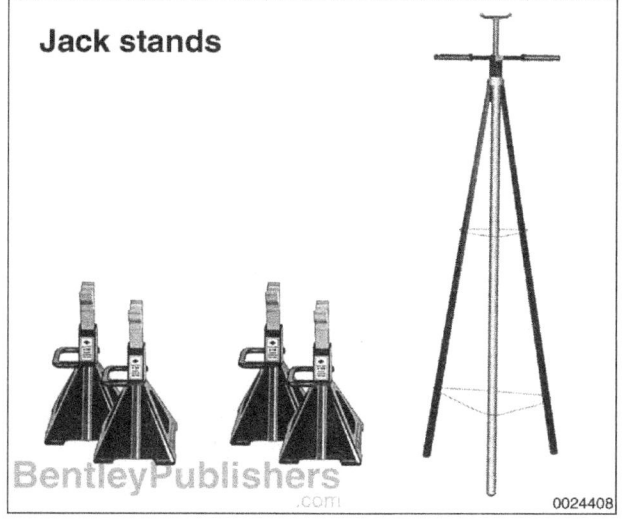

0024408

EMERGENCIES

Towing

Tow vehicles covered by this manual with a tow truck using flat bed equipment. Do not tow the vehicle on all four wheels except for very short distances to move it to a safe place.

> **CAUTION—**
> - *Do not tow with sling-type equipment.*
> - *Do not tow with front or rear axle raised individually.*
> - *Do not use tow hook to tow vehicle faster than 30 mph (50 kph) or for a distance greater than 95 miles (150 km).*
> - *Automatic transmission fluid (ATF) does not circulate when the vehicle is towed. Severe transmission damage may result.*

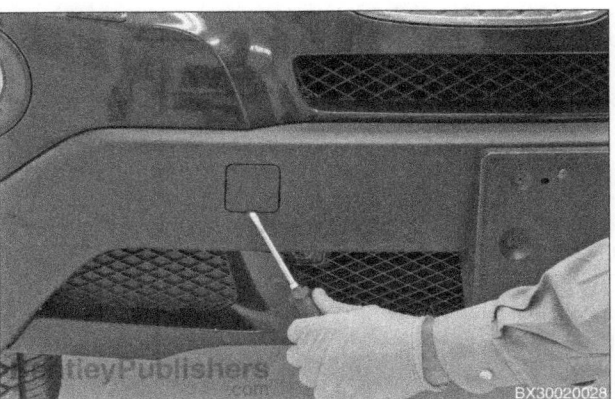

◄ To access threaded towing eye socket, pry open trim on front or rear bumper.

– Remove towing eye from cargo compartment tool kit. Towing eye is located under small carpeted panel on the left side of the cargo compartment.

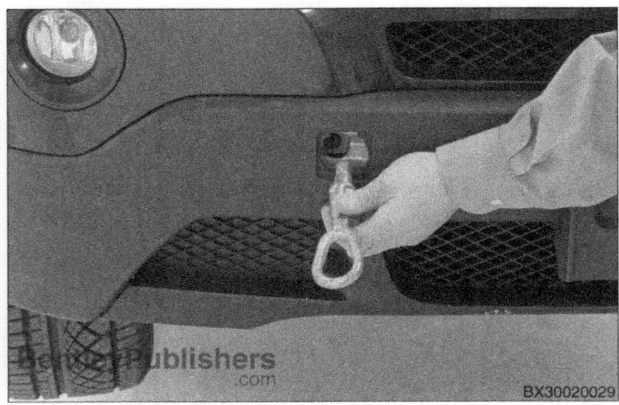

◄ Screw towing eye into threaded hole in bumper until tight.

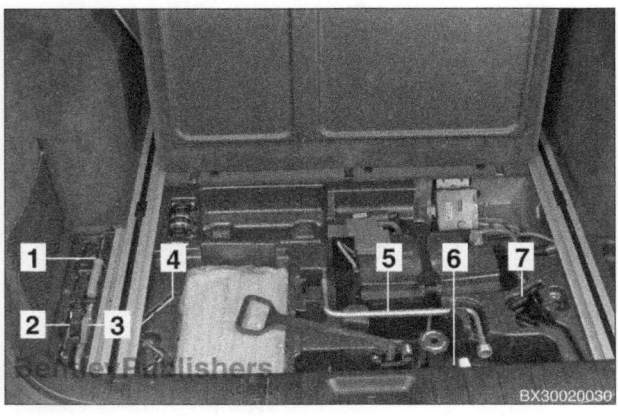

◄ Emergency equipment is located in the cargo compartment beneath the load floor.

1. Screwdriver
2. Open end wrench (13mm, 10mm combination)
3. Towing eye
4. Allen wrench for emergency closing of panorama sunroof
5. Lug wrench
6. Jack
7. Wheel chock

Spare tire, removing

The X3 is equipped with a compact spare tire, mounted beneath the rear of the vehicle.

– Open rear cargo load floor. Remove jack and jack handle, if required.

◄ Open locking nut by fully unscrewing counterclockwise (**inset**) and set aside. Then lift up on folding handle (**arrow**).

◄ Turn handle to left to unlock (**arrow**). Then slowly lower handle as far as possible.

NOTE—

• *Turning handle releases the compact spare tire lock. Weight of tire is approx. 18 lbs. It must be held up by the handle once the lock is released.*

◄ Take out compact spare towards rear.

Changing a tire

Comply with all safety guidelines and regulations. Change the wheel only on a level, non-slippery firm surface. The vehicle or the jack could slip to the side if you attempt to raise the vehicle on a soft or slippery surface such as snow or ice.

> **WARNING—**
> * If a tire goes flat while driving, pull well off the road. Changing a tire on a busy street or highway is very dangerous. If necessary, drive a short distance on the flat tire to get to a safe place. It is better to ruin a tire or rim than to risk being hit.

— Park vehicle as far as possible from passing traffic. Park on a firm, flat, surface.

— Switch on hazard warning flashers. Set out flares or emergency markers well behind vehicle. Chock wheel diagonally opposite to the one being changed.

> **WARNING—**
> * All passengers should be outside the vehicle and well away from your immediate working area, behind a guardrail, for instance.

— Lock steering wheel in straight-ahead position. Engage parking brake and engage first gear, reverse gear or selector-lever setting P

— Take jack, tools and spare tire out of cargo compartment, Lower and remove spare tire. See **Spare tire, removing** in this repair group.

— Loosen lug bolts while vehicle is on ground, but leave them a little snug.

> **WARNING—**
> * To avoid serious or fatal injury: never lie under the vehicle. Never start the engine while it is supported by the jack.

BX56020017

◄ Place jack into position, making sure base of jack is resting on flat, solid surface. Position jack so that jack is positioned squarely under jacking pad.

> **WARNING—**
> * If the hard rubber jacking pad is missing from the body, do not raise the car using the car jack. The jack can slip out of position. Replace missing jacking pad at the earliest opportunity.

— Raise vehicle just until wheel is fully off ground and then remove lug bolts and wheel.

— Install spare wheel. Install lug bolts and tighten hand tight using lug wrench.

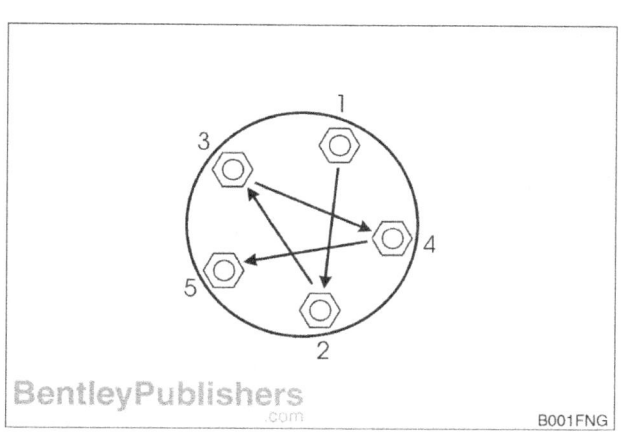

B001FNG

◄ Lower vehicle. With all wheels on ground, fully tighten lug bolts in a crisscross pattern. Check inflation pressure of newly installed spare tire.

Tightening torque	
Wheel to wheel hub	140 Nm (103 ft-lb)

– Replace jack and tools in cargo area. Stow defective wheel in cargo area.

***NOTE*—**

• *A full size tire will not fit into the compact spare tire area.*

– Check tire inflation pressure at the earliest opportunity.

Jump starting

Jump start vehicle with discharged or dead battery using the good battery from another vehicle. See owner's manual for proper instruction on jump starting.

***CAUTION*—**

• *Jump starting is not a recommended practice. Sensitive electronics can be damaged by voltage spikes. The best method is to disconnect and slow charge the dead battery.*

– In emergency situations, first switch off engine of vehicle with good battery. Switch off any electrical systems and components in both vehicles.

◄ Attach jumper cables to engine compartment B+ junction and ground lug. Start car with good battery and let idle. Then start vehicle.

***WARNING*—**

• *Do not jump-start engine if you suspect that the battery is frozen. Trapped gas may explode. Allow the battery to thaw first.*

***CAUTION*—**

• *Do not quick-charge the battery (for boost starting) for longer than one minute, and do not exceed 16.5 volts at the battery with the boosting cables attached. Wait at least one minute before boosting the battery a second time.*

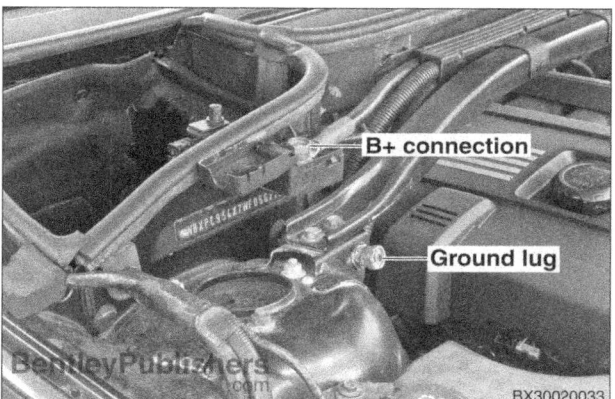

B+ connection

Ground lug

BX30020033

Indicator and warning lights

Many vehicle systems are self-monitored for faults while driving. Generally, a red warning lamp that comes on during driving should be considered serious. If you cannot immediately determine the seriousness of the warning light, stop the vehicle in a safe place and turn the engine off as soon as possible. Consult the owner's manual for additional information on the warning light and the recommended action.

If the malfunction indicator light (MIL) (Check Engine or Service Engine Soon warning light) comes on or flashes, it indicates that an emissions-related fault has occurred. Faults such as a bad oxygen sensor or a dead fuel injector can cause exhaust or evaporative emissions to exceed a specified limit. When these limits are exceeded, the MIL illuminates. The engine can be safety driven with the light on, but check the emission control systems as soon as possible. See **OBD On–Board Diagnostics** for more information on the MIL and the on-board diagnostic system.

ENGINE COMPARTMENT

Remove upper and lower engine covers as required and check engine compartment for signs of fluid leaks. Fluid leaks attract dust making them easier to spot. Many expensive repairs can be avoided by prompt repair of minor fluid leaks.

Visually inspect for oil and ATF leaks at engine and transmission. Also inspect cooling, fuel, heating and air-conditioning systems for leakage. Visually inspect hoses and hose connections for leaks, worn areas, porosity and brittleness.

Check that all fluid levels are between MIN and MAX marks.

M54 engine compartment

1. **Windshield washer reservoir cap**

2. **Oil filler cap**

3. **Oil dipstick**

4. **B+ junction**

5. **Grounding lug**

6. **Brake fluid reservoir**

7. **Intake air filter housing**

8. **Coolant reservoir cap**

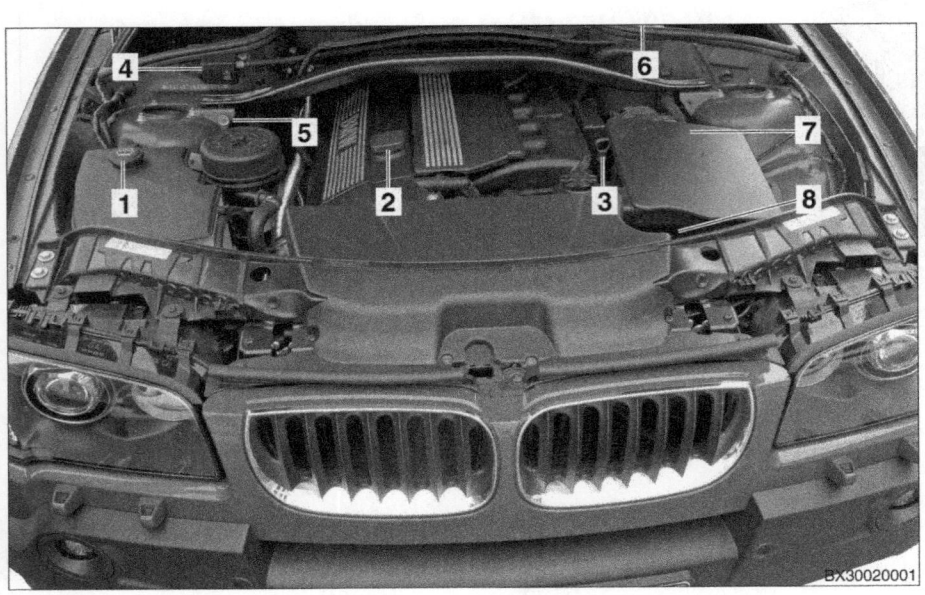

BX30020001

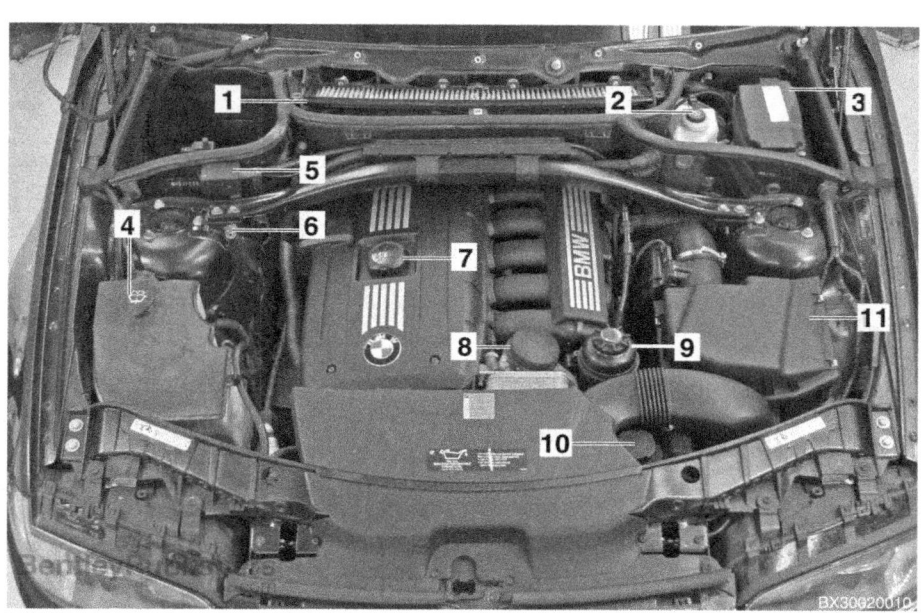

BX30020010

N52 engine compartment

1. Cabin air microfilter

2. Brake fluid reservoir

3. Electronics box (E-box)

4. Windshield washer reservoir cap

5. B+ junction

6. Grounding lug

7. Oil filler cap

8. Oil filler cap

9. Power steering fluid reservoir cap

10. Coolant reservoir cap

11. Intake air filter housing

Engine and transmission covers, removing

X3 vehicles are equipped with plastic panels in the engine compartment, both above and underneath the engine. Following are the methods for removing them.

Engine upper covers

BX30020009

◀ Remove plastic rivets and unfasten wiring loom from strut brace (**center arrows**). Remove bolts holding strut brace to strut towers (**outer arrows**). Remove brace.

NOTE —

• *N52 engine shown, M54 is similar.*

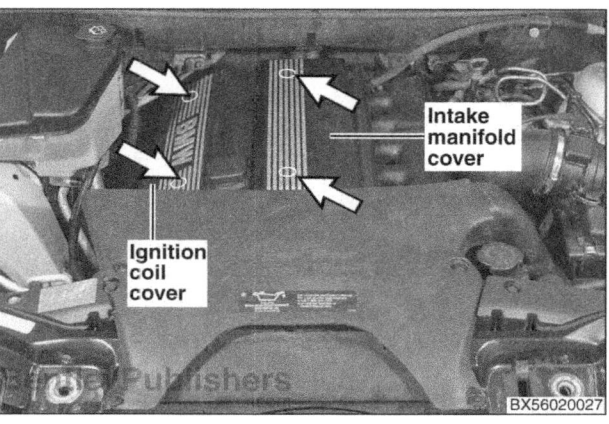

Intake manifold cover

Ignition coil cover

BX56020027

◀ **M54 engine**: Remove plastic trim caps (**arrows**). Remove cover mounting fasteners below caps and lift off covers.

NOTE —

• *X5 engine compartment shown.*

Engine Compartment

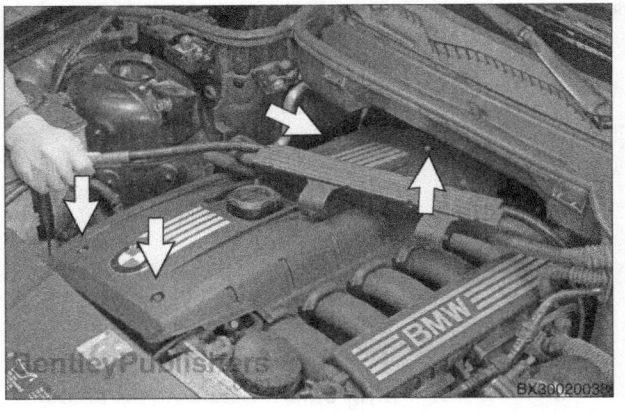

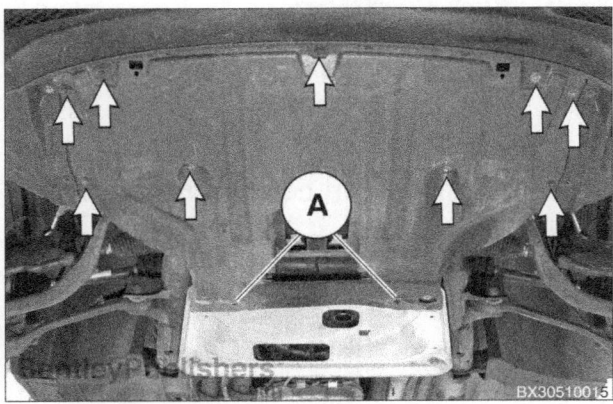

◄ **N52 engine**: Remove cover fasteners (**arrows**) and lift up cover.

– Installation is the reverse of removal.

Tightening torque	
Strut brace to strut towers	19 Nm (14 ft-lb)

Engine splash shield

◄ Remove engine splash shield cover fasteners and plastic rivets (**arrows**). Remove shield clips (**A**). Remove engine splash shield.

Transmission splash shield

◄ Remove transmission splash shield cover fasteners and plastic rivets (**arrows**). Remove transmission splash shield.

Front intake cowl, removing and installing

Removal of the intake air cowl is required in order inspect and access the front of the engine. For example inspecting and replacing the drive belt.

◄ Remove fasteners (**arrows**) and remove front intake cowl from radiator support.

◄ Remove intake cowl from radiator:
- Carefully unclip and remove intake elbow (**A**).
- Remove fasteners (**arrows**).
- Lift up rear of intake duct and remove from radiator support.

AIR FILTER SERVICE

The specified replacement intervals for the air filter are based on normal use. If the vehicle is operated primarily in dusty conditions, service air filter more frequently.

Air filter element, replacing

NOTE —
- *N52 engine shown. M54 engine similar.*
- *N52 engine uses an additional active carbon filter element in the lid of the air filter housing. A replacement interval is not specified for this filter.*

◄ Working at air filter housing:
- Disconnect mass air flow sensor connector (**A**). Loosen hose clamp at mass air flow sensor intake pipe.
- Release 4 upper air filter housing clips (**arrows**).
- Remove cover and replace air filter element.

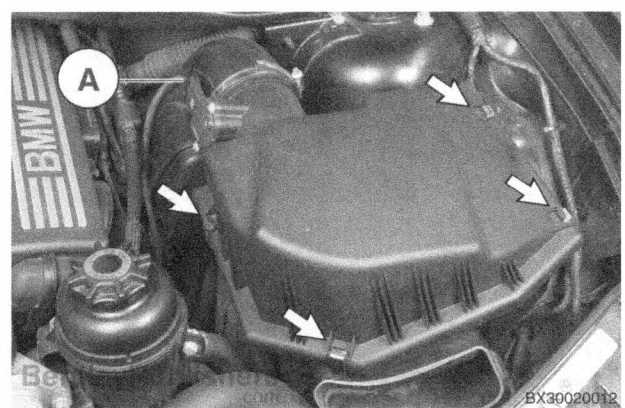

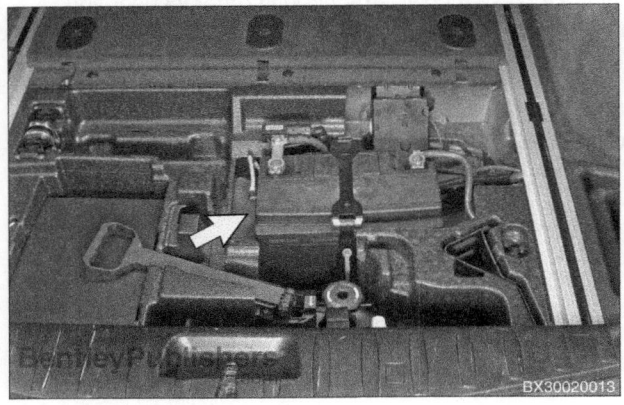

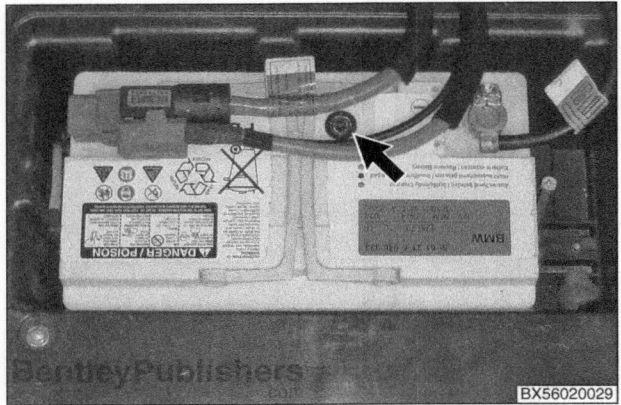

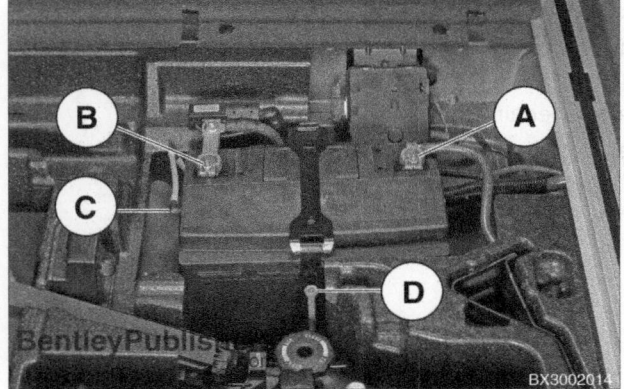

BATTERY SERVICE

The original equipment battery in E83 vehicles is maintenance free. The electrolyte will normally last the entire service life of the battery under moderate climate conditions.

> **CAUTION—**
> * Prior to disconnecting the battery, read the battery disconnection cautions given in **001 Warnings and Cautions**.

◀ Battery is located under cargo floor (**arrow**).

Battery, checking

◀ Original equipment BMW battery is equipped with built-in hydrometer "magic eye" (**arrow**). Battery condition is determined by eye color:

* Green: Adequate charge
* Black: Inadequate charge, recharge
* Yellow: Defective battery, replace

Simple maintenance of the battery and its terminal connections ensures maximum starting performance, especially in winter when colder temperatures reduce battery power.

Make sure terminals, cable clamps and battery case are free of white deposits that indicate corrosion and acid salts. Even a thin layer of dust containing conductive acid salts can cause battery discharge. Clean terminals as necessary.

> **WARNING—**
> * Take care to keep battery acid from contacting eyes, skin, or clothing. Wear eye protection. Extinguish all smoking materials and do not work near any open flames.

Battery, removing and installing

If replacing battery, replace with one of equal or higher rating.

> **CAUTION—**
> * Prior to disconnecting the battery, read the battery disconnection cautions given in **001 Warnings and Cautions**.

◀ Working in cargo compartment, open cargo load floor.

* Disconnect negative cable (**A**) first.
* Disconnect positive cable (**B**).
* Disconnect battery vent hose at side of battery (**C**).
* Remove hold down bolt at front of battery and lift battery out of cargo compartment (**D**).

— Clean away corrosion in and around battery tray and on cables ends.

— When reinstalling battery, reconnect negative cable last.

BRAKE SERVICE

Brake system maintenance includes maintaining brake fluid in the reservoir, checking pad thickness, checking parking brake function, and inspecting the system for fluid leaks and damage:

- Check that brake hoses are correctly routed to avoid chafing.
- Inspect unions and brake calipers for signs of fluid leaks.
- Inspect rigid lines for corrosion, dents, or other damage.
- Inspect flexible hoses for cracking.
- Replace faulty hoses or lines.

WARNING—

- *Incorrect installation or overtightening of hoses, lines and unions may cause chafing or leakage. This can lead to brake system failure.*

Brake fluid level, checking

Brake fluid absorbs moisture. This affects brake performance and reliability. BMW recommends replacing the brake fluid every two years. See **340 Brakes** for brake fluid flushing and bleeding.

When replacing or adding brake fluid, use only new fluid from previously unopened containers. Do not use brake fluid that has been bled from the system, even if it is new.

The brake fluid reservoir is located in the rear of the engine compartment on the driver's side.

WARNING—

- *Brake fluid is poisonous. Do not ingest. Wash thoroughly with soap and water if it comes into contact with skin.*

CAUTION—

- *Use only new, previously unopened brake fluid conforming to DOT 4.*
- *Do not let brake fluid come in contact with paint. Wash immediately with soap and water.*
- *Brake fluid absorbs moisture from the air. Store in an airtight container.*
- *Do not use DOT 5 (silicone) brake fluid.*
- *Do not mix mineral oil products such as gasoline or engine oil with brake fluid. Mineral oil damages rubber seals in the brake system.*
- *Dispose brake fluid as a hazardous waste.*

 Check that fluid level is between **MIN** and **MAX** marks on brake fluid reservoir. Fluid level drops slightly as brake pad material wears. Add fluid if fluid level is below the MIN mark.

Brake fluid application	
BMW preferred fluid	Low viscosity DOT 4 brake fluid
DOT 4 and low viscosity DOT 4 brake fluid can be mixed.	

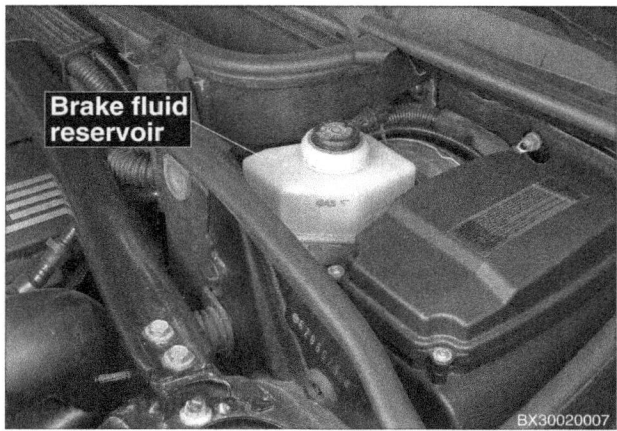

Brake fluid reservoir

BX30020007

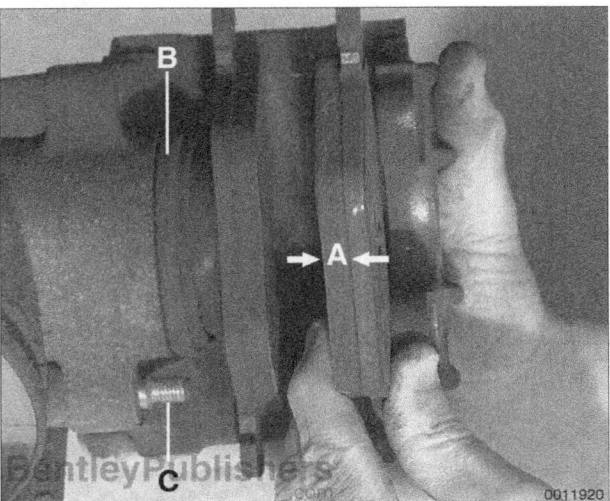

Brake pad and rotor wear, checking

Disc brakes are fitted at all four wheels. Although the brakes are equipped with a brake pad wear system, the system only monitors one wheel per axle. Check brake pad thickness whenever wheels are off or brake work is being done.

◄ Disc brake pad wear can be checked through opening in caliper once wheel is removed:

* Measure pad friction lining thickness (**A**). Compare to specification below.

◄ Unbolt caliper from steering arm to properly inspect:

* Brake pad thickness (**A**)
* Brake rotor
* Condition of caliper seal (**B**)
* Condition of caliper slider bolts (**C**)

Brake pad lining minimum thickness	
Dimension **A**	3.0 mm (0.12 in)

See **340 Brakes** for additional techniques for checking brakes and for brake pad, rotor and caliper replacement procedures.

Clutch fluid, checking

The hydraulic clutch and the brake system share the same reservoir and the same brake fluid. Clutch fluid level and brake fluid level are checked at the same time.

Parking brake, checking

The parking brake system is independent of the main braking system and may require periodic adjustment depending on use. Adjust the parking brake if the brake lever can be pulled up more than 8 clicks. Check that the cable moves freely. See **340 Brakes** for parking brake adjustment procedure.

The parking brake may lose some of its effectiveness if it is not used frequently. This is due to rust build-up on the parking brake drum. To remove rust, apply the parking brake just until it begins to grip, then pull the lever up one more stop (click). Drive the vehicle approximately 400 meters (1,300 ft.) and release the brake.

COOLING SYSTEM SERVICE

Routine cooling system maintenance consists of maintaining the coolant level and inspecting hoses. Coolant anticorrosion and antifreeze additives gradually lose their effectiveness over time. Replace long-life coolant every four years. For additional cooling system information, see **170 Radiator and Cooling System**.

> **CAUTION—**
> • Use only BMW phosphate-free antifreeze when filling the cooling system.

Coolant level, checking

 Unscrew radiator reservoir cap (**arrow**). Float in radiator overflow reservoir indicates coolant level. Inspect while coolant is cold. Use care not to overfill.

• When upper mark on float (**MIN**) is level with top of filler neck, coolant is at minimum allowable level.

• When lower mark on float (**MAX**) is level with top of filler neck, coolant is at maximum level.

Replacement of coolant every 4 years is recommended. Use BMW coolant and distilled water. **Table b** lists cooling system capacity.

Table b. Cooling system capacity

Engine	Capacity
M54: • Automatic transmission • Manual transmission	10.6L (11.20 US qt) 10.0L (10.56 US qt)
N52: • Automatic transmission • Manual transmission	10.2L (11.20 US qt) 10.0L (10.56 US qt)

Antifreeze concentration, checking

 Use a coolant hydrometer to determine antifreeze concentration.

Coolant mixture recommendations

Concentration	Cold protection
50% antifreeze / 50% distilled water	-35°C (-31°F)
60% antifreeze / 40% distilled water	-40°C (-40°F)

Do not use a higher concentration of antifreeze than a 60% mixture. Coolant heat transfer decreases with higher concentrations.

KALT / COLD

max

min

BX30020008

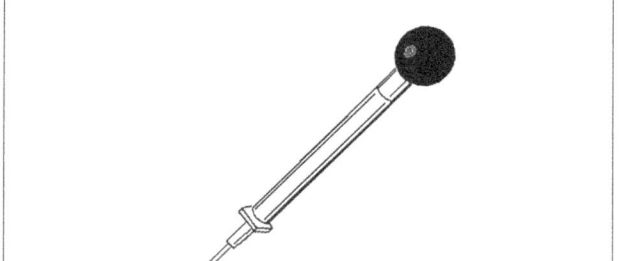

BentleyPublishers
.com

PB0419048

Cooling system hoses, inspecting

Inspect hoses and connections for leaks. Coolant seepage indicates that either the hose connection is faulty, hose is damaged, or connection is corroded. Dried coolant has a chalky appearance.

 Check hose condition by a visual and tactile inspection, making sure it is firm and springy. Replace hoses that exhibit conditions noted. (Illustration courtesy of Gates Rubber Company, Inc.)

- Leakage: Dripping, moisture, or seepage at end connectors.
- Electromechanical degradation: Difficult to see, but detectable by squeezing hose and feeling for cracks, weak areas, and voids.
- Oil damage: Soft and spongy to touch, visible bulges and swelling.
- Abrasion damage: Wear, abrasion, or scuffing, often due to contact with components in engine compartment.
- Heat damage: Internal and external damage, generally due to high underhood temperatures or overheating. Internal heat damage is often indicated by swelling with external damage marked by hardened and cracked areas.
- Ozone damage: Small, parallel cracks in outer layers, but without hardening. Due to exposure to atmospheric conditions.

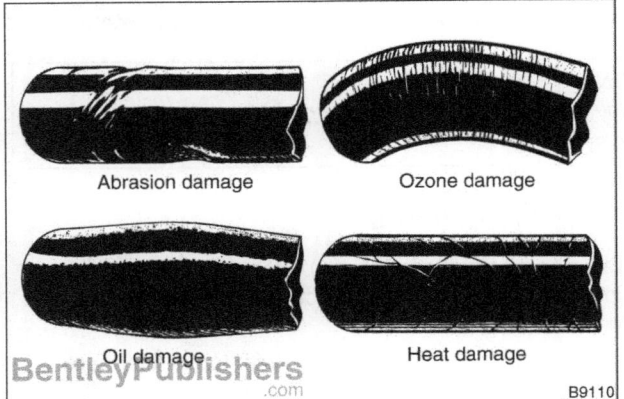

Abrasion damage

Ozone damage

Oil damage

Heat damage

B9110

ENGINE ACCESSORY BELT SERVICE

Inspect belt and belt tensioners with engine off. If belt shows signs of wear, cracking, glazing, or missing bits, replace immediately. To reduce the chance of belt failure, replace belts every four years.

Carefully inspect that tensioner pulleys are aligned and running true to the belt. If the pulley deviates in any degree from the belt, the tensioner assembly should be replaced immediately.

Accessory belts, replacing (M54 engine)

Two belts are used to drive M54 engine accessories:
- Outer (front) belt: A/C compressor
- Inner (rear) belt: Alternator, coolant pump, steering pump

Prior to removing the inner belt, the outer (A/C compressor) belt must first be removed.If planning to reinstall old belt(s), mark direction of rotation prior to removal.

Two types of automatic belt tensioners are used; a hydraulic version and a mechanical version.The procedure for releasing the tension on the belt is similar for both types.

 M54 accessory belts
1. Crankshaft pulley
2. A/C belt tensioner
3. A/C compressor pulley
4. Coolant pump pulley
5. Alternator pulley
6. Accessory belt tensioner
7. Idler pulley
8. Power steering pump pulley

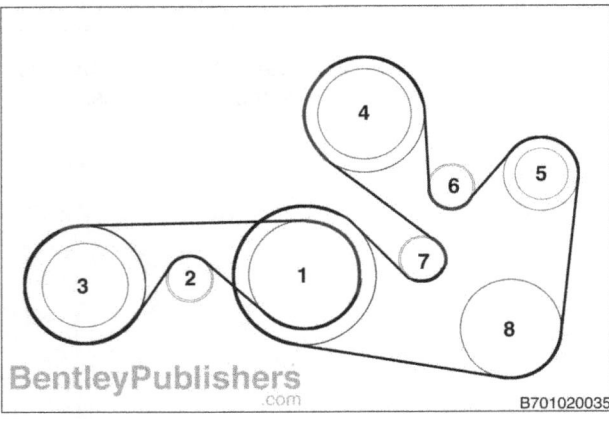

B701020035

 To remove A/C compressor belt:

- Use hex head (**left arrow**) or Torx socket to rotate A/C belt tensioner away from belt.
- Slip belt off pulleys and remove belt.
- Check belt for cracks and coolant or oil residue. Replace if necessary.

– To reinstall A/C compressor belt:

- Rotate A/C belt tensioner in direction of **lower arrow**.
- Route belt over pulleys and release tensioner.

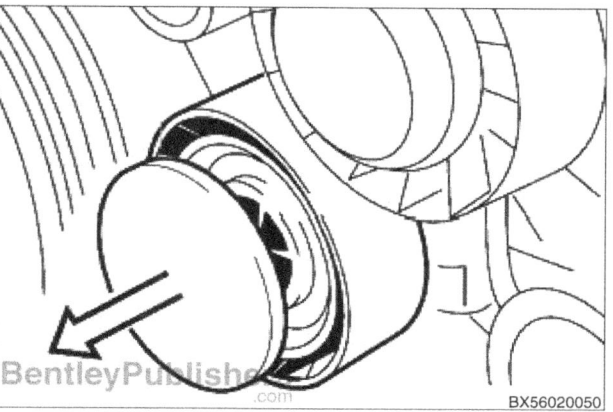

◄ To remove accessory belt:

- Remove A/C compressor belt
- Remove cap from accessory belt tensioner.

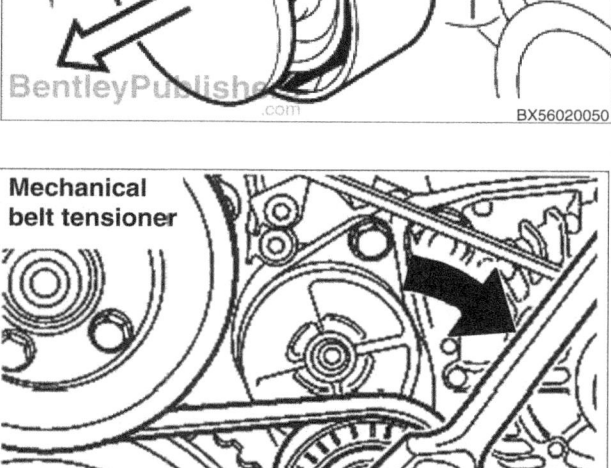

Mechanical belt tensioner

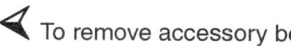

◄ Use long-handled wrench (8 mm hex bit), lever center bolt in tensioner pulley (**A**) clockwise, away from belt (**arrow**) to release belt tension.

> **WARNING—**
> - *Observe care when replacing belts. Personal injury could result if a tensioner springs back into position uncontrollably.*
> - *Belt tension should release easily. Excessive force should not be required. Always move the tensioner pulley away from the belt to relieve belt tension.*

NOTE—

Mechanical belt tensioners have a cast hex boss on tensioner body. Alternatively, use a 17mm wrench on hex boss to release belt tension.

– With tension released, slide belt off pulleys.

– When installing a new belt, gently pry it over the pulleys. Too much force can damage belt or the accessory.

– When reinstalling belt, check that it is correctly positioned on pulleys. If reinstalling old belt, pay attention to direction of rotation marks made previously.

Hydraulic belt tensioner

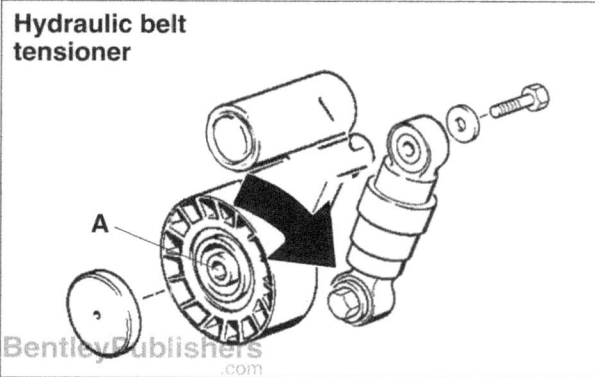

Tightening torques	
Belt tensioner to cylinder block	30 Nm (22 ft-lb)
Idler pulley to alternator bracket (M10)	42 Nm (31 ft-lb)

Accessory belt, replacing (N52 engine)

The accessory belt and pulleys transfer power from the engine crankshaft to the alternator, A/C compressor and power steering pump. The engine coolant pump and engine cooling fan are both electric. If planning to reinstall old belt(s), mark direction of rotation prior to removal.

> **CAUTION—**
> • *Do not use steel fasteners on aluminum-magnesium alloy N52 engines. Use aluminum fasteners only.*
> • *For reliable identification, test fasteners for aluminum composition with magnet. Replace aluminum bolts each time they are loosened.*

◀ **N52 accessory belt**

1. Alternator
2. Idler pulley
3. Air conditioning compressor
4. Power steering pump
5. Vibration damper
6. Idler pulley
7. Idler pulley
8. Belt tensioner with pulley
9. Drive belt

BX30020004

Note that excessive engine movement due to a defective left side engine mount can lead to accessory belt damage. This is usually caused by contact between the power steering pump pulley and the front axle carrier. The belt may become dislodged from pulleys or broken when traveling over curbs, speed bumps or at a high rate of speed.

If accessory belt, power steering pump pulley or front axle carrier are found to be damaged, replace these parts as well as the left engine mount with updated parts.

◀ Remove fasteners (**arrows**) and remove front intake cowl from radiator support.

BX30170028

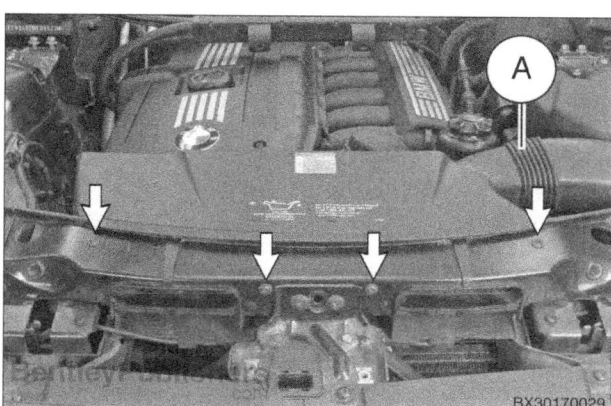

◀ Remove intake cowl from radiator:
  • Remove intake duct (**A**).
  • Remove fasteners (**arrows**).
  • Lift up rear of intake duct and remove from radiator support.

— Remove engine splash shield. See **Engine splash shield, removing** in this repair group.

— If planning to reinstall old belt, be sure to mark direction of rotation.

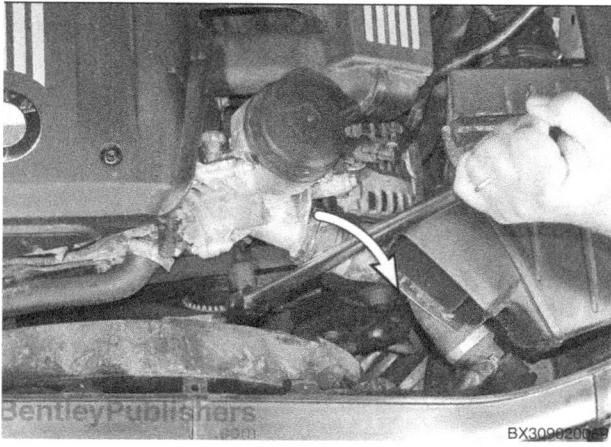

◀ Use T60 Torx socket to rotate belt tensioner clockwise (**arrow**). This releases belt tension.

◀ If necessary lock tensioner in released position using BMW special tool 11 3 340.

> **WARNING—**
> • *Observe care when working with tensioner. Personal injury could result if tensioner springs back into position uncontrolled.*

— Work belt off pulleys and remove.

N52 engine

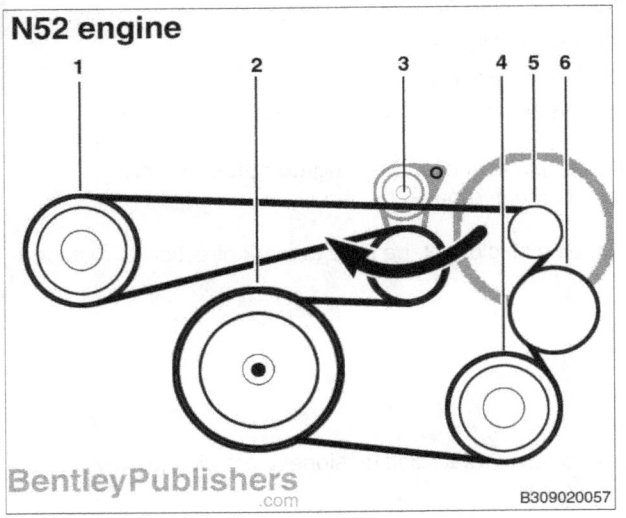

B309020057

 If replacing belt tensioner:

- Remove locking tool 11 3 340, if installed.
- Pry of dust cap from front of tensioner. Remove center bolt (**3**) and remove tensioner.
- Install new tensioner. Replace bolt with new.
- Using Torx socket, rotate new belt tensioner clockwise and lock in released position using special tool 11 3 340.

— If reinstalling used belt, follow direction-of-rotation mark made previously.

1. A/C compressor pulley
2. Vibration damper (crankshaft pulley)
3. Tensioner pulley
4. Power steering pump pulley
5. Alternator pulley
6. Idler pulley

Tightening torque	
Accessory belt tensioner to engine block M11 x 65 mm	25 Nm (18 ft-lb) + 90° (¼ turn)
Idler pulley to alternator housing M10 x 45	40 Nm (30 ft-lb)

ENGINE OIL SERVICE

> *CAUTION—*
> - *Use BMW specified oil to top off engine between oil changes.*
> - *Do not use engine oil additives.*

— BMW recommends the following engine oil.

Engine oil specification, E83	
BMW Long-life rating LL-01 synthetic oil (0W-30, 0W-40, 5W-30, 5W-40)	API rating SM or higher

Engine oil, checking level (M54 engine)

The M54 engine uses a dipstick to check oil level.

— Check oil level with vehicle on level surface, after engine has been stopped for at least a few minutes.

 Check level by pulling out dipstick and wiping it clean. Reinsert all the way and withdraw again.

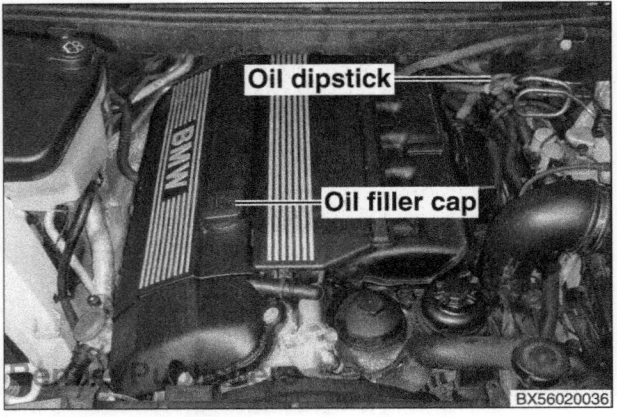

Oil dipstick

Oil filler cap

BX56020036

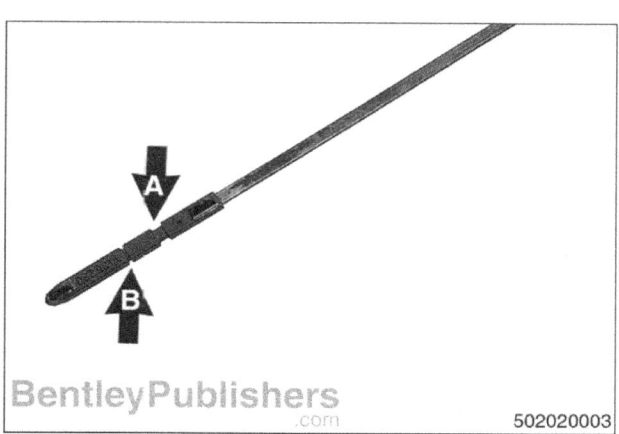

◀ Oil level is correct if it is between two marks (**A** and **B**) near end of dipstick.

– If oil level is low, add oil. Add only amount needed to bring oil level to upper mark on dipstick, using correct viscosity and grade oil.

Engine oil, checking level (N52 engine)

Oil level is measured dynamically when the engine is running and at operating temperature. Start up engine and drive at least 6.5 miles (10 km). Once oil is fully warmed up, oil level may be displayed while driving or while the vehicle is at a stand still on a level surface with the engine running.

If oil level is low, add oil at oil filler in cylinder head cover. Use correct viscosity and grade oil.

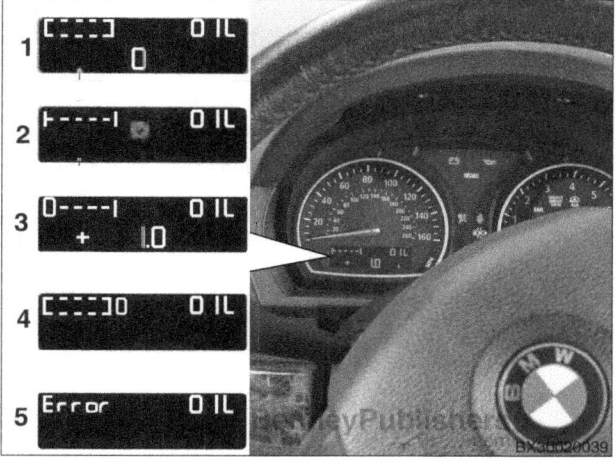

◀ Press the right button at the base of the instrument cluster (**arrow**). The oil level will display for 15 seconds. One of the following graphics will be displayed:

1. Oil level OK.

2. Oil level being checked (clock symbol).
   This can take about 3 minutes if vehicle is at a standstill on a level surface, or about 5 minutes if vehicle is underway.

3. Oil level down to minimum.
   Add 1 US quart or 1 liter of engine oil as soon as possible.

4. Oil level too high.
   Too much oil is harmful to engine. Have vehicle checked without delay.

5. Oil level sensor defective.
   Do not add engine oil. Have system checked as soon as possible.

Engine oil and filter, changing

> **CAUTION—**
> - In the case of vehicles that accumulate very low mileage per year, change engine oil once a year at a minimum, regardless of whether mineral or synthetic based oil is used.
> - In the interest of engine longevity, use half the recommended engine oil change interval.

A complete oil change requires the following:

- Oil filter cover wrench or socket (36mm socket for M54 engine, 88mm cover wrench for N52 engine)
- 17 mm drain plug socket or box wrench
- New oil and filter insert kit, (kit normally includes filter, O-rings, and drain plug sealing washer).

— Run engine for a few minutes to warm engine oil. Switch engine OFF.

◄ Loosen and remove oil filter housing cover (**arrow**). Allow oil in filter housing to drain into oil sump.

- **M54 engines**: Use 36mm socket to remove oil filter housing cover.
- **N52 engine**: Use 86mm oil filter cover removal tool to remove oil filter housing cover.

— Raise vehicle and support safely.

> **WARNING—**
> - Make sure vehicle is stable and well supported at all times. Use a professional automotive lift or jack stands. A floor jack is not adequate support.

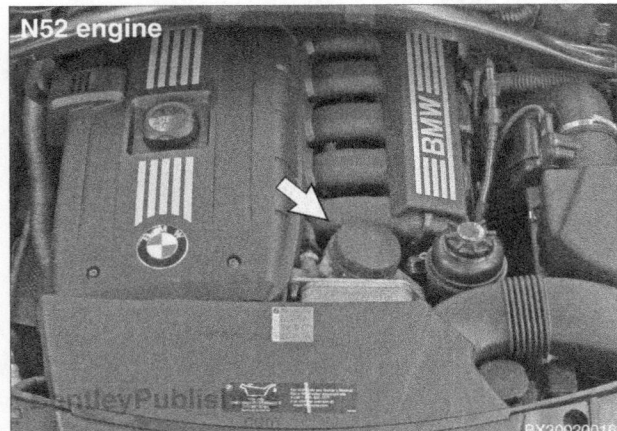

◄ Working under engine, place drain pan under oil drain plug. Using a 17mmm socket or box wrench, loosen drain plug. Remove plug by hand and let oil drain into pan.

> **WARNING—**
> - Pull loose plug away from hole quickly to avoid being scalded. Oil will run out quickly when the plug is removed. Use gloves to protect your hands.

— When oil flow has diminished to an occasional drip, reinstall drain plug with a new metal sealing washer and torque plug.

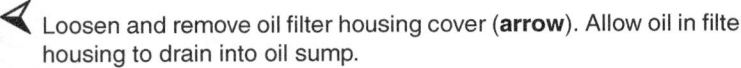

Tightening torque	
Engine oil drain plug to oil pan	25 Nm (18 ft-lb)

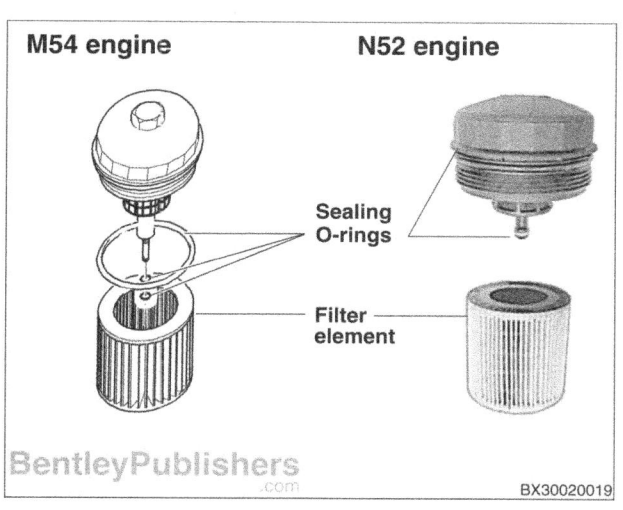

M54 engine   N52 engine

Sealing
O-rings

Filter
element

BentleyPublishers
.com

BX30020019

◁ Lubricate and install new oil filter O-rings and new filter element in oil filter housing. Install and tighten housing cover.

Tightening torque	
Cover to oil filter housing	25 Nm (18 ft-lb)

− Refill crankcase with oil. Approximate oil capacity is listed in **Table c**.

Table c. Engine oil capacity	
Engine	**Approx. capacity (incl.oil filter)**
M54, N52	6.5 liters (7.0 US qt)

− Start engine and check that oil pressure warning light immediately goes out.

− Check for correct oil level:

  • Park on horizontal surface.

  • Run engine until it reaches operating temperature. Increase engine speed to 1100 rpm and maintain for 3 minutes.

  • Read engine oil level using instrument cluster display. See **Engine oil, checking level** in this repair group.

FUEL FILTER SERVICE

The fuel filter is located in the right side of the fuel tank. It is a lifetime filter, as specified by BMW. The filter with integral fuel pressure regulator is available as a replacement part. See**160 Fuel Pump and Fuel Tank** for additional information.

CABIN AIR MICROFILTER

E83 models are equipped with a cabin air microfilter to filter dust and pollen from the incoming cabin air. Filter is located at the base of the windshield under a cover.

Cabin air microfilter, replacing

− Open engine hood.

◁ Release quick-release fasteners (**arrows**), pivot microfilter cover up and slide out microfilter.

− Check that microfilter housing drain holes are free of obstructions before closing compartment. Clean and vacuum housing if necessary.

BentleyPublishers

BX3002037

POWER STEERING FLUID

Power steering fluid, checking level

The power steering system is permanently filled and does not have a drain. Routinely adding fluid is not required unless the system is leaking.

NOTE—

- *The type of power steering fluid used is marked on the power steering reservoir cap. Most X3s use CHF 11S hydraulic fluid. Some early cars use ATF. See* **320 Steering and Wheel Alignment** *for additional information.*

◄ To check power steering fluid level:

- Park vehicle on level ground with engine off.
- Remove cap with dipstick from reservoir. Level is correct if it is between **MIN** and **MAX** marks on dipstick.
- If level is below **MIN** mark, add fluid to reservoir to bring level up.

— Hand-tighten reservoir cap.

SPARK PLUG SERVICE

Both the M54 engine and the N52 engine use a coil-over-spark plug configuration, with one ignition coil above each spark plug.

The recommended spark plug replacement interval for these is 100,000 miles. The spark plug electrode gap is not adjustable.

Spark plug applications	
M54 engine	
• Bosch	FGR7DQP
• NGK	BKR6EQUP
N52 engine	
• Bosch	FR7NPP33
• NGK	ILZFR6D11
Check for correct application with authorized BMW dealer parts department.	

Spark plugs, replacing

WARNING—

- *To avoid personal injury, be sure engine is cold before beginning work.*

NOTE—

- *N52 engine shown. M54 engine is similar.*

— With ignition key removed, remove engine cover. See **Engine and transmission covers, removing** in this repair group.

◄ Unlock ignition coil connector (**curved arrow**). Pull connector off coil (**straight arrow**).

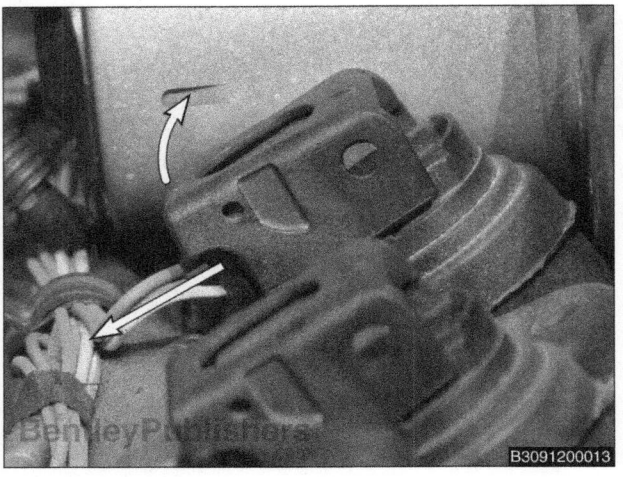

◀ Slide rod-shaped ignition coil straight out of spark plug hole.

> **CAUTION—**
> • *Maintain cleanliness when servicing ignition coils. Fuel and oil residue can cause a breakdown in the electrical resistance of the silicone encased coil, resulting in ignition coil failure.*

◀ Remove spark plugs, using thin-walled spark plug socket.

◀ **N52 engine**: if thin-walled spark plug socket is not available, carefully remove slotted ignition coil sleeves from cylinder head cover holes, then remove spark plugs.

Other Mechanical Maintenance

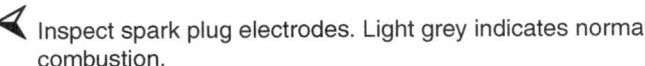

◀ Inspect spark plug electrodes. Light grey indicates normal combustion.

– Installation is reverse of removal, bearing in mind the following:
  • Lightly lubricate new spark plug threads with copper-based anti-seize compound.
  • Thread plugs into cylinder head by hand to prevent cross-threading.
  • Reinsert or replace slotted ignition coil sleeves if removed.
  • Carefully insert ignition coils in spark plug wells and reattach electrical connectors.

Tightening torque	
Spark plug to cylinder head	23 ± 3 Nm (18 ± 2 ft-lb)

OTHER MECHANICAL MAINTENANCE

Differential oil level, checking

The E83 front and rear differentials are filled with lifetime oil that ordinarily does not need to be changed. BMW recommends using only a specially formulated synthetic gear oil (SAF-XO) that is available through an authorized BMW dealer parts department.

See **311 Front Axle Differential** or **331 Rear Axle Differential** for differential fluid service.

Transfer case oil, checking

The E83 transfer case is filled with lifetime oil that ordinarily does not need to be changed. If an oil wear fault is present, the oil should be changed and VTG adaptations reset. See **270 Transfer Case** for more information.

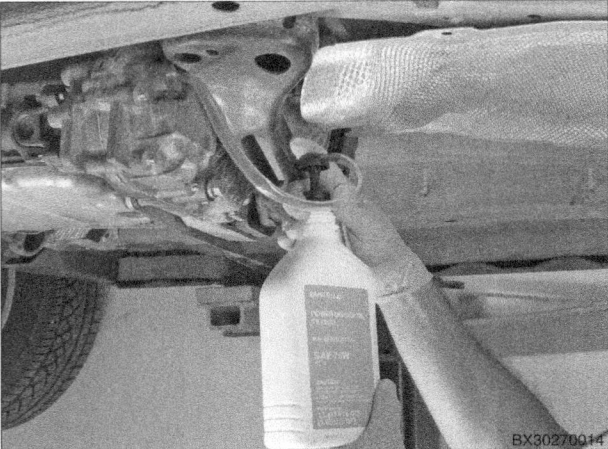

◀ BMW recommends using only a specially formulated lubricant TF0870 (BMW part no. 83 22 0 397 244), available through an authorized BMW dealer parts department.

Drive axle joint (CV joint) boots, inspecting

Inspect CV joint protective boots for cracks and damage. If the rubber boots fail, water and dirt that enter the joint quickly damage it.

Areas where leaks are most likely to occur are around drive shaft and drive axle mounting flanges.

CV boot replacement is covered in **331 Rear Axle Differential**.

Exhaust system, inspecting

Exhaust system life varies widely according to driving habits and environmental conditions. Scheduled maintenance of the exhaust system is limited to inspection.

Check that rubber hangers are in good condition and that system does not contact body.

Check for restrictions due to dents or kinks. Check for weakness or perforation. See **180 Exhaust System**.

Fuel tank and fuel lines, inspecting

– Inspect fuel tank and fuel lines for damage or leaks.

– Check for fuel leaks in engine compartment or fuel odors in passenger compartment.

– Check for evaporative emissions hoses that may have become disconnected. Check carefully at charcoal canister and leakage diagnosis pump. See **130 Fuel Injection** and **160 Fuel Tank and Fuel Pump** for component locations and additional information.

Oxygen sensors

Replacement of oxygen sensors at specified intervals ensures that the engine and emission control system continue to operate as designed. If any of the four oxygen sensors become sluggish or fail, the check engine light will be illuminated and a DTC will be stored in the DME. Oxygen sensor replacement is covered in **180 Exhaust System**.

Suspension and steering, inspecting

Check suspension and steering moving parts for wear and excessive play. Inspect ball joint and tie-rod rubber seals and boots for cracks or tears that allow the entry of dirt and water.

See also:

• **310 Front Suspension**.

• **320 Steering and Wheel Alignment**

• **330 Rear Suspension**

Tires, checking inflation pressure

Correct tire pressures are important to handling and stability, fuel economy, and tire wear. Tire pressure changes with temperature. Check tire pressures often during seasonal temperature changes. Correct inflation pressures can be found on driver door pillar and in the owner's manual. Note that tire pressure specifications are higher when the vehicle is more heavily loaded.

WARNING—

• *Do not inflate any tire to a pressure higher than maximum inflation pressure listed on the sidewall. Use care when adding air to warm tires. Warm tire pressures can increase as much as 4 psi (0.3 bar) over their cold pressures.*

Tires, rotating

BMW does not recommend tire rotation. Due to the vehicle's suspension design, the front tires begin to wear first at the outer shoulder and the rear tires begin to wear first at the middle of the tread or inner shoulder. Rotating the tires may adversely affect road handling and tire grip.

Transmission fluid service

Automatic transmission fluid has a service interval of approximately 100,000 miles. If service or repairs have to be made to the transmission or ATF cooler, use only the approved transmission fluid.

Check ATF level if there is evidence of a leak, a complaint related to fluid level or after transmission repairs.

 The automatic transmission is not equipped with a dipstick. Checking ATF level is an involved procedure that includes measuring and maintaining a specified ATF temperature during the checking procedure. See **240 Automatic Transmission** for fluid service information.

Manual transmissions are provided with lifetime lubrication. No oil change is required for the entire service life of these transmissions. If repairs have to be made to the transmission or transmission oil cooler, use only the approved lifetime lube oil. See **230 Manual Transmission** for fluid service information.

Wheels, aligning

BMW recommends checking the front and rear alignment once a year and whenever new tires are installed.

See **320 Steering and Wheel Alignment**.

BX30240002

BODY AND INTERIOR MAINTENANCE

Body, hinges, locks, lubricating

— Lubricate door locks and lock cylinders with an oil that contains graphite.

— Lubricate body and door hinges, hood latch and door check rods with SAE 30 or SAE 40 engine oil.

— Lubricate seat runners with multipurpose grease.

— If door weather-strips are sticking, lubricate them with silicone spray or talcum powder.

— Lubricate engine hood release and hood release cable with spray grease.

> **CAUTION—**
> • *Do not apply oil to rubber parts.*

Exterior washing

The longer dirt is left on the paint, the greater the risk of damaging the finish, either by scratching or by the chemical effect dirt particles may have on the painted surface.

— Wash with a mixture of lukewarm water and vehicle wash product.

— Rinse using plenty of clear water.

— Wipe body dry with a soft cloth towel or chamois to prevent water-spotting.

> **CAUTION—**
> • *Do not wash vehicle in direct sunlight.*
> • *If engine hood is warm, allow it to cool.*
> • *Beads of water not only leave spots when dried rapidly by the sun or heat from the engine, but also can act as small magnifying glasses and burn spots into the finish.*

Polishing

— Use paint polish only if finish assumes a dull look after long service.

— Use polish to remove tar spots and tarnish. Afterwards apply coat of wax to protect clean finish.

> **CAUTION—**
> • *Do not use abrasive polish or cleaners on aluminum trim or accessories.*

Waxing

— For a long-lasting, protective and glossy finish, apply a hard wax after the vehicle has been washed and dried. Use carnauba or synthetic based products.

Waxing is not needed after every washing. You can tell when waxing is required by looking at the finish when it is wet. If the water coats the paint in smooth sheets instead of forming beads that roll off, a new coat of wax is needed. Do not apply wax to black trim pieces, rubber, or other plastic parts.

Interior care

— Remove dirt spots on upholstery with lukewarm soapy water or dry foam cleaner.

— Use spot remover for grease and oil spots. Do not pour cleaning liquid directly on carpet or fabric. Dampen clean cloth and rub carefully, starting at edge of the spot and working inward.

WARNING—
• *Do not use gasoline, naphtha, or other flammable substances.*

Leather upholstery and trim

Clean leather upholstery periodically. Use slightly damp cotton or wool cloth to get rid of dirt in creases and pores that can cause brittleness and premature aging. On heavily soiled areas, use a specially formulated leather cleaner. Dry trim and upholstery completely using a soft cloth. Regular use of a good quality leather conditioner reduces drying and cracking of leather.

Seat belts

Dirt and other abrasive particles may damage seat belt webbing. To clean seat belts, use a mild soap solution. Inspect condition of belt webbing and function of retractor mechanisms. See **720 Seat Belts**.

WARNING—
• *Do not clean seat belt webbing using dry cleaning chemicals, bleach or other strong cleaning agents.*
• *Allow wet belts to dry before allowing them to retract.*

Special cleaning

Remove tar and insect spots with a bug and tar remover. Do not use gasoline, kerosene, nail polish remover, or other unsuitable solvents. A bit of baking soda dissolved in the wash water will facilitate their removal. This method can also be used to remove tree sap spots.

Underbody visual inspection

Inspect the following for leaks or damage:

- Engine
- Transmission
- Fuel system
- Cooling and heating systems
- Brake system
- Exhaust system

A small amount of dampness is considered normal in some cases, especially around axle and pulley seals since the leaking fluid helps the seal work properly. On the other hand, expensive repairs can be avoided by prompt repair of minor fluid leaks. Judgement and experience are required to distinguish among the different kinds of fluid leaks.

Inspect underside of vehicle for damage caused by normal wear and tear or by driving over road debris. Whenever vehicle is raised on a lift, inspect underbody, wheel wells and sill or rocker panels for damage to underbody sealants and coatings. Also inspect after major repairs to vehicle systems.

Repair damage or defects found. Only use wax-based or tar-based anti-corrosion compounds as specified. Do not use oil-based anti-corrosion sprays due to possible incompatibility with factory applied protection.

Washing chassis

Periodically wash underside of vehicle, especially in winter, to help prevent accumulation of road salt and rust.

The best time to wash the underside is just after the vehicle has been driven in wet conditions. Spray the chassis with a powerful jet of water. Commercial or self-service vehicle washes may not be best for this, as they may recycle the salt-contaminated water.

Windshield wiper blade maintenance

Common problems with windshield wipers include streaking or sheeting, water drops after wiping, and blade chatter. Streaking is usually caused when wiper blades are coated with road film or vehicle wash wax. Clean blades using soapy water. If cleaning the blades does not cure the problem, they should be replaced. BMW recommends replacing the wiper blades twice a year, before and after the cold season.

 To replace wiper blades:

- Switch ignition ON. Turn wipers ON briefly to bring wiper blades to center of windshield. Switch ignition OFF and remove ignition key.
- Pivot wiper arm off windshield.
- Position wiper blade approximately perpendicular to wiper arm.
- Depress retaining tab (**arrow**) and slide blade out of arm.

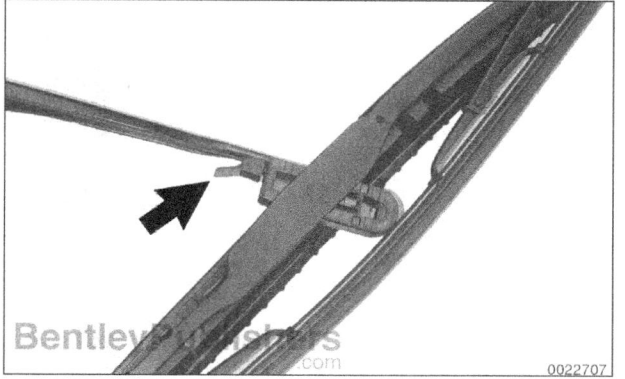

See **611 Wipers and Washers** for more information.

MAINTENANCE TABLES

The service indicator (SIA IV) signals the need for maintenance and inspection. See **Service interval indicator (SIA IV)** at the beginning of this repair group for additional information.

Oil service tasks are listed in **Table d**. Inspection I tasks are listed in **Table e**. Inspection II includes Inspection II plus additional tasks. Inspection II tasks are in **Table f**.

For reference, Inspection I is normally due at intervals with a maximum of 30,000 miles or 24 months. Inspection II is normally due at intervals with a maximum of 60,000 miles or 48 months.

Except where noted, the maintenance items listed apply to all models and model years covered by this manual. The number in the "additional repair information" column refers to the repair group in this manual where additional information can be found.

Table d. Oil service

	Tools required	New parts required	Warm engine required	Dealer service recommended	Additional repair information
Engine compartment maintenance					
Change oil and oil filter.	*	*	*		020
Replace cabin air microfilter.		*			020
Under vehicle maintenance					
Check overall thickness of front and rear brake pads. If replacing: Examine brake disc surface. Clean brake pad contact points in calipers. Grease wheel centering hubs. Check thickness of parking brake linings when replacing rear brake pads. Check operation of parking brake and adjust as necessary.	*				340
Check and adjust tire pressures, including spare.	*				020
Reset service indicator.	*				020

Table e. Inspection I service

	Tools required	New parts required	Warm engine required	Dealer service recommended	Additional repair information
Engine compartment and under vehicle maintenance					
Read out on-board diagnostic (OBD II) fault codes.	*				100, OBD
Change oil and oil filter.	*	*	*		020
Check transmission, differentials and transfer case for external leaks.	*				240, 270
Check CV joint boots for damage or leaks.					311, 331
Visually check fuel tank, fuel lines, and connections for leaks.					160

Table e. Inspection I service (continued)

	Tools required	New parts required	Warm engine required	Dealer service recommended	Additional repair information
Check condition, position, and mounting of exhaust system. Visually check and adjust if necessary.					180
Check power steering system for leaks. Check power steering fluid level and adjust if necessary.					020, 320
Check steering rack and tie rods for tightness. Check condition of front axle joints and boots, steering linkage, and steering shaft joints.	*				320
Check overall thickness of front and rear brake pads. If replacement is necessary: Examine brake disc surface. Clean brake pad contact points in calipers. Grease wheel centering hubs. Check thickness of parking brake linings when replacing rear brake shoes. Check operation of parking brake and adjust as necessary.	*				340
Check brake system connections and lines for leaks, damage, and incorrect positioning.					340
Check front control arm bushings for damage or wear.					310
Inspect entire body according to terms of rust perforation limited warranty. (Must be performed at least every two years).					
Check engine cooling system and heater hose connections for leaks. Check coolant level and antifreeze protection level. Add coolant as necessary.					170
Check condition of engine accessory belts. Replace if necessary.					020
Check washer fluid level and antifreeze protection. Add washer fluid as necessary.					611
Replace cabin air microfilter. (Note: reduce replacement intervals in dusty operation conditions).		*			020
Body/electrical					
Check battery state of charge.	*				121
Check operation of: headlights, parking lights, back-up lights, license plate lights, interior lights, glove box illumination, engine compartment light, trunk light, turn signals, emergency flashers, brake lights.					630
Check operation of horn and headlight dimmer switch					630
Check wipers and windshield washer system. Check aim of washer jets and adjust if necessary.					611
Check condition and function of seat belts.					720
Visually examine airbags for torn covers, obvious damage or attachment of decals, decorations or accessories.					721
Check central locking system and double lock.					515
Check operation and condition of doors, hood, and tailgate.					410, 515
Check air-conditioner operation.					640
Check heater, air-conditioner blower and rear window defogger operation.					640

Maintenance Tables

Table e. Inspection I service (continued)

	Tools required	New parts required	Warm engine required	Dealer service recommended	Additional repair information
Check warning and indicator lights, Check Control.					620
Check operation of rear view mirrors.					
Check and adjust tire pressures, including spare. Check condition of tires, tread wear pattern; in case of uneven wear, perform wheel alignment.	*				020
Road test					
Check braking performance, steering, heating and air-conditioner operation.					
Check clutch / manual transmission or automatic transmission operation.					
Reset service indicator.	*				020

Table f. Inspection II service (includes all service from Inspection I)

	Tools required	New parts required	Warm engine required	Dealer service recommended	Additional repair information
Engine compartment maintenance					
Replace air filter element. (Note: reduce replacement intervals in dusty operating conditions).		*			020
Brake system maintenance					
Replace brake fluid every 2 years (time interval begins from vehicle production date).	*	*		*	340
Cooling system service					
Replace coolant every 4 years (time interval begins from vehicle production date).	*	*			170
Oxygen sensor service					
Replace oxygen sensor every 120,000 miles.	*	*			180
Spark plug service					
Replace spark plugs every 100,000 miles.	*	*			020
Automatic transmission fluid service					
Replace every 100,000 miles.					
xDrive transfer case service					
Change oil based on VTG oil wear monitoring displayed on factory scan tool	*	*	*	*	270

100 Engine–General

GENERAL

This section covers general information on engines and engine components. See **Table a** for engine application information and specifications.

For specific repair procedures, refer to:

- **020 Maintenance** for engine compartment views and accessory belt service, oil change and air filter service
- **110 Engine Removal and Installation**
- **113 Cylinder Head Removal and Installation**
- **117 Camshaft Timing Chain**
- **119 Lubrication System** for lubrication system description and crankcase seal service
- **120 Ignition System** for ignition coil, camshaft sensor, crankshaft sensor and knock sensor service
- **130, 131 Fuel Injection** for engine management system description and component replacement (based on engine type)
- **170 Radiator and Cooling System** for radiator, coolant pump and coolant service
- **180 Exhaust System** for exhaust manifold, oxygen sensor service

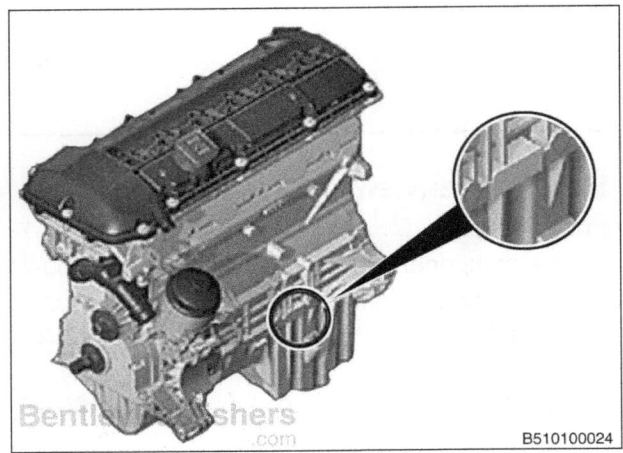

B510100024

Engine ID tag

◄ M54 engine ID tag with engine serial number is on left side of engine block, above engine oil pan.

Engine serial number

B510020074

◄ N52 engine ID tag with engine serial number is on left side of engine block, underneath intake manifold.

Engine applications

Table a. X3 engine applications and specifications							
Year, model	Engine code, type	Displacement cc (cid)	Bore x stroke mm (in)	Comp. ratio	Torque lb-ft @ rpm	Horsepower hp @ rpm	Engine management
2.5 liter 6-cylinder							
2004 - 2006 2.5i	M54B25, double VANOS	2494 (152)	84 x 75 (3.31 x 2.95)	10.5 : 1	180 @ 3500	189 @ 6000	Siemens DME MS 45
3.0 liter 6-cylinder							
2004 - 2006 3.0i	M54B30, double VANOS	2979 (182)	84 x 89.6 (3.31 x 3.53)	10.2 : 1	221 @ 3500	228 @ 5900	Siemens DME MS 45
2007 - 2010 3.0si, xDrive 30i	N52KB30, double VANOS, Valvetronic	2996 (183)	85.0 x 88.0 (3.35 x 3.46)	10.7 : 1	225 @ 2500	260 @ 6600	Siemens MSV80

M54 ENGINE OVERVIEW

Engine introduction

X3 (E83) 2.5 and 3.0 models introduced to the North American market in 2004 came equipped with in-line 6-cylinder normally-aspirated M54 engines. Two levels of performance were available:

- 2494 cc (152 cid) displacement engine in 2.5 models
- 2979 cc (182 cid) displacement engine in 3.0 models

Exhaust
manifolds

Clutch

B510100008

Cylinder block and crankshaft

The cylinder block is cast aluminum alloy ($AlSi_9Cu_3$) with cast iron cylinder liners. The cylinders are exposed on all sides to circulating coolant.

Connecting rods and pistons

The forged steel connecting rods use replaceable split-shell bearings at the crankshaft end and solid bushings at the piston pin end. Connecting rods weight classes are indicated by a color code system.

The pistons are equipped with three rings with two upper compression rings and a lower one-piece oil scraper ring. Full floating piston pins are retained with circlips.

Graphite coating is used on piston skirts to reduce friction and noise.

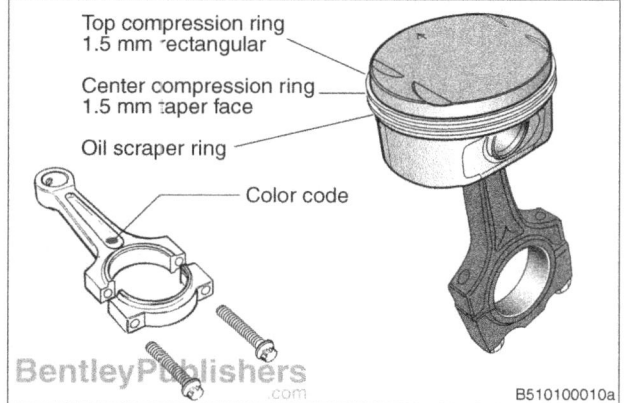

Top compression ring
1.5 mm rectangular

Center compression ring
1.5 mm taper face

Oil scraper ring

Color code

B510100010a

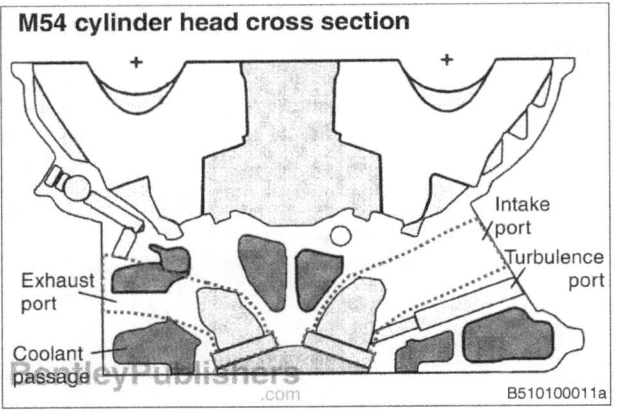

M54 cylinder head cross section

Intake port

Turbulence port

Exhaust port

Coolant passage

B510100011a

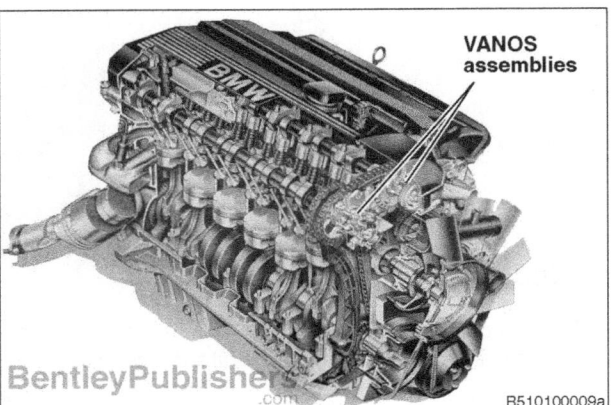

VANOS assemblies

B510100009a

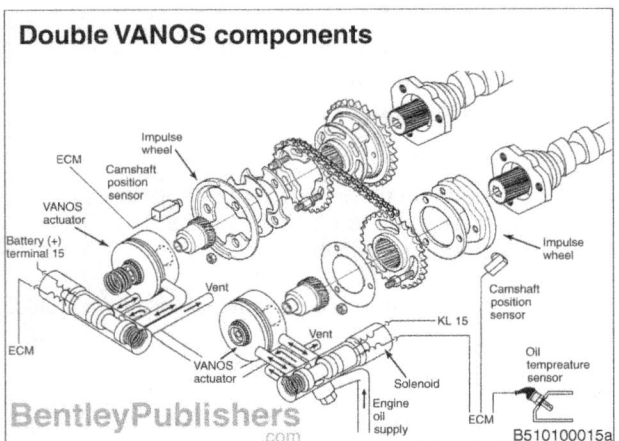

Double VANOS components

ECM

Impulse wheel

Camshaft position sensor

VANOS actuator

Battery (+) terminal 15

Vent

ECM

VANOS actuator

Vent

Solenoid

Engine oil supply

KL 15

Impulse wheel

Camshaft position sensor

Oil tempreature sensor

ECM

B510100015a

Cylinder head and valvetrain

◀ Cooling passages in the M54 cylinder head are designed for optimum coolant circulation, allowing the head to operate at lower temperatures than the cylinder block.

The aluminum cylinder head uses chain-driven double overhead camshafts and four valves per cylinder. The cylinder head employs a crossflow design for greater power and efficiency. Intake air enters the combustion chamber from one side while exhaust gasses exit from the other. The spark plugs are centrally located down the middle of the cylinder head.

Double VANOS

◀ M54 engines are equipped with compact, infinitely variable vane-type VANOS units for both intake and exhaust camshafts. The VANOS system (from the German words *VAriable NOckenwellen Steuerung*) electrohydraulically adjusts valve timing for enhanced mid-range performance and improved emissions. VANOS is controlled by the engine control module (ECM), using engine speed, engine load and engine coolant temperature as the primary inputs. Engine oil pressure is used for powering camshaft adjustment.

◀ Engine oil pressure is used to position the VANOS actuators. Oil pressure is fed from the engine oil pump up to the VANOS solenoids; oil drains back to the sump as the camshafts are adjusted during engine operation.

With the engine off, the base setting of the camshafts is as follows:
- Intake camshaft: Retarded
- Exhaust camshaft: Advanced

This is also the fail-safe position in case of an electronic control failure. Both camshafts are held in these positions by oil pressure from the engine oil pump. The exhaust camshaft is held additionally by a spring in the VANOS actuator.

The engine is equipped with static Hall-effect camshaft sensors so that camshaft positions are recognized as soon as the ignition is switched ON, before the engine is started.

With the engine running, the ECM makes an initial camshaft timing adjustment based on oil temperature, oil pressure and engine rpm. Following this initial setting, engine rpm, throttle position signal, intake air temperature and engine coolant temperature are used to adjust camshaft timing.

When the ECM detects that the camshafts are in the desired position, the solenoids are modulated at 100 - 220 Hz, maintaining oil pressure on both sides of the actuators to maintain camshaft timing.

In addition to increasing engine power output, double VANOS offers the following advantages:

• Increased torque at lower and medium rpm ranges

• More efficient combustion and improved idle quality

• Internal EGR in part-load range for lower NO$_x$ emissions

• Quicker warm-up cycle for catalytic converter and faster reduction in emissions

• Overall improved fuel economy

See **117 Camshaft timing chain** for VANOS system repairs.

Intake system

◀ The intake manifold, made of molded plastic, is configured as two sets of three runners. This design enhances low end torque by changing the intake air flow configuration for varying engine speeds. This helps achieve optimum torque throughout the entire rpm range.

During engine operation, a closed resonance valve gives the intake air charge the dynamic effect of long intake runners at low to mid-range engine speeds (up to 3750 rpm). This helps increase torque.

During mid-range to high speed operation (above 4100 rpm), the solenoid is de-energized and the resonance valve is sprung open. This allows intake air to be drawn through both resonance tubes, providing the air volume necessary for additional power at the upper rpm range.

The rpm for resonance valve activation varies slightly depending on temperature.

In addition, when the valve is closed, a dynamic effect is produced. For example, as intake air is flowing into cylinder 1, intake valves close. This blocks onrushing air. Cylinder 1 air flow stops and expands backward (resonance back pulse) to fill cylinder 5. The resonance wave along with the intake velocity enhances cylinder filling.

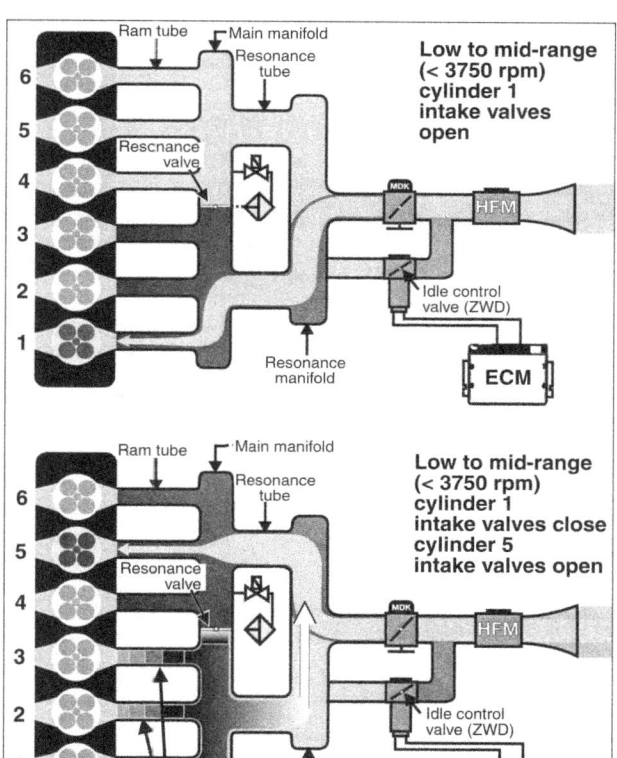

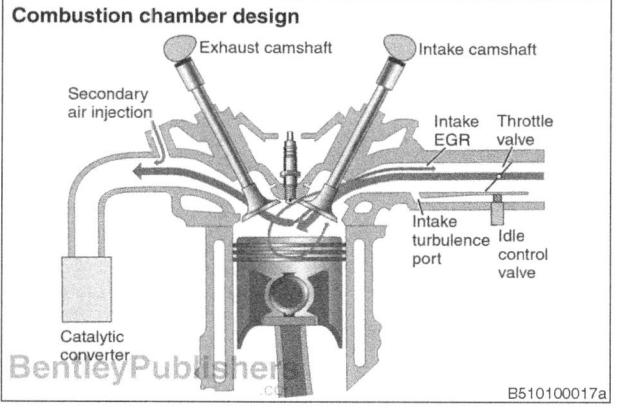

◀ The intake manifold includes intake turbulence ports. The 5.5 mm (0.217 in.) turbulence ports channel idle and low speed air directly from the idle speed control valve to one intake valve of each cylinder.

Routing intake air to one intake valve per cylinder causes the air charge to swirl in the cylinder. Together with the high flow rate of intake air across the small (5.5 mm) port, intake fluctuations are reduced for more stable combustion.

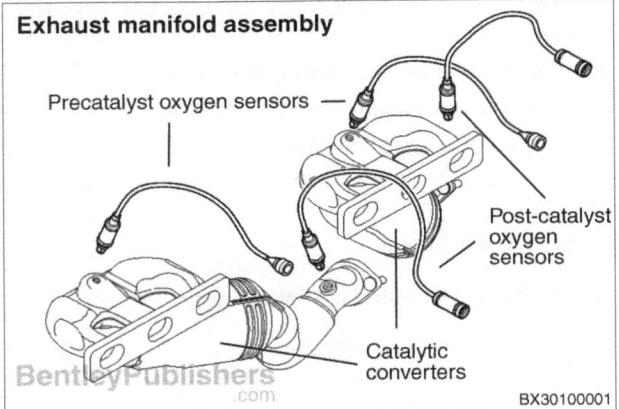

Exhaust manifold assembly

Precatalyst oxygen sensors

Post-catalyst oxygen sensors

Catalytic converters

BX30100001

Exhaust manifolds

◄ Each exhaust manifold assembly incorporates a catalytic converter. The converters are mounted close to the engine for faster heat up and light off. Pre- and post-catalyst oxygen sensors are a mounted in each exhaust manifold.

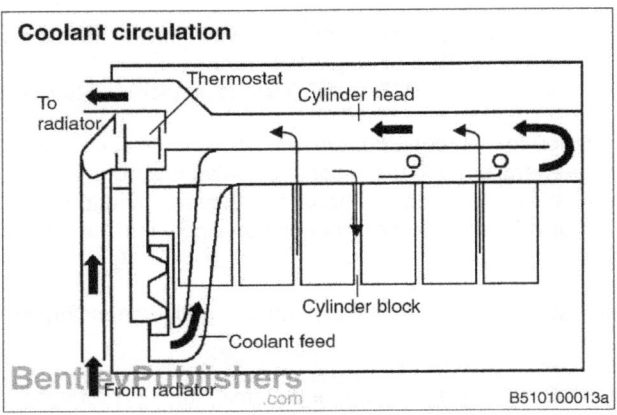

Coolant circulation

Thermostat

To radiator

Cylinder head

Cylinder block

Coolant feed

From radiator

B510100013a

Cooling system

◄ The cooling system is designed so that coolant flows directly from the coolant pump to the cylinder head. The coolant is fed from the coolant pump through a cast coolant feed passage to the rear of the cylinder head. From there it flows forward to the thermostat housing, radiator and heater valve.

X3 models are equipped with a DME-controlled electric cooling fan. See **170 Radiator and Cooling System** for additional information

Lubrication system

The lubrication system is pressurized whenever the engine is running. The oil pump draws oil through a pickup in the bottom of the oil pan, then forces it through a replaceable oil filter and into the engine oil passages.

Oilways in the cylinder head provide lubrication for the camshafts and valvetrain.

◄ The chain-driven oil pump is bolted to the bottom of the cylinder block inside the oil pan. A pressure relief valve limits the maximum system pressure. A bypass valve prevents the oil filter from bursting and insures engine lubrication should the filter become plugged.

See **119 Lubrication System** for additional information.

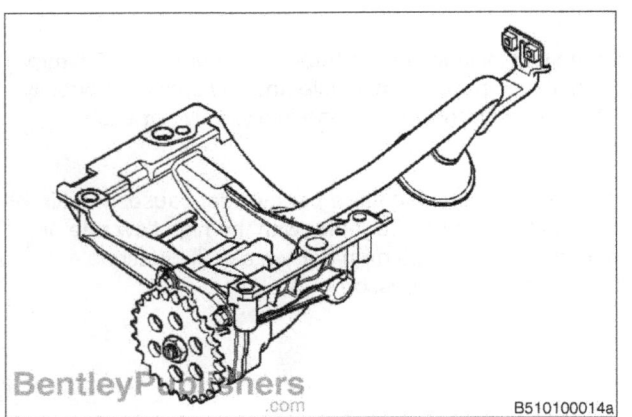

B510100014a

N52 ENGINE OVERVIEW

Engine introduction

 Beginning with the introduction of the mid life cycle update (LCI), X3 models were equipped with a 3.0 liter in-line 6-cylinder normally-aspirated N52 engine.

The N52 engine features the following:

- 4-valves-per-cylinder friction-optimized components
- Two-piece crankcase
- Composite magnesium-aluminum engine block structure
- Trapezoidal weight-optimized connecting rods
- Aluminum silicon (AluSil) cylinder head
- Timing case integrated in crankcase and cylinder head
- Cylinder head gasket with silicon sealing lip
- Valvetronic system
- Weight-optimized double VANOS system
- Volumetric flow-controlled oil pump
- Electrically controlled coolant pump
- Crankcase ventilation with integrated heater
- 3-stage variable intake manifold or DISA

Crankcase components

Crankcase

◀ The upper section of the crankcase consists of an aluminum / silicon (AluSil) insert cast in a magnesium alloy. The timing chain housing is cast as an integral part of the engine block.

N52 engine

BentleyPublishers
.com

B510100001

Timing chain housing

BentleyPublishers
.com

B510100005

Crankcase components

◁ The AluSil cylinder bores are not equipped with iron cylinder liners. Therefore, the cylinder bores cannot be machined.

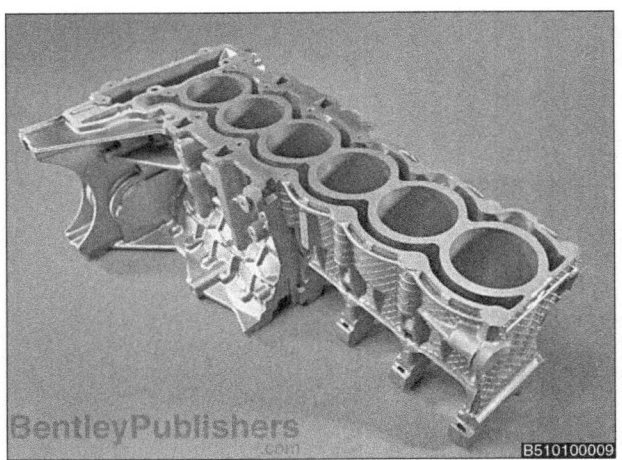

◁ The AluSil insert has threaded bores for transmission, cylinder head and crankshaft main bearing bolts.

The insert provides coolant passages as well. This is to prevent coolant contact with the magnesium portion of the engine block.

Machined groove

◁ The lower section of the crankcase is a bedplate structure made of magnesium with sintered steel inlays (**arrow**) for main bearing support. The magnesium structure is used to increase crankcase rigidity and the steel inlays take up forces which are not suitable for magnesium alone.

A liquid sealant is injected under high pressure into a machined groove between upper and lower crankcase sections. This detail is critical to understand in service applications. As an example, when the crankcase main seals are replaced, a special sealant is injected into the seal grooves and crankcase seams.

Crankshaft

 The crankshaft is cast iron with 7 main bearing journals. The trigger wheel for the crankshaft sensor is between cylinders 5 and 6. Due to the design of the timing chain housing (one piece with the crankcase), the crankshaft snout is modified to facilitate timing chain module removal and installation during service.

Connecting rods

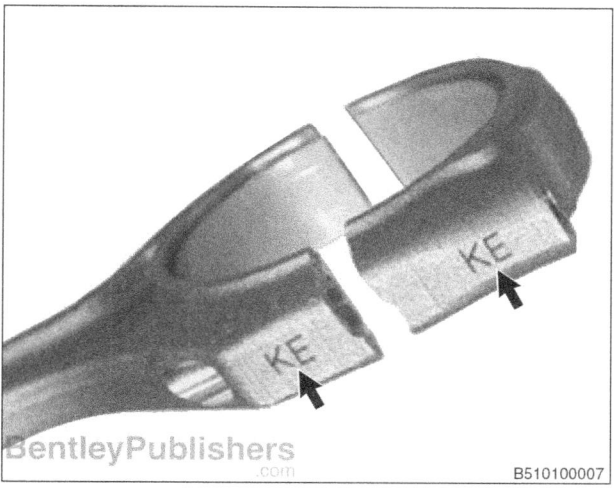

 The big end of each connecting rod is cracked to allow centering of the bearing cap without the use of dowel pins. This contributes to the overall weight reduction.

Pairing codes (**arrows**) are stamped on each connecting rod to match the correct rod cap to the connecting rod.

The small end of the rod is tapered, reducing weight without affecting strength.

The connecting rods are separated into weight categories and can only be replaced as a set.

Pistons

The pistons are manufactured from aluminum and have 4 valve reliefs. The undersides of the pistons are cooled with oil spray jets.

Cylinder head and valvetrain

Cylinder head

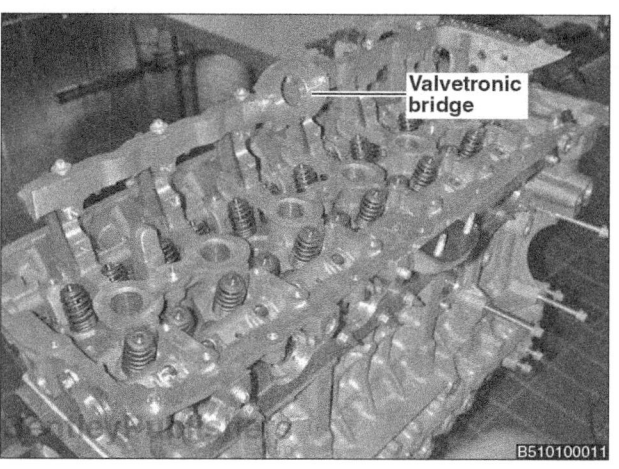

Valvetronic bridge

The N52 engine uses an AluSil cylinder head with a cast bridge to mount the Valvetronic actuator motor.

VANOS unit

Front view   Rear view

BentleyPublishers.com

B510100004

Variable camshaft timing (VANOS)

◄ N52 engines are equipped with compact, infinitely variable vane-type VANOS units for both intake and exhaust camshafts. The VANOS system (from the German words *VAriable NOckenwellen Steuerung*) electrohydraulically adjusts valve timing for enhanced mid-range performance and improved emissions. VANOS is controlled by the engine control module (ECM), using engine speed, engine load and engine coolant temperature as the primary inputs. Engine oil pressure is used for powering camshaft adjustment.

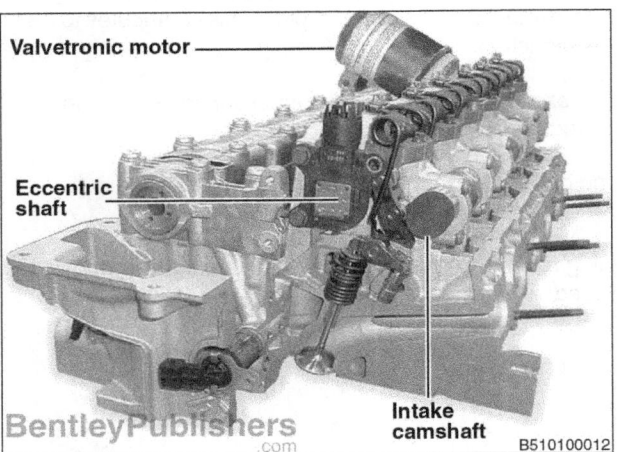

Valvetronic motor

Eccentric shaft

Intake camshaft

BentleyPublishers.com

B510100012

Valvetronic

◄ N52 engine load is controlled via the valve timing gear. This system, called Valvetronic, varies valve lift rather than throttle valve opening to control engine power and torque. It offers the following:

- Increased engine efficiency.
- Improved emission values.
- Top engine speed to 7,000 rpm.
- Power output of 85 hp / liter displacement.
- Engine torque of 100 Nm / liter displacement over a broad engine speed range.
- Reduced CO_2 emissions.

Intake manifold

Variable intake manifold (DISA)

◄ X3 models with N52 engines are equipped with 3-stage variable intake runners in a system known as DISA.

Valves in the intake manifold are driven by DISA electric motors and gear mechanisms. DISA actuators are driven by pulse width-modulated signals from the engine control module (ECM). Each valve has only two possible positions: Open or closed.

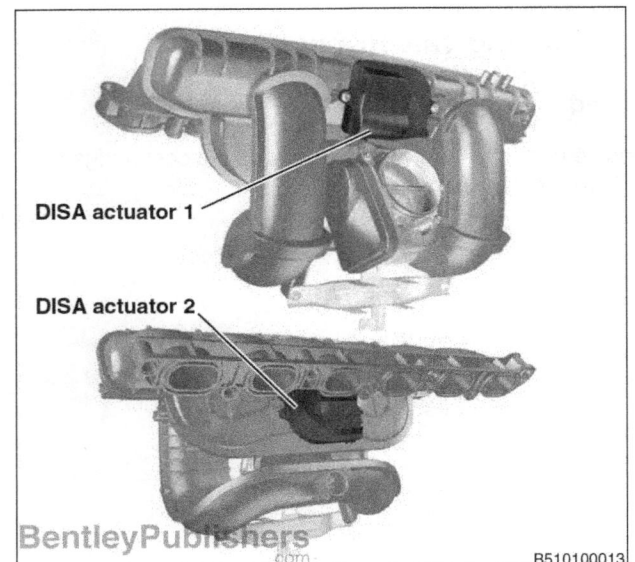

DISA actuator 1

DISA actuator 2

BentleyPublishers.com

B510100013

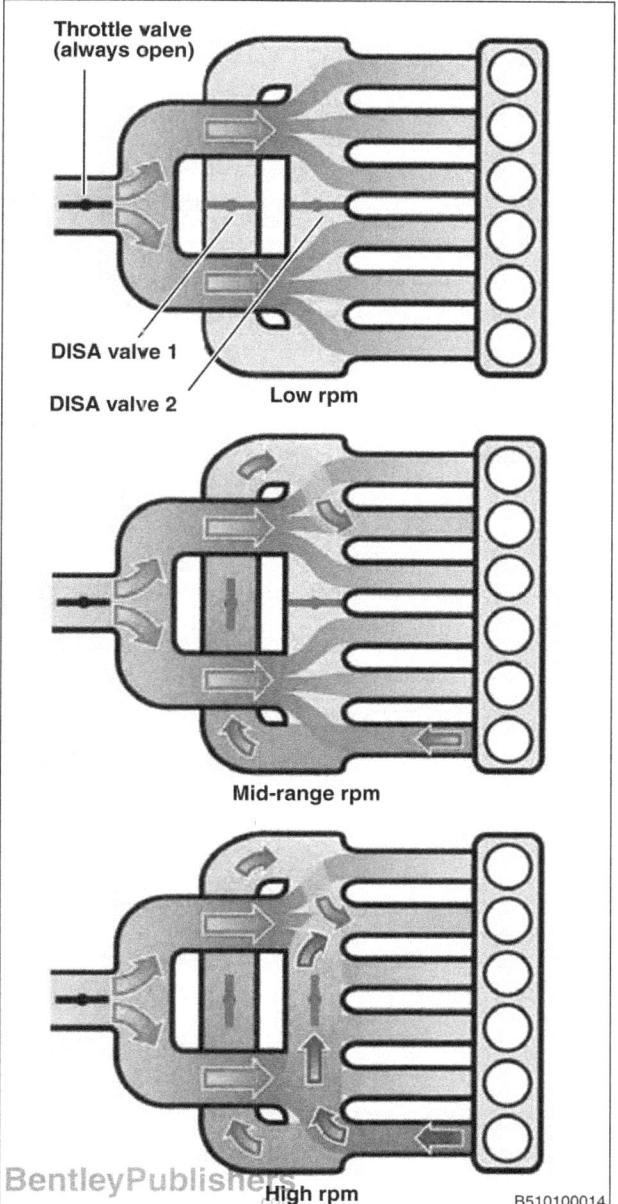

Throttle valve
(always open)

DISA valve 1

DISA valve 2

Low rpm

Mid-range rpm

High rpm

B510100014

◀ Switched-length intake manifold runners help achieve a high torque over the entire engine speed range using two DISA valves and an overflow pipe in the intake.

- **Stage 1**: Idle and low engine speed range. Both DISA valves closed. Intake air flows past throttle valve into resonance pipe. Air flow is split in resonance pipe and is further routed via collector runner and intake resonating runners into individual cylinders. In this way, a relatively large air mass is made available to cylinders.

- **Stage 2**: Medium engine speed range. DISA valve 2 open. (In this example, cylinder 1 intake valves are just closing.) Air flow produces pressure peaks at closing intake valves. This resonates to next cylinder in firing order, thus improving charge of next cylinder.

- **Stage 3**: High engine speed range. Both DISA valves open. (Again, In this example, cylinder 1 intake valves are just closing.) Pressure peaks ahead of closing intake valves are also utilized in this case. Intake air mass is now routed via resonance, overflow and manifold runners.

Lubrication, vacuum and cooling systems

Lubrication and vacuum systems

VANOS requires a large volume of oil, particularly at low engine speeds. To meet the oiling requirements of the engine, a high volume volumetric-flow controlled oil pump is utilized. The pump is designed to provide the high volume when needed. See **119 Engine Lubrication**.

Valvetronic engine load control requires a wide open throttle under most engine operating conditions, resulting in minimal intake manifold vacuum. In order to operate the brake vacuum booster, an auxiliary vacuum pump is fitted to the engine.

A chain assembly is used to drive the oil pump and brake booster auxiliary vacuum pump sprockets.

1. Auxiliary vacuum pump sprocket bolt
2. Crankshaft sprocket
3. Auxiliary vacuum pump drive sprocket
4. Auxiliary vacuum pump
5. Oil pump sprocket bolt
6. Oil pump drive sprocket
7. Oil pump

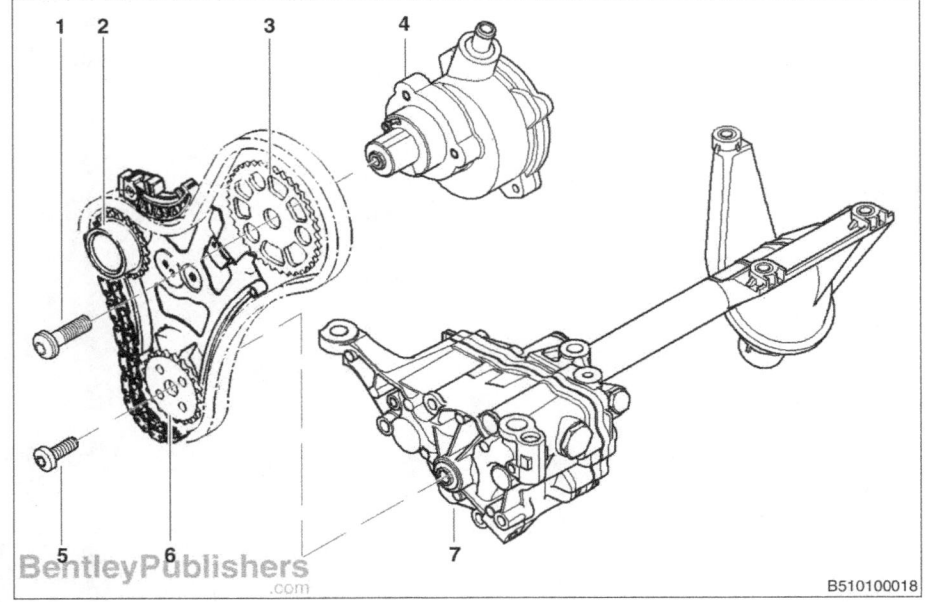

B510100018

Cooling system

◀ The cooling system utilizes a DME-controlled electric coolant pump that minimizes engine power losses and allows for increased fuel economy by a more efficient method of engine heat management.

B510170001

110 Engine Removal and Installation

110

GENERAL

This repair group includes an overview of M54 engine removal and installation.

Transmission removal is required before the engine can be removed.

See also:

- **020 Maintenance for engine cover removal**
- **100 Engine–General for engine codes and applications**
- **121 Battery, Starter, Alternator**
- **170 Radiator and Cooling System**
- **180 Exhaust System**
- **230 Manual Transmission**
- **240 Automatic Transmission**
- **260 Driveshafts**
- **310 Front Suspension**
- **410 Fenders, Engine Hood**

Engine identification

Engine applications and specifications are detailed in **100 Engine–General**.

Table a. Engine identification		
Engine designation	**Year, model**	**Identifying feature**
M54	2004 - 2006 2.5i, 3.0i	2 upper engine covers
N52	2007 - 2010 3.0si, xDrive 30i	Black plastic cylinder head cover

Warnings and Cautions

WARNING—

- *The fuel system is designed to retain pressure even when the ignition is OFF. When working with the fuel system, loosen fuel lines slowly to allow residual fuel pressure to dissipate. Avoid spraying fuel.*

- *Before beginning any work on the fuel system, place a fire extinguisher in the vicinity of the work area.*

- *Fuel is highly flammable. When working around fuel, do not disconnect any wires that could cause electrical sparks. Do not smoke or work near heaters or other fire hazards.*

- *Loosen the fuel tank cap to release pressure in the tank before working on the tank or lines.*

- *When disconnecting a fuel hose, wrap a shop towel around the end of the hose to prevent fuel spray.*

- *Do not use a work light with an incandescent bulb near any fuel. Fuel may spray on the hot bulb causing a fire.*

- *Make sure the work area is properly ventilated.*

CAUTION—

- *If the MIL (malfunction indicator light, also called Check Engine or Service Engine Soon light) is illuminated, see* **OBD On-Board Diagnostics** *for DME fault code information.*

- *If other system faults are indicated by an illuminated ABS, SRS or DSC warning light, see the appropriate repair group in this manual or an authorized BMW dealer for more information on fault codes.*

- *Magnesium crankcase requires aluminum fasteners.*

- *Steel fasteners may not be used in place of aluminum fasteners due to the threat of corrosion.*

- *Aluminum fasteners may be marked with blue paint. Use a magnet to identify.*

- *Replace aluminum fasteners each time they are loosened.*

ENGINE REMOVAL AND INSTALLATION

Be sure to cover painted surfaces before beginning the removal procedure. As an aid to installation, label components, wires and hoses before removing them. Do not reuse gaskets, O-rings or seals during reassembly.

> **WARNING—**
> • Due to risk of personal injury, be sure the engine is cold before beginning the removal procedure.

Engine, removing and installing (M54 engine)

NOTE—
• The following procedure shows an M54 engine, N52 engine removal is similar.

— Place hood in service position. See **410 Fenders, Engine Hood**.

— Disconnect negative (–) cable from battery.

> **CAUTION—**
> • Prior to disconnecting the battery, read the battery disconnection cautions in **001 Warnings and Cautions**.

— Remove air cleaner housing and fresh air ducts. See **130 Fuel Injection**.

— Remove brace from strut towers. See **310 Front Suspension**.

— Remove Housing for interior ventilation microfilter. See **640 Heating and Air-conditioning**.

◄ Working in E-box, detach engine wiring harness connectors from ECM, transmission control module, engine electronics fuse carrier and other connectors (**arrows**).

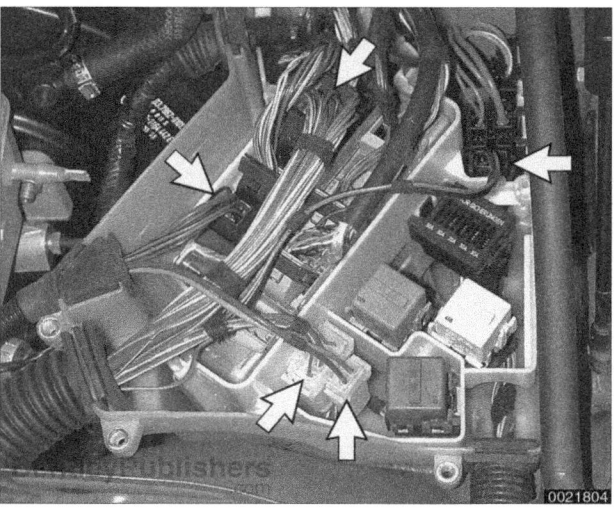

Engine, removing and installing (M54 engine)

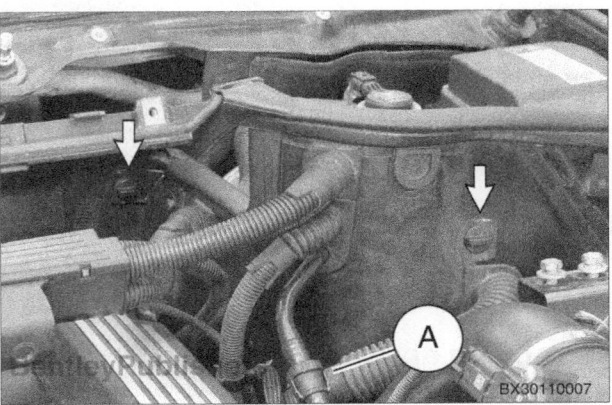

◀ Remove left partition wall:

- Remove rubber seal from top of heater bulkhead.
- Release vacuum line (**A**) for power brake booster. Disconnect line from power brake booster and remove from partition wall with electrical wiring.
- Release plastic locks (**arrows**) and pull trim slightly forward.
- Pull partition wall up to remove.

◀ Remove heater bulkhead:

- Remove fasteners (**arrows**).
- Lift heater bulkhead out and up to remove.

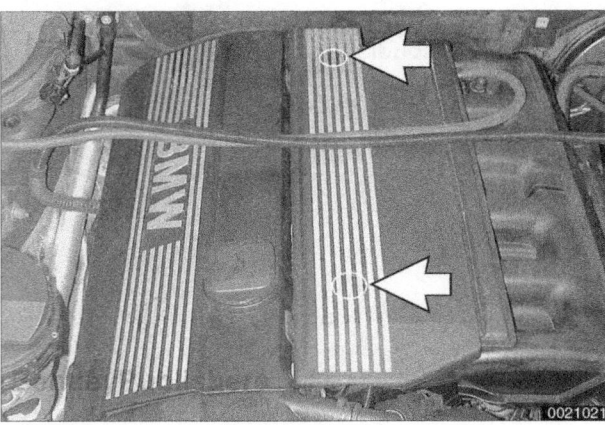

◀ Remove engine cover.

– Raise vehicle and support safely.

> **WARNING—**
> • *Make sure vehicle is stable and well supported at all times. Use a professional automotive lift or jack stands.*

– Remove underbody splash shield.

– Remove front suspension reinforcement plate. See **310 Front Suspension**.

– Remove exhaust system. See **180 Exhaust System**.

– Remove transmission. See **230 Manual Transmission**, or **240 Automatic Transmission**.

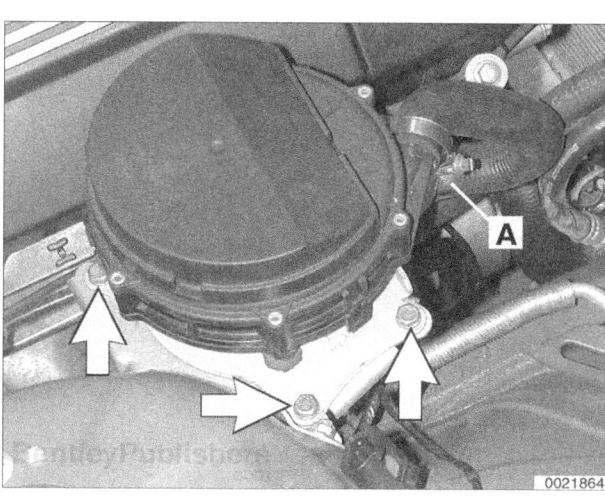

◀ Remove secondary air pump.

- Remove hose at one way valve (**A**).
- Remove bolts at bracket (**arrows**).
- Disconnect electrical harness from bottom of secondary air pump.

◀ Vehicles with automatic transmission:

- Remove transmission fluid line clamping bracket (**arrow**) on left side of engine oil sump.

— Drain engine oil.

— Drain engine coolant.

— Remove electric cooling fan and cowl. See **170 Radiator and Cooling System**.

— Remove radiator. See **170 Radiator and Cooling System**.

— Remove engine accessory belt. See **020 Maintenance**.

— Remove suction and pressure lines from powersteering pump.

- Be prepared to catch dripping fluid. Plug open fluid ports.
- If necessary, remove power steering reservoir for additional clearance when lifting engine.

— Remove pre-catalyst and post-catalyst oxygen sensors. See **180 Exhaust System**.

— Remove windshield washer reservoir. See **611 Wipers and Washers**.

◀ Remove vacuum line (**A**) from vacuum reservoir.

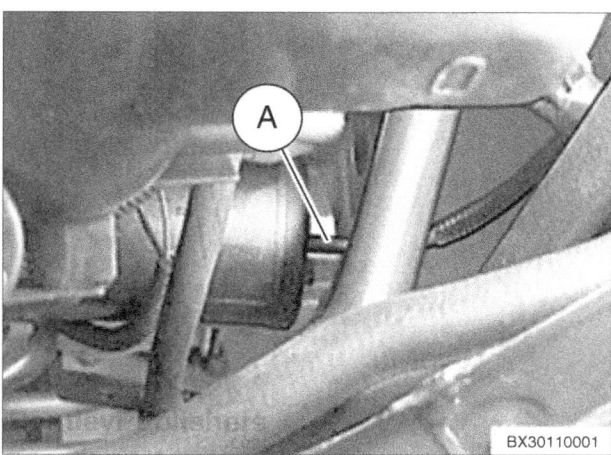

Engine, removing and installing (M54 engine)

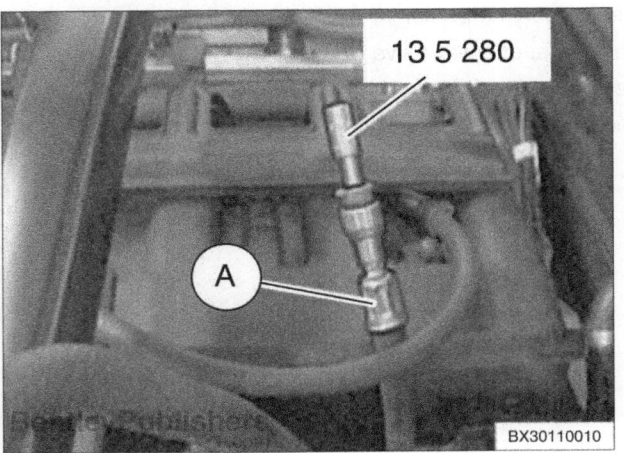

BX30110010

◀ Release fuel line from fuel rail.

- Cap open line using BMW special tool 13 5 280 or equivalent.

> **WARNING—**
> - *Wrap a clean shop towel around fitting before disconnecting. Residual fuel pressure may be present in fuel lines.*

– Disconnect vapor line from fuel tank vent valve.

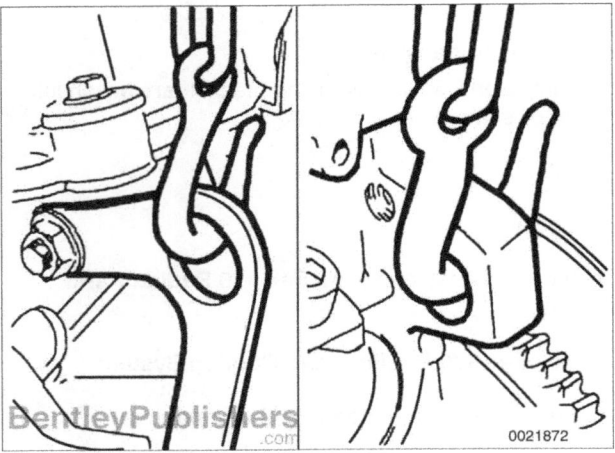

0021872

◀ Install engine lifting device (BMW 11 0 020 or equivalent) to front and rear engine supports. Raise engine until its weight is supported.

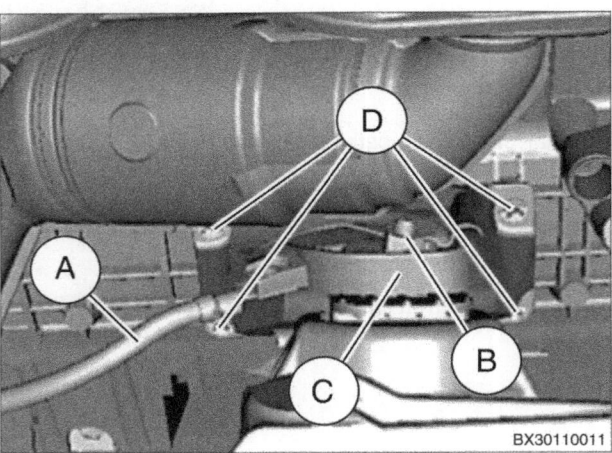

BX30110011

◀ Working at right side engine mount bracket:

- Remove ground cable (**A**) from engine mount suppoprt arm (**C**).
- Remove nut (**B**).
- If necessary, remove fasteners (**D**) and remove support arm.

Engine, removing and installing (M54 engine)

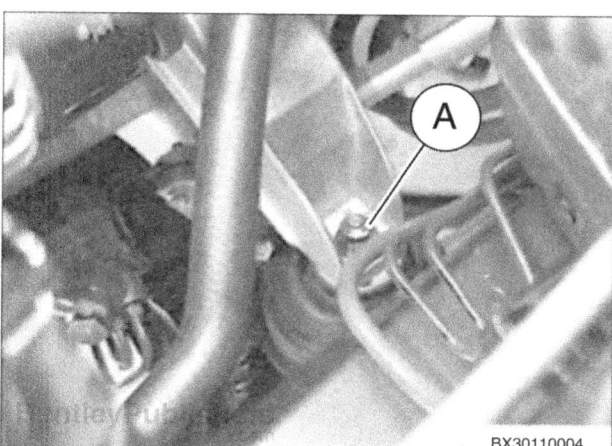

BX30110004

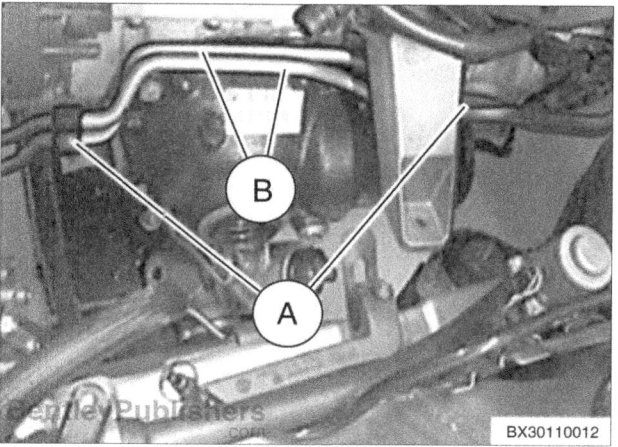

BX30110012

◄ Working at left side of engine, remove nut on left engine mount.

◄ Vehicles equipped with automatic transmission:

- Raise engine about 10 cm (4 in).
- Remove fasteners (**A**).
- Disconnect ATF cooler lines (**B**) from ATF cooler and remove from vehicle. See **170 Cooling System**

— Carefully raise engine out of engine compartment, checking for any wiring, fuel lines, or mechanical parts that might become snagged as engine is removed.

NOTE—

- *Steering shaft area is tight during engine removal. If necessary, disconnect steering shaft from steering gear for additional clearance.*

— Installation is reverse of removal, noting the following:

- Replace gaskets, O-rings and seals.
- Use new fuel injector seals.
- Check that engine drive belts properly engage pulley grooves.
- Inspect O-ring seal between mass air flow sensor and air filter housing. To facilitate reassembly, coat seal with acid-free grease.
- Change engine oil filter, refill oil and check all other fluid levels. See **020 Maintenance**.
- Refill and bleed cooling system. See **170 Radiator and Cooling System**.

CAUTION—

- *Use new fasteners for reinstalling front end reinforcement.*
- *When reattaching throttle assembly harness connector, connector is fully tightened when arrows on connector and plug line up.*

Tightening torques	
Engine mount to support arm (nut)	56 Nm (41 ft-lb)

113 Cylinder Head Removal and Installation

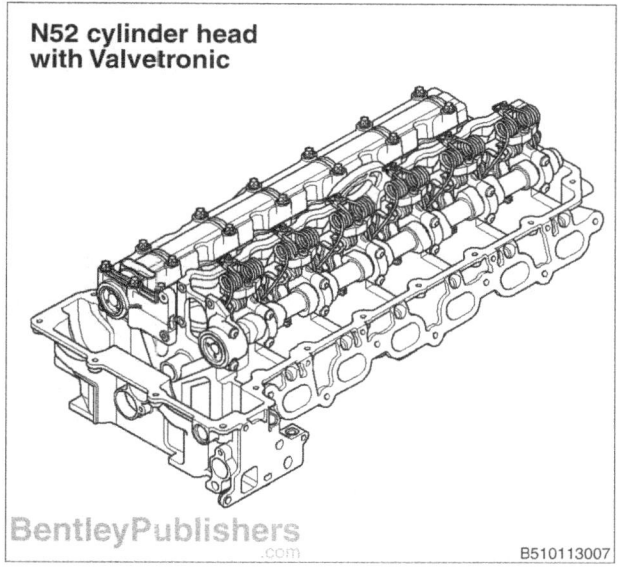

N52 cylinder head with Valvetronic

B510113007

GENERAL

◁ This repair group provides removal and installation procedures for the cylinder head and associated components.

The cylinder head is equipped with variable camshaft timing (referred to as VANO). Special tools and procedures are required to remove and install camshaft adjustment units and to time camshafts. Be sure to read each procedure through before starting work.

See also:

- **020 Maintenance**
- **100 Engine–General** for engine code and application information.
- **117 Camshaft Timing Chain** for camshaft timing chain and camshaft adjuster (VANOS) service
- **130, 131 Fuel Injection** for air filter housing and intake manifold removal
- **170 Radiator and Cooling System**

Engine identification

Engine applications and specifications are detailed in **100 Engine–General**.

Table a. Engine identification

Engine designation	Year, model	Identifying feature
M54	2004 - 2006 2.5i, 3.0i	2 upper engine covers
N52	2007 - 2010 3.0si, xDrive 30i	Black plastic cylinder head cover

Warnings and Cautions

WARNING—

- *To avoid personal injury, be sure the engine is cold before beginning work on engine components.*

- *Use extreme caution when draining and disposing of engine coolant. Coolant is poisonous and lethal to humans and pets. Pets are attracted to coolant because of its sweet smell and taste. Seek medical attention immediately if coolant is ingested.*

- *The fuel system is designed to retain pressure even when the ignition is OFF. When working with the fuel system, loosen fuel lines slowly to allow residual fuel pressure to dissipate. Avoid spraying fuel. Use shop towels to capture leaking fuel.*

- *Before beginning work on the fuel system, place a fire extinguisher in the vicinity of the work area.*

- *Fuel is highly flammable. When working around fuel, do not disconnect wires that could cause electrical sparks. Do not smoke or work near heaters or other fire hazards.*

- *Wear eye protection and protective clothing to avoid injuries from contact with fuel.*

- *Unscrew the fuel tank cap to release pressure in the tank before working on fuel lines.*

- *Do not use a work light with an incandescent bulb near fuel. Fuel may spray on the hot bulb causing a fire.*

- *Make sure the work area is properly ventilated.*

CAUTION—

- *To avoid electrochemical corrosion to engine components made of aluminum-magnesium alloy, do not use steel fasteners. Use aluminum fasteners only.*

- *Aluminum fasteners can be identified by blue paint markings. For reliable identification, test fasteners for aluminum composition with magnet.*

- *Replace aluminum bolts each time they are loosened.*

- *Follow torque instructions, including angle of rotation specifications, when installing aluminum fasteners.*

CYLINDER HEAD (M54 ENGINE)

Cylinder head cover, removing and installing (M54 engine)

— Make sure ignition is OFF. Remove ignition key.

— Remove brace from strut towers. See **310 Front Suspension**.

— Remove housing for interior ventilation microfilter.
See **640 Heating and Air-conditioning**.

— Remove upper engine covers. See **020 Maintenance**.

◄ Working at left front of cylinder head cover, pinch crankcase breather hose clip (**arrows**) and detach hose from cover.

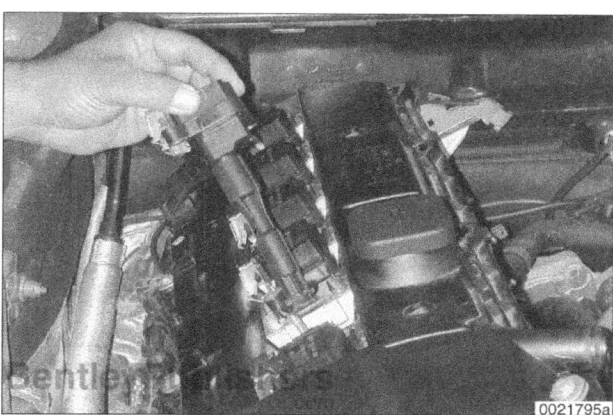

◄ Remove ignition coils:

• Disconnect ignition coil harness connectors.

• Remove coil mounting fasteners.

• Remove coils.

• Remove ground straps.

• Set coil harness to side of engine compartment.

> **CAUTION—**
> • *Note location of ground wires. Failure to reinstall grounds can result in permanent damage to engine control module or ignition system components.*

— Remove cylinder head cover mounting fasteners and remove cylinder head cover.

> **NOTE—**
> • *Make note of arrangement of fasteners during removal so that they can be reinstalled in their original locations.*

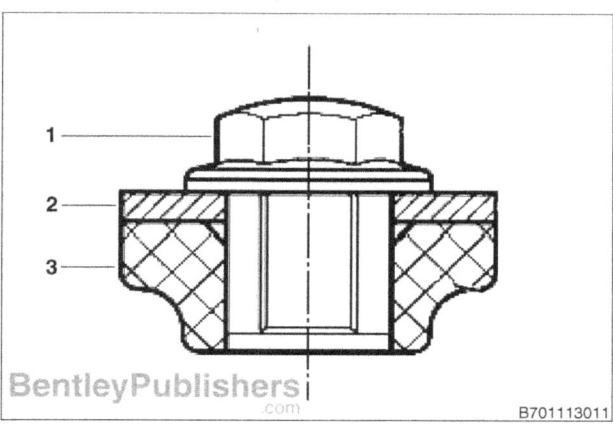

◄ Inspect cylinder head cover fasteners. Replace as necessary.

1. Cap nut
2. Washer
3. Rubber seal

— Clean gasket residue from cylinder head sealing surface. Apply thin beads of 3-Bond 1209® or equivalent sealer at timing chain cover seams.

— Remove inner and outer gaskets from cylinder head cover and clean gasket residue from grooves.

— Coat cylinder head cover grooves with thin layer of anti-friction compound such as glycerine. Press inner and outer gaskets in place, making sure gaskets are not stretched at any point.

Cylinder head cover, removing and installing (M54 engine)

B701113050

◀ Use a small amount of 3-Bond 1209® or equivalent sealer at corners of half-moon seals, and at left and right corners of cylinder head where cylinder head cover and VANOS units meet.

— Reinstall cylinder head cover.

- Coat cylinder head and gasket contact surfaces with thin layer of anti-friction compound such as glycerine.
- Check for correct seating of half-moon seals in back of cylinder head cover.
- Install cylinder head cover fasteners and tighten gradually in crisscross pattern, starting with inside fasteners.

Tightening torques	
Cylinder head cover to cylinder head (M6)	11 Nm (97 in-lb)

— Remainder of assembly is reverse of removal.

CYLINDER HEAD REMOVAL AND INSTALLATION (M54 ENGINE)

The 6-cylinder engine cylinder head is equipped with double VANOS. To remove the cylinder head, special tools and procedures are required for removing the VANOS unit. Read the entire procedure before beginning the repair.

> **CAUTION—**
> - *Disassembly, removal and assembly of camshafts or cylinder head without special tools poses the risk of damage or breakage. The valves may be bent by contact with the piston crown; camshafts may break if stressed incorrectly during removal or installation.*

> **NOTE—**
> - *VANOS or variable camshaft timing is from the German words VAriable NOckenwellen Steuerung.*
> - *VANOS service is covered in* **117 Camshaft Timing Chain**.

Cylinder head removal and installation procedures are described separately. Remove the intake manifold before removing the cylinder head. See **130 Fuel Injection**.

If you remove a cylinder head and determine that it requires significant reconditioning work, a remanufactured cylinder head is available from an authorized BMW dealer.

Cylinder head, removing (M54 engine)

> **WARNING—**
> • Due to risk of personal injury, be sure the engine is cold before beginning the removal procedure.

– Disconnect negative (–) cable from battery.

> **CAUTION—**
> • Prior to disconnecting the battery, read the battery disconnection cautions in **001 Warnings and Cautions**.

– Remove upper engine covers. See **020 Maintenance**.

– Detach air hose and vacuum line from secondary air valve on right side of cylinder head.

◄ Working above engine, disconnect the following:
  • Vent line from cylinder head cover. To remove, pinch clip (**arrows**).
  • Electrical harness connector from VANOS solenoid valve (**A**).

– Remove both exhaust manifolds. See **180 Exhaust System**. After removing exhaust manifolds, reinstall engine support arm and engine mount.

– Remove air filter housing and ducts. See **130 Fuel Injection**.

– Remove cylinder head cover. See **Cylinder head cover, removing and installing (M54 engine)** in this repair group.

– Remove spark plugs. Plug spark plug bores to prevent debris from falling into engine.

– Remove intake manifold. See **130 Fuel Injection**. Plug cylinder head intake ports to prevent debris from falling into engine.

> **WARNING—**
> • Unscrew fuel tank cap to release pressure in tank before working on the fuel line.
> • Wrap shop towels around fuel line fitting before disconnecting.
> • Plug open fuel lines and fittings.

– Raise car and support safely.

> **WARNING—**
> • Make sure car is stable and well supported at all times. Use a professional automotive lift or jack stands. A floor jack is not adequate support.

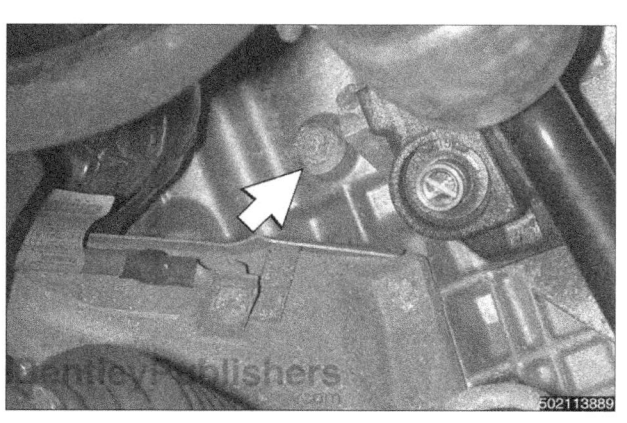

◄ Drain engine coolant:
  • Remove expansion tank cap on radiator.
  • Place a 3 gallon pail underneath engine to capture coolant.
  • Remove coolant drain plug (**arrow**) located on exhaust side of cylinder 2 on engine block.

Cylinder head, removing (M54 engine)

◀ Drain radiator into a 3 gallon pail by removing plastic drain plug (**arrow**) completely.

– Remove engine cooling fan and radiator. See **170 Radiator and Cooling System**.

◀ Remove thermostat housing:

- Disconnect electrical harness connector at thermostat housing.
- Remove hoses from thermostat housing by releasing locks (**arrows**).
- Unbolt (4 bolts) and remove thermostat housing.

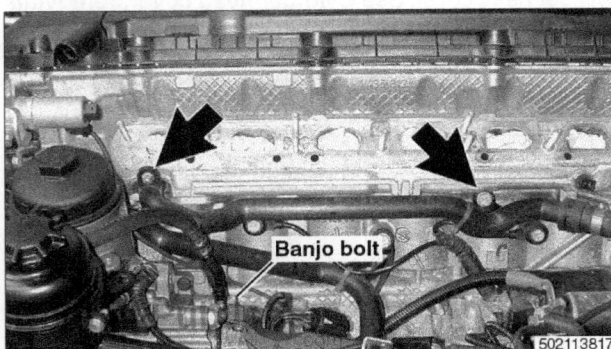

◀ Remove fasteners (**arrows**) from heater bypass tube. Pull tube out of cylinder head and set to side, leaving heater hose connected.

- If necessary, loosen oil pressure line banjo bolt and carefully push oil line aside.

◀ Remove oil baffle cover from above intake camshaft.

Cylinder head, removing (M54 engine)

◀ Remove banjo bolt from VANOS unit oil pressure line. Use banjo bolt to attach BMW special tool 11 3 450 (compressed air fitting) to VANOS unit.

• Be prepared to catch dripping oil. Do not allow oil to contaminate accessory belts.

◀ Cover oil bore (**arrow**) in VANOS unit with shop towel to capture oil which sprays when compressed air is applied.

— Connect compressed air line to air fitting. Apply air pressure set to 2 – 8 bar (30 – 115 psi).

◀ With compressed air line connected, use crankshaft vibration damper bolt to rotate engine in direction of rotation (clockwise) at least twice, until cylinder 1 intake and exhaust camshaft lobes face each other (**arrows**) in top dead center (TDC) position for cylinder 1.

CAUTION—
• *Do not rotate engine counterclockwise to reach TDC. If engine rotates past TDC, complete another two complete rotations.*

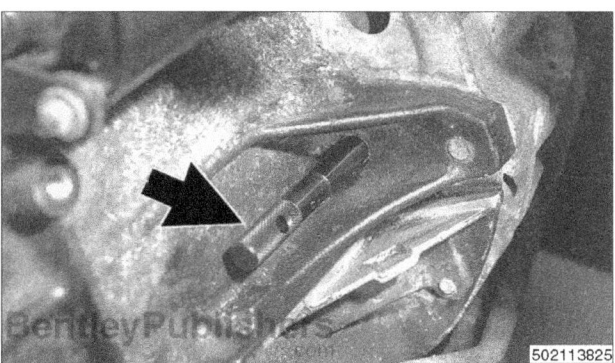

◀ Remove sealing plug from special tool bore on lower left side of engine block near flywheel. Secure crankshaft in TDC position with BMW special tool 11 2 300 (**arrow**).

Cylinder head, removing (M54 engine)

◀ Unscrew and remove two cylinder head cover studs (**arrows**) at rear of cylinder head.

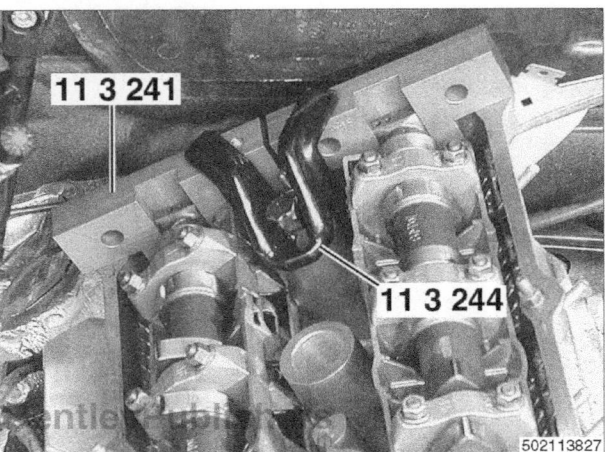

◀ Secure camshafts in TDC position using BMW special tool set 11 3 240 (includes 11 3 241 and 11 3 244).

– Remove VANOS unit from front of cylinder head. See **117 Camshaft Timing Chain**.

– Remove crankshaft locking tool from transmission bell housing.

◀ Lift primary chain and hold under tension. Use crankshaft vibration damper bolt to rotate engine in direction opposite to normal rotation (counterclockwise) approximately 30°.

> **CAUTION—**
> • *By turning crankshaft 30° counterclockwise, pistons are moved away from TDC. This prevents piston-to-valve interference during camshaft servicing.*

– Remove camshaft locking tools (BMW special tool set 11 3 240) from rear of cylinder head.

– Remove camshafts and camshaft bearing carriers. See **117 Camshaft Timing Chain**.

◀ Remove intake camshaft sensor (**arrow**) from side of cylinder head.

◄ Remove secondary chain lower guide bolts (**arrow**). Remove chain guide.

◄ Remove bolts (**arrows**) holding timing chain cover to cylinder head. (Photo shows camshafts and camshaft bearing caps in place).

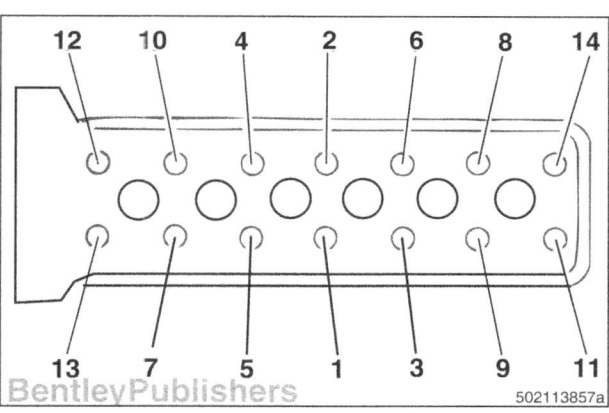

◄ Using BMW special tool 11 2 250 or equivalent, loosen cylinder head bolts in several stages, in sequence from 14 to 1. Discard head bolts after removing.

NOTE—

• *BMW special tool 11 2 250 is a thin-walled Torx E12 socket with an extended reach. The cylinder head bolts are recessed into the head below the camshaft carriers with little working space.*

— Lift off cylinder head.

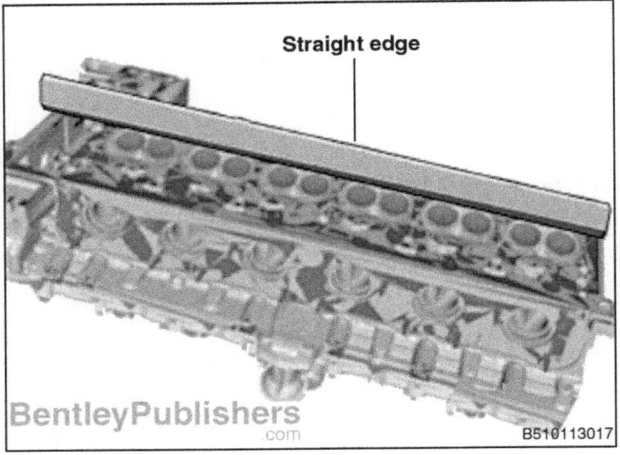

Straight edge

B510113017

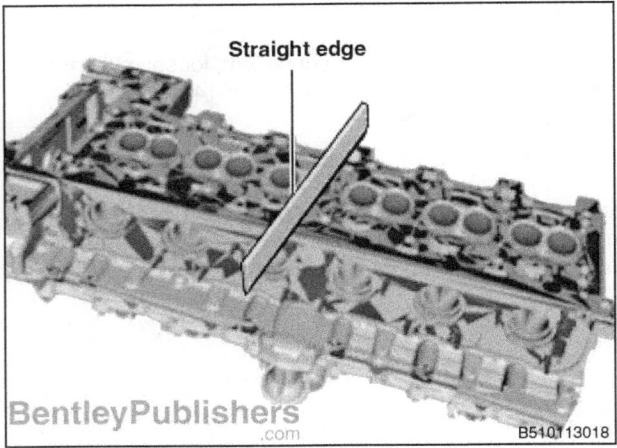

Straight edge

B510113018

502113888

Cylinder head, installing (M54 engine)

— Clean cylinder head and gasket surfaces of cylinder block and timing chain covers.

> **CAUTION—**
> • *Remove foreign matter and liquid from bolt holes. Trapped oil or coolant in bolt holes can cause damage to the engine block.*
> • *Do not use a metal scraper or wire brush to clean the aluminum cylinder head or pistons. If necessary, use a hard wooden or plastic scraper. Also available are abrasive discs to be used with an electric drill.*

— Inspect cylinder head for visible cracks or other defects.

— To check cylinder head for warpage:
  • Remove intake and exhaust camshafts and intermediate intake levers.

> **CAUTION—**
> • *Keep components in separate compartments and mark them for reassembly in their original positions.*

◄ Use straight edge to check evenness of cylinder head sealing surface in longitudinal direction.

◄ Use straight edge to check evenness of cylinder head sealing surface in transverse direction.

Cylinder head warpage specifications	
Maximum warpage allowed • Longitudinal • Transverse	 0.10 mm (0.0039 in) 0.05 mm (0.0020 in)

— Have cylinder head tested for coolant leaks and cracks.

— If cylinder head is warped but otherwise sound, machine a maximum of 0.3 mm (0.011 in) off sealing surface.

— If cylinder head is machined, use a special cylinder head gasket available from an authorized BMW dealer. The gasket is 0.3 mm (0.011 in) thicker than standard and is marked accordingly.

— Lubricate camshafts, camshaft carriers, bearing caps, hydraulic lifters and friction washers with assembly lubricant prior to installation.

◄ Check that two cylinder head aligning sleeves (**arrows**) are correctly positioned in block and are not damaged.

— Apply elastic sealing compound 3-Bond 1209® to corner joints and seam on cylinder block to timing chain cover.

— Place new cylinder head gasket on cylinder block.

> **NOTE—**
> • *The word "OBEN" or "TOP" printed on gasket faces up. The cylinder head gasket fits correctly in only one orientation.*

— Set cylinder head in position, guiding primary chain through cylinder head opening.

— Prior to installing cylinder head bolts, keep in mind the following:
  • Do not reuse cylinder head bolts. They are stretch-type bolts and are replaced whenever loosened.
  • Check that head bolt washers are in place before installing bolts. Some washers are staked to the cylinder head.

— Lightly lubricate **new** cylinder head bolts and washers with oil. Install cylinder head bolts and bolts for cylinder head to lower timing chain cover finger tight.

 Tighten cylinder head bolts in correct sequence (1 – 14).

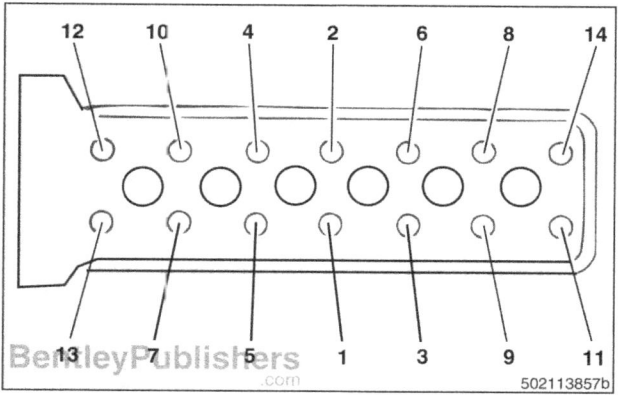

> **CAUTION—**
> • Tighten bolts in three stages as listed below. The final stages require the use of a BMW special tool 11 2 110 or a suitable protractor to tighten bolts to a specified torque angle.

Tightening torque	
Cylinder head to engine block	
• Stage 1	40 Nm (30 ft-lb)
• Stage 2	+90°
• Stage 3	+90°

 Install intake camshaft sensor (**arrow**).

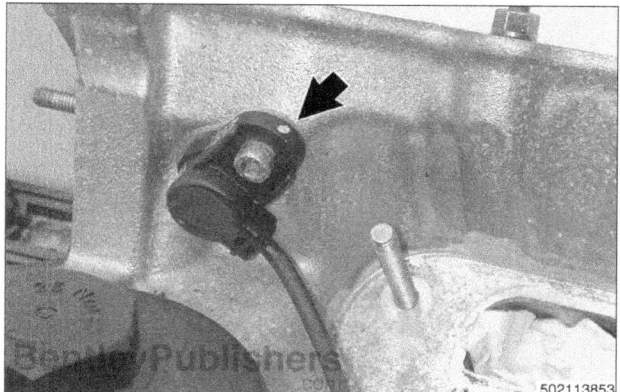

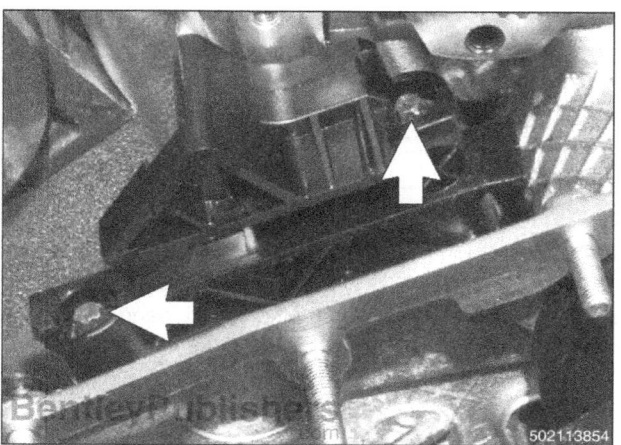

◄ Install lower secondary chain guide. Tighten torx bolts (**arrows**) to specifications. Bolt on intake camshaft side is long and extends into engine block.

Tightening torque	
Secondary chain guide to cylinder head (M6)	10 Nm (89 in-lb)

Cylinder head, installing (M54 engine)

◀ Tighten bolts (**arrows**) for cylinder head to lower timing chain cover. (Photo shows camshafts in place).

Tightening torque	
Cylinder head to lower timing chain cover (M6)	10 Nm (89 in-lb)

— Reinstall camshafts. See **117 Camshaft Timing Chain**.

> **CAUTION—**
> • *Make sure the crankshaft, which was rotated approximately 30° opposite the direction of engine rotation from TDC, is still in that position before reinstalling camshafts. This ensures that pistons are out of TDC position and prevents piston-valve interference when the camshafts are installed.*
> • *After the camshafts are installed, a minimum waiting time is required for the hydraulic lifters to bleed down before bringing the crankshaft and pistons back to TDC. When the camshafts are removed, the hydraulic lifters may expand. This expansion can cause increased valve lift when the camshafts are bolted down, possibly resulting in piston-valve interference.*

— Reinstall double VANOS unit. See **117 Camshaft Timing Chain**.

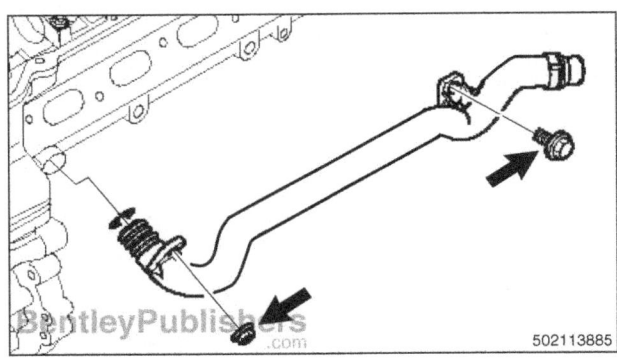

◀ Install coolant pipe fasteners at base of cylinder head and tighten fasteners (**arrows**).

> **NOTE—**
> • *Use new sealing O-ring on coolant pipe.*

— Attach oil line to VANOS unit using banjo bolt with new seals.

Tightening torque	
Oil line to VANOS unit (banjo bolt)	32 Nm (24 ft-lb)

— Install intake camshaft cover and cylinder head cover. See **Cylinder head cover, removing and installing (M54 engine)** in this repair group.

Tightening torque	
Cylinder head cover to cylinder head (M6)	10 Nm (89 in-lb)

— Install exhaust manifolds using new gaskets and nuts. Coat manifold studs with copper paste prior to installing nuts. See **180 Exhaust System**.

Tightening torque	
Exhaust manifold to cylinder head (M7)	20 Nm (15 ft-lb)

— Install electrical harness connectors for oil pressure sender and coolant temperature sensor before installing intake manifold.

— Reinstall intake manifold. See **130 Fuel Injection**.

> **CAUTION—**
>
> • *When reattaching throttle harness connector, connector is fully tightened when arrows on connector and plug align.*

— Installation of remaining parts is reverse or removal, noting the following:

- Refill and bleed cooling system. See **170 Radiator and Cooling System**.
- Change engine oil and filter. See **020 Maintenance**.
- Reconnect battery.

> **CAUTION—**
>
> • *To prevent damaging engine electronic systems, install ground wires previously removed, including ground wires for ignition coils.*
>
> • *Prior to starting engine, be sure to remove crankshaft lock tool.*

Tightening torque	
Coolant drain plug to cylinder block	25 Nm (18 ft-lb)
Radiator cooling fan to coolant pump	40 Nm (30 ft-lb)
Radiator drain screw to radiator	2.5 Nm (22 in-lb)
Spark plug to cylinder head	25 Nm (18 ft-lb)

CYLINDER HEAD (N52 ENGINE)

Cylinder head cover components (N52 engine)

1. Valvetronic motor mounting bolt (M6 x 16 mm)
   - Tighten to 10 Nm (7 ft-lb)
2. Valvetronic motor
3. Gasket
4. Cylinder head cover
5. Cylinder head cover fastener
6. Cylinder head cover gasket–outer
7. Cylinder head cover gasket–inner (spark plug holes)
8. Crankcase breather hose

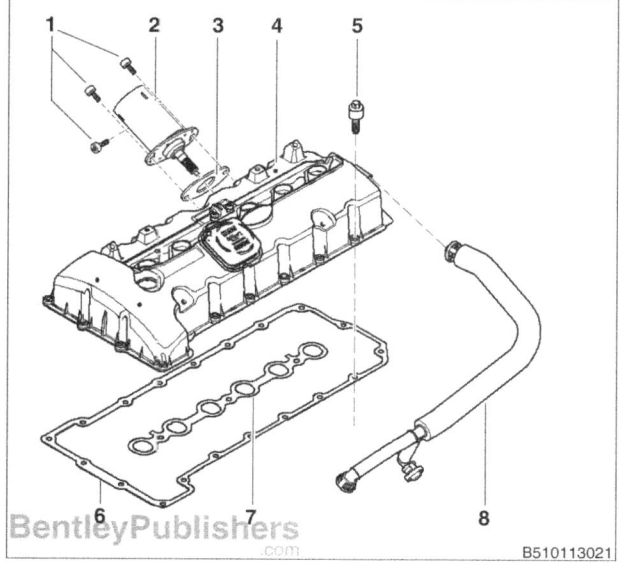

B510113021

Cylinder head cover, removing and installing (N52 engine)

Cylinder head cover, removing and installing (N52 engine)

— Use scan tool to read out and record ECM fault memory.

— Switch ignition OFF and remove key.

— Remove brace from strut towers.
  See **310 Front Suspension**.

— Remove Housing for interior ventilation microfilter.
  See **640 Heating and Air-conditioning**.

— Remove ignition coil cover (upper engine cover). See
  020 Maintenance.

— Detach ignition coil connectors. Unclip ignition coil harness from
  cylinder head cover and lift aside.

— Remove ignition coils. See **120 Ignition System**.

◄ Working at cylinder head cover:
  • Remove valvetronic motor mounting bolts (**arrows**). To disengage
    valvetronic motor, see **131 Fuel Injection**.

— Detach crankcase breather hose.

◄ Remove cylinder head cover fasteners (**A**, **B**).
  • Note position of different length fasteners, where applicable.

— Lift off cylinder head cover and discard old gaskets.

— Clean gasket residue from cylinder head and cylinder head cover
  sealing surfaces (**A**, **B**).

> **CAUTION—**
> • *Do not use metal scraping tool to clean aluminum surfaces.*

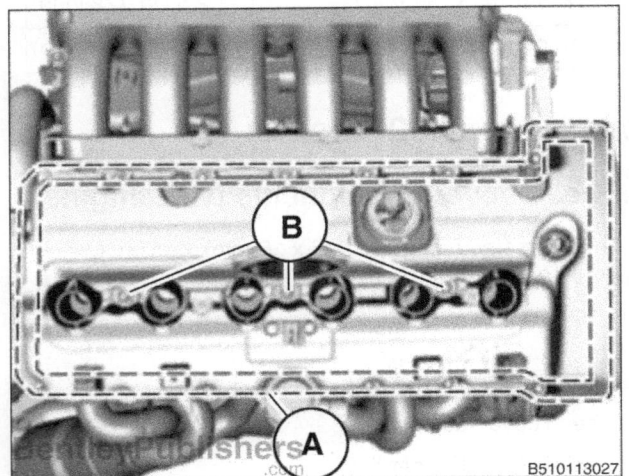

◄ Remove and replace slotted ignition coil sleeves in cylinder head
  cover.

— Coat cylinder head cover grooves with thin layer of anti-friction
  compound such as glycerine. Press gaskets in place, making sure
  they are not stretched at any point.

— Reinstall cylinder head cover:

• Coat cylinder head contact surfaces with thin layer of anti-friction compound such as glycerine.

• Place small quantity of silicone sealant at metal-to-metal seams (such as timing cover to engine block) and half moon gasket area.

• Replace aluminum fasteners where removed.

• Tighten gradually in crisscross pattern, starting with inside fasteners.

Tightening torques	
N52 engine cylinder head cover to cylinder head (plastic cover, steel M7 fasteners)	9 Nm (7 ft-lb)
Valvetronic motor to cylinder head cover (M6 x 16 mm bolts)	10 Nm (7 ft-lb)

— Remainder of assembly is reverse of removal. Make sure cabin microfilter housing seals correctly.

Tightening torques	
Ignition coil cover to cylinder head cover (M6)	4 Nm (35 in-lb)

Cylinder head and timing chain (N52 engine)

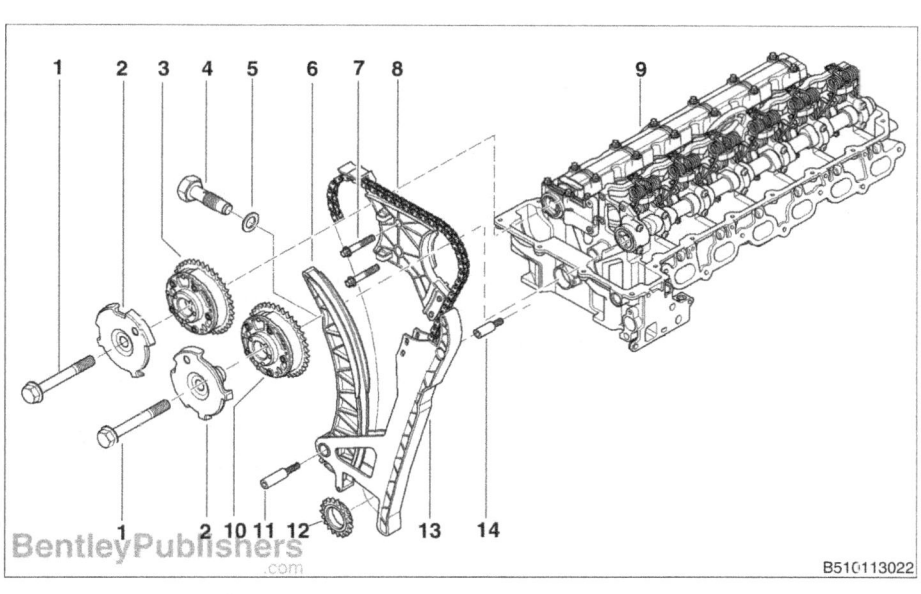

B510113022

1. Camshaft adjustment unit mounting bolt (M10 x 94 mm)
   • Replace with new
   • Tighten in 2 stages
     Stage 1: 20 Nm (15 ft-lb)
     Stage 2: Additional 180°

2. Camshaft impulse wheel

3. Exhaust camshaft adjustment unit

4. Chain tensioner (M22 x 1.5)
   • Tighten to 55 Nm (41 ft-lb)

5. Sealing O-ring
   • Install new

6. Chain tensioner rail

7. Chain module mounting bolts (M6 x 35 mm Torx)
   • Tighten to 8.5 Nm (6 ft-lb)

8. Timing chain

9. Cylinder head with camshafts

10. Intake camshaft adjustment unit

11. Chain tensioner rail mounting bolt (M8)
    • Tighten to 20 Nm (15 ft-lb)

12. Crankshaft sprocket

13. Chain guide

14. Chain guide mounting bolt (M7)
    • Tighten to 14 Nm (10 ft-lb)

Cylinder head, removing and installing (N52 engine)

Cylinder head, removing and installing (N52 engine)

When removing and installing the cylinder head, special tools and procedures are required to remove and install camshaft adjustment units and valvetronic eccentric shaft and to time camshafts. Read the entire procedure before beginning repairs.

> **CAUTION—**
> - *Disassembly, removal and assembly of camshafts, camshaft adjustment units or cylinder head without special tools poses the risk of damage or breakage: Valves may be bent by contact with the piston crowns.*

> **NOTE —**
> - *Camshaft timing is covered in* **117 Camshaft Timing Chain**.

Remanufactured cylinder heads are available from an authorized BMW dealer.

Cylinder head, removing (N52 engine)

The cylinder head stretch bolts are aluminum. Replace them any time they are removed. Use angle protractor to torque.

> **WARNING —**
> - *To avoid personal injury, be sure the engine is cold before beginning the removal procedure.*

— Disconnect negative (–) cable from battery.

> **CAUTION—**
> - *Prior to disconnecting the battery, read the battery disconnection cautions in* **001 Warnings and Cautions**.

— Raise vehicle and support safely.

> **WARNING —**
> - *Make sure vehicle is stable and well supported at all times. Use a professional automotive lift or jack stands. A floor jack is not adequate support.*

— Remove engine compartment splash shield. See **020 Maintenance**.

— With exhaust system fully cooled off, remove exhaust system and both exhaust manifolds. See **180 Exhaust System**.

— Drain engine coolant. See **170 Radiator and Cooling System**.

— Drain engine oil. See **020 Maintenance**.

— Remove ignition coil cover (upper engine cover). See **020 Maintenance**.

— Remove air filter housing, engine air intake ducts and intake manifold. See **131 Fuel Injection**.

> **WARNING —**
> - *Unscrew the fuel tank cap before working on fuel lines.*

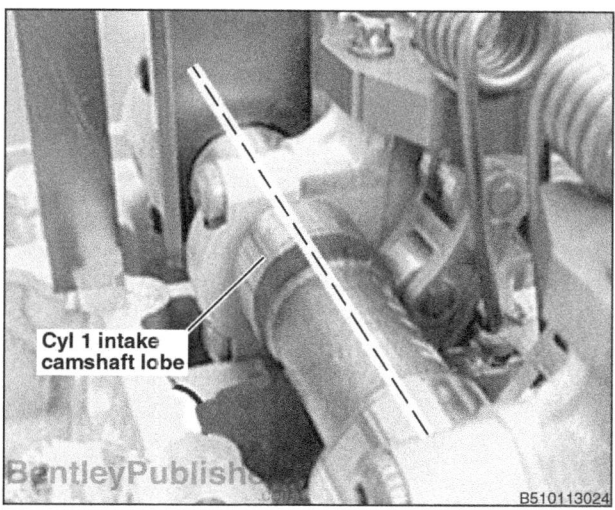

— Remove cylinder head cover. See **Cylinder head cover, removing and installing (N52 engine)** in this repair group.

— Detach coolant hoses from cylinder head.

◀ Using vibration damper bolt, rotate crankshaft to place cylinder 1 in TDC firing position. In this position, cylinder 1 intake camshaft lobe points upward at an angle.

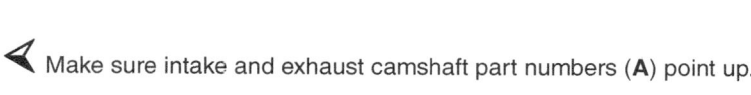

◀ Make sure intake and exhaust camshaft part numbers (**A**) point up.

◀ Cylinder 1 in TDC firing position: Cylinder 6 exhaust camshaft lobe (**A**) points downward at an angle (**dashed line**). Cam follower (**B**) is not actuated.

NOTE—

• *Use a mirror to check exhaust camshaft lobe position.*

Cylinder head, removing (N52 engine)

◀ Working underneath engine, slide out protective plug at lower left of engine bell housing flange. Install BMW special tool 11 0 300 (crankshaft locking tool) through bell housing flange port into flywheel (**A**) hole. If necessary, rock flywheel slightly back and forth to line up holes with tool. This locks crankshaft at TDC.

> **CAUTION—**
> • *Automatic transmission model: A short distance before the flywheel special tool bore for TDC position, there is a large bore that can be confused with the special tool bore. If the flywheel is locked using the correct bore, the engine can no longer be rotated at the vibration damper bolt.*

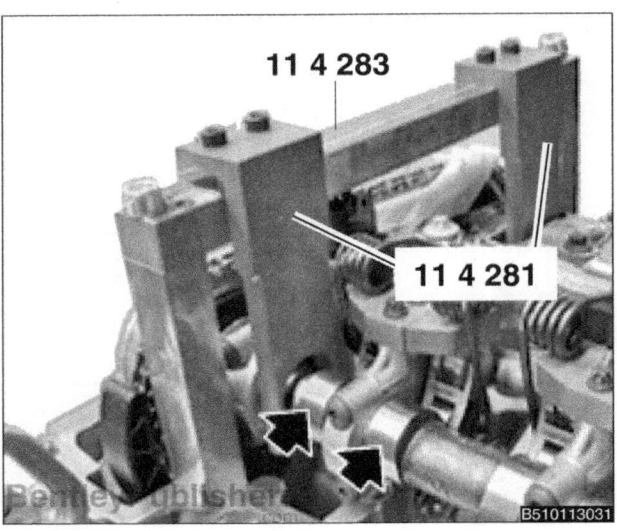

◀ Using BMW special tool set 11 4 280, lock down camshafts.

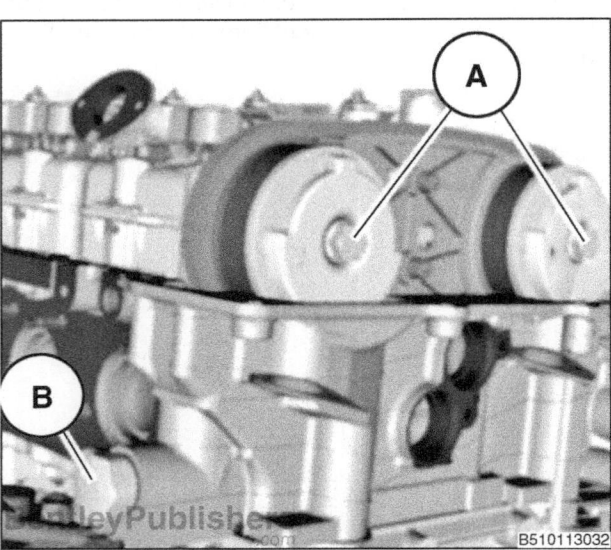

◀ Remove intake and exhaust camshaft adjustment units:

• Loosen and remove adjustment unit mounting bolts (**A**). Discard bolts.

• Remove timing chain tensioner (**B**). Be prepared to catch dripping oil with a shop towel. Do not allow oil to contaminate accessory belt.

• Disengage timing chain from camshaft adjustment unit sprockets. Remove adjustment units and set aside.

> **NOTE—**
> • *Illustration does not show special tool set 11 4 280 in place.*

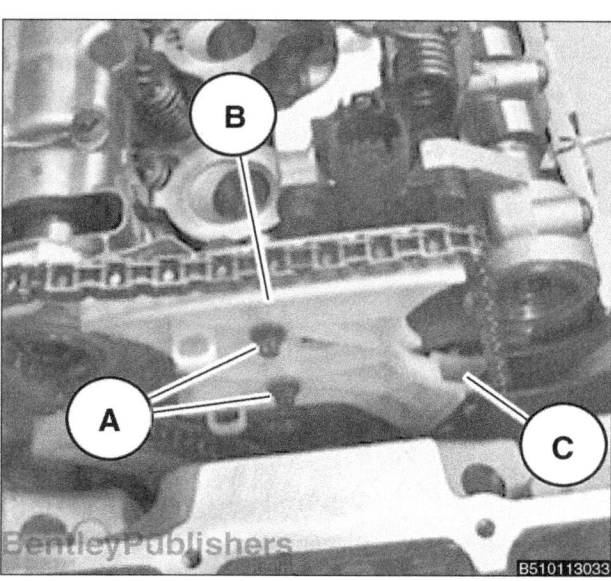

◀ Working at front of cylinder head:
- Remove timing chain module mounting bolts (**A**).
- Unclip chain module (**B**) at junction (**C**) and lift out.
- Place timing chain in cylinder head opening.

> **CAUTION—**
> - *Do not remove crankshaft locking tool. Rotating crankshaft may cause the timing chain to jam or jump teeth.*

◀ Unbolt and remove valvetronic eccentric shaft sensor mounting bolts (**A**). Slide sensor (**B**) forward (**arrow**) to remove.

> **CAUTION—**
> - *Use care when removing eccentric shaft sensor. Sensor is easily damaged.*

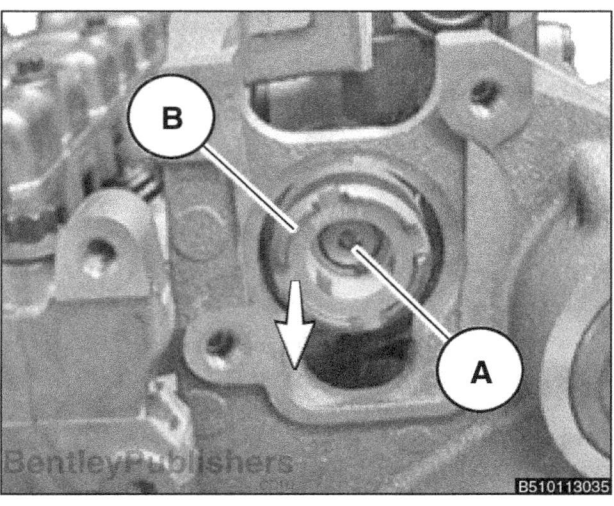

◀ Remove eccentric shaft magnet wheel mounting bolt (**A**). Slide magnet wheel (**B**) forward (**arrow**) to remove.

> **CAUTION—**
> - *Magnet wheel mounting bolt is non-magnetic. Do not allow it to fall into engine.*
> - *Magnet wheel is highly magnetic. Protect against metal filings by storing in sealed plastic bag.*

Cylinder head, removing (N52 engine)

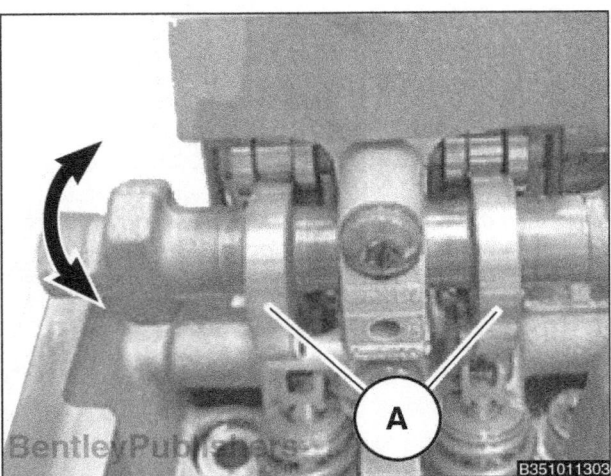

◀ Pretension eccentric shaft up (**arrow**). Remove stop screw between cylinders 1 and 2 (**A**).

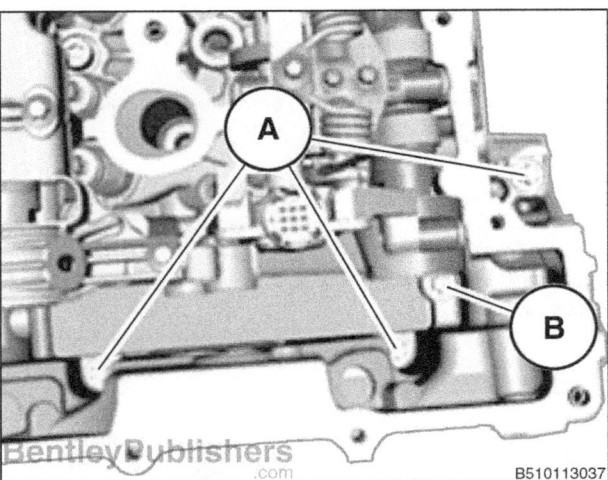

◀ Remove cylinder head bolts (**A**, **B**) at timing chain housing. Press timing chain rail forward slightly to remove bolt **B**. Discard aluminum bolts.

> **CAUTION—**
> • *Use mechanical gripper to prevent lower bolt(s) from falling down inside crankcase.*
> • *Measure and note down different bolt lengths for correct reinstallation.*

◀ Use BMW special tools 11 4 420 (Torx T50) and 11 8 580 (Torx T60) to loosen and remove M9 and M10 cylinder head bolts. (Intake and exhaust camshafts removed for purpose of illustration.)

• Loosen M9 bolts first.

• Loosen M10 bolts in crisscross pattern, starting with outside bolts.

• Note different bolt lengths.

• Discard aluminum bolts.

— Bolt lifting handles to cylinder head. Lift off head with help of assistant.

> **CAUTION—**
> • *Cylinder head weighs approx. 40 kg (88 lb).*
> • *Place cylinder head on work bench on its side. Putting it down on sealing surface risks damage to the valves.*
> • *Be sure to clean antifreeze out of cylinder head bolt holes in crankcase immediately.*

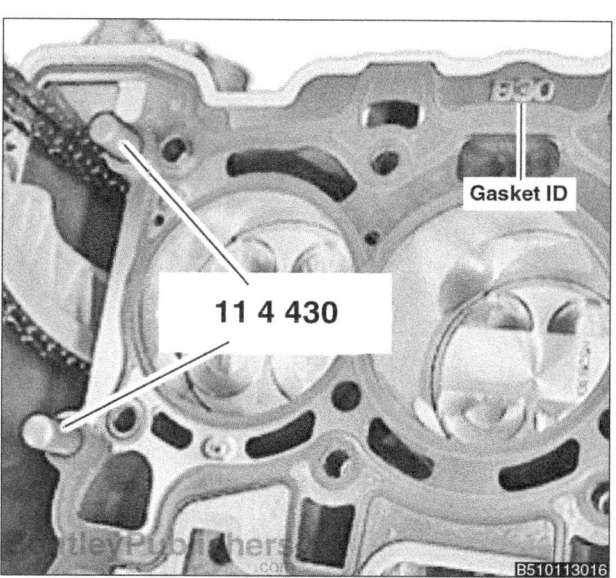

Gasket ID

11 4 430

B510113016

Cylinder head, installing (N52 engine)

◀ Before cleaning engine block sealing surface, insert plugs (BMW special tools 11 4 430 or equivalent) into oil passages.

- Note cylinder head gasket ID at right front edge of gasket.

– Clean cylinder head and gasket surfaces of engine block and timing chain housing.

> **CAUTION—**
> - *Remove foreign matter and liquid from bolt holes. Trapped oil or coolant in bolt holes can cause damage to the engine block.*
> - *Do not use a metal scraper or wire brush to clean sealing surfaces. If necessary, use a hard wooden or plastic scraper. Also available are abrasive discs to be with an electric drill.*

– Inspect cylinder head for visible cracks or other defects.

– To check cylinder head for warpage:

- Remove intake and exhaust camshafts and intermediate intake levers.

> **CAUTION—**
> - *Keep components in separate compartments and mark them for reassembly in their original positions.*

◀ Use straight edge to check evenness of cylinder head sealing surface in longitudinal direction.

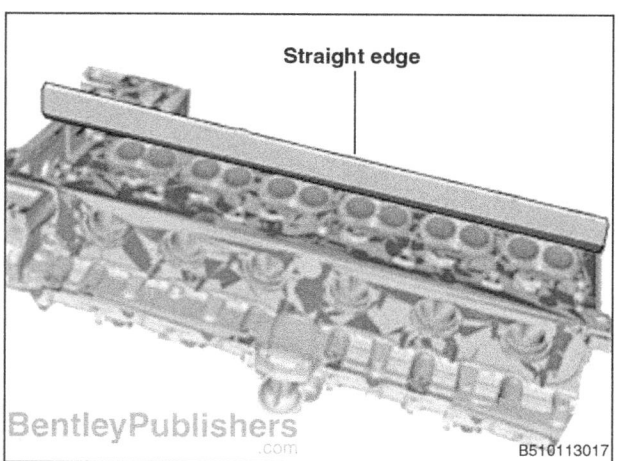

Straight edge

B510113017

◀ Use straight edge to check evenness of cylinder head sealing surface in transverse direction.

Cylinder head warpage specifications	
Maximum warpage allowed	
• Longitudinal	0.10 mm (0.0039 in)
• Transverse	0.05 mm (0.0020 in)

– Have cylinder head tested for coolant leaks and cracks.

– If cylinder head is warped but otherwise sound, machine a maximum of 0.3 mm (0.011 in) off sealing surface.

– Reassemble cylinder head, or use reconditioned BMW cylinder head. See **117 Camshaft Timing Chain**.

Tightening torques	
Oil spray nozzle to valvetronic guide block (M6 x 30 mm bolt)	10 Nm (7 ft-lb)

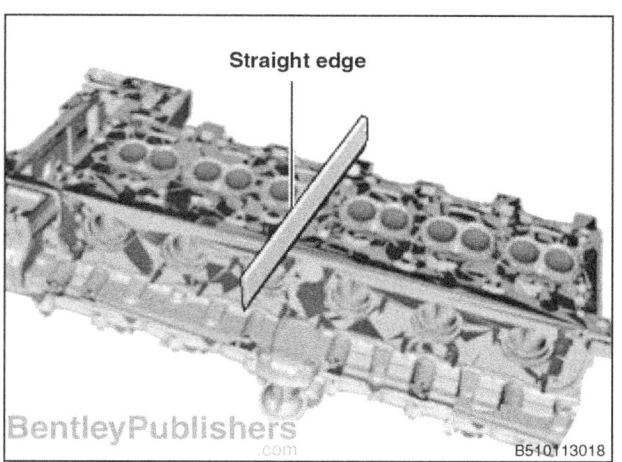

Straight edge

B510113018

113

Cylinder head, installing (N52 engine)

B510113019

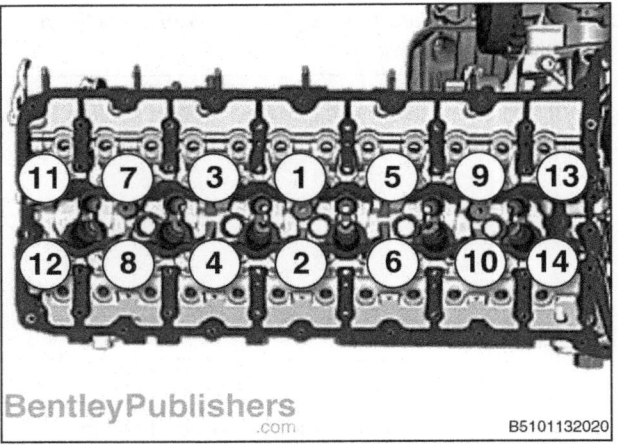

B5101132020

Tightening torques	
Valvetronic guide block to timing chain housing (M6 x 23 mm bolt)	10 Nm (7 ft-lb)
Valvetronic torsion spring to cylinder head (M6 x 20 bolt)	10 Nm (7 ft-lb)
Camshaft bearing strip to camshaft (M7 x 70 mm 10.9 steel bolt) • Stage 1 • Stage 2	8 Nm (71 in-lb) additional 60°

◄ Check that two cylinder head aligning sleeves (**arrows**) are correctly positioned in engine block and are not damaged.

– Replace cylinder head gasket.

– If cylinder head is machined, use a special cylinder head gasket available from an authorized BMW dealer. The gasket is 0.3 mm (0.011 in) thicker than standard and is marked accordingly.

– Place cylinder head on engine block and fit to aligning sleeves.

◄ Insert new aluminum cylinder head bolts:
- Bolts 1 - 10: M10 x 125 mm
- Bolts 11 - 14: M9 x 95 mm and M9 x 125 mm. Insert correct length bolts, as marked previously.

NOTE—
- *Graphic shows intake and exhaust camshafts removed.*

– Use BMW special tool 11 8 850 (Torx T60) to tighten bolts 1 - 10 in sequence shown below.

– Use BMW special tool 11 4 420 (Torx T50) to tighten bolts 11 - 14 in sequence shown below.

Tightening torques and sequence	
Cylinder head to engine block: • Stage 1: All bolts, 1 - 14 • Stage 2: All bolts, 1 - 14 • Stage 3: Only bolts 1 - 10 • Stage 4: All bolts 1 - 14	30 Nm (22 ft-lb) additional 90° additional 90° additional 45°

CAUTION—
- *Stage 3 applies to M10 bolts (1 - 10) only.*

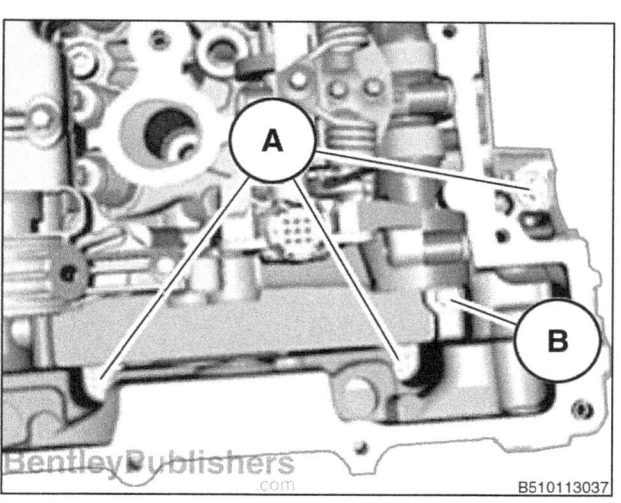

◄ Use new aluminum bolts (**A**, **B**) to attach cylinder head to timing chain housing. Press timing chain rail forward slightly to install lower bolt(s).

CAUTION—

• *Use mechanical gripper to prevent lower bolt(s) from falling down inside crankcase.*

• *Place different bolt lengths in correct bores.*

Tightening torques	
N52 engine cylinder head to timing chain housing (M9 x 30 mm): • Stage 1 • Stage 2	 10 Nm (7 ft-lb) additional 90°
N52 engine cylinder head to timing chain housing (M9 x 70 mm): • Stage 1 • Stage 2	 10 Nm (7 ft-lb) additional 135°

— Reinstall eccentric shaft stop screw.

Tightening torque	
Eccentric shaft stop screw to cylinder head (M6)	10 Nm (7 ft-lb)

— Replace eccentric shaft magnet wheel.

— Reinstall eccentric shaft sensor.

— Use wire hook to retrieve timing chain from inside timing chain housing. Place chain over chain module and clip module to lower chain rail. Reinstall chain module mounting bolts.

Tightening torque	
Chain module to cylinder head (M6 x 35 mm Torx)	8.5 Nm (6 ft-lb)

113

Cylinder head, installing (N52 engine)

B510113023

◄ Use new bolts to reattach camshaft adjustment (VANOS) units. Note that exhaust and intake units are different and so marked. Camshaft sensor impulse wheel for intake and exhaust are the same.

> **CAUTION—**
> • *Use special tools shown in* **117 Camshaft Timing Chain** *to lock down camshafts.*

Tightening torque

Camshaft adjustment (VANOS) unit to camshaft (use new M10 x 94 mm bolt): • Stage 1 • Stage 2	20 Nm (15 ft-lb) additional 180°

— Install chain tensioner and set camshaft timing. See **117 Camshaft Timing Chain**.

> **CAUTION—**
> • *If chain tensioner is reused, drain its oil chamber. Place tensioner on level working surface and compress slowly. Repeat twice.*
> • *No sealing ring is fitted to chain tensioner at the factory. When reassembling engine, be sure to use new sealing O-ring.*

Tightening torque

Timing chain tensioner to cylinder head (M22 x 1.5) (use new sealing O-ring)	55 Nm (41 ft-lb)

— Remainder of installation is reverse of removal. Remember to:

  • Remove camshaft and crankshaft locking tools.

  • Assemble cylinder head cover with new gasket.

  • Reattach and tighten any ground cables removed.

  • Reassemble fuel rail using new O-ring seals.

  • Change engine oil and filter. See **020 Maintenance**.

  • Fill and bleed cooling system. See **170 Radiator and Cooling System**.

117 Camshaft Timing Chain

GENERAL

This repair group provides removal and repair information for crankshaft vibration damper, engine timing chain and camshaft adjustment (VANOS) units. Camshaft timing procedure is also included.

The X3 engine is equipped with variable camshaft timing or VANOS. Special tools and procedures are required to remove and install camshaft adjustment units and to time camshafts. Be sure to read each procedure through before starting work.

Repair procedures in this repair group assume that the engine is installed in the engine bay.

See also:

• **020 Maintenance**

• **100 Engine–General** for engine code and application information.

• **113 Cylinder Head Removal and Installation** for cylinder head cover removal

• **119 Lubrication System** for crankshaft seal replacement

• **130 Fuel Injection** for air filter housing and intake manifold removal

• **170 Radiator and Cooling System**

Engine identification

Engine applications and specifications are detailed in **100 Engine–General**.

Repair procedures in this manual are broken down by engine version. Engine versions are identified by their BMW engine designation number.

Table a. Engine identification

Engine designation	Year, model	Identifying feature
M54	2004 - 2006 2.5i, 3.0i	2 upper engine covers
N52	2007 - 2010 3.0si, 30i	Black plastic cylinder head cover

Variable camshaft timing (VANOS)

Performance, torque, idle characteristics and exhaust emissions reduction are improved by variable camshaft timing or VANOS.

VANOS units are mounted on the front of the camshafts and adjust the timing of the intake and exhaust camshafts from retarded to advanced. The engine control module (ECM) controls the operation of the VANOS solenoids which regulate oil pressure to rotate the VANOS units. Engine rpm, load and temperature inputs are used to regulate VANOS activation.

VANOS mechanical operation is dependent on engine oil pressure applied to the VANOS units. When oil pressure is applied to the units, the camshaft hubs are rotated in the timing chain drive sprockets, thus advancing or retarding intake and exhaust camshaft timing.

The VANOS system is fully variable. When the ECM, using camshaft sensor signals, detects that the camshafts are in the optimum positions, the solenoids maintain oil pressure on the VANOS units to hold the camshaft timing.

M54 engine
Double VANOS components

Impulse wheel
ECM
Camshaft position sensor
VANOS actuator
Battery (+) terminal 15
Vent
Impulse wheel
Camshaft position sensor
ECM
KL 15
Vent
VANOS actuator
Solenoid
Engine oil supply
Oil temperature sensor
ECM

BentleyPublishers.com

B510100015a

N52 engine

Exhaust camshaft adjustment (VANOS) unit

Intake camshaft adjustment (VANOS) unit

Intake camshaft sensor

Exhaust camshaft sensor
Exhaust VANOS solenoid

Intake VANOS solenoid

B309117036

VANOS solenoids

◄ Separate VANOS solenoids control oil flow to intake and exhaust camshaft VANOS units.

VANOS solenoid operations are regulated according to OBD II requirements for emission control.

N52 engine VANOS solenoid

BentleyPublishers
.com

B309117037

N52 engine

Camshaft sensor impulse wheel

Camshaft sensor

BentleyPublishers
.com

B309117038

Camshaft sensors and impulse wheels

◄ Intake and exhaust camshaft sensors are mounted at the front of the cylinder head and monitor the impulse wheels which are bolted to the VANOS units.

The sensors are supplied power via engine electronics fuses. Ground is supplied via the ECM. The Hall effect sensors provide the ECM with a 5 volt square wave signal indicating camshaft position.

Camshaft sensor replacement is covered in **120 Ignition System**.

VANOS fault diagnosis

> **CAUTION—**
> • *A small amount of silicone introduced into VANOS actuator or solenoid can set faults.*

◄ A sticky VANOS solenoid may set a VANOS, camshaft or camshaft sensor fault code. To test for this problem:

• Swap VANOS solenoid positions.

• Clear and recheck for fault codes. If fault code swaps position, a solenoid is at fault.

— Remove faulty solenoid and use shop air to gently blow out particles and contaminants. Reinstall and retest.

N52 engine

Intake VANOS solenoid
Exhaust VANOS solenoid

B309117042

Warnings and cautions

WARNING—

- *To avoid personal injury, be sure the engine is cold before beginning work on engine components.*

- *The fuel system is designed to retain pressure even when the ignition is OFF. When working with the fuel system, loosen fuel lines slowly to allow residual fuel pressure to dissipate. Avoid spraying fuel. Use shop towels to capture leaking fuel.*

- *Before beginning work on the fuel system, place a fire extinguisher in the vicinity of the work area.*

- *Fuel is highly flammable. When working around fuel, do not disconnect wires that could cause electrical sparks. Do not smoke or work near heaters or other fire hazards.*

- *Wear eye protection and protective clothing to avoid injuries from contact with fuel.*

- *Unscrew fuel tank cap before working on fuel lines.*

- *Do not use a work light with an incandescent bulb near fuel. Fuel may spray on the hot bulb causing a fire.*

- *Make sure the work area is properly ventilated.*

CAUTION—

- *To avoid electrochemical corrosion to engine components made of aluminum-magnesium alloy, do not use steel fasteners. Use aluminum fasteners only.*

- *The end faces of aluminum fasteners are usually painted blue. For reliable identification, test fasteners for aluminum composition with magnet.*

- *To avoid camshaft damage, counter hold hexagon casting at rear of camshaft whenever loosening or tightening camshaft adjuster (VANOS) unit.*

- *Replace aluminum bolts each time they are loosened.*

VIBRATION DAMPER

Vibration damper, removing and installing (M54 engine)

The M54 engine uses a 1-piece crankshaft vibration damper, integrated with the hub.

— Raise front of vehicle and support in a safe manner.

WARNING—

- *Make sure vehicle is stable and well supported at all times. Use a professional automotive lift or jack stands.*

— Working from below, remove front splash guard. See **020 Maintenance**.

— Remove electric cooling fan and cowl. See **170 Radiator and Cooling System**.

NOTE—

- *Protect radiator from damage with a piece of thin plywood.*

Vibration damper, removing and installing (M54 engine)

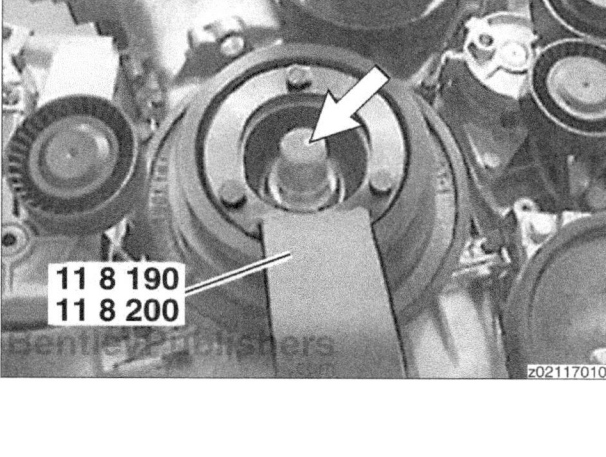

— With engine fully cooled off, mark direction of rotation on engine accessory belts. Remove belts. See **020 Maintenance**.

 Bolt BMW special tools 11 8 190 and 11 8 200 together. Insert fingers of specia tool 11 8 200 in vibration damper openings. Use this tool setup to counterhold vibration damper hub while loosening vibration damper mounting bolt (**arrow**).

> **CAUTION—**
> • *Make sure an assistant holds special tool.*
> • *If assistant is not available, rest handle of tool on front subframe. Protect subframe from damage with a piece of wood.*
> • *Do not use flywheel locking tool to hold crankshaft stationary to loosen or tighten vibration damper mounting bolt.*

— Remove vibration damper mounting bolt and discard.

— Pull off vibration damper using BMW special tools 11 8 210 and 11 8 200.

— Inspect front crankshaft seal for leaks. For seal replacement, see **119 Lubrication System**.

— When reinstalling:
  • Align vibration damper groove to crankshaft woodruff key.
  • Insert new vibration damper mounting bolt and washer.

> **CAUTION—**
> • *Inspect woodruff key for damage before installing vibration damper. Replace if necessary*

— Use BMW special tools 111 8 190 and 11 8 200 to counterhold vibration damper while tightening mounting bolt.

> **CAUTION—**
> • *Do not use flywheel locking tool to hold crankshaft stationary to loosen or tighten vibration damper bolt. Use the recommended special tools, or equivalent tools for counterholding the pulley.*

Tightening torque	
Vibration damper to crankshaft (replace damper bolt)	410 Nm (300 ft-lb)

Vibration damper, removing and installing (N52 engine)

Crankshaft vibration damper may also be referred to as front pulley.

— Raise vehicle and support safely.

> **WARNING—**
> • *Make sure vehicle is stable and well supported at all times. Use a professional automotive lift or jack stands.*

— Working from below, remove front splash guard. See **020 Maintenance**.

— Remove electric cooling fan and cowl. See **170 Radiator and Cooling System**.

> **NOTE—**
> • *Protect radiator from damage with a piece of plywood.*

— With engine fully cooled off, mark direction of rotation on engine accessory belt. Remove belt. See **020 Maintenance**.

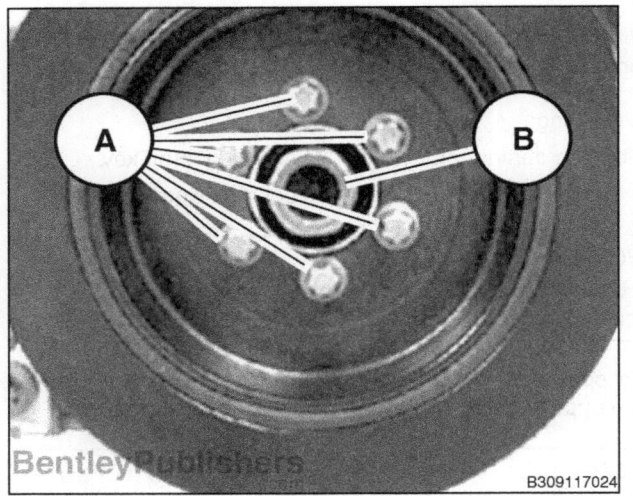

◄ Remove vibration damper mounting Torx bolts (**A**) and discard. Lift off vibration damper.

> **CAUTION—**
> • *Do not remove vibration damper hub bolt (**B**). If this bolt is removed, the timing chain drive sprocket becomes free to rotate, resulting in valve damage.*

— Installation is reverse of removal.

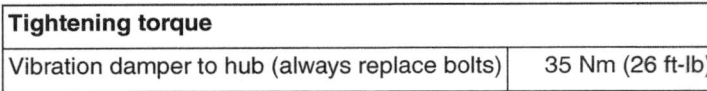

Tightening torque	
Vibration damper to hub (always replace bolts)	35 Nm (26 ft-lb)

TIMING CHAIN SERVICE (M54 ENGINE)

The M54 engine uses a pair of chains to drive the camshafts. A primary chain is driven off the crankshaft and drives the primary sprocket on the exhaust camshaft. The secondary chain drives the intake camshaft. Each chain is tensioned by a hydraulic tensioner.

Intake and exhaust camshaft timing is variable and is controlled by the engine control module (ECM). This system is known as double VANOS.

Camshaft timing chain service and repair requires the removal of front crankshaft vibration damper, double VANOS unit, engine oil pan and timing chain housing cover. Be sure to read the procedures before starting work.

Double VANOS unit components (M54 engine)

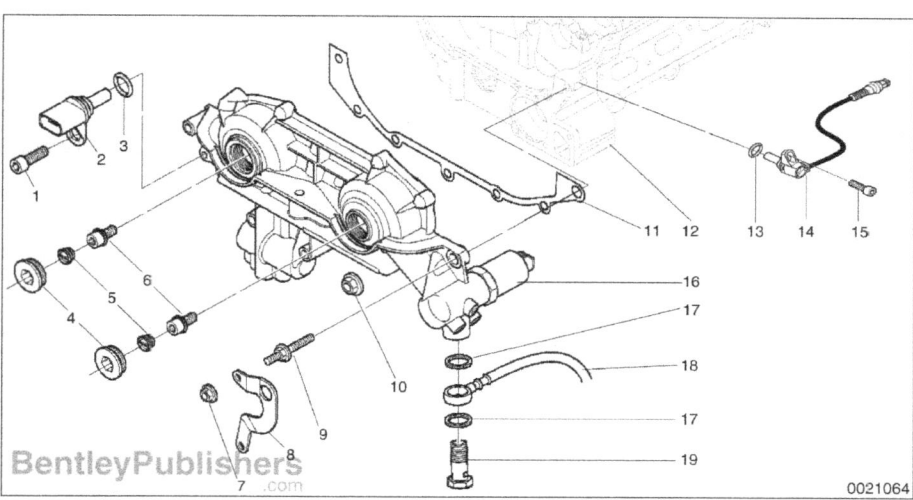

0021064

1. Bolt (M6)

2. Exhaust camshaft sensor

3. Sealing ring

4. Camshaft end sealing plug
   • Tighten to 50 Nm (37 ft-lb)

5. Camshaft seal cap

6. VANOS hydraulic piston set screw
   • Left hand thread
     Tighten to 10 Nm (7 ft-lb)

7. Nut (M7)
   • Tighten to 14 Nm (10 ft-lb)

8. Engine lifting hook

9. Stud (M7)

10. Nut (M6)
    • Tighten to 10 Nm (7 ft-lb)

11. Gasket

12. Cylinder head

13. Sealing ring

14. Intake camshaft sensor

15. Bolt (M6)

16. VANOS unit

17. Copper sealing ring

18. VANOS oil feed line

19. Banjo bolt
    • Tighten to 32 Nm (24 ft-lb)

Double VANOS unit, removing (M54 engine)

> **WARNING—**
> • Due to risk of personal injury, be sure engine is cold before beginning the removal procedure.

> **CAUTION—**
> • Special BMW service tools are required to remove and install the VANOS unit. Read the procedure through before starting.
> • If camshafts are not properly timed, the pistons can contact the valves, causing engine damage.

— Disconnect negative (–) cable from battery.

> **CAUTION—**
> • Prior to disconnecting the battery, read the battery disconnection cautions in **001 Warnings and Cautions**.

— Remove air filter housing with mass air flow sensor. See **130 Fuel Injection**.

Double VANOS unit, removing (M54 engine)

— Remove electric cooling fan and cowl. See **170 Radiator and Cooling System**.

NOTE —

• *Protect radiator from damage with a piece of plywood.*

— Remove engine covers and cylinder head cover. See **113 Cylinder Head Removal and Installation**.

— Remove spark plugs. Plug spark plug bores to prevent debris from falling into engine.

◀ Remove oil baffle cover from above intake camshaft.

◀ Remove banjo bolt from VANOS unit oil pressure line. Use banjo bolt to attach BMW special tool 11 3 450 (compressed air fitting) to VANOS unit.

• Be prepared to catch spraying oil. Do not allow oil to contaminate accessory belts.

◀ Cover oil bore (**arrow**) in VANOS unit with shop towel to capture oil which sprays when compressed air is applied.

— Connect compressed air line to air fitting. Apply air pressure set to 2 – 8 bar (30 – 115 psi).

◀ With compressed air line connected, use crankshaft vibration damper bolt to rotate engine in direction of rotation (clockwise) at least twice, until cylinder 1 intake and exhaust camshaft lobes face each other (**arrows**) in top dead center (TDC) position for cylinder 1.

CAUTION —

• *Do not rotate engine counterclockwise to reach TDC. If engine rotates past TDC, continue another two complete rotations.*

Double VANOS unit, removing (M54 engine)

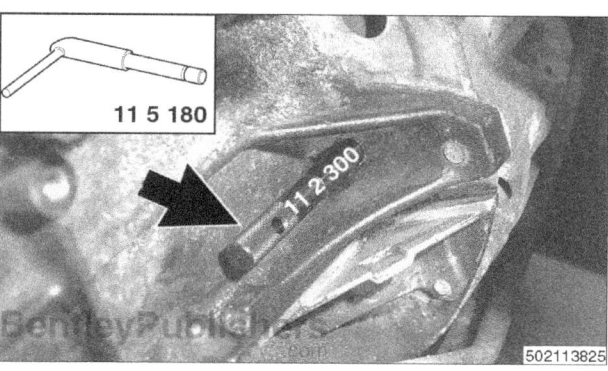

◅ Remove sealing plug from special tool bore on lower left side of engine block at flywheel bellhousing. Secure crankshaft in TDC position with BMW special tool 11 5 180 (**arrow**).

NOTE—

• BMW special tool 11 2 300 (shown) used on non-X3 M54 engines.

◅ Unscrew and remove two cylinder head cover studs (**arrows**) at rear of cylinder head.

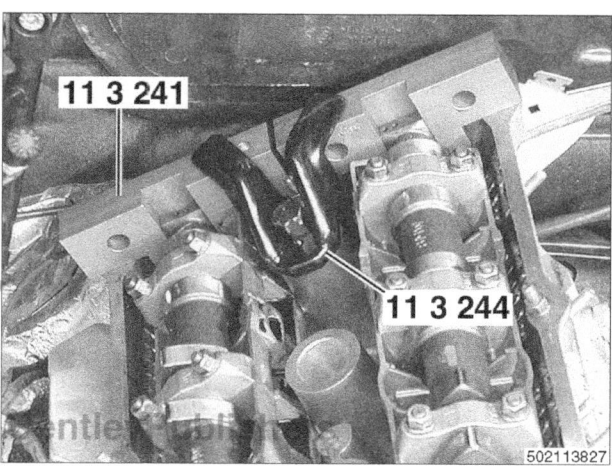

◅ Secure camshafts in TDC position using BMW special tool set 11 3 240 (includes 11 3 241 and 11 3 244).

— Disconnect compressed air line, leaving compressed air fitting attached to VANOS unit.

 • Be prepared to catch dripping oil. Do not allow oil to contaminate accessory belts.

◅ Unscrew sealing plugs (**arrows**) from VANOS unit.

Double VANOS unit, removing (M54 engine)

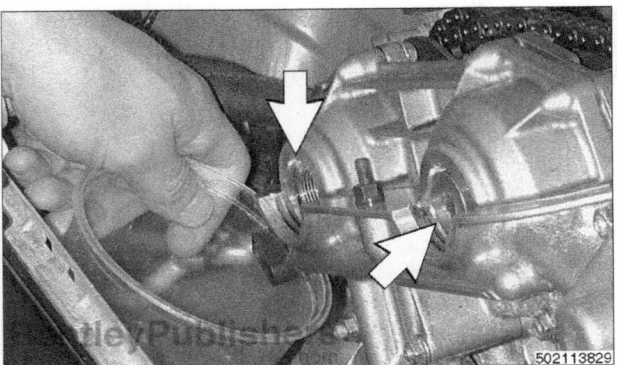

◄ Be prepared to catch dripping oil. Do not allow oil to contaminate accessory belts.

◄ Pull sealing caps straight out of VANOS unit with BMW special tool 11 6 170, or with short needle-nosed pliers.

• Additional oil may drain from VANOS unit.

◄ Remove set screws on ends of intake and exhaust camshafts.

CAUTION—
• *Set screws have left hand threads. Unscrew clockwise.*

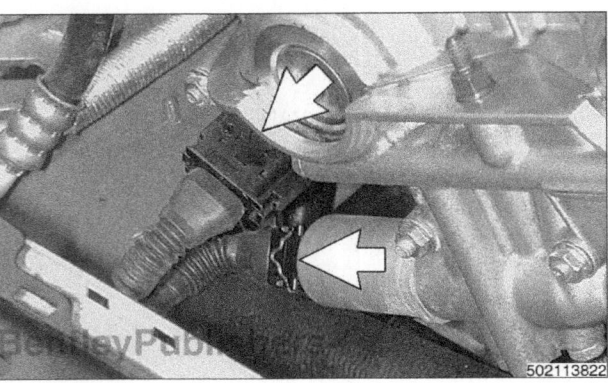

◄ Detach harness connectors at exhaust camshaft position sensor and exhaust camshaft VANOS control valve (**arrows**).

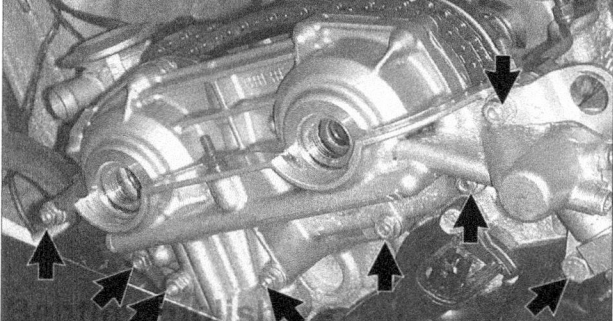

◀ Remove VANOS unit:

- Remove fasteners from engine support eye.
- Remove VANOS mounting nuts (**arrows**) from cylinder head. Slide VANOS unit and metal gasket off.
- The VANOS unit contains residual oil. Place shop towels underneath when removing.

> **CAUTION—**
> - Do not crank the engine with VANOS unit removed. Damage to engine may result from piston-to-valve interference.

Double VANOS unit, installing (M54 engine)

◀ Clean contact edges of cylinder head face and VANOS unit and apply a thin coat of permanently elastic 3-Bond 1209® or equivalent to surfaces.

> **CAUTION—**
> - Check locating dowel (**A**) and dowel sleeve (**B**) at top of cylinder head for damage or incorrect installation.
> - Make sure gasket material is removed from face of cylinder head. Clean sealing face and keep free of oil. If foreign material is present on the sealing surface, camshaft timing will be incorrect.

— Using new gasket, install VANOS unit to cylinder head.

- Reinstall engine support eye.

Tightening torques	
VANOS unit to cylinder head	
• M6 nut	10 Nm (7 ft-lb)
• M7 nut	14 Nm (10 ft-lb)

◀ Insert and tighten VANOS hydraulic piston set screws on intake and exhaust camshafts.

Tightening torque	
Hydraulic piston to splined shaft (Left-handed set screw)	10 Nm (7 ft-lb)

> **CAUTION—**
> - Set screws have left-hand threads. Tighten counterclockwise.

Double VANOS unit, installing (M54 engine)

◀ Replace sealing caps inside VANOS unit with BMW special tool 11 6 170 or short needle-nosed pliers.

◀ Insert and secure VANOS sealing plugs (**arrows**), using new sealing O-rings.

Tightening torque	
Sealing plug to VANOS unit	50 Nm (37 ft-lb)

– Remove compressed air fitting from VANOS unit.

– Fit VANOS oil line banjo bolt with new seals. Attach oil line to VANOS unit.

Tightening torque	
Oil line to VANOS unit (banjo bolt)	32 Nm (24 ft-lb)

– Connect electrical harness connectors to camshaft position sensors and VANOS solenoid valves.

– If VANOS unit is replaced, or if repair operations are completed that affect camshaft timing, recheck and adjust camshaft timing. See **Camshaft timing, checking and adjusting (M54 engine)**.

– Remove BMW special locking tools from rear of cylinder head.

– Remove crankshaft locking tool and replace sealing plug.

◀ Install intake camshaft baffle and cylinder head cover.

• Check for correct seating of half-moon seals (**A**) in back of cylinder head cover.

• Use a small amount of 3-Bond 1209® or equivalent sealant at corners (**B**) of half-moon cutouts.

• Similarly, seat gasket and seal corners in front of cylinder head, at VANOS unit.

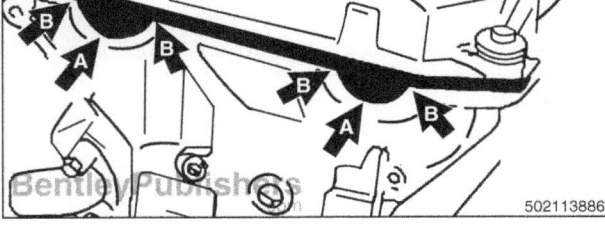

Tightening torque	
Cylinder head cover to cylinder head (M6)	10 Nm (7 ft-lb)

– Remainder of installation is reverse of removal.

Tightening torques	
Spark plug to cylinder head	25 Nm (18 ft-lb)

– After completing work, check VANOS operation using BMW scan tool.

Timing chain components (M54 engine)

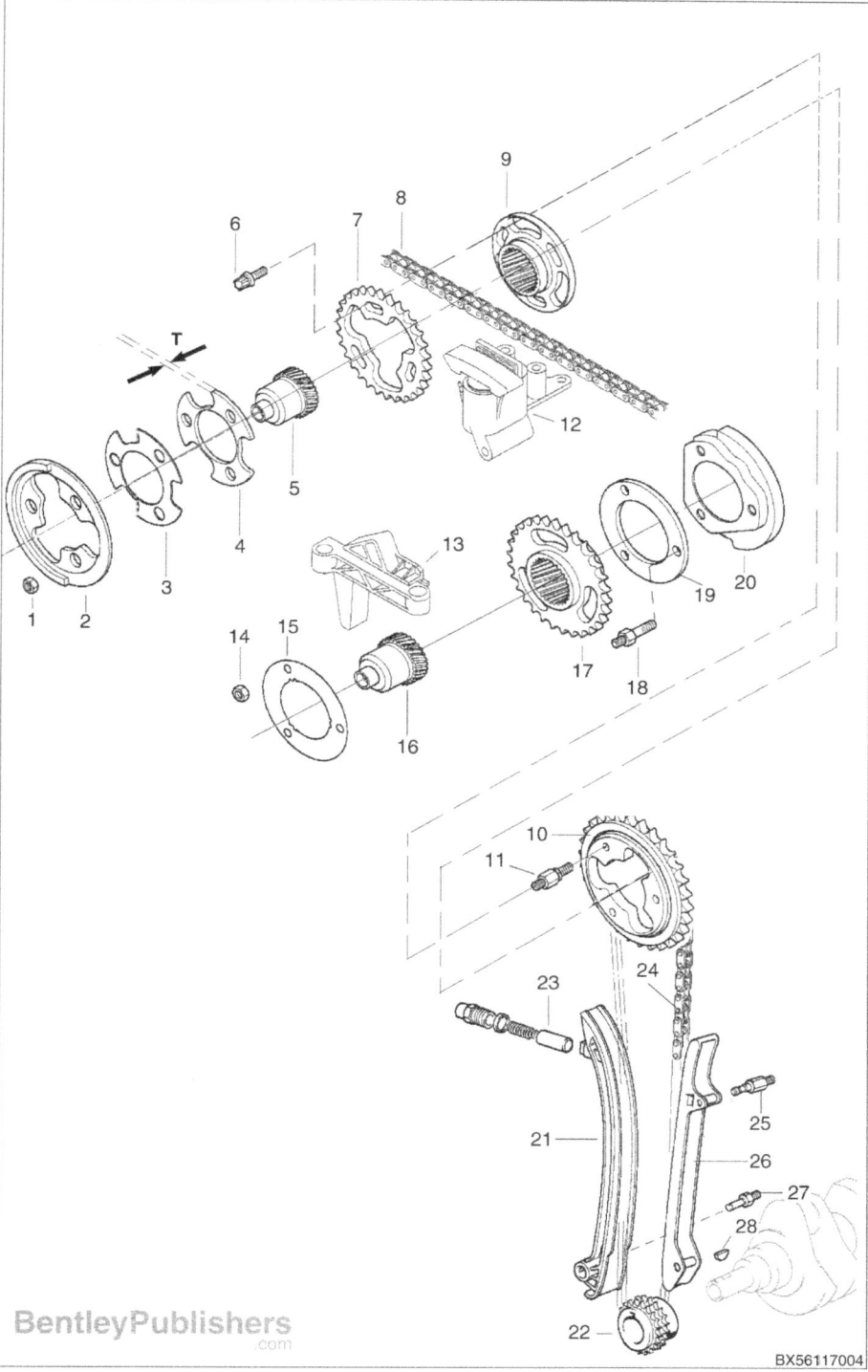

1. Impulse wheel mounting nut
2. Exhaust camshaft impulse wheel
3. Spring plate
4. Thrust spacer
   • Thickness (T) = 3.5 mm
5. Splined shaft
6. Torx screw
7. Exhaust secondary sprocket
8. Secondary timing chain
9. Splined sleeve
10. Primary sprocket
11. Threaded locating stud
12. Secondary chain tensioner
13. Secondary chain lower guide
14. Sprocket mounting nut
15. Spring plate
16. Splined shaft
17. Intake camshaft sprocket
18. Locating stud
19. Thrust spacer
20. Intake camshaft impulse wheel
21. Chain tensioner rail
22. Crankshaft sprocket
23. Primary chain tensioner
24. Primary chain
25. Locating stud
26. Guide rail
27. Locating stud
28. Woodruff key

BX56117004

Timing chains, removing (M54 engine)

Special BMW service tools are needed for camshaft disassembly and timing chain removal and installation. These tools assure proper timing of the valvetrain. Precise marks to set the timing on the camshafts are not provided for reassembly. Read the procedures through before beginning the procedure.

> **WARNING—**
> • Due to risk of personal injury, be sure engine is cold before beginning the removal procedure.

> **CAUTION—**
> • If camshafts are not properly timed, the pistons can contact the valves, causing engine damage.

— Disconnect negative (–) cable from battery.

> **CAUTION—**
> • Prior to disconnecting the battery, read the battery disconnection cautions in **001 Warnings and Cautions**.

— Remove air filter housing. See **130 Fuel Injection**.

— Remove electric cooling fan and cowl.
  See **170 Radiator and Cooling System**.

— Mark direction of engine rotation on accessory belts. Remove belts. See **020 Maintenance**.

— Remove coolant pump pulley.

— Remove engine covers and cylinder head cover. See **113 Cylinder Head Removal and Installation**.

— Remove spark plugs. Plug spark plug bores to prevent debris from falling into engine.

— Remove VANOS unit. See **Double VANOS unit, removing (M54 engine)** in this repair group.

— Raise car and support safely.

> **WARNING—**
> • Make sure car is stable and well supported at all times. Use a professional automotive lift or jack stands. A floor jack is not adequate support.

— Drain engine cooling system. See **170 Radiator and Cooling System**.

— Drain engine oil and remove oil pan. See **119 Lubrication System**.

◄ Make sure camshafts are locked in TDC position using BMW special tool set 11 3 240. See **Double VANOS unit, removing (M54 engine)** in this repair group.

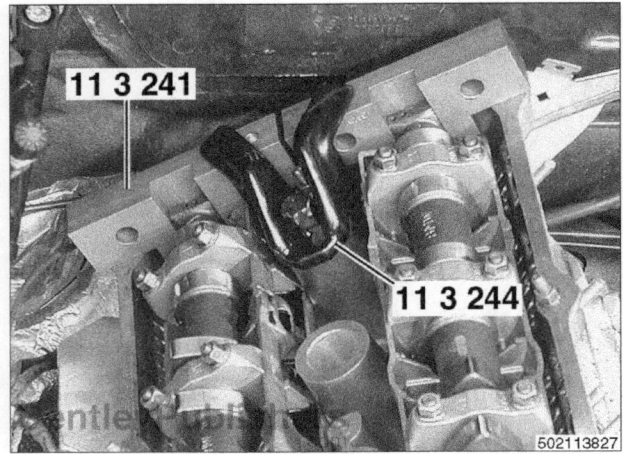

Timing chains, removing (M54 engine)

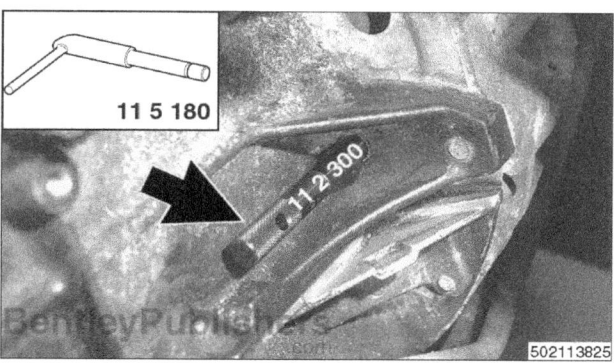

◄ Make sure crankshaft is still locked with BMW special tool 11 5 180. See **Double VANOS unit, removing (M54 engine)** in this repair group.

NOTE—

• *BMW special tool 11 2 300 (shown) used on non-X3 M54 engines.*

◄ Remove primary camshaft chain tensioner (**arrow**) from timing chain cover.

> **CAUTION—**
>
> • *Chain tensioner piston is under spring pressure.*

◄ Press down on secondary chain tensioner and lock into place using BMW special tool 11 3 292 or a similar size pin tool.

◄ Remove exhaust camshaft impulse wheel mounting nuts (**arrows**). Remove impulse wheel (**A**).

Timing chains, removing (M54 engine)

◀ Remove spring plate (**A**).

◀ Remove intake camshaft sprocket mounting nuts (**arrows**) and remove spring plate (labeled **FRONT**).

◀ Remove torx bolts (**arrows**) from exhaust camshaft sprocket.

◀ Lift off exhaust and intake sprockets with secondary chain, thrust spacer (**A**) and splined shaft (**B**).

> **CAUTION—**
> • *Intake and exhaust camshaft splined shafts share the same part number. Be sure to mark splined shafts so they can be reinstalled in their original positions.*

◄ Remove exhaust camshaft splined sleeve (**A**) and shaft (**B**).

◄ Remove secondary chain tensioner mounting bolts (**arrows**). Remove tensioner while keeping locking pin in place.

◄ Remove primary chain sprocket mounting studs (**arrows**) on exhaust camshaft.

Timing chains, removing (M54 engine)

◄ Lift primary chain sprocket off exhaust camshaft. Remove sprocket from chain.

◄ Hang timing chain on exhaust camshaft end.

◄ Working in cylinder head cavity, remove timing chain cover bolts (**arrows**).

◄ Remove secondary chain lower guide mounting bolts (**arrows**). Remove chain guide.

NOTE—

• *Bolt on intake camshaft side is long and extends into timing chain cover.*

— Remove crankshaft vibration damper. See **Vibration damper, removing and installing (M54 engine)** in this repair group.

> **CAUTION—**
> - *Do not use flywheel locking tool to hold crankshaft stationary to loosen or tighten vibration damper mounting bolt. Use only the special tools specified, or equivalent hub holding tool.*
> - *Do not allow crankshaft to rotate while timing chains are loosened or removed. The pistons can contact the valves, causing engine damage.*

◄ Using a 5 mm or smaller drift, drive two locating dowels (**insets**) in lower timing cover toward rear of car.

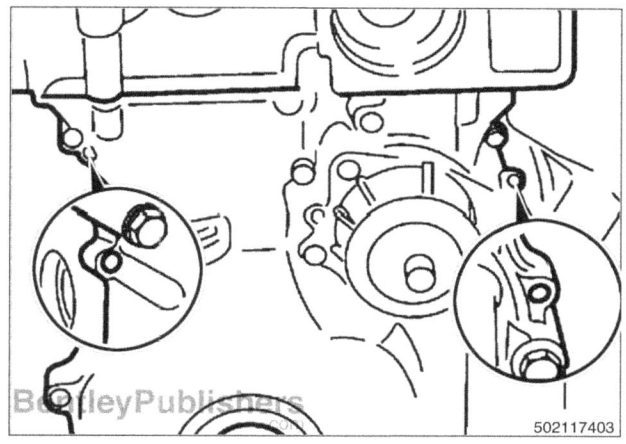

502117403

◄ Remove timing cover mounting bolts (**arrows**). Slide cover with coolant pump forward to remove.

> **CAUTION—**
> - *Use care when removing the cover from the cylinder head gasket. If the cover is stuck, use a sharp knife to separate it from the head gasket.*
> - *If cylinder head gasket is damaged, remove cylinder head and replace head gasket. See* **113 Cylinder Head Removal and Installation***.*
> - *Use care when detaching front timing cover from coolant pipe at rear of cover.*

> **NOTE—**
> - *For clarity, front timing cover is illustrated with coolant pump removed.*

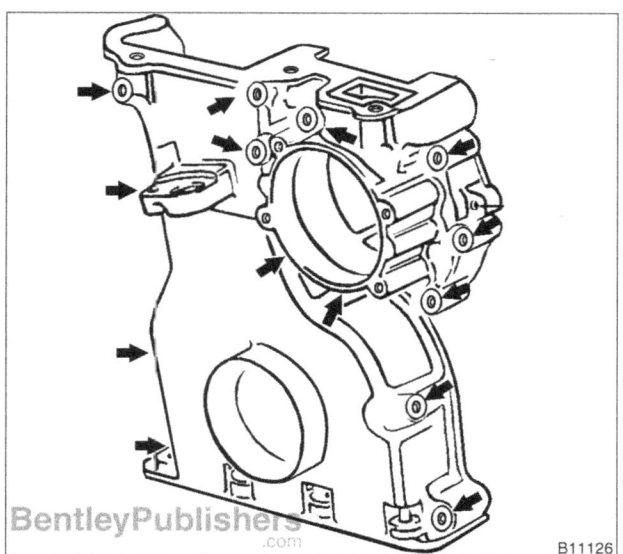

B11126

— Push primary chain tensioner guide rail aside and remove chain.

Timing chains, installing (M54 engine)

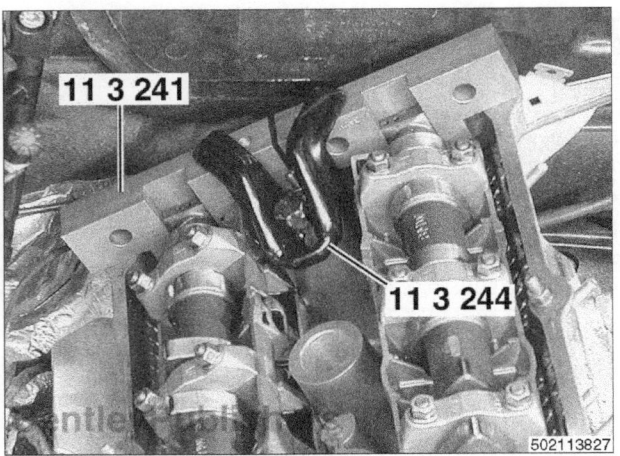

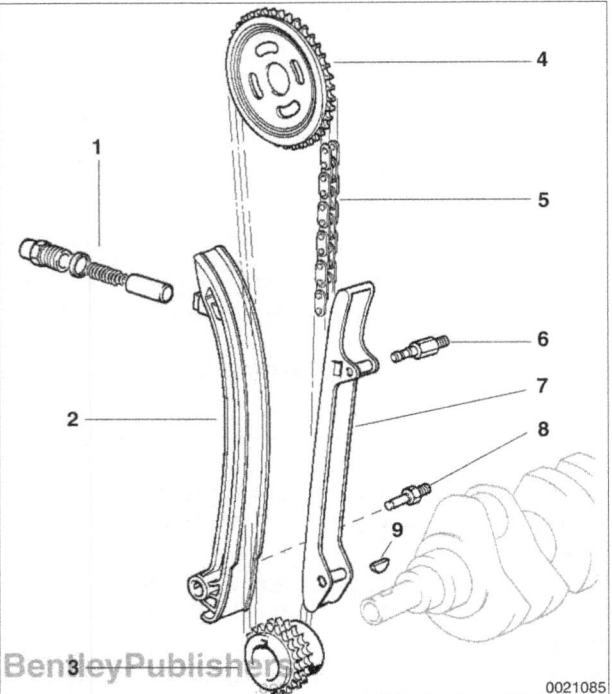

Timing chains, installing (M54 engine)

◀ Make sure camshafts are locked in TDC position using BMW special tool set 11 3 240.

— Inspect timing chain sprockets. Inspect guide rail and tensioner rail for damage. Replace any part that is worn or damaged.

NOTE —

• *If any sprockets are replaced due to wear, also replace chain.*

◀ Primary timing chain assembly

1. Primary chain tensioner
2. Chain tensioner rail
3. Crankshaft sprocket
4. Exhaust camshaft sprocket
5. Primary chain
6. Anchor bolt
7. Guide rail
8. Anchor bolt
9. Woodruff key

— Install primary timing chain to crankshaft sprocket and hang upper end from exhaust camshaft.

— If necessary, replace crankshaft front seal in timing chain cover. See **119 Lubrication System**.

— To install lower timing chain cover:

• Clean cover and cylinder block sealing surfaces.

• Use new gaskets and coolant pipe O-ring.

• Remove timing chain cover dowel pins from engine block.

• Drive dowels into cover until they just protrude slightly from sealing surface.

• Apply a small bead of silicon sealer (3-Bond 1209® or equivalent) to corners of cylinder head where timing cover meets cylinder head and engine block.

• Tap cover into position until firmly seated.

• Install all bolts hand tight, including two Torx bolts from above.

• Install secondary chain lower guide.

• Tighten cover mounting bolts alternately and in stages.

Tightening torque	
Lower timing cover to cylinder block (M6)	10 Nm (7 ft-lb)

Timing chains, installing (M54 engine)

– Install oil pan with new gasket. See **119 Lubrication System**.

Tightening torques	
Oil pan to engine block (M6) • 8.8 grade • 10.9 grade	 10 Nm (7 ft-lb) 12 Nm (9 ft-lb)

– Reinstall crankshaft vibration damper. See **Vibration damper, removing and installing (M54 engine)** in this repair group.

> **CAUTION—**
>
> • *Do not use BMW special tool 11 5 180 to hold crankshaft stationary to tighten vibration damper mounting bolt. Use only the special tools specified, or equivalent hub holding tool.*
>
> • *Have a second person hold special tool 11 8 190 while tightening vibration damper mounting bolt.*

Tightening torque	
Vibration damper hub to crankshaft (use new bolt)	410 Nm (300 ft-lb)

◄ Remove crankshaft locking tool (**arrow**).

> **NOTE—**
>
> • *BMW special tool 11 2 300 (shown) used on non-X3 M54 engines.*

◄ Fit top sprocket to primary timing chain and install on exhaust camshaft so that pointer on sprocket (**arrow**) lines up with cylinder head sealing surface (**dashed line**).

– Position sprocket so that chain slack is on tensioner rail side.

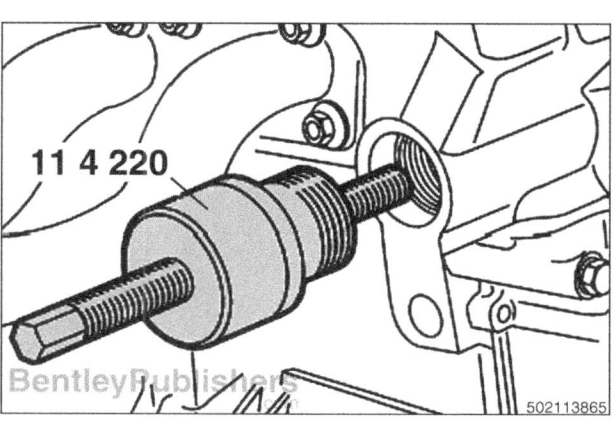

◄ Insert BMW special tool 11 4 220 in cylinder head and screw in adjustment screw by hand just until it contacts tensioning rail and chain slack is removed.

> **NOTE—**
>
> • *BMW special tool 11 4 220 is an adjustable dummy tensioner that simulates the function of the primary chain tensioner.*

– Make sure arrow on upper primary sprocket still lines up with upper edge of cylinder head. Reposition sprocket if necessary.

Timing chains, installing (M54 engine)

◀ Install and tighten down threaded locating studs (**arrows**) in end of exhaust camshaft.

Tightening torque	
Exhaust camshaft locating stud	20 Nm (15 ft-lb)

◀ Install secondary chain tensioner on cylinder head (**arrows**). Keep tensioner compressed using BMW special tool 11 3 291 or suitable pin tool.

◀ Fit exhaust camshaft splined sleeve, aligning gap in sleeve splines with corresponding gap on camshaft splines (**arrows**).

◄ Slide splined shaft on exhaust camshaft. Be sure that locating tooth of shaft fits into spline gaps of camshaft and splined sleeve (**arrows**).

• Push splined shaft in further to rotate splined sleeve until three threaded holes in primary chain sprocket are centered in splined sleeve slots (**dashed lines**).

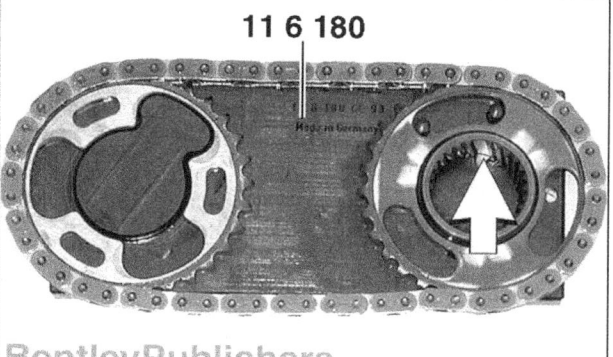

◄ Time intake to exhaust sprockets using BMW special tool 11 6 180. Position spline gap on intake sprocket (**arrow**) as shown and place secondary chain on sprockets.

◄ Remove chain and sprockets from tool and slide sprockets on camshafts, aligning gap in intake sprocket splines with corresponding gap in camshaft splines (**arrow**).

CAUTION—

• *Do not alter position of sprockets with respect to chain when removing from special tool 11 6 180.*

◄ Slide splined shaft onto intake camshaft until approx. 1 mm (0.04 in) of splines (**arrows**) are visible.

Timing chains, installing (M54 engine)

◀ Install intake camshaft spring plate so that **FRONT** mark is visible. Install mounting nuts (**arrows**) finger tight.

◀ Insert sprocket mounting bolts (**arrows**) on exhaust side camshaft assembly.

- Initially tighten to approx. 5 Nm (44 in-lb) and then back off by half a turn.

◀ Fit thrust spacer (**A**) on exhaust camshaft.

◀ Install spring plate (**A**) to exhaust camshaft. Make sure that **F** mark is visible.

NOTE—

- *If **F** mark is no longer visible, install spring plate as shown in inset: convex side facing forward.*

Timing chains, installing (M54 engine)

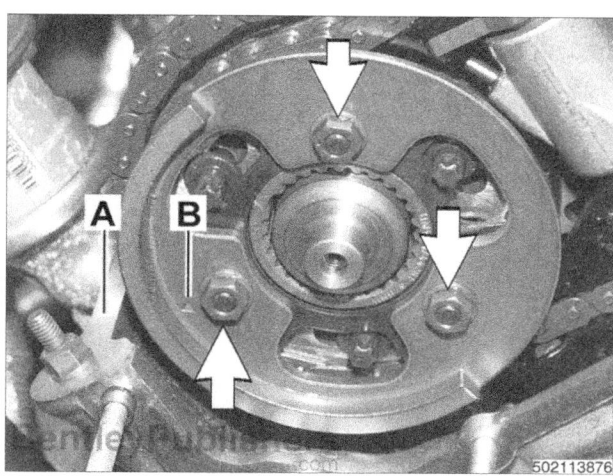

◄ Install exhaust camshaft impulse wheel, aligning pointer (**B**) with top edge of cylinder head (**A**). Install mounting nuts (**arrows**) finger tight.

◄ Pull out exhaust camshaft splined shaft to stop (**arrow**).

– Press down on secondary chain tensioner and remove tensioner lock-down tool.

◄ Preload primary chain:

• Tighten adjusting screw on BMW special tool 11 4 220 to specified torque.

Tightening torque	
Primary chain tensioner preload	0.7 Nm (6 in-lb)

Timing chains, installing (M54 engine)

◀ Preload exhaust camshaft spring plate by pressing on impulse wheel while tightening mounting nuts (**arrows**) finger tight.

◀ Install BMW special tool 11 6 150 (VANOS setup bracket) to front of cylinder head timing case. Install nuts (**arrows**) finger tight, then tighten down uniformly until special tool is in full contact with cylinder head.

> **CAUTION—**
> • *Make sure gasket material is removed from face of cylinder head. Clean sealing face and keep free of oil. If foreign material is present on the sealing surface, camshaft timing will be incorrect.*

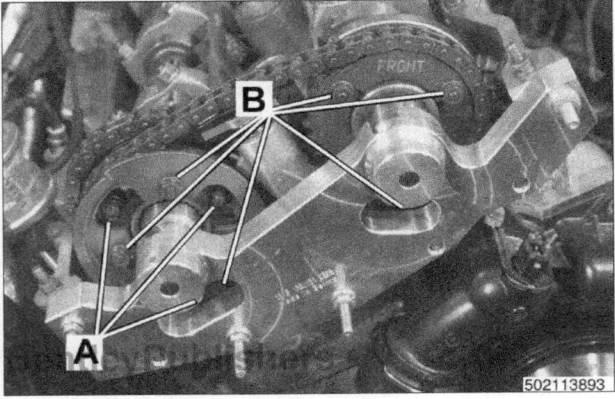

◀ Secure camshaft sprockets and impulse wheels:

- Tighten mounting screws (**A**) on exhaust camshaft impulse wheel to approx. 5 Nm (44 in-lb).
- Tighten mounting nuts (**B**) on exhaust and intake sprocket assemblies to approx. 5 Nm (44 in-lb).
- Torque down mounting screws (**A**) and nuts (**B**) to final specifications.

Tightening torques	
Sprocket assembly wheel to camshaft (initial torque)	5 Nm (44 in-lb)
Sprocket assembly wheel to camshaft • M7 torx screws (**A**) • M6 mounting nuts (**B**)	20 Nm (15 ft-lb) 10 Nm (8 ft-lb)

— Remove crankshaft locking tool so that crankshaft is no longer secured in TDC position.

— Remove camshaft locking tools from cylinder head.

◀ Turn engine over twice in direction of rotation until cylinder 1 intake and exhaust camshaft lobes (**arrows**) face each other.

— Secure crankshaft in TDC position with BMW special tool 11 5 180.

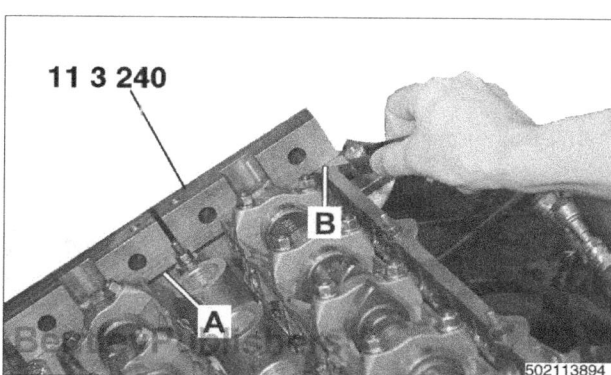

Place BMW special tool set 11 3 240 over camshafts and measure clearances.

- Due to VANOS unit tolerances and play, intake side of special tool 11 3 240 (**B**) may be up to 1 mm (0.04 in) above surface of cylinder head. This is normal. Reassemble engine.

- Otherwise, reset camshaft timing. See **Camshaft timing, checking and adjusting (M54 engine)** in this repair group.

> **CAUTION—**
> - *If exhaust side of tool (**A**) is not flush with cylinder head, camshaft timing is incorrect. Reset camshaft timing.*

— Remove BMW special tool 11 6 150 from front of cylinder head.

— Reinstall VANOS unit. See **Double VANOS unit, installing (M54 engine)** in this repair group.

— Remove BMW special tool 11 4 220 (adjustable dummy tensioner). Reinstall primary chain tensioner.

Tightening torque	
Primary chain tensioner to timing chain cover (M26 x 1.5)	70 Nm (52 ft-lb)

— Install intake camshaft oil baffle.

 Install cylinder head cover:

- Check for correct seating of half-moon seals (**A**) in back of cylinder head cover.

- Use a small amount of 3-Bond 1209® or equivalent sealant at corners (**B**) of half-moon cutouts. Seal corners in front of cylinder head at VANOS unit.

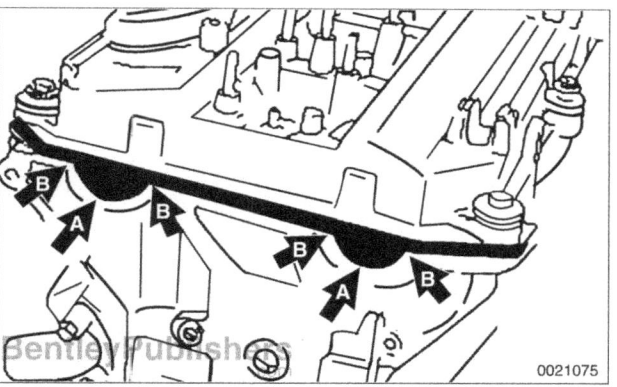

Tightening torque	
Cylinder head cover to cylinder head	10 Nm (7 ft-lb)

— Remainder of assembly is reverse of removal, noting the following:

- Secure all coolant hoses, thermostat housing, engine coolant drains.

- Install new engine oil filter and oil. See **119 Lubrication System**.

- Refill and bleed cooling system. See **170 Radiator and Cooling system**.

- Use scan tool to check VANOS operation with engine idling.

Tightening torques	
Coolant drain plug to cylinder block	25 Nm (18 ft-lb)
Radiator drain screw to radiator	2.5 Nm (22 in-lb)
Vibration damper hub to crankshaft (use new bolt)	410 Nm (300 ft-lb)

Camshaft timing, checking and adjusting (M54 engine)

Camshaft timing, checking and adjusting (M54 engine)

— Remove engine top covers and cylinder head cover. See **113 Cylinder Head Removal and Installation**.

◀ Remove oil baffle cover from above intake camshaft.

— Remove engine drive belts and cooling fan. See **170 Radiator and Cooling System**.

— Remove spark plugs. Plug spark plug bores to prevent debris from falling into engine.

◀ Remove primary camshaft chain tensioner cylinder (**arrow**).

> **CAUTION—**
> • *Chain tensioner piston is under spring pressure.*

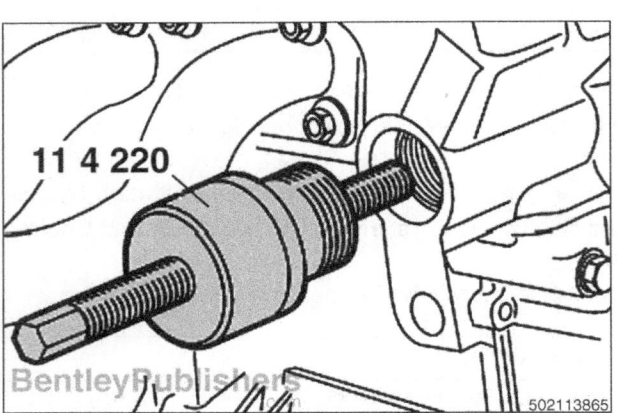

◀ Insert BMW special tool 11 4 220 in cylinder head and screw in adjustment screw by hand just until it contacts tensioning rail and chain slack is removed.

NOTE—
• *BMW special tool 11 4 220 is an adjustable dummy tensioner that simulates the function of the primary chain tensioner.*

Camshaft timing, checking and adjusting (M54 engine)

 Preload primary chain tensioner rail:

• Tighten adjusting screw on BMW special tool 11 4 220.

Tightening torque	
Primary chain tensioner preload	0.7 Nm (6 in-lb)

 Remove banjo bolt from VANOS unit oil pressure line. Use banjo bolt to attach BMW special tool 11 3 450 (compressed air fitting) to VANOS unit.

• Be prepared to catch dripping oil. Do not allow oil to contaminate accessory belts.

 Cover oil bore (**arrow**) in VANOS unit with shop towel to capture oil which sprays when compressed air is applied.

– Connect compressed air line to air fitting. Apply air pressure set to 2 – 8 bar (30 – 115 psi).

With compressed air line connected, use crankshaft vibration damper bolt to rotate engine in direction of rotation (clockwise) at least twice, until cylinder 1 intake and exhaust camshaft lobes face each other (**arrows**) in top dead center (TDC) position for cylinder 1.

> **CAUTION—**
> • *Do not rotate engine counterclockwise to reach TDC. If engine rotates past TDC, complete another two complete rotations.*

Camshaft timing, checking and adjusting (M54 engine)

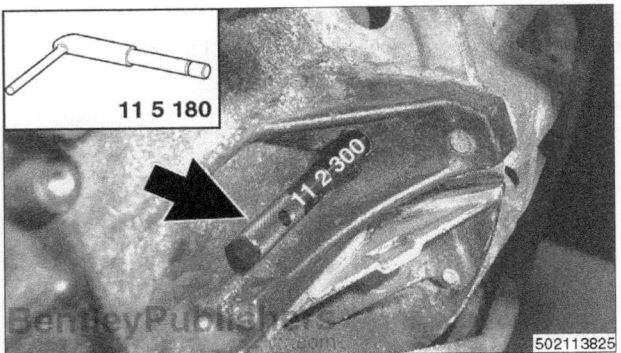

◀ Remove sealing plug from special tool bore on lower left side of engine block near flywheel. Secure crankshaft in TDC position with BMW special tool 11 5 180 (**arrow**).

NOTE —

• BMW special tool 11 2 300 (shown) used on non-X3 M54 engines.

◀ Unscrew and remove two cylinder head cover studs (**arrows**) at rear of cylinder head.

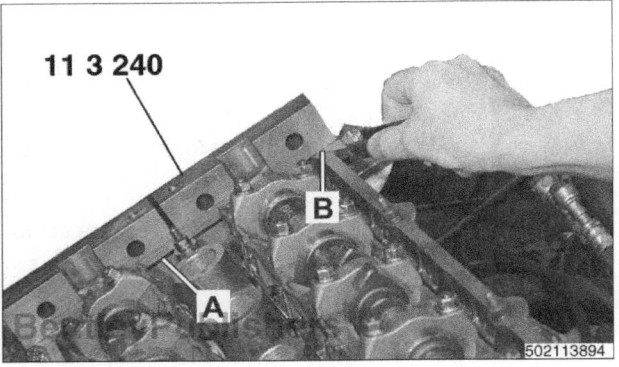

◀ Place BMW special tool set 11 3 240 over camshafts and measure clearances.

• Due to VANOS unit tolerances and play, intake side of special tool 11 3 240 (**B**) may be up to 1 mm (0.04 in) above surface of cylinder head. This is normal. Reassemble engine.

• Otherwise, continue with camshaft timing adjustment procedure.

CAUTION—

• If exhaust side of tool (**A**) is not flush with cylinder head, camshaft timing is incorrect. Reset camshaft timing.

Adjusting camshaft timing (M54 engine)

— Remove double VANOS unit. See **Double VANOS unit, removing (M54 engine)** in this repair group.

◀ Press down on secondary chain tensioner and lock into place using BMW special tool 11 3 292 or equivalent pin or drift.

◀ Loosen intake camshaft sprocket mounting nuts (**arrows**) by 1 turn.

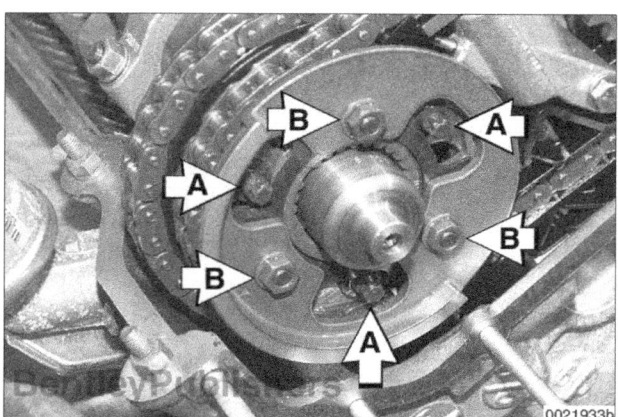

◀ Loosen exhaust camshaft sprocket mounting fasteners:
  • Release bolts **A** ½ turn.
  • Release nuts **B** 2 turns.

◀ Pull out intake camshaft splined shaft out so that approx. 1 mm (0.04 in) of splines (**arrows**) can be seen.

◀ Pull out exhaust camshaft splined shaft to stop (**arrow**).

– Make sure camshafts are secured in TDC position using BMW special tools 11 3 240 and 11 3 244.

Camshaft timing, checking and adjusting (M54 engine)

 Make sure chain tensioning rail is preloaded.

Tightening torque	
Primary chain tensioner preload	0.7 Nm (6 in-lb)

◄ Preload exhaust camshaft spring plate by pressing on impulse wheel. Tighten mounting nuts (**arrows**) by hand. Do not tighten fully.

◄ Install BMW special tool 11 6 150 (VANOS setup bracket) to front of cylinder head timing case. Tighten nuts (**arrows**) by hand, and then tighten down uniformly until special tool contacts cylinder head firmly.

> **CAUTION—**
> * *Make sure gasket material is removed from face of cylinder head. Clean sealing face and keep free of oil. If foreign material is present on the sealing surface, camshaft timing will be incorrect.*

Camshaft timing, checking and adjusting (M54 engine)

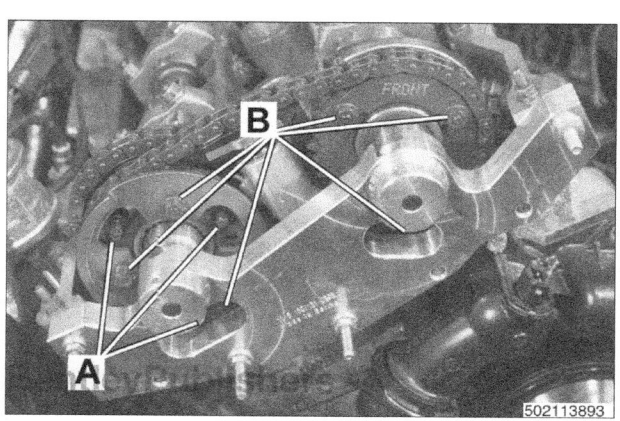

◀ Secure camshaft impulse sprockets and wheels:

- Pretighten Torx screws (**A**) on exhaust camshaft impulse wheel to approx. 5 Nm (44 in-lb).
- Pretighten mounting nuts (**B**) on exhaust and intake sprocket assemblies to approx. 5 Nm (44 in-lb).
- Torque down Torx screws (**A**) and nuts (**B**) to final specifications.

Tightening torques	
Sprocket assembly to camshaft (initial torque)	5 Nm (44 in-lb)
Sprocket assembly to camshaft • M7 Torx screw (**A**) • M6 mounting nut (**B**)	20 Nm (15 ft-lb) 10 Nm (7 ft-lb)

- Remove flywheel locking tool from transmission bellhousing so that crankshaft is no longer locked.

- Remove camshaft locking tools from rear of cylinder head.

- Use crankshaft vibration damper bolt to crank engine over twice by hand in direction of rotation until cylinder 1 intake and exhaust camshaft lobes face each other again.

- Secure crankshaft with BMW special tool 11 5 180.

◀ Place BMW special tool set 11 3 240 over camshafts and measure clearances.

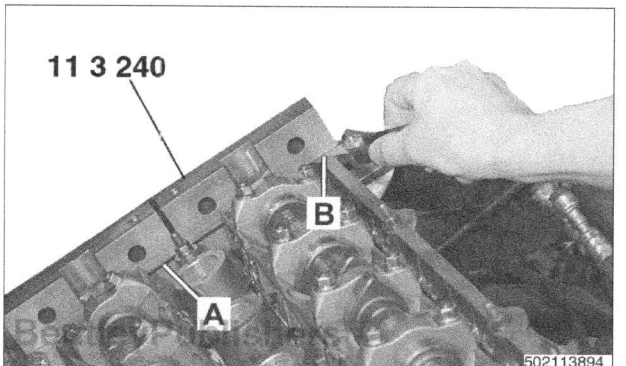

- Due to VANOS unit tolerances and play, intake side of special tool 11 3 240 (**B**) may be up to 1 mm (0.04 in) above surface of cylinder head. This is normal. Reassemble engine.
- Otherwise, repeat camshaft timing adjustment procedure.

> **CAUTION—**
> • *If exhaust side of tool (**A**) is not flush with cylinder head, camshaft timing is incorrect. Reset camshaft timing.*

- Remove camshaft locking tools from rear of camshafts.

- Remove BMW special tool 11 4 220 (adjustable dummy tensioner). Reinstall primary chain tensioner.

Tightening torque	
Primary chain tensioner to timing chain cover (M26 x 1.5)	70 Nm (52 ft-lb)

- Remove crankshaft locking tool from transmission bellhousing. Reinstall sealing plug.

- Remove VANOS setup bracket from front of cylinder head.

- Install VANOS unit. See **Double VANOS unit, installing (M54 engine)** in this repair group.

- Remove compressed air line adapter (BMW special tool 11 3 450) from VANOS unit.

Camshaft sprockets assembly (M54 engine)

— Fit VANOS oil line banjo bolt with new seals. Attach oil line to VANOS unit.

Tightening torque	
Oil line to VANOS unit (banjo bolt)	32 Nm (24 ft-lb)

— Remainder of installation is reverse of removal. Note the following:
  • Install spark plugs.
  • Install intake camshaft plastic baffle prior to installing cylinder head cover. Install ignition coil packs and connect electrical harness connectors.
  • Install accessory belts, radiator cooling fan and cooling fan shroud.
  • Install upper engine covers.

Tightening torques	
Cylinder head cover to cylinder head	10 Nm (7 ft-lb)
Spark plug to cylinder head	25 Nm (18 ft-lb)

CAMSHAFT SERVICE (M54 ENGINE)

Camshaft sprockets assembly (M54 engine)

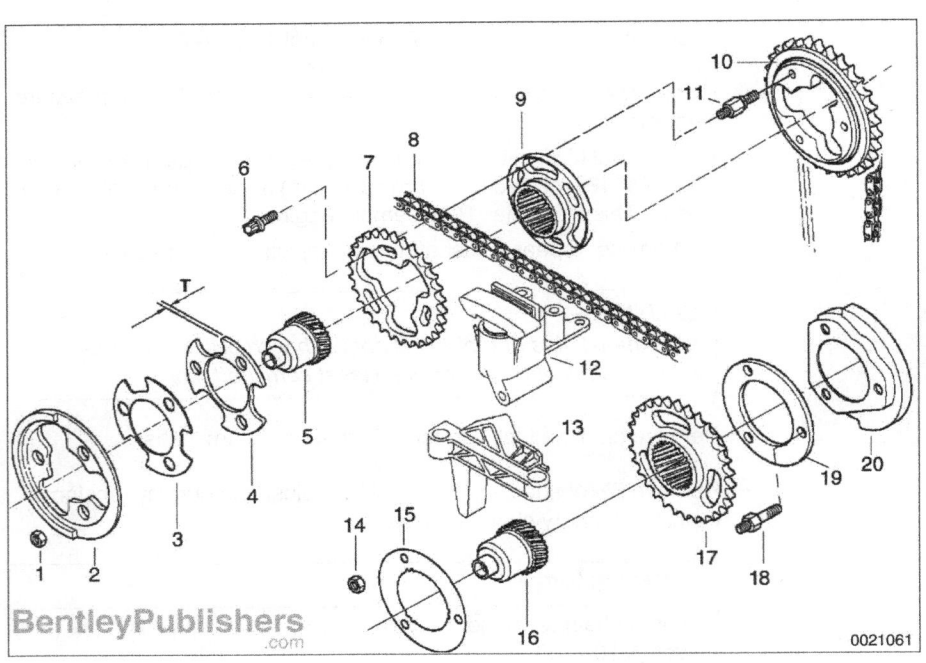

1. Impulse wheel mounting nut
2. Exhaust camshaft impulse wheel
3. Spring plate, exhaust
4. Thrust spacer (T = 3.5 mm)
5. Splined shaft
6. Torx screw
7. Exhaust camshaft secondary sprocket
8. Secondary timing chain
9. Splined sleeve
10. Primary sprocket
11. Threaded locating stud
12. Secondary chain tensioner
13. Secondary chain lower guide
14. Sprocket mounting nut
15. Spring plate, intake
16. Splined shaft
17. Intake camshaft sprocket
18. Locating stud
19. Thrust spacer
20. Intake camshaft impulse wheel

Camshafts, removing (M54 engine)

> **WARNING—**
> • Due to risk of personal injury, be sure engine is cold before beginning removal procedure.

> **CAUTION—**
> • Special BMW service tools are required to remove and install camshafts and VANOS units. Read procedure through before starting.
> • If camshafts are not properly timed, pistons can contact valves, causing engine damage.

— Disconnect negative (–) cable from battery.

> **CAUTION—**
> • Prior to disconnecting the battery, read battery disconnection cautions in **001 Warnings and Cautions**.

— Remove air filter housing and ducts. See **130 Fuel Injection**.

— Remove electric cooling fan and cooling fan shroud. See **170 Radiator and Cooling System**.

— Remove engine covers and cylinder head cover. See **113 Cylinder Head Removal and Installation**.

— Remove spark plugs. Plug spark plug bores to prevent debris from falling into engine.

— Remove VANOS unit. See **Double VANOS unit, removing (M54 engine)** in this repair group.

◀ Remove primary camshaft chain tensioner cylinder (**arrow**).

> **CAUTION—**
> • Chain tensioner piston is under spring pressure.

◀ Press down on secondary chain tensioner and lock into place using BMW special tool 11 3 291, or a thin drift or pin.

◁ Remove exhaust camshaft impulse wheel mounting nuts (**arrows**). Remove impulse wheel (**A**).

◁ Remove spring plate (**A**).

◁ Remove intake camshaft sprocket mounting nuts (**arrows**) and remove spring plate (labeled **FRONT**).

◁ Remove Torx bolts (**arrows**) from exhaust camshaft sprocket.

◄ Lift off exhaust and intake sprockets together with secondary chain, thrust spacer (**A**), and splined shaft (**B**).

> **CAUTION—**
> • *Intake and exhaust camshaft splined shafts share the same part number. Be sure to mark splined shafts so they can be reinstalled in their original positions.*

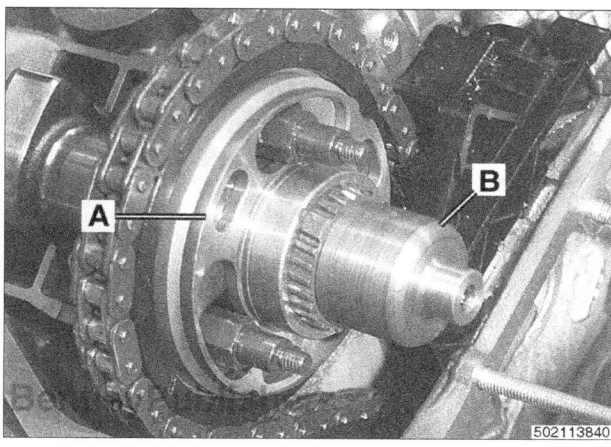

◄ Remove exhaust camshaft splined sleeve (**A**) and shaft (**B**).

◄ Remove secondary chain tensioner mounting bolts (**arrows**) and remove tensioner with retaining pin in place.

Camshafts, removing (M54 engine)

◀ Remove sprocket mounting studs (**arrows**) from exhaust camshaft.

◀ Lift primary chain sprocket off exhaust camshaft. Remove sprocket from chain.

◀ Place timing chain on end of exhaust camshaft.

◀ Remove locating studs (**arrows**) from intake camshaft. Lift off intake camshaft thrust spacer (**A**) and impulse wheel (**B**).

◄ Do not remove Torx screws (**arrows**) from camshafts.

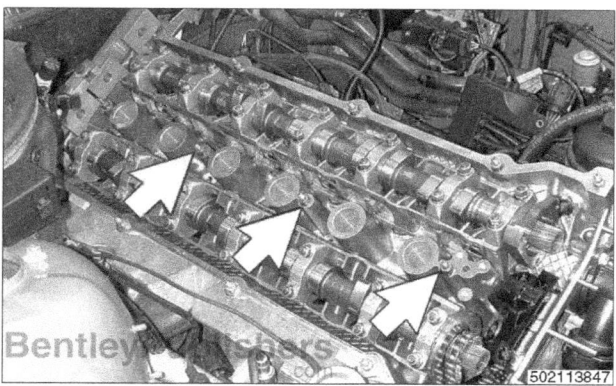

◄ Remove cylinder head cover mounting studs (**arrows**) from center of cylinder head.

− Remove crankshaft locking tool.

◄ Lift primary chain and hold under tension. Use crankshaft vibration damper bolt to rotate engine in direction opposite to normal rotation (counterclockwise) approximately 30°.

> **CAUTION—**
> • *By turning crankshaft 30° counterclockwise, pistons are moved away from top dead center. This prevents piston-to-valve interference during camshaft servicing.*

− Remove camshaft locking tools (BMW special tool set 11 3 240) from rear of cylinder head.

◄ Remove intake camshaft bearing cap 1 fasteners (**arrows**). Remove bearing cap.

> **CAUTION—**
> • *Do not remove camshaft bearing caps 2 - 6 at this time.*

Camshafts, removing (M54 engine)

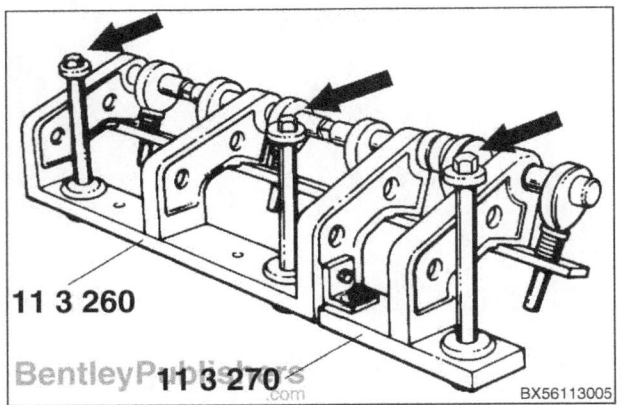

◄ Fit BMW special tools 11 3 260 and 11 3 270 to cylinder head and screw long bolts (**arrows**) into spark plug threads. Align tensioning pins on tool with bearing caps on camshaft.

> **CAUTION—**
> • *Do not overtighten bolts in spark plug holes.*

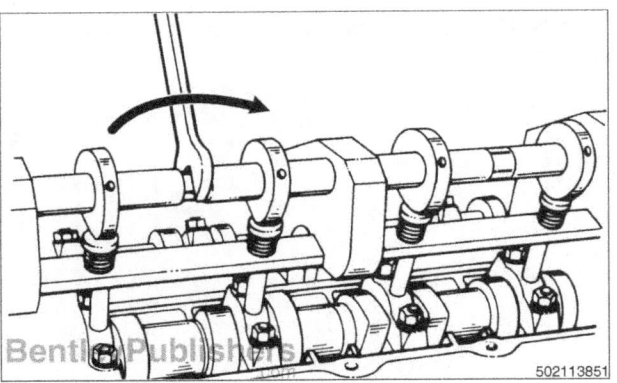

◄ Rotate eccentric shaft of special tool (**arrow**) to pretension intake camshaft bearing caps. Remove remaining intake camshaft bearing cap fasteners.

– Slowly release tension on eccentric shaft and remove BMW special tools. Remove bearing caps and set aside in order. Remove camshaft and store safely.

– Repeat procedure for exhaust camshaft.

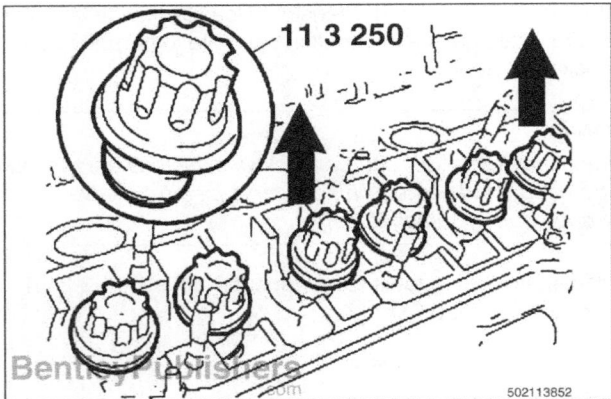

◄ If cylinder head is being removed, secure hydraulic lifters in lifter bores using BMW special tool set 11 3 250, or remove lifters using a magnetic pick-up tool. With lifters secure or removed, lift out camshaft bearing carriers from cylinder head.

> **CAUTION—**
> • *Do not let hydraulic lifters fall out as camshaft carrier is removed.*
> • *Mark hydraulic lifters so that they can be reinstalled in their original lifter bores.*
> • *Store hydraulic lifters in an upright position.*

Camshafts, installing (M54 engine)

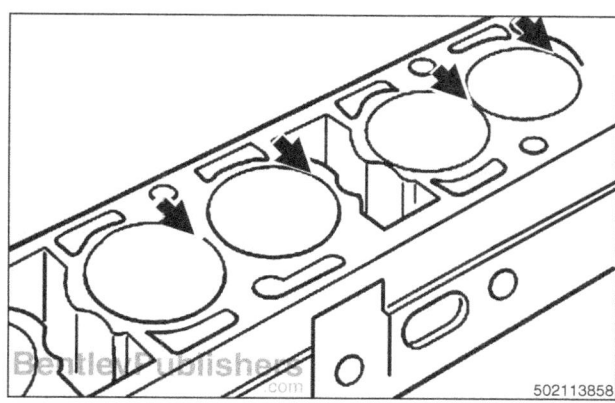

◄ Before installing camshaft carriers, examine hydraulic lifter bore bearing points (**arrows**) on underside of camshaft carriers for signs of wear.

– Lubricate camshafts, camshaft carriers, bearing caps, hydraulic lifters and friction washers with assembly lubricant.

◄ Center camshaft carrier with hydraulic lifters on pins (**arrows**) at bearing positions 2 and 7.

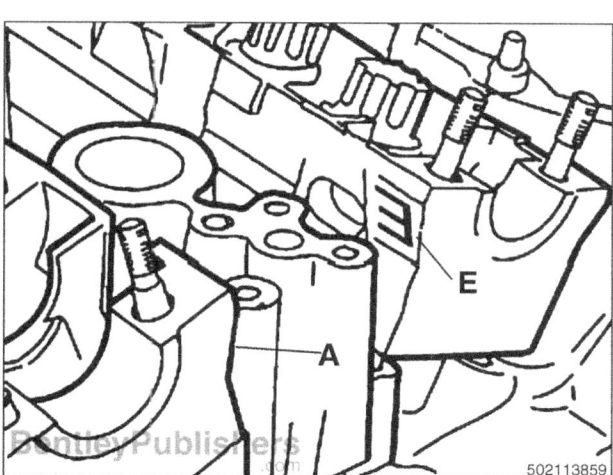

◄ Note marks on camshaft carriers: **E** for intake side and **A** for exhaust side.

– Lift timing chain and place exhaust camshaft on exhaust camshaft carrier. Place intake camshaft on intake camshaft carrier.

◄ Place bearing caps on camshafts and install retaining nuts (**arrows**) finger tight.

• Note that each bearing cap is marked (**inset**):
E1 to E7 for intake (front to rear)
A1 to A7 for exhaust (front to rear)

> **CAUTION—**
> • *Make sure crankshaft, which was rotated approximately 30° opposite direction of engine rotation from TDC, is still in that position.*

Camshafts, installing (M54 engine)

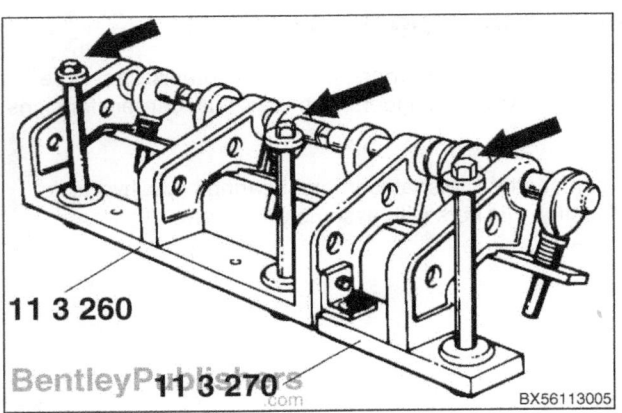

◀ Fit BMW special tools 11 3 260 and 11 3 270 to cylinder head and screw long bolts (**arrows**) into spark plug threads. Align tensioning pins on tool with bearing caps on intake camshaft.

> **CAUTION—**
> • *Do not overtighten bolts in spark plug holes.*

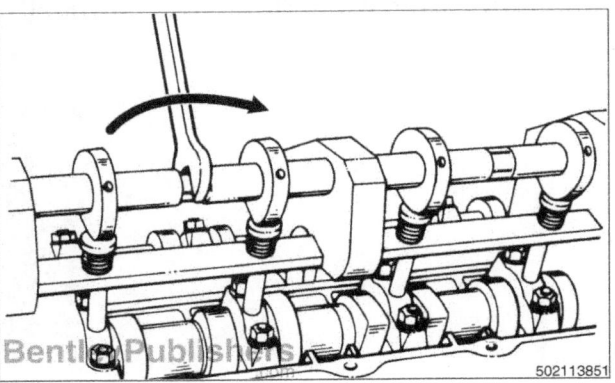

◀ Rotate eccentric shaft of special tool (**arrow**) to pretension bearing caps. Torque bearing cap nuts.

Tightening torque	
Camshaft bearing cap to cylinder head (M7)	14 Nm (10 ft-lb)

− Release tension on eccentric shaft and remove special tools.

− Repeat procedure for exhaust camshaft.

> **CAUTION—**
> • *A minimum waiting time is required for hydraulic lifters to bleed down before bringing crankshaft and pistons back to TDC. When camshafts are removed, the hydraulic lifters may expand. This expansion can cause increased valve lift when camshafts are bolted down, possibly resulting in interference.*

Hydraulic lifter bleed down waiting times	
68°F (20°C) and higher	4 minutes
50° − 68°F (10° − 20°C)	11 minutes
32° − 50°F (0° − 10°C)	30 minutes

Grind off

◀ Using 27 mm open-end wrench, rotate camshaft into position. If necessary, grind off outer edges of wrench jaws to prevent damage to cylinder head.

◀ Rotate camshafts until intake and exhaust lobes for cylinder 1 face each other (**arrows**).

Camshafts, installing (M54 engine)

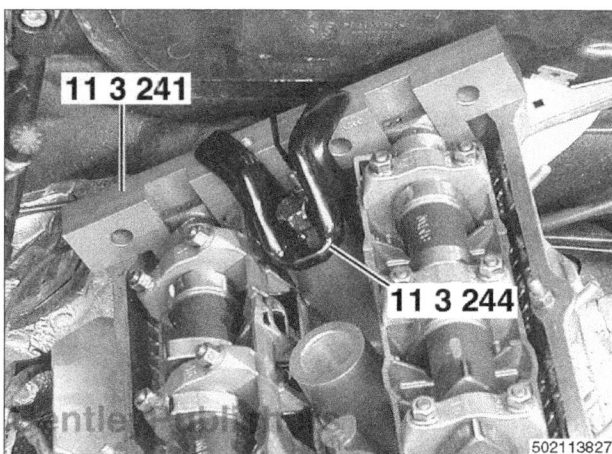

◄ Secure camshafts in TDC position using BMW camshaft TDC tools 11 3 241. Align camshafts so that camshaft TDC tools rest solidly on cylinder head upper surface. Lock down with special tool 11 3 244 bolted to a spark plug bore.

◄ Lift timing chain and hold under tension.

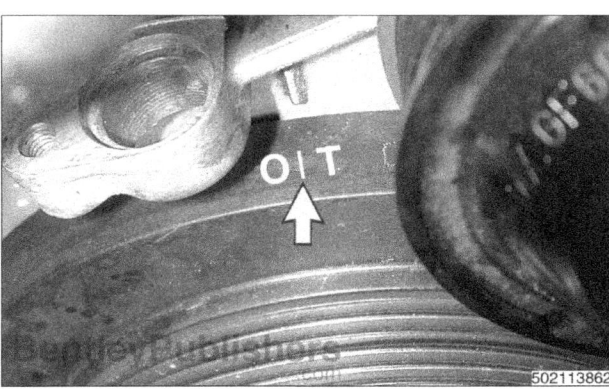

◄ While maintaining tension on timing chain, use crankshaft vibration damper bolt to rotate crankshaft in direction of rotation (clockwise) until cylinder 1 is at TDC position. **OIT** (**arrow**) on front pulley lines up with boss on lower timing chain cover.

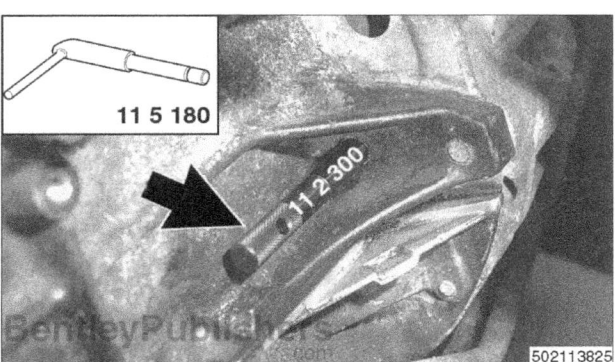

◄ Secure crankshaft in TDC position with BMW special tool 11 5 180 (**arrow**).

NOTE—
• *BMW special tool 11 2 300 (shown) used on non-X3 M54 engines.*

Camshafts, installing (M54 engine)

◄ Slide impulse wheel on intake camshaft, aligning boss with raised portion on camshaft (**arrow**).

◄ Fit thrust spacer (**A**) to intake camshaft (**B**) and tighten down with threaded locating studs. Place longer threaded end of studs into camshaft (**arrows**).

Tightening torque	
Impulse wheel studs to intake camshaft	20 Nm (15 ft-lb)

◄ Fit primary sprocket to primary timing chain and install on exhaust camshaft so that pointer on sprocket (**arrow**) lines up with cylinder head sealing surface (**dashed line**).

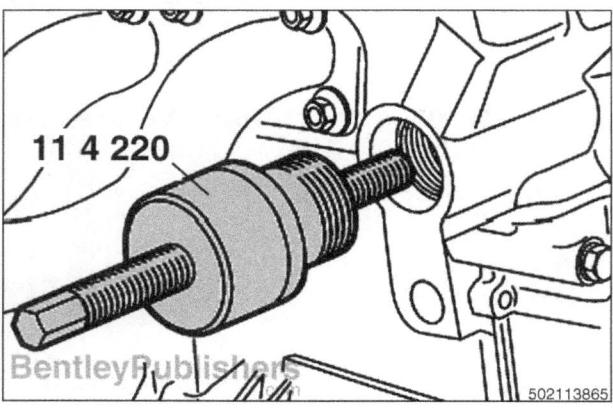

◄ Insert BMW special tool 11 4 220 into timing chain tensioner bore and bring center spindle into contact with tensioning rail. Tighten until slack is removed, but do not pretension timing chain.

NOTE—

- *BMW special tool 11 4 220 is an adjustable dummy tensioner and simulates the function of the primary chain tensioner.*

– Make sure arrow on upper primary sprocket still lines up with upper edge of cylinder head. Reposition sprocket if necessary.

◄ Insert and tighten down threaded locating studs (**arrows**) in end of exhaust camshaft. Note installed position of studs.

Tightening torque	
Exhaust camshaft locating stud	20 Nm (15 ft-lb)

◄ Install secondary chain tensioner on cylinder head (**arrows**). Keep tensioner compressed using BMW special tool 11 3 291 or suitable pin tool.

◄ Install exhaust camshaft splined sleeve. Confirm that gap in sleeve splines aligns with corresponding gap in camshaft splines (**arrows**).

Camshafts, installing (M54 engine)

◄ Slide splined shaft on exhaust camshaft (locating tooth of shaft fits into spline gaps of camshaft and splined sleeve (**arrows**)).

• Push splined shaft in further to rotate splined sleeve until three threaded holes in primary chain sprocket are centered in splined sleeve slots (**dashed lines**).

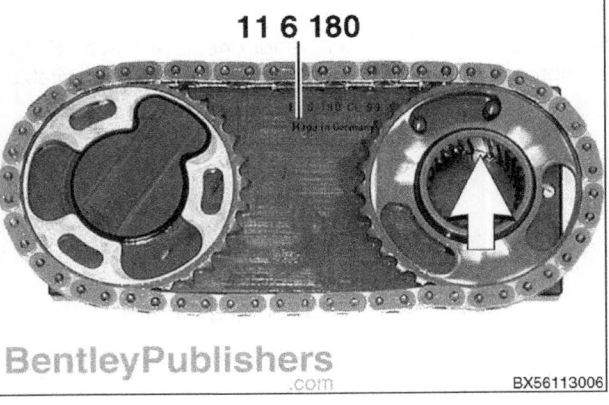

◄ Time intake to exhaust sprockets using BMW special tool 11 6 180. Position spline gap on intake sprocket (**arrow**) as shown and place secondary chain on sprockets.

◄ Remove chain and sprockets from tool and slide sprockets on camshafts, aligning gap in intake sprocket splines with corresponding gap in camshaft splines (**arrow**).

> **CAUTION—**
> • *Do not alter position of sprockets with respect to chain when removing from special tool 11 6 180.*

◄ Slide splined shaft onto intake camshaft until approx. 1 mm (0.04 in) of splines (**arrows**) are visible.

◄ Install intake camshaft spring plate so that **FRONT** mark is visible. Install mounting nuts (**arrows**) finger tight.

◄ Insert sprocket mounting bolts (**arrows**) on exhaust side camshaft assembly.

   • Initially tighten to approx. 5 Nm (44 in-lb) and then back off by half a turn.

◄ Fit thrust spacer (**A**) on exhaust camshaft.

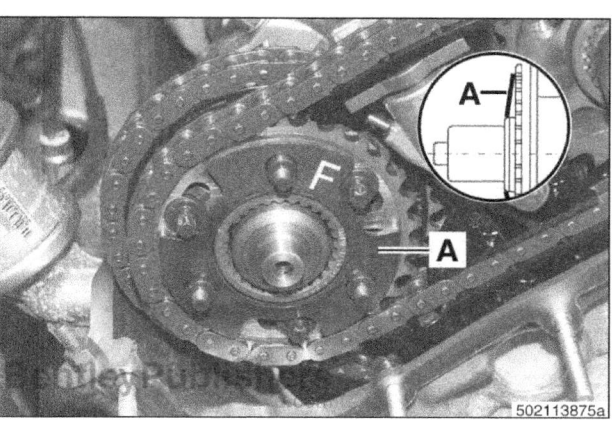

◄ Install spring plate (**A**) to exhaust camshaft. Make sure that **F** mark is visible.

NOTE—

   • *If* **F** *mark is no longer visible, install spring plate as shown in inset: convex side facing forward.*

Camshafts, installing (M54 engine)

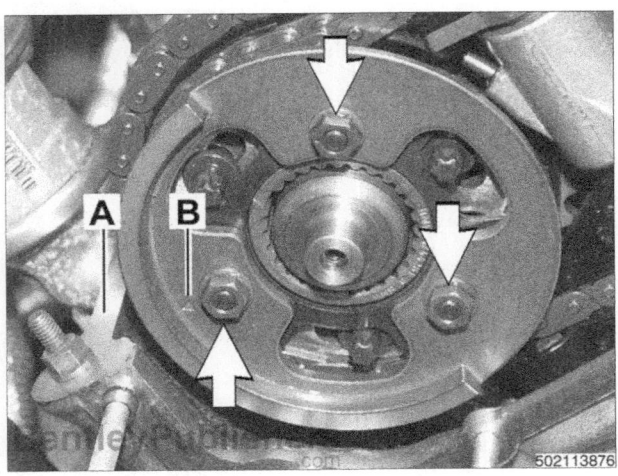

◁ Install exhaust camshaft impulse wheel, aligning pointer (**B**) with top edge of cylinder head (**A**). Install mounting nuts (**arrows**) finger tight.

◁ Pull out exhaust camshaft splined shaft to stop (**arrow**).

– Press down on secondary chain tensioner and remove tensioner lock-down tool.

◁ Preload primary chain:

• Tighten adjusting screw on BMW special tool 11 4 220 to specified torque.

Tightening torque	
Primary chain tensioner preload	0.7 Nm (6 in-lb)

– Preload exhaust camshaft spring plate by pressing on impulse wheel while tightening mounting nuts (**arrows**) finger tight.

◀ Install BMW special tool 11 6 150 (VANOS setup bracket) to front of cylinder head timing case. Install nuts (**arrows**) finger tight, then tighten down uniformly until special tool is in full contact with cylinder head.

> **CAUTION—**
> • Make sure gasket material is removed from face of cylinder head. Clean sealing face and keep free of oil.

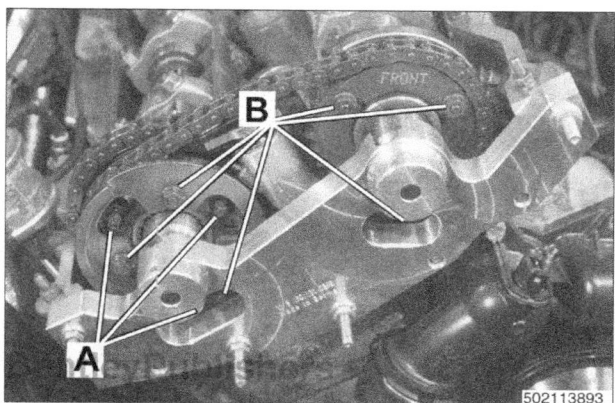

◀ Secure camshaft sprockets and impulse wheels:
  • Tighten mounting screws (**A**) on exhaust camshaft impulse wheel to approx. 5 Nm (44 in-lb).
  • Tighten mounting nuts (**B**) on exhaust and intake sprocket assemblies to approx. 5 Nm (44 in-lb).
  • Torque down mounting screws (**A**) and nuts (**B**) to final specifications.

Tightening torques	
Sprocket assembly wheel to camshaft– (initial torque)	5 Nm (44 in-lb)
Sprocket assembly wheel to camshaft • M7 torx screws (**A**) • M6 mounting nuts (**B**)	20 Nm (15 ft-lb) 10 Nm (8 ft-lb)

– Remove crankshaft locking tool so that crankshaft is no longer secured in TDC position.

– Remove camshaft locking tools from cylinder head.

◀ Turn engine over twice in direction of rotation until cylinder 1 intake and exhaust camshaft lobes (**arrows**) face each other.

– Secure crankshaft in TDC position with BMW special tool 11 5 180.

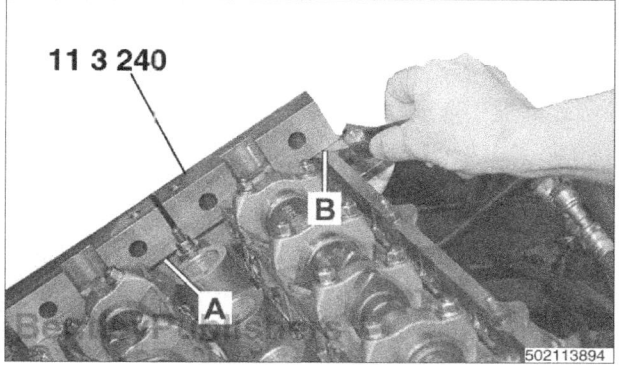

◀ Place BMW special tool set 11 3 240 over camshafts and measure clearances.
  • Due to VANOS unit tolerances and play, intake side of special tool 11 3 240 (**B**) may be up to 1 mm (0.04 in) above surface of cylinder head. This is normal. Reassemble engine.
  • Otherwise, reset camshaft timing. See **Camshaft timing, checking and adjusting (M54 engine)** in this repair group.

> **CAUTION—**
> • If exhaust side of tool (**A**) is not flush with cylinder head, camshaft timing is incorrect. Reset camshaft timing.

– Remove BMW special tool 11 6 150 from front of cylinder head.

– Reinstall VANOS unit. See **Double VANOS unit, installing (M54 engine)** in this repair group.

– Remove camshaft and crankshaft locking tools.

– Reassemble engine. Be sure to top off and bleed cooling system.

Camshaft timing chain components (N52 Engine)

TIMING CHAIN SERVICE (N52 ENGINE)

Camshaft timing chain components (N52 Engine)

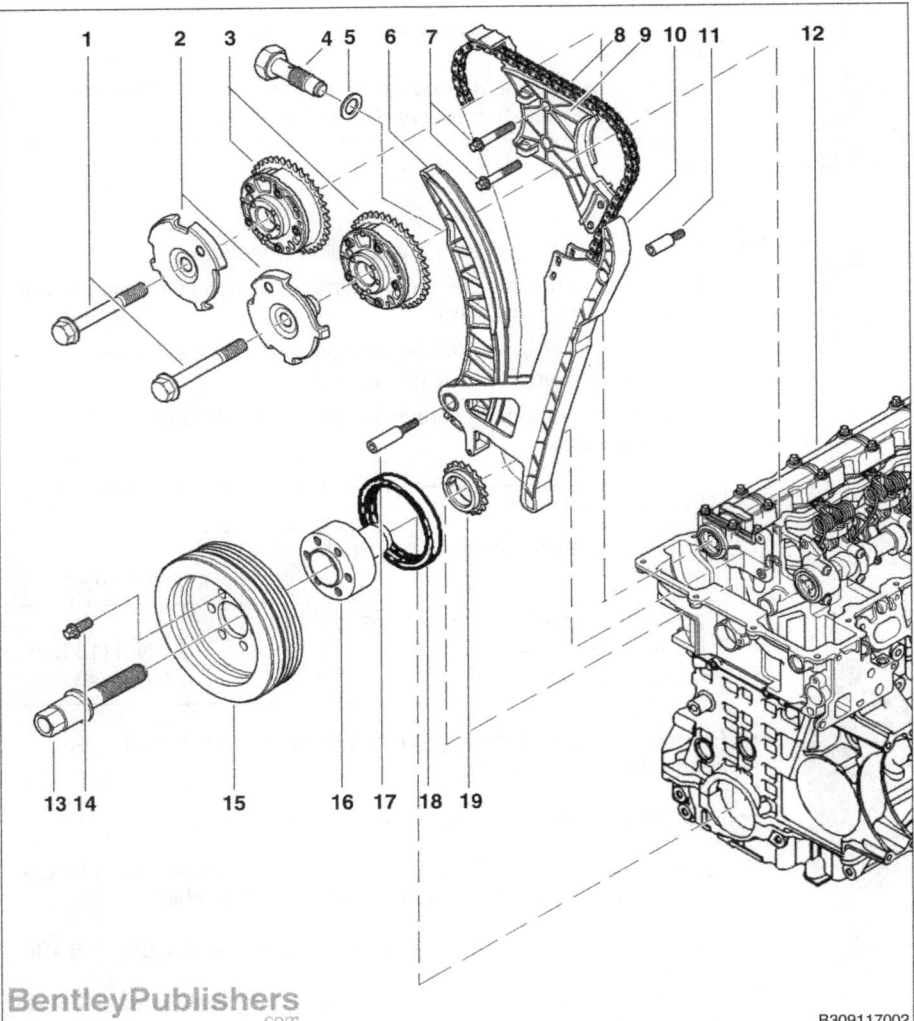

B309117002

1. VANOS unit mounting bolt (M10 x 94 mm)
   - Replace with new
   - Tighten in 2 stages
     Stage 1: 20 Nm (15 ft-lb)
     Stage 2: Additional 180°

2. Camshaft impulse wheel

3. VANOS unit
   - Different intake and exhaust adjustment units

4. Chain tensioner (M22 x 1.5)
   - Tighten to 55 Nm (41 ft-lb)

5. Sealing O-ring

6. Chain tensioner rail

7. Chain assembly mounting bolts (M6 x 35 mm Torx)
   - Tighten to 8.5 Nm (6 ft-lb)

8. Timing chain

9. Chain assembly

10. Chain guide

11. Chain guide mounting bolt (M7)
    - Tighten to 14 Nm (10 ft-lb)

12. Cylinder head with camshafts

13. Vibration damper hub mounting bolt (M16 x 80 mm)
    - Replace with new
    - Tighten in 2 stages
      Stage 1: 100 Nm (74 ft-lb)
      Stage 2: Additional 360°

14. Vibration damper mounting bolt (M8 x 16 mm Torx)
    - Tighten to 35 Nm (26 ft-lb)

15. Vibration damper (front pulley)

16. Vibration damper hub

17. Chain tensioner rail mounting bolt (M8)
    - Tighten to 20 Nm (15 ft-lb)

18. Crankshaft front seal

19. Crankshaft sprocket

VANOS units, removing and installing (N52 engine)

Special tools and procedures are required to remove and install VANOS units and to time camshafts. Read the entire procedure before beginning repairs.

> **WARNING** —
> • To avoid personal injury, be sure engine is cold before beginning.

> **CAUTION**—
> • Disassembly, removal and assembly of VANOS units without special tools poses the risk of damage or breakage: Valves may be bent by contact with the piston crowns.
> • Throughout this procedure, unless otherwise specified, crankshaft and camshafts remain locked against rotation using BMW special tools.
> • Keep VANOS components free of silicone sealant. A small amount of silicone in VANOS actuator or solenoid can set faults.

— Use scan tool to read out and record ECM fault memory.

— Switch ignition OFF and remove key.

— Remove engine cover and cylinder head cover.
See **113 Cylinder Head Removal and Installation**.

— Raise vehicle and support safely.

> **WARNING** —
> • Make sure vehicle is stable and well supported at all times. Use a professional automotive lift or jack stands. A floor jack is not adequate support.

— Working from below, remove engine compartment splash shield.
See **020 Maintenance**.

— Remove electric cooling fan and cowl.
See **170 Radiator and cooling system**.

◀ Using vibration damper bolt, rotate crankshaft to place cylinder 1 at TDC firing position. In this position, cylinder 1 intake camshaft lobe points upward at an angle.

Cyl 1 intake camshaft lobe

B309113024

VANOS units, removing and installing (N52 engine)

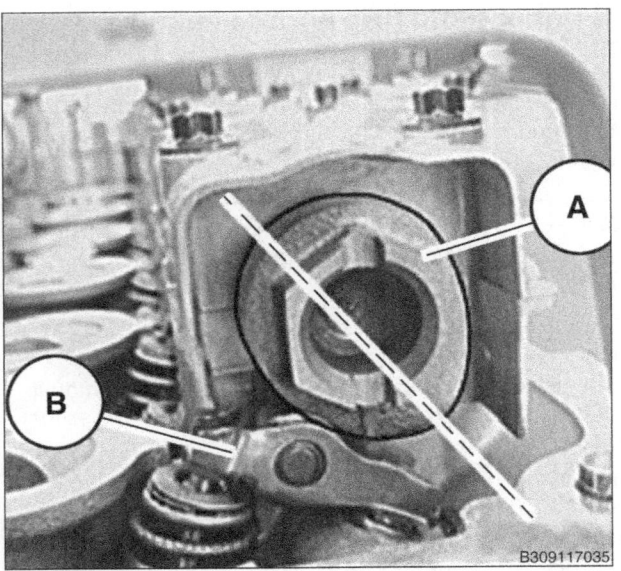

◄ Cylinder 1 in TDC firing position: Cylinder 6 exhaust camshaft lobe (**A**) points downward at an angle (**dashed line**). Cam follower (**B**) is not actuated.

NOTE—

• *Use mirror to check exhaust camshaft lobe position.*

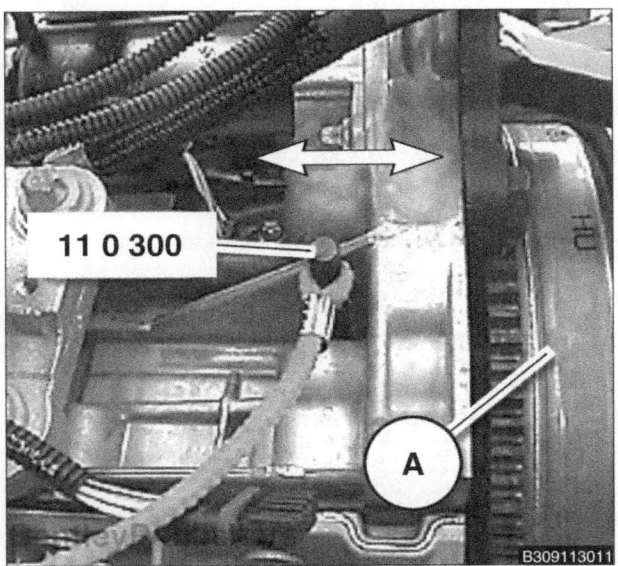

◄ Working underneath engine, slide out protective plug at lower left of engine bell housing flange. Install BMW special tool 11 0 300 (crankshaft locking tool) through bell housing flange port into flywheel (**A**) hole. If necessary, rock flywheel slightly back and forth to line up holes with tool. This locks crankshaft at TDC.

CAUTION—

• *Models with automatic transmission: In the flywheel (torque plate), a short distance before the bore for TDC position, there is a large bore which can be confused with the special tool bore. If the flywheel is locked using the correct bore, the engine can no longer be rotated at the vibration damper bolt.*

• *If special tool 11 0 300 does not slide easily into the bell housing flange bore, sand paint off the tool. Do not enlarge the bore.*

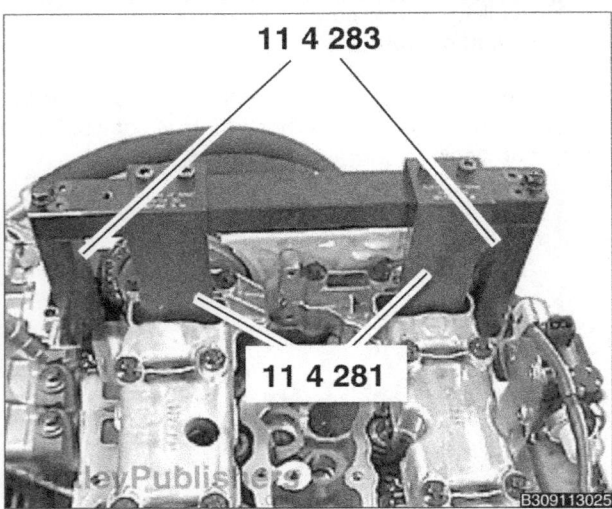

◄ Use BMW special tool set 11 4 280 to lock down camshafts.

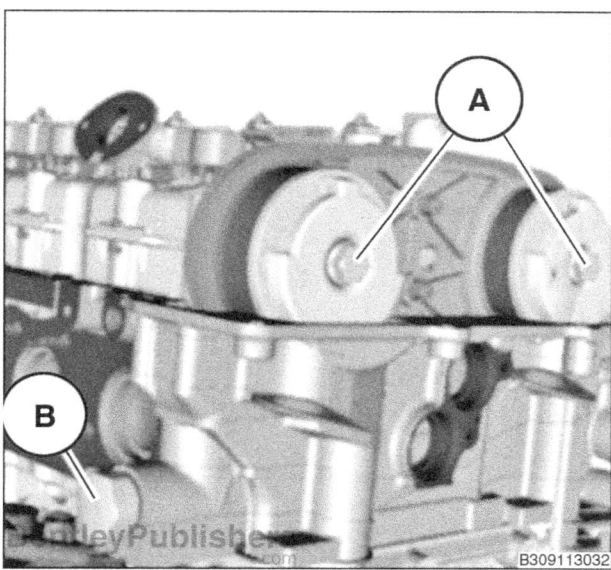

◀ Working at right front of cylinder head, remove timing chain tensioner (**B**). Be prepared to catch dripping oil with a shop towel. Do not allow oil to contaminate accessory belt.

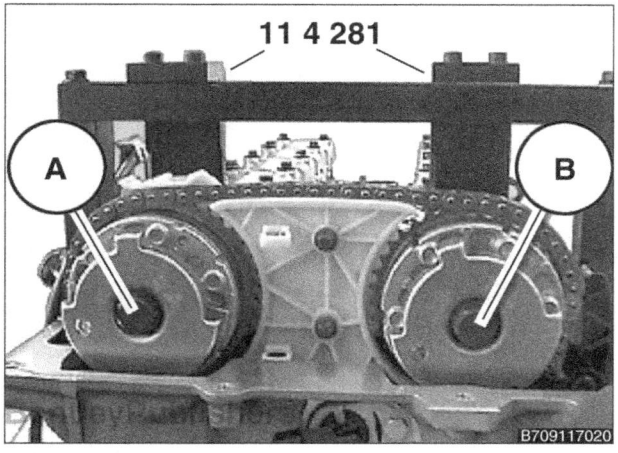

◀ Working at front of camshafts:

- Loosen and remove exhaust and intake VANOS unit mounting bolts (**A**, **B**). Discard bolts.
- Disengage timing chain from camshaft adjustment unit sprockets.
- Tilt VANOS units down to remove.

◀ Use new bolts to reattach VANOS units.

- Note that exhaust and intake units are different and so marked.
- Camshaft sensor impulse wheel for intake and exhaust are the same.
- VANOS units and sensor wheels may be installed in any position initially. Finger-tighten mounting bolts for now.

Camshaft timing chain, removing and installing (N52 engine)

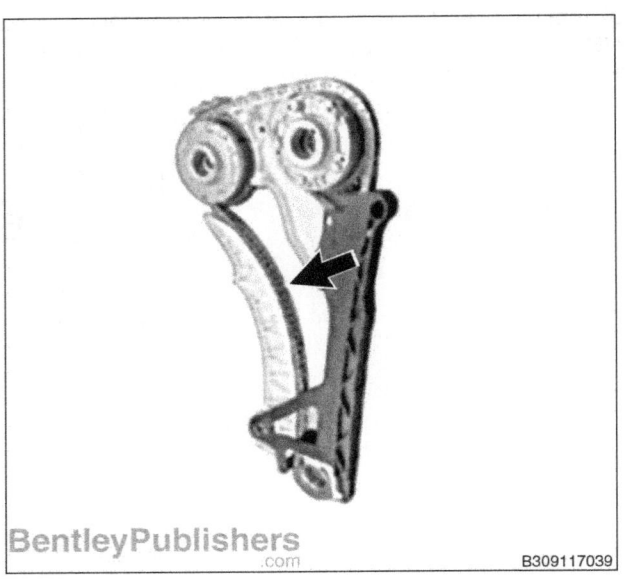

◀ Press chain into chain tensioner rail (**arrow**) by hand to make sure it is routed correctly. (Chain assembly and VANOS units shown removed from engine for purpose of illustration.)

— Adjust camshaft timing. See **Camshaft timing, adjusting (N52 engine)** in this repair group. Then torque VANOS mounting bolts.

Tightening torque	
VANOS unit to camshaft (use new M10 x 94 mm bolt): • Stage 1 • Stage 2	 20 Nm (15 ft-lb) additional 180°

— Install chain tensioner. See **Timing chain tensioner (N52 engine)** in this repair group.

> **CAUTION—**
> • *If chain tensioner is reused, drain its oil chamber. Place tensioner on level working surface and compress slowly. Repeat twice.*
> • *No sealing ring is fitted to chain tensioner at the factory. When reassembling engine, be sure to use new sealing O-ring.*

Tightening torque	
Timing chain tensioner to cylinder head (M22 x 1.5) (use new sealing O-ring)	55 Nm (41 ft-lb)

— Reassemble engine.

> **CAUTION—**
> • *Remove crankshaft and camshaft locking tools before rotating or starting engine.*

Camshaft timing chain, removing and installing (N52 engine)

When removing and installing the camshaft timing chain, special tools and procedures are required to remove and install VANOS units and to time camshafts. Read the entire procedure before beginning repairs.

> **WARNING—**
> • *To avoid personal injury, be sure the engine is cold before beginning the procedure.*

> **CAUTION—**
> • *Disassembly, removal and assembly of camshafts or VANOS units without special tools poses the risk of damage or breakage: Valves may be bent by contact with the piston crowns.*
> • *Throughout this procedure, unless otherwise specified, crankshaft and camshafts remain locked against rotation using BMW special tools.*

— Use scan tool to read out and record ECM fault memory.

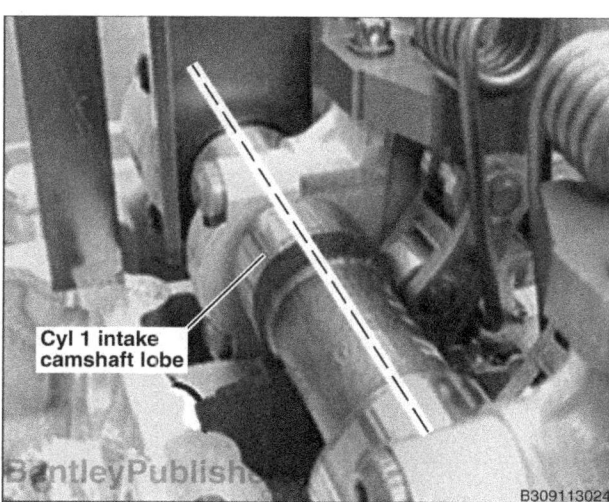

Cyl 1 intake
camshaft lobe

B309113024

- Switch ignition OFF and remove key.

- Remove cylinder head cover. See **113 Cylinder Head Removal and Installation**.

- Remove spark plugs.

◀ Using vibration camper bolt, rotate crankshaft to place cylinder 1 in TDC firing position. In this position, cylinder 1 intake camshaft lobe points upward at an angle (**dashed line**).

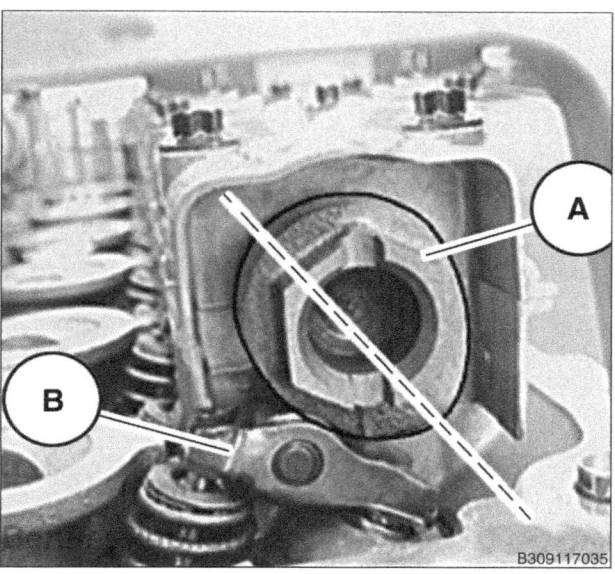

B309117035

◀ N52 engine: Cylinder 1 in TDC firing position: Cylinder 6 exhaust camshaft lobe (**A**) points downward at an angle (**dashed line**). Cam follower (**B**) is not actuated.

NOTE —

- *Use mirror to check exhaust camshaft lobe position.*

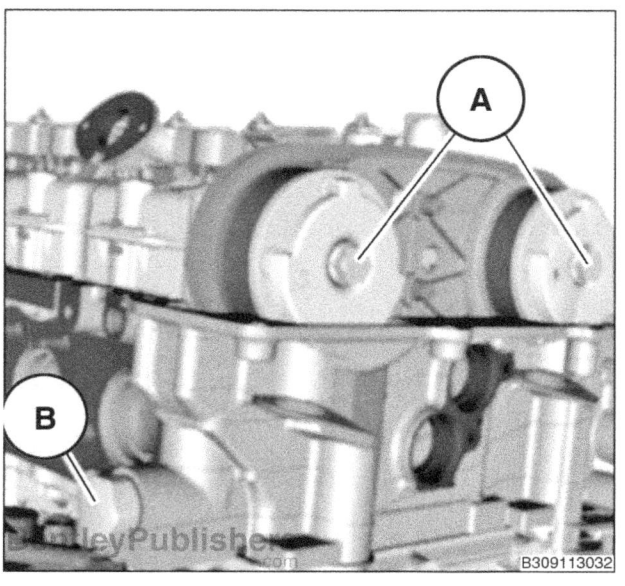

B309113032

◀ Working at right front of cylinder head, remove timing chain tensioner (**B**). Be prepared to catch dripping oil with a shop towel. Do not allow oil to contaminate accessory belt.

- Raise vehicle and support safely.

> **WARNING** —
> - *Make sure vehicle is stable and well supported at all times. Use a professional automotive lift or jack stands. A floor jack is not adequate support.*

- Working from below, remove engine compartment splash shield. See **020 Maintenance**.

- Remove engine accessory belt. See **020 Maintenance**.

- Remove vibration damper (front pulley). See **Vibration damper, removing and installing (N52 engine)** in this repair group.

- Remove crankshaft front seal. See **119 Lubrication System**.

Camshaft timing chain, removing and installing (N52 engine)

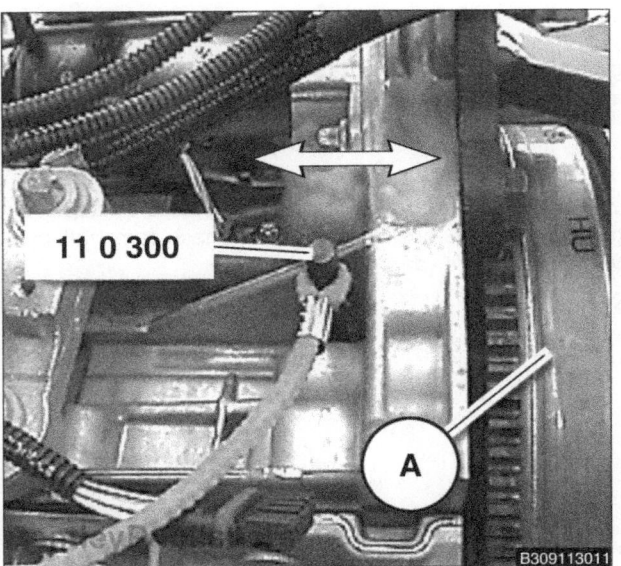

◄ Working underneath engine, slide out protective plug at lower left of engine bell housing flange. Install BMW special tool 11 0 300 (crankshaft locking tool) through bell housing flange port into flywheel (**A**) hole. If necessary, rock flywheel slightly back and forth to line up holes with tool. This locks crankshaft at TDC.

> **CAUTION—**
>
> • *Models with automatic transmission: In the flywheel (torque plate), a short distance before the bore for TDC position, there is a large bore which can be confused with the special tool bore. If the flywheel is locked using the correct bore, the engine can no longer be rotated at the vibration damper bolt.*
>
> • *If special tool 11 0 300 does not slide easily into the bell housing flange bore, sand paint off the tool. Do not enlarge the bore.*

◄ Remove vibration damper hub:

• Bolt BMW special tool 11 9 280 (counter hold tool) to hub.

• With help of assistant counter holding hub, loosen and remove hub bolt (**A**). Discard bolt.

• Pull hub off crankshaft, sliding it out of timing chain lower sprocket.

> **CAUTION—**
>
> • *Counter hold hub securely. Do not rely on flywheel lock (special tool 11 0 300) to counter hold against crankshaft rotation.*

◄ Unscrew plug (**arrow**) at upper left of timing chain housing.

Camshaft timing chain, removing and installing (N52 engine)

◄ Unscrew plug (**arrow**) at lower right of timing chain housing.

◄ Remove chain guide mounting bolt (**arrow**) at upper left of timing chain housing.

◄ Remove chain tensioning rail mounting bolt (**arrow**) at lower right of timing chain housing.

Camshaft timing chain, removing and installing (N52 engine)

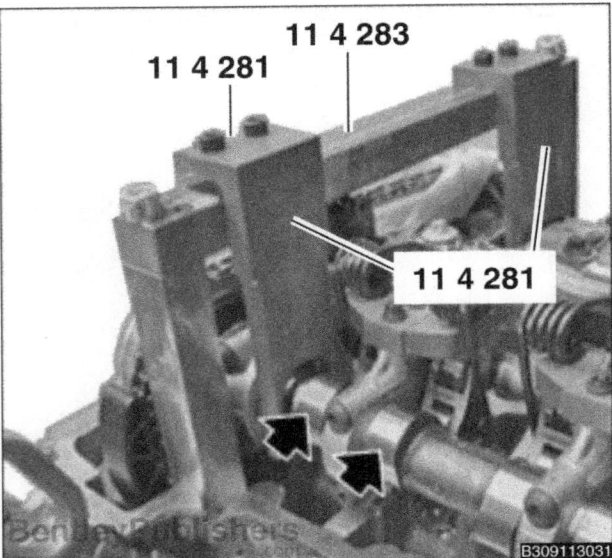

◄ Use BMW special tool set 11 4 280 to lock down camshafts.

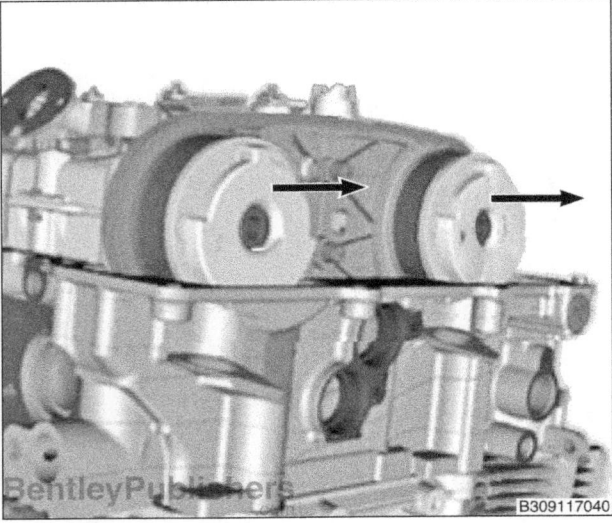

◄ Remove intake and exhaust VANOS units:
- Loosen and remove VANOS unit mounting bolts. Discard bolts.
- Disengage timing chain from VANOS unit sprockets.
- Remove VANOS units (**arrows**) and set aside. See **VANOS units, removing and installing (N52 engine)** in this repair group.

NOTE—
- *Illustration does not show special tool set 11 4 280 in place.*

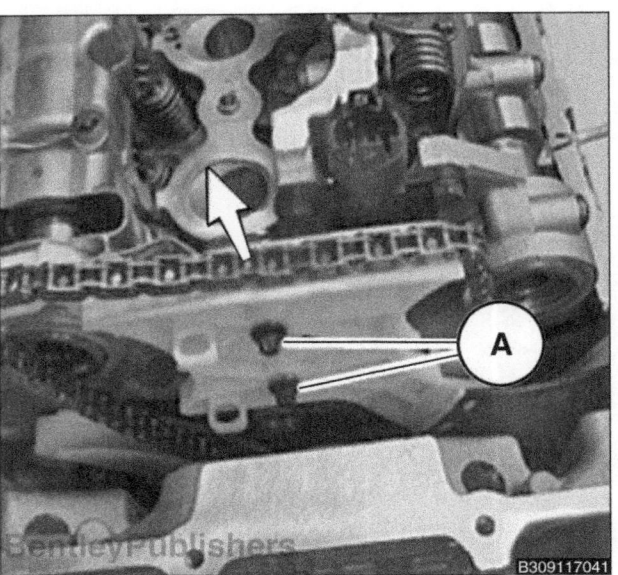

◄ Working at front of cylinder head:
- Remove timing chain assembly mounting bolts (**A**).
- Lift timing chain, timing chain assembly with crankshaft sprocket straight up (**arrow**) out of timing chain housing.

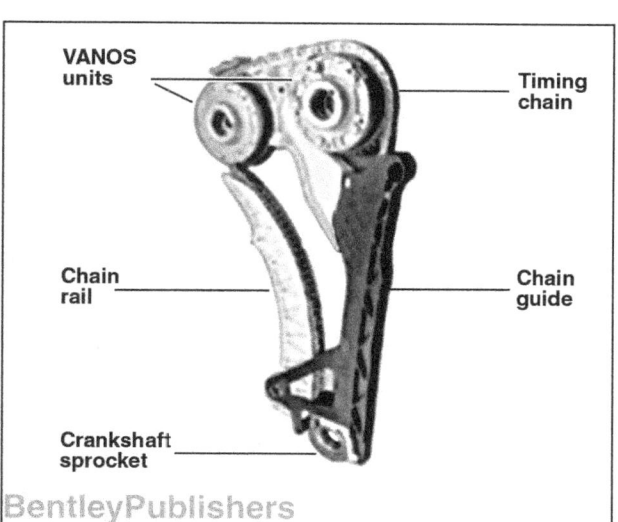

VANOS units

Timing chain

Chain rail

Chain guide

Crankshaft sprocket

BentleyPublishers
.com

B309117008

◄ Chain, chain assembly and crankshaft sprocket. VANOS units shown installed on assembly for purposes of illustration.

– Disengage timing chain from guide and rail assembly and crankshaft sprocket and fit new chain.

– Inspect timing chain guide rails for signs of wear or damage. Replace complete guide rail assembly if damage is present.

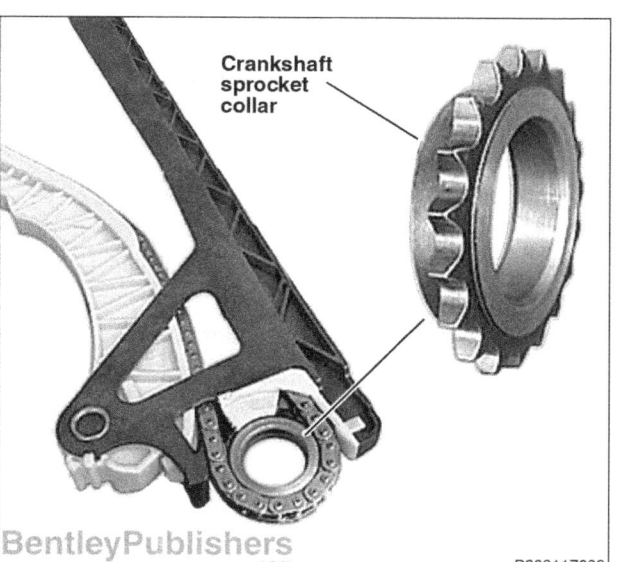

Crankshaft sprocket collar

BentleyPublishers
.com

B309117009

◄ Fit crankshaft sprocket to chain in orientation shown, with collar pointing to engine.

> **CAUTION—**
> • *Incorrect sprocket assembly results in engine damage.*

– Pull timing chain taut until sprocket engages chain guide. Install timing chain and chain assembly in chain housing in this position, holding chain under tension at all times.

– Install and torque timing chain assembly, rail and guide bolts.

Tightening torques	
Timing chain guide to cylinder head (M7)	14 Nm (10 ft-lb)
Timing chain assembly to cylinder head (M6 x 35 mm Torx)	8.5 Nm (6 ft-lb)
Timing chain rail to crankcase (M8)	20 Nm (14 ft-lb)

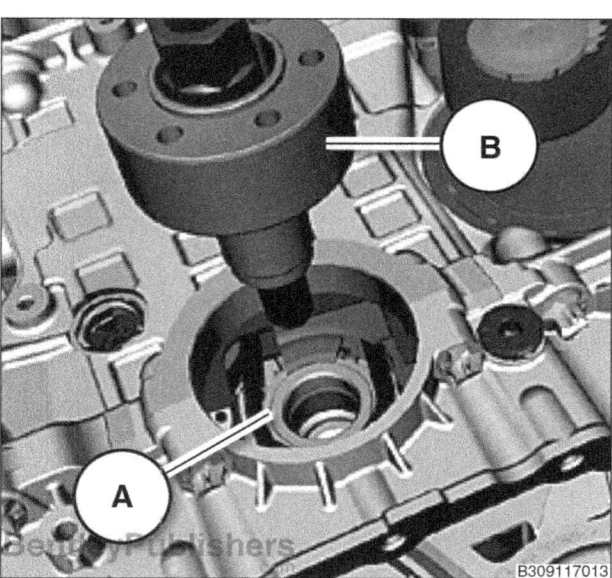

B

A

BentleyPublishers
.com

B309117013

◄ Line up timing chain and oil pump chain sprockets (**A**) inside crankcase bore, then insert vibration damper hub (**B**), sliding it through chain sprockets. Using new vibration damper bolt, attach hub finger tight to crankshaft.

117

Camshaft timing chain, removing and installing (N52 engine)

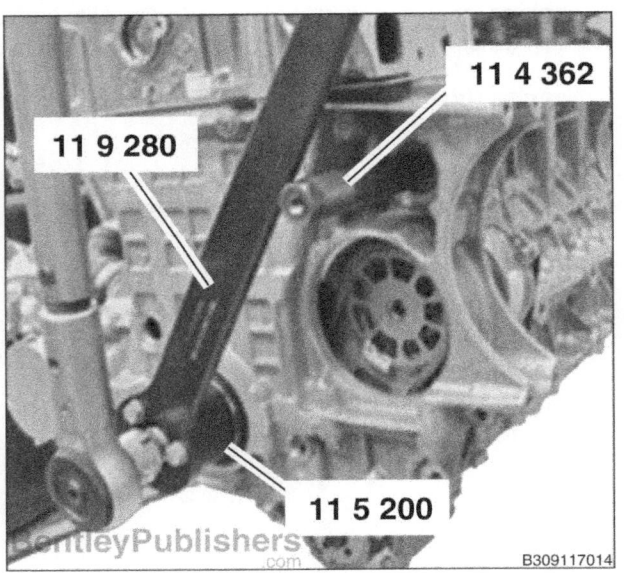

◄ To achieve final torque on vibration damper hub:

- Remove belt tensioner and screw in special tool 11 4 362.
- Bolt special tool 11 5 200 to vibration damper hub.
- Bolt special tool 11 9 280 to tool 11 5 200.
- Rest tool 11 9 280 against tool 11 4 362.
- Tighten to initial tightening torque.

Tightening torque	
Vibration damper hub to crankshaft • Stage 1	100 Nm (74 ft-lb)

CAUTION—
- *Do not rely on flywheel lock (special tool 11 0 300) to counter hold against crankshaft rotation.*

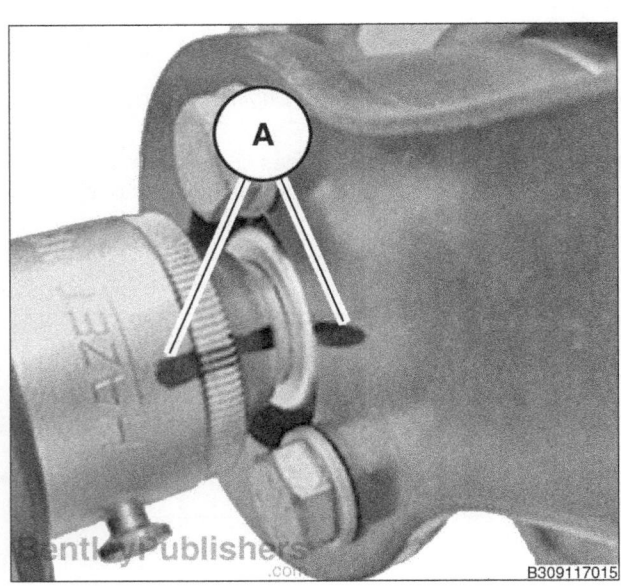

◄ Mark special tool 11 9 280 and socket wrench (**A**).

- Tighten hub bolt to final torque with assistant helping to counter hold tool 11 9 280.

Tightening torque	
Vibration damper hub to crankshaft • Stage 2	Additional 360°

— Install crankshaft front seal. See **119 Lubrication System**.

◄ Use new bolts to reattach VANOS units. Note that exhaust and intake units are different and so marked. Camshaft sensor impulse wheel for intake and exhaust are the same. See **VANOS units, removing and installing (N52 engine)** in this repair group.

Tightening torque	
VANOS unit to camshaft (use new M10 x 94 mm bolt): • Stage 1 • Stage 2	 20 Nm (15 ft-lb) additional 180°

— Install chain tensioner. See **Timing chain tensioner (N52 engine)** in this repair group.

> *CAUTION—*
> - *If chain tensioner is reused, drain its oil chamber. Place tensioner on level working surface and compress slowly. Repeat twice.*
> - *No sealing ring is fitted to chain tensioner at the factory. When reassembling engine, be sure to use new sealing O-ring.*

Tightening torque	
Timing chain tensioner to cylinder head (M22 x 1.5) (use new sealing O-ring)	55 Nm (41 ft-lb)

— Remove crankshaft and camshaft locking tools and rotate engine 2 full revolutions. Then check and, if necessary, reset camshaft timing. See **Camshaft timing, adjusting (N52 engine)** in this repair group.

> *CAUTION—*
> - *Remove crankshaft and camshaft locking tools before rotating or starting engine.*

— Reassemble engine.

Camshaft timing, adjusting (N52 engine)

> *WARNING—*
> - *To avoid personal injury, be sure engine is cold before beginning.*

— Use scan tool to read out and record ECM fault memory.

— Switch ignition OFF and remove key.

— Remove cylinder head cover.
   See **113 Cylinder Head Removal and Installation**.

— Remove electric cooling fan and cowl.
   See **170 Radiator and Cooling System**.

— Raise vehicle and support safely.

> *WARNING—*
> - *Make sure vehicle is stable and well supported at all times. Use a professional automotive lift or jack stands. A floor jack is not adequate support.*

— Remove engine compartment splash shield. See **020 Maintenance**.

◀ Using vibration damper bolt, rotate crankshaft to place cylinder 1 at TDC firing position. In this position, cylinder 1 intake camshaft lobe points upward at an angle (**dashed line**).

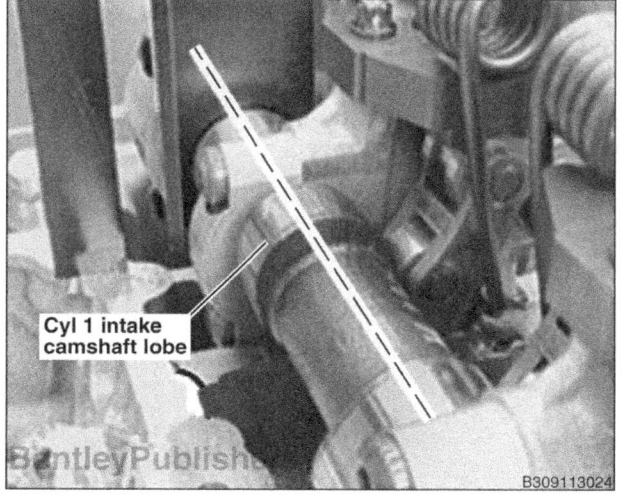

Cyl 1 intake camshaft lobe

B309113024

Camshaft timing, adjusting (N52 engine)

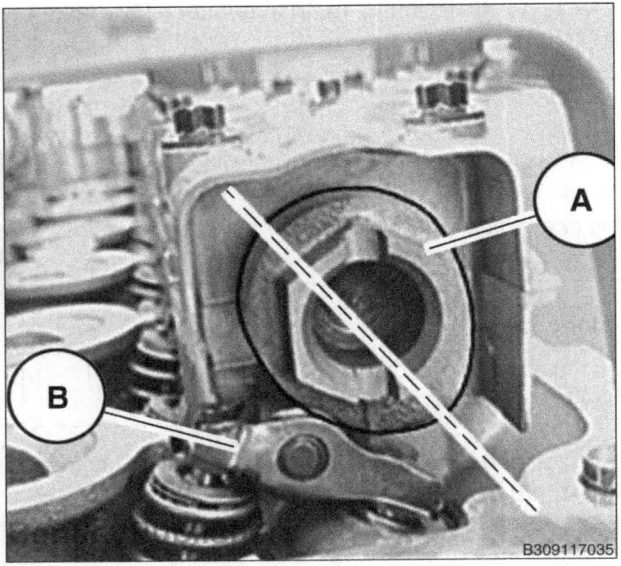

◀ Cylinder 1 in TDC firing position: Cylinder 6 exhaust camshaft lobe (**A**) points downward at an angle (**dashed line**). Cam follower (**B**) is not actuated.

NOTE —

• *Use mirror to check exhaust camshaft lobe position.*

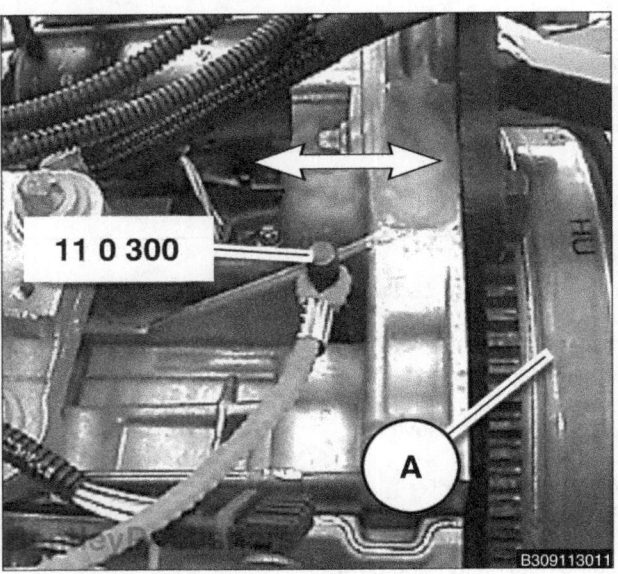

◀ Working underneath engine, slide out protective plug at lower left of engine bell housing flange. Install BMW special tool 11 0 300 (crankshaft locking tool) through bell housing flange port into flywheel (**A**) hole. If necessary, rock flywheel slightly back and forth to line up holes with tool. This locks crankshaft at TDC.

CAUTION—

• *Models with automatic transmission: In the flywheel (torque plate), a short distance before the bore for TDC position, there is a large bore which can be confused with the special tool bore. If the flywheel is locked using the correct bore, the engine can no longer be rotated at the vibration damper bolt.*

• *If special tool 11 0 300 does not slide easily into the bell housing flange bore, sand paint off the tool. Do not enlarge the bore.*

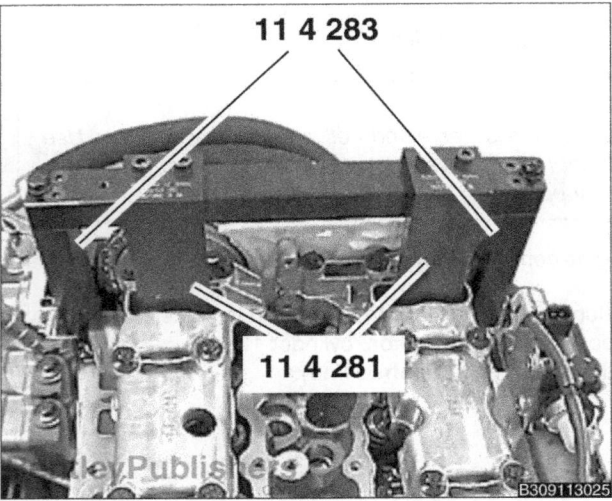

◀ Use BMW special tool set 11 4 280 to lock down camshafts.

— With crankshaft locked, if special tool 11 4 281 fits, camshaft timing is correct. Remove special tools and reassemble engine.

— If special tool 11 4 281 does not fit, proceed with camshaft timing procedure below.

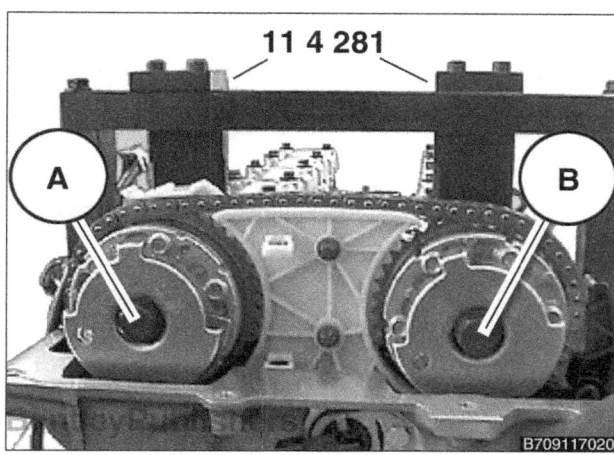

◄ Working at front of camshafts:

- Loosen exhaust and intake camshaft adjustment (VANOS) unit mounting bolts (**A**, **B**).
- Discard bolts and replace with new.
- Tighten bolts finger tight.
- Using hexagon casting at rear of camshafts, rotate camshafts until BMW special tool 11 4 281 can be installed.

◄ Install BMW special tool 11 8 520.

- Place tool up against VANOS unit sensor gears.
- Rotate sensor gears (**arrows**) until locating pins on tool line up with bores in sensor gears.
- Push tool firmly against sensor gears and lock down with M6 x 45 mm bolts (**A**).

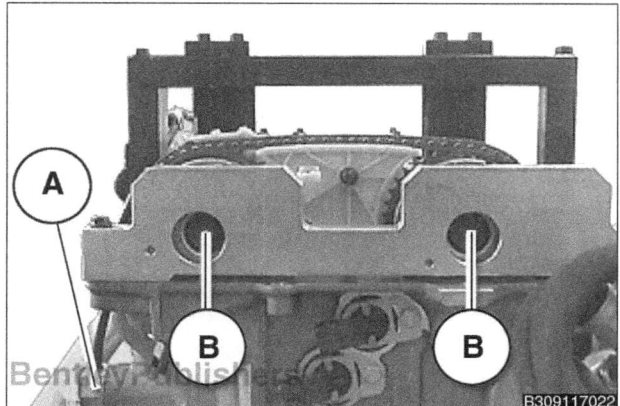

◄ Working at front of cylinder head:

- Remove timing chain tensioner (**A**). Be prepared to catch dripping oil. Do not allow oil to contaminate accessory belt.
- Screw BMW special tool 11 9 340 (dummy chain tensioner) into cylinder head. Using BMW special tool 00 9 250 (low-torque torque wrench), rotate stud of special tool 11 9 340 to pretension timing chain to 0.6 Nm (5.3 in-lb).
- Tighten VANOS unit mounting bolts (**B**).

Tightening torque	
VANOS unit to camshaft: • Stage 1 • Stage 2	 20 Nm (15 ft-lb) additional 180°

— Remove special tools. Reinstall chain tensioner using new sealing O-ring. See **Timing chain tensioner (N52 engine)** in this repair group.

Tightening torque	
Timing chain tensioner to cylinder head (M22 x 1.5) (use new sealing O-ring)	55 Nm (41 ft-lb)

— Rotate engine two full revolutions and recheck timing.

— Reassemble engine.

Timing chain tensioner (N52 engine)

B309117023

Timing chain tensioner (N52 engine)

The timing chain tensioner is screwed into the right front of the cylinder head. When it is removed be sure to catch dripping oil in a shop towel. Do not allow oil to contaminate accessory belt.

◄ If chain tensioner is reused, drain its oil chamber. Place tensioner vertically on level working surface and compress slowly (**arrow**). Repeat twice.

> **CAUTION—**
> • *No sealing ring is fitted to chain tensioner at the factory. When reassembling engine, be sure to use new sealing O-ring.*

Tightening torque	
Timing chain tensioner to cylinder head (M22 x 1.5) (use new sealing O-ring)	55 Nm (41 ft-lb)

119 Lubrication System

GENERAL

This repair group covers lubrication system service and repair, including crankshaft seal replacement.

See also:

• **020 Maintenance** for oil and oil filter change

• **100 Engine–General** for engine identification and application.

Table a. Engine identification

Engine designation	Year, model	Identifying feature
M54	2004 - 2006 2.5i, 3.0i	2 upper engine covers
N52	2007 - 2010 3.0si, 30i	Black plastic cylinder head cover

Warnings and cautions

> **WARNING—**
> • Due to risk of personal injury, be sure the engine is cold before beginning work on engine components.

> **CAUTION—**
> • Prior to disconnecting the battery, read the battery disconnection cautions in **001 Warnings and Cautions**.
> • To avoid electrochemical corrosion to engine components made of aluminum-magnesium alloy, do not use steel fasteners. Use aluminum fasteners only. For reliable identification, test fasteners for aluminum composition with magnet.
> • Replace aluminum bolts each time they are loosened.
> • Follow torque instructions, including angle of rotation specifications, when installing aluminum fasteners.
> • Cover alternator with shop towel to protect from oil drips.

ENGINE LUBRICATION

Engine lubricant

Engine oil specification	
BMW long-life rating (LL-01) synthetic oils for US market	API rating SM or higher

Engine oil capacity	
Engine	**Approximate capacity (incl. oil filter)**
M54	6.2 liters (6.5 US qt)
N52	6.5 liters (6.9 US qt)

Engine lubrication (M54 engine)

Oil pressure is generated by a gear-type pump bolted to the bottom of the engine block. The oil pump is chain driven off the front of the crankshaft.

1. Drive chain
2. Nut M10x1left-hand thread
3. Oil pump sprocket
4. Inner rotor
5. Outer rotor
6. Oil pressure relief valve assembly
7. Bolt M8
8. Oil pump housing
9. Locating dowels
10. Sealing O-ring
11. Oil pick-up pipe
12. Bolt M6

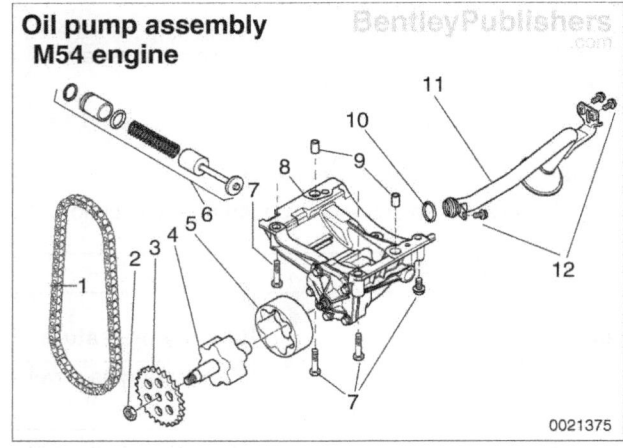

Oil pump assembly M54 engine

0021375

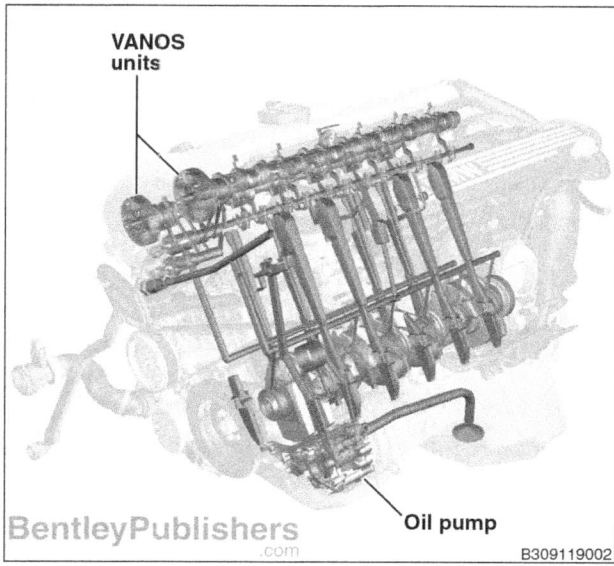

VANOS units

Oil pump

BentleyPublishers.com

B309119002

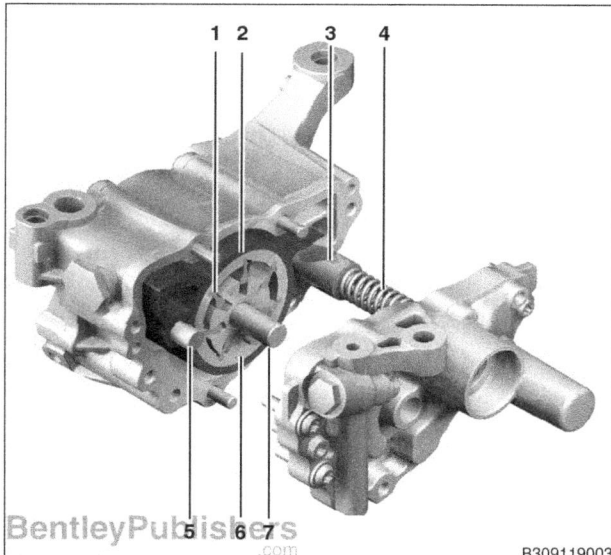

1 2   3 4

5 6 7

BentleyPublishers.com

B309119003

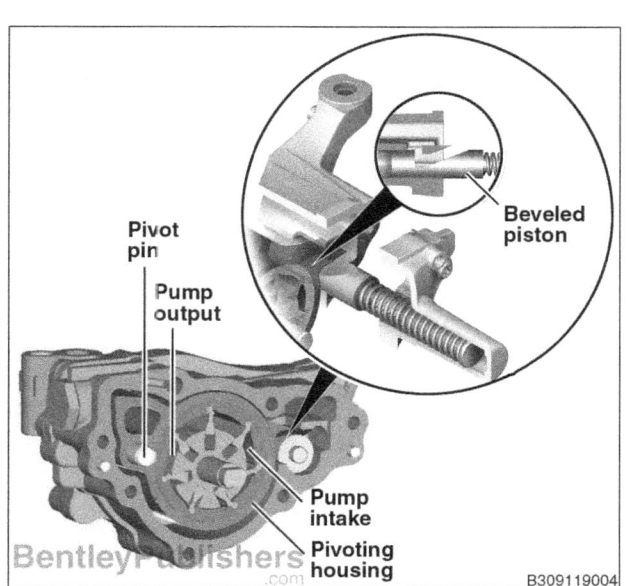

Pivot pin

Pump output

Beveled piston

Pump intake

Pivoting housing

BentleyPublishers.com

B309119004

Engine lubrication (N52 engine)

 To meet the oiling requirements of N52 engines, a chain-driven volumetric-flow controlled oil pump is utilized. The VANOS system requires a large volume of oil, particularly at low engine speeds.

The volumetric-flow controlled pump design allows:

• Increased power output
• Reduced weight
• Optimized fuel consumption
• Reduced exhaust emissions

Engine oil pump (N52 engine)

1. Sliding vane valve
2. Pivoting rotor housing
3. Beveled control piston
4. Compression spring
5. Pivot pin
6. Rotor
7. Pump shaft

The volumetric-flow controlled oil pump delivers only as much oil as is necessary. No surplus quantities of oil are delivered in low load operating ranges. This reduces the fuel consumption of the engine and slows down the oil wear rate.

The pump is designed with sliding vane valves. The pump shaft and rotor are positioned off-center in the pivoting rotor housing and the vanes are displaced radially during rotation. The vanes form chambers of differing volume depending on the position of the rotor housing.

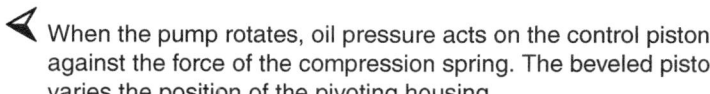 When the pump rotates, oil pressure acts on the control piston against the force of the compression spring. The beveled piston varies the position of the pivoting housing.

When the housing is centered on the rotor, changes in intake and output chamber volumes are small: Delivered oil volume is low. When the rotor housing is off-center in relation to the rotor, changes in input and output chamber volumes are greater: Delivered oil volume is high.

When the oil volume required by the engine increases, for example during VANOS operation, oil pressure in the lubricating system drops, reducing pressure on the beveled piston. In response, the compression spring presses the beveled piston against the pivoting housing control dog, forcing the housing further off-center and increasing oil volume. The opposite occurs as engine oil pressure increases and the need for delivered oil volume drops.

Oil pressure, checking

BX30119023

OIL PRESSURE WARNING SYSTEM

The oil pressure warning system consists of an oil pressure switch mounted in the oil circuit and an instrument panel warning light. Other safety features include:

- Dynamic oil level warning
- Engine oil temperature monitoring
- A filter bypass to provide lubrication should the oil filter become clogged
- An oil pump pressure relief valve to prevent excessive system pressure.

> **CAUTION—**
> * If the red oil pressure warning comes on or flashes on while driving, always assume the oil pressure is low.

When the ignition is turned on, the oil pressure warning light comes on. When the engine is started and the oil pressure rises slightly, the oil pressure switch opens and the warning light goes out. Make sure the oil level is correct before making tests.

— Turn ignition switch on.
  - Warning light on instrument panel must light up.

— Remove connector from oil pressure switch.
  - Warning light on instrument panel must go out.

Oil pressure, checking

Test oil pressure by removing oil pressure switch and installing oil pressure gauge in its place.

> **CAUTION—**
> * Running the engine with the oil pressure switch disconnected may set a fault code (DTC).

— Loosen oil filter cover to allow engine oil to drain back down into oil pan. Tighten cover.

◀ M54 engine: Access to oil pressure warning switch (**arrow**) is restricted (intake manifold removed for purposes of photo).

0021537a

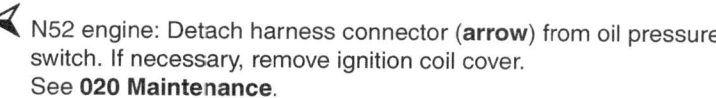

Oil filter cover

◀ N52 engine: Detach harness connector (**arrow**) from oil pressure switch. If necessary, remove ignition coil cover. See **020 Maintenance**.

— Remove switch. Be prepared to catch leaking oil with a shop towel.

> **CAUTION—**
> • *Thoroughly clean around the oil pressure switch before removing.*

— Install pressure gauge in place of oil pressure switch. If necessary, use BMW special adapter 11 4 050 in place of oil pressure switch.

— With gauge installed, start engine and allow to reach operating temperature. Check oil pressure. See **Table a**.

> *NOTE—*
> • *For the most accurate test results, make sure the engine oil and filter are new and the oil of the correct grade.*

Table b. Engine oil pressure	
At idle, engine at operating temperature • M54 engine • N52 engine	0.5 bar (7 psi) 1.5 bar (22 psi))
Maximum regulated pressure, engine at operating temperature • M54 engine • N52 engine	4 ± 0.5 bar (58 ± 7 psi) 4.0 - 6.0 bar (58 - 87 psi)

— Remove pressure gauge and reinstall pressure switch with new sealing washer.

Tightening torque	
Oil pressure switch to oil filter housing M54 engine (M12 x 1.5)	27 Nm (20 ft-lb)
Oil pressure switch to oil filter housing N52 engine (M12 x 1.5)	20 Nm (15 ft-lb) additional 16°

If testing shows low oil pressure, one or more of the following conditions may be indicated:

• Worn or faulty oil pump or faulty pump pressure relief valve

• Worn or damaged engine bearings

• Severe engine wear

Any of these conditions indicate the need for major repairs.

Oil pressure warning switch, replacing

◄ M54 engine: Access to oil pressure warning switch (**arrow**) is restricted (intake manifold removed for purposes of photo).

Oil filter cover

◄ N52 engine: If necessary, remove ignition coil cover. See **020 Maintenance**.

– Loosen oil filter cap to allow engine oil to drain back down into oil pan.

– Disconnect harness connector from oil pressure switch and remove switch. Be prepared to catch leaking oil with a shop towel.

> *CAUTION—*
> • *Thoroughly clean around the oil pressure switch before removing it.*

– Installation is reverse of removal. Tighten oil filter housing cap and top off oil, if necessary.

Tightening torque	
Oil pressure switch to oil filter housing M54 engine (M12 x 1.5)	27 Nm (20 ft-lb)
Oil pressure switch to oil filter housing N52 engine (M12 x 1.5)	20 Nm (15 ft-lb) additional 16°

OIL MONITORING

Oil level and temperature sensor (M54 engine)

Engine oil level and temperature is measured by the oil level and temperature sensor located in the oil pan, and indicated in the instrument cluster or central information display.

Oil condition information is processed by the engine control module (ECM), then routed via PT-CAN and K-CAN buses to the instrument cluster and central information display. The ECM software determines the optimal time for oil change interval.

Checking oil level is covered in **020 Maintenance**.

Oil condition sensor (OZS) (N52 engine)

Engine oil level is measured by the oil condition sensor (OZS) and indicated in the instrument cluster or central information display. Engine oil temperature and condition are also monitored by the OZS. N52 engines are not equipped with a dipstick.

Oil condition information is processed by the engine control module (ECM), then routed via PT-CAN and K-CAN buses to the instrument cluster and central information display. The ECM software determines the optimal time for oil change interval.

Checking oil level is covered in **020 Maintenance**.

OZS electronic circuitry features a self-diagnosis function. In case of a fault in the sensor, an error message is sent to the ECM. The fault can be viewed using a BMW scan tool.

OZS operation (N52 engine)

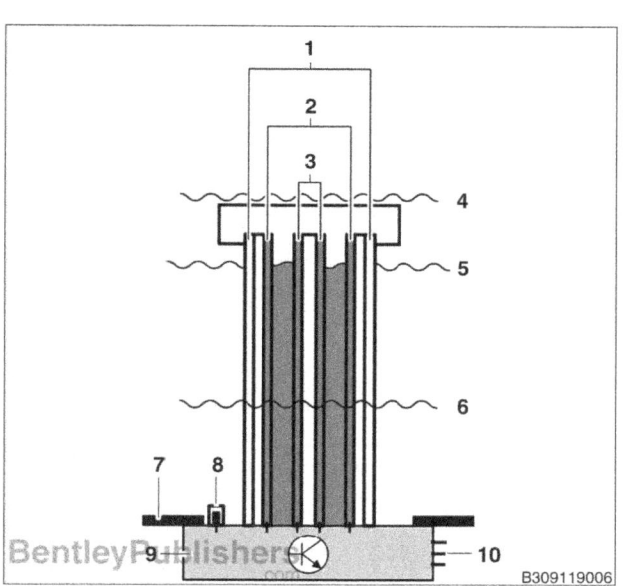

1. Housing
2. Outer metal tube
3. Inner metal tube
4. Engine oil (maximum)
5. Engine oil (average)
6. Engine oil (minimum)
7. Oil pan
8. Oil temperature sensor
9. Sensor electronics
10. Sensor connector

OZS consists of two cylindrical capacitors arranged one above the other. Oil condition is determined by the lower, smaller capacitor. Two metal tubes (**1**, **2**), arranged one inside the other, serve as capacitor electrodes. The dielectric is the engine oil between the electrodes. The electrical property of engine oil changes with age and break-down of oil additives, changing the OZS capacitance. This change is processed in the sensor electronics (**9**) and converted to a digital signal. The digital sensor signal is transferred to the ECM, which uses it to calculate the next oil change service due.

Engine oil level is determined by the capacitor of the OZS. As oil level drops, sensor capacitance changes accordingly. This change is processed in the sensor electronics (**9**) and converted to a digital signal. The digital sensor signal is transferred to the ECM and displayed to the driver.

A platinum temperature sensor (**8**) is installed at the base of the oil condition sensor.

Engine oil level, temperature and condition are monitored continuously as long as voltage is applied at terminal 15 (ignition ON). OZS is powered via terminal 87.

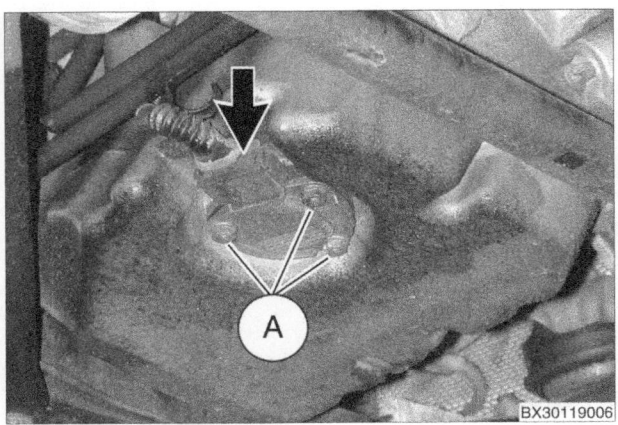

Oil level and temperature sensor, replacing (M54 engine)

Oil level warning switch is located at bottom of engine oil pan.

— Raise vehicle and support safely.

> **WARNING—**
> • *Make sure vehicle is stable and well supported at all times. Use a professional automotive lift or jack stands.*

— Remove front suspension reinforcement plate. See **310 Front Suspension**.

— Drain engine oil. See **020 Maintenance**.

◀ Disconnect electrical connector (**arrow**) and remove mounting nuts (**A**). Lower level sensor. be prepared to catch dripping oil.

— When reinstalling, replace sealing O-ring.

— Be sure to refill engine and check for leaks after work is completed.

OZS, replacing (N52 engine)

— Raise vehicle and support safely.

> **WARNING—**
> • *Make sure vehicle is stable and well supported at all times. Use a professional automotive lift or jack stands.*

— Remove front suspension reinforcement plate. See **310 Front Suspension**.

— Drain engine oil. See **020 Maintenance**.

◀ With engine fully cooled off, disconnect OZS electrical connector (**A**) and remove mounting nuts (**B**). Lower level sensor. Be prepared to catch dripping oil.

— When reinstalling, replace sealing O-ring.

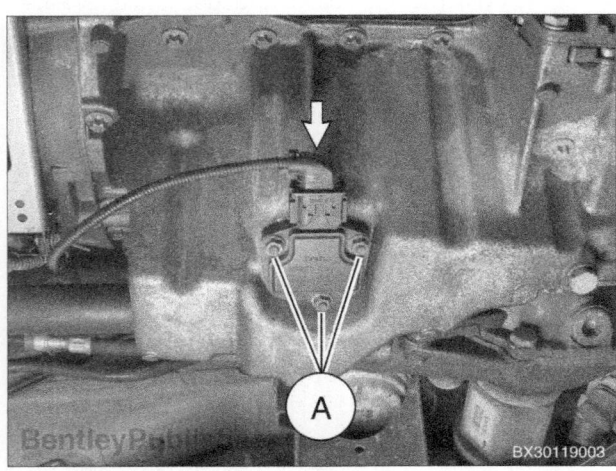

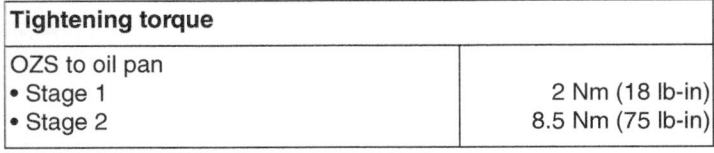

Tightening torque	
OZS to oil pan	
• Stage 1	2 Nm (18 lb-in)
• Stage 2	8.5 Nm (75 lb-in)

— Refill engine with oil and check for leaks after work is completed.

CRANKSHAFT SEALS (M54 ENGINE)

Crankshaft front oil seal, replacing (M54 engine)

– With engine fully cooled off, remove electric cooling fan and cowl, engine accessory belts and crankshaft vibration damper and pulley. Be sure to mark belts with direction of rotation. See **117 Camshaft Timing Chain**.

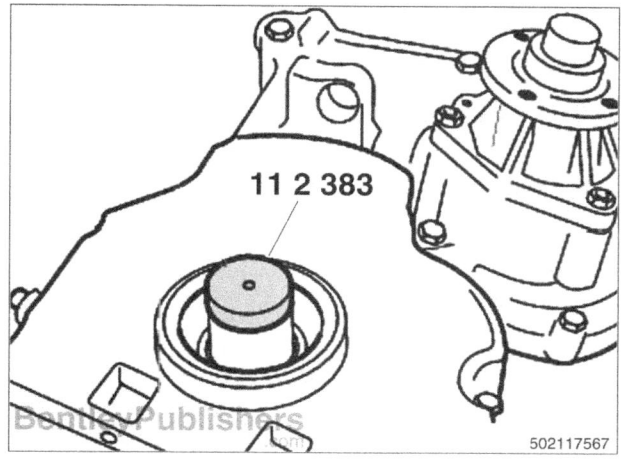

◄ Install cap (BMW special tool 11 2 383) on end of crankshaft.

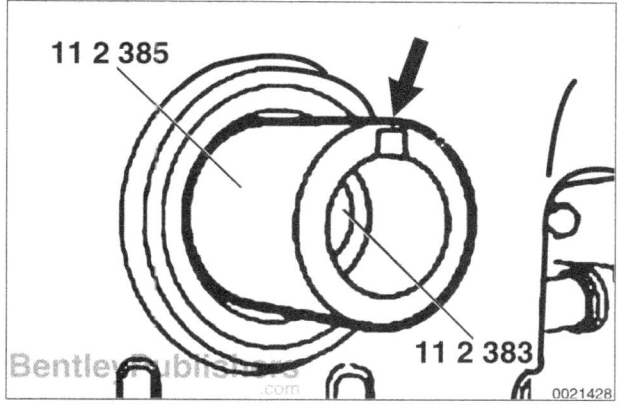

◄ Install seal guide (BMW special tool 11 2 385) over end of crankshaft. Be sure to align groove with keyway on crankshaft (**arrow**).

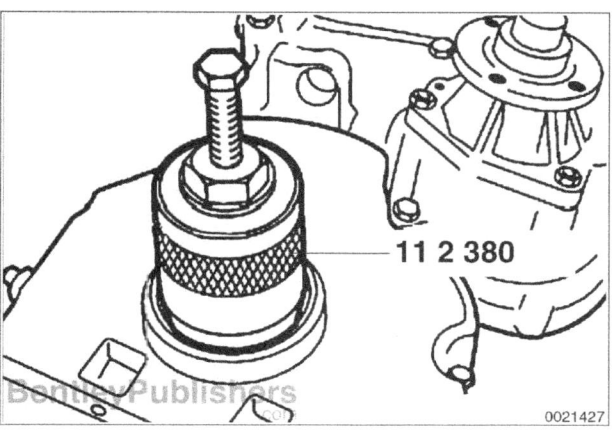

◄ Install oil seal puller (BMW special tool 11 2 380) and screw in body of puller until it contacts seal. Tighten bolt in center of tool to draw seal out of cover.

Crankshaft rear main seal, replacing (M54 engine)

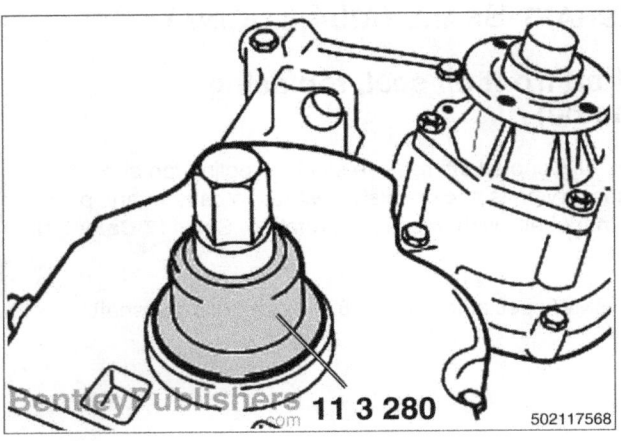

◀ Coat new seal with oil and position in timing chain cover. Use BMW special tool 11 3 280 and crankshaft center bolt to draw seal in flush with timing case cover.

— Reinstall crankshaft vibration damper and pulley.

Tightening torque	
Vibration damper hub to crankshaft (use new bolt)	410 Nm (302 ft-lb)

— Remainder of installation is reverse of removal, noting the following:
  • Install engine accessory belts. See **020 Maintenance**.
  • Install cooling fan. See **170 Radiator and Cooling System**.

Crankshaft rear main seal, replacing (M54 engine)

Crankshaft rear main seal (flywheel seal) replacement requires removal of the transmission and flywheel.

— Remove transmission. See **230 Manual Transmission**, or **240 Automatic Transmission**.

— Manual transmission vehicles: Remove clutch pressure plate and disc. See **210 Clutch**.

— Remove flywheel. See **210 Clutch** or **240 Automatic Transmission**.

— Drain engine oil.

◀ Remove seal carrier bolts from oil pan (**arrows**). Loosen all oil pan bolts.

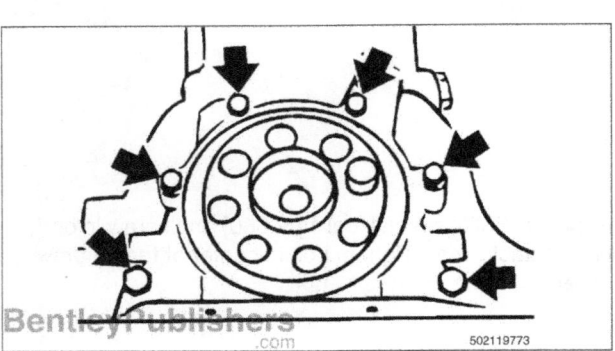

◀ Remove remaining seal carrier bolts (**arrows**) and carefully remove seal carrier without damaging oil pan gasket.

CAUTION—
  • *After removing seal carrier, check oil pan gasket for damage. If gasket is damaged during removal, remove oil pan and replace gasket. See **Oil pan, removing and installing (M54 engine)**.*

NOTE—
  • *BMW offers the rear main seal carrier and seal in a kit. A plastic installation sleeve, required for sliding the seal over the crankshaft, is included with the kit.*

— Install new seal carrier to crankcase. Remember to:
  • Check locating sleeves and bores in lower seal housing for damage.
  • Replace main seal carrier gasket.
  • Apply thin coat of 3 Bond® 1209 or equivalent sealant to oil pan gasket sealing surfaces.
  • Do not kink or damage sealing lip. Do not touch with fingers.
  • Lubricate crankshaft seal contact surface.

Crankshaft rear main seal, replacing (M54 engine)

◄ Use plastic support bushing (**A**) that comes with seal kit as an installation guide when fitting seal over end of crankshaft. Use care to push seal carrier and installation sleeve on straight, without tilting sideways. Remove installation sleeve.

− Install seal carrier bolts and torque to specifications.

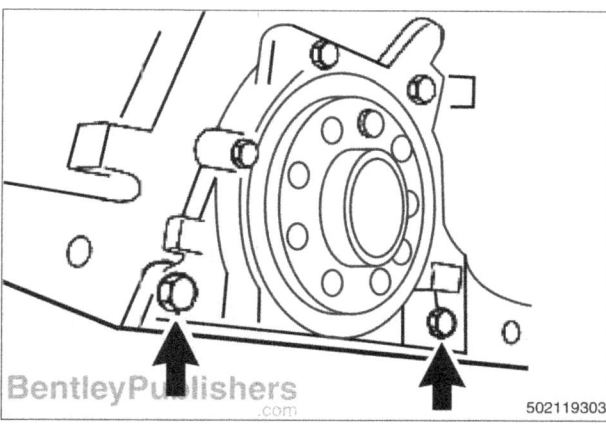

◄ Use new bolts (**arrows**) at base of seal carrier. Coat threads with sealing compound before installing.

− Install and tighten oil pan bolts.

− Remainder of assembly is reverse of disassembly.
  • Install flywheel, clutch or torque converter and transmission.
  • Fill engine with oil.
  • Run engine and check for leaks.

Tightening torques	
Oil drain plug to oil pan (M12)	25 Nm (18 ft-lb)
Oil pan to engine block or seal carrier • M6 (8.8 grade) • M6 (10.9 grade) • M8 (8.8 grade)	 10 Nm (89 in-lb) 12 Nm (9 ft-lb) 22 Nm (16 ft-lb)
Rear main seal carrier to crankcase • M6 • M8	 10 Nm (89 in-lb) 22 Nm (16 ft-lb)

CRANKSHAFT SEALS (N52 ENGINE)

Crankshaft front seal, removing and installing (N52 engine)

> **WARNING—**
> • To avoid personal injury, be sure the engine is cold before beginning the procedure.

> **CAUTION—**
> • When the crankshaft seal is replaced, its grooves and crankcase seams are filled with special Loctite® sealant to avoid oil leaks. Read entire procedure before starting work.

— Raise vehicle and support safely.

> **WARNING—**
> • Make sure vehicle is stable and well supported at all times. Use a professional automotive lift or jack stands.

— Remove splash shield underneath engine. See **020 Maintenance**.

— Remove engine accessory belt. See **020 Maintenance**.

◀ Remove vibration damper (front pulley). See **117 Camshaft Timing Chain**.

> **CAUTION—**
> • Do not remove vibration damper hub bolt. If this bolt is removed, the timing chain drive sprocket becomes free to rotate, resulting in valve damage.

◀ Place BMW special tool 11 9 221 against vibration damper hub and tighten down using bolts (special tool 11 9 224). This pushes crankshaft seal inward approx. 1 mm, thus loosening it for subsequent removal.

Tightening torque	
Special tool 11 9 221 to vibration damper hub	20 Nm (15 ft-lb)

— Remove special tools.

Crankshaft front seal, removing and installing (N52 engine)

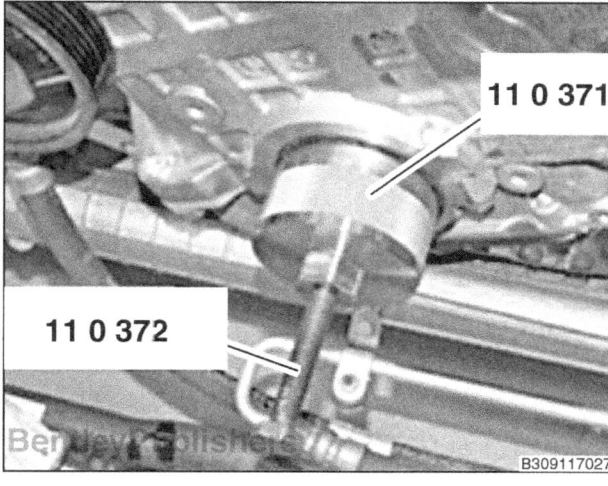

 Screw BMW special tool 11 0 371 into crankshaft seal with approx. 80 Nm (59 ft-lb) of torque. Then rotate special tool 11 0 371 clockwise to pull out seal. Repeat process if necessary.

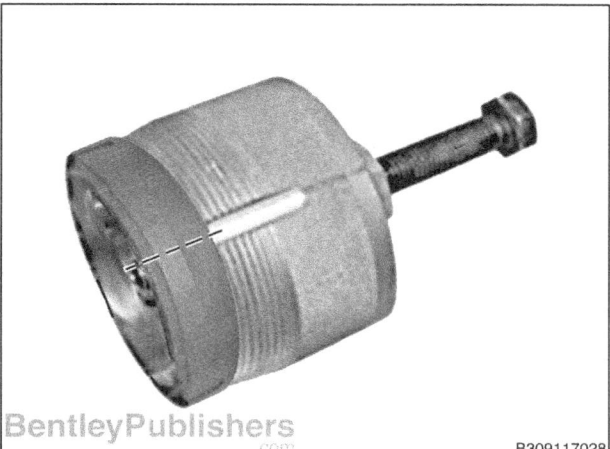

 Carefully saw seal at **dashed line** and remove from tool.

 Working at crankcase opening:

  • Clean crankshaft seal seating surface (**A**).
  • Degrease thoroughly area around crankcase seam (**arrows**).
  • Lightly oil sealing surface (**B**) on vibration damper hub.

Crankshaft front seal, removing and installing (N52 engine)

◄ Attach BMW special tool 11 9 232 to vibration damper hub using bolts (special tool 11 9 234).

◄ Place crankshaft seal and installation sleeve over tool and against crankcase opening.

- Plastic guide sleeve is supplied with seal.
- Coat both grooves on seal with Loctite® 171000 (primer). Allow to dry for approx. 1 minute.
- Make sure seal grooves center on crankcase seam (**arrows**).

◄ Use BMW special tools 11 9 231 and 11 9 233 to press in seal.

119

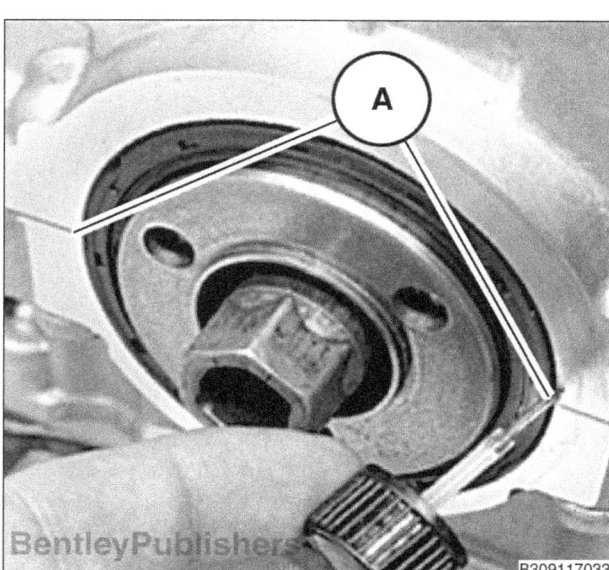

◀ Use brush to coat seal grooves and crankcase seams (**A**) with Loctite® 171000 (primer).

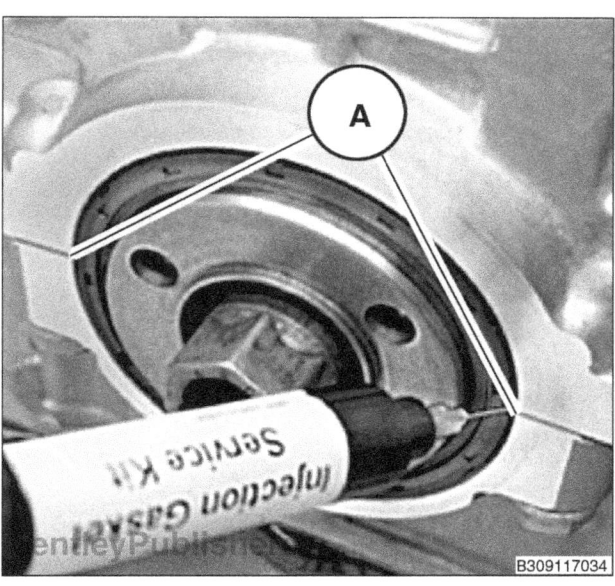

◀ Use injector kit to fill seal grooves and crankcase seams (**A**) with Loctite® 128357 (sealant).

– Coat sealed areas with Loctite® 171000 (primer) to bind sealant.

– Reinstall crankshaft vibration damper.

Tightening torque	
Vibration damper to vibration damper hub (M8 x 16 mm Torx)	35 Nm (26 ft-lb)

– Remainder of assembly is reverse of disassembly.

Crankshaft rear main seal, removing and installing (N52 engine)

Crankshaft rear main seal (flywheel seal) replacement requires removal of the transmission and flywheel.

> **CAUTION—**
> • When the crankshaft seal is replaced, its grooves and crankcase seams are filled with special Loctite® sealant to avoid oil leaks. Be sure to read the entire procedure before starting work.

– Remove transmission. See **230 Manual Transmission,** or **240 Automatic Transmission**.

– Manual transmission vehicles: Remove clutch pressure plate and disc. See **210 Clutch**.

Crankshaft rear main seal, removing and installing (N52 engine)

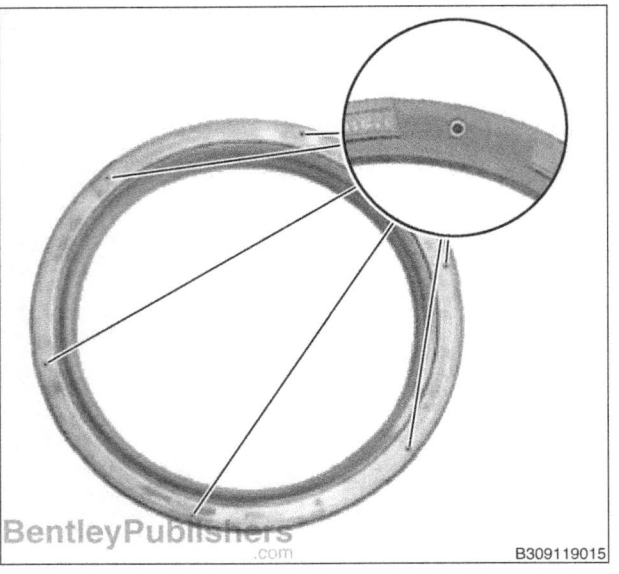

- Remove flywheel. See **210 Clutch** or **240 Automatic Transmission**.

- Drain engine oil.

◀ Crankshaft rear main seal has six removal openings (**inset**). If necessary, scrape off rubber coating to expose openings.

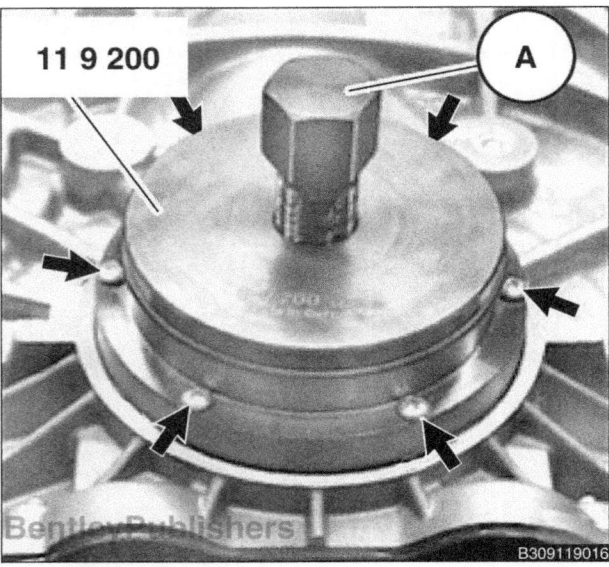

◀ Fit BMW seal puller, special tool 11 9 200, to seal.
  • Insert sheet metal screws (**arrows**) into seal removal openings. Tighten snugly but do not overtighten.
  • Screw in seal remover spindle (**A**) slowly to pull out seal.

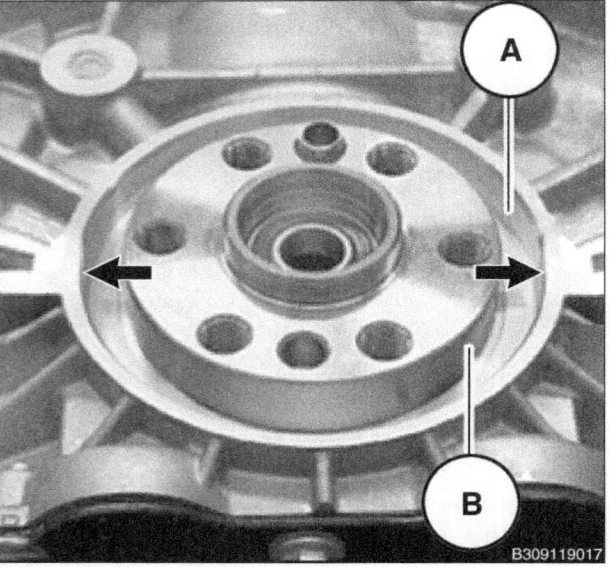

◀ Before installing new seal:
  • Clean seal seating surface (**A**).
  • Degrease crankcase seams (**arrows**) thoroughly.
  • Apply light coat of engine oil to seal lip running surface (**B**) on crankshaft flange.

Crankshaft rear main seal, removing and installing (N52 engine)

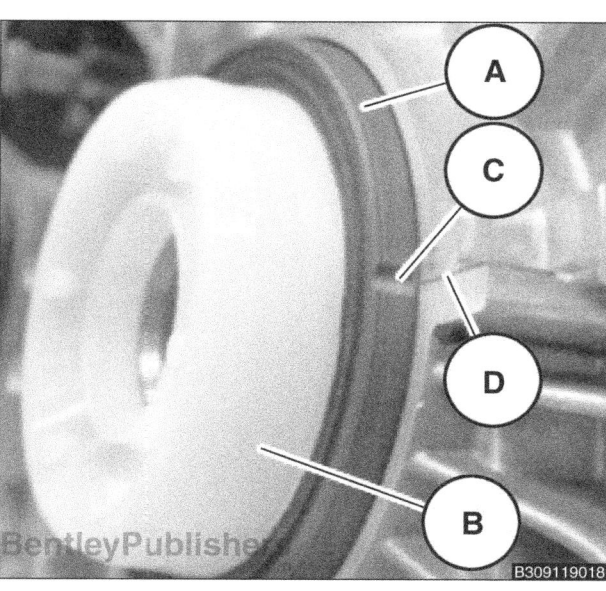

◄ Place crankshaft seal (**A**) and installation sleeve (**B**) against crankcase opening.

> **CAUTION—**
> • Do not kink or damage sealing lip. Do not touch with fingers.

- Plastic guide sleeve is supplied with seal.
- Coat both grooves on seal with Loctite® 171000 (primer). Allow to dry for approx. 1 minute.
- Make sure seal grooves (**C**) center on crankcase seams (**D**).
- Press in seal as far as possible by hand, then remove installation sleeve.

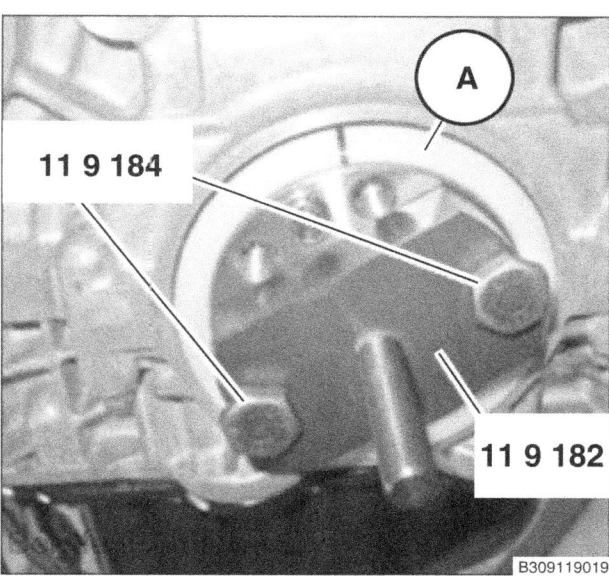

◄ Fit BMW special tools 11 9 182 and 11 9 184 to crankshaft flange.
- Fit spacer ring (**A**) over seal. Spacer ring is supplied with seal.

◄ Use BMW special tools 11 9 181 and 11 9 183 to press in seal.

– Remove special tools and spacer ring.

Crankshaft rear main seal, removing and installing (N52 engine)

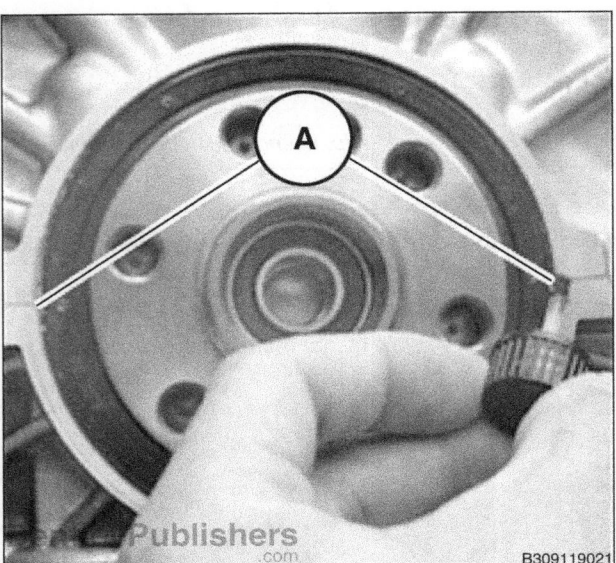

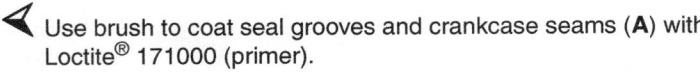 Use brush to coat seal grooves and crankcase seams (**A**) with Loctite® 171000 (primer).

◄ Use injector kit to fill seal grooves and crankshaft seams (**A**) with Loctite® 128357 (sealant).

– Coat sealed areas with Loctite® 171000 (primer) to bind sealant.

– Remainder of assembly is reverse of disassembly.
  • Install flywheel, clutch or torque converter and transmission.
  • Fill engine with oil.
  • Run engine and check for leaks.

OIL PAN AND OIL PUMP

Oil sump and front differential (M54 engine)

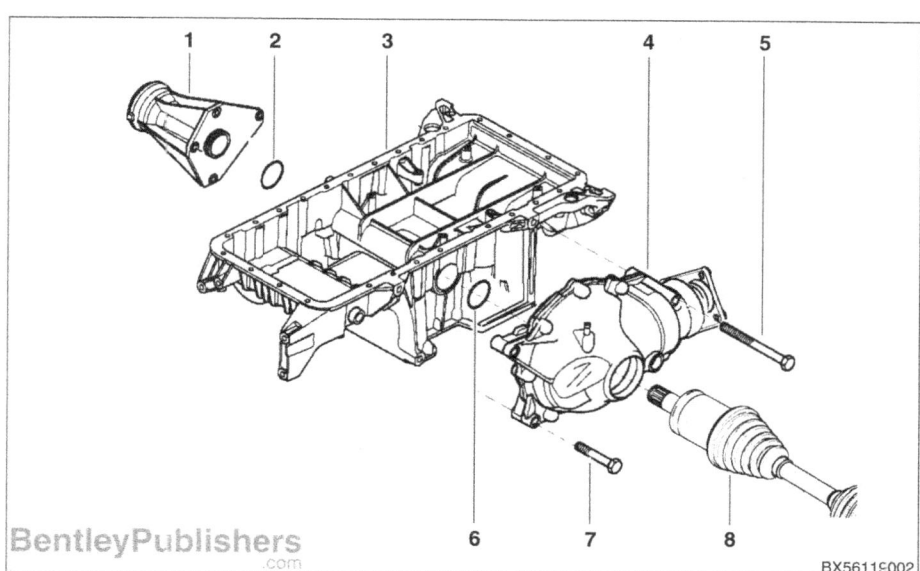

1. **Right drive axle inner bearing pedestal**
2. **Sealing O-ring**
3. **Oil pan**
4. **Front differential**
5. **Bolt**
6. **Sealing O-ring**
7. **Bolt**
8. **Left drive axle**

BX56119002

Oil sump, removing and installing (M54 engine)

The front differential is bolted to the left side of the oil pan. The right front drive axle inner bearing pedestal is bolted to the right side of the oil pan. When removing the oil pan, lower the front suspension subframe and remove the front differential. Read the procedure through before starting work.

— Disconnect negative (-) battery cable.

> **CAUTION—**
> • Prior to disconnecting the battery, read the battery disconnection cautions in **001 Warnings and Cautions.**

— Raise engine hood into assembly position.
See **410 Fenders, Engine Hood.**

— Remove brace from strut towers.
See **310 Front Suspension.**

— Remove Housing for interior ventilation microfilter.
See **640 Heating and Air-conditioning.**

— Remove air filter housing and duct.
See **130 Fuel Injection.**

— Remove electric cooling fan and cowl.
See **170 Radiator and Cooling System.**

— Remove upper engine covers. See **020 Maintenance.**

— Mark direction of rotation on alternator belt, then remove belt. See **020 Maintenance.**

Oil sump, removing and installing (M54 engine)

— Raise car and support safely.

> **WARNING —**
> • *Make sure vehicle is stable and well supported at all times. Use a professional automotive lift or jack stands.*

— Remove underbody splash shield

— Remove front suspension reinforcement plate. See **310 Front Suspension**

— Drain engine oil. See **020 Maintenance**.

◄ Install engine support brace across engine bay. Raise engine slightly to release load on engine mounts.

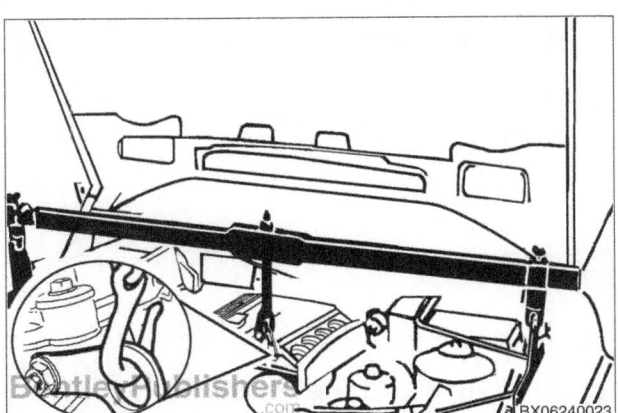

— Unbolt power steering pump and hang to side using stiff wire. See **320 Steering and Wheel Alignment**

> **NOTE —**
> • *Do not detach power steering fluid lines.*

— Lower front suspension subframe from body. See **310 Front Suspension**.

— Remove front differential and right drive axle inner bearing pedestal. See **311 Front Axle Differential**.

— Detach electrical harness connector at oil level sensor. Disconnect return hose from crankcase breather oil separator. Vehicles with automatic transmission:
> • Release transmission oil cooler lines from guides.

— Make sure all wiring and fluid lines are detached from oil pan.

— Remove oil pan screws to engine crank case.

◄ Remove bellhousing bolts.

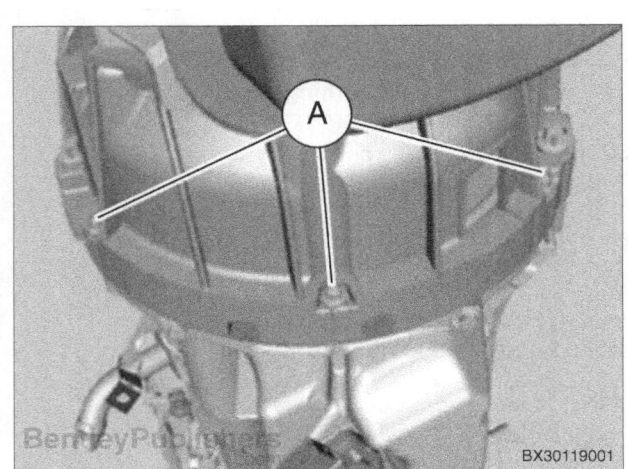

> **NOTE —**
> • *Different length bolts are used to secure the oil pan and transmission bellhousing. Note position when removing.*

— Lower oil pan and slide backward to remove.

> **CAUTION—**
> • *If oil pan does not separate easily from engine block, tap lightly with a rubber mallet to break it free. Do not use prying tools.*

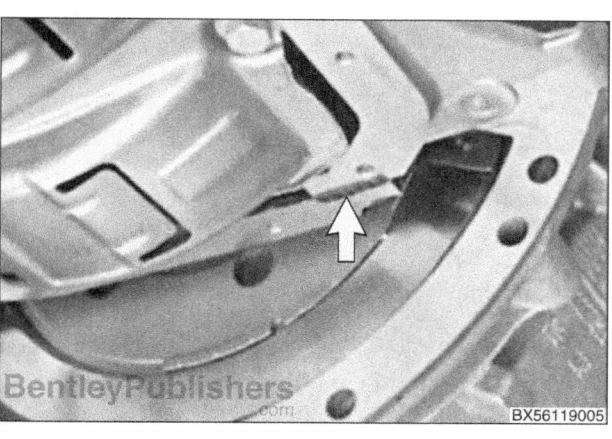

◄ Clean sealing surface of engine block, then apply beads of 3-Bond® 1209 or equivalent approx. 3 mm high and 2 mm wide (**arrow**) to timing cover and rear main seal carrier seams.

— When reinstalling oil sump:
  • Thoroughly clear old gasket material from oil sump sealing surface and use a new gasket.
  • Insert oil pan bolts. Tighten front oil sump bolts first. Tighten transmission bellhousing bolts last.

Torques	
Oil drain plug to oil sump (M12)	25 Nm (18 ft-lb)
Oil sump to engine block: • M6 (8.8) • M6 (10.9) • M8	 10 Nm (89 in-lb) 12 Nm (106 in-lb) 22 Nm (16 ft-lb)
Transmission bellhousing to oil sump: • M8 Allen • M8 Torx	 24 Nm (17 ft-lb) 21 Nm (33 ft-lb)

— Remainder of installation is reverse of removal. Fill engine with oil, run engine and check for leaks.

> **CAUTION—**
> • *Follow correct installation procedure for front end reinforcement plate using new bolts. See* **310 Front Suspension**.

Oil pump, removing and installing (M54 engine)

The M54 engine oil pump is driven by the crankshaft via chain and sprocket assembly. To remove the oil pump, the front suspension must be lowered while supporting the engine from above. Read the procedure through before starting.

◄ 6-cylinder engine oil pump assembly:

1. Drive chain
2. M10 x 1 nut (left hand threads)
   • Tighten to 25 Nm (18 ft-lb)
3. Oil pump sprocket
4. Inner pump rotor
5. Outer pump rotor
6. Pressure relief valve
7. M8 bolt
   • Tighten to 23 Nm (17 ft-lb)
8. Oil pump housing
9. Locating dowels
10. Pick-up tube sealing O-ring
11. Pick-up tube
12. Pickup tube mounting bolts (M6)
    • Tighten to 10 Nm (7 ft-lb)

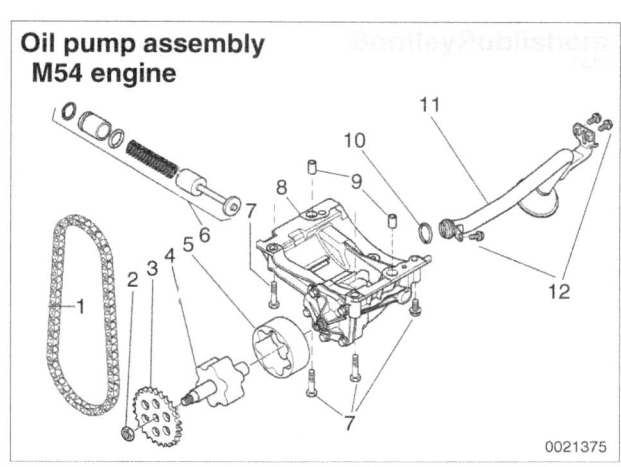

Oil pump assembly M54 engine

Oil pressure relief valve (M54 engine)

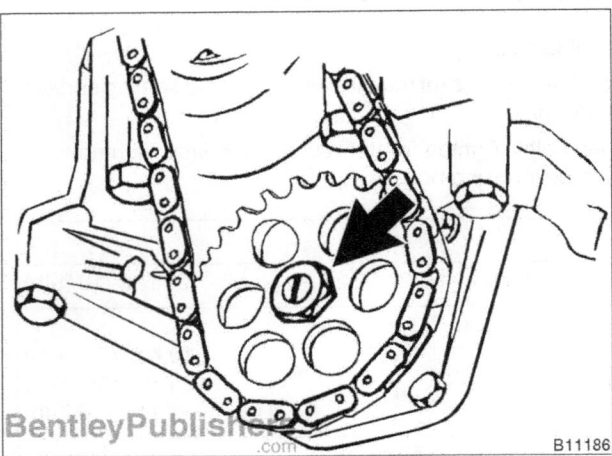

— Remove oil sump. See **Oil pan, removing and installing (M54 engine)** in this repair group.

◄ Remove oil pump sprocket mounting nut (**arrow**).

> **CAUTION—**
> • *Oil pump sprocket nut has left hand threads. Turn clockwise to loosen.*

— Lift sprocket off pump together with drive chain.

— Unbolt oil pump from engine block.
  • Remove oil pump pick-up tube bolts and remove pick-up tube before removing pump.
  • Remove mounting bolts from oil pump. Withdraw pump.
  • Be sure to record location of spacers between pump and engine block, if applicable.

— Spin oil pump shaft and check that gears turn smoothly. Replace pump if gears spin with difficulty.

— Inspect oil pressure relief valve.
  See **Oil pressure relief valve (M54 engine)** in this repair group.

— Installation is reverse of removal, noting the following:
  • Inspect pump locating dowels for damage and correct positioning.
  • Replace oil pick-up and return tube sealing O-rings.
  • Align sprocket splines to oil pump shaft splines before tightening sprocket nut.

> **CAUTION—**
> • *Oil pump sprocket nut has left hand threads. Turn counterclockwise to tighten.*

Tightening torques	
Oil pump sprocket to oil pump shaft (M10 x 1) (left hand thread)	25 Nm (18 ft-lb)
Oil pump to crankcase (M8)	23 Nm (17 ft-lb)

— Fill engine with oil, run engine and check for leaks.

Oil pressure relief valve (M54 engine)

— Remove oil pump. See **Oil pump, removing and installing (M54 engine)**. The oil pump pressure relief valve is held in the side of the oil pump with a circlip.

◄ Inspect oil pump relief valve components and bore for scoring or other damage.
  1. Control plunger
  2. Spring
  3. Sealing O-ring
  4. Sleeve
  5. Circlip

— Install using a new circlip.

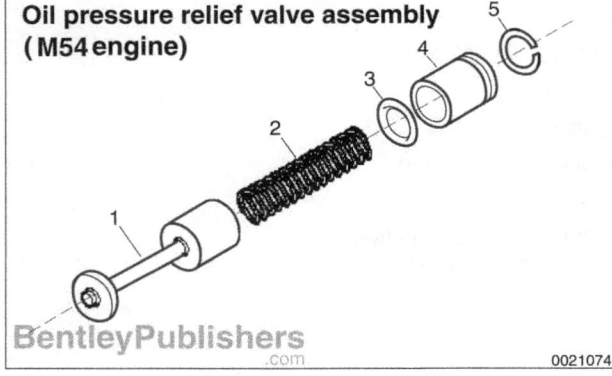

Oil pressure relief valve assembly (M54 engine)

Oil sump and front differential (N52 engine)

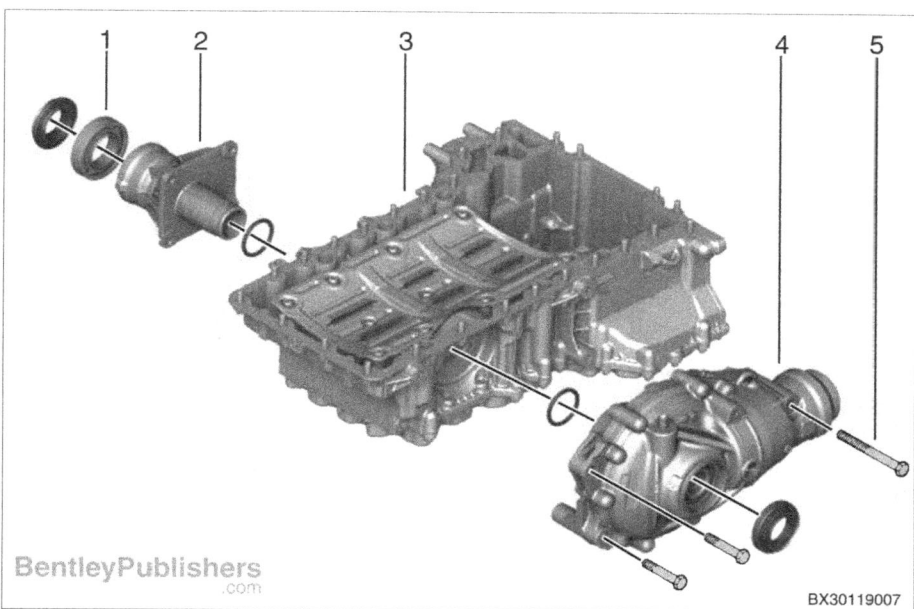

1. Bearing
2. Right drive axle inner bearing pedestal
3. Oil Pan
4. Front differential
5. Bolt

BentleyPublishers
.com

BX30119007

Oil sump, removing and installing (N52 engine)

The front differential is bolted to the left side of the oil sump. The right front drive axle inner bearing pedestal is bolted to the right side of the oil sump. When removing the oil sump, lower the front subframe and remove the front differential. Read the procedure through before starting work.

— Disconnect negative (-) battery cable.

> **CAUTION—**
> • Prior to disconnecting the battery, read the battery disconnection cautions in **001 Warnings and Cautions**.

— Raise engine hood into assembly position. See **410 Fenders, Engine Hood**.

— Remove brace from strut towers. See **310 Front Suspension**.

— Remove housing for interior ventilation microfilter. See **640 Heating and Air-conditioning**.

— Remove air filter housing and duct. See **130 Fuel Injection**.

— Remove electric cooling fan and cowl. See **170 Radiator and Cooling System**.

— Remove upper engine covers. See **020 Maintenance**.

— Mark direction of rotation on alternator belt, then remove belt. See **020 Maintenance**.

Oil sump, removing and installing (N52 engine)

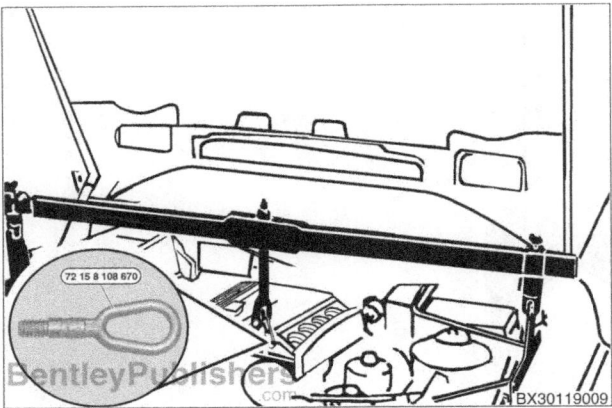

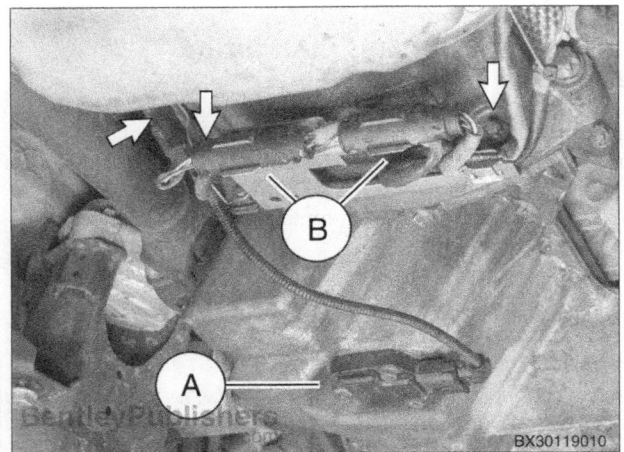

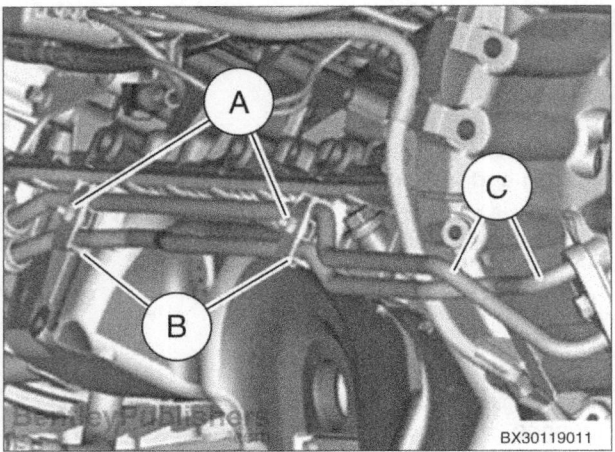

— Raise car and support safely.

> **WARNING—**
> • *Make sure vehicle is stable and well supported at all times. Use a professional automotive lift or jack stands.*

— Remove underbody splash shield

— Remove front suspension reinforcement plate. See **310 Front Suspension**

— Drain engine oil. See **020 Maintenance**.

◀ Install engine support brace across engine bay.

  • Support engine using vehicle tow hook (72 15 8 108 670) screwed into front of cylinder head.

  • Raise engine slightly to release load on engine mounts.

— Lower front subframe from body. See **310 Front Suspension**.

— Remove front differential and right drive axle inner bearing pedestal. See **311 Front Axle Differential**.

◀ Detach electrical harness connector at oil level sensor (**A**).

  • Disconnect oxygen sensor connectors (**B**).

  • Remove sensor lines from bracket.

  • Remove three e-Torx fasteners (**arrows**) between transmission bell housing and oil sump.

◀ Vehicles with automatic transmission:

  • Remove transmission cooler line fasteners (**A**).

  • Release holders (**B**).

  • Move cooler lines (**C**) away from oil sump.

Oil sump, removing and installing (N52 engine)

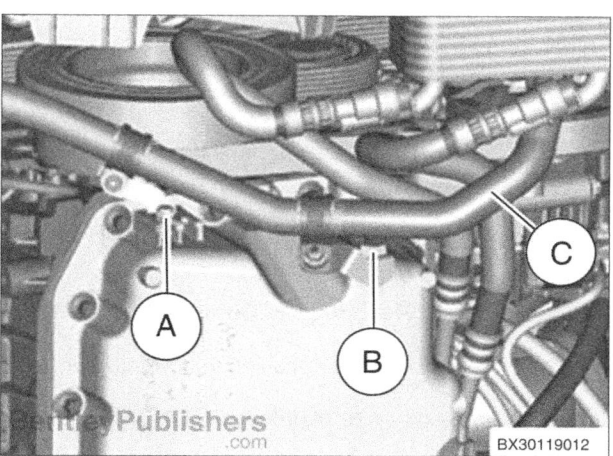

◄ Remove fasteners (**A**, **B**) and release holders with coolant lines from oil sump.

– Make sure all wiring and fluid lines are clear of oil sump.

– Remove oil pan screws to engine crank case.

NOTE—

• Different length bolts are used to secure the oil pan and transmission bellhousing. Note position when removing.

– Lower oil pan and remove.

CAUTION—

• If sump does not separate easily from cylinder block, tap lightly with a rubber mallet to break it free. Do not use prying tools.

– When reinstalling oil sump:

• Thoroughly clean old gasket material from oil sump sealing surface and use a new gasket.

• Replace aluminum fasteners. Install in correct locations as noted previously.

• Tighten front oil sump bolts first. Tighten transmission bellhousing bolts last.

Tightening torques	
Oil drain plug to oil sump (M12)	25 Nm (18 ft-lb)
Oil pan to engine block: • M8x36, M8x92 • Stage 1 • Stage 2 (angle torque)	 8 Nm (70 in-lb) 90°
Transmission bellhousing to oil sump: • M8x50	 19 Nm (14 ft-lb)
Transmission cooler line bracket: • M6	 8 Nm (70 in-lb)
Coolant line bracket: • Hexagon nut (M6) • Hexagon bolt (M10x18)	 9 Nm (80 in/lb) 21 Nm (15.5 ft-lb)

– Remainder of installation is reverse of removal. Fill engine with oil, run engine and check for leaks.

CAUTION—

• Follow correct installation procedure for front end reinforcement plate using new bolts. See **310 Front Suspension**.

NOTE—

• It is not necessary to realign the front end after this procedure.

Engine oil cooler, removing and installing (N52 engines)

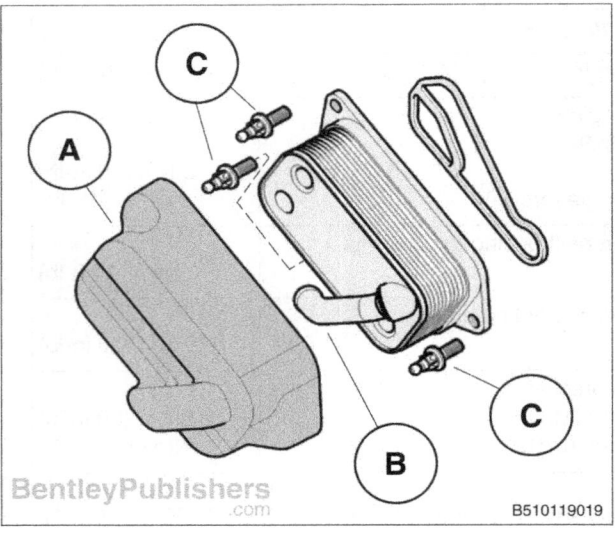

OIL COOLER

Engine oil cooler, removing and installing (N52 engines)

N52 engines may be equipped with an optional engine oil cooler mounted to the front of the oil filter housing.

◄ Oil cooler location on N52 engine (**arrow**).

− Drain engine coolant. See **170 Radiator and Cooling System**.

− Loosen oil filter cover to allow oil in filter housing to flow into pan.

− Remove engine upper cover. See **020 Maintenance**.

◄ Unclip cover (**A**) from cooler.

− Remove coolant line from hose fitting on cooler (**B**). Use a shop rag to catch coolant.

− Remove bolts (**C**) and remove oil cooler. Use a shop rag to catch oil.

− Installation is reverse of removal, noting the following.
  • Clean mating surfaces and replace seal.
  • Tighten fasteners to specified torque to avoid damaging seals.

Tightening torques	
M8	22 Nm (16 ft-lb)

  • Refill coolant, see **170 Radiator and Cooling System**.
  • Check and top off oil, see **020 Maintenance**.

OIL FILER HOUSING

Oil filter housing bracket, removing and installing (M54 engine)

— Disconnect battery negative cable.

— Remove air cleaner housing and fresh air ducts. See **130 Fuel Injection**.

— Loosen oil filter cover to allow oil in filter housing to flow into oil pan.

— Remove drive belt and unbolt alternator from oil filter housing bracket. See **121 Battery Starter, Alternator**.

— Empty power steering reservoir tank and then unbolt tank and move to one side (lines remain connected).

— Unbolt power steering pump from oil filter housing bracket pump (lines remain connected). See **320 Steering and Wheel Alignment**.

— Unbolt and remove alternator drive belt tensioner.

— Disconnect harness connector from oil pressure switch.

— Disconnect harness connector for oil temperature switch.

— Working at oil filter housing, disconnect oil pressure line for VANOS adjustment unit.

◄ Remove bolts (**arrows**) and remove complete oil filter housing bracket.

B510119024

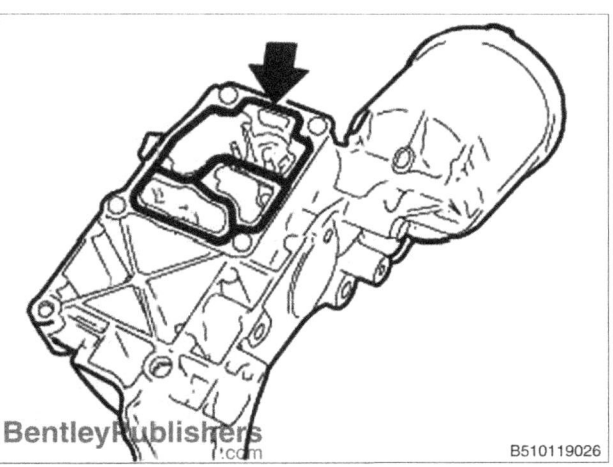

◄ Remove old profile gasket and install new gasket (**arrow**).

B510119026

Oil filter housing, removing and installing (N52 engines)

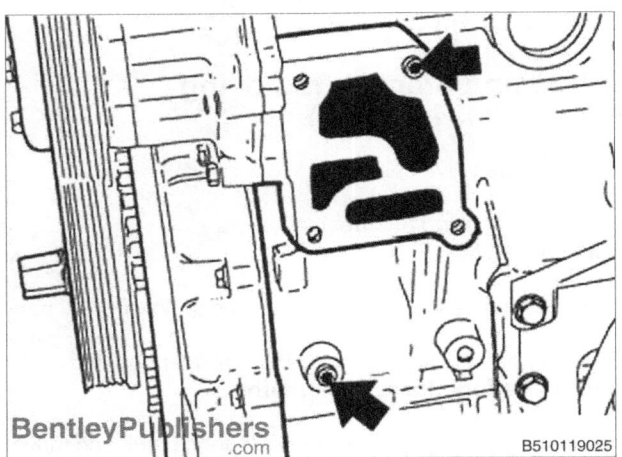

◄ Installation is reverse of removal. Keep in mind the following:

• A unique torque is not given for the oil filter housing bracket bolts. General tightening torque based on bolt grade is given below.

• Be sure to align bracket to locating dowels (**arrows**).

• Reconnect all harness connectors previously removed.

• Check engine oil level and power steering fluid level upon job completion.

• Reconnect battery negative cable.

NOTE —

• *Bolt grade is marked on bolt head.*

Tightening torques	
M8 (8.8 grade)	24 Nm (18 ft-lb)
M8 (10.9 grade)	34 Nm 25 ft-lb)

Oil filter housing, removing and installing (N52 engines)

— Drain engine coolant. Remove electric cooling fan. See **170 Radiator and Cooling System**.

— Loosen oil filter cover to allow oil in filter housing to flow into pan.

— Remove intake manifold, see **130 Fuel Injection**.

NOTE —

• *Intake manifold removal is required to access a difficult-to-reach oil filter housing fastener (bolt **D**). This bolt is located at right side of oil filter housing under intake manifold. It may be possible to access this bolt without removing the intake manifold using a combination of universal joints and an e-torx socket.*

— If necessary, remove oil cooler from oil filter housing. See **Engine oil cooler, removing and installing (N52 engine)** given earlier.

◄ Working at oil filter housing:

• Disconnect coolant line from housing (**A**).

• Remove oil pressure sensor (**B**).

• Remove bolts **C** and **D** and remove oil filter housing from engine.

— Installation is reverse of removal, noting the following:

• Clean mating surfaces and replace o-rings and seals.

• Be sure not to over tighten fasteners to avoid damaging seals.

Tightening torques	
M8	22 Nm (16 ft-lb)

• Refill coolant, see **170 Radiator and Cooling System**.

• Check and top off oil, see **020 Maintenance**.

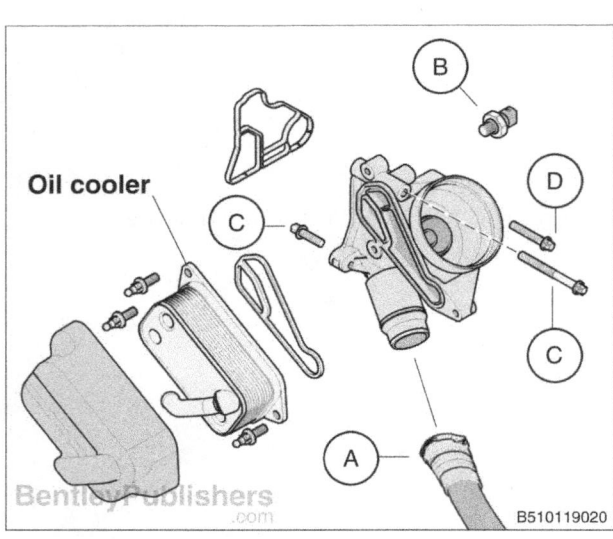

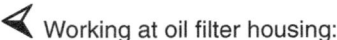

120 Ignition System

GENERAL

This repair group covers ignition component troubleshooting and replacement.

See also:

- **020 Maintenance** for spark plug replacement
- **100 Engine—General** for engine applications
- **130, 131, 132, 133 Fuel Injection**
- **ECL Electrical Component Locations**
- **ELE Electrical Wiring Diagrams**
- **OBD On-Board Diagnostics**

Ignition firing order

◀ **BMW 6-cylinder engine:** Cylinder 1 is at the front of the engine.

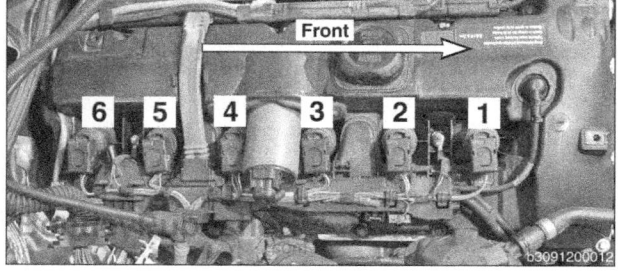

Table a. Ignition firing order	
6-cylinder engine	1-5-3-6-2-4

Disabling ignition system

The ignition system operates in a lethal voltage range. Disable the ignition system any time engine service or repair work is being done that requires the ignition to be switched ON.

One way of disabling the ignition is to remove the DME main relay. The relay is located in the electronics box (E-box) in the right rear of the engine compartment. DME fuse, relay and power supply information is in **130**, **131 Fuel Injection**.

> **CAUTION—**
> • Relay locations vary. Use care when identifying relays. See **ECL Electrical Component Locations**.

Warnings and cautions

> **WARNING —**
> • Do not touch or disconnect any cables from the ignition coils while the engine is running or being cranked by the starter.
> • The ignition system produces high voltages that can be fatal. Avoid contact with exposed terminals. Use caution when working on a car with the ignition switched ON or the engine running.
> • Connect and disconnect the DME system wiring and test equipment leads when the ignition is OFF.
> • Before operating the starter without starting the engine (for example when testing compression), disable the ignition. See **Disabling ignition system** in this repair group.

> **CAUTION—**
> • Do not attempt to disable the ignition by removing the coils from the spark plugs.
> • Do not connect any test equipment that delivers a 12-volt power supply to terminal 15 (+) of the ignition coil. The current flow may damage the engine control module (ECM).
> • Connect or disconnect ignition system wires, multiple wire connectors and ignition test equipment leads only while the ignition is OFF. Switch multimeter functions or measurement ranges with test probes disconnected.
> • Do not disconnect the battery while the engine is running.
> • Prior to disconnecting the battery cables, read the battery disconnection cautions in **001 Warnings and Cautions**.
> • Wait at least 1 minute after switching the ignition OFF before removing the ECM connector. If the connector is removed before this time, residual power in the system relay may damage the control module.
> • Use a digital multimeter for electrical tests. Use an LED test light for quick tests.
> • To avoid electrochemical corrosion to engine components made of aluminum-magnesium alloy, do not use steel fasteners in place of aluminum. For reliable identification, test fasteners with a magnet for aluminum composition.
> • Replace aluminum fasteners each time they are loosened.
> • Follow torque instructions, including angle of rotation specifications, when installing aluminum fasteners.

DIGITAL MOTOR ELECTRONICS (DME) IGNITION SYSTEM

BMW X3 models are equipped with digital motor electronics (DME), also known as Motronic. In these systems, fuel injection and ignition are controlled by an integrated engine control module (ECM). Application information for DME systems is in **Table b**.

Most DME functions are described in **130, 131 Fuel Injection**. Functions associated with ignition are given here.

Table b. Engine management applications

Year, model	Engine code	Engine management	Features
2004-2006 2.5i, 3.0i	M54	Siemens DME MS 45	double VANOS
2007-2010 3.0si, 30i	N52KP	Siemens MSV80 ULEV II	Valvetronic, double VANOS

Ignition coils

◀ X3 engines use a distributorless ignition system with individual ignition coils (**numbered**) for each cylinder (N52 engine shown in photo),

◀ Each coil is separately controlled and monitored by the ECM.

> **CAUTION—**
> • *Maintain a high level of cleanliness when servicing ignition coils. Fuel / oil residue can cause a breakdown in the electrical resistance qualities of silicone used in production. This in turn can result in ignition coil failure.*

NOTE—

• *Schematic diagrams shown are for illustrative purposes only. See* **ELE Electrical Wiring Diagrams** *for engine management specific wiring information.*

Ignition timing is electronically mapped and not adjustable. The ECM uses engine load, engine speed, coolant temperature, knock detection, and intake air temperature as the basic inputs for timing control.

The initial ignition point is determined by the crankshaft sensor during cranking. Once the engine is running, the ECM refers to the stored map to continually adjust ignition timing based on operating conditions.

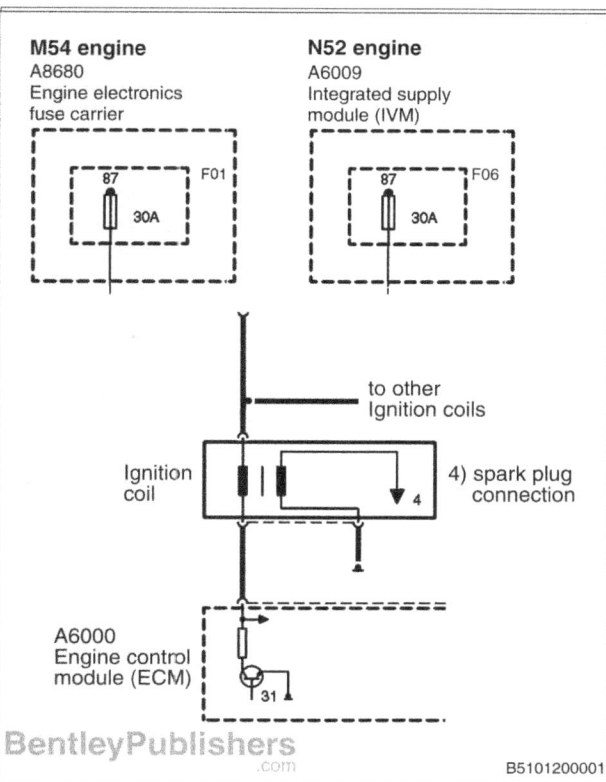

Crankshaft sensor

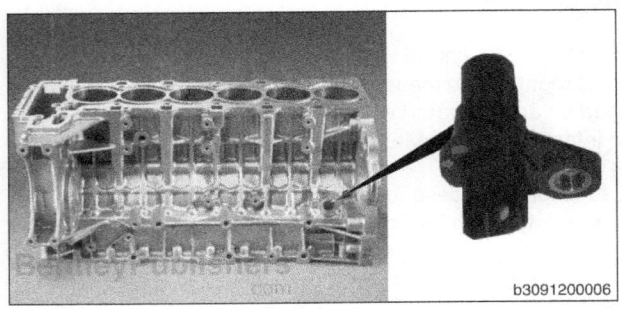

b3091200006

Crankshaft sensor

The crankshaft sensor detects crankshaft position and rotation speed via a toothed pulse wheel mounted on flywheel. If the ECM does not receive an impulse signal from the crankshaft sensor during cranking, the engine does not start. If the OBD II system misfire detection protocol detects a catalyst damaging fault due to a malfunction in crankshaft sensor components, the malfunction indicator light (MIL) is illuminated.

The crankshaft position sensor is supplied 12 volts from the engine electronics fuses and ground from the ECM The crankshaft sensor is mounted in the block at the left rear near starter motor.

Camshaft sensors

Each camshaft sensor responds to an impulse wheel mounted at the end of the camshaft. The signal from camshaft sensors are used by the ECM for cylinder recognition, spark timing, sequential fuel injection, VANOS (camshaft timing) and Valvetronic (variable valve lift) control. If a fault with the camshaft sensor is detected the malfunction indicator light (MIL) is illuminated

The camshaft position sensor is supplied 12 volts from the engine electronics fuses and ground from the ECM.

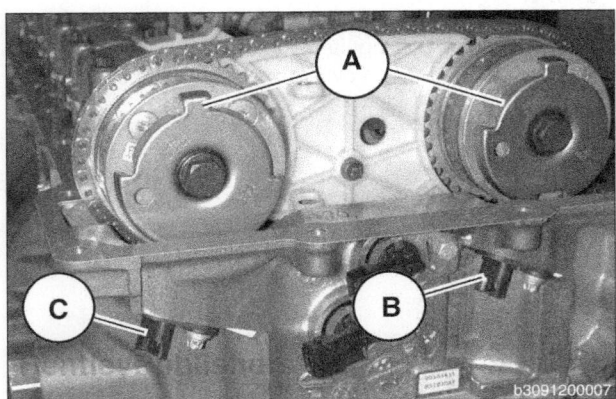

b3091200007

◄ Camshaft sensors on N52 engine:
- Intake camshaft sensor (**B**): Left front of cylinder head.
- Exhaust camshaft sensor (**C**): Right front of cylinder head.

NOTE—
- *N52 engine: A malfunctioning or sticking VANOS solenoid may set camshaft position sensor fault codes. If you suspect this, swap VANOS solenoid from bank with fault code to the other bank. If the camshaft position sensor fault code follows the location of the solenoid, the solenoid is at fault.*

Knock sensors

Knock sensors monitor the combustion chambers for engine-damaging knock. A knock sensor is a piezoelectric microphone tuned to the frequencies of engine knock or detonation. If engine knock is detected, ignition spark is retarded by the ECM. If a knock sensor fault is detected the malfunction indicator light (MIL) is illuminated.

Knock sensors are bolted to left side of cylinder block under intake manifold. They share a common electrical connector (**A**)and must be replaced as a pair.

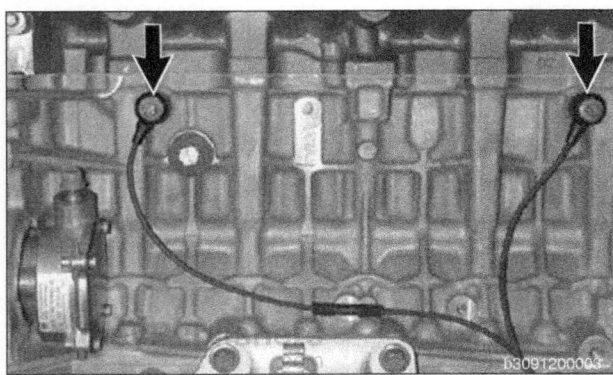

b3091200003

◄ Knock sensors (**arrows**). N52 engine shown.

BX30120001

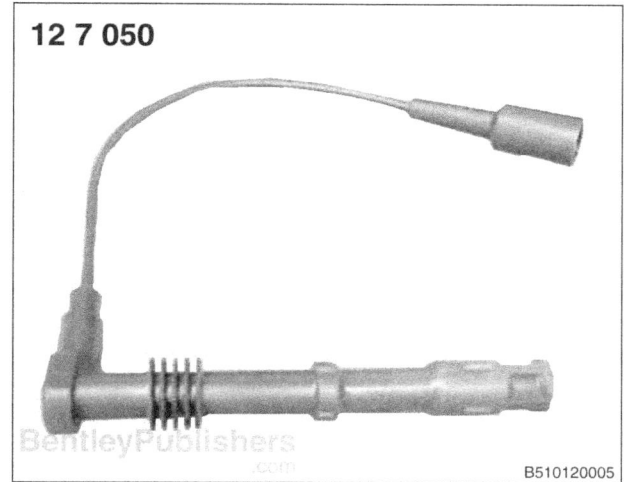

12 7 050

B510120005

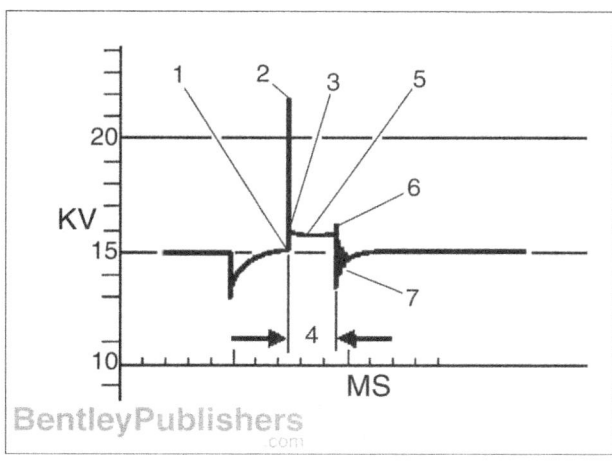

TROUBLESHOOTING

On-board diagnostics

◄ If faults arise, or if the malfunction indicator light (MIL) is illuminated, begin troubleshooting by connecting a BMW scan tool to the data link connector (DLC or OBD II plug). For information on how to access diagnostic trouble codes (DTCs), see **020 Maintenance**.

Misfire detection

Engine misfire in one or more cylinders may be caused by malfunctions in various subsystems. The OBD II system incorporated into the engine management systems is designed to detect and warn of misfire faults during engine operation. See **OBD On-Board Diagnostics.**

> **WARNING—**
> • Ignition misfires can cause high hydrocarbon emissions and catalytic converter damage. If a severe misfire is detected, the fuel injector to the cylinder is switched OFF and the MIL is illuminated. A misfire may also overheat the catalytic converters, a fire hazard.

Oscilloscope diagnostic diagrams

One way to diagnose faulty engine management components or functions is to use an oscilloscope to analyze spark quality with the engine running.

◄ BMW engines covered in this manual use a rod type ignition coil. Use BMW special adapter 12 7 050 to chek coil scope patterns

Table c lists common ignition coil voltage faults and related causes.

Table c. Ignition secondary voltage diagnostics		
	Secondary voltage low	Secondary voltage high
Spark plug electrode gap	Too small	Too big
Electrode condition		Worn / burnt
Electrode temperature	Too high	Too low
Engine compression	Too low	Too high
Spark plug wires		Faulty
Fuel air mixture		Too lean

◄ Normal scope trace of spark at idle

1. Start of ignition voltage peak
2. Level of ignition voltage
3. Level of combustion voltage
4. Period of combustion
5. Combustion curve characteristics
6. Start of spark decay
7. Termination oscillations

Oscilloscope diagnostic diagrams

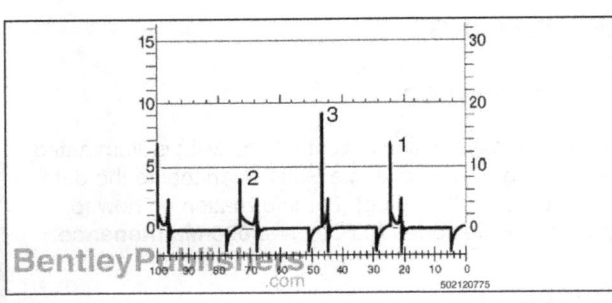

◀ Ignition spark at idle speed

1. Normal ignition voltage peak: Good spark plug.
2. Low voltage peak: Closed plug gap.
3. High voltage peak: Open plug gap.

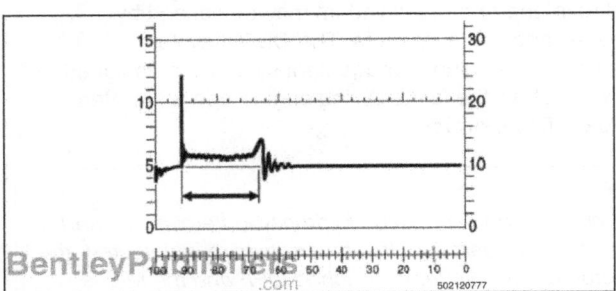

◀ Long combustion period: Small spark plug gap.

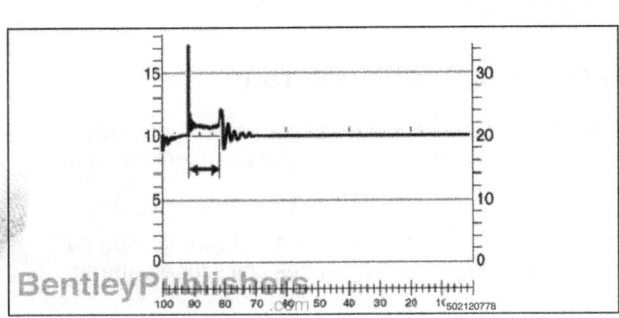

◀ Short combustion period: Large spark plug gap.

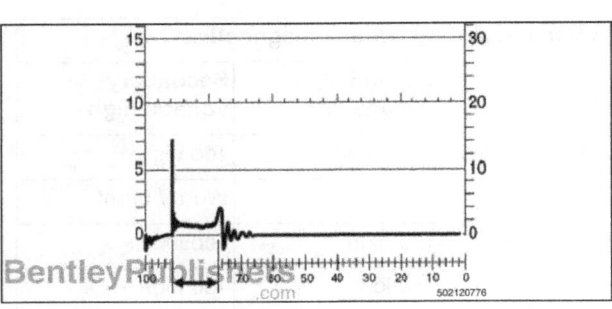

◀ Normal combustion period at idle.

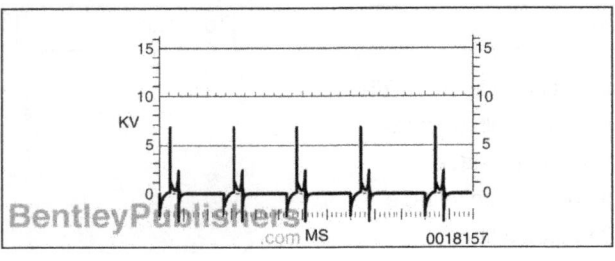

◀ Normal oscilloscope pattern for ignition system at idle.

Oscilloscope diagnostic diagrams

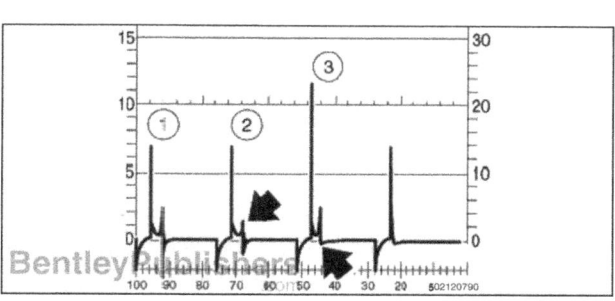

◀ Ignition voltage peaks at idle

1. Normal ignition peaks.
2. Downward peak (**arrow**) shortened: Ignition coil defective.
3. Downward peak (**arrow**) missing completely: Ignition coil defective.

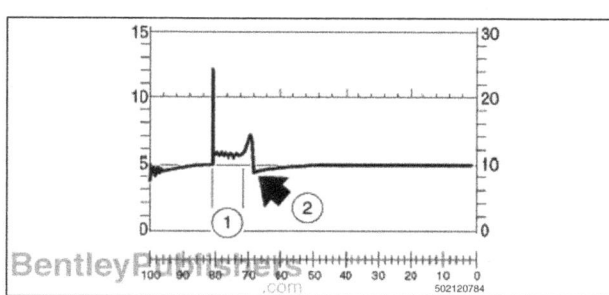

◀ Defective ignition coil

1. Short spark period.
2. Spark voltage line (**arrow**) with very slight drop.

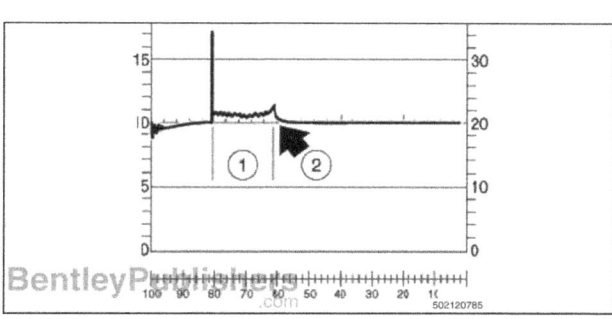

◀ Defective ignition coil

1. Normal combustion period.
2. Spark voltage line (**arrow**) absent.

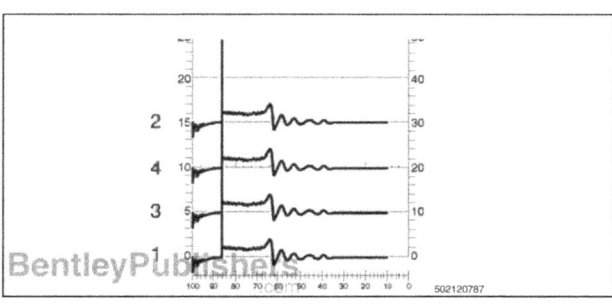

◀ Normal secondary voltage patterns (4–cylinder pattern shown).

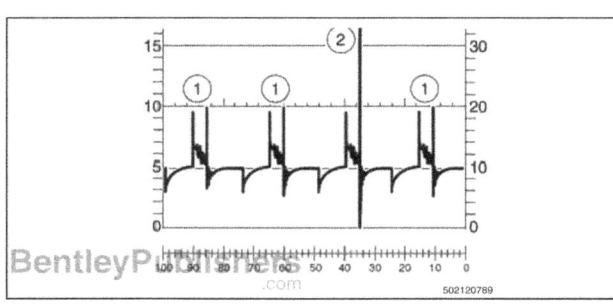

◀ Ignition voltage peaks in response to sudden acceleration load:

1. Normal ignition pattern. Beginning of dying out pattern is not much higher than ignition voltage peak.
2. Beginning of dying out pattern considerably higher than ignition voltage peak. Fault in injection system:
   • Lean fuel mixture
   • Defective fuel injector
   • Low compression in cylinder.

120

IGNITION COIL SERVICE

There is a separate ignition coil above each spark plug. Spark plug replacement is covered in **020 Maintenance**.

> **CAUTION—**
> • *Maintain a high level of cleanliness when servicing ignition coils. Fuel / oil residue can cause a breakdown in the electrical resistance qualities of silicone used in production. This in turn can result in ignition coil failure.*

Ignition coil, replacing (M54 engine)

— Make sure ignition is switched OFF.

— Remove upper engine cover. See **020 Maintenance**.

◄ Lift up on lock (**A**) and release ignition coil electrical connector.

— Remove fasteners (**B**). Note position of coil ground wire.

◄ Remove ignition coil by pulling straight up and off spark plug.

— Installation is reverse of removal. Be sure to reattach ground cables or wires.

— Check and clear fault codes from ECM memory.

Ignition coil, replacing (N52 engine)

— Make sure ignition is switched OFF.

— Remove upper engine cover. See **020 Maintenance**.

◄ Unlock (**curved arrow**) ignition coil connector. Pull (**straight arrow**) connector off coil.

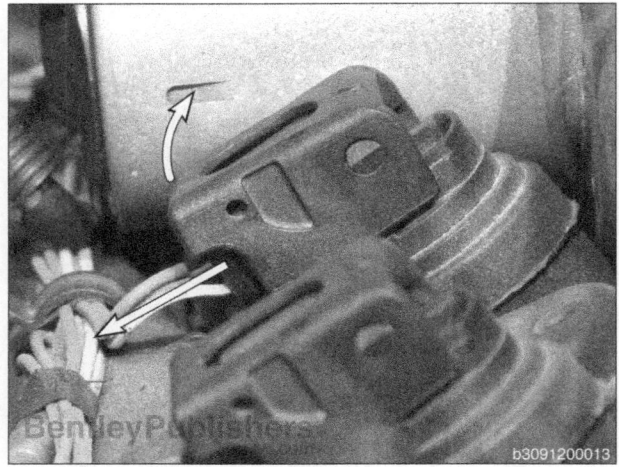

◄ Slide rod-shaped ignition coil straight out of spark plug hole.

— Installation is reverse of removal.

— Check and clear fault codes from ECM memory.

CRANKSHAFT SENSOR SERVICE

Crankshaft sensor, replacing (M54 engine)

Crankshaft sensor in M54 engine is on left rear of engine block, underneath intake manifold and starter motor.

— Make sure ignition is OFF.

— Raise car and support in a safe manner.

> **WARNING**—
> • Make sure car is stable and well supported at all times. Use a professional automotive lift or jack stands.

— Remove front end reinforcement plate. See **310 Front Suspension**.

◄ Working underneath starter:

• Cut off wire tie securing crankshaft sensor harness connector (**arrow**) to sensor.

• Disconnect harness connector.

◄ Remove sensor mounting fastener (**arrow**) and remove sensor from cylinder block.

— Installation is reverse of removal.

• Use new sealing O-ring when installing sensor.

• Replace self-locking mounting bolt.

• Be sure wiring is rerouted as before.

Tightening torque	
Crankshaft sensor to engine block (M6, replace with new)	10 Nm (7 ft-lb)

— Check and clear fault codes from ECM memory.

Crankshaft sensor, replacing (N52 engine)

Crankshaft sensor is on left rear of engine block, underneath intake manifold and starter motor.

− Make sure ignition is OFF.

− Raise car and support in a safe manner.

> **WARNING—**
> • *Make sure car is stable and well supported at all times. Use a professional automotive lift or jack stands. A floor jack is not adequate support.*

− Remove front end reinforcement plate. See **310 Front Suspension**.

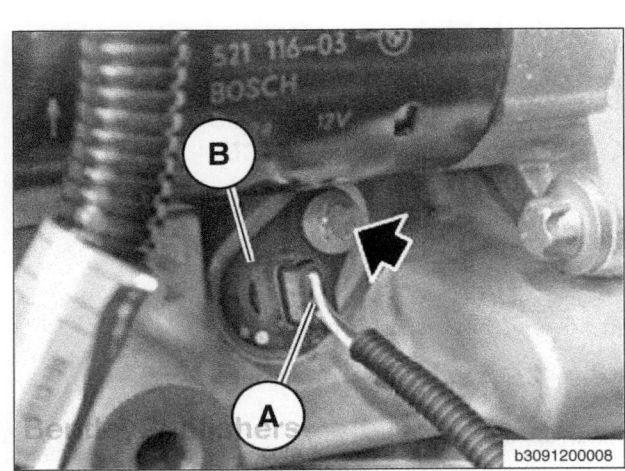

◀ Working underneath starter:
   • Disconnect crankshaft sensor harness connector (**A**) from sensor (**B**).

− Remove sensor mounting fastener (**arrow**) and remove sensor from cylinder block. Be prepared to catch dripping oil.

− Installation is reverse of removal. Remember to:
   • Use new sealing O-ring when installing sensor.
   • Replace mounting bolt.
   • Be sure wiring is routed as before.
   • Check and clear fault codes from ECM memory.

Tightening torque	
Crankshaft sensor to engine block (M6, replace with new)	8 Nm (6 ft-lb)

CAMSHAFT SENSOR SERVICE

Intake camshaft sensor, replacing (M54 engine)

Intake camshaft sensor on M54 engine is mounted at left side of cylinder head near front.

– Make sure ignition is OFF.

– Remove upper engine covers. See **020 Maintenance**.

– Remove air filter housing and ducts. See **130 Fuel Injection**.

◄ Working at left side of cylinder head:

• Detach engine vent hose from cylinder head cover by pinching spring clips (**arrows**).

• Detach VANOS solenoid electrical connector (**A**).

• Unscrew VANOS solenoid.

• If necessary, unfasten oil supply line on VANOS adjustment unit. Be prepared to catch dripping oil.

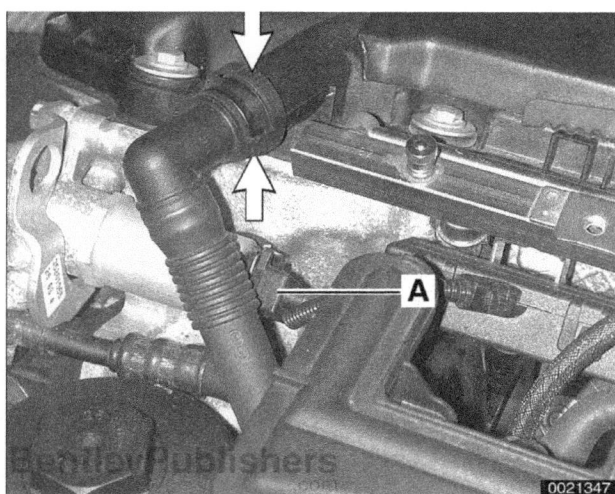

◄ Remove camshaft sensor mounting bolt. Remove sensor (**arrow**) from cylinder head.

– Reach under intake manifold to disconnect camshaft sensor harness.

NOTE—

• *Prior to removal, attach a stiff piece of wire to connector to aid in routing of harness during reinstallation.*

– Installation is reverse of removal. Remember to:

• Replace camshaft sensor mounting bolt.

• Use new sealing O-rings when installing sensor, VANOS solenoid and VANOS oil supply line.

• Be sure sensor harness is rerouted as before.

Tightening torques	
Intake camshaft sensor to cylinder head (M6, replace bolt)	10 Nm (7 ft-lb)
Oil supply line to VANOS unit (banjo bolt)	32 Nm (24 ft-lb)
VANOS solenoid to VANOS unit	30 Nm (22 ft-lb)

– Check and clear fault codes from ECM memory.

Exhaust camshaft sensor, replacing (M54 engine)

Exhaust camshaft sensor on M54 engine is mounted at right side of cylinder head near front.

— Make sure ignition is OFF.

◄ Working at front of engine on exhaust (right) side, detach exhaust camshaft sensor electrical harness connector (**arrow**).

— Remove sensor mounting bolt and remove sensor. Be prepared to catch dripping oil.

— Installation is reverse of removal.
  • Replace camshaft sensor mounting bolt.
  • Use new sealing O-ring when installing sensor.

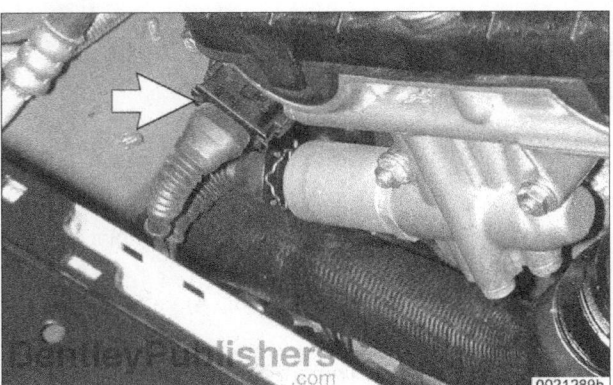

Tightening torque	
Exhaust camshaft sensor to cylinder head (M6, replace bolt)	10 Nm (7 ft-lb)

— Check and clear fault codes from ECM memory.

Intake camshaft sensor, replacing (N52 engine)

Intake camshaft sensor is mounted to left front of cylinder head.

— Make sure ignition is OFF.

— Remove upper engine covers. See **020 Maintenance**.

— Remove air filter housing and ducts. See **130, 131 Fuel Injection**.

◄ Detach camshaft sensor electrical connector (**A**).

— Remove camshaft sensor mounting bolt (**arrow**). Remove sensor (**B**) from cylinder head. Be prepared to catch dripping oil.

— Installation is reverse of removal. Remember to:
  • Replace camshaft sensor mounting bolt.
  • Use new sealing O-rings when installing sensor.
  • Be sure sensor harness is routed as before.
  • Check and clear fault codes from ECM memory.

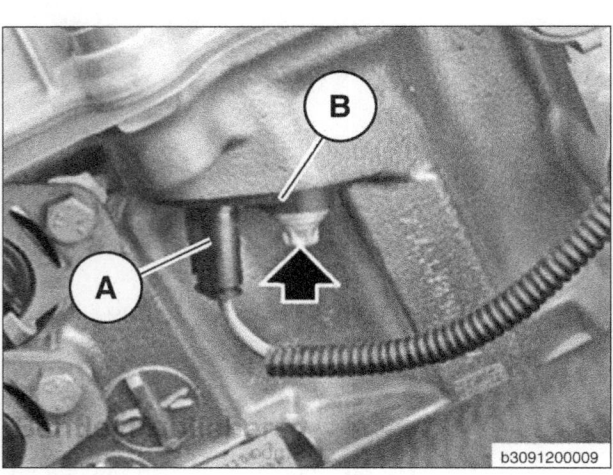

Tightening torques	
Intake camshaft sensor to cylinder head (M6, replace with new)	9 Nm (6.5 ft-lb)

Exhaust camshaft sensor, replacing (N52 engine)

Exhaust camshaft sensor is mounted to right front of cylinder head.

– Make sure ignition is OFF.

– Remove upper engine covers. See **020 Maintenance**.

– Remove air filter housing and ducts. See **131**, **132 Fuel Injection**.

◄ Detach camshaft sensor electrical connector (**A**).

– Remove camshaft sensor mounting bolt (**arrow**). Remove sensor (**B**) from cylinder head. Be prepared to catch dripping oil.

– Installation is reverse of removal. Remember to:
  • Replace camshaft sensor mounting bolt.
  • Use new sealing O-rings when installing sensor.
  • Be sure sensor harness is routed as before.
  • Check and clear fault codes from ECM memory.

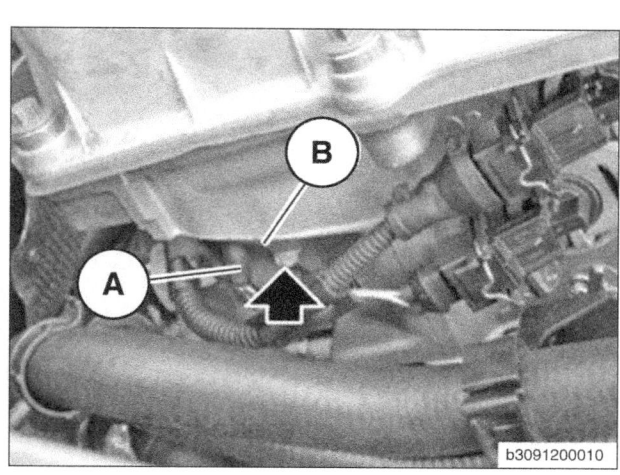

Tightening torques	
Intake camshaft sensor to cylinder head (M6, replace bolt)	9 Nm (6.5 ft-lb)

KNOCK SENSOR SERVICE

Knock sensors, replacing (M54 engine)

M54 engine knock sensors are under the intake manifold on the left side of the cylinder head.

– Disconnect negative (-) battery cable and cover battery terminal to keep cable from accidentally contacting terminal.

> **CAUTION—**
> • Prior to disconnecting battery, read battery disconnection cautions given in **001 Warnings and Cautions**.

– With engine fully cooled, remove intake manifold. See **130 Fuel Injection**.

◄ Disconnect knock sensor electrical harness connector (**A**) on left side of engine block.
  • Remove knock sensor mounting bolts (**arrows**) on side of cylinder block.
  • Remove sensors.

> **CAUTION—**
> • Note installed angle of knock sensor on block before removing it. Reinstall sensor in same position. Use a torque wrench when tightening sensor mounting bolt. Do not overtighten knock sensor bolt.

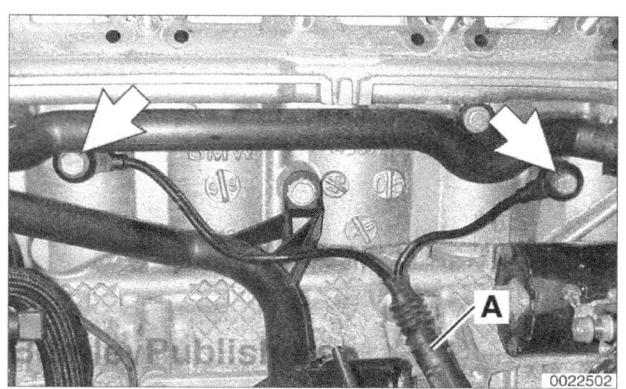

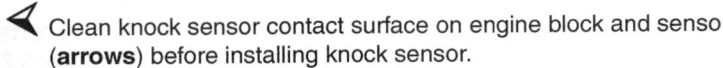 Clean knock sensor contact surface on engine block and sensor (**arrows**) before installing knock sensor.

Tightening torque	
Knock sensor to engine block (M8)	20 Nm (15 ft-lb)

— Check and clear fault codes from ECM memory.

Knock sensors, replacing (N52 engine)

N52 engine knock sensors are under the intake manifold on the left side of the cylinder head.

— Disconnect negative (-) battery cable and cover battery terminal to keep cable from accidentally contacting terminal.

> **CAUTION—**
> • *Prior to disconnecting the battery, read the battery disconnection cautions given in* **001 Warnings and Cautions**.

— With engine fully cooled, remove intake manifold. See **131 Fuel Injection**.

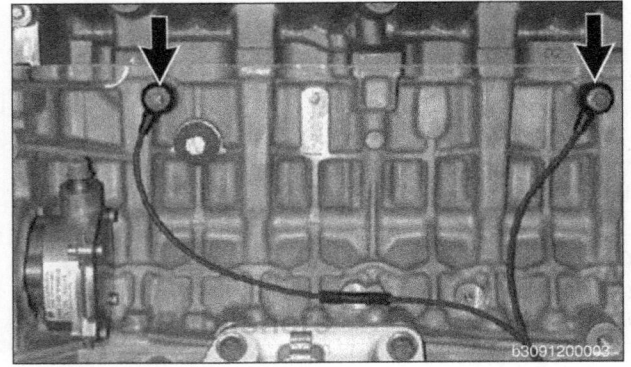

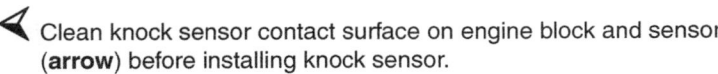 Disconnect knock sensor electrical harness connector.

• Remove knock sensor mounting bolts (**arrows**) on side of cylinder block. Remove sensors.

> **CAUTION—**
> • *Note installed angle of knock sensor on block before removing it. Reinstall sensor in same position. Use a torque wrench when tightening sensor mounting bolt. Do not overtighten knock sensor bolt.*

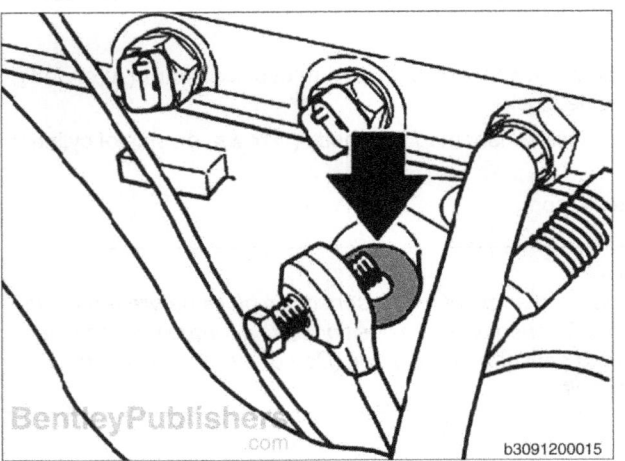

◀ Clean knock sensor contact surface on engine block and sensor (**arrow**) before installing knock sensor.

> **CAUTION—**
> • *Do not overtighten knock sensors.*

— Installation is reverse of removal. Remember to:
• Replace knock sensor mounting bolt.
• Be sure sensor harness is routed as before.

— Check and clear fault codes from ECM memory.

121   Battery, Starter, Alternator

GENERAL

This repair group covers the battery, alternator, starter and associated components of the electrical system.

Troubleshooting information for these components is found in **Table a**. For additional electrical troubleshooting information, see **600 Electrical System–General.**

See **020 Maintenance** for battery replacement procedure.

Engine electrical system

The alternator and starter are wired directly to the battery. To prevent accidental shorts that might blow a fuse or damage wires and electrical components, always disconnect the negative (–) battery cable before working on the electrical system.

Various versions of alternators, voltage regulators, starters, and batteries are used in X3 models. Replace components according to the original equipment specification

Battery safety terminal

 A battery safety terminal (BST) is combined as part of the positive battery terminal clamp. The BST is controlled by the multiple restraint system (MRS) control module.

BX30121004

Warnings and Cautions

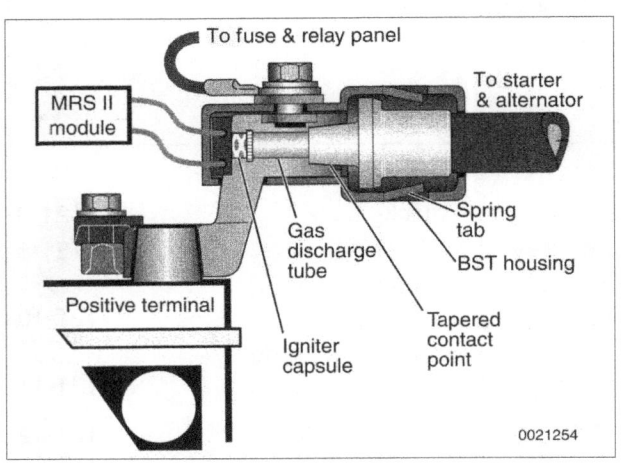

To fuse & relay panel

MRS II module

To starter & alternator

Spring tab

Gas discharge tube

BST housing

Positive terminal

Tapered contact point

Igniter capsule

0021254

◀ The battery safety terminal system disconnects electrical power to the engine compartment in the event of a significant impact. The MRS system fires an encapsulated pyrotechnic device in the positive (+) battery terminal clamp that disconnects power to the engine compartment, but maintains power to the exterior lights and interior of the vehicle.

Table a. Battery, alternator and starter troubleshooting

Symptom	Probable cause	Corrective action
Engine does not crank	Fault in immobilizer system (EWS).	Try another ignition key. If problem persists, contact your authorized BMW dealer.
Engine cranks slowly or not at all, solenoid clicks when starter is operated.	Battery cables loose, dirty or corroded.	Clean or replace cables.
	Battery discharged.	Charge battery and test. Replace if necessary.
	Battery to body ground cable in trunk loose, dirty or corroded	Inspect ground cable. Clean, tighten or replace if necessary.
	Poor connection at starter motor terminal 30.	Check connections at starter motor.
	Starter motor or solenoid faulty.	Test starter.
Battery will not stay charged more than a few days.	Short circuit draining battery.	Test for excessive current drain with everything electrical off.
	Short driving trips and high electrical drain on charging system does not allow battery to recharge.	Evaluate driving style. Where possible, reduce electrical consumption when making short trips.
	Engine accessory belt loose, worn or damaged.	Inspect or replace accessory belt. See **020 Maintenance**.
	Battery faulty.	Test battery and replace if necessary.
	Battery cables loose, dirty or corroded.	Clean or replace cables.
	Alternator or voltage regulator faulty.	Test alternator and voltage regulator.

Warnings and Cautions

WARNING—
- *Wear goggles, rubber gloves, and a rubber apron when working around the battery or battery acid (electrolyte).*
- *Battery acid contains sulfuric acid and can cause skin irritation and burning. If acid is spilled on your skin or clothing, flush the area at once with large quantities of water. If electrolyte gets into your eyes, flush them with large quantities of clean water for several minutes and call a physician.*
- *A battery that is being charged or is fully charged gives off explosive hydrogen gas. Keep sparks and open flames away. Do not smoke.*

CAUTION—

- *Only use a digital multimeter when testing automotive electrical components.*

- *If a repair procedure specifies disconnecting the battery, follow the instruction for safety reasons.*

- *Prior to disconnecting the battery, read the battery disconnection cautions in* **001 Warnings and Cautions**.

- *Disconnecting the battery cables may erase fault codes stored in ECM memory.*

- *Always disconnect the negative (–) battery cable first and reconnect it last. Cover the battery post with an insulating material whenever the cable is removed.*

- *Do not disconnect battery, alternator or starter wires while the engine is running.*

- *Never reverse battery cables. Even a momentary wrong connection can damage the alternator or other electrical components.*

- *Do not depend on the color of insulation to tell battery positive and negative cables apart. Label cables before removing.*

- *Power windows and slide-tilt sunroof may fail to function properly after reconnecting the battery. See* **512 Door Windows** *and* **540 Sunroof** *to reintialize.*

BATTERY

A maintenance free battery is mounted in the cargo area under the floor trim panel. BMW batteries are rated by ampere / hours (Ah) and cold cranking amps (CCA), listed on the battery. Always replace the battery with one having the same or higher ratings.

Battery testing

Battery testing determines the state of battery charge. Check that the cables are tight and free of corrosion before testing.

Hydrometer testing

A hydrometer measures the specific gravity of the electrolyte. Follow the manufacturer's instructions when testing hydrometer. The state of battery charge based on specific gravity values are given in **Table b**.

NOTE—

- *Electrolyte temperature affects hydrometer reading. The table below is based on a battery temperature of 27°C (80°F).*

Table b. Specific gravity of battery electrolyte at 27°C (80°F)	
Specific gravity	**State of charge**
1.265	Fully charged
1.225	75% charged
1.190	50% charged
1.155	25% charged
1.120	Fully discharged

If the specific gravity is at or above 1.225, but the battery lacks power for starting, determine the battery's service condition with a load voltage test. If the average specific gravity of the six cells is below 1.225, remove the battery from the vehicle and recharge.

Battery open-circuit voltage test

— Before testing, load battery with 15 amperes for one minute with battery load-tester or turn on headlights for one minute without engine running. Connect digital voltmeter across battery terminals. Open-circuit voltage levels are given in **Table c**.

— If open-circuit voltage is OK but battery still lacks power for starting, perform a load voltage test.

— If open-circuit voltage is below 12.4 volts, recharge battery and retest.

Table c. Open-circuit voltage and battery charge	
Open-circuit voltage	**State of charge**
12.6 or more	Fully charged
12.4	75% charged
12.2	50% charged
12.0	25% charged
11.7 or less	Fully discharged

Battery load voltage test

A battery load tester is required for a load voltage test. The test is made by applying a high resistive load to the battery terminals and then measuring battery voltage. The battery should be fully charged for the most accurate results. The battery cables must be disconnected before making the test. Replace the battery if the voltage is below that listed in **Table d**.

> **WARNING—**
> • *Always wear protective goggles and clothing when performing a load test.*

Table d. Battery load test–minimum voltage	
Ambient temperature	**Voltage***
27°C (80°F)	9.6
16°C (60°F)	9.5
4°C (40°F)	9.3
-7°C (20°F)	8.9
-18°C (0°F)	8.5
* Measure after applying a 200 amp load for 15 seconds.	

Battery parasitic draw, testing

If the vehicle battery continually discharges for unknown reasons, perform the parasitic draw test designed to detect excessive current flow from the battery when everything in the vehicle is shut down. This is also known as a closed circuit current measurement.

The following test is generally completed overnight using a battery isolation switch and a multimeter with a recording function.

− Check that battery voltage is 12 volts or higher. If lower, recharge battery.

− Switch off electrical consumers (interior lights, telephone, aftermarket equipment, or others).

◄ Remove negative cable and install battery isolation switch (OTC tool 7645 or equivalent).

− Close switch. Connect digital multimeter in series across switch. Set meter to milliamp (mA) scale.

NOTE—

• *Set multimeter to record average readings.*

• *If possible, turn off powersaving features of multimeter which prevent a long term (overnight) test by automatically powering down meter.*

− Turn rear hatch lock to locked position using screwdriver or similar (simulates rear hatch being closed).

− To simulate normal parasitic draw conditions: Switch ignition ON and activate an electrical consumer. Switch ignition OFF. Open and close driver's door (simulates somebody getting out).

− Lock car, arming alarm if installed. With exception of rear hatch, keep all other doors and lids closed.

− Wait at least 16 minutes for consumer cut-off.

NOTE—

• *Automatic transmission cars: amber shifter LED goes out at consumer cut-off.*

− Open battery isolation switch and monitor current draw.

− Maximum allowable parasitic draw after waiting: Approx. 40 mA.

− If draw exceeds maximum allowable, find consumer(s) at fault by removing individual fuses and noting change in parasitic draw. Repair or replace component(s) found at fault.

Fuse locations and applications are in **ECL Electrical Component Locations**.

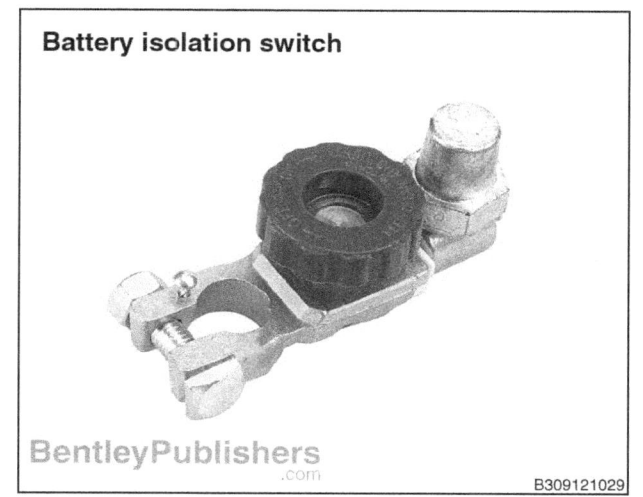

Battery isolation switch

Battery charging

Recharge batteries using a battery charger. Remove battery from vehicle during charging.

Prolonged charging causes electrolyte evaporation to a level that can damage the battery. It is best to use a low-current charger (6 amperes or less) to prevent battery damage caused by overheating.

Battery removal and installation is covered in **020 Maintenance**.

> ***WARNING—***
> • *Hydrogen gas given off by the battery during charging is explosive. Do not smoke. Keep open flames away from the top of the battery, and prevent electrical sparks by turning off the battery charger before connecting or disconnecting it.*

> *CAUTION—*
> • *Battery electrolyte (sulfuric acid) can damage the car. If electrolyte is spilled, clean the area with a solution of baking soda and water.*
> • *Always allow a frozen battery to thaw before attempting to recharge it.*
> • *Always disconnect both battery cables and remove battery from vehicle during battery charging. Do not exceed 16.5 charging voltage at the battery.*

Battery safety terminal, replacing

 The battery safety terminal (BST) (**A**) is part of the battery positive cable that runs along the passenger side of the vehicle.

Replacement of the BST involves running a new battery positive cable under the vehicle carpet from the battery to the bulkhead behind the passenger dash panel.

– The following components must be removed in order to gain access to battery positive cable routing:
See **513 Interior Trim, 520 Seats**

• Right side cargo compartment side trim panel.

• Instrument panel trim.

• Right front seat

• Right side front door pillar trim.

• Cover for central bass speaker.

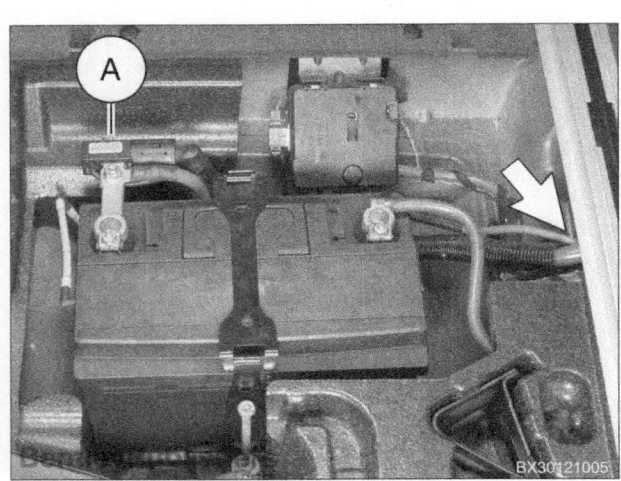

BX30121005

Tightening torques	
Battery cables to battery terminals	5 Nm (44 in-lb)
Battery positive lead to BST	15 Nm (11 ft-lb)
Battery positive cable to lug on bulkhead	19 Nm (14 ft-lb)

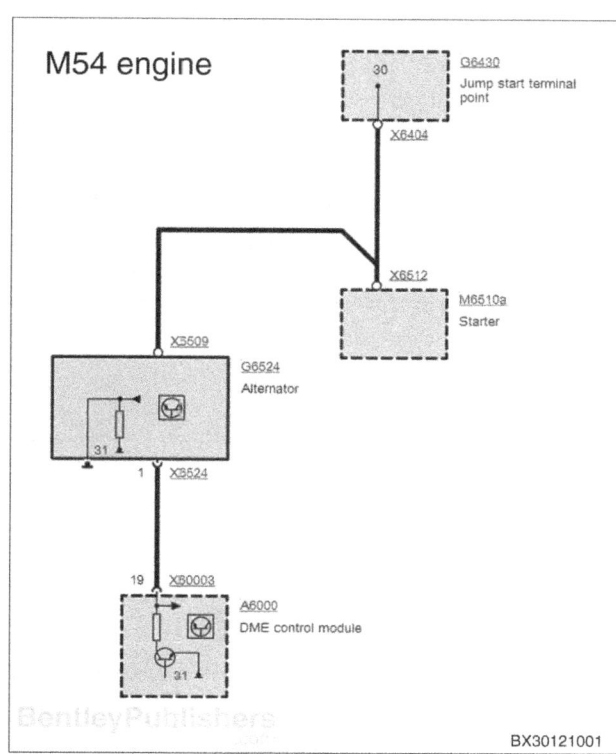

M54 engine

BX30121001

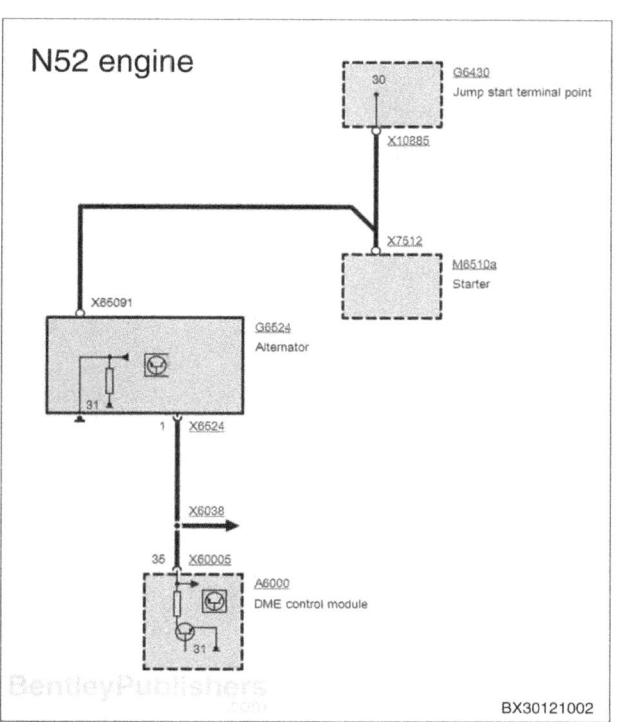

N52 engine

BX30121002

ALTERNATOR (GENERATOR)

Alternator with BSD interface

The alternator communicates with the engine control module (ECM) via bit-serial data (BSD) interface. This single wire connection allows the ECM to adapt ts calculations and control data to alternator output. The ECM controls the following functions:

- Alternator activation and deactivation.
- Informing the voltage regulator of the nominal voltage value to be set.
- Alternator load response control.
- BSD line diagnosis.
- Alternator fault code storage.
- Charge indicator light activation in instrument cluster via CAN bus.

The following possible defects and malfunctions can be identified based on ECM fault code entries:

- Controlled load reduction at high temperatures: The alternator is overloaded and the alternator voltage is reduced as a precautionary measure; it remains at a reduced level until the alternator has cooled. The charge indicator lamp does not light up
- Mechanical fault: The alternator is physically seized or the belt drive is no longer operational.
- Electrical fault: Defective field diodes, interruption in generation of field current, overvoltage.
- Communications failure: Defect in wiring between engine-management control unit and alternator.

NOTE —

- *Open windings or a short circuit can not be identified by the ECM, and therefore will not set a fault code.*

Charging system troubleshooting

Some charging system tests require special test equipment. If the test equipment is not available, charging system fault diagnosis can be performed by an authorized BMW dealer or other qualified repair shop. See **Table a** for general electrical component troubleshooting.

Before checking the alternator, make sure the battery is fully charged and capable of holding a charge. Check that the battery terminals are clean and tight and the alternator drive belt is properly tensioned and not severely worn.

Charging system quick-check

Use a digital multimeter to measure voltage across the battery terminals with ignition OFF and then again with engine running. Battery voltage should be about 12.6 volts with key OFF and between 13.5 and 14.5 volts with engine running.

NOTE—

• *The regulated voltage (engine running) should be between 13.2 and 14.5, depending on temperature and operating conditions. If the voltage is higher than 14.8, the voltage regulator is most likely faulty.*

Check for clean and tight battery cables. Check ground cable running from negative (–) battery terminal to chassis and ground cable running from engine to chassis. Check accessory belt condition and tension.

Charging system, checking

> *CAUTION—*
> • *Do not disconnect the battery while the engine is running. Damage to the alternator or engine electronic systems may result.*
> • *Only use a digital multimeter when testing charging system components.*

◀ Turn ignition ON. Check that battery warning light (**arrow**) comes on.

NOTE—

• *If the warning light does not come ON, repair bulb or wiring faults before continuing to check the charging system.*

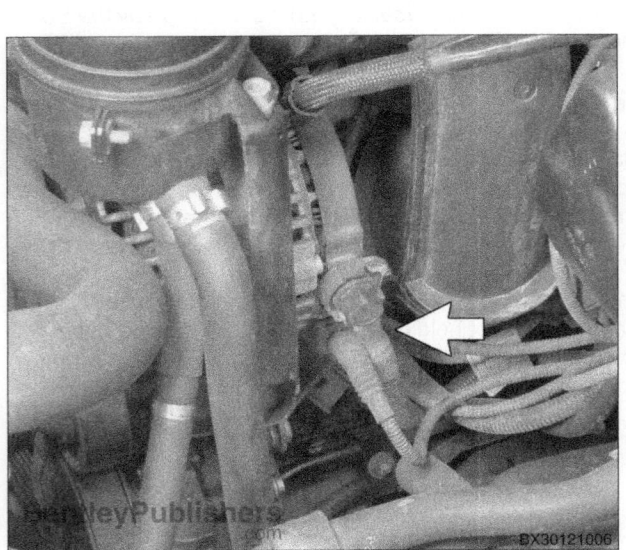

◀ Check for battery voltage at alternator terminal 30 (B+):

• Carefully pierce insulating cover at terminal 30 (**arrow**) at rear of alternator.

• Connect voltmeter between terminal 30 and ground and check for battery voltage. If voltage is not present, check wiring for faults.

NOTE—

• *N52 engine shown, M54 is similar,*

— Connect oscilloscope across battery terminals to check alternator function.

— Connecting oscilloscope:

• Positive test lead of oscilloscope to positive battery terminal.

• Negative test lead of oscilloscope to negative battery terminal

• Set oscilloscope to A/C volts and a time base of 500ms.

◀ Normal alternator pattern.

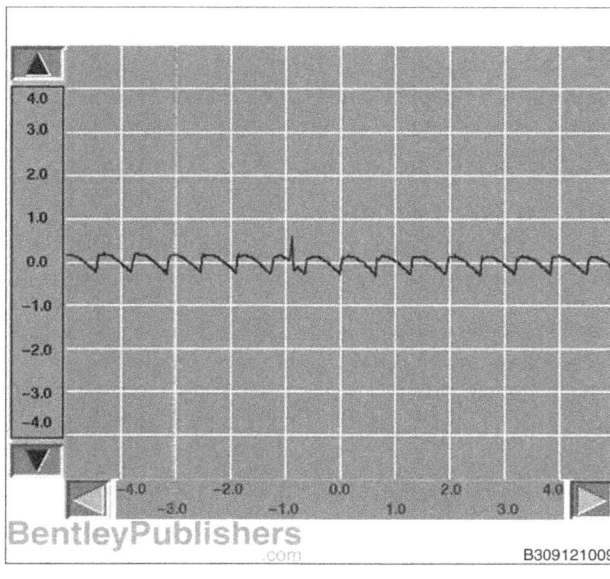

B309121009

◀ Alternator with defective diode.

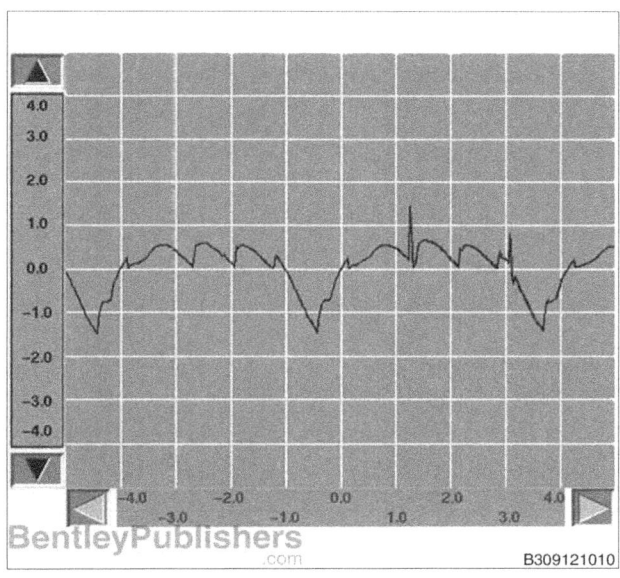

B309121010

◀ Alternator with broken winding.

– If test indicate a defective alternator, replace unit. Repair parts are not available for the alternator.

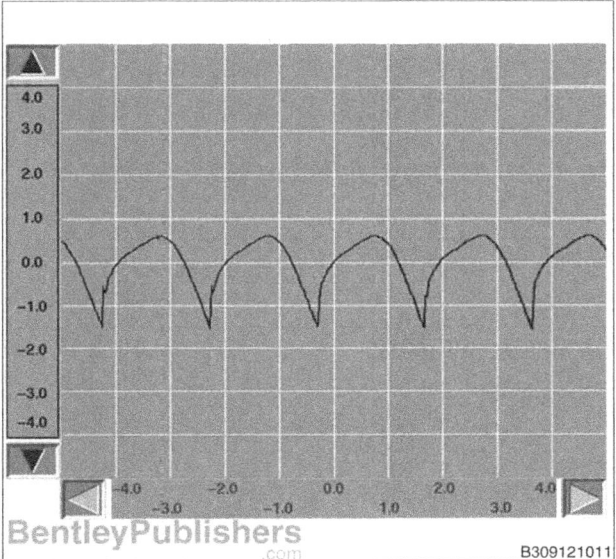

B309121011

Alternator, removing and installing (M54 engine)

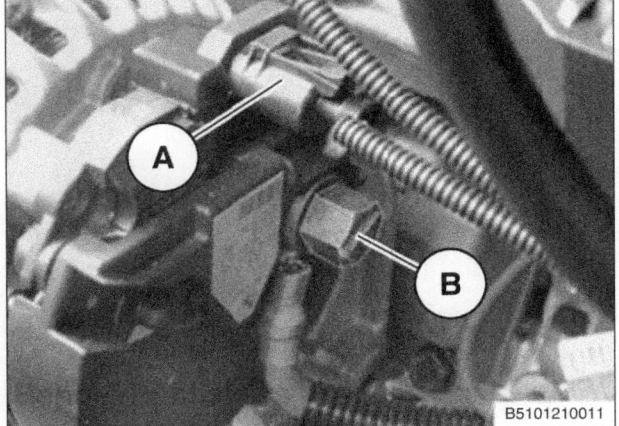

B5101210011

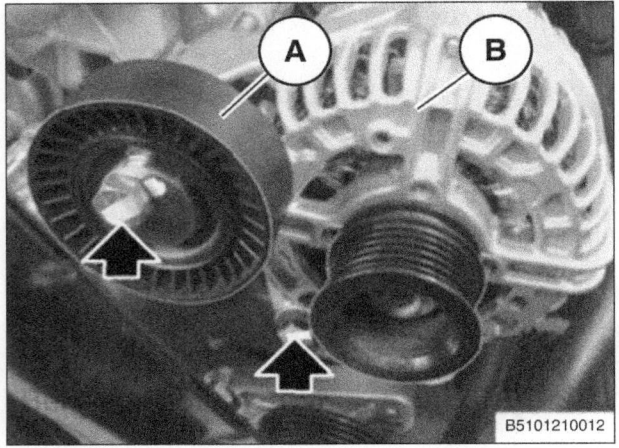

B5101210012

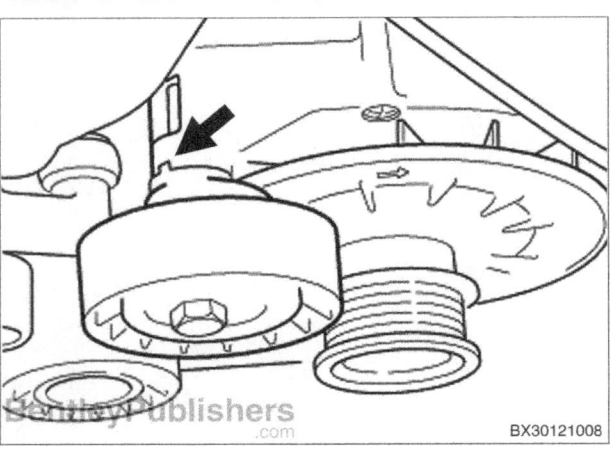

BX30121008

Alternator, removing and installing (M54 engine)

A replacement alternator should have the same rating as the original. Alternator manufacturer and ampere rating are normally marked on the alternator housing.

– Switch ignition OFF. Disconnect negative (–) battery cable and cover battery terminal to keep cable from accidentally contacting terminal.

> **CAUTION—**
> • Prior to disconnecting the battery, read the battery disconnection cautions in **001 Warnings and Cautions**.

– Remove air intake duct and filter housing. See **130 Fuel Injection (M54 engine)**.

– Remove engine accessory belt. See **020 Maintenance**. Mark direction of rotation on belt before removing.

◄ Working at rear of alternator, remove electrical connector (**A**) and battery positive cable fastener (**B**).

◄ Working at front of alternator (**B**), remove cover from idler pulley (**A**) and remove alternator fasteners (**arrows**).

– Rotate alternator forward and then up and out of engine compartment, using care to not damage radiator.

> **CAUTION—**
> • Protect radiator with heavy cardboard or sheet metal.

– Installation is reverse of removal. Reinstall accessory belt using previously made direction-of-rotation marks. Be sure accessory belt grooves engage pulleys correctly.

◄ Check that idler pulley locating tab (**arrow**) engages alternator notch correctly.

Tightening torques	
Terminal 30 (B+) wire to alternator (M8)	13 Nm (10 ft-lb)
Alternator or idler pulley to alternator bracket (M10)	42 Nm (31 ft-lb)

– After reconnecting battery, see **Battery reconnect ion notes** in this repair group.

Alternator, removing and installing (N52 engine)

— Switch ignition OFF. Disconnect negative (–) battery cable and cover battery terminal to keep cable from accidentally contacting terminal.

> **CAUTION—**
> • *Prior to disconnecting the battery, read the battery disconnection cautions in* **001 Warnings and Cautions**.

— Remove engine accessory belt. See **020 Maintenance**. Mark direction of rotation on belt before removing.

— Remove air intake duct and filter housing. See **131 Fuel Injection (N52 engine)**.

— Unbolt power steering reservoir from bracket and move reservoir to side.

• Power steering hydraulic lines remain connected.

◄ Working at rear of alternator:

• Detach harness connector (**A**)

• Remove nut (**B**) and detach alternator cable.

• Remove alternator mounting bolts (**arrows**) and discard (aluminum bolts).

• Lift out alternator.

> **NOTE—**
> • *Power steering reservoir bracket is bolted to alternator. Remove bracket with alternator mounting bolts.*

◄ With alternator on work bench:

• Remove idler pulley (**C**) fastener plastic cover, if applicable.

• Remove idler pulley and transfer to new alternator.

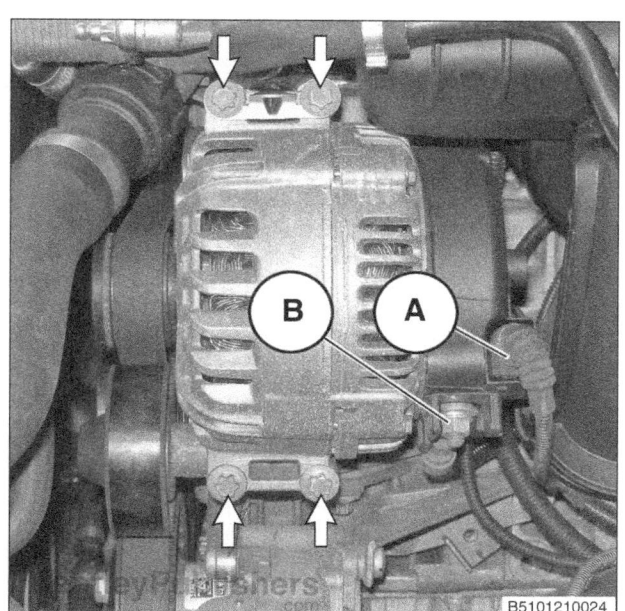

B5101210024

Tightening torques	
• Idler pulley to alternator	40 Nm (30 ft-lb)

— Reinstall alternator using new aluminium bolts. Reattach electrical harnesses.

Tightening torques	
Alternator cable to alternator (M8)	19 Nm (14 ft-lb)
Alternator to engine block (M8 x 82 mm aluminum bolts, replace with new) • Stage 1 • Stage 2	10 Nm additional 180°

B5101210025

— Reassemble front of engine. Remember to:

• Reinstall accessory belt using previously made direction-of-rotation marks. Make sure accessory belt grooves engage pulleys correctly.

• After reconnecting battery, see **Battery reconnection notes** in this repair group.

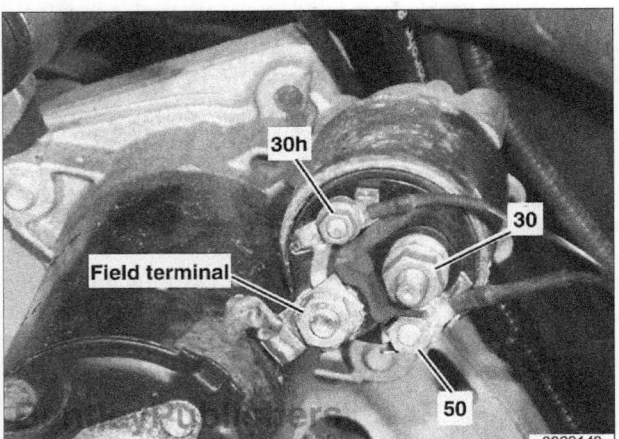

STARTER

Starter troubleshooting

◄ M54 engine starter wiring terminal identification is shown. Large wire at terminal 30 (not shown in photo) is direct battery voltage. Smaller wire at terminal 50 operates starter solenoid via ignition switch.

— If starter turns engine slowly when ignition is in START position:

• Check battery state of charge.

• Inspect wires, terminals, and ground connections for good contact. Be sure ground connections between battery, body and engine are clean and tight.

• If no faults are found, starter may be faulty and should be replaced.

— If starter fails to operate, check EWS (drive-away protection system). Try another ignition key. If no faults can be found, have the EWS system checked using BMW scan tool equipment.

• Check gear position switch.

NOTE —

• *EWS or driveaway protection is used on X3 models. The system prevents operation of the starter if the coded ignition key is not used.*

• *There is no separate neutral-safety switch. The automatic transmission range switch (gear position switch) signals EWS to prevent the engine from starting in gear positions other than PARK or NEUTRAL.*

— Check for battery voltage at terminal 50 of starter motor with key in START position. If voltage is not present, check wiring between ignition switch and starter terminal. Check EWS system and other inputs that disrupt terminal 50 power to starter. See **ELE Electrical Wiring Diagrams**. If voltage is present and no other visible wiring faults can be found, problem is most likely in starter motor.

Starter, removing and installing (M54 engine)

— Disconnect negative (–) battery cable.

> ***CAUTION—***
> • *Prior to disconnecting the battery, read the battery disconnection cautions in* **001 Warnings and Cautions**.

— Raise vehicle and support safely.

> ***WARNING—***
> • *Make sure car is stable and well supported. Use a professional automotive lift or jack stands. A floor jack is not adequate support.*

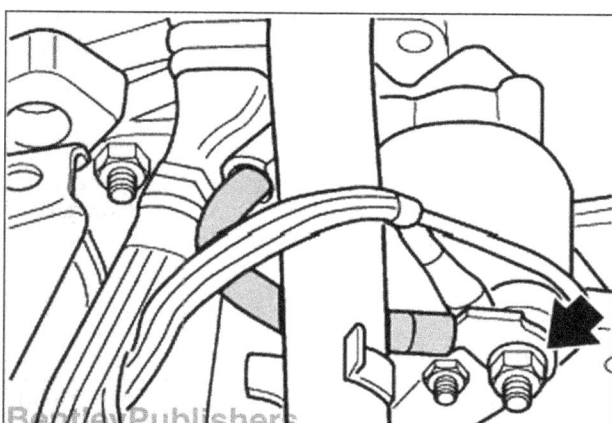

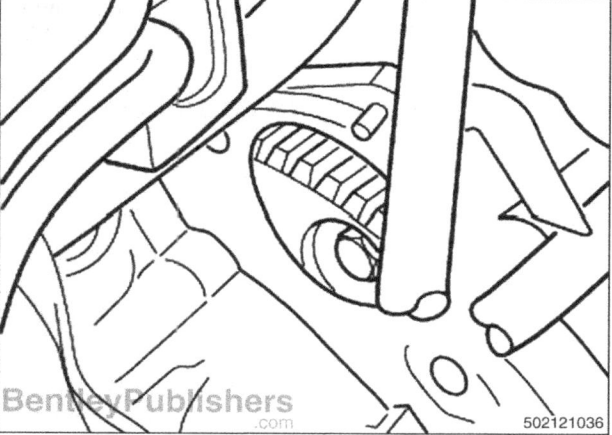

— Working underneath intake manifold:
  • Remove lines and vacuum components to gain access to starter.
  • Remove heat shield from starter (if equipped).

◄ Working underneath vehicle, disconnect battery positive (+) lead from starter (**arrow**).

NOTE—
  • *Note routing for cables. Cable routing can vary. When reinstalling, make sure cables do not chafe.*

— Using a long extension and universal joint from output end of transmission, remove bolts fastening starter to transmission bell housing and engine block.

— Pull starter out of transmission bell housing and remove remaining starter wiring.

— Remove starter from below.

◄ Check starter pinion gear and flywheel teeth for damage.

— Installation is reverse of removal.

Tightening torques	
Starter to transmission bell housing	45 Nm (33 ft-lb)
Wire terminals to starter • M5 • M6 • M8	 5 Nm (44 in-lb) 7 Nm (62 in-lb) 13 Nm (10 ft-lb)

Starter, removing and installing (N52 engine)

— Switch ignition OFF. Disconnect negative (–) battery cable and cover battery terminal to keep cable from accidentally contacting terminal.

CAUTION—
  • *Prior to disconnecting the battery, read the battery disconnection cautions in* **001 Warnings and Cautions**.

— Remove engine air filter housing and ducts. See **131 Fuel Injection**.

— Remove ignition coil cover. See **020 Maintenance**.

— Remove intake manifold. See **131 Fuel Injection**.

CAUTION—
  • *Do not detach fuel lines or injectors.*

◄ Working at starter solenoid electrical connections:
  • Remove fastener (**A**) and detach B+ cable from solenoid.
  • Press in wire clip (**arrow**) to release solenoid wire connector.

Solenoid switch, removing and installing

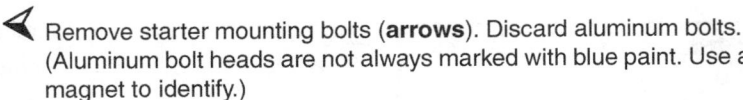 Remove starter mounting bolts (**arrows**). Discard aluminum bolts. (Aluminum bolt heads are not always marked with blue paint. Use a magnet to identify.)

— Lift out starter motor.

— Before installing new starter, rotate engine and inspect flywheel or torque plate gear teeth through starter hole. Replace if damaged. See **210 Clutch** or **240 Automatic Transmission**.

— Reinstall starter and reattach electrical connectors.

Tightening torques	
B+ cable to starter (M8)	13 Nm (10 ft-lb)
Starter to bell housing (replace M10 aluminum bolts) • Stage 1 • Stage 2	 20 Nm (15 ft-lb) additional 180°

Solenoid switch, removing and installing

— Remove starter as described previously.

— Disconnect field winding strap between starter motor and solenoid switch.

NOTE—
• *If the field winding strap is damaged or burned, a new or rebuilt starter motor is needed.*

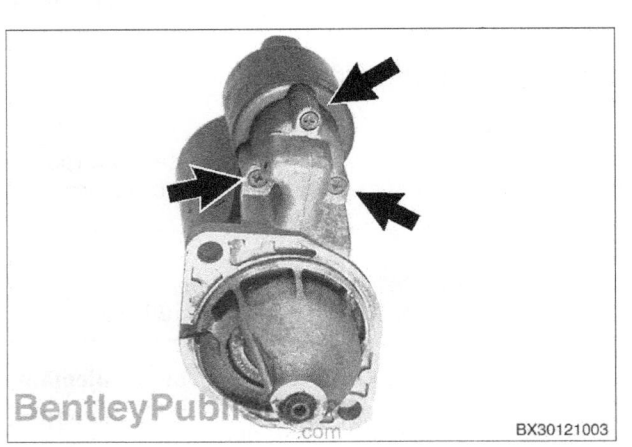

Remove solenoid switch mounting screws (**arrows**), and separate solenoid from starter.

• Unhook solenoid plunger from lever in starter drive.

— Installation is reverse of removal. Lubricate solenoid piston with light grease.

CAUTION—
• *When installing field winding strap to starter, position it so that it does not contact the starter body.*

Tightening torque	
Field strap to starter	13 Nm (10 ft-lb)

130 Fuel Injection (M54 Engine)

GENERAL

This repair group covers service and repair of the fuel injection system for X3 models with M54 engine. See **131 Fuel Injection (N52 engine)** for N52 fuel injection system.

See also:

• **020 Maintenance** for air filter, fuel filter and spark plug replacement

• **100 Engine–General** for engine identification

• **120 Ignition System** for ignition coil, camshaft sensor, crankshaft sensor and knock sensor service

• **160 Fuel Tank and Fuel Pump** for fuel pump and fuel pump relay service, fuel pressure tests and fuel pressure regulator replacement

• **180 Exhaust System** for oxygen sensor service

• **ECL Electrical Component Locations**

• **ELE Electrical Wiring Diagrams**

• **OBD On-Board Diagnostics**

DME applications

BMW X3 models are equipped with digital motor electronics (DME). In these systems, fuel injection and ignition are controlled by a engine control module (ECM). Application information for DME systems is in **Table a**.

Table a. X3 engine management applications

Year, model	Engine code	Engine management	Features
2004-2006			
2.5i	M54B25	Siemens MS 45.0	Double VANOS
3.0i	M54B30	Siemens MS 45 / MS 45.1*	Double VANOS

*MS 45.1 is used on 3.0 liter vehicles with automastic transmission. This system functions that same a the MS 45.0 system, with an added mass air flow sensor at the secondary air pump and new style wide-band pre-cat oxygen sensors.

Warnings and Cautions

WARNING—

- *The fuel system is designed to retain pressure even when the ignition is OFF. When working with the fuel system, loosen the fuel lines slowly to allow residual fuel pressure to dissipate. Avoid spraying fuel. Use shop towels to capture leaking fuel.*

- *Fuel in fuel lines is under pressure (approx. 3 - 5 bar) and may be expelled forcibly. Do not smoke or work near heaters or other fire hazards. Keep a fire extinguisher handy.*

- *Unscrew the fuel tank cap to release pressure in the tank before working on fuel lines.*

- *Plug open fuel lines and fittings.*

- *Before beginning work on the fuel system, place a fire extinguisher in the vicinity of the work area.*

- *Work only on the fuel system when engine temperature is below 40°C (104°F).*

- *Fuel is flammable. Do not disconnect wires that could cause electrical sparks. Do not smoke or work near heaters or other fire hazards.*

- *Wear eye protection and protective clothing to avoid injuries from contact with fuel.*

- *When working on an open fuel system, wear suitable hand protection, as prolonged contact with fuel can cause illnesses and skin disorders.*

- *Unscrew the fuel tank cap to release pressure in the tank before working on fuel lines.*

- *Do not use a work light with an incandescent bulb near fuel. Fuel may spray on the hot bulb causing a fire.*

- *Make sure the work area is properly ventilated.*

- *The ignition system produces high voltages that can be fatal. Use caution when working on a car with the ignition switched ON or the engine running.*

CAUTION—

- *Renew fuel system hoses, clamps and O-rings any time they are removed.*

- *Prior to disconnecting the battery, read the battery disconnection cautions in* **001 Warnings and Cautions**.

- *Connect and disconnect the DME system wiring and test equipment leads only when the ignition is switched OFF.*

- *Wait at least 1 minute after switching the ignition OFF before disconnecting engine control module (ECM) connectors. If the connectors are removed before this time, residual power in the system relay may damage the control module.*

- *Tests or repair procedures in this section may set fault codes (DTCs) in the ECM and illuminate the MIL. After repairs are completed, access and clear DTC memory using a BMW scan tool. See* **On-board diagnostics** *in this repair group.*

- *Fuel system cleaners and other chemical additives other than those specifically recommended by BMW may damage catalytic converters, oxygen sensors or other fuel supply components.*

- *Do not connect any test equipment that delivers a 12-volt power supply to terminal 15 (+) of the ignition coils. The current flow may damage the ECM. Connect test equipment only as specified by BMW or the equipment maker.*

- *Relay positions can vary. Be sure to confirm relay location and function by identifying the wiring in the socket using the wiring diagrams found in* **ELE Electrical Wiring Diagrams**.

- *Use a digital multimeter for electrical tests. Use an LED test light for quick tests.*

DRIVEABILITY TROUBLESHOOTING

The self-diagnostic DME engine management systems monitor and store diagnostic trouble codes (DTCs). If the malfunction indicator light (MIL) illuminates, it indicates that an emissions-related fault has occurred and that one or more DTCs are stored in the engine control module (ECM).

 If faults arise, or if the MIL is illuminated, begin troubleshooting by connecting a suitable scan tool to the OBD II plug under the dashboard. The capabilities of OBD II software has the potential to save diagnostic time and avoid incorrect component replacement. See **On-board diagnostics** in this repair group.

Basic engine settings

Idle speed, idle mixture (%CO), and ignition timing are not adjustable. The DME system is adaptive and automatically compensates for changes in the engine due to age, minor wear or small problems such as a disconnected vacuum hose. However, the adaptive range is limited. Once the limits are exceeded, driveability problems become noticeable.

Poor initial driveability may be encountered when the battery is disconnected and reconnected. When the battery is disconnected, ECM adaptive memory may be reset. The system readapts after about ten minutes of driving.

BX30120001

System voltage

Digital motor electronics (DME) requires that the system (battery) voltage be maintained within a narrow range of DC voltage. DC voltage levels beyond or below the operating range, or any AC voltage in the electrical system can cause driveability issues.

When troubleshooting an illuminated MIL, make sure the battery is charged and capable of delivering all its power to the electrical system. An undercharged battery can amplify AC alternator output ripple.

To make a quick check of battery charge, measure voltage across battery terminals with all cables attached and ignition OFF. A fully charged battery measures 12.6 volts or slightly more, compared to 12.15 volts for a battery with a 25% charge. Check battery terminals for corrosion or loose cable connections. See **121 Battery, Starter, Alternator**.

The DME system is sensitive to small increases in resistance. The electrical system is subject to corrosion, vibration and wear. Faults or corrosion in the wiring harness and connectors can lead to fault codes being set in the DME as well as difficult to diagnose driveability issues.

Loose or damaged connectors can cause intermittent problems, especially small terminals in ECM connectors. Disconnect wiring harness connectors to check for corrosion, and use electrical cleaning spray to remove contaminants.

Main grounds

Good grounds are critical to DME operation. If a ground point has no visible faults but is still suspect, measure the voltage drop across the connection. A large voltage drop means high resistance. Clean or repair the connection and retest. For voltage drop testing, see **600 Electrical System-General**. For ground locations, see **ECL Electrical Component Locations**.

On-board diagnostics

On-board diagnostics (OBD II) software and hardware is incorporated in the engine management systems. The OBD II system monitors components that influence exhaust and evaporative emissions. If a problem is detected, the OBD II system stores the a diagnostic trouble code (DTC) and condition.

If vehicle emissions levels exceed Federally mandated criteria, the OBD II system illuminates the malfunction indicator light (MIL) in the instrument cluster.

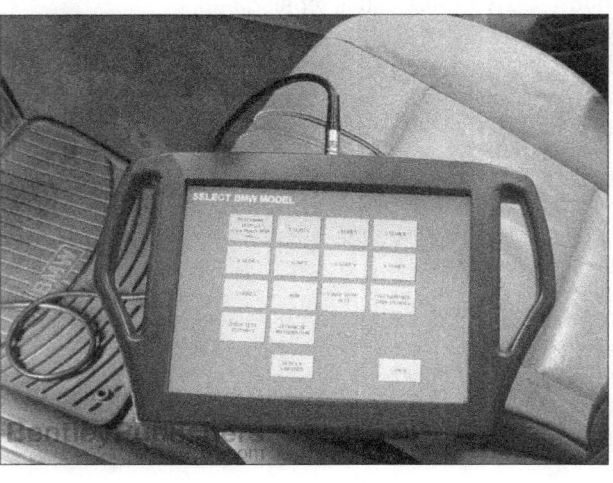

◄ Professional diagnostic scan tools include the factory BMW ISTA system, Autologic Diagnostics and a small number of aftermarket BMW-specific tools.

In addition to professional scan tools, there are inexpensive generic OBD II scan tool units available. Although these have limited capabilities, they can greatly aid the diagnosis of engine related faults.

NOTE—

- *DTCs must erased using a scan tool. Removing the ECM connector or disconnecting the battery does not erase DTC memory.*

ENGINE MANAGEMENT POWER SUPPLY

Power supply fuses

See **ECL Electrical Component Locations** for fuse panel access information.

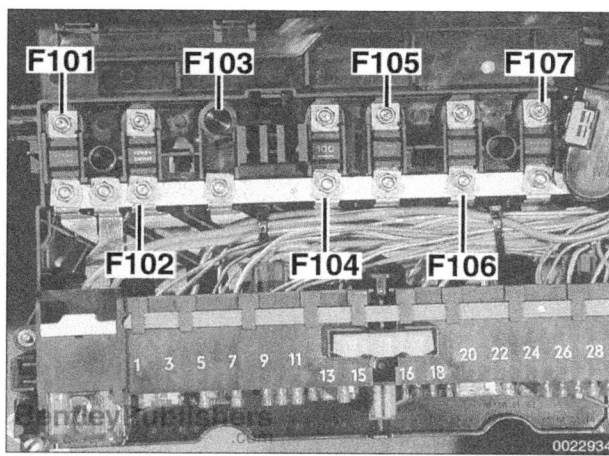

◄ **A41**: fuse and relay panel, behind glove compartment:

- **F102** 80A:
  Engine control module (ECM) (A6000)
  ECM main relay (K6300)
  F29 5A:
  Engine control module (ECM) (A6000)

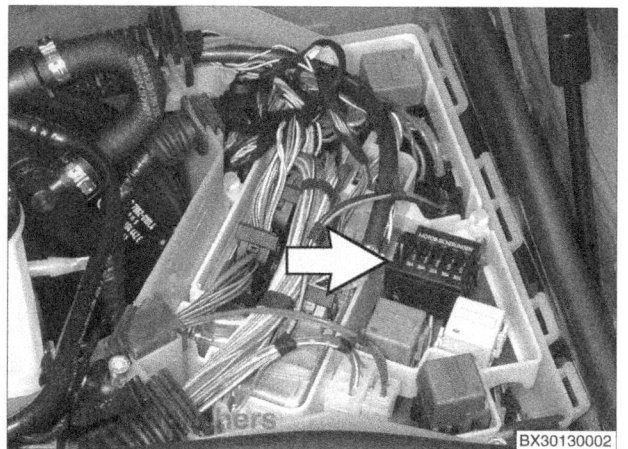

◄ **A8680**: fuse carrier, engine electronics, in electronics box (E-box), left rear of engine compartment:

- **F01** 30A: Power supply to ignition coils.

- **F02** 30A: Power supply to engine control module (ECM), VANOS solenoid valves, characteristic map thermostat, fuel tank vent valve, idle actuator.

- **F03** 20A: Power supply to reverse light relay, hot-film air mass meter, crankshaft position sensor, camshaft position sensors, secondary air pump relay, fuel pump relay, exhaust flap, AC compressor relay, steering angle sensor, diagnostic module for fuel tank leakage (DMTL), E-box fan.

- **F04** 30A: Power supply to oxygen sensors, transmission control module (A7000a) (if equipped).

- **F05** 30A: Power supply to fuel injector relay.

Relay for fuel injectors

◄ The relay for fuel injection (**K6327**) is located in the e-box, and supplies battery positive (B+) power to the fuel injectors. The fuel injectors are ground circuit controlled by the DME.

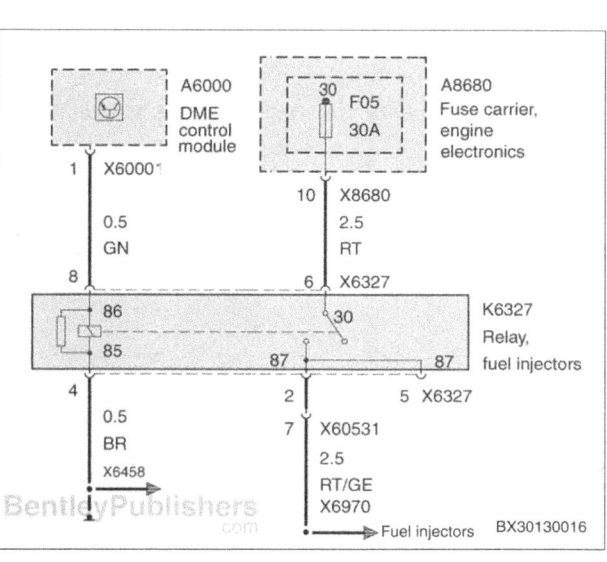

DME power supply circuit

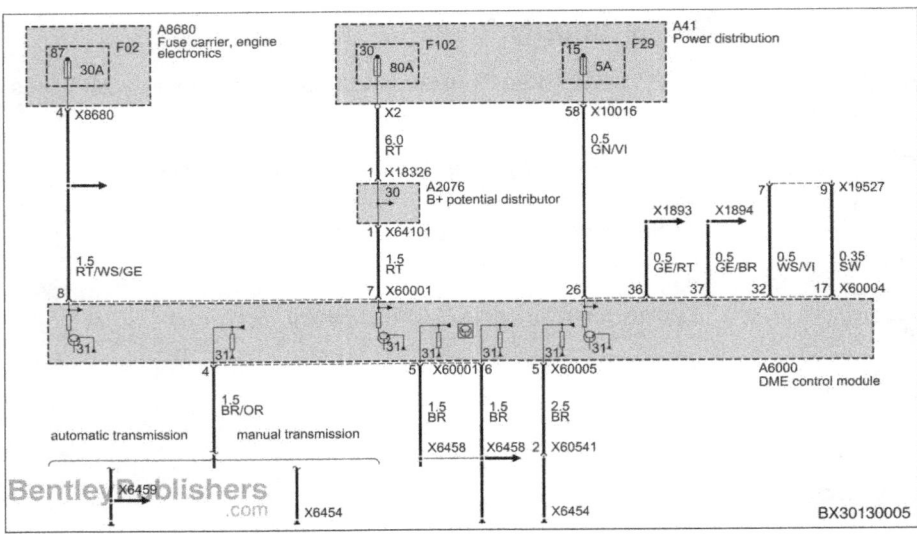

BX30130005

DME main relay

◄ DME main relay (**K6300**) is located in electronics box (E-box), left rear of engine compartment.
See **Electrical Component Locations** for E-box access.

NOTE—

• *Relay locations vary. Confirm relay identification by matching wiring colors and terminal numbers. See* **ELE Electrical Wiring Diagrams**.

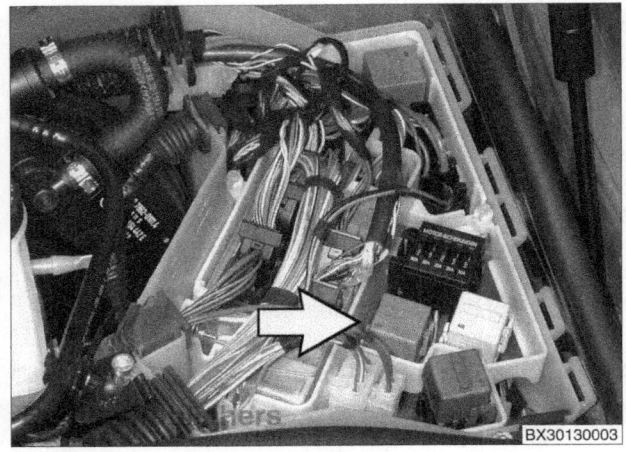

BX30130003

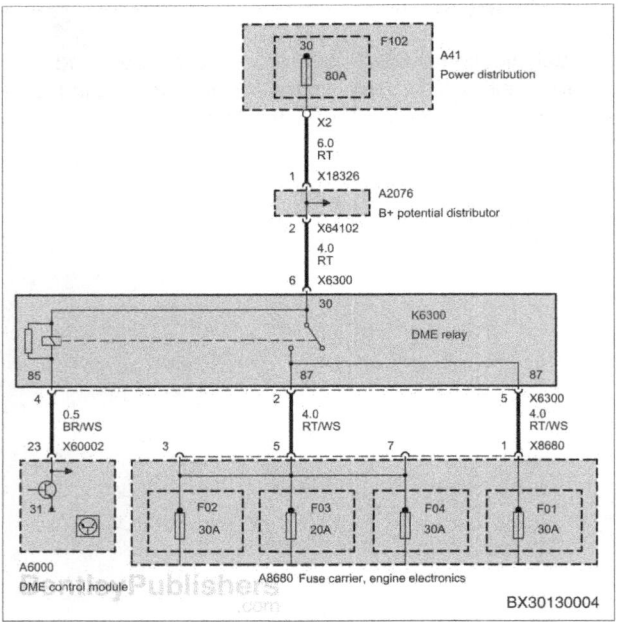

BX30130004

◄ The DME main relay is energized via the ECM and supplies battery positive (B+) power to the following:

• Fuse 01- fuse 04 in fuse carrier for engine electronics (A8680).

If the DME main relay is faulty, the engine does not start.

DME main relay testing

— With ignition off, remove DME main relay (**K6300**) in electronics box (E-box) at left rear of engine compartment.

NOTE—

> • *Relay locations vary. Confirm relay identification by matching wiring colors and terminal numbers. See* **ELE Electrical Wiring Diagrams**.

◄ Check for voltage at relay socket **30**.

— If battery voltage is present, continue testing.

— If battery voltage is not present, check the following:

  • Large red wire in relay socket.

  • Fuse **F102** on fuse and relay panel (**A41**), behind glove compartment.

  • See **ELE Electrical Wiring Diagrams** for more details.

— Check for ground at relay socket **85** with ignition ON.

— If ground is present, continue testing.

— If ground is not present, signal from ECM is missing. Check wire between relay and ECM pin 23 on connector X60002. See **ECM pin assignments** in this repair group.

— If no faults are found:

  • Check ECM grounding.

  • ECM may be defective.

— Reinstall relay. With ignition ON, check for battery voltage at relay socket **87** (check from underside of relay socket).

NOTE—

> • *Some relays may have an additional terminal 87 (labeled terminal 87a).*

— If battery voltage is present, relay circuit is functioning correctly.

— If battery voltage is not present and all earlier tests are OK, relay is faulty. Replace.

— If no faults are found during relay testing but power is not reaching ECM or other components, check fuses **F01** - **F05** in front power distribution box (**A400a**).

— When finished testing, check for fault codes and reset ECM memory.

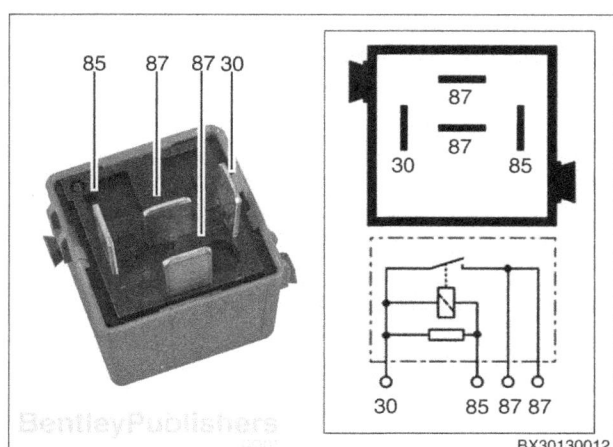

BX30130012

SIEMENS DME MS45 (M54 ENGINE)

DME MS45 system description

DME MS45 manages and monitors the following functions:

Air

- Idle speed valve
- Electronic throttle
- Hot film mass air flow sensor
- Resonance-turbulence variable intake manifold

Fuel

- Fuel supply (returnless)
- Fuel injection

Ignition

- Direct ignition
- Knock control
- Primary / secondary ignition monitoring

Emissions

- OBD II compliance
- Secondary air injection and monitoring
- Pre- and post-catalyst oxygen sensors
- Electrically heated DME-mapped thermostat
- Misfire detection
- Evaporative emission control and leak detection
- Ambient pressure sensing
- Malfunction indicator light (MIL)

Performance controls

- Double VANOS control
- Electric radiator cooling fan
- E-box cooling fan
- CAN-bus communication
- Immobilizer system communication (EWS)
- Cruise control
- Comfort start
- ECM programming
- Alternator interface (BSD)
- Dynamic stability control (DSC) interface

Engine control module (ECM)

The ECM (**arrow**) is mounted in the electronics box (E-box) at left rear of engine compartment.

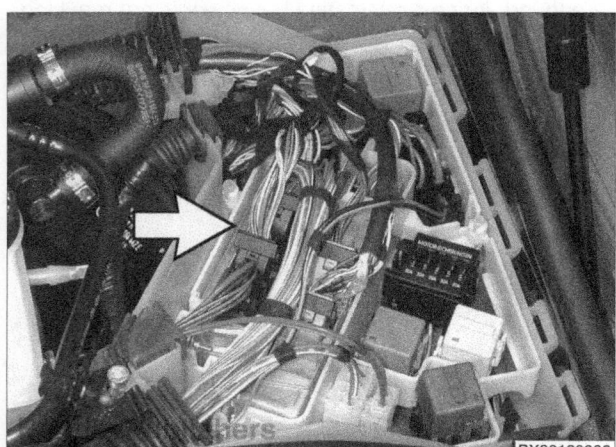

BX30130006

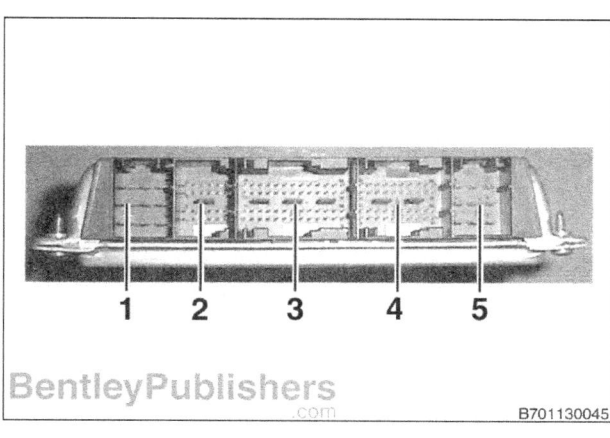

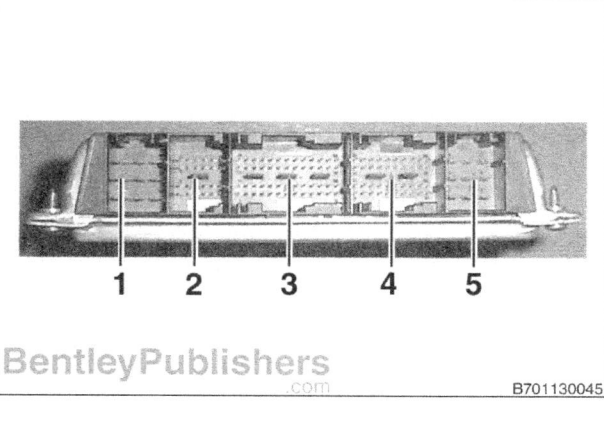

◁ The MS45 ECM is flash-programmable and features 5 electrical harness connectors with a total of 134 pins.

- **Connector 1:** Voltages and grounds
- **Connector 2:** Ancillary signals (oxygen sensors, etc.)
- **Connector 3:** Engine signals
- **Connector 4:** Vehicle signals
- **Connector 5:** Ignition signals

The EEPROM (chip) in the MS45 ECM is coded to the vehicle. It can be flashed (reprogrammed) up to 13 times.

Fuel metering

The ECM meters pressurized fuel by changing the opening time (pulse width) of the fuel injectors. The exact amount of fuel injected is determined by the amount of time the injectors are open. To ensure that injector pulse width is the only factor that determines fuel metering, fuel pump pressure is maintained by a pressure regulator. The injectors are mounted to a common fuel rail.

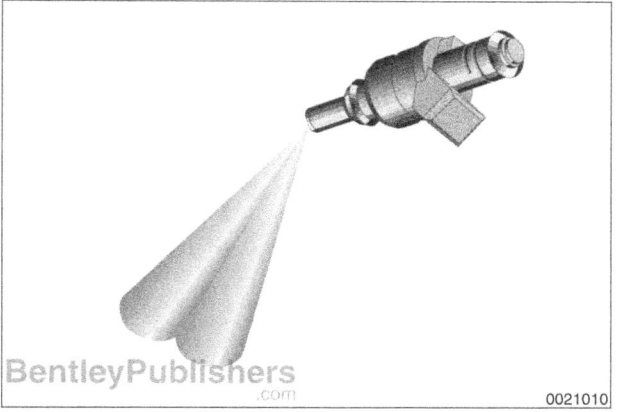

◁ The fuel-injectors inject fuel at an angle in a dual cone spray pattern.

The ECM monitors engine operating conditions to determine injector opening duration. Each injector can be individually controlled for cylinder selective fuel trim.

Air intake

Air entering the engine passes through a pleated paper element in the air filter housing. Intake air mass is then measured by a mass air flow sensor. A reference current is used to heat a thin film in the sensor when the engine is running. The current needed to hold the temperature of the film constant is the basis of the electronically converted voltage measurement corresponding to the mass of the intake air.

Idle speed control

Idle speed is electronically controlled via the idle speed control valve by bypassing varying amounts of air around the closed throttle valve. Idle speed is not adjustable. The ECM determines idle speed by controlling a dual-winding rotary idle control valve.

If the ECM detects a fault in the idle control valve, it increases or decreases air flow, depending on the nature of the fault:

- If the fault causes decreased air flow (idle control valve closed), the electronic throttle control compensates to maintain idle.
- If the fault causes increased air flow (idle control valve failed open), VANOS and knock control are deactivated. This reduces engine performance noticeably.

Throttle control

In order to integrate the driver's wish with the requirements of the traction control system (DSC) and cruise control, DME systems feature electronic throttle control (EDK). There is no throttle cable between the accelerator pedal and the throttle housing

Knock (detonation) control

Knock sensors monitor and control ignition knock through the ECM. Knock sensors function like microphones and are able to convert mechanical vibration (knock) into electrical signals. The ECM is programmed to react to frequencies that are characteristic of engine knock and adapt the ignition timing point accordingly.

Knock sensor replacement is covered in **120 Ignition System**.

Secondary air injection

The secondary air system pumps ambient air into the exhaust stream after a cold engine start to reduce catalytic converter warm-up time and to reduce HC and CO emissions. The ECM controls and monitors the secondary air injection system.

The electric air pump draws in ambient air and supplies it to the secondary air valve. The secondary air valve is bolted to the right front of the cylinder head. Cast passageways within the cylinder head duct the secondary air directly into the cylinder head exhaust ports.

Secondary air injection system components

 3.0L engine with automatic transmission:

1. Air pump
2. Filter air duct
3. air duct hose clamp
4. Mini mass air flow sensor (only 3.0 with A/T)
5. Air pump filter
6. Pressure hose
7. Secondary air valve
8. Air pump brackets

BX30130008

Secondary air injection system components

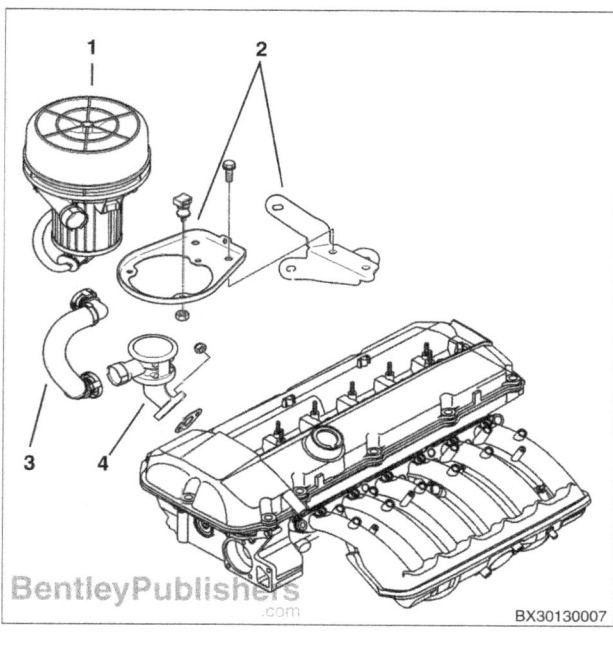

BX30130007

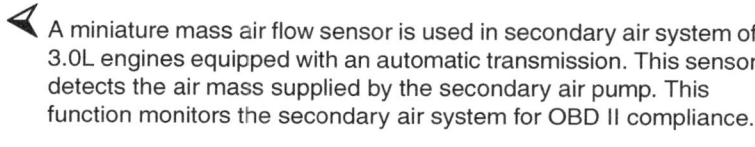

Except 3.0L engine with automatic transmission:

1. Air pump
2. Air pump bracket
3. Pressure hose
4. Secondary air valve

130

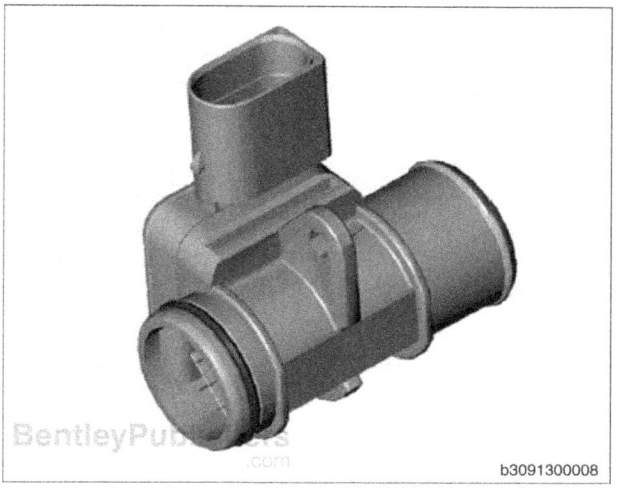

b3091300008

A miniature mass air flow sensor is used in secondary air system of 3.0L engines equipped with an automatic transmission. This sensor detects the air mass supplied by the secondary air pump. This function monitors the secondary air system for OBD II compliance.

When the mini mass air flow sensor detects no or insufficient air flow, a fault is stored in the ECM and the malfunction indicator light (MIL) is illuminated.

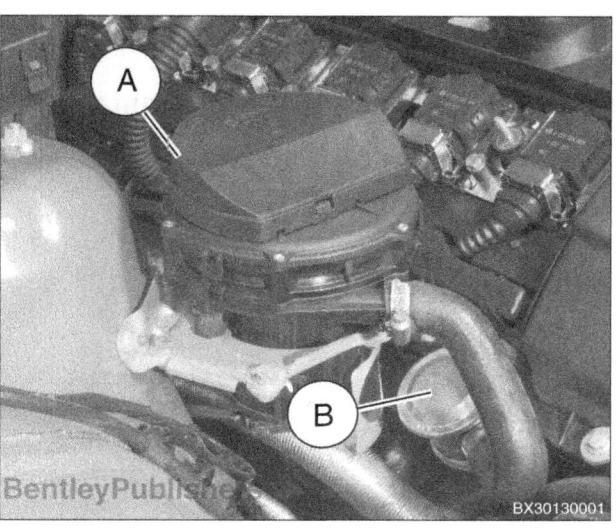

BX30130001

Secondary air pump (**A**) and secondary air valve (**B**) on right side of engine.

Air filter housing and ducts, removing and installing

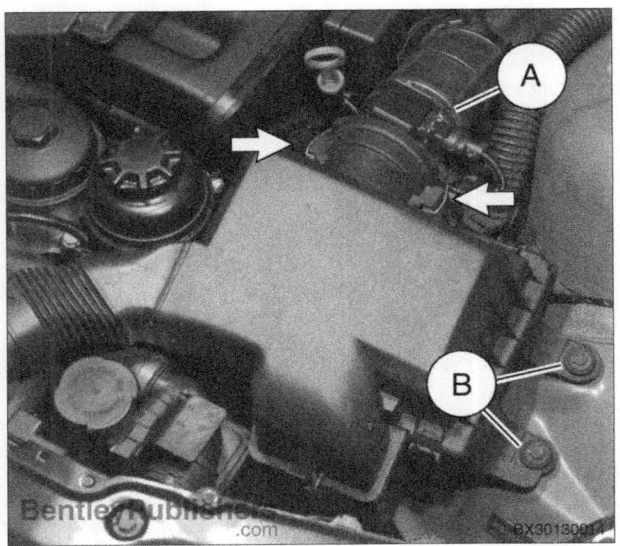

Air filter housing and ducts, removing and installing

For air filter servicing, see **020 Maintenance**.

◄ Disconnect mass air flow sensor connector (**A**).

• Release mass air flow sensor clips (**arrows**).

• Remove filter housing mounting bolts (**B**).

– Disconnect air duct and lift complete air filter housing out of engine compartment, pulling it forward away from mass air flow sensor.

– Working at throttle body, loosen duct clamp. Remove duct from throttle body.

– Installation is reverse of removal.

– After reinstalling, check and clear fault codes from ECM memory.

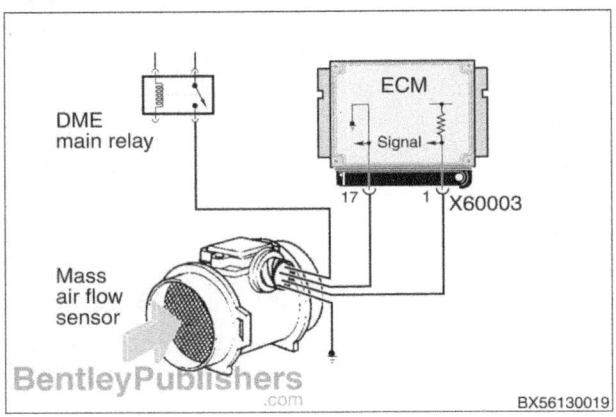

Mass air flow, measurement

◄ The hot film mass air flow sensor sends a varying voltage (approx. 0.5 - 4.5 V) to the ECM representing the measured intake air. The air mass input signal is produced using an electrically heated metal film in the air flow stream.

The DME main relay provides the operating voltage to the air flow sensor. As air flows through the sensor, the film is cooled. To maintain the film at a constant temperature, additional current is necessary. It is this additional current that is the basis for the input signal.

If there is no output signal from the air flow sensor, the ECM operates the engine using throttle position and engine rpm inputs. A faulty air flow sensor illuminates the MIL.

A faulty air flow sensor can produce the following problems:

• Difficult to restart when engine is hot

• Engine starts then stalls

• Engine starts and runs only with accelerator pedal depressed

Mass air flow sensor, removing and installing

– Switch ignition OFF and remove key.

◄ Working at left front of engine compartment:

• Remove intake air filter housing.

• Loosen air duct clamp (**arrow**).

• Remove MAF sensor.

– If air flow sensor is to be reused, visually inspect for damaged, missing or blocked screen. (Screen affects air flow calibration.)

– Check intake ducts for cracks and vacuum leaks.

– Installation is reverse of removal.

130

Accelerator pedal module (PWG)

There is no mechanical (cable) link between the accelerator pedal and the throttle plate.

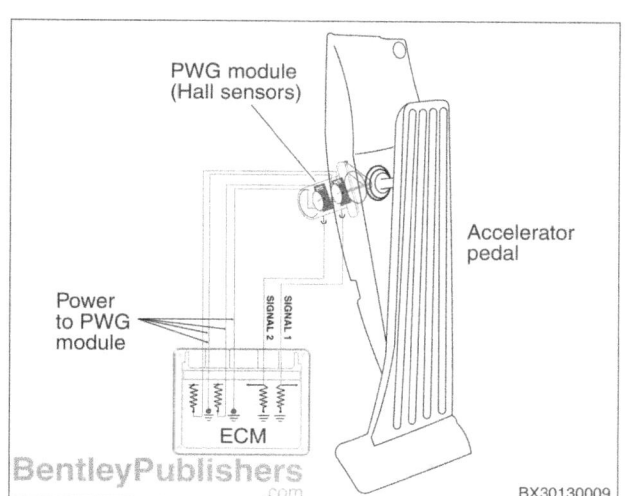

The accelerator pedal module (PWG) at the pedal assembly communicates pedal position directly to the ECM. The module provides two variable voltage signals (via two Hall sensors) to the ECM for pedal position and rate of movement.

The ECM provides an independent voltage and ground supply for each Hall sensor. Each Hall sensor is provided with 5 volts and ground. As the accelerator pedal is moved from rest to full throttle, the sensors produce a variable voltage signal. The output of the Hall sensors is checked for plausibility. The voltage range of Hall sensor 1 is approximately 0.5 to 4.5 volts. Hall sensor 2 ranges from approximately 0.5 to 2.5 volts.

The ECM adapts to throttle angle voltage at idle speed. If the accelerator pedal module must be replaced, ECM adaptation values must be reset and a throttle angle adaptation procedure must be performed using a factory BMW scan tool or the vehicle will not start.

Throttle housing (EDK), removing and installing

The throttle valve plate is electronically operated by the ECM to regulate intake air flow.

The EDK motor is pulse width modulated by the ECM to open and close the throttle plate. The throttle plate is also closed by a fail-safe return spring. Two integrated potentiometers in the EDK housing provide feedback to the ECM for throttle plate angle as the EDK motor is operated.

The throttle housing unit (EDK) is nonadjustable. If found to be faulty, replace as a complete unit. After replacing the throttle housing, use BMW scan tool to reset adaptation values

– Switch ignition OFF and remove key.

– Remove air filter housing and air intake ducts. See **Air filter housing and ducts, removing and installing** in this repair group.

◄ Working at side of intake manifold, disconnect electrical connectors:
  • Intake manifold resonance valve (**A**)
  • Idle speed control valve (**B**)

– Disconnect electrical connectors at oil pressure sender and oil temperature sender at base of oil filter housing.

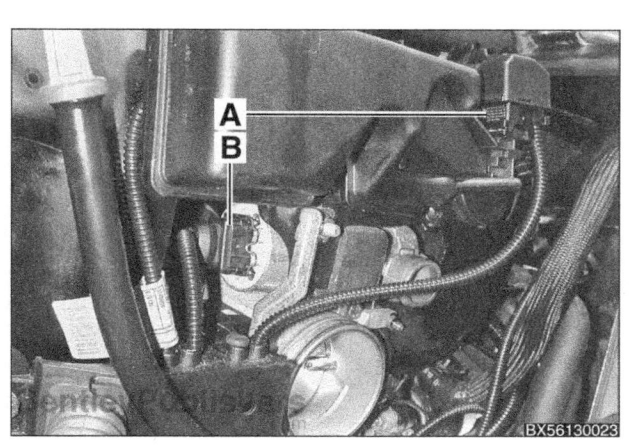

Throttle housing (EDK), removing and installing

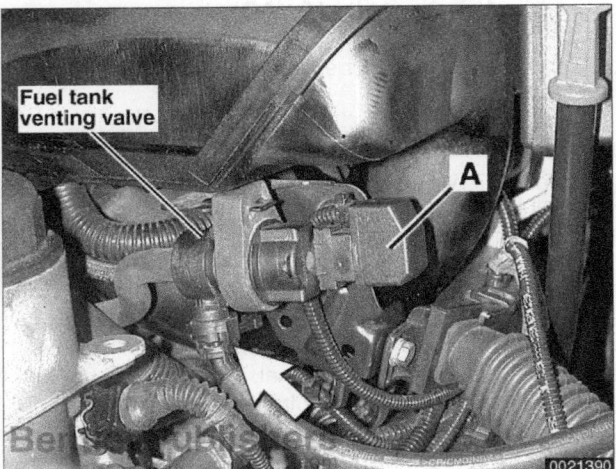

◀ Working at left side and underneath intake manifold:

• Detach electrical connector (**A**) at fuel tank venting valve.

• Disconnect hose at quick disconnect fitting (**arrow**).

• Remove valve from manifold and set aside.

◀ Remove wiring harness housing mounting fasteners (**arrows**) and pull housing away from throttle assembly.

— Remove engine oil dipstick tube.

◀ Working at throttle housing, unscrew harness plug counterclockwise (**arrow**) to disconnect.

Idle speed control valve, removing and installing

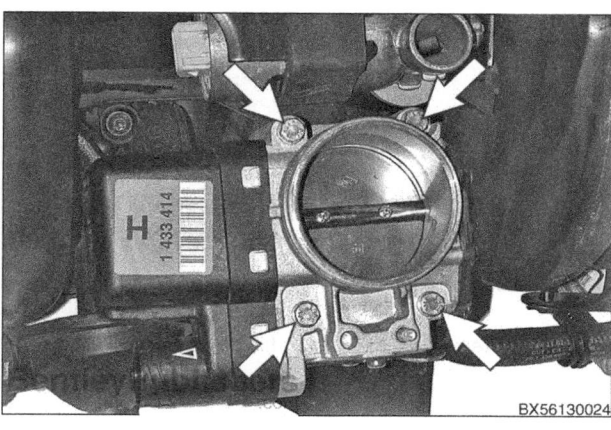

BX56130024

◀ Remove throttle housing mounting fasteners (**arrows**) and pull assembly off manifold.

– Installation is reverse of removal.
  - Replace profile gasket (sealing O-ring) between throttle assembly and intake manifold.
  - Reattach throttle assembly connector with care. Arrow on fully tightened connector must line up with corresponding arrow on throttle assembly housing.

– Use BMW scan tool to:
  - Check and clear fault codes from ECM memory.
  - Reset throttle adaptation values.

> **CAUTION—**
> - If the adaptation process is not completed correctly, the engine does not start.

Idle speed control valve, removing and installing

The idle speed control valve, mounted directly above the throttle housing, regulates idle speed by redirecting air around the throttle valve. The valve, supplied with battery voltage from the DME main relay, incorporates a two-coil rotary actuator. Coil grounds are pulsed simultaneously by the ECM. The duty cycle of each circuit is varied to achieve the required idle speed.

A faulty idle speed control valve sets a DTC. The MIL illuminates if OBD II fault criteria are exceeded.

– Switch ignition OFF and remove key.

– Disconnect battery negative (-) cable in cargo compartment.

> **CAUTION—**
> - Prior to disconnecting the battery, read the battery disconnection cautions in **001 Warnings and Cautions**.

– Remove air filter housing and air intake ducts. See **Air filter housing and ducts, removing and installing** in this repair group.

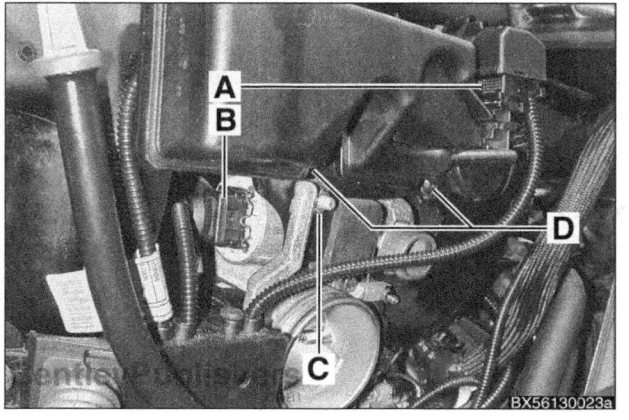

BX56130023a

◀ Working at side of intake manifold:
  - Disconnect electrical connector to intake manifold resonance valve (**A**).
  - Disconnect electrical connector to idle speed control valve (**B**).
  - Remove upper wiring harness housing mounting fastener (**C**). Pull harness housing back slightly.
  - Remove idle speed valve mounting bracket screws (**D**).
  - Pull idle regulator off intake manifold. It is fitted to manifold using a sealing grommet.

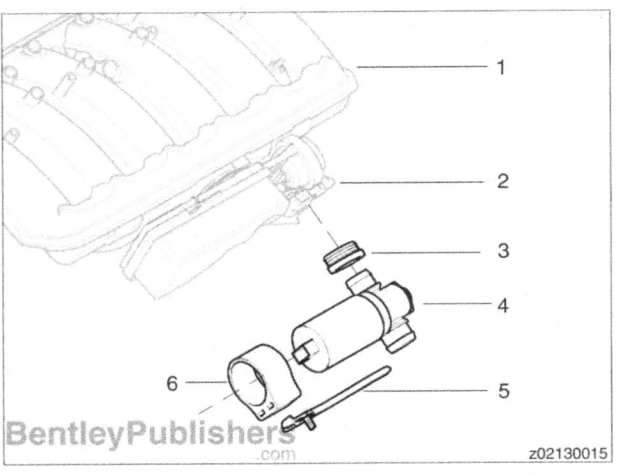

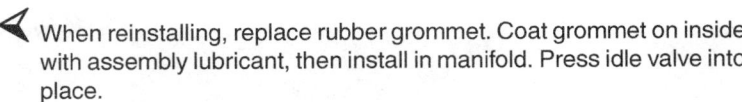

When reinstalling, replace rubber grommet. Coat grommet on inside with assembly lubricant, then install in manifold. Press idle valve into place.

1. Intake manifold
2. Intake manifold resonance valve
3. Sealing grommet
4. Idle speed control valve
5. Mounting bracket
6. Rubber mounting

— Reattach wiring harnesses. Reinstall air filter assembly and ducts.

— Check and clear fault codes from ECM memory.

Fuel rail and injectors, removing and installing

Fuel injectors are electrically controlled solenoid valves that provide precisely metered and atomized fuel into the engine intake ports.

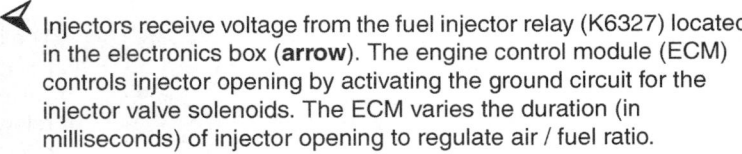

Injectors receive voltage from the fuel injector relay (K6327) located in the electronics box (**arrow**). The engine control module (ECM) controls injector opening by activating the ground circuit for the injector valve solenoids. The ECM varies the duration (in milliseconds) of injector opening to regulate air / fuel ratio.

— To access injectors, remove engine covers. See **020 Maintenance**.

— For a quick check of injectors, run engine and touch each injector with a screwdriver or stethoscope. You should feel a vibration or hear a buzzing. Switch engine OFF.

— Disconnect battery negative (-) cable.

> **CAUTION—**
> • *Prior to disconnecting battery, read the battery disconnection cautions in* **001 Warnings and Cautions**.

— Remove upper engine covers. See **020 Maintenance**.

Working above engine, detach the following:

• **B** Resonance valve electrical connector
• **C** Oxygen sensor connectors
• **D** Electrical connector for intake air temperature sensor
• **E** Manifold vacuum line
• **F** VANOS solenoid electrical connector

> **CAUTION—**
> • *Be sure to mark oxygen sensor connectors so that they can be reassembled as before.*

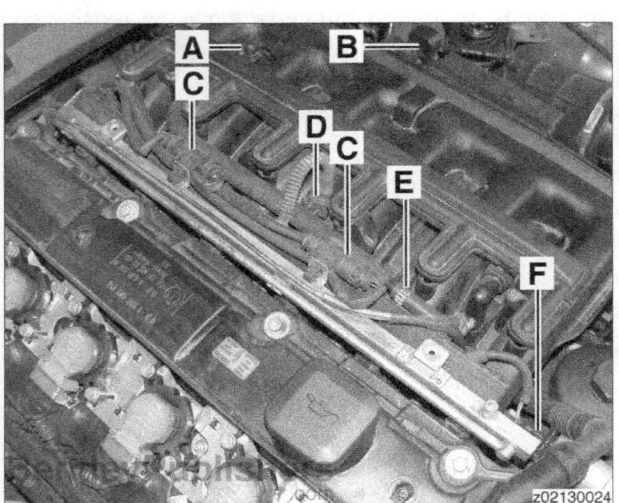

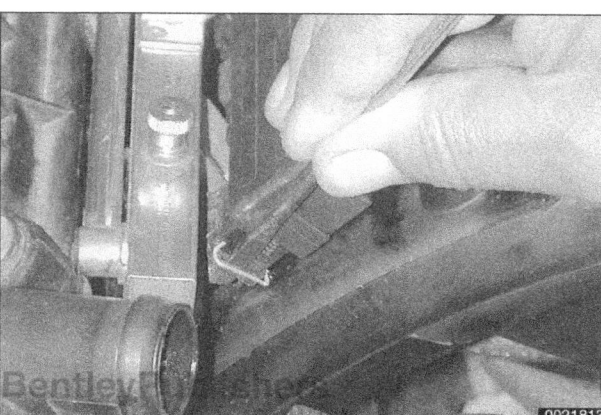

◄ Disconnect fuel injector electrical connectors from injectors:

- Use small screwdriver to pry one corner of wire lock clip on fuel injector 1 connector.
- Repeat for all injectors.
- Lift off connector loom and set aside.

◄ Unscrew Schræder valve cap (**arrow**) from fuel rail.

- Unscrew fuel tank cap to release pressure.
- Using a brief burst of compressed air (maximum of 3 bar or 43.5 psi), blow fuel back into fuel tank.

> **WARNING—**
> - *Wrap a clean shop towel around fitting before removing Schræder valve. Fuel in lines and rail is under pressure (approx. 3 - 5 bar or 45 - 75 psi) and may be expelled forcibly.*
> - *Unscrew the fuel tank cap to release pressure in the tank before working on the fuel line.*
> - *Do not smoke or work near heaters or other fire hazards. Keep a fire extinguisher handy.*
> - *Plug open fuel lines and fittings.*

◄ Working at rear of manifold, use BMW special tool 16 1 050 or equivalent to press locking clip inside end of fuel line fitting (**arrow**) to disconnect fuel supply line from fuel rail.

> **WARNING—**
> - *Wrap a clean shop towel around fitting before disconnecting. Residual fuel pressure may be present in fuel lines.*

◄ Remove fuel rail mounting bolts (**arrows**).

- Carefully pry fuel rail and injectors off manifold.
- Separate fuel line support bracket at rear of intake manifold.
- Guide fuel line(s) out of rear of engine compartment while lifting fuel rail out.

Intake manifold, removing and installing

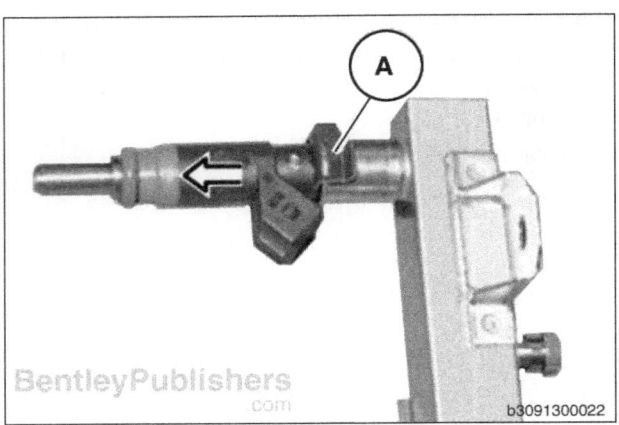

 Remove individual injectors:
- Pry retaining clip from injector (**A**).
- Pull injector from rail.

– Installation is reverse of removal. Remember to:
- Fit new sealing O-rings when installing injectors. For ease of installation, lightly lubricate O-rings with assembly lubricant.
- Check that injector electrical connections are correctly fitted and that injectors are fully seated prior to installing fuel rail mounting bolts.
- Check fuel line rubber O-rings and replace as necessary. For ease of installation, lightly lubricate O-rings with assembly lubricant.
- Replace wire ties.

Tightening torque	
Fuel rail to cylinder head	10 Nm (7 ft-lb)

– Check and clear fault codes from ECM memory.

Intake manifold, removing and installing

– Place hood in service position. See **410 Fenders, Engine Hood**.

– Disconnect negative (–) cable from battery.

> **CAUTION—**
> • *Prior to disconnecting the battery, read the battery disconnection cautions in* **001 Warnings and Cautions**.

– Remove air cleaner housing and fresh air ducts.
See **Air filter housing and ducts** in this repair group.

– Remove brace from strut towers.
See **310 Front Suspension**.

– Remove Housing for interior ventilation microfilter.
See **640 Heating and Air-conditioning**.

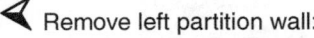 Remove left partition wall:
- Remove rubber seal from top of heater bulkhead.
- Release vacuum line (**A**) for power brake booster. Disconnect line from power brake booster and remove from partition wall with electrical wiring.
- Release plastic locks (**arrows**) and pull trim slightly forward.
- Pull partition wall up to remove.

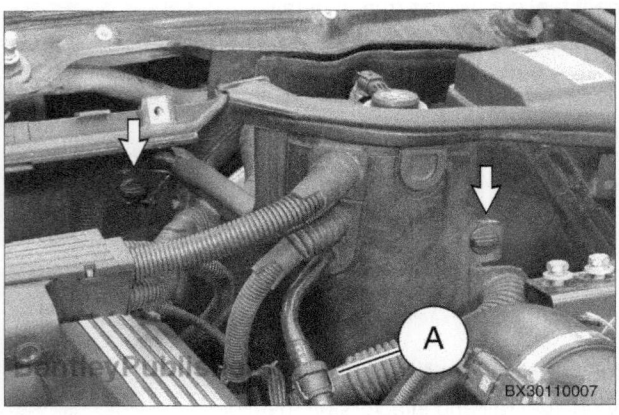

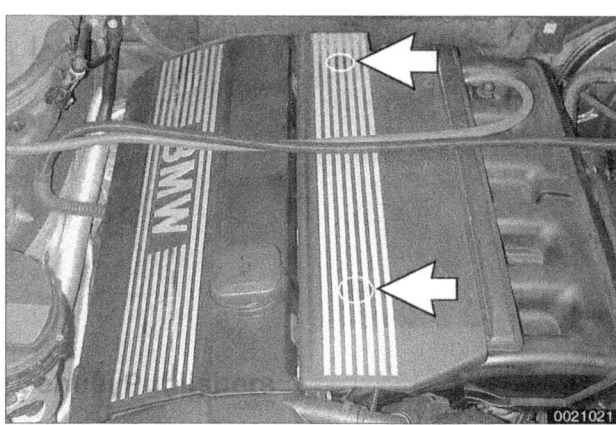

◄ Remove engine design cover.

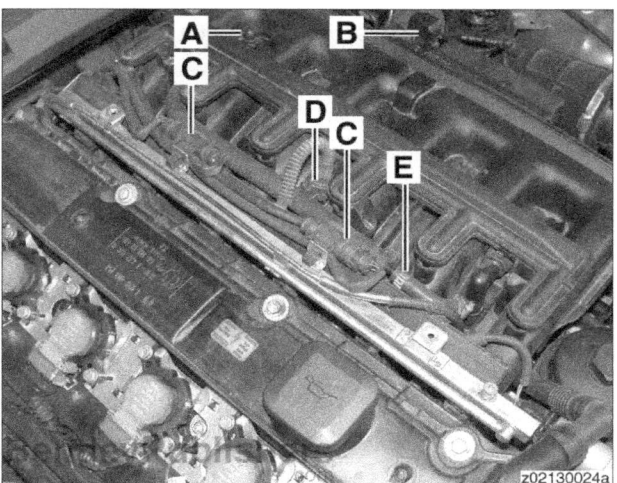

◄ Working above engine, detach the following:

• **A** B+ lead bracket
• **B** Resonance valve electrical connector
• **C** Oxygen sensor connectors
• **D** Electrical connector for intake air temperature sensor
• **E** Manifold vacuum line

> **CAUTION—**
> • *Be sure to mark oxygen sensor connectors so that they can be reassembled as before.*

◄ Working at left side of cylinder head:

• Detach engine vent hose from cylinder head cover by pinching spring clips (**arrows**).
• Detach VANOS solenoid electrical connector (**A**).

Intake manifold, removing and installing

◄ Detach fuel injector electrical connectors from injectors:

- Use small screwdriver to pry one corner of wire lock clip on fuel injector 1 connector.
- Repeat for all injectors.
- Remove two main harness hold-down fasteners. Lift off entire harness and lay aside.

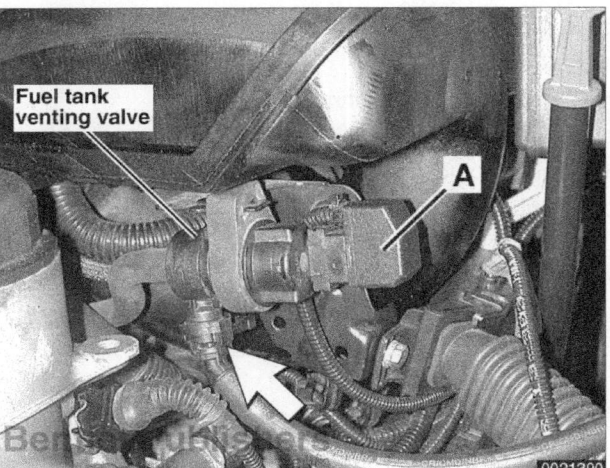

Fuel tank venting valve

◄ Working at left side and underneath intake manifold:

- Detach electrical connector (**A**) at fuel tank venting valve.
- Disconnect hose at quick disconnect fitting (**arrow**).
- Remove valve from manifold and set aside.

◄ Disconnect electrical connector (**arrow**) at idle speed control valve.

– Remove throttle housing. See **Throttle housing (EDK), removing and installing** in this repair group.

◀ Unscrew Schræder valve cap (**arrow**) from fuel rail.

- Unscrew fuel tank cap to release pressure.

- Using a brief burst of compressed air (maximum of 3 bar or 43.5 psi), blow fuel back into fuel tank.

> **WARNING**—
> - Wrap a clean shop towel around fitting before removing Schræder valve. *Residual fuel pressure is present in the fuel rail.*

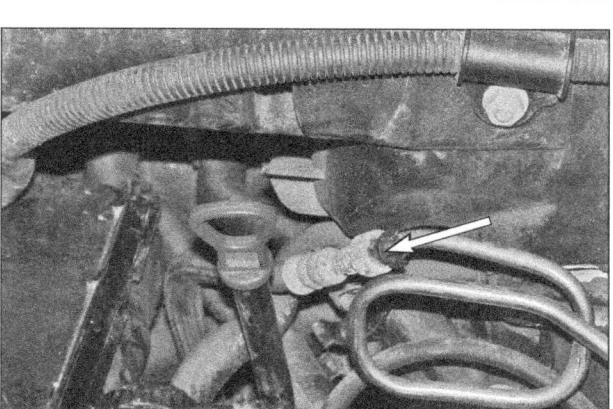

◀ Working at rear of manifold, use BMW special tool 16 1 050 or equivalent to press locking clip inside end of fuel line fitting (**arrow**) to disconnect fuel supply line from fuel rail.

> **WARNING**—
> - Wrap a clean shop towel around fitting before disconnecting. *Residual fuel pressure is present in the fuel line.*

◀ Working underneath car, remove lower intake manifold support mounting bolt (**arrow**), located adjacent to left engine mount.

— Detach knock sensor connector from bracket at base of manifold.

— Remove manifold lower support nuts.

◀ Remove intake manifold mounting nuts (**arrows**).

— Remove intake manifold from cylinder head while carefully checking for electrical connections or hoses that might become snagged.

> **CAUTION**—
> - Plug open intake ports to prevent parts or debris from falling into the engine intake.

Crankcase breather valve components

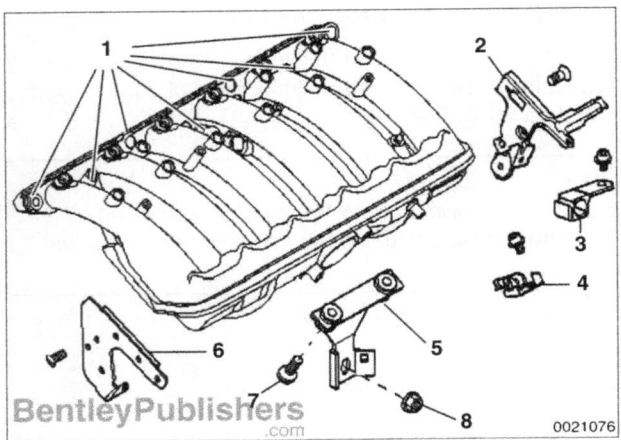

◀ Note intake manifold brackets and mounts:

1. Manifold mounting nuts
   • tighten to 15 Nm (11 ft-lb)
2. Fuel pipe bracket
3. Fuel pipe bracket
4. Vacuum pump bracket
5. Manifold mounting bracket
6. Tank venting valve bracket
7. Mounting bracket to manifold bolt (M6)
   • tighten to 10 Nm (7 ft-lb)
8. Mounting bracket to engine block nut (M10)
   • tighten to 47 Nm (33 ft-lb)

— Intake manifold installation is reverse of removal.

   • Use new fuel injector seals.

   • Carefully check intake manifold gaskets and replace if necessary.

   • Check condition of rubber seals at throttle housing and idle speed control valve. Replace as necessary.

   • Inspect O-ring seal between mass air flow sensor and air filter housing. To facilitate reassembly, coat seal with assembly fluid.

> **CAUTION—**
> • *When reattaching throttle assembly harness connector, make sure arrows on connector and plug line up when fully tightened.*

Tightening torques	
Intake manifold to cylinder head (M7)	15 Nm (11 ft-lb)
Mounting bracket to engine block (M10)	47 Nm (33 ft-lb)
Mounting bracket to intake manifold (M6)	10 Nm (7 ft-lb)

Crankcase breather valve components

1. Cylinder head cover
2. Connecting hose
3. Oil return hose
4. Breather valve
5. Vacuum hose
6. Dipstick guide tube vent hose
7. Dipstick guide tube
8. Vent pipe
9. Screw

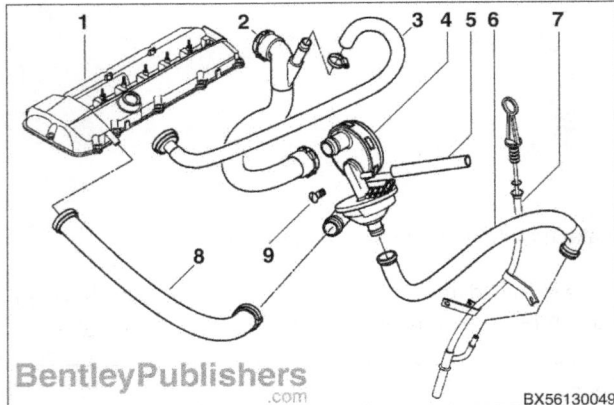

The M54 engine crankcase is ventilated by breather valve under the intake manifold. If the diaphragm valve in the breather housing leaks, full intake vacuum may be applied to the crankcase, resulting in excessive oil consumption, irregular idle, whistling or howling noises or oil smoke in the exhaust.

Crankcase breather valve, removing and installing

Engine breather hoses become brittle over time. Replace all hoses along with crankcase breather valve when removing.

— Disconnect battery negative (-) cable in cargo compartment.

> **CAUTION—**
> • *Prior to disconnecting the battery, read the battery disconnection cautions in* **001 Warnings and Cautions**.

— Remove throttle housing. See **Throttle housing (EDK), removing and installing** in this repair group.

◀ Working at left side of cylinder head, detach engine vent hose from cylinder head cover by pinching spring clips (**arrows**).

◀ Working between cylinder 1 and cylinder 2 intake manifold runners, detach engine vent hose from crankcase breather hose by pinching spring clips (**arrows**).

◀ Working between cylinder 1 and cylinder 2 intake manifold runners, detach engine vent hose from intake manifold by pinching spring clips (**arrows**).

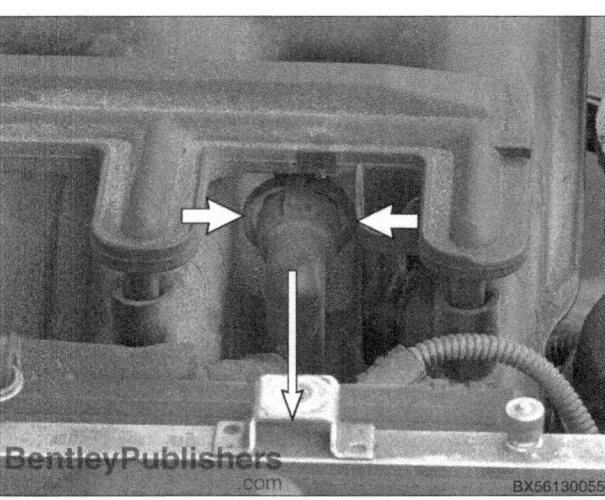

Crankcase breather valve, removing and installing

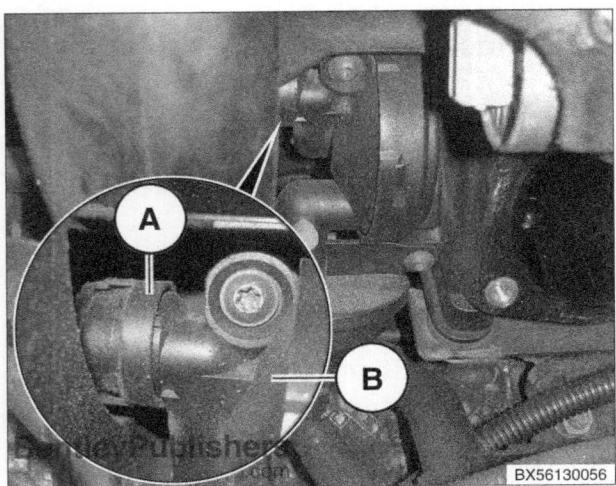

◄ Working under center of intake manifold, use a small pick or flat blade screwdriver to detach breather hose (**A**) from crankcase breather valve (**B**).

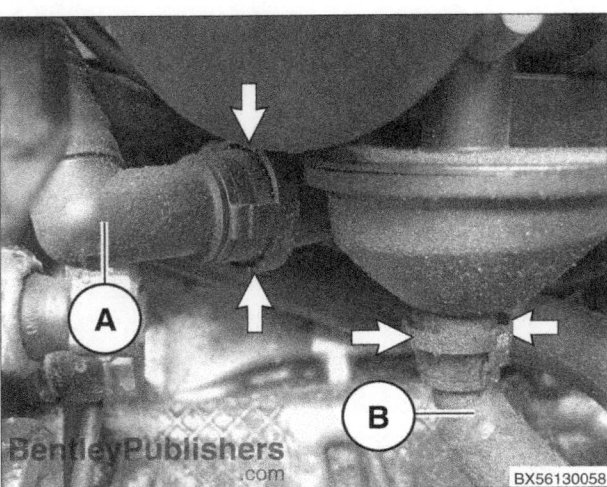

◄ Working under center of intake manifold:
- Detach engine vent hose (**A**) from crankcase breather by pinching spring clips (**arrows**).
- Detach crankcase breather drain hose (**B**) from crankcase breather by pinching spring clips (**arrows**).

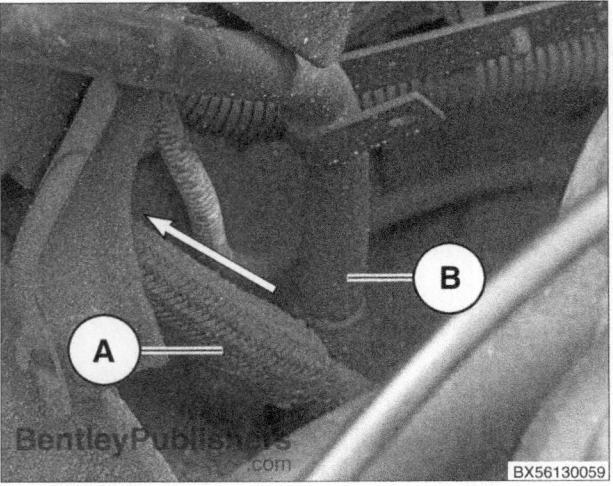

◄ Remove crankcase breather drain hose (**A**) from dipstick tube (**B**).

− Check that dipstick tube drain for crankcase breather valve is clear of obstructions.

◀ Remove crankcase breather fasteners (**arrows**) and remove crankcase breather valve (**A**) from intake manifold.

− Installation is reverse of removal. Remember to:
  • Check with parts supplier for updated or revised part numbers.
  • Replace engine vent hoses with new.
  • Listen for an audible click when installing engine vent hoses.

Engine coolant temperature (ECT) sensor, replacing

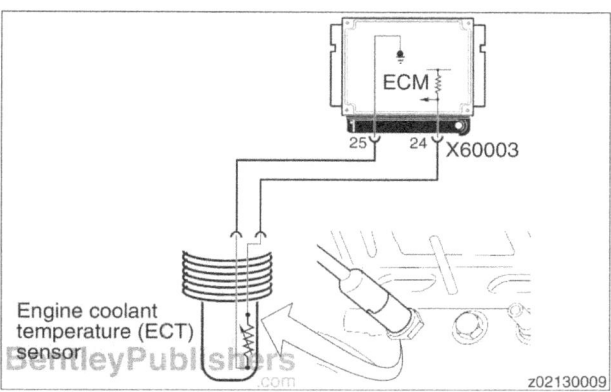
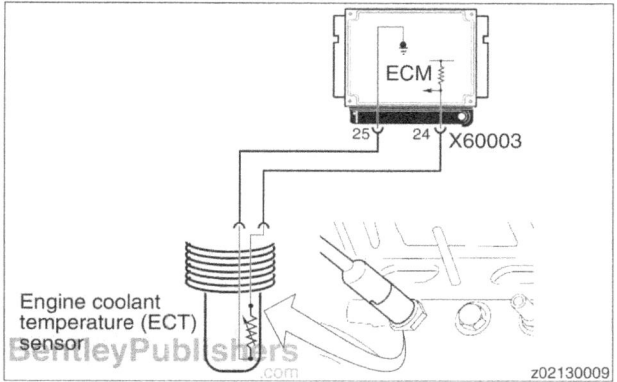

◀ The ECT sensor is an NTC (negative temperature coefficient) sensor. As coolant temperature rises, resistance through the sensor decreases.

The ECM varies ignition timing and air / fuel mixture based on engine coolant temperature. The ECT sensor is supplied a 5 volt reference voltage. The voltage drop across the sensor varies as the coolant temperature (sensor resistance) changes.

If the ECT sensor input is faulty or not plausible, the MIL is illuminated. The ECM assumes a substitute value (80°C / 176°F) to maintain engine operation. The ignition timing is set to a safely conservative basic setting.

The ECT sensor is located below cylinder 6 intake port at the rear of the engine, underneath the intake manifold.

− With engine fully cooled off, remove intake manifold. See **Intake manifold, removing and installing** in this repair group.

◀ Disconnect ECT sensor connector (**arrow**).

− Unscrew ECT sensor from cylinder head. Be prepared to catch small amount of coolant.

− Installation is reverse of removal:
  • Use new copper sealing washer when installing sensor.
  • Replace lost coolant.
  • Check and clear fault codes from ECM memory.

Tightening torque	
Temperature sensor to cylinder head	13 Nm (10 ft-lb)

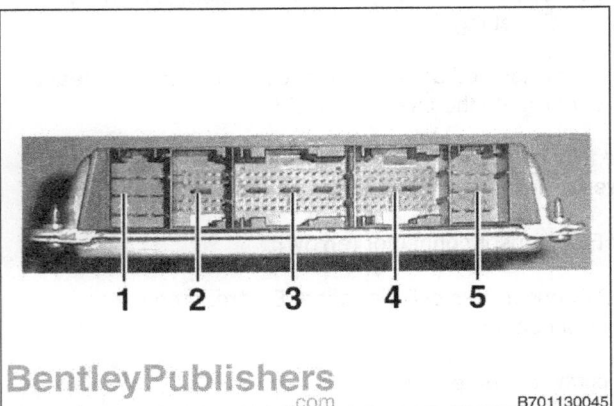

Radiator outlet coolant temperature sensor

◄ The radiator outlet temperature sensor (**inset**) is an NTC (negative temperature coefficient) sensor. As coolant temperature rises, resistance through the sensor decreases.

The ECM varies cooling fan speed based on radiator outlet coolant temperature. The radiator outlet coolant temperature sensor is supplied a 5 volt reference voltage. The voltage drop across the sensor varies as the coolant temperature (sensor resistance) changes.

The radiator outlet temperature sensor is located in the lower radiator hose on the right side of the radiator.

ECM pin assignments (Siemens DME MS45)

◄ The engine control module (ECM) (**arrow**) is located in the left rear of the engine compartment in the E-box.

◄ The ECM has 5 electrical connectors with a total of 134 pins:
- Connector **1** (X60001), 9 pins: Power and grounds
- Connector **2** (X60002), 24 pins: Ancillary signals (oxygen sensors, CAN-bus, etc.)
- Connector **3** (X60003), 52 pins: Engine signals
- Connector **4** (X60004), 40 pins: Vehicle signals
- Connector **5** (X60005), 9 pins: Ignition signals

ECM pin assignments for Siemens DME MS45 are given in **Table b**. This information can be helpful when diagnosing faults to or from the ECM.

Generally, absence of voltage or continuity means there is a wiring or connector problem. Test results with incorrect values do not necessarily mean that a component is faulty. Check for loose, broken or corroded connections and wiring before replacing components. For engine management system electrical schematics, see **ELE Electrical Wiring Diagrams**.

When making checks at the ECM, use a break-out box to allow tests to be made with the connector attached to the ECM. This prevents damage to the small terminals in the connector. As an alternative, the connector housing can be separated so that electrical checks can be made from the back of the connector.

130

> **CAUTION—**
> • Wait at least one minute after switching ignition OFF before removing connector from the ECM. If the connector is removed before this time, residual power may damage the ECM.
> • Connect or disconnect meter probes with the ignition OFF.

Table b. Siemens DME MS45 ECM pin assignments

Connector X60001 9-pin (power, grounds)

Pin	Type	Component or function	Note
1	Terminal 15	Relay, fuel injectors	
2	-	Not used	
3	input / output	TXD signal	Solder connector
4	ground	ECM	
5	ground	ECM	
6	ground	ECM	
7	Terminal 30	Power supply (fuse F105)	Battery voltage (B+) at all times
8	Terminal 87	Power supply (fuse F2)	
9	-	Not used	

Connector X60002 24-pin (ancillary signals)

Pin	Type	Component or function	Note
1	output	Oxygen sensor heater (pre-catalyst cyl. 1-3)	Negative activation
2	output	Oxygen sensor heater (pre-catalyst cyl. 4-6)	Negative activation
3	input / output	Signal CAN bus low	
4	input / output	Signal CAN bus high	
5	-	Not used	
6	output	Oxygen sensor heater (post-catalyst cyl. 1-3)	Negative activation
7	input	Oxygen sensor (pre-catalyst, cyl. 1-3)	Negative Signal
8	input	Oxygen sensor (post-catalyst, cyl. 4-6)	Negative Signal
9	input	Oxygen sensor (pre-catalyst, cyl. 4-6)	Negative Signal
10	input	Oxygen sensor (post-catalyst, cyl. 1-3)	Negative Signal
11	-	Not used	
12	output	Oxygen sensor heater (post-catalyst cyl. 4-6)	Negative activation
13	input	Oxygen sensor (pre-catalyst, cyl. 1-3)	Signal
14	output	Oxygen sensor (post-catalyst, cyl. 4-6)	Signal
15	output	Oxygen sensor (pre-catalyst, cyl. 4-6)	Signal
16	output	Oxygen sensor (post-catalyst, cyl. -3)	Signal
17	-	Not used	
18	-	Not used	
19	input	Oxygen sensor (pre-catalyst, cyl. 1-3)	Signal
20	input	Oxygen sensor (pre-catalyst, cyl. 1-3)	Signal
21	input	Oxygen sensor (pre-catalyst, cyl. 4-6)	Signal

ECM pin assignments (Siemens DME MS45)

Connector X60002 24-pin (ancillary signals) (continued)

Pin	Type	Component or function	Note
22	input	Oxygen sensor (post-catalyst, cyl. 4-6)	Signal
23	Terminal 87	DME system power supply	Battery voltage from DME main relay
24	-	Not used	

Connector X60003 52-pin (engine signals)

Pin	Type	Component or function	Note
1	input	Mass air flow sensor	Signal
2	-	Not used	
3	input	Crankshaft sensor	Signal
4	output	Mass air flow sensor	Voltage supply
5	output	Throttle valve (EDK)	Voltage supply
6	output	Fuel injector 2	Pulsed ground
7	output	Fuel injector 4	Pulsed ground
8	output	Fuel injector 6	Pulsed ground
9	output	VANOS solenoid exhaust	Signal
10	output	VANOS solenoid intake	Signal
11	output	Fuel injector 5	Pulsed ground
12	output	Thermostat heating	Signal
13	output	Fuel injector 1	Pulsed ground
14	ground	Mass air flow sensor	
15	ground	Throttle valve (EDK)	
16	input	Oil pressure switch	Signal
17	-	Not used	
18	-	Not used	
19	input / output	Alternator BSD	Interface
20	-	Not used	
21	output	Fuel tank vent valve	Signal
22	output	Idle speed control valve	Signal
23	output	Idle speed control valve	Signal
24	-	Not used	
25	-	Not used	
26	output	Fuel injector 3	Pulsed ground
27	input	Intake air temperature sensor	Signal
28	input	Coolant temperature sensor	Signal
29	input	Camshaft position sensor 1	Signal
30	input	Camshaft position sensor 2	Signal
31	input	Throttle position signal	Throttle valve (EDK)
32	input	Throttle position signal	Throttle valve (EDK)
33	input	Knock sensor, cyl. 1 - 3	Double knock sensor
34	input	Knock sensor, cyl. 4 - 6	Double knock sensor

Connector X60003 52-pin (engine signals) (continued)

Pin	Type	Component or function	Note
35	ground	Coolant temperature sensor	
36	ground	Camshaft position sensor 1	
37	ground	Crankshaft position sensor	
38	-	Not used	
39	-	Not used	
40	output	DISA changeover valve	Signal
41	-	Not used	
42	output	Throttle valve (EDK)	Signal
43	output	Throttle valve (EDK)	Signal
44	input	Oil temperature sensor	Signal
45	ground	Oil temperature sensor	Signal
46	input	Knock sensor, cyl. 1 - 3	Double knock sensor
47	input	Knock sensor, cyl. 4 - 6	Double knock sensor
48	-	Not used	
49	ground	Camshaft position sensor 2	
50	input	Oil level sensor	Signal
51	-	Not used	
52	-	Not used	

Connector X60004 40-pin (vehicle signals)

Pin	Type	Component or function	Note
1	-	Not used	
2	output	Diagnostic module tank leak (DM-TL) detection	Signal
3	output	Secondary air injection pump relay	Signal
4	output	Activation, electric cooling fan	Signal
5	ground	Mass air flow sensor	
6	-	Not used	
7	ground	Pedal position sensor	
8	input	Pedal position sensor 1	Signal
9	output	Pedal position sensor	Voltage supply
10	output	Activation, fuel pump relay	Signal
11	-	Not used	
12	ground	Pedal position sensor	
13	input	Pedal position sensor 2	Signal
14	output	Pedal position sensor	Voltage supply
15	Input	Mass air flow sensor, secondary air pump (MS 45.1)	Signal
16	-	Not used	

ECM pin assignments (Siemens DME MS45)

Connector X60004 40-pin (vehicle signals) (continued)

Pin	Type	Component or function	Note
17	output	Crankshaft speed signal	OBD II connector or 20-pin DLC
18	output	Exhaust flap	Signal
19	output	E-box cooling fan	Signal
20	output	Diagnostic module tank leak (DM-TL) detection	Signal
21	-	Not used	
22	input	Wheel speed sensor	Signal
23	input	Clutch pedal position switch	Signal
24	input	Brake light switch	Signal
25	-	Not used	
26	Terminal 15	Wake up signal (fuse F29)	Switched power
27	input	Vehicle speed control	Signal
28	input	Brake light switch	Signal
29	output	Activation, A/C compressor relay	Signal
30	output	Fuel tank leakage diagnosis pump (DM-TL)	Signal
31	-	Not used	
32	input / output	Diagnostic link TXD	Signal, diagnostic connector
33	input	Signal for electronic vehicle immobilization	Signal, EWS module
34	-	Not used	
35	-	Not used	
36	input / output	CAN-bus high	Signal
37	input / output	CAN-bus low	Signal
38	ground	Radiator coolant outlet temperature sensor	
39	input	Radiator coolant outlet temperature sensor	Signal
40	-	Not used	

Connector X60005 9-pin (ignition signals)

Pin	Type	Component or function	Note
1	output	Ignition coil 5	Signal
2	-	Not used	
3	-	Not used	
4	output	Ignition coil 3	Signal
5	ground	ECM ground	
6	output	Ignition coil 1	Signal
7	output	Ignition coil 2	Signal
8	output	Ignition coil 4	Signal
9	output	Ignition coil 6	Signal

131 Fuel Injection (N52 Engine)

GENERAL

This repair group covers service and repair of the engine management system for 2007 - 2010 X3 models with N52 engine. See **130 Fuel Injection (M54 engine)** for M54 engine management.

See also:

• **020 Maintenance** for air filter, fuel filter and spark plug replacement

• **100 Engine–General** for engine identification and application information

• **120 Ignition System** for ignition coil, camshaft sensor, crankshaft sensor and knock sensor service

• **160 Fuel Tank and Fuel Pump** for fuel pump and fuel pump relay service, fuel pressure tests and fuel pressure regulator replacement

• **180 Exhaust System** for oxygen sensor service

• **ECL Electrical Component Locations**

• **ELE Electrical Wiring Diagrams**

• **OBD On-Board Diagnostics**

DME applications

BMW X3 models are equipped with digital motor electronics (DME), also known as Motronic. In these systems, fuel injection and ignition are controlled by an integrated engine control module (ECM). Application information for DME systems is in **Table a**.

Table a. X3 engine management applications			
Year, model	Engine code	Engine management	Features
2007 - 2010			
3.0si, 30i	N52	Siemens MSV80	Valvetronic, Double VANOS

Warnings and cautions

> *WARNING—*
>
> • *The fuel system is designed to retain pressure even when the ignition is OFF. When working with the fuel system, loosen the fuel lines slowly to allow residual fuel pressure to dissipate. Avoid spraying fuel. Use shop towels to capture leaking fuel.*
>
> • *Fuel in fuel lines is under pressure (approx. 3 - 5 bar or 45 - 75 psi) and may be expelled forcibly. Do not smoke or work near heaters or other fire hazards. Keep a fire extinguisher handy.*
>
> • *Unscrew the fuel tank cap to release pressure in the tank before working on fuel lines.*
>
> • *Plug open fuel lines and fittings.*
>
> • *Before beginning work on the fuel system, place a fire extinguisher in the vicinity of the work area.*
>
> • *Work only on the fuel system when engine temperature is below 40°C (104°F).*
>
> • *Fuel is highly flammable. When working around fuel, do not disconnect wires that could cause electrical sparks. Do not smoke or work near heaters or other fire hazards.*
>
> • *Wear eye protection and protective clothing to avoid injuries from contact with fuel.*
>
> • *When working on an open fuel system, wear suitable hand protection, as prolonged contact with fuel can cause illnesses and skin disorders.*
>
> • *Unscrew the fuel tank cap to release pressure in the tank before working on fuel lines.*
>
> • *Do not use a work light with an incandescent bulb near fuel. Fuel may spray on the hot bulb causing a fire.*
>
> • *Make sure the work area is properly ventilated.*
>
> • *The ignition system produces high voltages that can be fatal. Avoid contact with exposed terminals. Use extreme caution when working on a car with the ignition switched ON or the engine running.*

DRIVEABILITY TROUBLESHOOTING

The self-diagnostic DME engine management systems monitor and store diagnostic trouble codes (DTCs). If the malfunction indicator light (MIL) illuminates, it indicates that an emissions-related fault has occurred and that one or more DTCs are stored in the engine control module (ECM).

◀ If faults arise, or if the MIL is illuminated, begin troubleshooting by connecting a suitable scan tool to the OBD II plug under the dashboard. The capabilities of OBD II software has the potential to save diagnostic time and avoid incorrect component replacement. See **On-board diagnostics** in this repair group.

Basic engine settings

Idle speed, idle mixture (%CO), and ignition timing are not adjustable. The DME system is adaptive and automatically compensates for changes in the engine due to age, minor wear or small problems such as a disconnected vacuum hose. However, the adaptive range is limited. Once the limits are exceeded, driveability problems become noticeable.

Poor initial driveability may be encountered when the battery is disconnected and reconnected. When the battery is disconnected, ECM adaptive memory may be reset. The system readapts after about ten minutes of driving.

System voltage

Digital motor electronics (DME) requires that the system (battery) voltage be maintained within a narrow range of DC voltage. DC voltage levels beyond or below the operating range, or any AC voltage in the electrical system can cause driveability issues.

When troubleshooting an illuminated MIL, make sure the battery is charged and capable of delivering all its power to the electrical system. An undercharged battery can amplify AC alternator output ripple.

To make a quick check of battery charge, measure voltage across battery terminals with all cables attached and ignition OFF. A fully charged battery measures 12.6 volts or slightly more, compared to 12.15 volts for a battery with a 25% charge. Check battery terminals for corrosion or loose cable connections. See **121 Battery, Starter, Alternator**.

The DME system is sensitive to small increases in resistance. The electrical system is subject to corrosion, vibration and wear. Faults or corrosion in the wiring harness and connectors can lead to fault codes being set in the DME as well as difficult to diagnose driveability issues.

Loose or damaged connectors can cause intermittent problems, especially small terminals in ECM connectors. Disconnect wiring harness connectors to check for corrosion, and use electrical cleaning spray to remove contaminants.

Main grounds

Good grounds are critical to DME operation. If a ground point has no visible faults but is still suspect, measure the voltage drop across the connection. A large voltage drop means high resistance. Clean or repair the connection and retest. For voltage drop testing, see **600 Electrical System-General**. For ground locations, see **ECL Electrical Component Locations**.

On-board diagnostics

On-board diagnostics (OBD II) software and hardware is incorporated in the engine management systems. The OBD II system monitors components that influence exhaust and evaporative emissions. If a problem is detected, the OBD II system stores the a diagnostic trouble code (DTC) and condition.

If vehicle emissions levels exceed Federally mandated criteria, the OBD II system illuminates the malfunction indicator light (MIL) in the instrument cluster.

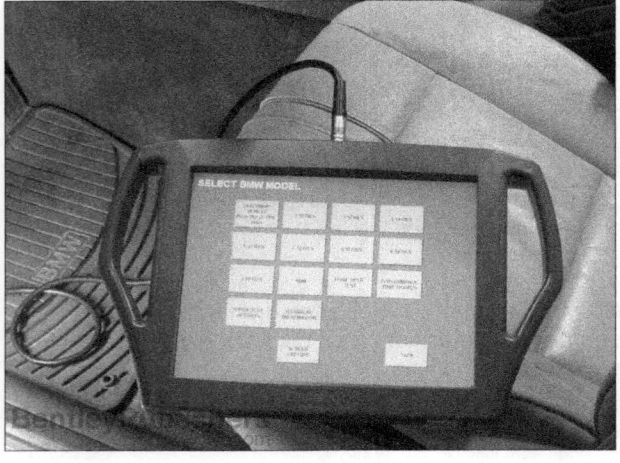

Professional diagnostic scan tools include the factory BMW ISTA system, Autologic Diagnostics and a small number of aftermarket BMW-specific tools.

In addition to professional scan tools, there are inexpensive generic OBD II scan tool units available. Although these have limited capabilities, they can greatly aid the diagnosis of engine related faults.

NOTE—

* *DTCs must erased using a scan tool. Removing the ECM connector or disconnecting the battery does not erase DTC memory.*

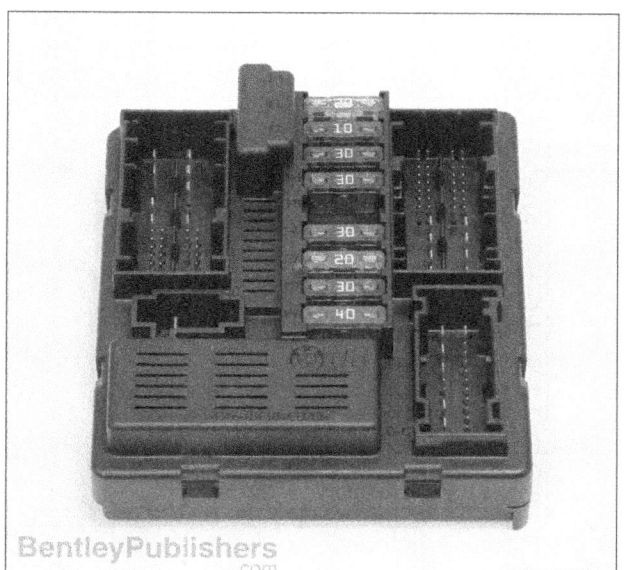

BX30131003

ENGINE MANAGEMENT POWER SUPPLY

Integrated voltage supply module (IVM)

The Integrated Voltage Supply Module (IVM) (A6009) serves as a central power supply for the engine control module (A6000), electronic transmission control (EGS), and dynamic stability control (DSC). The relays contained within the IVM are non-replaceable. If a faulty relay is suspected the complete IVM must be replaced. The following relays are contained as part of the IVM:

- DME main relay
- Variable valve timing relay
- Fuel injector relay
- Reversing light relay

See also:

- **Power supply fuses** in this repair group for IVM fuse applications.
- **ECL Electrical Component Locations** for E-box access information.

DME power supply circuit

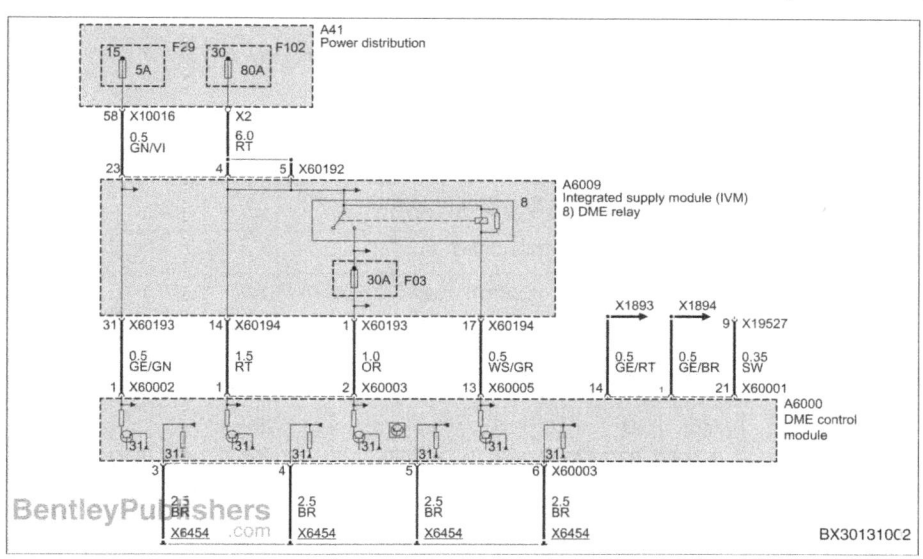

BX30131002

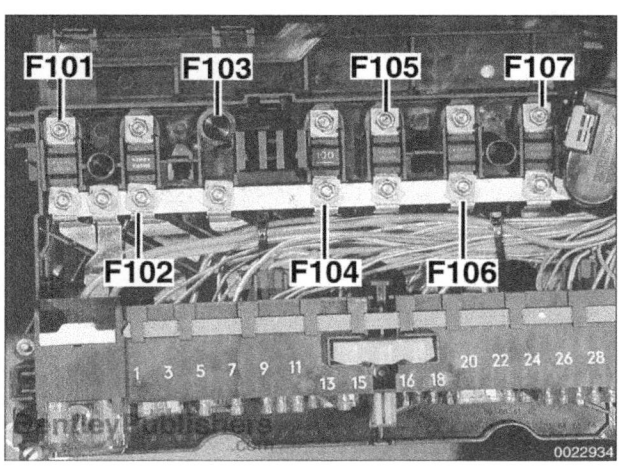

0022934

Power supply fuses

◀ **A41**: fuse and relay panel, behind glove compartment:
- **F102** 80A:
  Integrated supply module (IVM) (A6009)
- **F29** 5A:
  Integrated supply module (IVM) (A6009)

Power supply fuses

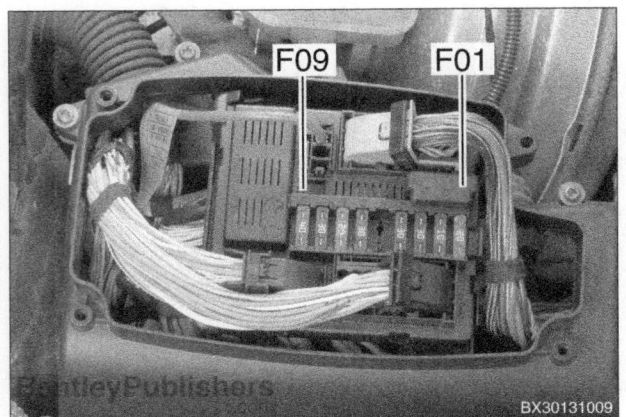

◄ Integrated voltage supply module (IVM) (A6009) is in the E-box, left rear engine compartment. IVM fuse ratings are in **Table b**.

Table b. Fuse applications, integrated voltage supply module (IVM) (A6009)

Fuse	Rating in amps	Protected circuits
F01	20	Crankshaft sensor (B6203a) Intake camshaft sensor (B6214a) Exhaust camshaft sensor B6224a) Vanos solenoid valve, intake (Y6275) Vanos solenoid valve, exhaust (Y6276) DISA controller 1 (Y6540) DISA controller 2 (Y6541) Heated air mass meter (B6207b) Characteristic map thermostat (Y6279) Electric coolant pump (M6035) Oil condition sensor (B62540a) Fuel tank vent valve (Y6120)
F02	10	Exhaust flap (Y198) Relay for A/C compressor (K19) DMTL pump (M119a), Power distribution (A41) Dynamic stability control (A65a) DSC sensor (B75) Steering angle sensor (A68) E-box fan (M6506)
F03	30	Relay, variable valve timing gear
F04	20	Crankshaft breather heating (E65390) Oxygen sensors
F05	-	not used
F06	30	Ignition coils (T6151 - T6156)
F07	20	Fuel injectors (Y6101 - Y6106)
F08	30	Electric coolant pump (M6035)
F09	40	Electronic control unit (ECU)

SIEMENS DME MSV80 (N52 ENGINE)

DME engine management system description

The DME manages and monitors the following functions:

Air
- Electronic throttle
- Mass air flow
- Resonance-turbulence intake control
- Valvetronic II

Fuel
- Fuel supply
- Fuel injection

Ignition
- Direct ignition
- Knock control
- Primary / secondary ignition monitoring

Emissions
- OBD II compliance
- Pre and post-catalyst oxygen sensors
- Electrically heated DME-mapped thermostat
- Misfire detection
- Evaporative emission control and leak detection
- Malfunction indicator light (MIL)

Performance controls
- Dual VANOS control
- Output of injection signal (TI) for fuel economy gauge
- Output of engine rpm (TD) for tachometer
- A/C compressor control
- Electric radiator cooling fan
- CAN-bus communication
- Immobilizer system communication (EWS)
- Dynamic stability control (DSC) interface
- Cruise control
- ECM programming

Engine control module (ECM)

◄ The engine control module (ECM) (**arrow**) is mounted in the electronics box (E-box) at the left rear of the engine compartment.

BX80131010

DME engine management system description

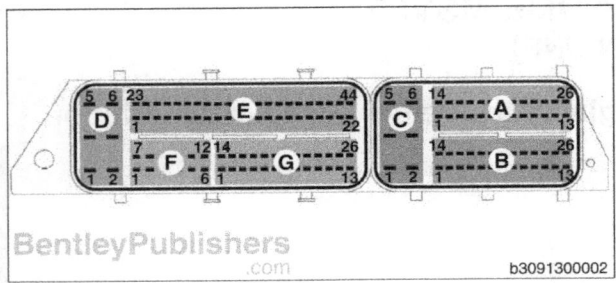

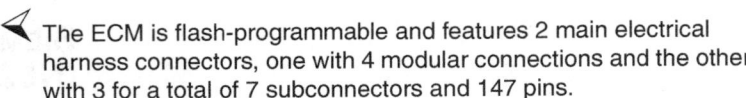 The ECM is flash-programmable and features 2 main electrical harness connectors, one with 4 modular connections and the other with 3 for a total of 7 subconnectors and 147 pins.

- **A:** X60001 (signals)
- **B:** X60002 (signals)
- **C:** X60003 (voltage, ground supply)
- **D:** X60004 (valvetronic)
- **E:** X60005 (signals)
- **F:** X60006 (ignition coils)
- **G:** X60007 (signals)

The EEPROM (chip) in the ECM is coded to the vehicle. The ECM cannot be swapped for testing purposes.

Fuel metering

The ECM meters pressurized fuel by changing the opening time (pulse width) of the fuel injectors. The exact amount of fuel injected is determined by the amount of time the injectors are open. To ensure that injector pulse width is the only factor that determines fuel metering, fuel pump pressure is maintained by a pressure regulator. The injectors are mounted to a common fuel rail.

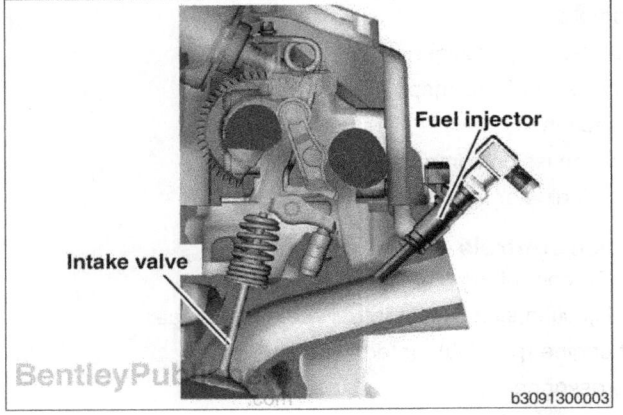

The fuel injectors are mounted into a machined bore in the cylinder head. This design allows the fuel injectors to be closely mounted to the intake valves. The injectors are a compact design with a resistance value of approximately 12 ohms each.

The ECM monitors engine operating conditions to determine injector opening duration. Each injector can be individually controlled for cylinder selective fuel trim.

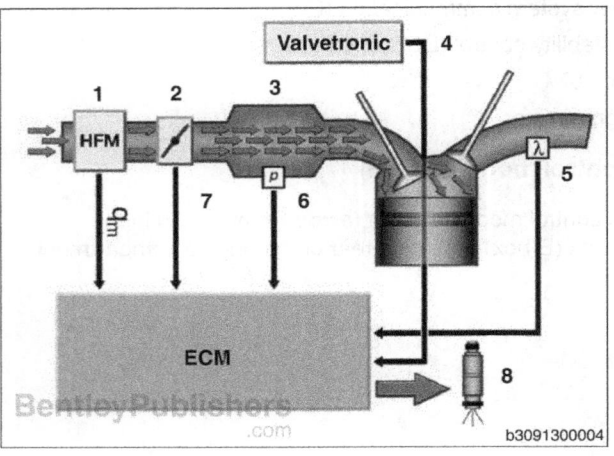

Air entering the engine passes through a pleated paper element in the air filter housing. Intake air mass is then measured by a mass air flow sensor. A reference current is used to heat a thin film in the sensor when the engine is running. The current needed to hold the temperature of the film constant is used to calculate the mass of the intake air.

1. Air mass measurement (HFM)
2. Throttle valve
3. Intake manifold
4. Variable intake valve lift (Valvetronic)
5. Residual oxygen measurement in exhaust
6. Intake manifold vacuum
7. Engine speed
8. Injection timing

Idle speed control

◄ The ECM controls Idle speed by varying intake valve lift via the Valvetronic system.

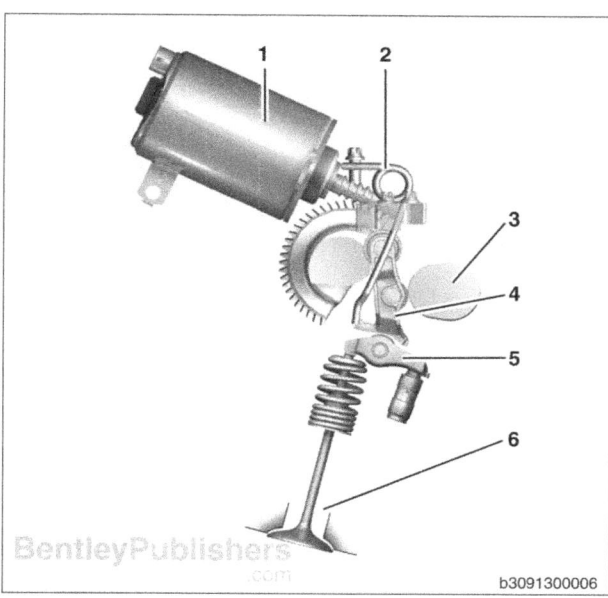

1. Valvetronic motor
2. Return spring
3. Intake camshaft
4. Intermediate lever
5. Intake rocker arm
6. Intake valve

Idle speed is not adjustable. The basic functions and parameters of idle speed control are as follows:

• Control of cold air intake volume.
• Smooth idle speeds regardless of load and inputs.
• Smooth transition from acceleration to deceleration.

Idle speed stabilization is active during the following conditions:

• Engine warm up
• Heating or A/C activation
• Drive gear selected (automatic transmission)
• Varying cooling fan speeds

Throttle control

 The throttle module (EDK) is not needed for engine load control, which is carried out by the Valvetronic function of the ECM. However, the throttle may be slightly closed to allow sufficient manifold vacuum for the crankcase ventilation and canister purge systems.

The EDK motor is pulse width modulated by the ECM to open and close the throttle plate. The throttle plate is also closed by a fail-safe return spring. Two integrated potentiometers in the EDK housing provide feedback to the ECM for throttle plate angle as the EDK motor is operated.

After replacing the throttle housing, use BMW scan tool to reset adaptation values.

Knock (detonation) control

Knock sensors monitor and control ignition knock through the ECM. The knock sensors function like microphones and are able to convert mechanical vibration (knock) into electrical signals. The ECM is programmed to react to frequencies that are characteristic of engine knock and adapt the ignition timing point accordingly.

Knock sensor replacement is covered in **120 Ignition System**.

Air filter housing and ducts, removing and installing

Air filter housing and ducts, removing and installing

For air filter element replacement, see **020 Maintenance**.

◄ Unclip fresh air intake tube at ends and remove.

◄ Working at air filter housing:

• Remove electrical connector (**A**) from mass air flow sensor.

• Loosen hose clamp (**arrow**) at mass air flow sensor and detach air intake duct from filter housing.

• Lift air filter housing straight up to release rubber grommets from plastic support mounts to remove.

◄ Loosen clamp (**arrow**). Remove intake duct from throttle housing elbow.

◄ Loosen clamp (**arrow**). Remove elbow from throttle housing

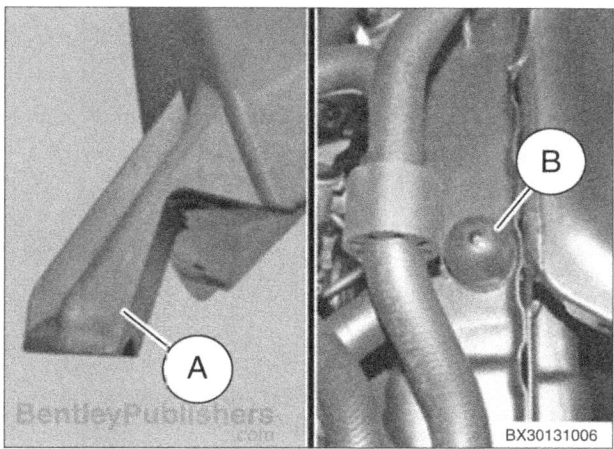

◄ Installation is reverse of removal, making sure to correctly position air cleaner housing (**A**) on rubber mount (**B**).

— After reinstalling, check and clear fault codes from ECM memory.

Mass air flow, measurement

The N52 engines utilize a digital mass air flow sensor. In this system, a duty cycle signal corresponds to changes in intake air mass. This eliminates the need for signal conversion in the ECM.

If there is no output signal from the air flow sensor, the ECM operates the engine using throttle position and engine rpm inputs. A faulty air flow sensor illuminates the MIL.

◄ The intake air temperature sensor is integrated into the mass air flow sensor. The sensor is an NTC thermistor that receives a 5 volt reference current and ground from the ECM.

A faulty air flow sensor can produce the following problems:
• Difficult to restart when engine is hot.
• Engine starts then stalls.
• Engine starts and runs only with accelerator pedal depressed.

Mass air flow sensor, replacing

— Switch ignition OFF and remove key.

◀ Working at left front of engine compartment at air filter housing:
  • Carefully lift clip and disconnect mass air flow sensor electrical connector (**A**).
  • Remove fasteners (**arrows**).
  • Remove mass air flow sensor (**B**).

— Check intake ducts for cracks and vacuum leaks.

— Installation is reverse of removal.
  • Inspect O-ring and replace if necessary.

— After reinstalling, check and clear fault codes from ECM memory.

Tightening torques	
Mass air flow sensor to housing	3 Nm (26 in-lb)

Accelerator pedal module (PWG)

There is no mechanical (cable) link between the accelerator pedal and the throttle plate.

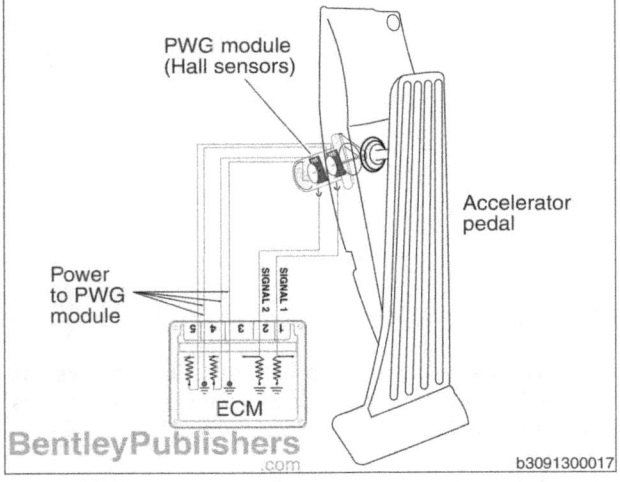

◀ The accelerator pedal module (PWG) at the pedal assembly communicates pedal position directly to the ECM. The module provides two variable voltage signals (via two Hall sensors) to the ECM for pedal position and rate of movement.

The ECM provides an independent voltage and ground supply for each Hall sensor. Each Hall sensor is provided with 5 volts and ground. As the accelerator pedal is moved from rest to full throttle, the sensors produce a variable voltage signal.

The output of the Hall sensors is checked for plausibility. The voltage range of Hall sensor 1 is approximately 0.5 to 4.5 volts. Hall sensor 2 ranges from approximately 0.5 to 2.5 volts.

The ECM adapts to throttle angle voltage at idle speed. If the accelerator pedal module must be replaced the ECM adaptation values must be reset and a throttle angle adaptation procedure must be performed using a factory BMW scan tool, or the vehicle will not start.

> **CAUTION—**
> • If the adaptation process is not completed correctly, the engine does not start.

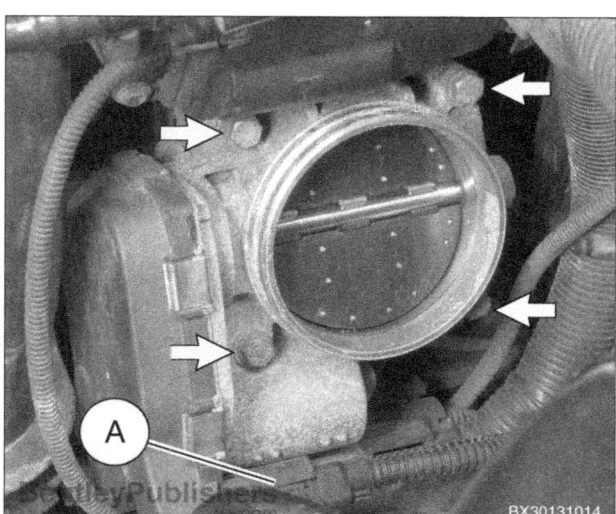

BX30131014

Throttle housing (EDK), replacing

– Switch ignition OFF and remove key.

– Remove air filter housing and air intake ducts. See **Air filter housing and ducts, removing and installing** in this repair group.

◀ Working at left side of intake manifold:
  • Disconnect electrical connector (**A**).
  • Remove fasteners (**arrows**) and remove throttle housing.

– Installation is reverse of removal.

– Replace profile gasket (sealing O-ring) between throttle assembly and intake manifold.

Tightening torques	
Throttle housing to intake manifold	9 Nm (80 in-lb)

– Reattach throttle assembly connector with care. It is possible to twist the connector before plugging it in. This can cause damage to the harness and connector.

– After reinstalling, check and clear fault codes from ECM memory. Reset throttle plate adaptation values following scan tool on-screen instructions.

Valvetronic motor, removing and installing

– Switch ignition OFF and remove key.

– Remove ignition coil cover. See **020 Maintenance**.

– Disconnect battery negative (-) cable.

> **CAUTION—**
> • *Prior to disconnecting the battery, read the battery disconnection cautions in* **001 Warnings and Cautions**.

◀ Disconnect electrical connectors from ignition coils and Valvetronic motor (**arrows**).

  • Remove ignition coils on either side of Valvetronic motor. See **120 Ignition System**

BX30131015

Valvetronic motor, removing and installing

◀ Slowly and carefully screw valvetronic motor in clockwise direction (**arrow**) until you feel the resistance of eccentric shaft stop.

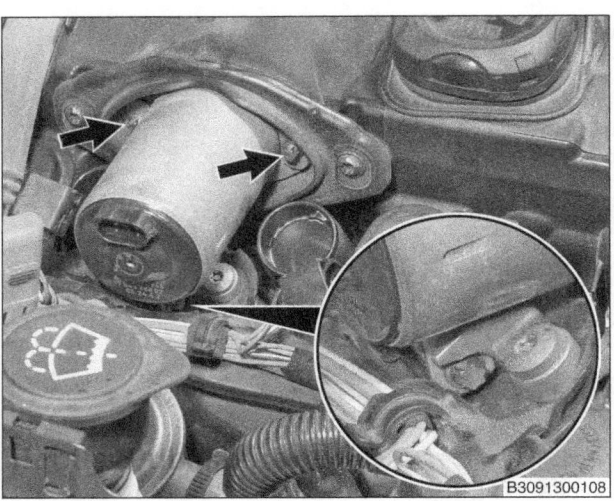

◀ Remove valvetronic motor fasteners (**arrows**) and Valvetronic motor support bracket fastener (**inset**).

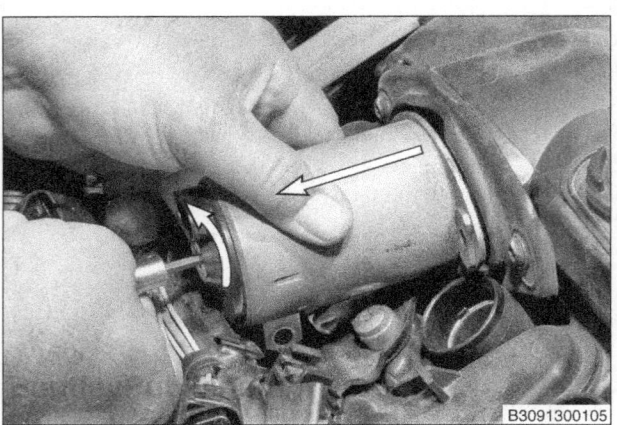

◀ Slowly and carefully screw valvetronic motor in counterclockwise direction while sliding motor out of cylinder head cover (**arrow**).

— Installation is reverse of removal. Remember to:
  - Replace aluminum fasteners.
  - Route ignition coil harness correctly

Tightening torque	
Valvetronic motor to valve cover / cylinder head	10 Nm (7 ft-lb)

— After reinstalling, check and clear fault codes from ECM memory.

Fuel rail and injectors, removing and installing

Fuel injectors receive voltage from the fuel injector relay, contained as part of the Integrated Voltage Supply Module (IVM). The engine control module (ECM) controls injector opening by activating the ground circuit for the injector valve solenoids.

– Switch ignition OFF and remove key.

– For a quick check of injectors, run engine and touch each injector with a screwdriver or stethoscope. You should feel a vibration or hear a buzzing. Switch engine OFF.

– Disconnect battery negative (-) cable.

> **CAUTION—**
> • Prior to disconnecting the battery, read the battery disconnection cautions in **001 Warnings and Cautions**.

– Remove upper engine covers. See **020 Maintenance**.

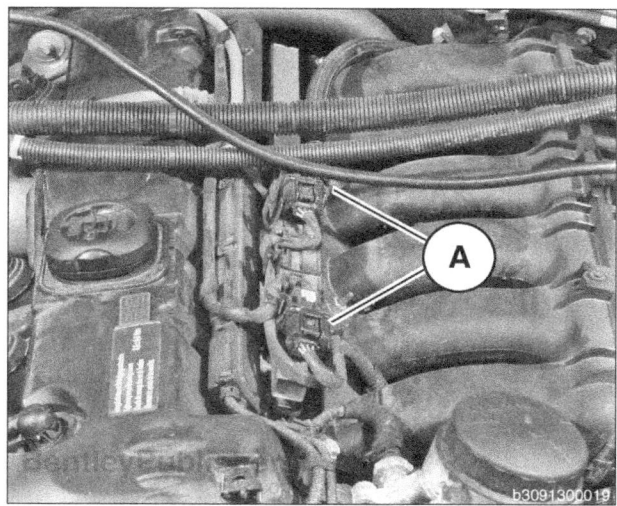

◄ Working above engine, detach oxygen sensor connectors (**A**) and unclip wiring harness from holder.

> **CAUTION—**
> • Be sure to mark oxygen sensor connectors so that they can be reassembled as before.

– Unclip oxygen sensor connector harness from fuel rail and remove.

◄ Unscrew Schræder valve cap (**arrow**) from fuel rail.
  • Unscrew fuel tank cap to release pressure.
  • Using a brief burst of compressed air (maximum of 3 bar or 43.5 psi), blow fuel back into fuel tank.

> **WARNING—**
> • Wrap a clean shop towel around fitting before removing Schræder valve. Fuel in lines and rail is under pressure (approx. 3 - 5 bar or 45 - 75 psi) and may be expelled forcibly.
> • Unscrew fuel tank cap before working on fuel lines.
> • Do not smoke or work near heaters or other fire hazards. Keep a fire extinguisher handy.
> • Plug open fuel lines and fittings.

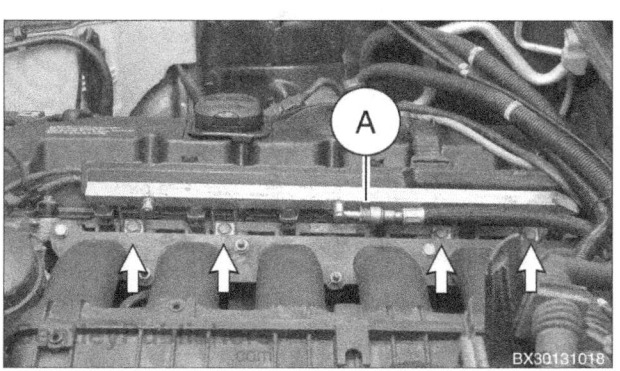

◄ Working at fuel rail:
  • Remove fuel line by pressing release clip (**A**) into fitting and pulling fuel line off of fuel rail.
  • Remove fasteners (**arrows**) and remove fuel rail.

> **WARNING—**
> • Wrap a clean shop towel around fitting before disconnecting. Residual fuel pressure may be present in fuel lines.

Intake manifold, removing and installing

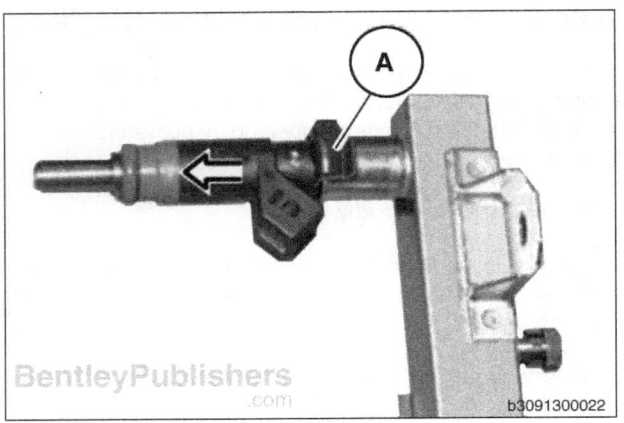

◀ Remove individual injectors:
- Pry retaining clip from injector (**A**).
- Pull injector from rail (**arrow**).

— Installation is reverse of removal. Remember to:
- Fit new sealing O-rings when installing injectors. For ease of installation, lightly lubricate O-rings with assembly lubricant.
- Check that injector electrical connections are correctly fitted and that injectors are fully seated prior to installing fuel rail mounting bolts.
- Replace wire ties.

Tightening torque	
Fuel rail to cylinder head	10 Nm (7 ft-lb)

— After reinstalling, check and clear fault codes from ECM memory.

Intake manifold, removing and installing

— Place hood in service position. See **410 Fenders, Engine Hood**.

— Disconnect negative (–) cable from battery.

> **CAUTION—**
> • *Prior to disconnecting battery, read battery disconnection cautions in* **001 Warnings and Cautions**.

— Remove air cleaner housing and fresh air ducts. See **130 Fuel Injection**.

— Remove brace from strut towers. See **310 Front Suspension**.

— Remove housing for interior ventilation microfilter. See **640 Heating and Air-conditioning**.

◀ Remove left partition wall:
- Remove rubber seal from top of heater bulkhead.
- Release vacuum line (**A**) for power brake booster. Disconnect line from power brake booster and remove from partition wall with electrical wiring.
- Release plastic locks (**arrows**) and pull trim slightly forward.
- Pull partition wall up to remove.

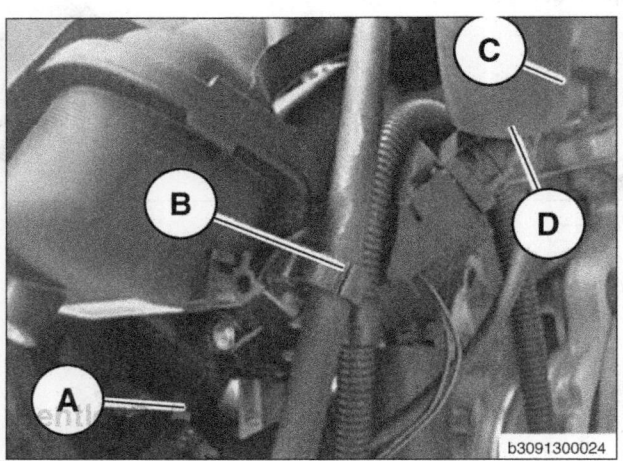

◀ Working at left side and underneath intake manifold:
- Open harness holder (**B**).
- Disconnect electrical connector (**A**).
- Release both crankcase breather connections (**C,D**).

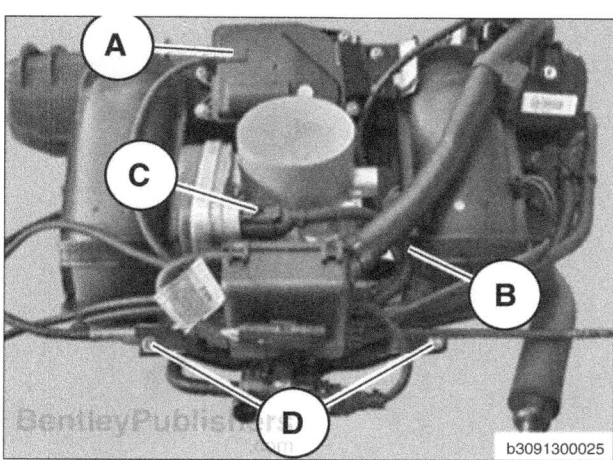

◄ Working at left side and underneath intake manifold:
- Disconnect electrical connectors (**A,C**).
- Remove fasteners (**D**).
- Detach engine wiring harness (**B**) from intake manifold and lay aside.

◄ Disconnect electrical connector (**A**) at oil pressure switch (**B**).

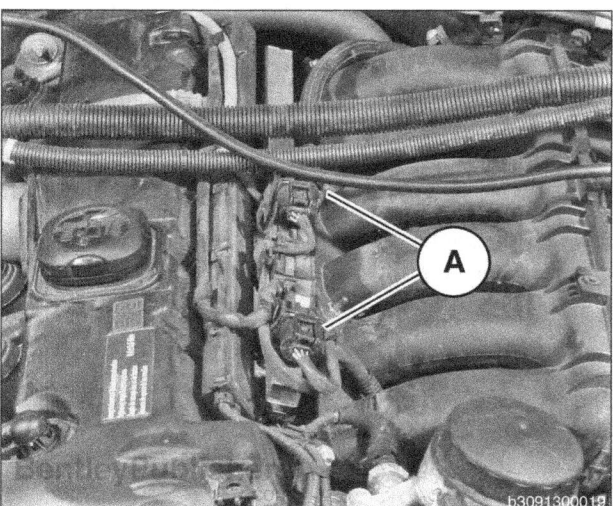

◄ Working above engine, detach oxygen sensor connectors (**A**) and unclip wiring harness from holder.

> **CAUTION—**
> - *Be sure to mark oxygen sensor connectors so that they can be reassembled as before.*

Crankcase breather valve

◄ Working above engine, remove fasteners (**arrows**)

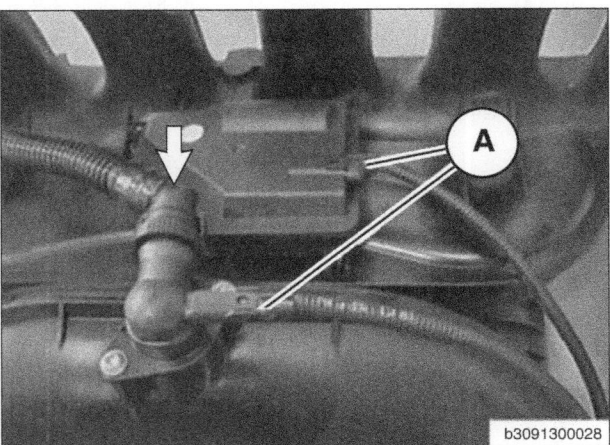

◄ Raise intake manifold approximately 10 cm (4 in). Working underneath:

- Disconnect electrical connector (**A**).
- Release fuel tank vent line (**arrow**) behind throttle valve assembly.
- Raise and remove intake manifold.

> **CAUTION—**
> - *Plug open intake ports to prevent parts or debris from falling into the engine intake.*

– Installation is reverse of removal. Remember to replace all seals.

Tightening torque	
Manifold to cylinder head	15 Nm (11 ft-lb)

Crankcase breather valve

◄ The N52 engine is equipped with an internal crankcase ventilation system inside the plastic cylinder head cover. The breather valve is part of the cover and not serviceable. See **113 Cylinder Head Removal and Installation** for cylinder head cover replacement.

If the diaphragm valve in the breather housing leaks, full intake vacuum may be applied to the crankcase, resulting in excessive oil consumption, irregular idle, whistling or howling noises or oil smoke in the exhaust.

A faulty crankcase breather valve causes significant deviations in crankcase pressure. Crankcase pressure can be measured using a digital automotive manometer.

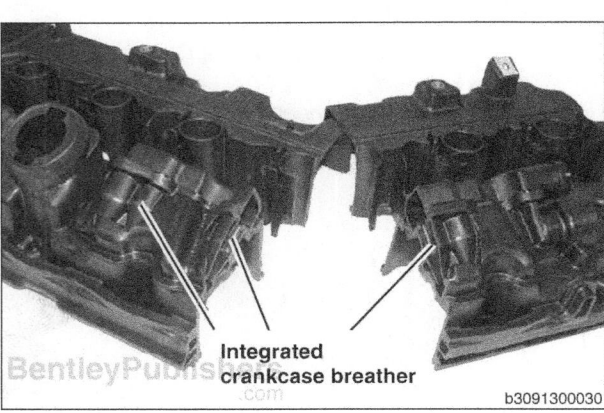

Integrated crankcase breather

Crankcase ventilation specifications (N52 engine)	
Operating pressure range	33±10% mbar
Deviation to ambient pressure:	+20 mbar to -60 mbar
Fault condition: • Clogged crankcase vent • Internal leak in crankcase vent	+100 mbar over ambient press. -170 mbar under ambient press,

Engine coolant temperature (ECT) sensor, replacing

The engine coolant temperature (ECT) sensor is an NTC (negative temperature coefficient) sensor. As coolant temperature rises, resistance through the sensor decreases.

The ECM varies ignition timing and air / fuel mixture based on engine coolant temperature. The ECT sensor is supplied a 5 volt reference voltage. The voltage drop across the sensor varies as the coolant temperature (sensor resistance) changes.

If the ECT sensor input is faulty or not plausible, the MIL is illuminated when OBD II fault criteria are exceeded. The ECM assumes a substitute value (80°C / 176°F) to maintain engine operation. The ignition timing is set to a safely conservative basic setting.

The ECT sensor is located in the left front of the engine near oil cooler.

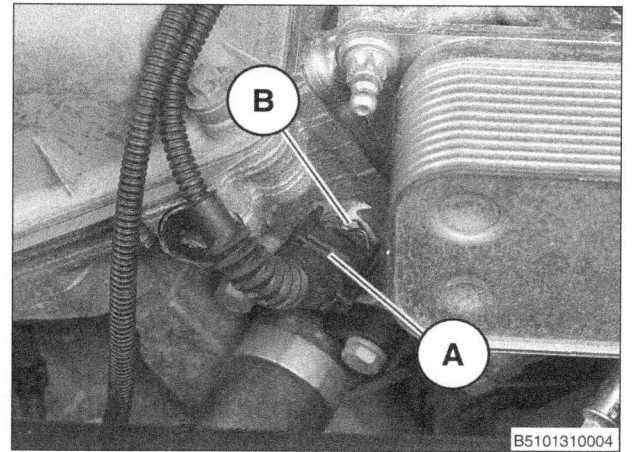

◄ With engine fully cooled off, disconnect ECT sensor connector (**A**).

− Unscrew ECT sensor (**B**) from cylinder head. Be prepared to catch small amount of coolant.

− Installation is reverse of removal:
  • Use new copper sealing washer when installing sensor.
  • Replace lost coolant.

Tightening torque	
Temperature sensor to cylinder head	18 Nm (13 ft-lb)

− After reinstalling, check and clear fault codes from ECM memory.

Engine vacuum pump, removing and installing

◄ To provide proper engine vacuum to the brake vacuum booster under all engine operating condiitons, a chain-driven vacuum pump is fitted to the engine. The vacuum pump is mounted beneath the intake maniold on the front left side of the engine.

BMW special tools are recommended to lock the sprocket in place when removing the sprocket center bolt.

− Remove engine drive belt and drive belt tensioner. See **020 Maintenance**.

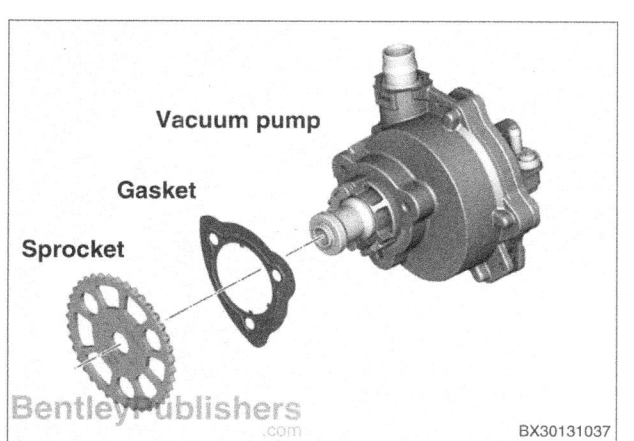

− Pry out sealing cover for vacuum pump from front of engine to access sprocket.

− Remove intake manifold. See **Intake manifold, removing and installing**.

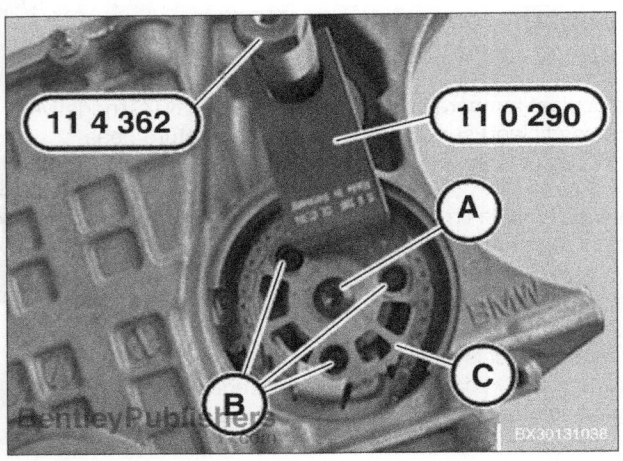

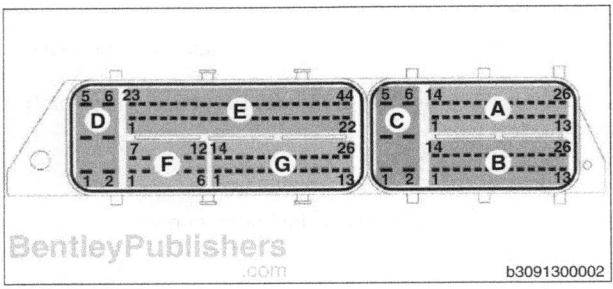

◄ Remove sprocket and pump

- Rotate crankshaft at vibration damper center bolt (in normal engine rotation) until holes in sprocket align with pump mounting bolts.
- Mount BMW special tool 11 4 362 to engine. Lock sprocket in place using BMW special tools 11 0 290.
- Remove sprocket mounting bolt (**A**).
- Remove pump mounting screws (**B**) while supporting pump from falling. Remove vacuum pump towards rear.

– Installation is reverse of removal. Replace gasket.

Tightening torque	
Vacuum pump to engine	10 Nm (7 ft-lb)
Vaccum pump sprocket to pump shaft	66 Nm (49 ft-lb)

ECM pin assignments

◄ The ECM has 2 main electrical harness connectors, one with 4 modular connections and the other with 3 for a total of 7 sub connectors and 147 pins.

- **A:** X60001 (signals)
- **B:** X60002 (signals)
- **C:** X60003 (voltage, ground supply)
- **D:** X60004 (valvetronic)
- **E:** X60005 (signals)
- **F:** X60006 (ignition coils)
- **G:** X60007 (signals)

ECM pin assignments are given in **Table c**. Test results with incorrect values do not necessarily mean that a component is faulty. Check for loose, broken or corroded connections and wiring before replacing components. For engine management system electrical schematics, see **ELE Electrical Wiring Diagrams**.

When making checks at the ECM, use great care not to distort or damage small terminals and pins. The connector housing can be separated so that electrical checks can be made from the back of the connector.

> **CAUTION—**
> - *Wait at least one minute after switching ignition OFF before removing connector from ECM. If connector is removed before this time, residual power in the system may damage the ECM.*
> - *Connect or disconnect meter probes with the ignition OFF.*

◄ The engine control module (ECM) (**arrow**) is located in the right rear of the engine compartment in the E-box.

Table c. Siemens DME MSV80 ECM pin assignments

Connector X60001 26-pin (signals)

Pin	Type	Component or function	Note
1	input/output	Signal PT-CAN low	Powertrain CAN-bus
2	-	Not used	
3	-	Not used	
4	input	Brake light signal	Brake light switch
5	output	Exhaust flap signal	Exhaust flap
6	-	Not used	
7	input	Accelerator pedal module signal	Accelerator pedal module
8	output	Electric fan signal	Electric engine cooling fan
9	output	Radiator shutter solenoid	Signal
10	ground	Accelerator pedal module	Accelerator pedal module
11	output	Accelerator pedal module supply voltage	Accelerator pedal module
12	-	Not used	
13	-	Not used	
14	input/output	Signal PT-CAN high	Powertrain CAN-bus
15	input	Signal, electronic vehicle immobilization	Electronic vehicle immobilizer (EWS)
16	input	Brake light test signal	Brake light switch
17	input	Right rear wheel speed sensor signal	Connector X10186 (right rear wheel speed sensor)
18	input	Clutch switch signal	Clutch switch module
19	-	Not used	
20	input	Accelerator pedal module signal	Accelerator pedal module
21	output	Speed signal	Diagnostic connector
22	-	Not used	
23	ground	Accelerator pedal module	Accelerator pedal module
24	output	Accelerator pedal module supply voltage	Accelerator pedal module
25	-	Not used	
26	output	E-box fan signal	E-box fan

Connector X60002 26-pin (signals)

Pin	Type	Component or function	Note
1	input	Wake up signal, terminal 15	Fuse F29
2	-	Not used	
3	-	Not used	
4	input	Signal, vehicle speed control	Volute spring
5	input	Oxygen sensor signal	Bank 2 sensor 1
6	input	Oxygen sensor signal	Bank 1 sensor 1
7	input	Oxygen sensor signal	Bank 2 sensor 1
8	input	Oxygen sensor signal	Bank 1 sensor 1
9	input	Oxygen sensor signal	Bank 2 sensor 1
10	ground	Oxygen sensor	Bank 1 sensor 1
11	ground	Oxygen sensor	Bank 2 sensor 1
12	input	Oxygen sensor heating	Bank 1 sensor 1

ECM pin assignments

Connector X60002 26-pin (signals) (continued)

Pin	Type	Component or function	Note
13	input	Oxygen sensor heating	Bank 2 sensor 1
14	-	Not used	
15	input	DMTL valve signal	Diagnosis module for fuel tank leakage
16	input	DMTL pump signal	Diagnosis module for fuel tank leakage
17	input	DMTL heating signal	Diagnosis module for fuel tank leakage
18	input	Oxygen sensor signal	Bank 1 sensor 1
19	input	Oxygen sensor signal	Bank 2 sensor 2
20	input	Oxygen sensor signal	Bank 1 sensor 2
21	output	Compressor enable from DME	Heating / air conditioning system
22	-	Not used	
23	ground	Oxygen sensor	Bank 1 sensor 2
24	input	Oxygen sensor	Bank 2 sensor 2
25	input	Oxygen sensor	Bank 2 sensor 2
26	output	Oxygen sensor	Bank 1 sensor 2

Connector X60003 6-pin (voltage, ground supply)

Pin	Type	Component or function	Note
1	input	Terminal 30	Integrated supply module (IVM)
2	input	Terminal 87	Fuse F03
3	ground	Ground	Ground point
4	ground	Ground	Ground point
5	ground	Ground	Ground point
6	ground	Ground	Ground point

Connector X60004 6-pin (valvetronic)

Pin	Type	Component or function	Note
1	input	Terminal 87	Integrated supply module (IVM)
2	input	Terminal 87	Integrated supply module (IVM)
3	output	Valvetronic actuator signal	Actuator, variable valve timing gear
4	output	Valvetronic actuator signal	Actuator, variable valve timing gear
5	output	Valvetronic actuator signal	Actuator, variable valve timing gear
6	output	Valvetronic actuator signal	Actuator, variable valve timing gear

Connector X60005 44-pin (signals)

Pin	Type	Component or function	Note
1	-	Not used	
2	-	Not used	
3	-	Not used	
4	input	Signal, mass air flow sensor	Mass air flow sensor
5	-	Not used	
6	-	Not used	
7	-	Not used	
8	-	Not used	

Connector X60005 44-pin (signals) (continued)

Pin	Type	Component or function	Note
9	-	Not used	
10	-	Not used	
11	-	Not used	
12	-	Not used	
13	output	DME main relay activation	DME main relay
14	output	Throttle valve voltage supply	Throttle valve
15	input	Throttle valve signal	Throttle valve
16	input	Throttle valve signal	Throttle valve
17	-	Not used	
18	output	DISA changeover valve signal	DISA controller 2
19	input	Knock sensor signal	Knock sensor
20	input	Knock sensor signal	Knock sensor
21	-	Not used	
22	input/output	Signal, CAN bus high	Integrated supply module (IVM)
23	output	Fuel tank vent valve signal	Fuel tank vent valve
24	-	Not used	
25	-	Not used	
26	-	Not used	
27	ground	Mass air flow sensor	Mass air flow sensor
28	input	Intake air temperature sensor signal	Intake air temperature sensor
29	input	Crankshaft position sensor signal	Crankshaft position sensor
30	ground	Crankshaft position sensor	Crankshaft position sensor
31	output	Intake manifold pressure sensor voltage supply	Intake manifold pressure sensor
32	ground	Intake manifold pressure sensor	Intake manifold pressure sensor
33	input	Intake manifold pressure sensor signal	Intake manifold pressure sensor
34	-	Not used	
35	input/output	BSD signal	BSD signal connector
36	input	Throttle valve signal	Throttle valve
37	input	Throttle valve signal	Throttle valve
38	ground	Throttle valve	Throttle valve
39	-	Not used	
40	output	DISA changeover valve signal	DISA controller 1
41	input	Knock sensor signal	Knock sensor
42	input	Knock sensor signal	Knock sensor
43	-	Not used	
44	input/output	Signal, CAN bus low	Integrated supply module (IVM)

Connector X60006 12-pin (ignition coils)

Pin	Type	Component or function	Note
1	output	Ignition coil signal	Ignition coil signal 1
2	output	Ignition coil signal	Ignition coil signal 2
3	output	Ignition coil signal	Ignition coil signal 3

ECM pin assignments

Connector X60006 12-pin (ignition coils) (continued)

Pin	Type	Component or function	Note
4	output	Ignition coil signal	Ignition coil signal 4
5	output	Ignition coil signal	Ignition coil signal 5
6	output	Ignition coil signal	Ignition coil signal 6
7	-	Not used	
8	-	Not used	
9	-	Not used	
10	-	Not used	
11	-	Not used	
12	-	Not used	

Connector X60007 26-pin (signals)

Pin	Type	Component or function	Note
1	output	Fuel injector signal	Fuel injector 1
2	output	Fuel injector signal	Fuel injector 2
3	output	Fuel injector signal	Fuel injector 3
4	input	Engine coolant temperature signal	Engine coolant temperature sensor
5	output	Intake VANOS solenoid signal	Intake VANOS solenoid
6	input	Eccentric shaft sensor signal	Eccentric shaft sensor
7	input	Eccentric shaft sensor signal	Eccentric shaft sensor
8	input	Eccentric shaft sensor signal	Eccentric shaft sensor
9	input	Eccentric shaft sensor signal	Eccentric shaft sensor
10	ground	Wire shielding	Eccentric shaft sensor
11	input	Camshaft position sensor 1 signal	Intake camshaft position sensor
12	input	Camshaft position sensor 2 signal	Exhaust camshaft position sensor
13	input	Oil pressure switch signal	Oil pressure switch
14	output	Fuel injector signal	Fuel injector signal 4
15	output	Fuel injector signal	Fuel injector signal 5
16	output	Fuel injector signal	Fuel injector signal 6
17	ground	Engine coolant temperature sensor	Engine coolant temperature sensor
18	output	Exhaust VANOS solenoid signal	Exhaust VANOS solenoid
19	input	Thermostat signal	Thermostat
20	ground	Eccentric shaft sensor	Eccentric shaft sensor
21	output	Eccentric shaft sensor voltage supply	Eccentric shaft sensor
22	input	Eccentric shaft sensor signal	Eccentric shaft sensor
23	output	Valvetronic actuator relay signal	Valvetronic actuator relay
24	ground	Camshaft position sensor 1	Intake camshaft position sensor
25	ground	Camshaft position sensor 2	Exhaust camshaft position sensor
26	input/output	BSD signal	Electric coolant pump

160 Fuel Tank and Fuel Pump

GENERAL

This repair group covers service information for the fuel supply system.

See also:

- **100 Engine–General** for model year, engine code, and DME applications
- **130 Fuel Injection (M54 Engine)**
- **131 Fuel Injection (N52 Engine)**
- **ECL Electrical Component Locations** for fuel pump fuse and relay access information

Fuel delivery systems

Fuel delivery systems

The fuel injectors are installed in machine-bored holes in the intake manifold. An in-tank electric fuel pump delivers pressure-regulated fuel to the fuel rail.

On M54 engines, the fuel pump is controlled by the DME via a fuel pump relay (K6301).

On N52 engines, the fuel pump is a variable speed pump controlled by the EKP (electric fuel pump control) module and delivers only the amount of fuel needed for engine operation.

Electric fuel pump

An electric fuel pump is mounted in the fuel tank in tandem with the right side fuel level sender. A suction-jet pump is located in the left side of the tank to transfer fuel to the right side. The combined fuel filter / pressure regulator delivers pressurized fuel to the fuel injection system. The system is a non-return design; there is one fuel line to the fuel injectors and excess fuel flows directly from the fuel filter / pressure regulator back into the tank.

Fuel tank

The saddle-shaped plastic fuel tank is mounted underneath the center of the car (under rear seat). Mounted in the fuel tank are the electric fuel pump, fuel filter, fuel pressure regulator, fuel level sending units and suction-jet pump. Connecting lines for the evaporative emission control system are also attached to the tank.

Fuel tank capacity for X3 is listed in **Table a**.

Table a. X3 fuel tank capacity	
Tank capacity	67 liters (17.7 US gal)
Reserve capacity	8 liters (2.1 US gal)

Fuel tank components

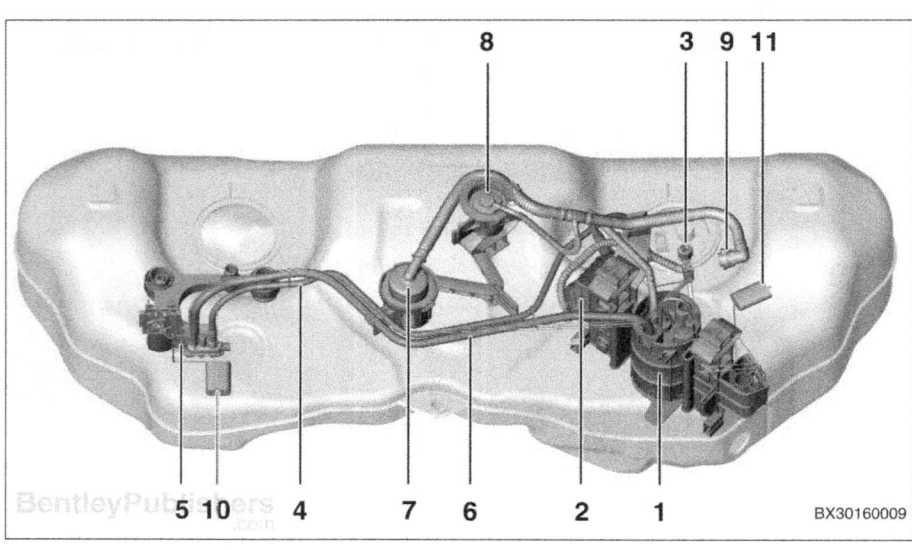

BX30160009

1. Electric fuel pump
2. Fuel filter with pressure regulator
3. Fuel feed
4. Return flow from pressure regulator to left suction-jet pump
5. Left suction-jet pump
6. Return flow from left suction-jet pump to fuel pump
7. Fuel filler breather valve
8. Service breather valve
9. Vent line
10. Left side fuel level sensor
11. Right side fuel level sensor

160

Warnings and Cautions

WARNING—

- *The fuel system is designed to retain pressure even when the ignition is OFF. When working with the fuel system, loosen the fuel lines slowly to allow residual fuel pressure to dissipate. Avoid spraying fuel. Use shop towels to capture leaking fuel.*

- *Before beginning work on the fuel system, place a fire extinguisher in the vicinity of the work area.*

- *Work only on the fuel system when engine temperature is below 40°C (104°F).*

- *Electric fuel pump starts each time a door is opened.*

- *Fuel is highly flammable. When working around fuel, do not disconnect wires that could cause electrical sparks. Do not smoke or work near heaters or other fire hazards.*

- *Wear eye protection, face shield and protective clothing to avoid injuries from contact with fuel.*

- *When working on an open fuel system, wear suitable hand protection, as prolonged contact with fuel can cause illnesses and skin disorders.*

- *Unscrew the fuel tank cap to release pressure in the tank before working on fuel lines.*

- *Do not use a work light with an incandescent bulb near fuel. Fuel may spray on the hot bulb causing a fire.*

- *Make sure the work area is properly ventilated.*

- *Due to risk of personal injury, be sure the engine is cold before beginning work on engine components.*

CAUTION—

- *Prior to disconnecting the battery, read the battery disconnection cautions given in* **001 Warnings and Cautions***.*

- *Before making any electrical tests with ignition switched ON, disable the ignition system as described in* **120 Ignition System***. Be sure the battery is disconnected when replacing components.*

- *To prevent damage to the ignition system or other DME components, including the engine control module (ECM), connect and disconnect wires and test equipment with ignition OFF.*

- *Cleanliness is essential when working with the fuel system. Thoroughly clean the fuel line unions before disconnecting any of the lines. Plug open fuel lines and ports.*

- *Use only clean tools. Keep removed parts clean and sealed or covered with a clean, lint-free cloth, especially if completion of the repair is delayed.*

- *Do not move the car while the fuel system is open.*

- *Avoid using high pressure compressed air to blow out lines and components. High pressure can rupture internal seals and gaskets.*

- *Use new seals, O-rings and hose clamps when replacing fuel system components*

- *Replace aluminum fasteners when loosened.*

- *For reliable identification test fastener with magnet for aluminum composition.*

BX30160001

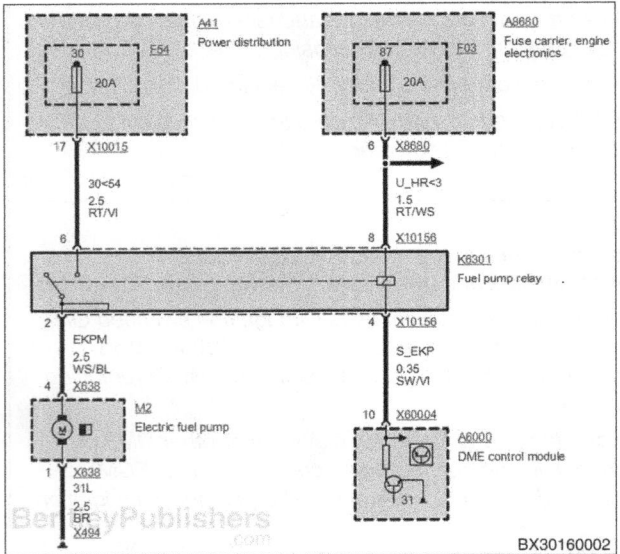

BX30160002

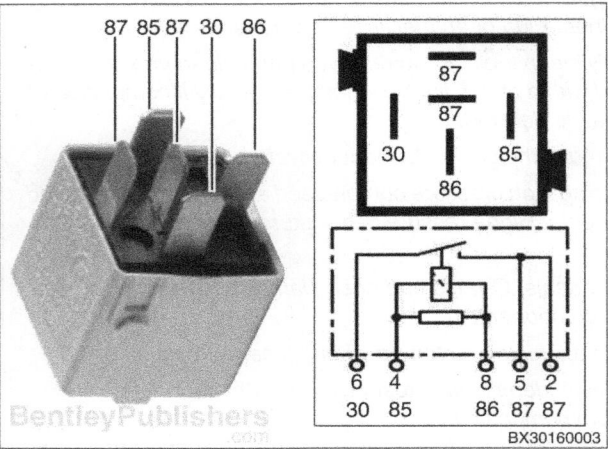

BX30160003

FUEL SYSTEM TROUBLESHOOTING

Fuel pump fuse and relay (M54 engine)

Begin troubleshooting fuel system faults by checking fuel pump fuse and relay. Also, check DME main relay and connections. \

◀ Fuel pump relay (**arrow**) is located behind glove compartment. See **ECL Electrical Component Locations** for access information.

> **CAUTION—**
> • Relay and fuse positions and wire colors vary. A good way to verify a relay position or wire colors is to compare the wiring colors at the relay socket to the colors indicated on the wiring diagrams in **ELE Electrical Wiring Diagrams**.

– The engine control module (ECM) supplies switched ground to the relay. During starting, the fuel pump runs as long as ignition switch is in START position and continues to run once engine starts. If power to fuel pump is interrupted, the engine does not run.

Fuel pump relay, testing (M54 Engine)

◀ Fuel pump supply circuit is fuse-protected by fuse F54 in power distribution box (A41) behind glove box. Also fuse F03 in engine electronics fuse carrier (A8680) in E-box.

– Remove fuel pump relay from socket. See **ECL Electrical Component Locations** for access information.

◀ With ignition in START position, check for battery voltage at relay connector terminals **6** and **8** (**red/violet** and **red/white** wires).

> **CAUTION—**
> • Ensure that manual transmission vehicles are not in gear, and automatic transmission vehicles are in Park or Neutral prior to operating ignition in START position.

– With ignition in START position, use digital multimeter to check for ground at terminal **4** (**black/violet** wire).

> **NOTE—**
> • Ground at terminal 4 is switched by the ECM. The ECM harness must be connected to check the switched ground connection.

— If no faults are found up to this point, turn ignition key off. Using a fused (14 gauge) jumper wire, connect relay connector terminal **6** to terminal **2**. The fuel pump should run.

- If pump runs and all other tests are as specified, fuel pump relay is likely faulty.

- If pump does not run, test fuel pump operation as described in **Operating fuel pump for tests** in this repair group

> *CAUTION*—
> - *The jumper wire should be 1.5 mm2 (14 ga.) and include an in-line fuse holder with a 15 amp fuse. To avoid fuse/relay panel damage from repeated connecting and disconnecting, also include a toggle switch.*

Fuel pump module and fuses (N52 engine)

◀ On the N52 engine, the ECM calculates the amount of fuel required at the given point in time and the electric fuel pump is activated as required. The total volume required is transmitted as a message to the EKP control module via PT-CAN.

The EKP module converts this message into an output voltage which controls the fuel pump. The fuel pump is capable of delivering up to 95 liters (25 gallons) per hour at a pressure of 5 bar (72.5 psi).

Begin troubleshooting fuel system faults by checking fuel pump control module (EKP). EKP module fuses are located in power distribution box (A41). See **ECL Electrical Component Locations** for access information.

EKP circuit diagram (N54 engine)

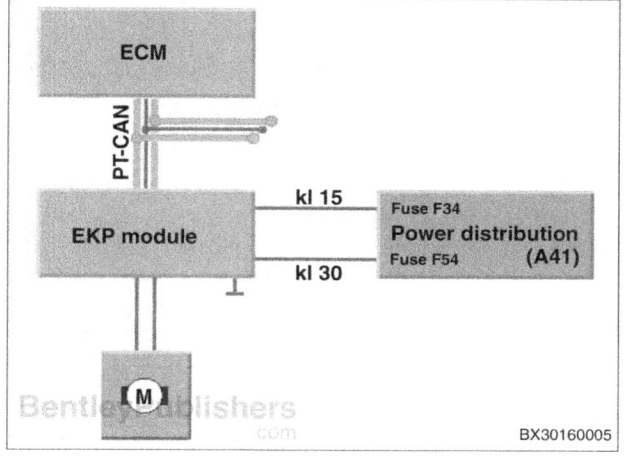

BX30160005

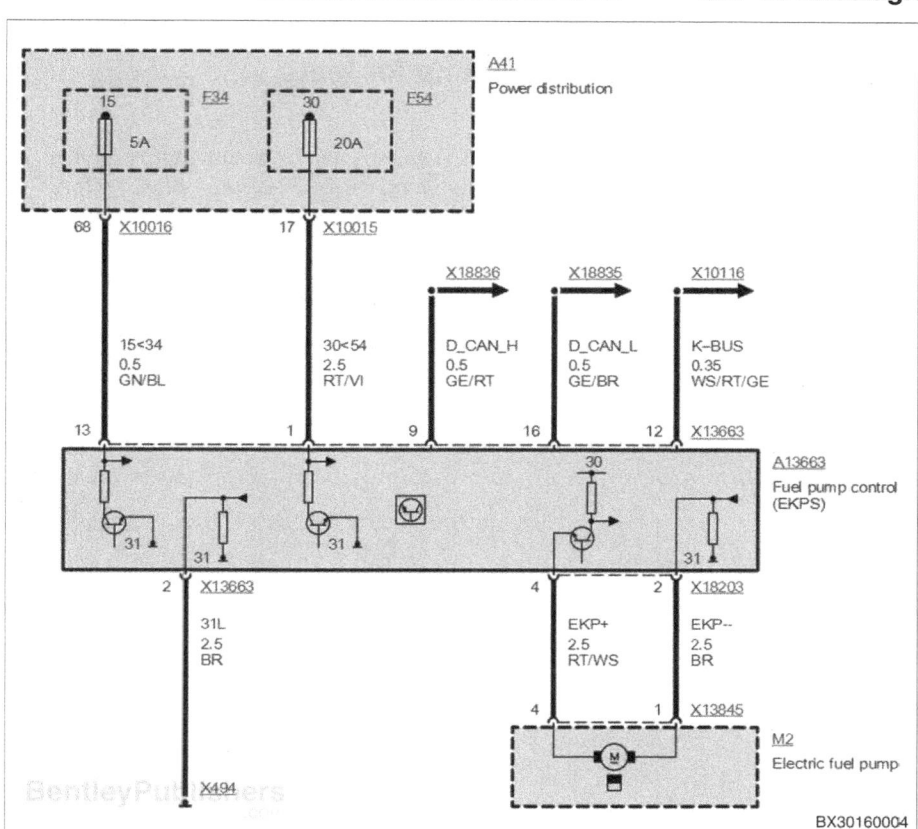

BX30160004

Operating fuel pump for tests (M54 engine)

Operating fuel pump for tests (M54 engine)

This procedure explains how to operate the fuel pump for testing purposes without having to run the engine.

◀ Remove fuel pump relay (**K6301**) located in relay panel behind glove compartment. Remove relay panel support bolt, and release panel from clip (**arrow**) to lower. See **ECL Electrical Component Locations** for additional access information.

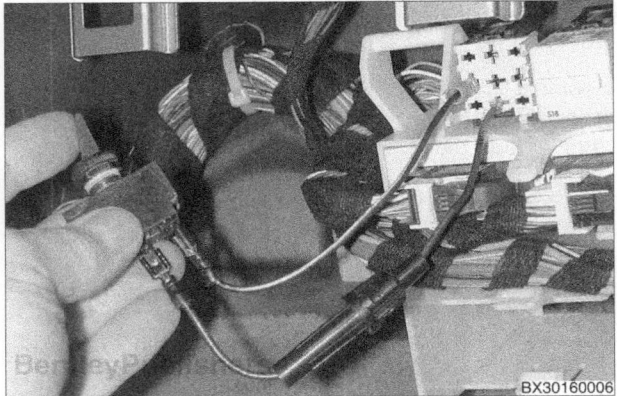

◀ Connect relay socket terminal 30 to relay socket terminal 87 with fused jumper wire.

 • Use 14 ga wire to make jumper and include an in-line fuse holder with a 15A fuse. To avoid relay socket damage from repeated connecting and disconnecting, also include a toggle switch in jumper harness.

 • Fuel pump operates as soon as jumper wire is attached.

— If pump does not run with jumper installed, fault could be in fuel pump, fuse F54, or wiring to pump. Check pump, fuses, and wiring. See **Fuel pump electrical circuit, testing** in this repair group.

— After completing tests, remove jumper harness and install relay.

> **WARNING—**
> • *Do not operate vehicle with jumper installed*

Operating fuel pump for tests (N52 engine)

Electronically controlled fuel pumps can be actuated through the electronic fuel pump control module (EKP) using a BMW factory scan tool or equivalent aftermarket scan tool.

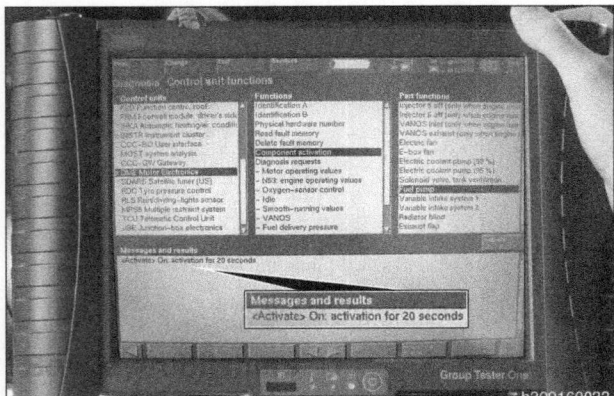

◀ When actuating fuel pump through EKP module using BMW scan tool the fuel pump will run at 100% (5 bar) for 20 seconds.

Fuel pump electrical circuit, testing

If fuel pump does not operate or there is no fuel pressure, first test fuel pump electrical circuit.

− Remove rear seat to access fuel pump and fuel level sender. See **Accessing fuel tank service cap** in this repair group.

◄ Slide electrical connector lock (in direction of **arrow**) and remove connector from fuel pump and fuel level sender.

◄ Connect voltmeter between fuel pump leads (**arrows**) on connector.

− Activate fuel pump. See **Operating fuel pump for tests** in this repair group.

− Use digital multimeter to test for battery voltage at fuel pump connector leads.

− If voltage and ground are present, fuel pump is likely faulty. If there is no voltage, check wiring between fuel pump and fuel pump relay or EKP module.

− After completing tests, reconnect fuel pump harness connector.

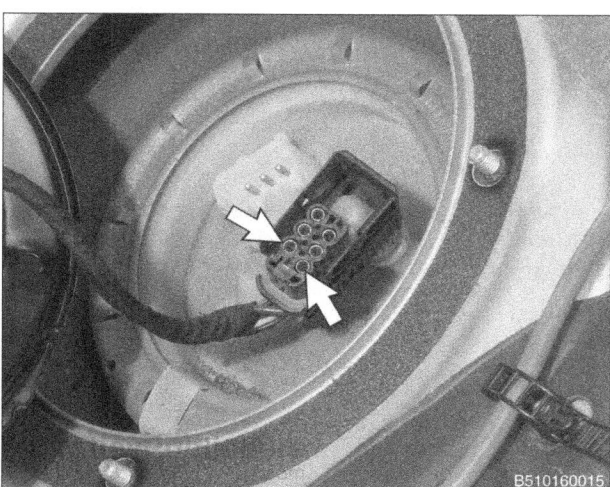

B510160016

b309160029

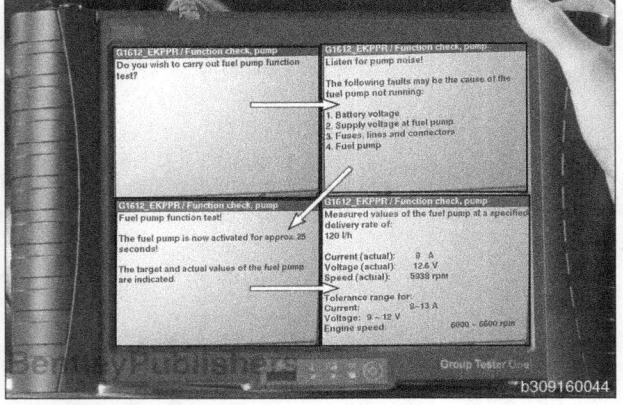

b309160044

Fuel pump power consumption, testing (M54 engine)

– Remove rear seat to access fuel pump and fuel level sender. See **Accessing fuel tank service cap** in this repair group.

◄ Disconnect harness connector from fuel pump.

– Use volt meter to verify voltage at fuel pump connector is 12.6 volts with fuel pump circuit actuated. See **Operating fuel pump for tests (M54 engine)**. Charge battery if necessary.

– Attach digital ammeter between pump lead and harness. Connect jumper wire between pump and harness.

> **CAUTION—**
> • *Do not allow the test leads to short to ground.*

– Activate fuel pump. See **Operating fuel pump for tests (M54 engine)** in this repair group.

◄ Compare ammeter reading with specification listed in table.

Fuel pump current (M54 engine)	
Current consumption	8 - 13 amps

– Higher than normal power consumption by fuel pump may indicate a worn pump, causing intermittent fuel starvation due to pump overheating and seizure. Replace pump.

– Lower than normal power consumption may indicate blockage in a fuel line. Before replacing fuel pump, be sure to check that return line and pump pickup (inside fuel tank) are not obstructed.

Fuel pump power consumption, testing (N52 engine)

If fuel delivery is erratic or poor, or if fuel pump makes abnormally loud noises, test pump power consumption. A BMW factory scan tool or equivalent can be used to measure fuel pump power consumption through the EKP module.

◄ Follow steps on screen to monitor fuel pump current.

Fuel pump current (N52 engine)	
Current consumption (fuel pump activated with BMW scan tool)	8 - 13 amps

An alternate method is to install a digital ammeter in fuel pump circuit using the following steps.

– Remove rear seat to access fuel pump and fuel level sender. See **Accessing fuel tank service cap** in this repair group.

◀ Slide locking connector in direction of arrow and remove electrical connector from fuel pump.

— Use voltmeter to verify battery voltage at fuel pump connector is 12.6 volts with fuel pump circuit actuated. See **Operating fuel pump for tests (N52 engine)** in this repair group. Charge battery if necessary.

— Attach digital ammeter between pump lead and harness. Connect jumper wire between pump and harness.

> **CAUTION—**
> • *Do not allow the test leads to short to ground.*

— Activate fuel pump. See **Operating fuel pump for tests (N52 engine)** in this repair group.

◀ Compare ammeter reading with specification listed in table.

Fuel pump current (N52 engine)	
Current consumption (fuel pump activated with scan tool)	8 - 13 amps

— Higher than normal power consumption by fuel pump may indicate a worn pump, causing intermittent fuel starvation due to pump overheating and seizure. Replace pump.

— Lower than normal power consumption may indicate blockage in a fuel line. Before replacing fuel pump, be sure to check that return line and pump pickup (inside fuel tank) are not obstructed.

Fuel pressure gauge, installing

Working in engine compartment, install fuel pressure gauge at Schræder valve on fuel rail.

— Remove upper engine covers. See **020 Maintenance**.

Use a fuel pressure gauge with a minimum range of 0 to 7 bar (0 to 100 psi).

> **WARNING—**
> • *The fuel system is designed to retain pressure even when the ignition is OFF. When working with the fuel system, loosen fuel lines slowly to allow residual fuel pressure to dissipate. Avoid spraying fuel. Use shop towels to capture leaking fuel.*
> • *Fuel pump starts (primes) each time door is opened.*
> • *Make sure the fuel pressure gauge is securely connected to the fuel rail to prevent it from coming loose under pressure.*

— Remove engine top cover. See **020 Maintenance**.

M54 engine

◄ Remove Schræder valve cap (**arrow**) at fuel rail and connect fuel pressure gauge.

N52 engine

◄ Remove Schræder valve cap (**arrow**) at fuel rail and connect fuel pressure gauge.

Fuel delivery, testing

Fuel pressure directly influences fuel delivery. There are two significant fuel delivery values to be measured:

• **System pressure** is created by fuel pump and maintained by pressure regulator.

• **Residual pressure** is pressure maintained in closed system after engine and fuel pump are shut off.

System pressure

— Attach fuel pressure gauge. See **Fuel pressure gauge, installing** in this repair group.

— Activate fuel pump. See **Operating fuel pump for tests** in this repair group. Compare fuel pressure to specifications in accompanying table.

Fuel system pressure specification	
M54 engine	3.5 ± 0.2 bar (50.76 ± 2.9 psi)
N52 engine	5 ± 0.2 bar (72.5 ± 2.9 psi)

CAUTION—

• *Fuel pump is capable of higher pressure than that regulated by the pressure regulator. Do not allow pressure to rise above 6.5 bar (94 psi). Damage to lines or system components could result.*

Residual pressure

For quick restarts and to avoid vapor lock when the engine is hot, the fuel injection system retains fuel pressure after the engine is shut off. This residual pressure is primarily maintained by the fuel pressure regulator and a check valve at the fuel pump outlet.

— Attach fuel pressure gauge. See **Fuel pressure gauge, installing** in this repair group.

— Start engine and allow it to run for approximately one minute. Note fuel pressure reading. Shut OFF engine.

— Note fuel pressure after approximately 20 minutes. Make sure pressure does not drop more than 0.5 bar from system pressure.

Fuel system pressure specification	
M54 engine	3.5 ± 0.2 bar (50.76 ± 2.9 psi)
N52 engine	5 ± 0.2 bar (72.5 ± 2.9 psi)

— When finished, disconnect pressure gauge and fitting, and replace Schræder valve cap. Check for faults and clear DME fault memory.

— If fuel system does not maintain pressure:
  • Visually check for leaks. Check for leaking injector(s).
  • Check for faulty fuel pump check valve.

FUEL SUPPLY COMPONENTS

Fuel filter

The fuel filter is a lifetime filter. It is located in the right side of the fuel tank.

Fuel pressure regulator

Fuel pressure is created by the fuel pump and maintained by the fuel pressure regulator. The fuel pressure regulator is integrated into the fuel filter in the right side of the fuel tank.

◀ Right side fuel pump assembly:

1. Fuel pressure regulator
2. Port for return line
3. Supply from electric fuel pump
4. Fuel filter
5. Supply to engine
6. Fuel pump
7. Fuel level sender

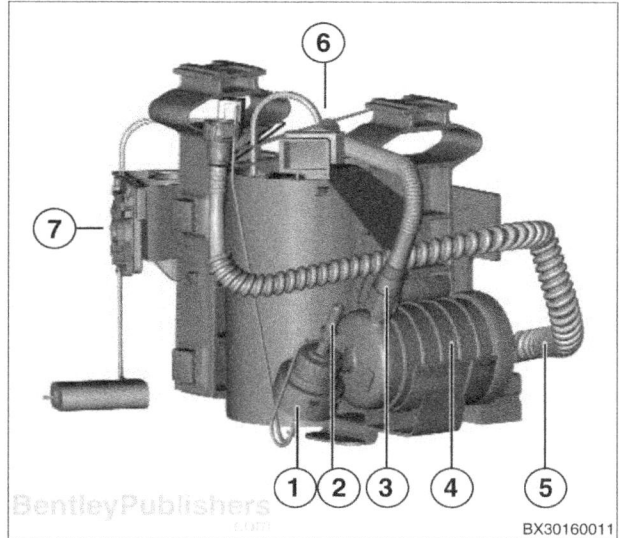

BX30160011

Fuel tank, draining

When draining fuel tank, use a safe storage unit and an approved fuel pumping device.

> **WARNING—**
> - *Before starting to work on tank removal, make sure hot components, such as the exhaust system, are completely cooled down.*
> - *Fuel may be spilled. Do not smoke or work near heaters or other fire hazards.*

— Start engine and allow to run 10 - 15 seconds to fill fuel compensating siphon assembly. This allows both lobes of fuel tank to be drawn off through fuel filler pipe.

— Disconnect negative cable from battery.

> **CAUTION—**
> - *Prior to disconnecting the battery, read the battery disconnection cautions given in* **001 Warnings and Cautions**.

— Remove fuel tank filler cap.

— Slide suction hose into filler neck about 130 cm (51 in), twisting as necessary. Withdraw fuel into storage unit.

— Monitor fuel level reduction in both lobes:
  - Remove rear seat cushion and access both fuel tank sender harness connectors. See **Accessing fuel pump and fuel level senders** in this repair group.
  - Use multimeter to measure resistance at both senders. Resistance should drop as fuel level drops.

— If siphoning mechanism is faulty, drain left tank lobe separately by removing sender cover and pumping fuel directly out of left lobe.

— Remove suction hose from tank filler neck carefully to avoid damaging filler neck baffle plate.

> **CAUTION—**
> - *After finishing repairs but before starting engine, be sure there is at least 5 liters (1.5 gallons) of fuel in tank. The fuel pump is damaged if run without fuel.*

Fuel pump (EKP) module, removing and installing (N52 engine)

- Working at right side of rear seat:
  - Lift seat belt trim cover up and pull to side with seat belt.
  - Pull side (c-pillar) bolster forward and lift up to remove.

◀ Working at fuel pump (EKP) module:
  - Remove electrical connectors (**A**).
  - Remove fasteners (**arrows**) and remove EKP module.

- Installation is reverse of removal.
  - Remember to code / program fuel pump (EKP) module if replaced. See **600 Electrical System-General** for information on coding and programming.

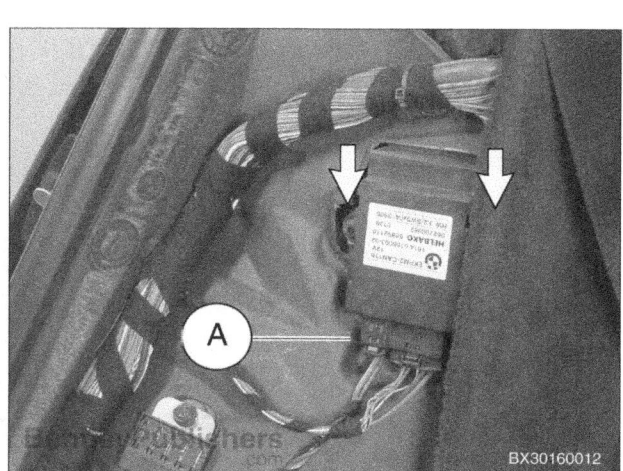

Tightening torques	
Fuel pump (EKP) module to body	8 Nm (5.9 ft-lb)

- Check and clear fault codes from ECM memory.

Fuel tank service cap, removing and installing

NOTE—
- *Right side fuel tank service cap shown. Accessing left side service cap is similar.*

- Disconnect negative cable from battery.

> *CAUTION—*
> - *Prior to disconnecting the battery, read the battery disconnection cautions given in* **001 Warnings and Cautions**.

- Remove rear seat cushion. See **520 Seats**.

- Peel back insulation to expose fuel sender service cover.

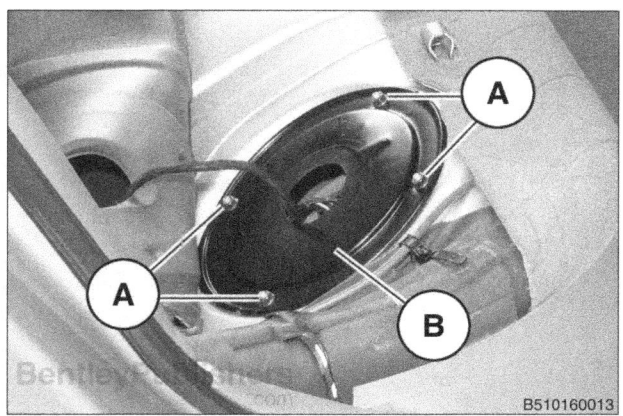

◀ Working at ride side fuel tank:
  - Remove rubber grommet for wiring harness from service cover (not shown).
  - Remove fasteners (**A**).
  - Remove fuel pump access cover (**B**).

- Drain fuel tank. See **Fuel tank, draining** in this repair group.

- Remove fuel pump access cover. See **Accessing fuel tank service cap** in this repair group.

◀ Slide electrical connector lock in direction of **arrow,** remove connector and fuel lines if equipped.

> *WARNING—*
> - *When disconnecting fuel hose, wrap shop towel around end of hose to prevent spray of fuel under pressure.*

Fuel tank service cap, removing and installing

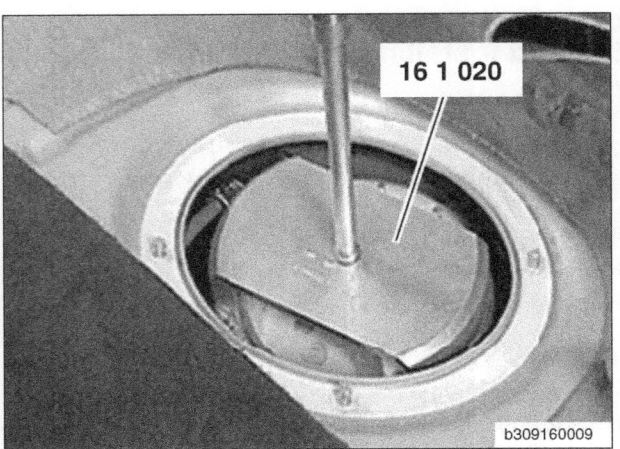

◀ Using BMW special tool 16 1 020, remove fuel pump service cap lock ring.

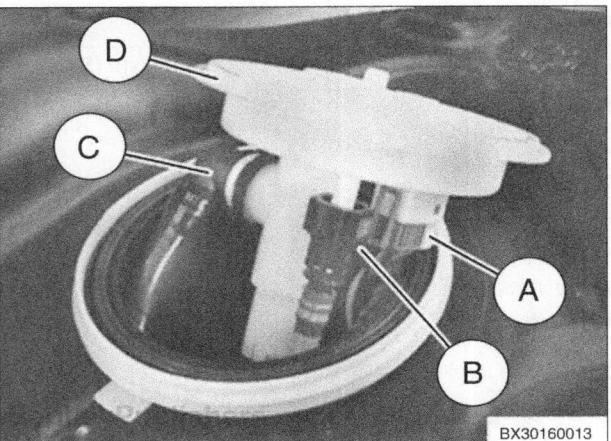

◀ Carefully raise service cap (**D**).

- Disconnect electrical connector (**A**).
- Press (pinch) and release fuel line connector (**B**).
- Squeeze lock ring and release vent line connector (**C**).

– Remove service cap.

> **CAUTION—**
> • *Be prepared to catch any dripping fuel.*

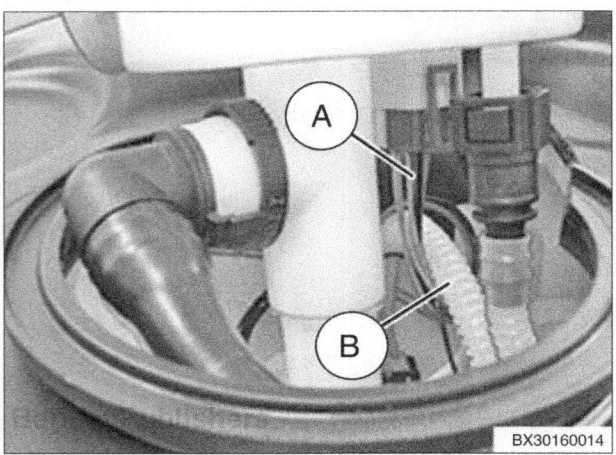

◀ When installing fuel tank service cap:

- Wiring harness (**A**) must be run in a loop around fuel line (**B**).
- Electrical harness must not be allowed to restrict movement of fuel level sender.
- All lines and connectors must snap audibly into place

Fuel tank service cap, removing and installing

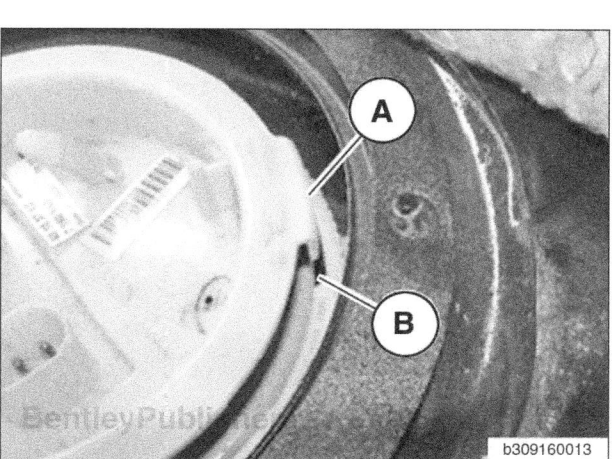

b309160013

◀ When installing service cap lock ring, check to see that service cap lug (**A**) engages with corresponding slot (**B**) of fuel tank.

– Install service cap lock ring hand tight.

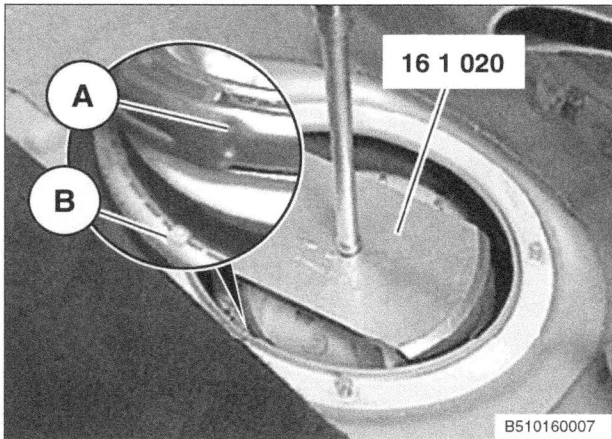

16 1 020

B510160007

◀ Using BMW special tool 16 1 020 tighten service cap lock ring until notch on lock ring (**A**) points to notch on fuel tank (**B**).

Tightening torque	
Service cap to fuel tank	45 ± 5 Nm (33 ± 3.6 ft-lb)

B510160020

◀ Connect electrical connector by sliding lock in direction of **arrow** and connect fuel lines.

– Install fuel tank access cover.

> **CAUTION—**
> • *After finishing repairs but before starting engine, be sure there is at least 5 liters (1.5 gallons) of fuel in the tank. The fuel pump is damaged if run without fuel.*

Fuel pump, removing and installing

Fuel pump, removing and installing

– Remove fuel tank service cap. See **Fuel tank service cap, removing and installing** given earlier.

◀ Using a screwdriver (**A**) carefully separate electrical connectors.

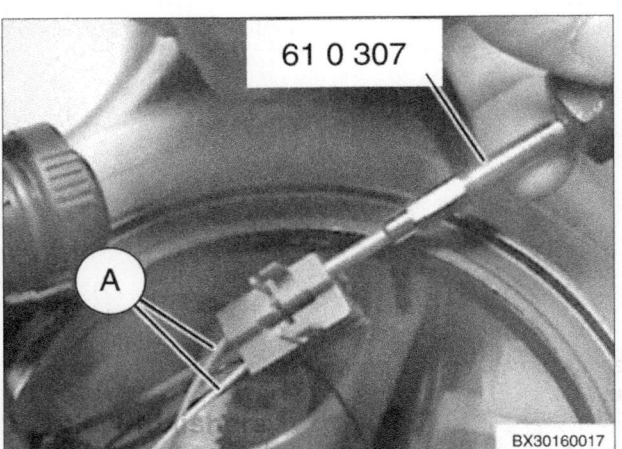

BX30160015

◀ Using BMW special tool 61 0 307, remove fuel pump wiring (**A**) from blue electrical connector inside tank.

NOTE—

• *Connector on fuel pump must not be removed. Replacement pump comes with electrical connector already installed.*

• *Record wiring position in blue connector for reassembly.*

61 0 307

A

BX30160017

◀ Working inside fuel tank:

• Press tabs (**A**) and detach line (**B**) in direction of arrow.

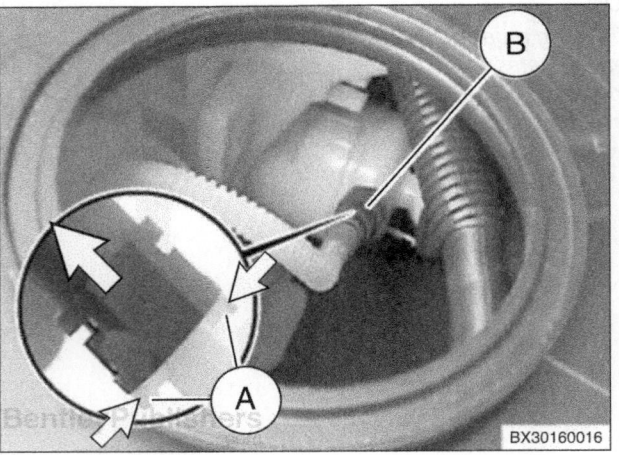

BX30160016

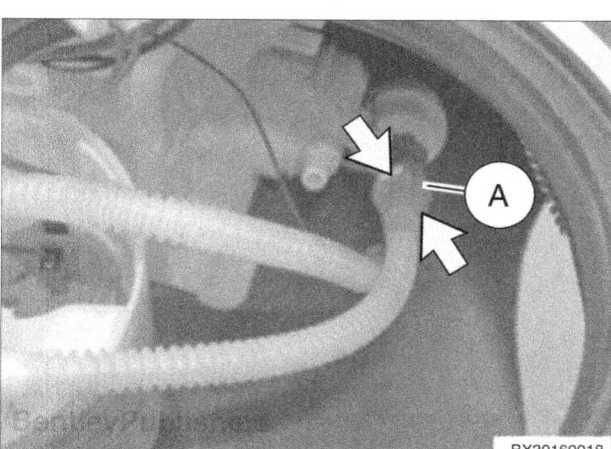

◀ Press tabs for quick release (**arrows**) and remove fuel line (**A**).

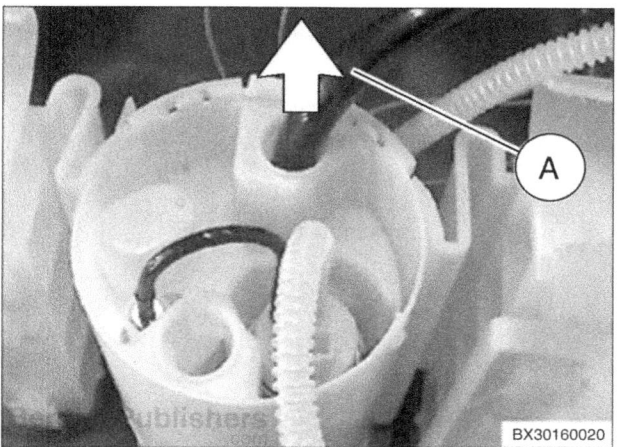

◀ Remove suction-jet line (**A**) in direction of arrow.

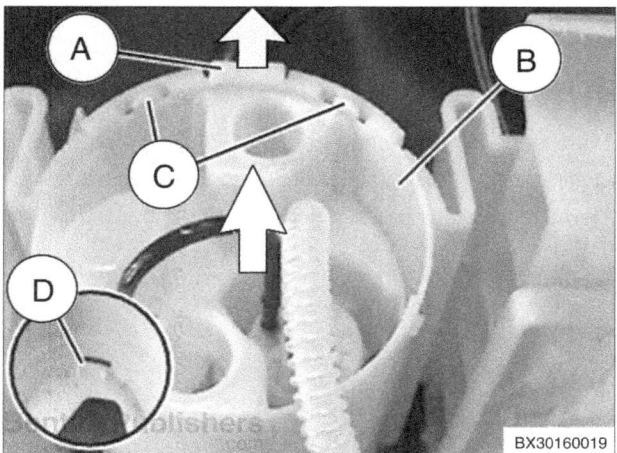

◀ Press retaining lug (**A**) towards the rear of the fuel tank (**arrow**) and lift remove fuel pump out as a unit with surge chamber (**B**).

– Installation is reverse of removal, noting the following:

• Fuel pump can be installed in only one position.

• Fuel pump must be positioned in guides (**C**), and mounting lug (**D**) must fully engage in fuel pump.

• Insert fuel pump electrical wiring into blue connector.

– Fuel line connectors must lock audibly into place.

> **CAUTION—**
> • *After finishing repairs but before starting engine, be sure there is at least 5 liters (1.5 gallons) of fuel in the tank. The fuel pump is damaged if run without fuel.*

Fuel level sender (right side), removing and installing

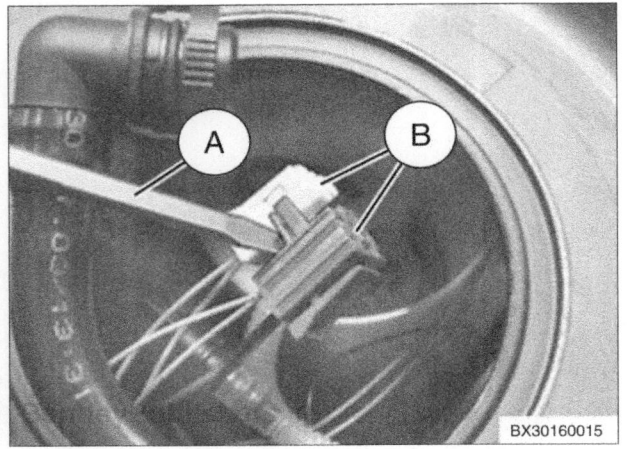

BX30160015

Fuel level sender (right side), removing and installing

– Remove fuel tank service cap. See **Fuel tank service cap, removing and installing** given earlier.

◄ Using a screwdriver (**A**) carefully separate electrical connectors.

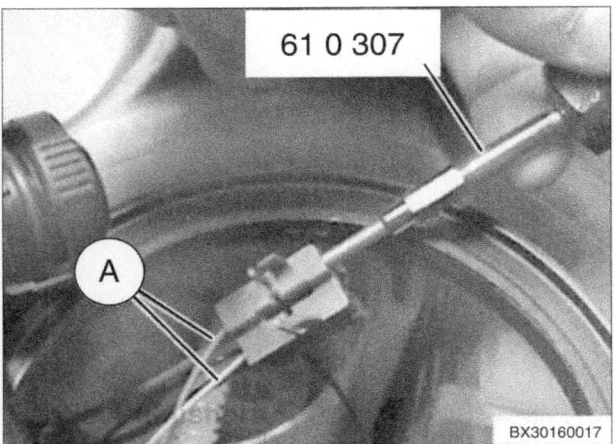

61 0 307

BX30160017

◄ Using BMW special tool 61 0 307, remove fuel level sender wiring (**A**) from blue electrical connector inside tank.

NOTE—

• *Record wiring position in connector for reassembly.*

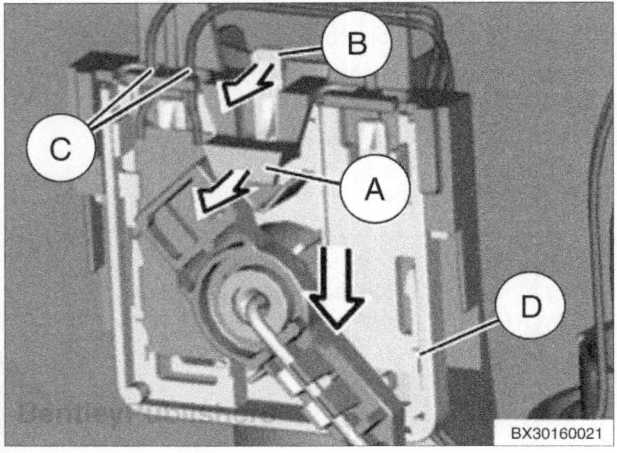

BX30160021

◄ Working inside fuel tank:

• Carefully remove fuel sender wiring from guides (**C**).

• Pull tab (**A**) and press tab (**B**) simultaneously in direction of arrows.

• Press fuel level sender downwards to remove to remove from guides (**D**).

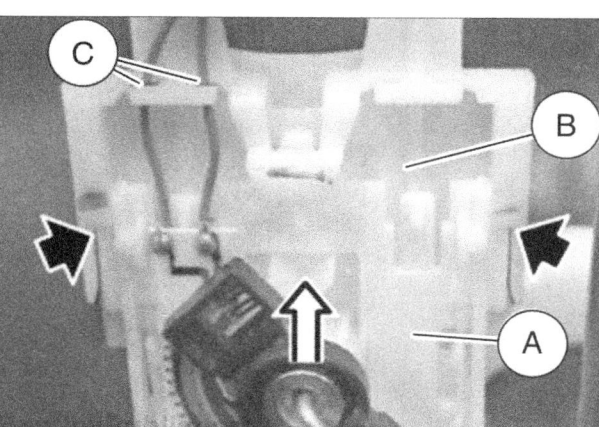

BX30160022

◄ When installing fuel level sender:

- Carefully slide fuel level sender (**A**) upwards into guides (**arrows**) on sender holder (**B**).
- Fuel level sender must snap audibly into place.
- Place level sender wiring in cable guides (**C**).

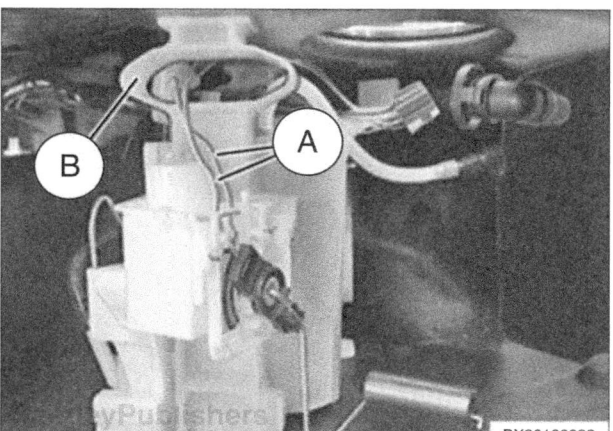

BX30160023

◄ Route level sender wiring (**A**) through upper loop of fuel tank support (**B**).

NOTE—

- *Fuel tank shown cutaway for illustration.*

– Insert fuel level sender wiring into blue connector.

– Remainder of installation is the reverse of removal.

> **CAUTION—**
> - *After finishing repairs but before starting engine, be sure there is at least 5 liters (1.5 gallons) of fuel in the tank. The fuel pump is damaged if run without fuel.*

Fuel level sender (left side), removing and installing

– Remove left side fuel tank service cap. See **Fuel tank service cap, removing and installing** given earlier.

◄ Disconnect electrical connector (**A**) for fuel level sender.

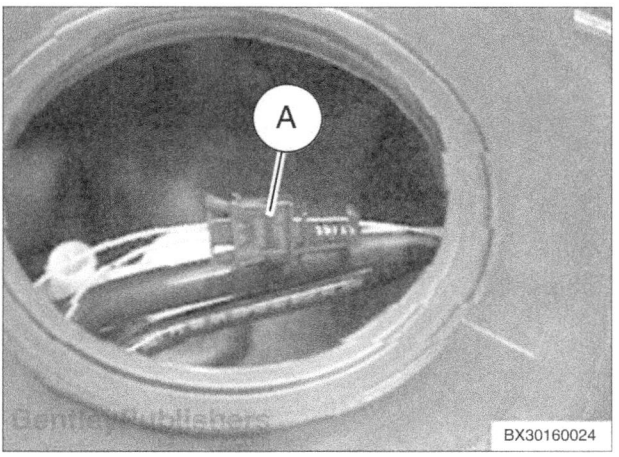

BX30160024

Fuel level sender (left side), removing and installing

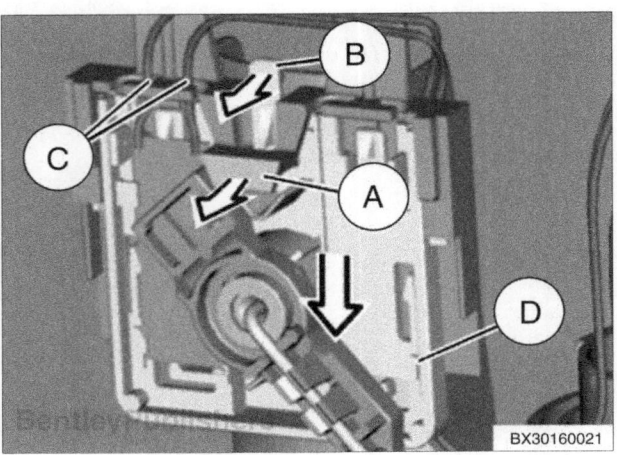

◄ Working inside fuel tank:

- Carefully remove fuel sender wiring from guides (**C**).
- Pull tab (**A**) and press tab (**B**) simultaneously in direction of arrows.
- Press fuel level sender downwards to remove to remove from guides (**D**).

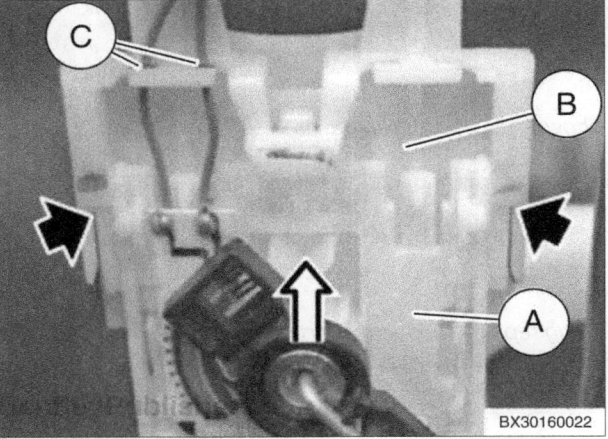

◄ When installing fuel level sender:

- Carefully slide fuel level sender (**A**) upwards into guides (**arrows**) on sender holder (**B**).
- Fuel level sender must snap audibly into place.
- Place level sender wiring in cable guides (**C**).

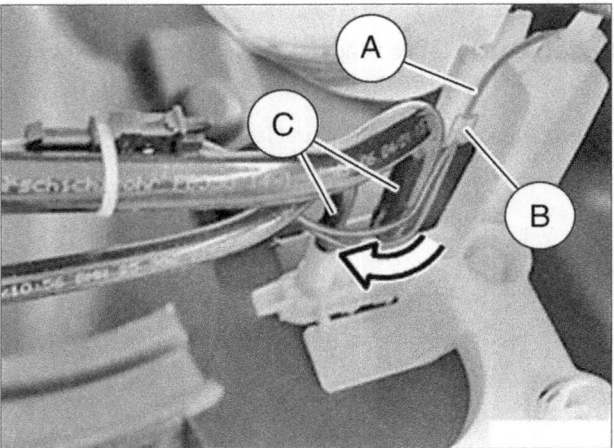

◄ Route level sender wiring (**A**) through cable guide (**B**), and lay behind lines (**C**).

NOTE—

- *Fuel tank shown cutaway for illustration.*
- *Level sender wiring must not be allowed to interfere with movement of level sender.*

− Reconnect fuel line electrical connector.

− Remainder of installation is the reverse of removal.

> **CAUTION**—
> - *After finishing repairs but before starting engine, be sure there is at least 5 liters (1.5 gallons) of fuel in the tank. The fuel pump is damaged if run without fuel.*

FUEL TANK EVAPORATIVE CONTROL SYSTEM

Evaporative control, also referred to as running losses control, is designed to prevent fuel system evaporative losses from venting into the atmosphere. The components of this system allow control and monitoring of evaporative losses by on-board diagnostic (OBD II) software incorporated into the engine control module (ECM).

Listed below are the main components of the evaporative control system and their functions:

- Carbon canister stores fuel vapors.
- Plumbing ducts vapors from fuel tank to canister and from canister to intake manifold.
- Carbon canister purge valve is controlled by engine control module (ECM).
- Pressure regulator shunts excess fuel volume directly back to fuel tank before it circulates through fuel lines.
- Leak detection unit (DMTL) pressurizes fuel tank and evaporative system to monitor system leaks.

Evaporative system troubleshooting

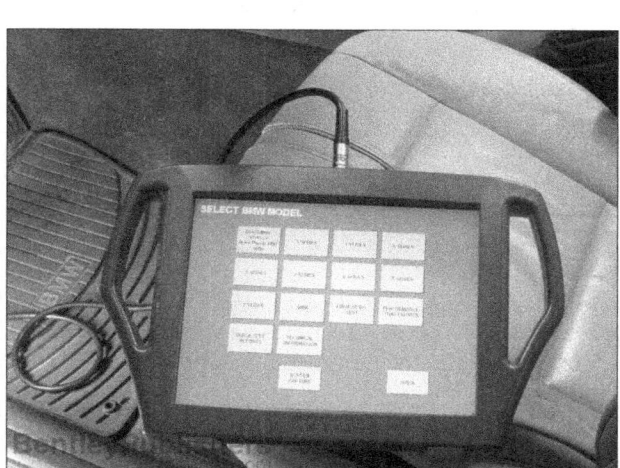

 Start by accessing diagnostic trouble codes (DTCs) using a factory BMW or equivalent scan tool.

- For purposes of OBD II emissions compliance, the DME system sets a diagnostic trouble code (DTC) when it detects a leak in the evaporative control system.
- Malfunction indicator light (MIL) is illuminated upon second recurrence of fault. See **OBD On-Board Diagnostics**.

— When leak testing, observe the following conditions to obtain plausible results:

- Fuel tank ¼ to ¾ full.
- Vehicle parked for at least 2 hours to allow fuel to reach ambient temperature. Ideal fuel temperature is 10°- 20°C (50° - 68°F).
- Do not refuel immediately before leak test.

— If a leak is detected, check the following areas:

- Fuel filler cap leaking or off.
- Fuel tank ventilation lines leaking at fuel tank or activated carbon canister.
- Tank ventilation valve leaking (in engine compartment).
- Fuel level sensor and fuel pump assembly cover leaking.

For evaporative system component replacement, see **Fuel Supply Components** in this repair group.

BX30160027

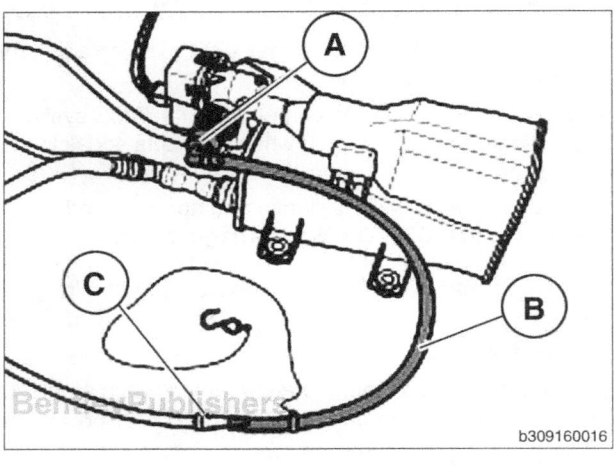

b309160016

Evaporative system leak test

Use the following leak test when diagnosing evaporative system leak fault codes.

— Working behind right rear inner fender liner: gain access to activated carbon canister. See **Activated carbon canister, removing and installing** in this repair group.

◄ Remove fresh air line (**inset**) from DMTL pump.

◄ Install BMW test adapter 83 30 0 433 207 (**B**) at DMTL fresh air connection (**A**).

— Connect evaporative system smoke machine (**C**) to test adapter (**B**).

NOTE —
   • *BMW recommends VACUTEC 625-522B (nitrogen pressure swing absorption technology).*

> *WARNING* —
> • *Use only smoke machine that utilizes nitrogen to pressurize fuel system. The fuel system may release a substantial amount of fuel-rich gasoline vapors during testing. Work in a well ventilated area.*

— Remove fuel filler cap.

— Activate smoke machine and fill fuel system with smoke until it escapes from fuel filler neck.

— Shut off smoke machine.

— Reinstall fuel filler cap.

— Reactivate smoke machine and fill fuel system with smoke.

> *WARNING* —
> • *Do not exceed a maximum fuel system pressure of 0.3 bar (4 psi) when using smoke machine.*

— Examine fuel system components for signs of escaping smoke. Repair or replace faulty components.

— After completing tests:
   • Attach DMTL fresh air line.
   • Check and clear fault codes from ECM memory.

Activated carbon canister, removing and installing

The carbon canister is on the right side behind the right rear wheel well liner.

— Raise rear end of car and support safely.

> **CAUTION—**
> • *Make sure car is stable and well supported at all times. Use a professional automotive lift or jack stands. A floor jack is not adequate support.*

— Remove right rear wheel.

— Remove right rear wheel well liner.

◄ Remove activated carbon canister:

- Remove line connections at carbon canister and fuel filler neck (**arrows**).
- Remove fasteners (**A**) and lower carbon canister slightly.
- Disconnect electrical connector from DMTL pump, and lever off harness guide clips from carbon canister mounts.
- Remove carbon canister from vehicle.

— Installation is reverse of removal.

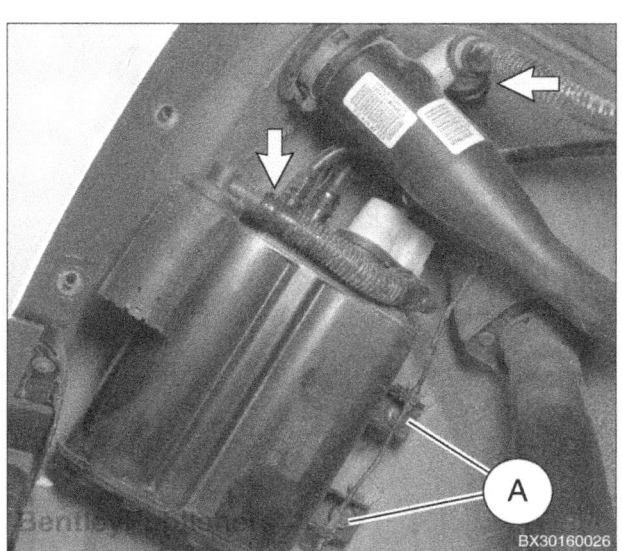

Tightening torque	
Carbon canister to body (M6)	9 Nm (80 in/lb)

Fuel tank leak detection module (DMTL), removing and installing

The DMTL is mounted to the activated carbon canister.

— Remove activated carbon canister. See **Activated carbon canister, removing and installing** in this repair group.

◄ Remove fasteners (**A**) and pull DMTL unit out of carbon canister in direction of **arrow**.

— Installation is reverse of removal.

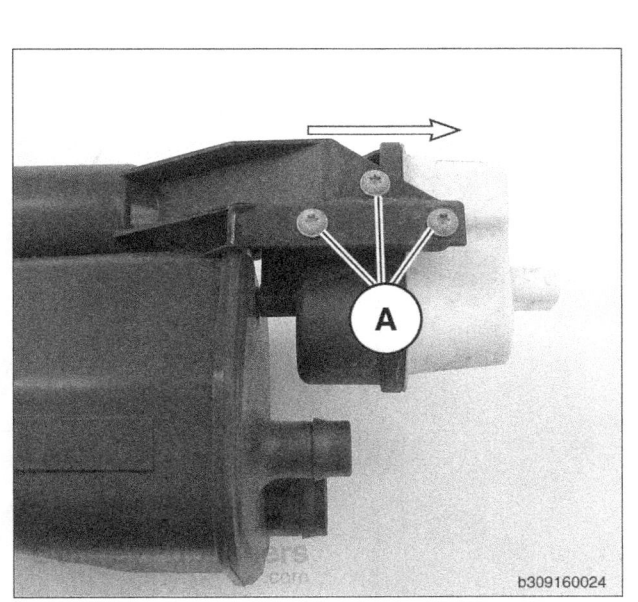

Tightening torque	
DMTL to carbon canister	2 Nm (18 in/lb)

170 Radiator and Cooling System

GENERAL

This repair group covers component repair information for the engine cooling system.

See also:

• **020 Maintenance** for coolant hose inspection

• **100 Engine–General** for engine code and application information

• **119 Lubrication** for engine oil cooler removal

• **130 Fuel Injection (M54 engine)** for engine coolant temperature (ECT) sensor service

• **131 Fuel Injection (N52 Engine)** for engine coolant temperature (ECT) sensor service

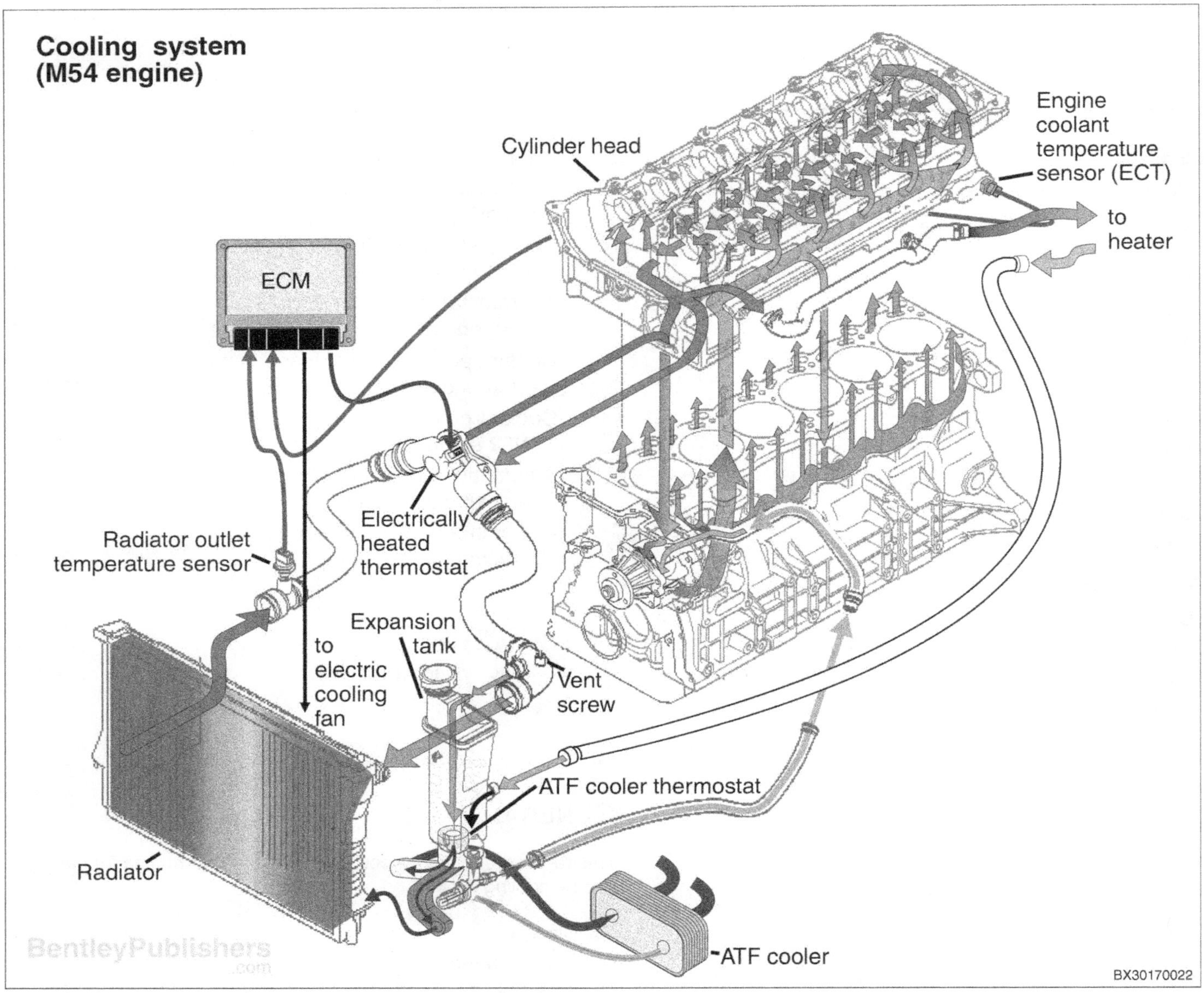

Cooling system (M54 engine)

Cylinder head

Engine coolant temperature sensor (ECT)

to heater

ECM

Radiator outlet temperature sensor

Electrically heated thermostat

to electric cooling fan

Expansion tank

Vent screw

ATF cooler thermostat

Radiator

ATF cooler

BX30170022

B510170001

Coolant pump

M54 engine

A conventional centrifugal coolant pump is mounted to the front of the engine. The belt-driven pump circulates coolant through the system whenever the engine is running.

N52 engine

◄ An electric coolant pump is bolted to the right front of the engine block. The electric pump allows for more efficient heating and cooling of the engine. It can operate regardless of whether the engine is ON or OFF.

A low coolant flow rate is used during cold start situations to speed engine warm-up. A high flow rate (including flow with engine OFF) is used for rapid cool-down. In this way the electric coolant pump helps ensure engine efficiency and longevity.

The pump is DME controlled. The DME uses engine load, engine operating range and various temperature sensors to determine coolant pump operation and speed.

The electric coolant pump is self-diagnosable and can identify and store the following faults:

• Impeller speed deviation
• Stiff operation or blocked by foreign objects
• Incorrect mixture ratio coolant / water
• Air in cooling system

Electrically heated thermostat

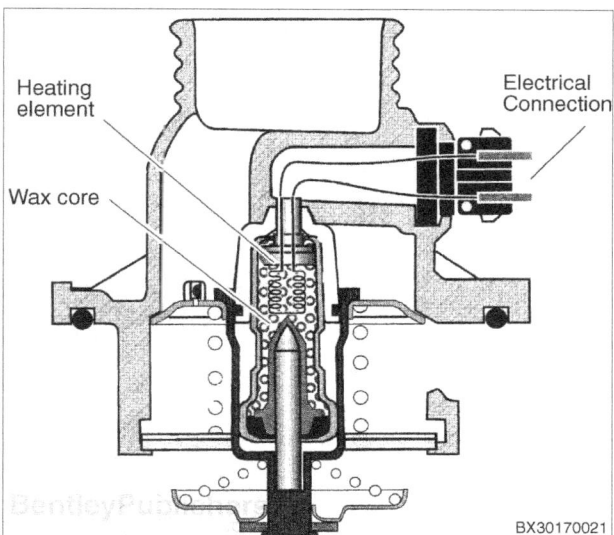

Heating element

Wax core

Electrical Connection

BX30170021

 An electrically heated, DME-controlled thermostat is externally mounted above the coolant pump. The engine control module (ECM) activates the thermostat to maintain engine coolant temperature within a narrow range.

If the electronics fail, the mechanical function of the thermostat acts as a fail-safe.

NOTE —

• *M54 thermostat shown, N52 thermostat is similar in function.*

Radiator and expansion tank

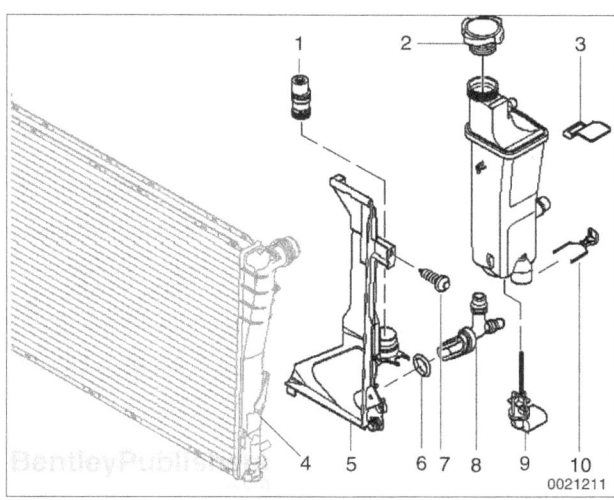

0021211

The radiator is a crossflow design. An expansion tank provides for coolant expansion at higher temperatures and easy monitoring of the coolant level. Automatic transmission fluid (ATF) is circulated through an additional heat exchanger (ATF cooler).

1. Thermostat (ATF heat exchanger)
2. Expansion tank cap
3. Label
4. Radiator
5. Mounting bracket
6. Sealing O-ring
7. Self-tapping screw
8. Connector (ATF heat exchanger)
9. Coolant level sensor
10. Locking clip

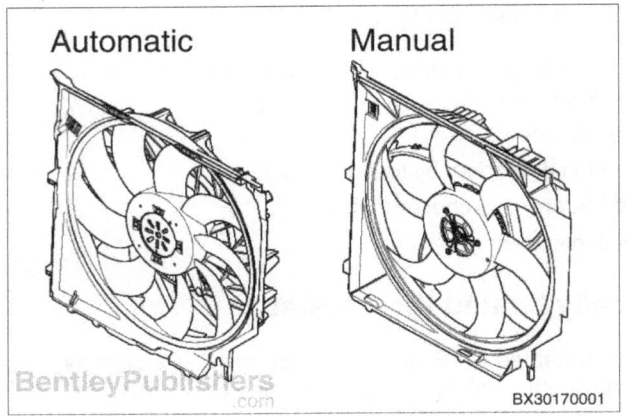

Automatic   Manual

BX30170001

Electric cooling fan

◀ X3 models use an electric cooling fan mounted on the engine side of the radiator. Two versions of cooling fans are used, one for automatic transmission vehicles, and one for manual transmission vehicles.

The electric cooling fan is controlled by the engine control module (ECM) via the output final stage.

The output final stage is mounted on the fan housing, next to the fan motor. The fan is operated using a pulse width modulated signal. Fan circuit wiring is protected by a high-amp fuse. Electric fan activation is based on the following inputs to the ECM:

• Radiator outlet temperature

• Calculated catalytic converter temperature

• Vehicle speed

• Battery voltage

• Calculated refrigerant pressure

When the vehicle is first started, the ECM activates the electric fan briefly at 20% of its maximum speed, then switches OFF. This is for diagnostic monitoring. The voltage generated by the fan when it slows down (acting as a generator) must match the stored rpm values in the fan output stage to confirm that the fan is operating correctly.

NOTE—

• If the ECM fault memory indicates a cooling fan fault, check that the fan is not seized and that it spins freely.

• When A/C is switched ON, the electric fan is not immediately turned on.

• After the engine is switched OFF, the fan may continue to run at varying speeds for up to 10 minutes, based on calculated catalyst temperature.

Automatic transmission fluid (ATF) cooler

ATF lines connect the transmission to the ATF cooler (heat exchanger) at back of radiator.

On cold engine start-up, the engine coolant is heated more quickly than the transmission fluid. Heat from engine coolant is used to warm up the ATF faster, reducing drag in the transmission and improving fuel mileage.

Once ATF reaches normal operating temperature, it is hotter than the engine coolant. The ATF heat exchanger then acts as a cooling device.

Engine oil cooler

◀ N52 engines may be equipped with an optional engine oil cooler as part of the cooling system. The engine oil cooler is mounted to the front of the oil filter housing.

Engine oil cooler removal is covered in **119 Lubrication system**.

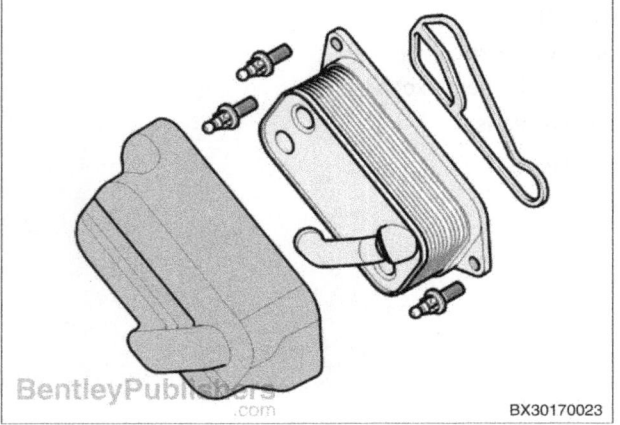

BX30170023

Warnings and Cautions

Observe the following warnings and cautions when working on the cooling system.

> **WARNING—**
> - *At normal operating temperature the cooling system is pressurized. Allow the system to cool as long as possible before opening (a minimum of one hour), then release the cap slowly to allow safe release of pressure.*
> - *Releasing cooling system pressure lowers the coolant boiling point. The coolant may boil suddenly. Use heavy gloves and wear eye and face protection to guard against scalding.*
> - *Use extreme care when draining and disposing of engine coolant. Coolant is poisonous and lethal to humans and pets. Pets are attracted to coolant because of its sweet smell and taste. Seek medical attention immediately if coolant is ingested.*

> **CAUTION—**
> - *Avoid adding cold water to the coolant while the engine is hot or overheated. If it is necessary to add coolant to a hot system, do so only with the engine running and coolant pump operating.*
> - *To avoid excess silicate gel precipitation in the cooling system and loss of cooling capacity, use BMW coolant or equivalent low silicate antifreeze.*
> - *If oil enters the cooling system, the radiator, expansion tank and heating circuit must be flushed with cleaning agent. BMW recommends removal of the radiator and expansion tank to flush.*
> - *When working on the cooling system, cover the alternator to protect it against coolant drips.*
> - *Prior to disconnecting the battery, read the battery disconnection cautions given in* **001 Warnings and Cautions**.
> - *Replace aluminum fasteners when loosened.*
> - *For reliable identification test fastener with magnet for aluminum composition.*

TROUBLESHOOTING

Begin the diagnosis of cooling system problems with a thorough visual inspection. If no visual faults are found, check the engine control module (ECM) fault memory for stored diagnostic trouble codes (DTCs) using BMW scan tool.

Common cooling system faults can be grouped into one of 4 categories:

- Cooling system leaks
- Poor coolant circulation
- Radiator cooling fan faults
- Electrical / electronic faults

Cooling system inspection

— Check operation of electric radiator fan:

- Start engine, turn A/C on, MAX setting. Electric fan should run.

— Check coolant hoses for cracks or softness. Check clamps for looseness. Check coolant level and check for evidence of coolant leaks from engine.

— Check that radiator fins are not blocked with dirt or debris. Clean radiator using low-pressure water or compressed air. Blow outward from engine side out.

— To check mechanical coolant pump (M54 engine):

- Remove cooling fan. See **Electric cooling fan, removing and installing** in this repair group.
- Remove accessory belt from coolant pump pulley. See **020 Maintenance**.
- Firmly grasp opposite sides of pulley and check for play in all directions.
- Spin pulley and check that shaft runs smoothly without play.

NOTE —

- *The coolant provides lubrication for the pump shaft, so an occasional drop of coolant leaking from the pump is acceptable. If coolant drips steadily from the vent hole, replace the pump.*

— Check operation of electric coolant pump (N52 engine):

- Turn ignition key on.
- Adjust heat to max. setting.
- Press accelerator pedal to floor.
- Pump should audibly run after about 10 seconds.

— At normal operating temperature, cooling system is pressurized. This raises boiling point of coolant. Leaks may prevent system from becoming pressurized. Pressure test cooling system to help pinpoint hard-to-find leaks. See **Cooling system pressure test**.

— If cooling system is full of coolant and holds pressure:

- Use an appropriate scan tool to interrogate engine control module (ECM) for radiator fan or DME faults.
- Check for failed thermostat or coolant pump impeller.
- Check for clogged / plugged radiator or coolant passages.

Cooling system pressure test

A cooling system pressure tester is used to test for coolant leaks, including internal ones. Common sources of internal coolant leaks are a faulty cylinder head gasket, a cracked cylinder head, or a cracked engine block.

> **WARNING—**
> • At normal operating temperature the cooling system is pressurized. Allow the system to cool before opening. Remove the cap slowly to allow safe release of pressure.

— With engine cold, install pressure tester (BMW special tools 17 0 101 / 17 0 113 or equivalent) to expansion tank. Pressurize system to specification listed in **Table a**.

  • Pressure should not drop more than 0.1 bar (1.45 psi) for at least two minutes.

  • If pressure drops rapidly and there is no sign of external leakage, cylinder head gasket may be faulty. Perform compression and leak-down tests.

  • Test expansion tank cap using pressure tester with correct adapter (BMW special tool 17 0 114 or equivalent). Replace faulty cap or cap gasket.

> **CAUTION—**
> • Exceeding specified test pressures could damage radiator or other system components.

Table a. Cooling system test pressures

Component	Test pressure
Radiator	1.5 bar (21.75 psi)
Radiator cap	2 bar (29 psi)

Combustion chamber leak test

— If you suspect that combustion chamber pressure is leaking into the cooling system past the cylinder head gasket, use an exhaust gas analyzer to test the vapors rising from the coolant at the expansion tank.

> **CAUTION—**
> • Use an extension tube above the reservoir neck to maintain distance between the top of the coolant and the gas analyzer nozzle. The gas analyzer is easily damaged if it is allowed to inhale liquid coolant.
> • While running engine to check for causes of overheating, observe coolant temperature carefully to avoid engine damage.

Thermostat

If the engine overheats or runs too cool and no other cooling system tests indicate trouble, the thermostat may be faulty. The electrically heated thermostat is monitored by the OBD II diagnostic software. The fault may lie in the DME software or hardware, or it may lie in the wiring to the thermostat. See **OBD On-Board Diagnostics**.

COOLING SYSTEM SERVICE

Coolant, draining and filling

> **WARNING—**
> • Allow the cooling system to cool before opening or draining the cooling system.

— Raise front of car and support safely.

> **WARNING—**
> • Make sure car is stable and well supported at all times. Use a professional automotive lift or jack stands. A floor jack is not adequate support.

— Remove splash shield from under engine. See **020 Maintenance**.

— Remove front suspension reinforcement plate. See **310 Front Suspension**.

— Remove fresh air duct above radiator.

◀ Remove cap from radiator expansion tank.

— Place 5-gallon pail underneath radiator.

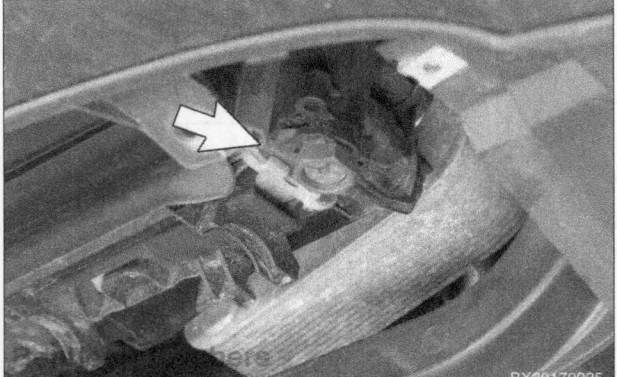

◀ Loosen drain plug (**arrow**) at bottom left radiator and allow coolant to drain.

> **NOTE—**
> • For radiators without drain plug, remove lower hose to drain radiator.

> **WARNING—**
> • Coolant is poisonous. It is especially lethal to pets. Clean up spills and rinse the area with water. If coolant is ingested, immediately seek medical attention.

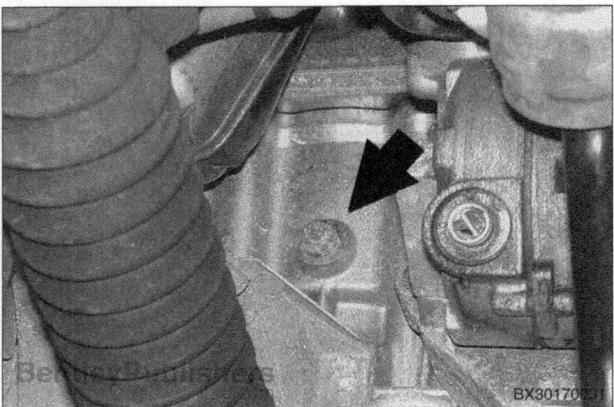

◀ M54 engine, additional drain plug is located on right side of engine block near cylinder 2.

— Place 5-gallon pail underneath engine block coolant drain plug.

— Remove engine block coolant drain plug and drain coolant.

- Before refilling radiator:
  - Switch ignition ON. Do not start engine.
  - Set temperature controls to full warm.
  - Set blower control to low.
  - Set seat heat control to maximum.

- Using a coolant mixture of 50% antifreeze and 50% distilled water, fill expansion tank slowly. Continue until coolant emerges from bleed screw. Cooling system capacities are in **Table b**.

NOTE—

- *Tap water may cause corrosion of radiator, engine and coolant hoses.*

- *Coolant can be reused provided it is clean and less than two years old. Do not reuse coolant when replacing damaged engine parts.*

- Bleed cooling system. See **Cooling system, bleeding** in this repair group.

Table b. Cooling system capacities	
Engine	**Capacity**
M54: • Automatic transmission • Manual transmission	10.6L (11.20 US qt) 10.0L (10.56 US qt)
N52: • Automatic transmission • Manual transmission	10.2L (11.20 US qt) 10.0L (10.56 US qt)

Tightening torques	
Drain plug to engine block: • M14 x 1.5 • M16 x 1.5 • M18 x 1.5	25 Nm (18 ft-lb) 35 Nm (26 ft-lb) 40 Nm (30 ft-lb)

Cooling system, bleeding

Trapped air in the cooling system can prevent proper coolant circulation and cause overheating. Whenever the coolant is drained and filled, bleed the cooling system.

Models equipped with the N52 engine feature an electric coolant pump. The bleeding procedure operates the coolant pump for approximately 12 minutes to remove trapped air and ensure that the cooling system is filled to capacity.

CAUTION—

- *Carry out this procedure when replacing cooling system components or refilling the cooling system. Failure to follow this procedure may result in incomplete filling of cooling system, overheating and engine damage.*

Cooling system, bleeding

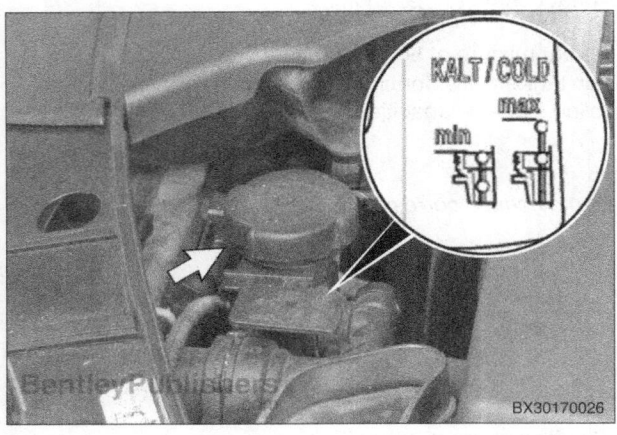

— Before refilling radiator:
- Switch ignition ON. (Do not start engine).
- Set temperature controls to full warm.
- Set blower control to low.

◄ Using a coolant mixture of 50% antifreeze and 50% distilled water, fill expansion tank slowly to MAX.

> **CAUTION—**
> • *Use genuine BMW coolant or its equivalent to avoid the formation of harmful, clogging deposits in the cooling system.*

◄ **Additional steps for N52 engine with electric coolant pump**:

1. Close cap on coolant expansion tank.
2. Connect vehicle power supply. See **600 Electrical System– General**.
3. Switch ignition ON, switch low-beam headlights ON.
4. Press accelerator pedal to floor for 10 seconds.
5. Bleeding procedure begins when accelerator pedal is pressed and takes approximately 12 minutes. (Electric coolant pump turns ON and OFF automatically after approx. 12 minutes).

> **CAUTION—**
> • *Do not open expansion tank cap until bleeding procedure has completed.*
> • *If bleeding procedure must be repeated, remove ignition key and wait at least three minutes before restarting procedure.*

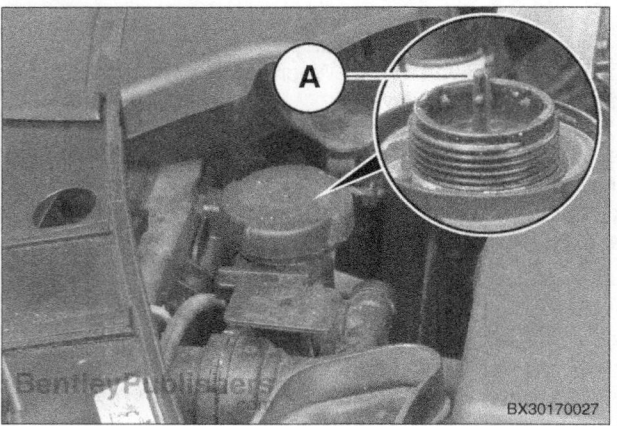

◄ After filling cooling system and performing bleeding procedure (N52 engine only), start engine and run at idle speed for one minute (cap open). Adjust coolant level to MAX (**A**). Close cap.

- Run engine until it reaches operating temperature.
- After engine has cooled, recheck coolant level.
- Top up so that coolant level indicator is at MAX.
- If trapped air cannot be bled manually, vacuum-bleed system using cooling system vacuum filler.

Front intake cowl, removing and installing

◄ Remove fasteners (**arrows**) and remove front intake cowl from radiator support.

◄ Remove intake cowl from radiator:
- Remove intake duct (**A**).
- Remove fasteners (**arrows**).
- Lift up rear of intake duct and remove from radiator support.

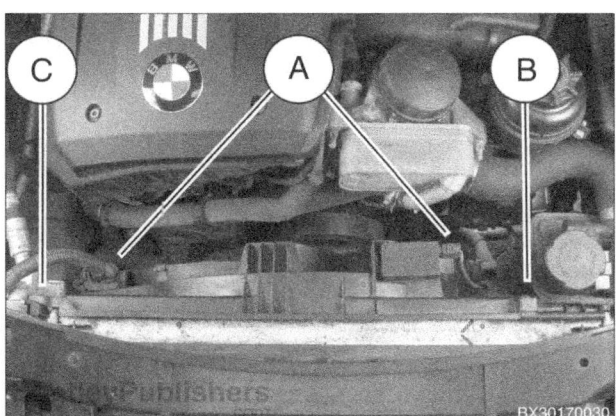

◄ Remove electrical connectors (**A**).
- Lever out expansion rivet (**B**).
- Remove fastener (**C**).

– Lift fan cowl up to remove.

– Installation is reverse of removal. Remember to:
- Electric cooling fan cowl clips securely at bottom.
- Correctly route all electric harnesses.
- Check and clear fault codes from ECM memory.

Radiator, removing and installing

— Raise car and support safely

> **WARNING—**
> • *Make sure the car is stable and well supported at all times. Use a professional automotive lift or jack stands. A floor jack is not adequate support.*

— Remove splash shield from under engine.

— Drain radiator. See **Coolant draining and filling** in this repair group.

> **WARNING—**
> • *Allow cooling system to cool before opening or draining system.*

— Remove electric cooling fan and cowl. See **Electric cooling fan and cowl, removing and installing** in this repair group.

◀ Release hose retaining clips and disconnect upper and lower coolant hose fittings (**A, B**).

◀ Working on ride side of radiator, release hose retaining clips (**A**) and disconnect lower coolant hose fitting from radiator (**B**).

— Working underneath radiator, disconnect harness connector from coolant level sensor in coolant expansion tank.

> **NOTE—**
> • *M54 engine cooling line shown with radiator outlet temperature sensor.*

Radiator, removing and installing

◀ Vehicles equipped with automatic transmission:

• Disconnect automatic transmission fluid (ATF) cooler lines from ATF cooler at quick disconnect unions (**arrows**) as follows:

• Push hose toward oil cooler.

• Press black locking ring into hose fitting while pulling hose off cooler.

CAUTION—

• *Be sure to have drain pan ready to catch spilled ATF.*

NOTE—

• *Alternatively, ATF cooler can be removed from radiator and left in vehicle by pulling up on quick release clips and pulling cooler from radiator tank.*

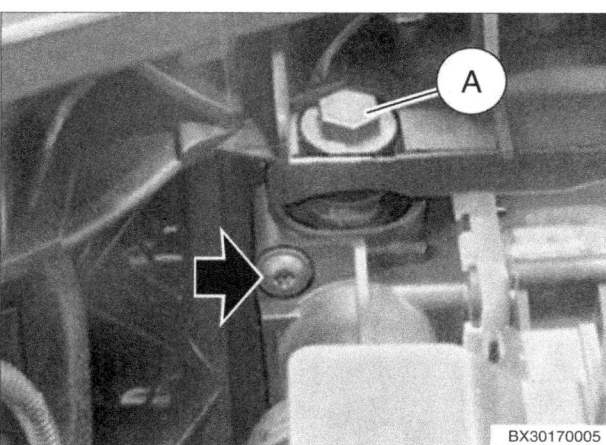

◀ Working at left side of radiator:

• Remove screw (**arrow**).

• Loosen fastener for radiator mount (**A**).

◀ Working at right side of radiator:

• Loosen fastener for radiator mount (**A**).

Coolant expansion tank, removing and installing

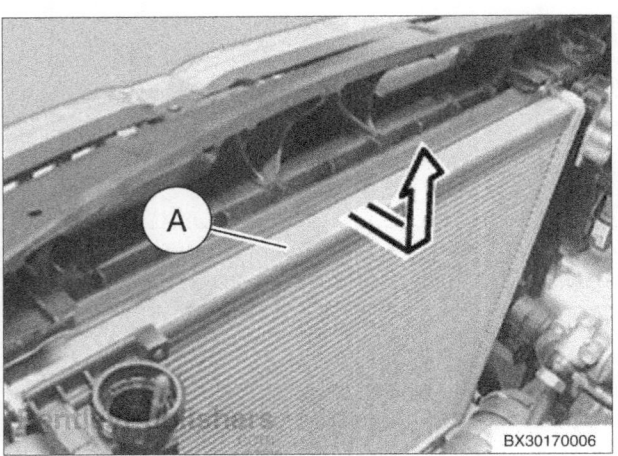

BX30170006

◀ Tilt radiator (**A**) inwards and lift out of engine compartment in direction of arrow.

– Installation is reverse of removal. Make sure:
  • Radiator seats firmly in lower mounts.
  • Electric cooling fan cowl clips securely at bottom.
  • Refill and bleed cooling system. See **Cooling system, bleeding** in this repair group.
  • Check cooling system for leaks.

Coolant expansion tank, removing and installing

– Drain cooling system. See **Coolant, draining and filling** in this repair group.

> **WARNING—**
> • *Allow cooling system to cool before opening or draining system.*

– Remove cooling fan and cowl. See **Electric cooling fan and cowl, removing and installing** in this repair group.

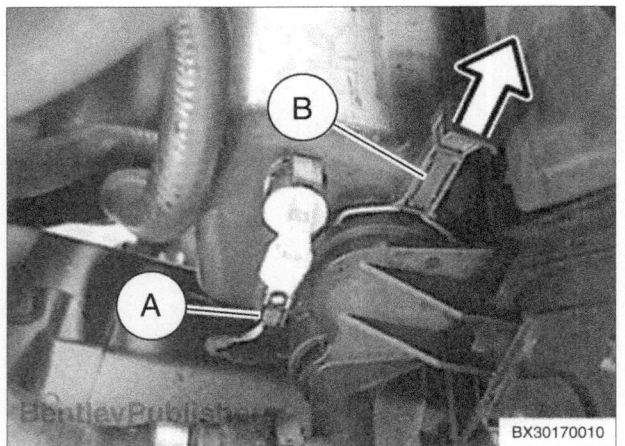

BX30170010

◀ Working at bottom of expansion tank:
  • Remove connector for level sensor (**A**).
  • Pull retaining clip (**B**) in direction of arrow to release.

Coolant expansion tank, removing and installing

◀ Release hose retaining clips and disconnect upper and lower coolant hose fittings (**A, B**).

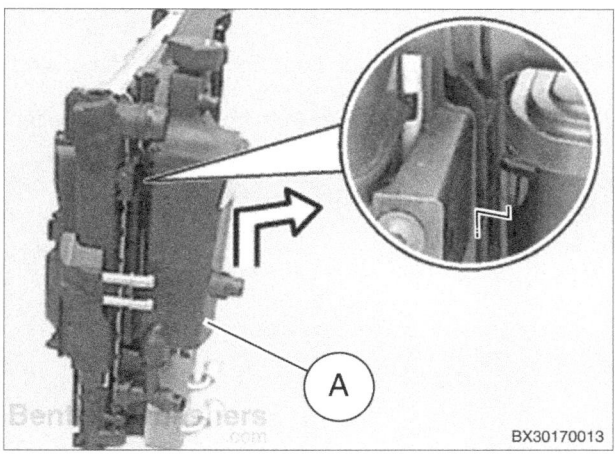

◀ Lift expansion tank (**A**) slightly upwards to release from mounting bracket (**inset**), then tilt tank towards rear and lift to remove.

— Installation is reverse of removal. Remember to:

 • Make sure tank is clipped securely in mounting bracket and retaining clip is fully engaged at bottom of tank.

 • Fill and bleed cooling system. See **Cooling system, bleeding** in this repair group.

 • Check cooling system for leaks.

Thermostat, removing and installing (M54 engine)

The electrically-heated thermostat is an integral part of the thermostat housing. The operation of the thermostat is monitored by the ECM. If a faulty thermostat is suspected, interrogate the ECM for stored fault codes using a BMW scan tool.

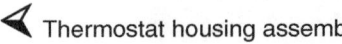 Thermostat housing assembly

1. Bolt M6
2. Bolt M8
3. Housing with heated thermostat
4. Gasket

— Drain radiator and engine block. See **Coolant, draining and filling** in this repair group.

> **WARNING—**
> • *Allow cooling system to cool before opening system.*

— Remove cooling fan and cowl. See **Electric cooling fan and cowl, removing and installing** in this repair group.

— Disconnect electrical harness connector from thermostat housing.

— Cover alternator to prevent damage from coolant.

◄ Lever out retaining clips (**arrows**) and pull hose fittings off housing.

— Unbolt and remove thermostat housing from front of engine. Loosen nut at top of engine lifting eye to facilitate removal.

— Installation is reverse of removal, noting the following:
  • Keep sealing faces free of oil.
  • Use new sealing gasket.

— Fill system with coolant and bleed. See **Coolant, draining and filling** in this repair group.

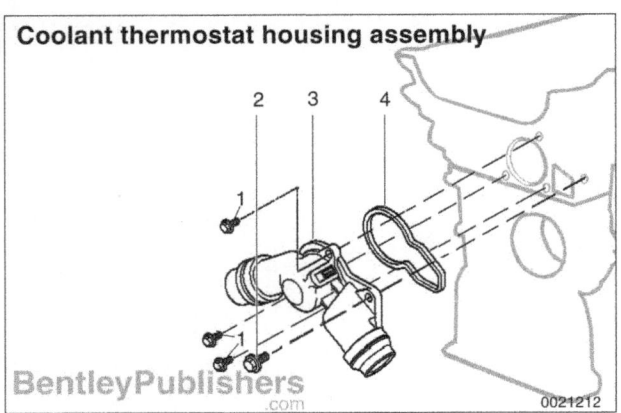

Coolant thermostat housing assembly

Thermostat, removing and installing (N52 engine)

— Raise car and support safely

> **WARNING—**
> • Make sure the car is stable and well supported at all times. Use a professional automotive lift or jack stands designed for the purpose. A floor jack is not adequate support.

— Remove splash shield from under engine.

— Remove cooling fan and cowl. See **Electric cooling fan and cowl, removing and installing** in this repair group.

— Drain cooling system. See **Coolant, draining and filling** in this repair group.

> **WARNING—**
> • Allow cooling system to cool before opening or draining system.

 Working above engine coolant pump, release hose clamps (**A**, **B**) and disconnect hoses.

— Unlock fasteners (**C**, **D**) and remove hoses.

— Disconnect electrical connector (**E**).

— Remove bolts (**F**) and remove thermostat (**G**).

— Installation is reverse of removal. Remember to:
  • Refill and bleed cooling system. See **Cooling system, bleeding** in this repair group.
  • Check cooling system for leaks.

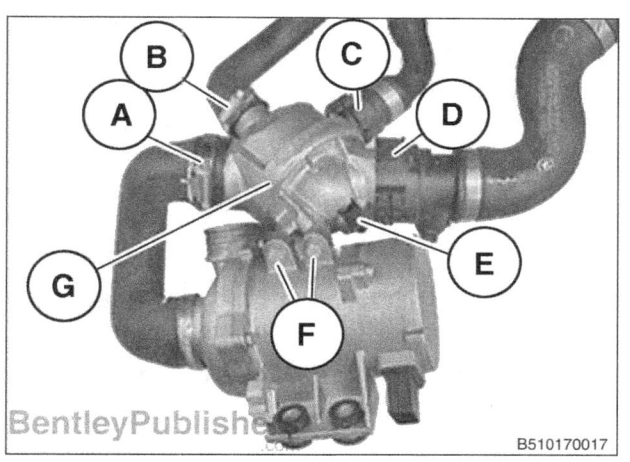

Tightening torques	
Thermostat to coolant pump	9 Nm (80 in-lb)

Coolant pump, removing and installing (M54 engine)

— Remove cooling fan and cowl. See **Electric cooling fan and cowl, removing and installing** in this repair group.

— Drain cooling system. See **Coolant, draining and filling** in this repair group.

> **WARNING—**
> • Allow cooling system to cool before opening or draining system.

— Cover alternator to prevent damage from coolant.

— Loosen coolant pump pulley bolts slightly but do not remove.

— Remove alternator drive belt. See **020 Maintenance**. Mark direction of rotation on belt.

Coolant pump, removing and installing (N52 engine)

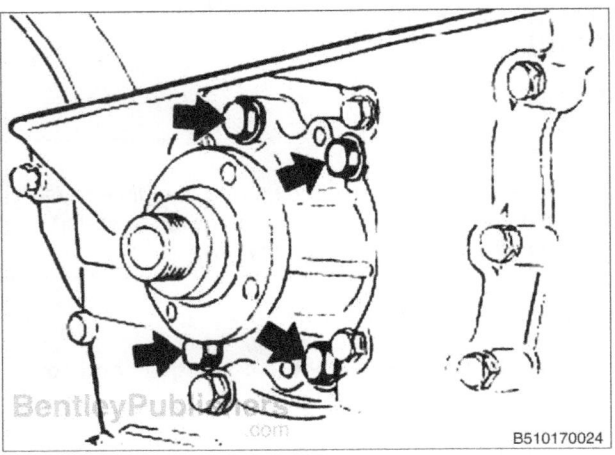

B510170024

B510170025

– Remove coolant pump pulley bolts the rest of the way and remove pulley from pump.

◀ Remove coolant pump fasteners (**arrows**).

◀ Insert two M6 screws (**arrows**) in tapped bores and tighten uniformly until pump is free from timing chain cover.

– Installation is reverse of removal. Remember to:
  • Replace sealing O-ring and gaskets.
  • Coat O-ring with lubricant during installation.
  • Refill and bleed cooling system. See **Cooling system, bleeding** in this repair group.
  • Check cooling system for leaks

Tightening torques	
Coolant pump to timing chain cover	10 Nm (89 in-lb)
Coolant pump pulley to coolant pump	10 Nm (89 in-lb)

Coolant pump, removing and installing (N52 engine)

– Remove splash shield from under engine.

– Remove cooling fan and cowl. See **Electric cooling fan and cowl, removing and installing** in this repair group.

– Drain cooling system. See **Coolant, draining and filling** in this repair group.

> **WARNING—**
> • *Allow cooling system to cool before opening or draining system.*

– Cover alternator to prevent damage from coolant.

– Remove coolant thermostat. See **Thermostat, removing and installing** in this repair group.

◀ Release hose clamps (**1**) and disconnect coolant hoses from back of pump.

– Disconnect electrical connector (**4**) at front of pump.

– Remove bolts (**5**) and remove pump from side of engine.

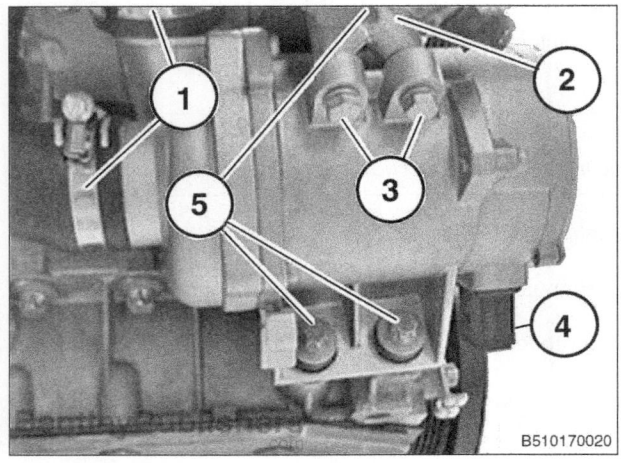

B510170020

170

> **CAUTION—**
> • If coolant pump is to be reused, fill with mixture of 50% antifreeze and 50% distilled water immediately after removing, and plug openings to avoid contamination.

– Installation is reverse of removal. Remember to:

  • Replace aluminum fasteners (fasteners with heads painted blue) with new.

> **CAUTION—**
> • Do not use steel fasteners in place of aluminum. Electrochemical corrosion will result.

  • Reinstall thermostat.

  • Refill and bleed cooling system. See **Cooling system, bleeding** in this repair group.

  • Check cooling system for leaks.

Tightening torques	
Thermostat to coolant pump	9 Nm (80 in-lb)
Coolant pump to engine block (replace aluminum fasteners with new and observe torque angle)	10 Nm (89 in-lb) + 90° turn

Automatic transmission fluid (ATF) cooler, removing and installing

– Remove splash shield from under engine.

– Remove cooling fan and cowl. See **Electric cooling fan and cowl, removing and installing** in this repair group.

– Drain cooling system. See **Coolant, draining and filling** in this repair group.

> **CAUTION—**
> • Cover alternator when working on oil, coolant or fuel circuits to protect from damage.

 Disconnect automatic transmission fluid (ATF) cooler lines from ATF cooler at quick disconnect unions (**arrows**) as follows:

  • Push hose toward oil cooler.

  • Press black locking ring into hose fitting while pulling hose off cooler.

BX30170003

Power steering fluid cooling loop, removing and installing

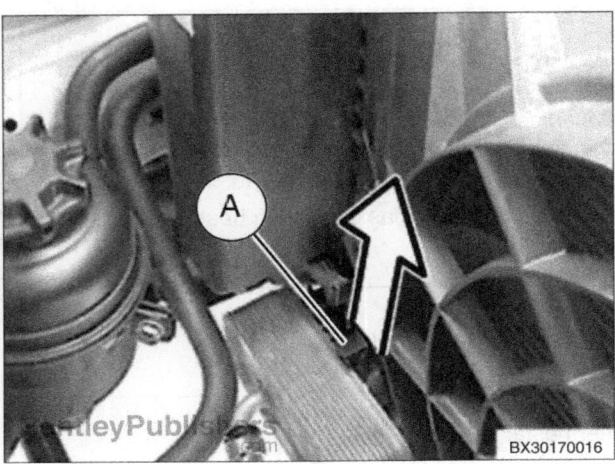

◄ Release lock (**A**) in direction of **arrow**. Pull ATF cooler away from radiator to remove.

– Installation is reverse of removal. Remember to:

• Replace all sealing rings.

• Press lock (**A**) downwards before installing ATF cooler.

• Lock (**A**) must snap audibly into place when installing ATF cooler.

• Check automatic transmission fluid level. See **240 Automatic Transmission**.

• Refill and bleed cooling system. See **Cooling system, bleeding** in this repair group.

• Check cooling system for leaks.

Power steering fluid cooling loop, removing and installing

– Raise car and support safely

> **WARNING** —
> • *Make sure car is stable and well supported at all times. Use a professional automotive lift or jack stands. A floor jack is not adequate support.*

– Remove splash shield from under engine.

– Drain radiator. See **Coolant draining and filling** in this repair group.

> **WARNING** —
> • *Allow cooling system to cool before opening or draining system.*

– Remove electric cooling fan and cowl. See **Electric cooling fan and cowl, removing and installing** in this repair group.

– Remove radiator. See **Radiator, removing and installing** in this repair group.

– Using a fluid recovery machine, suction fluid from power steering fluid reservoir.

◄ Remove expansion rivet (**A**) from left side of A/C condenser.

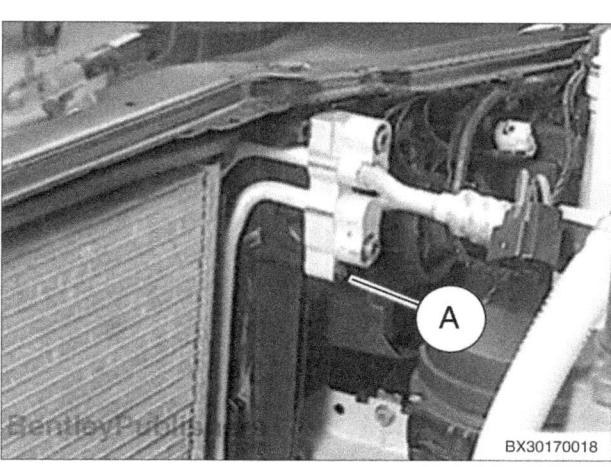

◄ Remove fastener (**A**) from right side of A/C condenser.

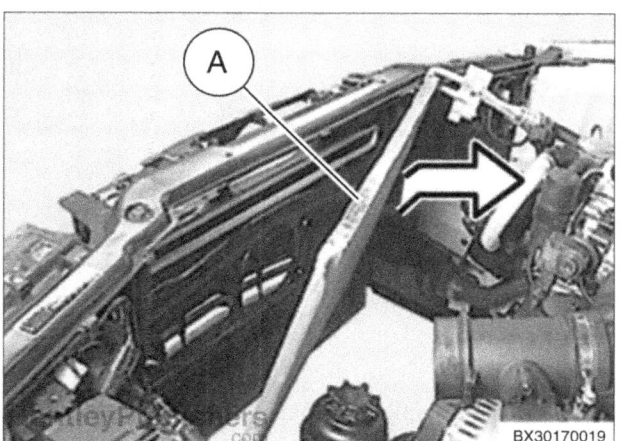

◄ Tilt A/C condenser towards engine and support in place.

> **CAUTION—**
> • *Do not disconnect A/C refrigerant lines.*

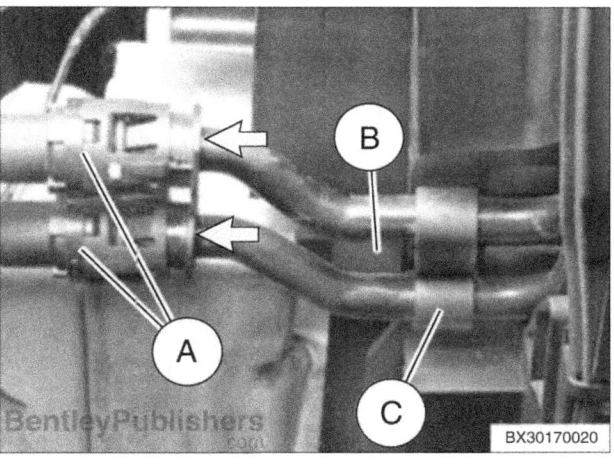

◄ Press hydraulic lines (**A**) towards cooling loop. Pull back on locking ring (**arrows**) and remove lines.

– Place a suitable container beneath power steering cooling loop connections to catch dripping fluid. Dispose of properly.

– Press lock (**B**), then remove cooling loop (**C**) from module carrier towards rear.

– Installation is reverse of removal. Remember to:

  • Make sure cooling loop hydraulic lines connect securely.

  • Check that cooling loop lines snap securely into holder (**A**).

  • Refill and bleed cooling system. See **Cooling system, bleeding** in this repair group.

  • Refill and bleed power steering system. See **320 Steering and Wheel Alignment**.

  • Check cooling system for leaks.

180 Exhaust System

GENERAL

This repair group covers removal and replacement of the exhaust system, including exhaust manifolds, and oxygen sensors.

Warnings and Cautions

> *WARNING—*
> * *Exhaust gases are colorless, odorless, and very toxic. Run the engine only in a well-ventilated area. Immediately repair any leaks in the exhaust system or structural damage to the car body that might allow exhaust gases to enter the passenger compartment.*
> * *The exhaust system and catalytic converter operate at very high temperatures. Allow components to cool before servicing. Wear protective clothing to prevent burns. Do not use flammable chemicals near a hot catalytic converter.*
> * *Corroded exhaust system components crumble easily and often have exposed sharp edges. To avoid injury, wear eye protection and heavy gloves when working with old exhaust system parts.*

> *CAUTION—*
> * *Prior to disconnecting the battery, read the battery disconnection cautions given in* **001 Warnings and Cautions**.
> * *Replace aluminum fasteners when loosened.*
> * *Use care not to drag or bang oxygen sensors. Oxygen sensors are easily damaged.*
> * *When detaching and reattaching oxygen sensor connectors, make sure front and rear connectors are not mixed up.*
> * *The exhaust system is heavy. Work with an assistant.*

Exhaust system components (M54 engine)

EXHAUST SYSTEM

The exhaust system is designed to be maintenance free, although regular inspection is warranted due to the harsh operating conditions. Under normal conditions, catalytic converters do not require replacement unless damaged

Use new fasteners, clamps, rubber mounts and gaskets when replacing exhaust components. A liberal application of penetrating oil to the exhaust system nuts and bolts in advance may make removal easier.

On both M54 and N52 engines, catalytic converters are integrated in each exhaust manifold.

N52 engines include downstream catalytic converters that are welded into the exhaust system and must be cut off to be replaced.

Exhaust system components (M54 engine)

1. Exhaust manifold, cyl 1-3
2. Exhaust manifold, cyl 4-6
3. Pre-catalyst oxygen sensor, cyl 1-3
4. Pre-catalyst oxygen sensor, cyl 4-6
5. Post-catalyst oxygen sensor, cyl 1-3
6. Post-catalyst oxygen sensor, cyl 4-6
7. Bracket

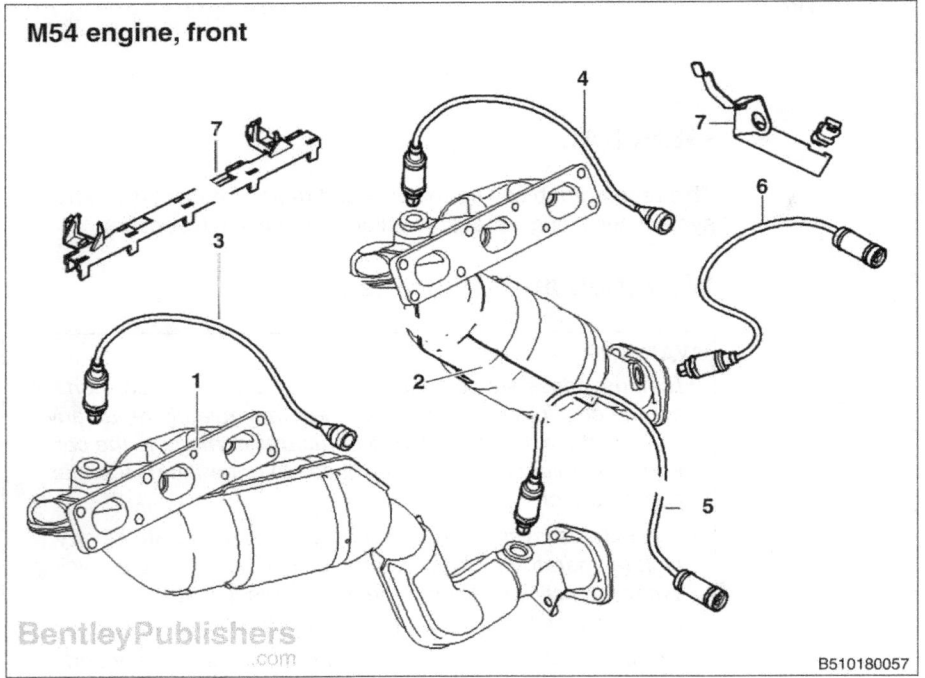

M54 engine, front

B510180057

M54 engine, center, rear

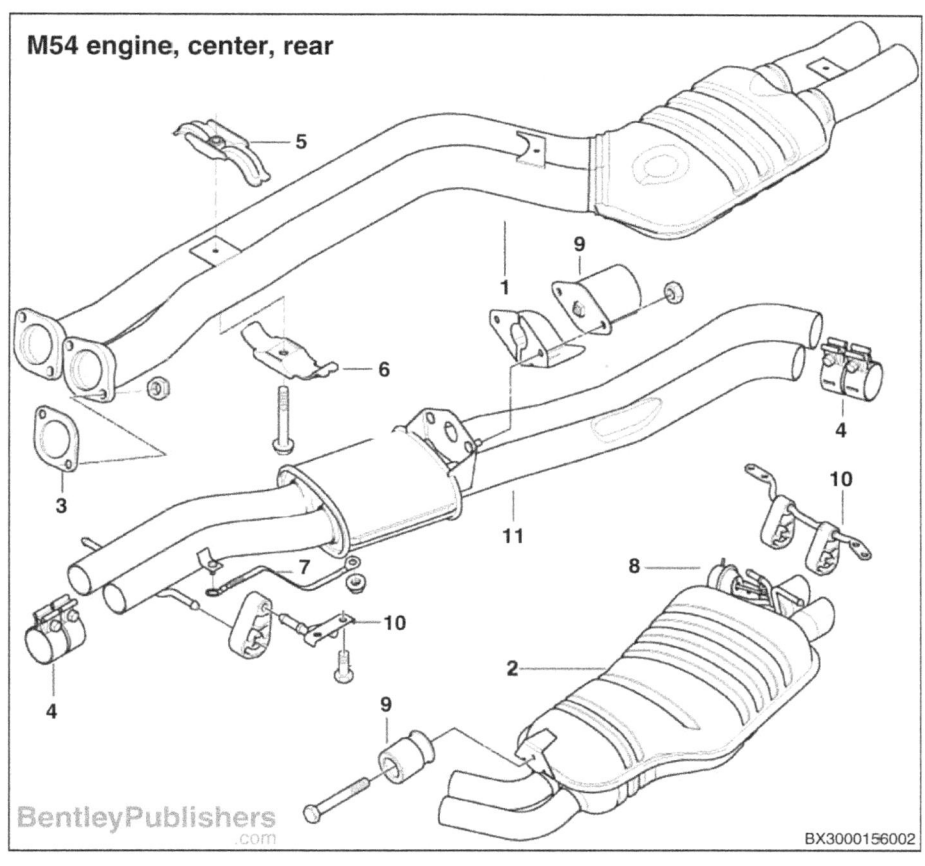

BX3000156002

BentleyPublishers.com

1. Mid pipe
2. Muffler
3. Gasket
4. Band clamp
5. Bracket
6. Bracket
7. Ground Strap
8. Muffler silencing flap
9. Vibration damper
10. Exhaust hanger
11. Rear pipe

Exhaust system components (N52 engine)

N52 engine, front

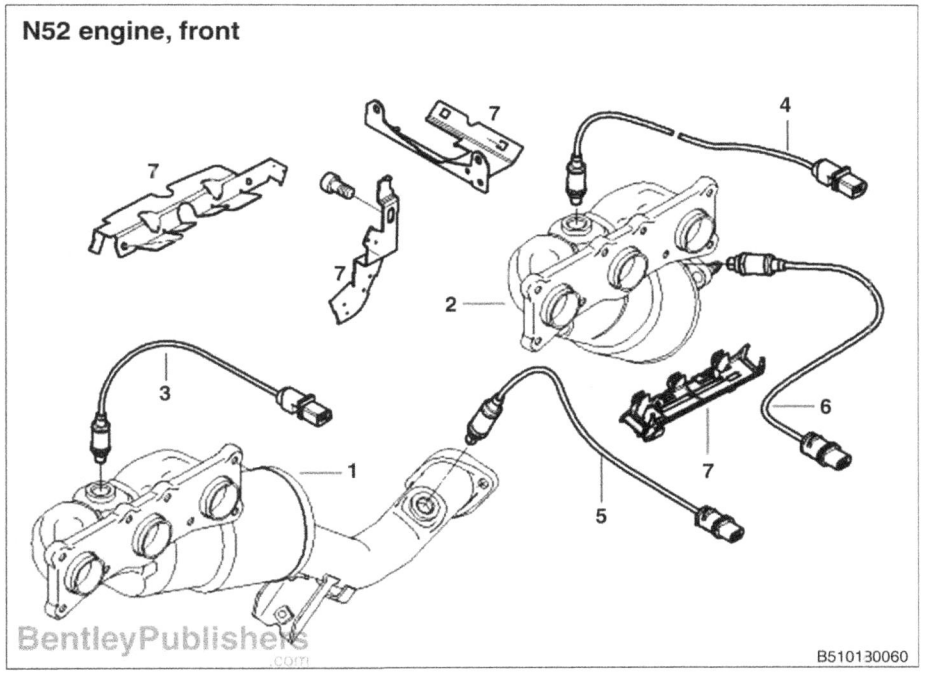

B510130060

BentleyPublishers.com

1. Exhaust manifold, cyl 1-3
2. Exhaust manifold, cyl 4-6
3. Pre-catalyst oxygen sensor, cyl 1-3
4. Pre-catalyst oxygen sensor, cyl 4-6
5. Post-catalyst oxygen sensor, cyl 1-3
6. Post-catalyst oxygen sensor, cyl 4-6
7. Bracket

Exhaust system, removing and installing

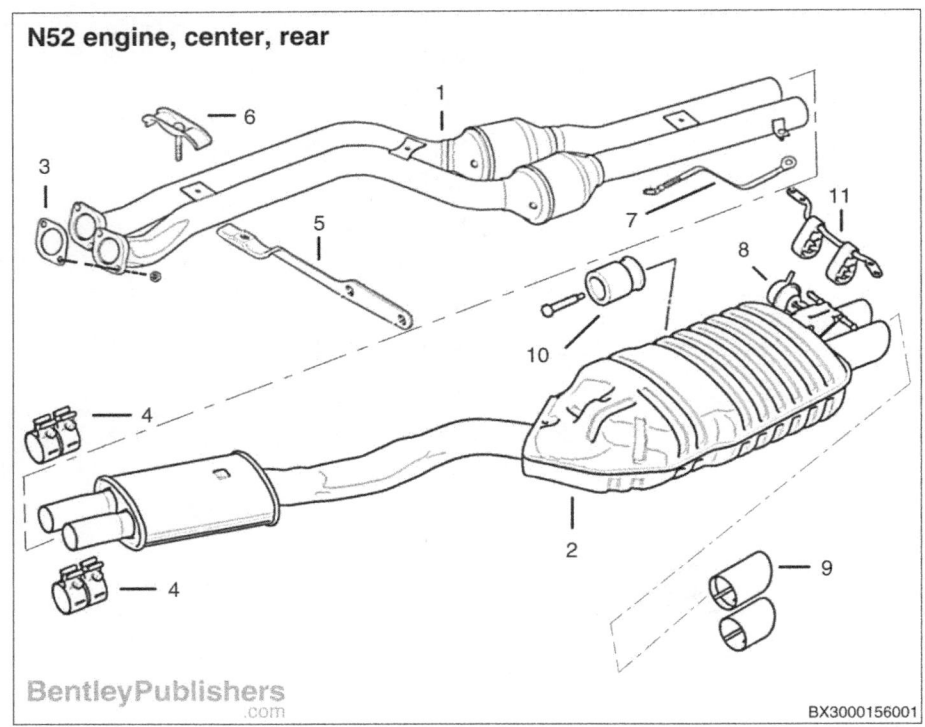

N52 engine, center, rear

1. Mid pipe with catalytic converters
2. Muffler
3. Gasket
4. Band clamp
5. Bracket
6. Bracket
7. Ground strap
8. Muffler silencing flap
9. Tail pipe trim
10. Vibration damper
11. Exhaust hanger

BX3000156001

Exhaust system, removing and installing

Remove exhaust system as a complete unit.

Once the complete system is removed from the car, replace individual pipes and mufflers. Rear muffler can be replaced without removing exhaust system.

– Raise vehicle and support safely.

> **WARNING—**
> • Make sure vehicle is stable and well supported at all times. Use a professional automotive lift or jack stands. A floor jack is not adequate support.

 Support exhaust system from below using a tall jack stand or other suitable jack.

BX30180041

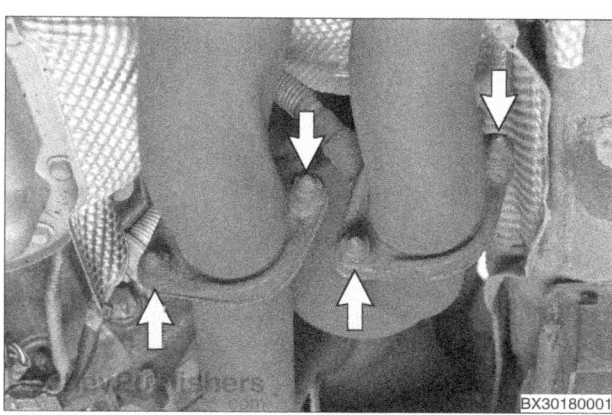

◄ Release nuts at exhaust manifolds (**arrows**).

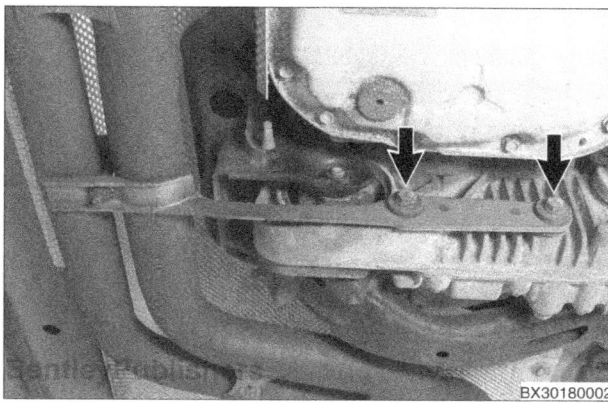

◄ Remove exhaust pipe support fasteners from transfer case (**arrows**). N52 engine. Release ground strap from exhaust.

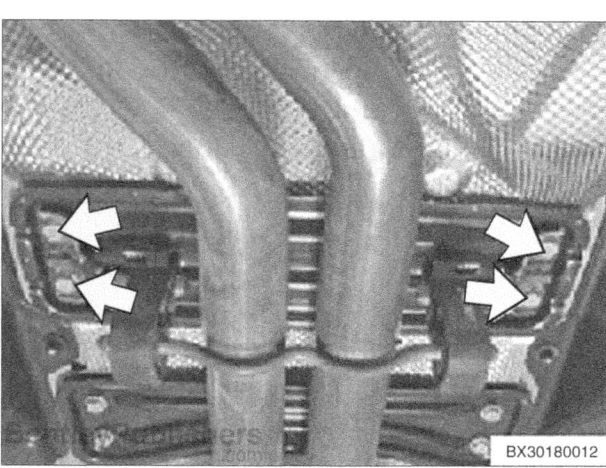

◄ Remove exhaust pipe support fasteners from body (**arrows**). M54 engine. Release ground strap from exhaust.

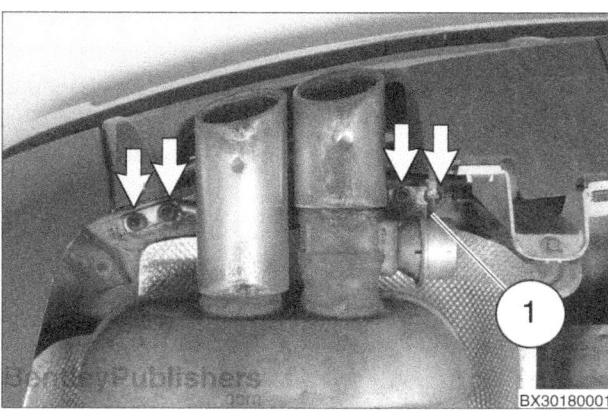

◄ Pull off vacuum hose (**1**) and unscrew nuts.

– Carefully lower complete exhaust system and remove.

Exhaust system components, removing and installing

— Installation is reverse of removal. Remember to:
  - Use new gaskets and hardware.
  - Coat hardware threads with anti-seize paste.
  - Loosely install exhaust system mounting hardware and hangers before tightening fasteners to their final torque.
  - Make sure there is sufficient clearance between exhaust system and vehicle underbody at every point.
  - Check exhaust system for leaks.

Tightening torques	
Exhaust pipe to manifold flange	45 Nm (33 ft-lb)
Front exhaust pipe support to transmission	20 Nm (15 ft-lb)
Exhaust system hanger to rear subframe	20 Nm (15 ft-lb)
Exhaust system hanger to rear subframe	20 Nm (15 ft-lb)

Exhaust system components, removing and installing

BMW offers individual exhaust components as replacement parts. Originally installed exhaust components are welded together at the factory and must be cut off to be replaced.

Muffler replacement is best accomplished by first removing the complete exhaust system. See **Exhaust system, removing and installing** in this repair group.

— Measure old exhaust system parts against replacement parts to locate cutting point.

◄ Use exhaust pipe cutter (BMW special tool 00 2 210 or equivalent) to cut pipe(s). Deburr cut ends.

00 2 210

BX30ele186213

◄ Assemble pipes using band clamps.

— Installation is reverse of removal. Remember to:
  - Use new gaskets and hardware.
  - Coat hardware threads with anti-seize paste.
  - Loosely install exhaust system mounting hardware and hangers before tightening fasteners to their final torque.
  - Make sure there is sufficient clearance between exhaust system and vehicle underbody at every point.
  - Check exhaust system for leaks.

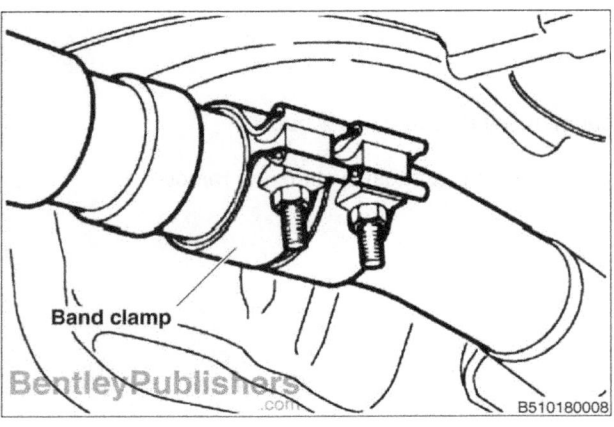

Band clamp

B510180008

Tightening torque	
Band clamp to exhaust pipes	45 Nm (33 ft-lb)

OXYGEN SENSORS

Oxygen sensors are installed at the front and rear of the catalytic converters. Prior to sensor removal, use BMW scan tool to read and clear ECM fault codes.

> **CAUTION—**
> * Use care not to drop or bang on oxygen sensors. Oxygen sensors are easily damaged.
> * To avoid possible engine damage, do not mix up oxygen sensor connectors. Mark connectors before disassembling.

Pre-catalyst oxygen sensors, removing (M54 engine)

BX3018021552

— Remove brace from strut towers. See **310 Front Suspension**.

— Remove housing for interior ventilation microfilter. See **640 Heating and Air-conditioning**.

— Remove engine covers. See **020 Maintenance**.

◄ Working on right side of engine. Label oxygen sensor harness connectors (**arrows**) then disconnect. Remove oxygen sensors (**A**) using 22mm crow-foot wrench.

— Installation is reverse of removal. Remember to:
  * Apply a small amount of anti-seize compound to sensor threads.
  * Make sure sensor electrical harness connectors are routed as before and connected correctly.

Post-catalyst oxygen sensors, removing (M54 engine)

BX30180013

— Remove brace from strut towers. See **310 Front Suspension**.

— Remove housing for interior ventilation microfilter. See **640 Heating and Air-conditioning**.

— Remove engine covers. See **020 Maintenance**.

◄ Working on top of engine. Label oxygen sensor harness connectors (**arrows**) then disconnect.

— Raise vehicle and support safely.

— Working from under engine, remove front end reinforcement plate. See **310 Front Suspension**.

> **WARNING—**
> * Be sure vehicle is stable and well supported at all times. Use a professional automotive lift or jack stands. A floor jack is not adequate support.

Pre-catalyst oxygen sensors, removing (N52 engine)

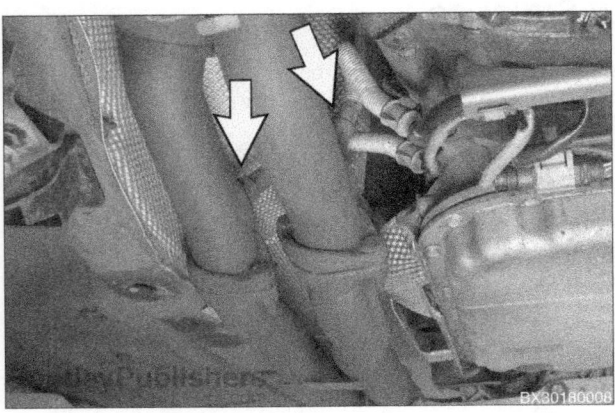

◀ Remove oxygen sensors (**arrows**) using 22mm crow-foot wrench. N52 engine shown, M54 engine similar.

– Installation is reverse of removal. Remember to:
  • Apply a small amount of anti-seize compound to sensor threads if not already present.
  • Make sure sensor electrical harness connectors are routed as before and connected correctly

Pre-catalyst oxygen sensors, removing (N52 engine)

– Remove engine covers. See **020 Maintenance**.

◀ Working on top of engine. Label oxygen sensor harness connectors (**arrows**).

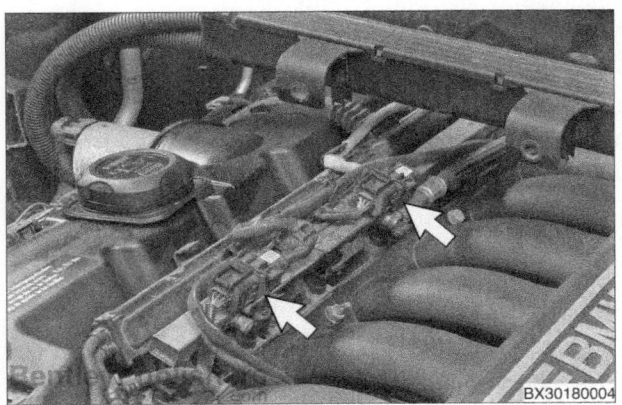

◀ Working at passenger side of engine above exhaust manifolds. Remove 2 Torx bolts (**arrows**) attaching bracket to exhaust manifold and remove bracket.

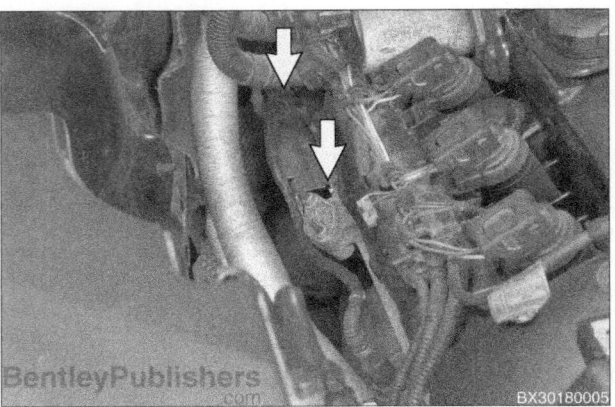

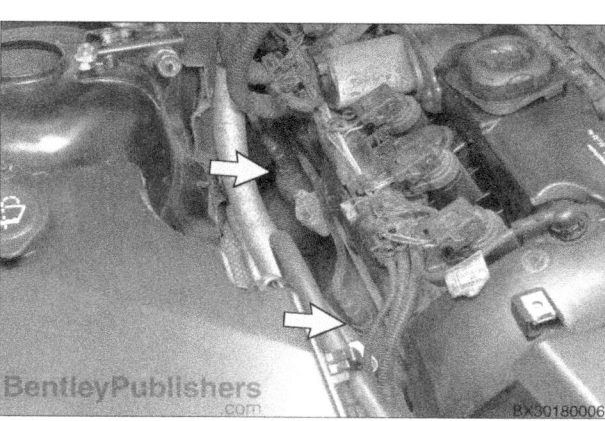

◀ Remove oxygen sensors (**arrows**) using 22mm crow-foot wrench.

– Installation is reverse of removal. Remember to:
  • Apply a small amount of anti-seize compound to sensor threads.
  • Make sure sensor electrical harness connectors are routed as before and connected correctly

Post-catalyst oxygen sensors (N52 engine)

– Raise vehicle and support safely.

– Working from under engine, remove front end reinforcement plate. See **310 Front Suspension**.

> **WARNING—**
> • *Make sure vehicle is stable and well supported at all times. Use a professional automotive lift or jack stands. A floor jack is not adequate support.*

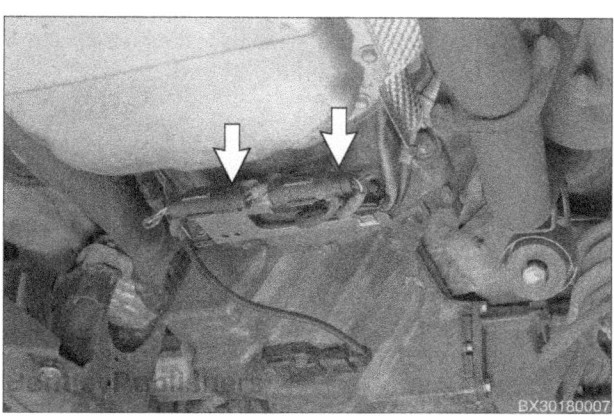

◀ Oxygen sensor connectors (**arrows**) are located under transmission bell housing between engine oil pan and transmission oil pan. Label oxygen sensor harness connectors then disconnect.

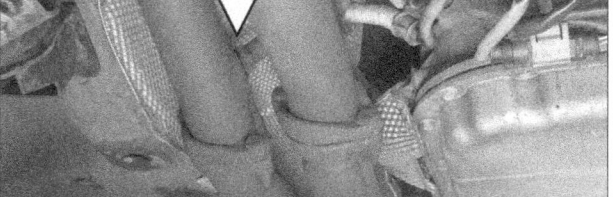

◀ Remove oxygen sensors (**arrows**) using 22 mm crow-foot wrench.

– Installation is reverse of removal. Remember to:
  • Apply a small amount of anti-seize compound to sensor threads.
  • Make sure sensor electrical harness connectors are routed as before and connected correctly.

> **CAUTION—**
> • *Do not overuse anti-seize paste. Do not contaminate tip of sensor with paste or lubricants.*

Tightening torques

Oxygen sensor to exhaust pipe:	
• Using BMW special tool 11 7 020	50 Nm (37 ft-lb)
• Using BMW special tool 11 7 030	47 Nm (35 ft-lb)

Exhaust manifolds (cylinders 1 - 3), removing and installing

EXHAUST MANIFOLDS

Each manifold includes an integral catalytic converter. Should the catalyst need replacing, replace the appropriate exhaust manifold / catalyst unit. See **Exhaust System Components** in this repair group.

Exhaust manifolds (cylinders 1 - 3), removing and installing

— Remove engine cover. See **020 Maintenance**.

◀ Support engine from above with suitable hoist. See **110 Engine removal and installation.**

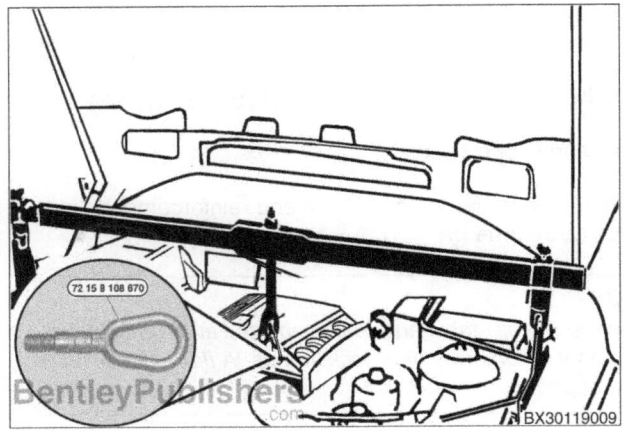

NOTE—
• *Use tow hook (BMW #72 15 8 108 670) to support **N52 engine** at front of cylinder head.*

— Working from under engine, remove front end reinforcement plate. See **310 Front suspension.**

— Remove complete exhaust system. See **Exhaust system, removing and installing** in this repair group.

— Remove ground cable from body.

— Evacuate and recover A/C system (N52 only). Remove screws and disconnect electrical connection. Disconnect pressure and suction A/C lines. See **640 Heating and Air-conditioning.**

— Remove oxygen sensors. See **Oxygen Sensors** in this repair group.

◀ **M54 engine**: Remove right engine support mount.
• Remove fastener for isolator (**A**).
• Remove bolts between mount and engine block (**B**).
• Remove mount and set aside.

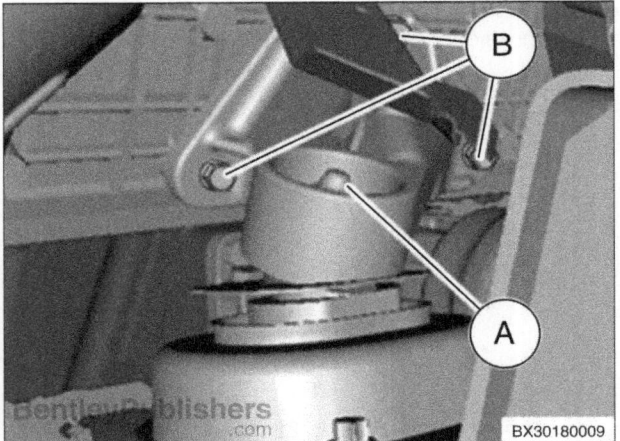

◀ **N52 engine**: Remove right engine support mount.
• Remove fastener for isolator (**A**).
• Remove bolts between mount and engine block (**B**).
• Remove mount and set aside.

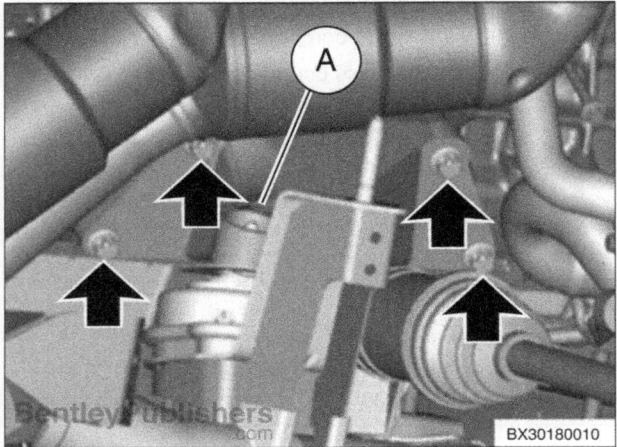

Exhaust manifold (cylinders 4 - 6), removing and installing

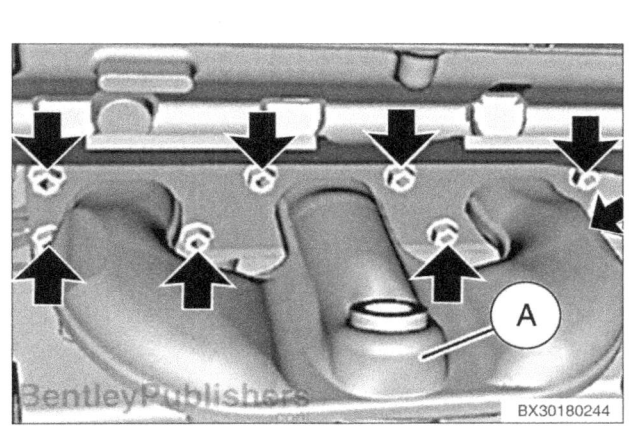

BX30180243

◀ Remove fasteners (**arrows**) and remove exhaust manifold (**A**).

- Installation is reverse of removal. Remember to:
  - Clean sealing surfaces of manifold and cylinder head.
  - Use new gaskets and hardware.
  - Check exhaust system for leaks.

Tightening torques	
Exhaust manifold to cylinder head	20 Nm (15 ft-lb)
Front pipe to exhaust manifold	45 Nm (33 ft-lb)
Oxygen sensor to exhaust manifold	50 Nm (37 ft-lb)

Exhaust manifold (cylinders 4 - 6), removing and installing

- Remove exhaust manifold for cylinders 1-3.

- Remove oxygen sensors. See **Oxygen Sensors** in this repair group.

- **M54 engine**: Remove secondary air pump.

◀ Remove fasteners (**arrows**) from rear exhaust manifold (**1**) and remove manifold.

- Installation is reverse of removal. Remember to:
  - Clean sealing surfaces of manifold and cylinder head.
  - Use new gaskets and hardware.
  - Check exhaust system for leaks.

Tightening torques	
Exhaust manifold to cylinder head	20 Nm (15 ft-lb)
Front pipe to exhaust manifold	45 Nm (33 ft-lb)
Oxygen sensor to exhaust manifold	50 Nm (37 ft-lb)

BX30180244

200 Transmission–General

200

GENERAL

This section provides general information for drivetrain components such as clutch, transmission, xDrive transfer case.

See also:

- **119 Lubrication System** for rear main seal replacement

- **210 Clutch** for clutch mechanical and hydraulic repairs and flywheel replacement

- **230 Manual Transmission** for manual transmission fluid service, seal replacement and transmission replacement

- **240 Automatic Transmission** for ATF change and transmission replacement

- **260 Driveshafts** for front and rear driveshaft repairs

- **270 Transfer Case** for xDrive transfer case replacement

- **311 Front Axle Differential** for front differential, front drive axles and front CV joints

- **331 Rear Axle Differential** for rear differential, rear drive axles and rear CV joints

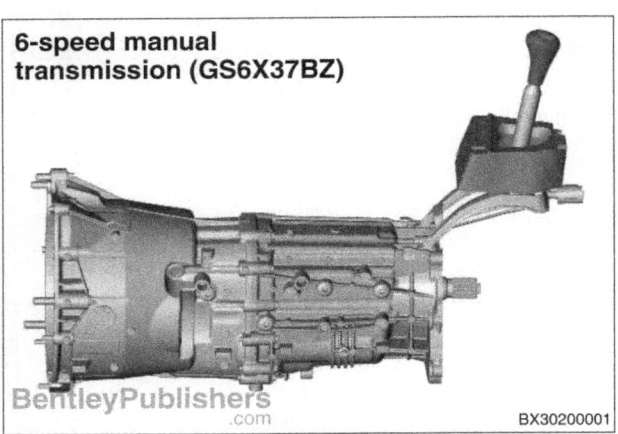

6-speed manual
transmission (GS6X37BZ)

BX30200001

DRIVETRAIN

X3 models are equipped with a longitudinal drivetrain. The transmission is bolted directly to the rear of the engine. A transfer case is mounted to the rear of the transmission, with drive shafts leading to front and rear differentials. Individual drive axles with integrated constant velocity joints transfer rotational power from the differentials to the drive wheels.

MANUAL TRANSMISSION

◄ A 6-speed manual transmission is standard on all models.

NOTE—

• *Manual transmission has metal ID plate mounted on side of transmission. Do not rely on numbers cast on transmission case for identification.*

Table a. Manual transmission applications

Model	Year	Transmission (6-speed)
2.5i, 3.0i (M54 engine)	2004 - 2006	GS6X37BZ - THET
3.0i, 3.0si (N52 engine)	2007 - 2010	GS6X37BZ - THRF / TJEO

Table b. Manual transmission gear ratios

Gear	GS6X37BG
1st	4.35
2nd	2.50
3rd	1.67
4th	1.23
5th	1.00
6th	0.85
Reverse	3.93
Final drive	3.73

◄ Manual transmission vehicles are equipped with a single-disc clutch and dual-mass flywheel.

1. Pilot bearing
2. Dual-mass flywheel
3. Clutch disc
4. Clutch pressure plate
5. Clutch release bearing

For further information, see **210 Clutch**.

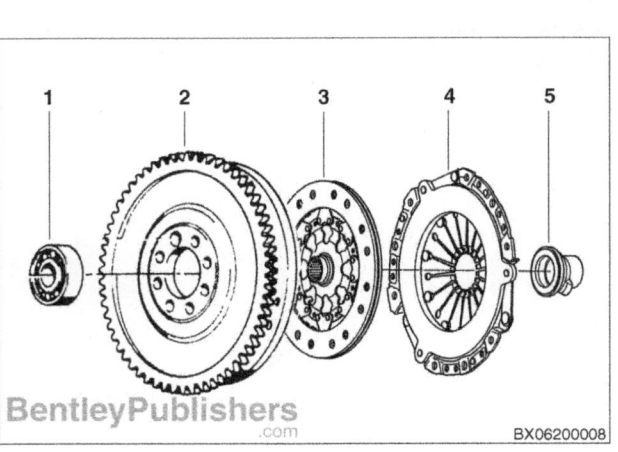

BX06200008

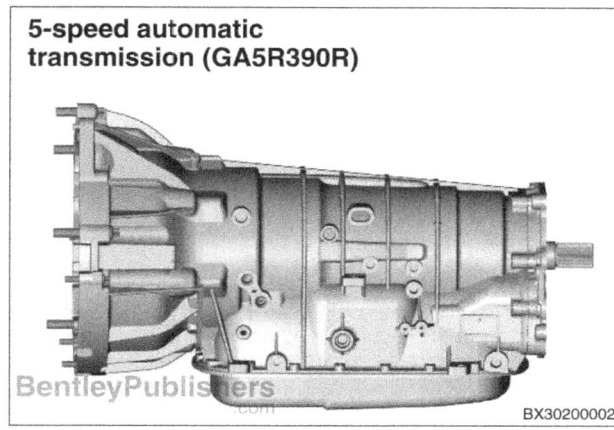

5-speed automatic transmission (GA5R390R)

BX30200002

BX56200014

AUTOMATIC TRANSMISSION

 The Steptronic automatic transmission offers a choice of Normal, Sport, and Manual mode. Sport mode is engaged by moving the shift lever out of Drive and into the Sport / Manual shift gate. In Sport mode, shifts occur at a higher rpm than normal. Additionally, the driver can tip the lever forward (downshifts) or backward (upshifts) to manually select a gear. Automatic transmission applications are in **Table b.**

Table c. Automatic transmission applications		
Model	**Year**	**Transmission**
2.5i, 3.0i (M54 engine)	2004 - 2006	A5S390R (5-speed)
3.0i, 3.0si (N52 engine)	2007 - 2010	GA6L45R (6-speed)

200

 GM transmission identification tag (**arrow**) is on left side of transmission, just above transmission pan, behind transmission selector cable.

xDRIVE

BMW's advanced all-wheel drive system is known as xDrive. It includes a transfer case with electronically controlled clutch that regulates the front to rear torque split for best traction.

Transfer case

The xDrive transfer case, bolted to the rear of the transmission, directs power from the transmission to both the front and rear differentials via driveshafts.

1. Transfer case input shaft
2. Transmission and transfer case mount
3. Fill plug
4. Front driveshaft output
5. Rear driveshaft output
6. xDrive clutch actuator / servomotor

xDrive transfer case

B309200010

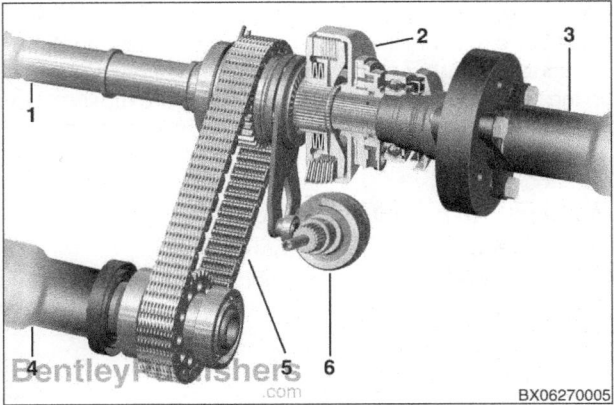

BX06270005

The electronically controlled xDrive clutch allows for infinitely variable distribution of front to rear torque for best traction.

 xDrive components consist of:

1. Transmission output shaft
2. Multidisc clutch
3. Rear driveshaft
4. Front driveshaft
5. Power transfer chain
6. xDrive clutch actuator (cam disc)

xDrive functions are integrated with ABS / DSC. If a wheel begins to slip or if the DCS steering angle sensor and acceleration sensors signal excessive "yaw" in the vehicle, xDrive reacts by transferring power to the wheel or wheels with best traction, usually before a wheel is able to spin. This significantly reduces the risk of under- or oversteer, improving agility and safety on the road.

Torque and engine power are redistributed by xDrive within a few milliseconds. As a result, the driver normally does not notice a change in power distribution.

In addition to controlling power distribution, xDrive and DSC may intervene via braking. If a wheel starts to spin without transmitting power, the brakes are applied at that wheel. In this case, the differential automatically supplies more power to the opposite wheel.

For additional information on xDrive and DSC functions, see **340 Brakes**.

DRIVETRAIN LUBRICANTS

> **CAUTION—**
> • *Consult an authorized BMW dealer parts department for the latest fluid and lubricant applications. Lubricants and fluids specifications and applications are subject to change over time.*

Transmission fluids

Manual transmissions are filled with lifetime lubrication. No oil change is required for the service life of the transmission.

Automatic transmission fluid change intervals are listed **020 Maintenance**.

If repairs have to be made to the transmission or transmission oil cooler, use only the recommended fluid to refill. See **Table d** or **Table e**.

 A label on manual transmission specifies original lubricant used at the factory.

B309230038

For manual transmission fluid service, see **230 Manual Transmission**.

Table d. Manual transmission fluids

Transmission	Fluid type
GS6X - 37BZ - THET	MTF-LT-2
GS6X - 37BZ - THRF / TJEO	MTF-LT-3

MTF-LT-2 (Lifetime fluid) BMW part no. 83 22 0 309 031
MTF-LT-3 (Lifetime fluid) BMW part no. 83 22 7 533 818

 ATF is specified cn colored label on automatic transmission sump. Fill or top off with the proper fluid only. Do not mix fluids types.

For automatic transmission fluid service, including checking fluid level and ATF filter replacement, see **240 Automatic Transmission**.

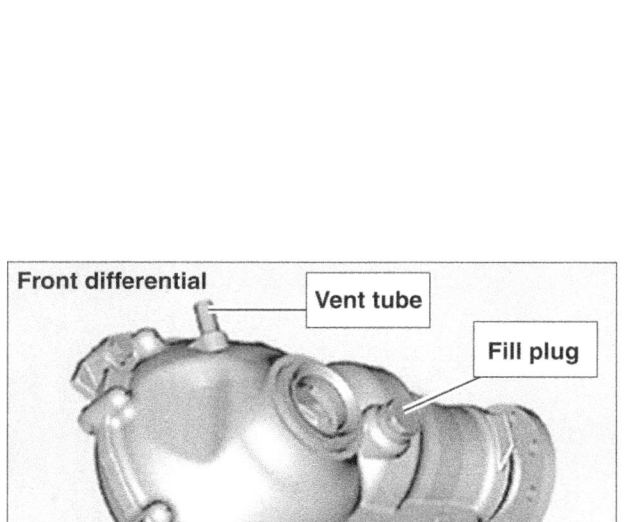

Table e. Automatic transmission fluids

Type	Fluid type
A5S390R (5-speed)	BMW ATF 2
GA6L45R (6-speed)	Dexron VI

Transfer case fluid

xDrive models: Transfer case fluid specifications are in **Table g**.

Table f. Transfer case fluid specifications

Type	BMW part no.
xDrive (all)	83 22 0 397 244

For transfer case fluid service, see **270 Transfer Case**.

Differential oil

Front and rear differentials are filled with lifetime lubrication. No oil change is required for the service life of the differential. If repairs have to be made to the differential, use only the recommended lifetime oil to refill. See **Table g**.

Table g. Differential oil (lifetime)

BMW specification	SAF-XO Synthetic

For front differential oil service, see **311 Front Axle Differential**. For rear differential oil service, see **331 Rear Axle Differential**.

 Front differential.

Front differential

Vent tube

Fill plug

Drain plug

210 Clutch

210

GENERAL

This repair group covers replacement of clutch mechanical and hydraulic components.

See also:

- **200 Transmission–General** for transmission application information

- **230 Manual Transmission** for transmission removal

- **270 Transfer Case** for xDrive transfer case removal

Warnings and Cautions

> *CAUTION—*
>
> - *When performing any repair which involves separating the engine and transmission, check that the bellhousing dowels are undamaged and properly in place before reassembly. If the alignment of the engine flywheel to the transmission input shaft or torque converter is incorrect any of the following complaints may result: Clutch slipping, shudder, or poor disengagement; noise from transmission input shaft; transmission popping out of gear; difficulty changing gears; or internal damage to the transmission.*
>
> - *For N52 engines with magnesium crankcase, only aluminum fasteners and dowels may be used. Consult with an authorized BMW dealer parts department for the correct fasteners and dowels for the engine and model concerned.*

Warnings and Cautions

CLUTCH HYDRAULICS

The clutch is hydraulically actuated by the master and slave cylinders. Clutch disc wear is automatically taken up through the self-adjusting clutch (SAC) pressure plate springs.

A soft or spongy feel to the clutch pedal, long pedal free-play, or grinding noises from the gears while shifting can all indicate problems with the clutch hydraulics. In these circumstances it is best to start with a clutch fluid flush, followed, if necessary, by replacement of hydraulic components.

The clutch hydraulic system shares the fluid reservoir and fluid with the brake hydraulic system.

Most early models are fitted with a metal slave cylinder. Later models (from 03/2008 production) are equipped with a plastic slave cylinder. Differences are noted in the text where they occur.

Clutch assembly and hydraulics

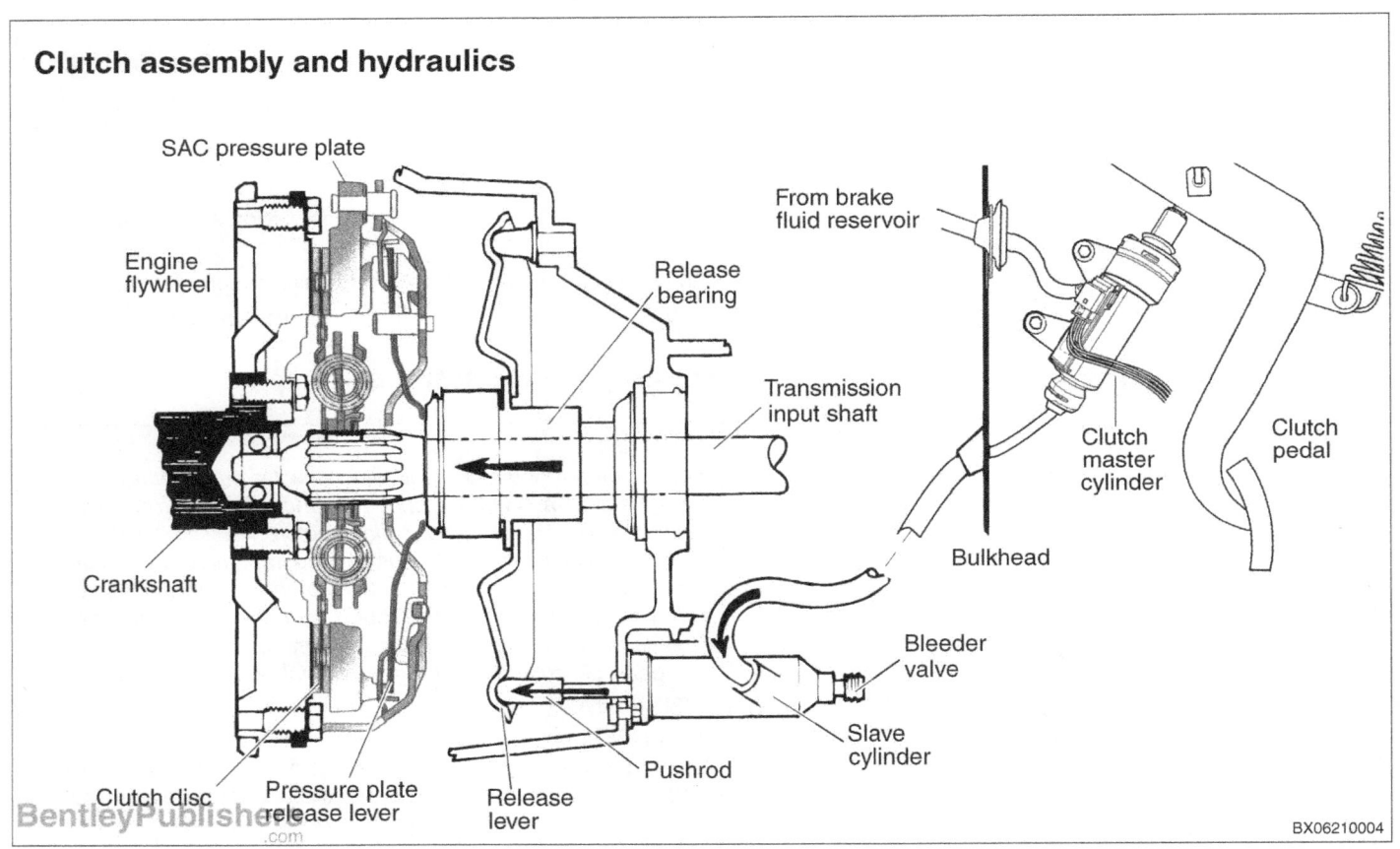

SAC pressure plate

Engine flywheel

Crankshaft

Clutch disc

Pressure plate release lever

Release lever

Pushrod

Release bearing

Transmission input shaft

From brake fluid reservoir

Clutch master cylinder

Clutch pedal

Bulkhead

Bleeder valve

Slave cylinder

BX06210004

Clutch hydraulic system, bleeding and flushing

If the clutch and brake fluid is murky or muddy, or has not been changed within the last two years, flush the system using a brake system pressure bleeder.

— Raise vehicle and support safely.

> **WARNING—**
> - *Make sure vehicle is stable and well supported at all times. Use a professional automotive lift or jack stands. A floor jack is not adequate support.*

— Remove splash shield under transmission. See **020 Maintenance**.

— Remove brake fluid reservoir cap. Using a clean syringe, remove brake fluid from reservoir. Refill reservoir with clean DOT4 low viscosity brake fluid.

◀ Attach pressure brake bleeder to fluid reservoir and pump bleeder a few times to pressurize hydraulic fluid system.

> **CAUTION—**
> - *Do not exceed 2 bar (29 psi) pressure at the fluid reservoir when bleeding or flushing the hydraulic system.*
> - *Brake fluid is poisonous, highly corrosive and dangerous to the environment. Wear safety glasses and rubber gloves when working with brake fluid. Do not siphon brake fluid with your mouth. Immediately clean away any fluid spilled on painted surfaces and wash with water, as brake fluid will remove paint.*
> - *Use new brake fluid from a fresh, unopened container. Brake fluid absorbs moisture from the air. This can lead to corrosion problems in the hydraulic systems, and also lowers the brake fluid boiling point. Dispose of brake fluid properly.*

Clutch hydraulics, bleeding

◀ Connect a length of hose from clutch slave cylinder bleeder valve (**arrow**) to a container.

— Open bleeder valve and allow brake fluid to expel until clean fluid comes out free of air bubbles.

— Close bleeder valve and disconnect pressure bleeding equipment.

— Slowly operate clutch pedal about 10 times. Fill reservoir with clean fluid as necessary.

Slave cylinder　**21 5 030**

BX06210012

Clutch hydraulics, bleeding using BMW special tool 21 5 030

◄ Working underneath vehicle, unbolt slave cylinder from transmission. Fit BMW special tool 21 5 030 to slave cylinder. Rotate threaded tool spindle to press slave cylinder pushrod completely into slave cylinder.

– Attach pressure brake bleeder to fluid reservoir.

– Hold slave cylinder so that bleeder valve is at highest point.

  • Open bleeder valve.

  • If bubble-free brake fluid emerges, use tool spindle to retract slave cylinder push rod slightly, then press in again.

  • If bubbles appear, repeat procedure until fluid runs clear and without bubbles. Once brake fluid appears without air bubbles, close bleeder valve.

  • Release pressure bleeder and detach special tool. Disconnect bleeder hose.

> **CAUTION—**
> • *Do not detach special tool from slave cylinder if fluid is pressurized. The slave cylinder push rod can blow out of cylinder.*

– Reinstall slave cylinder to transmission. Add clean brake fluid to reservoir as necessary. Check clutch operation.

Tightening torque	
Clutch slave cylinder to transmission	22 Nm (16 ft-lb)

Clutch master cylinder, replacing

The clutch master cylinder is mounted to the pedal assembly directly above the clutch pedal.

– Remove brake fluid reservoir cap. Using a clean syringe, remove brake fluid from reservoir.

◄ Disconnect clutch fluid supply line (**1**) from brake fluid reservoir. Place a pan under hose to catch dripping fluid.

– Working at pedal cluster, remove lower left trim panel under dashboard (pedal cluster trim). See **513 Interior Trim**.

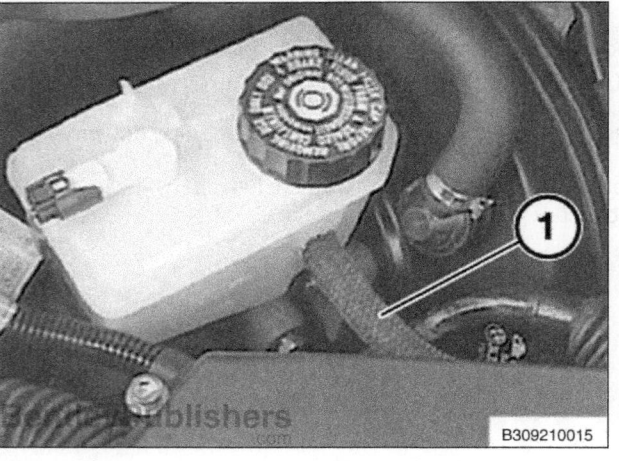

B309210015

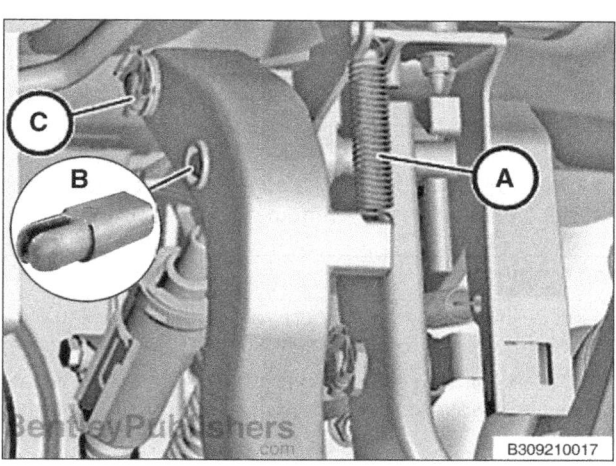

◁ Remove clutch pedal return spring (**A**).

– Remove locking clip (**B**) to release clutch pedal and master cylinder from bearing block.

– Using a stubby screwdriver, press pin (**C**) in and remove pin so that master cylinder is free from clutch pedal.

NOTE —

• *Note flat side cn pin (C). Flat faces up when installing.*

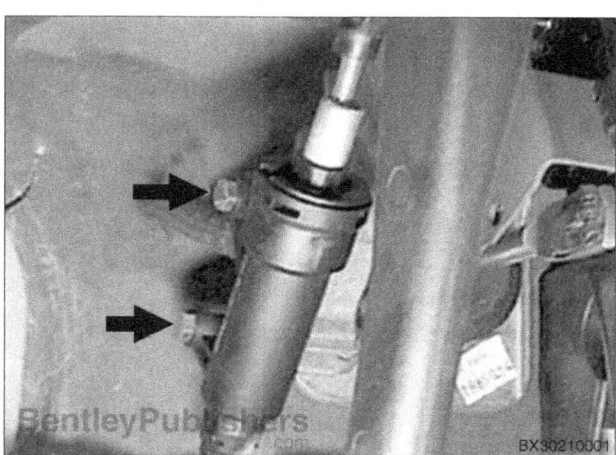

◁ Remove fasteners (**arrows**) on master cylinder.

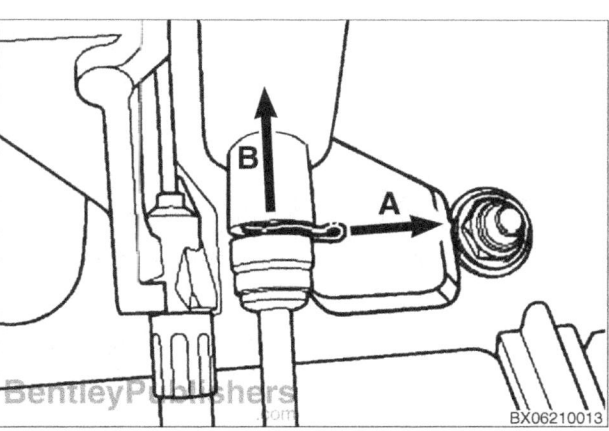

◁ Remove pressure line locking clip (**A**) and pull master cylinder (**B**) off line.

CAUTION—

• *To prevent brake fluid spill, wrap clutch master cylinder with shop towels when removing hydraulic fluid lines from master cylinder.*

• *Brake fluid damages paint and stains carpets. Clean off any brake fluid on or in vehicle immediately.*

– Remove supply hose from master cylinder. Do not pull supply hose into vehicle interior.

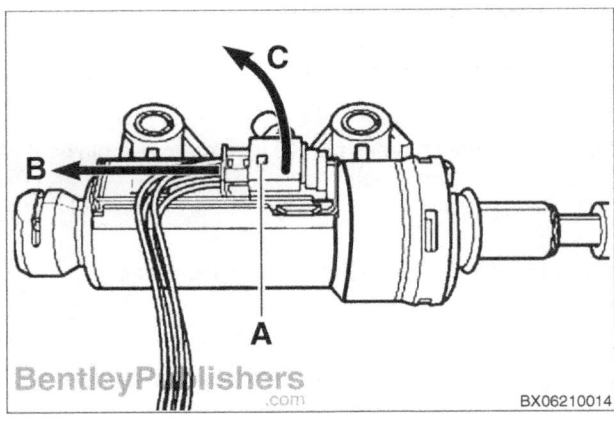

BX06210014

◀ Remove switch module from master cylinder.
  • Press locking button (**A**) to release harness connector.
  • Pull harness connector (**B**) off switch module.
  • Use screwdriver to lever off switch module (**C**).

— Installation is reverse of removal. Make sure switch module snaps audibly into place on master cylinder housing.

Tightening torques	
Clutch master cylinder to pedal support	22 Nm (16 ft-lb)

— Fill brake fluid reservoir with clean fluid and bleed clutch hydraulics. See **Clutch hydraulic system, bleeding and flushing** in this repair group.

Clutch switch, replacing

The clutch switch is a single module, attached to the clutch master cylinder. It performs cruise control and starter immobilization functions.

— Remove driver side footwell trim. See **513 Interior Trim**.

◀ Remove switch module from master cylinder.
  • Press locking button (**A**) to release harness connector.
  • Pull harness connector (**B**) off switch module.
  • Use screwdriver to lever off switch module (**C**).

— Installation is reverse of removal. Make sure switch module snaps firmly into place.

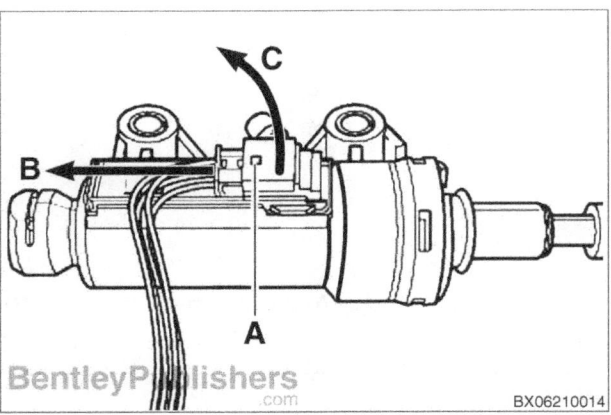

BX06210014

Clutch slave cylinder, replacing

— Working on left side of engine compartment, remove brake fluid reservoir cover.

◀ Use BMW special tool 13 3 010 or equivalent hose clamping tool to pinch off brake reservoir to clutch master cylinder supply hose.

— Raise vehicle and support safely.

> **WARNING—**
> • *Make sure vehicle is stable and well supported at all times. Use a professional automotive lift or jack stands. A floor jack is not adequate support.*

— Remove lower engine and transmission splash shields as necessary. See **020 Maintenance**.

13 3 010

B309210022

- **Models with metal slave cylinder:** Working underneath transmission, disconnect fluid line from slave cylinder on side of transmission. Place pan under hose to catch dripping fluid.

◀ Remove slave cylinder mounting nuts (**arrow**) from clutch bellhousing and remove cylinder.

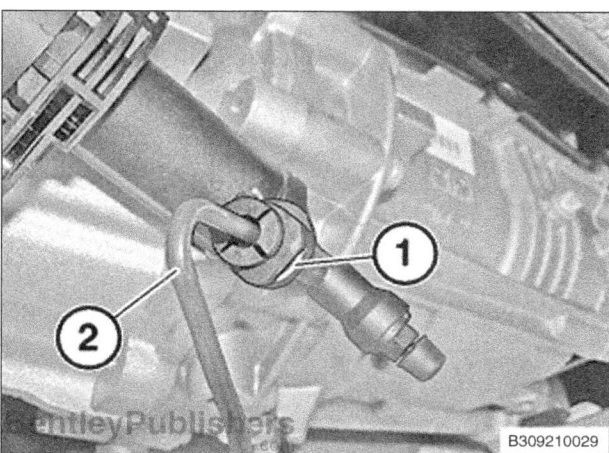

◀ **Models with plastic slave cylinder:** Remove slave cylinder mounting nuts from clutch bellhousing and remove cylinder.

- Working underneath transmission, release retaining clip (**1**) and remove hydraulic line (**2**). Place pan under hose to catch dripping fluid.

◀ To reinstall, press cylinder piston in by hand. Reconnect hydraulic line with cylinder fully depressed.

- Working at brake fluid reservoir, remove hose clamp tool (BMW special tool 13 3 010 or equivalent) from hydraulic line.

Clutch slave cylinder, replacing

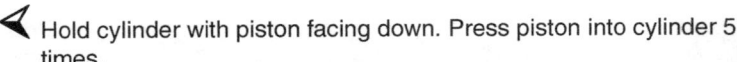 Hold cylinder with piston facing down. Press piston into cylinder 5 times.

- **All models:** Remainder of installation is reverse of removal. Note the following:
  - Check for wear on slave cylinder. Any wear except on tip is caused by misalignment of clutch components.
  - Lightly coat pushrod tip with molybdenum disulfide grease (Molykote® Longterm or equivalent).
  - During installation be sure pushrod tip engages recess in clutch release lever.
  - Make sure spacer (if equipped) between fuel line and hydraulic line remains in installed position.
  - Fill brake fluid reservoir with clean fluid and bleed clutch hydraulics. See **Clutch hydraulic system, bleeding and flushing** in this repair group.

Tightening torques	
Clutch slave cylinder to transmission (use new self locking nuts)	22 Nm (16 ft-lb)
Fluid line to slave cylinder	14.5 Nm (11 ft-lb)

CLUTCH MECHANICAL

Clutch replacement requires removal of the transfer case and transmission.

Clutch disc, pressure plate and release bearing are usually replaced during a clutch overhaul. Check flywheel for wear and scoring. Replace if necessary.

Be sure to check the bottom of the bellhousing for oil. If engine oil is found, check for faulty rear crankshaft (rear main) oil seal. Rear main seal replacement is covered in **119 Lubrication System**.

If reinstalling a used self-adjusting clutch (SAC), special tools will be need. Read the procedure through before beginning the procedure.

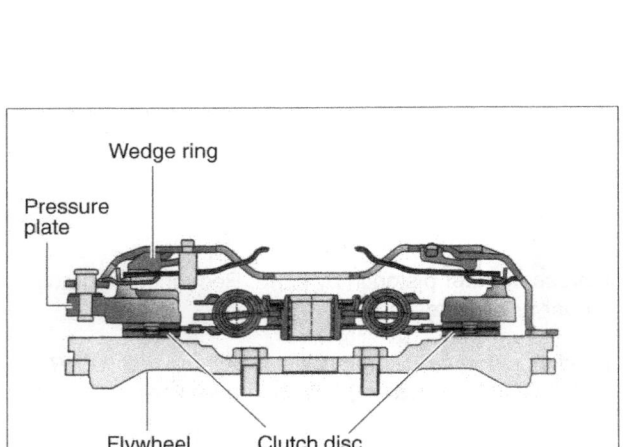

Wedge ring

Pressure plate

Flywheel   Clutch disc

Clutch, removing

— Raise vehicle and support safely.

> **WARNING** —
> • Make sure vehicle is stable and well supported at all times. Use a professional automotive lift or jack stands. A floor jack is not adequate support.

— Remove splash shield under transmission. See **020 Maintenance**

— Remove intermediate muffler and heat shield. See **180 Exhaust System**.

> **WARNING** —
> • Exhaust system must be fully cool before starting removal.

— Detach front and rear driveshaft. Tie to side. See **260 Driveshafts**.

— Remove transmission from engine. See **230 Manual Transmission**.

◄ Lock flywheel in position using BMW special tool 11 9 260 or equivalent.

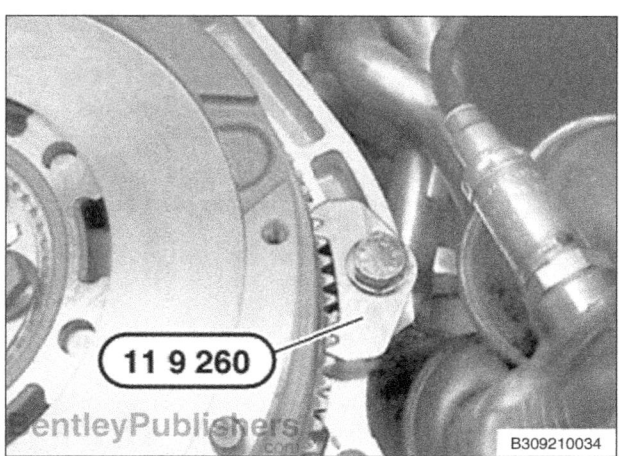

◄ Loosen 6 clutch mounting bolts (**arrows**) evenly in stages.

— Remove pressure plate and clutch disc.

> **WARNING** —
> • Friction material in clutch disc produces dangerous dust. Do not breathe in dust. Use water to wet down components and collect dripping mixture in a shop towel.

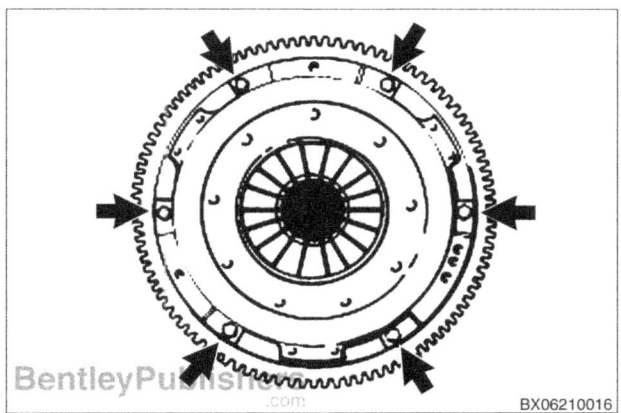

◄ Remove clutch release bearing / lever module from transmission input shaft as a complete unit.

— Remove release module (**1**) from spring clip in direction of **arrow**.

> **CAUTION** —
> • To avoid installing incorrectly, do not disassemble bearing from combined release bearing / lever module.

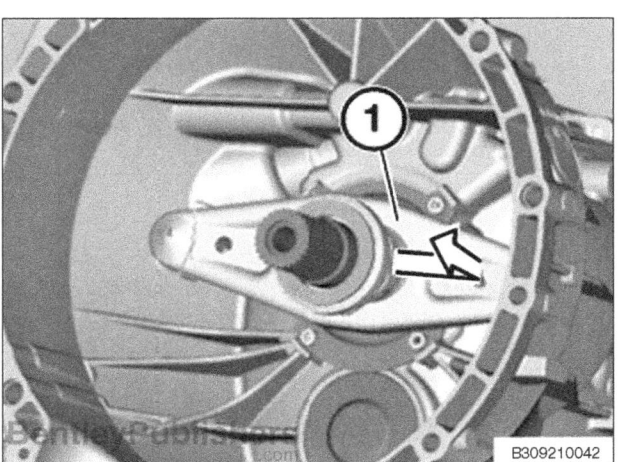

Clutch components, inspecting

— Inspect clutch disc for wear, cracks, loose rivets, contamination or excessive runout (warping). Replace if necessary.

— Measure depth of clutch lining at lining rivets. If shallowest rivet depth is less than 1 mm (0.04 in), replace clutch disk.

— Inspect flywheel for scoring, hot spots, cracks or loose or worn guide pins. Replace flywheel if any faults are found. See **Flywheel, removing and installing** in this repair group.

> **CAUTION—**
> • *If flywheel is removed from engine, install using new bolts.*

— Check to make sure transmission pilot bearing rotates smoothly without play. Replace if faulty. See **Transmission pilot bearing, replacing** in this repair group.

— Inspect and clean release bearing module.

◀ Check release bearing ball stud and spring retainer. Replace if damaged or worn.

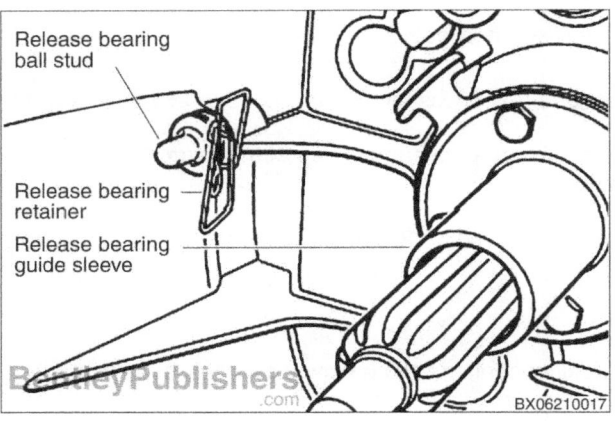

Release bearing ball stud

Release bearing retainer

Release bearing guide sleeve

BX06210017

— Clean release bearing guide sleeve.

> **CAUTION—**
> • *Do not grease release bearing module or guide sleeve. If guide sleeve is greased, release bearing may stick to it.*

Clutch, installing (new SAC components)

The SAC pressure plate, when new, comes from the factory with a lock plate at the center which maintains spring tension on the self-adjusting springs. Do not remove lock plate until the pressure plate is securely installed on the flywheel with clutch disk in place.

> **CAUTION—**
> • *Avoid contaminating clutch friction surfaces with oil or grease. Do not touch these surfaces.*

◀ Center clutch disc on flywheel using the appropriate BMW (or equivalent) centering tool.

> **CAUTION—**
> • *Be sure clutch disc is facing the correct way. The disc is marked "engine side" or "transmission side".*

NOTE —

• *The large bolt in the clutch disc centering tool is used to install and remove the tool only. Once the disc is in place on the flywheel, remove the bolt to make room for the SAC pressure plate.*

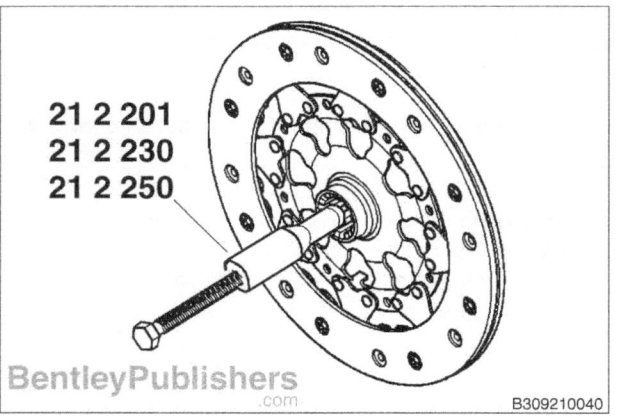

21 2 201
21 2 230
21 2 250

B309210040

— Lock flywheel in position using BMW special tool 11 9 260 or equivalent.

Clutch, installing (new SAC components)

– Install SAC pressure plate on dowel pins at flywheel. Install clutch mounting bolts and tighten each one turn at a time until pressure plate is fully seated.

Tightening torque	
M54 engine • 8.8 bolt (use new M8 ZNS bolts)	25 Nm (18 ft-lb)
N52 engine Clutch to flywheel (use new M8 ZNS bolts) • Stage 1 • Stage 2 (torque angle)	 15 Nm (11 ft-lb) additional 90° ± 5°

◀ Use 14 mm Allen wrench to unscrew (clockwise or counterclockwise) lock plate in center of pressure plate.

NOTE—

• *The spring lock plate may make snapping noises during removal.*

– Using large bolt, pull out clutch disc centering tool.

– Remove flywheel locking tool.

– Inspect and clean clutch release bearing / lever module.

◀ Install clutch release bearing / lever module (**1**).

– Install transmission. See **230 Manual Transmission**.

BX06210025

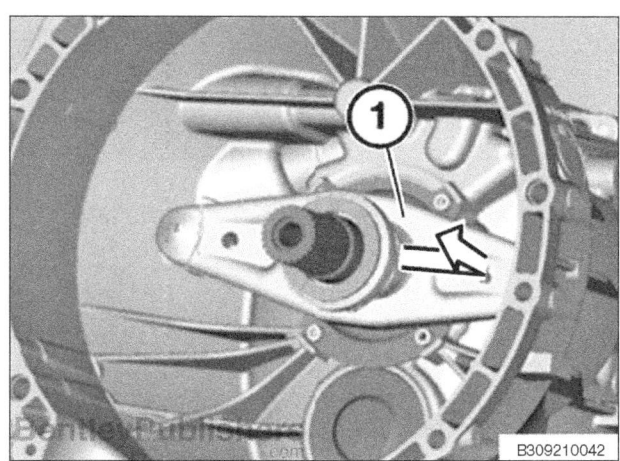

B309210042

CAUTION—
• *Replace aluminum bolts each time they are loosened.* • *Follow torque instructions when installing aluminum fasteners.*

Tightening torques	
Slave cylinder to transmission	22 Nm (16 ft-lb)
Transmission crossmember to rubber mounts (M12)	73 Nm (54 ft-lb)

Transmission to engine
M54 engine
• M8 bolt
• M12 bolt
N52 engine (use new alum. bolts)
• M10 x 30 mm
  Stage 1
  Stage 2
• M10 x 85 mm
  Stage 1
  Stage 2
• M12
  Stage 1
  Stage 2
	
	19 Nm (14 ft-lb)
	66 Nm (49 ft-lb)
	
	20 Nm
	additional 90° - 110°
	
	20 Nm
	additional 180° - 200°
	
	25 Nm
	additional 130° + 20°

210

Clutch, installing (used SAC components)

When reinstalling a previously used self-adjusting clutch (SAC), special tools are needed to reset the self-adjusting ring to its original position.

– Place SAC pressure plate on clean work surface.

◄ Place BMW special tool 21 2 180 on pressure plate.
  • Note that locating hooks of special tool engage pressure plate adjusting ring openings (**inset**).
  • Grip tool firmly and squeeze special tool handles together.
  • Tighten down special tool knurled screws (**arrows**).
  • SAC adjustment ring is now in its original position.

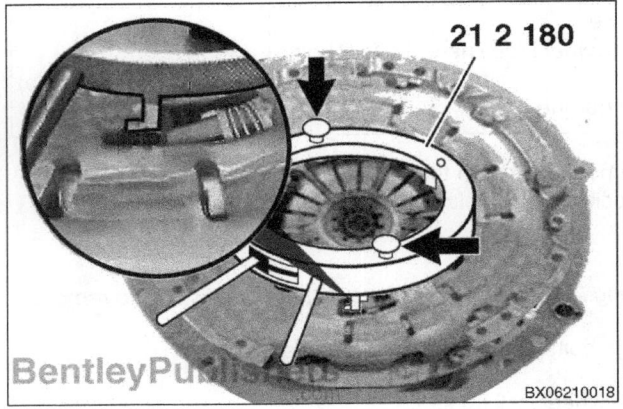
BX06210018

◄ Install BMW special tool 21 2 170 on SAC pressure plate.
  • Fit fingers of special tool in slots above dowel pin bores.
  • Tighten down knurled nut (**arrow**) finger-tight.
  • Screw in T-handle until pressure plate diaphragm spring is pretensioned to stop.

> **CAUTION—**
> • *Avoid contaminating clutch friction surfaces with oil or grease. Do not touch these surfaces.*

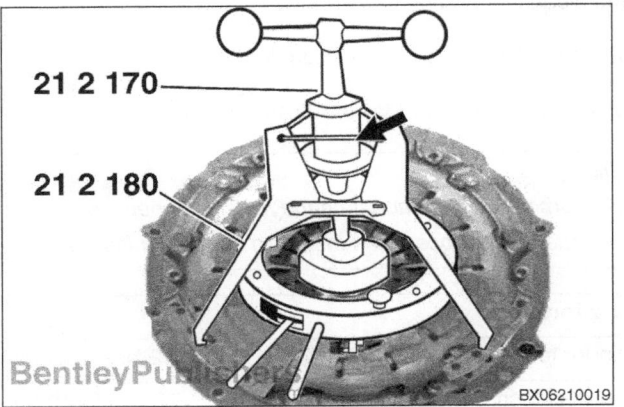
BX06210019

◄ Center clutch disc on flywheel using the appropriate BMW (or equivalent) centering tool.

> **CAUTION—**
> • *Be sure clutch disc is facing the correct way. The disc is marked "engine side" or "transmission side".*

> **NOTE—**
> • *The large bolt in the clutch disc centering tool is used to install and remove the tool only. Once the disc is in place on the flywheel, remove the bolt to make room for the SAC pressure plate.*

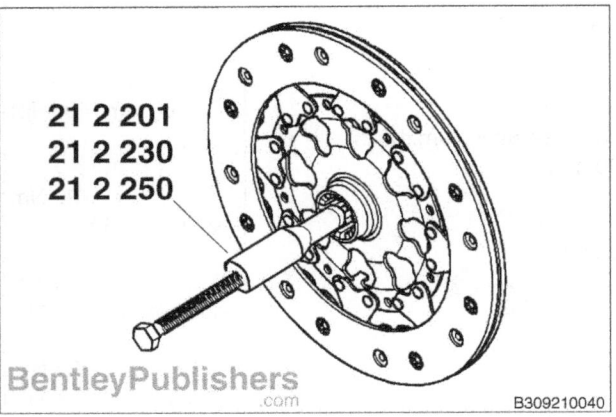
B309210040

– Lock flywheel in position using BMW special tool 11 9 260 or equivalent.

– Install SAC pressure plate on dowel pins at flywheel. Install clutch mounting bolts and tighten each one turn at a time until pressure plate is fully seated. Torque to specification in 2 stages.

– Using large bolt, pull out clutch disc centering tool.

Clutch, installing (used SAC components)

Tightening torque	
M54 engine • 8.8 bolt (use new M8 ZNS bolts)	25 Nm (18 ft-lb)
N52 engine Clutch to flywheel (use new M8 ZNS bolts) • Stage 1 • Stage 2 (torque angle)	 15 Nm (11 ft-lb) additional 90° ± 5°

— Remove flywheel locking tool.

— Inspect and clean release bearing lever.

◄ Install clutch release bearing / lever module (**1**).

— Install transmission. See **230 Manual Transmission**.

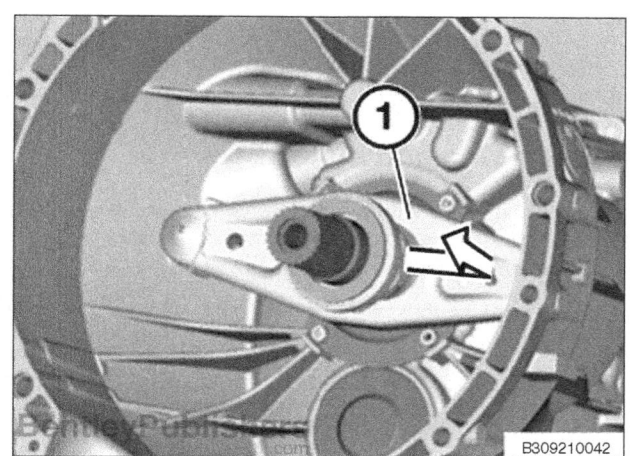

B309210042

> **CAUTION—**
> • *Replace aluminum bolts each time they are loosened.*
> • *Follow torque instructions when installing aluminum fasteners.*

Tightening torques	
Slave cylinder to transmission	22 Nm (16 ft-lb)
Transmission crossmember to rubber mounts (M12)	73 Nm (54 ft-lb)

Transmission to engine
M54 engine
• M8 Torx bolt
• M12 Torx bolt
N52 engine (use new alum. bolts)
• M10 x 30 mm
  Stage 1
  Stage 2
• M10 x 85 mm
  Stage 1
  Stage 2
• M12
  Stage 1
  Stage 2
	
	19 Nm (14 ft-lb)
	66 Nm (49 ft-lb)
	
	20 Nm
	additional 90° - 110°
	
	20 Nm
	additional 180° - 200°
	
	25 Nm
	additional 130° + 20°

Self-adjusting clutch (SAC), breaking in

In normal driving, approx. 800 to 1000 gearshifts are needed for a new SAC clutch lining to be fully broken in. To ensure correct operation and long life, break in the SAC gradually, with light to medium loads. Fast sports-style driving and abrupt clutch engagement may destroy a new clutch. The following procedure helps to break in the clutch.

— Drive at 20 mph (30 kph) on level grade. Start, upshift and downshift through the gears at approx. 2000 rpm.

— Increase speed. Upshift and downshift through the gears at approx. 3500 - 4000 rpm.

— On medium grade (approx. 12% and up): Start off at approx. 2500 rpm 3 - 5 times.

Flywheel, removing and installing

This procedure is for vehicles with manual transmission. Flywheel and torque plate removal for automatic transmission vehicle is covered in **240 Automatic Transmission**.

> **WARNING—**
> • *Make sure exhaust system is fully cooled off.*

— Detach front (xDrive models) and rear driveshaft. Tie to side. See **260 Driveshafts**.

— Remove transmission. See **230 Manual Transmission**.

— Remove clutch. See **Clutch, removing** in this repair group.

— Inspect flywheel for scoring, hot spots, cracks or loose or worn guide pins. Replace flywheel if any faults are found.

◀ Lock flywheel in position using BMW special tool 11 9 260 or equivalent.

— Loosen and remove flywheel mounting bolts. Remove flywheel.

— Clean flywheel bolt threads in crankshaft.

— All engines: Check flywheel location dowel sleeve for damage and correct installation.

11 9 260

B309210034

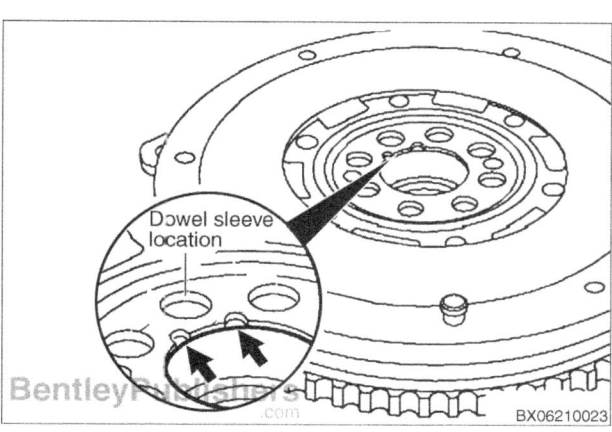

Dowel sleeve location

BX06210023

◀ When reinstalling flywheel, position dowel sleeve next to two locating notches (**arrows**).

– Install flywheel using new self-locking bolts.

Tightening torque	
Flywheel to crankshaft (use new self-locking bolts) • M54 engine • N52 engine	105 Nm (77 ft-lb) 120 Nm (89 ft-lb)

CAUTION—

• *Use new self-locking bolts to install flywheel. Do not reuse the old stretch-type bolts. Do not install bolts with Loctite® or similar thread-locking compound.*

Transmission pilot bearing, replacing

– Remove splash shield under transmission. See **020 Maintenence.**

– Remove exhaust and heat shield. See **180 Exhaust System.**

WARNING—

• *Make sure exhaust system is fully cooled off before starting removal.*

– Detach front and rear driveshaft. Tie to side. See **260 Driveshafts.**

– Remove transfer case. See **270 Transfer Case.**

– Remove transmission. See **230 Manual Transmission.**

– Remove clutch. See **Clutch, removing** in this repair group.

– Remove flywheel. See **Flywheel, removing and installing** in this repair group.

◀ Use hydraulic press and BMW special tool 21 2 051 to press transmission pilot bearing out of dual-mass flywheel. Press from engine side of flywheel.

CAUTION—

• *Do not drive bearing in or out using a chisel or punch.*

– Place new pilot bearing on BMW special tool 21 2 052. Use hydraulic press to press bearing into flywheel as far as it will go. Press from clutch side of flywheel.

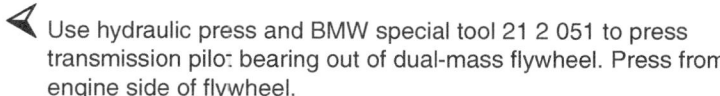

21 2 051

BX06210024

230 Manual Transmission

230

GENERAL

This repair group covers external service of manual transmission, including transmission removal and installation. Internal transmission repair is not covered. Special tools and procedures are required to disassemble and service the internal geartrain.

See also:
- **210 Clutch**
- **250 Gearshift Linkage**
- **260 Driveshafts**
- **270 Transfer Case**

CAUTION—
- *When performing any repair which involves separating the engine and transmission, check that the bellhousing dowels are undamaged and correctly positioned before reassembly. If the alignment of the engine flywheel to the transmission input shaft or torque converter is incorrect any of the following complaints may result: Clutch slipping, shudder, or poor disengagement; noise from transmission input shaft; transmission popping out of gear; difficulty changing gears; or internal damage to the transmission.*
- *The magnesium crankcase on the N52 engine requires aluminum fasteners (and dowels) exclusively. Aluminum fasteners must be replaced any time they are loosened. Aluminum fasteners are usually marked blue, but not always. Consult with an authorized BMW dealer parts department for the correct replacement fasteners and dowels.*

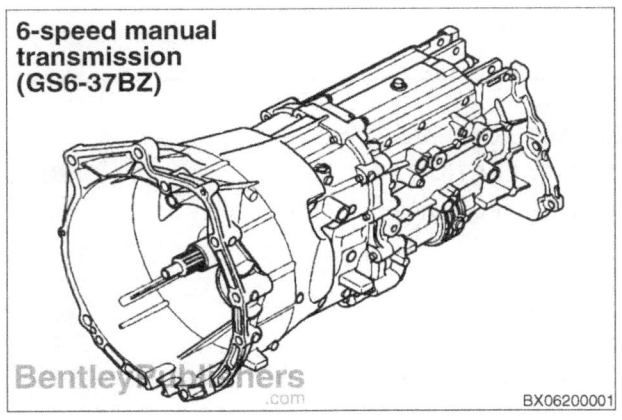

6-speed manual transmission (GS6-37BZ)

BX06200001

Manual transmission applications

Table a lists manual transmission applications.

Table a. Manual transmission applications

Model model year	Transmission	Manufacturer id
2.5i, 3.0i 2004 - 2006	GS6X-37BZ - THET	ZF type H
3.0i, 3.0si 2007 - 2010	GS6X-37BZ - THRF / TJEO	ZF type H

TRANSMISSION FLUID SERVICE

Manual transmissions are filled with lifetime lubrication. No oil change is required for the service life of these transmissions. If repairs have to be made to the transmission, use only the recommended lifetime fluid to refill.

Oil type is identified with a colored label near transmission fill plug.

B309230038

Table b. Manual transmission fluid type

Transmission	Year range	Fluid type
ZF GS637BZ - THET	2004 - 2006	MTF-LT-2
ZF GS637BZ - THRF / TJEO	2007 - 2010	MTF-LT-3
MTF-LT-2 (Lifetime fluid) BMW part no. 83 22 0 309 031 *MTF-LT-3 (Lifetime fluid) BMW part no. 83 22 7 533 818*		

Transmission fluid level, checking

– Drive vehicle for a few miles to warm transmission.

– Raise and safely support vehicle to access transmission filler plug. Make sure vehicle is level.

> **WARNING—**
> • *Make sure vehicle is stable and well supported at all times. Use a professional automotive lift or jack stands. A floor jack is not adequate support.*

Remove fill plug (**2**). Be prepared to catch dripping fluid.

– Wearing protective glove, insert finger in fill hole to check fluid level.
  • If fluid level is up to bottom of fill hole, level is correct.
  • If level is low, fill transmission with fluid until fluid overflows fill hole.

– Install and torque fill plug.

Tightening torque	
Drain or fill plug to transmission (M18 x 1.5)	35 Nm (26 ft-lb)

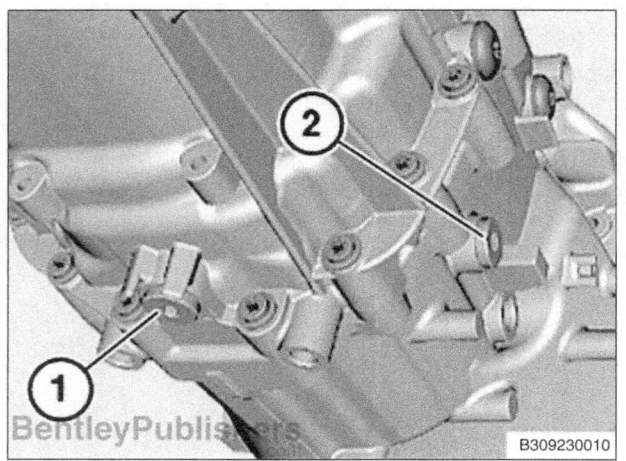

B309230010

Transmission fluid, replacing

— Drive vehicle for a few miles to warm transmission.

— Raise and safely support vehicle to access drain plug.

> **WARNING—**
> • *Make sure vehicle is stable and well supported at all times. Use a professional automotive lift or jack stands. A floor jack is not adequate support.*

 Place drain pan under transmission and
  • Remove fill plug (**2**) from side of transmission.
  • Remove drain plug (**1**) at bottom of transmission and drain fluid.
  • Install and torque drain plug.
  • Slowly fill transmission with fluid until fluid overflows fill hole.

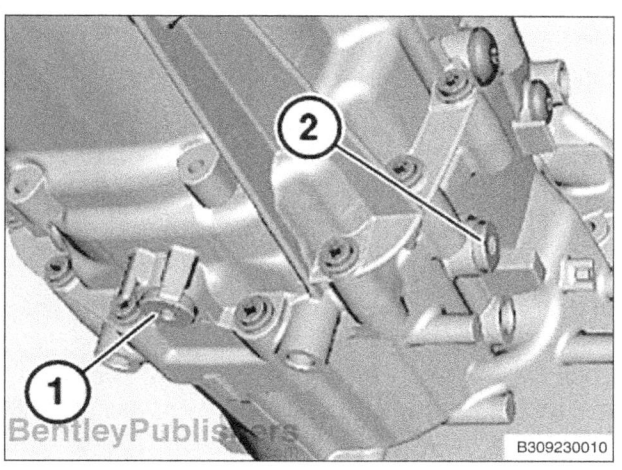

Table c. Manual transmission fluid capacities

Transmission	Initial fill, new or rebuilt unit	Fluid change
ZF GS6-37BZ	1.6 liter (1.7 US qt)	1.5 liter (1.6 US qt)

— Install and torque fluid fill plug.

Tightening torque	
Drain or fill plug to transmission case: • M18 x 1.5	35 Nm (26 ft-lb)

TRANSMISSION EXTERNAL SERVICE

Back-up light switch, replacing

— Raise and safely support vehicle to access back-up light switch.

> **WARNING—**
> • *Make sure vehicle is stable and well supported at all times. Use a professional automotive lift or jack stands. A floor jack is not adequate support.*

 Unscrew switch (**1**) from transmission.

— Install new switch.

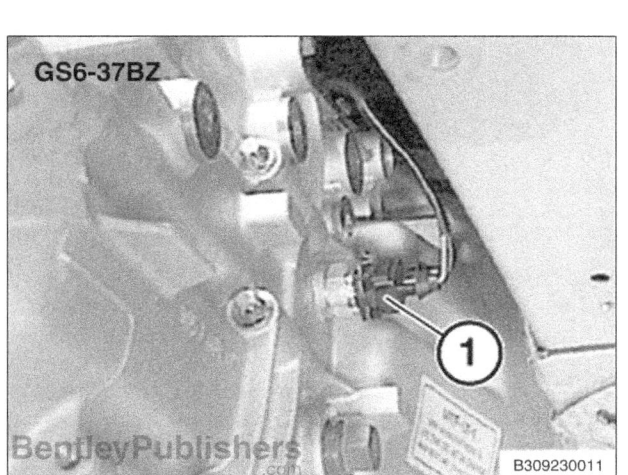

GS6-37BZ

Tightening torque	
Back-up light switch to transmission	16 Nm (12 ft-lb)

— Check transmission fluid level before lowering vehicle. Top off as necessary. See **Transmission Fluid Service** in this repair group.

Selector shaft seal, replacing

This repair can be done with transmission installed in vehicle.

— Place transmission into second gear.

— Raise vehicle and support safely.

> **WARNING—**
> • *Make sure vehicle is stable and well supported at all times. Use a professional automotive lift or jack stands. A floor jack is not adequate support.*

— Remove transmission splash shields. See **020 Maintenence**.

— Support transmission from below and remove transfer case. See **270 Transfer Case**.

> **CAUTION—**
> • *To prevent damage to rear driveshaft joint, do not allow driveshaft to hang unsupported.*

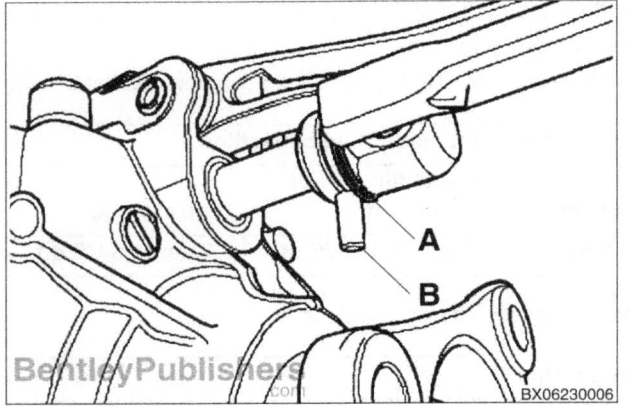

◄ Working at top rear of transmission at shifter console, pry locking spring (**A**) out of groove and press pin (**B**) out of shift coupling.

  • Detach shift coupling and shift linkage from selector shaft and tie aside.

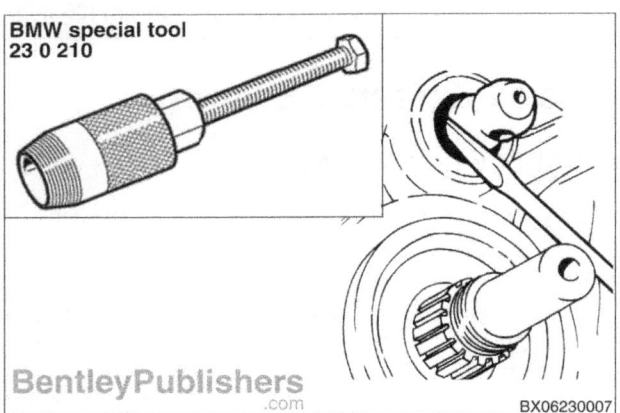

◄ Carefully pull out selector shaft oil seal with BMW special tool 23 0 210, or with a narrow seal remover.

◄ Coat new selector shaft seal with transmission fluid. Drive new seal in flush with housing. Use a proper sized seal installation tool (BMW special too 23 0 220) and a soft-faced (plastic) hammer.

— Remainder of installation is reverse of removal. Check transmission and transfer case oil level, topping up as necessary.

Tightening torques	
Transfer case to transmission	43 Nm (31 ft-lb)

Transmission input shaft seal, replacing

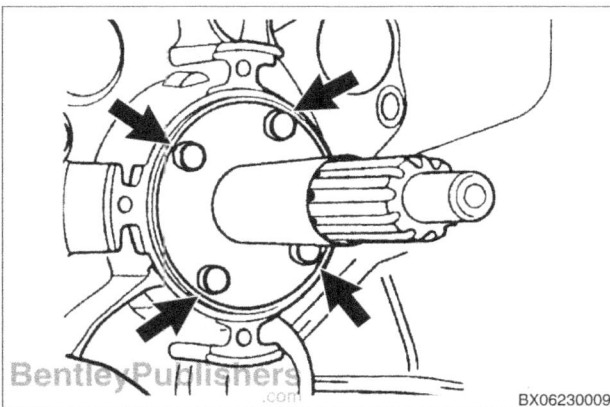

— Remove transmission from vehicle. See **Transmission, removing and installing** in this repair group.

— Remove clutch release bearing / release lever module from inside bellhousing. See **210 Clutch**.

◄ Remove bolts (**arrows**) for clutch release-bearing guide sleeve. Remove guide sleeve.

◄ Push in and turn seal puller (BMW special tool 23 3 151) onto seal Withdraw and remove seal by turing threaded screw in (**arrow**).

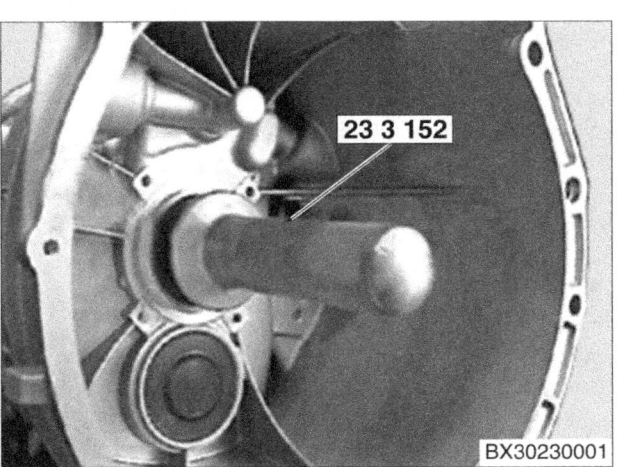

◄ To install new seal:

- Coat sealing lip of new seal with transmission oil.
- Push radial seal onto BMW special tool 23 3 152.
- Slide tool onto input shaft.
- Use plastic hammer to drive in seal until fully seated.

— Thoroughly clean clutch release bearing guide sleeve mounting bolts, sealing surfaces, and threads. Reinstall guide sleeve and spacer (if equipped).

Tightening torque	
Guide sleeve to transmission housing (M6)	10 Nm (7 ft-lb)

TRANSMISSION REMOVAL AND INSTALLATION

Removal and installation of the transmission is best accomplished with the vehicle on a lift. A transmission jack and an engine support bar is also required to do the job properly and safely.

The procedure outlined below removes the transmission together with the transfer case. Transfer case removal is covered in **270 Transfer Case**.

> **WARNING—**
> • *Removal of the transmission may upset the balance of the vehicle on the lift.*

Transmission, removing and installing

— Disconnect negative (–) cable from battery.

> **CAUTION—**
> • *Prior to disconnecting the battery, read the battery disconnection cautions given in* **001 Warnings and Cautions**.

— Raise and safely support vehicle.

> **WARNING—**
> • *Make sure vehicle is stable and well supported at all times. Use a professional automotive lift or jack stands.*

— Remove underbody splash shields. See **020 Maintenence**.

— Remove compete exhaust system. Remove exhaust system heat shields.See **180 Exhaust System**.

> **WARNING—**
> • *Exhaust system should be fully cooled off before removing.*

— Remove front drive shaft from transfer box and tie off to one side. See **260 Driveshafts**.

◀ Remove rear driveshaft from output flange on transfer case.
  • Remove flex-disc mounting bolts (**arrows**).
  • Remove driveshaft center bearing support fasteners. Support center of driveshaft.
  • Lower center of driveshaft sufficiently to disengage flex-disc from transfer case flange. Tie driveshaft to side.

> **CAUTION—**
> • *To prevent damage to driveshaft joint, do not allow driveshaft to hang unsupported.*

— Support weight of engine and transmission from above using engine lifting equipment.

— Disconnect harness connector from back-up light switch on transmission.

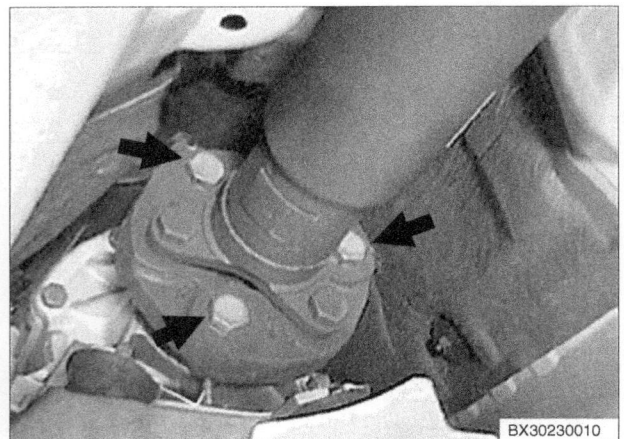

BX30230010

- **N52 engine only**: Disconnect oxygen sensor harness connectors at base of bellhousing.

  • Unbolt and remove connector bracket as well.

◄ Disconnect harness connectors from servomotor on transfer case (**1** and **2**).

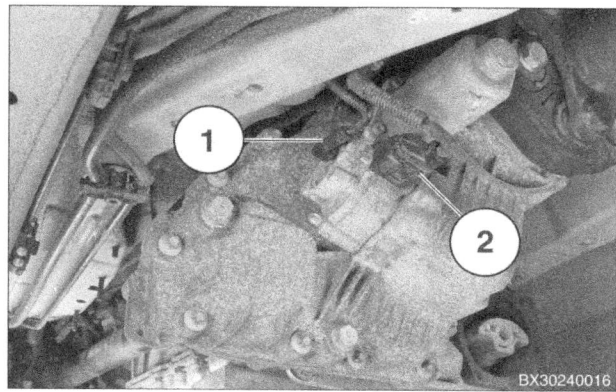

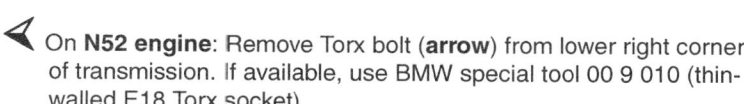

◄ On **N52 engine**: Remove Torx bolt (**arrow**) from lower right corner of transmission. If available, use BMW special tool 00 9 010 (thin-walled E18 Torx socket).

◄ On **M54 engine**: Remove cover bolt and remove cover.

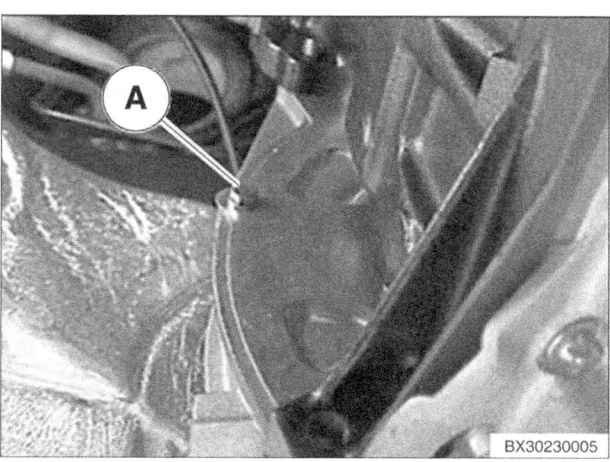

230

Transmission, removing and installing

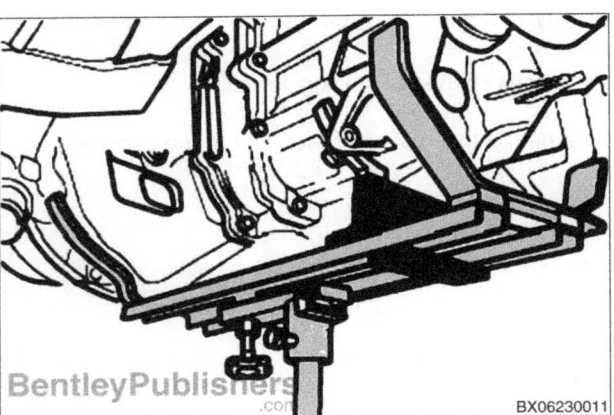

◄ Support transmission /transfer case on transmission jack. Secure transmission to jack.

◄ Working from below, remove transmission crossmember fasteners (**arrows**) and remove crossmember. (Automatic transmission vehicle shown.)

– Lower transmission jack slowly, allowing engine and transmission assembly to tilt down slightly.

> **CAUTION—**
>
> • Tilting engine to lower transmission can lead to damage to engine compartment components due to lack of clearance at rear of engine. Lower transmission carefully while checking engine clearance.

– Unbolt clutch slave cylinder from side of transmission. Do not disconnect fluid hose. Suspend slave cylinder from chassis using stiff wire.

> **CAUTION—**
>
> • Unbolt clutch slave cylinder slowly and evenly.
>
> • Do not operate clutch pedal with slave cylinder removed from transmission.

◄ Remove shift rod clip and disconnect shift linkage from selector shaft coupling.

– Disconnect shift console from top of transmission. See **250 Gearshift Linkage**.

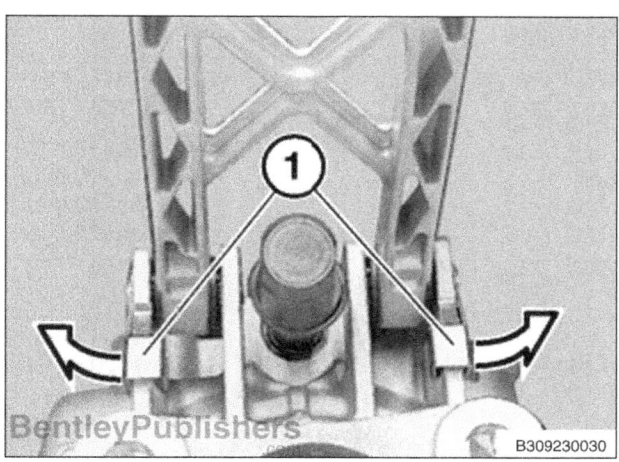

◀ Release locking clips (**1**) and lift out shift arms.

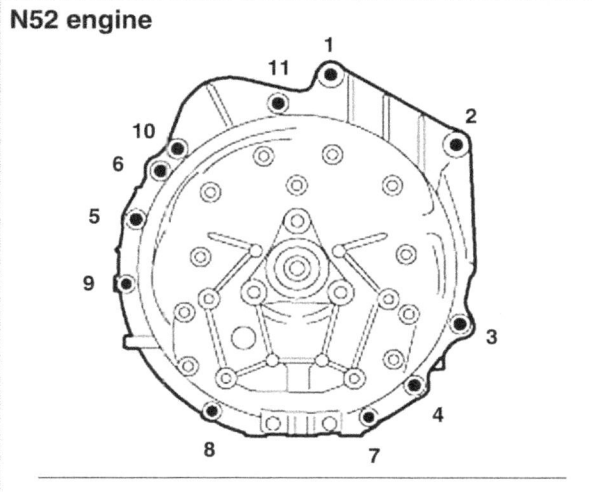

N52 engine

M54 engine

◀ Remove transmission mounting Torx-head bolts (**arrows**). Note length and location of bolts.

- On N52 engine, discard aluminum fasteners.

CAUTION—
- *Number, size and location of fasteners varies.*

— Remove transmission by pulling backward until transmission input shaft clears clutch disc splines, then pull downwards. Lower transmission jack to remove transmission.

CAUTION—
- *Do not allow transmission to hang from input shaft.*

— Prior to installing transmission:

- Inspect clutch, clutch release bearing and flywheel. See **210 Clutch**. Repair as necessary.
- Check and repair transmission seals. See **Transmission External Service** in this repair group.
- Be sure dowels on bellhousing are correctly positioned. Replace damaged sleeves.

— Reinstall transmission with transfer case, keeping in mind the following:

- Check transfer case and transmission fluid level. Top off as necessary.
- On N52 engine: use new aluminum fasteners to mount transmission to engine.
- Use new fasteners on front and rear driveshafts.
- If installing a new transmission, transfer parts over from old transmission.
- Thoroughly clean input shaft and clutch disc splines of old grease. Lightly lubricate transmission input shaft splines before installing.

Tightening torques	
Slave cylinder to transmission	22 Nm (16 ft-lb)
Transmission to engine (**M54 engine**) • M6 Allen bolt • M8 Torx bolt • M10 Torx bolt • M12 Torx bolt	 9 Nm (7 ft-lb) 22 Nm (16 ft-lb) 43 Nm (32 ft-lb) 72 Nm (53 ft-lb)
Transmission to engine (**N52 engine**) M10 • stage 1 • stage 2 (angle torque) M12 • stage 1 • stage 2 (angle torque)	 20 Nm (15 ft-lb) 90 - 110° 25 Nm (18 ft-lb) 130 ° + 20°
Crossmember to chassis (M8)	19 Nm (14 ft-lb)
Crossmember to rubber mount (M12)	68 Nm (50 ft-lb)

— Reinstall driveshafts using new bolts and self-locking nuts.
  See **260 Driveshafts**.

Tightening torques	
Front driveshaft to front differential / transfer case (M10 10.9, use new bolts) • stage 1 • stage 2 (angle torque)	 40 Nm (30 ft-lb) 45°

Rear driveshaft flex-disc to transfer case flange (ZNS fasteners)
• 2004-2006 (with single stage flex disc - 96mm bolt hole pattern)
  stage 1
  stage 2 (angle torque)
• 2007-2010 (with two-stage flex disc - 110mm bolt hole pattern, ribbed teeth)
  stage 1
  stage 2 (angle torque)
	
	55 Nm (40 ft-lb)
	+90°
	
	30 Nm (22 ft-lb)
	+90

Crossmember to chassis (M8)	19 Nm (14 ft-lb)
Crossmember to rubber mount (M12)	68 Nm (50 ft-lb)

240 Automatic Transmission

240

GENERAL

This repair group covers maintenance and replacement of the automatic transmission. Automatic transmission internal repairs are not covered. Transmission repairs require special service equipment and knowledge. If transmission internal service is required, consult an authorized BMW dealer about a factory reconditioned unit or a transmission rebuild.

See also:

• **119 Lubrication System** for crankshaft rear main (flywheel) seal.
• **170 Radiator and Cooling System** for ATF cooler and heat exchanger.
• **200 Transmission–General** for drivetrain information.
• **260 Driveshafts** for front and rear driveshaft.
• **270 Transfer Case** for removal and installation.

> *CAUTION—*
> • *The magnesium crankcase on the N52 engine requires aluminum fasteners (and dowels) exclusively. Aluminum fasteners must be replaced any time they are loosened. Aluminum fasteners are usually marked blue, but not always. Consult with an authorized BMW dealer parts department for the correct replacement fasteners and dowels.*

Automatic transmission applications

Automatic transmissions are configured with adaptive transmission control and Steptronic. Automatic transmission applications are in **Table a**.

Table a. Automatic transmission applications

Model	Year	Transmission
2.5i, 3.0i (M54 engine)	2004 - 2006	A5S390R (5-speed)
30i, 3.0si (N52 engine)	2007 - 2010	GA6L45R (6-speed) with Mechatronics

Steptronic

 The Steptronic function makes it possible to shift the automatic transmission manually. Manual mode is engaged when the selector lever is moved left from automatic gate into manual gate. In manual mode, pressing the selector lever forward or backward closes electrical contacts, resulting in upshift or downshift.

BX30240010

5-speed automatic transmission overview

 The automatic transmission for the 2004 through 2006 X3 (2.5i and 3.0i models) is the A5S-390R (General Motors) transmission with GS 20 AGS control and Steptronic shifter.

The 134-pin transmission control unit is located in the electronics box in the engine compartment and is on the PT-CAN.

System features:

- Torque rating of 390Nm.
- Gradual torque converter lock up providing a controlled degree of clutch slippage and smooth transition to full lock.
- Torque converter variable lock up control can occur in 3rd, 4th and 5th gears.
- AGS shift program logic
- Adaptive hydraulic pressure control
- Reverse lock out function
- Shift solenoid control (all freewheel shifts).
- Shift lock solenoid control
- Downshift inhibit control
- Failsafe operation (emergency program)
- CAN communication with all drivetrain control modules and the instrument cluster. This feature reduces individual signal circuits dramatically and improves reliability.
- Scan tool communication for diagnosis and programming.

5-speed automatic

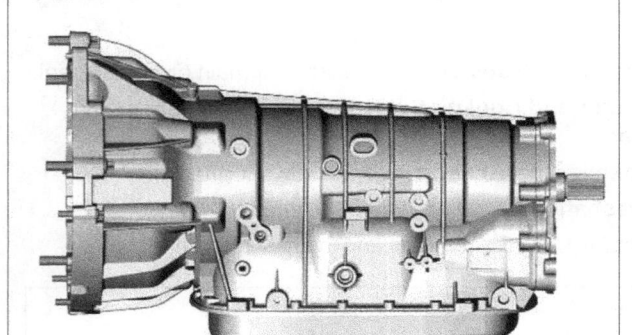

BX30240001

6-speed automatic transmission overview

The automatic transmission for the 2007 through 2010 X3 (3.0si and 30i models) is the 6-speed GA6L45R (General Motors) with Mechatronics.

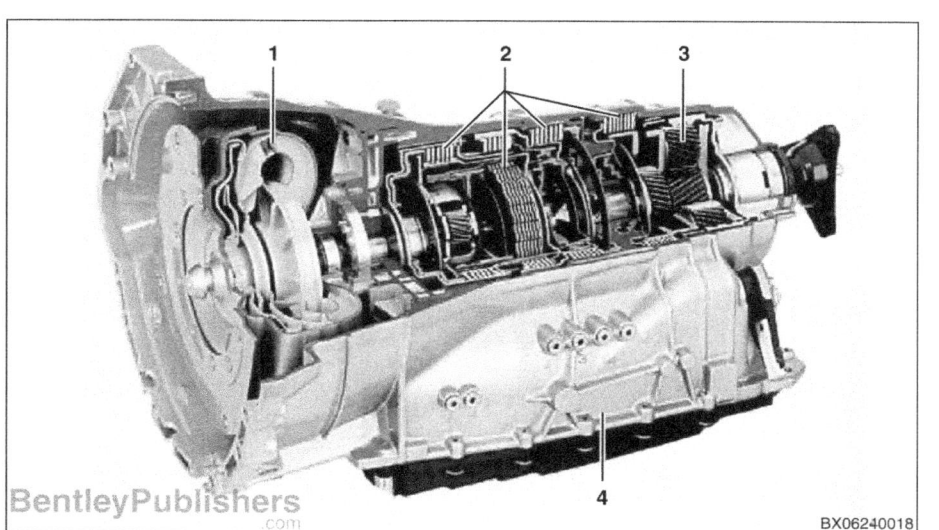

1. Torque converter
   • Capable of torque multiplication
2. Multi-plate clutch packs
3. Planetary gear assembly
4. Mechatronics module
   • Valve body (hydraulic unit)
   • Transmission control module (A7000a)

240

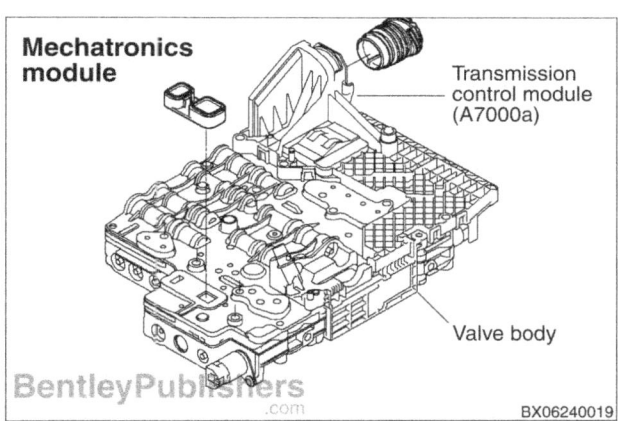

Mechatronics module

Transmission control module (A7000a)

Valve body

BX06240019

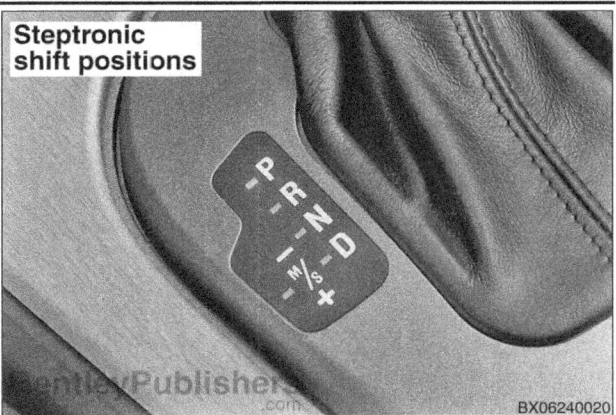

Steptronic shift positions

BX06240020

The 6-speed automatic transmission system utilizes the following components:

• Mechatronics module inside transmission housing, combining hydraulic unit (valve body) and transmission control module (TCM)(A7000a).

• Instrument cluster displaying shift selector range and drive program.

• Brake light switch signal affects function of selector lever shiftlock.

• Engine control module (ECM) signals engine speed, torque and other parameters. TCM signals current transmission operating status back to ECM.

• DSC control module signals cornering, acceleration and traction data.

• Accelerator pedal module signals driver power demand data.

Troubleshooting

Minor automatic transmission problems may be corrected by changing the automatic transmission fluid (ATF) and filter. Begin by checking ATF level and condition. Check to see if the fluid is dirty or has a burned odor indicating overheated fluid. The burned odor may be the results of burned discs in the clutch packs. Friction material from the burned disc can clog valve body passages.

Software in the transmission control module (TCM) monitors transmission operation for faults and alerts the driver by illuminating the transmission fault indicator on the instrument panel. The self-diagnostic software stores diagnostic trouble codes (DTCs) which may be accessed as follows:

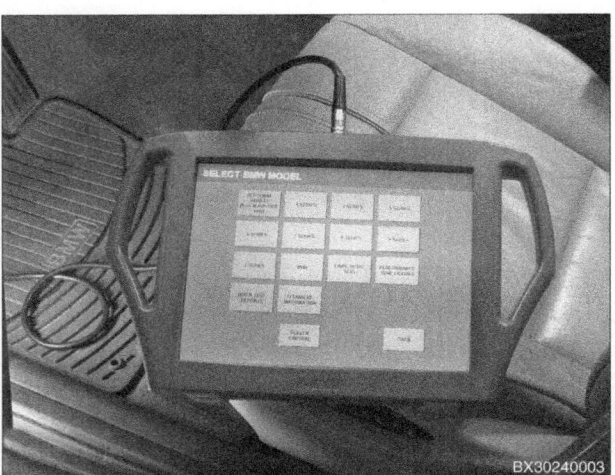

◄ Connect BMW diagnostic scan tool to OBD 2 plug on left door post. (Plug is behind plastic trim.)

– Place transmission selector lever in PARK or NEUTRAL. Engage parking brake.

– Switch ignition ON. Follow scan tool instructions as they appear on scan tool screen to check for fault codes.

Cautions

> **CAUTION—**
>
> • When performing any repair which involves separating the engine and transmission, check that the bellhousing dowels are undamaged and properly in place before reassembly. If the alignment of the engine flywheel to the transmission input shaft or torque converter is incorrect, shudder, noise and internal damage to the transmission may result.
>
> • For N52 engines with a magnesium crankcase only aluminum fasteners and dowels may be used. Consult with an authorized BMW dealer parts department for the correct fasteners and dowels for the engine and model concerned.
>
> • Do not mix BMW transmission oils, and do not replace with another oil.
>
> • ATF does not circulate unless the engine is running. When transporting the vehicle, use a flat bed truck or raise the wheels off the ground.

BX30240003

AUTOMATIC TRANSMISSION FLUID (ATF) SERVICE

Automatic transmission fluid has a service interval of approximately 100,000 miles. If service or repairs have to be made to the transmission or ATF cooler, use only the approved transmission fluid.

Check ATF level if there is evidence of a leak, a complaint related to fluid level or after transmission repairs.

The automatic transmission is not equipped with a dipstick. Check ATF level while monitoring ATF temperature with special equipment. Make sure transmission is at operating temperature and vehicle is level throughout tests.

Be sure necessary equipment, catch bin, transmission fluid and fluid pump are available before starting the fluid level checking procedure.

ATF level, checking

Transmission fluid expands with temperature. BMW requires that the ATF transmissions be checked when fluid temperature is between 30 - 50°C (86 - 122°F).

— Drive vehicle to warm up ATF to operating temperature.

◀ Connect BMW diagnostic scan tool to OBD 2 plug on left door post. (Plug is behind plastic trim.) Set scan tool to measure ATF temperature.

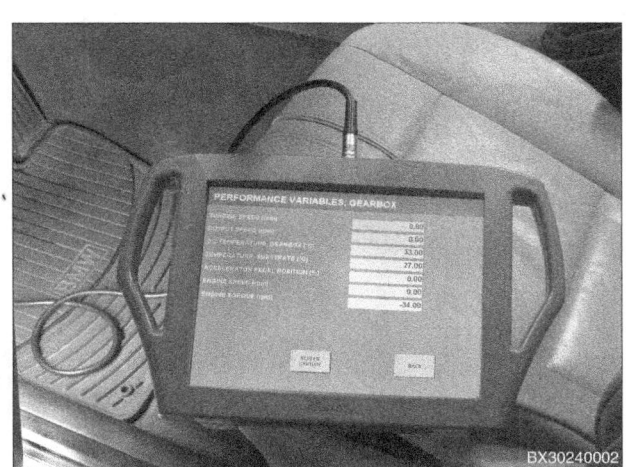

— With engine running, switch on air-conditioning to increase engine idle speed.

— Apply parking brake.

— While applying foot brake firmly move gear shift selector lever through all gear positions, pausing in each gear briefly.

— Raise and safely support vehicle. Be sure vehicle is level. Place oil drip pan underneath.

> **CAUTION—**
> • Make sure vehicle is stable and well supported at all times. Use a professional automotive lift or jack stands. A floor jack is not adequate support.

◀ With engine running, selector lever in PARK and temperature as specified, remove fill plug (**arrow**).

> **WARNING —**
> • Hot ATF can scald. Wear eye protection and protective clothing and gloves during the check. If the transmission is overfilled, hot ATF spills from the fill hole when the fill plug is removed.

Drain plug

ATF level checking	
Fluid temperature	30° - 50°C (86° - 120°F)

NOTE—

• *For best results, check fluid level with a fluid temperature of 30°C (85°F).*

• *An accurate level check is not possible if fluid temperature rises above 50ºC (120°F).*

— Level is correct if small stream of fluid runs out of fill hole.

— If no fluid runs out, add fluid until it starts to overflow.

CAUTION—

• *Transmission fluid specifications are subject to change and supersession. Consult an authorized BMW center for the latest Do not mix BMW transmission oils, and do not replace with another oil.*

Automatic transmission fluid

Type	BMW part no.	Fluid type
A5S390R	83 22 2 305 396	BMW ATF 2
GA6L45R	83 22 2 305 396	BMW ATF 2

— Install fill plug using new sealing ring.

Tightening torques

Fill plug to transmission sump: • A5S390R (M14) • GA6L45R (M18)	18 Nm (13 ft-lb) 19 Nm (14 ft-lb)

— Connect BMW diagnostic tool and call up "Service functions (drive)." Follow the on-screen instructions to complete fluid level check.

ATF, draining and filling (A5S390R)

— Raise vehicle and support safely.

WARNING—

• *Make sure vehicle is stable and well supported at all times. Use a professional automotive lift or jack stands. A floor jack is not adequate support.*

— Remove splash shield under transmission. If necessary to improve access, remove splash shield and exhaust brackets.

◄ Remove ATF drain plug (**arrow**) and drain fluid into container.

WARNING—

• *Make sure ATF is warm when draining. Hot ATF can scald. Wear eye protection, protective clothing and gloves.*

— Remove transmission sump mounting bolts and remove sump.

— Clean sump and sump magnet using a lint-free cloth. Remove sump gasket and clean gasket sealing surface.

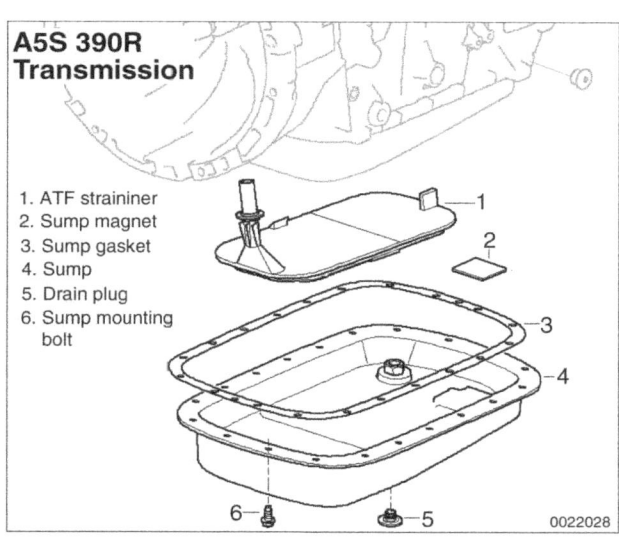

**A5S 390R
Transmission**

1. ATF strainer
2. Sump magnet
3. Sump gasket
4. Sump
5. Drain plug
6. Sump mounting bolt

0022028

◀ Pull ATF fluid strainer from transmission pump housing. If strainer sealing ring remains in pump housing remove using a seal puller.

– Use new ATF sump bolts purchased from BMW. Alternatively, clean old bolts and coat with Loctite® thread locking compound or equivalent.

– Install all bolts snug until seated to oil sump. Then torque going from one bolt to the next (not necessary to use diagonal order).

Tightening torque	
ATF sump to transmission (M6)	10 Nm (7 ft-lb)

– Replace drain plug with new.

Tightening torques (A5S390R)	
Drain plug to transmission sump (M14)	18 Nm 13ft-lb)
Fill plug to transmission sump (M14)	18 Nm (13 ft-lb)

– Top off transmission through fill plug and check fluid level. See **ATF level, checking** in this repair group.

Automatic transmission fluid (A5S390R)		
Type	BMW part no.	Fluid type
A5S390R	83 22 2 305 396	BMW ATF 2

Table b. ATF capacity (A5S390R)	
with torque converter drained	approx. 9.0 liters (9.5 US qt)

NOTE—

• *If not draining torque converter, measure fluid removed and replace with same amount. A rule of thumb is to have 7 liters of fluid on hand, although 6 liters is normally sufficient. Check fluid level using the method described under* **ATF level, checking**.

ATF, draining and filling (GA6L45R)

– Raise vehicle and support safely.

> **WARNING—**
>
> • *Make sure vehicle is stable and well supported at all times. Use a professional automotive lift or jack stands. A floor jack is not adequate support.*

– Remove splash shield under transmission. See **020 Maintenence**. If necessary to improve access, remove exhaust brackets.

◀ Remove ATF drain plug (**arrow**) and drain fluid into container.

> **WARNING—**
>
> • *Make sure ATF is warm when draining. Hot ATF can scald. Wear eye protection, protective clothing and gloves.*

– Remove transmission sump mounting bolts and remove sump.

BX30004

ATF, draining and filling (GA6L45R)

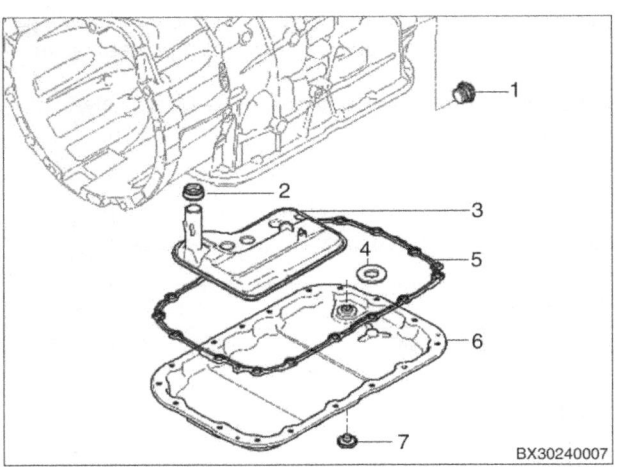

◄ GA6L45R sump and ATF strainer assembly

1. Fill plug
2. ATF strainer seal
3. ATF strainer (filter)
4. Gasket
5. Magnet
6. Sump
7. Drain plug

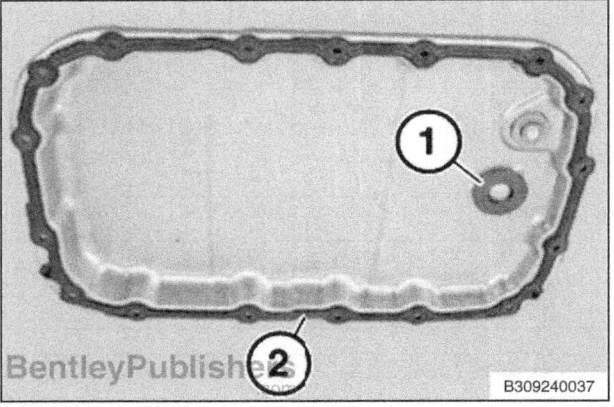

◄ Clean sump and sump magnet (**1**) using a lint-free cloth. Remove sump gasket (**2**) and clean gasket sealing surface.

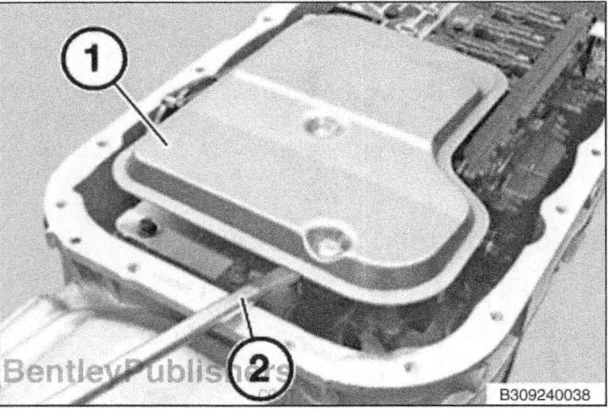

◄ Lever ATF strainer (**1**) from transmission pump housing using a prying tool (**2**). If strainer seal remains in pump housing, remove using a seal puller or small hooked tool.

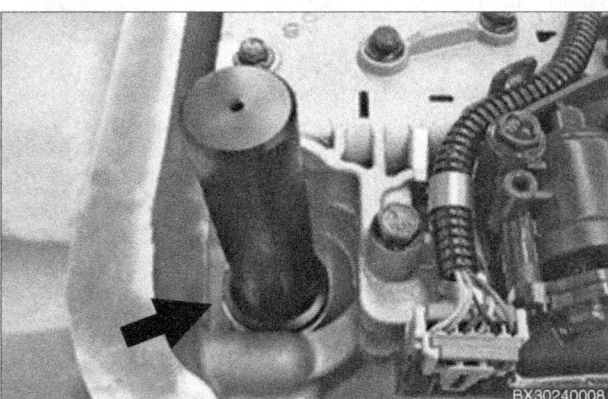

◄ Install new seal into transmission pump housing, using seal installer (**arrow**) (BMW special tool 24 4 400 or equivalent).

– Install ATF strainer.

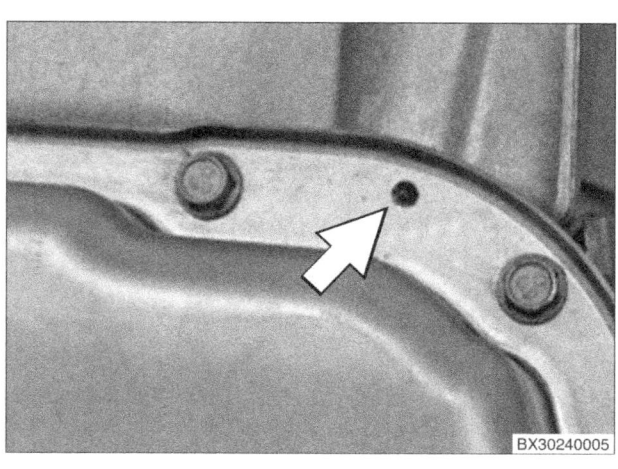

BX30240005

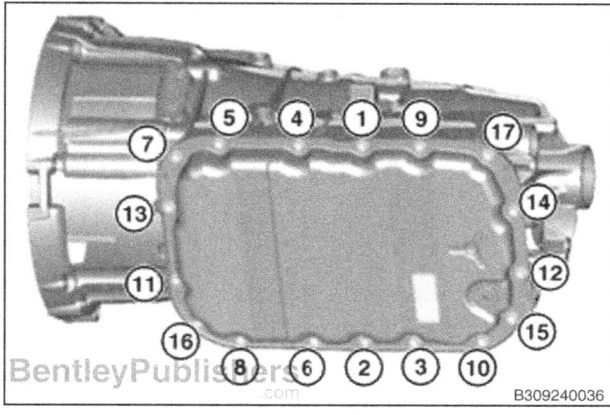

B309240036

◀ Install transmission sump using new gasket. Be sure locating tab of gasket engages hole in sump.

— Use new ATF sump bolts purchased from BMW. Alternatively, clean old bolts and coat with Loctite® thread locking compound or equivalent.

◀ Tighten transmission pan bolts using order shown, gradually and in several stages.

Tightening torque	
ATF sump to transmission (M6)	10 Nm (7 ft-lb)

— Replace drain plug using new sealing ring.

Tightening torques (GA6L54R)	
Drain plug to transmission sump (M12)	14 Nm (10 ft-lb)
Fill plug to transmission sump (M18)	19 Nm (14 ft-lb)

— Top off transmission and check fluid level. See **ATF level, checking** in this repair group.

Automatic transmission fluid (GA6L54R)		
Type	BMW part no.	Fluid type
GA6L45R	83 22 2 305 396	BMW ATF 2

Table c. ATF capacity (GA6L54R)	
with torque converter drained	approx. 9.5 liters (10 US qt)

NOTE—

• *If not draining torque converter, measure fluid removed and replace with same amount. A rule of thumb is to have 7 liters of fluid on hand, although 6 liters is normally sufficient. Always check fluid level using the method described under* **ATF level, checking***.*

TRANSMISSION REMOVAL AND INSTALLATION

Removal and installation of the transmission is best accomplished on a lift using a transmission jack. Use caution and safe workshop practices when working underneath vehicle and lowering transmission. Be sure to have appropriate tools on hand before starting the job.

> **CAUTION—**
> * N52 engines: replace aluminium fasteners each time they are released. Do not use steel fasteners in place of aluminium. Electrochemical corrosion will result.
> * Magnesium crankcase (N52 engines) requires aluminum fasteners exclusively.
> * When replacing aluminium fasteners, follow tightening torque and angle of rotation specification strictly.

Transmission, removing and installing

Automatic transition removal varies slightly depending on installed transmission. The following procedure is specific to the GM GA6L45R 6-speed transmission. It should be used as a guide used as a guide for removing the GM A5S390R 5-speed transmission.

> **WARNING—**
> * Allow engine and transmission to cool down before starting work on the transmission.

Transmission, removing

— Disconnect negative (-) cable from battery.

> **CAUTION—**
> * Prior to disconnecting the battery, read the battery disconnection cautions given in **001 Warnings and Cautions**.

— Remove electric radiator fan. See **170 Radiator and Cooling System**.

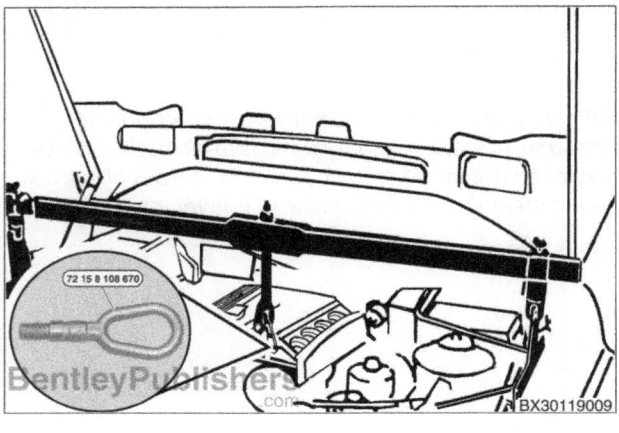

◄ Support weight of engine from above using engine support brace.
  * **N52 engine**: Screw tow hook into cylinder head.

— Raise and safely support vehicle.

> **WARNING—**
> * Make sure vehicle is stable and well supported at all times. Use a professional automotive lift or jack stands. A floor jack is not adequate support.

— Remove splash shields and supporting brackets under engine and transmission. See **020 Maintenence**.

— Remove front aluminum reinforcement plate from front suspension subframe. Discard bolts.

— Remove exhaust system. See **180 Exhaust System**.

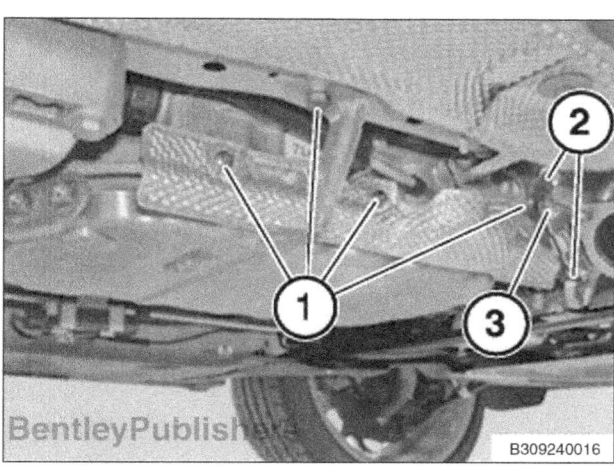

◀ Remove exhaust heat shields and support bracket:

- Remove fasteners (**1**) and remove heat shield.
- Unclip lines (**2**) and remove support bracket (**3**).

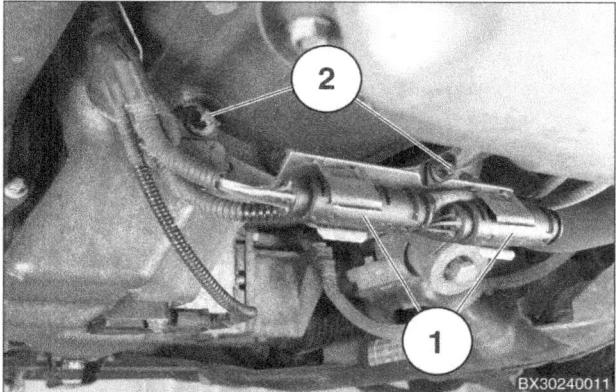

◀ **N52 engine**: Separate oxygen sensor electrical connectors (**1**). Remove fasteners (**2**) and remove connector retaining plate..

◀ Remove bellhousing fastener (**arrow**) next to electrical connector brackets (E18 socket).

Transmission, removing and installing

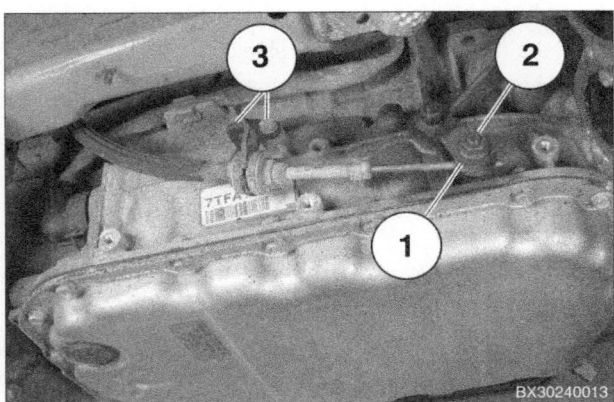

◀ Counterhold clamping sleeve (**1**) and loosen nut (**2**). Remove retaining bracket bolts (**3**) and set cable aside.

◀ Remove transmission fluid cooler hydraulic lines hold-down bolt (**arrow**).

NOTE —

• *Front driveshaft removed for clarity.*

◀ Remove nut (**arrow**) and bracket holding hydraulic lines to engine. Disconnect transmission fluid cooler hydraulic lines from transmission.

CAUTION—

• *Be prepared to catch dripping fluid.*

• *Make sure hydraulic line O-rings are removed with line and discarded. Always replace O-rings with new.*

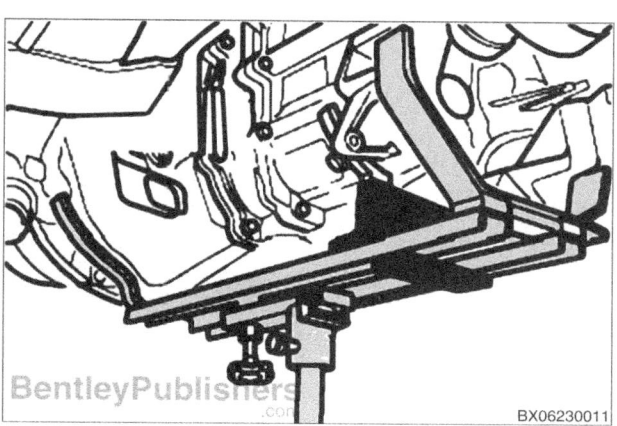

◀ Support transmission from below with suitable jack.

◀ Remove fasteners (**arrows**) and remove transmission cross-member.

– Remove front drive shaft. See **260 Driveshafts**.

– Rear driveshaft:

• Remove driveshaft center bearing support fasteners. Support center of driveshaft.

• Detach rear driveshaft flex-disc from transfer case.

• Lower center of driveshaft sufficiently to disengage flex-disc from transfer case flange. Tie driveshaft to side. See **260 Driveshafts**.

> *CAUTION—*
> • *To prevent damage to rear driveshaft CV joint, do not allow driveshaft to hang down unsupported.*

◀ Disconnect harness connectors from servomotor on transfer case (**1** and **2**).

Transmission, removing and installing

◄ Crank engine by hand in direction of rotation using bolt on crankshaft dampener until fastener (**1**) is visible through access hole in transmission bell housing.

— Remove fastener (**1**). Continue to rotate engine and remove remaining torque converter fasteners.

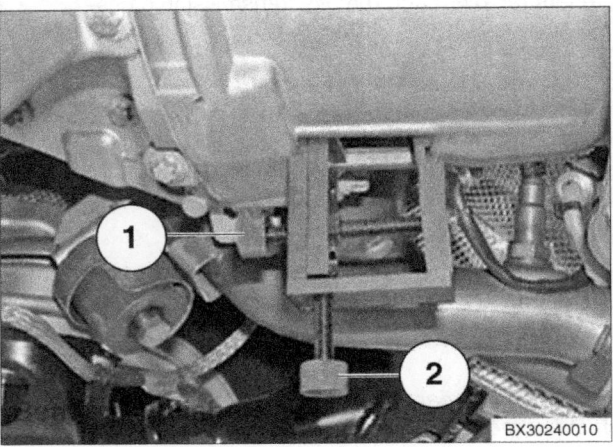

◄ Insert torque converter locking tool (BMW special tool 24 4 160). Raise clamping bar up (**adjuster 1**) to secure torque converter, then securely clamp tool to transmission housing (**adjuster 2**).

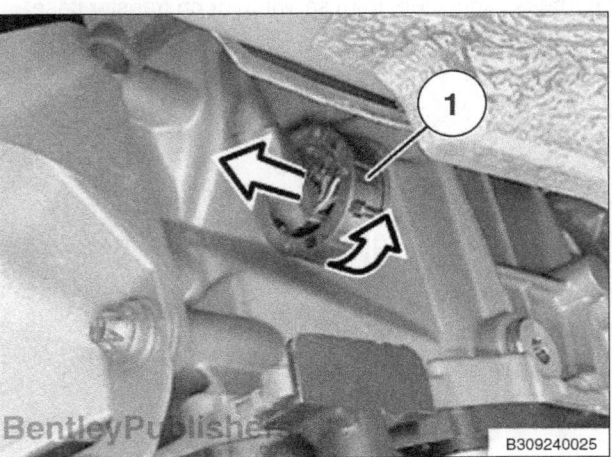

◄ Release mechatronics electrical connector bayonet lock (**1**) in direction of curved arrow. Carefully pull connector off pins.

— Insert BMW special tool 24 2 390 (protective cover) in place of mechatronics connector to pins.

> **CAUTION—**
> • *Use care not to touch or damage electrical pins in connector.*

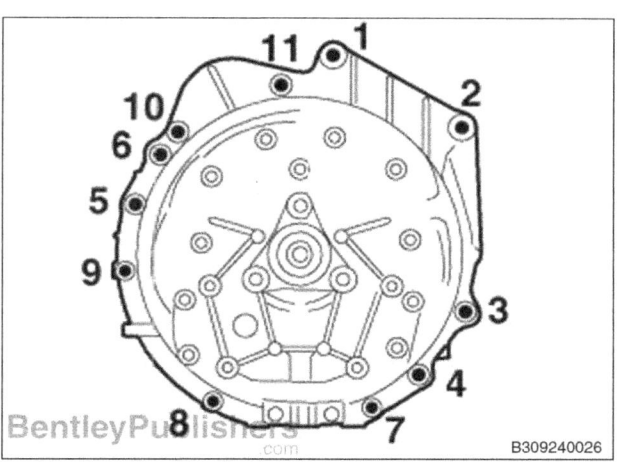

B309240026

◄ Remove remainder of fasteners from transmission bell housing.

– Remove transmission by pulling back and down. Lower jack slowly while watching carefully to make sure no lines, hoses or wires become snagged.

> **WARNING—**
> • Be sure the vehicle is properly supported. The removal of the transmission may upset the balance of the vehicle on the lift.

> **CAUTION—**
> • Tilting the engine to remove the transmission can lead to damage to various components due to lack of clearance.
> • Do not allow the torque converter to fall off the transmission input shaft. Use BMW special tool 24 1 370 or equivalent to hold torque converter in place during transmission removal.

– Blow out oil cooler lines with low-pressure compressed air and flush cooler with clean ATF twice.

> **CAUTION—**
> • Wear safety glasses when working with compressed air.
> • Do not reuse ATF used for flushing.

– Inspect engine drive plate and flywheel for cracks or elongated holes. Replace if necessary.

– If torque converter seal is leaky, or torque converter position on transmission input shaft was disturbed during removal, replace torque converter seal. See **Torque converter oil seal, removing and installing** in this repair group.

Transmission, installing

◄ Rotate flywheel until bore (**1**) is accessible through opening in engine oil pan.

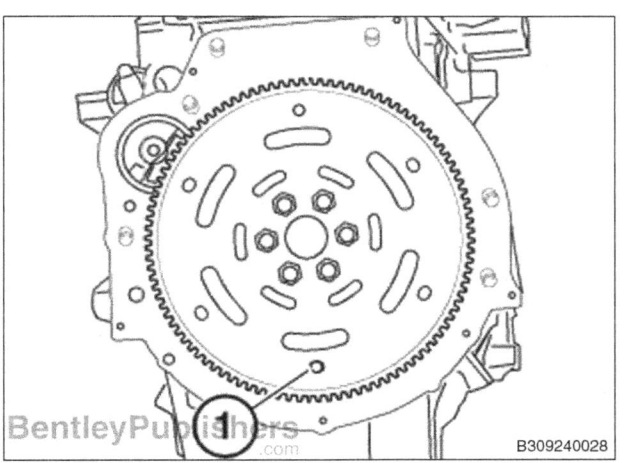

B309240028

Transmission, removing and installing

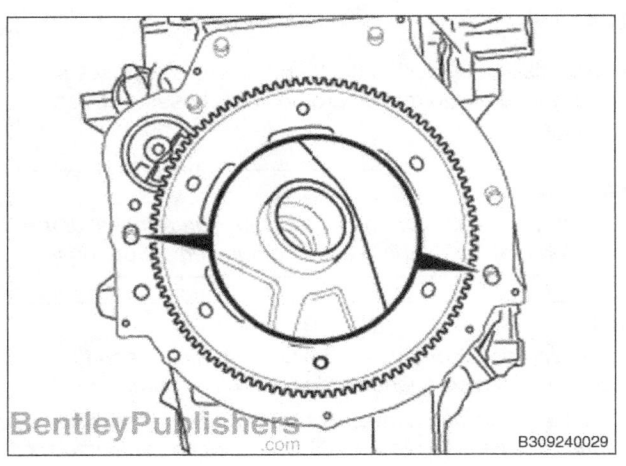

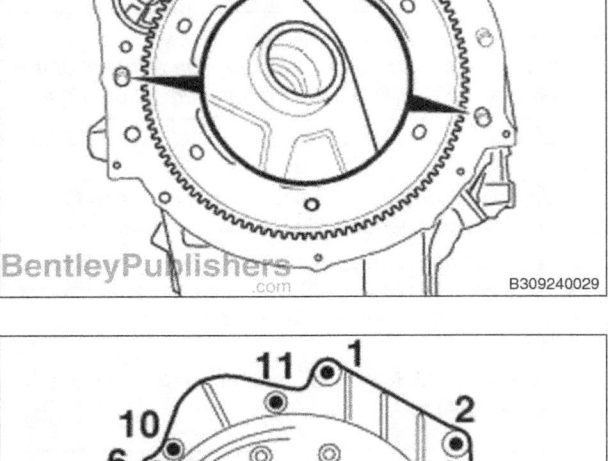

◀ Check that dowel sleeves are in good shape and correctly seated. Replace if needed.

– Check that torque converter is seated correctly in transmission.

– Rotate torque converter until bore in converter is flush with bore in driving disk.

– Join transmission to engine.

◀ When attaching transmission, replace all aluminium fasteners and follow tightening sequence.

– Tighten bolts at bell housing to initial torque.

> **CAUTION—**
> • On N52 engines, use new aluminum fasteners.

– Remainder of installation is reverse of removal. Remember to:
  • Tighten fasteners to final torque
  • Install new sealing washers or O-rings on ATF cooling line fittings.
  • Check gearshift mechanism, adjusting if necessary.
  • Fill transmission with clean ATF. See **ATF, draining and filling** in this repair group.

Automatic transmission fluid		
Type	**BMW part no.**	**Fluid type**
A5S390R	83 22 2 305 396	BMW ATF 2
GA6L45R	83 22 2 305 396	BMW ATF 2

ATF capacities (with torque converter drained)	
• A5S390R	approx. 9.0 liters (9.5 US qt)
• GA6L45R	approx. 9.5 liters (10 US qt)

Tightening torques	
Fill plug to transmission sump: • A5S390R (M14) • GA6L45R (M18)	18 Nm (13 ft-lb) 19 Nm (14 ft-lb)
Transmission to engine (**M54 engine**) • M6 Allen bolt • M8 Torx bolt • M10 Torx bolt • M12 Torx bolt	9 Nm (6.6 ft-lb) 22 Nm (16 ft-lb) 43 Nm (32 ft-lb) 72 Nm (53 ft-lb)

Tightening torques	
Transmission to engine (**N52 engine**) M10 • stage 1 • stage 2 (angle torque) M12 • stage 1 • stage 2 (angle torque)	20 Nm (15 ft-lb) 90 - 110° 25 Nm (18 ft-lb) 130 ° + 20°
Torque converter to flywheel: • M8 • M10 (8.8) • M10 (10.9)	26 Nm (19 ft-lb) 45 Nm (33 ft-lb) 56 Nm (41 ft-lb)
Transfer case crossmember • to transfer case (M12 through bolt) • to body (M8)	68 Nm (50 ft-lb) 19 Nm (14 ft-lb)
Heat shield to oil sump (N52 engine)	8 Nm (6 ft-lb)
Cover plate to transmission (N52 engine)	10 Nm (7 ft-lb)
Front reinforcement plate to front suspension subframe (use new bolts)	74 Nm (55 ft-lb)
Driveshaft center bearing support to body	21 Nm (15 ft-lb)
Driveshaft clamping sleeve to driveshaft	10 Nm (7 ft-lb)
Front driveshaft to front differential / transfer case (M10 10.9, use new bolts) • stage 1 • stage 2 (angle torque)	40 Nm (30 ft-lb) 45°
Rear driveshaft flex-disc to transfer case flange (ZNS fasteners) • 2004-2006 (with single stage flex disc - 96mm bolt hole pattern) stage 1 stage 2 (angle torque) • 2007-2010 (with two-stage flex disc - 110mm bolt hole pattern, ribbed teeth) stage 1 stage 2 (angle torque) • Rear driveshaft flex-disc to driveshaft flange (ZNS fasteners) stage 1 stage 2 (angle torque)	55 Nm (40 ft-lb) +90° 30 Nm (22 ft-lb) +90° 55 Nm (40 ft-lb) +90°

240

Torque converter, removing and installing

– Remove transmission. See **Automatic transmission, removing and installing** in this repair group.

◄ Screw BMW special tools 24 4 000 into torque converter. Pull converter straight off transmission input shaft (**arrow**).

> **CAUTION—**
> • *When torque converter is removed, transmission fluid will drain out. Be prepared to catch dripping fluid.*

– Remove torque converter slowly and set down vertically to avoid spilling additional transmission fluid.

– Reinstall torque converter, taking care to not damage new seal. Lightly oil converter seal surface and rotate converter during installation, applying slight pressure until recesses in converter locates audibly in ATF pump. Then press converter in firmly.

◄ After fitting torque converter, measure distance between mating surface and surface of threaded hole (**1**) in torque converter.
- **A5S390R transmission**: Measured value must be greater than 30 mm (1.18 in)
- **GA6L45R transmission**: Measured value must be greater than 25 mm (0.98 in).

> **CAUTION—**
> • *If torque converter is not installed correctly, impeller driver in converter is destroyed when transmission is mated to engine.*

Torque converter oil seal, removing and installing (A5S390R)

ATF leaking from the torque converter seal usually collects at the bottom of the bellhousing and drips out. Torque converter oil seal leakage is often caused by a worn or scored bushing in the torque converter hub. A damaged bushing rapidly wears the new seal.

◄ Remove two bolts holding seal cover to converter housing. Remove seal cover. Remove seal using a seal puller.

– Install new seal into position. Install seal cover and tighten bolts even in stages.

Tightening torque	
Seal cover to torque converter housing (M4)	3 Nm (26 in-lb)

– Reinstall torque converter, taking care to not damage new seal. Lightly oil converter seal surface and rotate converter during installation, applying slight pressure until recesses in converter locate audibly in ATF pump. Then press converter in firmly. See **Torque converter, removing and installing**.

> **CAUTION—**
> • *If torque converter is not installed correctly, impeller driver in converter is destroyed when transmission is mated to engine.*

Torque converter oil seal, removing and installing (GA6L45R)

ATF leaking from the torque converter seal usually collects at the bottom of the bellhousing and drips out. Torque converter oil seal leakage is often caused by a worn or scored bushing in the torque converter hub. A damaged bushing rapidly wears the new seal.

– Remove transmission. See **Transmission, removing and installing** in this repair group.

– Carefully slide torque converter off transmission input shaft. Be prepared to catch ATF as it flows out of torque converter.

– Check converter bushing surface for scoring or wear.
  • Remove sharp edges and burrs with fine emery cloth.
  • If hub is deeply scored, replace torque converter.

◄ Use small screwdriver to pry out seal retaining circlip (**arrow**) from ATF pump.

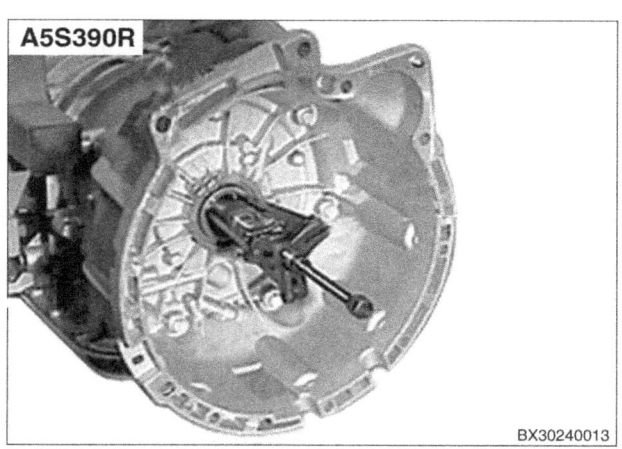

A5S390R

BX30240013

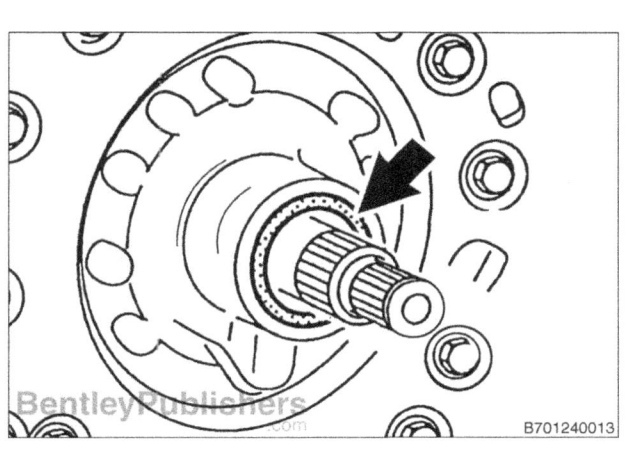

B701240013

240

Torque converter oil seal, removing and installing (GA6L45R)

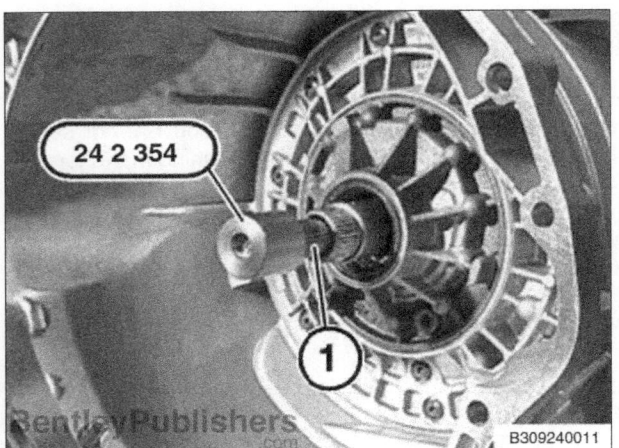

◄ Attach BMW special tool (24 2 354) to transmission input shaft (**1**).

◄ Screw BMW special tool 24 2 351 into seal. Use BMW special tool 24 2 352 to gradually draw out seal.

◄ Coat sealing lips of new seal with transmission fluid. Use BMW special tool (24 2 400) and soft-faced hammer to drive seal into transmission as far as it will go.

— Reinstall retaining circlip (if equipped).

— Reinstall torque converter, taking care to not damage new seal. Lightly oil converter seal surface and rotate converter during installation, applying slight pressure until recesses in converter locate audibly in ATF pump. Then press converter in firmly.

> **CAUTION—**
> • *If torque converter is not installed correctly, impeller driver in converter is destroyed when transmission is mated to engine.*

Torque plate and flywheel, removing and installing

Crankshaft rear main (flywheel) seal replacement is covered in **119 Lubrication System**.

- Remove transmission. See **Transmission, removing and installing** in this repair group.

◀ Use BMW special tool 11 9 260 or equivalent to lock flywheel.

- Loosen and remove flywheel bolts (**arrows**) and discard.

- Remove torque plate and flywheel.

- Clean bolt threads in crankshaft.

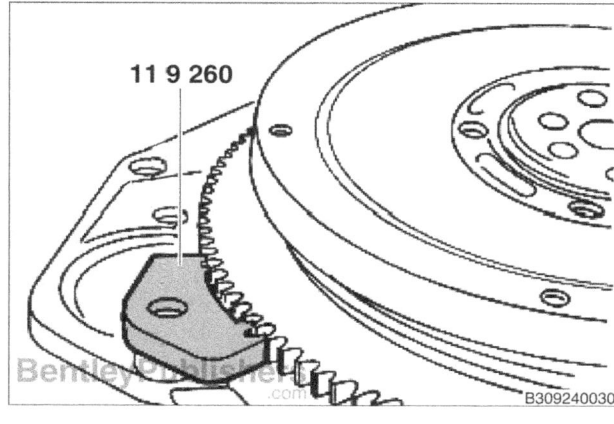

11 9 260

B309240030

B701240016

◀ When installing:

- Note that flywheel is located with dowel sleeve (**arrow**).
- Make sure torque converter mounting holes in torque plate and flywheel line up.
- Use new flywheel bolts.

Tightening torque	
Flywheel and torque plate to crankshaft **A5S390R transmission** (use new bolts)	121 Nm (89 ft-lb)
GA6L45R transmission (use new bolts)	joining - 30 Nm (22 ft-lb) final - 120 Nm (88 ft-lb)

240

250 Gearshift Linkage

250

GENERAL

This repair group covers transmission gearshift service for manual and automatic transmission models.

To gain access to the complete gearshift mechanism, remove the transfer case, the exhaust system, and rear driveshaft. See:

- **180 Exhaust System**
- **260 Driveshafts**
- **270 Transfer Case**
- **310 Front Suspension** for front end reinforcement

Neutral safety switch function

In models with automatic transmission, the electronic immobilizer function (EWS) prevents starter operation unless the gear position is (P)ARK or (N)EUTRAL. This serves as the neutral safety switch.

Gearshift knob and boot, removing and installing

Gearshift knob removal is the same on manual and automatic models. Make sure engine is OFF when removing gearshift knob.

 On manual transmission models, gently press in on both sides of shift boot frame (side **arrows**) and unclip boot from center console.

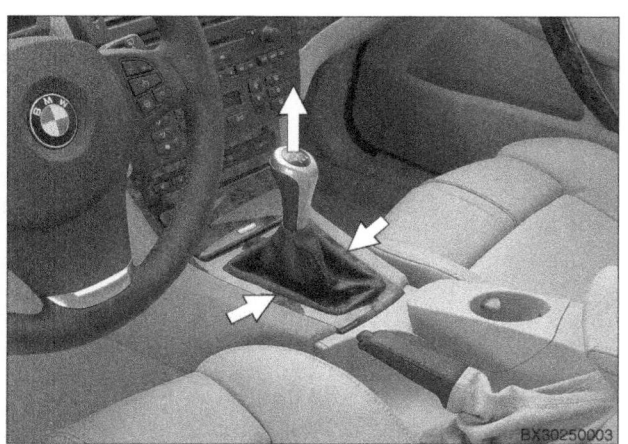

BX30250003

Gearshift knob and boot, removing and installing

◄ On automatic models, pull boot taut on leather, then gently press frame inwards until catch at top left is released (**arrows**). Continue to press in on frame and lift out boot with frame.

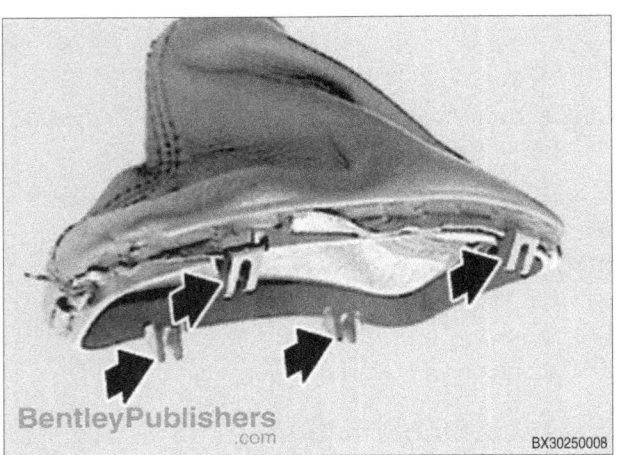

◄ Installation is reverse of removal. Check that no retaining lugs (**arrows**) are missing or damaged.

— Pull gearshift knob straight up (top **arrow**) to remove. It may require up to 90 lbs. of force.

> **CAUTION—**
> • *To prevent damage to shift knob locating tabs, do not twist knob during removal.*

MANUAL TRANSMISSION GEARSHIFT

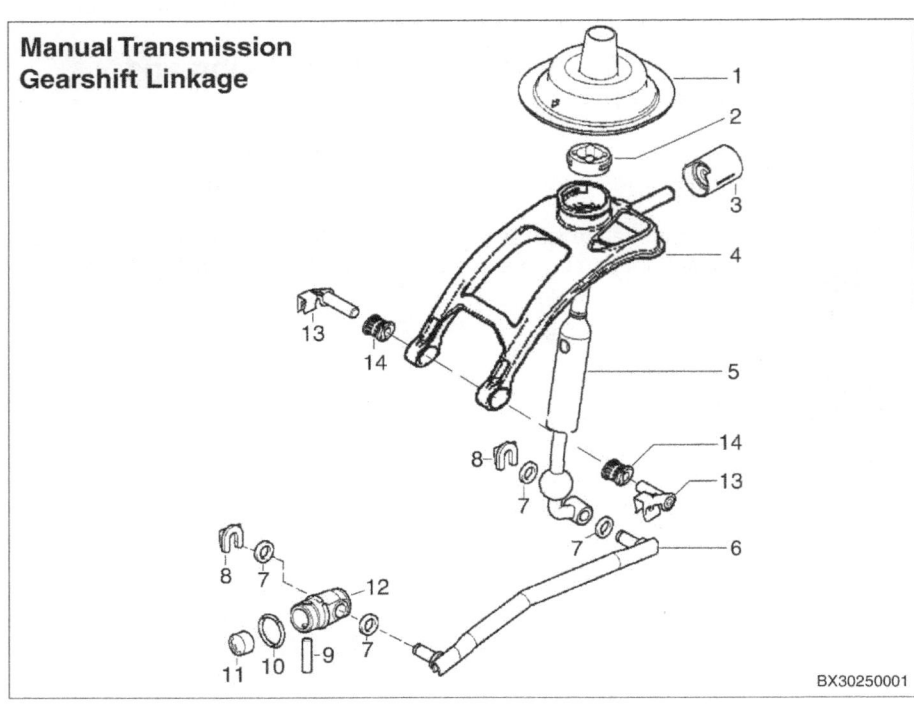

Manual Transmission Gearshift Linkage

Manual gearshift linkage

1. Rubber boot
2. Shift lever bearing
3. Shift arm bearing
4. Shift arm
5. Shift lever
6. Selector rod
7. Spacer ring
8. Locking clip
9. Dowel pin
10. Lock ring
11. Washer
12. Gear selector rod joint

Gearshift lever, removing and installing (manual transmission)

— Remove shift boot and shift knob. See **Gearshift knob and boot, removing and installing** in this repair group.

— Remove sound insulation at base of shift lever.

— Raise vehicle to gain access to underside of vehicle.

> **WARNING —**
> • *Make sure vehicle is stable and well supported at all times. Use a professional automotive lift or jack stands. A floor jack is not adequate support.*

— Remove exhaust system and heat shields. See **180 Exhaust System**.

— Support transmission from below with a suitable jack.

◄ Remove transfer case crossmember member support bracket bolts (**arrows**).

> **NOTE —**
> • *Auto transmission shown.*

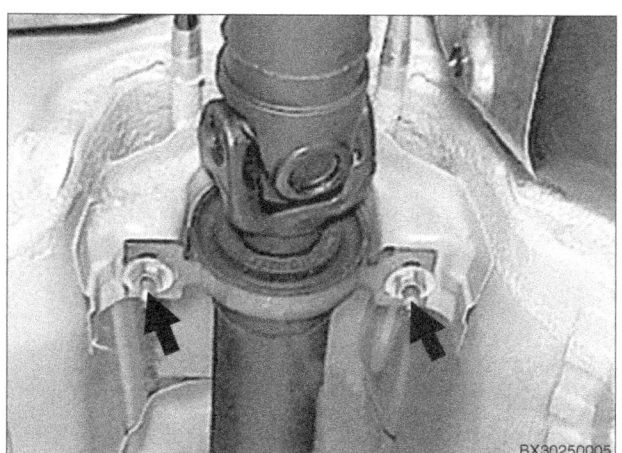

◄ Release fasteners (**arrows**) at driveshaft center support and lower support.

— Lower transmission slightly to gain access to gearshift lever.

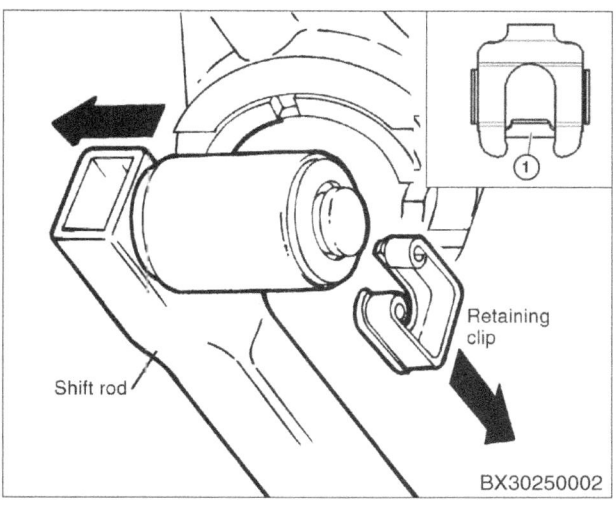

◄ Working above transmission, disconnect selector rod:
 • Pull off selector rod retaining circlip (**arrow**).
 • Disengage selector rod from gearshift lever, noting position of washers.

> **NOTE —**
> • *A revised shift rod clip is fitted as of 04/2008 (inset). Use new shift rod clip when reassembling. Be sure retaining lug (1) is seated behind shift rod pin during installation.*

Gearshift lever, removing and installing (manual transmission)

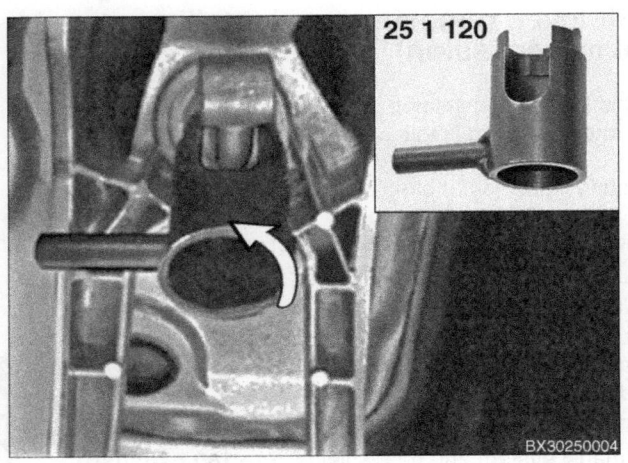
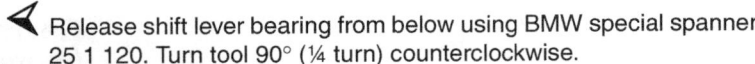

◀ Release shift lever bearing from below using BMW special spanner 25 1 120. Turn tool 90° (¼ turn) counterclockwise.

• Push shift lever and bearing up to remove from shift arm.

— Lower vehicle. Working from inside passenger compartment, pull up on shift lever to remove it together with inner rubber boot and shift lever bearing.

— Clean old grease from shift lever ball and mounting ring. Also clean shift arm bowl. Lubricate with molybdenum disulfide grease.

— Insert shift lever together with inner boot and bearing into shift arm. Position boot so that arrow on boot points to front of vehicle.

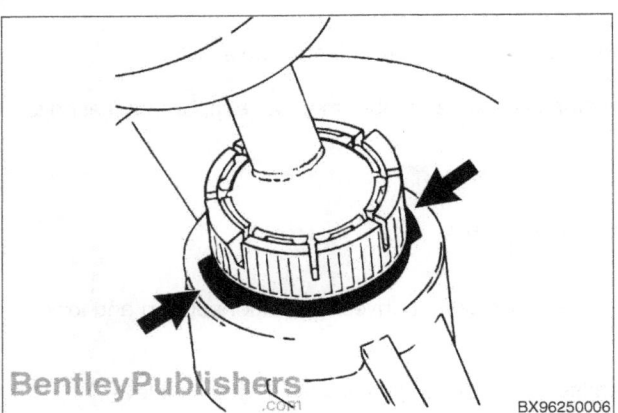

◀ When installing shift lever bearing:

• Align locking tabs with slots (**arrows**) in shift arm bowl.

• Make sure arrow on shift lever bearing points to front of vehicle.

• Press down until bearing snaps into place.

— Remainder of installation is reverse of removal.

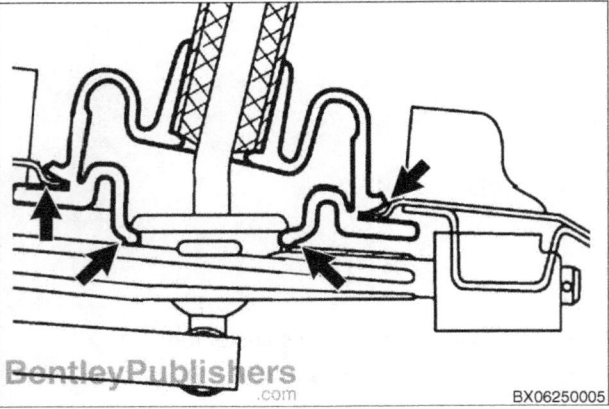

◀ Pull inner rubber boot over shift arm bowl (**arrows**) to seal base of shift lever. Install rubber boot with arrow pointing toward front of vehicle.

— Remainder of installation is reverse of removal.

Tightening torques	
Rear driveshaft to transfer case flange	See **260 Driveshafts**
Driveshaft center support to body	21 Nm (15.5 ft-lb)
Transfer case crossmember • to transfer case (M12 through bolt) • to body (M8)	 74 Nm (55 ft-lb) 22 Nm (16 ft-lb)
Heat shield to oil sump (N52 engine)	8 Nm (6 ft-lb)

AUTOMATIC TRANSMISSION GEARSHIFT

Steptronic gearshift assembly

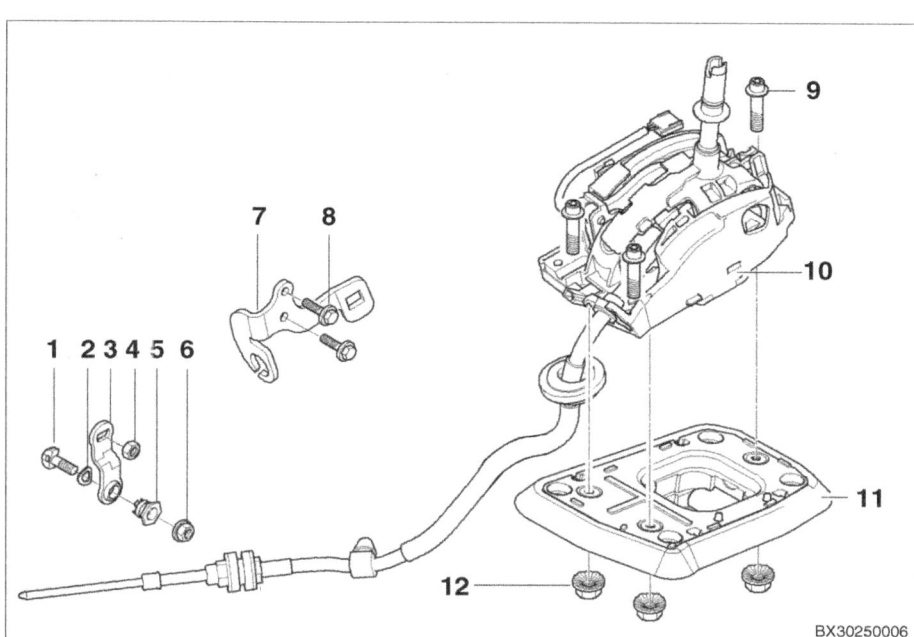

BX30250006

1. Clamping bolt
2. Washer
3. Transmission shift arm on side of transmission
4. M8 self-locking nut
5. Bushing
6. M6 bolt
7. Support bracket
8. Bracket mounting bolt
9. M6 Torx screw
10. Steptronic assembly with shift cable
11. Base mounting plate
12. Nut

250

Gearshift mechanism, adjusting

NOTE—

• Gearshift mechanism varies with transmission. Adjustment is similar.

— Position gearshift lever in P(ARK).

— Raise vehicle to gain access to shift linkage.

> **WARNING—**
> *• Make sure vehicle is stable and well supported at all times. Use a professional automotive lift or jack stands.*

 Working at transmission selector lever at side of transmission:

• Remove heat shield.
• Counterhold cable clamping bushing (**A**).
• Loosen cable clamping nut (**B**).
• Push transmission shift arm forward toward engine (**arrow 1**) (PARK position).
• Push shifter cable end backward away from engine (**arrow 2**). Release pressure on cable.
• Tighten clamping nut.

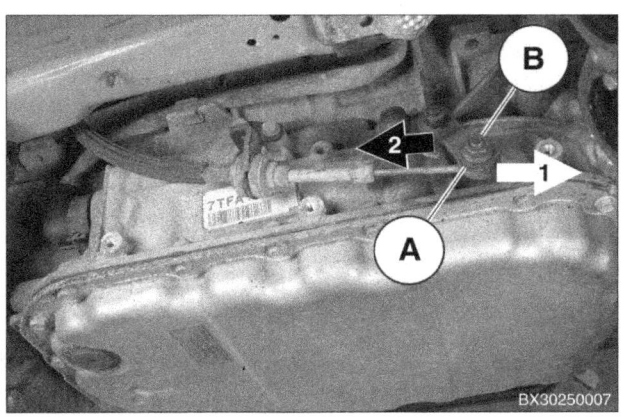

BX30250007

> **CAUTION—**
> *• Do not overtighten nut (do not allow cable to twist).*

Tightening torque	
Shift cable clamping nut	10 Nm (7 ft-lb)

Automatic shiftlock, checking function

The automatic shiftlock uses an electric solenoid to lock the selector lever in P(ARK) or N(EUTRAL). Depressing the foot brake with the ignition ON energizes the solenoid, allowing the lever to be moved into R(EVERSE) or D(RIVE).

The solenoid is energized only when engine speed is below 2,500 rpm and vehicle speed is below 3 mph (5 kph). The solenoid is mounted in the selector lever housing and not separately available from BMW.

— Automatic shiftlock prevents drive gear selection until brake pedal is depressed.
  • With engine running and vehicle stopped, place selector lever in P.
  • Without depressing brake pedal, check that selector lever is locked in P.
  • Depress brake pedal firmly and listen to solenoid clicking audibly.
  • Check that selector lever can now be moved out of P.

NOTE—

• *Perform the next test in an open area with the parking brake ON and with caution.*

— With selector lever in P and brake pedal depressed, raise engine above 2,500 rpm. Check that selector lever cannot be moved out of P.

— If any faults are found:
  • Check electrical operation of shiftlock solenoid
  • Check for wiring faults to or from transmission control module (TCM). See **ECL Electrical Component Locations** and **ELE Electrical Wiring Diagrams**.

NOTE—

• *The solenoid is controlled via the transmission control module (TCM), using brake pedal position, engine speed, and road speed as controlling inputs.*

Ignition interlock cable, removing and installing

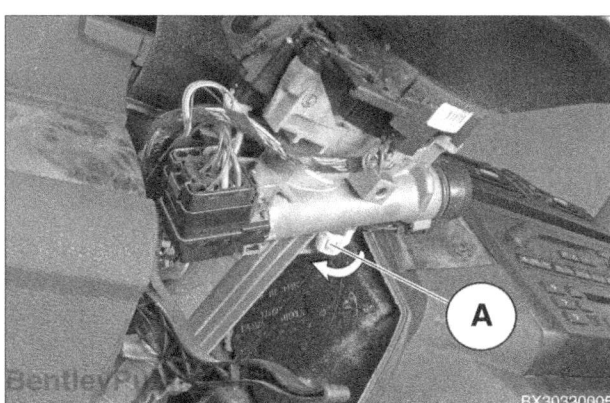

— Remove lower steering column trim. See **513 Interior Trim**.

— Remove gearshift knob and boot. See **Gearshift knob and boot, removing and installing** in this repair group.

— Remove center switch panel from dashboard, see **513 Interior trim.**

◀ Working near the shifter, remove fastener (**A**) to release cable holder (**B**).

  • Press interlock cable to driver's side and remove toward front of vehicle (**arrow**).

◀ Loosen and disconnect interlock cable (**A**) from ignition lock assembly by turing approximately 45°.

— Tie chase cord to interlock cable at shifter.

  • Remove interlock cable by pulling out in direction of steering column.

  • Untie chase cord from old interlock cable and attach it to new interlock cable.

  • Pull cord in direction of shifter to carefully feed new cable into position. Taking care to avoid kinks.

— The remainder of installation is reverse of removal.

Tightening torque	
Interlock cable to gearshift bracket bolt.	7 Nm (5 ft-lb)

Ignition interlock cable, adjusting

— Remove drive selection plate. See **Gearshift knob and boot, removing and installing** in this repair group.

— Remove center switch panel from dashboard. See **513 Interior Trim**.

◀ Place selector lever in PARK:

  • Loosen cable mounting fastener (**A**), do not remove.

— Press down on interlock lever (**arrow**) and tighten cable mounting fastener (**A**).

260 Driveshafts

260

GENERAL

This repair group covers repair and replacement of front and rear driveshafts and driveshaft components.

A transfer case is bolted to the rear of the transmission with front and rear driveshafts.

Front driveshaft repairs are limited to replacement of the complete driveshaft. Rear driveshaft repairs consist of replacement of the flex-discs, center mount and bearing. If rear driveshaft universal joints are defective, replace the complete driveshaft.

On vehicles are equipped with aluminium driveshafts and ZNS (shiny zinc-coated) fasteners. Always replace ZNS fasteners with same.

See also:
- **270 Transfer case**
- **310 Front Suspension** for front end components
- **311 Front Axle Differential** for front drive axle repairs
- **331 Rear Axle Differential** for rear drive axle repairs

Driveshaft assemblies

1. Transfer case
2. Front driveshaft
3. Front driveshaft universal joint
4. Rear driveshaft center bearing
   • Rubber mounted
5. Rear driveshaft flex-disc

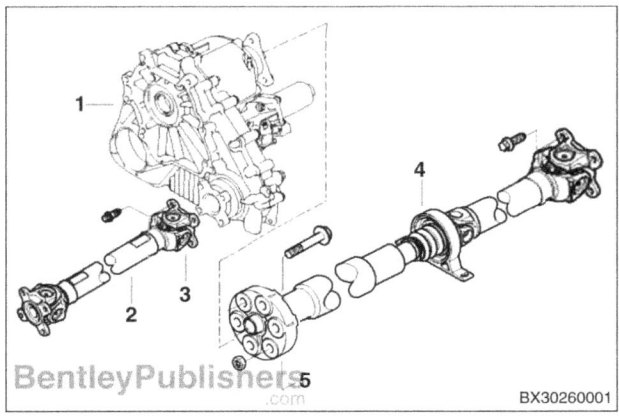

BX30260001

Cautions

> **CAUTION—**
> - *Be sure the wheels are off the ground before removing the driveshaft. Set the parking brake before removing the driveshaft.*
> - *Use only ZNS (zinc-coated) fasteners with aluminium driveshaft components. ZNS fasteners are designed to be used only once. Replace during reassembly.*
> - *Do not move vehicle using engine power once a driveshaft or driveaxle is removed. If the vehicle has been moved under engine power with a non-functioning drive system (e.g. front driveshaft no longer engaging front differential or a drive axle no longer engaging with front or rear differential), the VTG transfer box must be recalibrated using a BMW scan tool (control unit function – function check – transfer box) after repairs are complete.*
> - *Driveshaft are balanced to close tolerances. Whenever driveshafts are removed or disassembled, mark mounting flanges and driveshaft sections with paint before proceeding with work. This ensures that the driveshaft can be reassembled and installed in exactly the original orientation.*

FRONT DRIVESHAFT SERVICE

If detecting vibration or noise from the front driveshaft, check front universal joints for play. Pull and twist driveshaft while watching universal joint. Specified tolerance for play is very small, so almost any noticeable play indicates a problem.

Universal joint play	
Maximum allowable	0.15 mm (0.006 in)

Front driveshaft, removing and installing

— Raise car and support safely.

> **WARNING—**
> - *Make sure car is stable and well supported at all times. Use a professional automotive lift or jack stands. A floor jack is not adequate support.*

— Remove splash guard under engine. working below engine, remove front reinforcement plate. See **310 Front Suspension**.

— If driveshaft is to be reinstalled, mark mounting flanges and driveshaft sections with paint to preserve original orientation.

◀ Front driveshaft components:

1. Transfer case
2. ZNS bolt (replace with new)
3. Driveshaft
4. Universal joint

— Working at front differential input flange, remove universal joint bolts.

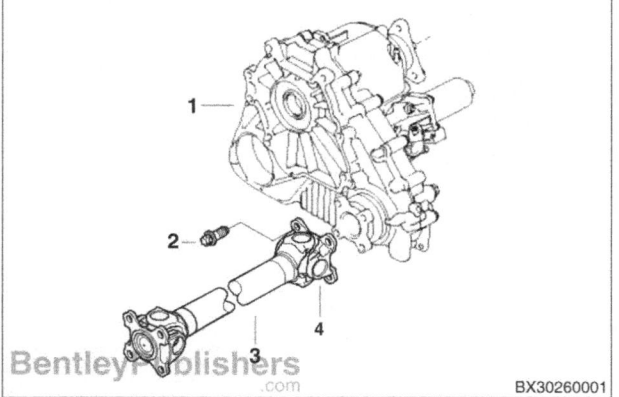

– Working at transfer case flange, remove universal joint bolts and remove driveshaft.

– Installation is reverse of removal. Remember to:
  • Observe marks made previously (if applicable).
  • Replace ZNS fasteners with new.

Tightening torque	
Front reinforcement plate to front suspension subframe (use new bolts)	74 Nm (55 ft-lb)
Front driveshaft to front differential / transfer case (M10 10.9, use new bolts) • stage 1 • stage 2 (angle torque)	 40 Nm (30 ft-lb) 45°

260

REAR DRIVESHAFT SERVICE

Rear driveshaft components

 Rear driveshaft components:

1. ZNS bolt (always replace)
2. Self-locking nut (always replace)
3. Centering sleeve
4. Flex-disc
5. ZNS bolt (replace)
6. Damper ring
7. Clamping sleeve (2004 - 2007)
   Boot (2007 - 2010)
8. ZNS bolt (always replace)
9. Center bearing and housing
10. Bolt
11. Damper ring
12. Circlip

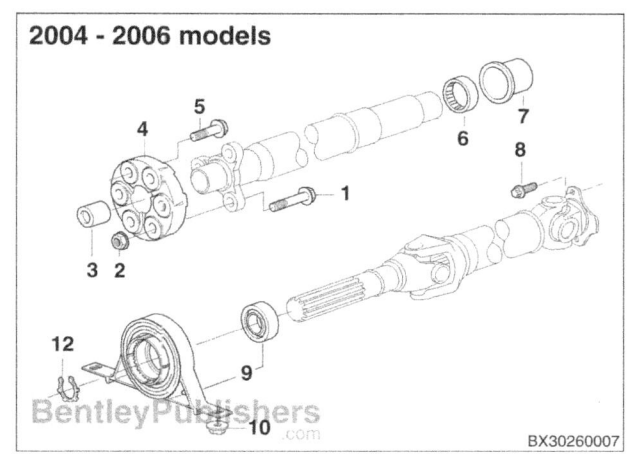

2004 - 2006 models

BX30260007

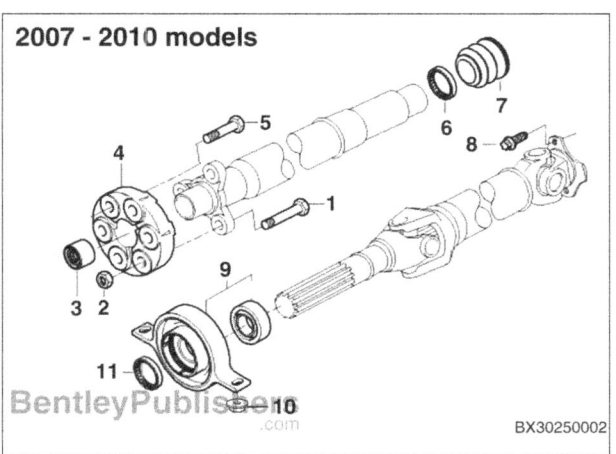

2007 - 2010 models

BX30250002

Troubleshooting

Sources of driveline vibrations and noise may be difficult to pinpoint. Engine, transmission, front or rear axle or wheel vibrations may be transmitted through the driveshafts to the car body.

Noises in the interior of vehicle may be caused by:

- Differential problems
- Faulty wheel bearings
- Damaged drive axle(s)
- Worn or improperly inflated tires

Driveshaft noise or vibrations are usually caused by worn or damaged components.

— To inspect or remove rear driveshaft, remove exhaust system and exhaust heat shield. See **180 Exhaust System**.

◄ Check driveshaft universal joint for play. Pull and twist driveshaft while watching universal joint. Specified tolerance for play is very small, so almost any noticeable play indicates a problem.

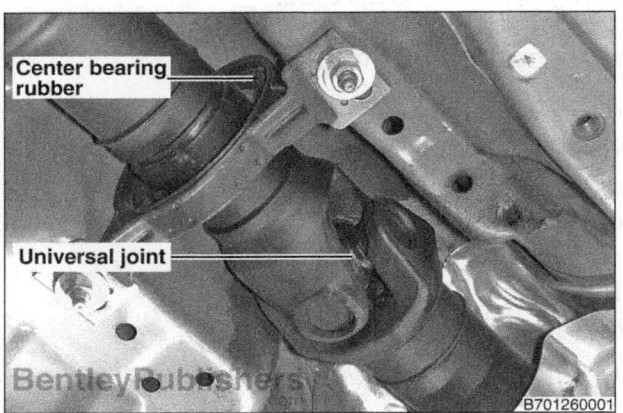

Universal joint play	
Maximum allowable	0.15 mm (0.006 in)

— Check for any loose fasteners at flange connections.

— Check flex-disc and center bearing rubber for deterioration or tearing.

— Check driveshaft for broken or missing balance weights. Weights are welded tabs on driveshaft tubes.

— Use paint to matchmark front and rear flanges. Remove driveshaft. See **Rear driveshaft, removing and installing** in this repair group.

— Check universal joints for wear or binding. If it is difficult to move or binds, replace driveshaft.

— Check centering sleeve at output flange for damage or misalignment.

— Check runout at transmission / transfer case output flange and output shaft, and at rear differential input flange.

Driveshaft flange wear limits	
Runout at transfer case output flange (max. allowable): • Axial play • Radial play	0.10 mm (0.004 in) 0.07 mm (0.003 in)
Rear differential input flange radial play (measured at driveshaft center lip)	0.07 mm (0.003 in)

— Check bolt bores at transmission / transfer case output flange and rear differential input flange for wear and elongation.

— Spin driveshaft center bearing and check for smooth operation without play.

If inspection reveals nothing wrong with driveshaft, it may need to be rebalanced. This can be done by a speciality driveshaft repair shop.

Sometimes a minor driveshaft vibration can be corrected by disconnecting at transfer case and repositioning it 90°, 180° or 270° in relation to differential input flange.

Table a lists symptoms of rear driveshaft problems and their probable causes. Most of the repair information is contained within this repair group. There are references to other repair groups, where applicable.

Table a. Rear driveshaft problems and causes

Symptom	Probable cause	Corrective action
Vibration when starting off (forward or reverse).	Center bearing rubber deteriorated.	Inspect center bearing and rubber. Replace if necessary. See **Center bearing assembly, replacing** in this repair group.
	Flex-disc damaged or worn.	Inspect flex-disc. Replace if necessary. See **Flex-disc, replacing** in this repair group.
	Engine or transmission mounts faulty.	Inspect engine and transmission mounts. Align or replace, if necessary.
	Front centering sleeve worn, or driveshaft mounting flanges out of round.	Check front centering sleeve and replace if necessary. See **Front centering sleeve, replacing** in this repair group. Also check runout of driveshaft flanges.
	Universal joint worn or seized.	Check universal joint play and movement. Replace driveshaft if necessary.
Noise during on / off throttle or when engaging clutch.	Differential components worn or damaged (excessive pinion-to-ring-gear clearance).	Remove differential and repair. See **311 Front Axle Differential** or **331 Rear Axle Differential**.
	Drive axle or CV joint faulty.	Inspect drive axles and CV joints. Repair or replace as necessary. See **311 Front Axle Differential** or **331 Rear Axle Differential**.
Vibration when driving under load.	Front centering sleeve worn, or driveshaft mounting flanges out of round or damaged.	Check front centering sleeve and replace if necessary. See **Front centering sleeve, replacing** in this repair group. Also check runout of driveshaft flanges.
	Universal joint worn or seized.	Check universal joint play and movement. Replace driveshaft if necessary.
	Flex-disc damaged or worn.	Inspect flex-disc. Replace if necessary. See **Flex-disc, replacing** in this repair group.
	Center bearing rubber deteriorated.	Inspect center bearing. Replace if necessary. See **Center bearing assembly, replacing** in this repair group.
	Mounting flange bolts loose or holes worn.	Remove rear driveshaft and check transfer case output flange and differential input flange. Replace if necessary.
	Rear driveshaft unbalanced.	Check driveshaft for loose or missing balance weights. Have driveshaft rebalanced or replace if necessary.
	Universal joint worn or seized.	Check universal joint play and movement. Replace rear driveshaft if necessary.
	Rear driveshaft center bearing faulty.	Replace center bearing. See **Center bearing assembly, replacing** in this repair group.
	Rear differential rubber bushing(s) faulty.	Inspect differential rubber bushing. Replace as necessary. See **331 Rear Axle Differential**.

Rear driveshaft, removing and installing

– Raise vehicle and support safely.

> **WARNING** —
> • *Make sure vehicle is stable and well supported at all times. Use a professional automotive lift or jack stands. A floor jack is not adequate support.*

– Remove exhaust system and exhaust heat shields. See **180 Exhaust System**.

> **WARNING** —
> • *Make sure exhaust system is fully cooled off before removing.*

– Mark mounting flanges and driveshaft sections with paint to preserve original orientation.

◀ Working at front flex-disc, remove three bolts (**arrows**) holding flex disc to transfer case flange. Discard old fasteners.

> **NOTE** —
> • *Dual stage flex disc (2007-2010 models) shown. Earlier single stage flex disc is similar. See Flex disc, replacing.*

◀ On 2004 - 2006 models, loosen threaded clamping sleeve on driveshaft a few turns.

– Working at driveshaft rear universal joint, remove Torx bolts at differential input flange. Discard bolts. If necessary, use pry bar at groove to pry universal joint free.

– Hang driveshaft rear section from body using stiff wire.

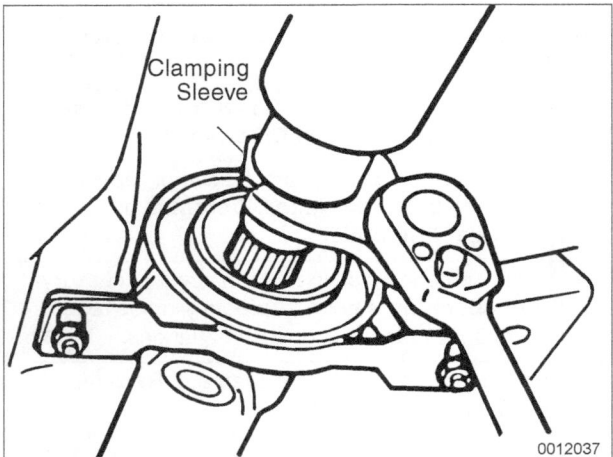

Clamping Sleeve

◀ Remove driveshaft center support bearing mounting nuts (**arrows**).

– Remove driveshaft by pulling down on center of driveshaft. If necessary, use pry bar to free flex disc from centering dowel on transfer case.

Rear driveshaft, removing and installing

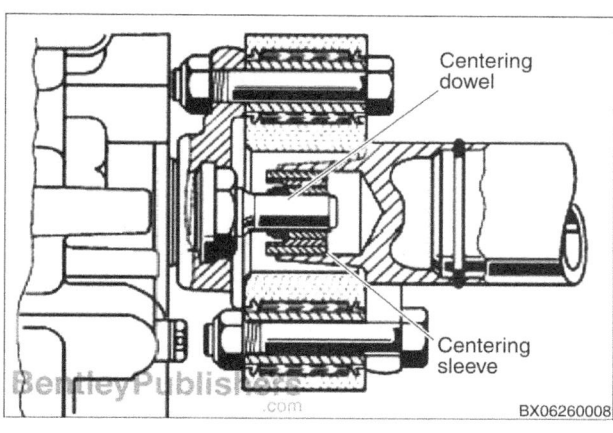

Centering
dowel

Centering
sleeve

BX06260008

260

◄ Prior to installation:
- Inspect centering dowel on transfer case output flange.
- Inspect centering sleeve inside driveshaft flex-disc.
- Replace damaged components. See **Front centering sleeve, replacing** in this repair group.
- When installing centering sleeve over centering dowel, apply thin coat of molybdenum disulfide grease (Molykote Longterm 2 Plus® or equivalent).

— Bend driveshaft at center universal joint to install.

— Align matchmarks on driveshaft to matchmarks on differential and transfer case flanges.

— Using new ZNS fasteners, alternately tighten bolts to draw joint evenly into flange. Once seated, tighten down bolts.

> **CAUTION—**
> - *Do not reuse fasteners. They are designed to be used only once.*
> - *Do not allow driveshaft to hang unsupported.*

Tightening torque

Rear driveshaft flex-disc to transfer case flange (ZNS fasteners)	
• 2004-2006 (with single stage flex disc - 96mm bolt hole pattern)	
stage 1	55 Nm (40 ft-lb)
stage 2 (angle torque)	+90°
• 2007-2010 (with two-stage flex disc - 110mm bolt hole pattern, ribbed teeth)	
stage 1	30 Nm (22 ft-lb)
stage 2 (angle torque)	+90°
• Rear driveshaft flex-disc to driveshaft flange (ZNS fasteners)	
stage 1	55 Nm (40 ft-lb)
stage 2 (angle torque)	+90°
Rear driveshaft to rear differential flange (M10 10.9, use new bolts)	
• stage 1	40 Nm (30 ft-lb)
• stage 2 (angle torque)	+45°
Driveshaft center bearing support to body	21 Nm (15 ft-lb)
Driveshaft clamping sleeve to driveshaft	10 Nm (7 ft-lb)

— Install heat shields. Install exhaust system. See **180 Exhaust System**.

— Road test vehicle and check for noise or vibration.

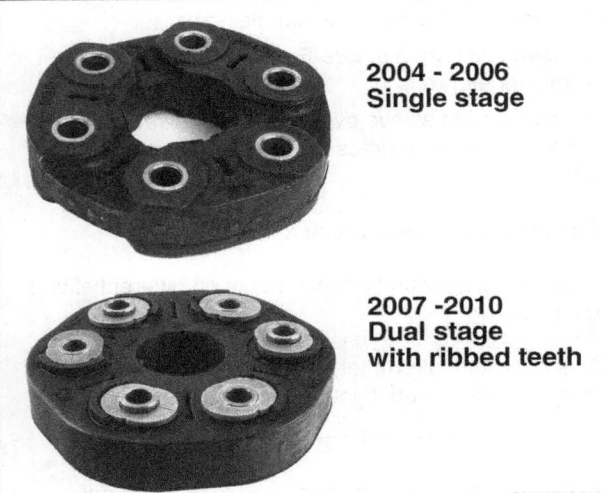

**2004 - 2006
Single stage**

**2007 -2010
Dual stage
with ribbed teeth**

BX30260004

BX30260008

Flex-disc, replacing

◄ Two types of flex disc are used, depending on model year. On 2004 - 2006 models, a single stage flex disc is used. On 2007 and later (LCI) models, a dual stage (with ribbed teeth inserts) flex disc is used.

The flex disc is mounted using one-time ZNS fasteners. Bolts and nuts should be replaced and time they are removed. Note also that toque settings differ based on type of flex disc installed.

− Check flex-disc for cracks, tears, missing pieces or distortion. Check for worn bolt hole bores in flange.

− Remove driveshaft center bearing support fasteners. Support center of driveshaft.

− Unbolt driveshaft flex-disc from transfer case flange. Note bolt position.

− Lower center of driveshaft sufficiently to disengage flex-disc from transfer case flange. Tie driveshaft to side.

− Remove fasteners and separate flex-disc from driveshaft. Hold bolts stationary while loosening nuts.

> **CAUTION—**
> • To avoid damaging rear driveshaft CV joint, do not allow driveshaft to hang unsupported.

◄ Install new flex-disc using new ZNS fasteners.
 • Counterhold bolts while tightening nuts.
 • Molded arrows (**arrow**) on flex-disc point toward flange arms.
 • Dual stage flex disc: raised ribbed inserts mount to transfer case flange.

> **CAUTION—**
> • To avoid damaging flex-disc rubber, hold bolts stationary while tightening nuts.

Tightening torque	
Flex-disc to transfer case flange (ZNS fasteners) • 2004-2006 (with single stage flex disc 96mm bolt hole pattern) stage 1 stage 2 (angle torque)	55 Nm (40 ft-lb) +90°
• 2007-2010 (with two-stage flex disc 110mm bolt hole pattern, ribbed teeth) stage 1 stage 2 (angle torque)	30 Nm (22 ft-lb) +90°
• Flex-disc to driveshaft flange (ZNS fasteners) stage 1 stage 2 (angle torque)	55 Nm (40 ft-lb) +90°
Driveshaft center bearing support to body	21 Nm (15 ft-lb)
Driveshaft clamping sleeve to driveshaft	10 Nm (7 ft-lb)

Center bearing assembly, replacing

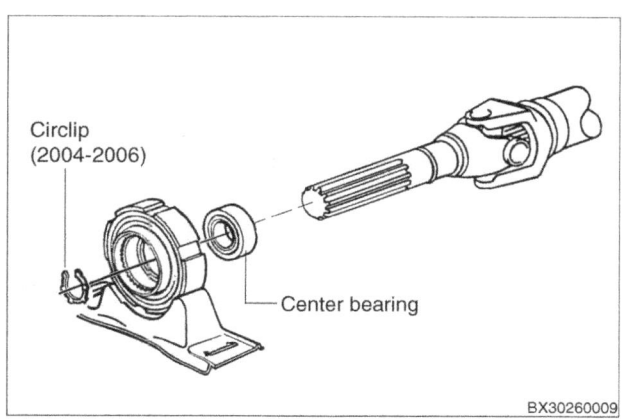

Circlip
(2004-2006)

Center bearing

BX30260009

The center bearing assembly consists of a grooved ball bearing in a rubber mount. The bearing assembly is pressed onto the front section of the driveshaft. On 2004-2006 cars, the bearing is secured by a circlip.

The rear driveshaft center bearing assembly consists of a grooved ball bearing in a rubber mount. The bearing assembly is pressed on the driveshaft.

- Remove driveshaft. See **Rear driveshaft, removing and installing** in this repair group.

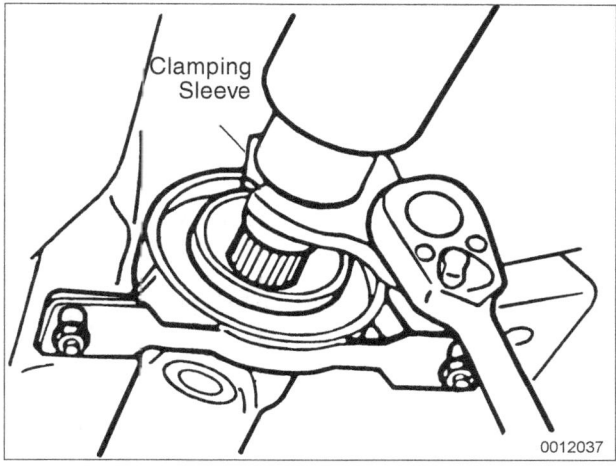

Clamping
Sleeve

0012037

◄ 2004 - 2006 models: loosen clamping sleeve fully.

- 2007 - 2010 models, separate rubber boot from front driveshaft section.

- Pull driveshaft sections apart.

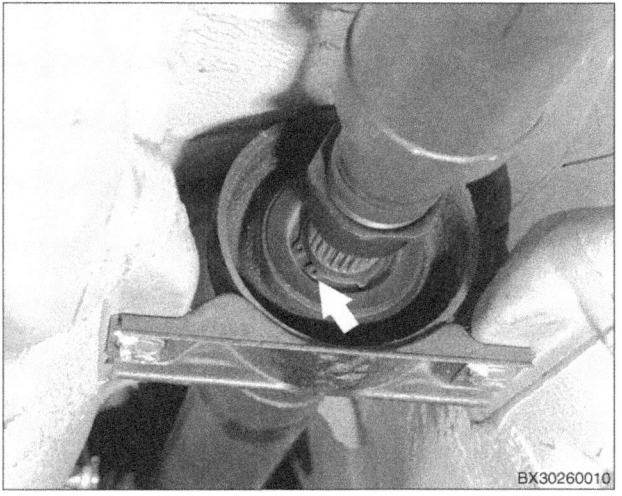

BX30260010

◄ On 2004-2006 models: Remove center bearing circlip (**arrow**).

- Use puller to remove center bearing assembly from driveshaft.

- On installation, drive new center bearing firmly to stop. On 2004 - 2006 models, install bearing circlip.

- Replace worn or damaged rubber and plastic parts. Lubricate splines with molybdenum disulfide grease (Molykote® Longterm 2 or equivalent). Reassemble driveshaft using matchmarks made prior to disassembly.

- Install driveshaft. See **Rear driveshaft, installing** in this repair group.

NOTE—

• *Do not tighten clamping sleeve until driveshaft is installed.*

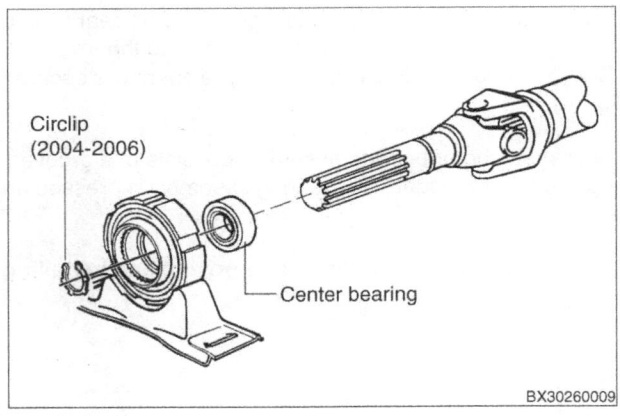

Circlip
(2004-2006)

Center bearing

BX30260009

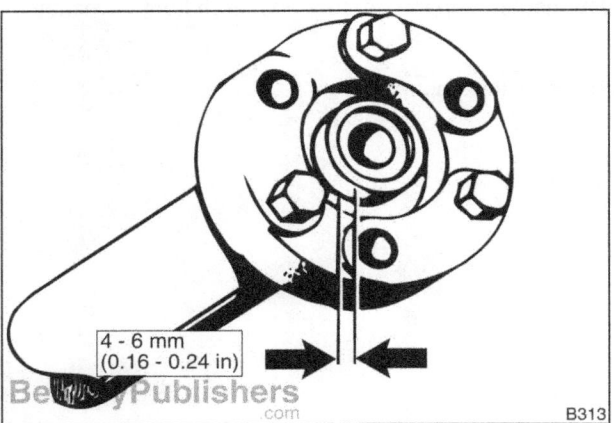

4 - 6 mm
(0.16 - 0.24 in)

B313

Front centering sleeve, replacing

◀ The front centering sleeve centers the rear driveshaft in relation to the transfer case flange. The sleeve is pressed into a cavity in the driveshaft tube and rides on a centering dowel on the transfer case output flange.

No specifications are given for wear of the sleeve. Check to make sure that the sleeve fits snugly over the dowel.

— Remove rear driveshaft. See **Rear driveshaft, removing and installing** in this repair group.

— Pack centering sleeve cavity with heavy grease until grease is flush with bottom edge of sleeve.

— Insert 14 mm (approximately $^{9}/_{16}$ in) diameter mandrel or metal rod into sleeve. Strike mandrel with hammer to force centering sleeve out. Make sure mandrel fits snugly in the centering sleeve so that grease cannot escape around the sides of the mandrel.

— Remove old grease from driveshaft, lubricate new centering sleeve with molybdenum disulfide grease (Molykote Longterm 2 Plus® or equivalent) and drive into driveshaft.

 • Sealing lip of sleeve faces outward.

 • Drive sleeve into driveshaft to a protrusion depth of 4 - 6 mm (0.16 - 0.24 in).

— Install driveshaft. See **Rear driveshaft, installing** in this repair group.

270 Transfer Case

270

. GENERAL

This repair group covers the all-wheel drive transfer case. Internal transfer case repair is not covered.

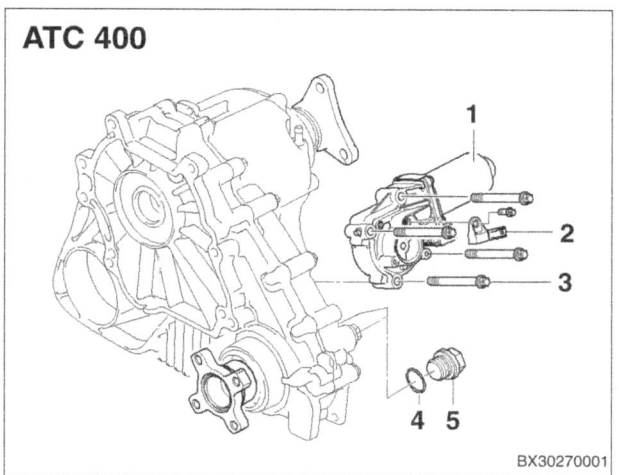

ATC 400

◄ The ATC 400 xDrive transfer case, bolted to the rear of the transmission, directs power from the transmission to both the front and rear differentials via driveshafts.

1. Servomotor with position sensor
2. Classification resistor
3. Fastener
   tighten to 22 Nm (16 ft-lb)
4. Drain / fill plug sealing washer
5. Drain / fill plug
   tighten to 33 Nm (24 ft-lb)

xDrive includes active torque control (ATC). ATC uses electronics via the VTG control module to control torque split and traction via a multidisc clutch.

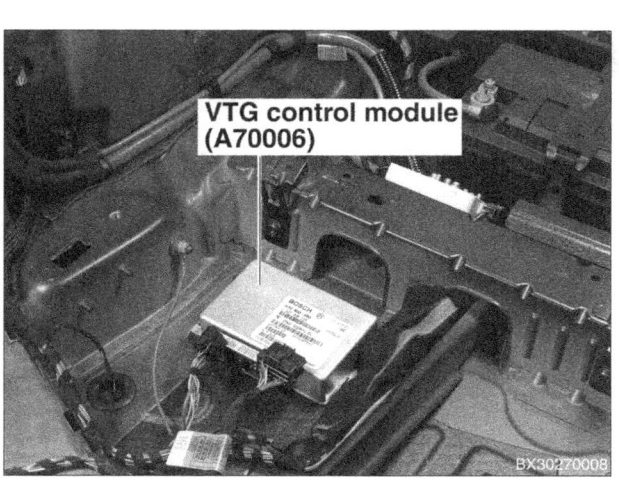

VTG control module (A70006)

◄ VTG (transfer case) control module (A70006) on rear floor panel under luggage compartment trim ahead of battery, passenger side.

For VTG ground and power supplies, see **ELE Electrical Wiring Diagrams**.

Additional information can also be found in **260 Driveshafts**.

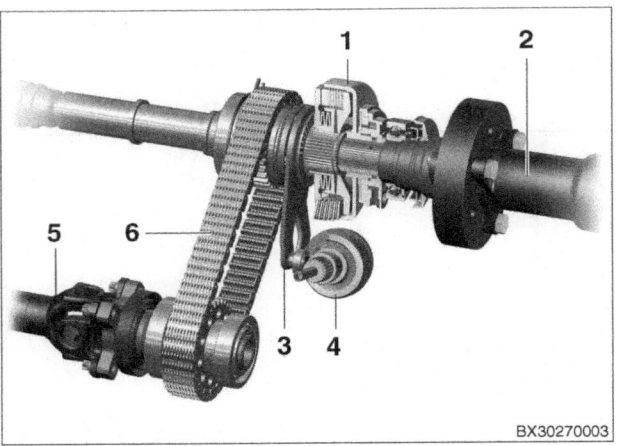

BX30270003

◄ When the multidisc clutch is open, no driving torque is transmitted to the front axle; instead, the entire driving torque is directed to the rear differential. When the clutch is fully closed, the front and rear axles turn at the same speed.

1. Multidisc clutch
2. Rear driveshaft
3. Adjusting levers with ball ramp
4. Cam disc (driven by servomotor)
5. Front driveshaft
6. Drive (power transfer) chain

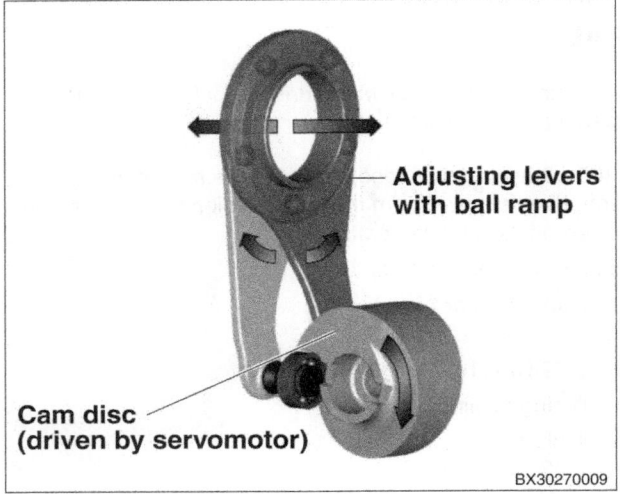

Adjusting levers with ball ramp

Cam disc (driven by servomotor)

BX30270009

◄ The VTG servomotor actuates the multidisc clutch via the cam disc and adjusting levers.

Classification resistor

xDrive servomotor

BX30270010

◄ Underneath vehicle at transfer case:
- **M8533**: xDrive (VTG) servomotor
- **R8554**: Classification resistor

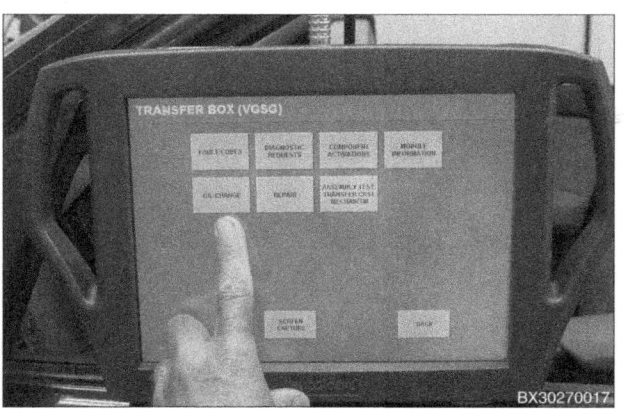

TRANSFER CASE SERVICE

The adaptive xDrive transfer case oil wear is monitored by the transfer case (VTG) control module to determine when an oil change is due.

◄ After changing worn transfer case oil, a BMW scan tool should be used to reset transfer case wear adaptations if "54C6 - VTG: Oil wear" fault code is present (including an illuminated 4 x 4 inactive warning lamp).

If the following xDrive driveline conditions/faults are present:

• Drivetrain vibrations, juddering and /or humming noises when traveling at speeds of 50 mph or more (particularly noticeable when coasting);

• Grabbing/juddering or chattering condition under hard acceleration in low gears;

• Vibrations when driving through turns at low speeds.

First check that tires are the same (brand, size, wear/ condition) at all four corners.

Next disconnect the harness connector at the VTG servomotor and test drive vehicle. If the issue is no longer present, change the transfer case fluid and reset the wear values in the VTG control module using a BMW factory scan tool.

If problems persist with new oil and a reset, the issue is likely related to the activation of the clutch in the VTG transfer case and additional transfer case diagnosis and service is required.

If the ABS, BRAKE and 4x4 inactive instrument panel warning lights are simultaneously illuminated and/or the transfer case actuator makes a clicking sound after shutting the engine off, the VTG servomotor is likely faulty.

◄ The cause of this fault can often be traced to a worn or cracked composite gear (**arrow**) within the servomotor housing. BMW does not sell the gear separately, although an aftermarket gear is available.

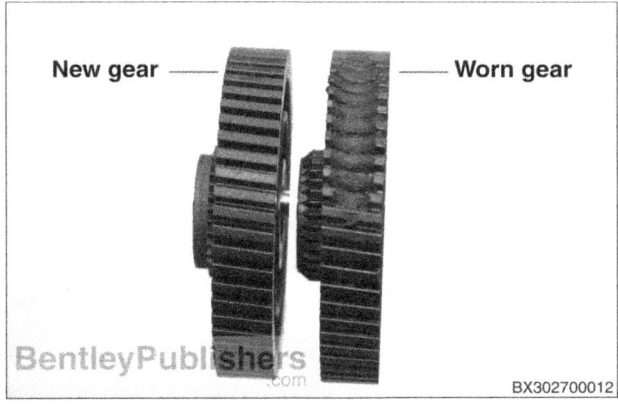

New gear ——————— Worn gear

◄ Gear (**arrow**) replacement requires removal and disassembly of the servomotor.

Transfer case fluid service

After performing work on transfer case, check fluid level. Be sure to use correct specification fluid.

> **CAUTION—**
> • *To prevent damaging transfer case, use only the recommended fluid.*

— Raise vehicle and support safely.

> **WARNING—**
> • *Make sure vehicle is stable and well supported at all times. Use a professional automotive lift or jack stands. A floor jack is not adequate support.*

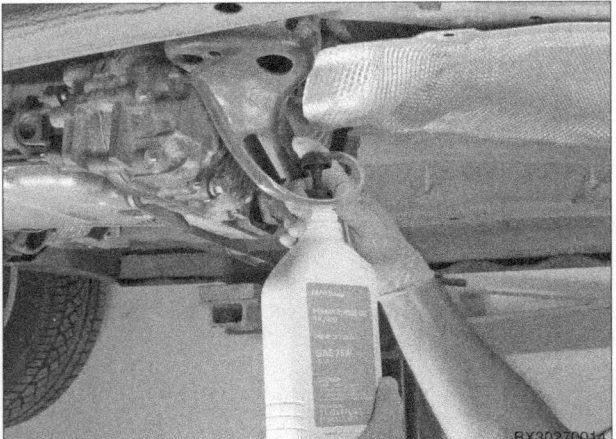

◄ Remove fill plug (**1**). Remove drain plug (**2**) and drain transfer case.

— Install and tighten drain plug using new sealing washer.

◄ Using fluid pump, fill transfer case until fluid begins to drip from lower edge of filler plug (**1**). Install and tighten fill plug using new sealing washer.

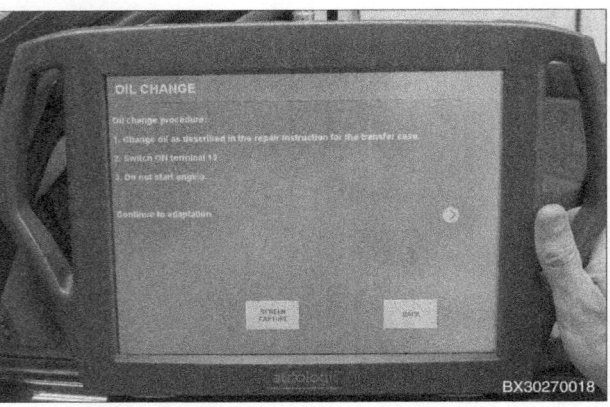

◄ If necessary, reset transfer case wear adaptations using a BMW scan tool and clear fault memory.

Transfer case fluid	
Capacity • drain and fill • refill	 0.69 ltr (0.73 qt) 0.80 ltr (0.85 qt)
Specification	Transfer case oil TF0870 BMW part no. 83 22 0 397 244

Tightening torque	
Drain / fill plug to transfer case (M18)	33 Nm (24 ft-lb)

Transfer case servomotor, removing and installing

— Raise vehicle and support safely.

> **WARNING—**
> • *Make sure vehicle is stable and well supported at all times. Use a professional automotive lift or jack stands. A floor jack is not adequate support.*

— Remove exhaust system and remove exhaust heat shields. See **180 Exhaust System**.

> **WARNING—**
> • *Make sure exhaust system is fully cooled off before removing.*

> **NOTE—**
> • *An alternative method to removing the complete exhaust system is to unbolt the heat shield, and gently bend and position it out of the way to access the servomotor harness connectors and mounting bolts. Removing the exhaust is the preferred method and offers the best access.*

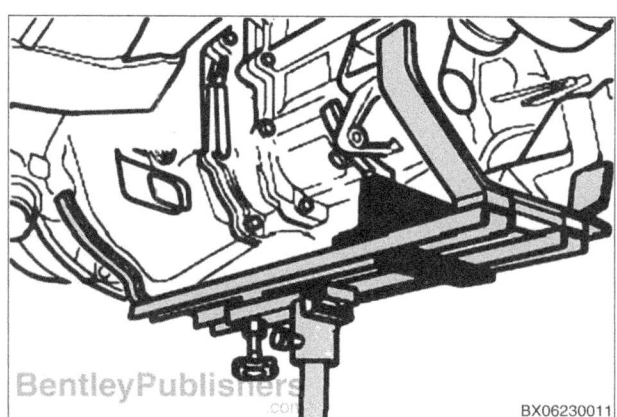

◄ Support transmission from below using transmission jack.

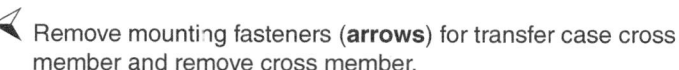

◄ Remove mounting fasteners (**arrows**) for transfer case cross member and remove cross member.

Transfer case, removing and installing

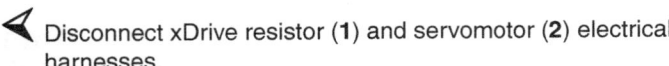

◀ Disconnect xDrive resistor (**1**) and servomotor (**2**) electrical harnesses.

— Remove servomotor mounting bolts. Pull servomotor from transfer case.

***NOTE*—**

- *To gain better access to mounting bolts at top of servomotor, lower transmission / engine assembly.*

— Installation is the reverse of removal, noting the following:

- Install exhaust system as described in **180 Exhaust System**
- After completion of work, check and top off fluid level. See **Transfer case fluid service** in this repair group. Drive vehicle approximately 200 meters (600 ft) and recheck fluid level.
- If new parts were installed, use BMW scan tool to carry out transfer case wear adaptation reset.

Tightening torques	
Servomotor to transfer case	22 Nm (16 ft-lb)
Classification resistor to servomotor	5 Nm (15 ft-lb)
Crossmember to chassis (M8)	19 Nm (14 ft-lb)
Crossmember to rubber mount (M12)	68 Nm (50 ft-lb)

Transfer case, removing and installing

— Raise vehicle and support safely.

***WARNING*—**

- *Make sure vehicle is stable and well supported at all times. Use a professional automotive lift or jack stands designed for the purpose. A floor jack is not adequate support.*

— Remove splash guard under engine. Remove front end reinforcement (if applicable). See **310 Front Suspension**.

— Remove exhaust system and exhaust heat shields. See **180 Exhaust System**.

***WARNING*—**

- *Make sure exhaust system is fully cooled off before removing.*

— Remove support brackets for heat and splash shields as needed.

◀ Working at transfer case, use paint to matchmark front driveshaft flanges. Remove front driveshaft from transfer case output flange. Tie driveshaft to side.

***CAUTION*—**

- *Use care when removing driveshaft from transfer case flange. Tap driveshaft flange gently to loosen it from transfer case flange. The flange is a slip fit and oil loss can occur if accidentally pulled out.*

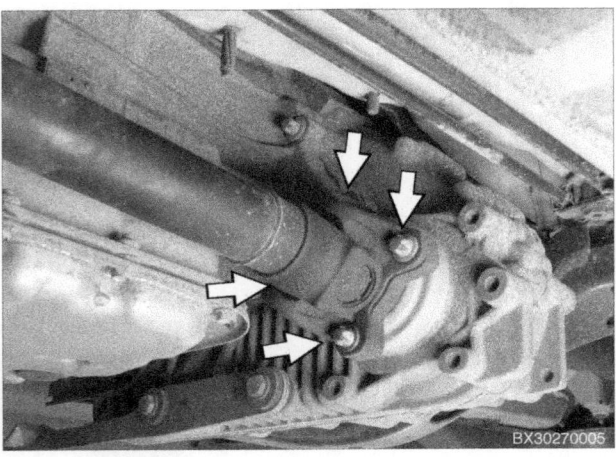

◁ Working at transfer case output flange, use paint to matchmark rear driveshaft flex-disc flanges. Then remove three bolts (**arrows**) holding flex disc to transfer case flange. Discard old fasteners.

— Remove driveshaft center bearing support fasteners. Lower center of driveshaft sufficiently to disengage flex-disc from transfer case flange. Tie driveshaft to side. See **260 Driveshafts**.

> **CAUTION—**
> • *To prevent damage to rear driveshaft CV joint, do not allow driveshaft to hang down unsupported.*

270

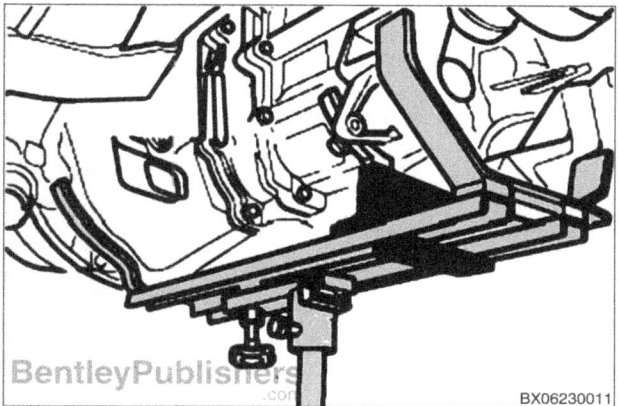

◁ Support transmission from below using transmission jack.

◁ Remove mounting fasteners (**arrows**) for transfer cross member and remove cross member.

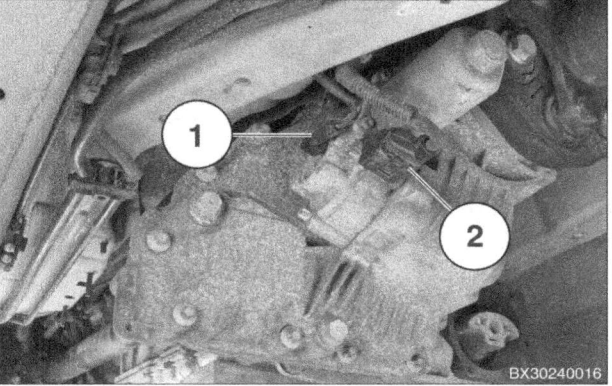

◁ Disconnect xDrive servo motor and resistor electrical harnesses (**1** and **2**).

Transfer case, removing and installing

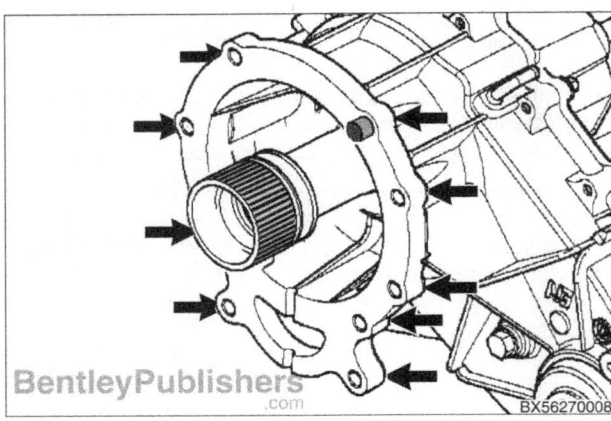

— While supporting transfer case, remove transfer case mounting bolts. Lower transfer case.

◄ When installing:

- Inspect dowel sleeves (**1**) and replace if damaged.
- Transfer covers and protective caps to new transfer case, as applicable.
- Replace transfer case input shaft sealing O-ring, if needed.
- Apply thin coat of Weicon® antiseize grease to dowel pin and input shaft splines.

CAUTION—
• *Do not reuse ZNS fasteners. They are designed to be used only once.*

Tightening torque	
Rear driveshaft flex-disc to transfer case flange (ZNS fasteners)	
• 2004-2006 (with single stage flex disc - 96mm bolt hole pattern)	
stage 1	55 Nm (40 ft-lb)
stage 2 (angle torque)	+90°
• 2007-2010 (with two-stage flex disc - 110mm bolt hole pattern, ribbed teeth)	
stage 1	30 Nm (22 ft-lb)
stage 2 (angle torque)	+90°
• Rear driveshaft flex-disc to driveshaft flange (ZNS fasteners)	
stage 1	55 Nm (40 ft-lb)
stage 2 (angle torque)	+90°
Rear driveshaft to rear differential flange (M10 10.9, use new bolts)	
• stage 1	40 Nm (30 ft-lb)
• stage 2 (angle torque)	+45°
Driveshaft center bearing support to body	21 Nm (15 ft-lb)
Driveshaft clamping sleeve to driveshaft	10 Nm (7 ft-lb)
Front driveshaft to front differential / transfer case (M10 10.9, use new bolts)	
• stage 1	40 Nm (30 ft-lb)
• stage 2 (angle torque)	45°
Transfer case to transmission (M10)	43 Nm (32 ft-lb)
Crossmember to chassis (M8)	19 Nm (14 ft-lb)
Crossmember to rubber mount (M12)	68 Nm (50 ft-lb)

— After completion of work, check and top off fluid level. See **Transfer case fluid service** in this repair group. Drive vehicle approximately 200 meters (600 ft) and recheck fluid level.

— If new parts were installed, use BMW diagnostic tool to carry out transfer case adaptation reset.

300 Suspension, Steering and Brakes– General

GENERAL

This repair group includes overview information for the front and rear suspension, braking, steering and traction control systems including antilock braking (ABS) and dynamic stability control (DSC). Also covered are wheel and tire specifications.

The X3 all-wheel drive system is integrated with the suspension. Front and rear drive axles are driven via a pair of differentials.

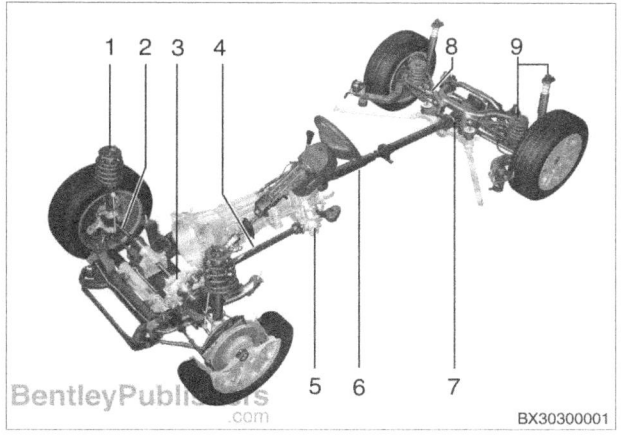

BX30300001

1. Front strut. See **310 Front Suspension**.
2. Front drive axles. See **311 Front Axle Differential**.
3. Front differential. See **311 Front Axle Differential**.
4. Front driveshaft. See **260 Driveshafts**.
5. Transfer case. See **270 Transfer Case**.
6. Rear driveshaft. See **260 Driveshafts**.
7. Rear differential. See **331 Rear Axle Differential**.
8. Rear drive axles. See **331 Rear Axle Differential**.
9. Rear spring and rear shock. See **330 Rear Suspension**.

In order to reduce vehicle weight, aluminum suspension components are used. A test with a magnet will easily reveal the metal used.

FRONT SUSPENSION

The X3 front suspension is a double-pivot, strut-type design with dual lower control arms. A subframe is used as a rigid mounting platform for the front suspension arms, stabilizer bar and steering gear. The suspension arms, known as lower control arms and tension struts, are connected to the subframe using rubber bushings. The arms are connected to the steering knuckles in a double pivot configuration.

Each front strut assembly includes a tubular strut and a coil spring. The upper strut mount includes a bearing. The lower end of each strut housing is fitted to the steering knuckle. The integral wheel bearing and hub are press fit in the steering knuckle.

Front suspension repairs are covered in **310 Front Suspension**.

The front differential is bolted to the left side of the engine oil pan. Drive axles with constant velocity (CV) joints at each end drive the front wheels.

Front differential and drive axle repairs are covered in **311 Front Axle Differential**.

REAR SUSPENSION

The rear suspension subframe (final drive carrier) is the main mounting point for the differential housing and rear suspension components. It is bolted to the vehicle undercarriage using four large bolts through rubber bushings.

Trailing arms locate the rear wheels together with upper and lower control arms. Aluminum is used for some parts of the rear suspension for weight saving.

Drive axles with constant-velocity (CV) joints at both ends transfer power from the differential to the road wheels. The differential is mounted to the subframe through rubber mounts and bushings to help isolate drivetrain noise and vibration.

Rear suspension repairs are covered in **330 Rear Suspension**.

Rear differential and drive axle repairs are covered in **331 Rear Axle Differential**.

Front suspension components

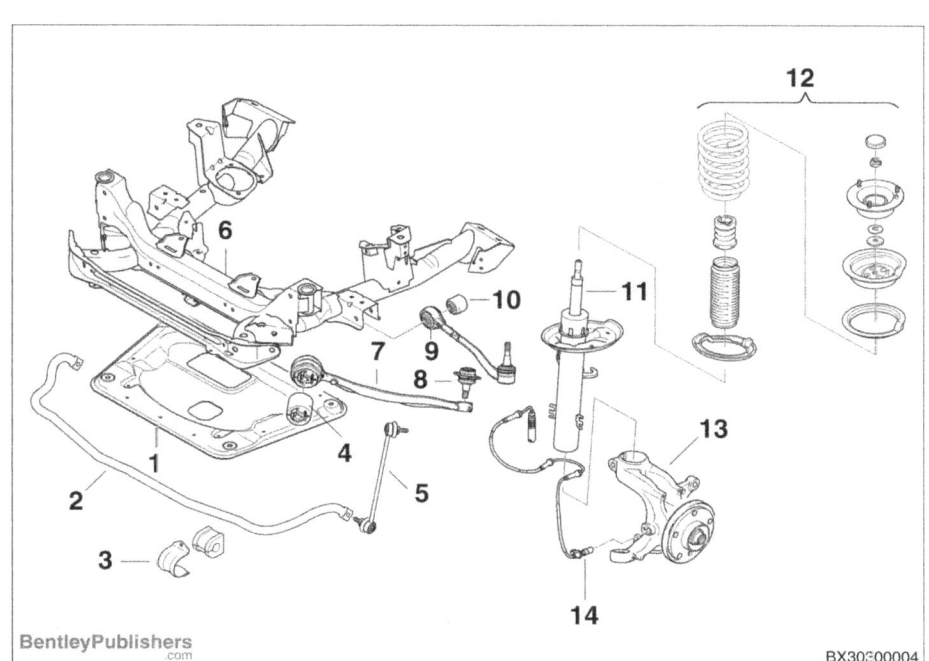

BX30300004

1. Front end reinforcement plate
2. Stabilizer bar
3. Stabilizer bar mount
4. Tension strut bushing
5. Stabilizer bar link
6. Suspension subframe
7. Tension strut
8. Tension strut ball joint
   • bolted to steering knuckle (13)
9. Control arm
10. Control arm bushing
11. Front suspension strut
12. Strut spring and mount assembly
13. Steering knuckle
14. Wheel speed sensor

Rear suspension components

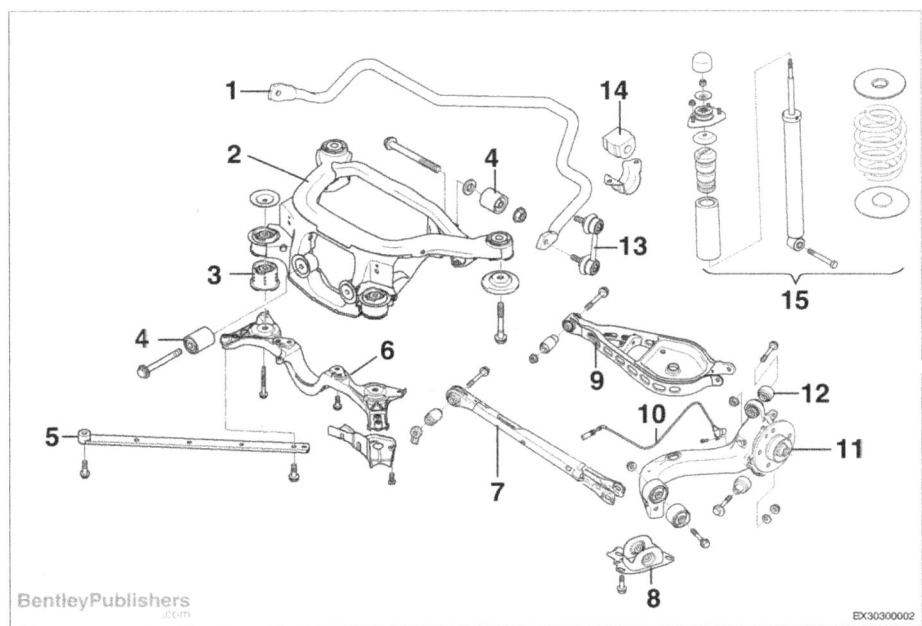

BX30300002

1. Stabilizer bar
2. Rear suspension subframe
3. Subframe mount (bushing)
4. Differential mount
5. Tension strut (bar)
6. Differential crossmember
7. Lower control arm
8. Trailing arm mount
9. Upper front control arm
10. Wheel speed sensor
11. Trailing arm
12. Upper control arm bushing (ball joint)
13. Stabilizer bar link
14. Stabilizer bar mount
15. Shock, shock mount and coil spring assembly

300

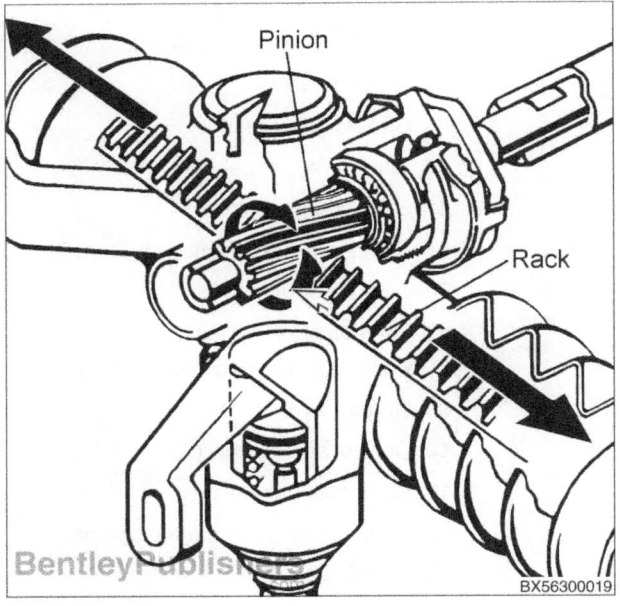

BX56300019

Pinion

Rack

STEERING

 The rack-and-pinion steering system features speed-sensitive variable power assist provided by an engine-driven hydraulic pump.

Servotronic was an available option. The servotronic control unit electro-hydraulically adjusts the amount of steering assistance based on the speed of the vehicle. An electromagnetic valve on the steering rack modulates the power assist for varying operating conditions. When parking, power assist is increased. The assist progressively decreases when the vehicle speeds up.

BRAKE SYSTEM

X3 vehicles are equipped with power disc brakes with integral antilock brakes (ABS) and dynamic stability control (DSC). The brake system is a hydraulic dual-circuit brake system with front/rear split vacuum boost power assist.

The parking brake is a dual-drum system integrated with the rear brake rotors.

Each disc brake uses a caliper with a single hydraulic cylinder. Brake pads in the left front and right rear contain wear sensors. When brake pads need replacement, the sensors illuminate a light on the dashboard.

Power assist is provided by a vacuum booster when the engine is running. The brake pedal pushrod is connected directly to the master cylinder, so failure of the vacuum booster does not normally result in total brake failure.

On M54 engines, manifold vacuum provides brake vacuum boost.

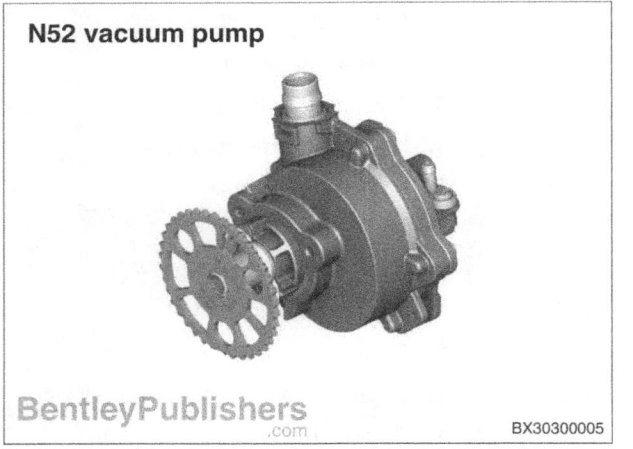

N52 vacuum pump

BX30300005

 On N52 (Valvetronic) engines, an additional vacuum pump is fitted, driven off the front of the engine.

WHEELS AND TIRES

Tire size is critical to the proper operation of the antilock brake and traction control systems. Several different styles of wheels in 17, 18 and 19 inch diameters are available from an authorized BMW dealer.

Use electronic alignment equipment to check and set camber and toe for all 4 wheels. Be sure to check and adjust ride height prior to attempting wheel alignment.

For ride height and alignment specifications and procedures, see **320 Steering and Wheel Alignment**.

ELECTRONIC BRAKE AND STABILITY CONTROL

X3 vehicles are equipped with antilock brakes (ABS) with dynamic stability control (DSC8).

ABS and DSC component replacement is covered in **340 Brakes**.

NOTE—

• *Steering angle sensor is covered in* **320 Steering and Wheel Alignment**.

Antilock brake system (ABS)

The electronically controlled antilock brake system (ABS) maintains vehicle stability and control during emergency braking by preventing wheel lock-up. ABS provides optimum deceleration and stability during adverse conditions. It automatically adjusts brake system hydraulic pressure at each wheel to prevent wheel lock-up.

Dynamic stability control (DSC)

DSC works in conjunction with ABS, the engine management system, and the transfer case (xDrive) electronics to enhance vehicle control. The main DSC function is to maintain contact between the tires and the road surface under all driving conditions. This is achieved through exact application and management of braking and drivetrain forces.

DSC is active throughout the driving range, helping to stabilize the vehicle in cornering and avoidance maneuvers by adjusting engine controls (throttle, ignition, fuel injection), the application of brake pressure (individually to wheels), and the distribution of driving torque to the front and rear axles (via regulation of the transfer case clutch).

The DSC control module uses various inputs to determine vehicle instability during braking, cornering, or reduced traction situations. Based upon these inputs the DSC control module sends outputs to the engine control module, the ABS / DSC hydraulic unit and the xDrive VTG control module to activate torque reduction protocols and braking intervention.

The ABS / DSC control module, operating through the ABS hydraulic control unit, modulates braking force at the wheels. In addition, DSC overrides throttle opening to reduce engine torque and maintain vehicle traction. Because throttle is controlled electronically, the driver cannot increase engine power output during DSC intervention regardless of how far the accelerator pedal is pushed.

Traction control also comes into operation during deceleration. Decelerating on snowy or icy road surfaces can lead to wheel slip. If a rear wheel starts to drag or lock up, DSC can limit the problem by adjusting front to rear driving torque, throttle, fuel injection and ignition timing.

DSC can be toggled ON and OFF by a switch mounted on the center console switching center. Turning DSC OFF does not disable ABS functions.

300

Dynamic stability control (DSC)

Brake and stability control systems

1. ECM (DME)
2. EGS (Transmission control module)
3. Yaw/transverse acceleration sensors
4. Steering angle sensor
5. Wheel speed sensor
6. Brake fluid level
7. DSC button
8. HDC (Hill decent control) button
9. RDW (tire pressure monitor) button
10. Transfer case control unit
11. DSC control unit
12. Transfer case clutch servomotor
13. instrument cluster
14. DSC hydraulic modulator

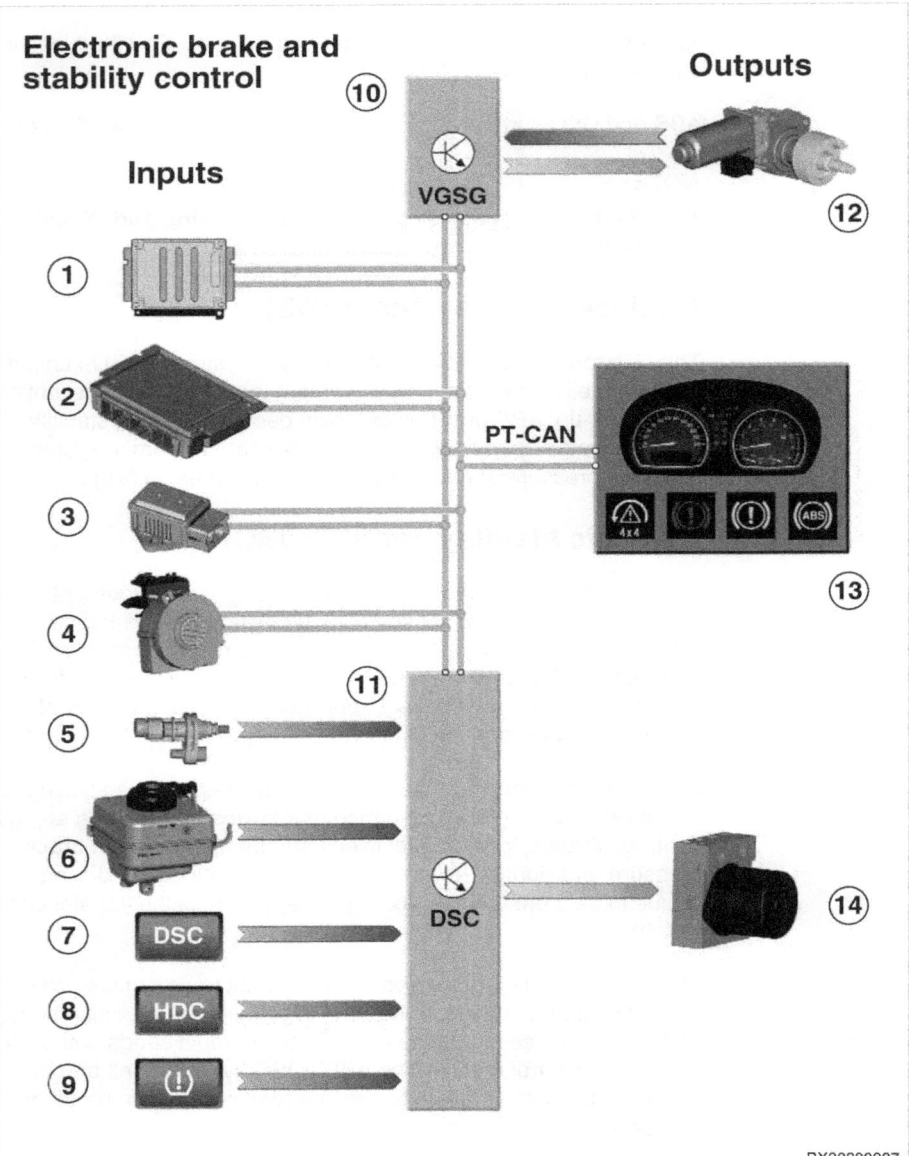

BX30300007

Transfer case clutch

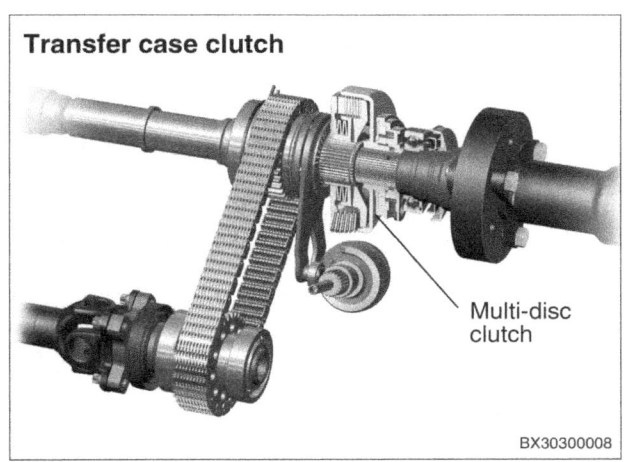

Multi-disc
clutch

BX30300008

xDrive operation

◄ The transfer case control unit (VTG) regulates the locking pressure of the multi-disc clutch in the transfer case. The driving torque on the front axle can be increased or decreased by actuating the clutch. When more driving torque is transmitted to the front axle, driving torque on the rear axle is proportionally reduced.

The transfer case control unit receives information from the DSC control unit. This information is then output as a corresponding rotary motion of the transfer case servomotor.

NOTE—

• *Even when DSC is deactivated, transfer case clutch remains active for maximum traction and driving dynamics.*

A clutch and oil wear calculation is also processed and stored in the VGSG. It increases the locking pressure as necessary in order to reduce friction. In the event of DSC failure, the VGSG incorporates a strategy for activating the transfer case clutch in order to maintain the four-wheel drive function.

The advantages of variable distribution of front-to-rear driving torque are:

• Optimum utilization of the cornering and longitudinal forces on the front and rear axles.

• DSC brake interventions occurs at a significantly later stage.

• xDrive significantly improves driving torque distribution when traction on the front and rear axles is notably different.

Hill descent control (HDC)

Hill descent control (HDC) is designed for off road use to automatically slow the vehicle and maintain a steady speed on steep gradients. This function allows the driver to focus on steering and controlling the vehicle without having to use the brakes to slow the vehicle.

◄ HDC is activated manually via the push button in the center console switching center. When activated, the DSC system pulses the brakes to maintain the vehicle speed to approximately 5 mph.

The following conditions are required for HDC to activate:

• Push button pressed, LED ON.

• Vehicle speed < 25 mph.

• Accelerator pedal pressed <15%.

• Downhill driving recognized from vehicle speed and engine load from ECM. PT-CAN bus communicates these inputs to DSC control module.

BX56300008

300

DSC acceleration sensor

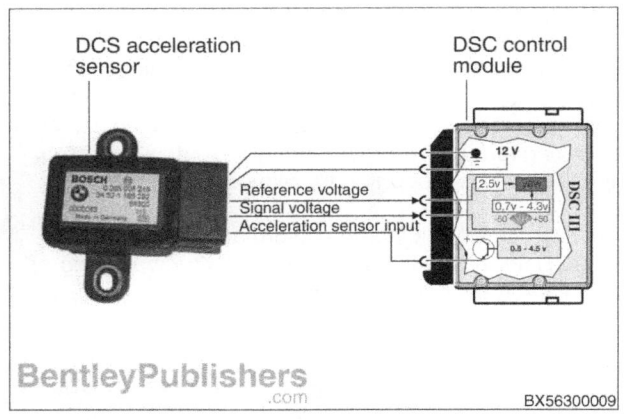

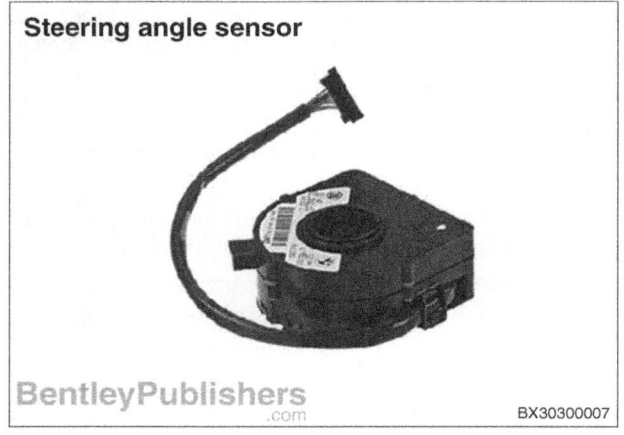

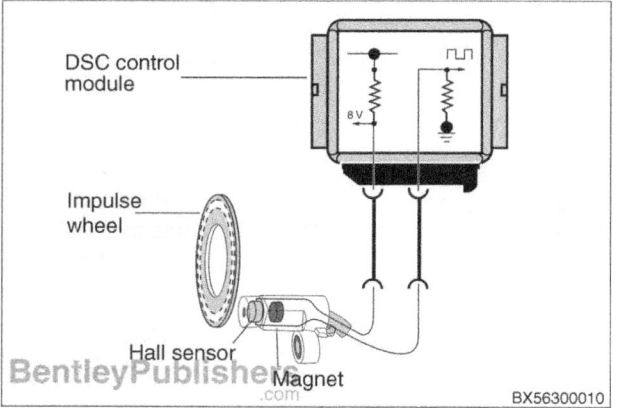

DSC acceleration sensor

The combined rotation rate and transverse acceleration sensor, under the center console, provide two inputs to the DSC control module.

◄ For rotational acceleration (yaw), the sensor produces a reference signal of 2.5 volts and a linear voltage signal from 0.7 to 4.3 volts. The sensor also produces a linear voltage signal for the lateral acceleration (G-force) that ranges from 0.5 to 4.5 volts. The DSC control module uses this input to determine the side forces acting on the vehicle.

Steering angle sensor

◄ The steering angle sensor, mounted at the bottom of the steering column, is equipped with a microprocessor and is directly linked via PT-CAN bus to the DSC control module.

The sensor utilizes two potentiometers to determine steering angle and rate of steering. These are the raw signals the microprocessor utilizes to create the steering angle signal for output on the PT-CAN bus.

DSC control module logic checks the plausibility of the steering angle sensor signal against other inputs such as wheel speeds and acceleration inputs. If battery voltage is interrupted, steering wheel rotation is recalculated by the DSC control module evaluating the wheel speeds.

NOTE —

- *After repairs to the steering or suspension system, the sensor requires a recalibration. A replacement steering angle sensor requires coding. Both service procedures require a BMW diagnostic scan tool. If replacing, recode sensor prior to recalibration.*

Wheel speed sensors

The active wheel speed sensors require a supply voltage for operation and output a constant non-speed dependent amplitude signal.

The wheel speed sensor at each wheel operates as follows:
- 2 wire Hall effect sensor (square wave generator) pulses 48 times per wheel revolution.
- Stabilized power supply to Hall element on one wire, ground path for sensor through second wire back to control module.
- Impulse wheel incorporated in wheel bearing seal for protection from contamination. Signal is generated by impulse wheel affecting voltage flow through Hall element.
- Right rear wheel speed sensor provides vehicle speed recognition.

310 Front Suspension

310

GENERAL

This repair group covers the repair and replacement of front suspension components.

All models are equipped with a rack and pinion type steering system mounted to a steel subframe. The subframe is strengthened by a front end reinforcement plate.

The front suspension shock absorbers on X3 models are MacPherson struts. The strut is a major component of the front suspension and supports the spring. Most strut assembly components are available as replacement parts. Replace struts and springs in pairs.

See **320 Steering and Wheel Alignment** for specifications on ride height.

> **WARNING—**
> • Do not reuse self-locking fasteners. Do not reuse aluminum fasteners. They are designed to be used only once and may fail if reused. Replace with new.

Front end reinforcement plate, removing and installing

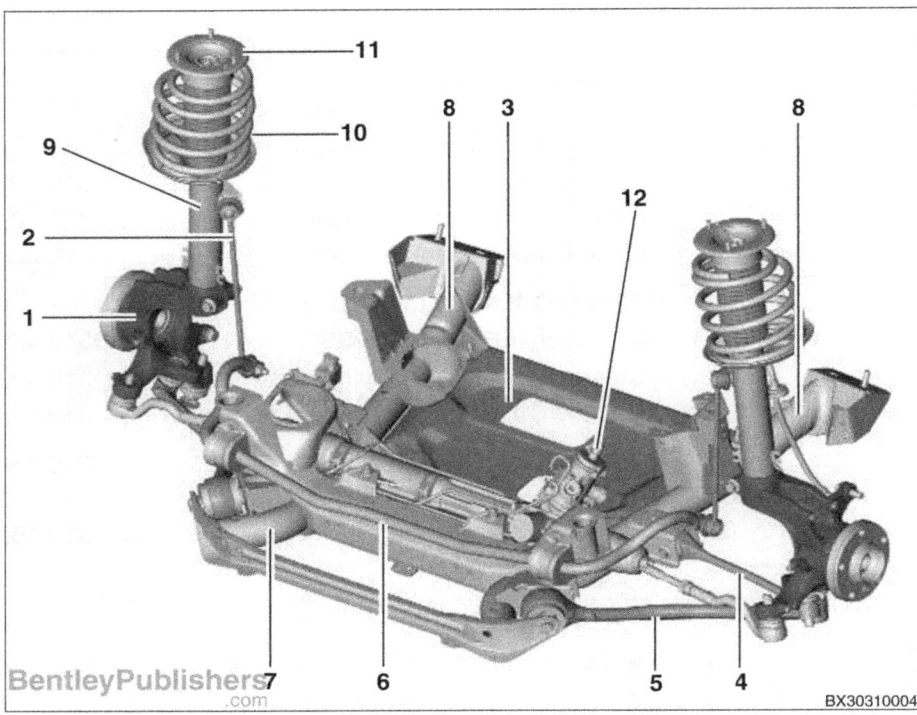

Front suspension components

1. Steering knuckle (swivel bearing)
2. Stabilizer bar link
3. Front end reinforcement plate
4. Control arm
5. Tension strut
6. Stabilizer bar
7. Front axle subframe
8. Front axle subframe rear mounts
9. Suspension strut
10. Coil spring
11. Strut mount (bearing)
12. Steering rack

Front end reinforcement plate, removing and installing

– Raise vehicle support safely.

> **WARNING—**
> • *Make sure vehicle is stable and well supported at all times. Use a professional automotive lift or jack stands. A floor jack is not adequate support.*

◀ Remove fasteners (**A**) and expansion rivets (**arrows**) to remove reinforcement plate.

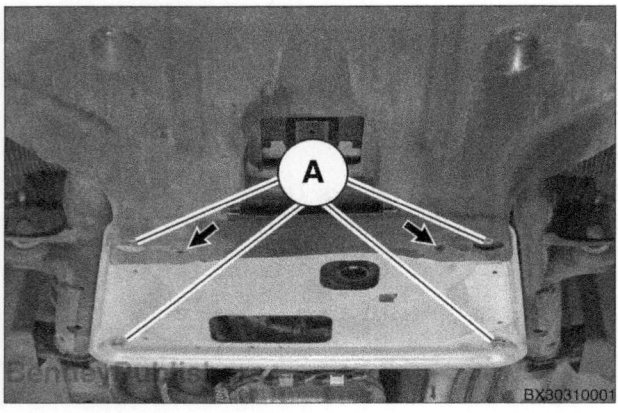

> **CAUTION—**
> • *Do not drive vehicle with front end reinforcement plate removed.*

– Installation is reverse of removal. Remember to replace fasteners with new components.

Tightening torque	
Front end reinforcement plate to subframe (use new fasteners)	74 Nm (55 ft-lb)

Strut brace, removing and installing

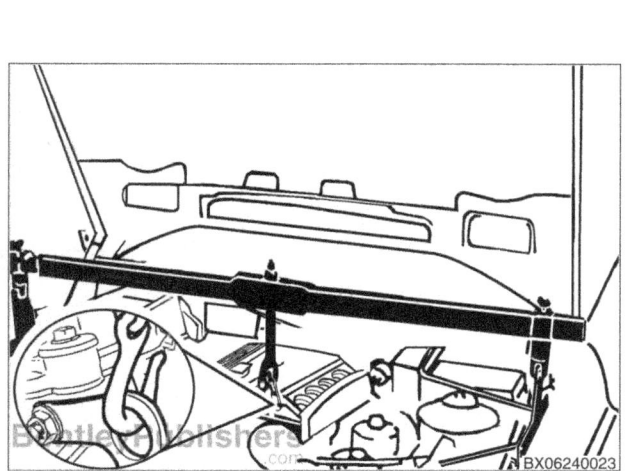

> **CAUTION—**
> • *Do not drive vehicle with strut brace removed.*

◄ To remove strut brace from strut towers:
  • Remove expansion rivets at wiring harness holder (**A**).
  • Remove fasteners (**arrows**) and remove tension strut.

— Installation is reverse of removal.

Tightening torque	
Strut brace to body (M8):	19 Nm (14 ft-lb)

Front suspension subframe, lowering

— Raise vehicle support safely.

> **WARNING—**
> • *Make sure vehicle is stable and well supported at all times. Use a professional automotive lift or jack stands. A floor jack is not adequate support.*

— Remove underbody splash shield. See **020 Maintenance**.

— Remove front suspension reinforcement plate.
  See **Front end reinforcement plate, removing and installing**.

— Partially remove front wheel housing liner. See **410 Fenders, Engine Hood**.

— Disconnect steering shaft from steering rack. See **320 Steering**.

◄ **M54 engine**: Install engine support brace across engine bay. Raise engine slightly to release load on engine mounts.

— **N52 engine**: Install engine support brace across engine bay.
  • Support engine using vehicle tow hook (72 15 8 108 670) screwed into front of cylinder head.
  • Raise engine slightly to release load on engine mounts.

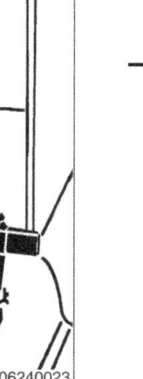

310

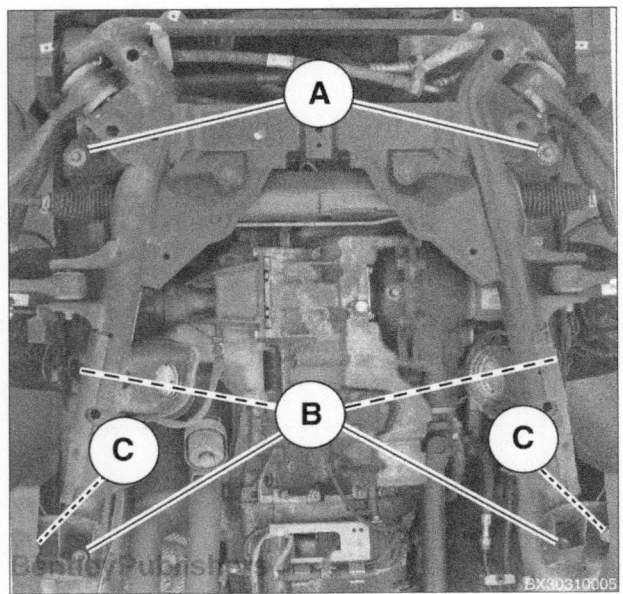

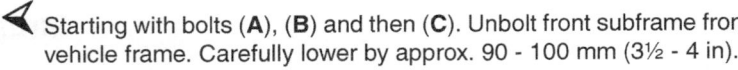

Starting with bolts (**A**), (**B**) and then (**C**). Unbolt front subframe from vehicle frame. Carefully lower by approx. 90 - 100 mm (3½ - 4 in).

> **CAUTION—**
> • *Lower subframe as far as possible without damaging power steering lines. Make sure subframe is adequately supported throughout the remainder of this procedure.*

— Installation is reverse of removal: Make sure power steering lines are not kinked, tensioned or bent.

• Replace all fasteners.

• Tighten down bolts in order of (**A**), (**B**) and then (**C**).

Tightening torques	
Front end of subframe to body bolts (**A**) • M12 10.9 (replace with new)	113 Nm (83 ft-lb)
Middle / rear subframe to body bolts (**B**) • M10 10.9 (replace with new)	50 Nm (37 ft-lb)
Rear subframe to body bolts (**C**) • M12 10.9 (replace with new)	100 Nm (74 ft-lb)

FRONT STRUT ASSEMBLY

Front strut assembly, removing and installing

Struts are marked right and left for installation. Front strut, upper strut mount or spring replacement is a two-step procedure:

1. Removal of strut assembly from vehicle.
2. Disassembly and replacement of components on work bench using special service tools.

— Raise car and remove front wheel.

> **WARNING—**
> • *Make sure vehicle is stable and well supported at all times. Use a professional automotive lift or jack stands. A floor jack is not adequate support.*

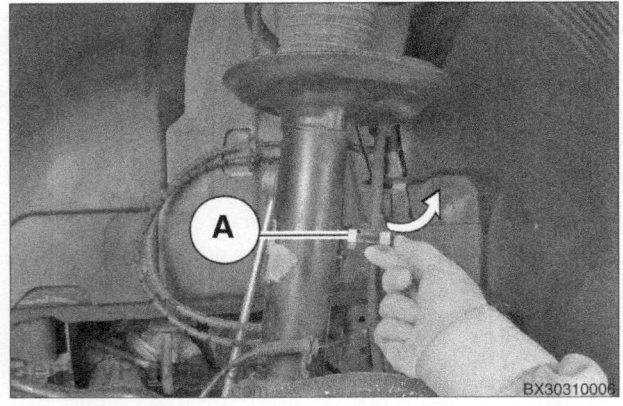

Remove clip (**A**) securing brake fluid hydraulic line to front strut.

Remove upper stabilizer bar connecting link mounting nut (**arrow**).

• Use a thin wrench to counterhold shaft of stabilizer bar link ball joint while removing nut.

Front strut assembly, removing and installing

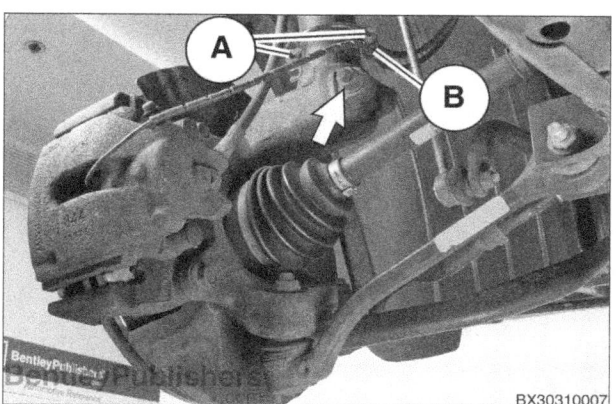

◄ Detach wheel speed sensor wire harness and brake pad wear sensor wire harness (**A**) and (**B**) from strut housing.

– Remove front strut pinch bolt (**arrow**).

– Support steering knuckle with suitable jack.

– Separate strut from knuckle.

> **CAUTION—**
> • Be sure to support steering knuckle to prevent over extension of CV axle joint or damage may occur.

◄ If necessary, use BMW special tool 31 2 230 to spread steering knuckle pinch collar (**A**).

– Installation:
  • Align strut in steering knuckle pinch collar with alignment pins (**B**).

> **NOTE—**
> • Keep steering knuckle pinch collar and strut free of oil and grease where they clamp together.

◄ Note position of strut centering pin (**A**).

> **CAUTION—**
> • If strut centering pin is missing from upper strut mount, mark position of studs to strut tower to maintain original camber.

– Secure spring strut against falling out.

– Remove upper strut mount nuts (**arrows**).

– Remove strut down out of wheel arch. If necessary, use a spring compressor to carefully compress coil spring to gain additional clearance for removal.

– Installation is reverse of removal. Remember to:
  • Install bolt head of steering knuckle pinch bolt in direction of travel.
  • Make sure steering knuckle aligns with pins on strut body.
  • Check alignment when job is complete.

Tightening torques	
Road wheel to hub	140 Nm 103ft-lb)
Stabilizer bar link to strut • flanged nut (replace with new)	65 Nm (48 ft-lb)
Strut assembly to steering knuckle • pinch bolt (replace with new)	100 Nm (74 ft-lb)
Strut mount to body • M8 nut (replace with new)	34 Nm (25 ft-lb)

310

Front strut assembly, disassembling and assembling

Front strut assembly

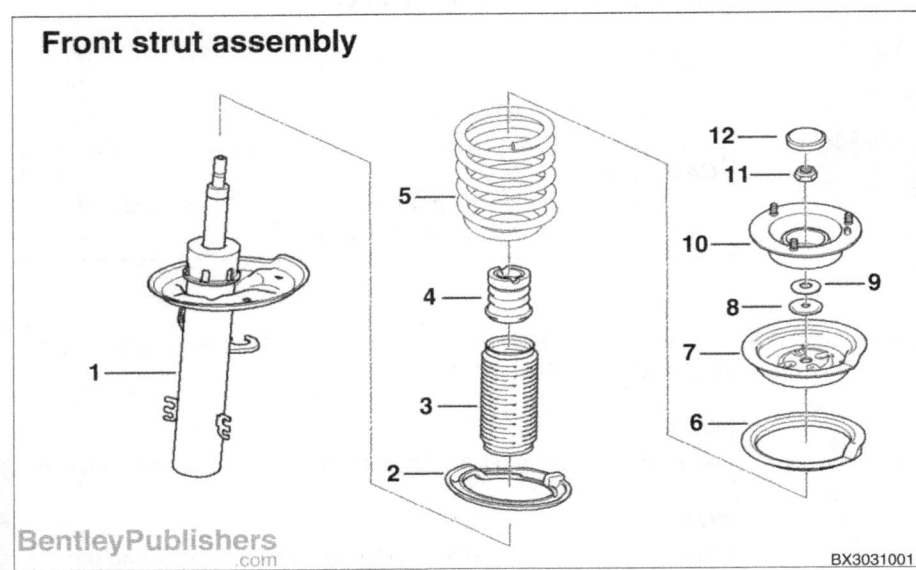

BentleyPublishers.com

BX30310011

Front strut assembly components

1. Strut with lower spring seat
2. Lower spring pad
3. Dust boot
4. Rubber stop
5. Coil spring
6. Upper spring pad
7. Upper spring seat
8. Washer
9. Strut mount collar
10. Upper strut mount
11. Self-locking nut
12. Cap

Front strut assembly, disassembling and assembling

Replacing the strut, upper strut mount or spring requires that the strut assembly first be removed from the car and disassembled. See **Front strut assembly, removing and installing** in this repair group.

◄ Clamp spring compressor (BMW special tool 31 3 340 or equivalent) in shop vise.

> **WARNING—**
> • Do not attempt to disassemble strut assembly without a spring compressor designed specifically for this job.
> • Prior to each use, check special tool for functionality.
> • Do not use a damaged tool. Do not make any modifications to tool.
> • Use correct size spring retainers when compressing coil spring.

RTI MAX 1100 KG.

502310993

◄ Position coil spring between spring holders so that 3 coils lie between spring holders (**arrows**). Compress spring.

> **WARNING—**
> • When tensioned, the spring coils must rest completely in the spring holder recess.
> • Do not tighten or loosen spring compressor with an impact tool.
> • Only tighten down the coil springs until stress on the thrust bearing is relieved.
> • Only loosen strut nut if spring coils are completely inserted in the spring holder grooves. If necessary, loosen compressor, reposition and recompress.

RTI MAX 1100 KG.

BentleyPublishers.com

502310996

Front strut assembly, disassembling and assembling

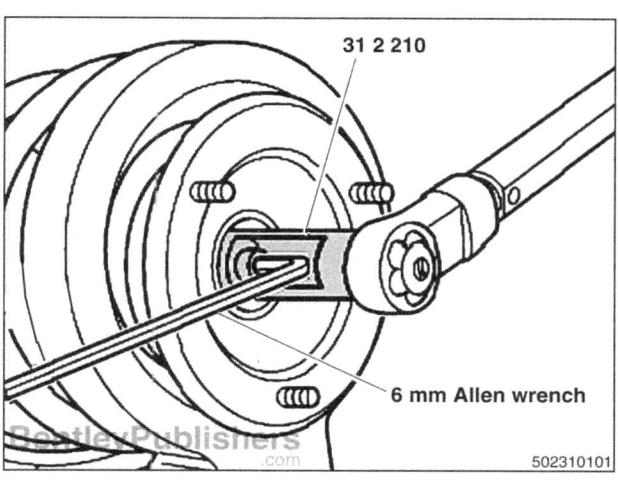

◀ Use BMW special tool 31 2 210 or equivalent to remove strut nut. Counterhold strut shaft using 6 mm Allen wrench.

> **CAUTION—**
> • *Do not remove strut nut with impact tool.*

— Remove upper strut bearing and related components.

— If a new coil spring is being installed, relieve tension on spring compressor and remove coil spring.

— Check strut dust boot, rubber stop and spring pads. Replace as necessary.

— Replace strut, upper strut mount or spring, as needed.

◀ Replace springs in matched pairs only. BMW ID number is stamped near end (**A**).

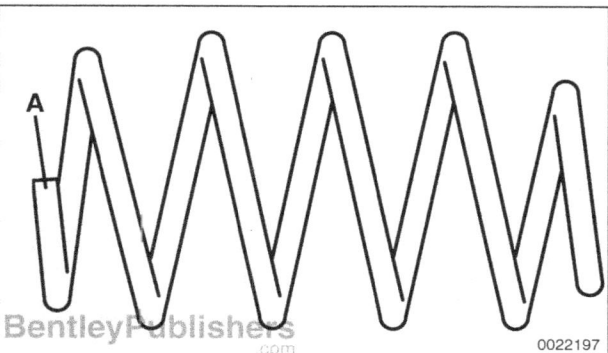

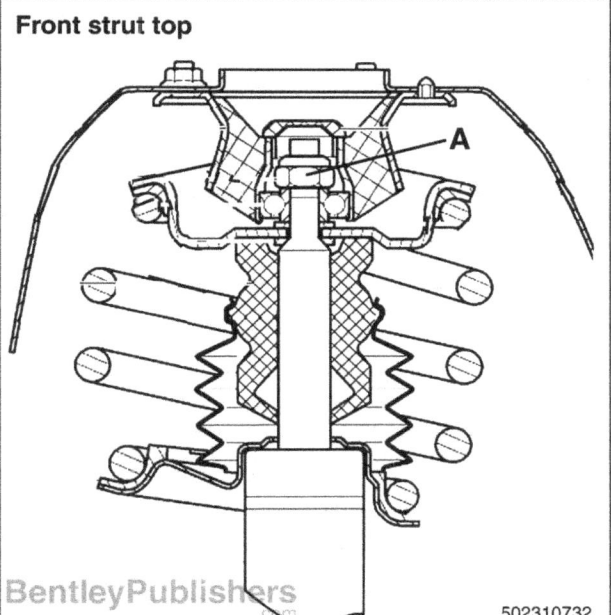

Front strut top

◀ Assembly is reverse of disassembly, noting the following:

• Use a new upper strut self-locking nut (**A**). Tighten nut fully before releasing spring compressor.

> **CAUTION—**
> • *Do not tighten strut nut with impact tool.*

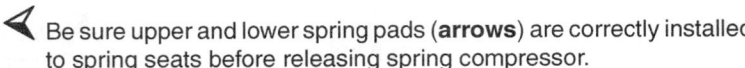

◀ Be sure upper and lower spring pads (**arrows**) are correctly installed to spring seats before releasing spring compressor.

- Release spring compressor carefully and evenly, allowing spring to expand slowly.

- Have car professionally aligned when job is complete.

Tightening torques	
Strut shaft to strut mount bearing (replace with new)	64 Nm (47 ft-lb)

FRONT SUSPENSION ARMS

Control arms and tension struts are attached to the front subframe through rubber bushings and to the steering knuckles by ball joints.

NOTE —

- *Tension struts are sometimes called thrust arms or thrust rods.*

- *Control arms are sometimes called lower rear arms.*

Inspect ball joints for wear and looseness. Inspect bushings for wear or fluid leaks. Certain ball joints can only be replaced as part of an entire suspension arm assembly. Some suspension arm bushings are available as replacement parts. Always replace in pairs.

NOTE —

- *Steering wheel vibration during braking (usually at road speeds of 50 to 60 mph) is often caused by faulty suspension arm bushings, not out-of-true brake rotors.*

Some special tools may be required to remove suspension arms and to replace bushings. Read procedures through before beginning the job.

Tension strut, removing and installing

— Raise car and remove front wheel.

> **WARNING —**
> - *Make sure vehicle is stable and well supported at all times. Use a professional automotive lift or jack stands. A floor jack is not adequate support.*

NOTE —

- *Tension strut to ball joint connection on knuckle was increased by 10mm on vehicles built after 12/2006. When replacing control arm on vehicles built before 12/2006, ball joint must also be replaced.*

— Remove underbody splash shield. See **020 Maintenance**.

◀ Working at steering knuckle, remove fasteners from ball joint (**arrows**). If needed loosen nut (**A**).

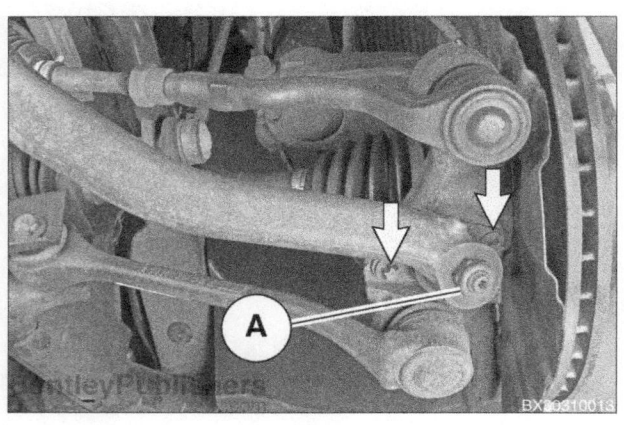

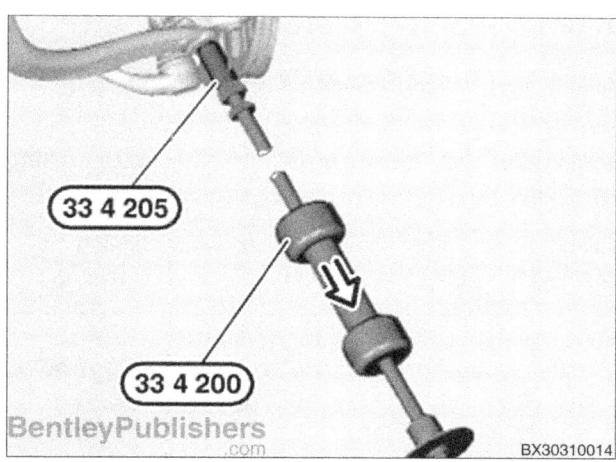

— Lower ball joint from steering knuckle.

◀ If ball joint is frozen in knuckle use BMW special tools 31 2 205 and 33 4 200 or equivalent to separate ball joint from steering knuckle.

NOTE—

• *Thread ball joint fasteners into steering knuckle a few turns to prevent ball joint from suddenly falling out.*

• *Ball joint must be replaced if driven out with special tools.*

◀ Remove control arm fastener through bolt (**arrow**). Lightly tap control arm mounting bolt out of front subframe.

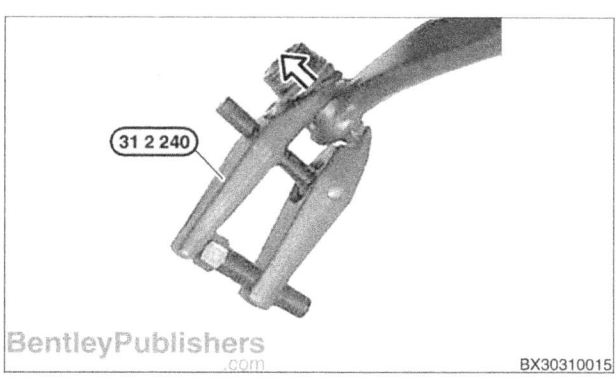

◀ Use BMW special tool 31 2 240 or equivalent to separate ball joint from tension strut.

— Installation is reverse of removal, noting the following:

• Make sure thread bores, bolts, nuts and mating surfaces are clean.

• Install bushing end of tension strut to subframe using new fasteners. Do not tighten nut at this time.

• Install tension strut ball joint to steering knuckle using new fasteners. Tighten fully.

• Install tension strut to ball joint using new fastener. Tighten fully.

• Install wheel and lower car.

• Tighten bushing end of tension strut to subframe with car on ground and loaded. Bounce suspension a few times before final tightening.

• Check vehicle alignment.

Tightening torques	
Ball joint to steering knuckle • M10 x 20 10.9 bolt (replace with new)	60 Nm (44 ft-lb)
Tension strut to ball joint • M14 self-locking nut (replace with new)	80 Nm (59 ft-lb)
Tension strut to subframe bolt • M14 10.9 bolt (replace with new)	165 Nm (122 ft-lb) + 90°
Road wheel to hub	140 Nm (103 ft-lb)

Tension strut bushing, replacing

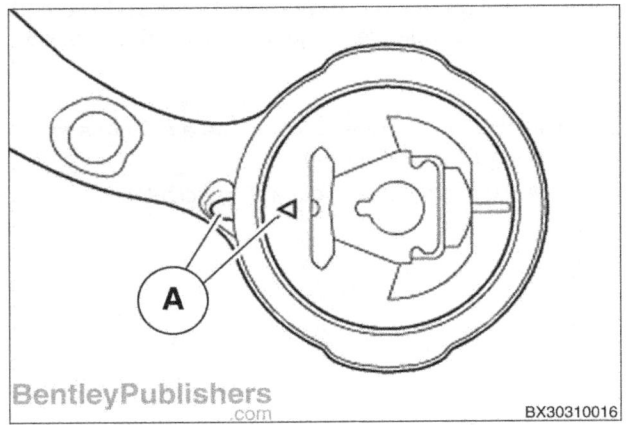

BX30310016

Tension strut bushing, replacing

Replace tension strut bushings in pairs. Bushings may only be replaced once.

— Remove tension strut. See **Tension strut, removing and installing** in this repair group.

◄ Clean bushing bore and press in new bushing while aligning mark on bushing with mark on tension strut (**A**).

> **CAUTION—**
> • *Draw in rubber mount from chamfered side of control arm bore.*
> • *To avoid damaging new bushing, press only on outer steel.*

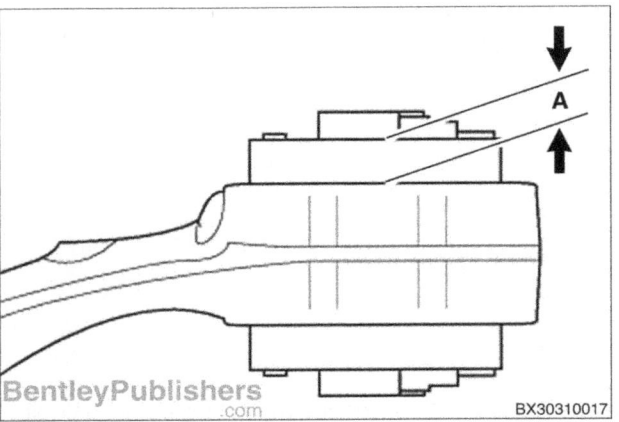

BX30310017

◄ Press bushing in so it protrudes equally from both sides of arm. **A** = approximately 12.5 mm (0.5 in).

— Install tension strut. See **Tension strut, removing and installing**.

> **CAUTION—**
> • *Tighten tension strut through-bolt to its final torque only with car on the ground and the suspension normally loaded.*

Control arm, removing and installing

— Raise car and remove wheel.

> **WARNING—**
> • *Make sure vehicle is stable and well supported at all times. Use a professional automotive lift or jack stands. A floor jack is not adequate support.*

— Remove underbody splash shield. See **020 Maintenance**

— On passenger side remove ride height sensor arm if equipped.

◄ Remove control arm strut fastener (**A**). Lightly tap control arm mounting bolt out of front subframe in direction of arrow.

— Loosen control arm ball joint nut (**B**).

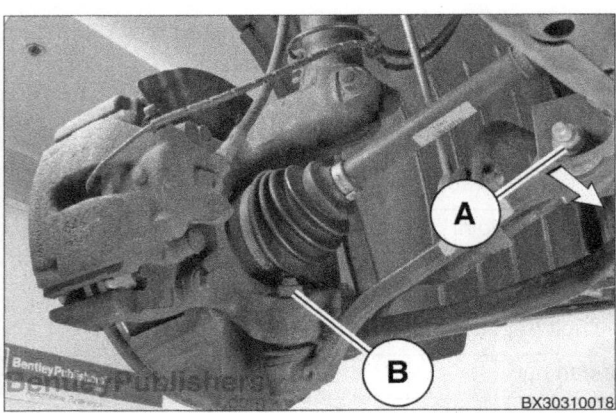

BX30310018

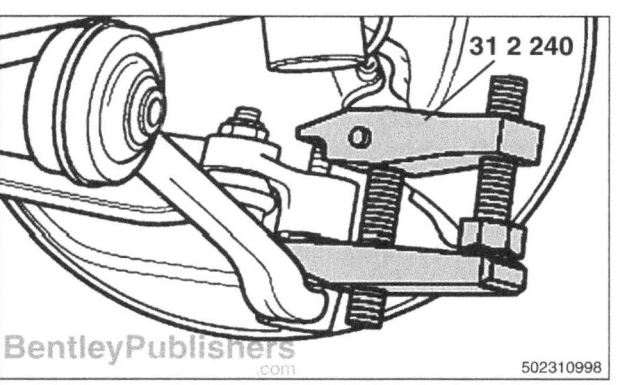

Use BMW special tool 31 2 240 or equivalent to separate ball joint from steering knuckle.

> **CAUTION—**
> • *Use care not to damage ball joint threads if control arm is to be reused.*

— Installation is reverse of removal, noting the following:

• Make sure thread bores, bolts, nuts and mating surfaces are clean.

• Install bushing end of control arm to subframe using new fasteners. Do not tighten nut at this time.

• Install control ball joint to steering knuckle using new self-locking nut. Tighten fully.

• Install wheel and lower car.

• Tighten bushing end of control arm to subframe with car on ground and loaded. Bounce suspension a few times before final tightening.

• Check vehicle alignment.

Tightening torques	
Control arm ball joint nut to steering knuckle • M14 x 1.5 (replace with new)	80 Nm (59 ft-lb)
Control arm to subframe • M12 10.9 (replace with new)	100 Nm (74 ft-lb) + 90° +/- 15°
Road wheel to hub	140 Nm (103 ft-lb)

Control arm bushing, replacing

Replace control arm bushings in pairs. Bushings may only be replaced once.

— Remove tension strut. See **Control arm, removing and installing** in this repair group.

— Using a service press and appropriate press tools, press bushing out of tension strut.

> **CAUTION—**
> • *Draw in rubber mount from chamfered side of control arm bore.*
> • *To avoid damaging the new bushing, press only on the outer steel sleeve during installation.*

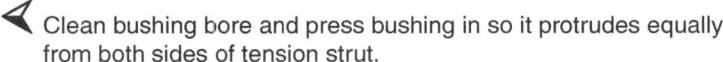

Clean bushing bore and press bushing in so it protrudes equally from both sides of tension strut.

— Install control arm.

> **CAUTION—**
> • *Tighten control arm through-bolt to its final torque only with car on the ground and the suspension normally loaded as described earlier.*

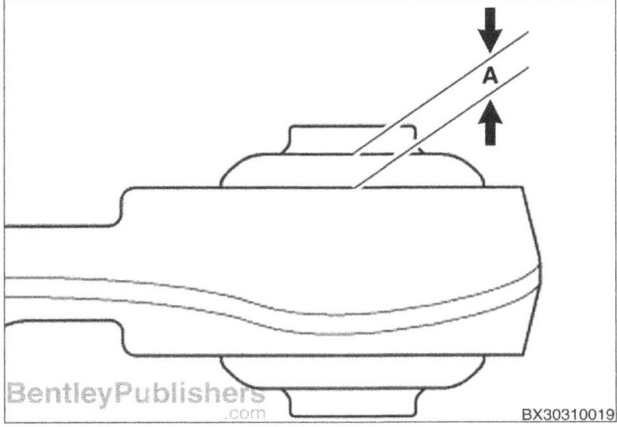

STEERING KNUCKLE AND FRONT WHEEL BEARINGS

The steering knuckle (also called swivel bearing) serves as the outboard attachment point for the suspension arms and as the wheel hub / wheel bearing carrier.

Wheel bearings are permanently sealed and require no maintenance. Wheel bearing replacement requires removal of steering knuckle. Wheel bearings are pressed onto the steering knuckle and require several special tools to remove. The bearing is destroyed when the wheel hub is removed. Steering knuckle removal requires multiple procedures to complete. Familiarize yourself with the other procedures before attempting removal of steering knuckle.

Steering knuckle, removing and installing

– Raise car and remove front wheel.

> **WARNING—**
> • *Make sure vehicle is stable and well supported at all times. Use a professional automotive lift or jack stands. A floor jack is not adequate support.*

◄ Using a suitable drift, release staked side of axle nut (**arrows**).

– Remove center cap and reinstall wheel. Lower vehicle to ground.

– With an assistant holding down brake, remove collar axle nut. Do not reuse collar nut.

– Raise car and remove front wheel.

– Remove underbody splash shield. See **020 Maintenance**.

– Unbolt brake caliper and hang to side with stiff wire. Do not disconnect brake hose. Remove front brake disc. Remove wheel speed sensor. See **340 Brakes**.

– Remove tie rod end from steering knuckle. See **320 Steering and Wheel Alignment**.

– Remove tension strut ball joint from steering knuckle. See **Tension strut, removing and installing**.

– Remove control arm from steering knuckle. See **Control arm, removing and installing**.

– Press drive axle out of steering knuckle and secure from falling. See **311 Front Axle Differential**.

– Remove front strut only from steering knuckle. See **Front strut removing and installing** in this repair group.

— Remainder of installation is reverse of removal. Remember to:

• Install bolt head of steering knuckle pinch bolt in direction of travel.

• Replace self locking fasteners with new.

• Make sure steering knuckle contacts stop on strut

• Using a suitable drift, stake side of axle nut to axle.

• Tighten tension strut and control arm busing end through bolts with car on ground and suspension loaded.

• Tighten drive axle collar nut to final torque with road wheel installed and vehicle lowered.

Tightening torques	
Road wheel to hub	140 Nm (103 ft-lb)
Tie rod end to steering knuckle (replace nut with new)	80 Nm (59 ft-lb)
Control arm ball joint nut to steering knuckle • M14 x 1.5 (replace with new)	80 Nm (59 ft-lb)
Tension strut ball joint to steering knuckle • M10 x 20 10.9 bolt (replace with new)	60 Nm (44 ft-lb)
Wheel hub to axle shaft (replace with new)	420 Nm (310 ft-lb)

Front wheel bearing, removing and installing

— Raise car and remove front wheel.

> **WARNING —**
> • *Make sure vehicle is stable and well supported at all times. Use a professional automotive lift or jack stands. A floor jack is not adequate support.*

— Remove underbody splash shield. See **020 Maintenance**.

— Remove steering knuckle. See **Steering knuckle, removing and installing**.

— Clamp steering knuckle in bench vice with aluminum clamping jaws.

◀ Remove wheel hub using BMW special tools 33 2 160 / 33 2 116 / 33 4 200 and 5 wheel lugs.

> **NOTE —**
> • *Position rounded inside edge of special tool 33 2 160 towards wheel hub.*

> **WARNING —**
> • *Bearing is destroyed when wheel hub is removed. Replace wheel bearing and wheel hub together.*

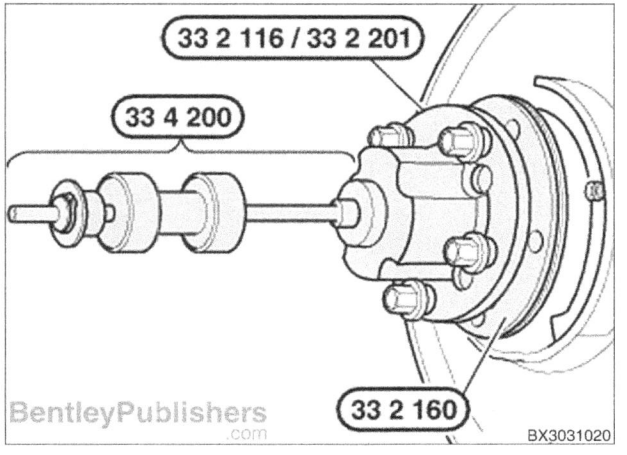

33 2 116 / 33 2 201

33 4 200

33 2 160

BX3031020

Front wheel bearing, removing and installing

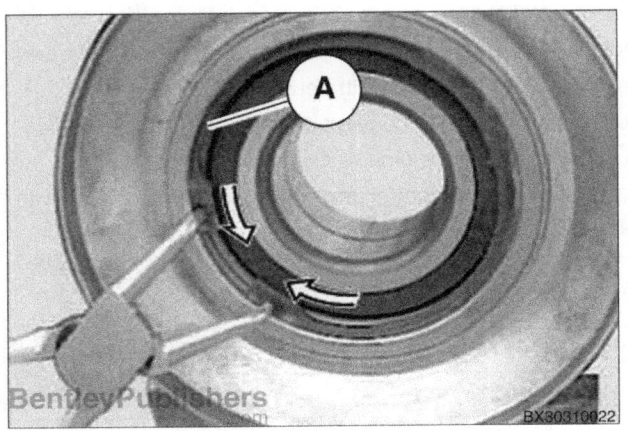

◄ Use snap ring pliers to remove wheel bearing circlip (**A**).

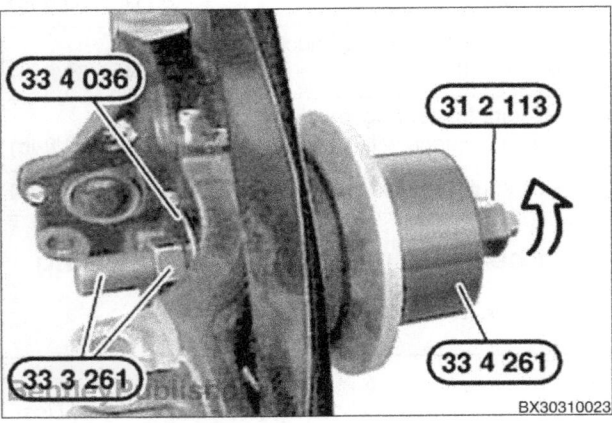

◄ Remove wheel bearing using BMW special tools 31 2 113 / 33 4 261 / 33 3 266 / 33 3 261.

– Check dust sleeve. Replace if necessary.

◄ Make sure steering knuckle bearing surface is clean and coat 50% of its length with Loctite 638®. Note that chamfer of bearing (**A**) points towards steering knuckle.

Stabilizer bar, links and bushings, removing and installing

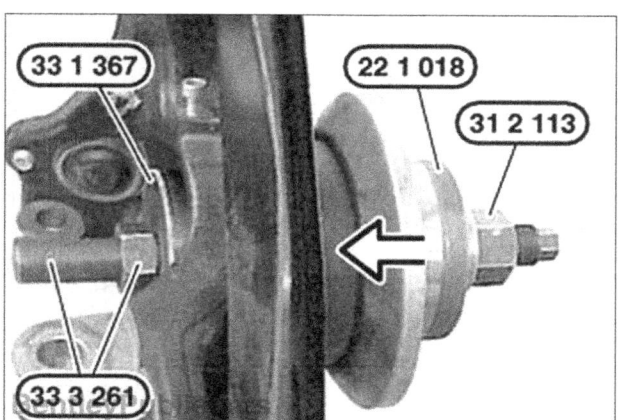

◄ With chamfer of bearing pointing towards steering knuckle, draw new bearing into hub using BMW special tools 31 2 113 / 22 1 018 / 33 4 262 / 33 3 261.

– Install new wheel bearing circlip. Make sure circlip is correctly seated.

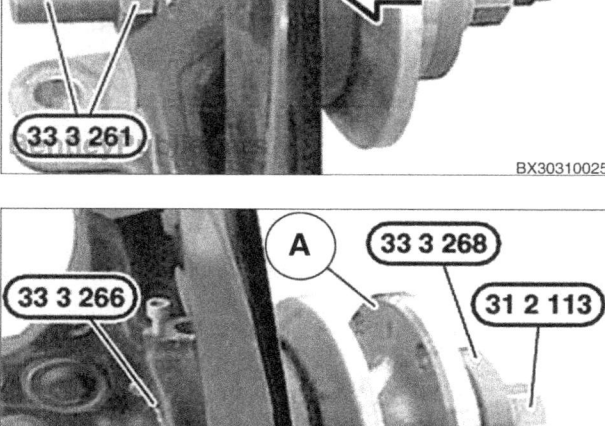

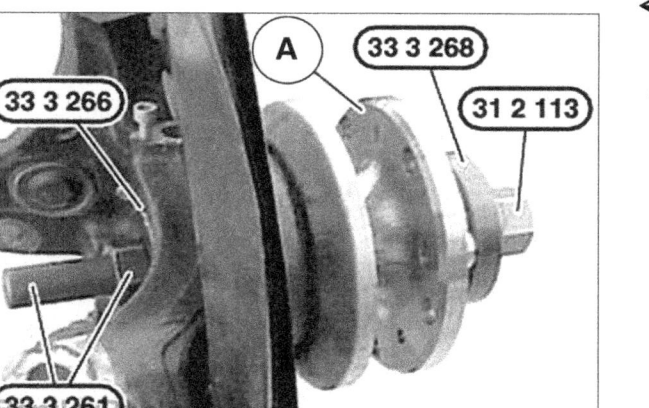

◄ Replace wheel hub (**A**) and draw into steering knuckle using BMW special tools 32 2 113 / 33 3 268 / 33 3 263 / 33 3 261.

– Install steering knuckle. See **Steering knuckle, removing and installing** in this repair group.

FRONT STABILIZER BAR

The stabilizer bar mounts to the front subframe. The front stabilizer bar links attach to the strut assemblies.

Stabilizer bar, links and bushings, removing and installing

– Raise car and remove front wheel.

> **WARNING**—
> • *Make sure vehicle is stable and well supported at all times. Use a professional automotive lift or jack stands. A floor jack is not adequate support.*

– Remove underbody splash shield. See **020 Maintenance**.

Bushings

– Fold back wheel housing liner. See **410 Fenders, Engine Hood**.

◄ Remove stabilizer bar bushing mount bolts (**arrows**) slide bushing out to remove.

– Installation is reverse of removal. Do not grease bushings.

Stabilizer bar, links and bushings, removing and installing

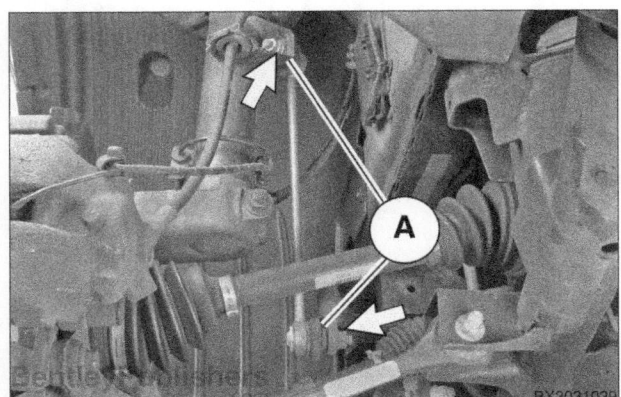

Stabilizer bar links

Raise car and remove front wheel.

> **WARNING—**
> • *Make sure vehicle is stable and well supported at all times. Use a professional automotive lift or jack stands. A floor jack is not adequate support.*

 Remove stabilizer bar connecting link mounting nut (**arrows**). Use a thin wrench to counterhold shaft (**A**) of stabilizer bar link ball joint while removing nut.

Stabilizer bar

— Raise car and remove front wheel.

> **WARNING—**
> • *Make sure vehicle is stable and well supported at all times. Use a professional automotive lift or jack stands. A floor jack is not adequate support.*

— Remove underbody splash shield. See **020 Maintenance**.

— Lower front subframe, See **Front subframe, lowering** in this repair group

— Remove stabilizer links from stabilizer bar.

 Remove stabilizer bar bracket bolts on right and left sides.

— Slide stabilizer out from front of vehicle.

— Installation is reverse of removal. Remember to:

  • Replace fasteners with new.

  • Check rubber mounts for damage. Replace as needed.

Tightening torques	
Stabilizer bar link to stabilizer bar	65 Nm (48 ft-lb)
Stabilizer bar link to strut	65 Nm (48 ft-lb)
Stabilizer bar brackets to frame • M10 10.9 bolts	56 Nm (41 ft-lb)

311 Front Axle Differential

GENERAL

This repair group covers service and replacement of front drive axles and front differential. Front differential internal repair is not covered.

For additional information, see also the following repair groups:

- **260 Driveshafts** for front driveshaft removal
- **310 Front Suspension**

Front differential and drive axles

1. Drive axle
2. Right drive axle inner bearing pedestal
3. Front differential
4. Shaft (through oil pan)
5. Inner CV joint
6. Outer CV joint

The front axle differential and the right side bearing pedestal bolt to each side of the oil pan. Power is transmitted to the front differential from the transfer case via a driveshaft, and out to front drive hubs through two drive axles. The right drive axle shaft extends through the oil pan into the front differential.

Warning

Front differential and drive axles

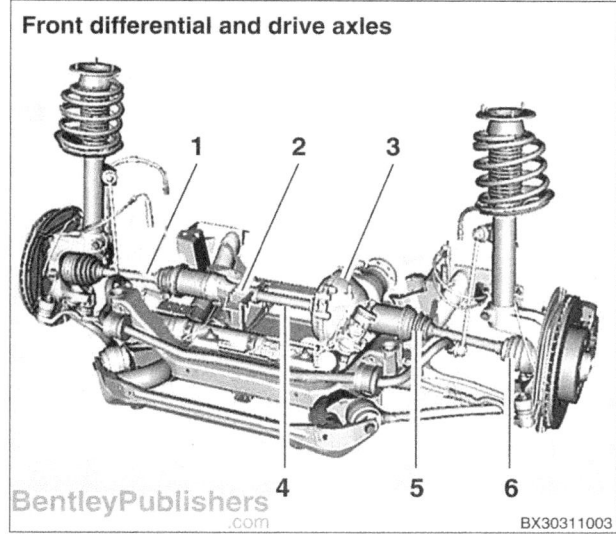

BX30311003

> **WARNING—**
> - *Do not reuse self-locking fasteners. They are designed to be used only once and may fail if reused. Replace with new.*

Drive axle, removing and installing

DRIVE AXLES

Front drive axles use two different types of CV joint.

- **Outer CV joint**: Traditional design allows power to be delivered from axle to wheel hub continuously while allowing suspension and steering motion.

- **Inner joint**: Triple roller bearing joint minimizes the amount of vibration and noise transmitted back through vehicle drivetrain while allowing axle to move in and out to compensate for suspension travel.

To replace a CV joint or boot, remove the drive axle from the vehicle.

Drive axle, removing and installing

— Raise car and remove front wheel.

> **WARNING—**
> • *Make sure vehicle is stable and well supported at all times. Use a professional automotive lift or jack stands. A floor jack is not adequate support.*

◄ Using a suitable drift, release staked side of axle nut (**arrows**).

— Remove center cap and reinstall wheel. Lower vehicle to ground.

— With an assistant holding down brake, remove collar axle nut. Do not reuse collar nut.

— Raise car and remove front wheel.

— Remove underbody splash shield. See **020 Maintenance**.

— Remove front end reinforcement plate. See **310 Suspension.**

— Unbolt brake caliper and hang to side with stiff wire. Do not disconnect brake hose See **340 Brakes.**

— Remove front brake disc. See **340 Brakes**.

— Remove wheel speed sensor. See **340 Brakes**.

— Remove tie rod end from steering knuckle. See **320 Steering and Wheel Alignment**.

— Remove tension strut from steering knuckle. See **310 Suspension**.

— Remove control arm from steering knuckle. See **310 Suspension**.

— Swivel steering knuckle and press drive axle shaft inward to disengage from steering knuckle.

> **CAUTION—**
> • *Do not pound on end of drive axle shaft.*

BX30310021

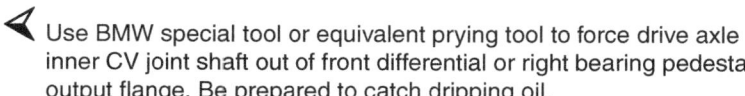

Front differential flange seal, replacing

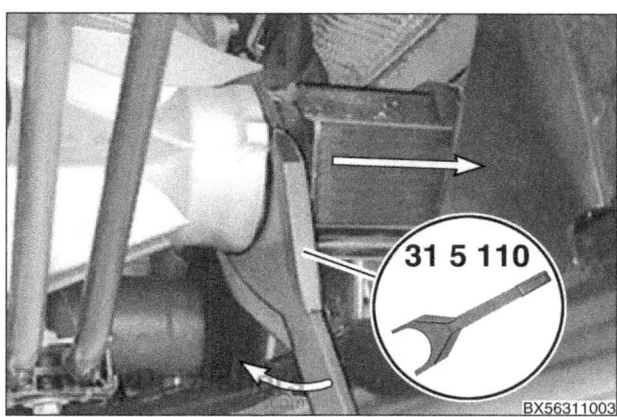

◄ Use BMW special tool or equivalent prying tool to force drive axle inner CV joint shaft out of front differential or right bearing pedestal output flange. Be prepared to catch dripping oil.

– Replace differential or bearing pedestal flange seal while axle is removed from vehicle. See **Front differential flange seal, replacing** in this repair group.

– Replace CV joint boots as necessary. See **Outer CV joint boot, replacing** or **Inner CV joint boot, replacing** in this repair group.

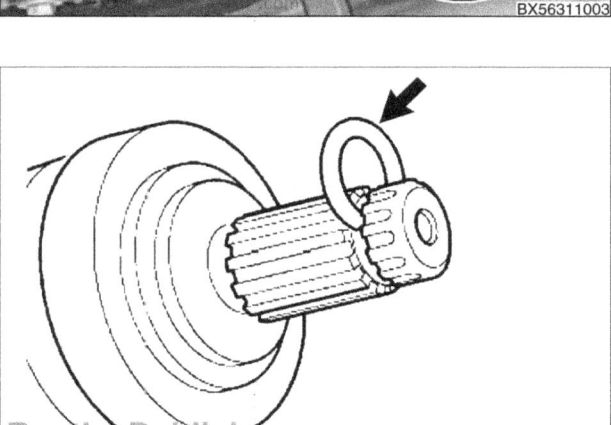

◄ Replace inner CV joint locking circlip (**arrow**).

– When installing:
  • Coat sealing lip of flange seal with transmission fluid.
  • Push inner CV joint shaft into differential or bearing pedestal flange until locking circlip snaps in place.
  • Use new collar nut at drive axle. Tighten drive axle collar nut to final torque with road wheel installed and vehicle lowered.
  • Install front end reinforcement plate using new fasteners. See **310 Front Suspension**.
  • Check front differential oil level. See **Differential fluid level, draining and filling** in this repair group.

Tightening torques	
Road wheel to hub	140 Nm (103 ft-lb)
Wheel hub to axle shaft (replace with new)	420 Nm (310 ft-lb)

Front differential flange seal, replacing

Front differential flange seal requires drive axle removal.

– Raise car and remove front wheel.

> **WARNING —**
> • *Make sure vehicle is firmly supported on jack stands. Place jack stands underneath structural chassis points. Do not place jack stands under suspension parts.*

– Remove left or right drive axle. See **Drive axle removing and installing**.

> **NOTE —**
> • Drive axle can remain with steering knuckle as a single unit. This will eliminate the need to remove the drive axle from the steering knuckle.

Left seal

◄ Use seal removal tool or screw driver to pry flange seal out of differential.

Front differential flange seal, replacing

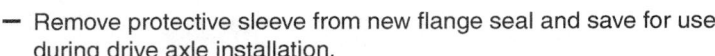

— Remove protective sleeve from new flange seal and save for use during drive axle installation.

NOTE —

• *Seal is equipped with a protective covering to prevent sealing lip from damage during axle installation.*

◄ Use BMW special tool or equivalent seal driver to drive flange seal into differential or bearing pedestal as far as it will go.

— Coat sealing lip of flange seal with gear oil.

— Insert protective sleeve into seal.

— Install drive axle:

• Insert inboard end of drive axle partially into differential housing or bearing pedestal.

• Withdraw protective sleeve from sealing lip, cut protective sleeve and remove sleeve.

• Continue pressing drive axle in until spring clip snaps audibly into place.

• Check front differential oil level. See **Differential fluid level, draining and filling** in this repair group.

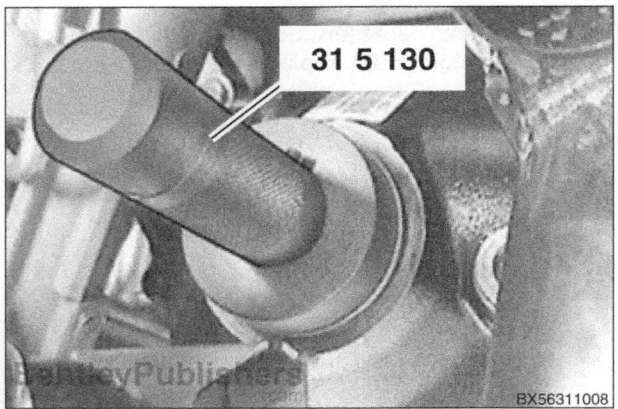

Right seal

◄ Use seal removal tool or screw driver (**B**) to pry flange seal (**A**) out of bearing pedestal (**C**).

— Remove protective sleeve from new flange seal and save for use during drive axle installation.

NOTE —

• *Seal is equipped with protective covering to prevent sealing lip from damage during axle installation.*

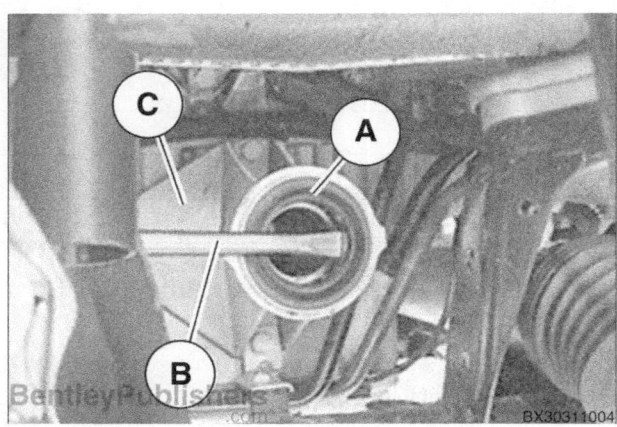

◄ Use BMW special tool or equivalent seal driver to drive flange seal into differential or bearing pedestal as far as it will go.

— Coat sealing lip of flange seal with gear oil.

— Insert protective sleeve into seal.

— Install drive axle:

• Insert inboard end of drive axle partially into differential housing or bearing pedestal.

• Withdraw protective sleeve from sealing lip, cut protective sleeve and remove sleeve.

• Continue pressing drive axle in until spring clip snaps audibly into place.

• Check front differential oil level. See **Differential fluid level, draining and filling** in this repair group

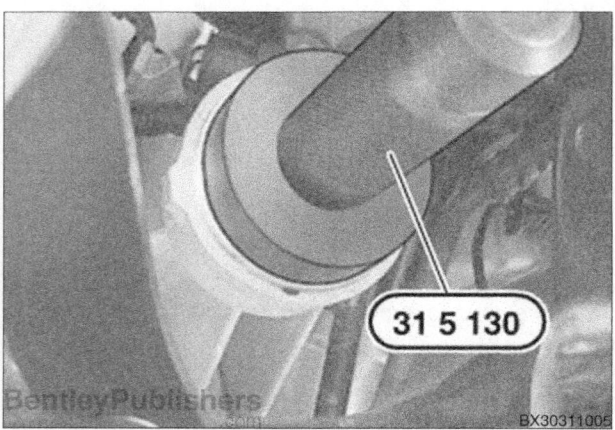

Outer CV joint boot, replacing

When replacing CV boot, use a complete boot repair kit available from an authorized BMW dealer parts department. The kit includes new boot, clamping bands, special lubricant and a new CV joint shaft circlip.

— Remove drive axle. See **Drive axle, removing and installing** in this repair group. Place axle in shop vice with aluminum jaws.

— Release boot clamps from both ends of outer CV boot. Cut off boot and discard.

— Using a soft-faced hammer, pound outer CV joint off drive axle.

— Using a flat blade screw driver, pry spring clip off drive axle splines.

— Clean old lubricant off axle splines.

— Inspect CV joint carefully.
  • Look for galling, pitting and other signs of wear or physical damage.
  • Polished surfaces or visible ball tracks alone are not necessarily cause for replacement.
  • Discoloration (overheating) indicates lack of lubrication.

— Place new clamping bands and CV boot over drive axle.

— Replace spring clip on splined end of drive axle.

— Pack joint with fresh CV joint grease.

CV joint lubricant capacity	
Outer CV joint	80 grams (2.8 oz)

— Tap CV joint onto splined end of drive axle until spring clip snaps audibly into place.

— Using clamp pliers, secure retaining clamp into position tightly sealing large end of boot against CV joint.

◀ Before installing small boot clamp:
  • Flex CV joint as far over as it will go.
  • Insert small screw-driver between boot and axle-shaft to "burp" boot.

— With outer boot full of grease, and any air eliminated from boot, secure small end of boot on CV joint by pinching clamp with pliers.

— Remainder of installation is reverse of removal. See **Drive axle, removing and installing** in this repair group.

— Check differential oil level. See **Differential fluid level, draining and filling** in this repair group.

BX56311009

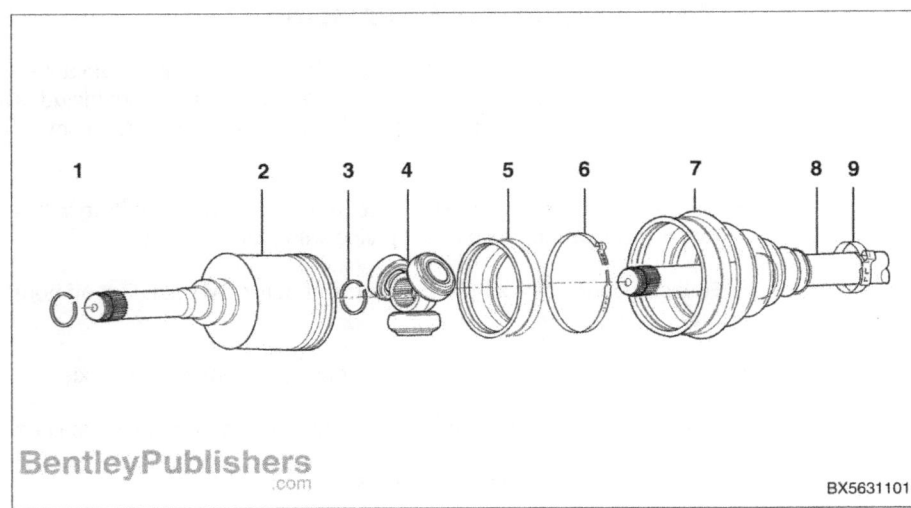

BX56311011

Inner CV joint (triple-roller)

1. Locking circlip
2. Inner CV joint housing
3. Circlip
4. Triple roller bearing
5. Inner CV joint boot adapter
6. Clamp
7. Inner CV joint boot
8. Drive axle shaft
9. Clamp

Inner CV joint boot, replacing

When replacing CV boot, use a complete boot repair kit. Kits includes new boot, clamps, special lubricant and a new circlip.

– Remove drive axle. See **Drive axle, removing and installing**.

– Release boot clamp on both ends of inner CV boot. Pull back inner boot and detach inner CV joint housing.

– Remove circlip retaining triple roller bearing and remove triple roller bearing.

– Slide boot off drive axle. Separate inner boot adapter from boot.

– Clean old lubricant off axle splines and triple roller bearing splines.

– Install new inner CV joint boot:
  • Place boot adapter in boot.
  • Slide retaining clamps and boot over drive axle.
  • Secure retaining clamp using clamp pliers, tightly sealing small end of boot against drive axle.

◀ Install triple roller bearing with flat edge of joint facing retaining circlip.

– Replace inner CV joint circlip.

– Pack triple roller bearing and boot with fresh CV joint grease.

CV joint lubricant capacity	
Inner CV joint	80 grams (2.8 oz)

– Insert triple roller bearing into inner CV joint housing.

– Secure boot connection to boot adapter using clamp supplied with boot kit.

– Remainder of installation is reverse of removal. See **Drive axle, removing and installing** in this repair group. Top off differential fluid. See **020 Maintenance**.

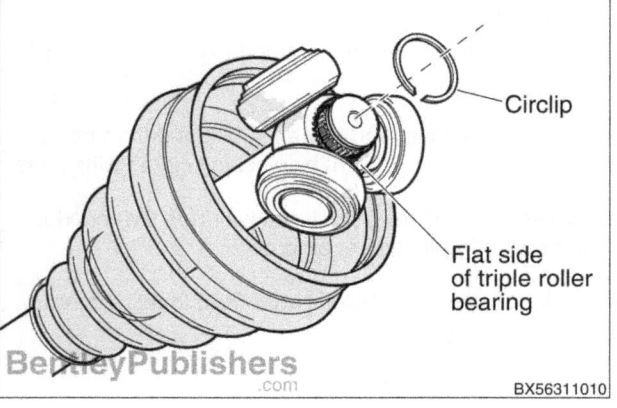

Circlip

Flat side of triple roller bearing

BX56311010

FRONT DIFFERENTIAL

Replacement of O-ring seal between engine oil pan and front differential is covered in **Front differential, removing and installing** in this repair group.

Replacement of O-ring seal between engine oil pan and right side bearing pedestal is covered in **Right axle bearing pedestal, removing and installing** in this repair group.

Differential oil level, draining and filling

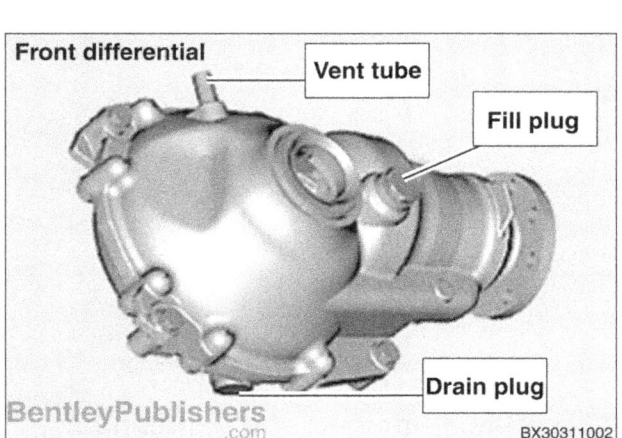

Front differential

Vent tube

Fill plug

Drain plug

BentleyPublishers
.com

BX30311002

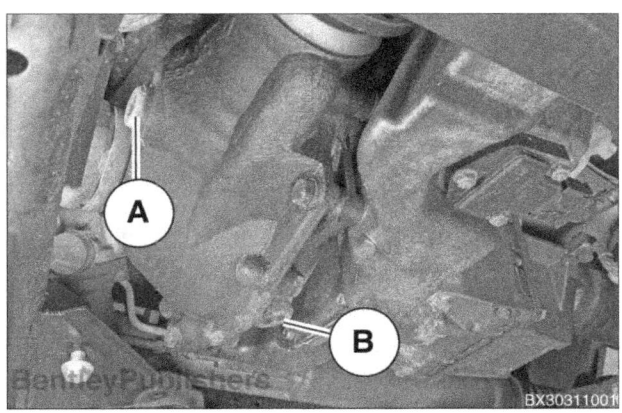

A

B

BentleyPublishers

BX30311001

◀ The E83 front differential is filled with lifetime oil that ordinarily does not need to be changed. BMW recommends using only a specially formulated synthetic gear oil (SAF-XO) that is available through an authorized BMW dealer parts department.

NOTE —

* *The front differential is filled below the top edge of the fill plug hole, making fluid level checking difficult. If in doubt, drain and fill differential using fresh fluid.*

NOTE —

* *Bring differential oil to operating temperature before draining.*

– Remove front end reinforcement plate. See **310 Front Suspension**.

◀ Front differential: Use 14 mm Allen socket to remove fill plug (**A**).

* Check oil level after removing fill plug (**A**).
* Level is correct when fluid just reaches edge of fill hole.
* If necessary, top up fluid.
* Replace fill plug sealing ring.
* Install and tighten oil fill plug when oil level is correct.
* Drain plug (**B**).

Tightening torque	
Fill or drain plug to front differential housing	60 Nm (44 ft-lb)

Front differential fluid capacity	
Fill and drain (differential warmed up)	600 ml (20.3 oz)

NOTE —

* *Do not fill differential to edge of fill hole. Although this is a normal practice, the differential will then contain approximately 700 ml (23.7 oz) of fluid. In some instances this amount would cause the fluid to overflow the vent tube. Filling with 600 ml (20.3 oz) of differential oil is the recommended fill.*

Front differential, removing and installing

Front differential and right bearing pedestal

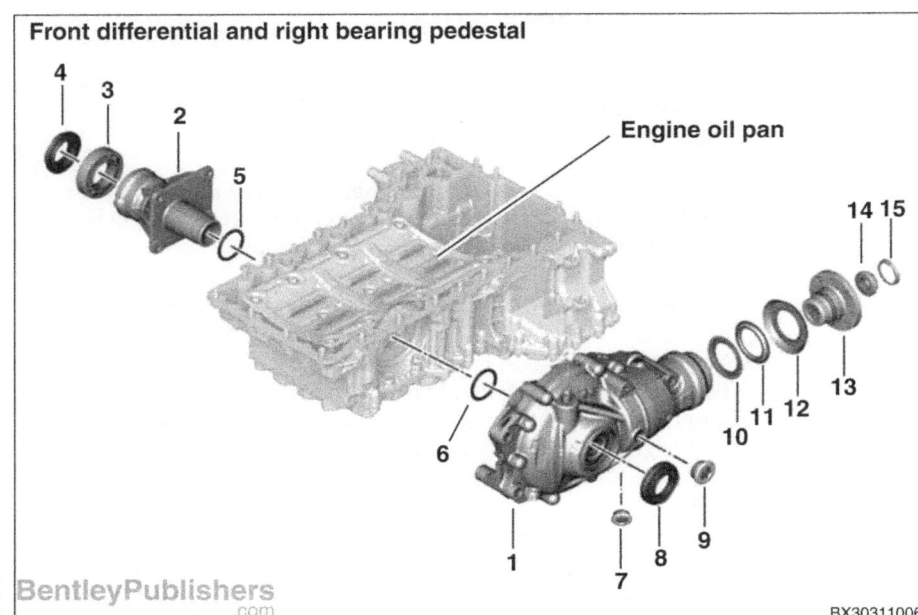

Engine oil pan

BX30311006

Front differential and right bearing pedestal

1. Front differential
2. Right bearing pedestal
3. Right bearing
4. Right drive axle seal
5. Right sealing O-ring
6. Left sealing O-ring
7. Drain plug
8. Left drive axle seal
9. Fill plug
10. Driveshaft seal
11. Small dust cover
12. Large dust cover
13. Drive flange
14. Drive flange lock nut
15. Securing plate for drive flange

Front differential, removing and installing

– Raise car and remove front wheel.

> **WARNING—**
> • *Make sure vehicle is firmly supported on jack stands. Place jack stands underneath structural chassis points. Do not place jack stands under suspension parts.*

– Remove underbody splash shield. See **020 Maintenance**.

– Remove front end reinforcement plate. See **310 Suspension.**

– Drain front axle differential oil. See **Front differential fluid level, draining and filling** in this repair group.

– Remove left drive axle. See **Drive axle removing and installing** in this repair group.

– Remove right drive axle from bearing pedestal approximately 7 to 8 cm. See **Drive axle removing and installing** in this repair group.

– Remove front drive shaft. See **260 Driveshafts.**

◄ Remove bolts (**arrows**) and lower differential carefully.

> **CAUTION—**
> • *Be sure to support front differential while removing bolts to prevent it from falling.*

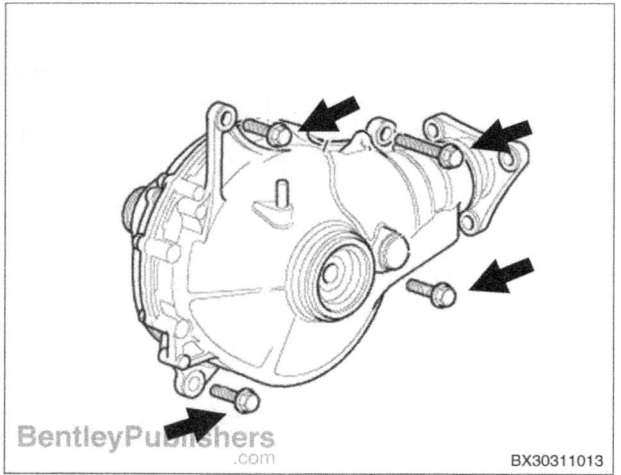

BX30311013

Right axle bearing pedestal, removing and installing

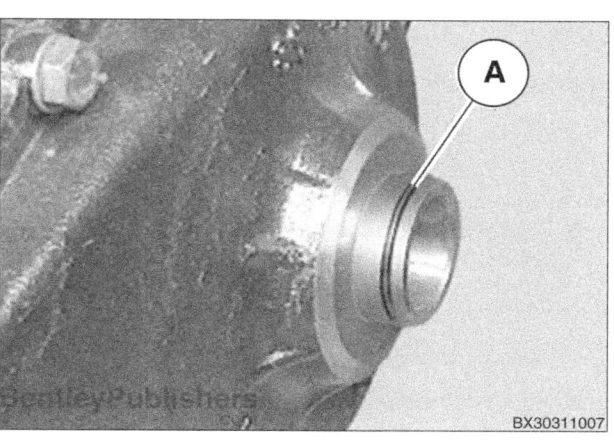

BX30311007

◄ Replace sealing O-ring (**A**) between oil pan and differential before reinstalling differential:

• Install new sealing O-ring (**A**), coating inside edge with front differential oil.

– Install differential to oil pan.

Tightening torques	
Front differential to oil pan	
• M10 10.9 with ribbed shim	65 Nm (48 ft-lb)
• M10 10.9 ex. with ribbed shim	55 Nm (41 ft-lb)

– Remainder of assembly is reverse of removal. Keep in mind:

• Replace drive axle flange seal before installing drive axle.

• Check differential oil level. See **Differential fluid level, draining and filling** in this repair group.

Right axle bearing pedestal, removing and installing

– Raise car and remove front wheel.

> **WARNING—**
> • *Make sure vehicle is firmly supported on jack stands. Place jack stands underneath structural chassis points. Do not place jack stands under suspension parts.*

– Remove underbody splash shield. See **020 Maintenance**.

– Remove front end reinforcement plate. See **310 Suspension**.

– Remove right drive axle. See **Drive axle removing and installing** in this repair group.

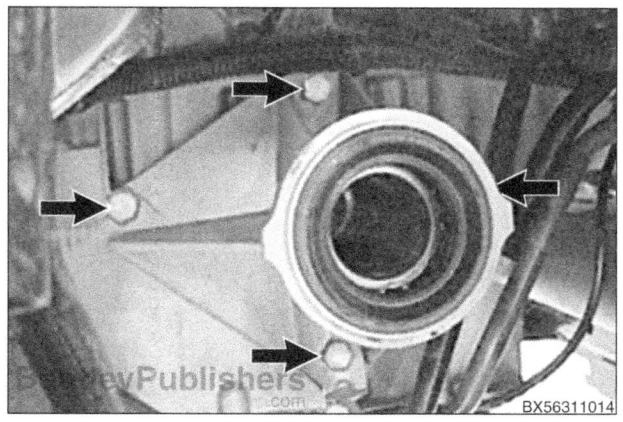

BX56311014

◄ Remove grounding strap and bearing pedestal mounting bolts (**arrows**) at side of oil pan. Lift off pedestal.

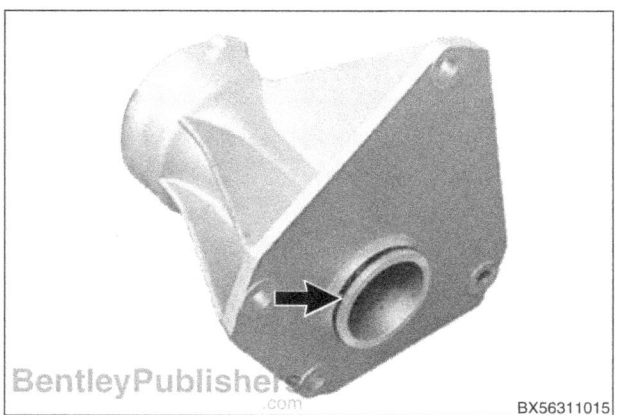

BX56311015

◄ When reinstalling:

• Replace sealing O-ring (**arrow**). Coat O-ring with differential oil.

• Replace drive axle flange seal before installing drive axle.

Tightening torques	
Bearing pedestal to oil pan	27 Nm (20 ft-lb)

Differential input flange seal, replacing

This procedure requires several special BMW service tools.

— Raise car and remove front wheel.

> **WARNING—**
> • *Make sure vehicle firmly supported on jack stands. Place jack stands underneath structural chassis points. Do not place jack stands under suspension parts.*

— Remove underbody splash shield. See **020 Maintenance**.

— Remove front end reinforcement plate. See **310 Suspension.**

— Drain front axle differential oil. See **Front differential fluid level, draining and filling** in this repair group.

— Remove front driveshaft. See **260 Driveshafts.**

— Pry out input flange retaining nut lock plate (**A**).

◄ Using a center punch, mark relation of input flange retaining nut to shaft (**arrow**).

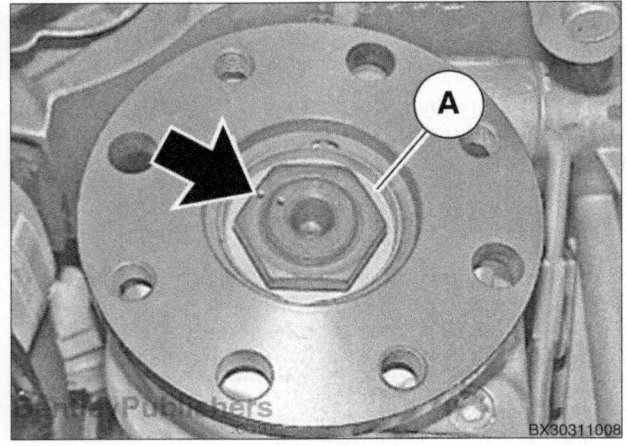

◄ Counterhold input flange using BMW special tool and remove nut (**A**).

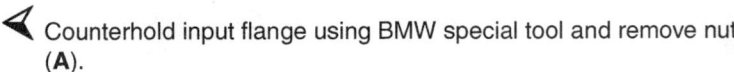

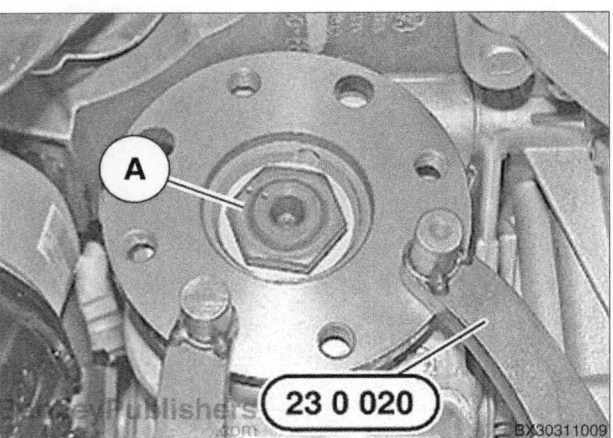

◄ Remove input flange with BMW special tool. Use M10 x 30 fasteners to attach to drive flange.

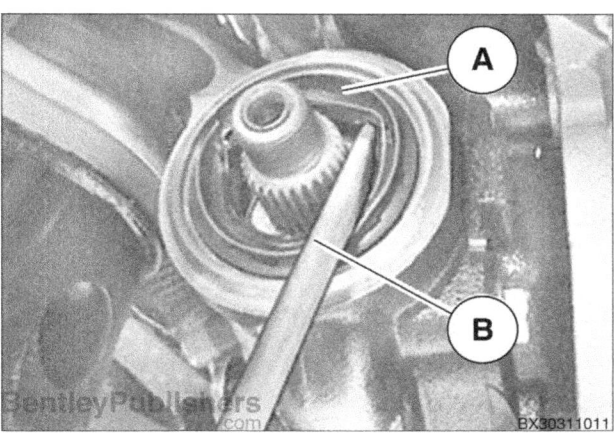

◄ Using a seal puller or flat screwdriver (**B**), pry seal (**A**) out of differential housing.

◄ Coat sealing edges of seal with differential oil and drive into differential housing using BMW special tool or equivalent drift.

– Clean input flange and install into differential housing.
  • Tighten down nut until punch marks align.
  • Install new input flange retaining nut locking plate.

> **CAUTION—**
> • *Do not torque input flange retaining nut beyond match marks. Over-torquing can damage differential internals.*
> • *Do not replace input flange or input flange locking nut.*

– Remainder of installation is reverse of removal. Check front differential oil level. See **Differential fluid level, draining and filling** in this repair group.

320 Steering and Wheel Alignment

GENERAL

This repair group covers steering wheel and column removal and steering system service, including wheel alignment information. For additional information, see:

- **513 Interior Trim** for steering column trim
- **612 Switches** for ignition lock cylinder, ignition switch, steering column stalk switches
- **721 Airbag System** for driver airbag

Steering system

X3 models are equipped with a power-assisted steering rack. Power boost for the steering is provided by an engine-driven hydraulic pump. Servotronic is an available option. Servotronic steering uses hydro-electronics to adjust the amount of power assistance based on road speed. Total ratio of the steering rack is 18.9:1.

The steering wheel connects to the steering rack via a manually adjustable steering column which incorporates a rubber coupling ("guibo") to dampen vibration and noise.

The steering system requires no maintenance other than alignment and periodic inspection for worn components. Inspect tie rod ends and end boots periodically for tears and wear. Replace faulty parts.

Warnings and Cautions

> *WARNING* —
> * *The airbag mounted in the steering wheel is an explosive device. Treat it with extreme caution. Follow the airbag removal procedure in* **721 Airbag System***.*
> * *Serious injury may result if airbag system service is attempted by persons unfamiliar with the BMW MRS and its approved service procedures.*
> * *Before performing any work involving airbags, disconnect the negative (-) battery cable.*
> * *BMW airbags are equipped with a back-up power supply inside the airbag control module. Observe a 5 second waiting period after disconnecting the battery cable to allow the reserve power supply to discharge.*
> * *Do not reuse self-locking nuts. They are designed to be used only once and may fail if reused. Replace with new.*
> * *Do not install bolts and nuts coated with undercoating wax, as correct tightening torque cannot be assured. Clean the threads with solvent before installation, or install new parts.*
> * *Do not attempt to weld or straighten steering components. Replace damaged parts.*

> *CAUTION* —
> * *When working with power steering components, maintain cleanliness to ensure proper operation of the hydraulic system.*
> * *Follow local, state and federal regulations for safe disposal of power steering fluid.*

STEERING WHEEL

* For airbag removal. See **721 Airbag System.**
* For ignition lock, ignition switch, steering column stalk and steering wheel switch removal. See **612 Switches**.

Steering wheel, removing and installing

— Center steering wheel with front wheels are pointed straight ahead.

— Disconnect negative (–) cable from battery.

> *CAUTION* —
> * *Prior to disconnecting the battery, read the battery disconnection cautions given in* **001 Warnings and Cautions***.*

— Carefully remove airbag from front of steering wheel. See **721 Airbag System**. Store airbag unit in a safe place.

◀ Remove steering wheel center bolt (**arrow**).

> *NOTE* —
> * *Steering column and steering wheel are match marked at the factory.*

BX30320001

BX30320002

CAUTION—

- *The MRS contact reel (also known as airbag contact ring) is integral with the steering column switch block. The contact reel is a wound wire coil that ensures continuous electrical contact for the airbag and steering wheel components. When the steering wheel is removed the contact reel is locked and its position must not be altered.*

◄ Check for proper alignment of steering column marks (**arrows**) before removing steering wheel.

– When installing steering wheel:
  - Align steering wheel and column match marks.
  - Align steering wheel to alignment pins located on steering column switch block.
  - Install steering column center bolt. Do not over-torque.

– Carefully install airbag. See **721 Airbag System**.

Tightening torques	
Steering wheel to steering shaft (M14)	62.5 Nm (46 ft-lb)

320

STEERING COLUMN

Steering column components

1. Upper steering column
2. Lower steering column with universal joint
3. Double joint with flex disc
4. Steering column adjustment lever
5. Column pivot bushing
6. Steering wheel to column bolt (M14 X 1.5)
7. Steering column mounting bracket
8. Bolt (M8 x 36)
9. Column return spring
10. Nut (M8)
11. Nut (M8)
12. Crash sleeve and disc
13. Bushing
14. Cup
15. Gasket ring
16. Frame
17. Nut
18. Steering angle sensor
19. Steering angle sensor bracket

Steering column assembly

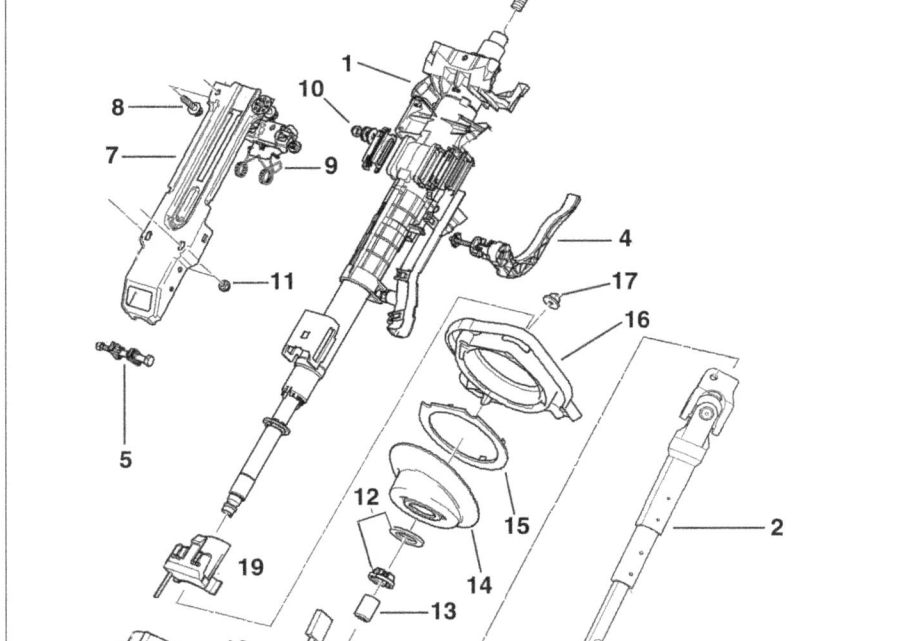

BX30320003

Steering column, removing and installing

The X3 steering column consists of three main parts. They must be removed and installed in specific order.

Double joint with flex disc, removing and installing

> **CAUTION—**
> • When the double joint is separated from the steering column / steering rack, the steering wheel is free to spin. Once separated, lock the steering wheel in position. Otherwise the MRS contact reel (coil of wire) could be damaged.

— Raise front of car and remove front left wheel.

> **WARNING—**
> • Make sure vehicle is stable and well supported at all times. Use a professional automotive lift or jack stands. A floor jack is not adequate support.

◄ It may be necessary to rotate steering wheel to access pinch bolts.

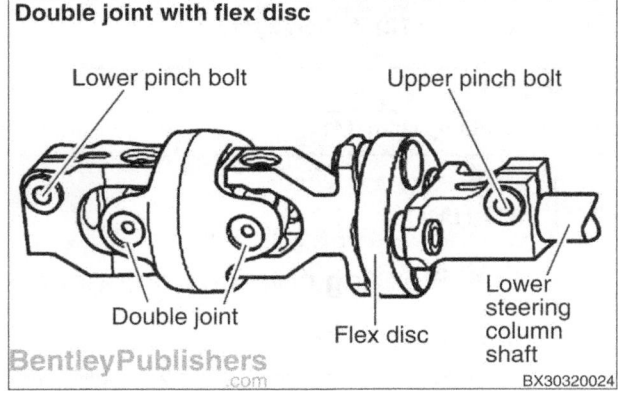

Double joint with flex disc

Lower pinch bolt   Upper pinch bolt

Double joint   Flex disc   Lower steering column shaft

BentleyPublishers.com

BX30320024

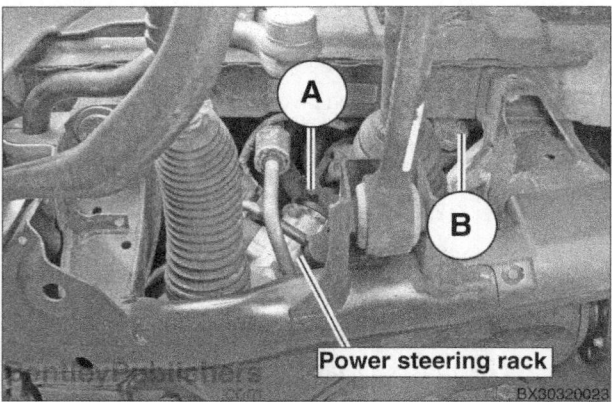

A   B

Power steering rack

BentleyPublishers

BX30320023

◄ Release pinch bolt (**A**) on steering rack and slide double joint off of steering rack.

— Release pinch bolt (**B**) at double joint on lower steering column shaft.

— Move steering wheel and front wheels to straight ahead position. Remove ignition key to lock steering wheel.

   • Remove double joint with flex disc.

— Installation:

   • If re-using double joint clean threads of pinch bolt holes to remove any thread lock residue.

   • Replace pinch bolts.

   • Pinch bolts must rest in groves of steering rack and lower steering column.

   • Carry out steering angle sensor adjustment using BMW scan tool. If replacing steering angle sensor, code using BMW scan tool before performing steering angle offset check.

Tightening torque	
Double joint to steering rack (replace pinch bolt)	22 Nm (16 ft-lb)
Double joint to lower steering column (replace pinch bolt)	28 Nm (21 ft-lb)

Lower steering column, removing and installing

> **CAUTION—**
> • When the double joint is separated from the steering column / steering rack, the steering wheel is free to spin. Once separated, lock the steering wheel in position. Otherwise the MRS contact reel (coil of wire) could be damaged.

— Raise front of car and remove front left wheel.

> **WARNING—**
> • Make sure vehicle is stable and well supported at all times. Use a professional automotive lift or jack stands. A floor jack is not adequate support.

— It may be necessary to rotate steering wheel to access pinch bolts.

◄ Working in engine compartment near rear bulkhead, release pinch bolt (**arrow**) at universal joint between upper and lower steering column.

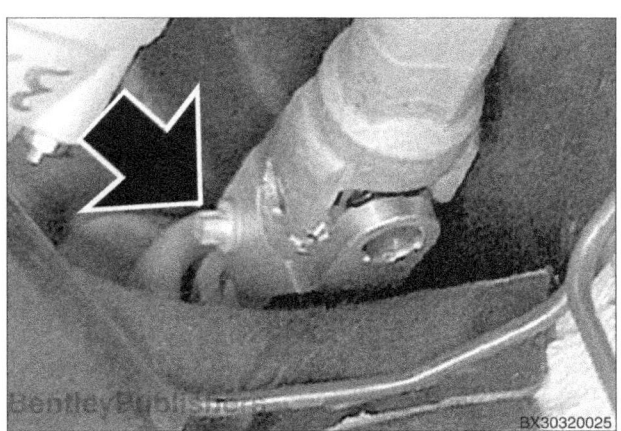

— Move steering wheel and front wheels to straight ahead position. Remove ignition key to lock steering wheel.

◄ Release pinch bolt (**B**) on double joint at lower steering column.

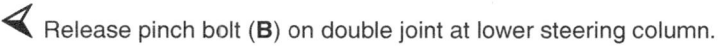

• Pull lower steering column (**A**) out of double joint and remove.

— Installation:

• Clean threads of pinch bolt holes to remove any thread lock residue.

• Replace pinch bolts.

• Pinch bolts must rest in groves of upper steering column and lower steering column.

• Carry out steering angle sensor calibration using a BMW diagnostic scan tool. If replacing steering angle sensor, code using BMW diagnostic scan tool before performing steering calibration.

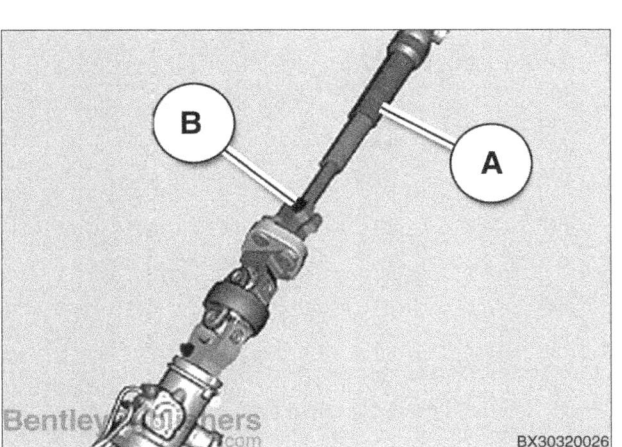

Tightening torque	
Lower steering column universal joint to upper steering column (replace pinch bolt)	22 Nm (16 ft-lb)
Lower steering column to double joint (replace pinch bolt)	28 Nm (21 ft-lb)

Upper steering column, removing and installing

— Remove lower section of steering column. See **Lower steering column, removing and installing** in this repair group.

— Remove trim above pedal assembly. See **513 Interior Trim**.

— Remove upper and lower steering column cover. See **513 Interior Trim**.

— Move steering wheel as far back and as low as possible.

— Disconnect negative (-) battery cable.

> **CAUTION—**
> • *Prior to disconnecting the battery, read the battery disconnection cautions given in* **001 Warnings and Cautions**.

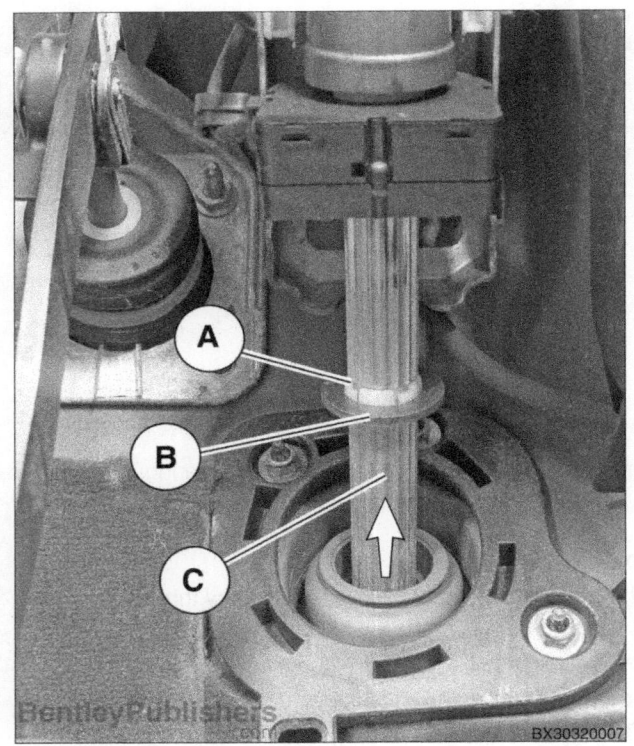

◄ Working under dashboard, press crash disc (**B**) of off crash sleeve (**A**).

  • Open crash sleeve (**A**) slightly and remove from upper steering column spindle.

— Slide steering spindle (**C**) into steering column.

— Installation: Replace crash sleeve.

— Remove steering wheel. See **Steering wheel, removing and installing** in this repair group.

— Remove steering column stalk switch assembly. See **612 Switches**.

— Disconnect ignition interlock cable from steering column. See **250 Gearshift Linkage**.

BX30320007

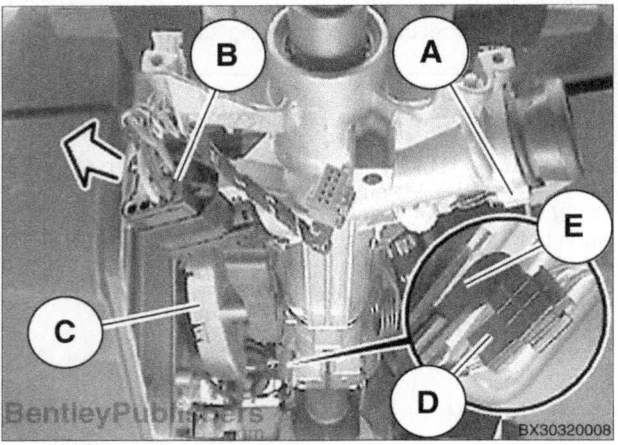

◄ Disconnect electrical connections (**A**) and (**B**).

  • Remove wiring harness from cable duct (**C**).

— Turn holder (**E**) approximately 45° down and remove to disconnect electrical connection (**D**).

BX30320008

◀ Remove mounting bolts (**arrows**) from upper part of steering column support frame.

◀ With an assistant helping to support steering column, remove mounting nuts (**arrows**) at bottom of steering column support frame.

– Installation is reverse of removal, noting the following:
  • Make sure interlock cable snaps into place.

Tightening torque	
Steering column to instrument panel support tube	21 Nm (15 ft-lb)
Bearing block of steering column to bulkhead (replace nuts)	21.4 Nm (16 ft-lb)

– Check steering for freedom of movement through entire steering column adjustment range.

– Carry out steering angle sensor calibration using a BMW diagnostic scan tool. If replacing steering angle sensor, code using BMW diagnostic scan tool before performing steering calibration.

Steering angle sensor, removing and installing

– Remove trim above pedal assembly, See **513 Interior Trim**.

– Disconnect lower steering column from upper steering column. See **Steering column, removing and installing** in this repair group.

> *CAUTION—*
> • *When the lower steering column is separated from the upper steering column, the steering wheel is free to spin. Once separated, lock the steering wheel in position. Otherwise the MRS contact reel (coil of wire) could be damaged.*

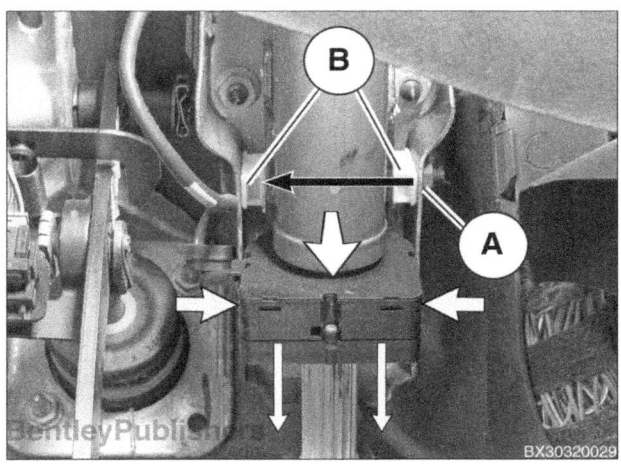

◀ Remove nut (**A**) and slide bolt out of steering column and bushings (**B**).

– Pull steering column down toward the floor.

320

Power steering system, bleeding and filling

— Remove crash sleeve with crash disc from upper steering column spindle and slide steering spindle into steering column. See **Upper steering column, removing and installing**.

— Pinch tabs on steering angle sensor (**arrows**) and slide down steering column spindle to remove.

— Trace electrical wire for steering angle sensor back to plug and disconnect.

— Installation is reverse of removal, noting the following:

  • Check steering system for freedom of movement through entire steering column adjustment range.

  • Replace crash sleeve.

  • Code steering angle sensor using BMW diagnostic scan tool before performing steering calibration.

Tightening torque	
Steering column to steering column support • M6 through bolt	9 Nm (80 in-lb)
Lower steering column universal joint to upper steering column (replace pinch bolt)	22 Nm (16 ft-lb)

POWER STEERING PUMP

Power assist is provided by a belt-driven pump at the lower left front of the engine. The power steering fluid reservoir is located at the left side of the engine compartment.

Power steering system, bleeding and filling

◄ With engine off, fill power steering fluid reservoir with clean fluid. Fill level to MAX mark on dip stick.

— Start engine. Turn steering wheel twice to left lock and right lock.

— Recheck fluid level with engine off. Fill to MAX.

NOTE—

• *The type of power steering fluid used is marked on the power steering reservoir cap. Most X3s use CHF 11S hydraulic fluid. Some early cars may use ATF. Refer to reservoir cap for proper fluid type.*

Power steering pump, removing and installing (M54 engine)

— Drain power steering fluid reservoir using clean syringe. Do not reuse fluid.

— Raise front of car and remove left front wheel.

> **WARNING—**
> • *Make sure vehicle is stable and well supported at all times. Use a professional automotive lift or jack stands. A floor jack is not adequate support.*

— Remove splash shield from under engine. See **020 Maintenance**.

— Remove accessory belt from power steering pump. See **020 Maintenance**. Mark direction of rotation if reusing belt.

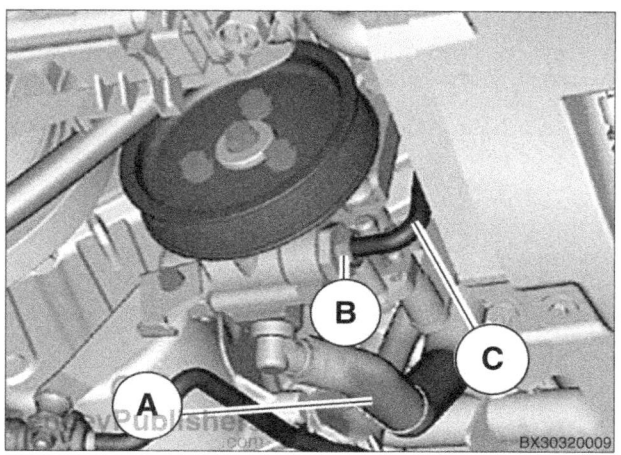

◀ Working under vehicle, detach fluid hoses from pump. Be prepared to catch dripping fluid.

• Remove clamp from suction hose (**A**) detach from pump.

• Remove pressure fitting (**B**) remove pressure line (**C**).

• Plug openings in pump and hose ends to prevent contamination.

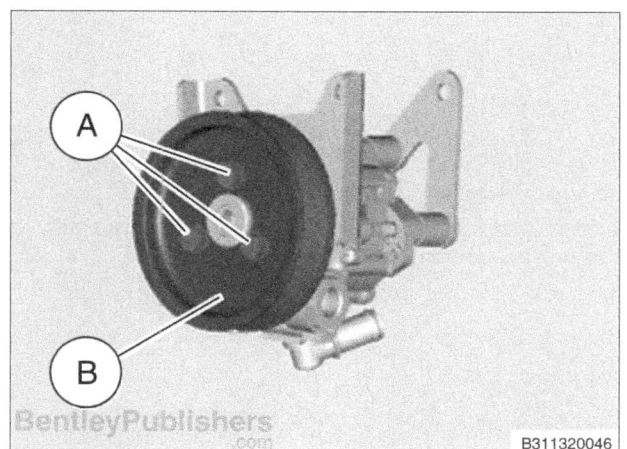

◀ Working at front of pump, remove fasteners (**A**) and remove power steering pulley (**B**) from pump.

— Remove idler pulley from alternator. See **121 Battery, Starter and Alternator**.

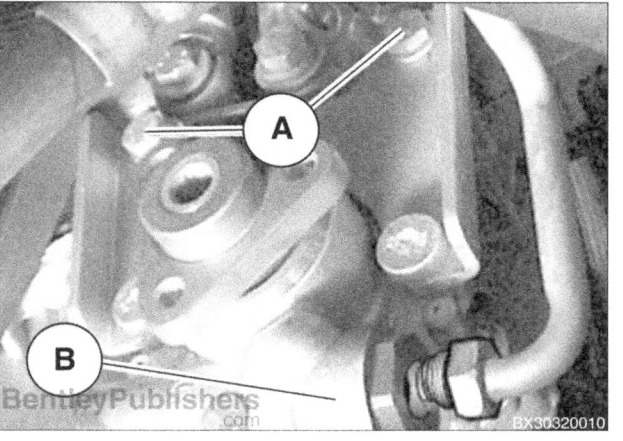

◀ Remove pump mounting bolts (**A**), noting any spacers or shims present. Remove pump (**B**) from engine compartment.

— Installation is reverse of removal. Replace pressure fitting seal and hose clamp on fluid lines.

— Fill and bleed power steering system. See **Power steering system, bleeding and filling** in this repair group.

Tightening torques	
Fluid pressure line to steering pump (banjo bolts, replace seal)	35 Nm (26 ft-lb)
Power steering pump bracket to engine block	21 Nm (15 ft-lb)
Belt pulley to power steering pump (M8)	28 Nm (21 ft-lb)

320

Power steering pump, removing and installing (N52 engine)

— Drain power steering fluid reservoir using clean syringe. Do not reuse fluid.

— Raise front of car.

> **WARNING—**
> • *Make sure vehicle is stable and well supported at all times. Use a professional automotive lift or jack stands. A floor jack is not adequate support.*

— Remove intake filter housing. See **131 Fuel injection**.

— Remove accessory belt from power steering pump.
See **020 Maintenance**. Mark direction of rotation if reusing belt.

◀ Working at front of pump, remove fasteners (**A**) and remove power steering pulley (**B**) from pump.

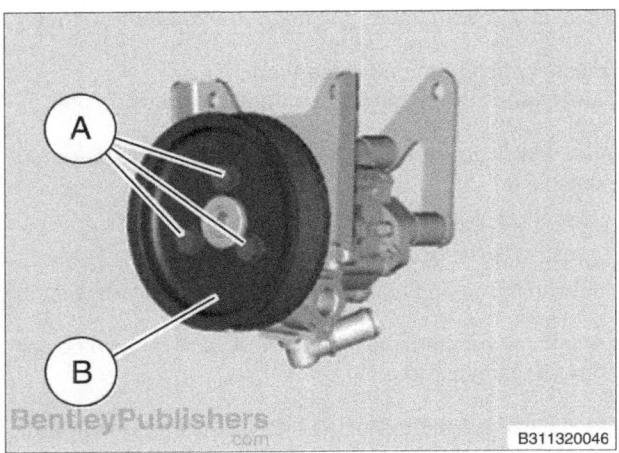

◀ Working inside engine compartment, detach hose clamp (**A**) and remove fluid suction hose (**B**) from pump.

• Be prepared to catch dripping fluid. Plug opening in pump and hose end to prevent contamination.

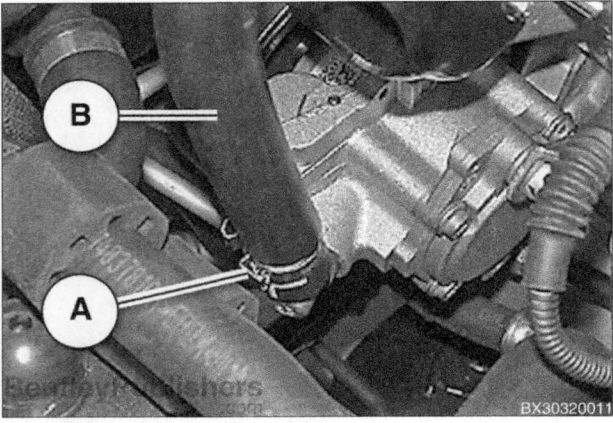

◀ Working at diver's side of engine block, remove pump mounting bolts (**A**).

— Remove splash shield from under engine. See **020 Maintenance**.

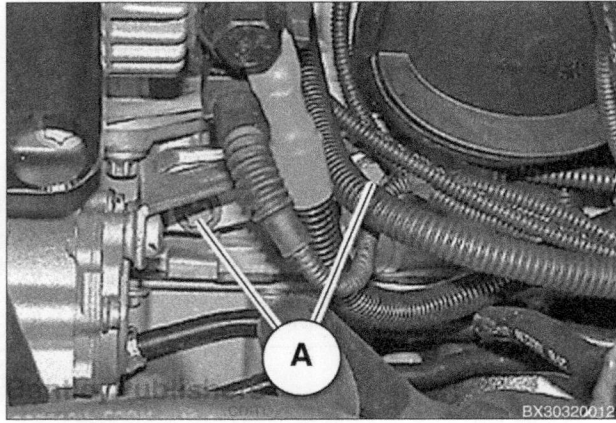

Servotronic (EH) converter, removing and installing

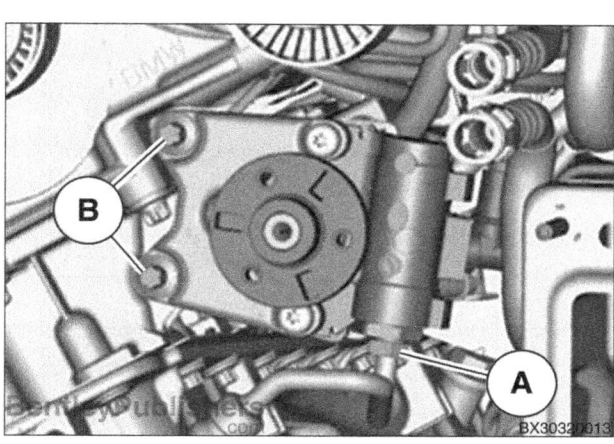

◄ Remove pressure fitting (**A**) remove pressure line.

– Remove pump mounting bolts (**B**), noting any spacers or shims present. Remove pump from engine compartment.

– When installing:
  • Make sure all thread bores, bolts, nuts, fluid couplings and mating surfaces are clean.
  • Use new sealing rings when reattaching power steering lines.
  • Make sure hoses have adequate clearance from chassis.
  • Use new aluminum fasteners and install pump according to torque sequence.
  1. Tighten all power steering pump fasteners to 2 Nm (18 in-lb).
  2. Tighten bolts on front of power steering pump to engine block according to torque spec and angle.
  3. Release fasteners on side of power steering pump and check for freedom of movement.
  4. Tighten bolts on side of power steering pump to engine block according to torque spec and angle.

Tightening torques	
Fluid pressure line to steering pump (banjo bolts, replace seals)	35 Nm (26 ft-lb)
Power steering pump bracket to engine block (M10 aluminum bolts, replace with new) • Stage 1 • Stage 2 • Stage 3	2 Nm (18 in-lb) 20 Nm (15 ft-lb) additional 90°
Belt pulley to power steering pump (M8)	28 Nm (21 ft-lb)

– Fill and bleed power steering. See **Power steering system, bleeding and filling** in this repair group.

Servotronic (EH) converter, removing and installing

The servotronic control unit is located behind glove box. See **ECL Electrical Component Locations.** The servotronic electro hydraulic (EH) converter is mounted to the steering rack.

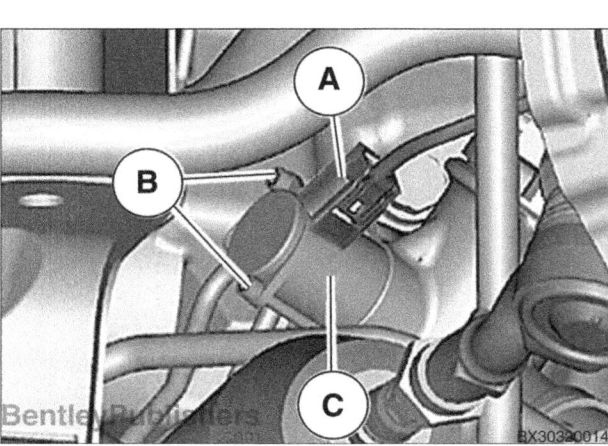

◄ Disconnect electric connection (**A**) on EH converter (**C**).

– Remove fasteners (**B**), and pull EH converter (**C**) out of steering rack. Be prepared to catch dripping fluid. Cover EH converter opening to prevent dirt from entering the system.

– Installation:
  • Align EH converter with steering gear when installing and press in until EH converter bottoms out.
  • Insert fasteners and tighten.
  • Fill and bleed power steering system. See **Power steering system, bleeding and filling** in this repair group.

Tightening torques	
Servotronic converter to power steering rack	3 Nm (26.5 in-lb)

MECHANICAL STEERING COMPONENTS

Steering rack, removing and installing

– Drain power steering fluid reservoir using clean syringe. Do not reuse fluid.

– Raise front of car and remove front wheels.

> **WARNING—**
> • *Make sure vehicle is stable and well supported at all times. Use a professional automotive lift or jack stands. A floor jack is not adequate support.*

– Remove splash shield from under engine. See **020 Maintenance.**

– Remove front end reinforcement plate. See **310 Front Suspension**.

– Remove outer tie rod ends. See **Outer tie rod ends, replacing** in this repair group.

– Remove stabilizer bar links from stabilizer bar. See **310 Front Suspension**.

◀ Remove double universal joint lower pinch bolt (**A**) and disengage from power steering rack.

> **CAUTION—**
> • *When the double joint is separated from the steering column / steering rack, the steering wheel is free to spin. Once separated, lock the steering wheel in position. Otherwise the MRS contact reel (coil of wire) could be damaged.*

– For servotronic equipped vehicles, remove electro hydraulic converter. See **Servotronic (EH) converter, removing and installing** in this repair group.

◀ Remove quick connect high pressure fittings (**A**) on power steering rack by turning and pushing inwards according to **arrows**.

– Remove line while pressing down on cap at same time.
  • Be prepared to catch dripping power steering fluid.

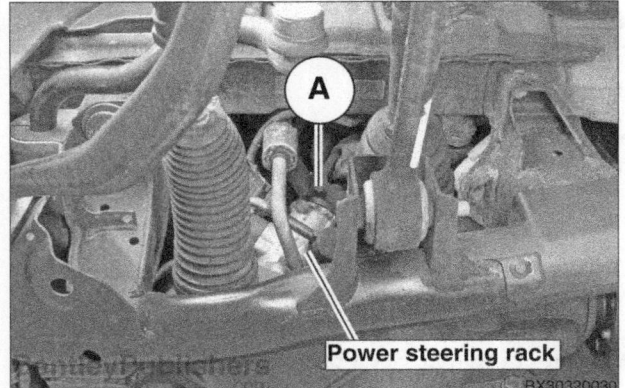

Power steering rack

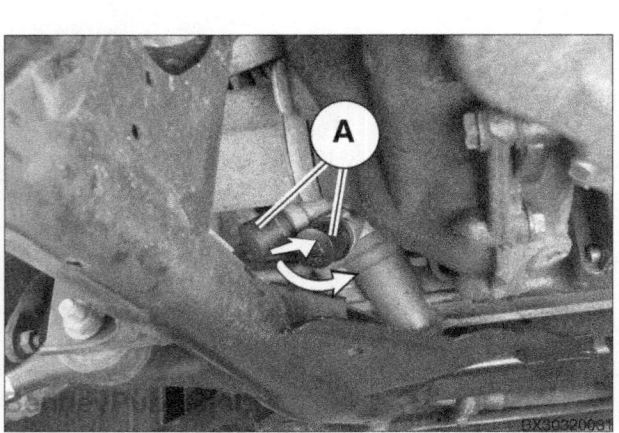

Steering rack, removing and installing

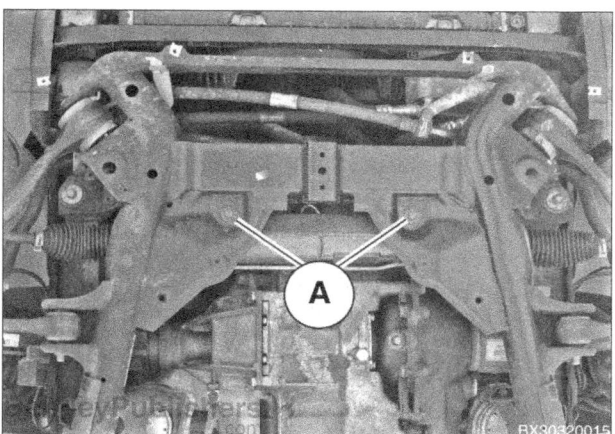

◄ Unbolt steering rack mounting Torx fasteners (**A**). Counterhold nuts above rack. Discard fasteners.

— If needed remove pressure line from front subframe.

— Twist left steering knuckle to the left.

— Slide steering rack to left side to remove, watching carefully to make sure no fluid lines or electrical harnesses are snagged.

— Installation is reverse of removal, keeping in mind the following:
  • Make sure all thread bores, bolts, nuts, splines and mating surfaces are clean.
  • Make sure power steering fluid lines are routed without tension and with sufficient spacing to nearby components.
  • Use new steering rack mounting bolts.
  • Replace steering spindle double joint with flex disc pinch bolt(s).
  • Use new self-locking fasteners wherever applicable.

Tightening torques	
Road wheel to hub	140 Nm (103 ft-lb)
Double joint to steering rack (replace pinch bolt)	22 Nm (16 ft-lb)
Steering rack to front subframe (replace Torx bolts and self-locking nuts)	100 Nm (74 ft-lb)
Tie rod to steering knuckle (replace nut with new)	80 Nm (59 ft-lb)

— Rotate steering wheel and check that steering spindle and steering double universal joint do not contact vehicle chassis or front subframe.

— After reassembling steering and front suspension:
  • Fill and bleed power steering. See **Power steering system, bleeding and filling** in this repair group.
  • Have car professionally aligned.
  • Carry out steering angle sensor calibration using BMW diagnostic scan tool.

320

Steering rack boot, replacing

– Raise front of car and remove front wheels.

> **WARNING—**
> • Make sure vehicle is stable and well supported at all times. Use a professional automotive lift or jack stands. A floor jack is not adequate support.

– Make length reference mark on tie rod, then remove outer tie rod end. See **Tie rod (outer), replacing**, in this repair group.

◀ Cut or remove steering rack boot band clamps (**A**) and slide off boot.

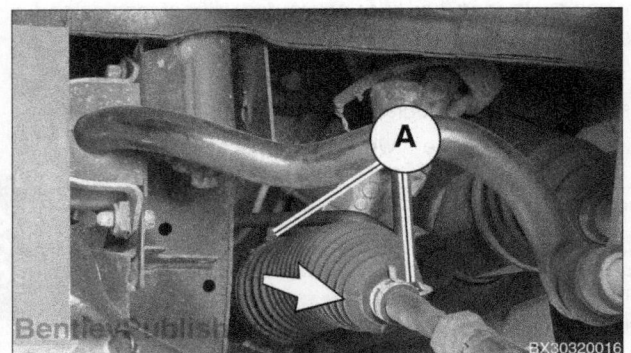

> **NOTE—**
> • New rack boot kit comes with new band clamps.

– Grease tie rod taper so that small end of rack boot slides on tie rod when tie rod is tightened, preventing rack boot from twisting.

– Slide new boot into position and replace band clamps. Reinstall tie rod end using previously made reference marks.

Tightening torques	
Tie rod end to tie rod (lock nut)	51 Nm (38 ft-lb)
Tie rod to steering knuckle (use new nut)	80 Nm (59 ft-lb)

– After reassembling steering:
  • Have car professionally aligned.
  • Carry out steering angle sensor calibration using BMW diagnostic scan tool.

Tie rod (outer), replacing

– Raise front of car and remove front wheels.

> **WARNING—**
> • Make sure vehicle is stable and well supported at all times. Use a professional automotive lift or jack stands. A floor jack is not adequate support.

◀ Make reference measurement (**A**) of outer tie rod end to tie rod. Record measurement.

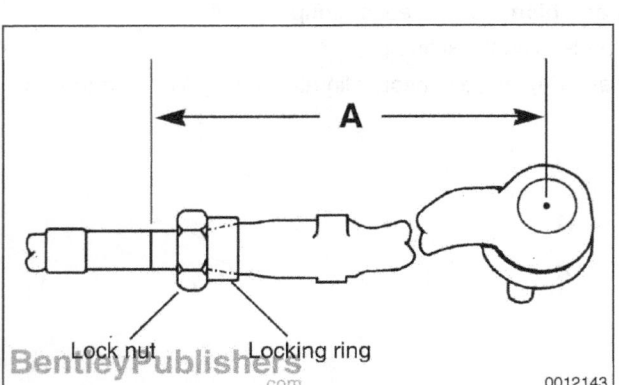

Lock nut   Locking ring

> **NOTE—**
> • Accurate measurement of tie rod end with reference to tie rod helps approximate correct wheel alignment when new parts are installed.
> • Note correct placement of inner taper on locking ring.

Tie rod (outer), replacing

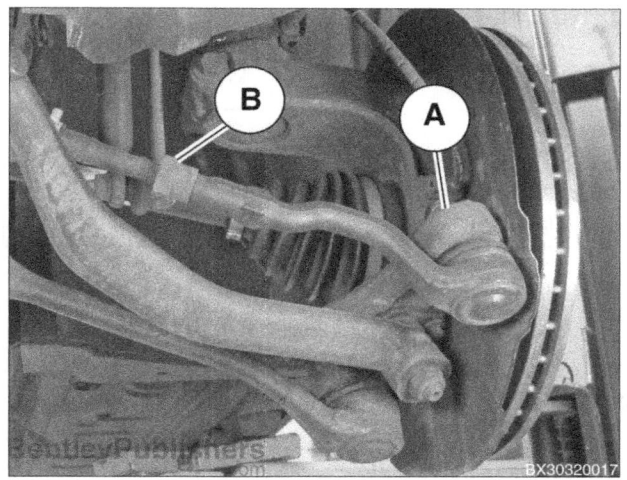

◀ Working at outer end of tie rod:

• Remove tie rod ball join lock nut (**A**) at steering knuckle.

• Loosen tie rod adjustment lock nut (**B**).

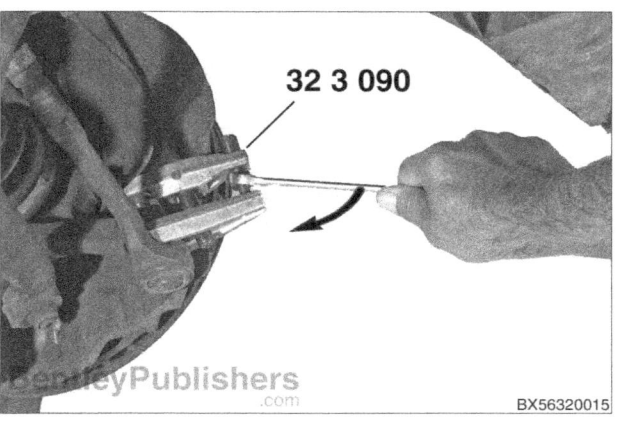

◀ Use BMW special tool 32 3 090 or equivalent to press tie rod end out of steering knuckle.

— Unscrew tie rod end from tie rod shaft.

— Installation is reverse of removal.

• Make sure threaded parts are clean.

• Use anti-seize paste on inner tie rod threads.

• Use new self-locking nuts where applicable.

• Use previously made reference marks to set toe temporarily.

Tightening torques	
Tie rod end to tie rod (lock nut)	51 Nm (38 ft-lb)
Tie rod to steering knuckle (use new nut)	80 Nm (59 ft-lb)

— After reassembling steering:

• Have car professionally aligned.

• Carry out steering angle sensor adjustment using BMW scan tool.

Tie rod (inner), replacing

— Raise front of car. Remove road wheel.

> **WARNING—**
> • *Make sure vehicle is stable and well supported at all times. Use a professional automotive lift or jack stands. A floor jack is not adequate support.*

— Make length reference mark on tie rod, then remove outer tie rod end. See **Tie rod (outer), replacing**, in this repair group.

— Cut or remove steering rack boot clamps and slide boot off. See **Steering rack book, replacing**, in this repair group.

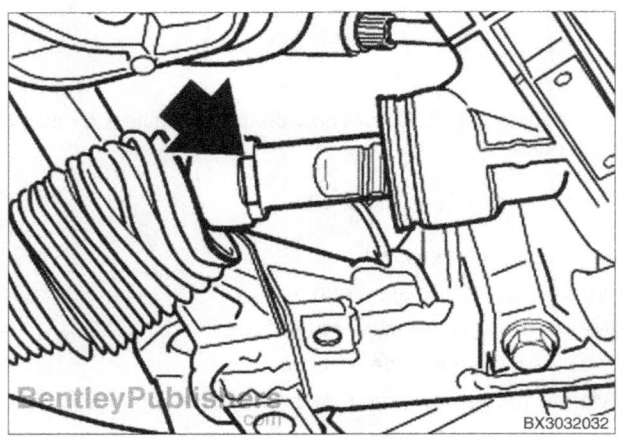

◄ Loosen and remove inner tie rod joint (**arrow**) shaft from steering rack.

> **CAUTION—**
> • *To avoid damage to steering rack while removing tie rod, turn steering until end of rack is as far as possible inside rack housing.*

— When reassembling, grease tie rod taper so that rack boot support buffer or small end of rack boot slides on tie rod when tie rod is tightened, preventing rack boot from twisting.

— Inspect boot for any signs of damage. Replace boot if necessary, using new band clamps.

> **NOTE—**
> • *New rack boot comes with new band clamps.*

— Installation is reverse of removal, noting the following:
  • Make sure threaded parts are clean.
  • Use anti-seize paste on inner tie rod threads.
  • Use new self-locking nuts where applicable.
  • Use previously made reference marks to set toe temporarily.

Tightening torques	
Tie rod adjustment lock nut	51 Nm (38 ft-lb)
Tie rod to steering knuckle (use new nut)	80 Nm (59 ft-lb)
Tie rod to steering rack	110 Nm (81 ft-lb)

— After reassembling steering:
  • Have car professionally aligned.
  • Carry out steering angle sensor adjustment using BMW scan tool.

WHEEL ALIGNMENT

The front axle is aligned in relation to the rear axle, then the front wheels are aligned in relation to one another. This is known as a four-wheel or thrust-axis alignment. BMW X3 vehicles use a sophisticated multi-link suspension at the front and rear of the car. Proper alignment requires computerized alignment equipment.

Preparing for alignment

The following conditions are necessary prior to wheel alignment:

• Correct wheels and tires in good condition and inflated correctly.

• Steering and suspension parts and bushings undamaged and showing no signs of abnormal wear.

• Wheel bearings in good condition.

• Ride height in accordance with specifications. See **Ride height** in this repair group.

• Vehicle in normal loaded position.

BMW defines vehicle normal loaded position as follows.

Normal loaded position	
Each front seat	68 Kg (150 lb)
Center of rear seat	68 Kg (150 lb)
Cargo compartment	21 Kg (46 lb)
Fuel tank	Full

Front toe, setting

Set front toe before adjusting camber. Camber and toe influence each other. Toe is the difference in the distance between the front of the wheels and the rear of the wheels. It is adjusted by altering the length of the tie rods.

Make toe adjustments with vehicle in normal loaded position. See **Preparing for alignment** in this repair group.

− Clean threads on tie rod.

◄ Loosen tie rod adjuster lock nut (**arrow**).

• Adjust toe by turning inner tie rod to change length.

NOTE—

• *Center steering rack by aligning centering mark on steering shaft with lug on steering rack.*

• *To keep steering wheel centered, adjust both tie rods equal amounts.*

• *Make sure the rack boot moves freely on the tie rod and does not become twisted.*

Tightening torque	
Tie rod adjustment lock nut	51 Nm (38 ft-lb)

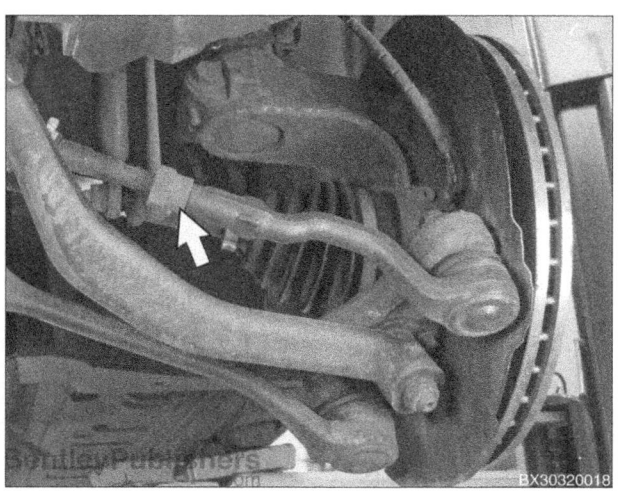

BX30320018

320

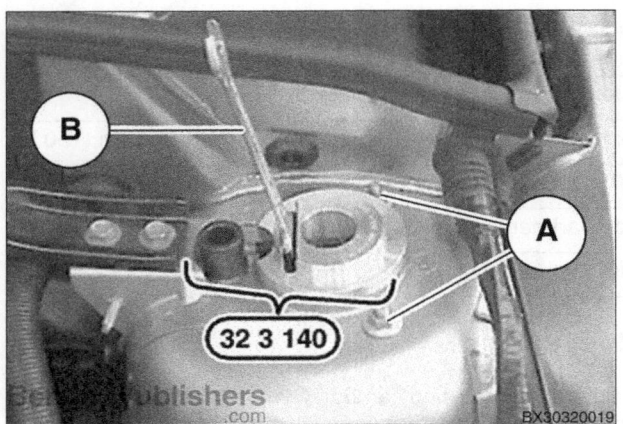

Front camber, adjusting

Set front toe before adjusting camber. Camber and toe influence each other. Camber is the deviation of each wheel from vertical. If necessary, adjust camber by removing front strut top centering pin.

> **CAUTION—**
> • *Do not attempt to correct accident-related alignment deviations by adjusting the camber.*

◄ Working at strut top bearing in engine compartment:
- Remove centering pin (**A**).
- Loosen strut top bearing mounting nut (**arrow**) 1 - 1½ turns.

— Raise vehicle until wheels are off ground. Support vehicle safely.

— Working below vehicle, use compressed air to clean off debris in wheel housing near strut top bearing.

◄ Fit BMW special tool 33 3 140 over inboard strut top nut.
- Replace outboard strut top bearing nuts (**A**). Reinstall finger tight.
- Lower vehicle on alignment rack and bounce vehicle to make sure suspension is in loaded position and free from tension.
- Turn nut with wrench (**B**) in special tool to adjust camber to specified value.
- Tighten down outboard strut top mounting nuts (**A**).
- Remove special tool and replace inboard strut top mounting nut.

Tightening torque	
Strut top bearing to chassis (replace with new)	34 Nm (25 ft-lb)

— Check directional stability of vehicle. If necessary, reset toe. See **Front toe, setting**.

Rear camber, adjusting

Adjust rear camber before setting toe. A camber change means a toe change as well. Camber is the deviation of each wheel from vertical.

— Raise vehicle and support safely.

— Working underneath rear suspension near rear knuckle:
- Replace nut (**B**) on swing arm eccentric bolt. Tighten to 5 Nm (finger tight).
- Lower vehicle on alignment rack and use eccentric bolt (**A**) to adjust camber (**curved arrow**).
- Tighten swing arm eccentric bolt to specification with vehicle in normal loaded position.

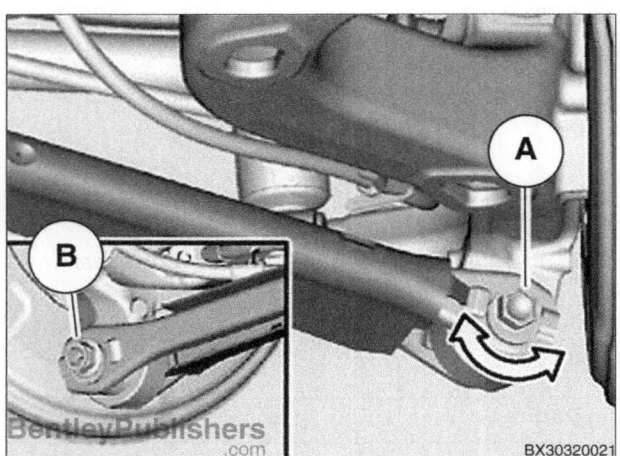

Tightening torque	
Swing arm eccentric fastener to rear subframe (replace nut, tighten with suspension loaded)	100 Nm (74 ft-lb)

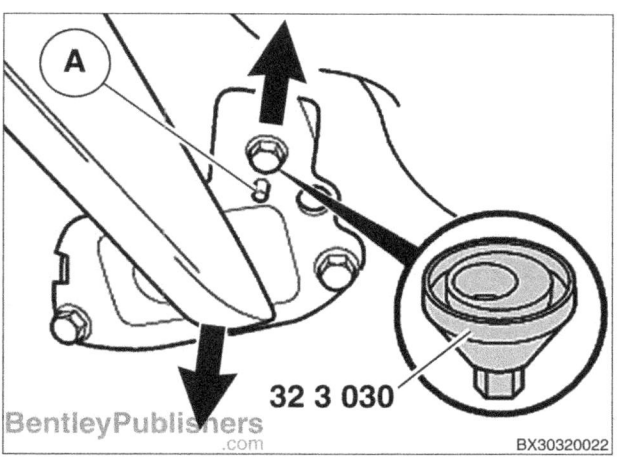

32 3 030

BentleyPublishers
.com

BX30320022

Rear toe, setting

Adjust rear camber before setting toe. A camber change means a toe change as well. Toe is the difference in the distance between the front of the wheels and the rear of the wheels.

◀ Working at upper trailing arm where it attaches to vehicle body:

- Loosen bolts on bearing block approximately 1 to 1.5 turns.
- Attach BMW special tool 32 3 330 to bolt head and pin (**A**).
- Turn special tool to adjust toe to desired value and tighten down bolts.

Tightening torque	
Trailing arm to rear body (tighten with suspension loaded)	77 Nm (57 ft-lb)

Caster

Front and rear caster are fixed and deviations are usually the result of worn or damaged suspension or body parts.

— Check front suspension arms and bushings for wear, damage and deformation if front caster problems are present.

— Check rear axle subframe and traction struts if rear caster problems are present.

Ride height

◀ Measure ride height (**A**) from center of fender arch to bottom of wheel rim.

- Car in normal loaded position on the ground. See **Preparing for alignment**.
- Specified tires and wheels, correct tire pressure, even tire wear.
- No play in wheel bearings.

— If ride height is outside specification listed, install new springs. Suspension spring removal and installation is covered in **310 Front Suspension** and **330 Rear Suspension**.

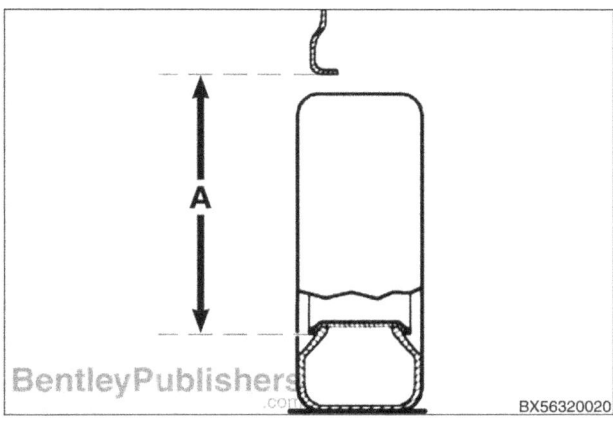

BentleyPublishers
.com

BX56320020

Table a. Ride height (measurement A)		
Wheel size	Front ride height in mm (in)	Rear ride height in mm (in)
17 inch	686 (27.01)	673 (26.49)
18 inch	699 (27.50)	685 (26.96)
19 inch	711 (27.99)	698 (27.48)
Maximum combined deviation from specification: 10 mm (0.4 in)		

NOTE—

- *Due to fender shape or model variation, ride height may vary by 1 mm (0.04 in) from specifications.*
- *These specifications do not apply to "low-slung" vehicles.*

Alignment specifications

Table b. X3 Alignment specifications	
Parameter	**Specification**
Front axle	
Total toe	0° 6' ± 12'
Adjustment total toe	0° 6' ± 4'
Toe angle (difference between left / right maximum)	30'
Camber (difference between left / right maximum 30')	- 20' ± 30'
Adjustment camber	- 20' ± 25'
Front caster (difference between left / right maximum 30'):	
With ± 20° wheel lock	2° 16' ± 30'
Front wheel displacement	0° ± 15'
Maximum wheel lock	
Inside wheel (approx.)	38°
Outside wheel (approx.)	31°
Rear axle	
Total toe	0° 16' ± 12'
Adjustment total toe	0° 16' ± 4'
Camber (difference between left / right maximum 15'):	-2° 00' ± 25'
Adjustment camber	-2° 00' ± 5'
Geometrical axis deviation	0° ± 12'

330 Rear Suspension

330

GENERAL

This repair group covers removal and replacement of E83 rear suspension components. For related information see:

- **300 Suspension, Steering and Brakes–General** for a general description of the E83 suspension.
- **320 Steering and Wheel Alignment** for ride height and alignment specifications.

Special service tools are required for some of the work described in this repair group. Most of these tools are specialized press jigs and pullers that may be replaced by standard pullers of various sizes. Read the procedures through before beginning any job.

Rear suspension description

◄ The X3 uses an independent rear suspension consisting of an upper and a lower control arm and a trailing arm on each side. The weight of the vehicle is supported by coil springs. There is a rear stabilizer bar attached to the upper control arms. Gas-pressure shock absorbers round out the rear suspension.

The rear subframe (final drive carrier) supports the rear differential and provides mounting points for the upper and lower control arms. The upper control arm on each side provides the lower spring perch for the coil spring. The upper and lower control arm on each side are attached to the trailing arm. Wheel bearings and drive hubs are pressed into trailing arms. Rear brake calipers are bolted to the trailing arms. Two tension arms provide additional mounts to the rear body (not shown in image).

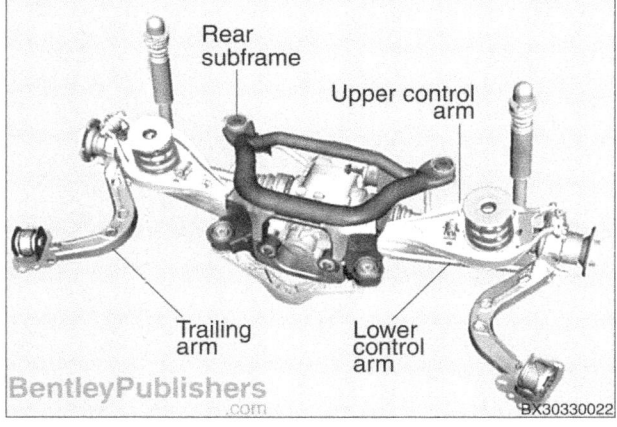

Rear subframe

Upper control arm

Trailing arm

Lower control arm

BX30330022

Warnings and Cautions

> **WARNING—**
> • Do not reuse self-locking nuts, bolts or fasteners. They are designed to be used only once and may fail if reused. Replace them with new self-locking fasteners.

> **CAUTION—**
> • E83 models are equipped with some aluminum suspension components. The following cautions apply:
> -Due to the chemical and corrosion characteristics of aluminum, do not bring into contact with battery acid.
> -Do not clean with wire brushes with brass or iron bristles. Only use brushes with stainless steel bristles.
> -Do not expose to flying sparks from grinding / cutting operations.
> -Do not subject to steel welding splashes.
> -Do not expose to temperatures over 80°C (176°F), even for short periods. Temperatures in painting facilities are not a problem.

REAR SHOCK ABSORBERS AND SPRINGS

Rear shock absorber and spring components

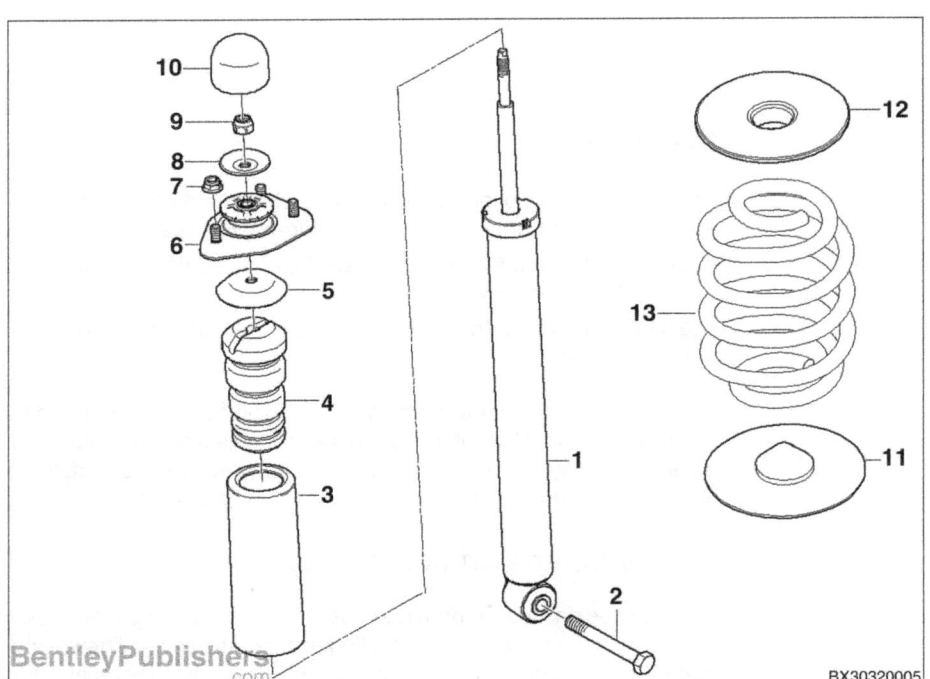

BX30320005

1. Rear shock absorber
2. Lower bolt with washer (M12x1 5x 63-10.9)
3. Dust cover
4. Bump stop
5. Bump stop plate
6. Shock absorber mounting plate
7. Self locking collar nut (M8)
8. Mounting plate washer
9. Self locking nut for shock piston (M10)
10. Dust cap
11. Lower spring pad
12. Upper spring pad
13. Coil spring

Rear shock absorber, removing and installing

— Replace shock absorbers in pairs only.

— Remove cargo area trim. See **513 Interior Trim**.

— Raise vehicle and remove rear wheels.

> **WARNING —**
> • Make sure vehicle is stable and well supported at all times. Use a professional automotive lift or jack stands. A floor jack is not adequate support.

◀ Support trailing arm from below using an adjustable jack stand. Remove shock absorber lower mounting bolt (**arrow**).

> **CAUTION—**
> • The shock absorber prevents the drive axle from dropping too far. Support the trailing arm before removing the lower shock absorber bolt to avoid damage to drive axle CV joints.

— Working in cargo area, open sound proofing insulation and remove dust cap.

◀ Support shock absorber from below while removing upper mounting nuts (**arrows**). Remove shock absorber out of wheel housing.

— Transfer shock absorber mounting plate, dust cover, bump stop and related components to new shock absorber. Inspect for damage and replace if necessary.

— Installation is reverse of removal, noting the following:
  • Make sure all threaded bolts, nuts and mating surfaces are clean.
  • Install shock absorber mounting plate to body using new self-locking nuts.
  • Tighten fasteners to final torque only after vehicle has been lowered and suspension has settled.
  • Check that rear drive axle is seated in differential.

Tightening torques	
Road wheel to hub	140 Nm (103 ft-lb)
Shock absorber piston to shock mounting plate (M10 replace self-licking nut)	14 Nm (10 ft-lb)
Shock absorber to trailing arm	100 Nm (74 ft-lb)
Shock absorber mounting plate to body. (M8, replace self-locking nut)	24 Nm (18 ft-lb)

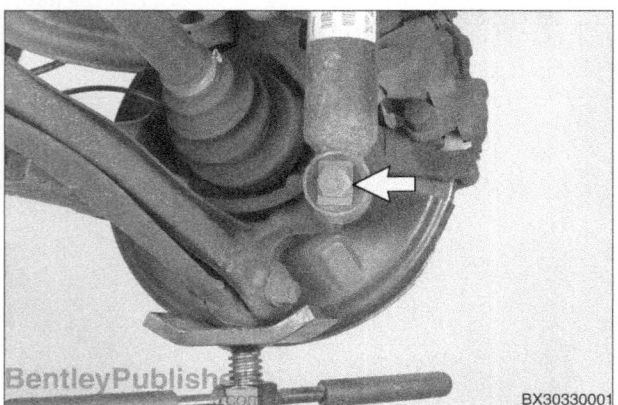

Coil spring, removing and installing

Replace coil springs in pairs only and replace spring pads at the same time.

– Raise vehicle and remove rear wheels.

> **WARNING—**
> • *Make sure vehicle is stable and well supported at all times. Use a professional automotive lift or jack stands. A floor jack is not adequate support.*

◄ Remove drive axle to differential mounting bolts (**arrows**).
  • Detach drive axle from differential.
  • Suspend drive axle from chassis using stiff wire.

◄ Remove stabilizer bar link from stabilizer bar (**arrow**).

– When working on passenger side, remove rod (**A**) for right height sensor.

◄ Remove rear brake line bracket mounting bolt (**arrow**). Detach bracket from trailing arm.

> **CAUTION—**
> • *Avoid damaging the brake hose by stretching when the trailing arm is lowered.*

◄ Support trailing arm from below using jack stand. Remove shock absorber lower mounting bolt (**arrow**).

– Lower jack stand slowly to relieve coil spring tension and remove spring from mounting position.

– Installation is reverse of removal.

Tightening torques	
Road wheel to hub	140 Nm (103 ft-lb)
Brake line bracket to trailing arm (M6)	9 Nm (80 in-lb)
Shock absorber to trailing arm	100 Nm (74 ft-lb)

Coil spring, removing and installing

REAR SUSPENSION ARMS AND BUSHINGS

A damaged suspension arm or worn bushings will alter the rear wheel alignment and may adversely affect handling and stability.

> **WARNING** —
> • Do not attempt to straighten a damaged suspension arms. Bending or heating may weaken the original part. Always replace a damaged suspension arm.

Suspension arm and bushing components

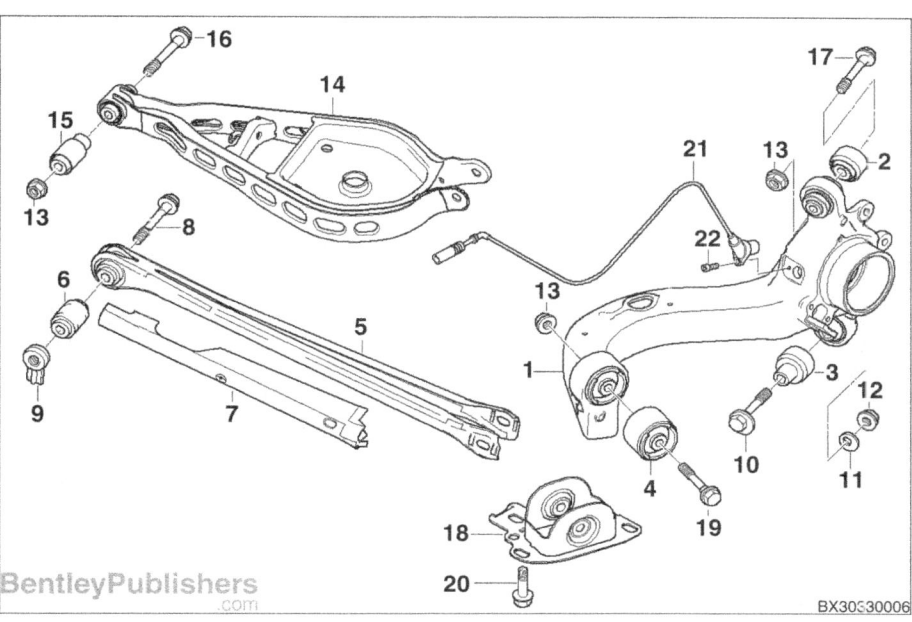

BX30330006

1. Trailing arm
2. Upper trailing arm bushing (ball joint)
3. Lower trailing arm bushing
4. Front trailing arm bushing
5. Lower control arm
6. Lower control arm bushing
7. Lower control arm plastic cover
8. Lower control arm bolt (M12)
   • Tighten with suspension in normal loaded position
9. Lock plate
10. Eccentric bolt (M12x1.5x81-10.9)
11. Eccentric flat washer (A12)
12. Nut (M12x1.5)
    • Always replace
    • Tighten with suspension in normal loaded position
13. Self locking collar nut M12x1.5)
    • Always replace
    • Tighten with suspension in normal loaded position
14. Upper control arm with spring seat
15. Upper control arm bushing
16. Bolt with washer (M12x1.5x88-10.9)
17. Collar bolt (M12x1.5x80 ZNS)
18. Trailing arm mounting bracket
19. Collar bolt (M12x1.5x70-10.9)
20. Collar bolt (M12x1.5x43 ZNS)
21. ABS rear wheel speed pulse sensor

330

Trailing arm, removing and installing

— Raise vehicle and remove rear wheels.

> **WARNING—**
> • *Make sure vehicle is stable and well supported at all times. Use a professional automotive lift or jack stands. A floor jack is not adequate support.*

— Remove rear underbody splash shields as applicable.

— Remove coil spring, see **Coil spring, removing and installing** in this repair group.

— Remove stabilizer bar links, see **Stabilizer bar, removing and installing** in this repair group.

— Remove drive axle. See **311 Rear Axle Final Drive**.

— Remove brake caliper, rotor and parking brake cable. See **340 Brakes**. Do not remove brake line from caliper. Suspend caliper from body using stiff wire.

◄ Remove rear brake line bracket mounting bolt (**arrow**). Detach bracket from trailing arm.

> **CAUTION—**
> • *Avoid damaging the brake hose by stretching when the trailing arm is lowered.*

— Remove wheel speed sensor from top of trailing arm. See **340 Brakes** if necessary.

— Unclip brake pad sensor harnesses (if applicable) from control arm and lay aside.

◄ Support trailing arm from below using an adjustable jack stand. Remove shock absorber lower mounting bolt (**arrow**).

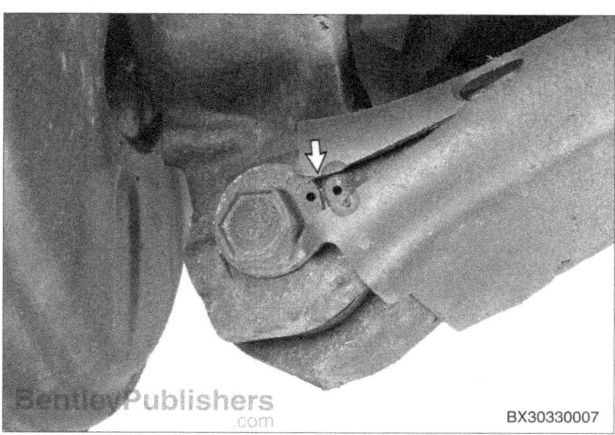

◄ Mark position of lower control arm eccentric bolt to control arm (**arrow**).

– With an assistant helping to support trailing arm:
  • Remove lower eccentric bolt, nut and washer.
  • Note direction of bolt installation for reassembly.

◄ With an assistant helping to support trailing arm:
  • Remove upper control arm bolt.
  • Note direction of bolt for reassembly.

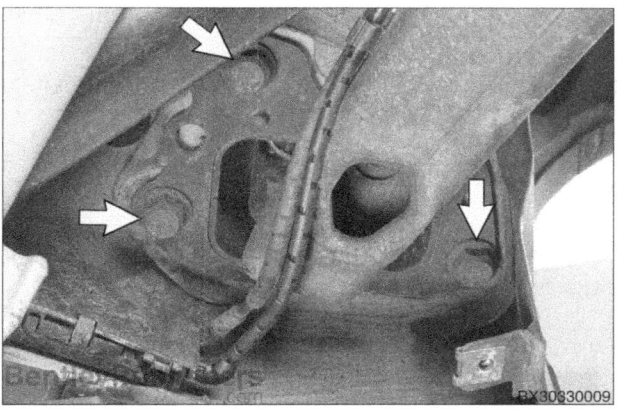

◄ With an assistant helping to support trailing arm, remove bolts from trailing arm bracket and remove from vehicle.
  • Mark position of trailing arm bracket to body to help with alignment when reinstalling.

– Working with trailing arm on workbench, detach front bracket from arm.

> **WARNING—**
> • *The trailing arm is heavy and awkward to handle. Use an assistant to help with supporting and removing from vehicle.*

Trailing arm front bushing, replacing

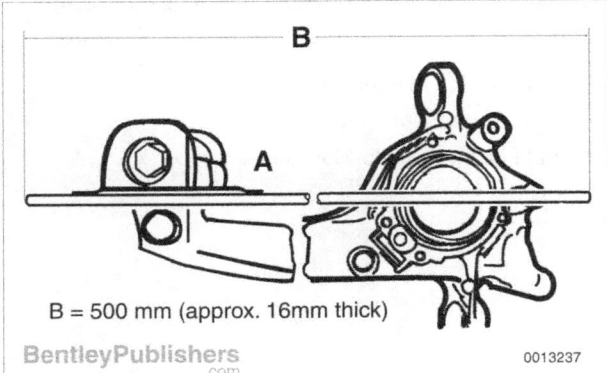

B = 500 mm (approx. 16mm thick)

BentleyPublishers.com

0013237

◄ Before installing trailing arm, preload trailing arm front bracket bushing:
  • Install bolt (**A**) through bracket and bushing and install nut finger tight.
  • Using bar stock as shown in illustration, align base of bracket so that it is parallel with center of wheel bearing bore on trailing arm.
  • Torque bracket bolt (**A**).

Tightening torques	
Trailing arm bushing to front bracket (M12)	100 Nm (74 ft-lb)

— Remainder of installation is reverse of removal, noting the following:
  • Align control arm eccentric mounting bolt and to marks earlier.
  • Use new self-locking nuts.
  • Transfer brake system components to new arm.
  • Tighten upper and lower trailing arm.
  • Have vehicle professionally aligned when job is complete.

NOTE—

  • *BMW-supplied replacement trailing arms come with control arm bushings installed. Install a new wheel bearing.*

Tightening torques	
Road wheel to hub	140 Nm (103 ft-lb)
Stabilizer link (M10 replace with new)	65 Nm (48 ft-lb)
Brake line bracket to trailing arm (M6)	9 Nm (80 in-lb)
Trailing arm front bracket to body	77 Nm (57 ft-lb)
Lower control arm to trailing arm (M12, tighten with suspension loaded)	100 Nm (74 ft-lb)
Upper control arm to trailing arm (M12, replace nut with new)	106 Nm (78 ft-lb)

Trailing arm front bushing, replacing

— Raise vehicle and remove rear wheels.

> ***WARNING—***
>
> • *Make sure vehicle is stable and well supported at all times. Use a professional automotive lift or jack stands. A floor jack is not adequate support.*

— Remove trailing arm. Be sure to mark position of trailing arm front bracket on body to facilitate resetting of rear toe. See **Trailing arm, removing and installing** in this repair group.

◄ Using appropriate press tools:
  • Press bushing out of trailing arm.
  • Clean trailing arm bore.
  • Press new bushing into trailing arm.
  • Line up slot in bushing with mark (**A**) on trailing arm bore.
  • Correctly installed bushing protrudes from trailing arm bore by measurement **B** = 2.5 mm (0.1 in).

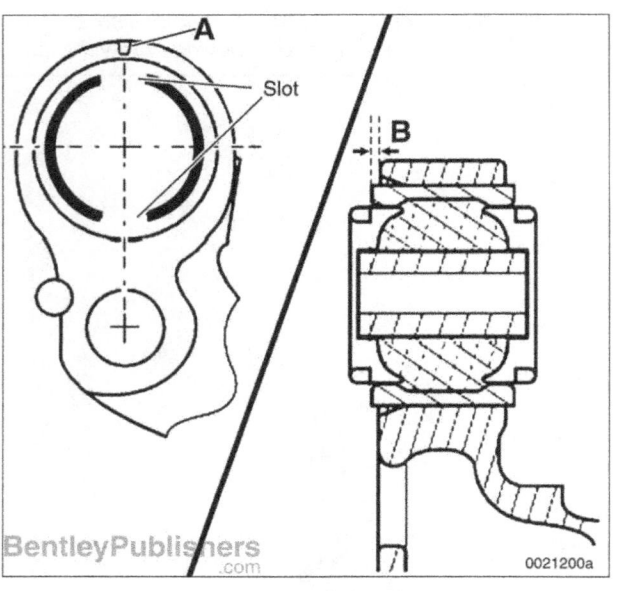

Slot

BentleyPublishers.com

0021200a

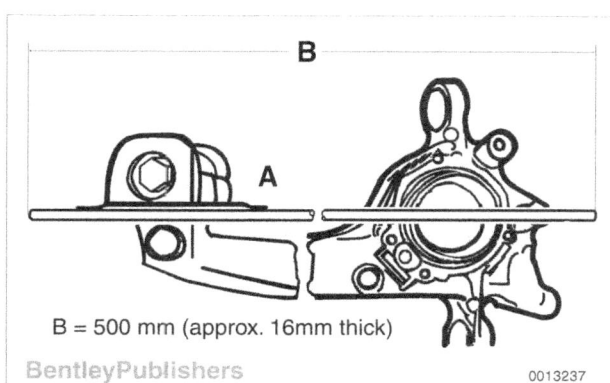

B = 500 mm (approx. 16mm thick)

◀ Before installing trailing arm, preload trailing arm front bushing:

- Install bolt (**A**) through bracket and bushing. Install nut finger tight.
- Using bar stock, align base of bracket so that it is parallel with center of wheel bearing bore on trailing arm.
- Torque bracket bolt (**A**).

Tightening torques	
Trailing arm bushing to front bracket (M12)	100 Nm (74 ft-lb)

– Reinstall trailing arm. See **Trailing arm, removing and installing**. Have vehicle professionally aligned when job is complete.

Upper control arm, removing and installing

– Raise vehicle and remove rear wheels.

> **WARNING—**
> - *Make sure vehicle is stable and well supported at all times. Use a professional automotive lift or jack stands. A floor jack is not adequate support.*

– Remove coil spring, see **Coil spring, removing and installing** in this repair group.

◀ After coil spring removal with trailing arm still supported by jack stand:

- Remove upper control arm bolt.
- Note direction of bolt installation for reassembly.

◀ To remove upper control arm:

- Remove stabilizer bar link from stabilizer bar (**arrow**).
- Remove rod (**A**) for right height sensor (passenger side only).
- Remove nut on reverse of bolt (**B**) and remove bolt toward rear of vehicle.

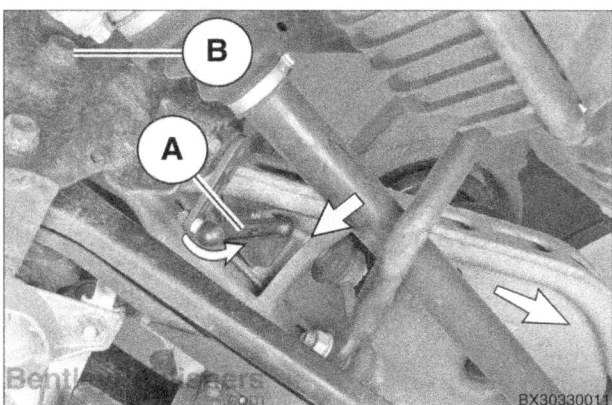

– Remove upper control arm out from under vehicle through wheel well.

– Installation is reverse of removal, noting the following:

- Use previously made marks to install eccentric bolt and fit eccentric washer.
- Use new self-locking nuts.
- Tighten fasteners to final torque only after vehicle has been lowered and suspension has settled.
- Have vehicle professionally aligned when job is complete.

Tightening torques	
Road wheel to hub	140 Nm (103 ft-lb)
Upper control arm to subframe (tighten with suspension loaded)	77 Nm (57 ft-lb)
Upper control arm to trailing arm (M12, replace nut with new)	106 Nm (78 ft-lb)
Stabilizer link (M10)	65 Nm (48 ft-lb)

330

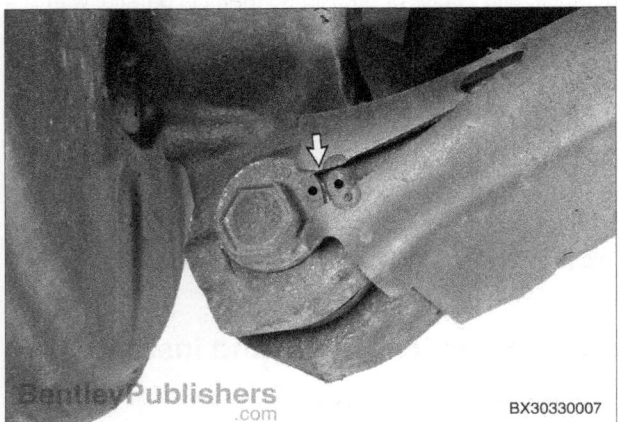

BX30330007

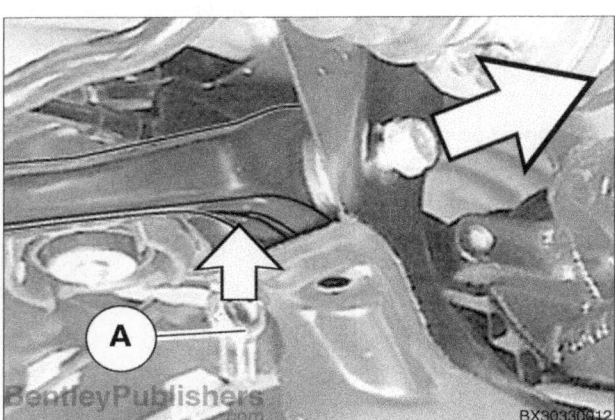

BX30330012

Lower control arm, removing and installing

— Raise vehicle and remove rear wheels.

> **WARNING—**
> • Make sure vehicle is stable and well supported at all times. Use a professional automotive lift or jack stands. A floor jack is not adequate support.

— Support trailing arm from below using an adjustable jack stand.

◀ Mark position (**arrows**) of lower control arm eccentric mounting bolt to control arm.

— Remove lower control arm plastic shield.

— Remove lower control arm mounting bolt at trailing arm. Note direction of bolt insertion.

◀ Remove lower control arm mounting bolt at subframe:
  • Slide bolt out and remove lock plate (**A**) from opposite end.

— Use soft hammer to tap control arm out of its mounting points.

> **NOTE—**
> • If additional clearance is needed to get through bolt out, unbolt differential from subframe and push it toward rear of vehicle.

— Installation is reverse of removal.
  • Welded seam of control arm faces up.
  • To install mounting hardware at subframe, insert lock plate into opening in subframe from below.
  • Line up eccentric bolt head with marks made previously.
  • Have vehicle professionally aligned when job is complete.

Tightening torques	
Road wheel to hub	140 Nm (103 ft-lb)
Lower control arm to subframe (tighten with suspension loaded)	77 Nm (57 ft-lb)
Lower control arm to trailing arm (M12, tighten with suspension loaded)	100 Nm (74 ft-lb)
Stabilizer link (M10)	65 Nm (48 ft-lb)

Upper or lower control arm outer bushing, replacing

— Upper control arm bushing (ball joint):

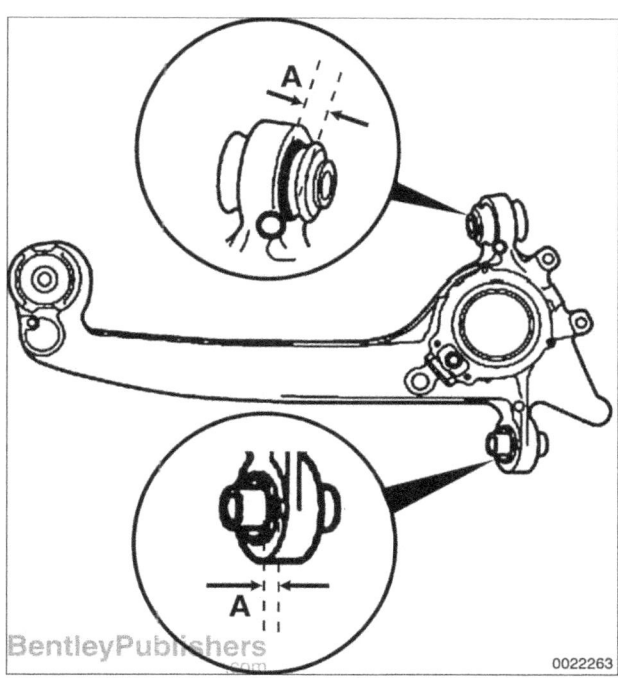

- Remove trailing arm. Be sure to mark position of trailing arm front bracket on body to facilitate resetting of rear toe. See **Trailing arm, removing and installing** in this repair group.

— Lower control arm bushing:

- Detach lower control arm from trailing arm. There is no need to remove trailing arm.
- Be sure to mark position of eccentric mounting bolt to facilitate resetting of rear camber.
- Note direction of bolt insertion.

◀ To replace bushing:

- Measure and record protrusion (**A**) of old bushing from trailing arm boss.
- Press old bushing out and install new bushing, using protrusion measurement **A** as a reference.
- Have vehicle professionally aligned when job is complete.

Tightening torques	
Road wheel to hub	140 Nm (103 ft-lb)
Lower control arm to trailing arm (M12, tighten with suspension loaded)	100 Nm (74 ft-lb)
Upper control arm to trailing arm (M12, replace nut with new)	106 Nm (78 ft-lb)

Upper control arm inner bushing, replacing

— Remove upper control arm. See **Upper control arm, removing and installing** in this repair group.

— Press old bushing out using appropriate press tools.

◀ Press new bushing starting at inner bevelled end (**arrow**) of control arm bore.

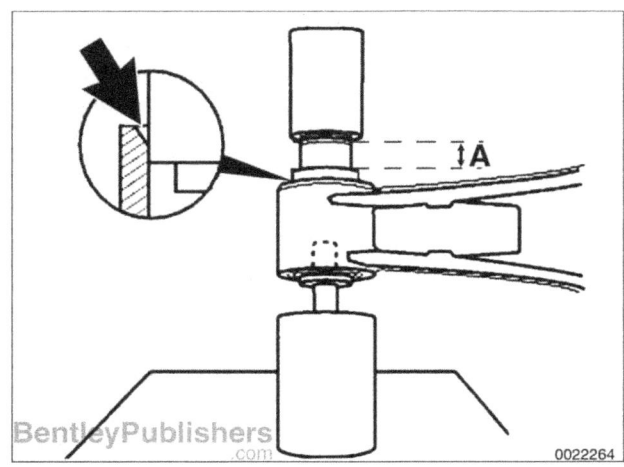

- Make sure that longer collar of bushing (**A**) is on same side as bevel in control arm.
- Make sure that outer bushing housing is flush with control arm bore when fully pressed in.

— Install upper control arm. See **Upper control arm, removing and installing**. Have vehicle professionally aligned when job is complete.

REAR SUBFRAME

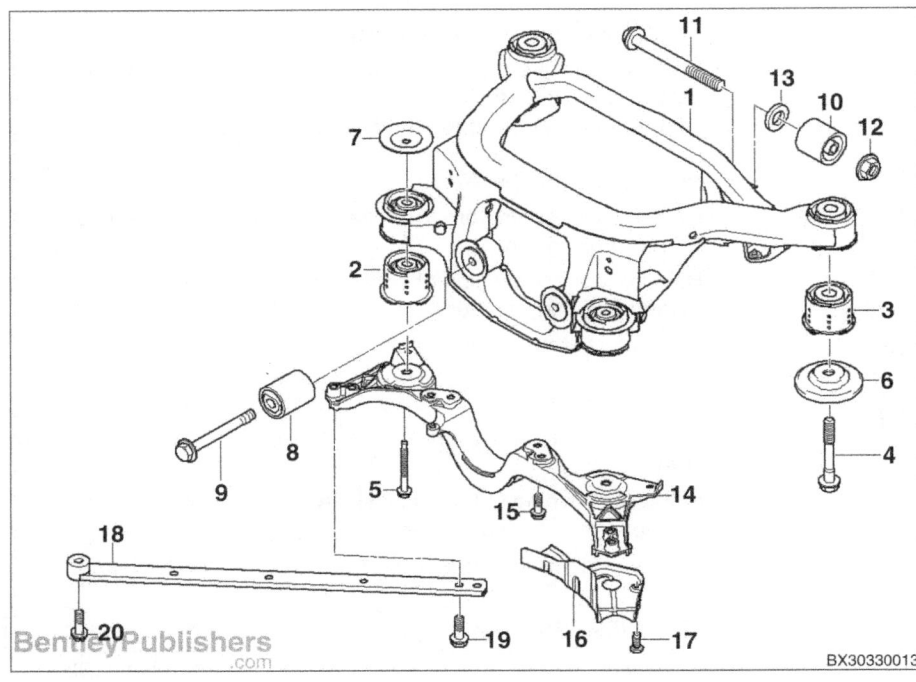

BX30330013

Rear subframe components

1. Rear subframe
2. Subframe bushing (front)
3. Subframe bushing (rear)
4. Mounting bolt (M12 x 1.5 x 116-8.8)
5. Mounting bolt (M12 x 1.5 x 127)
6. Rear stopper plate
7. Front stopper plate
8. Differential bushing (front)
9. Differential mounting bolt (M12 x 1.5 x 80)
10. Differential bushing (rear)
11. Differential mounting bolt (M14 x 1.5 x138)
12. Self-locking collar nut
13. Washer
14. Rear subframe brace
    See **331 Rear Axle Differential** for removal
15. Mounting bolt (M8X20.5 8.8)
16. Heat shield
17. Self taping screw (M6x13)
18. Tension strut
19. Torx bolt self taping (M10x35 10.9)
20. Torx bolt self taping (M10x40 10.9)

Rear subframe, removing and installing

In case of damage to the subframe, or if a pressed-in bushing is worn, remove subframe. Use a shop press and suitable tools to replace pressed in bushings. Removal of rear subframe requires use of workshop jacks to support the subframe and vehicle when removing.

— Raise vehicle and remove rear wheels.

> **WARNING—**
> • *Make sure vehicle is stable and well supported at all times. Use a professional automotive lift or jack stands. A floor jack is not adequate support.*

— Remove rear underbody splash shields as applicable.

— Remove spare tire carrier tray.

— Detach rear driveshaft from rear differential. See **260 Driveshafts**.

— Remove lower shock absorber bolts. See **Shock absorbers, removing and installing** in this repair group.

Rear subframe, removing and installing

— Remove coil springs see **Coil springs, removing and installing** in this repair group.

— Remove exhaust system. See **180 Exhaust System**.

— Remove tension struts (crossbars) from rear suspension and body.

— Remove drive axle. See **311 Rear Axle Final Drive**.

◄ Remove rear brake line bracket mounting bolt (**arrow**). Detach bracket from trailing arm.

— Remove wheel speed sensor from trailing arm and disconnect pad wear sensor wire.

— Remove brake caliper, rotor and parking brake cable. See **340 Brakes**. Do not remove brake line from caliper. Suspend caliper from body using stiff wire.

— Unbolt trailing arms from body. See **Trailing arms, removing and installing** in this repair group.

◄ Remove fasteners (**A**) on heat shield (**B**) to remove from front of subframe.

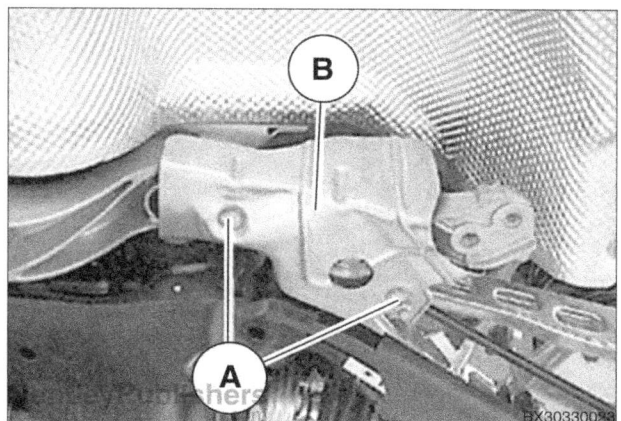

— Support subframe and rear differential with appropriate workshop jack.

◄ Remove 4 rear suspension subframe mounting bolts (**arrows**).

> **WARNING—**
> • *Removing the rear subframe alters the vehicle's center of gravity. Make sure vehicle remains securely in place on lift or jacks. Strap vehicle to lift arms.*

— Carefully lower rear suspension subframe away from body to remove.

> **NOTE—**
> • *Photo shows compression strut removed at front of subframe.*

— To install, jack subframe into position. Install and tighten subframe mounting bolts. Replace stop plates in their original position.

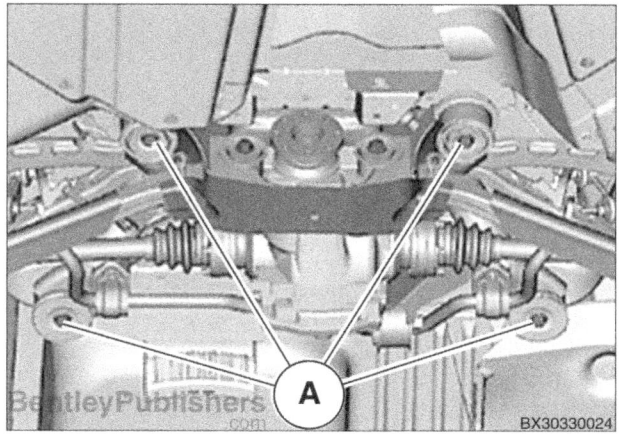

Tightening torque	
Rear subframe to body (M12x1.5)	77 Nm (57 ft-lb)
Brake line bracket to trailing arm (M6)	9 Nm (80 in-lb)

> **NOTE—**
> • *In case of damage to subframe mounting stud threads in body, repair using Helicoil thread insert M12 x 1.5 x 18.*

Rear wheel bearing replacing

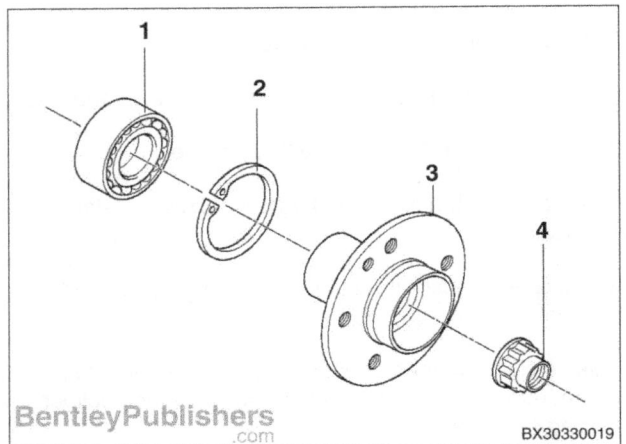

REAR WHEEL BEARINGS

Rear wheel bearing is pressed into the trailing arm and then the wheel hub is pressed into the bearing. Wheel bearing is destroyed when drive hub is removed and cannot be reused.

Special press tools, to be used with the trailing arm attached to the vehicle, are required to replace a wheel bearing. Read the procedure through before beginning the job.

Rear wheel bearing components

1. Wheel bearing
2. Snap ring
3. Wheel hub
4. Collar nut (axle nut)
   • Tighten to 300 Nm (222 ft-lb)

Rear wheel bearing replacing

— Raise vehicle and remove rear wheel.

> **WARNING—**
> • *Make sure vehicle is stable and well supported at all times. Use a professional automotive lift or jack stands. A floor jack is not adequate support.*

◄ Using a suitable drift, release staked side of axle nut (**arrows**).

— Remove center cap and reinstall wheel. Lower vehicle to ground.

— With an assistant holding down brake, remove collar axle nut. Do not reuse collar nut.

— Raise vehicle and remove rear wheel.

◄ Remove rear brake line bracket mounting bolt (**arrow**). Detach bracket from trailing arm.

— Remove brake calipers and brake discs. Hang brake calipers aside with stiff wire. Do not disconnect brake fluid hoses. See **340 Brakes**.
  • Unclip brake pad sensor (if applicable) harnesses from control arm and lay aside.

— Remove wheel speed sensor from trailing arm.

— Remove rear drive axle. See **331 Rear Axle Differential**.

Rear wheel bearing replacing

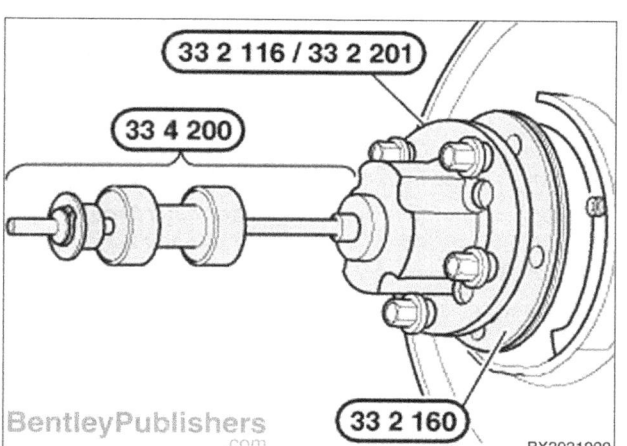

◀ Remove wheel hub using BMW special tools and 5 wheel bolts.

NOTE —

- *Position rounded inside edge of special tool 33 2 160 towards wheel hub.*

WARNING —

- *Bearing is destroyed when wheel hub is removed. Replace wheel bearing and wheel hub together.*

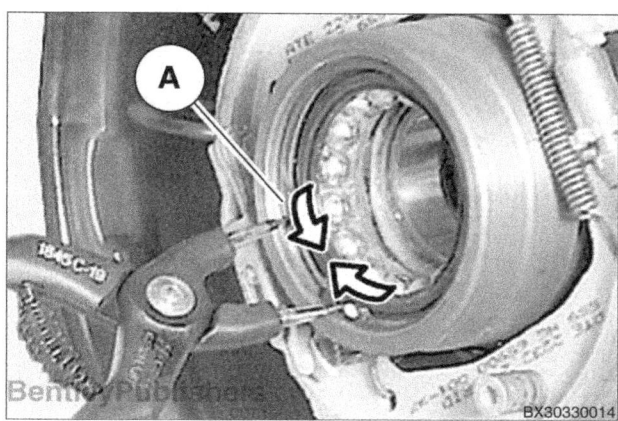

◀ Use snap ring pliers to remove wheel bearing circlip **(A)**.

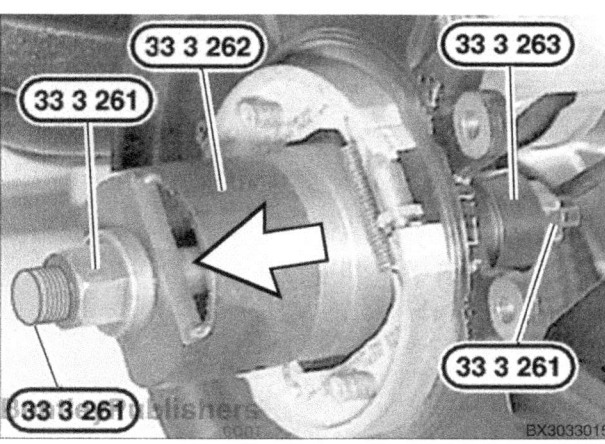

◀ Using BMW bearing extraction tools, pull bearing assembly out of trailing arm bearing housing.

− Inspect bearing housing for damage or contamination.

- Clean housing bore thoroughly before installing bearing.
- Make sure mating surfaces are clean.

Rear wheel bearing replacing

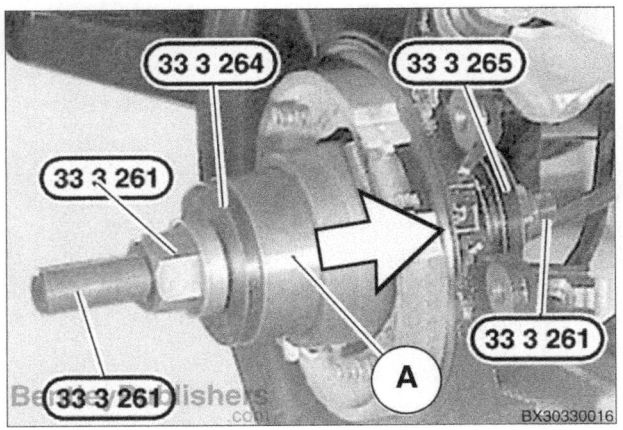

◀ Install new bearing assembly using BMW press tools.

– Install new circlip.

> **CAUTION—**
> • *Apply force only to outer race when installing bearing.*
> • *Make sure that the bearing is pressed in far enough to contact the shoulder at the back side of the housing and that the circlip is fully seated in its groove.*
> • *Always use a new circlip.*

◀ Press wheel hub into bearing using BMW press tools.

> **CAUTION—**
> • *BMW specifies special tools to pull the drive flange through the wheel bearing into position. If using alternative tools, be sure to support the bearing inner race when pressing or pulling the drive flange into place.*

– Installation is reverse of removal. Remember to:
   • Adjust parking brake.
   • Tighten drive axle collar nut to final torque with road wheel installed and vehicle lowered.

Tightening torque	
Wheel hub to drive axle collar nut (replace with new)	300 Nm (222 ft-lb)
Brake line bracket to trailing arm (M6)	9 Nm (80 in-lb)
Road wheel to hub	140 Nm (103 ft-lb)

REAR STABILIZER BAR

The rear stabilizer bar is mounted to the rear subframe and attached to the swing arms with stabilizer bar links.

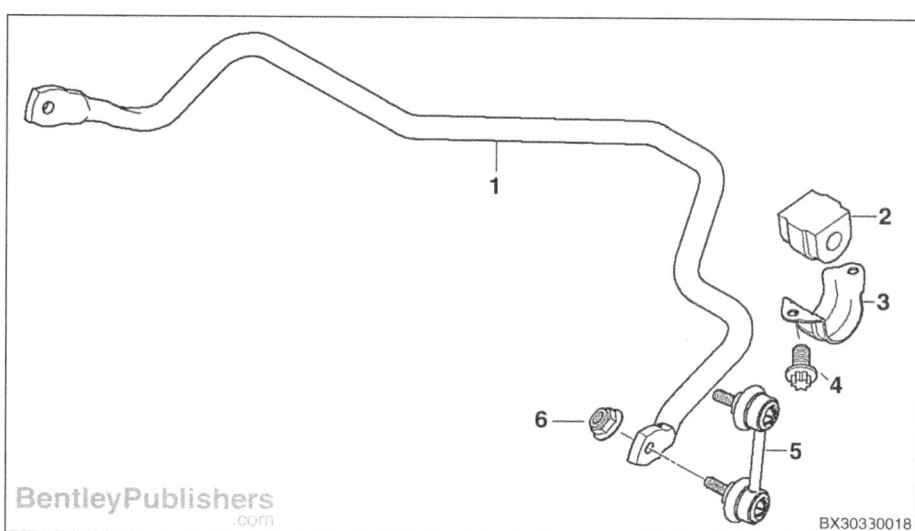

BX30330018

Rear stabilizer bar components

1. Stabilizer bar
2. Stabilizer bushing
3. Stabilizer bracket
4. Torx bolt (M8x22)
5. Stabilizer link
6. Self-locking nut (M10)

Stabilizer bar link, removing and installing

– Raise vehicle.

> **WARNING —**
> • Make sure vehicle is stable and well supported at all times. Use a professional automotive lift or jack stands. A floor jack is not adequate support.

◄ Remove stabilizer bar link fasteners from bar and upper control arm. (**arrows**)

– Installation is reverse of removal.

Tightening torques	
Stabilizer link (M10 replace with new)	65 Nm (48 ft-lb)
Stabilizer bar bracket to subframe (M8)	21 Nm (16 ft-lb)

BX30330004

330

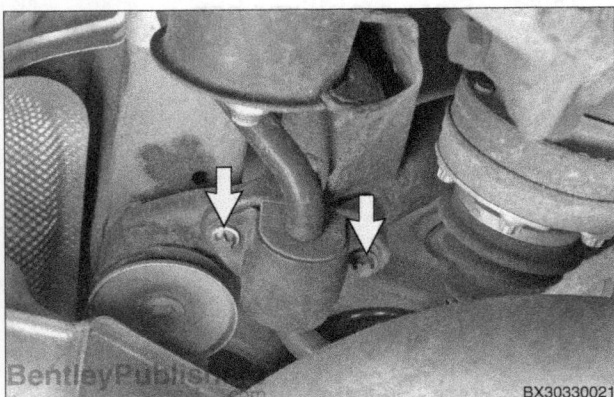

BX30330021

Stabilizer bar and bushings, removing and installing

— Raise vehicle.

> **WARNING—**
> • *Make sure vehicle is stable and well supported at all times. Use a professional automotive lift or jack stands. A floor jack is not adequate support.*

— Remove spare tire carrier tray.

— If removing stabilizer bar:

  • Remove stabilizer bar brackets on both sides. See **Stabilizer bar link, removing and installing**.

◀ Remove stabilizer support bracket fasteners (**arrows**) on each side.

— Remove stabilizer bar.

— Check rubber mounts. Replace if necessary by prying off of stabilizer bar.

— Installation is reverse of removal.

Tightening torques	
Stabilizer link (M10) replace with new)	65 Nm (48 ft-lb)
Stabilizer bar bracket to subframe (M8)	21 Nm (16 ft-lb)

331 Rear Axle Differential

331

GENERAL

This repair group covers removal and repair information for the rear differential (final drive), axle shafts, CV joints, CV joint boots, and differential seal replacement.

Internal repairs of the differential assembly are not covered in this manual.

Special tools

BMW recommends several special tools for the removal of the drive axles as well as the installation of differential input and output drive flange seals, and differential mounts. Some common pullers and drifts can often be substituted for these tools.

 The E83 rear axle differential consists of a final drive (rear differential) and output drive axles to the rear wheels. Rear drive axles have sliding CV-joints on both wheel side and rear differential side to accommodate suspension movement up and down. For strength and sound damping final drive consist of a cast iron housing with an aluminum cover. Life cycle impulse (LCI) vehicles received updated final drive (rear differential) with improved efficiency and torque capacity.

NOTE—

• *Right and left drive axles can not be interchanged.*

BX30331002

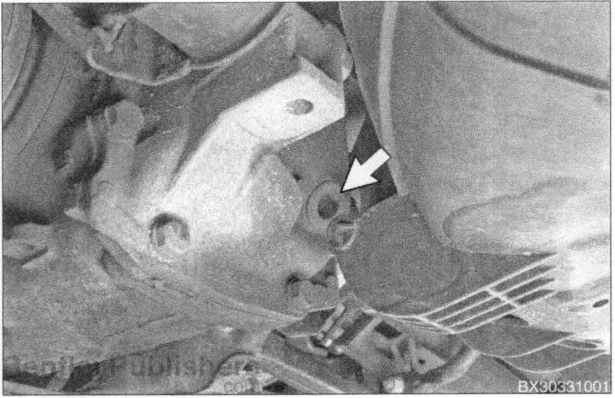

REAR DIFFERENTIAL

Differential oil, draining and filling

The X3 rear differential is filled with lifetime oil that ordinarily does not need to be changed. BMW recommends using only a specially formulated synthetic gear oil (SAF-XO) that is available through an authorized BMW dealer parts department. For additional information on this lubricant and any other lubricants that may be compatible, contact an authorized BMW dealer service department.

– Operate vehicle to warm differential oil.

– If necessary remove spare tire carrier tray.

 Remove differential plug (**arrow**). Using a suction gun, remove fluid from differential.

– Drain oil into a suitable container.

– Replace plug and seal.

– Add rear differential oil and check level. See **Differential oil level, checking** in this repair group.

Tightening torque	
Fill / drain plug to rear differential housing: • Plug with sealing O-ring	60 Nm (44 ft-lb)

Table a. Rear differential fluid capacity	
2004 - 2006 • M54 engine, 2.5i (type 168K) • M54 engine, 3.0i (type 188K)	approx. 1.0 liter approx. 0.9 liter
2007 - 2010 • N52 engine, 3.0si (type 188L)	approx. 1.0 liter

Differential oil level, checking

 Check lubricant level with vehicle on a level surface:

• Remove differential plug (**arrow**).

• Level is correct when fluid just reaches edge of plug hole.

• If necessary, top up fluid.

• Replace plug and seal.

– Install and tighten oil filler plug when oil level is correct.

Tightening torque	
Fill / drain plug to rear differential housing: • Plug with sealing O-ring	60 Nm (44 ft-lb)

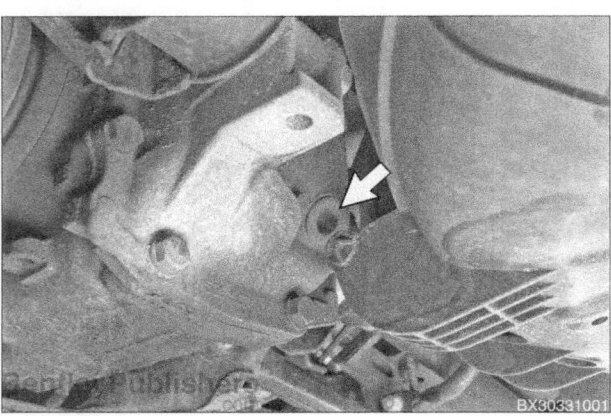

Rear subframe brace, removing and installing

Many procedures in this repair group require the removal of the subframe brace to access other components. The subframe brace is also called the compression strut.

◀ To remove rear subframe brace (compression strut).

- Remove left and right tension struts.
- Remove heat shield at drivers side.
- Remove two subframe mounting bolts that pass through brace.
- Remove 4 M8 subframe brace mounting bolts. Remove subframe brace.
- Re-install and tighten subframe mounting bolts and tighten until the rear subframe brace is reinstalled.

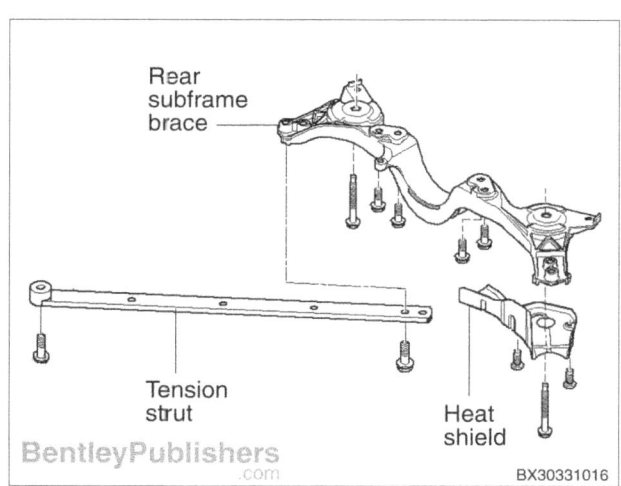

Tightening torques	
Tension strut to body / subframe brace	60 Nm (44 ft-lb)
Subframe brace to body (M8)	21 Nm (16 ft-lb)
Rear subframe / subframe brace to body (M12)	77 Nm (57 ft-lb)

Differential, removing and installing

— Raise car and support safely.

> **WARNING—**
> • *Make sure vehicle is stable and well supported at all times. Use a professional automotive lift or jack stands. A floor jack is not adequate support.*

— If necessary remove spare tire carrier tray.

— Lower or remove exhaust. **See 180 Exhaust**.

— Disconnect rear drive shaft from differential. See **260 Driveshaft**.

◀ Remove drive axle CV joint bolts (**arrows**) at left and right sides. Suspend drive axles from body using stiff wire.

— Support differential from below using workshop jack.

— Remove rear subframe brace. See **Rear subframe brace, removing and installing**. Reinstall rear subframe mounting bolts.

◀ WIth differential supported by a workshop jack, remove bolts (**A**).

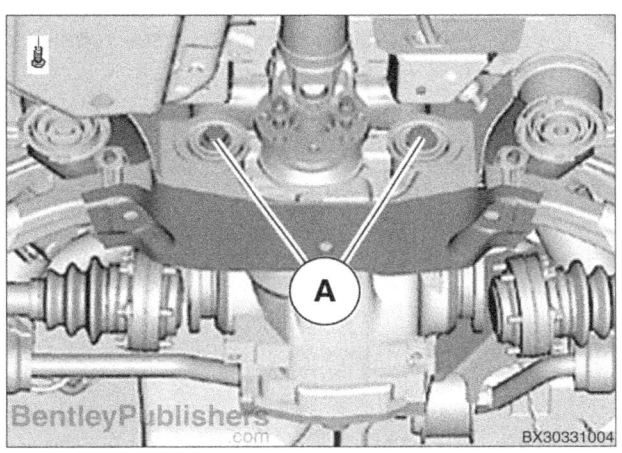

Differential input shaft seal, replacing

◄ WIth differential supported by a workshop jack, remove rear mounting nut and bolt (**arrows**).

– Lower differential out of subframe.

– To install, use workshop jack to lift differential into place:
  • Install mounting bolts finger tight (replace nuts and bolts).
  • Re-install rear subframe brace. See **Rear subframe brace, removing and installing**.
  • Lower workshop jack.
  • Tighten both front mounting bolts.
  • Tighten rear mounting bolt.

– Remainder of installation is reverse of removal. Remember to check differential oil. See **Differential oil level, checking** in this repair group.

Tightening torques	
Differential to rear subframe (front)	100 Nm (74 ft-lb)
Differential to rear subframe (rear)	165 Nm (122 ft-lb)
Drive axle to differential flange: • Torx M8 (replace bolts and washers) • Torx M10 (replace bolts and washers)	52 Nm (38 ft-lb) 80 Nm (59 ft-lb)
Tension strut to body / subframe brace	60 Nm (44 ft-lb)
Subframe brace to body (M8)	21 Nm (16 ft-lb)
Rear subframe / subframe brace to body (M12)	77 Nm (57 ft-lb)

Differential input shaft seal, replacing

– Raise car and support safely.

> **WARNING—**
> • *Make sure vehicle is stable and well supported at all times. Use a professional automotive lift or jack stands. A floor jack is not adequate support.*

– Remove exhaust system. See **180 Exhaust System**.

– Remove drive shaft. See **260 Driveshaft**.

– Support differential with work shop jack. See **Differential, removing and installing** in this repair group.

– Remove rear subframe brace. See **Rear subframe brace, removing and installing**. Reinstall rear subframe mounting bolts.

◄ Lift out collar nut locking plate (**arrow**).

– Mark position of collar nut (**B**) to pinion shaft (**B**) and drive flange (**C**) with a center punch or paint marker.

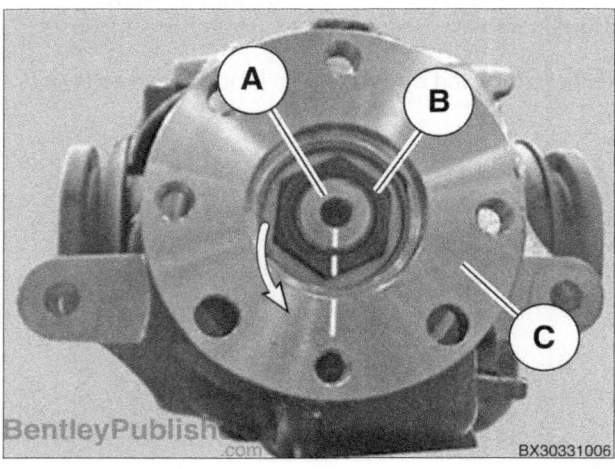

Differential input shaft seal, replacing

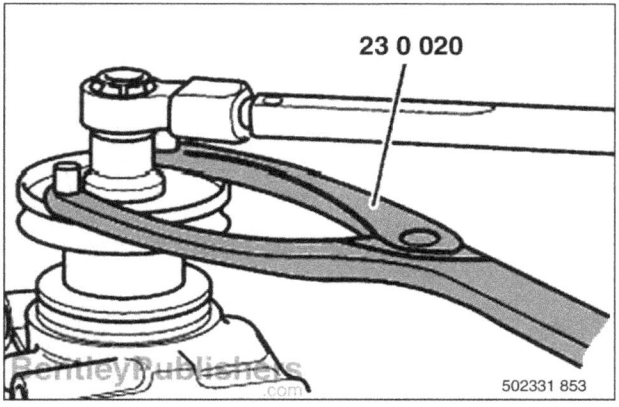

502331 853

◄ While counterholding drive flange with special BMW tool, loosen and remove collar nut.

NOTE—
• For clarity, illustration shows differential removed.

− Remove differential input flange pinion shaft using an appropriate puller.

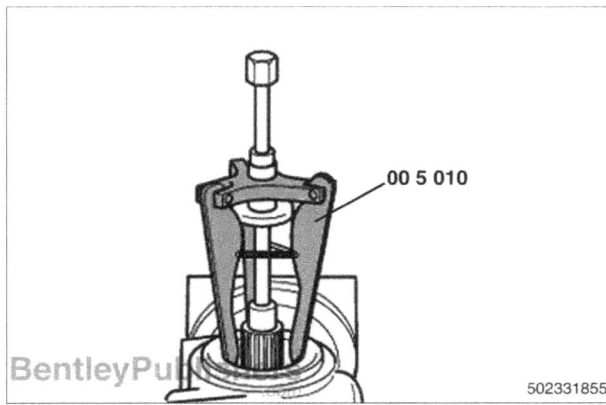

502331855

◄ Using BMW special tool to remove seal from differential housing.

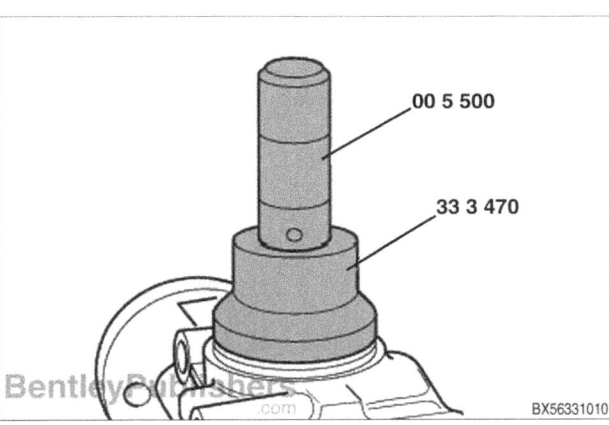

BX56331010

◄ Drive new seal into place until fully seated using BMW special tools.

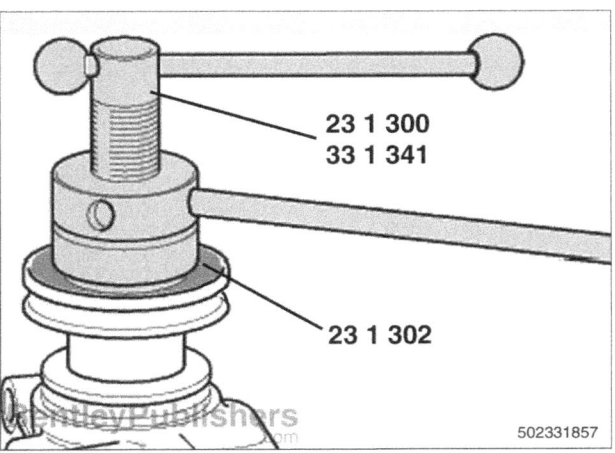

502331857

◄ Coat drive flange sealing area and seal lip with differential oil:
• Install drive flange on pinion shaft.
• Using BMW special tools press drive flange on pinion shaft just far enough to allow collar nut to be installed.

Differential output shaft seals, replacing

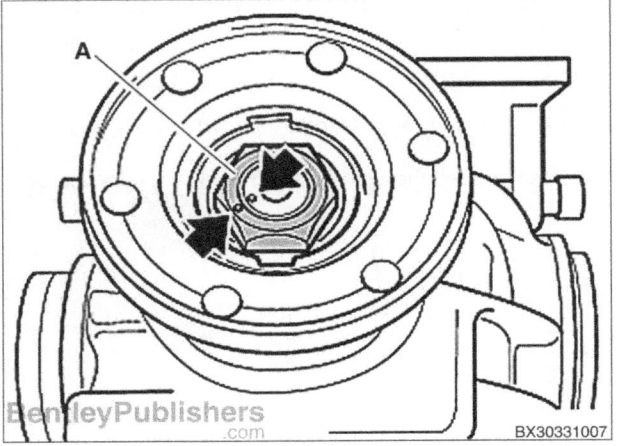

BX30331007

◄ Tighten collar nut only until previously marked points are aligned (**arrow**).

> **CAUTION—**
> • *Do not under any circumstances tighten collar nut beyond the marked points, otherwise clamping sleeve inside differential housing will have to be replaced.*

— Using a suitable drift, install new collar nut locking plate. Stake plate in place.

— Remainder of installation is reverse of removal.

— Check differential oil level. See **Differential oil level, checking** in this repair group.

Tightening torque	
Drive axle to differential flange:	
• Torx M8 (replace bolts and washers)	52 Nm (38 ft-lb)
• Torx M10 (replace bolts and washers)	80 Nm (59 ft-lb)

Differential output shaft seals, replacing

— Remove exhaust system (if necessary). See **180 Exhaust System**.

BX30330006

◄ Remove drive axle CV joint bolts (**arrows**) at left and right sides. Suspend drive axles from body using stiff wire.

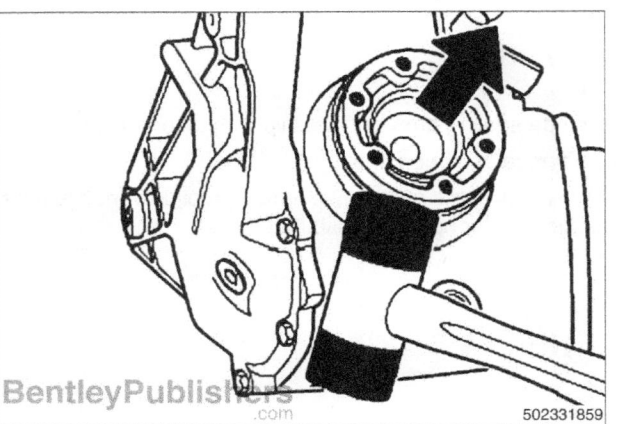

502331859

◄ Drive out differential output flange using soft faced hammer. Be careful not to damage output flange dust covers (if applicable).

— Press off output flange dust cover (if applicable).

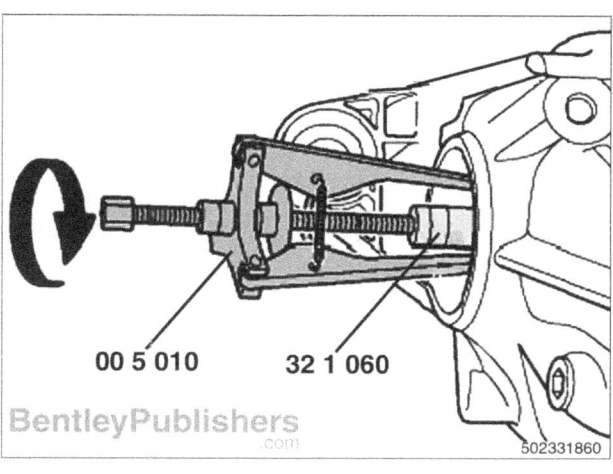

◀ Remove seal using BMW special tool 00 5 010 and 32 1 060 or equivalent.

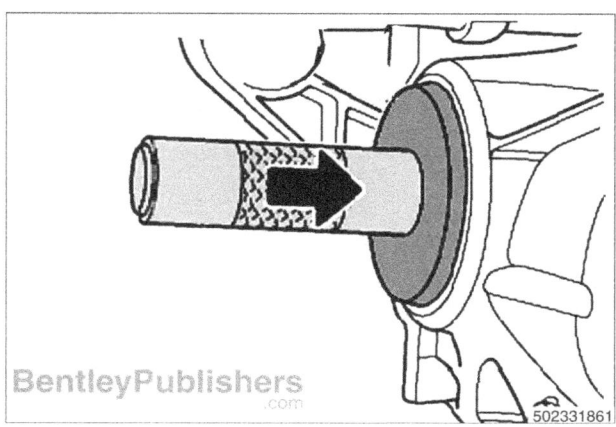

◀ Coat seal with differential oil and drive into place using BMW special tools 00 5 500 and 33 4 240 or equivalent.

– Replace output flange dust cover (if applicable).

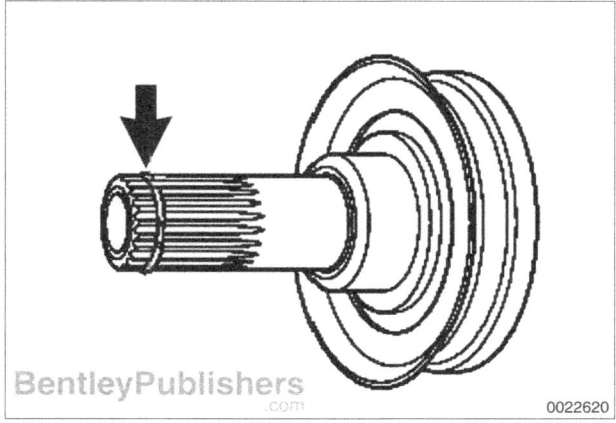

◀ Replace snap ring (**arrow**) on differential output flange shaft:
- Coat output flange shaft with differential oil where it contacts shaft seal.
- Push output flange into differential until flange splines engage splines of differential gear and snap ring can be heard to snap into place.

– Remainder of installation is reverse of removal. Remember to:
- Check differential oil level. See **Differential oil level, checking** in this repair group.

Tightening torques	
Drive axle to differential flange: • Torx M10 (replace bolts and washers)	80 Nm (59 ft-lb)

Differential cover, removing and installing

— Drain rear differential oil to a suitable container.

— Remove stabilizer bar. See **330 Rear Suspension**.

— Lower differential. See **Differential, removing and installing**.

— Remove 8 fasteners from rear cover and remove cover:
  • Clean cover and differential housing sealing surfaces.
  • Install new gasket with cover.

— Installation is reverse of removal. Refill differential with oil. See **Differential oil, draining and filling** in this repair group.

Tightening torque	
Differential cover to differential housing: • M10 x 25 (10.9 grade)	55 Nm (41 ft-lb)

Differential mounts, replacing

— Remove differential. See **Differential, removing and installing** in this repair group.

— Remove rear subframe if necessary. See **330 Rear Suspension**.

Rear differential mount

◀ Remove rear differential rubber mounts using BMW special tools or equivalent.

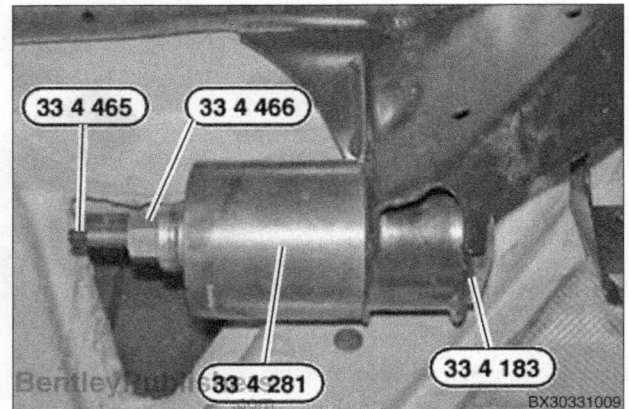

33 4 465   33 4 466
33 4 281   33 4 183
BX30331009

◀ Compress rubber mount (**A**) using BMW special tools.

A
33 4 455   33 4 456
33 4 450
BX30331010

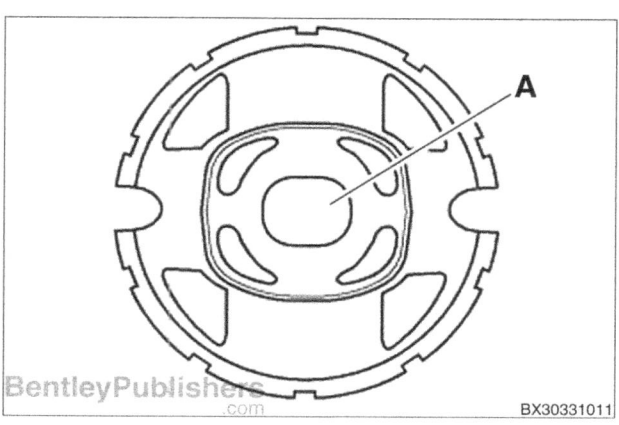

◀ Coat new mount with Circolight® anti-friction agent and install, noting the following:

• Align elongated bore hole horizontally.

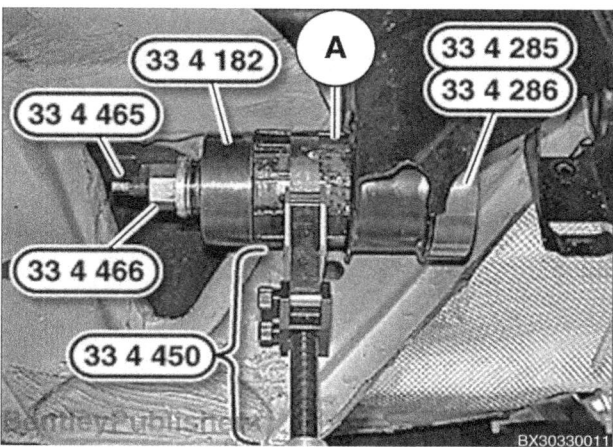

◀ Draw mount in firmly using BMW special tools until bushing is flush with rear subframe.

331

Front differential mount

◀ Remove front differential mount using BMW special tools.

Differential mounts, replacing

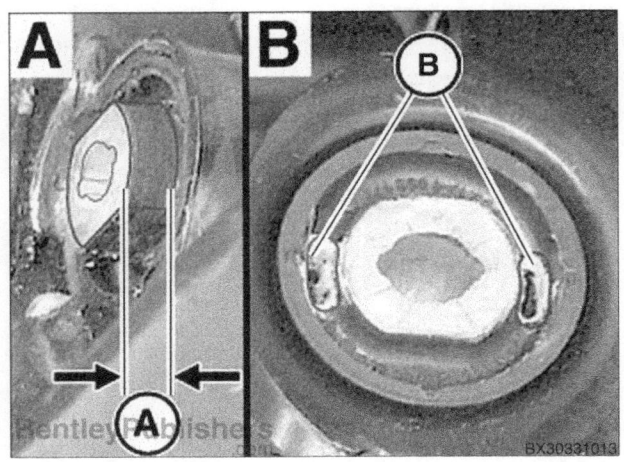

◄ Bushing protrudes (**A**) to rear of vehicle.

– Position slot (**B**) horizontally in rear axle support.

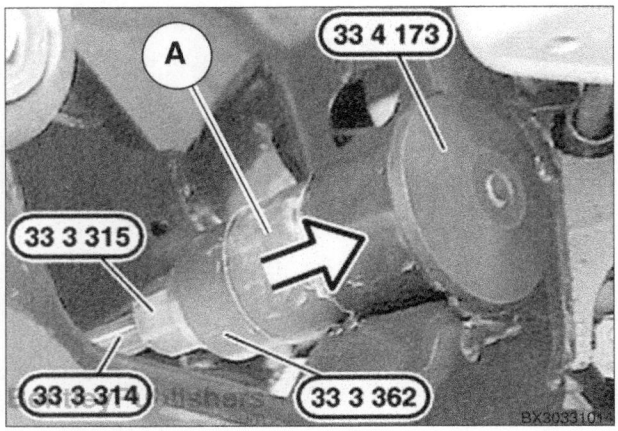

◄ Draw rubber mount (**A**) in firmly with BMW special tools as far as it will go.

– Remainder of installation is reverse of removal.

DRIVE AXLES

Drive axles use constant-velocity (CV) joints on both ends. For replacement parts, only CV joint boots or complete axles are offered by BMW.

Drive axle assembly

1. Drive axle
2. Reinforcement plate
3. Torx bolt
4. Drive axle collar nut.
5. Inner CV boot kit
6. Outer CV boot kit

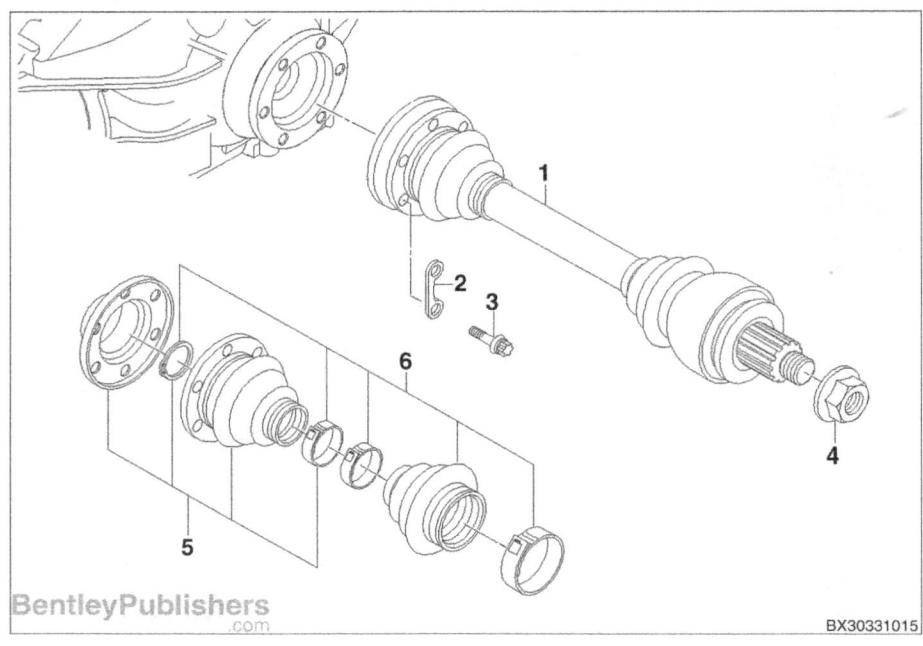

Drive axle, removing and installing

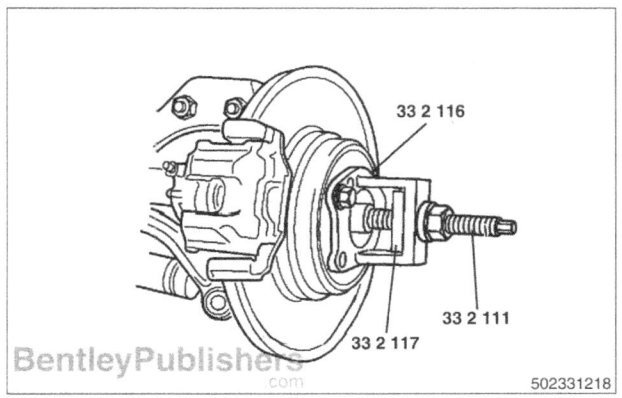

NOTE —
- *Right and left drive axles can not be interchanged.*

− Raise car and remove front wheel.

◄ Using a suitable drift, release staked side of axle nut (**arrows**).

− Remove center cap and reinstall wheel. Lower vehicle to ground.

− With an assistant holding down brake, remove collar axle nut. Do not reuse collar nut.

− Raise car and remove front wheel.

− If necessary remove spare tire carrier tray.

− Remove stabilizer bar. See **Stabilizer bar, removing and installing** in this repair group.

− Lower or remove exhaust. See **180 Exhaust**.

◄ Remove drive axle CV joint bolts (**arrows**) and if necessary free from differential drive flange using a suitable pry tool.

◄ Press drive axle from drive flange at wheel side using a suitable press tool and remove axle toward middle of vehicle.

− Installation is reverse of removal, noting the following:
  - Use a new collar nut.
  - Apply a light coating of oil to contact face of collar nut and tighten firmly, but not to final torque.
  - Install road wheel and lower car to ground.
  - With an assistant applying brakes, tighten drive axle collar nut to its final torque. Stake collar nut.

Tightening torques	
Drive axle collar nut to wheel hub (M27)	300 Nm (221 ft-lb)
Drive axle to differential flange: • Torx M8 (replace bolts and washers) • Torx M10 (replace bolts and washers)	 52 Nm (38 ft-lb) 80 Nm (59 ft-lb)
Road wheel to hub	140 Nm (103 ft-lb)

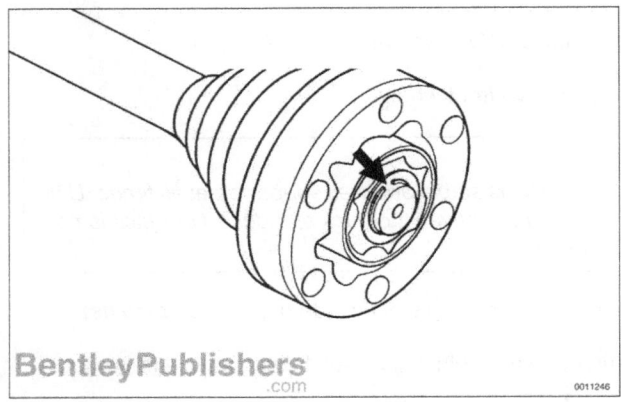

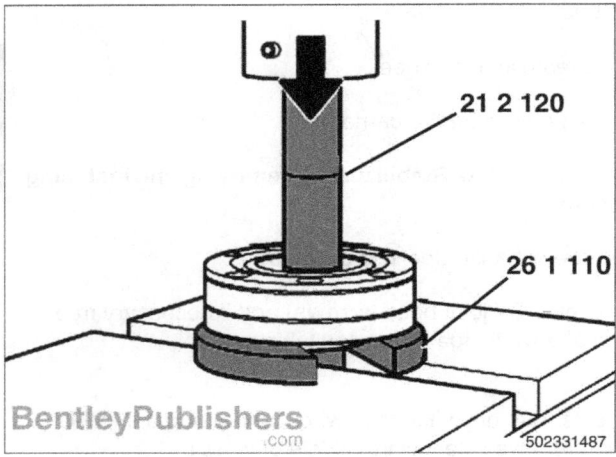

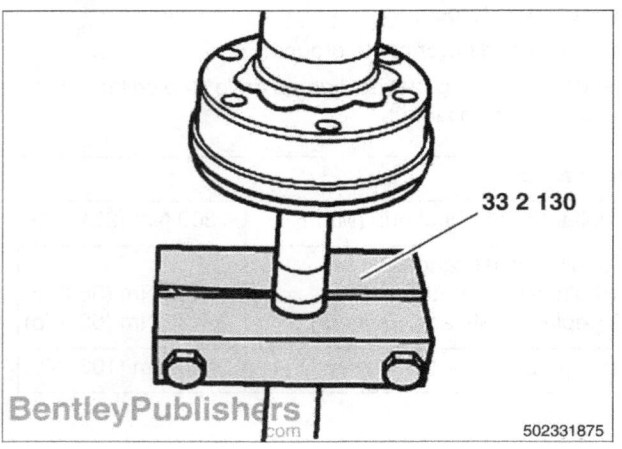

CV joint boots

When replacing a CV joint boot, use a complete CV joint boot repair kit. The kit will include a new boot, clamping bands, special lubricant, and a new inner CV joint circlip.

NOTE—
- *To replace outer CV boot, remove the inner joint and boot first.*

— Remove axle shaft. See **Drive axle, removing and installing** in this repair group.

— Working with axle shaft at bench, cut off old boot clamps and remove boot. Clean old grease off joint and shaft.

◄ Remove dust cover from CV joint and remove circlip (**arrow**) retaining joint inner hub to axle shaft. Press off joint cap.

◄ Support inner hub with BMW special tool and press axle shaft out of joint.

— Clean all old lubricant off shaft splines and inner joint splines and inspect for damage. Replace joint if wear heavy wear is present.

> *CAUTION—*
> - *If disassembling CV joint, matchmark inner and outer race and intermediate ball cage for purposes of reassembly.*

— Slide CV joint boot on axle shaft.

— Apply Loctite® 270 or an equivalent heavy-duty locking compound to drive axle splines. Position new CV joint on shaft so that raised or taller side of hub is facing shaft.

> *CAUTION—*
> - *Do not let the locking compound contact the balls in the joint. Apply only a thin coat to cover the splines.*

◄ While supporting axle shaft, press inner hub of CV joint onto shaft. Install a new circlip.

— Install new boot clamps.

— Use sealing gel to seal dust cover to CV joint prior to reinstallation.

NOTE—
- *Do not let ball hub pivot too far in outer ring of the joint. The balls will fall out.*
- *Before installing each small boot clamp be sure to "burp" the boot by flexing the CV joint. A small screwdriver inserted between the boot and the axle shaft will help the process.*

— Install axle shaft. See **Drive axle, removing and installing** in this repair group.

340 Brakes

340

GENERAL

This repair group covers service for the brake system and for electronic braking and stability control (traction control) systems.

See also:

- **020 Maintenance** for basic brake system checks.
- **300 Suspension, Steering and Brakes–General** for ABS and DSC system descriptions.
- **320 Steering Wheel and Alignment** for steering angle sensor
- **612 Switches** for brake light switch.
- **ECL Electrical Component Locations** for fuse and component access.
- **ELE Electrical Wiring Diagrams**.

Brake system

BMW E83 models are equipped with vacuum power-assisted four-wheel disc brakes with integral antilock braking system (ABS) and dynamic stability control (DSC). Single-piston calipers act on vented front and rear rotors. A brake pad wear sensor for each axle indicates when brake pads need replacement. The dual drum-type parking brake system is integrated with the rear brake rotors.

Electronic braking and stability control

E83 models were introduced with Dynamic Stability Control (DSC). DSC is a computer controlled traction control system that uses the ABS system in conjunction with engine management controls to control wheel spin during acceleration and maintain vehicle stability while braking.

For DSC descriptions, see **300 Suspension, Steering and Brakes—General**.

Troubleshooting

Brake performance is mainly affected by three factors:

• Level and condition of brake fluid

• Ability of brake system to create and maintain pressure

• Condition of friction components

Air in brake fluid makes the brake pedal feel spongy during braking or increases the brake pedal force required to stop. Fluid contaminated by moisture or dirt corrodes the system. Inspect the brake fluid inside the reservoir. If it is dirty or murky, or is more then two years old, replace fluid. See **Brake system, bleeding** in this repair group.

To check the function of the master cylinder, hold the brake pedal down hard with the engine running. If the pedal slowly falls to the floor, either the master cylinder is leaking internally or fluid is leaking externally.

Inspect the brake rotors for glazing, discoloration and scoring. Steering wheel vibration while braking at speed is often caused by warped rotors, but can also be caused by worn suspension components.

When troubleshooting, keep in mind that tire inflation, wear and temperature can all have an affect on braking. See **300 Suspension, Steering and Brakes—General** for additional suspension and brake system troubleshooting.

Table a lists symptoms of brake problems, probable causes, and suggested corrective actions. Unless noted otherwise, relevant repairs are described later in this repair group.

Table a. Brake system troubleshooting

Symptom	Probable cause	Repairs
Steering wheel shake when braking at speed (> 50 mph)	Worn control arm bushings	Check front bushings. Replace work parts. See **310 Front Suspension**.
	Brake rotors out of true	Replace brake rotors.
Brake squeal	Brake pad carriers dirty or corroded or pads loose (poor fit) in pad carrier	Remove brake pads and clean calipers. Use original equipment pads for proper fit and use BMW anti-squeal compound during installation.
	Brake pads heat-glazed or oil-soaked	Replace brake pads. Clean rotors. Replace leaking calipers as required.
	Wheel bearings worn (noise most pronounced when turning)	Replace worn bearings. See **310 Front Suspension** or **330 Rear Suspension**.
	Incorrectly installed brake pads, parking brake shoes, or brake parts	Check component installation. Check/replace anti-rattle springs.
Pedal goes to floor when braking	Brake fluid loss due to system leaks	Check fluid level and inspect for signs of leakage.
	Master cylinder or traction control system faulty	Replace master cylinder. Diagnose traction control system using factory or compatible diagnostic tool.
Low pedal after system bleeding	Master cylinder faulty	Replace master cylinder.
Pedal spongy or brakes work only when pedal is pumped	Air in brake fluid	Bleed system using factory or compatible diagnostic tool.
	Master cylinder or traction control system faulty	Replace master cylinder. Diagnose traction control system using factory or compatible diagnostic tool.
Excessive braking effort	Brake pads wet	Use light pedal pressure to dry pads while driving.
	Brake pads heat-glazed or fluid-soaked	Replace brake pads and rotors. Replace leaking calipers.
	Vacuum booster or vacuum hose connections to booster faulty	Inspect vacuum lines. Test vacuum booster and replace as required. Test brake booster check valve for one-way flow.
Brakes pulsate, chatter or grab	Warped brake rotors	Resurface or replace rotors.
	Brake pads worn	Replace brake pads.
	Brake pads heat-glazed or oil-soaked	Clean rotors. Replace leaking calipers.
Uneven braking, car pulls to one side, rear brakes lock	Incorrect tire pressures or worn tires	Inspect tire condition. Check and correct tire pressures.
	Brake pads on one side of car heat-glazed or fluid-soaked	Replace brake pads. Clean rotors. Replace leaking calipers.
	Caliper or brake pads binding	Clean and recondition brakes.
	Worn suspension components	Inspect for worn or damaged suspension components. See **310 Front Suspension** or **330 Rear Suspension**.
Brakes drag, bind or overheat	Brake caliper or brake pads binding	Clean or replace caliper.
	Master cylinder or traction control system faulty	Replace master cylinder. Diagnose traction control system using factory or compatible diagnostic tool.

Warnings and Cautions

> **WARNING—**
> - *Make sure that the brake system is bled using the BMW service tool. See* **Bleeding Brakes** *in this repair group.*
> - *Semi-metallic and metallic brake friction materials in brake pads or shoes produce dangerous dust. Treat all brake dust as a hazardous material. Do not create dust by grinding, sanding, or cleaning brake friction surfaces with compressed air.*
> - *Brake fluid is poisonous, corrosive and dangerous to the environment. Wear safety glasses and rubber gloves when working with brake fluid. Do not siphon brake fluid with your mouth. Dispose of brake fluid properly.*
> - *Do not reuse self-locking nuts, bolts or fasteners. They are designed to be used only once and may fail if reused. Replace them with new self-locking fasteners.*
> - *A car with electronic stability control is still subject to normal physical laws. Avoid excessive speeds for the road conditions encountered.*

> **CAUTION—**
> - *Brake fluid damages paint. Immediately clean brake fluid spilled on painted surfaces and wash with water.*
> - *Use new brake fluid from a fresh, unopened container. Brake fluid absorbs moisture from the air. This can lead to corrosion problems in the braking system and also lowers the fluid boiling point.*
> - *When working on brake fluid lines:*
>   *-Do not mix up fluid lines at the master cylinder, hydraulic unit or precharge pump. Label unions before disconnecting.*
>   *-Do not kink brake lines.*
>   *-Plug open lines and brake fluid ports to prevent contamination.*
> - *Tighten brake hoses on front wheels with wheels in straight ahead position.*
> - *If carrying out electric welding work, be sure to disconnect electrical harness connector from electronic control module.*
> - *Do not expose electronic control modules to high sustained heat. Maximum heat exposure:*
>   *-95°C (203°F) for short periods of time*
>   *-85°C (185°F) for long periods of time (approx. 2 hours)*

BLEEDING BRAKES

> **WARNING—**
> • *The BMW traction control system uses electronic controls and a sophisticated hydraulic unit in the brake system. Once air enters the hydraulic unit, it is very difficult to remove using traditional methods. For this reason, use BMW service tool to pressure bleed brakes.*
> • *When flushing brake fluid from the system, use extreme care to not let the brake fluid reservoir run dry. If air enters the hydraulic unit, be sure to use the BMW service tool to bleed the brake system before the vehicle is driven.*

Brake bleeding is usually done for one of two reasons:

• To replace old brake fluid as part of routine maintenance

• To expel trapped air in the system that resulted from opening the brake hydraulic system during repairs.

BMW recommends completely replacing the brake fluid at least once every two years. When replacing brake fluid or bleeding brakes, use the correct specification brake fluid according to application table below.

Brake fluid application	
BMW preferred fluid	Low viscosity DOT 4 brake fluid
DOT 4 and low viscosity DOT 4 brake fluid can be mixed.	

When adding or replacing brake fluid, add new brake fluid from an unopened container. It is important to bleed the entire system when any part of the hydraulic system is opened.

If you are certain no air was introduced into the master cylinder or DSC hydraulic unit, bleed the brakes at the calipers using a pressure bleeder. See **Brake calipers, bleeding** in this repair group.

However, if air enters the DSC hydraulic unit, bubbles may adhere to the edges and internal valves of the unit and these cannot be removed via conventional flushing. In that case it is necessary to bleed brakes using a BMW service tool. The special tool creates pulsations or vibrations which loosen and flush the bubbles.

Therefore, if you are in any doubt about introduced air into the brake system, use a BMW diagnostic scan tool to bleed the system or have the brakes bled by an authorized BMW dealer. See **Brake system, bleeding** in this repair group.

When bleeding the brakes, start at the wheel farthest from the master cylinder and progress in the following order:

• right rear brake

• left rear brake

• right front brake

• left front brake

340

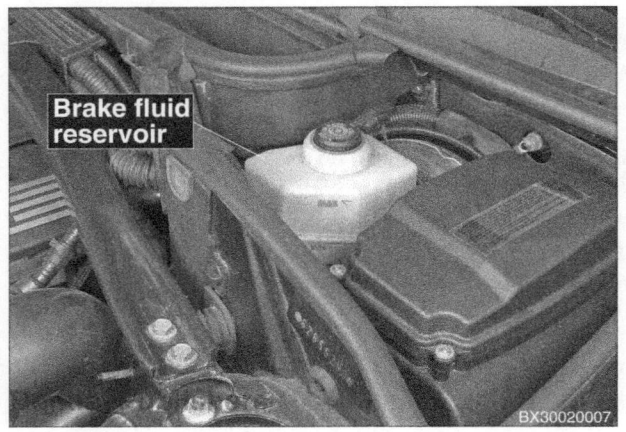

Brake calipers, bleeding

◄ Top off brake fluid reservoir.

Brake fluid application	
BMW preferred fluid	Low viscosity DOT 4 brake fluid
DOT 4 and low viscosity DOT 4 brake fluid can be mixed.	

– Connect pressure bleeder to reservoir. Pressurize system to approximately 2 bar (29 psi).

> **CAUTION—**
> • *Do not exceed a pressure of 2 bar (29 psi) when pressure bleeding the brake system. Excessive pressure damages the brake fluid reservoir.*

◄ Connect bleeder hose and bottle to **right rear** caliper bleeder screw (**arrow**). Have a helper hold brake pedal down.

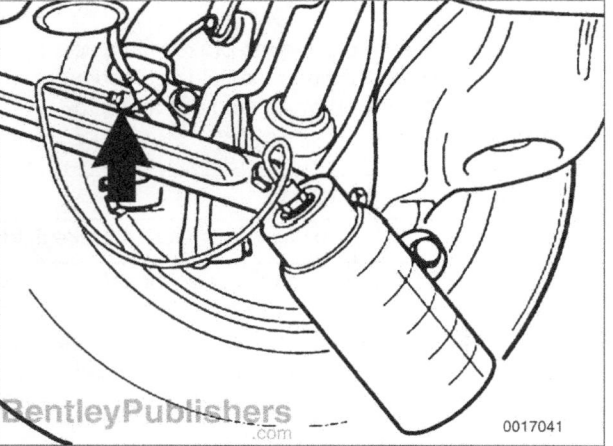

◄ Remove rubber cap and open bleeder screw (**arrow**). Have helper slowly pump brakes about 10 times with bleeder screw open, holding pedal down on last pump. When escaping fluid is free of air bubbles, close bleeder screw.

> **CAUTION—**
> • *Be sure bleeder hose remains submersed in clean brake fluid whenever the bleeder valve is open.*

– Close bleeder screw and release brake pedal. Remove pressure bleeder tool, refill brake fluid reservoir and proceed to left rear wheel.

– Continue bleeding remaining wheels in the following order:
• **left rear, right front, left front**

Tightening torques	
Bleeder to caliper: • 7 mm screw • 9 mm screw • 11 mm screw	 3 - 5 Nm (2 - 4 ft-lb) 7 - 11 Nm (5 - 8 ft-lb) 12 - 16 Nm (9 - 12 ft-lb)

Brake system, bleeding

The procedure below requires the use of BMW service tool.

◀ Top off brake fluid reservoir.

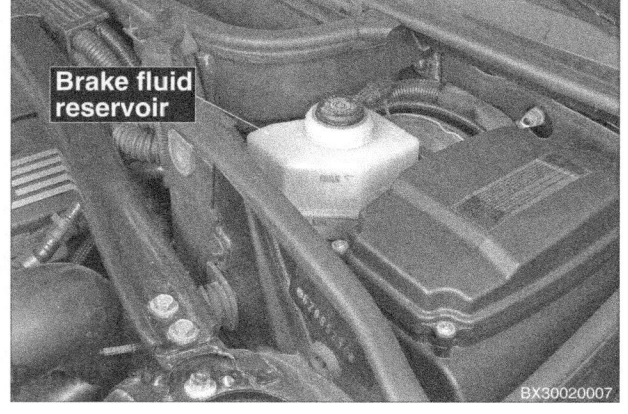

Brake fluid application	
BMW preferred fluid	Low viscosity DOT 4 brake fluid
DOT 4 and low viscosity DOT 4 brake fluid can be mixed.	

— Connect pressure bleeder to reservoir. Pressurize system to approximately 2 bar (29 psi).

> **CAUTION—**
> • *Do not exceed a pressure of 2 bar (29 psi) when pressure bleeding the brake system. Excessive pressure damages the brake fluid reservoir.*

◀ Connect diagnostic scan tool to OBD II plug on underside of dash in left footwell.

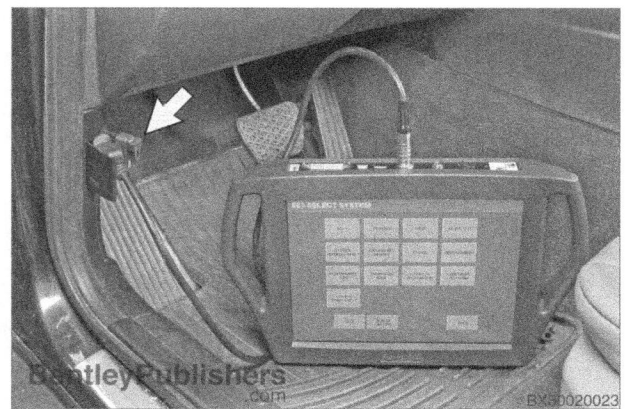

— Set tool to service function Bleeding ABS / DSC.

◀ Connect bleeder hose and bottle to **right rear** caliper bleeder screw (**arrow**). Have a helper hold brake pedal down.

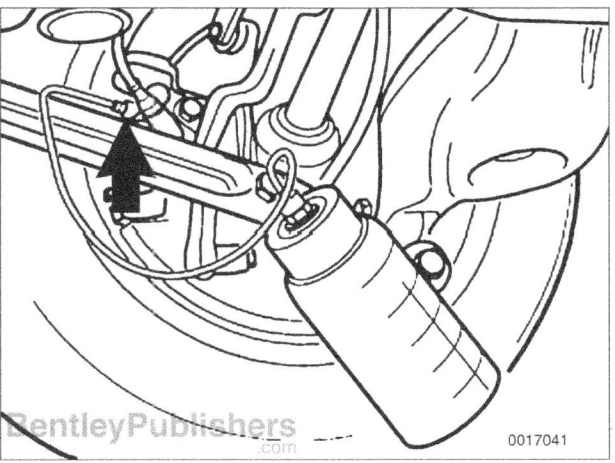

340

Braking system components

◄ Open bleeder screw. Carry out bleeding procedure using BMW service tester on-screen instructions until clear, bubble-free fluid flows.

− After BMW service tool bleeding routine has finished, press brake pedal to floor 5 times until clear, bubble-free fluid flows. Close bleeder.

> **CAUTION—**
> • *Make sure bleeder hose remains submersed in clean brake fluid whenever the bleeder valve is open.*

− Repeat procedure at **left rear** brake, then **right front** brake, then **left front** brake.

− Close bleeder screw and release brake pedal. Remove pressure bleeder tool, refill brake fluid reservoir.

Tightening torques	
Bleeder to caliper:	
• 7 mm screw	3 - 5 Nm (2 - 4 ft-lb)
• 9 mm screw	7 - 11 Nm (5 - 8 ft-lb)
• 11 mm screw	12 - 16 Nm (9 - 12 ft-lb)

BRAKE PADS, CALIPERS AND ROTORS

Braking system components

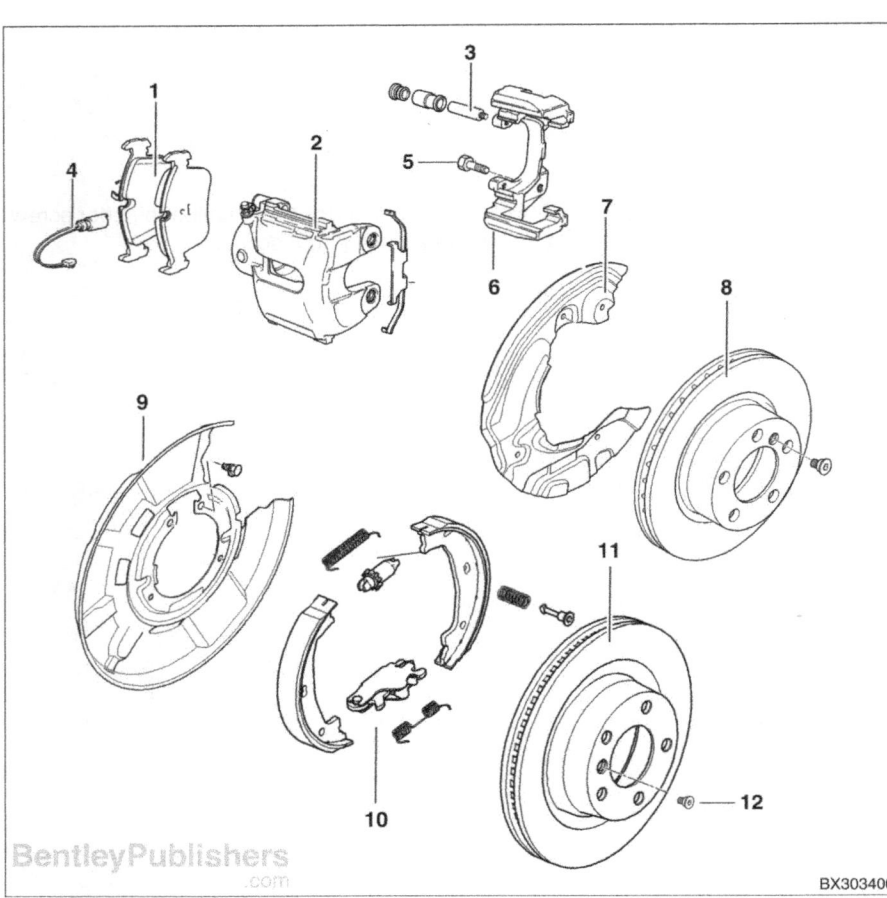

1. Brake pads
   • Wear limit: 3 mm (0.12 in).

2. Brake caliper

3. Brake caliper guide bolt
   • Tighten to 30 ˉ5 Nm (22 ˉ4 ft-lb)

4. Brake pad wear sensor
   • On left front, right rear inner pad.
   • Replace with new pads
   • Replace if warning light is illuminated

5. Brake caliper bracket bolt
   • Tighten to 110 Nm (81 ft-lb)

6. Caliper bracket (brake pad carrier)

7. Front brake backing plate

8. Front brake rotor
   • Clean off preservative before installing new rotor

9. Rear brake backing plate

10. Parking brake shoes with hardware

11. Rear brake rotor

12. Brake rotor retaining screw
    • Tighten to 16 Nm (12 ft-lb)

BX30340001

Brake pads, checking and replacing

Brake pads can be replaced without disconnecting the brake fluid hose from the caliper or having to bleed the brakes. The rotors can be replaced without disassembling wheel hub and bearing. Front and rear brake pad replacement procedures are similar.

Replace pads in sets.

— Raise car and support safely. Remove wheels.

Brake pad wear sensor

BX30020032

> **WARNING—**
> * Make sure vehicle is stable and well supported at all times. Use a professional automotive lift or jack stands. A floor jack is not adequate support.

◀ Disc brake pad wear can be checked through opening in caliper once wheel is removed:

* Measure pad friction lining thickness (**A**). Compare to specification below. See **Table b**.

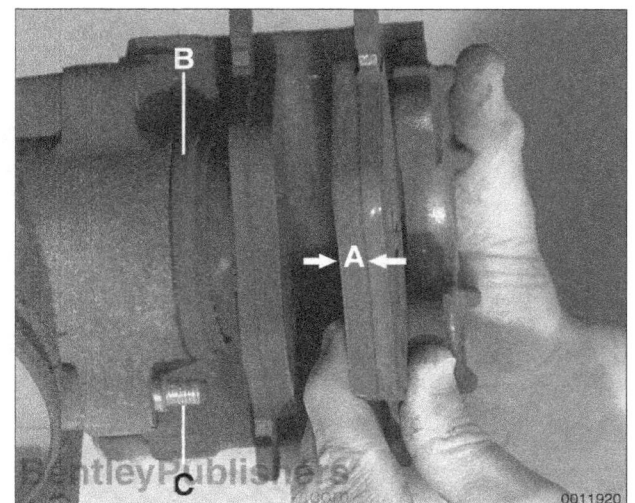

0011920

◀ Unbolt caliper from steering knuckle to further inspect:

* Brake pad thickness (**A**)
* Brake rotor
* Condition of caliper seal (**B**)
* Condition of caliper slider bolts (**C**)

Table b. Brake pad lining minimum thickness	
Minimum pad thickness, front or rear (dimension **A**)	3.0 mm (0.12 in)

— After inspection, replace parts as needed:

* See **Brake caliper and bracket removing and installing** and **Brake rotor removing and installing** in this repair group.

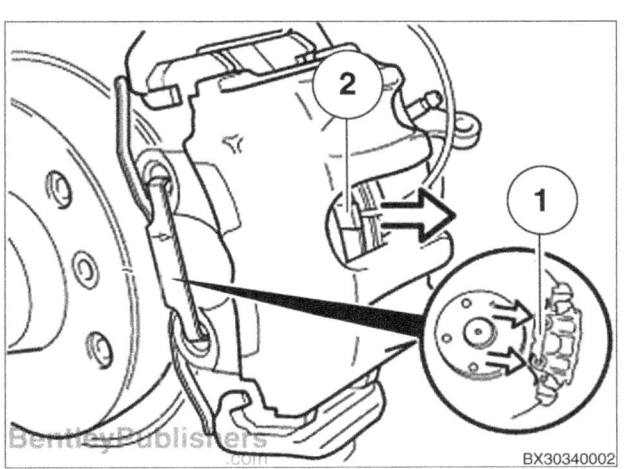

BX30340002

◀ Pry off brake caliper anti-rattle spring (**1**).

— Using your fingers, carefully remove brake pad wear sensor (**2**) from brake pad.

340

Brake pads, checking and replacing

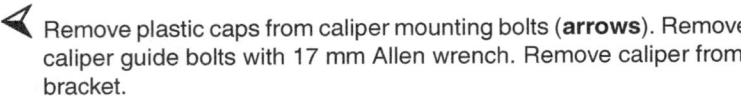

◀ Remove plastic caps from caliper mounting bolts (**arrows**). Remove caliper guide bolts with 17 mm Allen wrench. Remove caliper from bracket.

> **CAUTION—**
> • *Do not let brake caliper assembly hang from the brake hose. Support caliper from chassis with strong wire.*

> **NOTE—**
> • *If there is a ridge on brake rotor edge, press caliper pistons back into caliper before removing caliper.*

— Check brake rotor thickness. Inspect for rust or damage. If necessary replace or machine brake rotors. See **Brake rotor, removing and installing** in this repair group.

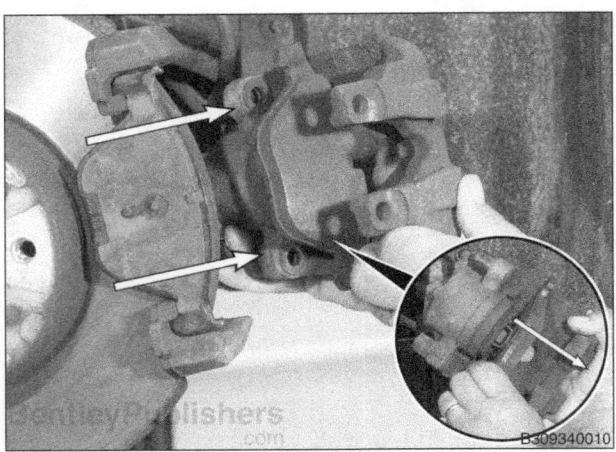

◀ Remove brake pads in direction of **arrows**.

> **NOTE—**
> • *Inner brake pad (**inset**) has a spring to locate it in the caliper piston.*

◀ Compress caliper piston using BMW special tool or equivalent.

> **CAUTION—**
> • *Pressing caliper pistons in may cause brake fluid reservoir to overflow. To prevent this, use a clean syringe to first remove some fluid from reservoir.*

— Check caliper dust boots for damage and replace if necessary.

— Clean contact surfaces between caliper and caliper carrier.

◄ Apply thin coating of BMW anti-squeal compound to caliper contact face (**arrows**).

• Do not apply grease to brake pad backing plate.

> **CAUTION**—
> • *Do not let caliper rubber dust sleeve come in contact with anti-squeal compound. The compound causes rubber to swell and deteriorate.*

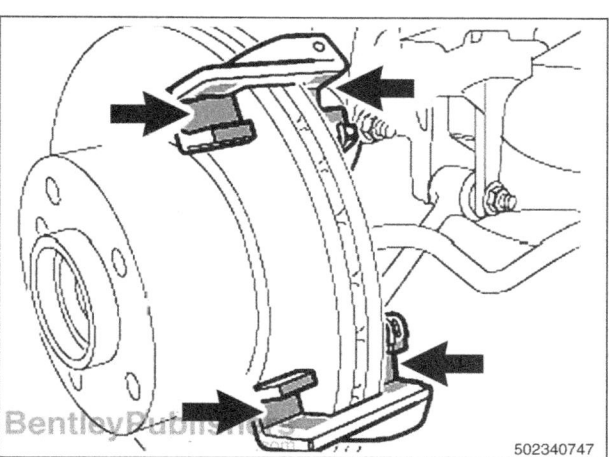

◄ Apply thin coating of BMW anti-squeal compound to brake pad rests (**arrows**) on pad carrier.

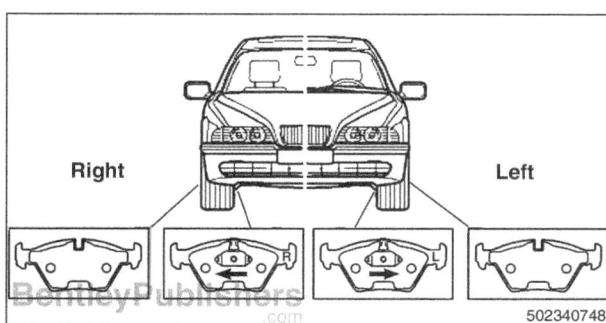

◄ When installing directional brake pads, install marked pads as shown.

> **NOTE**—
> • *BMW-supplied (OEM) front brake pads may be marked as directional pads. Aftermarket brands are generally not labeled as directional. When installing directional pads, be sure to install them as indicated in the illustration.*

— Where applicable, insert brake pad wear sensor into cutout in new pad. Push sensor into pad cutout until it locks into place.

> **NOTE**—
> • *If brake pad wear sensor light illuminated prior to brake pad replacement, replace wear sensor.*

— Route pad wear sensor wiring through caliper opening and under bleeder dust cap.

— Remainder of installation is reverse of removal.

- Clean brake caliper guide bolts (7 mm Allen). Replace if not in perfect condition. Do not grease.
- Top off brake fluid to MAX marking.
- Before driving car, pump brake pedal several times so that brake pads contact brake rotors.
- Check that brake fluid level is correct. Top off if necessary.
- Hold ignition key for at least 30 seconds in accessory position without starting engine. This clears fault codes in memory and turns brake pad warning light OFF.

Tightening torques	
Brake caliper to caliper bracket (7 mm Allen)	30 - 5 Nm (22 - 4 ft-lb)
Road wheel to hub	140 Nm (103 ft-lb)

Brake caliper and bracket, removing and installing

Front and rear caliper removal are similar unless otherwise noted.

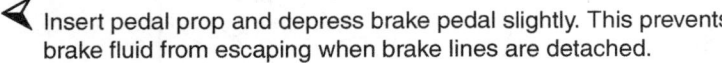 Insert pedal prop and depress brake pedal slightly. This prevents brake fluid from escaping when brake lines are detached.

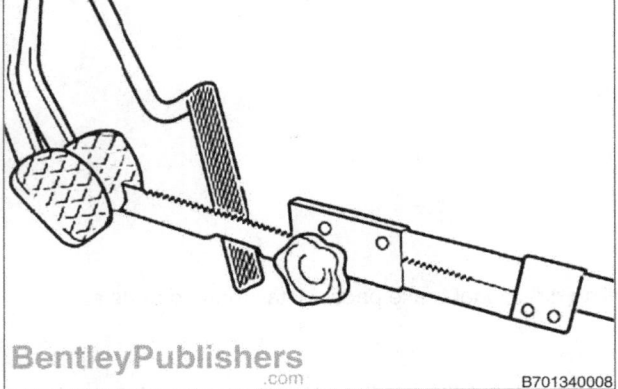

BentleyPublishers.com

B701340008

— Raise car and support safely. Remove wheels.

> **WARNING—**
> - *Make sure vehicle is stable and well supported at all times. Use a professional automotive lift or jack stands. A floor jack is not adequate support.*

Wear sensor removal

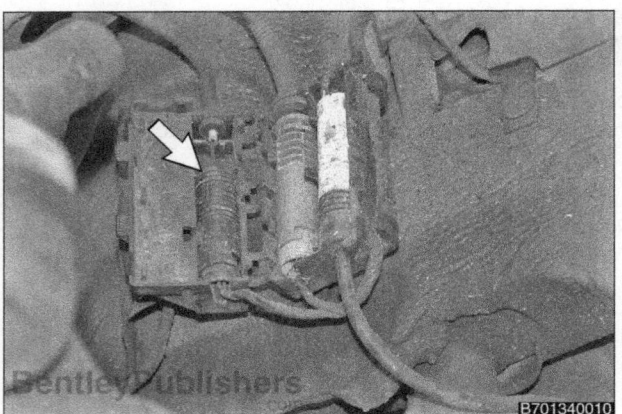

BentleyPublishers.com

B701340010

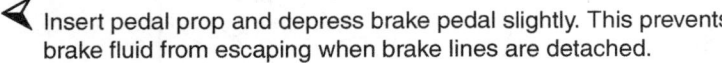 **Left front wheel**: Working in junction box in wheel housing, separate brake pad warning sensor electrical harness (**arrow**).

— **Right rear wheel**: Remove small underbody plastic cover if necessary.

◄ Working in junction box (**1**) under body near trailing arm mount, separate brake pad warning sensor electrical connector (**2**) and unclip harness from trailing arm (**3**).

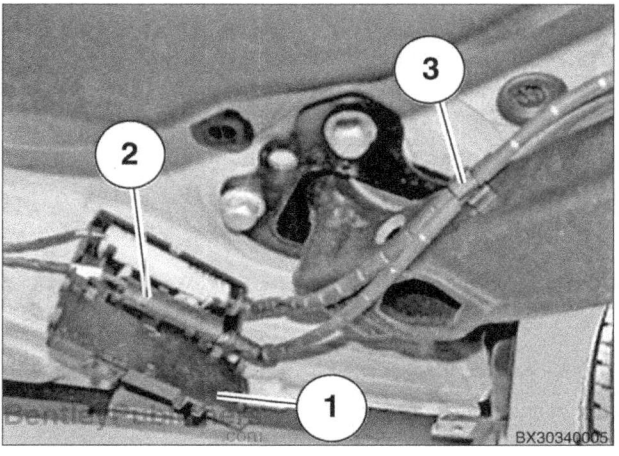

Brake hose removal

◄ **Front brakes**: Remove clip (**A**) securing brake hose to front strut.

◄ **Rear brakes**: Remove bracket (**arrow**) securing brake hose to trailing arm.

Brake rotors, replacing

BX30340004

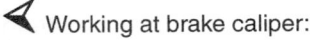 Working at brake caliper:

- Loosen brake hose fitting at caliper. Use shop towels to catch dripping brake fluid.
- Remove caliper bracket mounting bolts (**arrows**) from steering knuckle (**front caliper**) or from trailing arm (**rear caliper**).

– Lift off caliper and spin assembly off hose. Plug open fluid lines and ports.

– Inspect brake caliper for signs of leakage. Check that caliper piston slides smoothly into caliper. Replace caliper if any faults are found.

– Installation is reverse of removal. Bleed entire brake system before driving car. See **Brake calipers, bleeding** in this repair group.

Tightening torques	
Brake hose bracket to trailing arm	9 Nm (7 ft-lb)
Brake fluid hose to caliper	19 Nm (14 ft-lb)
Front caliper bracket to steering knuckle	110 Nm (81 ft-lb)
Rear caliper bracket to trailing arm	65 Nm (50 ft-lb)
Road wheel to hub	140 Nm (103 ft-lb)

Brake rotors, replacing

Front and rear brake rotor, removing and installing is similar. Replace brake rotors in pairs per axle.

– Raise car and support safely. Remove wheels.

> **WARNING—**
> - *Make sure vehicle is stable and well supported at all times. Use a professional automotive lift or jack stands. A floor jack is not adequate support.*

 Remove brake caliper carrier bolts (**arrows**). Suspend brake caliper from chassis using stiff wire.

> **NOTE—**
> - *Brake hose remains connected.*

BX30340004

◀ Remove brake rotor mounting screw (**arrow**) and remove rotor.

— Inspect rotor for cracks, signs of overheating and scoring.

— Minimum allowable thickness (MIN TH) is stamped on rotor hub. Measure rotor braking surface with a micrometer at eight to ten different points and use the smallest measurement.

— If rotor does not pass minimum thickness requirements or is damaged, replace rotor.

  • Clean rotor with brake cleaner before installing.

  • When installing new rear brake rotors, adjust parking brake. See **Parking brake, adjusting** in this repair group.

Tightening torques	
Brake rotor to hub	16 Nm (12 ft-lb)
Front caliper bracket to steering knuckle	110 Nm (81 ft-lb)
Rear caliper bracket to trailing arm	65 Nm (50 ft-lb)
Road wheel to hub	140 Nm (103 ft-lb)

MASTER CYLINDER

The brake master cylinder is mounted to the front of the vacuum booster on the driver side bulkhead.

> **WARNING—**
> • Make sure that the brake system is bled using the BMW service tool. See **Bleeding Brakes** in this repair group.

Master cylinder, removing and installing

> **CAUTION—**
> • Brake fluid is highly corrosive and dangerous to the environment. Dispose of it properly.

— Remove heater bulkhead and partition wall near reservoir. See **640 Heating and Air-conditioning**.

◀ Working at brake fluid reservoir at left rear of engine compartment:

  • Detach brake fluid level sensor connector.

  • Remove reservoir cap.

  • Using a clean syringe, empty brake fluid reservoir.

  • **Manual transmission:** Disconnect clutch master cylinder supply line from fluid reservoir. Be prepared to catch dripping fluid. Secure supply line in vertical position to prevent excessive fluid loss.

  • Plug open brake fluid lines and ducts to prevent fluid leakage and contamination.

— Remove brake fluid reservoir by pulling vertically out of master cylinder.

Brake fluid reservoir

Brake booster check valve, checking

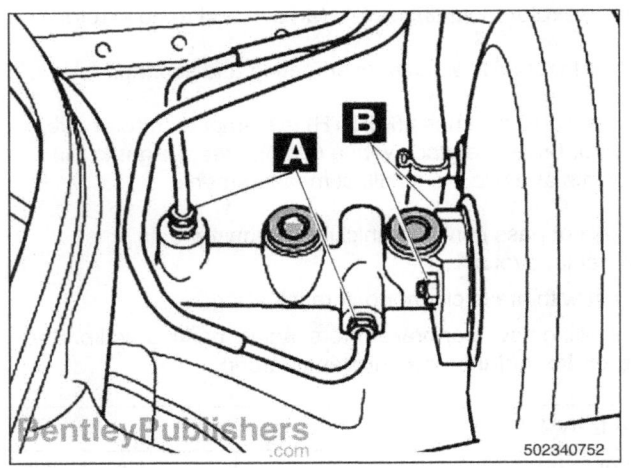

502340752

◄ Disconnect master cylinder brake lines (**A**).

  • Plug open brake lines to prevent contamination.

  • Remove master cylinder mounting nuts (**B**) and remove cylinder.

– During reinstallation, make sure all nuts, fluid couplings, thread bores, and mating surfaces are clean.

– Mount master cylinder to brake booster using new sealing O-ring and new self-locking nuts.

– Connect brake fluid lines to master cylinder.

– Reinstall fluid reservoir using new sealing grommets.

> **CAUTION—**
> • *Be sure to align master cylinder pushrod and booster pushrod.*
> • *Do not over-torque master cylinder mounting nuts. This could damage the brake booster and prevent proper vacuum build-up.*

Tightening torque	
Brake master cylinder to brake booster (replace nuts with new)	26 Nm (19 ft-lb)
Brake lines to master cylinder	17 Nm (12.5 ft-lb)

– Reconnect clutch fluid supply hose, if applicable.

– Remainder of installation is reverse of removal.

  • Top up with fresh brake fluid.

  • Bleed entire brake system. See **Brake system, bleeding** in this repair group.

Brake booster check valve, checking

The check valve in the brake booster vacuum line prevents contamination from engine backfires and other sources from entering the brake booster. The check valve is in brake booster.

– Pump brake pedal a few times to reduce vacuum in brake booster. This makes removal of check valve easier.

– Remove or loosen hose clamp(s) at check valve.

– Disconnect hoses. Remove valve to test or replace. If valve is pressed into grommet in vacuum booster, pry it out carefully.

– Reinstall valve using new hose clamps. Install valve so that molded arrow is pointing toward intake manifold.

Vacuum pump (N52 engine)

To provide proper engine vacuum to the brake vacuum booster under all engine operating conditions, a chain-driven vacuum pump is fitted to the engine. The vacuum pump is mounted beneath the intake manifold on the front left side of the engine. For removing and installing, see **131 Fuel Injection (N52 engine)**.

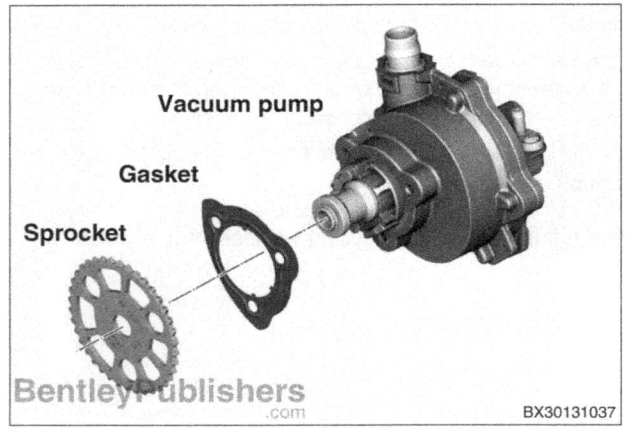

Vacuum pump

Gasket

Sprocket

BX30131037

PARKING BRAKE

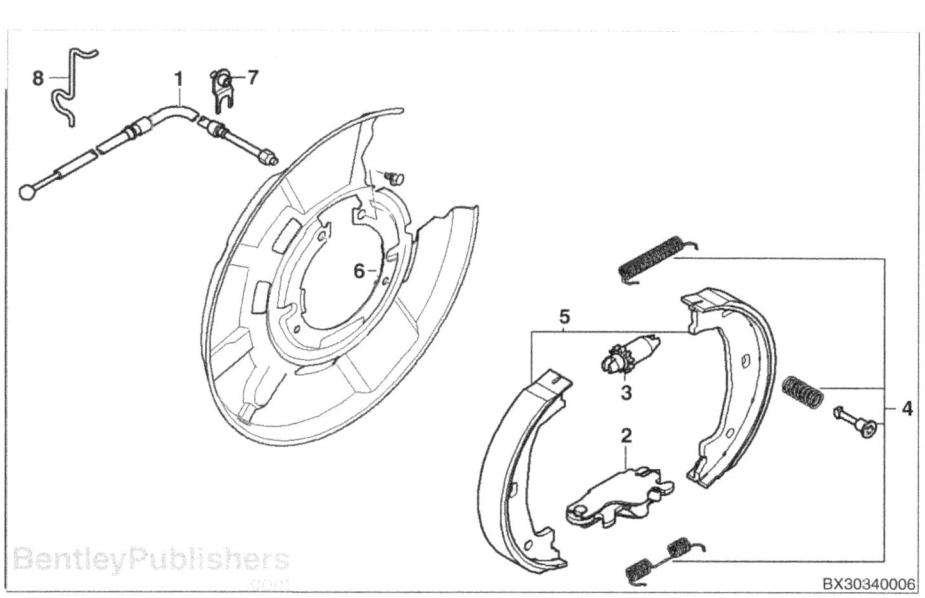

BX30340006

Parking brake components

1. Parking brake bowden cable
2. Expanding lock
3. Adjuster
4. Brake shoe hardware
5. Brake shoes
6. Backing plate
7. Spring clip
8. Bowden cable bracket

Parking brake, adjusting

The parking brake is a brake drum system integrated into the rear brake rotors. Adjust with rear of car raised off the ground and the wheels installed.

Adjusting parking brake under the following circumstances:

• After replacing parking brake shoes.

• After replacing rear brake rotors.

• Excessive stroke of parking brake handle required for actuation (more then 10 clicks).

• After replacement of brake shoe adjuster or parking brake cable(s).

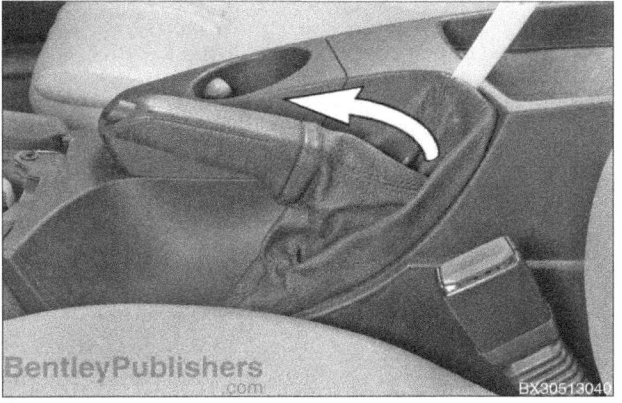

◄ Working at the parking brake handle use a suitable prying tool to unclip boot from catches.

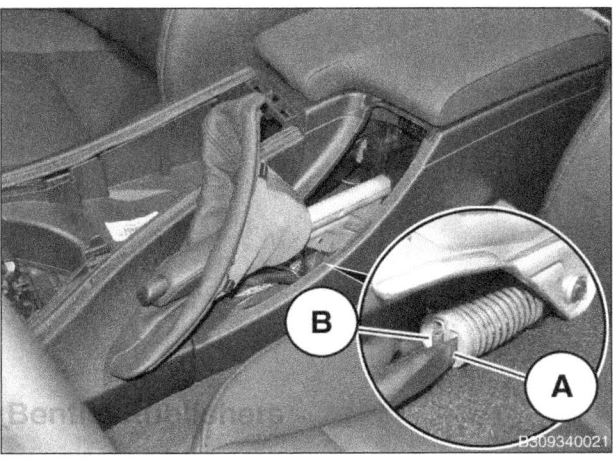

◄ Relieve parking brake cable tension: Using a screwdriver, lock parking brake handle adjuster by pressing spring (**A**) back to engage lock (**B**). **Inset** shows lock engaged.

NOTE —

• *E90 shown in photo, E83 parking brake handle is similar.*

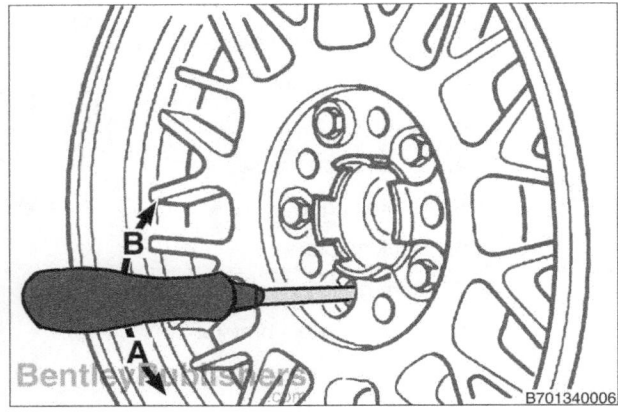

— Raise car and support safely.

> **WARNING—**
> • *Make sure vehicle is stable and well supported at all times. Use a professional automotive lift or jack stands. A floor jack is not adequate support.*

— Remove one lug bolt from each rear wheel. Turn road wheel until lug bolt hole lines up with parking brake adjuster.

◄ Use flat-bladed screwdriver to reach into brake drum through lug bolt hole and turn brake adjuster.
  • Left rear wheel: Turn adjuster in direction **A** to spread brake shoes.
  • Right rear wheel: Turn adjuster in direction **B** to spread brake shoes.

— Turn adjuster until wheel no longer turns. Back adjuster off 6 notches.

Parking brake adjusting (initial)	
Back off adjuster through wheel lug bolt hole	6 notches

◄ Unlock parking brake handle adjuster by levering out lock (**arrow**) with a screwdriver.

> **NOTE—**
> • *E90 shown*

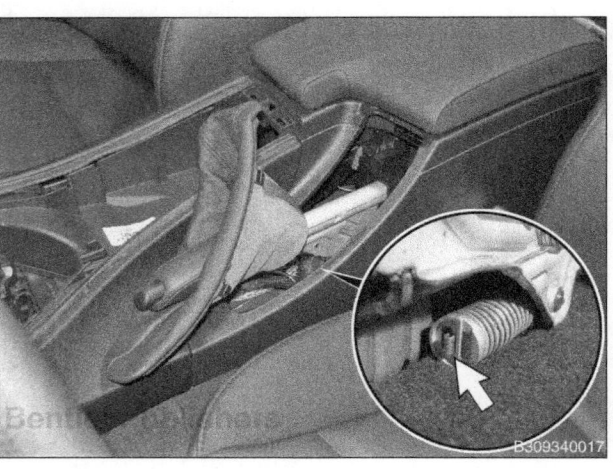

— Working inside car, set parking brake several times to seat brakes.

— Release lever and make sure rear wheels turn freely.

— Switch ignition ON. Pull up parking brake lever 1 notch and make sure that parking brake warning light comes on. If not, adjust parking brake warning light contact switch.

— Install parking brake lever boot. Install road wheel lug bolts.

Tightening torque	
Road wheel to hub	140 Nm (103 ft-lb)

Parking brake shoes, removing and installing

Replace parking brake hardware when replacing shoes.

— Raise car and support safely. Remove rear wheels.

> **WARNING—**
> • *Make sure vehicle is stable and well supported at all times. Use a professional automotive lift or jack stands. A floor jack is not adequate support.*

— Without disconnecting brake fluid hose, remove rear brake calipers from trailing arms. Remove rear brake rotors. See **Brake rotor, removing and installing** in this repair group.

> **CAUTION—**
> • *Do not let the brake caliper assembly hang from the brake hose. Support caliper from chassis with strong wire.*

◀ Working at the parking brake handle use a suitable prying tool to unclip boot from catches.

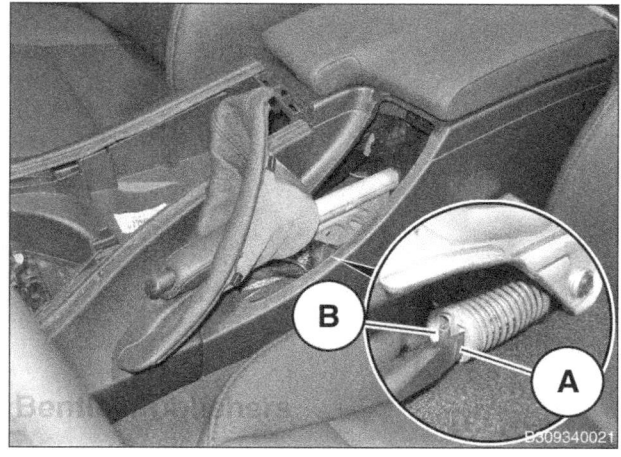

◀ Relieve parking brake cable tension: Using a screwdriver, lock parking brake handle adjuster by pressing spring (**A**) back to engage lock (**B**). **Inset** shows lock engaged.

> **NOTE—**
> • *E90 shown in photo, E83 parking brake handle is similar.*

◀ Working at rear brake, unhook return springs (**arrows**) from brake shoes.

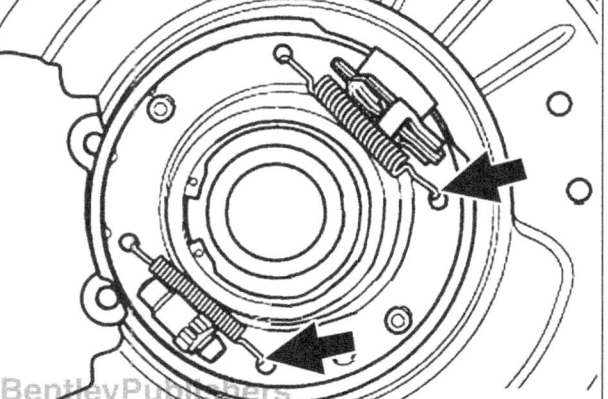

340

◀ Rotate hub flange to align lug hole with return spring. Remove brake shoe retaining pins using 6 mm allen wrench.

- Rotate retainer 90º to release.
- Spread shoes apart and lift out.
- Apply thin coat of grease to sliding parts and pins before reassembly.

— Installation is reverse of removal.

- Install rear brake rotor as described in **Brake rotor, removing and installing**.
- Adjust parking brake cables. See **Parking brake, adjusting**.

Parking brake cable, replacing

The parking brake is actuated by two separate Bowden cables. Each cable can be replaced separately.

— Working inside car, gain access to base of parking brake handle by removing center console storage tray and center armrest, as necessary. See **513 Interior Trim.**

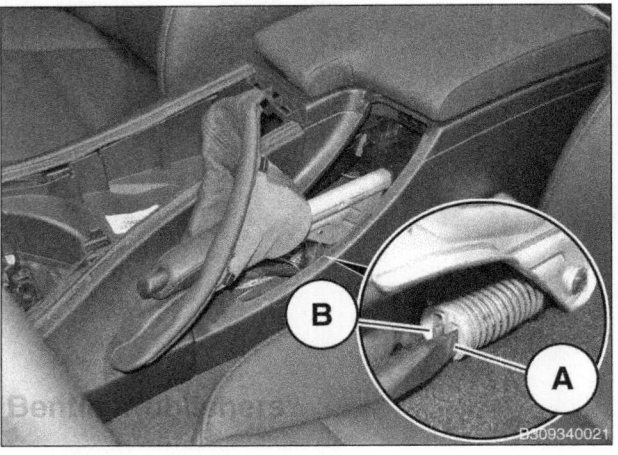

◀ Relieve parking brake cable tension: Using a screwdriver, lock parking brake handle adjuster by pressing stop (**A**) spring back to engage hook (**B**). **Inset** shows hook engaged.

NOTE—
- *E90 shown*

— Raise car and support safely. Remove rear wheels.

> *WARNING—*
> - *Make sure vehicle is stable and well supported at all times. Use a professional automotive lift or jack stands. A floor jack is not adequate support.*

— Without disconnecting brake fluid hose, remove rear brake calipers from trailing arms. Remove rear brake rotors. See **Brake rotor, removing and installing** in this repair group.

> *CAUTION—*
> - *Do not let the brake caliper assembly hang from the brake hose. Support caliper from chassis with strong wire.*

— Remove complete exhaust system. See **180 Exhaust System**.

— Remove center tunnel heat shield.

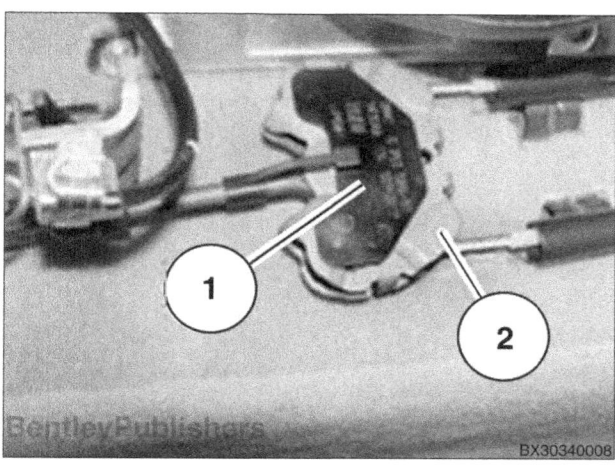

◀ Working inside center console area, unclip cover (**1**) from balance bar (**2**).

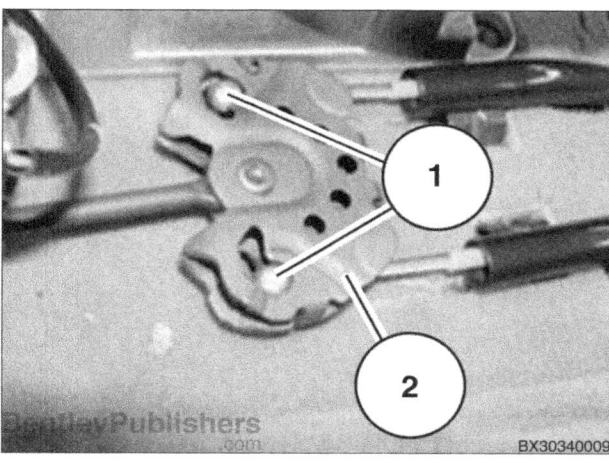

◀ Remove parking brake cables (**1**) from balance bar (**2**).

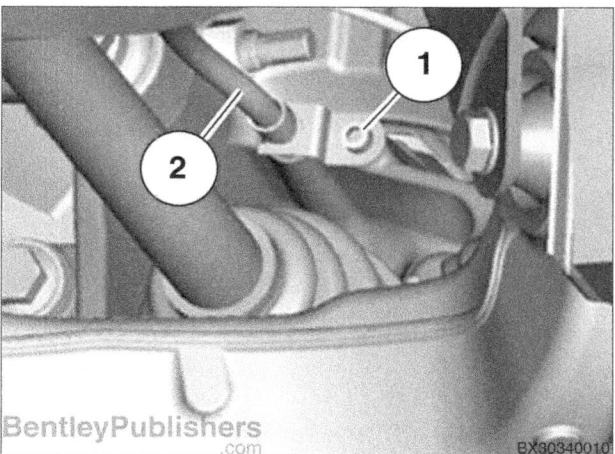

◀ Working at trailing arm, remove cable fastener and cable hold down (**1**) for parking brake cable (**2**).

Parking brake cable, replacing

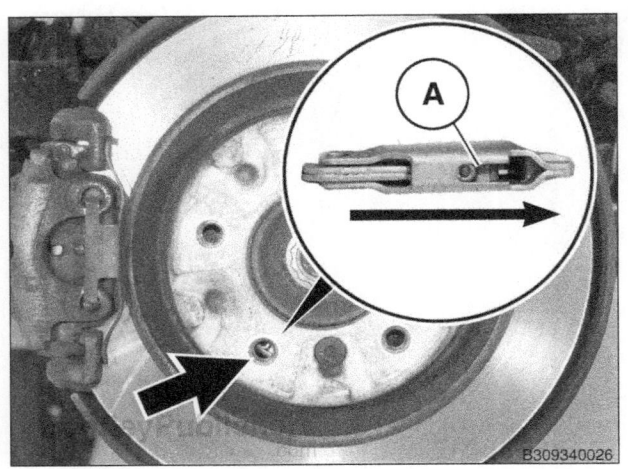

◀ Rotate brake rotor to align stud hole until cable end and expander are visible through hole (**arrow**).

− Press and release spring (**A**) in direction of **arrow** while pulling parking brake cable out of expander and backing plate.

NOTE—
• *E90 shown in photo, E83 rear brake assembly is similar.*

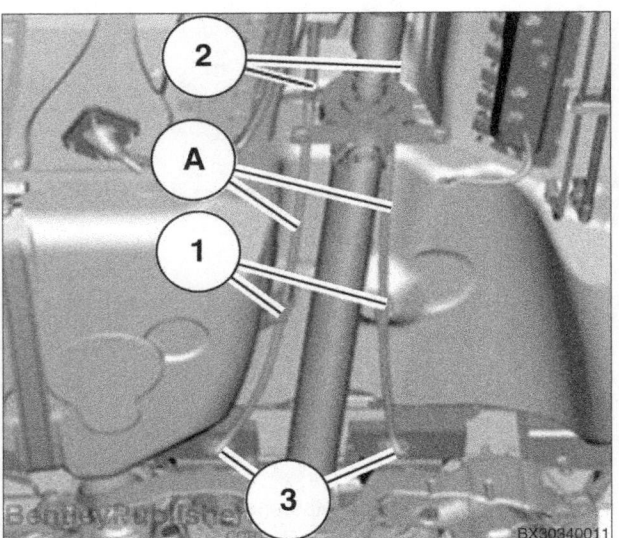

◀ Unclip parking brake cables (**A**) from mounts (**1**).

− Pull parking brake cables out of guide (**2**).

− Feed parking brake cables out of rear subframe (**3**) to remove.

− Remainder of installation is reverse of removal. Adjust parking brake. See **Parking brake, adjusting** in this repair group.

DSC COMPONENTS AND REPAIRS

> **CAUTION—**
> • *If the tires on the car are of different makes, the DSC system may overreact. Only fit tires of the same make and tread pattern.*

X3 vehicles are equipped with antilock brakes (ABS) with dynamic stability control (DSC8). This system is also known as DXC (with VTG xDrive electronics).

DSC works in conjunction with ABS, the engine management system, and the transfer case (xDrive) electronics to enhance vehicle control. The main DSC function is to maintain contact between the tires and the road surface under all driving conditions. This is achieved through exact application and management of braking and drivetrain forces.

For DSC system descriptions, see **300 Suspension, Steering and Brakes–General**.

On-board diagnosis, coding

DSC systems are self-diagnosing and store fault codes (diagnostic trouble codes or DTCs) in the DSC control module. For information on how to access DTCs, see **020 Maintenance**.

DSC components are coded to each other and to the vehicle using a BMW diagnostic scan tool. When replacing DSC components, a scan tool may be required to finish the job, including recalibration of the steering angle sensor. A BMW dealer service department or other qualified shop with the correct equipment can code the DCS system.

DSC power supply

See **ECL Electrical Component Locations** for fuse panel access information.

DSC controls

 Lower dashboard above center console:
• **HDC** (hill decent control) switch
• **DSC** (dynamic stability control) switch

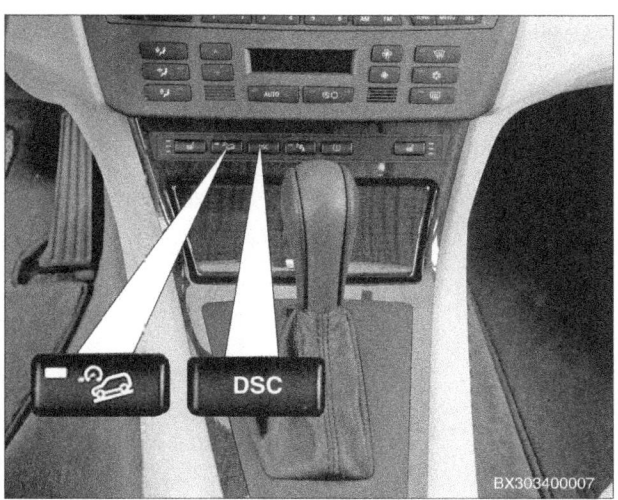

340

Wheel speed sensor, replacing

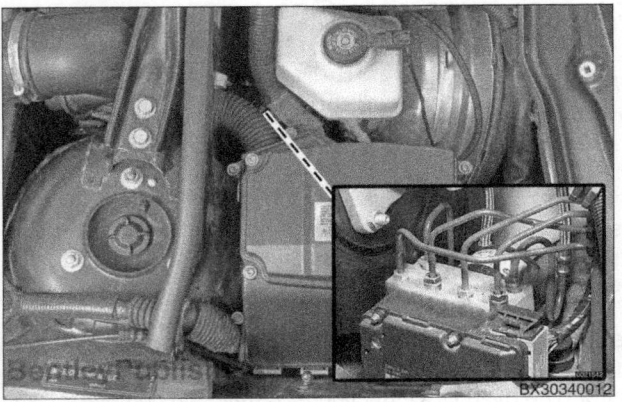

◀ Left side engine compartment under brake master cylinder:
  • Combined DXC control module / hydraulic unit.

> **CAUTION—**
> • *Replacement of the DSC (DXC) hydraulic control unit requires the use of a BMW diagnostic scan tool to code the new unit, bleed the system of air, and recalibrate the steering angle sensor. The new part cannot be safely replaced without the use of the factory diagnostic scan tool.*

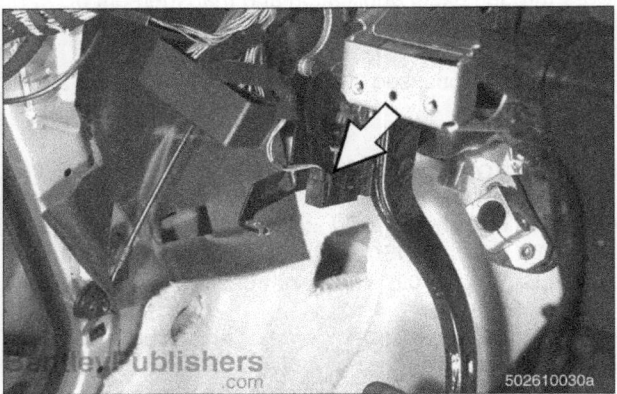

◀ Above brake pedal (**arrow**), underneath left side dashboard:
  • **S29** Brake light switch.

Wheel speed sensor, replacing

– Raise car and support safely. Remove rear wheels.

> **WARNING—**
> • *Make sure vehicle is stable and well supported at all times. Use a professional automotive lift or jack stands. A floor jack is not adequate support.*

Front wheel speed sensor

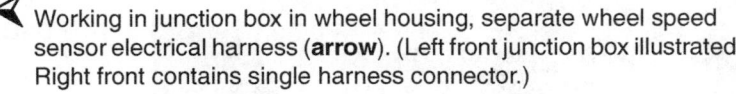

◀ Working in junction box in wheel housing, separate wheel speed sensor electrical harness (**arrow**). (Left front junction box illustrated. Right front contains single harness connector.)

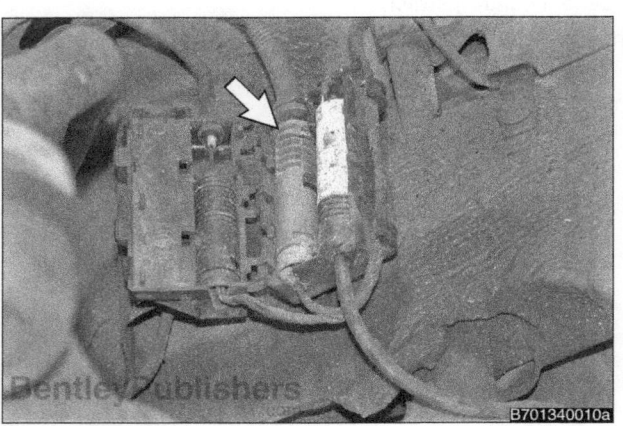

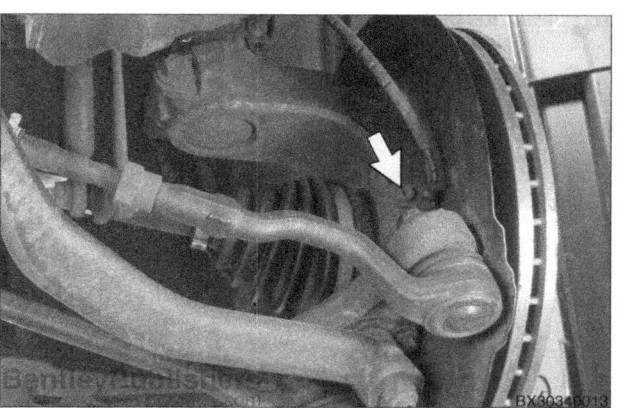

◄ Unscrew sensor mounting bolt (**arrow**) at steering knuckle.

– During installation, apply thin coat of Staburags®NBU 12/K or equivalent grease to speed sensor and housing.

– Installation is reverse of removal.

Tightening torque	
ABS wheel speed sensor to steering knuckle	8 Nm (6 ft-lb)

Rear wheel speed sensor

– Remove small underbody plastic cover if necessary.

◄ Working in junction box (**1**) under body near trailing arm mount, separate ABS sensor electrical connector (**2**) and unclip harness from trailing arm (**3**) (Left rear contains single harness connector.)

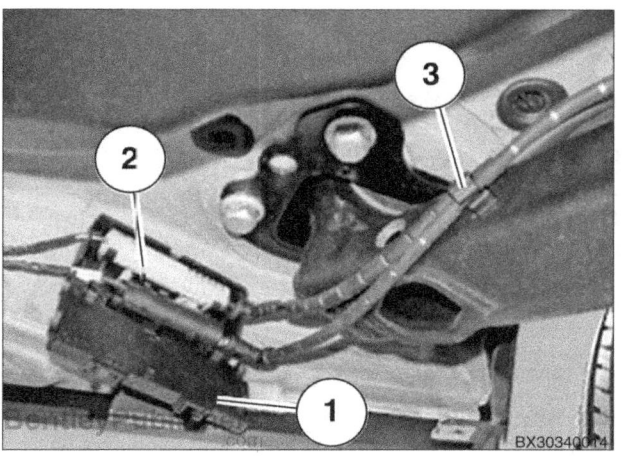

◄ Unscrew mounting bolt (**arrow**) in rear wheel bearing carrier.

– During installation, apply thin coat of Staburags®NBU 12/K or equivalent grease to speed sensor and housing.

– Installation is reverse of removal.

Tightening torque	
ABS wheel speed sensor to rear wheel bearing carrier	8 Nm (6 ft-lb)

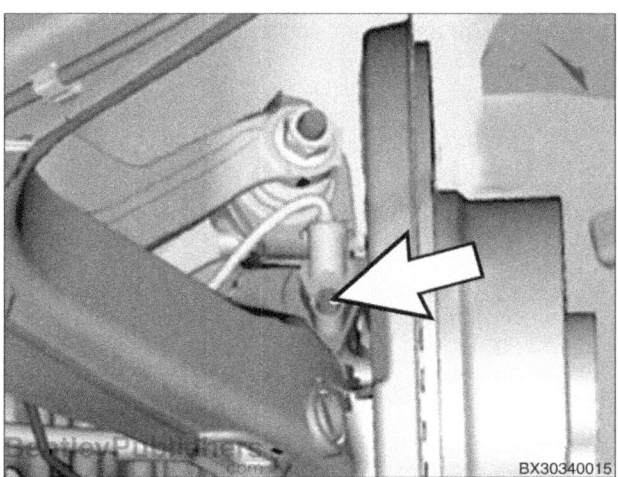

ABS impulse wheel

The front and rear ABS impulse wheels are integral with the inner wheel bearing seal and not available as separate parts. See **310 Front Suspension** or **330 Rear Suspension** for wheel bearing replacement procedures.

DSC acceleration sensor, replacing

The DSC system is equipped with an acceleration sensor that provides vehicle transverse acceleration and rotational rate (yaw) data to the DSC control module.

DSC sensor is mounted underneath the center console, behind the MRS III control module. The sensor is isolated from chassis vibrations by a rubber mount.

– Remove center console. See **513 Interior Trim**.

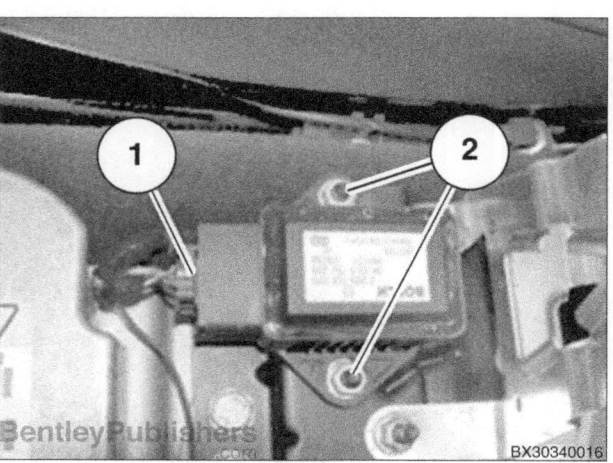

BX30340016

◄ Detach electrical connector (**1**) and remove sensor mounting bolts (**2**).

– Lift sensor away from bracket.

– Installation is reverse of removal.

> **CAUTION—**
> • *Be sure to tighten the DSC acceleration sensor and mounting bracket to the specified torques. The sensor is vibration sensitive and causes DSC malfunctions if installed improperly.*

Tightening torques	
Acceleration sensor to bracket	8 Nm (6 ft-lb)
Sensor bracket to body	8 Nm (6 ft-lb)

– Calibrate system (steering angle sensor) using BMW diagnostic scan tool.

400 Body–General

GENERAL

This chapter covers system descriptions and general information for the repair groups in partitions **4 Body** and **5 Body Equipment**.

The E83 (X3) chassis was manufactured from model year 2004 to 2010. For the 2007 model year, the X3 received a mid-life update, referred to as the Life Cycle Impulse (LCI).

400

BX304000004

BODY ASSEMBLY

Technical data

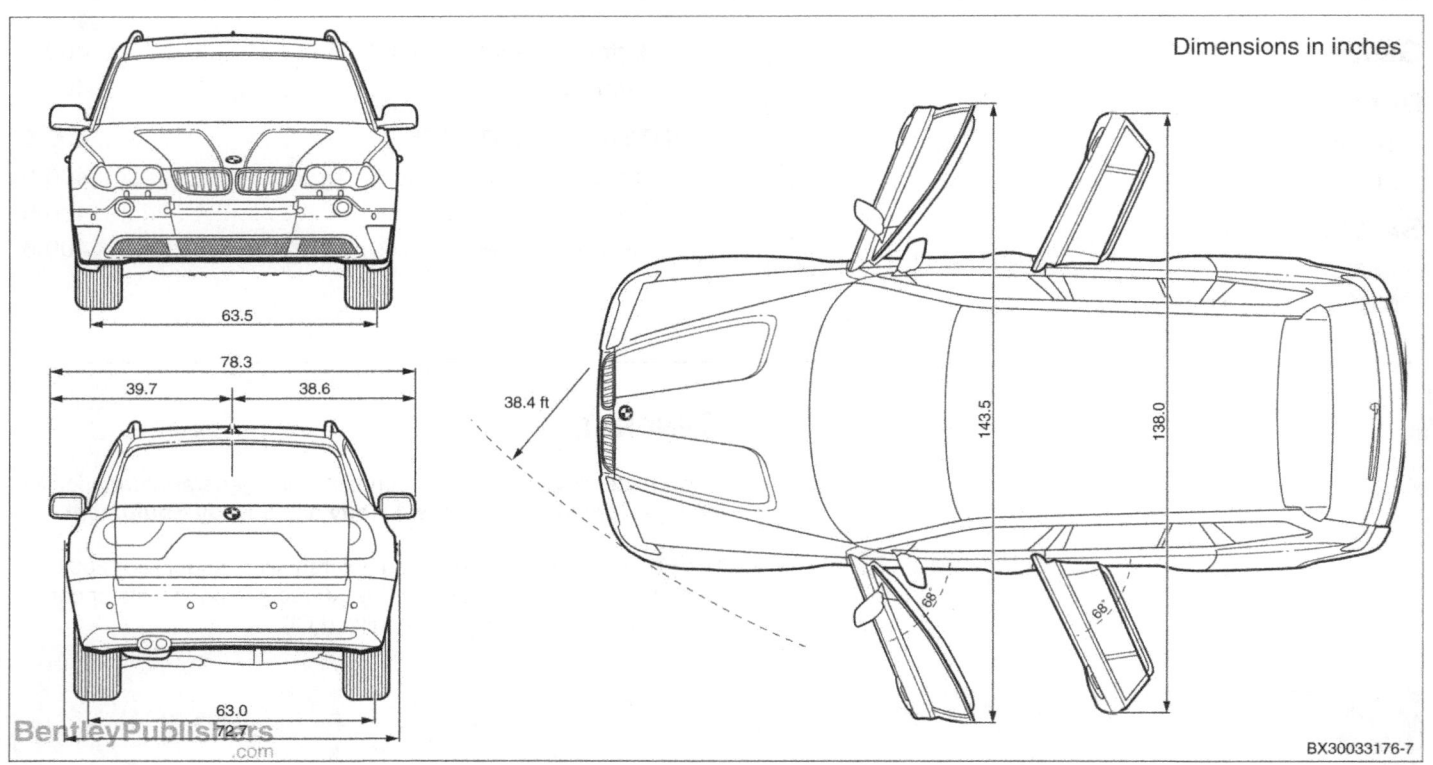

Dimensions in inches

BX30033176-7

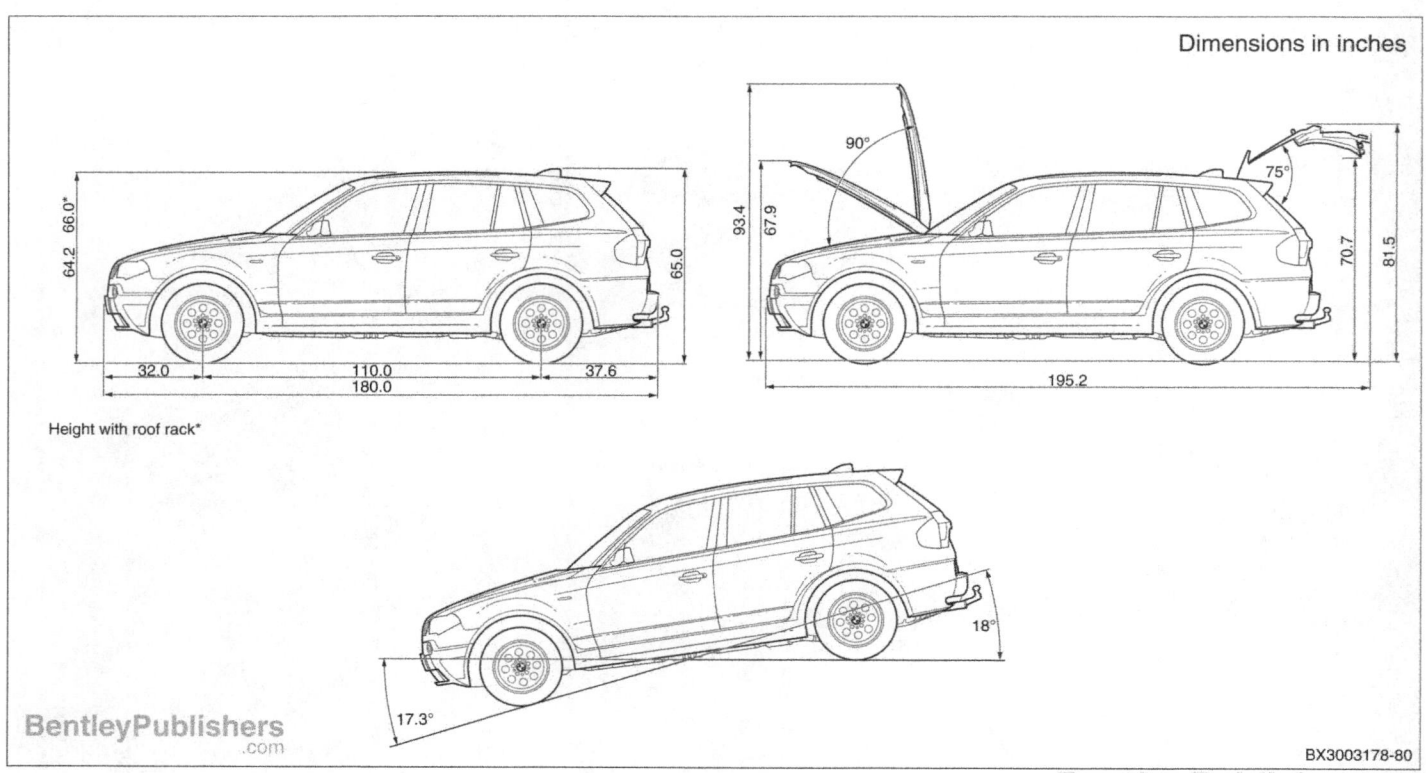

Dimensions in inches

Height with roof rack*

BX3003178-80

Weight

Curb weight	
Model	**Weight in lbs(kg)**
2.5i • Manual transmission • Automatic transmission	4001(1815) 4045 (1835)
3.0I (M54) • Manual transmission • Automatic transmission	4023(1825) 4067(1845)
3.0I (N52) • Manual transmission • Automatic transmission	4012(1820) 4067 (1845)

Body design

 The E83 (X3) design was conceived as smaller addition to the X family of SAV's. Based on the E46 (3 series) sportwagon, its size, weight and capabilities more closely match those of the E53 (X5). Almost 35% of the parts were designed specifically for the E83. The chassis and many other parts are taken either directly or in modified form from the E46 or the E53. The E83 is much heavier than the E46.

The front axle is bolted the chassis at 8 points. The front end is stabilized with a suspension cross-brace with a load factor higher than the E46 M3. Seat crossmembers and reinforcement plates in the B-pillars provide additional protection in the event of a side impact and the rear engine brackets are made of high-tensile but light steel.

BX304000003

 The body shell panels are stamped and assembled by Magna Steyr in Graz, Austria.

The engine in the E83 is lower than in the E46. To ensure sufficient clearance for the manifold heat shield, the left engine bracket is shorter than the right. The hood has a side support to prevent it from moving in the event of a crash. This helps prevent the hood from damaging the windshield during a collision.

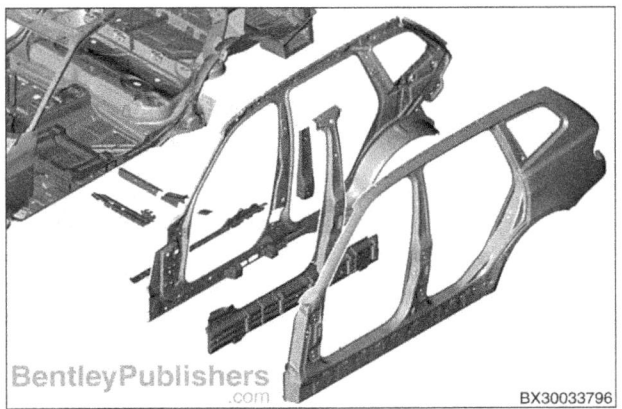

BX30033796

400

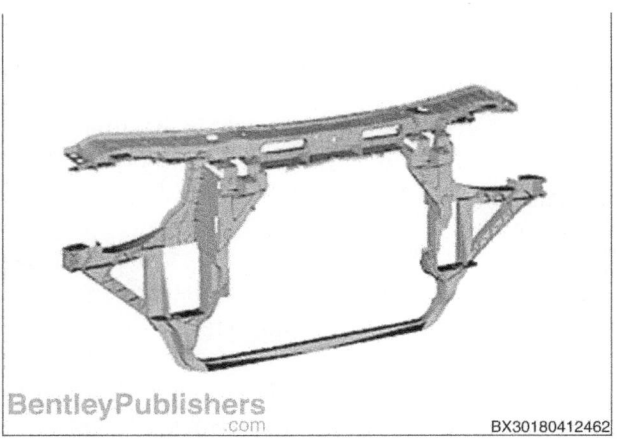

BX30180412462

◄ To reduce weight, the front bulkhead (radiator support) of the E83 is made of a hybrid steel injection-molded with plastic. The air ducts are cast on to the bulkhead. If the bulkhead is damaged in an accident it cannot be repaired and must be replaced.

SAFETY AND SECURITY

Seat belts

The pyrotechnic seatbelt tensioner has the task in the event of a crash to minimize any belt slack in the pelvic and shoulder region. The seatbelt tensioner is located on the driver's and passenger seat. In combination with the mechanical force limiter in the inertia reel, this reduces the chest load for the seat occupants. See **720 Seat Belts**.

MRS (airbag) system

Front airbags, side airbags, pyrotechnic seat belt tensioners, seat occupancy detector and the battery safety terminal (BST) are integrated into the multiple restraint system (MRS). On 2008 and later models, active front head restraints were added to the MRS system.

Smart two-stage front passenger and driver airbags include a seat sensor to help prevent the unnecessary deployment of the passenger airbag if the seat is unoccupied.

On the E83, a curtain airbag is standard equipment. When deployed, it extends from the A-pillar to the C-pillar covering the entire side-window area.

Airbag deployment automatically triggers fuel shutoff, alternator shutoff, switches the hazard lights ON and unlocks the doors.

For additional information, see:
- **720 Seat belts**
- **721 Airbag System (SRS)**

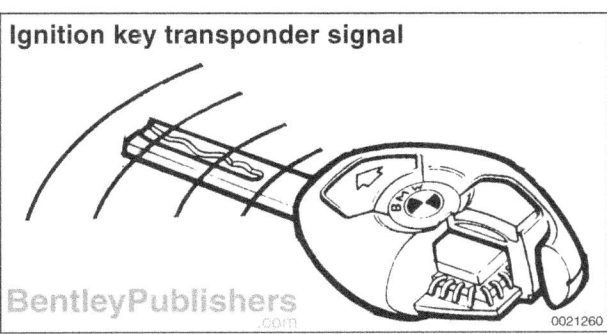

Battery safety terminal (BST)

◄ A pyrotechnic (explosive charge) device automatically disconnects the battery positive terminal during impacts. Key features, like power windows and door locks, remain operational.

For more information, see **121 Battery, Starter, Alternator**.

Security

Electronic immobilization (EWS)

◄ E83 vehicles incorporate an electronic immobilization system known as EWS. This system uses a wireless communication link between a transponder chip in the ignition key and the ring antenna surrounding the ignition switch. The EWS control module blocks the starting of the vehicle unless the correct coded ignition key is used.

NOTE —

• EWS is sometimes referred to as the driveaway protection system.

Ignition key transponder signal

Antitheft alarm (DWA)

In cars equipped with the factory alarm, the DWA system monitors door lock contacts and trunk and engine hood locks and sounds an alarm if it detects tampering. Included in the system is a tilt sensor to protect against the vehicle being towed away, and an interior motion sensor.

For more information, see **515 Central Locking and Anti-theft**.

INTERIOR FEATURES

◄ Interior and cargo volume is only slightly reduced compared to the E53.

400

BX30400002

Instruments and controls

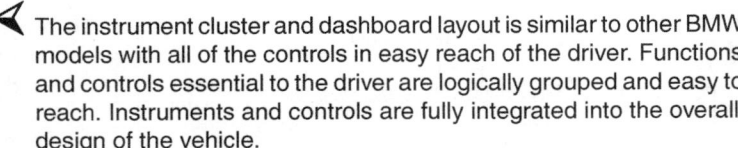 The instrument cluster and dashboard layout is similar to other BMW models with all of the controls in easy reach of the driver. Functions and controls essential to the driver are logically grouped and easy to reach. Instruments and controls are fully integrated into the overall design of the vehicle.

• Multifunction steering wheel contains two key pads containing controls for the sound system, telephone and cruise control.

Padded dashboard houses the instrument cluster and the ventilation and heating system.

For more information see **620 Instruments**.

Seats

Ergonomically engineered seats are constructed from polyurethane foam containing areas or zones of different firmness. They offer superior lateral support without constricting the occupant.

In cars equipped with memory seats, three different seat configurations can be memorized by the seat control module. Seat memory coordinates with outside mirror memory. These functions are controlled by the seat memory module.

For additional information, see **520 Seats**.

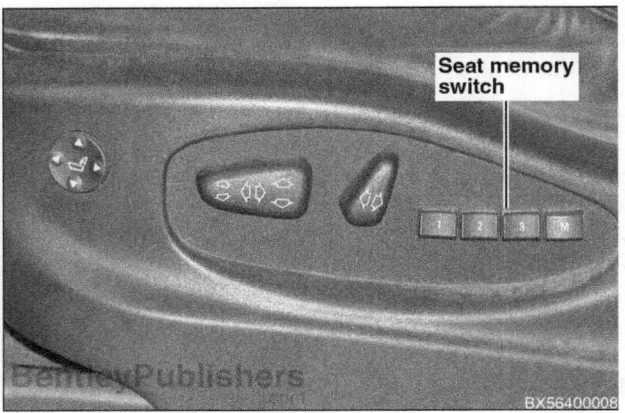

Seat memory switch

BX56400008

Central body electronics

E83 vehicles are equipped with an multitude of electronic modules connected mostly via the K-bus. The K-bus links the components of the general vehicle electrical system, the information and communications systems and the safety system. The majority of the systems and components have been taken from other models and adapted to the E83.

Additional central body electronics details can be found in:
• **512 Door Windows**
• **515 Central Locking and Anti-theft**
• **520 Seats**
• **540 Sunroof**
• **600 Electrical System–General**.
• **611 Wipers and Washers**
• **620 Instruments**

410 Fenders, Engine Hood

GENERAL

This repair group covers replacement of the front fenders and removal and installation of the engine hood.

> **CAUTION—**
> * The body is painted at the factory after assembly. Realignment of body panels may expose unpainted metal. Paint all exposed metal once the work is complete.

For additional information, see:
* **400 Body-General** for gap dimensions.

Special tools

Most body repairs can be performed using regular automotive service tools. Special BMW tools are required to set engine hood into service position.

FRONT FENDERS

Front wheel housing liner, removing and installing

— Raise front of vehicle and remove wheel.

> **WARNING—**
> * Make sure that car is firmly supported on jack stands. Place jack stands beneath structural chassis points. Do not place jack stands under suspension parts.

Front and rear fender liner removal and installation are similar.

Ambient temperature sensor

◀ Remove rivets (**arrows**) from fender edge by driving center pins out with a punch. Then pry out rivets with plastic prying tool. See **510 Body equipment.**

> **NOTE—**
> * Rivets are not reusable. Be sure to have more on hand.
> * Driver's side: unclip ambient temp sensor from bottom of liner.

Front fender, removing and installing

◀ Remove wheel housing liner screws.

– Pull liner out from behind fender trim piece and remove.

Front fender, removing and installing

– Raise hood to service position. See **Engine hood, raising to service position** in this repair group.

– Remove front wheel housing liner. See **Front wheel housing liner, removing and installing** in this repair group.

◀ Remove plastic rivets from under side of rocker panel trim and pull trim gently away from body. Remove hidden fastener (**arrow**) for fender trim from behind rocker panel trim.

NOTE —

• *Rocker panel trim removal is covered in* **510 Exterior Trim, Bumpers**.

◀ Pull fender trim away from body, releasing from blind fasteners (**arrows**).

Front fender, removing and installing

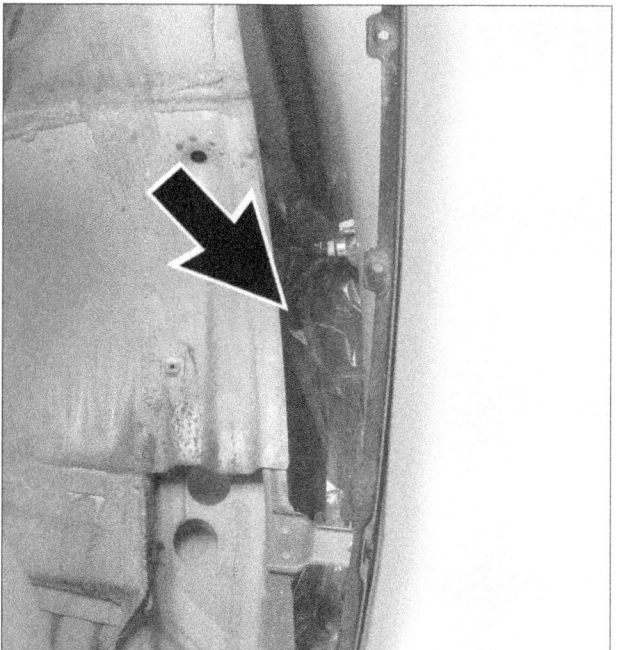

◄ Working between fender and wheelhousing, pull foam sound insulation out from A-pillar (**arrow**) to expose inner fender bolt.

◄ Remove inner fender bolt at rear of wheel housing.

410

Front fender, removing and installing

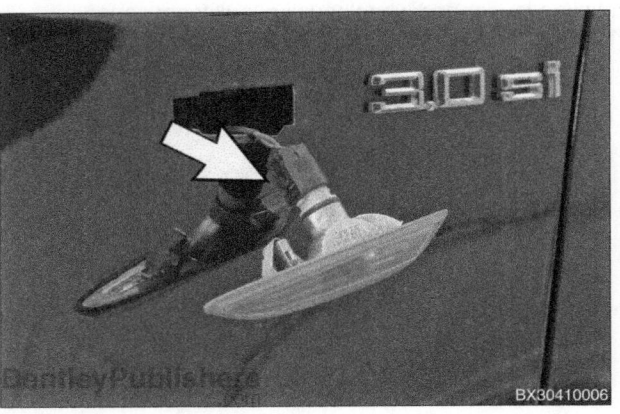

◄ Remove side turn indicator light by sliding it forward and lifting out. Disconnect electrical harness.

◄ Remove lower fender attaching bolts (**arrows**) at rear of wheel housing.

◄ With door open, remove bolt (**arrow**) attaching upper fender to door post.

◄ Remove torx bolt (**arrow**) at front of fender to loosen from bumper.

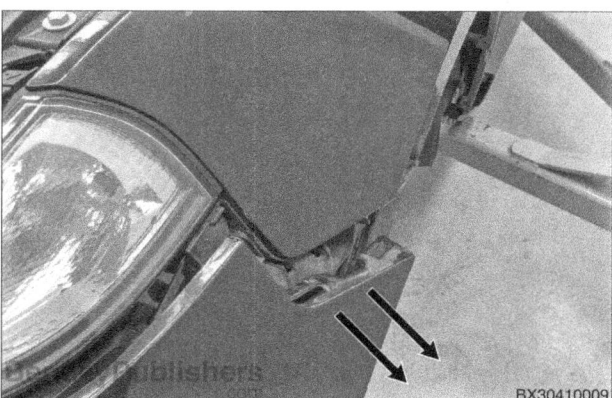

◄ Unclip and release bumper from bracket by levering away from fender with suitable plastic prying tool.

◄ Remove bolt (**arrow**) at front of fender.

◄ Remove bolts (**arrows**) along top edge of fender.

– Carefully remove fender from body.

– Installation is reverse of removal, noting the following:

  • Before installing new fender, clean old sealant and protective coating from mounting surfaces.

  • Position new fender and loosely install all mounting bolts.

  • Align fender with door pillar and inner fender, then tighten bolts.

  • Repair any paint damage and paint any exposed metal.

  • Reseal and apply protective coating to mounting surfaces.

410

ENGINE HOOD

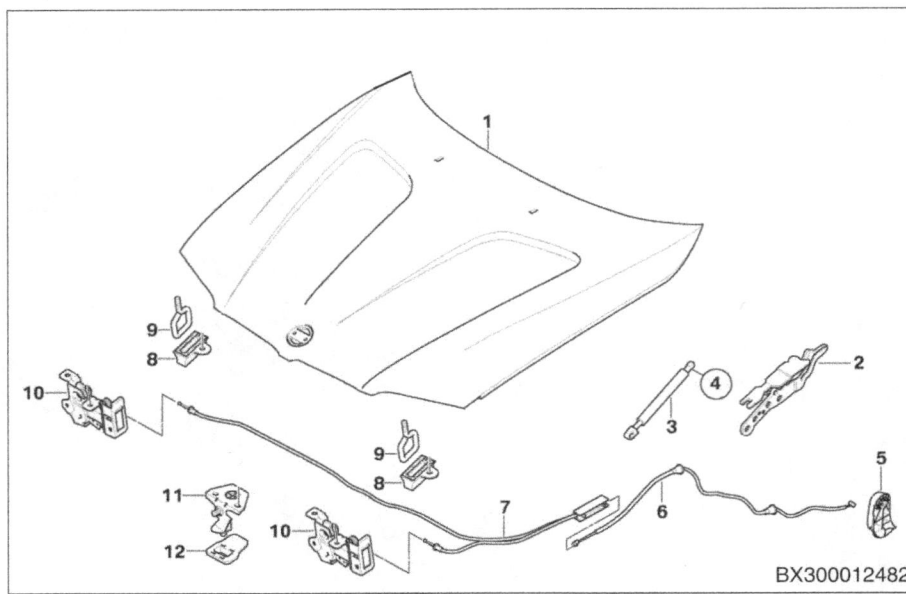

BX300012482

Engine hood latch components

1. Engine hood
2. Hinge
3. Gas pressurized spring
4. Ball pin, M8 x 13
5. Hood release lever
6. Bowden cable (part 1 of 2)
7. Bowden cable (part 2 of 2)
8. Locking cover
9. Catch bracket
10. Lock
11. Hood catch
12. Hood catch end support

Engine hood, raising to service position

◄ With hood open and help of an assistant, support hood and remove retaining clips on end of pressurized lifting struts. Strut can be mounted in opposite direction.

– Slide BMW special tool 51 2 040 over housing of gas strut then clip ball socket of special tool on ball stud on hood. Special tool can be used in both directions.

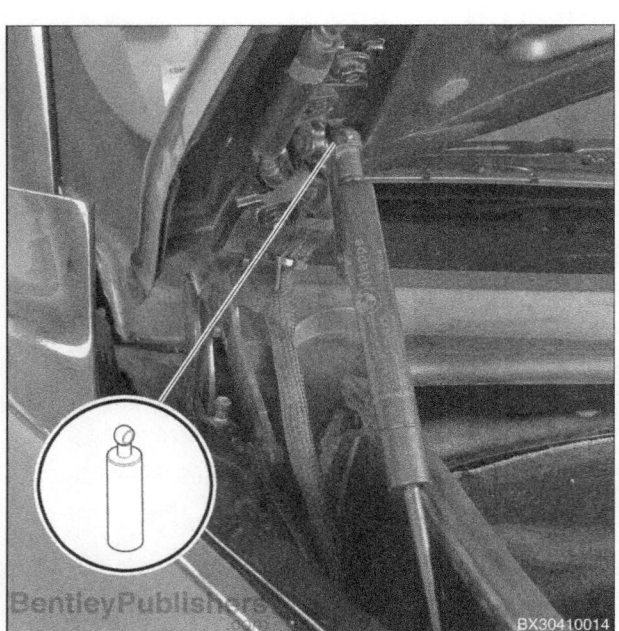

BX30410014

Engine hood, removing and installing

> **WARNING —**
> • The hood is heavy. Before loosening and removing hood bolts, be sure to have an assistant help support the hood.

– Open hood. Working at rear of engine hood, remove round plastic covers at left and right sides.

◄ Disconnect right and left electrical harness connectors and windshield washer hoses (**arrows**).

– Remove grommet and pull hood harness out of hood. Leave harness connected to hood hinge.

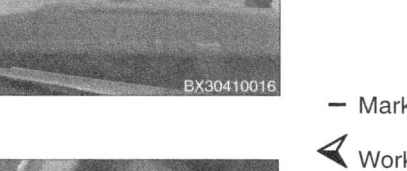

– Mark position of hood hinge mounting plates to hood.

◄ Working with a helper, loosen upper hinge mounting bolts (**black arrow**) and remove lower bolts (**white arrow**) at left and right himges. Lift hood off carefully.

– Installation is reverse of removal noting the following:
  • Repair any pain: damage and paint any exposed metal.
  • Check hood alignment. See **Engine hood, aligning** in this repair group.

Hood harness

BX30410016

BX30410017

Engine hood, aligning

Engine hood, aligning

When installing hood, align hinges as close to original painted surface as possible. Movement of hood on its attaching hardware may require touch up paint.

• See, **400 Body-General** for gap dimensions

◀ Align the hood so the gap (**arrows**) to fender is as even as possible.

◀ If height adjustment at rear of hood is off, adjust height using adjusting screw in lower hinge (**arrow**). Loosen and reposition as necessary.

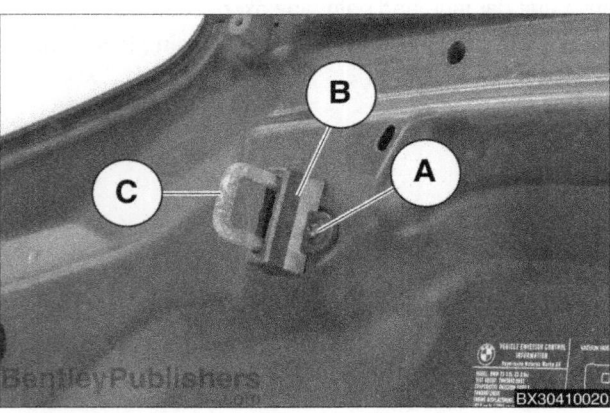

◀ If front height adjustment is off, adjust hood lock springs:
• Remove screw (**A**).
• Remove cover (**B**).
• Adjust height by turning latch (**C**).

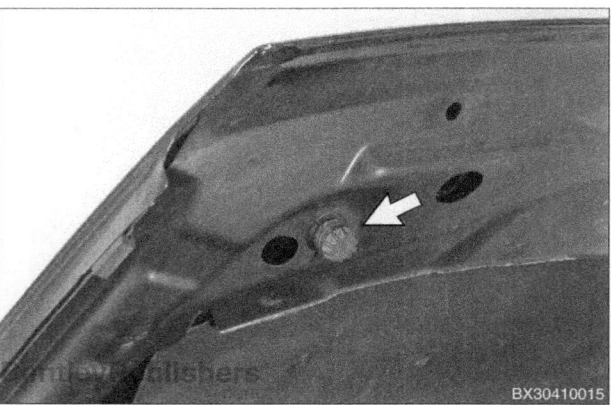

◀ If height adjustment of engine hood lid to front fenders is off, turn front buffer stops (**arrow**) on left and right.

> **CAUTION—**
> • *To avoid excessive wind noise, make sure hood does not protrude beyond front fenders.*

411 Doors

GENERAL

This repair group covers front and rear door repair information and includes door trim panel service.

> **CAUTION—**
> - The body is painted at the factory after assembly. Realignment of body panels may expose unpainted metal. Paint exposed metal once work is complete.

For additional information, see:

- **400 Body-General** for gap dimensions
- **512 Door Windows** for power door windows and door glass replacement.
- **515 Central Locking and Anti-theft** for power door locks
- **721 Airbag System (SRS)** for airbag removal and installation

Warnings and Cautions

> **WARNING—**
> - E83 cars are fitted with side-impact airbags in the doors. When servicing doors, always disconnect the negative (-) battery terminal. See **721 Airbag System (SRS)** for cautions and procedures relating to the airbag system.

> **CAUTION—**
> - Prior to disconnecting the battery, read the battery disconnection cautions given in **001 Warnings and Cautions**.
> - To avoid damaging plastic interior trim, use a plastic prying tool or a screwdriver with the tip wrapped with masking tape.

411

DOORS

Door check, replacing

Front and rear door check replacement are similar.

— Close door window completely.

— Disconnect negative (-) battery cable.

> **CAUTION—**
> • *Prior to disconnecting the battery, read the battery disconnection cautions given in* **001 Warnings and Cautions.**

— Remove interior door panel. See **Door trim panel, removing and installing** in this repair group.

— Where applicable, remove side-impact airbag from door. See **721 Airbag System (SRS)**. Remove door vapor barrier.

◀ Peel back door check seal (**C**).

— Release door check Torx-bolts (**A** and **B**).

B309411002

◀ Working inside door, remove door check assembly. (**A**)

— Installation is reverse of removal.

  • Lubricate door check before installing.
  • Do not damage rubber seal.
  • Use new mounting bolts if reinstalling side-impact airbag to door.

B510411009

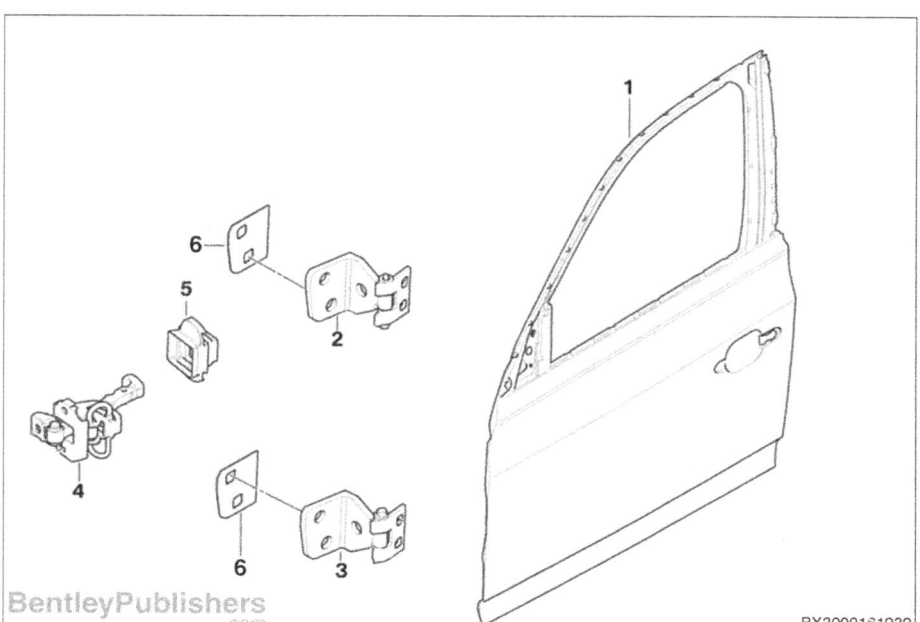

Door hinge assembly, front

1. Front door
2. Upper hinge
3. Lower hinge
4. Door check
5. Door check seal
6. Spacer plate

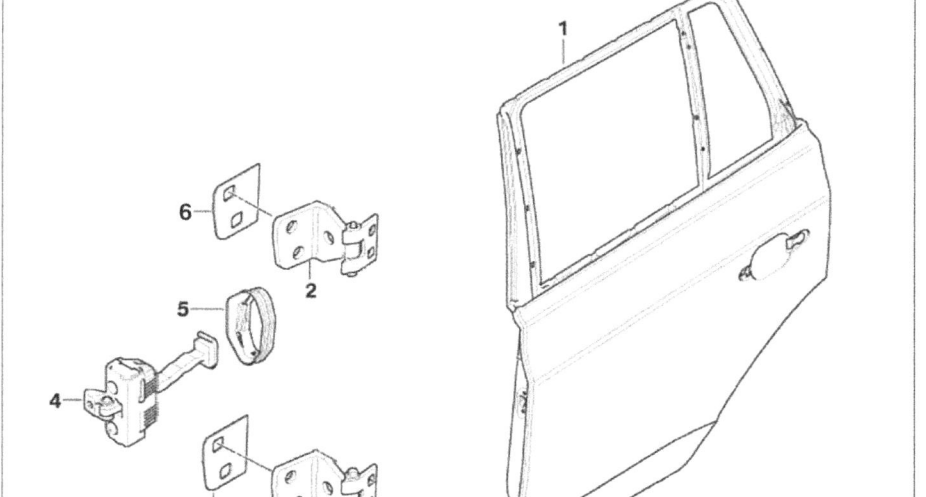

Door hinge assembly, rear

1. Rear door
2. Upper hinge
3. Lower hinge
4. Door check
5. Door check seal
6. Spacer plate

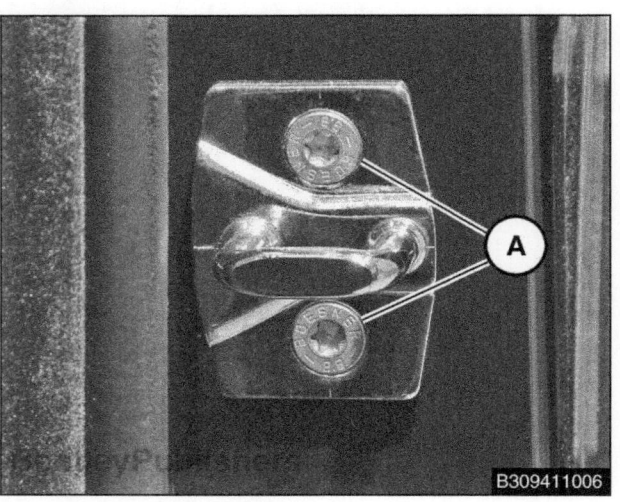

Door, adjusting

Front and rear door adjustment procedure are similar.

◄ If the installed door is uneven or out of parallel, loosen bolts at door hinges (**arrows**) to adjust at top and bottom.

– If more adjustment is necessary, spacers (or shims) can be used to correct its position. Spacers are placed behind hinge.

◄ Check that adjoining body parts are flush in terms of height (**arrows**) and correct if necessary. After adjustment, tighten hinge nuts and screws.

◄ Loosen Torx-screws (**A**) to adjust lock striker.

NOTE—

• *When door is closed, lock striker must not touch or brush against door lock. Avoid scratching door.*

Tightening torques	
Door to door hinge	18.5 Nm (14 ft-lb)
Door hinge to body	56 Nm (41 ft-lb)
Lock striker to body • M18 screw • M20 screw	 25 Nm (18 ft-lb) 18.5 Nm (14 ft-lb)

Door, removing and installing

Front and rear door removal and installation are similar.

Disconnect negative (-) battery cable.

> **CAUTION—**
> • *Prior to disconnecting the battery, read the battery disconnection cautions given in* **001 Warnings and Cautions**.

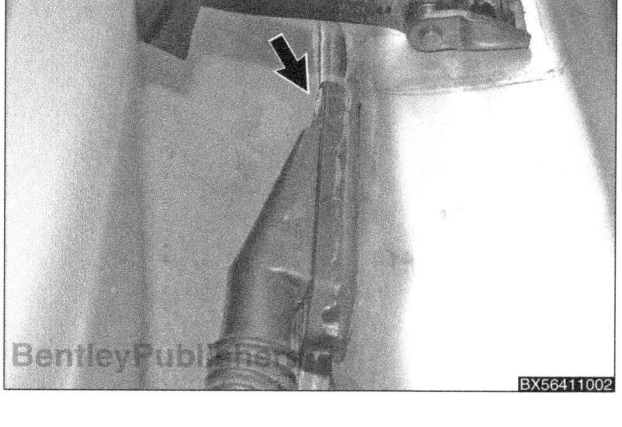

◄ Remove harness connector mounting bolt (**arrow**) at door pillar.

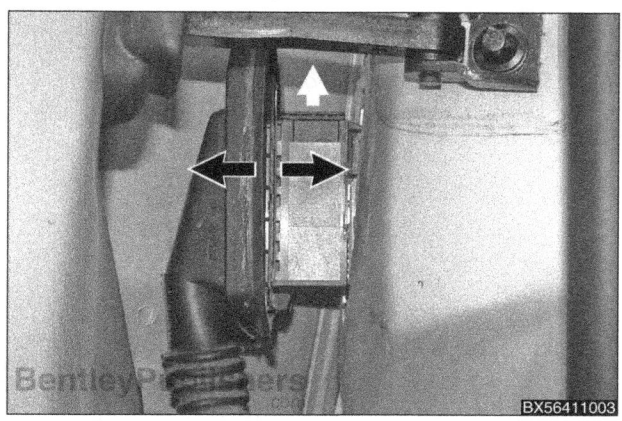

◄ Pull plug connection from door pillar by lifting it up and out.

– Slide lock up (white **arrow**) and separate connection (black **arrows**).

◄ With door fully open, unscrew door hinge pin bolts (**arrows**) from top and bottom hinges.

Door trim panel, removing and installing

◀ Remove door check mounting bolt (**arrow**).

− Remove door by lifting up off lower hinge halves.

− Installation is reverse of removal. Keep in mind the following:
  • Mount and align rear doors first, followed by the front doors.
  • Align door so that panel gaps are equal on either side. If necessary, adjust door hinges. See **Door, adjusting** in this repair group.
  • Adjust door striker so that trailing edge of front door is slightly higher than leading edge of rear door.
  • Repair paint damage and paint exposed metal.

DOOR PANELS

Front and rear door panel removal and installation are similar. 2007 X3 shown, other years similar.

Door trim panel, removing and installing

> **WARNING**—
> • E83 cars are fitted with side-impact airbags in the front and possibly rear *doors. When servicing doors, always disconnect the negative (-) battery terminal. See* **721 Airbag System (SRS)** *for cautions and procedures relating to the airbag system.*

− Disconnect negative (-) battery cable.

> **CAUTION**—
> • *Prior to disconnecting the battery, read the battery disconnection cautions given in* **001 Warnings and Cautions**.

◀ Pry out airbag emblem and clip on door trim panel (**arrows**) using plastic prying tool and release Torx bolts underneath.

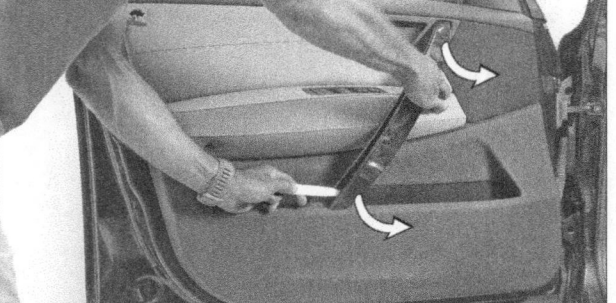

◀ Pry off door handle cover in direction of arrows.

◀ Release Torx bolts (**arrows**)

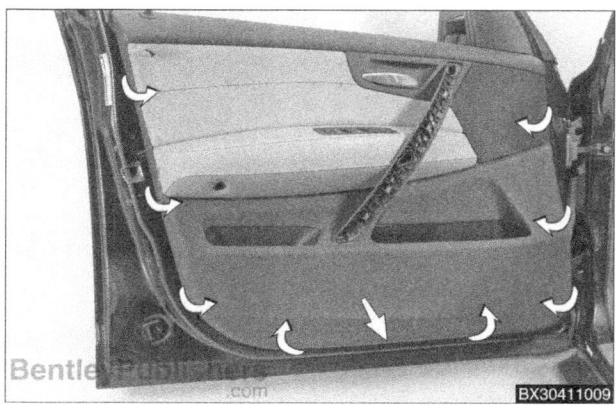

◀ Unclip door trim panel starting at bottom. Unclip door trim panel clips using plastic prying tool working around panel edge.

◀ Carefully unclip door trim panel from retainers by pulling straight out.

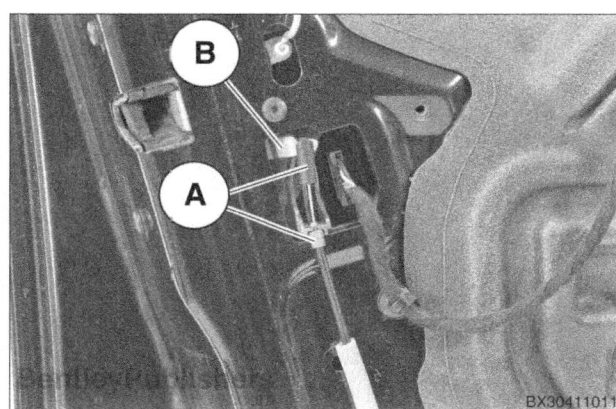

◀ Unhook Bowden cable (**A**) from inner door opener by unlatching tab (**B**).

– Disconnect side airbag harness connector.

– Disconnect wiring harness for window switch panel and remove door trim panel.

– Disconnect speaker from wiring harness.

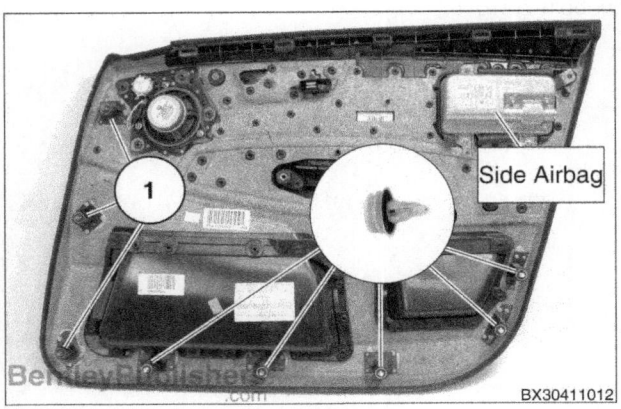

Side Airbag

BX30411012

◀ Clips (**1**) are gray in color and longer than white clips.

— Fit all clips with sealing ring (**inset**).

— Installation is reverse of removal

Replace broken clips, including sealing ring. Check door lock mechanism and window for ease of movement and proper function.

Tightening torques	
Door trim panel to door (screw under airbag emblem)	8 Nm (72 ft-lb)
Door trim panel to front door (screw to armrest or door handle)	8 Nm (72 ft-lb)

412 Tailgate

GENERAL

This repair group covers tailgate lock, tailgate removal, installation and adjustment.

> **CAUTION—**
> * The body is painted at the factory after assembly. Realignment of body panels may expose unpainted metal. Paint exposed metal once work is complete.

For additional information, see:

• **513 Interior Trim** for tailgate and cargo area trim removal.

• **400 Body-General** for gap dimensions.

• **515 Central locking** for tailgate lock removing and installing.

TAILGATE

Tailgate, adjusting

Buffer Stops

◀ If necessary, adjust buffer stops.

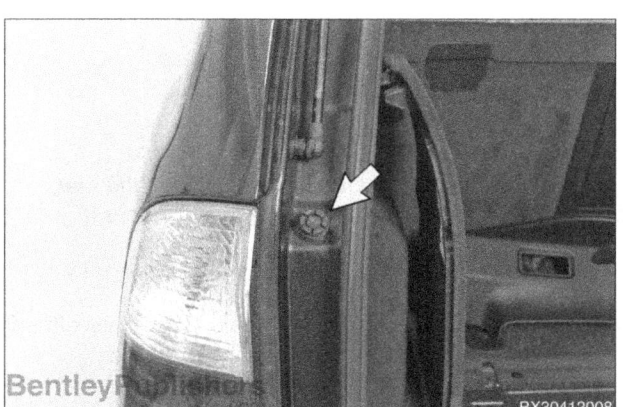

BX30412008

Tailgate, adjusting

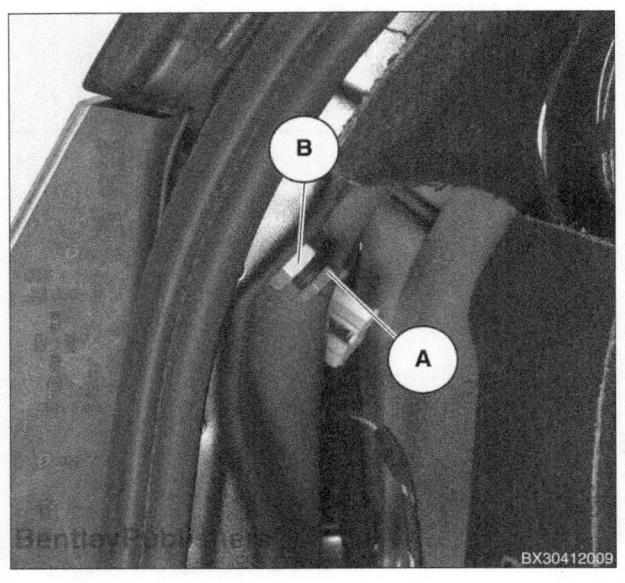

◁ To adjust buffers, remove inner trim panel and loosen lock nut (**A**). Nut (**B**) remains tightened. For trim removal, see **Tailgate lock, removing and installing** in this repair group.

– Use allen key to adjust buffer stops until closed tailgate rests on buffer stops. Then tighten one turn and tighten lock nut. Tailgate must not rest higher than side panels.

Striker

◁ Working at tailgate, pry off plastic cover around striker.

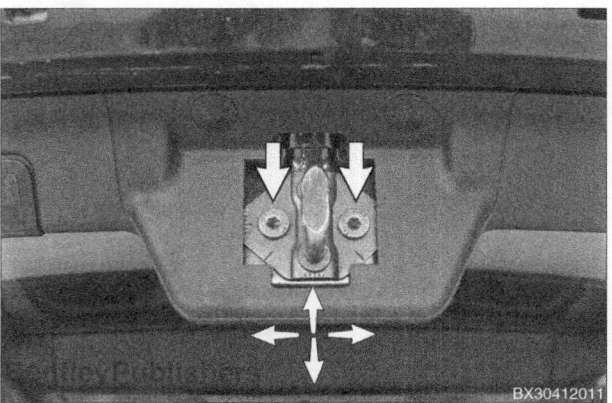

◁ Loosen screws on striker until it is just able to move.

NOTE —

• *Striker must not scrape against the lower section of the rear tailgate lock. Check striker for damage, replace if necessary.*

– Close tailgate. This automatically adjusts the striker correctly.

– Open tailgate. Tighten down screws on strikers. Check adjustment of tailgate and striker, repeating adjustment if necessary.

Hinges

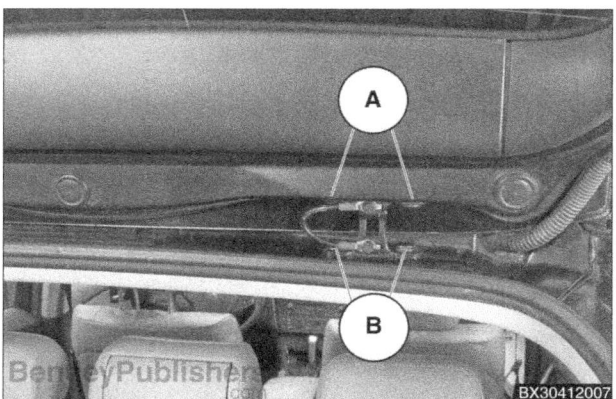

◄ Release screws (**A**) on both hinges. If adjustment range is not enough slacken screws (**B**) on both hinges. Tighten screws after adjustment.

Tailgate, removing and installing

> **WARNING**—
> • *Support tailgate before removing struts.*

– Remove tailgate trim. See **513 Interior Trim**.

– Secure tailgate against dropping closed.

◄ Remove retaining clip (**arrow**) on upper end of pressurized lifting struts and then detach struts.

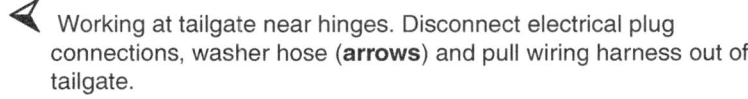

◄ Working at tailgate near hinges. Disconnect electrical plug connections, washer hose (**arrows**) and pull wiring harness out of tailgate.

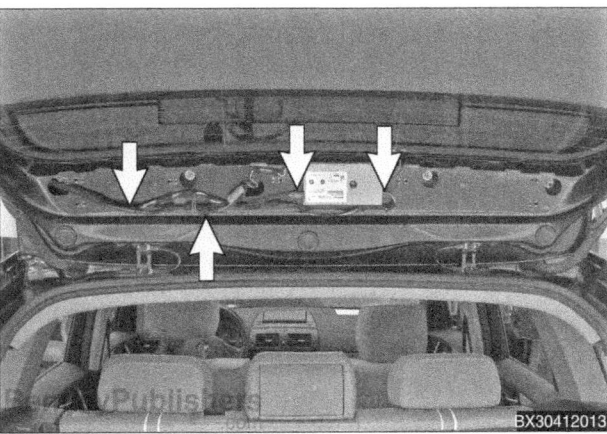

Tailgate, removing and installing

◀ Working at rear of tailgate. Disconnect electrical plug connections (**arrows**) and pull wiring harness out of tailgate.

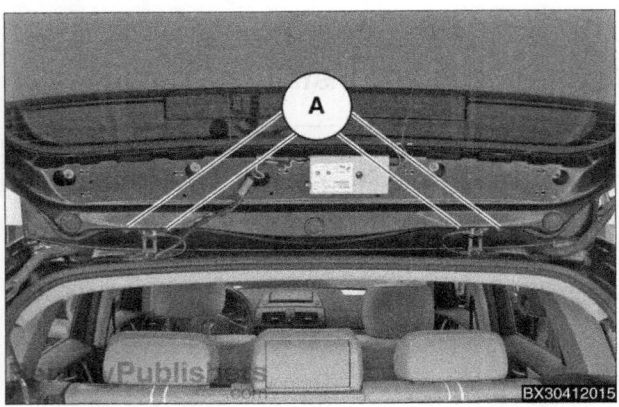

◀ Remove screws (**A**) from upper hinges. Remove upper tailgate.

– Installation is reverse of removal. If necessary adjust tailgate. See **Tailgate, adjusting** in this repair group.

510 Exterior Trim, Bumpers

GENERAL

This repair group includes repair information for the outside rear view mirrors, front and rear bumpers, and the easily removable exterior trim parts.

See also:

• **411 Doors** for door panels
• **721 Airbag System (SRS)** for side airbag warnings

OUTSIDE REAR VIEW MIRROR

Many of the mirror components are separately available from an authorized BMW dealer, including the glass and outside plastic housing.

Two types of outside mirrors are available on X3 models, standard, which are power adjusted and heated. Optional mirrors offer power adjustment, heating and power folding. Both versions have automatic dip (automatic curb monitor, passenger side).

To activate the passenger side exterior mirror tilt function, move the mirror adjustment switch to the DRIVER'S MIRROR position. When the transmission is placed in REVERSE, the passenger side mirror tilts downward to help the driver monitor the area directly adjacent to the car during parking (curbs, etc.). To deactivate this feature, set the mirror adjustment switch to the passenger's mirror position.

Mirror functions are controlled by the General Module (GM5 Redesign). The GM5RD sends mirror movement instructions to the electronics in the mirrors. Potentiometers in the mirror electronics monitor position. The mirror switch in the driver door module (SBFA) communicates with the GM5RD via the LIN bus.

510

Outside mirror glass, removing and installing

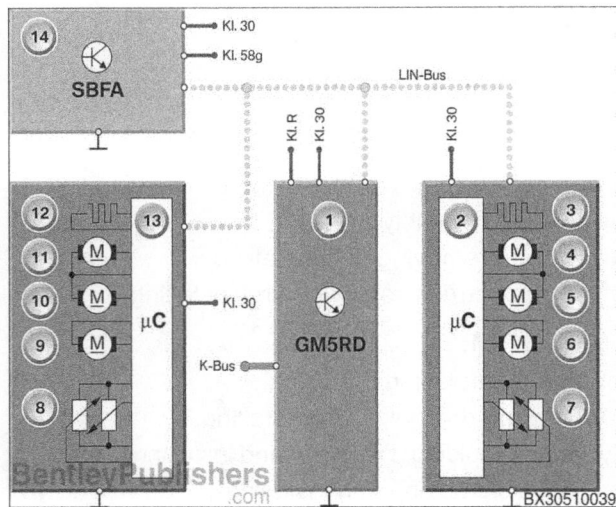

BX30510039

General module 5 redesign (GM5RD)

1. Mirror electrics, right
2. Mirror heating, right
3. Mirror vertical motor, right
4. Mirror horizontal motor, right
5. Mirror fold motor, right
6. Mirror potentiometer, right
7. Mirror potentiometer, right
8. Mirror fold motor, left
9. Mirror horizontal motor, left
10. Mirror vertical motor, left
11. Mirror heating, left
12. Mirror electrics, left
13. Driver's door module (SBFA)

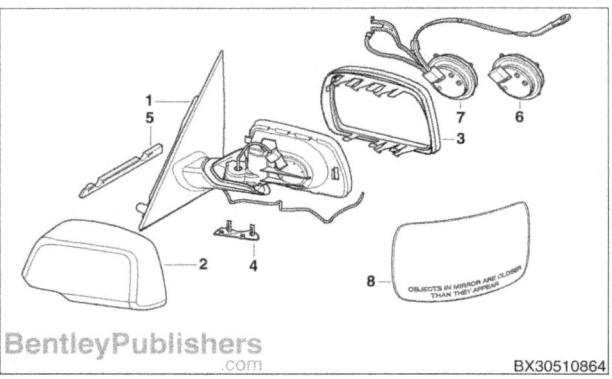

BX30510864

Outside mirror assembly

1. Outside mirror
2. Outside mirror cover cap
3. Mirror frame
4. Covering cap
5. Gasket
6. Mirror drive unit w/o memory
7. Mirror drive unit with memory
8. Mirror glass

Outside mirror glass, removing and installing

Extra force is often required to free the glass from the mounting base, making it difficult to remove without breaking. For added protection, cover glass completely with masking tape or wear hand protection when removing.

> **CAUTION—**
> • *Make sure mirror glass is at or above room temperature before removing. Otherwise, small plastic parts or glass may break.*

— Tilt mirror housing out.

— With mirror glass squarely positioned in housing frame, push one side fully into housing.

◄ Insert plastic wedge under center of glass and gently pry until glass disengages from retaining clips.

— Lift glass out and disconnect wiring plug connections. Store mirror glass in a safe place.

— When installing:
  • Reattach wiring.
  • Position mirror glass in housing while aligning plastic retainers. Carefully push mirror glass down to engage retaining clip.

BX30510001

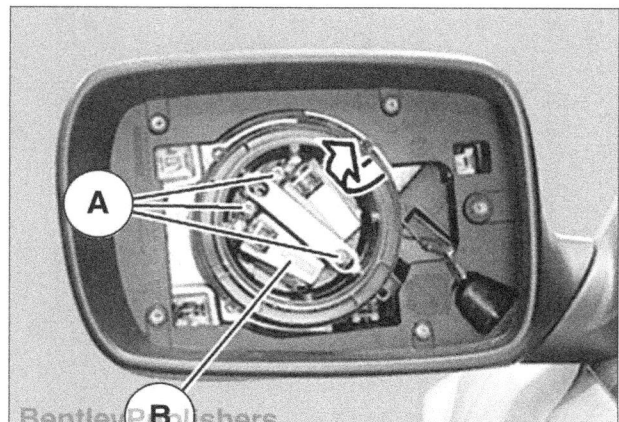

Outside mirror drive unit (without memory), removing and installing

− Remove mirror glass. See **Outside mirror glass, removing and installing**.

◀ Remove screws (**A**).

− Fold out drive unit (**B**) for mirror in direction of arrow.

◀ Disconnect plug connection (**A**) and remove drive unit for mirror (**B**).

NOTE —

• *Coat plug housing (**A**) at cable and connection ends with dielectric grease during installation to prevent corrosion.*

− Installation is reverse of removal.

Outside mirror drive unit (with memory), removing and installing

− Remove mirror glass. See **Outside mirror glass, removing and installing**.

− Remove mirror from door. See **Outside mirror housing, removing and installing**.

◀ Remove screws (**A**)

• Fold out drive unit (**B**) for mirror in direction of arrow.

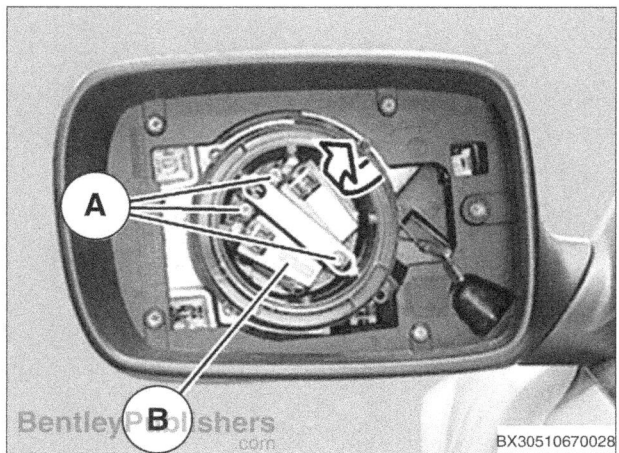

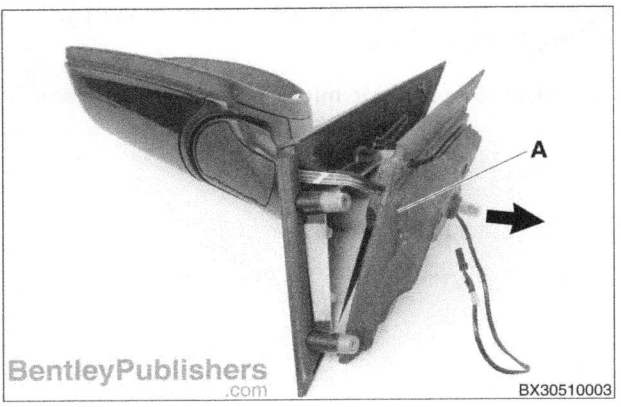

BX30510003

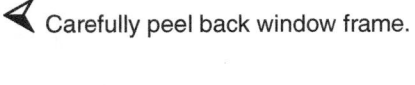 Remove sound insulation (**A**) from mirror.

  • Feed out ribbon cable (**arrow**) from mirror housing.

— Installation is reverse of removal.

Outside mirror housing, removing and installing

— Remove door trim panel. See **411 Doors**.

NOTE —

• *Mirror with memory function shown, others similar.*

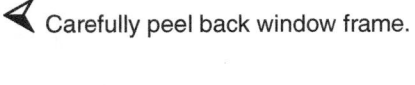 Remove push clip (**arrow**) on window frame.

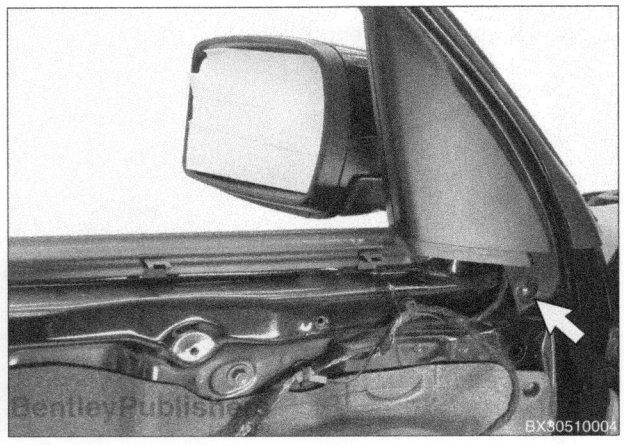

BX30510004

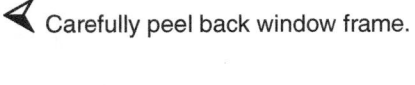 Carefully peel back window frame.

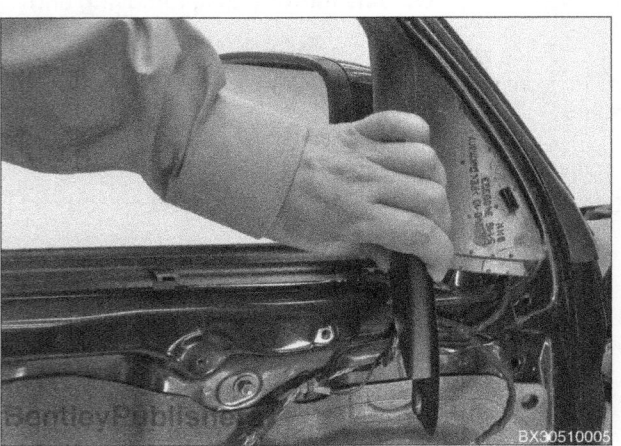

BX30510005

Outside mirror housing, removing and installing

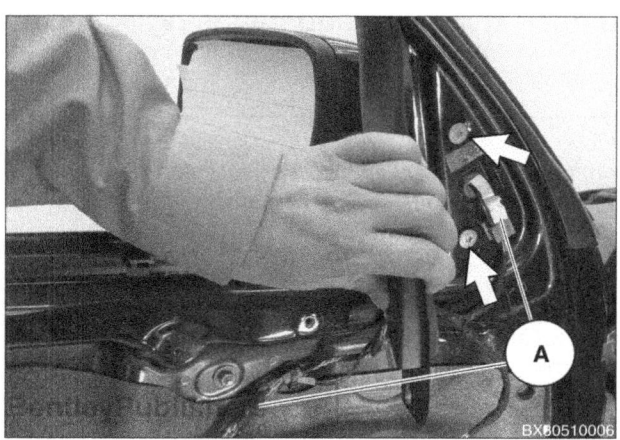

◄ Pull back foam insulation to window frame.

– Follow mirror electrical harnesses to door and disconnect (**A**). If necessary, carefully cut wire ties around wiring.

– Removed Torx bolts (**arrows**).

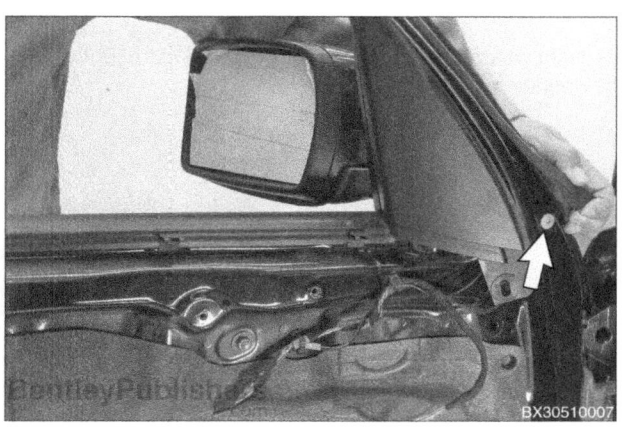

◄ While supporting mirror, peel back rubber door seal to access and remove Torx bolt (**arrow**).

– Lift mirror to free from door. Feed mirror electrical harnesses through opening to remove.

– Installation is reverse of removal.

Tightening torque	
Outside mirror to door (M6)	6 Nm (4.5 ft-lb)

BUMPERS

Different bumpers assemblies are used depending on model year. 2004 - 2006 (pre-LCI) models use a 2-piece bumper. 2007 and later (LCI) models use a 3-piece bumper. Early and late Bumper designs are similar.

Front bumper assembly (LCI)

1. Front bumper trim panel
2. Front grills
3. Front bumper trim panel, top
4. Front bumper carrier
5. Crash box
6. Front bumper grid
7. Center grid
8. Right closed grid
9. Left open grid
10. Front bumper trim panel bottom
11. Front license plate bracket
12. Bumper mount
13. Head lamp sprayer cover cap
14. Front tow hook cover
15. Side marker
16. Bumper bracket

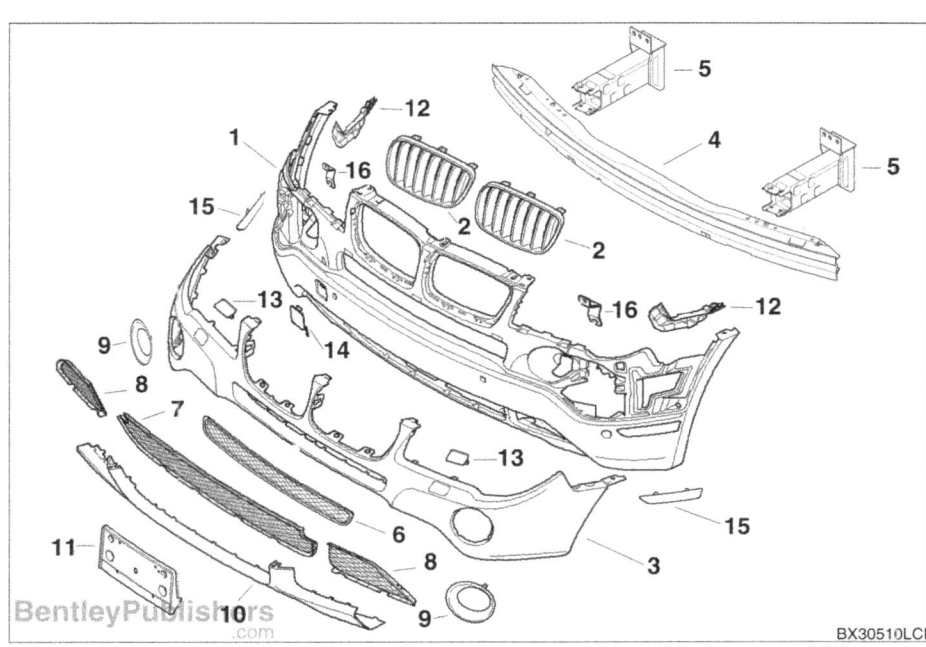

Front bumper, removing and installing

– Raise and properly support vehicle.

> **WARNING—**
> • *Make sure that car is firmly supported on jack stands. Place jack stands under structural chassis points. Do not place jack stands under suspension parts.*

> **NOTE—**
> • *Bumper removal shown on a 2007 model year X3 non-M sport, other years similar.*

– Remove front wheels.

– Open engine hood.

◀ Remove headlight washer covers. Use a plastic prying to gently pull up headlight washer nozzles.

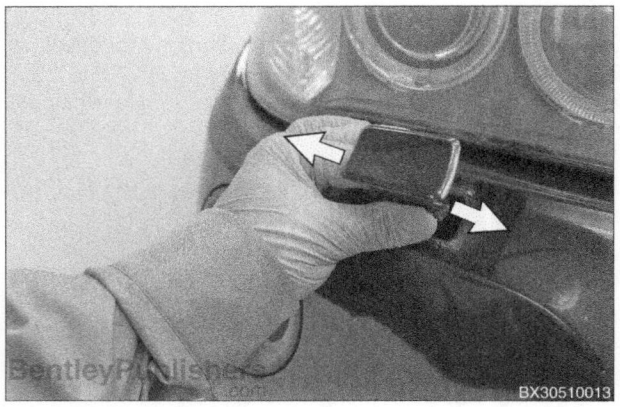

◀ Gently pull apart tabs in direction of (**arrows**) to remove cover.

◀ Remove wheel housing liner bolts (**arrows**). On driver's side unclip ambient temperature sensor (**A**).

– Fold back both wheel liners.

◄ With wheel liners folded back, remove Torx bolt (**arrow**) at front of both fenders to loosen bumper.

◄ Working inside front bumper, unclip harness plug from fog lamps (**arrows**). Release screws from headlight washer jets (**A**) to remove from bumper.

◄ Working at front of engine compartment. Remove fasteners (**arrows**) and remove front intake cowl from radiator support.

510

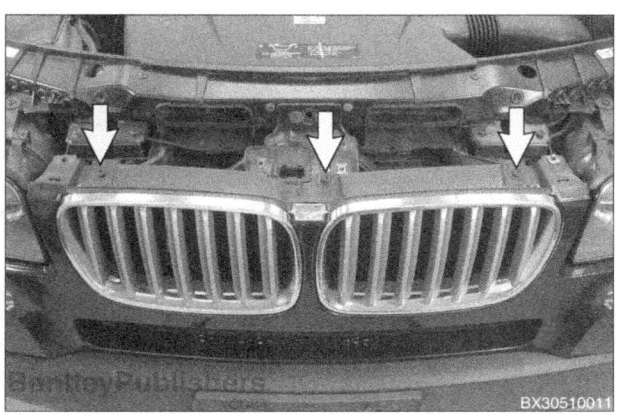

◄ Release screws on bumper trim.

Front bumper, removing and installing

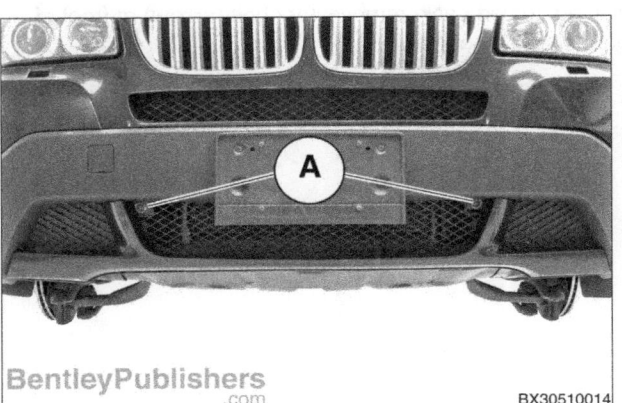

◀ Release lower screws on bumper trim (**A**).

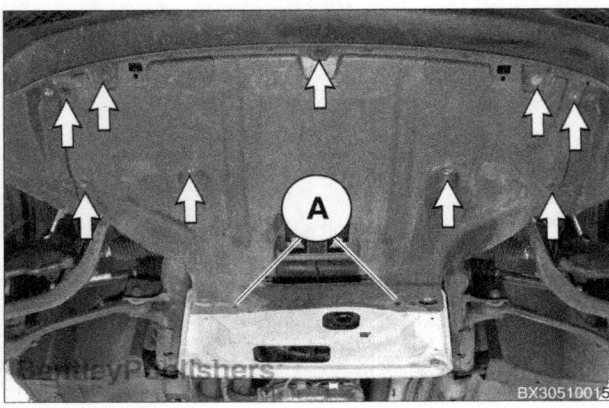

◀ Remove engine splash shield cover fasteners (**arrows**). Remove shield clips (**A**). Remove splash shield.

◀ Release bumper from both bumper brackets by giving it a firm pull outward.

– Unclip headlight washer hose inside front bumper trim.

– Using an assistant, slide bumper cover straight off and remove.
  • If necessary, disconnect plug connections on ultrasonic sensors.

Front bumper, carrier removing and installing

— Remove bumper. See **removing front bumper** in this repair group.

◁ Remove hi and low tone horn brackets (**arrows**) and remove horns form carrier.

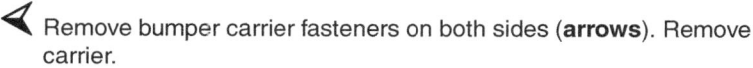

◁ Remove bumper carrier fasteners on both sides (**arrows**). Remove carrier.

— Installation is reverse of removal.

510

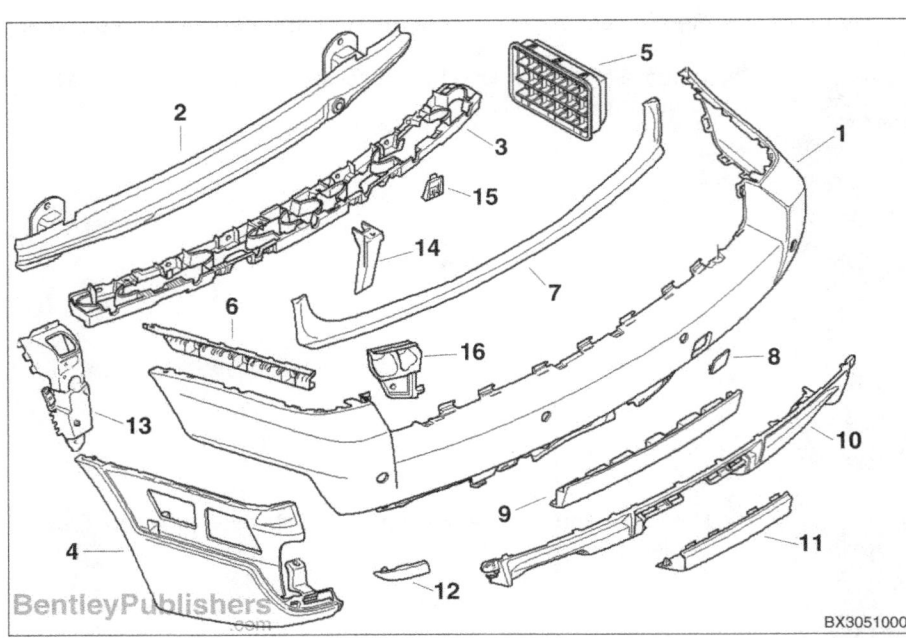

BX3051000R

Rear bumper assembly (LCI)

1. Rear bumper trim panel
2. Rear bumper carrier
3. Rear bumper support
4. Covering (qty. 2)
5. Rear breather covering
6. Rear bumper mount (qty. 2)
7. Loading sill cover
8. Impact absorber
9. Bumper cover support
10. Bottom cover
11. Trailer hitch flap
12. Reflector (qty. 2)
13. Bumper support (qty. 2)
14. Rear bumper bracket
15. Inner cover
16. Rear bumper corner mount (qty. 2)

Rear bumper, removing and installing

– Open tailgate.

◄ Working at rear bumper, remove sill trim from bumper.

> **NOTE** —
> • *LCI model shown, pre - LCI model is similar unless otherwise noted.*
> • *LCI (life cycle impulse) models were introduced for MY2007.*

– Pry out sill trim (**A**) along bumper to remove.

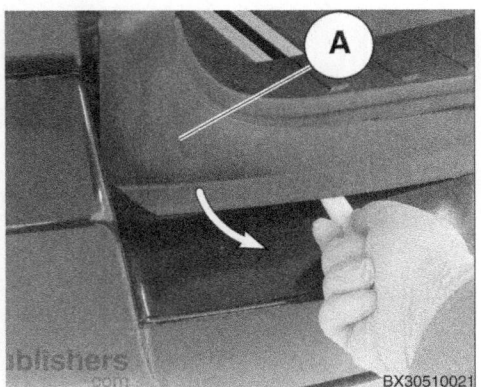

BX30510021

2004 - 2006 (pre - LCI) vehicle

◄ Remove corner sill trim on bumper. Release fasteners from bumper (**B**) on both sides.

> **NOTE** —
> • *Pre - LCI model only has two fasteners on either side of bumper.*

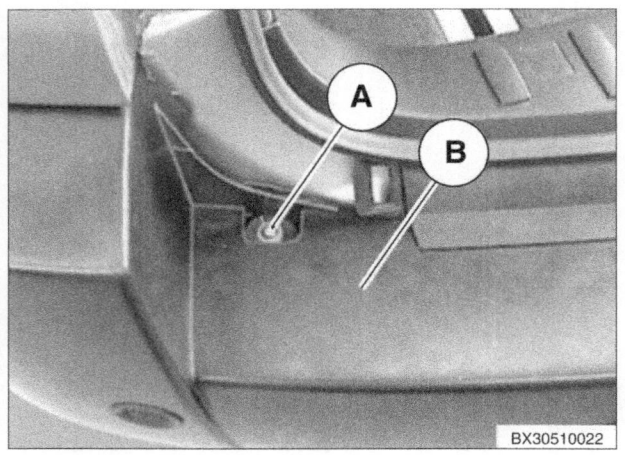

BX30510022

2007 - 2010 (LCI) vehicle

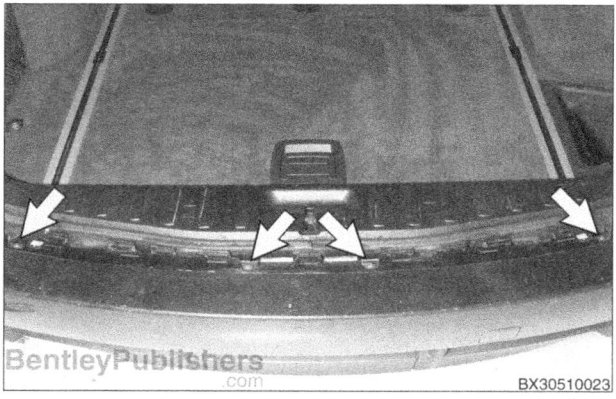

◄ Remove Torx fasteners on top of rear bumper.

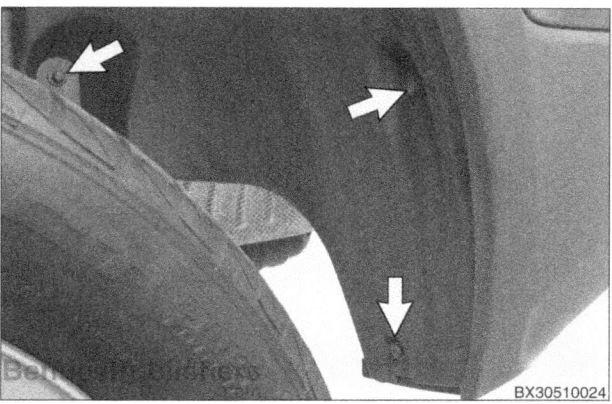

◄ Working in rear wheel well, remove fasteners (**arrows**) and then fold housing liner back on left and right sides.

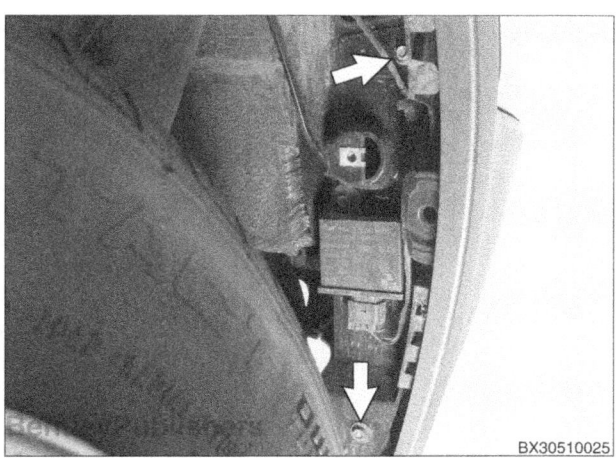

◄ Remove fasteners on left and right bumper bracket.

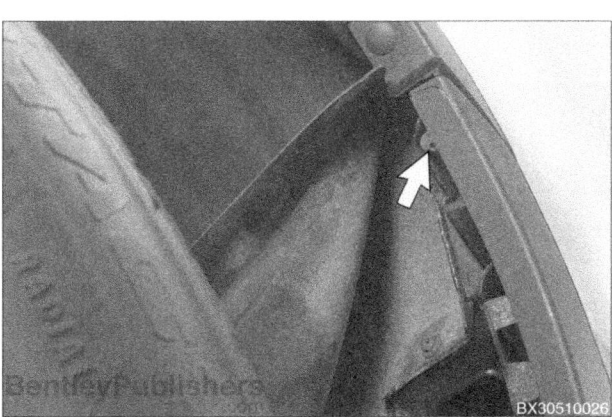

◄ Release fastener on left and right sides of bumper.

510

Rear bumper, removing and installing

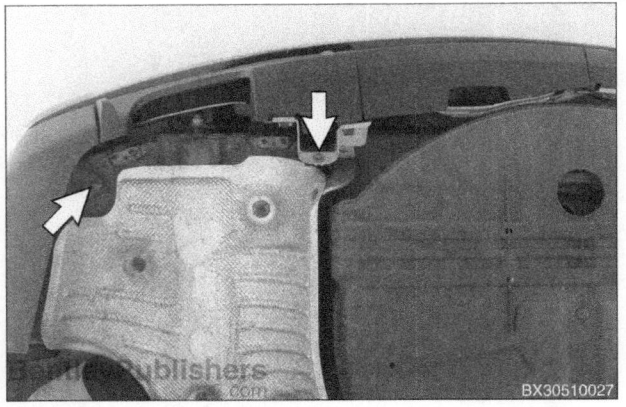

◄ Working on driver's side of bumper near muffler area. Remove fasteners.

NOTE —

• *Exhaust system shown removed.*

◄ Working under the bumper on the passenger side remove fastener.

◄ Pull bumper cover at sides to release from brackets.

− Remove bumper cover by pulling straight off vehicle.

− Installation is reverse of removal.

Rear bumper carrier, removing and installing

– Remove bumper. See **Rear bumper, removing and installing** in this repair group.

◀ Remove fasteners (**arrows**) holding impact absorber to body on both sides. Pull absorber from body.

– Installation is reverse of removal.

Tightening torques	
Bumper to impact absorber (M12)	55 Nm (41 ft-lb)
Impact absorber to chassis (M8 nut)	24 Nm (17 ft-lb)

EXTERIOR TRIM

Exterior trim is attached to the body with plastic rivets, clips and fasteners that may be damaged during removal. Be sure to have necessary fasteners on hand when reinstalling exterior trim pieces.

Plastic rivets, replacing

Plastic rivets are used to hold different exterior trim panels on the body. Rivets are generally non-reusable.

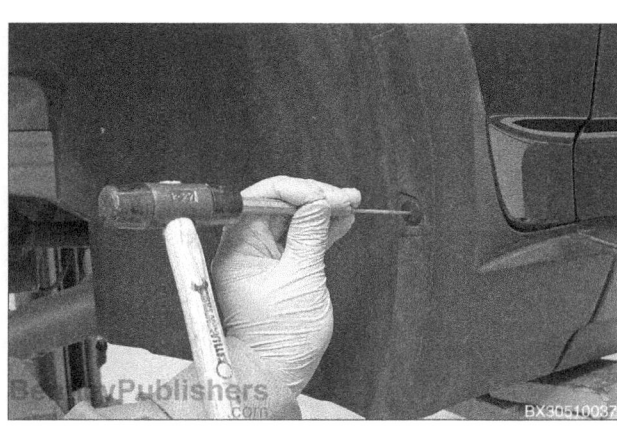

◀ Remove rivets by driving center pin out with punch, then prying out clip with plastic prying tool.

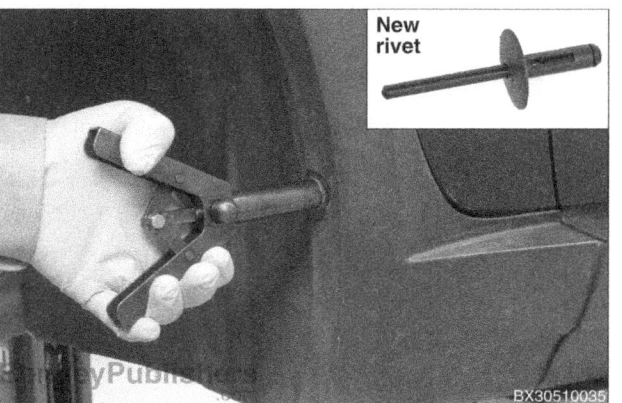

New rivet

◀ Use a plastic rivet tool to install new rivets.

510

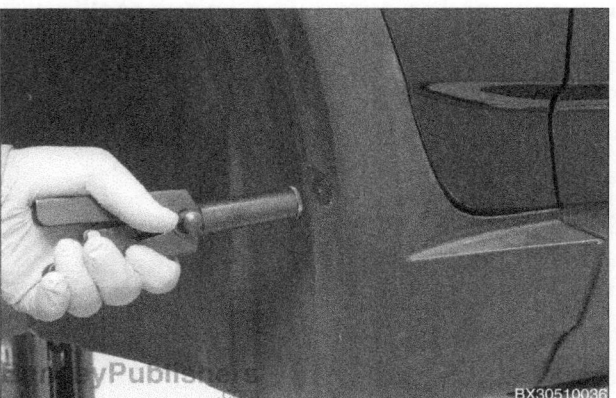

◀ Squeezing the tool sets the rivet in place.

NOTE—

• Removing a wheel and raising vehicle may be required to access all rivet locations.

> **WARNING—**
>
> • Make sure that car is firmly supported on jack stands designed for the purpose. Place jack stands beneath structural chassis points. Do not place jack stands under suspension parts.

BMW emblem, removing and installing

The procedure given below applies to both front and rear emblems.

— Wrap end of a pair of thin screwdrivers with tape.

> **CAUTION—**
>
> • Protect hood paint by covering area around emblem with tape.

◀ Pry up emblem carefully on either side (**arrows**).

— Installation is reverse of removal.
  • Replace plastic inserts in body if damaged.
  • If emblem fits loosely, use a small amount of body molding tape or adhesive on rear of emblem before installing.

Body side sill molding, removing and installing.

NOTE—

• Rivets are not reusable, so make sure you have more on hand.

• 2007 model year X3 shown, others similar.

• Vehicle shown on lift, but not necessary for side sill removal.

— See **Plastic rivet removing and installing** in this repair group.

◀ Working under body, remove rivets (**inset**) from underside of side sill by driving center pin out with a punch, then prying out clip with a plastic prying tool.

Body side sill molding, removing and installing.

◁ Working in at rear wheel well. Remove rivets (**arrows**) from trim by driving center out with a suitable sized punch, then prying out clip with suitable plastic prying tool.

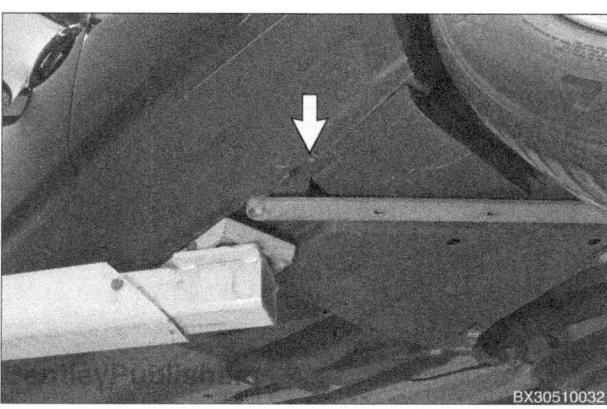

◁ Working under side sill, remove fastener (**arrow**).

◁ With both side doors open, pull side sill away from body to release from clips and remove.

– Installation is reverse of removal, noting the following:
  • If necessary, replace any loose or missing clips.

510

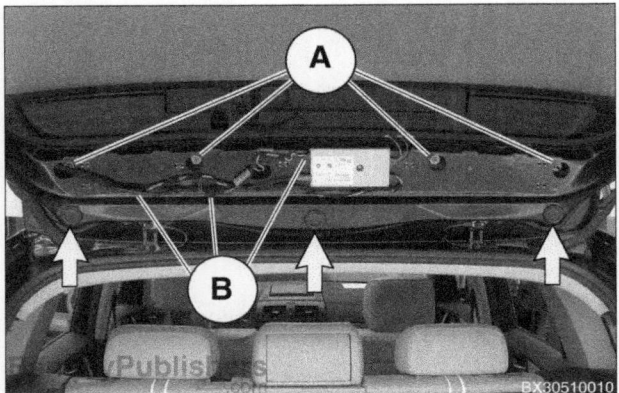

Rear spoiler, removing and installing

— Open upper tailgate.

— Remove tailgate trim. See **513 Interior trim**

◀ Working from underside of tailgate, pry out rubber plugs at left, right and center. Remove mounting fasteners from left, right and center of tailgate (**arrows**).

— Remove mounting fasteners (**A**).

— Disconnect washer hose and electrical connections (**B**). Unclip harness from tailgate or cut tape.

— Carefully slide spoiler cover towards rear of vehicle and lift off. Feed harness out of tailgate.

— Installation is reverse of removal, noting the following:
  • If necessary, replace any loose or missing adhesive (double-sided tape) buffers.
  • Check to make sure cover is correctly aligned before tightening mounting screws.
  • Tighten center screw first, then outer fasteners.

Tightening torques	
Rear spoiler cover to upper tailgate	3 Nm (27 in-lb)

512 Door Windows

GENERAL

This repair group covers door glass and window regulator repair information. The windshield, rear window, and fixed rear door glass are bonded using special adhesives and tools. For bonded glass replacement, see an authorized BMW service facility or an automotive glass installer.

See also:

- **411 Doors** for door trim panel
- **515 Central Locking and Anti-theft**
- **612 Switches** for electric window switch replacement
- **721 Airbag System (SRS)** for side-impact airbag information

Power window features

- Door window motors controlled by the General Module 5 Redesign (GM5RD) and/or door switch modules.
- One-touch operation in both directions on all four windows.
- Anti-trap protection integrated into power window motors.
- Convenience closing / opening (one-touch) of windows from driver's lock cylinder or opening only from remote (FZV) key.
- Window operation can be customized with car memory function. See **515 Central Locking and Anti-theft**.
- After ignition is switched OFF, electric windows can be operated until a door is opened, or until 1 minute has elapsed.
- One-touch function in the close direction as well as convenience locking are disabled in the event of implausible values from the jamming protection sensor.

512

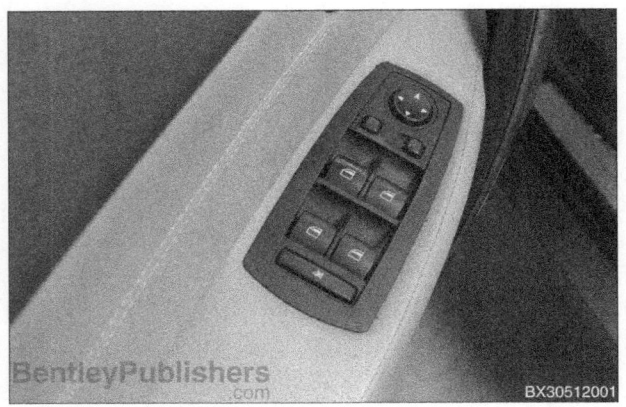
BX30512001

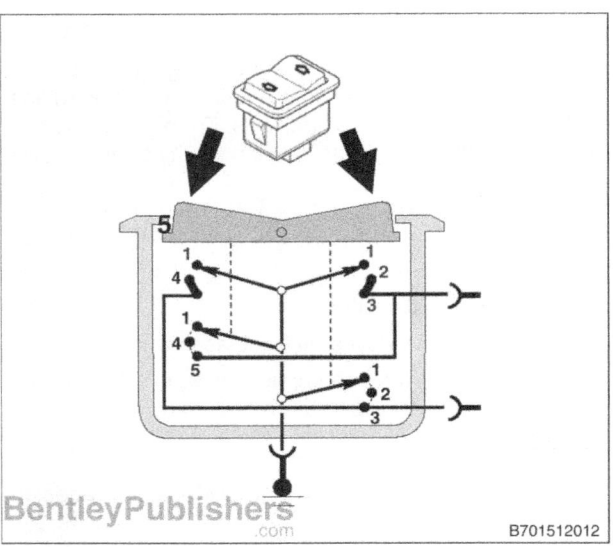
B701512012

BX30512002

Drivers door switch module (SBFA)

The SBFA (drivers door switch module) incorporates switches for all power windows. Communication with the General Module 5 Redesign takes place across the LIN bus. The passenger door switch and both rear door switch assemblies are connected directly via hard wire to the GM5RD.

The push-pull type window switch provides the GM5RD with a coded ground signal. Holding a switch at the first detent provides a single ground signal on one wire requesting the GM5RD to open the window. When released, the ground signal is removed and the window motor stops.

Momentarily pushing the switch to the second detent and releasing provides an additional ground signal on the second wire requesting "one touch mode". The GM5RD lowers the window automatically until it reaches the end position.

The switch functions in the same manner for window closing but the ground signal sequence is reversed.

Window switch positions

1. Off
2. Open
3. One touch open
4. Close
5. One touch close

Rear window child lockout switch

The rear window child lockout switch (**arrow**) is incorporated in the SBFA. When activated, it provides a constant ground signal to the GM5RD, preventing the windows from being operated from the rear door switches.

- The lockout switch ground signal is overridden by the general module if a multiple restraint system (MRS) crash signal is received.

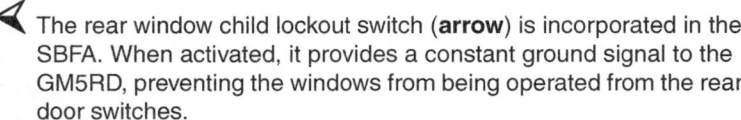

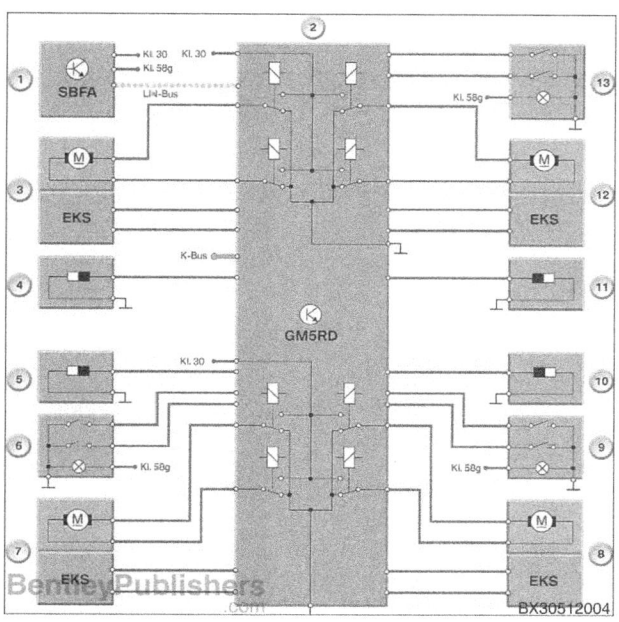

BX30512004

General module 5 redesign (GM5RD)

6. Drivers door switch module (SBFA)
7. General Module 5 Redesign (GM5RD)
8. Driver's power window motor
9. Driver's door contact
10. Driver's side rear door contact
11. Driver's side rear window switch
12. Driver's Side rear power window motor
13. Passenger rear door power window motor
14. Passenger rear window switch
15. Passenger door rear contact switch
16. Passenger door front contact switch
17. Passenger front power window motor
18. Passenger front window switch

Warnings and Cautions

> **WARNING—**
>
> - *E83 X3 models are fitted with side-impact airbags in the front doors. Some models are also equipped with airbags in the rear doors. When servicing the door windows on cars with side-impact airbags, always disconnect the negative (–) battery cable. See* **721 Airbag System (SRS)** *for cautions and procedures relating to the airbag system.*
>
> - *Always wear hand and eye protection when working with broken glass.*
>
> - *If a window is broken, all of the glass bits should be vacuumed out of the door cavity. Use a blunt screwdriver to clean out any remaining glass pieces from the window guide rails.*
>
> - *When servicing the door windows, the harness connector to the window regulator should always be disconnected to prevent pinching fingers in the moving window mechanism.*

> **CAUTION—**
>
> - *Prior to disconnecting the battery, read the battery disconnection cautions given in* **001 Warnings and Cautions**.

512

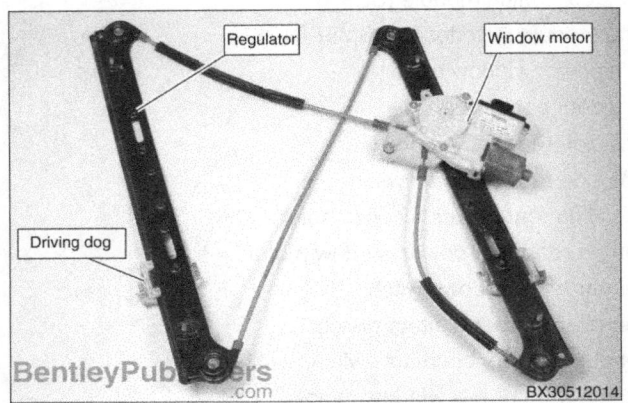

BX30512014

POWER WINDOW MOTORS

◄ The window motors are mounted on cable regulators. The window motor control circuit consists of two wires for operating the motor in both directions.

— Common power window motor faults include:

- Power window is noisy/grinds while going up and down.
- Window does not move, but sound can be heard from regulator / motor.
- Window can be moved by hand or does not stay closed.

These faults are often the result of broken or damaged driving dog(s) on the window regulator. See **Window regulator driving dog, replacing** at the rear of this repair group.

The window motors are activated by relays in the GM5RD. The relays provide either power or ground depending on the direction of window travel. The GM5RD controls the polarity based on a request to run the window from a window switch or a convenience opening / closing signal.

Convenience opening / closing

The GM5RD provides the convenience open / close feature, providing control of the power windows (and sunroof) from outside the vehicle with the key in the driver's door lock. The remote key provides the same function for window opening only.

Anti-trap (EKS) protection is active during convenience closing from the driver's door lock.

If the GM5RD receives a request to operate convenience closing or opening for more than 110 seconds, the function is deactivated and a fault code is stored.

Window anti-trap (EKS) protection

EKS electronics are included in the window motors. EKS monitors load on the electric lift motor to determine if the window lift path is obstructed. When an obstruction is detected, the window reverses direction.

Window anti-repeat circuit

If repeated window activation (up / down cycles) exceeds one minute, the GM5RD deactivates the window motor. The general module provides motor activation after a short period, but not for the full one minute monitoring cycle, allowing the motor to cool down.

Window motors, initializing

Initialization must be performed if the window motor malfunctions, is replaced or is disconnected from power. Initialization is performed on the power window switch of the relevant door.

Be sure the battery has a sufficient charge. Connect a power supply if necessary. Initialization comprises of first erasing prior initialization and then reinitialization,

Erasing prior initialization:

• With door window fully closed, open window fully.

• Hold switch in "open" position (second position) for 15 and 20 seconds.

This erases initialization of the power window. Anti-trapping and convenience opening are inactive. Confirm by pulling window switch into first position. Window should not close automatically.

Reinitialization:

— Close door window, release switch when closed. Then hold switch in "close" position (second position) for 1 second.

— Open door window, release switch when opened. Then hold switch in "open" position (second position) for 1 second.

— Close door window, release switch when closed. Then hold switch in "close" position (second position) for 1 second.

Initialization is now complete, check that convenience close and anti-trapping feature are working.

WINDOWS

Front door window, removing and installing

> **CAUTION—**
> • *A MRS airbag system fault will be set whenever the ignition is turned on with the door panel and door air bag disconnected. A BMW diagnostic scan tool will be required to reset the fault memory after the door is reassembled. See **721 Airbag System**.*

◄ Working carefully with a plastic prying tool, remove window trim strip (**1**) from door.

• Slide window trim (**1**) towards rear and feed out of guide (**2**) and door mirror (**3**).

— Disconnect negative (–) cable to battery and remove door panel. See **411 Doors**.

> **WARNING—**
> • *Prior to disconnecting the battery, read the battery disconnection cautions given in **001 Warnings and Cautions**.*

BX30512003

Front door window, removing and installing

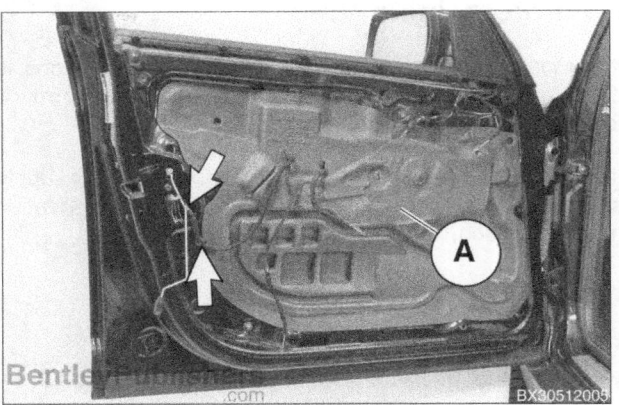

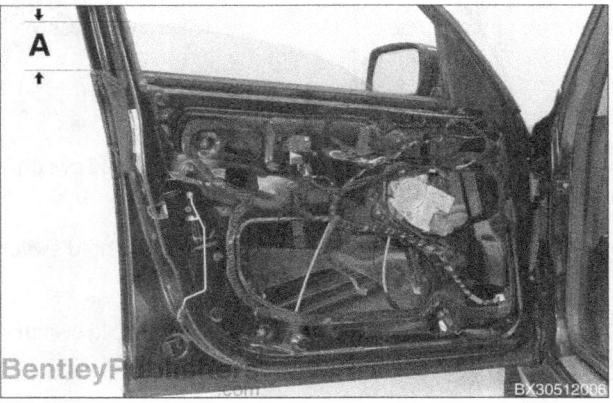

◄ Disconnect plug at door lock and harness clip (**arrows**).

- Remove vapor barrier (**A**) from inside of door. Feed out wires from vapor barrier.

> **CAUTION—**
> - *Use care when peeling back vapor barrier. Damaged vapor barrier should be replaced to prevent possible water leaks.*

— Reconnect negative (–) cable to battery.

◄ Reconnect window switch. Turn ignition on and lower window 105 mm (4.1 in.) (**A**). Turn ignition off and disconnect window switch.

> **CAUTION—**
> - *A MRS airbag system fault will be set when the ignition is turned on. A BMW diagnostic scan tool will be required to reset the fault memory. See **721 Airbag System**.*

— Disconnect negative (–) cable from battery.

◄ Working inside door, carefully pry out both catches on front window driving dogs in direction of arrow.

◄ Carefully remove window glass from regulator. Tilt glass inside door cavity and lift out of door toward rear top corner of door frame.

BX30512008

◀ Installation is reverse of removal, noting the following:

- Window driving dog, catch or buffer stop (**arrows**) must not be damaged or missing.
- Be sure that window is properly seated in channels.
- Be sure to correctly seal vapor barrier to prevent water leaks.
- Initialize window after reconnecting battery. See **Window motors, initializing**.

Rear door window, removing and installing

– Open window.

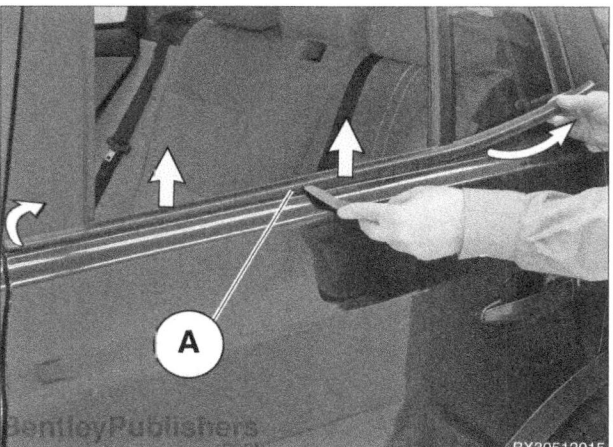

BX30512015

◀ Working carefully with a plastic prying tool, remove window trim strip (**A**) from door.

– Gently pull window trim (**A**) up feed out of door.

– Disconnect negative (–) cable from battery.

> **WARNING—**
> • Prior to disconnecting the battery, read the battery disconnection cautions given in **001 Warnings and Cautions**.

– Remove door panel. See **411 Doors**.

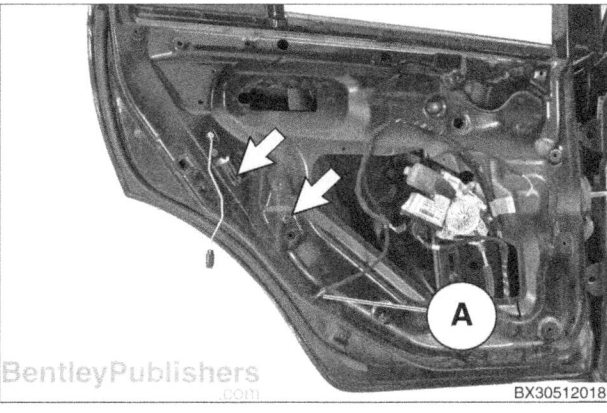

BX30512018

◀ Disconnect plug (**A**) at door lock and harness clip (**arrows**).

- Remove vapor barrier from inside of door. Feed out wires from vapor barrier.

> **CAUTION—**
> • Use care when peeling back vapor barrier. Damaged vapor barrier should be replaced to prevent possible water leaks.

512

Rear door window, removing and installing

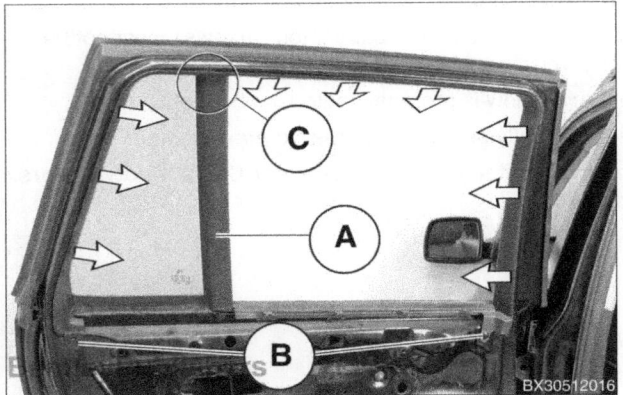

◄ Remove push clips (**B**). Unclip rest of cover (**A**) in direction of arrows.

CAUTION—

• Use car not to tear cover at window guide (**C**).

> **NOTE—**
>
> • Rubber guide is one piece and should be replaced after removal.

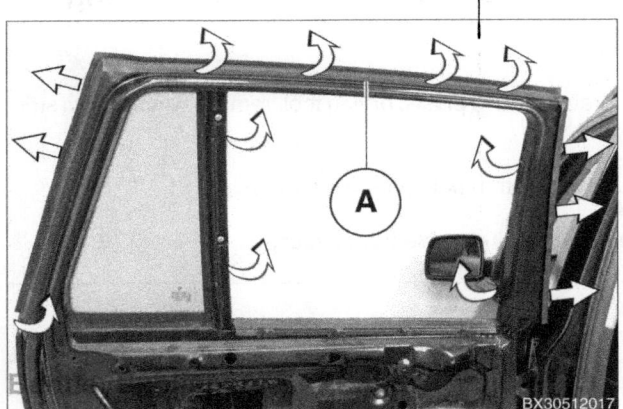

◄ Pry off rubber guide (**A**) on door window frame and feed out towards top.

> **NOTE—**
>
> • For Installation close window glass slightly. Push rubber guide onto door window glass and into window guide channel. Lubricate with water to ease installation.

— Reconnect negative (–) cable to battery.

◄ Reconnect window switch. Turn ignition on and raise window to 105 mm (4.1 in.) (**A**). Turn ignition off and disconnect window switch.

CAUTION—

• A MRS airbag system fault will be set when the ignition is turned on. A BMW diagnostic scan tool will be required to reset the fault memory. See **721 Airbag System**.

— Disconnect negative (–) cable from battery.

WARNING—

• Prior to disconnecting the battery, read the battery disconnection cautions given in **001 Warnings and Cautions**.

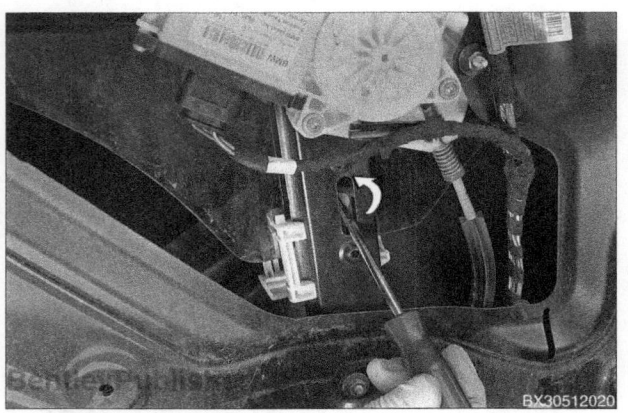

◄ Working inside the door carefully pry out catch on rear window drive dog in direction of arrow.

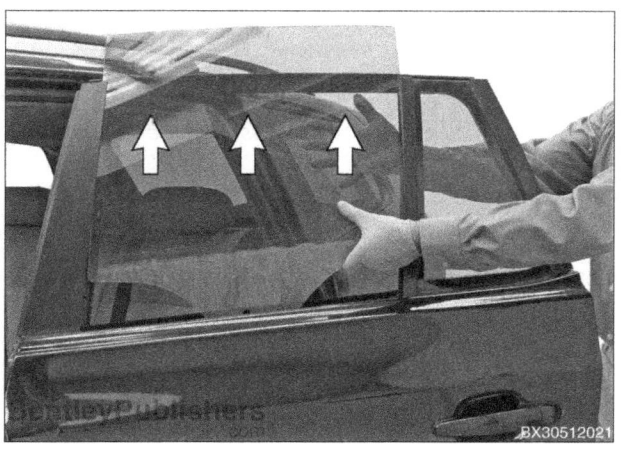

◀ Carefully remove window glass from regulator. Lift glass straight up and guide out of door.

◀ Installation is reverse of removal, noting the following:

  • Window driving dog, catch and buffer stop, (**arrows**) must not be damaged or missing.

  • Be sure that window is properly seated into run channels.

  • Be sure to correctly seal vapor barrier to prevent water leaks.

− Initialize window after reconnecting battery. See **Window motors, initializing**.

WINDOW REGULATORS

NOTE—

  • *The electronically-controlled window motor does not have mechanical end positions. For this reason the motor can be removed and installed with the window in any position.*

Tightening torques	
Motor to regulator	3 Nm (2.2 ft-lb)
Front window regulator to door	8 Nm (5.9 ft-lb)
Rear window regulator to door	8.2 Nm (6 ft-lb)

Front window regulator, removing and installing

NOTE—

  • *Remove window regulator and motor as one unit. If necessary, separate the two on the bench.*

− Remove front panel. See **411 Doors**.

− Disconnect negative (−) cable from battery.

Front window regulator, removing and installing

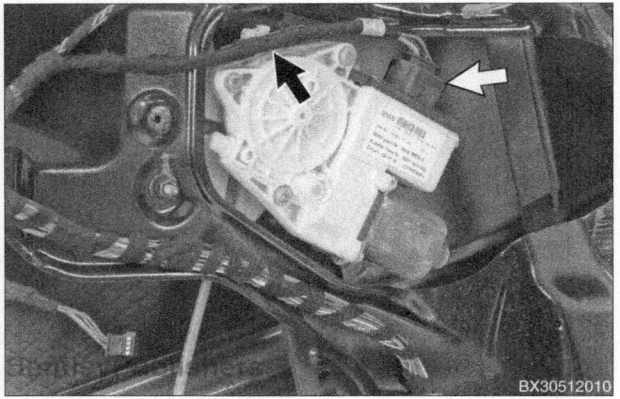

– Remove vapor barrier from door.

> **CAUTION—**
> • *Use care when peeling back vapor barrier. Damaged vapor barrier should be replaced to prevent possible water leaks.*

– Remove window from door. See **Front door window, removing and installing** in this repair group.

◄ Disconnect electrical harness connector at window motor (**arrows**).

◄ Remove fasteners (**arrows**).

◄ Feed rear section out of door cavity, then feed out front section with drive motor.

– Installation is reverse of removal, noting the following:
  • Route wiring harnesses to keep them away from moving window mechanism. Use new wire ties as necessary.
  • Be sure to correctly seal vapor barrier to prevent water leaks.
  • Initialize window after reconnecting battery. See **Window motors, initializing**.

Rear window regulator, removing and installing

NOTE—

- *Remove window regulator and motor as one unit. If necessary, separate the two on the bench.*

– Remove front panel. See **411 Doors**.

– Disconnect negative (–) cable from battery.

– Remove vapor barrier from door.

> **CAUTION—**
> - *Use care when peeling back vapor barrier. Damaged vapor barrier should be replaced to prevent possible water leaks.*

– Remove window from door. See **Rear door window, removing and installing** in this repair group.

◄ Disconnect electrical harness connector at window motor (**arrows**).

◄ Remove fasteners (**arrows**).

◄ Rotate regulator and feed out of door cavity.

– Installation is reverse of removal, noting the following:

- Route wiring harnesses to keep them away from moving window mechanism. Use new wire ties as necessary.

- Be sure to correctly seal vapor barrier to prevent water leaks.

- Initialize window after reconnecting battery. See **Window motors, initializing**.

512

Window motor, removing and installing

Front and rear window motors are similar.

— Remove door panel. See **411 Doors**.

— Remove vapor barrier from door.

> **CAUTION—**
> • *Use care when peeling back vapor barrier. Damaged vapor barrier should be replaced to prevent possible water leaks.*

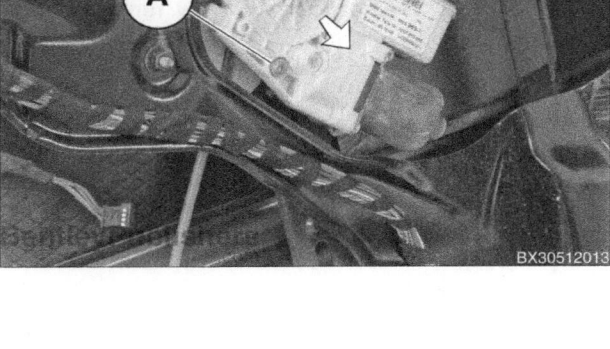

◄ Disconnect plug connections and harness (**arrows**).

— Remove fasteners (**A**), detach motor in direction of arrow pulling straight off of the regulator.

— Installation is reverse of removal noting the following:
  • Be sure motor gear engages teeth of guide wheel.
  • Route wiring harnesses free from moving window mechanism. Use new wire ties as necessary.
  • Be sure to correctly seal vapor barrier to prevent water leaks.
  • Initialize window after reconnecting battery. See **Window motors, initializing**.

Window regulator driving dog, replacing

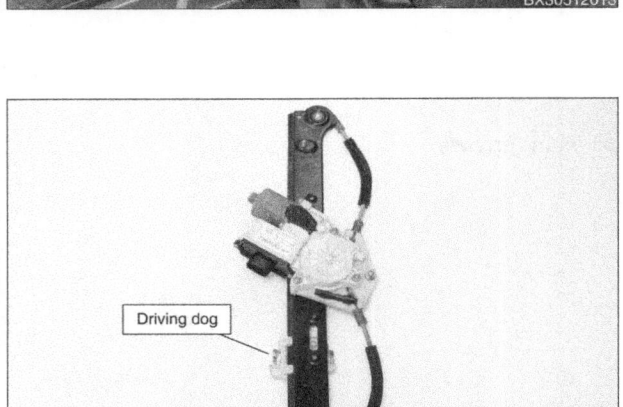

Driving dog

◄ The driving dog is a white plastic slider made from a brittle plastic that over time can break off of the regulator cable wire. Replacement driving dogs are available separately from a BMW parts center.

> **NOTE—**
> • *Front windows have two driving dogs - replace in pairs.*

— Remove window regulator from door. See **Front window regulator, removing and installing** or **Rear window regulator, removing and installing** in this repair group.

> **NOTE—**
> • *Optionally, this repair can be completed with the regulator in place, although space is limited.*

> **CAUTION—**
> • *If replacing driving dog while regulator is still in the door, secure window in place with strong tape to prevent from falling.*

Removing driving dog:

◄ Working with regulator on a flat surface and driving dog(s) facing upward, twist driving dog (**1**) upward on regulator rail.

Window regulator driving dog, replacing

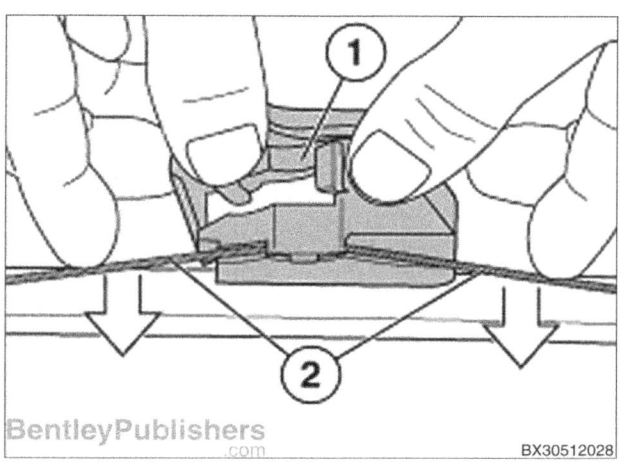

◄ Hold driving dog (**1**) in position, press wire cable (**2**) away from driving dog to unclip from retainer.

Installing driving dog

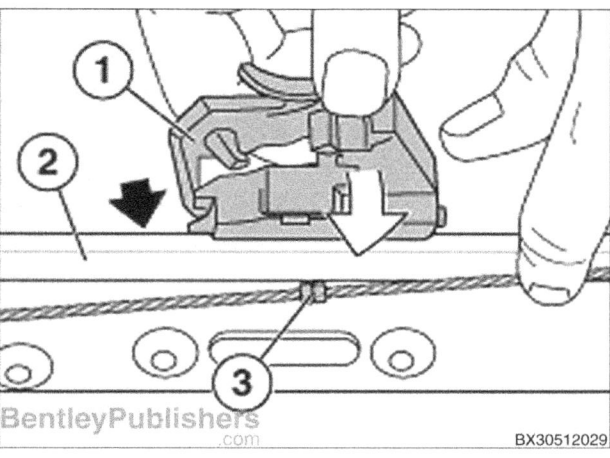

◄ Position driving dog (**1**) on regulator (**2**) adjacent to cable wire drive lug (**3**).

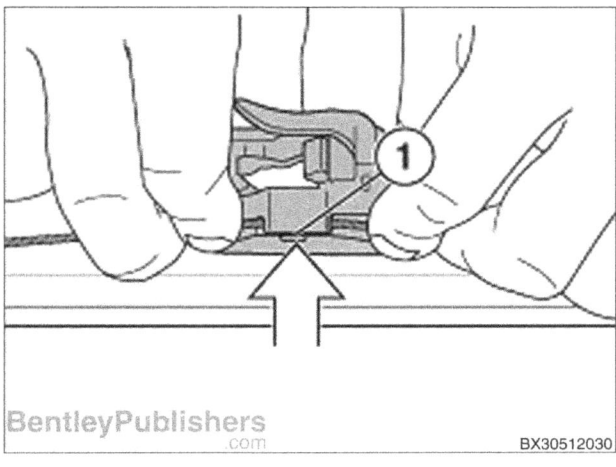

◄ With both hands use index fingers and press cable into retainer on driving dog (**1**).

• Make sure cable and drive lug are fully seated and driving dog is correctly seated on regulator.

— Install window regulator. See **Front window regulator, removing and installing** or **Rear window regulator, removing and installing** in this repair group.

512

513 Interior Trim

GENERAL

This repair group covers interior trim removal and installation.

Photos in this repair group illustrate a 2007 model year X3. Other models are similar.

Trim clips

Interior trim and finish panels are held in place with clips and plastic rivets. Be sure to have spare replacements on hand before beginning the job.

 Many trim clips may be reused if removed carefully.

- Pry out center locking pin.
- Lever out clip using removal tool.

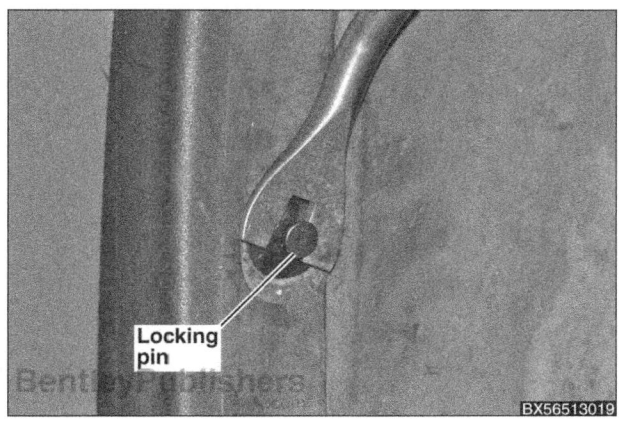

Locking pin

BX56513019

513

Warnings and cautions

> **WARNING—**
> - *Serious injury may result if airbag system service is attempted by persons unfamiliar with the BMW MRS and its approved service procedures.*
> - *Before performing any work involving airbags, disconnect the negative (-) battery cable. See* **721 Airbag System.**
> - *BMW airbags are equipped with a back-up power supply inside the airbag control module. Observe a 5 second waiting period after disconnecting the battery cable to allow the reserve power supply to discharge.*

> **CAUTION—**
> - *When working on electrical switches or lights, disconnect the negative (-) battery cable and insulate the cable end to prevent accidental reconnection.*
> - *Prior to disconnecting the battery, read the battery disconnection cautions given in* **001 Warnings and Cautions.**
> - *To prevent marring the trim, work with a plastic prying tool or wrap a screwdriver tip with masking tape before prying out trim panels, switches or electrical accessories.*

DASHBOARD

Right lower dashboard trim, removing and installing

This panel is above the right footwell, underneath the glove compartment.

– Move front passenger seat fully towards rear.

◀ Working in right footwell, press right lower dashboard panel trim (**1**) forwards slightly and feed down out of guides (**2**).

– Lower sufficiently to detach courtesy light from electrical harness and remove right lower dashboard trim.

– Installation is reverse of removal.

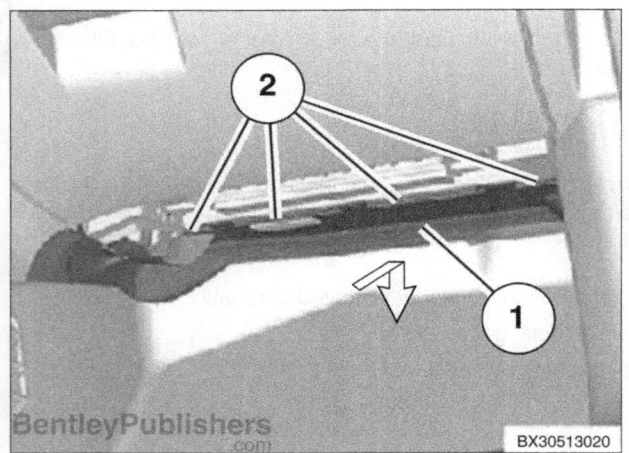

BX30513020

Left lower dashboard trim, removing and installing

This panel is above the foot pedals.

◄ Working in left footwell, remove lower dashboard trim screws (**A**) and plastic fastener (**B**). Disengage trim from anchors near steering column (**arrows**) and remove in direction of arrow.

– Installation is reverse of removal.

Center air vent grill, removing and installing

◄ Use a suitable prying tool, unclip center air vent grill from dashboard.

◄ Pull back center air vent grill to unclip bowden cable (**arrow**) and remove.

◄ Disconnect central locking and hazard switch at connector (**arrow**) and remove center air vent.

– Installation is reverse of removal.

513

Left air vent grill, removing and installing

◄ Us suitable prying tool to unclip right air vent grill and remove (**arrows**).

– Installation is reverse of removal.

Right air vent grill, removing and installing

◄ Use suitable prying tool to unclip right air vent grill and remove (**arrows**).

– Installation is reverse of removal.

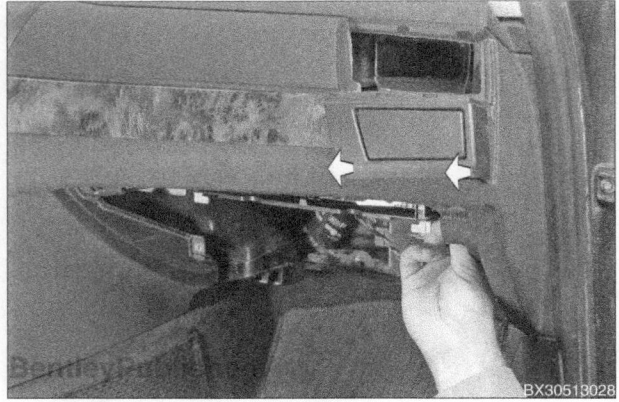

Dashboard cup holder, removing and installing

– Remove glove compartment. See **Glove compartment carrier, removing and installing** in this repair group.

◄ Working inside glove compartment carrier opening, remove screw or unclip cup holder and push out from behind to remove.

– Installation is reverse of removal.

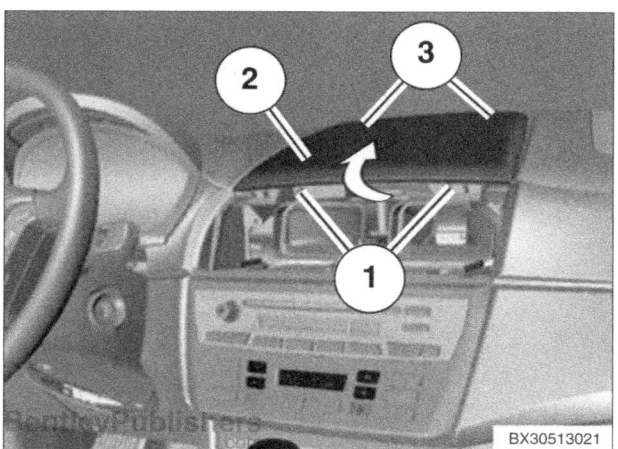

BX30513021

Dashboard storage compartment, removing and installing

NOTE—

- *For center information display (CID) removing and installing, see* **650 Radio**.

— Remove center air vent grill see **Center air vent grill, removing and installing** in this repair group.

◄ Remove fasteners (**1**) and lift off to remove storage compartment (**2**) from top guides (**3**).

Dashboard, removing and installing

Dashboard, removing

— Move front seats fully rearward.

— Lower steering column and extend out fully.

— Disconnect negative (-) battery cable and cover battery terminal to keep cable from accidentally contacting terminal.

> *CAUTION—*
> - *Prior to disconnecting the battery, read the battery disconnection cautions given in* **001 Warnings and Cautions**.

— Remove both upper and lower A-pillar trim panels. See **Covers and Trim Panels** in this repair group.

— Remove light switch. See **612 Switches**.

— Remove instrument cluster. See **620 Instruments**.

— Remove steering wheel upper and lower trim. See **Covers and Trim Panels** in this repair group.

— Remove steering wheel. See **320 Steering and Wheel Alignment**.

— Remove steering column stalk switch. See **612 Switches**.

— Remove left and right air vents grills.

— Remove radio. See **650 Radio**.

— Remove passenger (right front) airbag. See **721 Airbags**.

— Remove center console. See **Center console, removing and installing** in this repair group.

— Remove both lower dashboard panels. See **Covers and Trim Panels** in this repair group.

— Remove center dash storage pocket or CID display.

— Remove glove compartment. See **Glove compartment carrier, removing and installing** in this repair group.

513

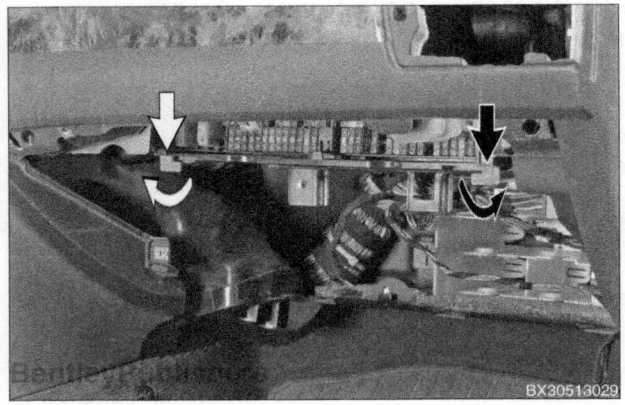

– Remove cup holder.

◄ With glove box removed; open locks (**arrows**) and fold down fuse block.

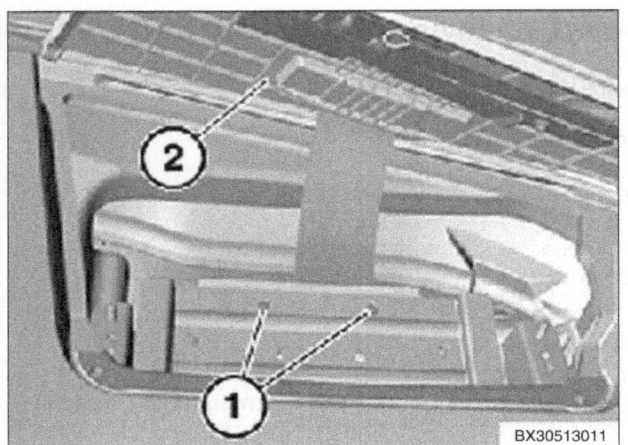

◄ Working at passenger side of dashboard, remove screws (**1**) remove passenger airbag cover (**2**) with mounting plate.

NOTE—

• *When removing screws mounting plate could fall into passenger footwell.*

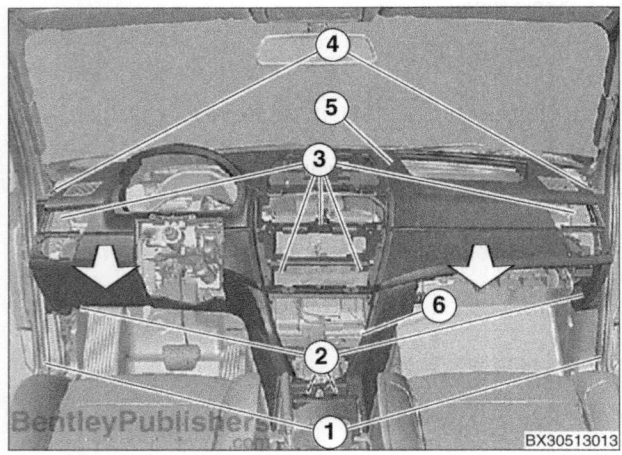

◄ Remove weather strip near dashboard trim (**1**).

– Release fasteners (**2**) and (**3**).

– Disconnect plug for solar sensor (**6**).

– Pull back dashboard trim (**5**) and remove.

– Installation: Make sure foam insulation (**4**) is properly seated.

Dashboard, installing

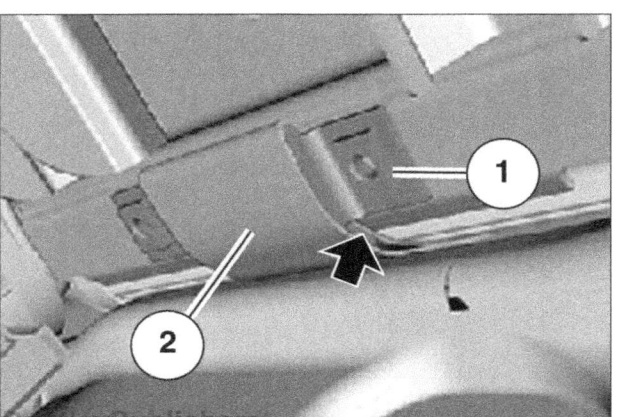

◄ Working inside passenger side of dashboard, make sure mounting plate (**1**) for retaining strap of front passenger airbag (**2**) is properly seated.

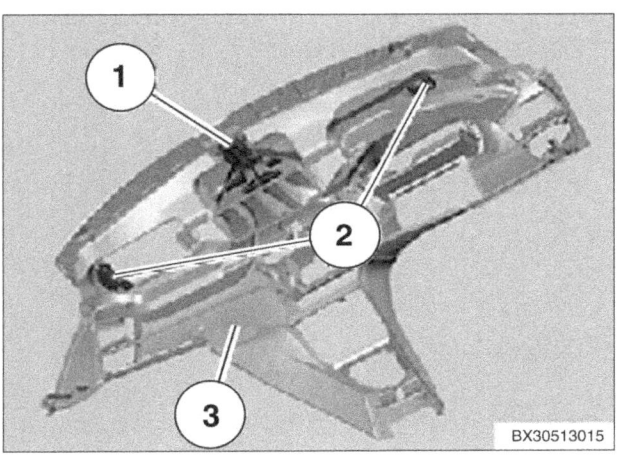

◄ When preparing to reinstall dashboard:

- Make sure guides (**1**) and (**2**) for instrument panel trim (**3**) are seated properly when installed.
- Make sure seals are correctly seated on air ducts.
- Remainder of installation is reverse of removal.

CENTER CONSOLE

NOTE—

- *2007 model year X3 shown without cd changer, other models similar.*

Center console, removing and installing

– Remove shift knob and boot or drive selection plate. See **250 Gearshift Linkage**.

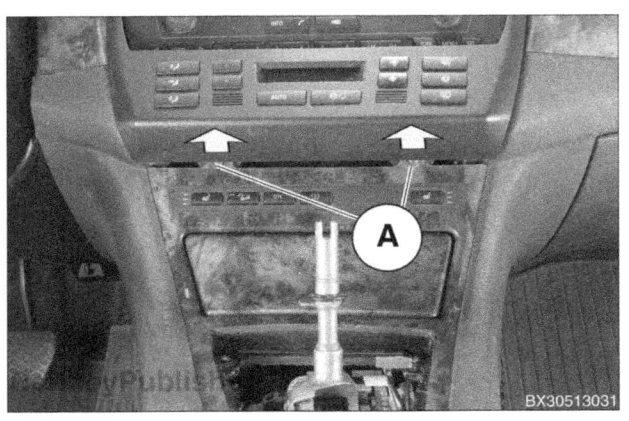

◄ Working at HVAC panel, use a suitable prying tool to unclip trim from the bottom only. Remove screws (**A**).

513

Center console, removing and installing

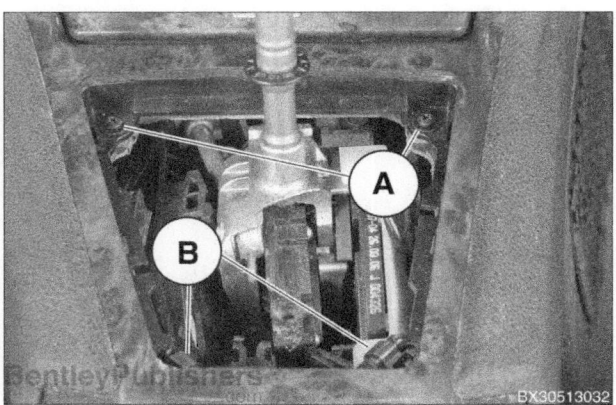

◀ Remove screws (**A**) and unclip spring clips (**B**). Taking care to not drop spring clips into shifter area.

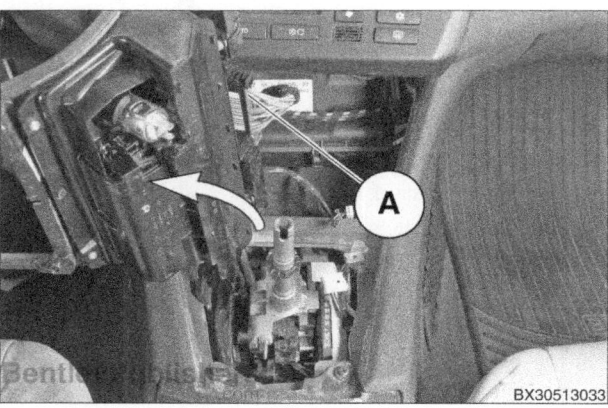

◀ Lift out trim and disconnect 12 volt socket and center switch panel connectors.

WARNING—
• *If vehicle shifter is in neutral to facilitate trim removal be sure car is on level ground and parking brake is engaged.*

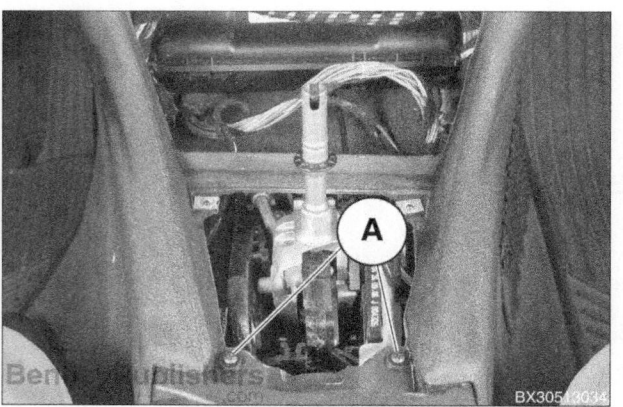

◀ Remove screws (**A**) at rear of shifter.

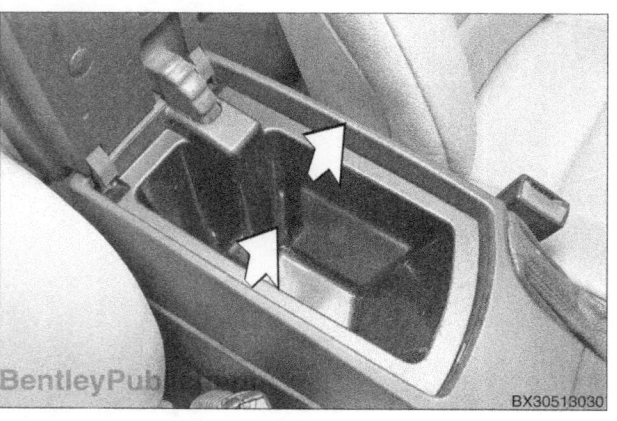

◀ Open center console armrest cover. Lift out storage compartment by hand.

Center console, removing and installing

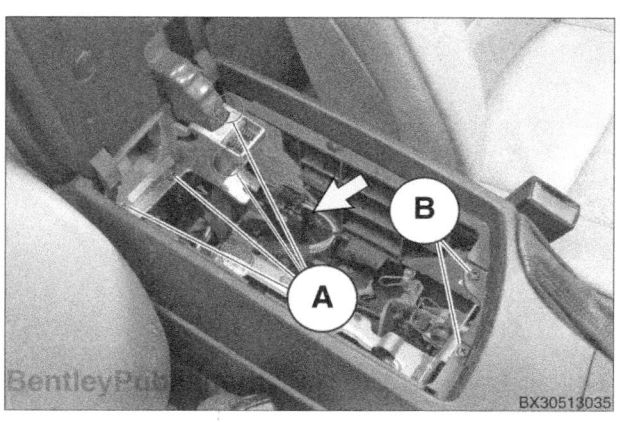

◀ Remove cap head screws (**A**) and unclip electrical connections to console lid arm rest and remove.

– Remove screws (**B**).

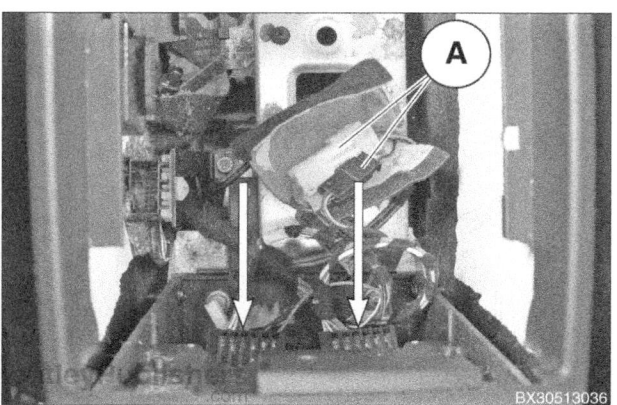

◀ Working inside at rear of center console. Disconnect electrical connector (**A**) for 12 volt socket and aux plug if equipped.

– Push on connector for rear heated seats to pop out switches from rear panel.

◀ Disconnect heated seat switches from harness (**arrows**) and remove panel.

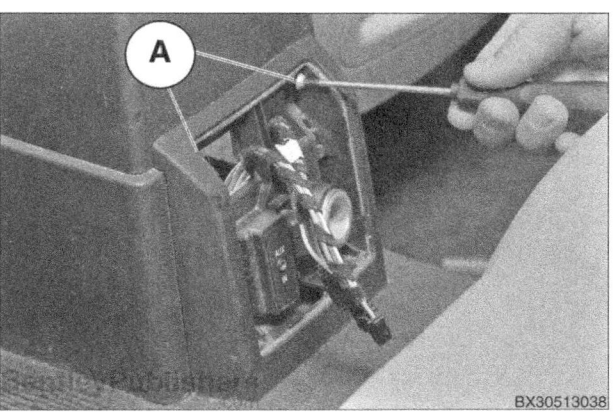

◀ Remove screws (**A**) from rear panel. Remove panel and feed out wiring.

513

Center console, removing and installing

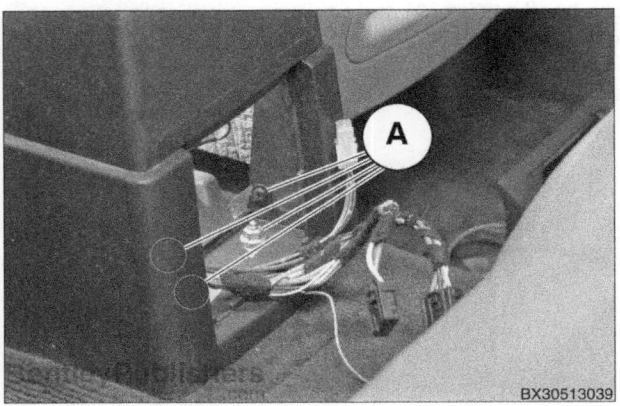

◄ Remove center console mounting nuts and screws (**A**) on both sides at bottom of storage bin opening.

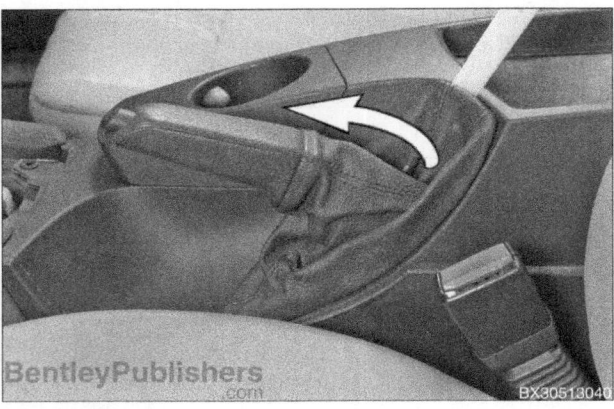

◄ Working at parking brake lever, use a suitable prying tool to unclip boot from catches.

◄ Lift console towards rear and upward over parking brake handle.

- If necessary lift parking brake handle up and feed center console over parking brake handle.

– Installation is reverse of removal.

- Take care to reconnect all connector plugs and keep wiring clear from any pinch points.

GLOVE COMPARTMENT

Glove compartment carrier, removing and installing

◀ Open glove box, remove any contents.

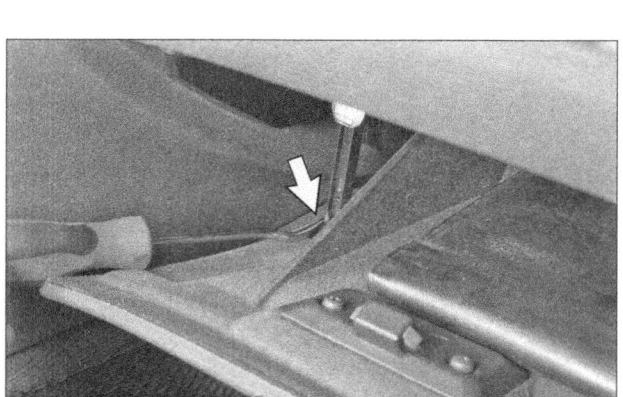

– While supporting glove compartment lid, use thin prying tool to pull out retaining pin (**arrow**) from retainer strap at right side of lid.

◀ While supporting glove compartment lid, use thin prying tool to pull out retaining pin (**arrow**) from damper piston at left side of lid.

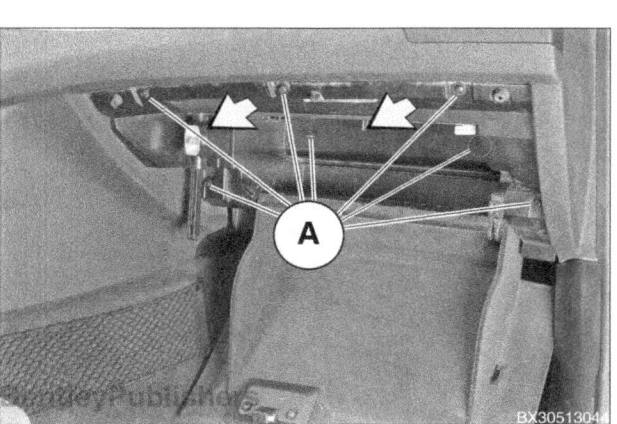

◀ Remove glove compartment carrier mounting screws (**arrows**).

– Disengage glove compartment carrier and lower from dashboard. Detach electrical connectors, then remove glove compartment carrier.

– Installation is reverse of removal.

513

COVERS AND TRIM PANELS

Steering column lower trim, removing and installing

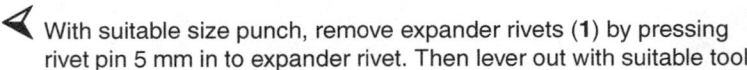

— Remove trim for pedal assembly.

— Extend steering column as far back and as high as possible.

◄ With suitable size punch, remove expander rivets (**1**) by pressing rivet pin 5 mm in to expander rivet. Then lever out with suitable tool.

NOTE —

• *Rivets can be reused. Insert rivet and push in pin until flush.*

— Lower adjusting lever for steering column. Grabbing hold of the opening pull off lower steering column trim downward to remove.

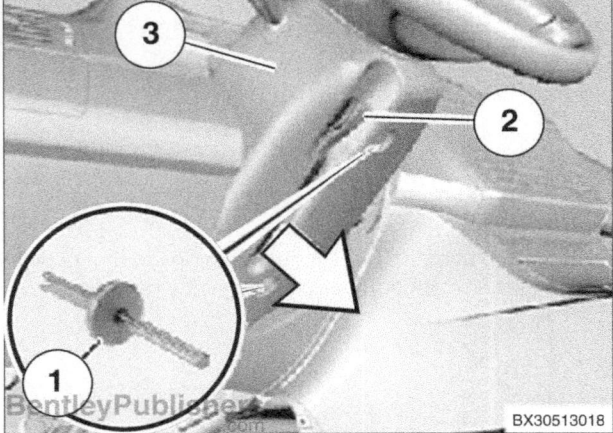

BX30513018

Installing

— Catch (**1**), guide (**2**), pins (**3**) and locks (**4**) must not be damaged.

◄ Working close to the steering wheel, first insert pins (**3**) until lower steering column trim engages with upper section lock (**4**).

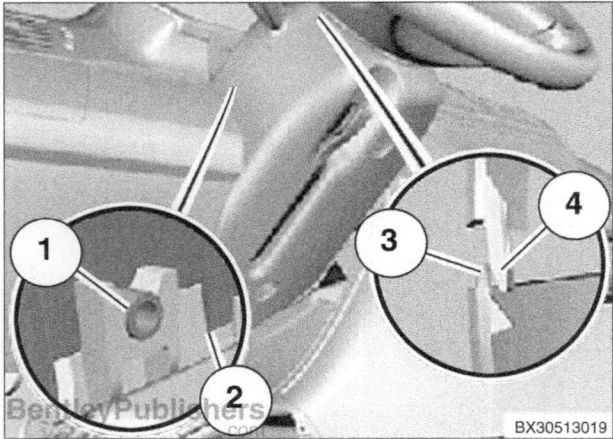

BX30513019

Steering column upper trim, removing and installing

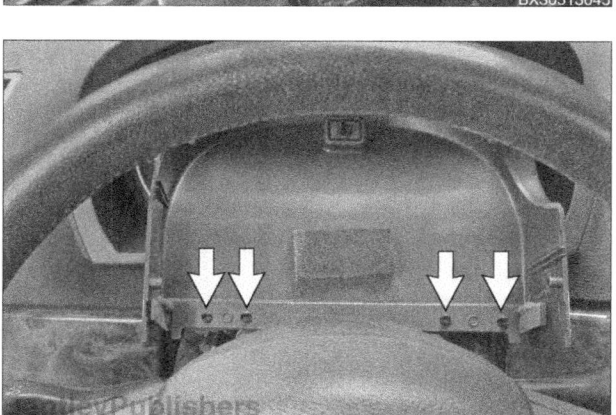

— Remove lower steering column trim.

— Extend steering column as far back and as low as possible.

◄ Remove plastic screw from (**arrow**) top of upper steering column cover.

◄ Tilt steering column trim up toward instrument cluster.

— Unclip steering column gap cover (**arrows**) from steering column trim.

— Installation is reverse of removal. Snap upper and lower steering column covers together.

  • Make sure steering column gap cover is in correct position for installation.

Door sill trim, removing

Front

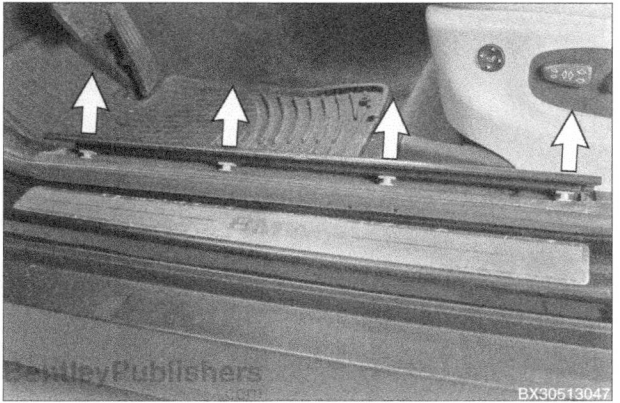

◄ Using plastic prying tool, pry door sill trim to disengage trim clips from body.

— Before reinstalling, replace damaged or broken clips.

A-pillar trim, removing and installing

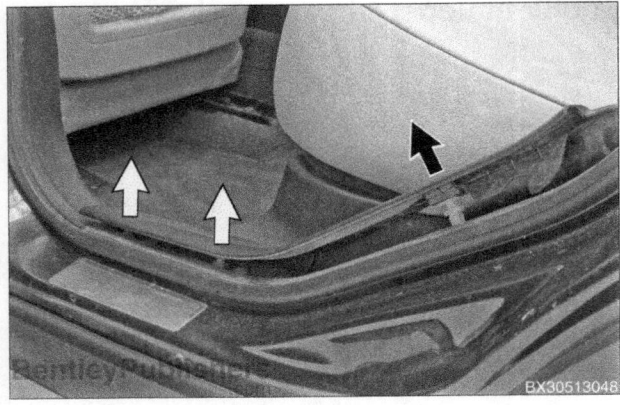

Rear

– Lift up rear seat bottom to ease with removal. See **520 Seats.**

◀ Using plastic prying tool, pry door sill trim to disengage trim clips from body.

– Before reinstalling, replace damaged or broken clips.

A-pillar trim, removing and installing

– Disconnect negative (–) battery cable and cover battery terminal to keep cable from accidentally contacting terminal.

> **WARNING—**
> • *Prior to removing A-pillar trim, read airbag warnings and cautions in* **721 Airbags**.

> **CAUTION—**
> • *To avoid damaging head protection airbag behind headliner, do not use sharp-edged tools to remove trim.*
> • *Prior to disconnecting the battery, read the battery disconnection cautions given in* **001 Warnings and Cautions**.

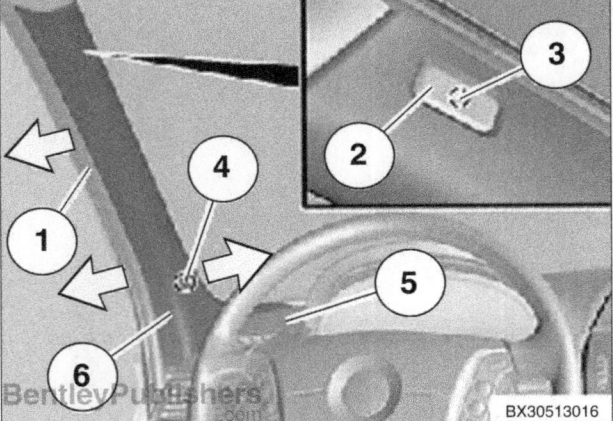

◀ Working at A-pillar:
• Peel back door edge trim (**1**) in direction of arrows.
• Unclip and remove protective cap (**2**) and remove screw (**3**)
• Unclip a-pillar trim (**6**) at hold point (**4**) and feed out from dashboard panel (**5**).

Installation

◀ Make sure guides (**3**) of a-pillar trim panel (**2**) are correctly seated in mounting holes.

– With clip (**1**) pre-installed, clip a-pillar trim panel (**2**) into place.

– When reinstalling, replace clip (**1**) if damaged.

– The rest of installation is reverse of removal.

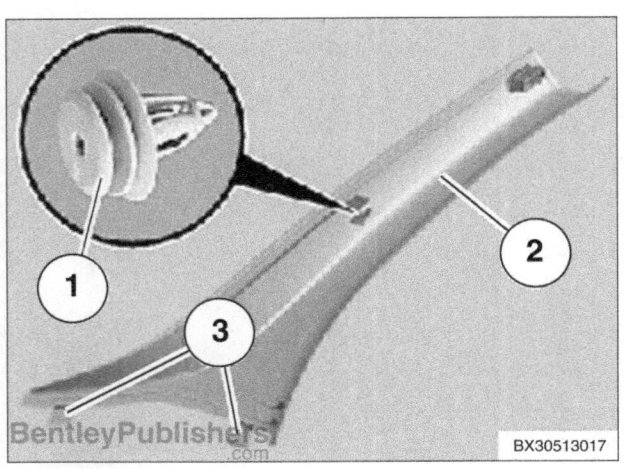

Tightening Torques	
A-pillar mounting screw	2.0 Nm

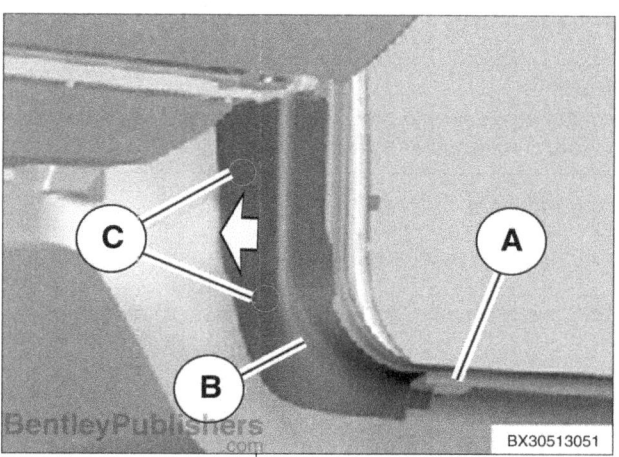

— Remove front door sill trim. See **Door sill trim, removing** in this repair group.

◀ Partially detach rubber edge protection (**A**) on lower A pillar trim (**B**).

— Unclip lower A-pillar trim (**B**) in direction of arrow from retaining points (**C**).

— Installation is reverse of removal. If necessary replace faulty clips.

B-pillar trim, removing and installing

CAUTION—
• *To avoid damaging head protection airbag behind headliner, do not use sharp-edged tools to remove trim.*

— Remove front door sill trim. See **Door sill trim, removing** in this repair group.

— Slide seat forward to ease with removal.

Lower trim

◀ Partially detach rubber edge protection area on b-pillar. Snap trim out of clips at bottom and carefully feed out bottom trim from top trim.

— Remove seat belt, see **720 Seatbelts**.

— Remove lower trim.

Upper trim

◀ Using suitable prying tool, remove expansion rivets on B-pillar panel.

— Pull off panel towards bottom. Feed out seat belt strap and remove.

— Installation is reverse of removal.

— When reinstalling, replace damaged clips or grommets.

Tightening torque	
Seat belt to height adjuster	31 Nm (23 ft-lb)
Seat belt to seat base	45 Nm (33 ft-lb)

513

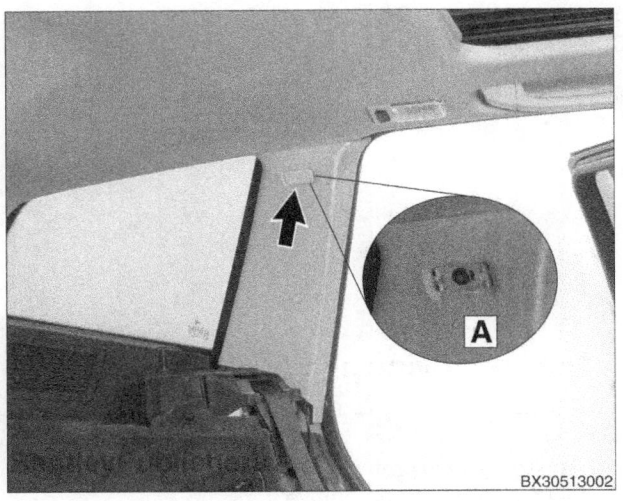

BX30513002

C-pillar trim, removing and installing

> **WARNING—**
> • *To avoid damaging head protection airbag behind headliner, do not use sharp-edged tools to remove trim.*

– Fold seat back forward.

– Remove rear seat belt reel cover by levering off.

◄ Pry out airbag emblem (**arrow**), remove fastener (**A**) at top of C-pillar trim.

– Pull back top of trim, then lift out.

– Installation is reverse of removal.

D-pillar trim, removing and installing

– Working in cargo area, swing up floor cover and remove.

– Remove left and right cargo lights from trim panel by levering out with suitable plastic prying tool. Unplug from harness.

◄ Working at sides of cargo area. Remove left and right covers by pushing release (**A**) and pulling down and outward.

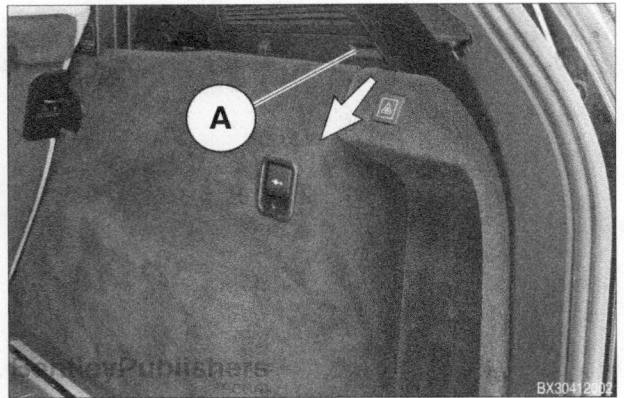

BX30412002

◄ Remove plastic covers (**arrows**) from above screws.

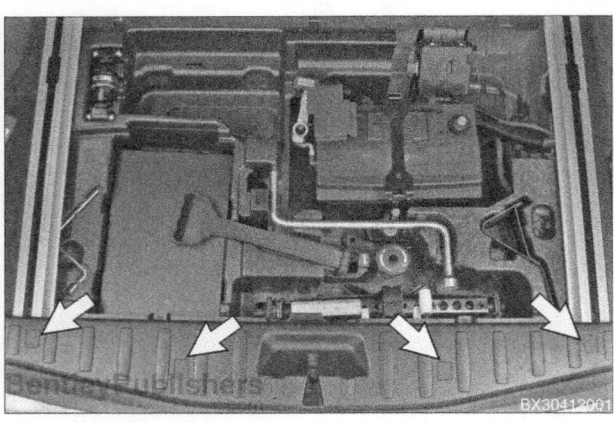

BX30412001

Front cargo floor cover removing and installing

◄ Remove screws and lift off tailgate lock trim cover.

◄ Release screws to remove left and right D-pillar trim panels by pulling to release from clips.

— When reinstalling, make sure plastic guides fit correctly. If necessary, replace mounting clips.

Front cargo floor cover removing and installing

— Remove rear seats and side bolster. See **520 Seats**.

— Working in cargo area, swing up floor cover and remove.

◄ Remove fasteners for front floor covering and remove.

513

Cargo compartment side panels, removing and installing

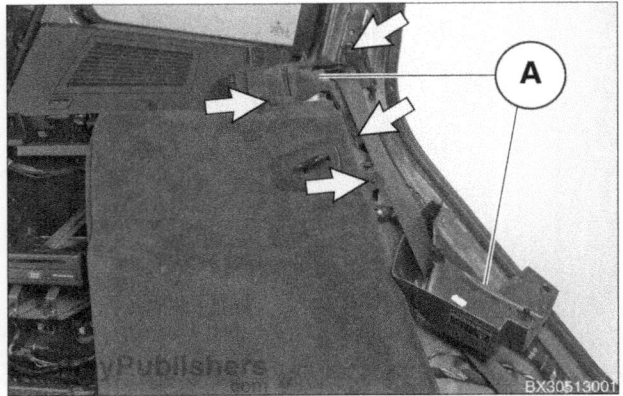

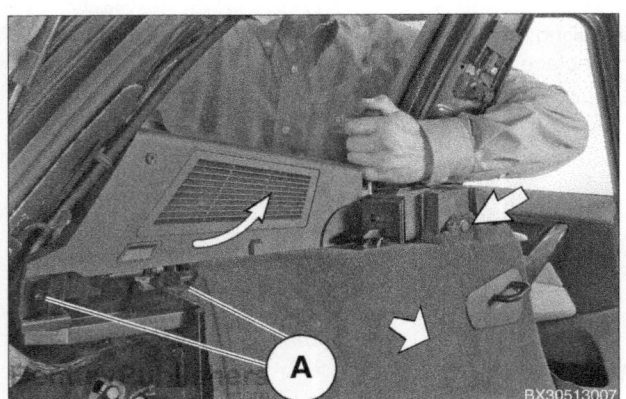

Cargo compartment side panels, removing and installing

– Working in the cargo area, swing up floor cover and remove.

– Remove rear seats and side bolster. See **520 Seats**.

– Remove front cargo floor cover see **Front cargo floor covering removing and installing** in this repair group.

◀ Remove C-pillar, D-pillar trim and Cargo compartment side panels. See **C-pillar trim, D-pillar trim and Cargo compartment side panels removing and installing** in this repair group.

– Remove cover (**A**) from seat belt reel by levering it off of base.

– Remove fasteners (**arrows**).

◀ Working between seat belt reel and upper trim remove fastener.

– Remove plastic push clip (**arrow**).

– Remove screws (**A**) and lift off upper trim panel.

– For passenger side pull back panel and detach electrical harness from 12v utility socket.

– Remove side panel.

– Installation is reverse of removal.

Cargo load rails, removing and installing

– Working in cargo area, swing up floor cover and remove.

– Remove rear seats and side bolster. See **520 Seats**.

– Remove front cargo floor covering see **Front cargo floor covering removing and installing** in this repair group.

– Remove C-pillar, D-pillar trim and Cargo compartment side panels. See **C-pillar trim, D-pillar trim and Cargo compartment side panels removing and installing** in this repair group.

◀ Working on passenger side remove fasteners (**arrows**) on cargo bucket and lift out of channel on load rail.

– Remove Torx bolts (**A**) inside of load rails.

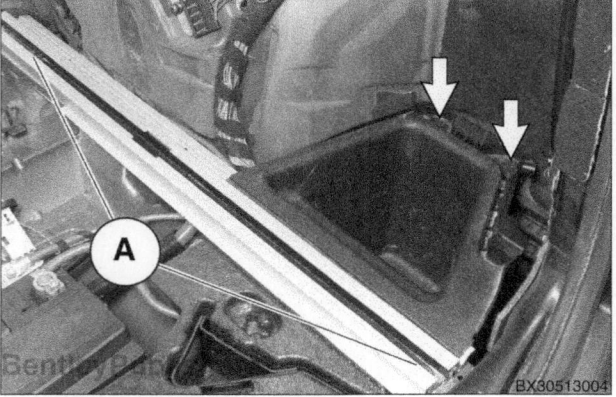

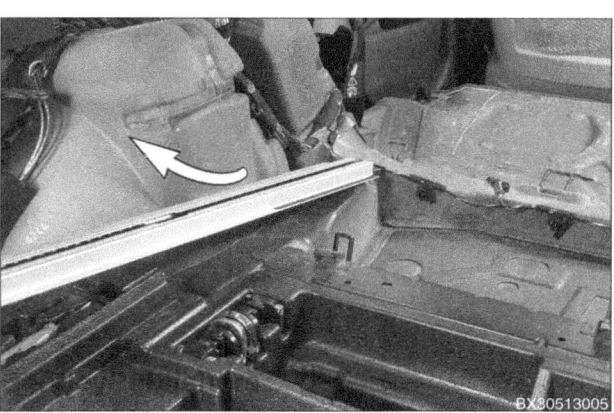

◄ Pull load rails to rear of car and lever up to disengage the lock.

— Installation is the reverse of removal.

Tailgate trim, removing and installing

— Lower trim can be removed without removing upper trim.

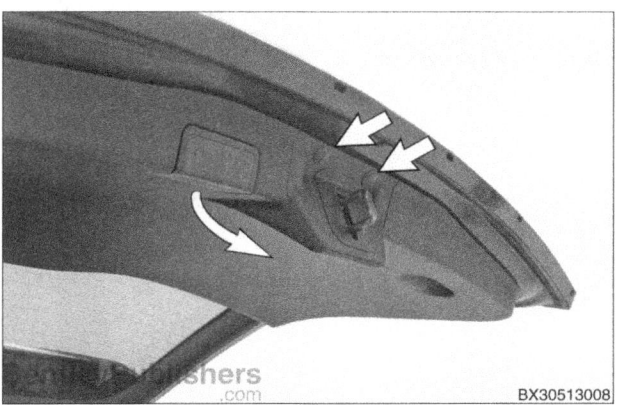

◄ Lower trim: Use plastic prying tool to remove cargo compartment light fixture. Detach electrical connectors.

— Remove expansion rivets (**arrows**) by driving center out with a suitable sized punch, then prying out clip with suitable prying tool.

NOTE—

• *Rivets are not reusable, so make sure you have more on hand.*

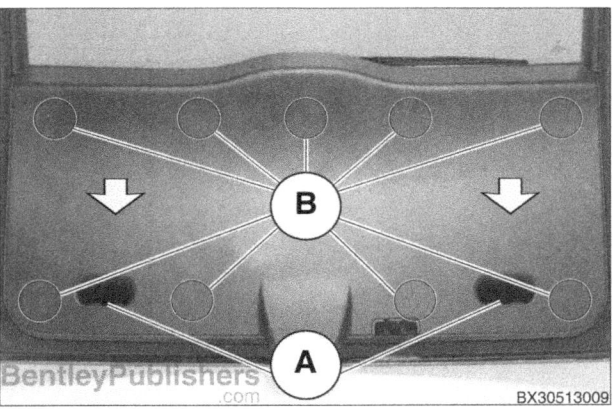

◄ Remove lower trim mounting screws (**A**).

— Pop trim off clips (**B**) remove trim towards bottom.
  • If necessary, replace broken clips.
  • Installation is reverse of removal.

513

Tailgate trim, removing and installing

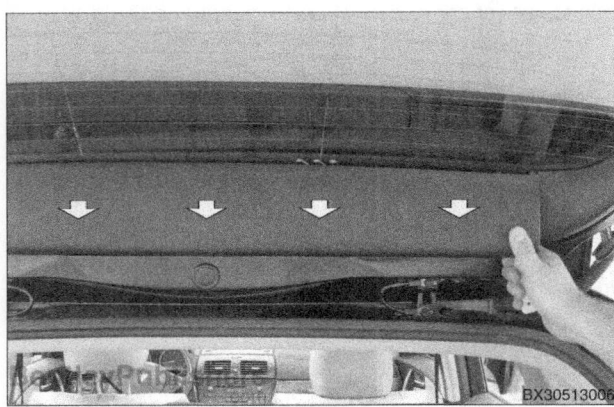

◄ Upper trim: Use plastic prying tool to release.

   • When installing, check clips and retainers. Replace if necessary.

– Installation is reverse of removal.

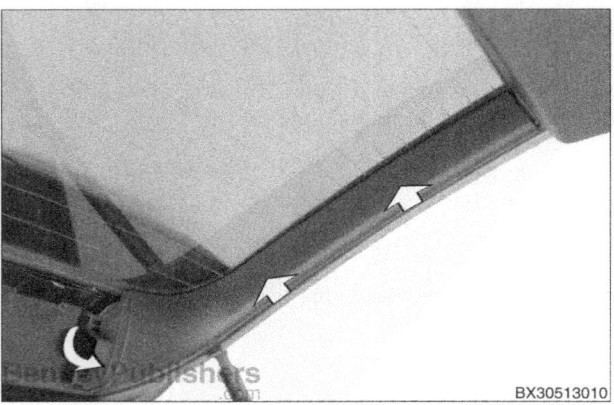

◄ Upper side trim: Use plastic prying tool to release in direction of arrows.

   • When installing, check clips and retainers. Replace if necessary.

– Installation is reverse of removal.

515 Central Locking and Anti-theft

GENERAL

This section covers repair information for door and tailgate locks, central locking, electronic immobilization (EWS) and anti-theft alarm (DWA).

X3 vehicles are equipped with self-diagnostic capabilities. When experiencing malfunctions relating to central locking, EWS or anti-theft systems, start with a diagnostic scan. An advanced BMW diagnostic scan tool can often pinpoint electrical faults quickly and safely.

See also:
- **411 Doors** for inner door trim removal
- **513 Interior Trim** for tailgate trim removal
- **600 Electrical System–General**
- **ECL Electrical Component Locations**
- **ELE Electrical Wiring Diagrams**

CENTRAL LOCKING

Central locking in X3 vehicles controls the door locks, tailgate lock and fuel filler door lock. The control module for the central body electronics system (ZKE) is called the General Module 5 ReDesign (GM5RD), and one of its many functions is to control central locking.

GM5RD manages the following central locking-related functions:
- Door, tailgate and fuel flap locking and unlocking
- Keyless entry
- Key memory
- DWA alarm system
- Diagnosis

For more information on ZKE, see **600 Electrical System–General**.

515

General module

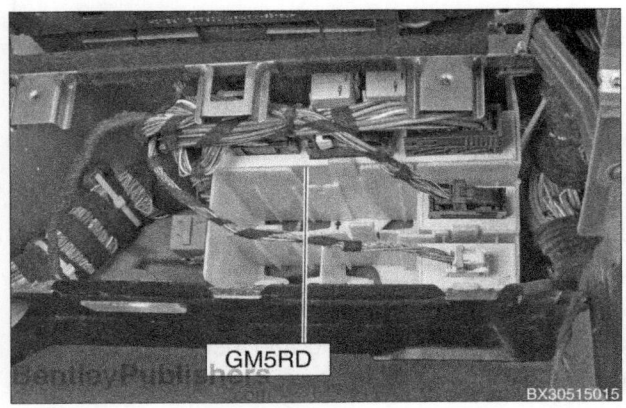

GM5RD

BX30515015

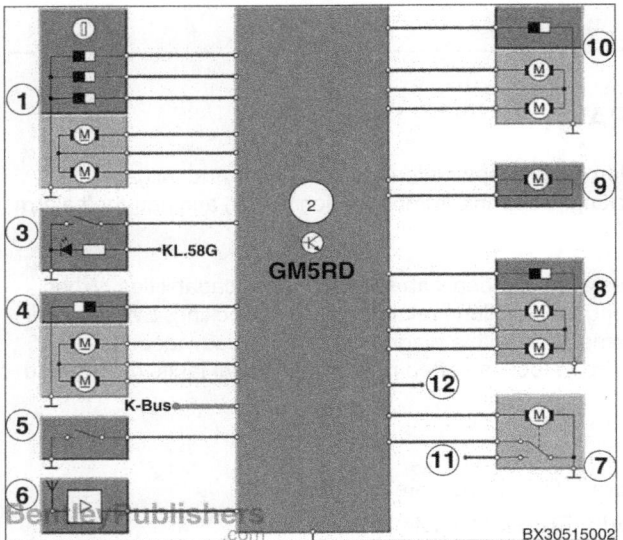

BX30515002

General module

◀ The General Module 5 ReDesign (GM5RD) is behind the glove compartment.

Based on input information, the GM5RD uses internal transistors to switch current flow (providing voltage or ground) through circuits and actuators (motors). Actuators are used to operate or control functions such as door locks.

NOTE—

There is a door lock key cylinder on the driver's door only.

Central locking features

GM5RD inputs and outputs

1. Central locking, driver's door w/hall sensor
2. GM5RD
3. Tailgate Release Button
4. Central locking, driver's side rear door w/hall sensor
5. Center lock button
6. Remote control antenna
7. Tailgate lock assembly
8. Passenger door rear, w/hall sensor
9. Fuel filler flap locking
10. Passenger door front, w/hall sensor
11. Luggage compartment light

Door locks and actuators

Door locks with integral lock actuators are sealed self contained units. If a lock actuator is faulty, the door lock unit will need to be replaced. The door actuators use Hall effect sensors in place of microswitches to provide door OPEN / CLOSED status signal.

NOTE—

• *Tailgate lock actuator and fuel filler door actuator are separately available replacement parts.*

Door lock actuators can be set to automatically lock when a road speed signal of 2.5 mph is detected by GM5RD via K-bus. The factory default coding for this feature is ON.

The GM5RD and electronic immobilization (EWS) interface via the K-bus to monitor double lock status and to initiate double lock override. This feature allows the doors to be opened from the inside if a key (accepted by EWS) is switched on in when the doors are double locked.

Continuous locking / unlocking initiates a timed arrest of the locking system. The GM5RD counts each time the locks are actuated. After approximately 12 cycles, lock operation is arrested to allow the lock actuators to cool down.

Central locking switch

◄ The central locking switch is located in the center of the dashboard between the center air vents. The switch locks all vehicle locks except for the fuel filler flap.

The switch provides a momentary ground input signal to the GM5RD. This input single locks each door and the tailgate. The fuel filler flap remains unlocked for refueling purposes.

Single lock and double lock function

Each door lock actuator incorporates two motors:

Single lock motor controls the mechanical lock mechanism when the central lock switch is pressed to single lock the vehicle. The lock mechanism is fully locked at this point but can still be opened from the interior by pulling the interior door handle twice or by pressing the central lock switch again. When single lock function is activated, the fuel filler flap actuator is not locked.

Double lock motor, also known as central arrest, is activated only when the vehicle is locked from the outside at the driver door lock with a key or when the GM5RD receives a lock request from the keyless entry (FZV) system. In this case the double lock motor is activated simultaneously with the single lock motor. The double lock motor mechanically offsets an internal rod in the lock actuator, preventing it from unlocking the vehicle from the interior. With double lock activated, the doors cannot be unlocked by any means except by an unlock request at the driver door lock cylinder or via the FZV key.

Car memory and key memory

A number of safety, security and comfort features and functions can be customized. The identity of the vehicle user is provided by a signal from the keyless entry system (FZV).

Car memory and key memory are two separate functions, although they are marketed as a combined feature.

Prior to vehicle delivery, the BMW diagnostic scan tool is used to code the driver preferences into the appropriate control modules. Thereafter these choices cannot be changed without a BMW scan tool.

The car memory functions that can be set include:

• Alarm system (DWA) features such as arming / disarming with keyless entry (FZV), activation of tilt sensor or interior sensor
• Interior light activation when central locking is used
• Convenience opening of windows and sunroof
• Interior and external lighting preferences
• Heating and A/C preferences (IHKA)
• Seat and mirror position preferences (triggered by key memory)
• Instrument cluster display units (km or miles)

515

Whenever an FZV key is used to lock or unlock the car, the specific key is identified by the GM5RD. A maximum of four keys can be programmed. If the vehicle is equipped seat memory, the use of the personalized key triggers automatic adjustment of the driver's seat and exterior mirror position as part of key memory.

NOTE—

Key memory is only activated when using keyless entry. If the driver door is unlocked manually, no electronic input is received at the GM5RD and car memory / key memory features are not activated.

Remote entry (FZV)

The remote (keyless) entry system (FZV) uses a radio transmitter in the vehicle key to lock and unlock the doors and the tailgate by remote control. There are a number of other features incorporated in FZV:

• Locking and unlocking of fuel filler flap

• Selective unlocking of driver's door

• Arming and disarming of DWA alarm system

• Remote unlocking of tailgate

• Comfort opening of windows and sunroof

• Interior lighting activation

• Panic mode alarm activation

Each key battery is automatically charged in the ignition lock during driving. It is recommended to use each key at least twice a year to maintain the charge.

 The GM5RD is connected to the AM/FM diversity antenna (in center top of tailgate, under trim). Locking and unlocking of doors and tailgate and convenience closing is carried out by the general module subsystem controlling the door lock, window and sunroof modules.

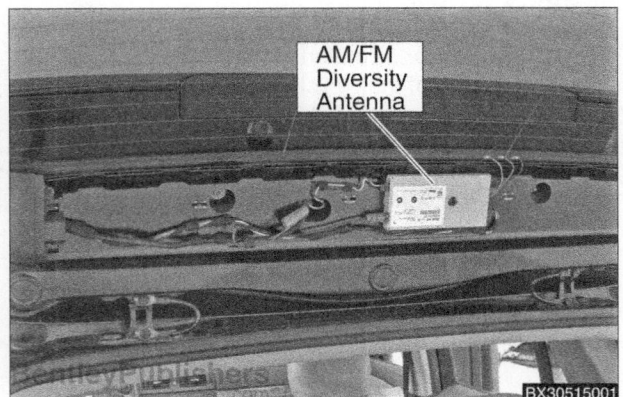

AM/FM Diversity Antenna

BX30515001

Remote (FZV) key, operation

◀ Remote (FZV) key button default functions:

— Unlocking:

A single unlock request by pressing button (**1**) with the FZV key unlocks the driver's door and fuel filler door only. A second unlock request unlocks the remaining doors and tailgate. Using Key memory programming capabilities, this feature can be modified to activate all lock actuators on the first click. If the vehicle is unlocked but no doors are opened the central locking system will automatically re-lock the car after a short time period.

Pressing button (**3**) unlocks the tailgate only.

— Convenience opening:

Press and hold button (**1**) windows and panorama glass sunroof are opened.

— Locking

Press button (**2**) hazard flashers flash once all doors and fuel lid lock. Pressing button (**2**) again right after locking will switch off the tilt alarm sensor and interior motion sensor if equipped.

— Panic mode (if fitted with anti-theft system):

Press and hold button (**3**) for at least 3 seconds to trigger panic alarm. To deactivate alarm press any buttons on key fob.

— Interior lighting:

With vehicle is locked press button (**2**). This will turn on interior lights.

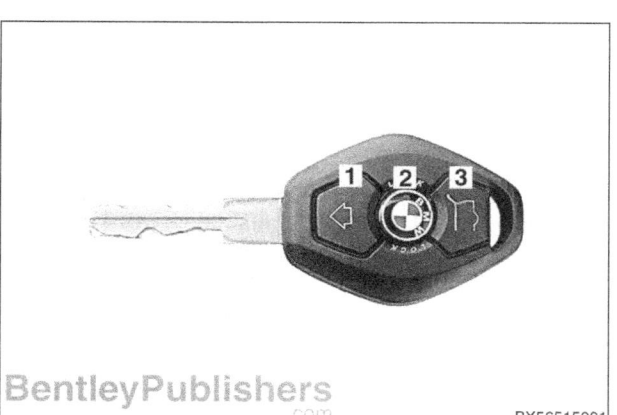

BX56515001

Remote (FZV) key, initializing

Up to four keys can be coded to operate the same system. Initialize all keys at the same time, following the order set out in the colored labels sheet which came with the vehicle. If the keys are not initialized in the original order, key memory is not assigned correctly.

◀ Close all doors and have all keys available. Make sure the vehicle is unlocked.

— Using key number 1, turn ignition switch to KL R (ACCESSORY), then switch OFF within 5 seconds and remove first key.

— Within 30 seconds of turning ignition switch to OFF, press and hold button **1**.

• While holding button **1**, press and release (tap) button **2** three times within 10 seconds.

• Release both buttons. GM immediately locks and unlocks doors to signal successful initialization.

— Initialize remaining keys, repeating steps above.

— If acknowledgement signal (doors locking / unlocking) does not follow initialization procedure, repeat process. If ignition is switched ON during process, procedure is cancelled.

BX56515001

515

EWS control module, location

ELECTRONIC IMMOBILIZER (EWS)

X3 vehicles are equipped with a passive theft-prevention system. The electronic immobilizer (EWS) makes it impossible to start the engine using any means other than the special keys furnished with the vehicle.

In the EWS system, the ignition key is embedded with a computer chip (EEPROM) and coded. The key communicates with the vehicle using a transponder in the key and a ring antenna surrounding the steering lock cylinder. Up to 6 replacement keys (in addition to the 4 originally supplied with the vehicle) can be coded. Only an authorized BMW dealer can provide replacement keys with proof of vehicle ownership.

If the starter engages, the following EWS inputs are functioning normally:

• Ignition key

• Code function

• Transmission range switch

• Engine speed sensor

NOTE—

• *The coded FZV key, the EWS control module and the DME control module must all communicate correctly for the vehicle to start. If either the DME module or the EWS module is replaced, a BMW diagnostic scan tool must be used to align the DME module to the EWS module. Without alignment, the engine does not start.*

• *Swapping a known good ECM into another vehicle for test purposes results in a no start situation. Similarly, once the ECM is programmed to the vehicle, it cannot be reprogrammed to another vehicle.*

• *If a vehicle key is lost or stolen, the electronic authorization for that key can be disabled using BMW diagnostic scan tool.*

EWS control module, location

◄ EWS control module (**arrow**) is located to left of steering column, below dashboard. To gain access, remove left dashboard panel above pedals. See **513 Interior Trim**.

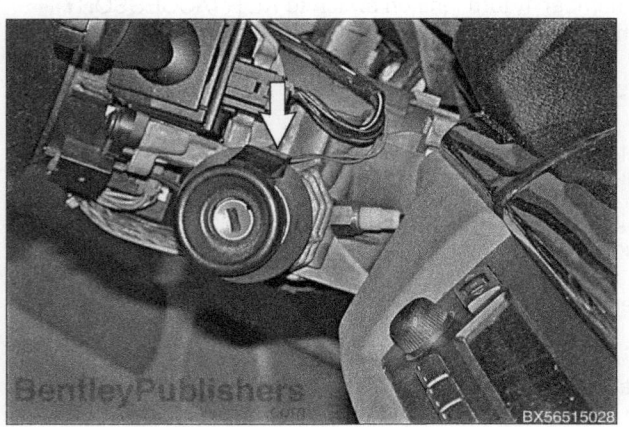

EWS ring antenna, removing and installing

◄ To remove ring antenna:

• Remove upper and lower steering column trim. See **513 Interior Trim**.

• Disconnect ring antenna harness connector (**arrow**).

• Pry off ring antenna using BMW special tool 61 3 300 or equivalent flattened prying tool.

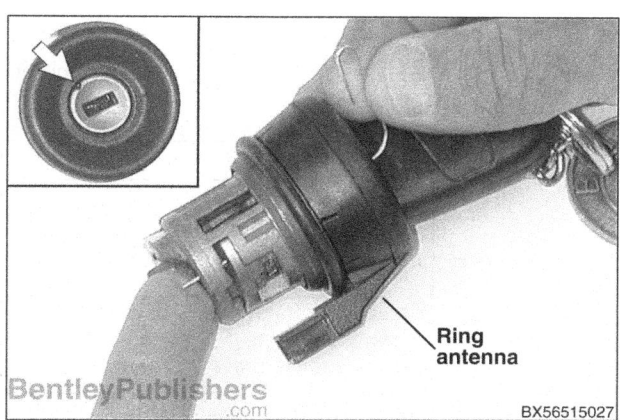

BX56515027

◄ Alternatively, remove ignition switch key cylinder:

- With ignition key in ON position (60° from LOCKED), insert thin piece of stiff wire into opening (**arrow**) in lock cylinder and pull lock cylinder out.
- Detach ring antenna harness connector.
- Gently work ring antenna off key cylinder.

— Installation is reverse of removal.

ANTI-THEFT SYSTEM (DWA)

DWA operation

NOTE—

- *DWA anti-theft alarm is not standard on the X3.*

The system is armed or disarmed from the driver's door lock cylinder or the remote transmitter (FZV key) when the vehicle is locked or unlocked. The interior compartment monitor is activated approximately 30 seconds after the vehicle is locked.

The system indicates that it is armed by flashing the hazard warning lights once and emitting a brief chirp from the siren.

◄ If the alarm is activated, the tailgate may still be opened using button **3** on the FZV key. The alarm resets when the tailgate is closed.

Following the triggering of an alarm, the system resets and can trigger again if further tampering to the vehicle is detected.

The control electronics for DWA are integrated in the GM5RD.

When the anti-theft system (DWA) is armed:

- The doors, hood, windows, and tailgate are monitored against forcible entry.
- A tilt sensor protects the vehicle from being jacked up or towed away.
- Movement inside the vehicle is monitored.
- Battery voltage is monitored.

The system responds to unauthorized vehicle entry or attempted theft by activating the following:

- Alarm siren sounds for 30 seconds.
- Hazard warning lights and high beams flash for approximately. 5 minutes.

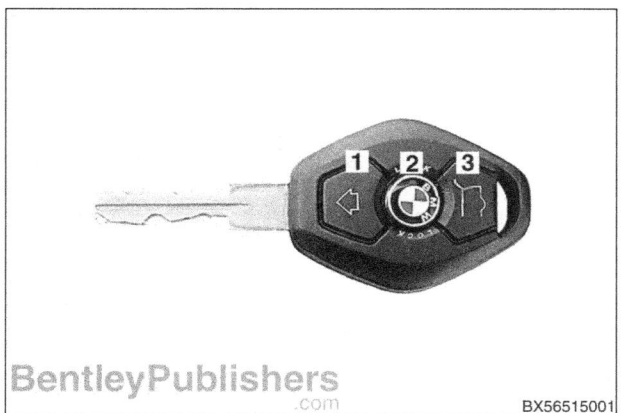

BX56515001

515

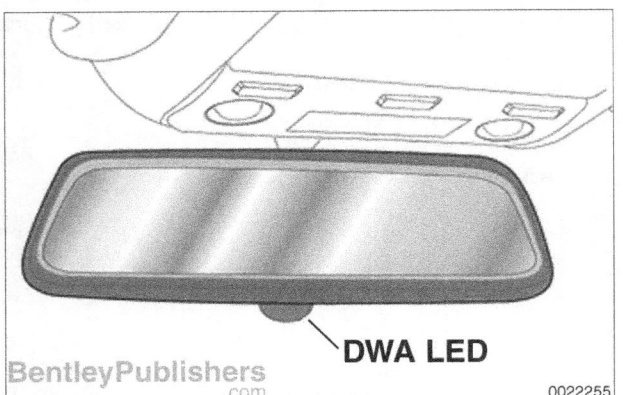

DWA LED

DWA LED display

 The DWA status LED (**arrow**) is below the interior rear view mirror. LED displays are listed in **Table a**.

Table a. DWA LED status	
DWA status	**LED signal**
Disarmed	OFF
Armed	Continual slow flash
Armed with tailgate or door not fully closed	Rapid flash for 10 second, then continual slow flash. Interior motion sensor not activated.
Alarm activated	Rapid flash for 5 minutes, then continual slow flash
Rearmed in less than 10 seconds	ON for 1 second
Disarmed after activated alarm	Rapid flash for 10 seconds, then OFF

DWA alarm siren

The DWA alarm siren is located behind the heater bulkhead on the passenger side area. The siren is powered by a separate rechargeable battery. This battery is recharged by the vehicle electrical system when DWA is not armed.

Tilt sensor

Tilt sensor is integrated with the DWA alarm siren. When flat-bed transporting the vehicle, lock the vehicle twice within 10 seconds to switch tilt sensor OFF.

Interior protection

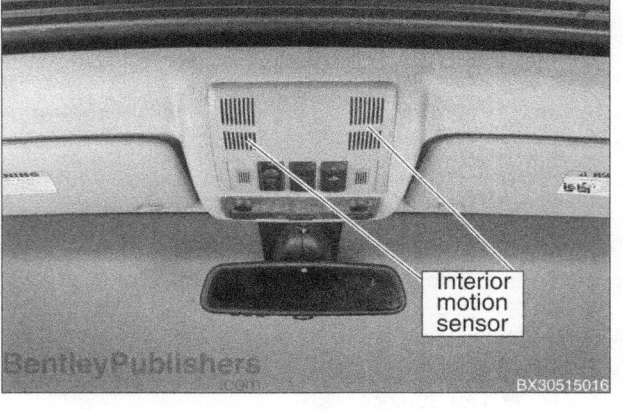

Interior motion sensor

The interior motion sensor (UIS) is located in the headliner above review mirror. As with the tilt sensor, when flat-bed transporting the vehicle, lock the vehicle twice within 10 seconds to switch interior motion sensor OFF.

The UIS system uses ultrasound to sense motion inside its detection cone. Every time DWA is armed, the UIS sensor adapts to whatever objects are stationary in the interior. UIS also checks for background hiss (wind noise through a partially open window) and adapts for this.

- If detected echoes and sounds are consistent, no movement is detected.
- If the echoes are altered (inconsistent), UIS determines motion in the interior compartment.
- If motion is detected, the UIS changes from a pulsed signal to a constant signal and the echo is compared again.
- If the inconsistency is still present the UIS sends an alarm ON signal to the GM5RD.

Emergency disarming

Emergency disarming occurs automatically when a recognized key is inserted into the ignition and is turned to the ON position. If the key is accepted by the EWS, a signal is sent to the GM to unlock the doors and deactivate the alarm.

DOOR HANDLES AND LOCKS

Components

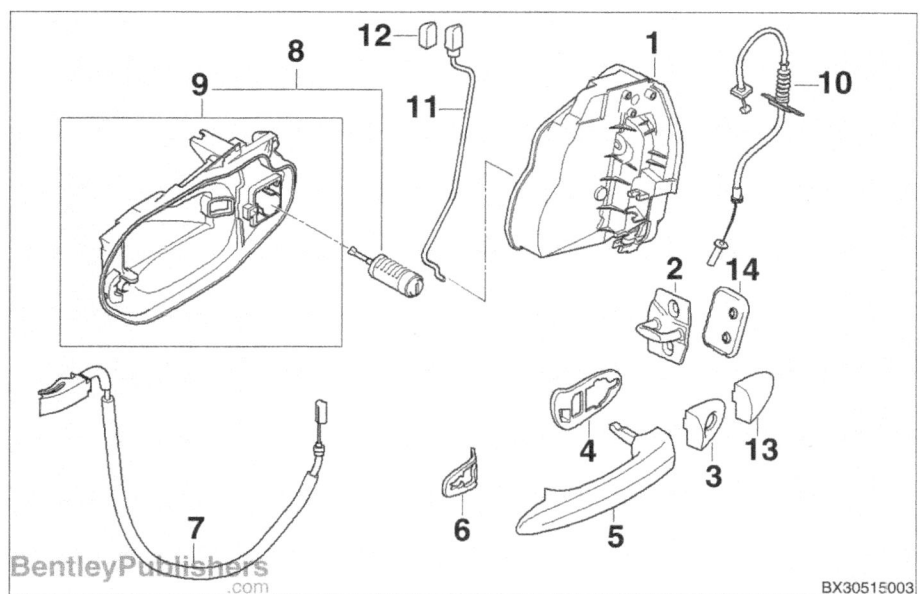

1. Door lock
   • With integrated door lock actuator
2. Door striker
3. Lock cylinder cap
4. Door handle base gasket
5. Door handle
6. Door handle base gasket
7. Bowden cable for door handle
8. Door handle carrier with lock cylinder
9. Door handle carrier
10. Door lock bowden cable
11. Interior door lock rod
12. Door lock rod button
13. Door handle cap
14. Lock plate

In the procedures that follow, door handle removal, door lock cylinder removal and door latch removal are covered for the left front door. Other doors are similar although simpler, due to the lack of lock cylinder.

Door handle, removing and installing

◄ Open door. Working at door rear edge, pry out rubber covers from access holes (**1**) and (**2**).

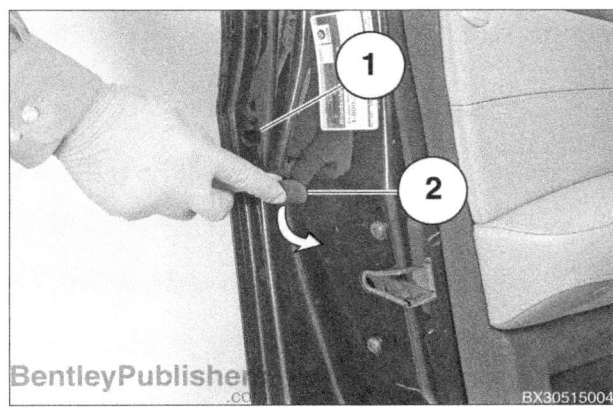

◄ Release cap head retaining screw inside access hole (**2**).

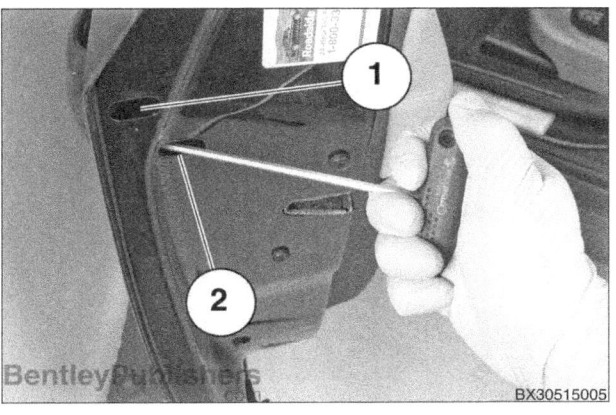

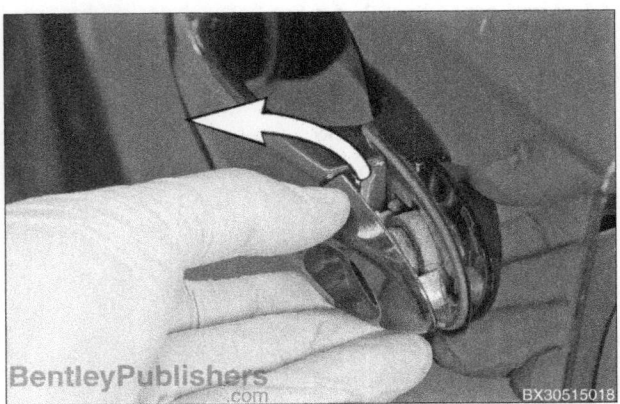

 Remove outer lock cylinder cap.

– Installation is reverse of removal, noting the following:
  • Be sure that handle is properly seated before tightening retaining screw.

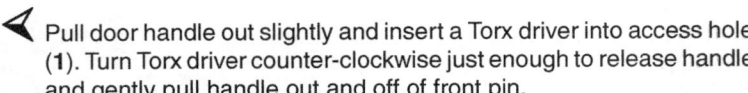 Pull door handle out slightly and insert a Torx driver into access hole (**1**). Turn Torx driver counter-clockwise just enough to release handle and gently pull handle out and off of front pin.

Door lock, removing and installing

NOTE—
  • *Electric door lock actuator is part of door lock unit and not separately available form BMW.*

– Door window should be closed.

– Remove door handle. See **Door handle, removing and installing**.

– Remove door panel. See **411 Doors**.

◁ Unclip electrical connection from door lock and wiring harness clip.

– Unclip lock rod from door lock.
  • Partially remove vapor barrier (**B**) from inside of door. Feed out wires from Vapor barrier.

CAUTION—
  • *Use care when peeling back vapor barrier. Damaged vapor barrier should be replaced to prevent possible water leaks.*

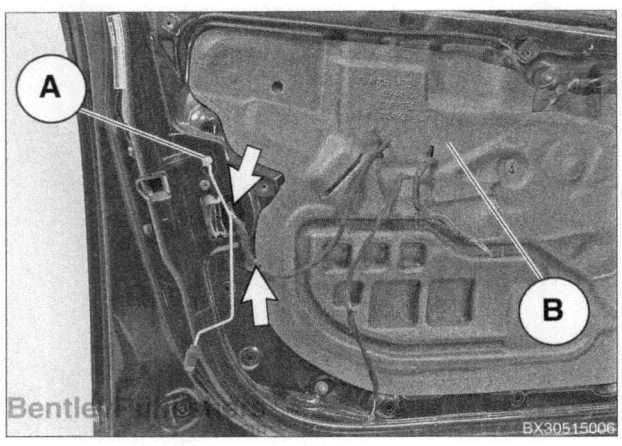

Door handle carrier, removing and installing

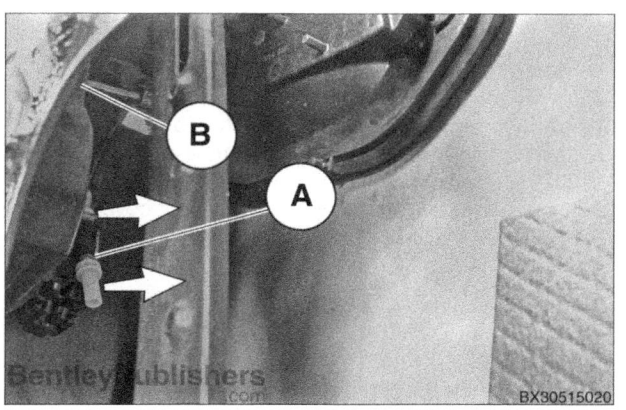

◁ Working inside door cavity, unclip bowden cable (**A**) from door lock assembly.

NOTE—
- *When reinstalling, be sure that lock cylinder drive (**B**) is properly seated.*

> **CAUTION**—
> - *Use care not to damage lock seal during removal.*

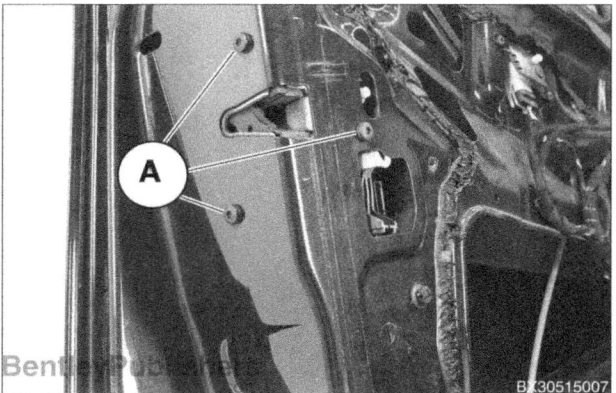

◁ Remove screws (**A**) and feed out door lock from inside of door cavity.

— Installation is reverse of removal.

Door handle carrier, removing and installing

— Door window should be closed.

— Remove Door Handle. See **Door handle removing and installing** in this repair group.

— Remove door trim panel. See **411 Doors**.

— Remove door lock. see **Door lock removing and installing** in this repair group.

◁ Working on outside of door, carefully remove rubber gaskets (**A**).

— Loosen carrier screw (**arrow**). Slide carrier to front of vehicle, remove carrier assembly from inside door cavity.

— Installation is reverse of removal.

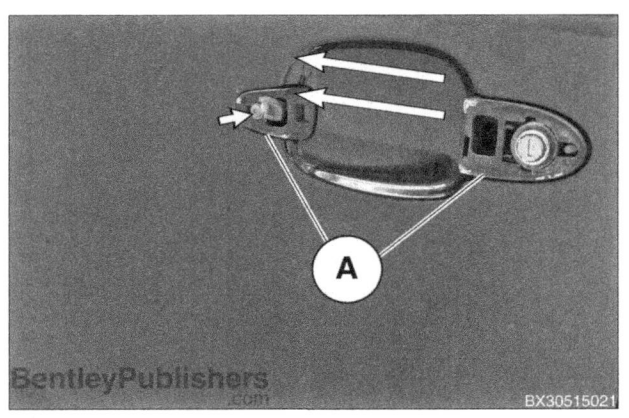

515

Tailgate lock, removing and installing

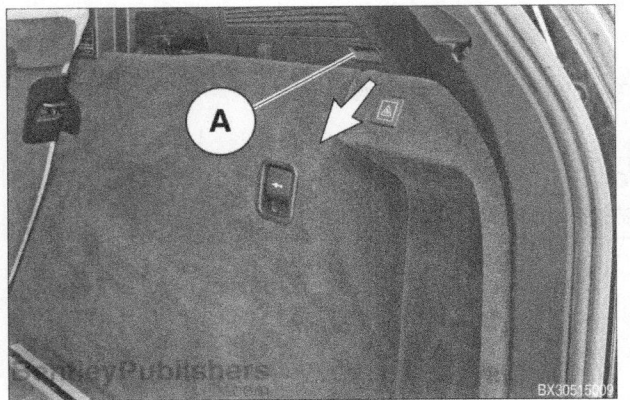

Tailgate lock, removing and installing

- Working in cargo area, swing up floor cover and remove.

- Remove left and right cargo lights from trim panel, by levering out with suitable plastic prying tool. Unplug from harness.

◄ Working at sides of cargo area. Remove left and right covers by pushing release (**A**) and pulling down and outward.

◄ Release screws to remove left and right D-pillar trim panels by pulling to release from clips.

◄ Remove plastic caps over screws and remove screw (**arrows**).

◄ Remove Torx bolts (**A**) and disconnect electrical connector on actuator drive (**arrow**) to remove lock.

- Installation is reverse of removal. Check lock contact points for wear. Replace worn parts. Make sure plastic guides on D-pillar trim fit correctly. If necessary, replace mounting clip.

520 Seats

GENERAL

This repair group covers removal and installation of the front and rear seats.

See also:

- **612 Switches** for seat heater and seat switches
- **ECL Electrical Component Locations.**
- **ELE Electrical Wiring Diagrams**
- **721 Airbag system**

Seat design and upholstery

 E83 front seats come in either manual or powered version. Seat construction is engineered to work together with the vehicle suspension to absorb vibration. Vinyl is the most common upholstery, and leather is an available option. Front and rear heated seats are optional. A characteristic double reflective strip on the seating surfaces is standard for the E83. Front seatback nets are standard.

Passenger seat occupancy (OC3) detector

E83 vehicles are equipped with a passenger seat occupancy sensor in the seat bottom. If OC3 is defective it must be replaced with the seat bottom as one unit. This device is part of the two-stage deployment MRS airbag system. See **721 Airbag** for more information.

520

Seat memory position, setting

Seat memory (seat, exterior mirror position) can be memorized and stored for three different users. The seat control module is integral with the front seat control switches.

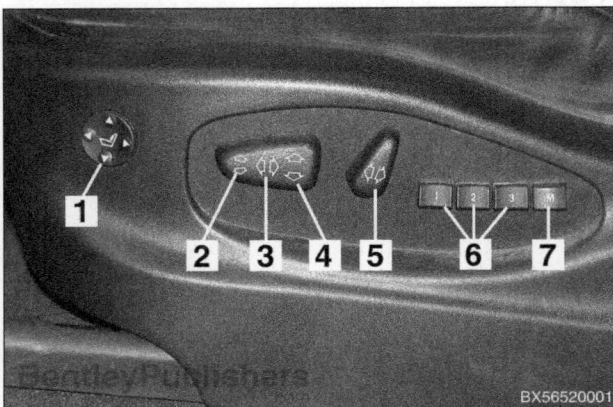

BX56520001

— With transmission range selector in P, switch ignition ON and adjust seat, mirrors and steering column to desired position.

◀ Press M (**7**) on memory switch and press one of the three memory switches (**6**).

• The current position of the mirrors and seat is now stored in memory.

Power seat controls.

• **1**— Lumbar support (optional)
• **2**— Seat tilt
• **3**— Longitudinal adjustment
• **4**— Cushion height
• **5**— Head restraint height and backrest angle
• **6**— Memory positions
• **7**— Memory activation

NOTE —

• *Seat memory is held in an EEPROM in the seat module prior to the vehicle going into sleep mode. Once the vehicle goes to sleep, the memory position is stored in the general module. If the battery is disconnected before the 16 minute sleep mode activation, seat memory positions are lost.*

FRONT SEATS

Seat repair and component replacement is possible once the seat has been removed from the vehicle. Before servicing front seats read safety regulations on handling pyrotechnic seatbelt tensioners. See **720 Seat Belts** and **721 Airbag System**.

WARNING —

• *The front seats are equipped with pyrotechnic seat belt tensioners. These tensioners are powerful devices and should be handled with extreme care. Incorrect handling can trigger off the tensioner and cause injury.*

• *BMW recommends that repair or replacement work on pyrotechnic devices be carried out by a qualified BMW technician.*

• *Be sure to disconnect the battery and wait 5 seconds before attempting to work on pyrotechnic devices.*

• *During body straightening and welding with an electric arc welder, disconnect the battery and the connection to the pyrotechnic gas generators.*

Front seats removing and installing

◄ Raise seat and move to its forward position. Working at base of seat near door, remove seat belt mounting bolt (**arrow**).

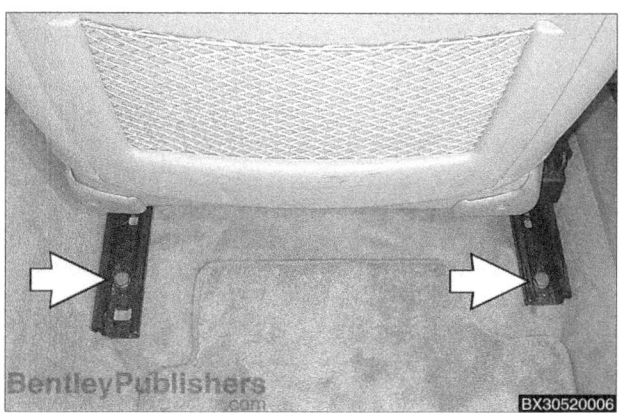

◄ Remove two mounting bolts (**arrows**) at rear of seat rails.

– Move seat to its rear most position, keeping it raised.

◄ Remove plastic caps over front seat mounting nuts, then remove mounting nuts (**arrows**).

– Disconnect negative (–) cable from battery.

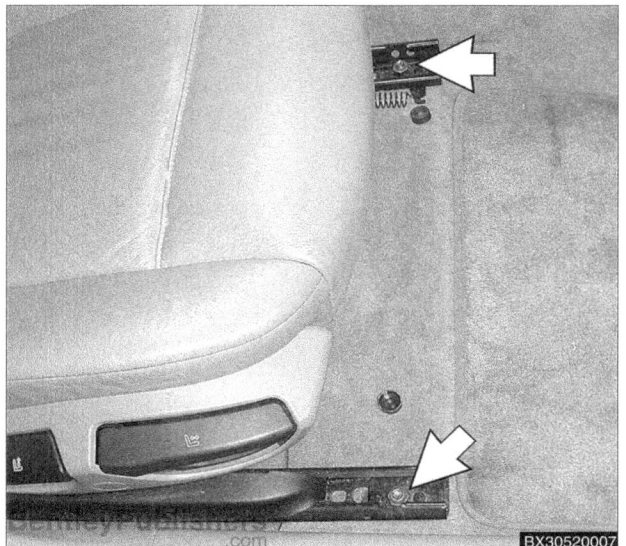

CAUTION—
• *Prior to disconnecting battery, read the battery disconnection cautions. See* **001 Warnings and Cautions**.

520

Rear seat configuration

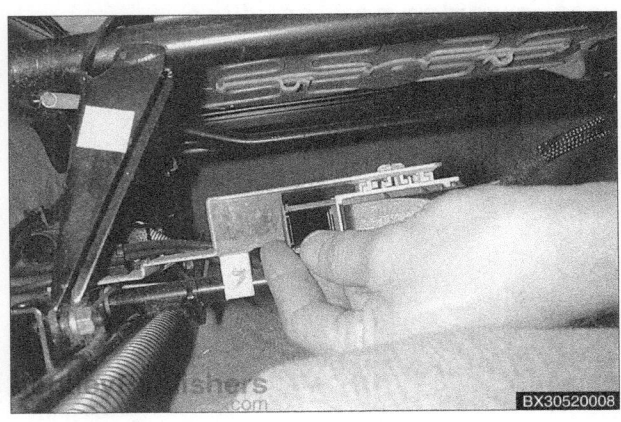

◄ Tilt seat back to access electrical harness connectors. Slide lock to release and disconnect. Cut or untwist wire ties as necessary.

– Remove seat from car. Headrests may be removed to provide additional clearance.

NOTE —

• *Use a blanket to protect door sill from scuffing by seat rail during seat removal.*

– Installation is reverse of removal.

• Use new seat mounting bolts.

• Use wire ties or equivalent means to keep seat harness wiring from fraying.

Tightening torques	
Seat belt to seat	31 Nm (23 ft-lb)
Front seat to vehicle floor	45 Nm (33 ft-lb) +90°

REAR SEATS

Rear seat configuration

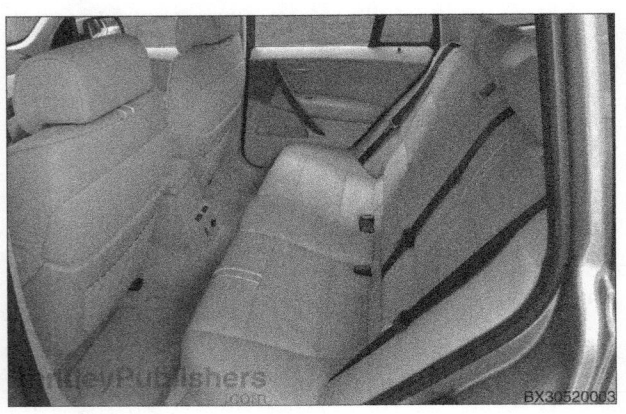

◄ Split rear folding seats are standard in the E83. They are split 60:40 left to right with a folding center armrest in the left portion.

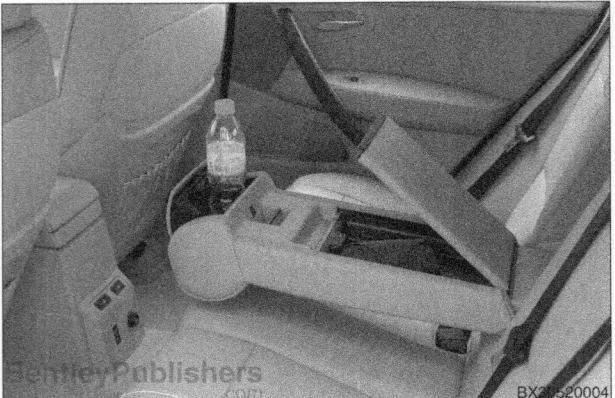

◄ The rear armrest, when folded down, is equipped with a storage compartment and cup holders.

Rear seat, removing and installing

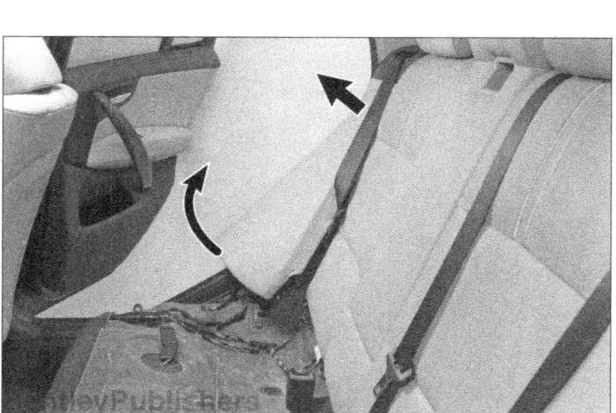

◀ Pull seat bottom up and away (**arrows**) from pedestal.

NOTE—

- *For models equipped with rear seat heaters be sure to disconnect electrical connectors before completely removing seat.*

◀ Pull top (**arrow**) of seatback side bolster forward.

− Lift bolster up to disengage bottom clip.
  - If necessary fold seat back down.

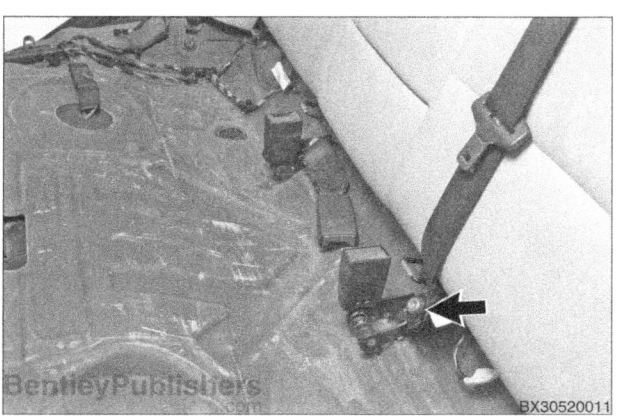

◀ Remove seat belt to body bolt for center seat belt.

Tightening torque	
Center seat belt to body	31 Nm (23 ft-lb)

− Fold down rear seats.

520

Rear seat, removing and installing

◄ Remove mounting bolts for rear seat backrest on both sides.

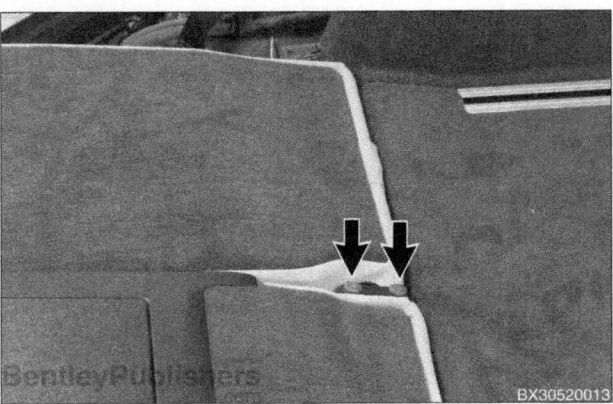

◄ Working at the 60:40 split remove both center bolts.

• With the help of an assistant lift out rear seats.

– Installation is reverse of removal.

540 Sunroof

GENERAL

This repair group covers basic panorama glass sunroof service. Removal and repair of the panorama glass sunroof cassette and other components inside the roof cavity is not covered in this manual.

◄ All E83 X3 vehicles are equipped with a fully automatic two-part panorama glass sunroof.

Panorama glass sunroof assembly consists of the following components:

- Multiple drive sunroof (MDS) control unit
- Sunroof drive motor
- Headliner drive motor
- Headliner (2-part)
- Glass covers
- Wind deflector

NOTE —

- *The general body module (GM5RD) signals MDS for convenience opening and closing of the panorama sunroof when using the remote key buttons or operating the driver's door lock.*

Multiple sunroof drive (MSD) module

The MDS module acts as the power supply for both the panorama sunroof motor and the floating headliner motor. MDS communication is though the K-Bus.

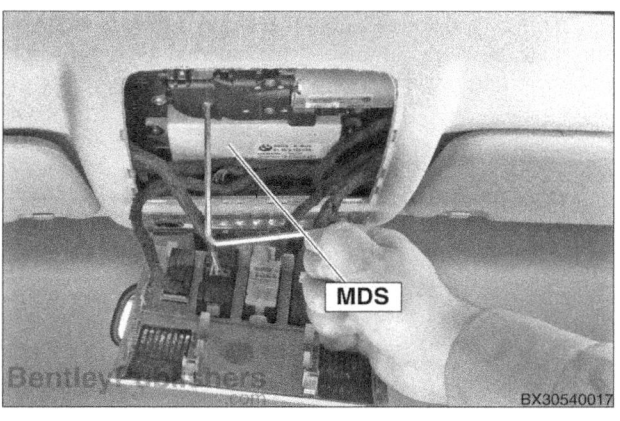

◄ MDS is located behind sunroof switch panel.

MDS contains the following components.

- Control electronics
- K-Bus interface
- Drive motor relay
- Hall sensor power supply

540

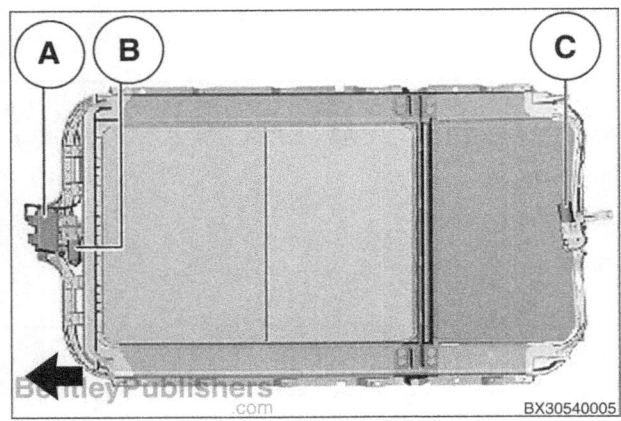

BX30540005

BX30540002

Drive motors

 Two DC Drive motors with integrated hall sensors are used to drive the roof mechanism.

- Motor (**B**) drives sliding and tilting of glass panels.
- Motor (**C**) controls floating headliner and wind deflector.

Hall sensor signals are sent to the MDS (**A**) for analysis. This allows the MDS to recognize position of glass panels and floating headliners.

NOTE—

- *Initialization is required after replacing one or both drive motors.*

Floating headliner (sun shade)

The floating headliner is a two part component (front and rear) controlled by a bowden cable. The headliner is synchronized to the function of the glass roofs. In other words, the headliner must be opened before the sunroof will open and the sunroof must be closed before headliner can close.

When opened, the front part of headliner moves over rear part of the headliner. This allows the headliner to be fully opened without opening or tilting of the glass sunroof.

 Floating headliner in vent position. Vent position reduces suction effect at road speed.

Glass panels

Two glass panels make up the panorama roof. The front glass panel is secured with six bolts. Four bolts secure the rear glass panel to the frame. Front glass panel can tilt and slide open, while rear panel can only tilt.

Wind deflector

Wind deflector is cable operated by headliner motor located at the rear of the sunroof cassette. Wind deflector operation is regulated according to road speed. When sunroof is opened while the vehicle is stopped, the wind deflector will remain in down position until MDS sees a road speed signal. Then wind deflector will be moved to an extended position. If road speed exceeds 84 mph it is retracted to an intermediate position. When road speed is reduced wind deflector returns to an extended position.

Anti-trap

Both glass panels and floating headliners are equipped with anti-trap protection. If MDS detects an obstruction the appropriate motor is stopped and activated in reverse direction.

CAUTION—
- *Anti-trapping feature can be overridden by pressing and holding the switch in the closed position.*

Panorama sunroof, initializing

Panorama sunroof initialization must be preformed anytime MDS looses positioning of glass panels or floating headliner or if any component of the sunroof cassette is replaced.

◀ Press sunroof control button in tilt position and hold for approximately 15 seconds. Continue to hold button down until sunroof begins to operate (initialize). Hold control button down for entire for duration of initialization. This process may take up to 2 minutes to complete.

During initialization sunroof will operate as follows:
- Both glass panels enter tilt position, floating headliners will enter vent mode
- Both parts of floating headliner will open
- Both glass panels will lower
- Front glass panel will open and then close
- Floating headliner will close, completing initialization.

NOTE—

- *Control button must be held in tilt position during entire initialization process.*

Panorama sunroof, emergency closing

If the panorama sunroof cannot be closed electrically, it can be closed manually using a supplied allen key. The allen key is stored in the tool kit beneath the cargo area floor.

◀ Pull cover down working from rear edge of cover. If necessary use a plastic pry tool.

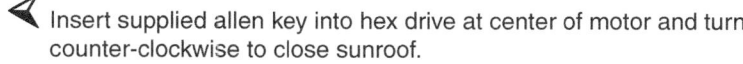

◀ Insert supplied allen key into hex drive at center of motor and turn counter-clockwise to close sunroof.

NOTE—

- *Panorama sunroof can also be opened manually by turning clockwise.*

540

PANORAMA SUNROOF ADJUSTMENTS

Adjusting

The sunroof is controlled by a set of cables that move the sunroof panel along guide rails when the motor is operated. The sunroof can be adjusted without removing it from the car.

NOTE —
* *Be sure to check drains in corners of sunroof carrier if water is entering car through headliner.*

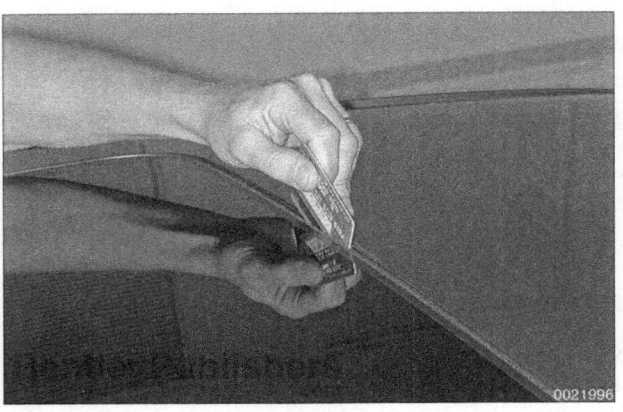

— Adjust sunroof panel under the following circumstances:
  * Sunroof misaligned with roof.
  * Sunroof does not close squarely.
  * Wind noise at high speeds (sunroof closed).
  * Sunroof has been removed and installed.

◄ For correct sunroof alignment:
  * Front slide/tilt glass panel must be adjusted first.
  * Sunroof must be fully closed.
  * Gap must be even all around edges of sunroof.
  * Front of sunroof must be flush to 1 mm (0.04 in.) below surface of roof.
  * Rear of sunroof must be flush to 1 mm (0.04 in.) above surface of roof.

NOTE —
* *Use credit card to measure gap. Card should insert through gap with equal resistance all around perimeter.*

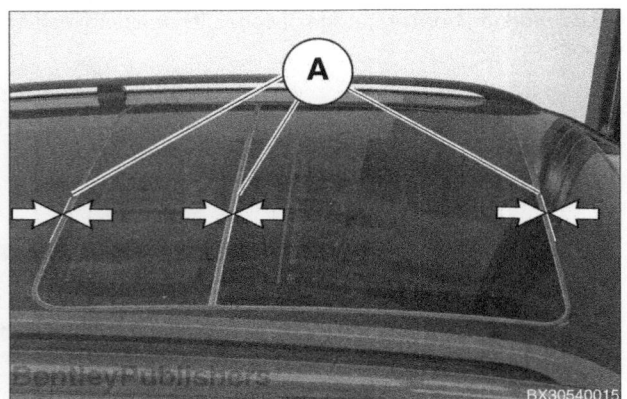

◄ Adjust panorama sunroof glass panels for consistent front and rear gaps (**A**).
  * Credit card can be used to check gap spacing.
  * **A** = 5.8 ± 0.3 mm (0.23 ± 0.012 in.).

◄ Open floating headliner to expose rubber bellows (**arrows**).

— Working from edges of bellows (**arrows**), carefully pull bellows off upper and lower channel on sunroof cassette.

CAUTION—
* *Use care around rubber bellows. They are easily damaged/torn.*

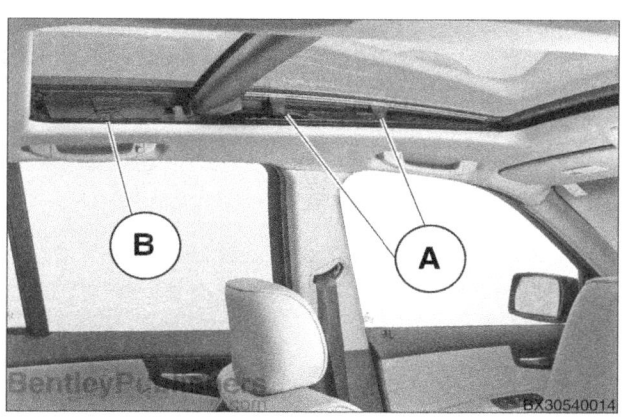

◄ Loosen mounting screws (**A**) on left and right sides so that front glass panel can be adjusted first.

– Loosen mounting screws (**B**) on left and right sides so that rear glass panel can be adjusted.

NOTE—

• *If adjusting both panels, always adjust front slide/tilt panel first.*

– Tighten mounting screws for glass panels.

Tightening torque	
Glass panel to sunroof frame	4 Nm (35 in-lb)

– Install rubber bellows.

SUNROOF MOTOR

Sunroof motor, replacing

This procedure is for replacing glass panel drive motor. Floating headliner drive motor replacement is similar but requires removing the vehicle headliner.

◄ Pull cover down working from rear edge of cover. If necessary use a plastic pry tool.

– Disconnect electrical connections from cover and set cover aside.

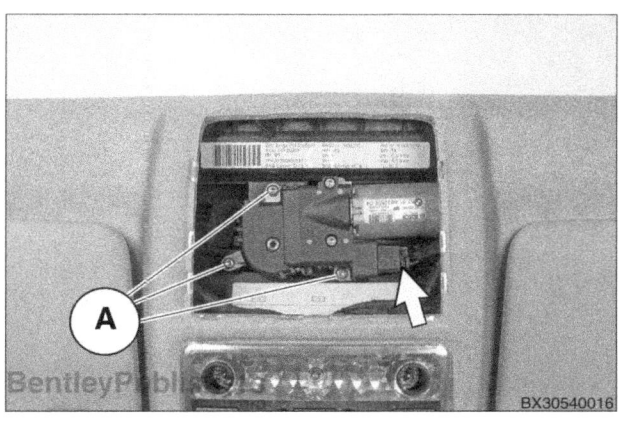

◄ Remove screws (**A**) from motor. Hold motor to prevent it from falling. Screws are captured in motor housing and will not come out fully.

– Disconnect electrical connection (**arrow**) and remove motor.

– Installation is reverse of removal. Be sure to properly engage sunroof motor drive gear sprocket into sunroof drive gear.

Tightening torque	
Sunroof motor to sunroof carrier	2.8 Nm (25 in-lb)

– Perform initialization procedure. See **Initializing** in this repair group.

600 Electrical System–General

GENERAL

This section presents a brief description of the principal parts of the electrical system. Also covered here are basic electrical system troubleshooting tips.

See also:

- **121 Battery, Starter, Alternator**
- **ECL Electrical Component Locations** for common BMW acronyms as well as component location information
- **ELE Electrical Wiring Diagrams**
- **OBD On-Board Diagnostics**

Electrical test equipment

Many electrical tests described in this manual call for measuring voltage, current or resistance using a digital multimeter. A digital meter is preferred for precise measurements and for electronics work because it is generally more accurate than an analog meter (swing-needle). An analog meter may draw enough current to damage sensitive electronic components.

An LED test light is a safe, inexpensive tool that can be used to perform many simple electrical tests that would otherwise require a digital multimeter. The LED indicates when voltage is present between any two test-points in a circuit.

The integrated safety, comfort, security and handling systems on X3 vehicles are designed with self-diagnostic capabilities. The quickest way to diagnose many problems is to start with a scan tool read-out of diagnostic trouble codes (DTCs).

600

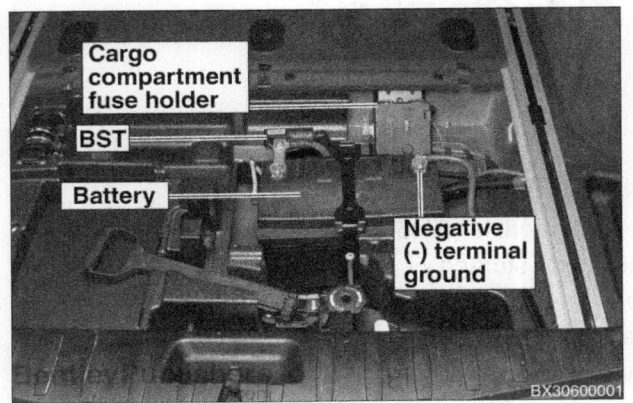

Cargo compartment fuse holder

BST

Battery

Negative (-) terminal ground

BX30600001

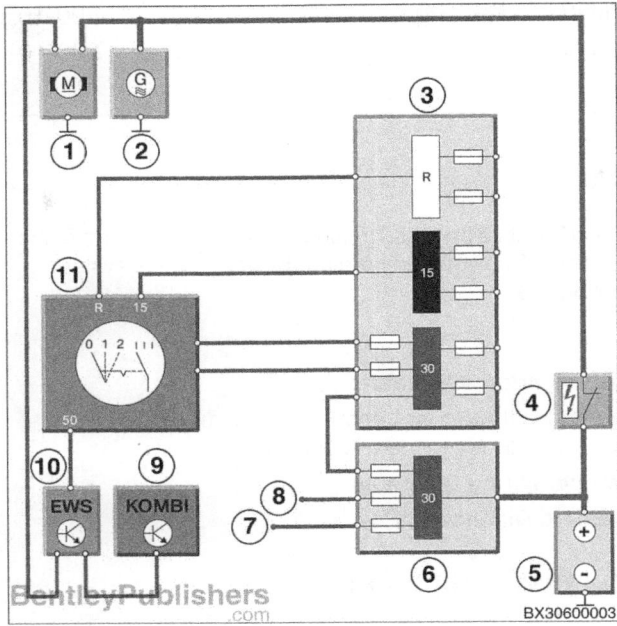

BX30600003

Fuse panel above glove compartment

BX30600003

Voltage and polarity

◀ The vehicle operates on a 12-volt direct current (DC) negative-ground system. Power is supplied by a lead-acid battery located under cargo compartment floor cover.

A voltage regulator controls system voltage at approximately 14 volts. All circuits are grounded by direct or indirect connection to the negative (-) terminal of the battery. A number of ground connections throughout the vehicle connect the wiring harness to chassis ground. These circuits are completed by the battery cable or ground strap between the body and the battery negative (-) terminal.

Wiring, fuses and relays

Electrical components connect using one of the following:
• Heavy cables with lug-type connectors (battery and starter).
• Electrical harnesses with keyed, push-on connectors that lock into place.
• Buses with modular connectors.

◀ Electrical power is routed from the battery through high-amperage fuses in the cargo compartment along the B+ battery cable on passenger side of interior to the fuse block above the glove compartment. Fuses are color coded to indicate current capacities.

1. Starter
2. Alternator
3. Glove box fuse holder
4. Battery safety terminal (BST)
5. Battery
6. Cargo compartment fuse holder
7. Valvetronic or common rail
8. Top HiFi amplifier, if equipped.
9. Instrument cluster (KOMBI)
10. Electronic immobilizer (EWS)
11. Ignition/starter switch

◀ Individual components are powered by fuses in the fuse panel above the glove compartment. Main fuses for DME and ignition/starter switch are located on rear side of glove box fuse holder.

Relays and control modules are mounted in various places throughout the vehicle. See **ECL Electrical Component Locations**.

Warnings and Cautions

> **WARNING—**
> - *Airbags and pyrotechnic seat belt tensioners utilize explosive devices. Handle with extreme care. See warnings and cautions in **721 Airbag System**.*
> - *The ignition system operates at lethal voltages. If you have a weak heart or wear a pacemaker, do not expose yourself to ignition system electric currents. Take extra precautions when working on the ignition system or when servicing the engine while it is running or the key is ON. See **120 Ignition System** for additional ignition system warnings and cautions.*
> - *Keep hands, clothing and other objects clear of the electric engine cooling fan when working on a warm engine. The fan may start at any time, even when the ignition is switched OFF.*

> **CAUTION—**
> - *Do not disconnect the battery with the engine running.*
> - *Prior to disconnecting the battery, read the battery disconnection cautions given in **001 Warnings and Cautions**.*
> - *Switch the ignition OFF and remove the negative battery cable before removing any electrical components. Connect and disconnect electrical connectors and ignition test equipment leads only while the ignition is switched OFF.*
> - *Relay and fuse positions are subject to change and may vary from vehicle to vehicle. If questions arise, an authorized BMW dealer is the best source for the most accurate and up-to-date information.*
> - *Use a digital multimeter for electrical tests. Switch the multimeter to the appropriate function and range before making test connections.*
> - *Many control modules are static sensitive. Static discharge damages them permanently. Handle the modules using proper static prevention equipment and techniques.*
> - *To avoid damaging harness connectors or relay panel sockets, use jumper wires with flat-blade connectors that are the same size as the connector or relay terminals.*
> - *Do not try to start the engine of a vehicle which has been heated above 176°F (80°C) (for example, in a paint drying booth). Allow it to cool to normal temperature.*
> - *Disconnect the battery before doing any electric welding on the vehicle.*
> - *Do not wash the engine while it is running, or any time the ignition is ON.*
> - *Choose test equipment carefully. Use a digital multimeter with at least 10 MΩ input impedance or an LED test light. An analog meter (swing-needle) or a test light with a normal incandescent bulb may draw enough current to damage sensitive electronic components.*
> - *Do not use an ohmmeter to measure resistance on solid state components such as control modules.*
> - *Disconnect the battery before making resistance (ohm) measurements on a circuit.*

600

BUS SYSTEMS

X3 vehicles are electrically complex. Many vehicle systems and subsystems are interconnected or integrated. In addition, the requirements of second generation on-board diagnostics (OBD II) are such that there are now many more circuits and wires in the vehicle than ever before. The components must exchange large volumes of data with one another in order to perform their various functions.

To handle this complexity effectively, X3 vehicles make extensive use of control module networking via bus systems. Signals are shared digitally among several control modules on a bus, eliminating the need for separate connections for each pair of control modules. The use of bus communication for controls and accessories reduces wiring complexity and improves system response time.

Data transfer over a bus is similar to a telephone conference. A control module on the bus transmits a stream of data which other modules receive at the same time. Each control module then decides to use or ignore this data.

The benefits of the bus method of data transfer are as follows:

- As data and programs are modified and extended, only software modifications are necessary.
- Continuous verification of transmitted data leads to low error rate.
- Sensors and signal wires can be simplified or eliminated due to the transmittal of multiplexed digital data.
- Control modules transfer data at a high rate.
- Control module sizes and connector sizes are smaller.
- Bus architecture conforms to international standards. This facilitates data interchange between control modules of different manufacture.

Bus systems and sub-bus systems are divided according to groups of control modules which share common functionality and information. BMW uses the following buses in X3 models:

- **K-bus** (body bus): General vehicle electrical system, information system, communications systems, safety systems.
- **PT-CAN-bus** (controller area network bus): Engine management, transmission, traction control, transfer case.
- **D-bus** (diagnosis bus): Fault codes.

Sub-bus systems

- **BSD** (Bit-serial data interface) connection of electronic engine management to alternator.
- **LIN-bus** (local interconnected network), headlights, GMR5, driver's door mirror switch block.
- **M-bus** (motor bus): IHKA/IHKR stepper motors

***NOTE*—**

- *Electrical component acronyms can be found at the front of the* **ECL Electrical Component Locations** *repair group.*

E83 Bus Chart (to 07/2006)

BX30600004

K-bus

K-bus transmit and receive serial information over one wire. The K-bus links components of the general vehicle electrical system including panorama sunroof (MDS). Information system, communications system and safety system (MRS4RD) are also linked by K-bus.

K-bus specifications	
Data transfer rate	9.6 Kbps

PT-CAN-bus

PT-CAN-bus data is transmitted over a pair of wires twisted together to ensure reliable communication among modules without conflicts or interference. The PT-Can links control units for drive and chassis systems including the transfer case.

PT-Can-bus specifications	
Data transfer rate	500 Kbps

600

D-bus

D-bus transmits fault code information between control modules and the BMW diagnostic scan tool. D-bus (diagnosis bus) connects with two leads to the overall bus system. Pin 7 is directed to DME and transfers all emissions data from the engine management system and automatic gearbox, Pin 8 connects to remaining control units either directly or using the instrument cluster as a gateway for communication.

D-bus specifications	
Data transfer rate	9.6 Kbps

Sub-bus systems

BSD (Bit-serial data interface) engine management (DME) must communicate with the alternator because the DME contains the software to regulate charging. See **Energy management** in this repair group.

LIN-bus (Local interconnected network) Adaptive headlights, bi-xenon headlights and driver's door mirror switch connect locally to the General Module 5 ReDesign (GM5RD) using the LIN-bus, because the GMR5RD is responsible for their control.

M-bus connects climate control stepper motors to the IHKA control module. See **640 Heating and Air-conditioning** for additional details.

CENTRAL BODY ELECTRONICS (ZKE)

X3 vehicles are equipped with an integrated complex of electronic modules connected mostly via K-bus. This system, called ZKE V, is primarily controlled by the General Module 5 ReDesign (GM5RD).

ZKE V directly controls the following functions:
- Windshield wiper / washer system. See **611 Wipers and Washers**.
- Central locking with power tailgate release. See **515 Central Locking and Anti-theft**.
- Keyless entry (FZV).
- Power window control. See **512 Door Windows**.
- Car Memory / Key Memory. See **515 Central Locking and Anti-theft**.
- Interior lighting. See **630 Lights**.
- Alarm system (DWA). See **515 Central Locking and Anti-theft**.
- Electronic consumer sleep mode. See **600 Electrical System General**.

Other functions not directly controlled by ZKE V but interconnected:
- Rain sensor (AIC). See **611 Wiper and Washers**.
- Sunroof operation. See **540 Sunroof**.
- Seat memory. See **520 Seats**.
- Outside rear-view mirror control and heating.
- Windshield washer jet heating.

General module (GM5RD)

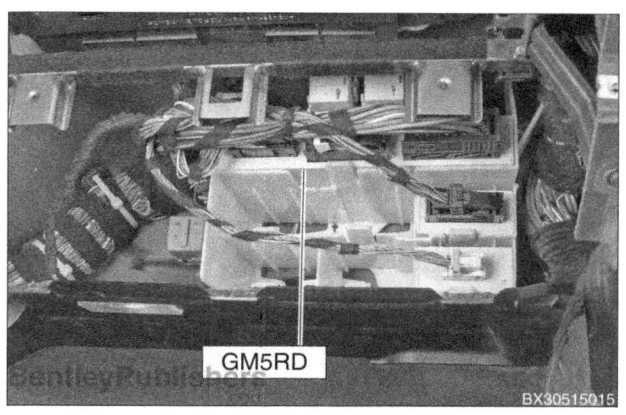

◀ The General Module 5 ReDesign (GM5RD) is the master controller for other ZKE system modules The GM5RD is in the relay carrier behind the glove compartment. See **513 Interior Trim** for glove compartment removal.

Car memory / key memory

A number of vehicle comfort features can be customized to the driver(s) preference via the GM5RD. The identity of the vehicle user is provided by a signal from the keyless entry system (FZV). See **515 Central Locking and Anti-theft** for further details.

Fault code storage

Scan tool fault codes or diagnostic trouble codes (DTCs) stored in the general module (GM) are accessible electronically through the OBD II plug.

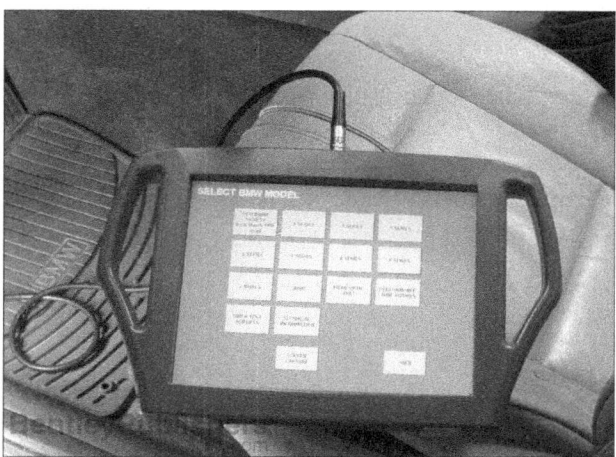

◀ Autologic scan tool connected to OBD II plug below left dashboard.

Consumer cutoff

Consumer current cutoff interrupts battery voltage to specific circuits, preventing inadvertent battery drain if one of these consumers remains ON after the engine is shut OFF.

For example, if one of the interior light control switches is left ON, consumer cutoff deactivates power (KL 30) to the light control module after 16 minutes (sleep mode).

The following circuits are controlled by consumer cutoff:

• Map and reading lights.
• Glove compartment and cargo compartment lights.
• Transmission range indicator light.
• Overload protection relay for power seat motors.

Sleep mode

To lower constant battery draw when the vehicle is parked, ZKE system goes into sleep mode 16 minutes after ignition is switched OFF and no further ZKE function is active.

Although electronic control modules in the ZKE system go into sleep mode, K-bus, which connects the GM5RD with door lock and seat control modules, remains active. No data transfer takes place until a wake-up request is received. The door modules or keyless remote module (FZV) and alarm can wake the system up.

600

Energy management

Software regulating the charging voltage is contained in the DME (engine management). If there is increased current consumption by the electrical system, the DME will raise the charging voltage by communicating with the alternator over BSD (bit -serial data) interface. Maximum charging voltage is 14.8v. Battery replacement does not required coding. The system also has the option of load/consumer shut down if it sees excessive current consumption.

ELECTRICAL TROUBLESHOOTING

Four things are required for current to flow in any electrical circuit:
• Voltage source.
• Wires or connections to transport voltage.
• Load or device that uses electricity.
• Connection to ground.

Most problems can be found using a digital multimeter (volt / ohm / ammeter) to check the following:
• Voltage supply.
• Breaks in the wiring (infinite resistance / no continuity).
• A path to ground that completes the circuit.

Electric current is logical in its flow, always moving from the voltage source toward ground. Electrical faults can usually be located through a process of elimination. When troubleshooting a complex circuit, separate the circuit into smaller parts. General tests outlined below may be helpful in finding electrical problems. The information is most helpful when used with wiring diagrams.

Be sure to analyze the problem. Use wiring diagrams to determine the most likely cause. Get an understanding of how the circuit works by following the circuit from ground back to the power source.

When making test connections at connectors and components, use care to avoid spreading or damaging the connectors or terminals. Some tests may require jumper wires to bypass components or connections in the wiring harness. When connecting jumper wires, use blade connectors at the wire ends that match the size of the terminal being tested. The small internal contacts are easily spread apart, and this can cause intermittent or faulty connections that can lead to more problems.

Voltage and voltage drop

Wires, connectors, and switches that carry current are designed with very low resistance so that current flows with a minimum loss of voltage. A voltage drop is caused by higher than normal resistance in a circuit. This additional resistance actually decreases or stops the flow of current. Some common sources of voltage drops are corroded or dirty switches, dirty or corroded connections or contacts, and loose or corroded ground wires and ground connections.

A voltage drop test is a good test to perform if current is flowing through the circuit but the circuit is not operating correctly. A voltage drop test helps pinpoint a corroded ground strap or a faulty switch.

Voltage and voltage drop

Normally, there should be less than 1 volt drop across most wires or closed switches. A voltage drop across a connector or short cable should not exceed 0.5 volt.

A voltage drop test is more accurate than a simple resistance check because the resistances involved are often too small to measure with most ohmmeters. For example, a resistance as small as 0.02 Ω results in a 3 volt drop in a typical 150 amp starter circuit. (150 amps x 0.02 Ω = 3 volts).

Keep in mind that voltage with ignition key ON and voltage with engine running are not the same. With ignition ON and engine OFF, fully charged battery voltage is approximately 12.6 volts. With engine running (charging voltage), normal voltage is approximately 14.0 volts. Measure voltage at battery with ignition ON and then with engine running to get exact measurements.

Voltage, measuring

◀ Connect digital multimeter negative lead to a reliable ground point on vehicle.

NOTE—

• *The negative (-) battery terminal is always a good ground point.*

– Connect digital multimeter positive lead to point in circuit you wish to measure.

– Check that voltage reading does not deviate more than 1 volt from voltage at battery. If voltage drop is more than this, check for a corroded connector or loose ground wire.

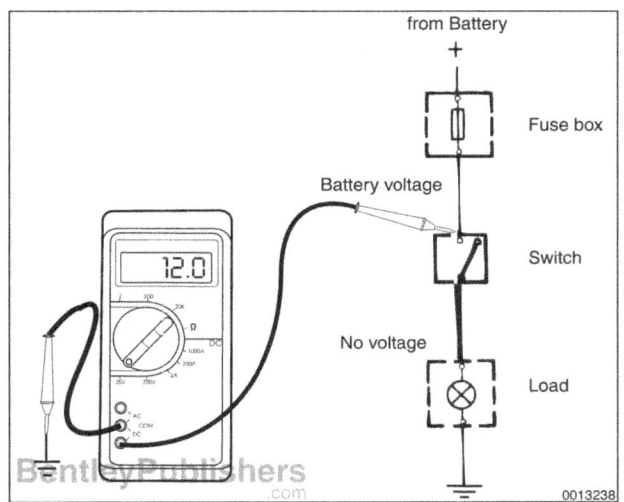

Voltage drop, testing

Check voltage drop only when there is a load on the circuit, such as when operating the starter motor or turning on the headlights. Use a digital multimeter to ensure accurate readings.

◀ Connect digital multimeter positive lead to positive (+) battery terminal or a positive power supply close to battery source.

– Connect digital multimeter negative lead to other end of cable or switch being tested.

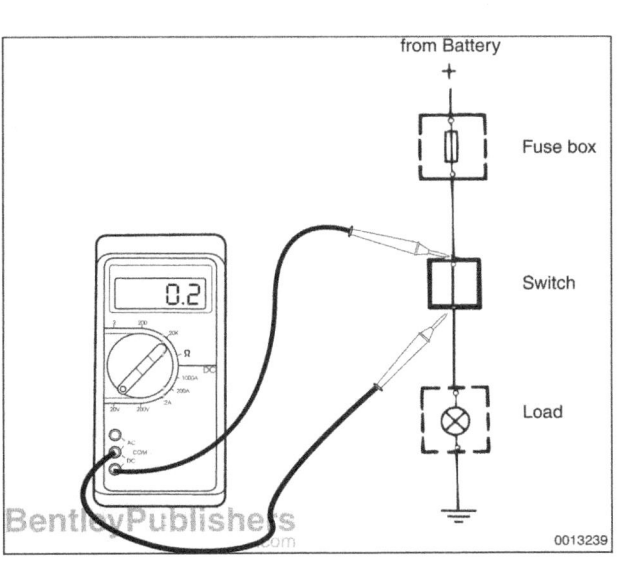

600

— With power switched ON and circuit working, meter shows voltage drop (difference between two points). This value should not exceed 1 volt. Maximum voltage drop in an automotive circuit, as recommended by the Society of Automotive Engineers (SAE), is as follows:

- 0 volt for small wire connections
- 0.1 volt for high current connections
- 0.2 volt for high current cables
- 0.3 volt for switch or solenoid contacts

— On longer wires or cables, the drop may be slightly higher. In any case, a voltage drop of more than 1.0 volt usually indicates a problem.

Continuity, checking

Use continuity test to check a circuit or switch. Because most automotive circuits are designed to have little or no resistance, a circuit or part of a circuit can be easily checked for faults using an ohmmeter. An open circuit or a circuit with high resistance does not allow current to flow. A circuit with little or no resistance allows current to flow easily.

When checking continuity, switch ignition OFF. On circuits that are powered at all times, disconnect battery. Using the appropriate wiring diagram, test circuit for faulty connections, wires, switches, relays and engine sensors by checking for continuity.

 Example: Test brake light switch for continuity:

- With brake pedal in rest position (switch open) there is no continuity (infinite Ω).
- With pedal depressed (switch closed) there is continuity (0 Ω).

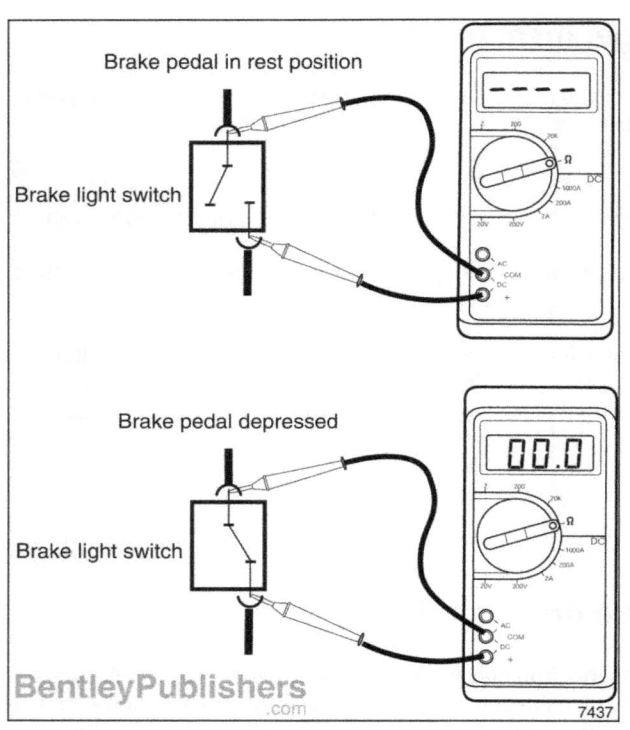

Short circuits, testing

The most common short that causes problems is a short to ground where the insulation on a positive (+) wire wears away and the metal wire is exposed. When the wire rubs against a metal part of the vehicle or other ground source, the circuit is shorted to ground. If the exposed wire is live (positive battery voltage), a fuse blows and the circuit may be damaged.

Use a digital multimeter to locate short circuits.

> **CAUTION—**
> - *In circuits protected with high rating fuses (25 amp and greater), wires or circuit components may be damaged before the fuse blows. Check for wiring damage before replacing fuses of this rating. Also, check for correct fuse rating.*

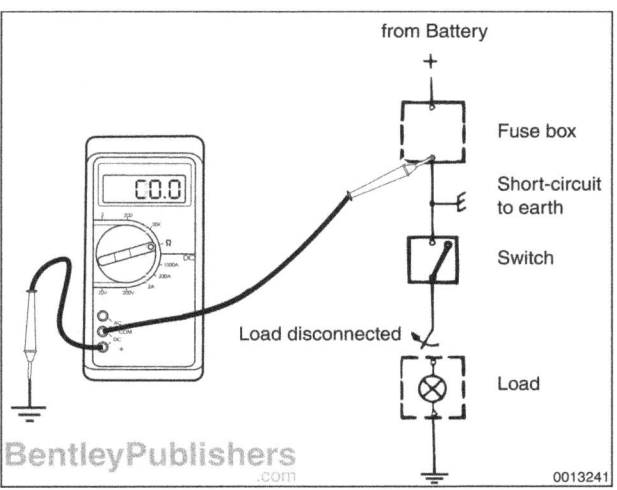

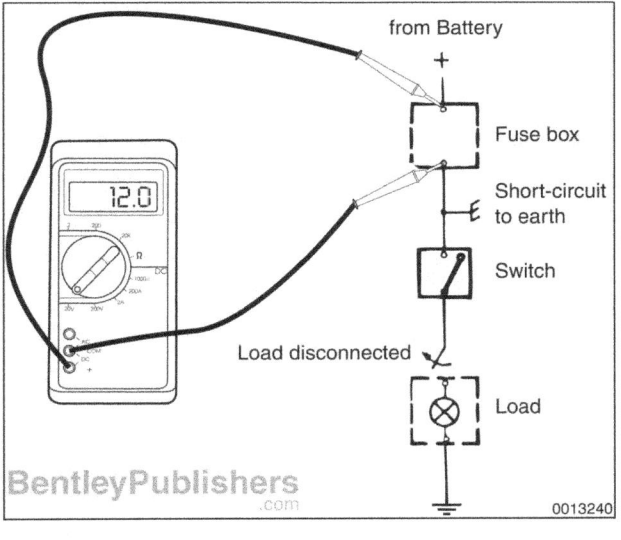

Testing with ohmmeter

— Remove blown fuse from circuit and disconnect cables from battery. Disconnect harness connector from circuit load or consumer.

◄ Using an ohmmeter, connect one test lead to load side of fuse terminal (terminal leading to circuit) and other test lead to ground.

— If there is continuity to ground, there is a short to ground.

— If there is no continuity, work from wire harness nearest to fuse and relay panel and move or wiggle wires while observing meter. Continue to move down harness until meter displays a reading. This is the location of the short to ground.

— Visually inspect wire harness at this point for any faults. If no faults are visible, carefully slice open harness cover or wire insulation for further inspection. Repair any faults found.

Testing with voltmeter

— Remove blown fuse from circuit. Disconnect harness connector from circuit load or consumer.

NOTE —

• *Most fuses power more than one consumer. Be sure all consumers are disconnected when checking for a short circuit.*

◄ Using a digital multimeter, connect test leads across fuse terminals. Make sure power is present in circuit. If necessary switch ignition ON.

— If voltage is present at voltmeter, there is a short to ground.

— If voltage is not present, work from wire harness nearest to fuse and relay panel and move or wiggle wires while observing meter. Continue to move down harness until meter displays a reading. This is the location of the short to ground.

Visually inspect wire harness at this point for any faults. If no faults are visible, carefully slice open harness cover or wire insulation for further inspection. Repair any faults found.

600

611 Wipers and Washers

GENERAL

This repair group covers repair information for windshield, headlight and rear window wiper and washer systems.

See also:
- **513 Interior trim**
- **612 Switches** for wiper and washer stalk switch replacement
- **ECL Electrical Component Locations**
- **ELE Electrical Wiring Diagrams**

Wiper and washer system operation

Wiper and washer functions in X3 vehicles are controlled by the General Module 5 ReDesign(GM5RD), located behind the glove compartment. GM5RD controls front wiper and washer functions including headlight washers. Rear wiper and washer functions are controlled by a wiper module directly hooked to the rear wiper switch.

 Driver input to wiper and washer system is via multi-function stalk switch to right of steering column.

BX30611014

611

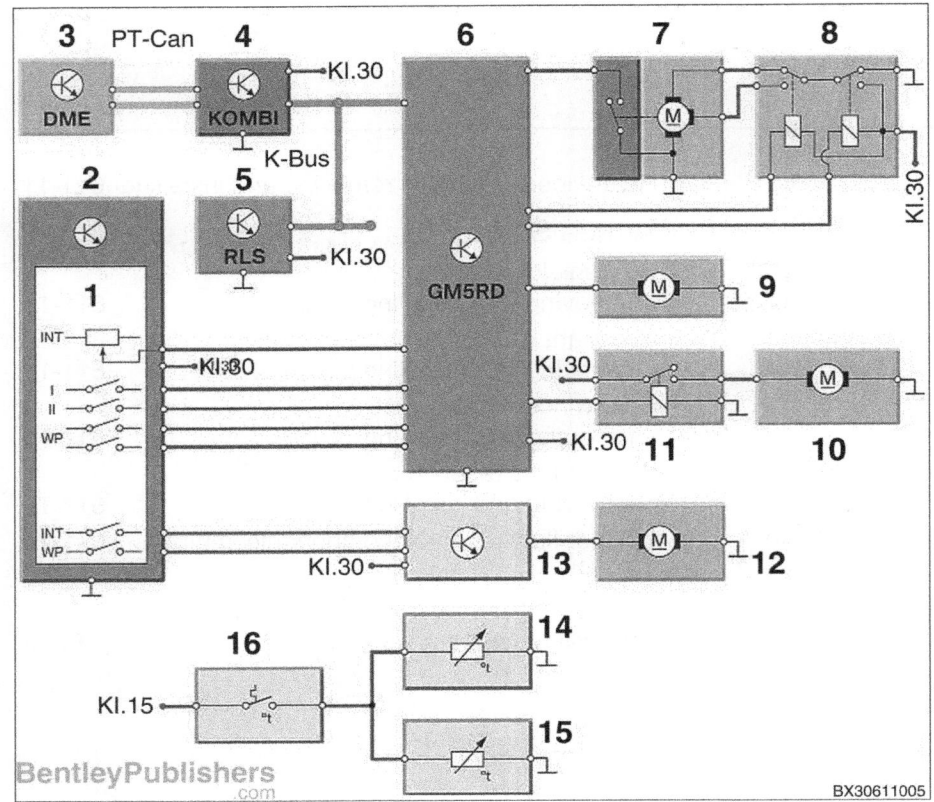

Wiper and washer system diagram

1. Wiper switch
2. Wiper switch electronics
3. Digital motor electronics (DME)
4. Instrument cluster (KOMBI)
5. Rain light sensor (RLS)
6. General module 5 redesign (GM5RD)
7. Wiper motor reset contact
8. Dual mode relay
9. Windshield washer pump
10. Headlight washer pump
11. Headlight washer relay (SRA)
12. Tailgate washer pump
13. Tailgate wiper electronics
14. Driver's side heated washer
15. Passenger's side heated washer
16. Ambient temperature switch

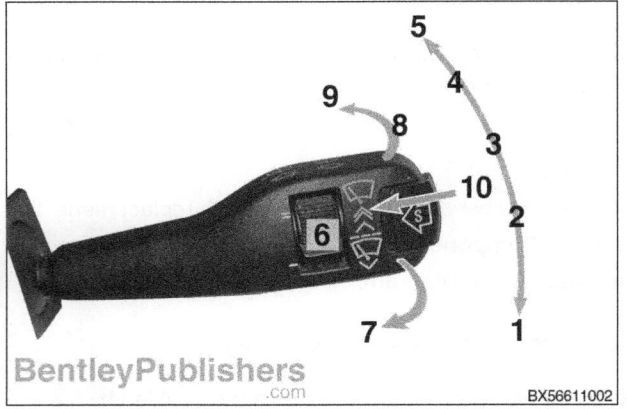

Wiper and washer switch operation

1. Single wipe (hold stalk switch down)
2. Off
3. Interval windshield wipe
4. Slow windshield wipe (automatically switches to interval when car is stopped)
5. Fast windshield wipe (automatically switches to slow speed when car is stopped)
6. 4-position thumb wheel for interval control
7. Washer (pull stalk toward driver)
8. Rear window wipe (push stalk away from driver)
9. Rear window wash (push stalk away from driver)
10. Headlight wash and cycled windshield wash and wipe

Wiper switch interval control

The interval control thumb wheel sets wiping interval. Wiping intervals are dependent on road speed. Interval time varies from 26 seconds with car at rest to 2 seconds at high speeds. As road speed increases, wiping interval is shortened. See **Table a**.

Table a. Wiper interval vs. road speed

Thumb wheel position	Vehicle speed (mph)					
	4	5 - 22	23 - 45	46 - 60	61 - 87	87
	Interval time (seconds)					
1	26	19	17	15	15	13
2	17	12	11	10	9	7
3	10	6	6	5	4	3
4	5	3	3	2	2	2

Slow and fast wiping speed are also dependent on road speed. Slow speed switches to intermittent when the vehicle is stopped. Fast speed switches to slow when the vehicle is stopped.

Wiper motor wiring and electrical contacts are configured to protect the motor from excessive load. For example, if a wiper arm is blocked for 16 seconds, the wiper motor switches OFF.

Wiper relay

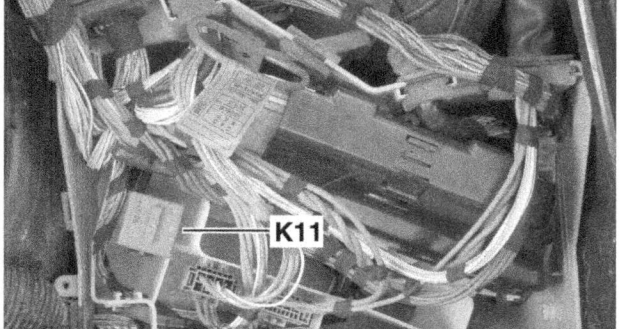

N52 engine

K11

BX30ecl015

 The dual wiper relay (K11) is located in the E-box. See **ECL Electrical Component Locations**.

- **M54 engine**: K11 relay located in left rear of E-box.
- **N52 engine**: K11 relay located in left front of E-box.

NOTE—

- *On N52 engine, some disassembly of the E-box is required to access K11 relay. See **ECL Electrical Component Locations**.*

Washer system

 Washer system fluid reservoir is in the right front of engine compartment. It is fitted is with three separate pumps (windshield, rear window and headlight washers) and the washer fluid level switch (not shown in photo). Washer fluid level switch is under the front of washer reservoir near head lamp.

Windshield washer jets are on the engine hood. With ignition switched ON, washer jets are automatically heated. The nozzle heaters, being of positive temperature coefficient (PTC) design, increase resistance as they heat up and automatically cut back on current consumption.

Washer resevoir

Windshield washer pump

Rear window washer pump

Headlamp washer pump

BX30611012

611

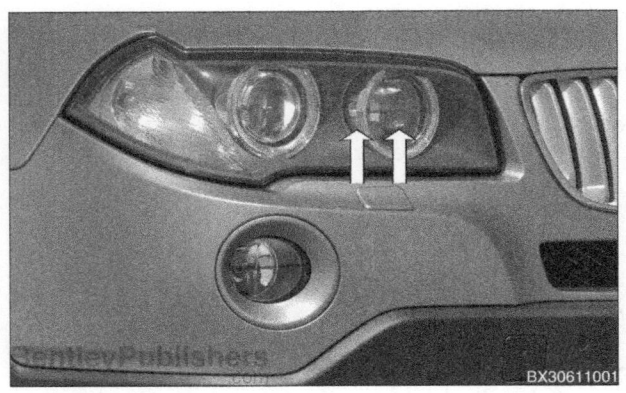

◀ **Headlight washer nozzles** are on top of the front bumper cover. 2004 - 2006 (pre-LCI) vehicles have two washer jet pedestals on each side of the bumper facing the headlights. On 2007 - 2010 (LCI) vehicles, headlight washers are concealed behind trim covers. When activated, the washers extend out with the trim covers. The headlight washer pump uses fluid from the washer fluid reservoir. If headlights are ON, they are cleaned every fifth time the windshield washers are activated.

Rain light sensor (optional)

The optional rain light sensor (RLS) system uses an infrared sensor at top of the windshield to detect water drops on the windshield. Sensor signal activates interval wipe cycle if the wiper switch interval control is ON. The rain light sensor is mounted on the windshield in front of the rear view mirror.

◀ The rain light sensor functions by aiming a beam of infrared light through the windshield at a set angle. The beam is reflected back and forth within the windshield until it is detected by the rain light sensor. Rain drops (or other impurities) on the outside of the windshield cause some of the infrared to be dissipated outside the windshield. As a result the sensor detects lower infrared intensity. This is interpreted as a need for the wipers to be turned ON.

Rain light sensor operation

◀ The rain light sensor continuously monitors the windshield for rain accumulation and signals the general module to activate the wipers based on the interval control position and how fast rain accumulates on the windshield.

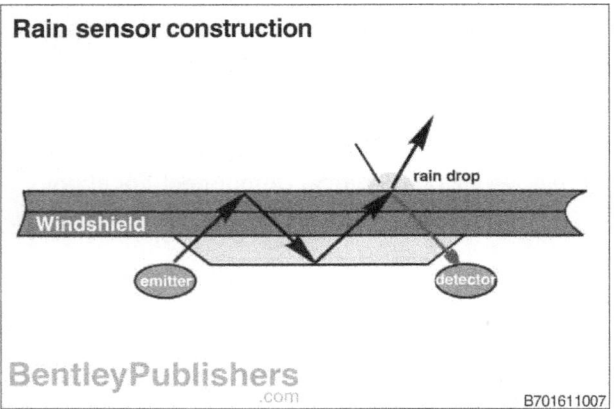

Rain sensor construction

The interval control signal informs the rain light sensor of the selected level of sensitivity:

• Position 1 (least sensitive) delays wiper activation signal.

• Position 4 (most sensitive) sends wiper activation signal to the general module sooner.

Depending on the intensity of rain the wipers can operate continuously as if set in a normal wiper stalk switch position (slow or fast) regardless of interval control setting. For this reason, vehicle speed signal is not utilized on the rain-sensor-equipped wiper system.

If ignition is switched OFF with wiper switch in intermittent position, the rain sensor becomes active after ignition is switched back ON and one of the following occurs:

• Stalk switch is moved from intermittent position and then back.

• Interval control thumb wheel is adjusted.

• Wash function is activated.

The rain light sensor control module, integrated with the rain light sensor, adapts to sensor optics as follows:

• **Windshield aging**: As the vehicle ages, windshield pitting in the rain sensor monitoring area may cause a loss of light in the optics system. The control module adapts for loss of light based on the intensity of the detected infrared light with a cleared windshield.

- **Dirty windows**: Rain sensor adaptation reacts less sensitively to a dirty windshield (dirt, road salt, wax residue) after a completed wipe cycle. A dirty windshield has a film on it that diminishes the ability of infrared to refract into water droplets that are present. This causes a delay in rain sensor detection and lengthens time intervals on an intermittent wipe. A dirty windshield can cause the rain sensor control module to set a fault due to approaching limits of its adaptation abilities.

> **CAUTION—**
> - On rain-sensor-equipped models, make sure wiper blades are in perfect condition and windshield is kept clean.

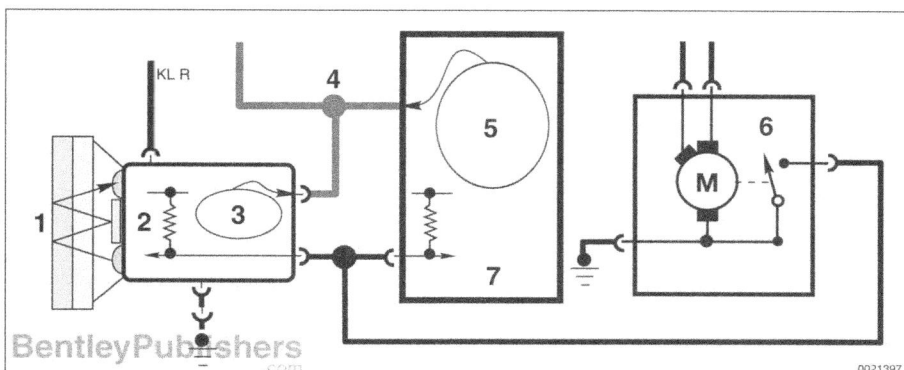

Rain sensor diagram

1. Windshield
2. Rain light sensor module
3. Wiper activation
4. K-Bus
5. Interval position selection
6. Wiper motor
7. General module

Rear window wiper / washer system

The rear wiper motor assembly is mounted in the tailgate through a sound-insulating rubber bushing.

The rear wiper / washer is controlled by the wiper / washer steering column stalk switch via ZKE V system. System functions are:

- Normal interval wipe
- Programmed interval wipe
- Continuous wipe
- Washing

611

Rear wiper/washer system

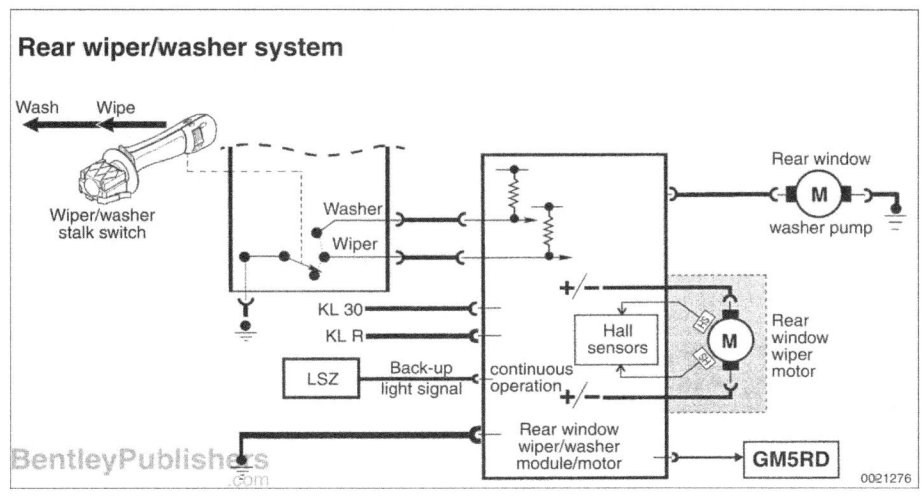

Normal operation is a timed interval of approximately 7 seconds. This is triggered by pressing stalk switch forward to first detent. Full sweep and park position of the wiper arm are recognized by two Hall sensors on motor assembly. If wiper is switched OFF, wiper arm returns to PARK position.

Programmed interval wipe:

• Quickly switch rear wiper ON and OFF.

• Wait the needed interval time.

• Switch rear wiper ON again.

The OFF time is the programmed interval, up to approximately 30 seconds.

Continuous wiping is activated any time rear wiper is ON and transmission is in reverse. Signal is provided by back-up light switch via LSZ (light control module).

Rear window washing is activated when the stalk switch is pushed forward past the first detent:

• Wash cycle 1. Washer pump ON for 1.5 seconds. Wiper ON 1 second later.

• Wash cycle 2. Washer pump ON for 0.5 second after 0.8 second delay. Wiper continues.

• Wash cycle 3. Washer pump ON for 0.5 second after 0.8 second delay. Wiper ON for two wipe-dry cycles.

NOTE —

• After washing, the rear wiper remains in interval (normal) wiping mode until switched OFF.

WIPER BLADES AND ARMS

Wiper blade cleaning problems

Common problems with the windshield wipers include streaking or sheeting, water drops after wiping, and blade chatter.

Streaking is usually caused when wiper blades are coated with road film or car wash wax.

— Clean blades using soapy water. If cleaning does not cure problem, replace blades.

NOTE —

• BMW recommends replacing the wiper blades twice a year, before and after the cold season.

Drops that remain behind after wiping are usually caused by oil, road film, or diesel exhaust residue on the glass.

— Use an alcohol or ammonia solution or other non-abrasive cleaner to clean windshield.

Chatter may be caused by dirty or worn blades, or by wiper arms that are out of alignment.

— Clean blades and windshield as described above.

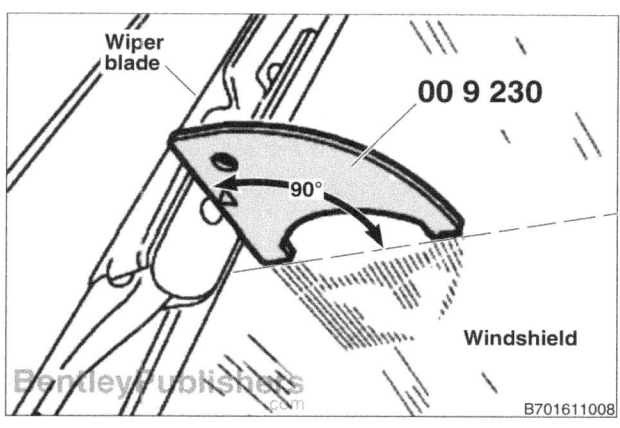

◄ Place BMW special tool 00 9 230 along wiper blade fulcrum and check for perpendicularity to windshield surface.

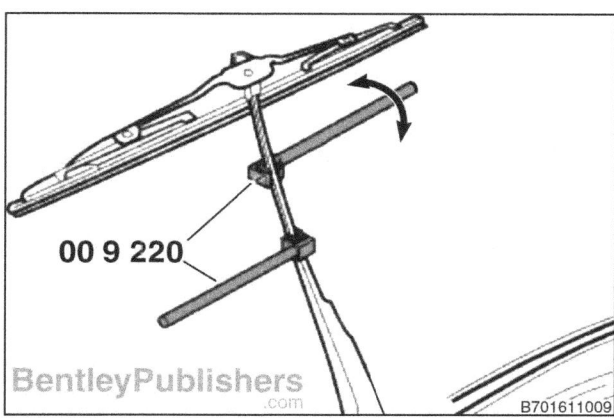

◄ Use BMW special tools 00 9 220 to adjust wiper arm twist so that there is even pressure along blade, and so that blade is perpendicular to windshield at rest.

— If problems persist, replace blades and wiper arms. See **Wiper blade, replacing** or **Front wiper arm, removing and installing** in this repair group.

Wiper blade insert, replacing

— Remove wiper blade. See **Wiper blade, replacing**.

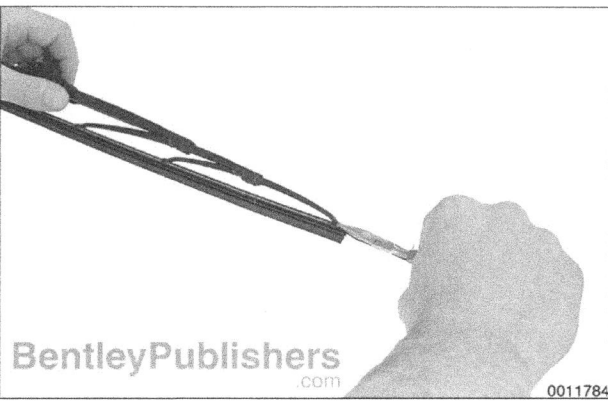

◄ Unhook wiper blade insert from wiper arm guides. If necessary, spread guide slightly using needle nose pliers.

— Pull old insert from wiper arm guides, noting installation position.

— Remove metal support strips from old insert and install into slots in new insert, noting installation direction of cutouts in support strips.

— Slide new insert through wiper blade guides. Lock insert in place at end guides.

NOTE —

• *Some wiper blade versions may have two retaining tabs.*

Wiper blade, replacing

— Switch ignition ON. Turn wipers ON briefly to bring wiper blades up to center of windshield. Switch ignition OFF and remove ignition key.

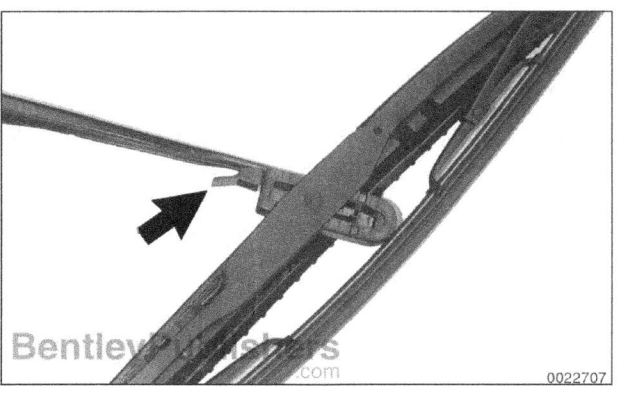

◄ To replace wiper blades:

• Pivot wiper arm off windshield.

• Position wiper blade approximately perpendicular to wiper arm.

• Depress retaining tab (**arrow**) and slide blade out of arm.

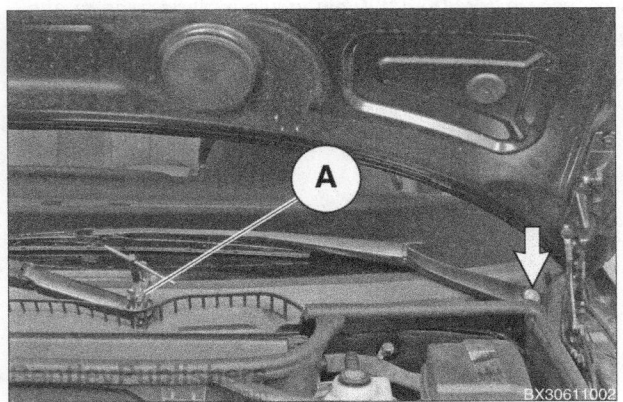

Front wiper arm, removing and installing

> **CAUTION—**
> • *Make sure wipers are parked (wiper stalk switch in OFF position) and the ignition is also OFF.*
> • *Use fender cover to protect windshield.*

— Open hood. Pry off wiper arm mounting nut cover.

◄ Remove wiper arm mounting nut (**arrow**).

— If necessary, use BMW special tool 61 6 060 or equivalent puller (**A**) to pull arm off pivot.

— Installation is reverse of removal. Make sure that each wiper blade is approximately 55 mm (2 in) from lower windshield edge when parked.

Tightening torque	
Front wiper arm to wiper shaft	30 Nm (22 ft-lb)

— Recheck torque on wiper arm fasteners after first use.

Rear wiper arm, removing and installing

> **CAUTION—**
> • *Make sure wipers are parked (wiper stalk switch in OFF position) and the ignition is also OFF.*

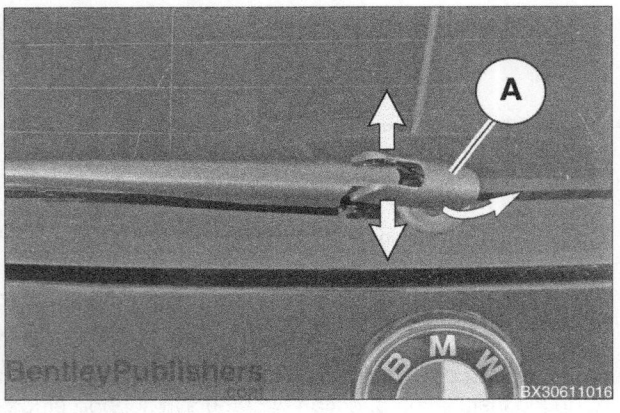

◄ Carefully pry off wiper arm cover (**A**). Spread cover apart to remove from mounting pins.

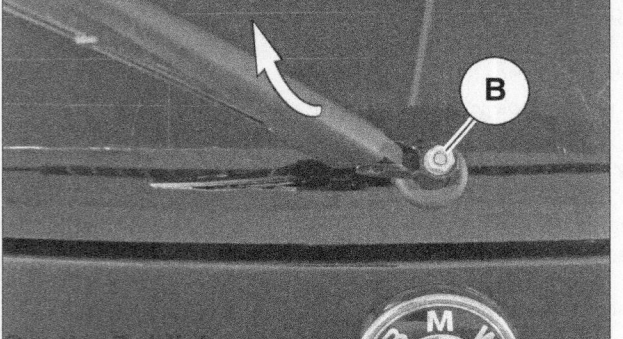

◄ Lift wiper arm off glass and remove wiper arm mounting nut (**B**).

— Remove wiper arm. If necessary use puller to remove from driveshaft.

— Installation is reverse of removal. Install wiper blade approximately 33 mm (1⅓ in) from lower rear window edge in parked position.

Tightening torque	
Rear wiper arm to wiper shaft (M8)	12 Nm (9 ft-lb)

WIPER ASSEMBLIES

Windshield wiper assembly, removing and installing

> **CAUTION—**
> * Make sure wipers are parked (stalk switch in OFF position) and the ignition is also OFF.
> * Use fender cover to protect windshield.
> * To avoid damaging the wiper arms and pivots, do not manually slide or force the wiper arms across the windshield.

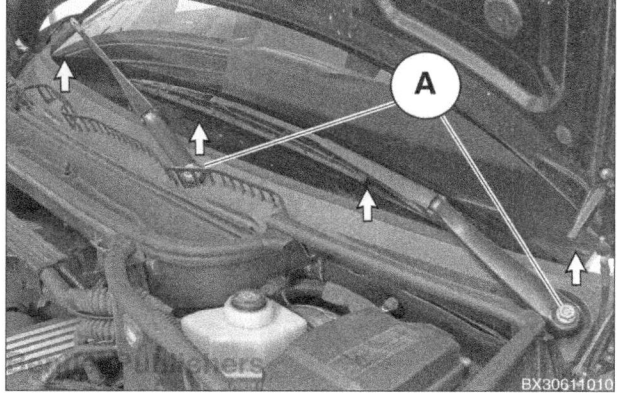

− Remove strut bar. See **310 Front Suspension**.

◅ Remove wiper arms (**A**). See **Front wiper arm, removing and installing** in this repair group.

− Release 3 fasteners 90° to loosen cabin cover. Lift cover and remove cabin. See **020 Maintenance** if necessary.

− Unclip cowl panel from blind fasteners and lift off of vehicle.

◅ Remove fasteners (**arrows**) at rear of plenum chamber and lift off of vehicle.

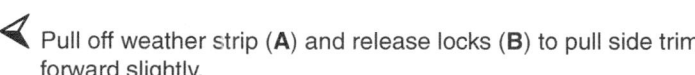

◅ Pull off weather strip (**A**) and release locks (**B**) to pull side trim forward slightly.

Windshield wiper assembly, removing and installing

◀ Remove fasteners (**arrows**) for heater bulkhead. Lift off and remove from vehicle.

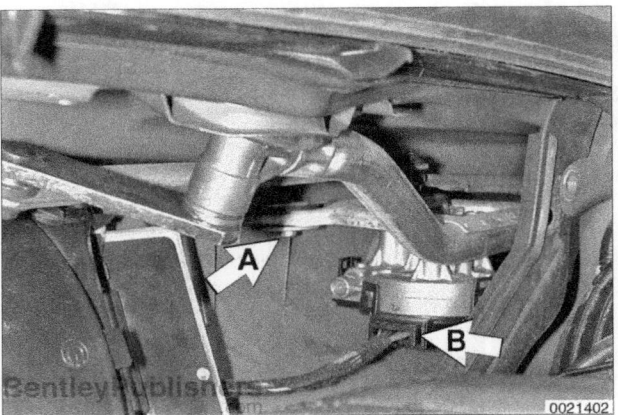

◀ Release wiper motor bracket from under cowl:

- Remove mounting bolt (**A**).
- Detach electrical connector (**B**).

◀ Remove large nut (**arrow**) base of wiper arm shafts on left and right sides.

— Remove wiper assembly.

— Prior to reinstallation, replace rubber mounting grommets as necessary.

— Install wiper motor bracket and tighten mounting bolt.

Tightening torques	
• Wiper bracket to body	10 Nm (7 ft-lb)
• Wiper shaft nut at cowl	10 Nm (7 ft-lb)

— Prior to reinstalling wiper arms:

- Reconnect wiper motor electrical connector.
- Briefly switch ignition ON with wiper switch in OFF position. Allow wiper pivots to reach PARK position.
- Reinstall wiper arms and blades, making sure that, when parked, each wiper blade is approximately 55 mm (2 in) from lower windshield edge.Check wiper blade contact angle. See **Wiper blade cleaning problems** in this repair group.

Rear wiper assembly, removing and installing

– Remove trim panel on tailgate. See **513 Interior Trim**.

– Remove rear wiper arm. See **Rear wiper arm, removing and installing** in this repair group.

◄ Detach electrical connector (**A**) and remove mounting bolts (**arrows**).

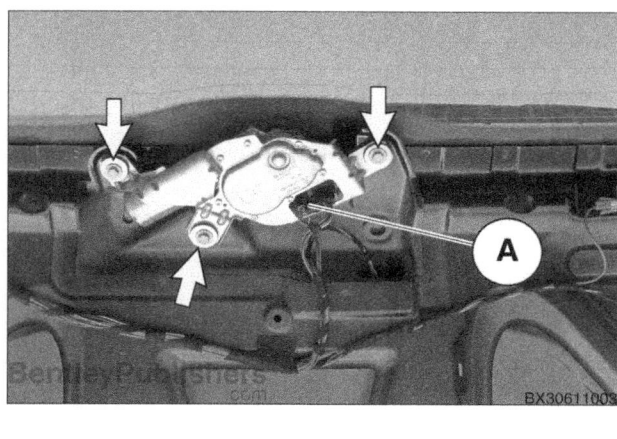

– Pull wiper motor out of grommet.

– Prior to reinstallation, replace rubber grommet. Make sure mark on grommet is horizontal.

– Insert wiper motor in grommet and install bolts finger-tight. Tighten bolts fully after centering wiper motor.

Tightening torque	
Rear wiper motor to tailgate	10 Nm (7 ft-lb)

WASHER SYSTEMS

The windshield washer system includes heated spray jets in the engine hood, the washer fluid pump, and washer fluid reservoir at right front of engine compartment.

The headlight washer system (optional) consists of front washer fluid reservoir (shared with windshield washer system), a separate washer pump, and washer jets in the front bumper.

The rear window washer consists of the fluid reservoir (shared with windshield washer system), a separate washer pump, and a washer jet at the top of the rear window.

Windshield washer jet, removing and installing

– Open engine hood. Working at rear of engine hood, remove round plastic covers at left and right sides.

◄ Disconnect right and left electrical harness connectors and windshield washer hoses (**arrows**).

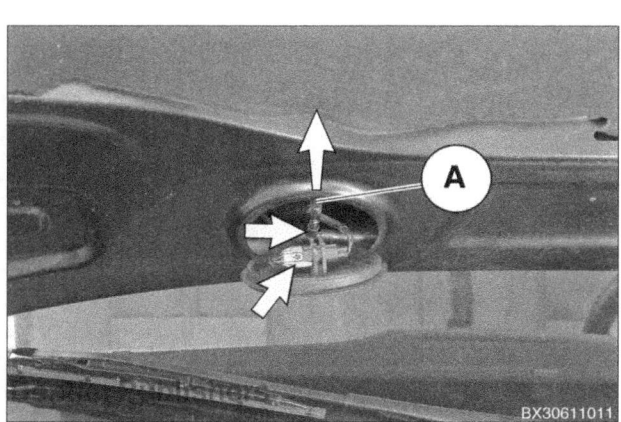

– Release washer nozzle by squeezing at (**A**) and pushing out of hood opening.

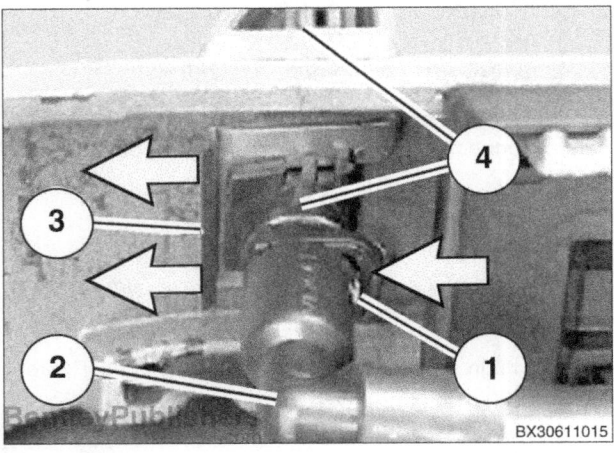

Headlight washer jet, removing and installing

– Removal and installation is similar for driver and passenger side.

– Remove front bumper see **510 Exterior trim**

◄ Working inside front bumper. Clamp feed hose to prevent washer fluid from leaking out.

– Press locking clip (**1**) to remove feed hose connection (**2**) from headlight spray nozzle.

– Pull retainer (**3**) out in direction of arrows and pull headlight washer (**4**) out from bumper trim.

◄ **2007 -2010 (LCI) vehicle**: Remove headlight washer covers. Use a plastic prying to gently pull up headlight washer nozzles.

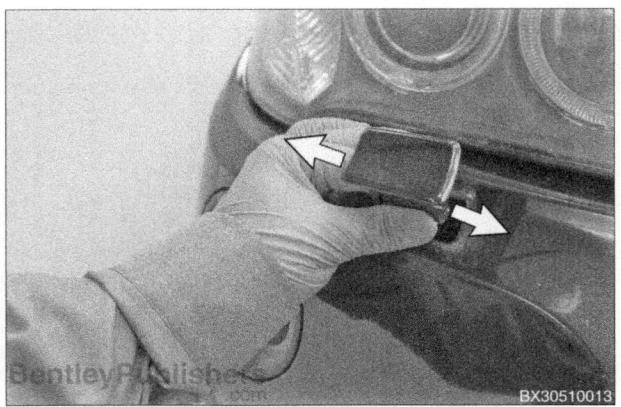

◄ **2007 -2010 (LCI) vehicle**: Gently pull apart tabs in direction of (**arrows**) to remove cover.

◄ Remove wheel housing liner bolts (**arrows**). On driver's side unclip ambient temperature sensor (**A**).

– Fold back both wheel liners.

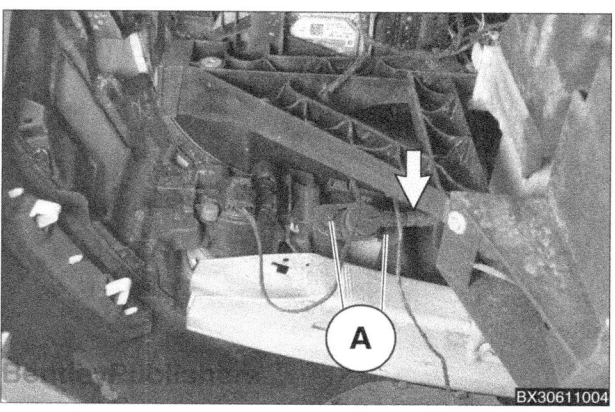

◄ Working inside front bumper. Clamp feed hose to prevent washer fluid from leaking out. Then remove feed hose from washer (**arrow**).

– Release screws from headlight washer jet (**A**) to remove from bumper.

– Installation is reverse of removal.

Rear window washer jet, removing and installing

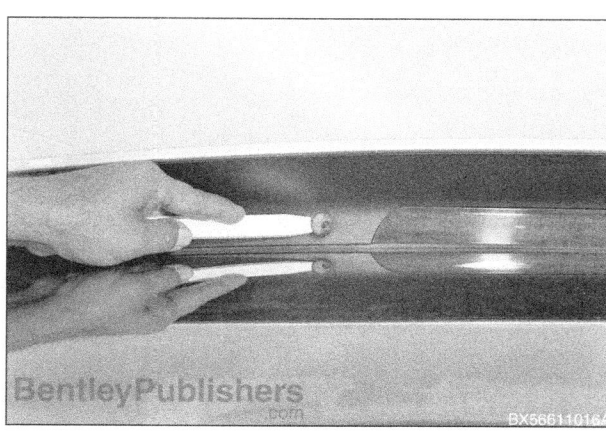

◄ Use plastic prying tool to lever rear window washer jet out of jet holder.

– Installation is reverse of removal. Be sure to insert locating lug of washer jet into groove of holder.

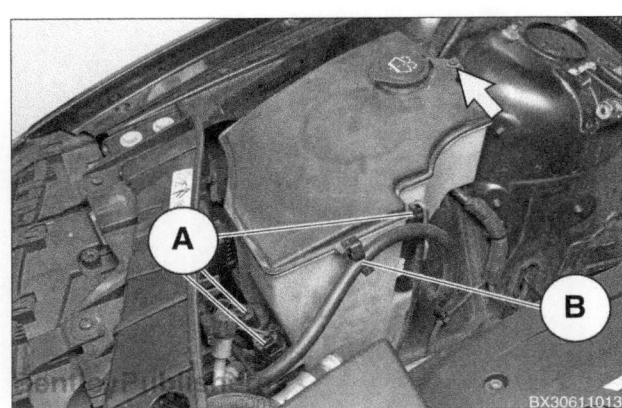

Washer fluid reservoir, removing and installing

— Open engine hood. Working at right front of engine compartment, siphon out washer fluid from reservoir.

◄ Remove reservoir:

- Remove mounting nut (**arrow**). Detach hoses and electrical connectors (**A**) from fluid pumps and fluid level switch.
- Unclip hose (**B**) and lift reservoir straight up out of mounting slot to remove. Be prepared to catch dripping fluid.

NOTE—

• Level switch is located under reservoir, not shown in photo.

— Installation is reverse of removal. remember to:

- Locate reservoir by placing lug at base into mounting slot.
- Make sure hoses are not kinked.
- Fill reservoir and check for leaks.

Washer fluid reservoir components service

— Open engine hood. Working at right front of engine compartment, siphon out washer fluid from reservoir.

— **Washer fluid level switch** replacement: Located under the washer reservoir near head lamp.

- Partially remove washer reservoir to ease with removal.
- Detach electrical connector.
- Carefully pry sensor out of reservoir. Be prepared to catch dripping fluid.

◄ **Headlight washer pump** replacement:

- Detach electrical connector.
- Detach hose from pump.
- Carefully pry pump out of reservoir. Be prepared to catch dripping fluid.

— **Rear window washer pump** or **windshield washer pump** replacement:

- Detach electrical connector.
- Detach hose from pump.
- Carefully pry pump out of reservoir. Be prepared to catch dripping fluid.

— Installation is reverse of removal, noting the following:

- Coat grommet at base of pump or sensor with anti-friction agent.
- After installation, check that fluid hoses are not kinked.
- Fill reservoir and check for leaks.

612 Switches

GENERAL

This repair group covers replacement of electrical switches at the steering wheel, steering column, dashboard, pedal cluster, center console and door panels.

See also the following sections:

- **250 Gearshift Linkage** for automatic shift lock
- **320 Steering and Wheel Alignment** for steering wheel and steering column components
- **520 Seats** for seat position control switches
- **540 Sunroof** for sunroof control switch
- **721 Airbag system** for airbag removal
- **ECL Electrical Component Locations**
- **ELE Electrical Wiring Diagrams**

612

CAUTION—

- *When working on electrical switches or lights, disconnect the negative (–) cable from the battery and insulate the cable end to prevent accidental reconnection.*
- *Prior to disconnecting the battery, read the battery disconnection cautions given in **001 Warnings and Cautions**.*
- *To prevent marring interior trim, work with plastic prying tools or wrap the tips of screwdrivers and pliers with tape before prying out switches or trim.*

STEERING WHEEL SWITCHES

X3 vehicles covered by this manual are equipped with the either multi-function (MFL) steering wheel or sports steering wheel. Incorporated into both steering wheels are:

• SRS airbag

• Horn contact

• Cellular telephone controls

• Radio controls

• Cruise control buttons

There is an early and late steering wheel switch design, Removal procedures vary.

NOTE—

• *The horn button is integrated with the airbag and not replaceable separately.*

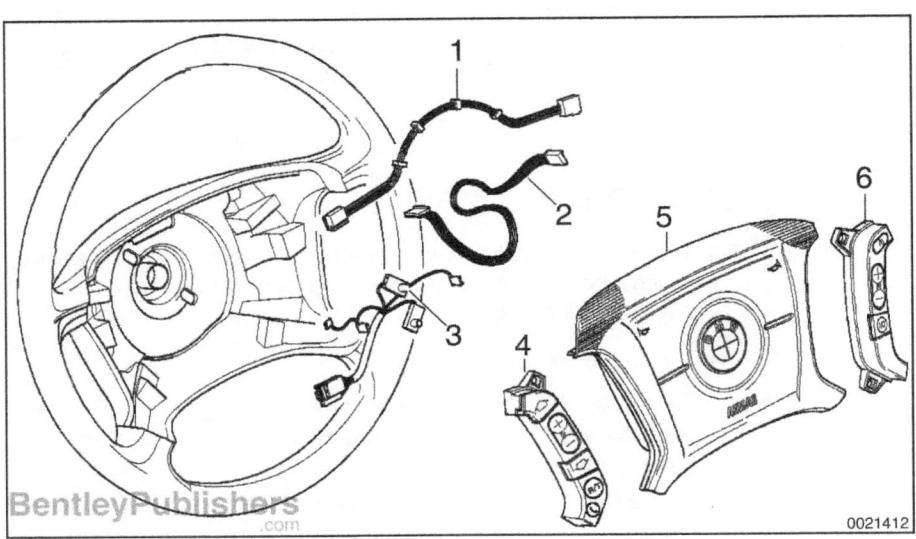

Multi-function steering wheel (2004 - 2006 models)

1. Cruise control, radio and telephone electrical harness

2. Horn button electrical harness

3. Airbag electrical harness

4. Radio and telephone control switches

5. Airbag unit and horn button

6. Cruise control switch set

Multifunction steering wheel switches, removing and installing (2004 -2006 models)

— Make sure ignition is switched OFF. Remove driver airbag in steering wheel. See **721 Airbag System.**

WARNING—

• *The steering wheel mounted airbag is an explosive device. Treat with extreme caution. Follow the airbag removal procedure in* **721 Airbag System.**

• *Airbag removal may set MRS fault codes. Do not cycle the ignition key with MRS components removed. The airbag fault indicator light remains ON until problems are corrected and fault memory cleared.*

◀ Disconnect switch electrical harness connectors (**arrows**).

Multifunction steering wheel switches, removing and installing (2007- 2010 models)

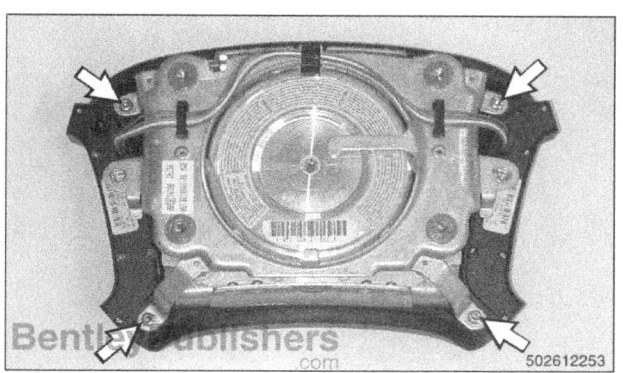

◄ Remove fasteners (**arrows**) from left or right rear of airbag pad to release switch pack, as necessary.

— Installation is reverse of removal.

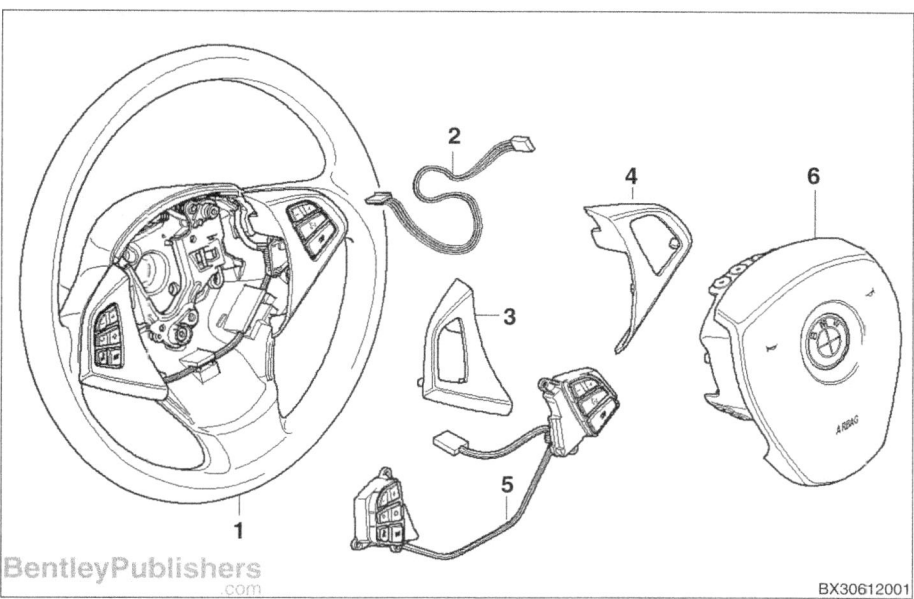

Multi-function steering wheel (2007 - 2010 models)

1. Steering wheel

2. Airbag electrical harness

3. Left steering wheels cover

4. Right steering wheel cover

5. Multi-function steering wheels switches

6. Airbag unit

Multifunction steering wheel switches, removing and installing (2007- 2010 models)

NOTE—

• *Sports steering wheel shown for this procedure.*

— Make sure ignition is switched OFF. Remove driver airbag in steering wheel. See **721 Airbag System.**

WARNING—

• *The steering wheel mounted airbag is an explosive device. Treat with extreme caution. Follow the airbag removal procedure in* **721 Airbag System**.

• *Airbag removal may set MRS fault codes. Do not cycle the ignition key with MRS components removed. The airbag fault indicator light remains ON until problems are corrected and fault memory cleared.*

— Remove steering wheel. See **320 Steering and Wheel Alignment**.

◄ Working on rear of steering wheel remove Torx screws (**A**) to release side covers.

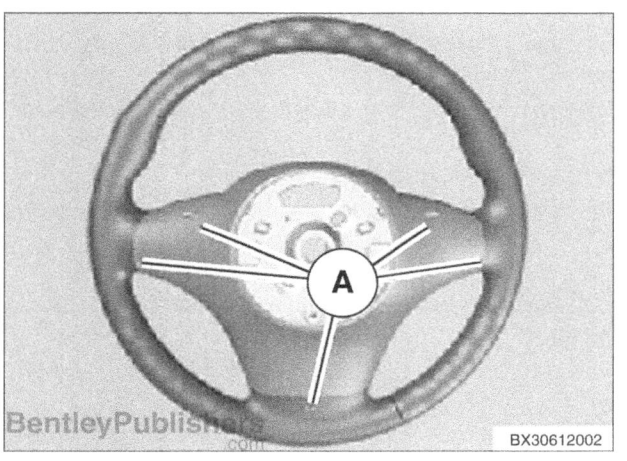

612

Ignition lock cylinder, removing and installing

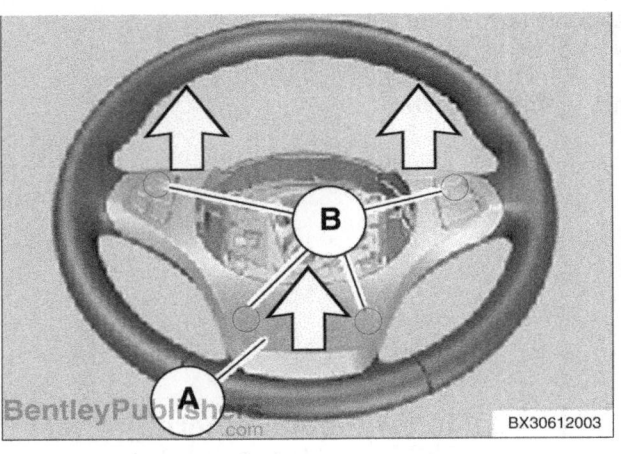

◄ Unclip cover trim(s) (**A**) from mounting points (**B**) in direction of arrows.

– Disconnect electrical connection for switches.

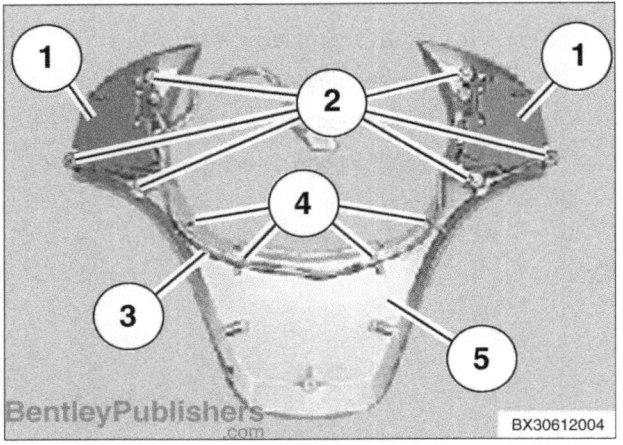

◄ To remove switches (**1**) loosen screws (**2**) remove both switches at the same time from trim (**5**).

– Installation is reverse of removal.
  • Be sure that wiring harness (**3**) is seated correctly inside of trim clips (**4**).

STEERING COLUMN SWITCHES

Ignition lock cylinder, removing and installing

– Disconnect negative (–) cable from battery.

> **CAUTION—**
> • *Prior to disconnecting the battery, read the battery disconnection cautions given in* **001 Warnings and Cautions**.

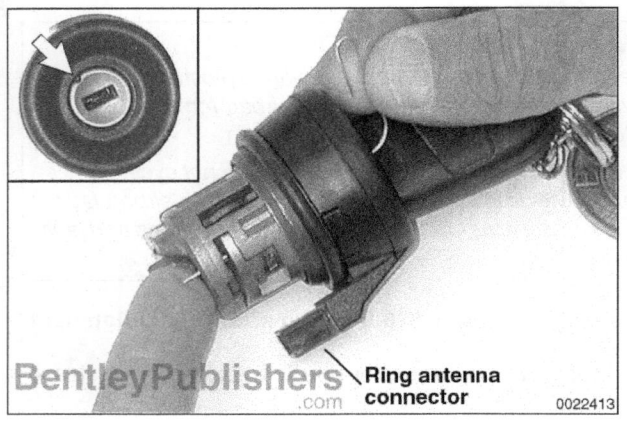

◄ With ignition key in ON position:
  • Insert BMW special tool 32 3 110 or a thin piece of stiff wire into opening (**arrow**) in lock cylinder.
  • Turn tool forward (clockwise) approximately 90° and remove lock cylinder.
  • Disconnect ring antenna harness connector.
  • Installation is reverse of removal.

> **NOTE—**
> • *Using the valet key during this procedure will provide better access to lock opening.*

Ring antenna connector

Ignition switch, removing and installing

— Disconnect negative (–) cable from battery and cover terminal with insulating material.

> CAUTION—
> • Prior to disconnecting the battery, read the battery disconnection cautions given **001 Warnings and Cautions**.

— Remove lower steering column cover. See **513 Interior Trim**.

◄ Remove protective paint covering ignition switch fasteners (**1**) and remove fasteners.

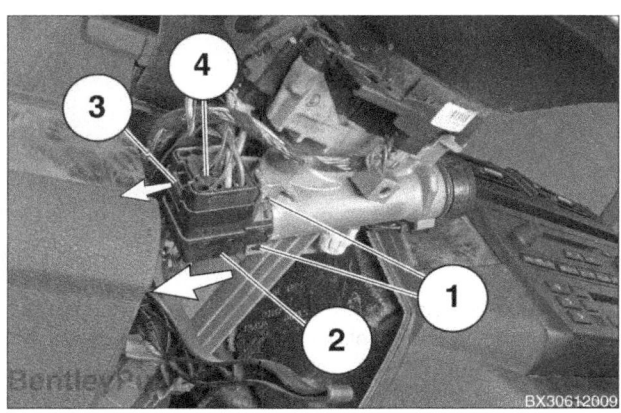

— Detach ignition starter switch (**2**) in direction of arrow.

— Open lock (**3**) in direction of arrow and disconnect plug (**4**) from ignition starter switch (**2**).

— Installation is reverse of removal, noting the following:

  • Correctly align switch drive to steering lock.

  • Secure switch fasteners with paint or lacquer after installation.

Steering column stalk switches, removing and installing

— Disconnect negative (–) battery cable.

> CAUTION—
> • Prior to disconnecting the battery, read the battery disconnection cautions given **001 Warnings and Cautions**.
> • The SRS contact reel (also known as airbag contact ring / slip ring) is integral with the steering column switch block. The contact reel is a wound coil of wire that ensures continuous electrical contact for the airbag and steering wheel electrical components. When the steering wheel is removed the contact reel is locked and its position must not be altered.

— Extend steering column back and up as far as it will go

— Remove driver airbag. See **721 Airbag System**.

— Remove steering wheel. See **320 Steering and Wheel Alignment**.

— Remove upper and lower steering column covers. See **513 Interior Trim**.

◄ Remove stalk switch carrier mounting screws (**arrows**). Lift off carrier and detach electrical connectors. Do not rotate the center part of switch carrier for any reason.

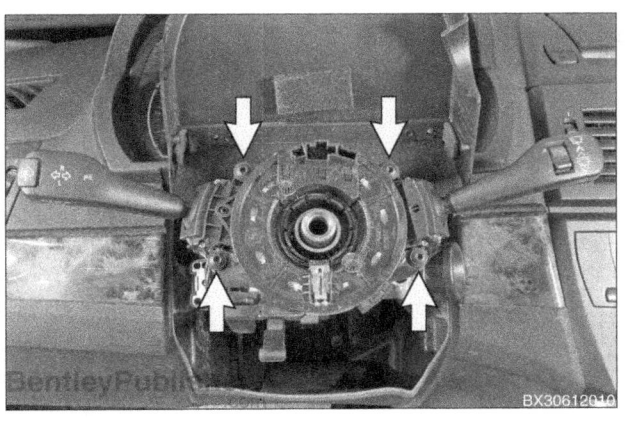

612

Light switch center, removing and installing

Wiper and washer switch

◄ Squeeze locking tabs (**arrows**) to release switch and slide out of carrier.

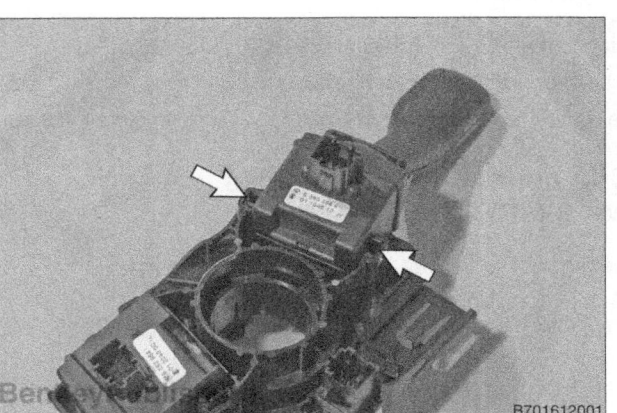

Turn signal and headlight dimmer switch

◄ Remove steering column positioning switch first. Squeeze locking tabs (**arrows**) to release headlight dimmer switch and slide out of carrier.

– Installation is reverse of removal.

DASHBOARD SWITCHES

Light switch center, removing and installing

The light switch center (LSZ) replacement requires vehicle coding because of redundant vehicle memory. See **620 Instruments** for more information.

NOTE—

- *Early (pre-LCI) models use a different light switch center than the later LCI models. The switches are not interchangeable.*

– Remove left dash air vent, see **513 Interior trim**.

◄ Using a plastic pry tool, carefully pry light switch assembly out of dashboard in direction of arrows.

NOTE—

- *After replacing the LSZ, use BMW factory scan tool to synchronize vehicle memory and mileage. If LSZ, EWS and instrument cluster are not synchronized, the tamper warning light illuminates, indicating possible tampering with vehicle mileage.*

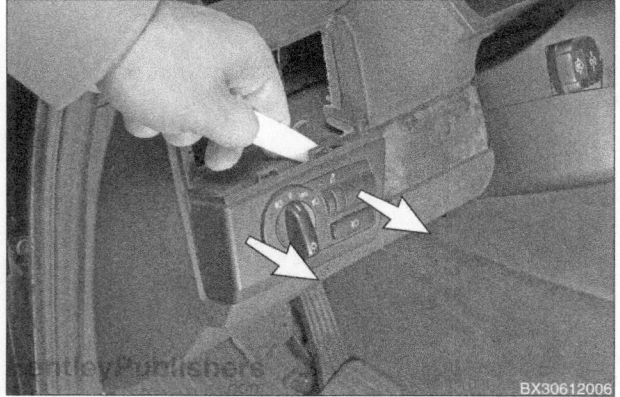

Switch unit in center console, removing and installing

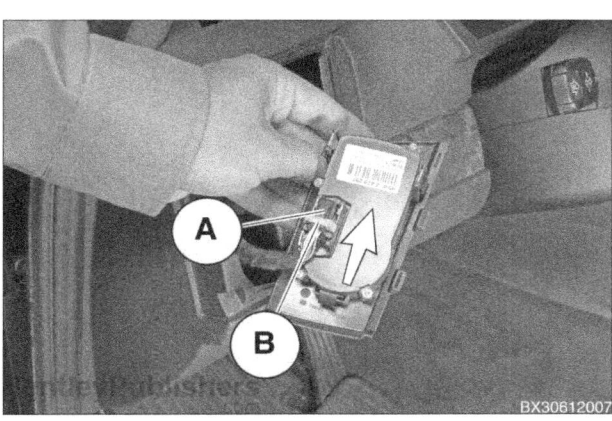

◀ Press in lock (**A**) on electrical connector, then push lock (**B**) in direction of arrow to unlock electrical connector.

– Installation is reverse of removal.

Switch unit in center console, removing and installing

The following switches (if applicable) are integrated in the switch unit in the center console:

- ABS / DSC
- Seat heaters
- Park distance control (PDC)
- Hill descent control (HDC)

– Remove shift knob and boot or drive selection plate. See **250 Gearshift Linkage**.

> **WARNING—**
> • *If vehicle shifter is in neutral to facilitate trim removal be sure car is on level ground and parking brake is engaged.*

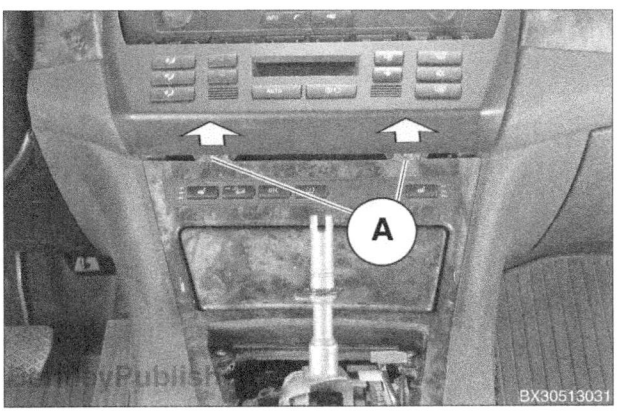

◀ Working at the HVAC panel, use a suitable prying tool to unclip trim from the bottom only. Remove screws (**A**).

◀ Remove screws (**A**) and unclip spring clips (**B**). Taking care to not drop spring clips into shifter area.

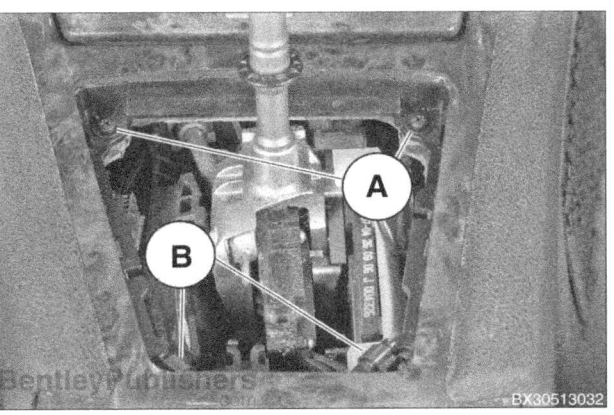

612

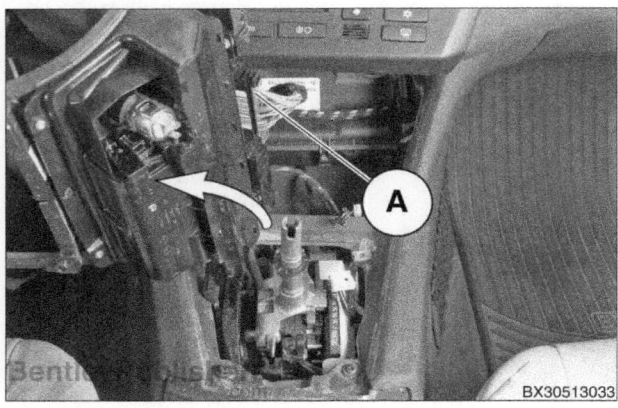

BX30513033

◄ Lift out trim and disconnect 12 volt socket and center switch panel connectors).

− Switch panel can now be removed from trim panel.

− Installation is reverse of removal.

OTHER SWITCHES

Back-up light switch

For manual transmission back-up light switch location, see **230 Manual Transmission**.

The automatic transmission range switch combines the following functions:

• Neutral safety switch.
• Back-up light switch.

See **240 Automatic Transmission**.

Brake light switch, removing and installing

− Remove left lower dashboard trim (above pedals). See **513 Interior Trim**.

◄ Working at pedal cluster, disconnect electrical harness connector (**arrow**) from brake light switch.

502610030a

Hazard warning and central locking switch, removing and installing

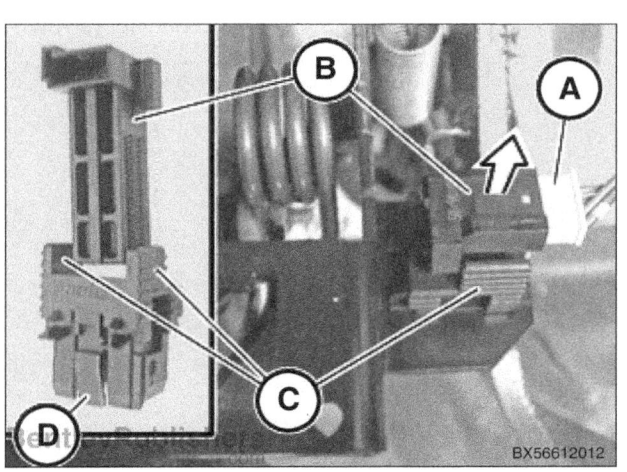

◄ Pull brake light switch (**B**) from holder in direction of **arrow**.

− To install, depress brake pedal and hold with suitable fixture.

− Slide brake light switch (**B**) as far as it will go into brake light switch holder (**C**).

− Attach harness connector (**A**).

− Grip brake light switch holder (**C**), slowly return brake pedal to rest position and pull switch back to stop.

− Check function of brake light switch with helper.

Hazard warning and central locking switch, removing and installing

◄ Use a suitable prying tool to unclip center air vent grill from dashboard.

◄ Pull back center air vent grill to unclip bowden cable (**arrow**) and remove.

612

 Disconnect central locking and hazard switch at connector (**arrow**).

– Switch can now be removed from trim by squeezing tabs.

– Installation is reverse of removal.

Driver door switch module (SBFA), removing and installing

NOTE—

• *Take care to avoid damaging door panel arm rests or window switches. A prying tool with a wide flat head works best.*

See **512 Door windows** for more information on window switch operation. This procedure only covers removal and installation.

◀ Using plastic prying tool, push in hidden locks (**black arrows**) Then pry complete assembly out of arm rest at in direction of white arrows.

– Disconnect electrical harnesses and remove module.

– Installation is reverse of removal.

Passenger door power window switch, removing and installing

NOTE—

• *Take care to avoid damaging door panel arm rests or window switches. A prying tool with a wide flat head works best.*

◀ Using plastic prying tool, push door switch to rear to release hidden locks and pry door switch unit from door arm rest.

– Disconnect harness connector from switch unit.

– Installation is reverse of removal.

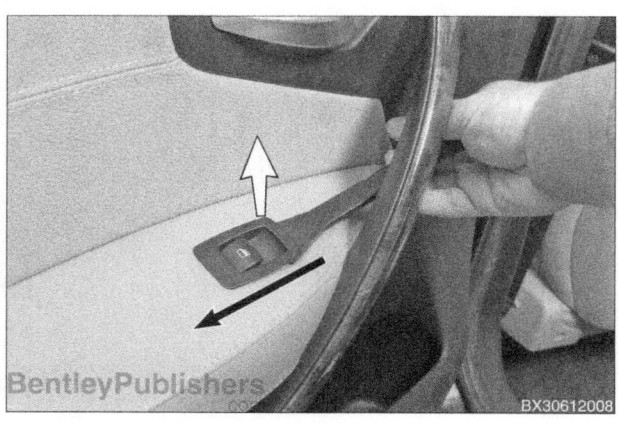

620 Instruments

GENERAL

This repair group covers removal and installation of the instrument cluster. X3 instrument cluster is a sealed unit and bulb replacement is not possible. Instrument cluster replacement requires coding with BMW diagnostic equipment.

INSTRUMENT CLUSTER

Instrument cluster functions

The instrument cluster is the control and information center for the X3 driver. It is connected to vehicle systems and sensors via bus networks. See **600 Electrical System—General** for information on bus systems.

Check Control displays safety and convenience system status and malfunctions and also provides a self-test system for the cluster electronics.

If the vehicle is equipped with **On-board Computer**, pushing the button at the end of the turn signal stalk switch brings up on the cluster information of interest to the driver:

• Time
• Outside temperature
• Average fuel consumption
• Cruising range
• Average vehicle speed

These functions are more fully explained in the owner's manual.

620

Redundant vehicle data storage

BX30620001

Instrument cluster layout

1. Speedometer
2. Indicator and warning lamps
3. Tachometer/indicator and warning lamps
4. Coolant temperature gauge
5. Fuel gauge
6. Button for
   - Displaying the time
   - Service interval display
   - Checking oil level
7. Selector lever and program displays for automatic transmission.
8. Button for
   - Resetting trip odometer, service interval
   - Setting time
9. Display for
   - Trip odometer/odometer
   - Time
   - Service interval
   - Computer
   - Checking oil level (2007 and later)

Redundant vehicle data storage

The instrument cluster module stores vehicle data such as total mileage and service interval. A parallel set of data is stored in the light control module and electronic vehicle immobilization unit (EWS). Redundant data storage allows information to be saved if a module is replaced.

After replacing the instrument cluster, use BMW diagnostic scan tool to synchronize vehicle memory and mileage. If LCM, EWS and instrument cluster are not synchronized, the tamper warning light (dot) will illuminate.

INSTRUMENT CLUSTER SERVICE

Instrument cluster, removing and installing

– Extend steering column as far back and down as it will go.

◄ Remove instrument cluster fasteners (**arrows**).

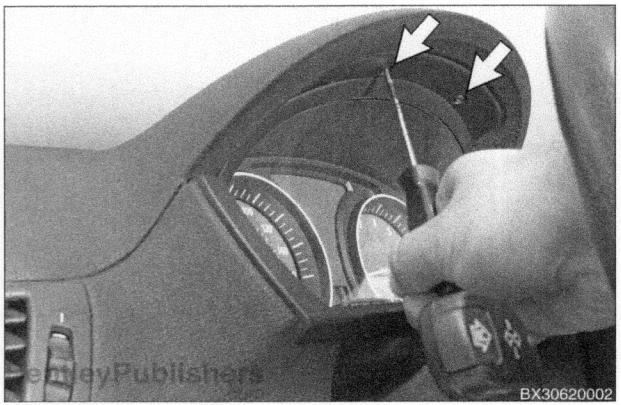

BX30620002

Instrument cluster, removing and installing

◀ Using a plastic prying tool, tilt cluster downward out of dashboard.

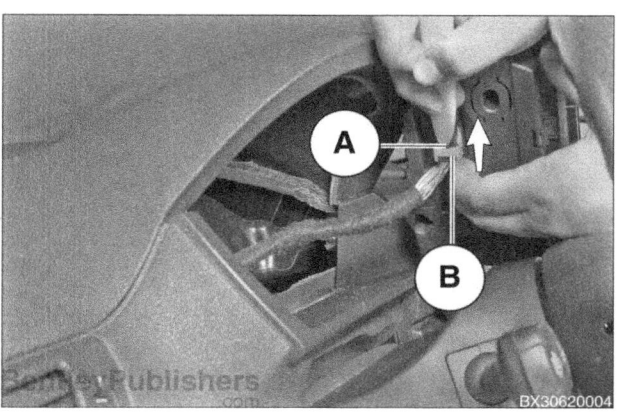

◀ Slide cluster sideways to clear steering wheel.

− Depress lock (**A**) and slide lock (**B**) over in direction of to release electrical connector from instrument cluster.

− Installation is reverse of removal, noting the following:
  • Make sure instrument cluster harness connector locking lever is in fully unlocked position before installing connector.
  • Recode replacement cluster using BMW diagnostic scan tool.

620

630 Lights

GENERAL

This repair group covers interior and exterior lights. Head lights are complete assemblies. Only light bulbs can be replaced.

See also:

- **611 Wipers and Washers** for headlight washer system
- **612 Switches** for light switch replacement
- **ECL Electrical Component Locations**
- **ELE Electrical Wiring Diagrams**

Bulb applications

Bulb applications are in **Table a**.

Table a. Bulb applications	
Location	**Type and wattage**
Headlights	
High beam, halogen	H7 55 w
Low beam, halogen	H7 55 w
Low beam, xenon	D2–S
Foglights	
Fog light bulb	H11 55 w

630

Table a. Bulb applications (continued)	
Turn signals and taillights	
Back-up	21 w
Brake light	21 w
Licence plate	5 w
Taillight	21 w
Turn signal • Front • Rear • Side	 21 / 5 w amber 21 / 5 w amber 5 w amber
Interior lights	
Dome lights • Front dome/map lights • Rear dome light	 6 w 6 w
Door lights • Courtesy (footwell)	 5 w
Glove compartment	10 w
Tailgate	5 w
Vanity mirror	10 w

Light switch center (LSZ)

◄ The light switch center (LSZ) has the following functions:

- Headlight / taillight / running light control switch
- Foglight switch
- Instrument dimmer control
- Light control module

In addition to normal light control, the LSZ provides the following functions:

- Hot and cold monitoring of the exterior bulbs
- Emergency lighting function
- Short circuit protection
- Redundant storage of mileage and service interval data
- Adaptive headlight control (2007 - 2010 vehicles)

Headlight versions

X3s are equipped with halogen headlights as standard equipment. Halogen bulb replacement is performed from the back (engine) side of the headlight assembly.

◄ Optional adaptive bi-xenon low-beam headlights illuminate the road ahead and to the sides in greater detail than conventional headlights. The high beam bulbs remain halogen bulbs. Vehicles equipped with adaptive bi-xenon headlights will have "BMW DYNAMIC XENON" written on the low beam lens holder.

NOTE—

- *Adaptive and bi-xenon headlights are a combined option on the X3.*

Sometimes referred to as High Intensity Discharge (HID) lights, xenon lights use less energy and last longer than other headlight bulbs.

Light switch center (LSZ)

BX30630001

BX30630012

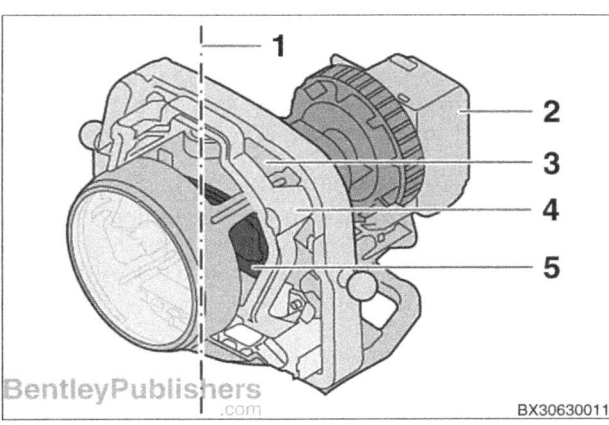

BX30630011

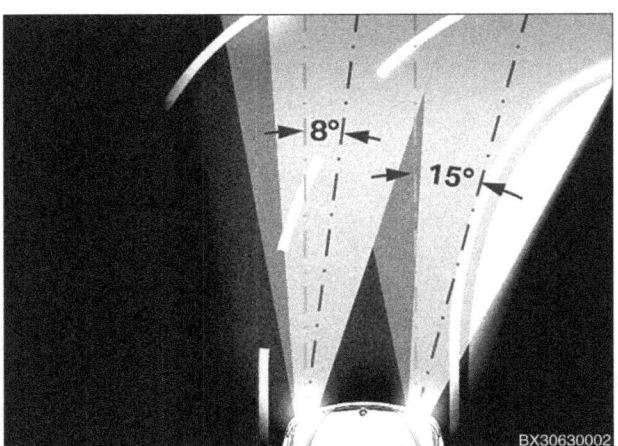

BX30630002

 Bi-xenon headlights provide greater visibility when using the high beam function. During high beam operation a shutter opens allowing light from the xenon low beam bulb to supplement the halogen high beam bulb giving better high beam illumination performance.

1. Axis of movement
2. Xenon ignition unit
3. Reflector
4. Positioning frame
5. Mechanical shutter

Adaptive headlights (AHL) description

 Optional adaptive headlights follow the road surface for better illumination. AHL functions on both high and low beams. The headlight on the inside of the curve will swivel a maximum of 15° away from the vehicle center. The headlight on the outside of curve will swivel a maximum of 8° inward to vehicle center during use. Adaptive headlights point straight ahead when reversing vehicle.

A combination of steering angle sensor and DSC sensor input provide information for horizontal headlight swivel to the AHL module. Ride height sensors are used as part of the AHL system and installed on the right front and right rear suspension. Ride height sensors provide signals to the AHL module for control of vertical aiming adjustment. This system accounts for ride height changes due to passenger or cargo carrying weight and also during braking and acceleration to keep headlights level. The system also receives a signal from the brake light switch when the brake pedal is pushed.

NOTE—

• *2004 - 2006 (pre-LC) vehicles use an AHL control module. On 2007 -2010 (LCI) vehicles, the software for AHL has been incorporated into the light switch center (LSZ).*

LCI vehicles incorporate a turning lamp function with adaptive headlights. Reflectors inside the fog lamp housings are designed to illuminate road sides when turning. Fog lamps act as the turning lamps and are switched on individually when needed. This happens automatically according to steering angle or turn signal position up to 43 mph. Turning lamp feature also functions when reversing the vehicle and turning at the same time.

Adaptive headlights are not serviceable and provided as complete assemblies only. Light bulbs are the only replaceable parts.

In case of a system failure, a fault light will illuminate in the instrument cluster and the green LED on the LSZ will flash. AHL function is then disabled. Depending on what component has failed headlights will be returned to the straight-ahead position, lowered or bi-xenon bulb will be disabled.

630

Rain / light sensor (RLS)

When the headlights are switched to the auto setting, headlights are turned on and off automatically by the rain / light sensor (RLS), depending on ambient light conditions.

For vehicles with adaptive head lights (AHL), the RLS will sense ambient light and signal the AHL control module. During "twilight" adaptive headlights will only self level as needed. Swivelling to follow the road is disabled. When the RLS senses "darkness" AHL swivelling is activated.

The rain sensor system is augmented by two additional optical sensors, both housed in the rear view mirror at the top of the windshield:

Surrounding-light sensor detects light intensity in a wide angle above the vehicle.

Frontal-light sensor detects light intensity in a narrow cone in front of the vehicle.

A microprocessor uses this data to determine when and whether to turn the lights ON or OFF in the following circumstances:
• Dawn or dusk
• Night
• Driving through a tunnel
• Precipitation such as rain or snow

Suspension level sensors

Vehicles equipped with adaptive bi-xenon headlights have two suspension level sensors that detect body loading. The sensors signal the AHL to adjust vertical headlight aim.

Bulb monitoring

The light switch center (LSZ) monitors the following bulbs in both hot and cold states:
• High / low beams
• Brake lights
• Turn signal lights
• Taillights
• Parking lights
• Side marker lights
• License plate lights

 Hot and cold monitoring of light bulbs allows the LSZ to detect defective bulbs. Hot monitoring checks the continuity of circuits while the lights are switched on. Cold monitoring consists of a brief pulse of current which is too short for the lights to illuminate. If the module detects a defective bulb, a signal is sent to the instrument cluster and Check Control is illuminated with the appropriate warning.

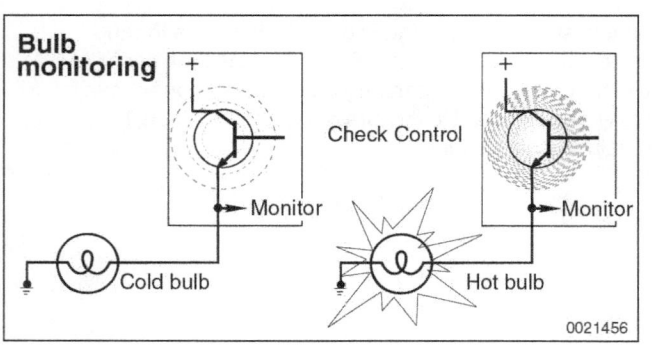

Bulb monitoring

Check Control

Monitor

Monitor

Cold bulb

Hot bulb

0021456

Home lighting

This convenience feature provides lighting for occupants to leave the vehicle and enter their house. The feature is switched on by activating the headlight flasher switch after the lights and ignition are switched OFF. The lights are switched OFF after the programmed time delay or by switching the ignition ON.

Emergency (failsafe) lighting

The light control module provides emergency lighting in case of an electronic module failure. Back up hardware allows the following lighting circuits to function:

• Low beam headlights

• Taillights

• Brake lights

The headlights and taillights come on as soon as the ignition is switched ON. The brake lights operate when the brake pedal is pressed.

Warnings and cautions

WARNING—

• *High voltage in xenon headlights is hazardous. Disconnect xenon headlight components from power supply before removing.*

• *Internal pressure of xenon glass bulb may exceed 100 bar (in operation). Bulb temperature may exceed 700 degrees Celsius. Always wear safety glasses and gloves when removing and installing an xenon bulb.*

• *Never look directly at an operating xenon bulb. The UV emissions of an xenon bulb are approximately 2.5 times that of a comparable halogen bulb.*

• *When working on electrical systems, remove the fuse protecting the circuit under repair. See* **Electrical Component Locations***.*

CAUTION—

• *Xenon bulbs and control modules are static-sensitive. Use an antistatic mat and work with caution.*

• *Do not operate the xenon control module unless a bulb is connected.*

• *Before servicing headlight system, switch off all electrical consumers. Switch ignition off and remove ignition key.*

• *To ensure bulb longevity, do not handle bulb glass with bare fingers. Dirt and skin oils cause a bulb to fail prematurely. If necessary, wipe bulb using a clean cloth dampened with rubbing alcohol.*

• *Use only original equipment replacement bulbs. Non-original equipment bulbs may cause false failure readings on the Check Control display.*

• *To avoid marring car paint or trim, work with plastic prying tools or wrap the tips of tools with tape.*

630

HEADLIGHTS

Halogen headlight components

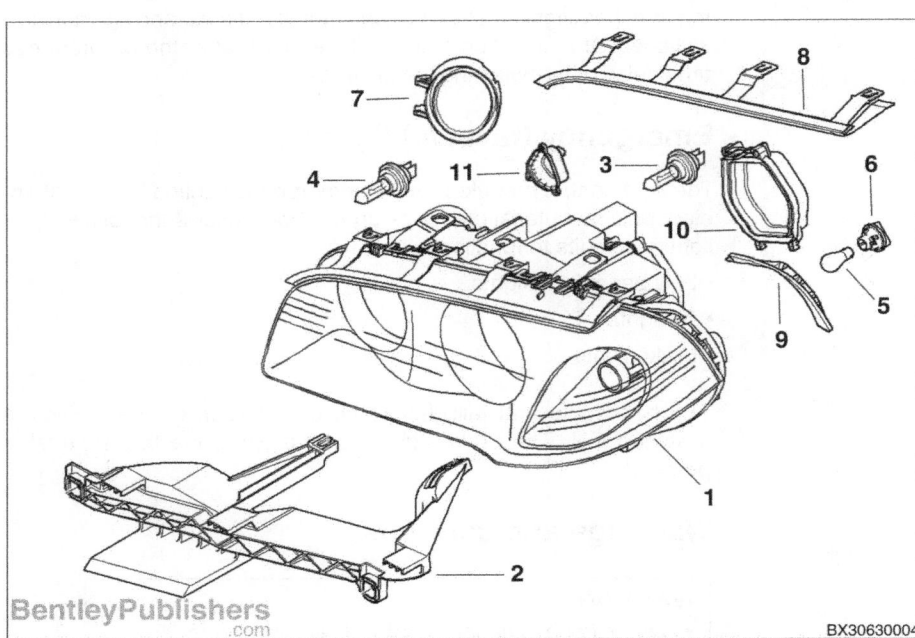

1. Headlight assembly
2. Headlight bracket
3. Low beam bulb
   • H7 55 w
4. High beam bulb
   • H7 55 w
5. Turn signal bulb
   • 12 v 21 w
6. Turn signal socket
7. High beam cover cap
8. Headlight weather strip
9. Headlight to fender gasket
10. Low beam cover cap
11. Head lamp leveling cover cap

BX30630004

Bi-xenon adaptive head light components

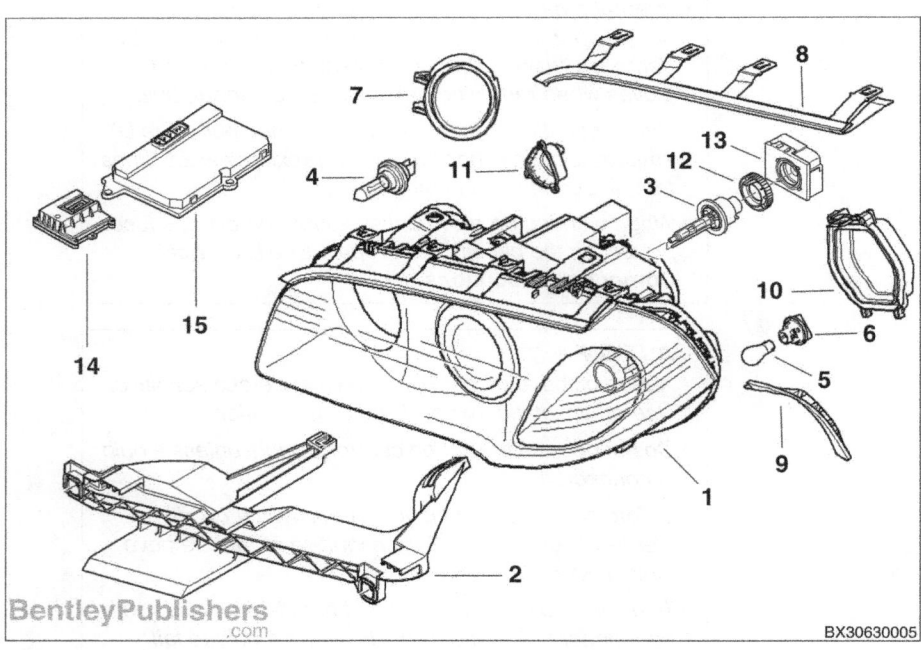

1. Headlight assembly
2. Headlight bracket
3. Low beam xenon bulb
   • D2-S 35 w
4. High beam bulb
   • H7 55 w
5. Turn signal bulb
   • 12 v 21 w
6. Turn signal socket
7. High beam cover cap
8. Headlight weather strip
9. Headlight to fender gasket
10. Low beam cover cap
11. Head lamp leveling cover cap
12. Xenon bulb support ring
13. Xenon bulb ignition unit
14. Control unit for headlight
15. Control unit for xenon light

BX30630005

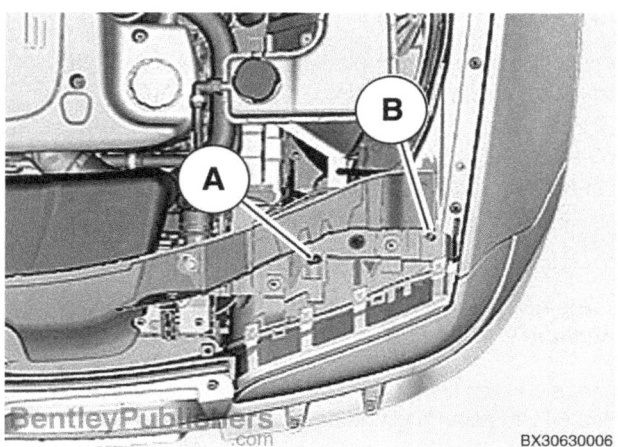

BX30630006

Headlight aim, adjusting

Adjust headlight aim with correct tire pressures, fuel tank full, and weight of one person (approximately 75 kg or 165 lb) in driver seat.

◄ Working at top of headlight housing, use knurled knobs or screws to adjust headlight aim:

• **A**: Vertical aim adjustment

• **B**: Lateral aim adjustment

Halogen headlight bulb, replacing

NOTE—

• Headlight shown removed for clarity.

Low beam

— For drivers side partially remove air box. See **020 Maintenance**.

— For passenger side partially remove washer fluid reservoir. See **611 Wipers and Washers**.

◄ Working in engine compartment behind headlight (**A**), unclip plastic bulb cover (**B**) in direction of arrow.

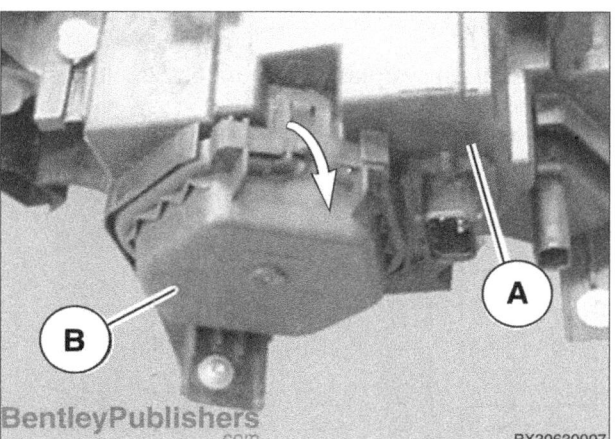

BX30630007

◄ Unclip bulb (**A**) by pressing connector (**B**). Disconnect bulb at plug and remove in direction of arrow.

— Installation is reverse of removal making sure that bulb is fully seated in headlight.

NOTE—

• Do not touch bulb surface with bare finger. Grease from skin can cause bulb to fail prematurely.

630

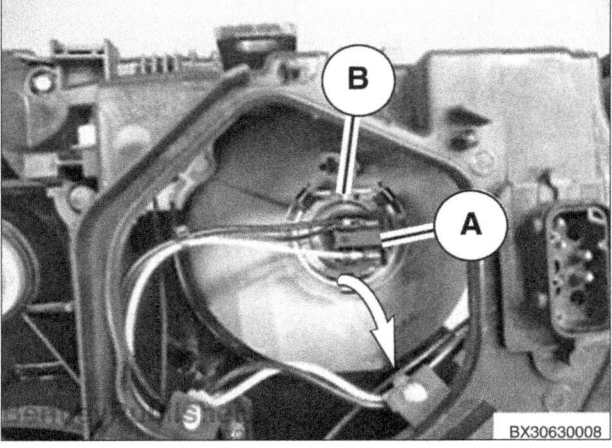

BX30630008

Xenon headlight bulb and ignition unit, replacing

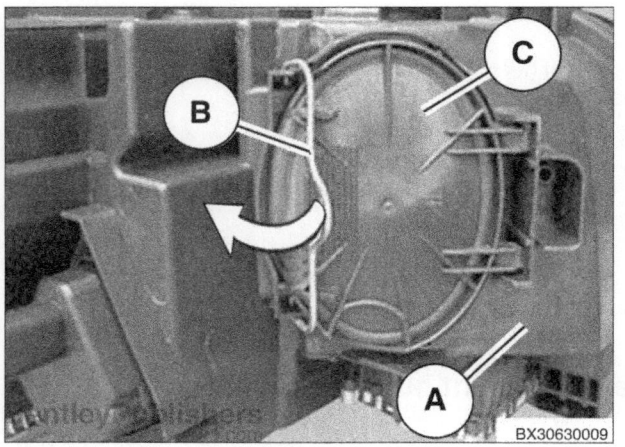

BX30630009

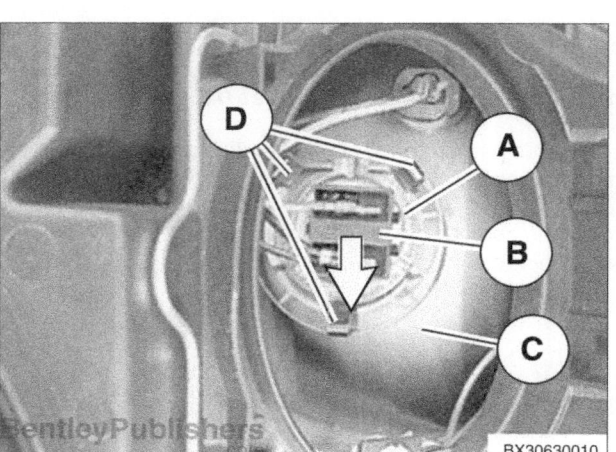

BX30630010

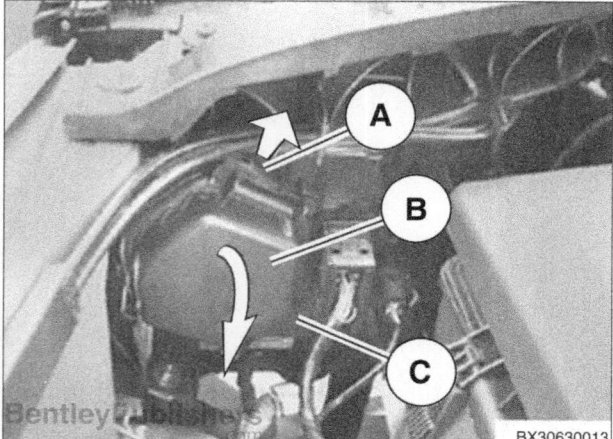

BX30630013

High beam

– High beam bulb is halogen and replacement is similar for both halogen and xenon equipped vehicles.

> **WARNING—**
> • *Danger to life due to high voltage! Disconnect all Xenon headlight components from power supply before servicing headlights.*

– For driver's side headlight, partially remove air filter housing. See **020 Maintenance**.

– For passenger side headlight, partially remove windshield washer reservoir. See **611 Wipers and washers.**

◀ Working in engine compartment behind headlight (**A**), unclip (**B**) plastic bulb cover (**C**) in direction of arrow.

◀ Unclip bulb (**A**) by pressing connector (**B**). Disconnect bulb at plug and remove in direction of arrow from headlight (**C**).

– Installation is reverse of removal making sure that bulb is fully seated in catches (**D**) on headlight.

> **NOTE—**
> • *Do not touch bulb surface with bare finger. Grease from skin can cause bulb to fail prematurely.*

Xenon headlight bulb and ignition unit, replacing

Vehicles equipped with the optional Xenon headlights utilize a special high voltage bulb and control unit for the low beam headlights. High beam bulbs are still conventional Halogens and removal is shown above.

> **WARNING—**
> • *Danger to life due to high voltage! Disconnect all Xenon headlight components from power supply before removing*

– For driver's side headlight, partially remove air filter housing. See **020 Maintenance**.

– For passenger side headlight, partially remove windshield washer reservoir. See **611 Wipers and Washers**.

2004 - 2006 (pre-LCI) vehicle

◀ Working in engine compartment behind headlight, unlock catch (**A**) in direction of **arrow** and remove cover (**B**) in direction of **arrow** from headlight (**C**).

Xenon headlight bulb and ignition unit, replacing

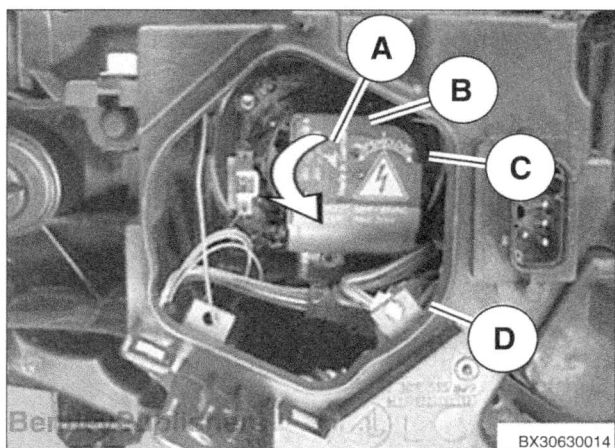

◄ Rotate ignition unit (**A**) for xenon headlight approximately 30º counter-clockwise and detach from headlight (**C**). Xenon bulb plug connection (**B**) is released automatically while turing ignition unit (**A**).

– Feed ignition unt (**A**) out of headlight opening (**D**) and remove.

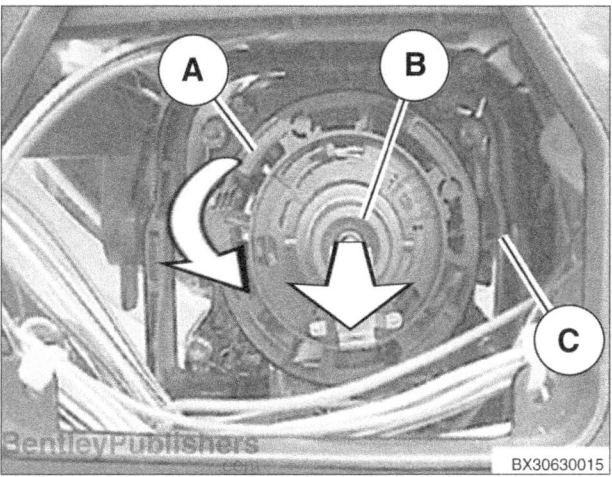

◄ Working at the back of the headlight housing inside opening.

• Rotate bulb retaining collar (**A**) counter-clockwise in direction of **arrow**. Pull xenon bulb (**B**) out of reflector (**C**) and replace. Do not touch bulb surface with bare finger. Grease from skin can cause bulb to fail prematurely.

– Installation is reverse of removal. Be sure that bulb is fully seated in headlight.

2007 - 2010 (LCI) vehicle

NOTE —

• *Xenon ignition unit and bulb are an assembly and should not be separated.*

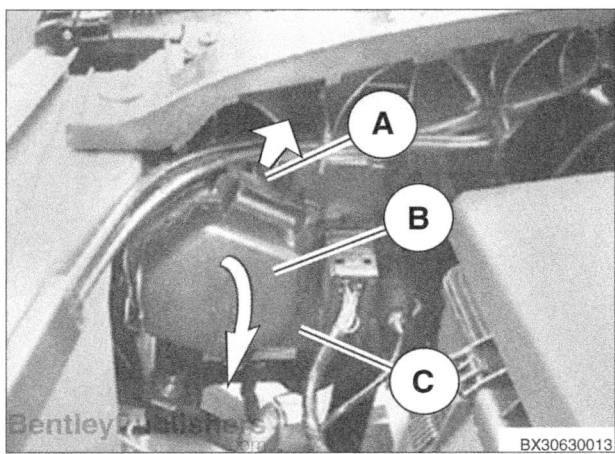

◄ Working in engine compartment behind headlight, unlock catch (**A**) in direction of **arrow** and remove cover (**B**) in direction of **arrow** from headlight housing (**C**).

630

Headlight assembly, removing and installing

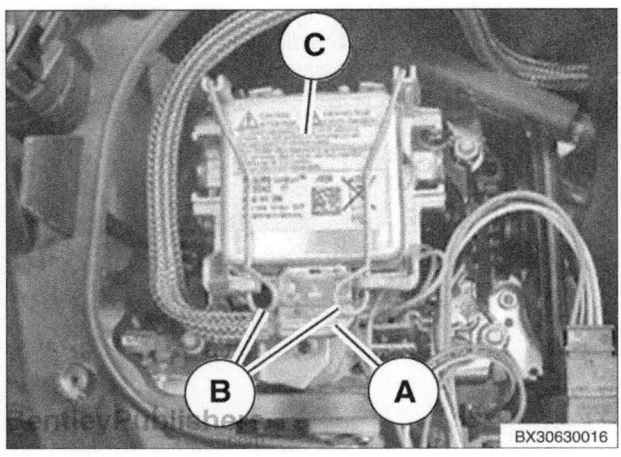

◄ Working at back of headlight housing inside opening, disconnect electrical connector (**A**) from ignition unit and bulb assembly.

— Unhook wire spring clips (**B**) to release ignition unit and bulb assembly (**C**) and remove from headlight housing. Do not touch bulb surface with bare finger. Grease from skin can cause bulb to fail prematurely.

— Installation is reverse of removal making sure that ignition unit and bulb assembly is fully seated in headlight.

Headlight assembly, removing and installing

Removal is similar for both driver and passenger Halogen and AHL headlights.

◄ Open engine hood:
• Remove front bumper See **510 Exterior Trim, Bumpers**.

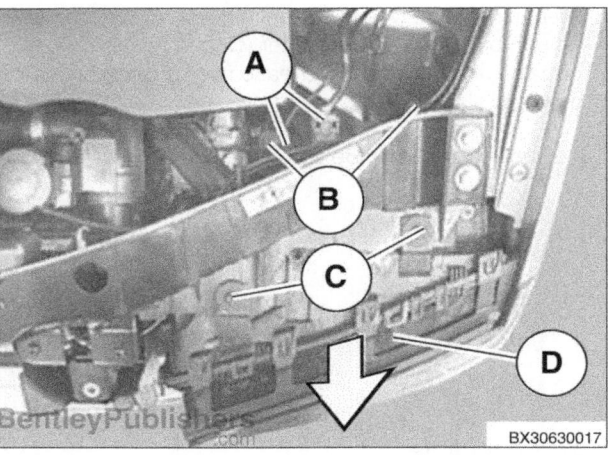

— Unplug headlight connectors (**A**). Working behind headlight remove fasteners (**B**).

— Remove fasteners (**C**) and slide headlight (**D**) in direction of arrow to remove from bracket.

— Installation is reverse of removal. Remember to:
• Set front headlight cover flush with engine hood and fender before tightening fasteners. Make sure that headlight is seated in bracket.
• Adjust headlight aim if necessary. See **Headlight aim, adjusting** in this repair group.

EXTERIOR LIGHTS

Front turn signal bulb, replacing

— Headlight removed for clarity.

◄ Working at back of headlight assembly near fender, remove turn signal bulb holder (**A**) counter-clockwise in direction of **arrow** from headlight (**B**).

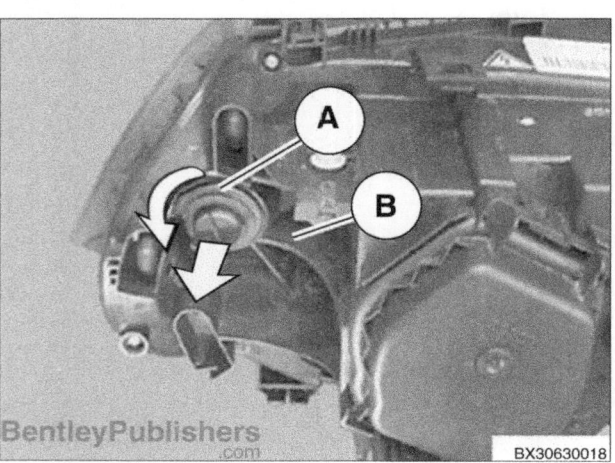

Side turn signal bulb, replacing

2004 - 2006 (Pre-LCI) vehicle

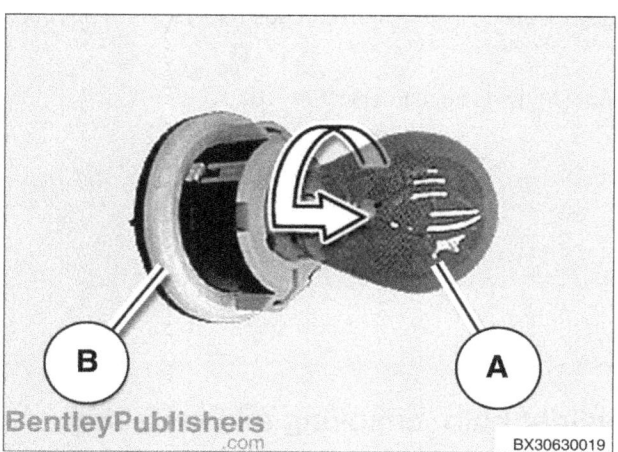

— With turn signal bulb and socket removed from headlight.

◄ Unscrew turn signal bulb from socket in direction of **arrow.**

2007 -2010 (LCI) vehicle

— With turn signal bulb and socket removed from headlight.

◄ Turn bulb in direction of **arrow** to unlock from socket (**A**) and remove.

— Installation: be sure that sealing ring (**C**) is correctly seated when reinstalling bulb holder (**B**).

Side turn signal bulb, replacing

◄ Remove side turn indicator light by sliding it forward and lifting out.

— Disconnect electrical harness.

— Rotate bulb socket and remove. Replace bulb.

— Installation is reverse of removal.

630

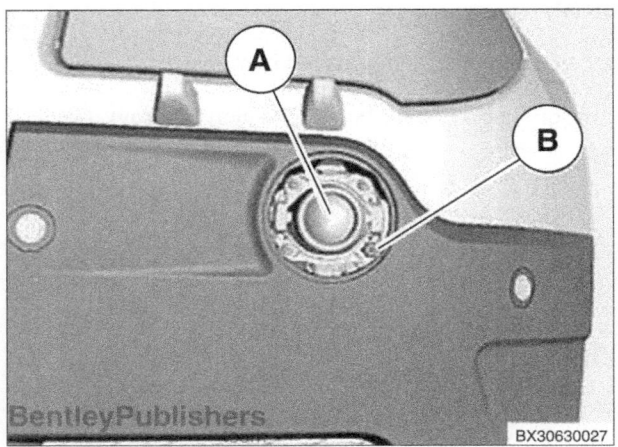

Front foglight aim, adjusting

– Remove foglight plastic trim ring from bumper. Use fingers to pull out trim ring.

◀ Adjust foglight (**A**) using adjustment screw (**B**).

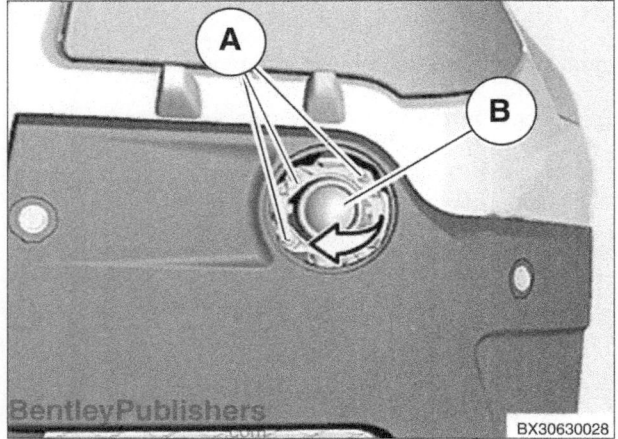

Front foglight bulb, removing and installing

– Remove foglight plastic trim ring from bumper. Use fingers to pull out trim ring.

◀ Remove foglight mounting screws (**arrows**) and slide assembly forward out of bumper.

– Detach electrical connector from rear of housing. Remove housing rear cover.

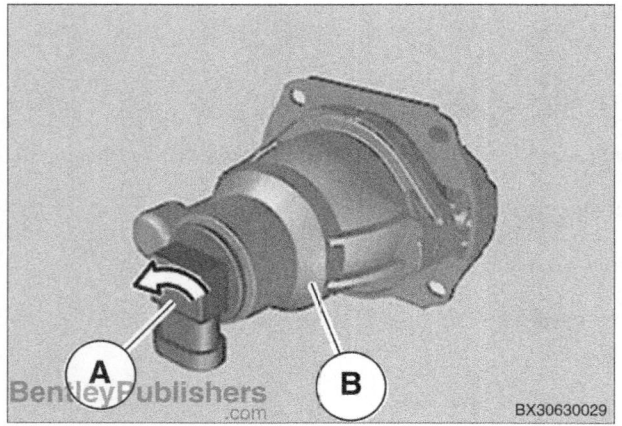

◀ Turn bulb in direction of **arrow** and remove from fog light.

– Replace bulb. Do not touch bulb surface with bare finger. Grease from skin can cause bulb to fail prematurely.

Pre-LCI taillight components

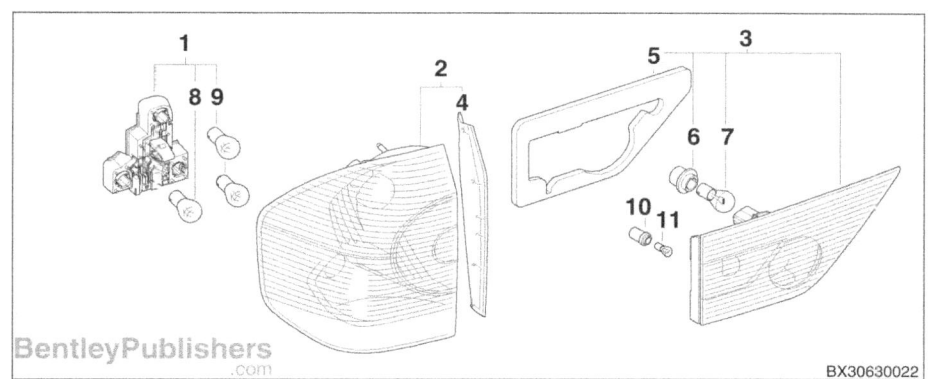

1. Bulb socket assembly
2. Taillight assembly
3. Tailgate light assembly
4. Taillight side panel seal
5. Tailgate light weather seal
6. Bulb socket
7. Marker bulb
   • 12v 21 w
8. Brake light bulb
   • 12 v 21 w
9. Directional light bulb
   • 12 v 21 w
10. Bulb socket
11. Reverse light bulb
    • 12 v 16 w

LCI taillight components

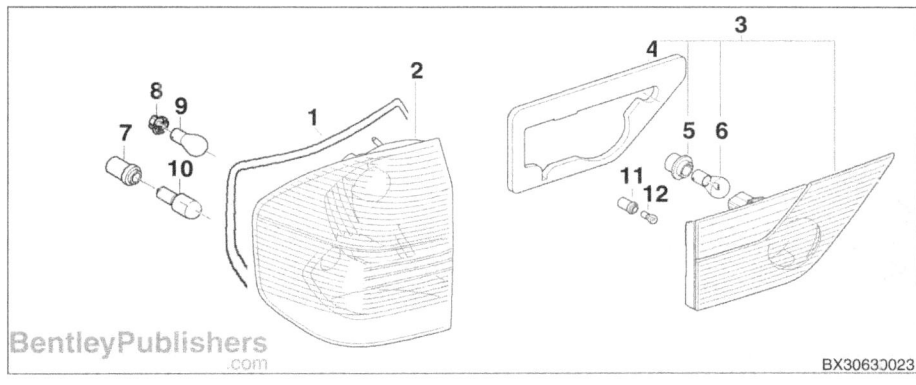

1. Taillight seal
2. LED Taillight assembly
3. Tailgate light assembly
4. Tailgate light weather seal
5. Bulb socket
6. Running light bulb
   • 12 v 21 w
7. Bulb socket
8. Bulb socket
9. Turn signal bulb
   • 12 v 21 w
10. Marker bulb
    • 12 v 16 w
11. Bulb socket
12. Reverse light
    • 12 v 16 w

630

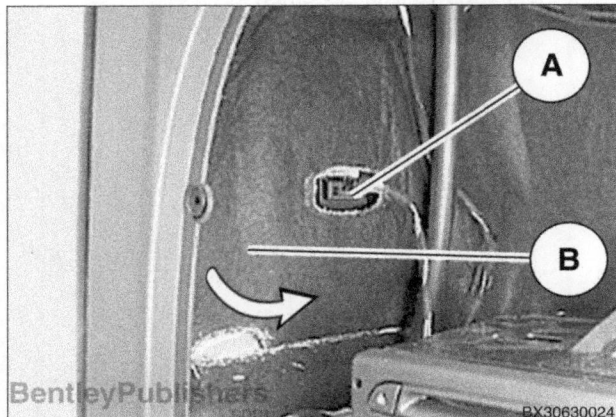

Taillight bulb, replacing

2004 - 2006 (pre-LCl) vehicle

Bulbs are mounted in a socket housing.

– Open tailgate and remove left or right side trim panel. See **513 Interior Trim**.

◀ Working inside the trim panel area unplug electrical connector for taillights (**A**).

– Pull back insulation (**B**) in direction of **arrow.**

◀ Unlock catch (**A**) and remove socket assembly (**B**) in direction of **arrow.**

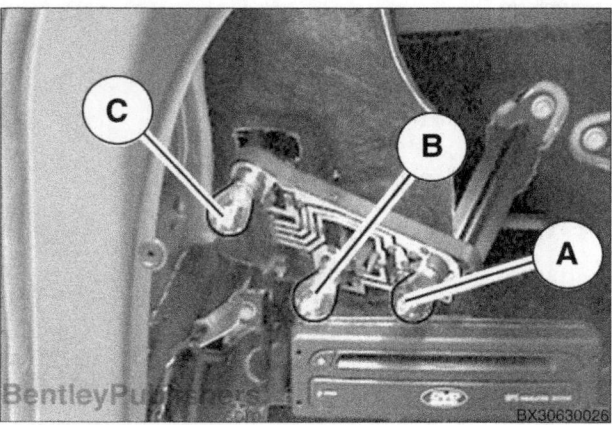

◀ Twist taillight bulbs as needed to remove from socket assembly:
- **A** Turn signal
- **B** Taillight/brake light
- **C** Taillight

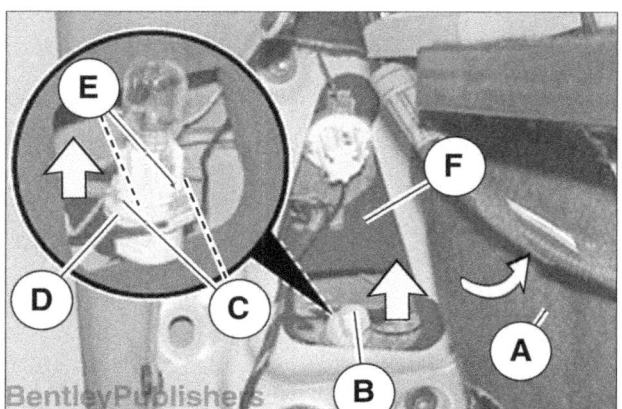

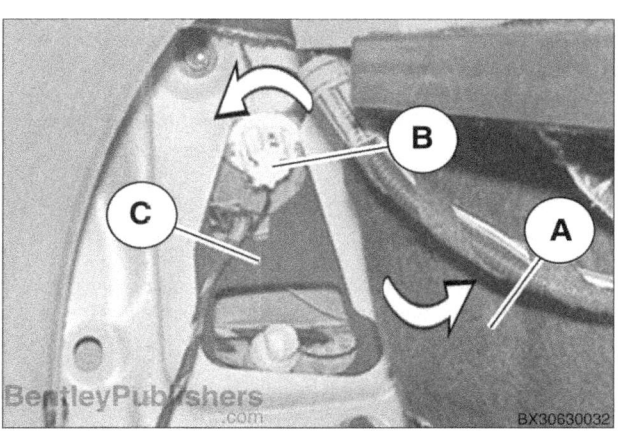

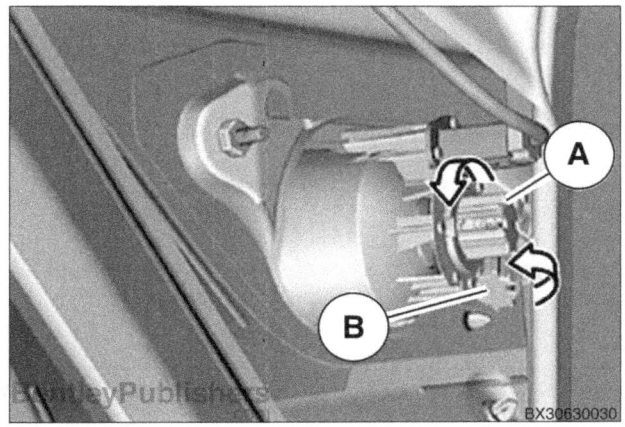

2007 - 2010 (LCI) vehicle

Brake light bulb, replacing

– Open tailgate and remove left or right side trim panel. See **513 Interior Trim**.

◄ Pull back insulation (**B**) in direction of **arrow.**

– Brake light bulb socket (**B**) is held by retaining lugs (**C**) on taillight housing (**F**). Unclip socket (**B**) from taillight (**F**) in direction of **arrow.**

– Working with socket (**B**) press in retaining lugs (**E**) to remove retaining ring (**D**) in direction of **arrow** to remove brake light bulb.

– Installation is reverse of removal making sure that socket is seated in rear light correctly.

Turn signal bulb, replacing

◄ Pull back insulation (**A**) in direction of **arrow.**

– Turn socket (**B**) for turn signal bulb in direction of **arrow** to remove from taillight housing (**C**) and remove bulb.

– Installation is reverse of removal making sure that socket is seated in rear light correctly.

Taillight bulbs, tailgate

2004 - 2006 (pre-LCI) vehicle

– Remove trim panel from inside tailgate. See **513 Interior Trim**.

◄ Twist bulb socket (**A**) and remove bulb.

– Replace bulb and install in reverse order of removal.

630

Taillight assembly, removing and installing

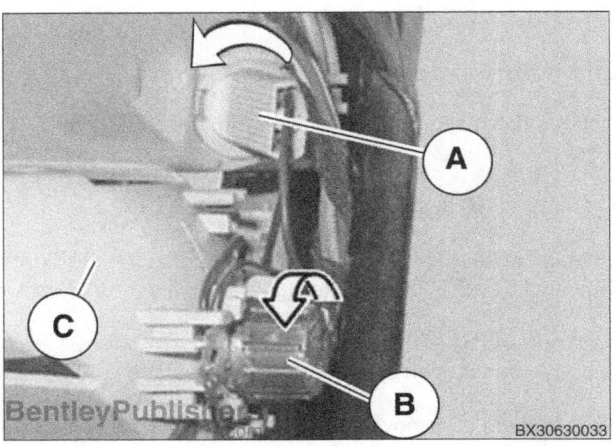

◄ Twist sockets (**A**) and (**B**) as needed in direction of arrows to remove from tailgate light (**C**).

– Replace taillight or rear fog light bulb as needed.

– Installation is reverse of removal making sure that socket is seated in rear light correctly.

Taillight assembly, removing and installing

2004 - 2006 (pre-LCI) vehicle

– Open upper and lower tailgate and remove left or right side trim panel. See **513 Interior Trim**.

– Remove socket assembly. See **Tail light bulb, replacing** in this repair group.

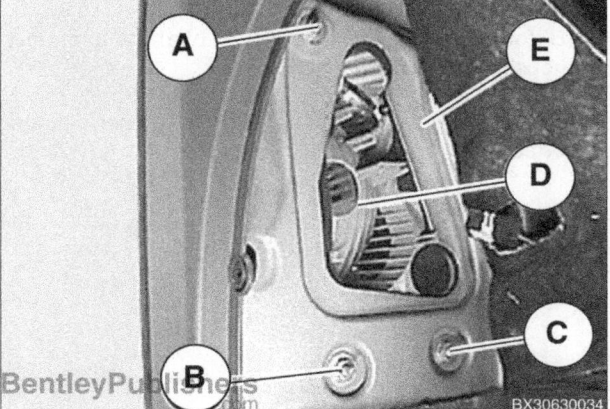

◄ Remove taillight assembly mounting fasteners (**A**)(**B**)(**C**) to remove taillight (**D**) from body (**E**).

– Installation: tighten fasteners in order A-B-C. Make sure light is correctly seated into body with sealing washers and weather-stripping.

2007 - 2010 (LCI) vehicle

– Open upper and lower tailgate and remove left or right side trim panel. See **513 Interior Trim**.

– Remove socket assembly see **Tail light bulb replacing** in this repair group. Fold back insulation (**E**).

– Disconnect electrical connector (**D**)

◄ Remove taillight assembly mounting fasteners (**A**)(**B**)(**C**) while gripping ends of threaded pins (**F**). Remove taillight from body.

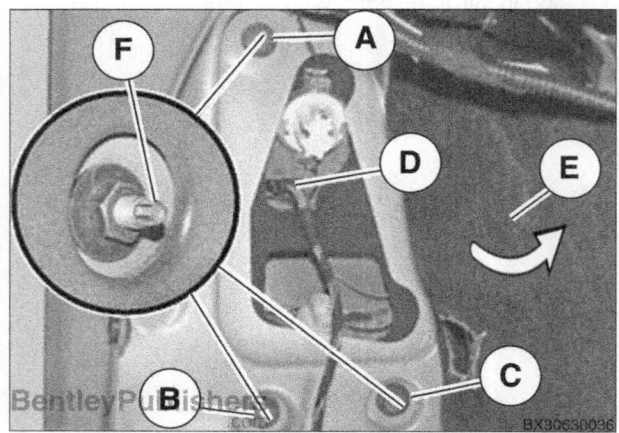

– Installation: tighten fasteners in order of A-B-C: Make sure light is correctly seated into body with sealing washers and weather-stripping.

Tightening torque	
Taillight to body	4 NM (2.9 ft lb)

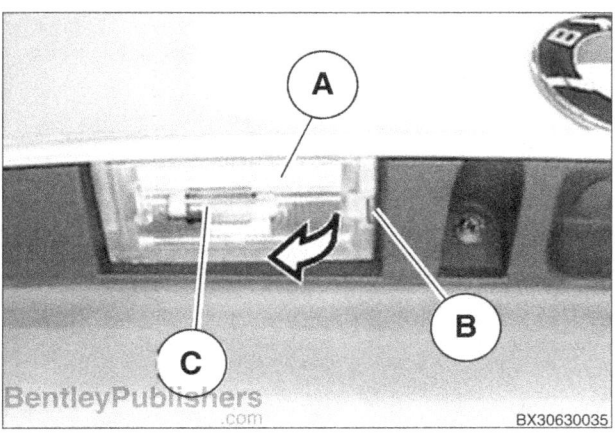

License plate light bulb, replacing

◀ Use small screwdriver in opening (**B**) to carefully pry out license plate light cover (**A**).

– Carefully remove license plate light bulb (**C**) and replace bulb.

– Installation is reverse of removal.

Center brake light, replacing

Center brake light is an LED assembly with no replaceable bulbs.

– Remove rear spciler. See **510 Exterior Trim, Bumpers**.

◀ Working with the rear spoiler off of the vehicle remove fasteners (**A**).

– Slide loose center brake light assembly (**C**) slightly out of rear spoiler.

– Installation: Make sure rear window washer hose (**B**) is seated correctly.

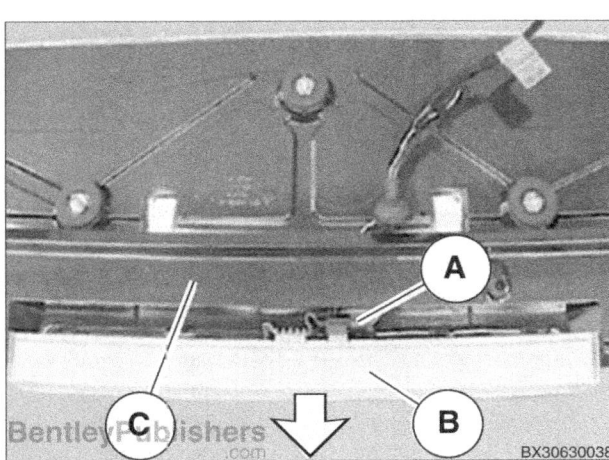

◀ Disconnect electrical connection (**A**) and remove center brake light (**B**) from rear spoiler (**C**) in direction of **arrow.**

630

INTERIOR LIGHTS

The general module 5 redesign (GM5RD) controls interior lighting automatically using input from several monitors. The lighting can also be manually controlled.

Each door lock actuator contains a Hall effect sensor to monitor door open or closed status. The sensor is activated by the position of the door lock rotary latch plate:

• **Door closed**: Current flow through Hall sensor < 5 mA.

• **Door open**: Current flow through Hall sensor > 12 mA.

A change in Hall sensor current flow informs the GM5RD when a door is opened or closed.

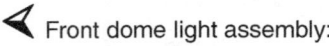

Front dome light assembly:

1. Front center interior light switch
   • Manual signal to GM5RD to switch interior light ON-OFF.
   • Workshop mode switch.
2. Right front map light switch
3. Left front map light switch
4. Left front map light
5. Interior light
6. Right front map light

The front and rear interior lights and door-mounted courtesy lights are switched ON by the GM5RD when a door is opened or by pressing the interior light switch (**1**) located on the front dome light assembly. The switch provides a momentary ground signal that the GM5RD recognizes as a request to switch the lights ON or OFF.

Interior light automatic controls

The GM5RD automatically switches the interior lighting circuit ON under the following conditions:

• Door contact Hall sensor active (door open)

• Ignition switched OFF after exterior lights are switched OFF

• Crash signal from airbag control module

• *Unlock* request received from driver door key lock Hall sensor (ignition switch OFF)

• *Unlock* request from FZV keyless entry system received via K- bus (ignition switch OFF)

• Lock button of remote key pressed with vehicle already locked (interior search function)

The GM5RD automatically switches the interior lighting circuit OFF under the following conditions:

• All doors closed with ignition ON

• After 20 seconds with all doors closed and ignition OFF

• 20 seconds after switching ignition OFF with lights OFF

• 8 seconds after keyless entry lock activation

• After 16 minutes with doors open (consumer cutoff function)

• Door locked

Interior light bulbs, removing and installing

Front dome light bulbs

◄ Use plastic prying tool at **arrows** to remove front dome light assembly.

— Disconnect harness connector.

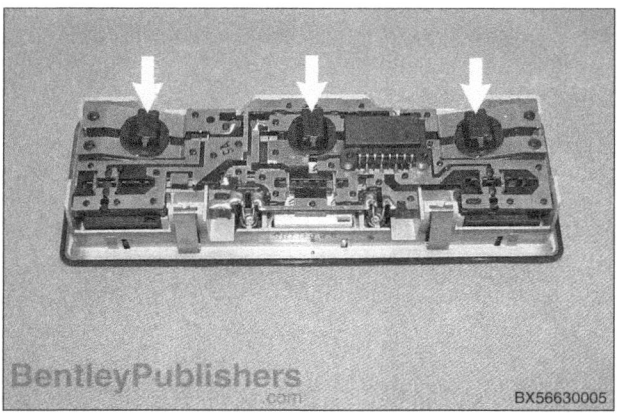

◄ Twist bulb holders (**arrows**) to remove. Replace bulbs as necessary.

— Installation is reverse of removal.

Mirror vanity light bulbs

◄ Use a suitable plastic prying to remove vanity mirror light lens (**A**).

— Replace bulbs as necessary.

— Installation is reverse of removal.

630

Interior light bulbs, removing and installing

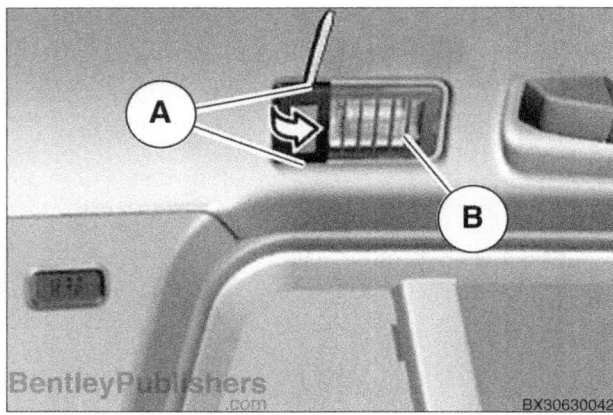
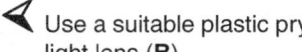

Rear dome light bulbs

◄ Use a suitable plastic prying tool at points (**A**) to remove rear dome light lens (**B**).

– Replace bulbs as necessary.

– Installation is reverse of removal.

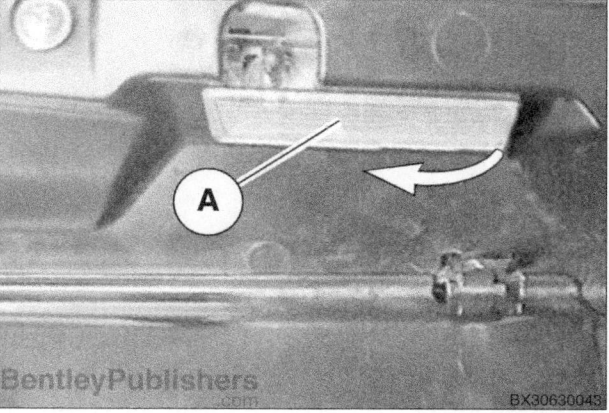

Glove box light bulb

◄ Use a suitable plastic prying tool to remove glove box light lens (**A**).

– Replace bulbs as necessary.

– Installation is reverse of removal.

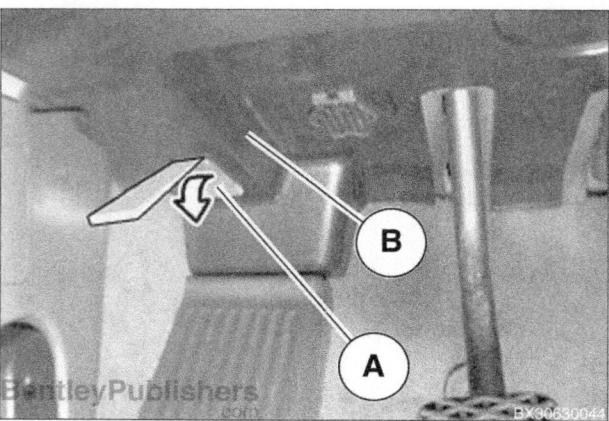

Driver's footwell light bulb

◄ Use a suitable plastic prying tool to remove footwell light (**A**) out of pedal assembly trim (**B**).

– Replace bulbs as necessary

– Installation is reverse of removal.

Interior light bulbs, removing and installing

Footwell light bulb

◀ Use a suitable plastic prying tool (**A**) to remove footwell light lens (**B**) out of holder (**C**).

– If necessary disconnect electrical connection (**D**) and replace bulb.

– Installation is reverse of removal.

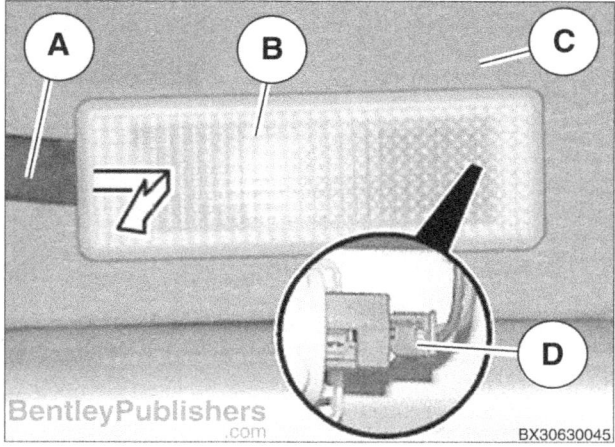

Door courtesy light bulb

◀ Working at bottom of door trim panel, use a suitable plastic prying tool (**A**) to remove courtesy light (**B**) from door panel (**C**).

– If necessary disconnect electrical connection (**D**) and replace bulb.

– Installation is reverse of removal.

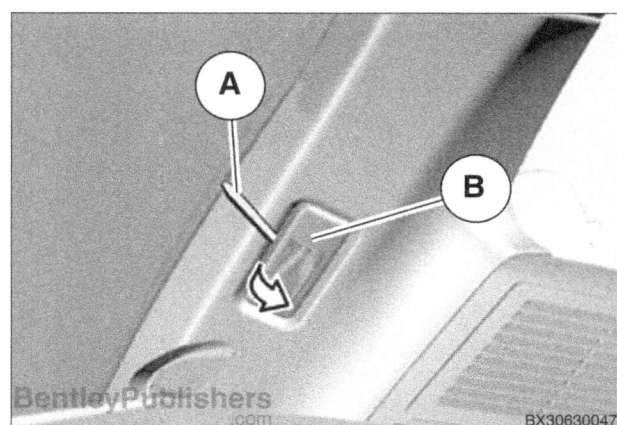

D-pillar light bulb replacing

◀ Use a suitable plastic prying tool (**A**) to remove footwell light (**B**) out of D-pillar trim.

– Replace bulb.

– Installation is reverse of removal.

630

Interior light bulbs, removing and installing

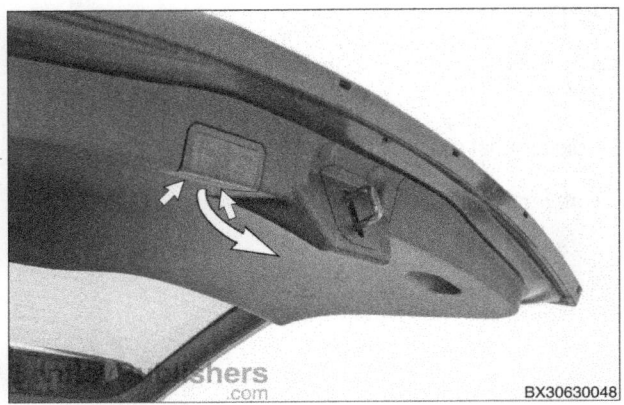

BX30630048

Rear hatch bulb, replacing

◄ Use a suitable plastic prying tool at **arrows** to remove footwell light out of tailgate trim.

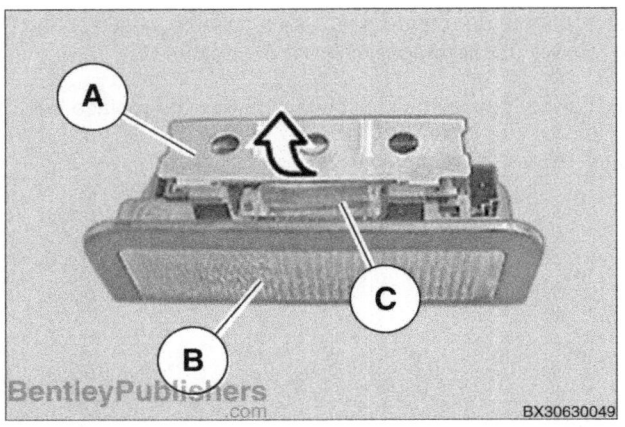

BX30630049

◄ Fold up cover (**A**) on luggage compartment light (**B**). Replace bulb (**C**).

– Installation is reverse of removal.

640 Heating and Air-conditioning

GENERAL

This repair group covers heating and air-conditioning operation and component replacement.

Many of the procedures given in this group require evacuation and recharging of A/C refrigerant using special equipment. Follow the equipment manufacturer's instructions during A/C system service.

See also:

- **020 Maintenance** for fresh air microfilter service.
- **170 Radiator and Cooling System** for cooling system service and electric cooling fan removal and installation.

A/C system fluids

The air-conditioning refrigerant is R134a, known chemically as *tetrachloroethane*. Strict regulations govern the handling and disposal of automotive refrigerants. Be sure to read **Warnings and Cautions** in this repair group if working with A/C and heating components.

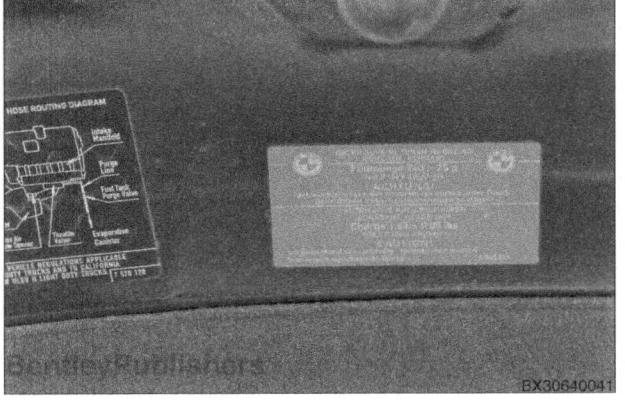

◄ A sticker on the engine hood gives the manufacturer's recommendation for refrigerant capacity.

A synthetic oil, *polyalkylene glycol* (PAG), is used to lubricate the A/C compressor. This type of oil is highly hygroscopic (attracts water). Be sure to immediately reseal an opened container after use.

BX30640041

640

Warnings and Cautions

> **WARNING—**
> - *Do not discharge or charge the A/C system without proper equipment and training. Damage to the vehicle and personal injury may result.*
> - *Wear hand and eye protection (gloves and goggles) when working around the A/C system.*
> - *If refrigerant come in contact with your skin or eyes:*
>   -*Do not rub skin or eyes.*
>   -*Immediately flush skin or eyes with cool water for 15 minutes.*
>   -*Rush to a doctor or hospital.*
>   -*Do not attempt to treat yourself.*
> - *Work in a well ventilated area. Switch on exhaust / ventilation systems when working on the refrigerant system.*
> - *Do not expose any component of the A/C system to high temperatures (above 80°C or 176°F) or open flames. Excessive heat causes a pressure increase which could burst the system.*
> - *Keep refrigerant away from open flames. Poisonous gas is produced if it burns. Do not smoke near refrigerant gases for the same reason.*
> - *The A/C system is filled with refrigerant gas which is under pressure. Pressurized refrigerant in the presence of oxygen may form a combustible mixture. Do not introduce compressed air into any refrigerant container (full or empty).*
> - *Electric welding near refrigerant hoses causes R-134a to decompose. Discharge system before welding.*
> - *At normal operating temperature the cooling system is pressurized. Allow the system to cool as long as possible before opening (a minimum of one hour), then release the cap slowly to allow safe release of pressure.*

> **CAUTION—**
> - *In the United States, any person who services a motor vehicle air-conditioner must, by law, be properly trained and certified, and use approved refrigerant recycling equipment. Technicians must complete an EPA-approved recycling course to be certified.*
> - *State and local governments may have additional requirements regarding air-conditioning servicing. Comply with state and local laws.*
> - *Do not top off a partially charged refrigerant system. Discharge system, evacuate and then recharge system.*
> - *The mixture of refrigerant oil (PAG oil) and refrigerant R-134a attacks some metals and alloys (for example, copper) and breaks down certain hose materials. Use only hoses and lines that are identified with a green mark (stripe) or marked with R-134a.*
> - *Immediately plug open connections on A/C components and lines to prevent dirt and moisture contamination.*
> - *Do not steam clean the A/C condenser or evaporator. Use only cold water or compressed air.*
> - *To avoid damaging plastic interior trim, use a plastic prying tool or a screwdriver with the tip wrapped with masking tape.*

CLIMATE CONTROL SYSTEM

Integrated heating and cooling system (IHKA)

X3 integrated automatic climate control system (IHKA) includes the following:

• Single heater core for temperature regulation.

• Maximum heating and cooling for defroster functions.

• Rear window defogger operation integrated into the heating / cooling system.

• Blower controlled through a final stage variable resistor.

• Road speed dependent air distribution and fresh air volume.

• Self-calibrating air distribution stepper motors.

• Fresh air microfilter system.

• Electronically regulated A/C compressor.

• Heater control personalization via car memory / key memory.

IHKA control panel and module functions

 Heating and air conditioning functions are programmed via the center console mounted control panel. The control panel has large, easy to use soft-touch controls and an LED display.

1. Air vent manual control (windshield, face level, foot level).

2. Interior air temperature sensor intake, driver side (small blower fan continuously draws interior air over temperature sensor).

3. Temperature control up or down.

4. Automatic operation assures that set temperature is reached as quickly as possible and then maintained using cooling or heating and air vent control as needed. Cooling function (A/C) is automatically activated in this mode.

5. LCD display panel, displays automatic blower speed mode, AUTO mode and actual blower speed, indicated numerically and by number of bars displayed. Also displays set temperature and current temperature.

6. Recirculation / automatic recirculation. Toggles system between fresh / recirculated air flap activation and automatic recirculation control (AUC). AUC system incorporates a sensor in the engine compartment that reacts to high levels exterior air pollution. When levels exceed set value stored in IHKA control module, system switches automatically to recirculation.

7. The blower rocker switch on the IHKA control panel is the master switch for the entire system. Selecting slower fan speeds eventually results in the following:
   • Blower motor OFF
   • All air distribution valves closed
   • LED and LCD displays OA/C compressor OFF.

8. Interior air temperature sensor intake, passenger side (small blower fan continuously draws interior air over temperature sensor).

9. Windshield defroster. Maximum windshield defrost overrides other distribution settings (also switches on cooling function A/C).

10. Cooling function control button (A/C). Turns Air conditioning on and off manually.

11. Rear window defroster.

BX30640003

640

IHKA control module

IHKA control module, integral with the front panel, includes an EEPROM chip for storage of diagnostic trouble codes (DTCs). Inputs to the module include:

- Heater core temperature sensor.
- A/C evaporator temperature sensor.
- Other programmed functions from Car Memory (such as rear window defrost timing).

The module can go into "sleep mode" to reduce power consumption when the ignition is switched OFF but still retain control panel settings and DTC information. If the control module is replaced, program and recode new unit using BMW diagnostic can tool.

Heat regulation

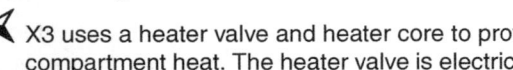

Heater valve

BX30640042

X3 uses a heater valve and heater core to provide passenger compartment heat. The heater valve is electrically pulsed to control the flow of coolant through the heater core.

Temperature regulation is based on the following inputs:

- Temperature control switch setting
- Interior temperature sensor signal
- Ambient temperature signal
- Heater core temperature sensor signal
- Evaporator temperature signal
- Solar sensor input (if applicable)

A rocker switch is used to select the desired cabin temperature, shown in the display matrix of the control panel. The range for temperature display is from 15° to 32°C (60° to 90°F). Even in the lowest setting, the interior temperature sensor continues to operate and the IHKA control panel continues to signal the heater valve for heat.

Regulated A/C compressor

The operation of the A/C compressor is regulated, eliminating noticeable on / off cycling. In order to reduce fuel consumption and improve vehicle performance, the system default is with the compressor OFF.

The A/C system uses a variable displacement compressor. The swash plate of the compressor is hinged so that is can vary piston travel based on output requirements of the system.

A/C compressor function is controlled by the Engine Control Module (ECM) based on inputs from the IHKA control panel. Pressing the "snowflake" button requests A/C activation. As long as the evaporator temperature is above 2°C (36°F), the IHKA signals the ECM to activate the compressor.

The IHKA control module sends the following signals to the ECM over the K-bus and CAN-bus via the instrument cluster:

- Request for A/C activation
- Load torque for switching the compressor
- Requested cooling fan speed

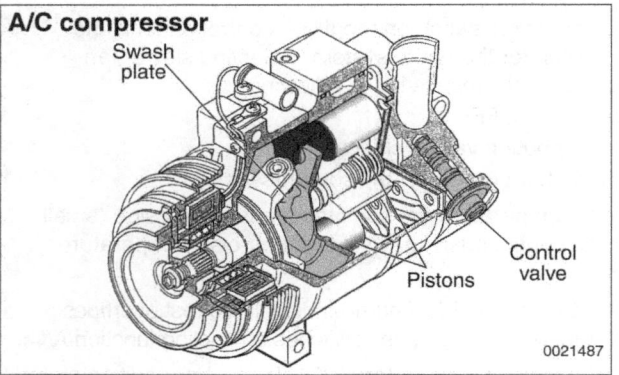

A/C compressor

Swash plate

Pistons

Control valve

0021487

The IHKA determines the load torque for compressor activation and required engine cooling fan speed from the pressure sensor mounted on the receiver-dryer. The pressure sensor provides a linear voltage input signal (0 - 5 volts) to the IHKA control module. The module processes this signal and determines the load torque of the system (0 - 30 Nm). The higher the pressure in the system, the higher the voltage input signal to the IHKA module. The output signal to the ECM enables the ECM to modify the idle speed, timing and fuel injection amount based on the load that is imposed when the compressor is activated.

Regulated engine cooling fan operation

◄ X3 models use an electric cooling fan mounted on the engine side of the radiator. Two versions of cooling fans are used, one for automatic transmission vehicles, and one for manual transmission vehicles. See **170 Radiator and Cooling System** for further details.

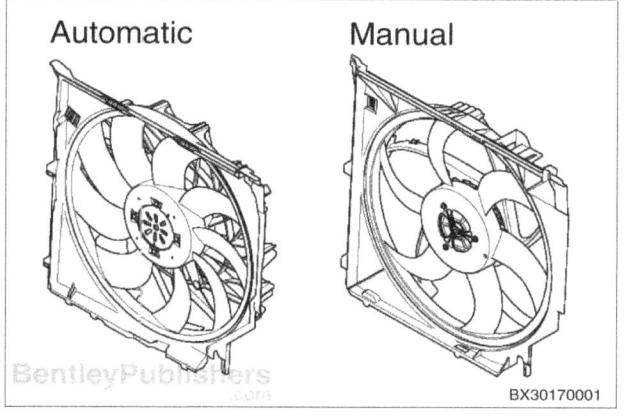

Automatic   Manual

BX30170001

IHKA air distribution control

◄ The IHKA system is equipped with stepper motors that control air distribution flaps. The motors are controlled by the IHKA control module via M-bus.

Air distribution stepper motors use a 4 pin connection with the IHKA control unit. Stepper motors are switched in series on the M-bus. Stepper motors are all identical. Each stepper motor is assigned a specific address: face level vents, defrost, etc. This unique address also allows the IHKA control unit to receive fault messages from and identify the faulty stepper motor. Where the stepper motors are plugged into the wiring harness determines it's assigned address. When replacing stepper motors only replace one at a time to avoid mixing up the stepper motor harness location.

Air distribution stepper motors must be re-addressed after replacement using a BMW diagnostic scan tool.

Air distribution motors

1. Face vent
2. Defrost
3. Footwell
4. Recirculation
5. Fresh air

0022835

640

IHKA control panel and module functions

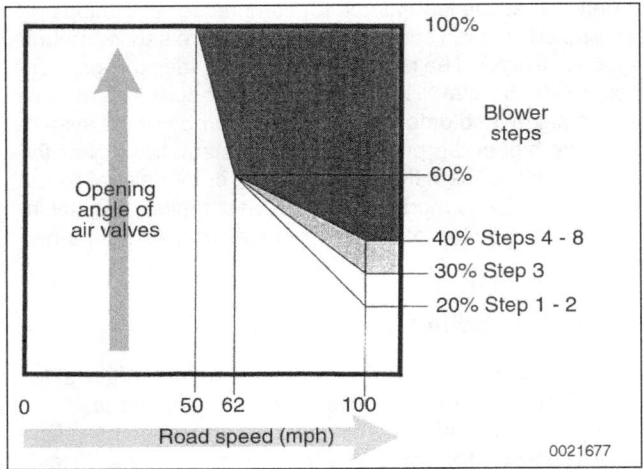

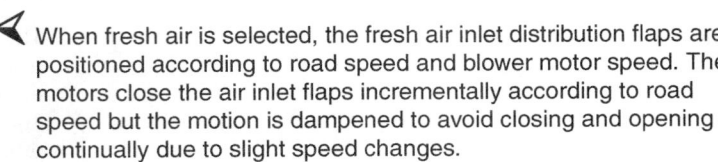 When fresh air is selected, the fresh air inlet distribution flaps are positioned according to road speed and blower motor speed. The motors close the air inlet flaps incrementally according to road speed but the motion is dampened to avoid closing and opening continually due to slight speed changes.

Automatic air recirculation

 Automatic recirculation control is available. This system uses an air quality sensor (**AUC**), located at the top right corner of the radiator, to detect high levels of air pollution and automatically switch the IHKA to recirculation of interior air. The recirculation button on the IHKA control panel can be toggled to allow automatic, manual or no recirculation.

Once recirculation is turned on, it runs until it is turned off using the button. Once the ignition is turned off, the recirculation setting is saved for 15 minutes, after which the IHKA system reverts to fresh air mode. This feature can be over-ridden using the car memory feature, so that recirculating interior air is automatically selected on engine start-up.

IHKA personalization

Car memory / key memory allows various functions and features of IHKA control to be tailored to the driver's wishes. IHKA functions that can be programmed using a BMW diagnostic scan tool include:

• Automatic activation of recirculation when vehicle is started.

• Blower speed adjustment (8-speed blower).

• Automatic opening of ventilation flaps with warm coolant.

• Automatic closing of footwell flaps with A/C activation.

• Automatic closing of defroster flaps with A/C activation.

• Adjustments to set temperature.

• Automatic activation of compressor control when ignition is switched ON.

• Auto program for blower control when ignition is switched ON.

Cabin micro filter system

 X3 cabin microfilter is housed below the fresh air inlet at the rear of the engine compartment. Service by releasing three-quick release screws and removing a plastic cover. See **020 Maintenance.**

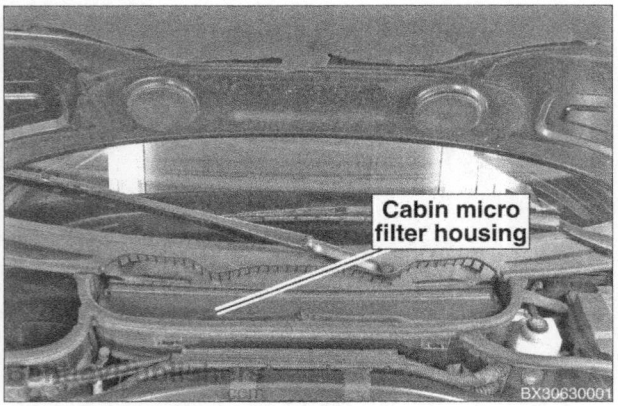

Rear window defogger

Electric rear window defogger switch is integrated in the IHKA control panel. Pressing the rear window defogger button activates the rear window heating element for about 17 minutes, although this can be changed through Car Memory. Pressing the button again activates a cycle of 40 seconds on / 80 seconds off for 5 minutes.

The defogger element in the rear glass is integrated with the radio antenna.

 Rear window defogger relay (**K13**) is on right side of cargo compartment behind the trim. see **ECL Electrical Component Locations.**

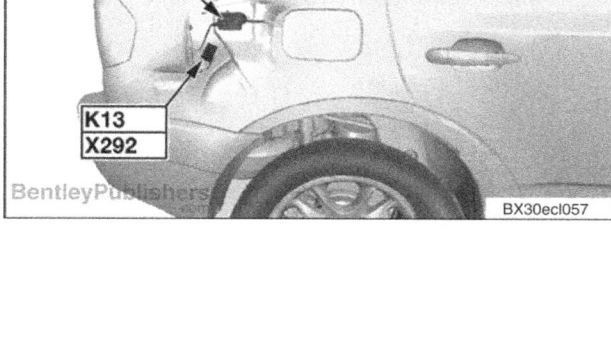

BX30ecl057

Solar sensor

The solar sensor relays data about the amount and intensity of solar heating to the IHKA control module. Climate control settings are changed to compensate for this additional influence.

 The solar sensor consists of a photoresistor installed in the right defroster outlet and a short harness.

The solar sensor receives power (5 volts) and ground from the IHKA control module. Voltage drop across the photoresistor increases as solar radiation increases. The control module calculates voltage drop across the photoresistor and determines the degree of solar heating based on the change in voltage. In response to the solar sensor signal, the IHKA module regulates interior climate settings using the following adaptations:

• Blower activation curve is changed.

• Opening angles of air distribution flaps are changed.

The control module processes the photoresistor input every 10 seconds and also checks it for plausibility based on mapped values. Values outside the limit indicate a malfunction and the solar sensor signal is ignored by the module. Troubleshoot solar sensor using a BMW diagnostic scan tool.

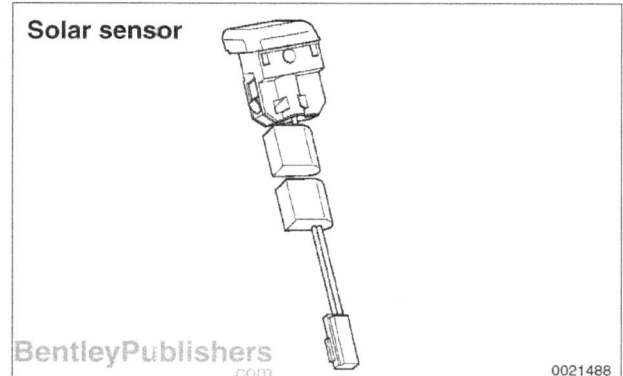

Solar sensor

0021488

640

Troubleshooting

Trouble with the heating and A/C system can be broken down into one or more of the following categories. Troubleshoot the IHKA system using a BMW diagnostic scan tool.

Mechanical problems

• Control panel malfunction
• Blower motor malfunction
• Noisy or seized compressor
• Noisy compressor clutch
• Malfunctioning belt

A/C belt replacement is covered in **020 Maintenance**.

Cooling system problems

• Coolant problems
• Cooling fan problems

Cooling system pressure testing and other diagnosis is covered in **170 Radiator and Cooling System**.

Refrigerant leak

Use diagnostic equipment to pinpoint refrigerant leaks. Replace leaky components or seals.

Odors

Mildew in the IHKA housing and in the evaporator fins can cause strong odors.

◄ Working under right side of dash, remove blower resistor pack (**arrow**). See **Blower resistor pack, replacing** in this repair group.

– Poke a spray wand through IHKA housing opening and spray commercially available cleaning agent on evaporator. Move wand back and forth to cover evaporator fins with liquid.

– Allow 5 minutes for liquid to drip through evaporator drain.

– Start car and run heater and A/C at maximum power for 5 minutes to dry out evaporator.

IHKA function problems

IHKA inputs and outputs are self-diagnosed. If a fault is detected, a diagnostic trouble code (DTC) is initially entered in IHKA control module RAM and then in EEPROM when the ignition is switched OFF, up to a maximum of six DTCs. The IHKA module is connected to the diagnostic link connector (DLC or OBD II) via the K-bus and instrument cluster. Access DTCs using a BMW diagnostic scan tool.

> **CAUTION—**
> • *When troubleshooting problems with the X3 IHKA, be sure to review car memory / key memory settings prior to condemning a component as faulty.*

Substitute value operation

If an input potentiometer, sensor or circuit fails or the signal from it is *not plausible*, the IHKA control module ignores the faulty signal and substitutes a programmed substitute value.

Table a. Substitute programmed values for IHKA component inputs

Input	Working range	Substitute value
Heat exchanger sensor	5° to 124°C (41° to 255°F)	55°C (131°F)
Evaporator sensor	-10° to 30°C (14° to 86°F)	0°C (32°F)
Interior temperature sensor	10° to 40°C (50° to 104°F)	20°C (68°F)
Exterior temperature		0°C (32°F)
Coolant temperature		100°C (212°F)
Specified temperature	16° to 32°C (61° to 90°F)	22°C (72°F)

NOTE—

• *The substitute value for the evaporator temperature sensor is below the A/C compressor cycling temperature (2°C / 34°F). If the evaporator temperature sensor signal is* not plausible, *the substitute value switches the A/C OFF.*

Table b lists resistance values and fault limits for IHKA temperature sensors.

Table b. Temperature sensor resistance values at 25°C (77°F)

Sensor	Resistance	Fault limit
Heater core	9 kΩ ± 2%	Temp > 125°C (257°F)
Evaporator	9 kΩ ± 2%	Temp > 120°C (248°F)
Interior	10 kΩ ± 2%	Temp ≤ −46°C (-51°F)

Table c lists A/C evaporator temperature-dependent resistance values.

Table c. A/C evaporator temperature sensor resistance values

Temperature °C (°F)	Resistance range kΩ
-5 (23)	11.7 - 11.9
0 (32)	8.8 - 9.2
5 (41)	6.8 - 7.2
10 (50)	5.3 - 5.6
15 (59)	4.2 - 4.5
20 (68)	3.3 - 3.6

640

Table c. A/C evaporator temperature sensor resistance values	
Temperature °C (°F)	Resistance range kΩ
25 (77)	2.6 - 2.9
30 (86)	2.1 - 2.3
35 (95)	1.7 - 1.9

lists A/C expansion valve pressure values.

Table d. Expansion valve pressure values	
Inlet pressure	14 bar (203 psi)
Outlet pressure	1.8 bar (26 psi)
Leak test with detector pressure	1 - 2 bar (14.5 - 29 psi)

CLIMATE CONTROL COMPONENTS

Climate control panel (IHKA), removing and installing

– Remove center dashboard fresh air grill see **513 Interior trim.**

– With ignition turned off, remove fuse F63 from fuse panel above glove box. See **ECL Electrical Component Locations.**

◄ Remove screws (**A**) from top of IHKA trim panel.

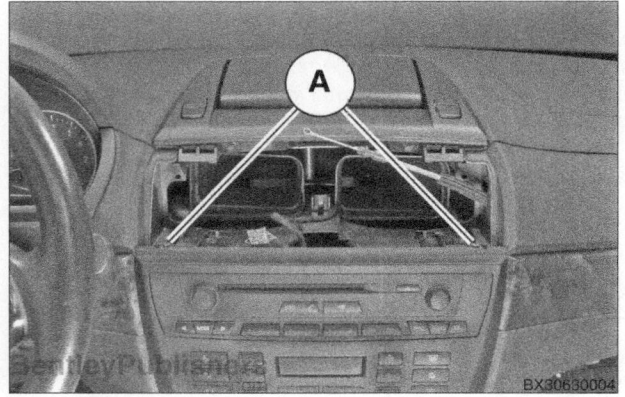

◄ Using a suitable plastic prying tool lift up from bottom of IHKA panel to release from retaining points.

– Disconnect plug connections and remove IHKA control panel.

– Installation is reverse of removal.

– Recode and program new IHKA control module using a BMW diagnostic scan tool.

NOTE—

• *Shifter assembly does not have to be removed for this procedure.*

Heater core temperature sensors, replacing

The heater core temperature sensor(s) are in the climate control housing above the heater core.

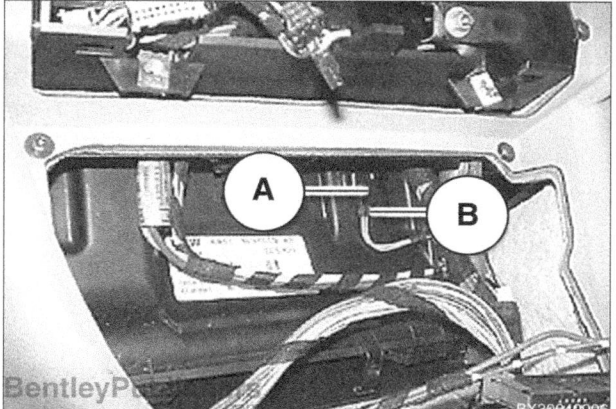

— Remove climate control panel. See **Climate control panel (IHKA), removing and installing** in this repair group.

— Remove switch unit in center console. See **612 Switches.**

◄ Remove temperature sensor (**A**) and disconnect electrical connection (**B**).

— Installation is reverse of removal.

Evaporator temperature sensor, replacing

The evaporator temperature sensor is under the left side of the dashboard on the side of the climate control housing.

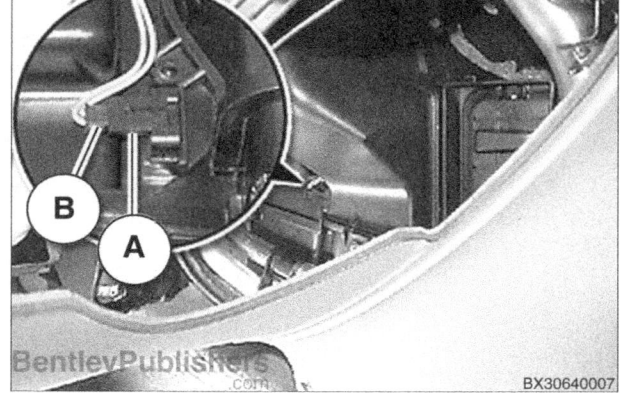

— Remove left lower dashboard trim above pedal assembly. See **513 Interior Trim.**

◄ Working at side of IHKA housing:

• Pull out evaporator temperature sensor (**A**) and disconnect electrical connection (**B**) to remove.

— Installation is reverse of removal; making sure sensor is seated correctly.

Air distribution stepper motors

The five air distribution motors are installed under the dashboard. They are made accessible by removing either the glove compartment and right footwell trim panel or the trim above pedal assembly and lower steering column cover as described below.

NOTE—

• Air distribution stepper motors must be re-addressed after replacement using a BMW diagnostic scan tool.

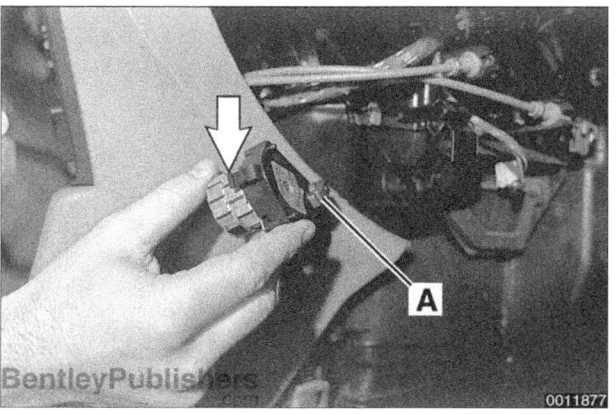

◄ Each motor can be removed after its electrical wiring harness connector has been removed.

• Squeeze plastic clip (**arrow**) to release motor.

• Tilt motor out of housing.

• Stepper motors are identical and should be replaced one at a time to avoid plugging them into the wrong harness connection.

— During installation, be sure to align air distribution flap and motor drive (**A**).

640

Air distribution stepper motors

Right side air distribution motors, accessing

Four of the air distribution motors are under the right side of the dashboard:

• Right side fresh air / recirculation
• Defroster
• Ventilation flaps
• Right footwell vent

— Disconnect negative (–) battery cable.

> **CAUTION—**
> • *Prior to disconnecting the battery, read the battery disconnection cautions given in* **001 Warnings and Cautions**.

— Remove glove compartment and right footwell trim panel for access. See **513 Interior Trim**.

— Remove footwell air duct.

Fresh air / recirculation motor

◄ Working inside dashboard, release screws (**A**) from stepper motor (**B**) with bracket.

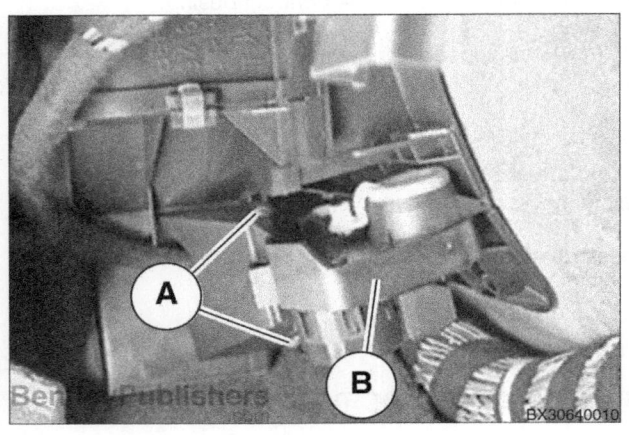

◄ Disconnect electrical connection (**A**) and remove adjusting lever (**B**).

— Then remove stepper motor and bracket (**C**).

Air distribution stepper motors

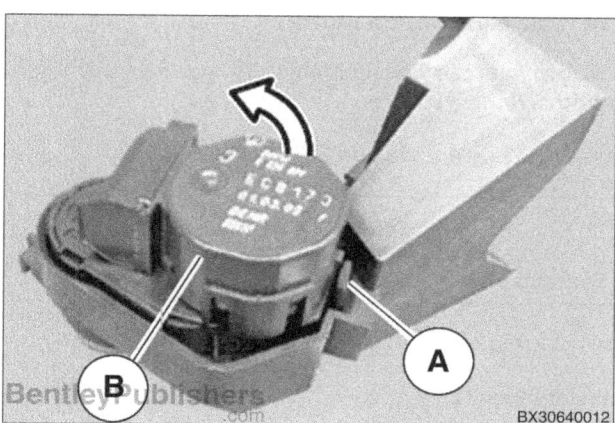

◄ Release lock (**A**) and remove stepper motor from bracket.

– Installation is reverse of removal.

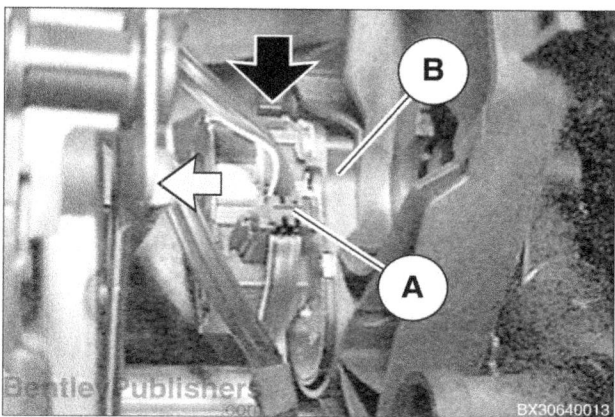

Ventilation distribution motor

◄ Disconnect electrical connection (**A**), unlock stepper motor (**B**) at **black arrow** and remove in direction of **white arrow.**

– Installation is reverse of removal.

Defroster distribution motor

– Remove ventilation distribution motor first.

◄ Unlock stepper motor (**A**) and feed out towards side.

– Disconnect electrical connection.

– Installation is reverse of removal.

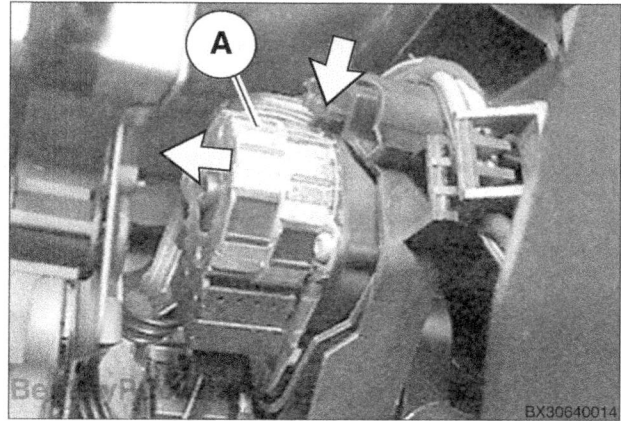

640

Air distribution stepper motors

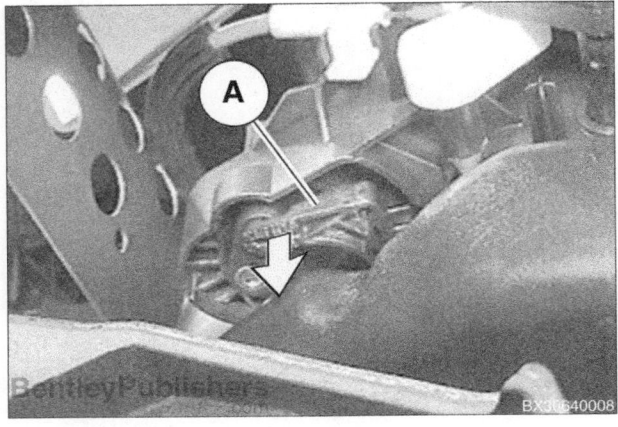

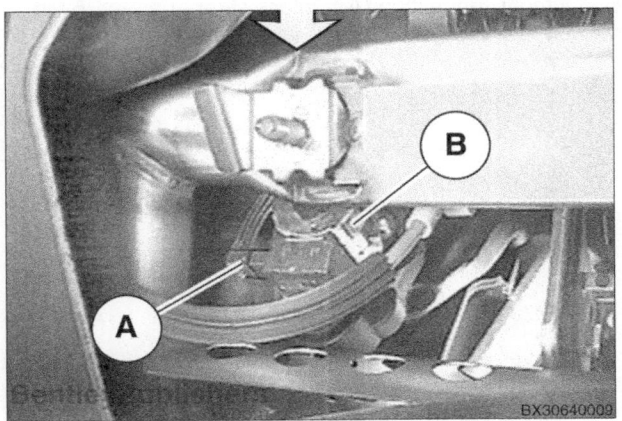

Footwell vent air distribution motor.

— Remove glove compartment and right footwell trim panel for access. See **513 Interior Trim**.

— Remove passenger side airbag. See **721 Airbag System**.

> **WARNING—**
> • *Prior to removing the airbag, read airbag cautions given in* **721 Airbag System**.

— Partially remove fuse box.

◄ Unhook actuator lever (**1**).

◄ Disconnect electrical connection (**A**). Remove stepper motor (**B**) towards rear.

Left side air distribution motor, accessing

The fresh air distribution motor is under the left side of the dashboard.

— Remove trim above pedal assembly for access. See **513 Interior Trim.**

> *NOTE—*
> • *Heater assembly is removed for clarity.*

◄ Reach up above accelerator pedal to gain access to fresh air distribution motor (**C**).

— Remove screw (**A**) and unclip adjusting clasp to remove stepper motor.

— Installation is reverse of removal.

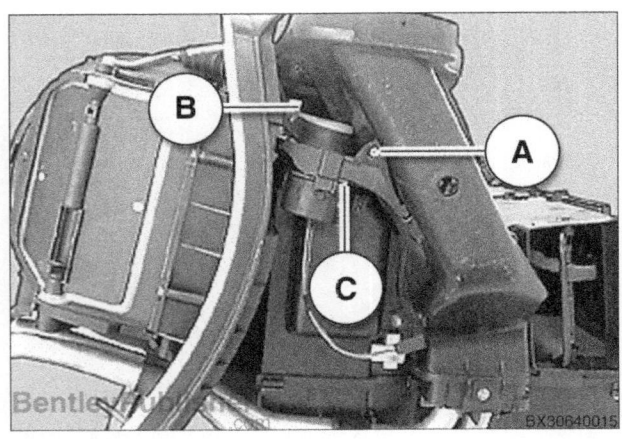

Blower motor, removing and installing

– Disconnect battery negative cable.

CAUTION—

• *Prior to disconnecting the battery, read the battery disconnection cautions given in* **001 Warnings and Cautions**.

– Remove strut bar. See **310 Front Suspension**.

◄ Remove wiper arms (**A**). See **611 Wipers and Washers**.

– Release fasteners (qty. 3) 90° to loosen cabin microfilter cover. Lift cover and remove microfilter. See **020 Maintenance.**

– Unclip cowl panel from blind fasteners and lift off of vehicle.

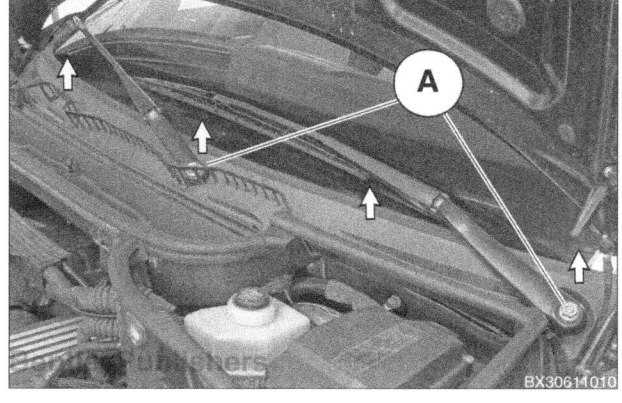

◄ Remove fasteners (**arrows**) at rear of plenum chamber and lift off of vehicle.

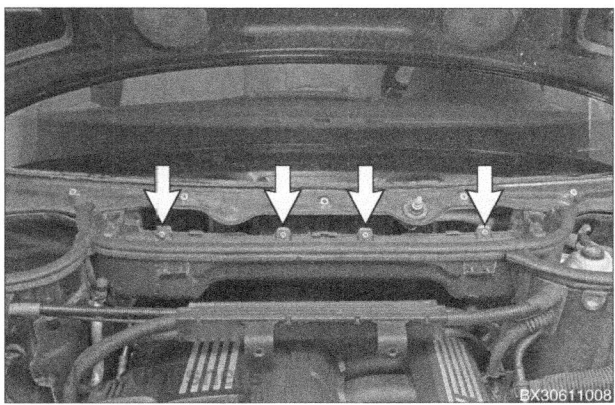

◄ Pull off weather strip (**A**) and release locks (**B**) to pull side trim forward slightly.

640

◀ Remove fasteners (**arrows**) for heater bulkhead. Lift off and remove from vehicle.

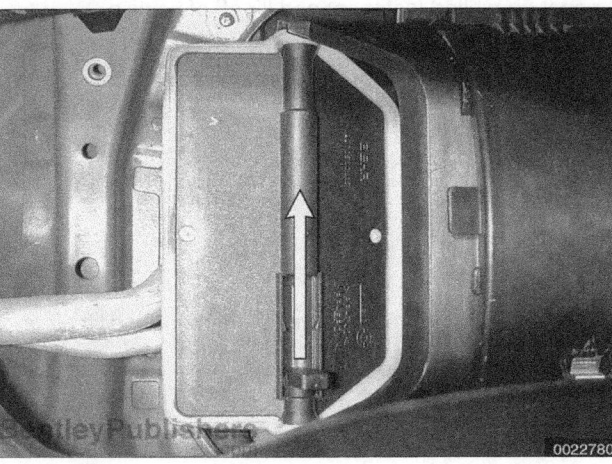

◀ Working inside right side of cowl, pull up on lever (**arrow**) and detach right air intake flap from blower housing.

◀ Pry off blower cover retaining clips (**A**). Remove screw (**B**) and lift off outer blower housing cover.

◀ Remove blower cover retaining screws (**arrows**). Lift off cover.

◀ Detach electrical harness connector (**arrow**).

– Pry off blower motor retaining strap in direction of (**arrow**) and pull blower motor forward to remove.

– Installation is reverse of removal: making sure to align slot in blower motor with mounting tab in blower motor housing.

Blower resistor, removing and installing

The blower resistor is also referred to as the blower output or final stage switch. It is located on the passenger side of IHKA housing inside the dashboard.

– Remove glove compartment and right footwell trim panel for access. See **513 Interior Trim**.

– Remove footwell air duct.

– Remove fresh air / recirculation motor. See **Air distribution stepper motors** in this repair group.

◀ To remove blower resistor pack from IHKA housing:
  • Remove mounting screws (**arrows**).
  • Detach electrical harness connector.
  • Press retaining clip away from switch to release switch.

– Installation is reverse of removal.
  • Make sure electrical harness is routed as before.
  • Align guides and clips correctly.

640

HEATER COMPONENTS

Climate control (IHKA) housing underneath the dashboard houses the heater core, the A/C evaporator, the heating and A/C blower and associated sensors and air distribution stepper motors.

Be sure to read **Warnings and Cautions** in this repair group.

Heater valve, replacing

— Remove air filter housing and intake duct. See **130 Fuel injection (M54 engine)** or **131 Fuel injection (N52 engine)**.

— Drain engine coolant. See **170 Radiator and Cooling System.**

> *WARNING —*
> • *Allow the engine to cool thoroughly before opening or draining the cooling system.*

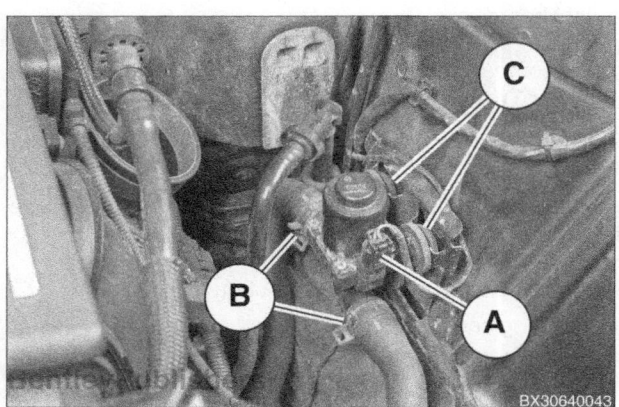

◄ Working in engine compartment at left strut tower:
  • Detach electrical connector (**A**) at heater valve.
  • Loosen hose clamps (**B**). Pull coolant hoses off valve. Use shop towels to catch dripping coolant.

— Pull heater valve out of rubber mounts (**C**).

— Installation is reverse of removal. Remember to:
  • Inspect hoses and rubber mounts. Replace as necessary. Use new hose clamps.
  • Fill and bleed cooling system. See **170 Radiator and Cooling System**.

IHKA housing, removing and installing

IHKA housing removal is a complex procedure that will require dashboard removal among other steps.

— Remove housing for interior ventilation micro filter and remove heater bulkhead cover. see **Blower motor removal** in this repair group.

> *CAUTION—*
> • *Removing the IHKA housing requires evacuating the A/C system. DO NOT attempt this procedure without proper tools and training.*
>
> • *Any person who services a motor vehicle air conditioner must, by law, be properly trained and certified, and use approved refrigerant recycling equipment. Technicians must complete an EPA-approved recycling course to be certified*

— Drain engine coolant. See **170 Radiator and Cooling System**.

> *WARNING —*
> *Allow the cooling system to cool before opening or draining the cooling system.*

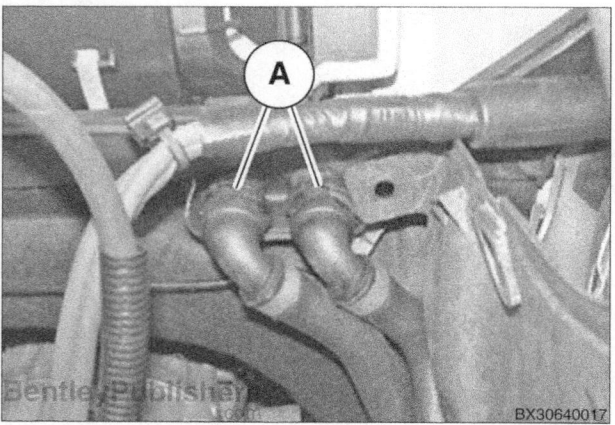

◄ Working at rear engine compartment bulkhead, loosen hose clamps (**A**) and detach heater hoses.

- Blow out excess coolant from heater core using compressed air at coolant lines.

- Following manufacturer's instructions, connect approved refrigerant recovery / recycling / recharging unit to A/C system and discharge system.

◀ Release fastener (**A**) and remove refrigerant line from expansion valve.

- If necessary remove intake flap from blower housing. See **Blower motor, removing and installing** in this repair group.

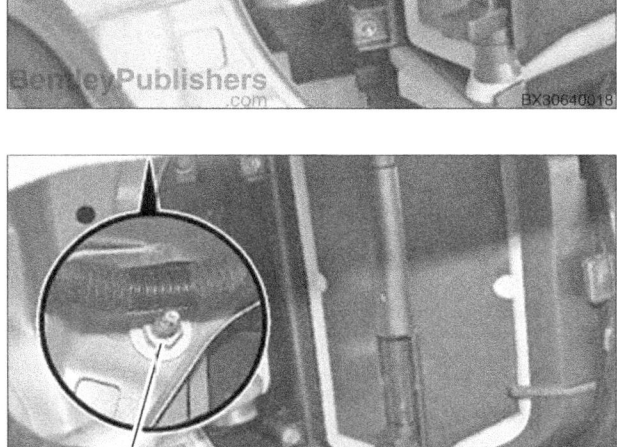

◀ Working inside heater cowl opening, remove fasteners (**A**) on both sides of sides of IHKA housing.

- Remove steering column and dashboard trim, see **513 interior Trim** and **320 Steering and Wheel Alignment**.

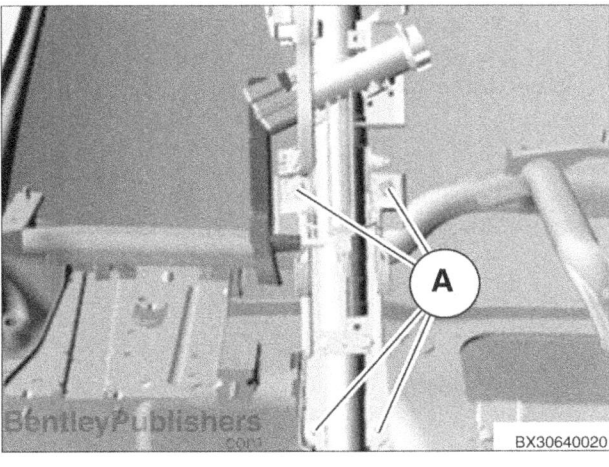

◀ Remove fasteners (**A**) and fold steering column down.

640

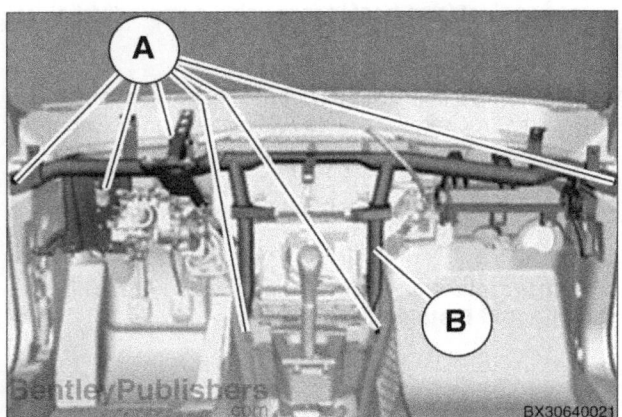

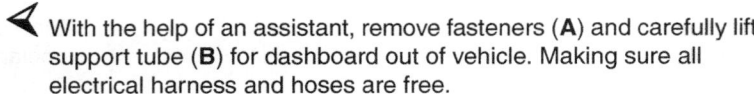

◀ With the help of an assistant, remove fasteners (**A**) and carefully lift support tube (**B**) for dashboard out of vehicle. Making sure all electrical harness and hoses are free.

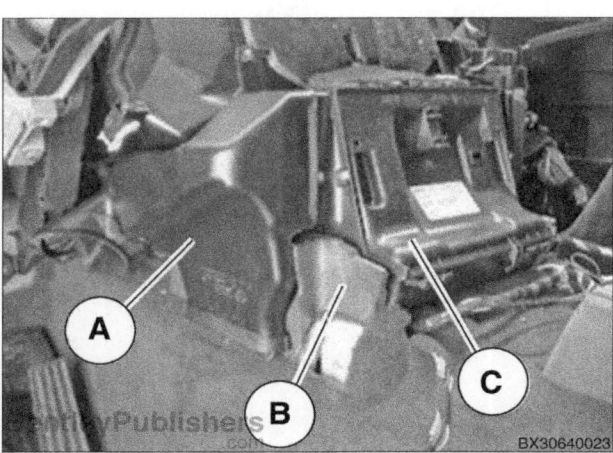

◀ Remove air ducts (**A**) on both sides of IHKA housing.

– Remove foam insulation (**B**).

– Then disconnect wiring harness and remove IHKA housing from vehicle with the help of an assistant.

– Installation is reverse of removal, noting the follow:
  • Make sure IHKA housing is properly seated on drain when installing.
  • Bleed cooling system and check for leaks.
  • Recharge A/C system with refrigerant.

Tightening torque	
Refrigerant lines to expansion valve (M6) (replace sealing O-rings)	8 Nm (6 ft-lb)
IHKA housing to bulkhead	6 Nm (5 ft-lb)

Heater core, removing and installing

– Remove IHKA housing. See **IHKA housing, removing and installing** in this repair group.

◀ Working with IHKA housing outside vehicle, remove temperature sensor (**A**) and unclip wiring harness (**B**).

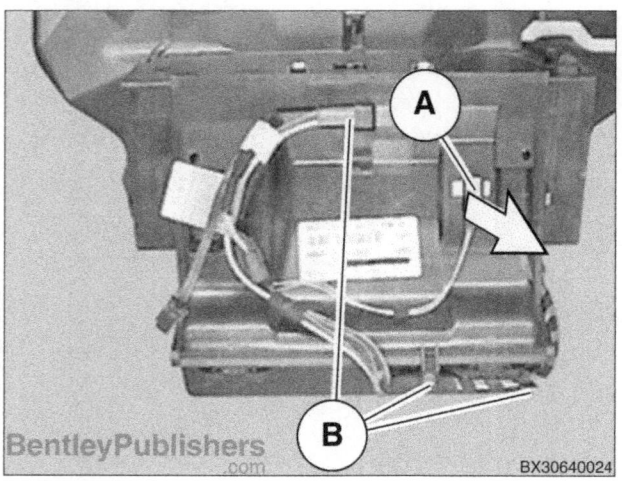

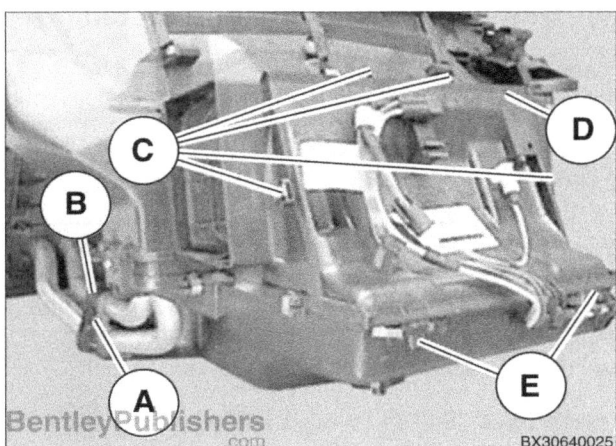

BX30640025

◄ Remove fastener (**A**) to remove bracket (**B**) from double pipe.

– Unclip retainers (**C**) and lift off cover (**D**) for heater core.

– When installing cover (**D**) for heater core, place in mounts (**E**) first.

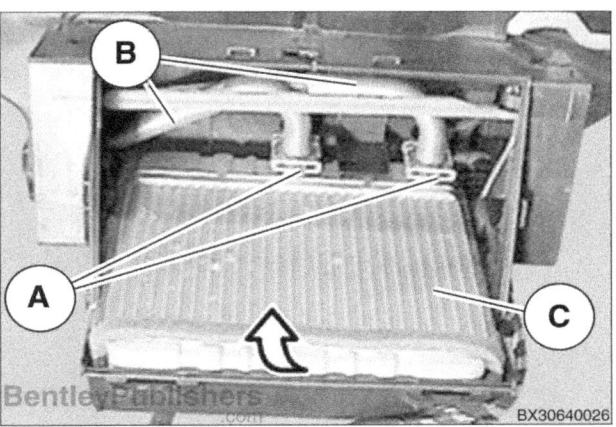

BX30640026

◄ Remove retainers (**A**) on heater core pipes (**B**) and lift up.

– Lift up heater core (**C**) in direction of arrow and remove from IHKA housing.

– Installation is reverse of removal, noting the following:
  • Replace sealing rings on heater core pipes (**B**) and coat with lubricant when installing to seat lines correctly.
  • Make sure IHKA housing is properly seated on drain when installing.
  • Bleed cooling system and check for leaks.
  • Recharge A/C system with refrigerant.

AIR-CONDITIONING COMPONENTS

This section covers removal and installation of air-conditioning refrigerant components. These procedures require evacuation and recharging of A/C refrigerant using special equipment. Follow the equipment manufacturer's instructions during A/C system service.

The refrigerant pressure sensor, A/C condenser, compressor and receiver-drier are installed in the engine compartment. The receiver-drier is inserted into the condenser.

The expansion valve and evaporator are installed in the climate control housing under the dashboard. Expansion valve replacement is covered here.

Be sure to read **Warnings and Cautions** in this repair group.

640

A/C expansion valve, removing and installing

A/C expansion valve, removing and installing

— Following manufacturer's instructions, connect an approved refrigerant recovery / recycling / recharging unit to A/C system and discharge system.

— Disconnect battery negative cable.

> **CAUTION—**
> • *Prior to disconnecting the battery, read the battery disconnection cautions given in* **001 Warnings and Cautions**.

— Remove strut bar. See **310 Front Suspension**.

— Remove wiper arms (**A**). See **611 Wipers and Washers**.

◀ Twist 3 quick-release fasteners (**B**) 90° to loosen cabin microfilter cover and remove microfilter. See **020 Maintenance**.

— Unclip cowl panel from blind fasteners and lift off of vehicle.

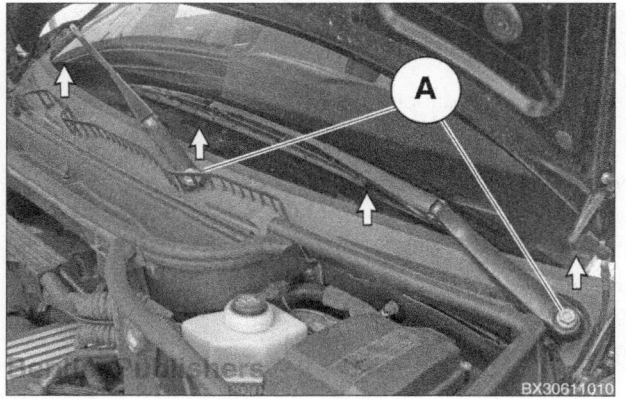

◀ Remove fasteners (**arrows**) at rear of plenum chamber and lift off of vehicle.

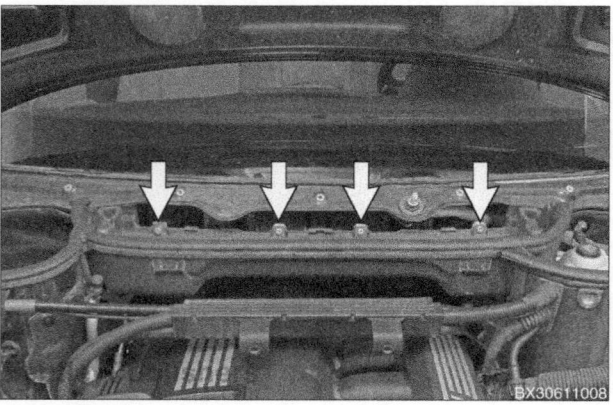

◀ Pull off weather strip (**A**) and release locks (**B**) to pull side trim forward slightly.

A/C expansion valve, removing and installing

◀ Remove fasteners (**arrows**) for heater bulkhead. Lift off and remove from vehicle.

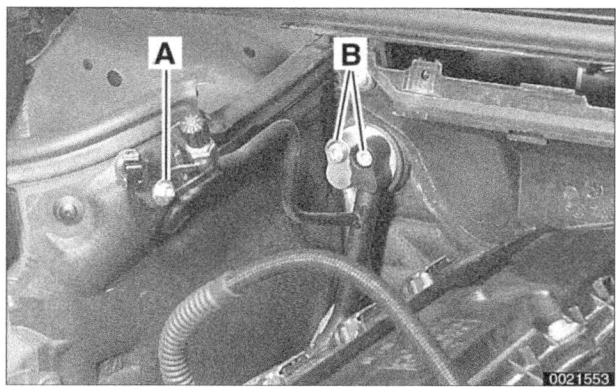

◀ Working in right rear of engine compartment, detach A/C lines:
  • Remove A/C recharging port bracket mounting nut (**A**).

— Remove allen bolts (**B**) at bulkhead. Release and plug open A/C lines.

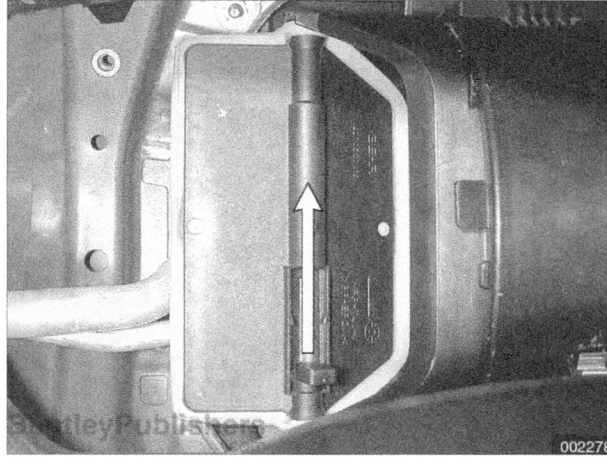

◀ Working inside right side of cowl, pull up on lever (**arrow**) and detach right air intake flap from blower housing.

640

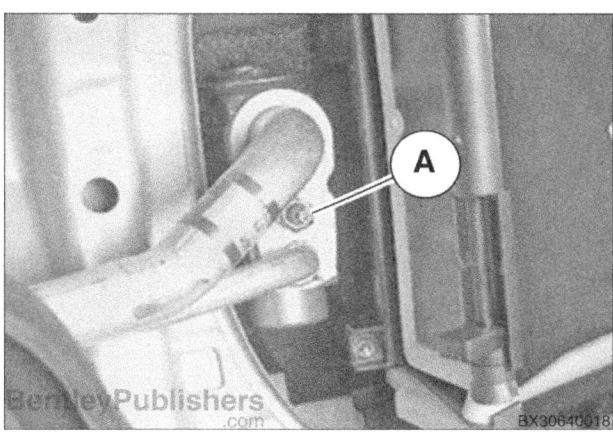

◀ Release fastener (**A**) and remove refrigerant line from expansion valve.

◄ Release fasteners (**arrows**) and remove expansion valve.

• Installation is reverse of removal.

Tightening torque	
Refrigerant lines (double pipe) (M8)	20 Nm (15 ft-lb)
Refrigerant lines to expansion valve (M6) (replace sealing O-rings)	8 Nm (6 ft-lb)
Expansion valve to IHKA housing (M5)	5.5 Nm (4 ft-lb)

— Recharge system following equipment manufacturer's instructions.

A/C evaporator, removing and installing

— Following manufacturer's instructions, connect an approved refrigerant recovery / recycling / recharging unit to A/C system and discharge system.

— Drain engine coolant. See **170 Radiator and Cooling System**.

— Remove complete IHKA housing. See **IHKA housing, removing and installing** in this repair group.

— Remove heater core. See **Heater core, replacing** in this repair group.

— Remove blower motor resistor. See **Blower motor resistor, replacing** in this repair group.

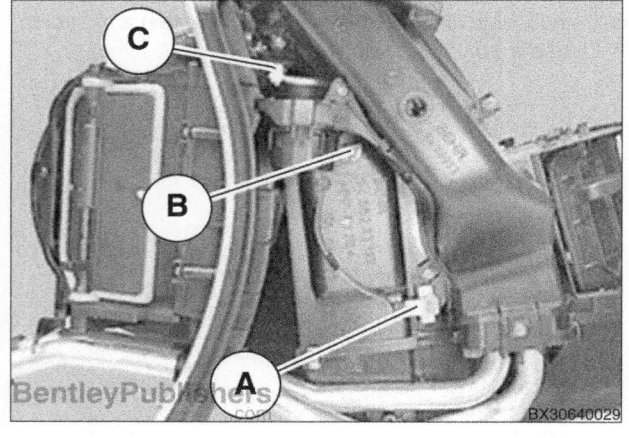

◄ Working with IHKA housing out of vehicle, remove temperature sensor (**A**) and disconnect electrical connection (**B**).

— Unclip linkage on stepper motor (**C**).

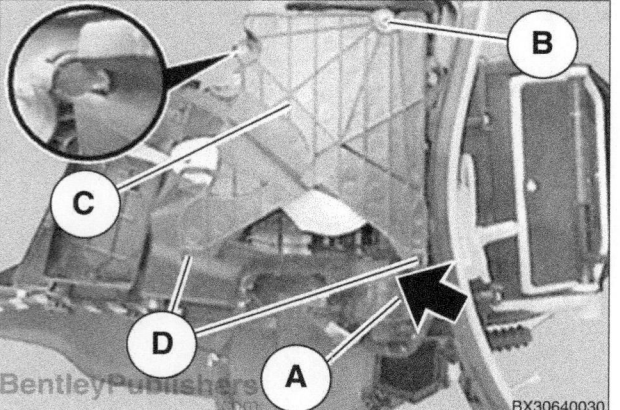

◄ Remove stepper motor (**A**) and disconnect from harness.

— Release screw (**B**) and unlock plate (**C**) from IHKA housing. Use locating tabs (**D**) when installing.

— Unclip wiring harness from IHKA housing.

A/C evaporator, removing and installing

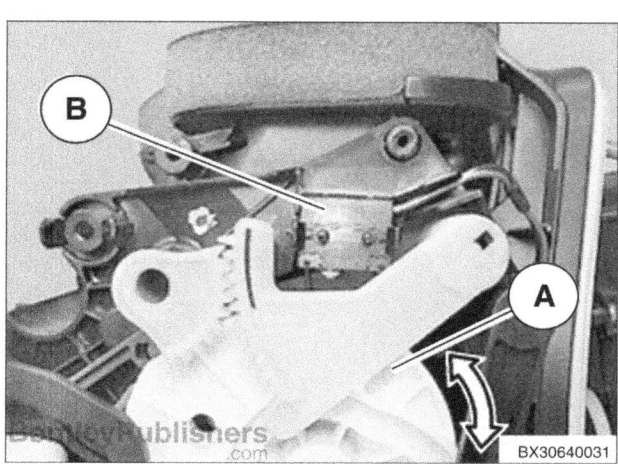

◀ Turn cam disc (**A**) until microswitch (**B**) is unclipped, then remove it.

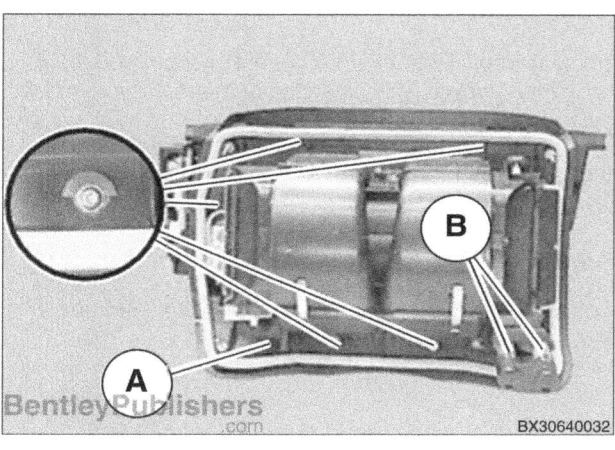

◀ Release screws on blower housing (**A**) and feed out double pipe (**B**).

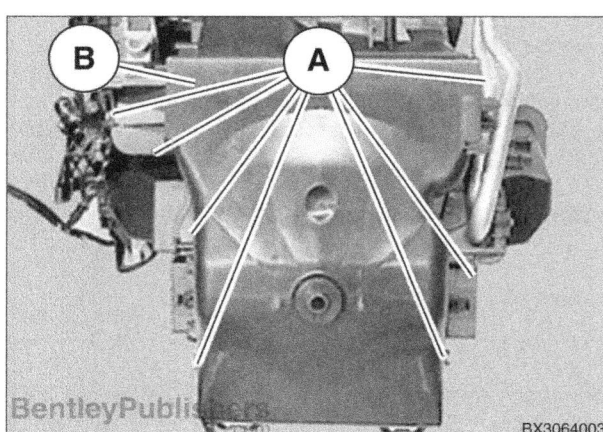

◀ Unclip clamps (**A**) on IHKA housing cover (**B**) and remove.

640

A/C pressure switch

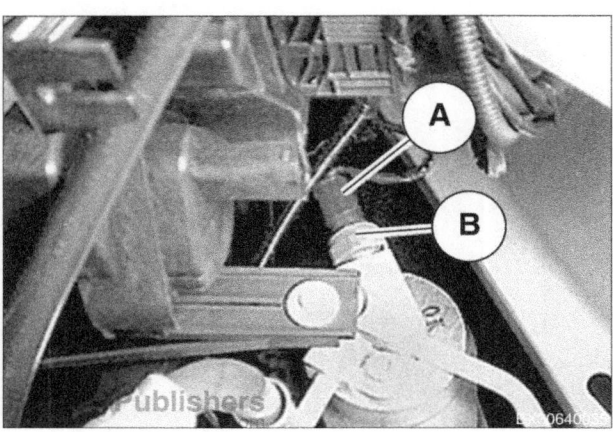

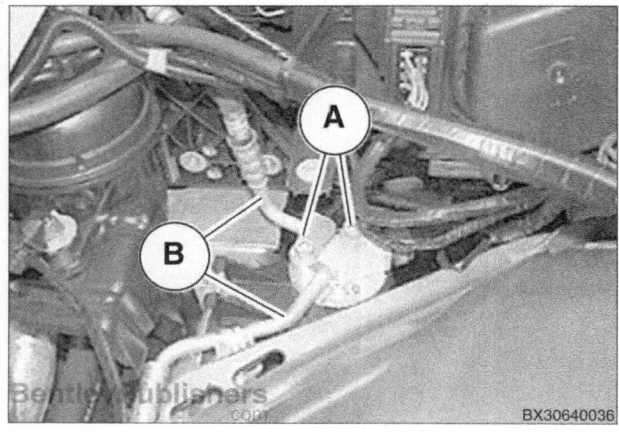

◀ Remove expansion valve (**B**). See **Expansion valve, removing and replacing** in this repair group.

— Remove evaporator (**A**).

— Installation is reverse of removal.

NOTE—
• *Always replace O-rings when reconnecting refrigerant lines.*

A/C pressure switch

— Following manufacturer's instructions, connect an approved refrigerant recovery / recycling / recharging unit to A/C system and discharge system.

— Remove windshield washer reservoir. See **611 Wipers and Washers**.

◀ Pressure switch is located at receiver dryer.

— Disconnect electrical location (**A**) and unscrew switch (**B**) from receiver dryer.

NOTE—
• *Always replace O-rings when reconnecting refrigerant lines.*

A/C receiver-drier, replacing

— Following manufacturer's instructions, connect an approved refrigerant recovery / recycling / recharging unit to A/C system and discharge system.

— Remove windshield washer reservoir, see **611 Wipers and Washers**.

◀ Remove fasteners (**A**) and remove refrigerant lines (**B**).

CAUTION—
• *Replace the receiver-drier when:*
  -There is dirt in the A/C system.
  -The compressor seized or is replaced.
  -The condenser or evaporator are replaced.
  -The A/C system is leaking and there is no more refrigerant.
  -The A/C system was open for 24 hours or more.

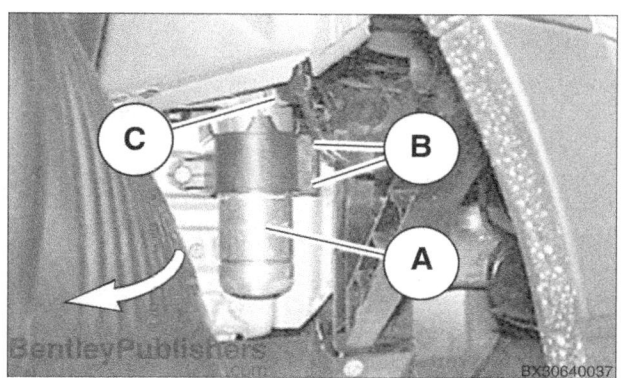

◄ Partially remove front fender liner. See **410 Fenders, Engine hood**.

– Loosen fasteners (**B**) and slide receiver dryer (**A**) towards top and disconnect electrical connection (**C**).

  • Installation is reverse of removal.

Tightening torque	
Refrigerant lines to receiver dryer(M8) (replace sealing O-rings)	20 Nm (15 ft-lb)

A/C compressor, replacing

M54 engine

– Following manufacturer's instructions, connect an approved refrigerant recovery / recycling / recharging unit to A/C system and discharge system.

– Raise car and support safely.

> **WARNING** —
> • Make sure car is stable and well supported at all times. Use a professional automotive lift or jack stands. A floor jack is not adequate support.

– Remove splash shield from under engine. See **020 Maintenance**.

– Mark A/C drive belt with direction of rotation and remove belt. See **020 Maintenance**.

– Remove windshield washer reservoir. See **611 Wipers and Washers**.

◄ Remove A/C pressure hose and suction hose flange bolts (**arrows**) from compressor. Plug hoses immediately.

> **NOTE** —
> • Working above right front of engine compartment, tie secondary air hose to aside to gain access to A/C compressor.

– Disconnect electrical harness connector from A/C compressor.

◄ Support compressor while removing mounting bolts (**arrows**). Remove compressor.

> **NOTE** —
> • Depending on model, compressor may be mounted with 3 or 4 bolts.

640

A/C compressor, replacing

– Installation is reverse of removal.

- Replace sealing O-rings when reconnecting refrigerant lines.

- If installing new compressor, or if compressor is off vehicle for more than 24 hours, replace receiver-drier unit. See **A/C receiver-drier, replacing**.

- Install and tension A/C drive belt, noting previously made direction mark. See **020 Maintenance**.

- Recharge A/C system following equipment manufacturer's instructions.

Tightening torque	
Refrigerant lines to compressor (M8) (replace sealing O-rings)	20 Nm (15 ft-lb)
A/C compressor to carrier (M8)	21 Nm (15.5 ft-lb)

– When starting a new compressor for the first time, carry out the following break-in procedure:

- Switch A/C system ON.
- Set air vents to OPEN.
- Start engine and allow to idle.
- Set blower output to 75% of maximum.
- Run A/C for at least 2 minutes at idle speed (under 1500 rpm).

> **CAUTION—**
> - *New compressor may be damaged if run at higher than idle speed at start-up.*

N52 engine

A/C compressor is mounted using aluminum fasteners that must be replaced. Be sure to have more on hand before removing and installing A/C compressor.

– Following manufacturer's instructions, connect an approved refrigerant recovery / recycling / recharging unit to A/C system and discharge system.

– Raise car and support safely.

> **WARNING—**
> - *Make sure car is stable and well supported at all times. Use a professional automotive lift or jack stands. A floor jack is not adequate support.*

– Remove splash shield from under engine. See **020 Maintenance**.

– Mark A/C drive belt with direction of rotation and remove belt. See **020 Maintenance**.

– Remove coolant thermostat. See **170 Radiator and Cooling System**.

◄ Remove A/C pressure hose and suction hose flange bolts (**arrows**) from compressor. Plug hoses immediately.

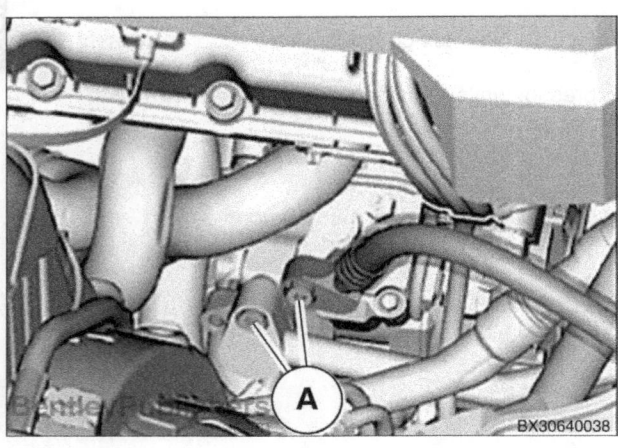

BX30640038

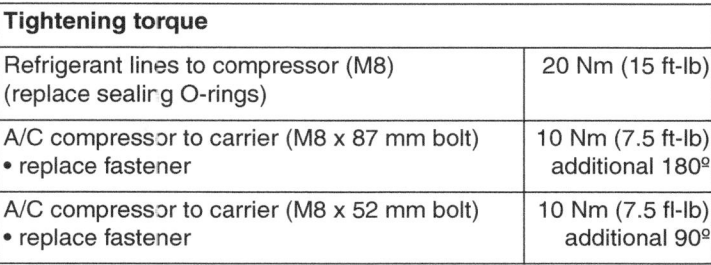

NOTE—
- *Working above right front of engine compartment, tie secondary air hose to aside to gain access to A/C compressor.*

– Disconnect electrical harness connector from A/C compressor.

◄ Support compressor (**C**) while removing mounting bolts (**A**) and (**B**). Remove compressor.

– Installation is reverse of removal.
- Replace aluminum fasteners.
- Replace sealing O-rings when reconnecting refrigerant lines.
- If installing new compressor, or if compressor is off vehicle for more than 24 hours, replace receiver-drier unit. See **A/C receiver-drier, replacing**.
- Install and tension A/C drive belt, noting previously made direction mark. See **020 Maintenance**.
- Recharge A/C system following equipment manufacturer's instructions.

Tightening torque	
Refrigerant lines to compressor (M8) (replace sealing O-rings)	20 Nm (15 ft-lb)
A/C compressor to carrier (M8 x 87 mm bolt) • replace fastener	10 Nm (7.5 ft-lb) additional 180º
A/C compressor to carrier (M8 x 52 mm bolt) • replace fastener	10 Nm (7.5 fl-lb) additional 90º

– When starting a new compressor for the first time, carry out the following break-in procedure:
- Switch A/C system ON.
- Set air vents to OPEN.
- Start engine and allow to idle.
- Set blower output to 75% of maximum.
- Run A/C for at least 2 minutes at idle speed (under 1500 rpm).

CAUTION—
- *The new compressor may be damaged if run at higher than idle speed at start-up.*

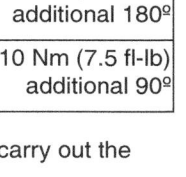
640

A/C condenser, replacing

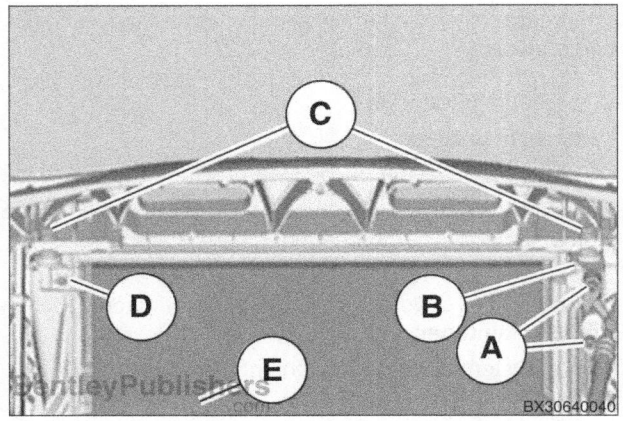

– Following manufacturer's instructions, connect an approved refrigerant recovery / recycling / recharging unit to A/C system and discharge system.

– Remove radiator. See **170 Radiator and Cooling System**.

◄ Remove fasteners (**A**) and remove refrigerant lines.

– Release screws (**B**) and remove spacers (**C**).

– Release retaining clip (**D**) and remove condenser.

– Installation is reverse of removal.

  • Replace sealing O-rings when reconnecting refrigerant lines.

  • If installing new condenser, or if condenser is off vehicle for more than 24 hours, replace receiver-drier unit. See **A/C receiver-drier, replacing**.

  • Recharge A/C system following equipment manufacturer's instructions.

Tightening torque	
Refrigerant lines to condenser (M8) (replace sealing O-rings)	20 Nm (15 ft-lb)

650 Radio

GENERAL

This section covers the BMW factory-installed sound system, including radio, amplifier, antenna and speakers. Information on cellular telephone and navigation equipment is also included.

Communication equipment

 Optional pop up Central Information Display (CID) Radio with navigation unit. X3 vehicles come standard with BMW business Radio with CD player and HiFi audio system. Top HiFi audio system and CD changer are optional for both Business radio with CD and CID radio with Navigation. A Telematic Control Unit (TCU) that includes bluetooth connectivity for hands free cell phone use is also optional.

X3 sound system, communication and navigation equipment			
Model	Hifi audio system	Top HiFi audio system	CDC
Business Radio w/CD	Standard	Optional	Optional
CID Radio w/Nav	Standard	Optional	Optional

650

Communication system features

Steering wheel. Basic radio and cellular telephone controls incorporated in multifunction steering wheel (MFL).

K-bus. Sound system components interconnected via K-bus.

Theft proofing. Radio code not required. Radio non-functional without K-bus connection and valid signal from instrument cluster.

Sound system features:

• Autostoring of stations.

• Speed dependent volume.

• Telephone muting.

CD changer. Sound system prewired for optional CD changer in center console.

Bluetooth. Optional Telematic control unit (TCU) provides bluetooth hands free cell phone use and emergency or break down calling function.

Navigation System

X3 vehicles are available with an optional DVD based navigation system. Vehicle navigation systems utilize signals from global positioning system (GPS) satellites. The navigation system also incorporates a dead reckoning system that compensates for driving in areas without a GPS signal.

Route maps are stored digitally on a navigational database DVD that is installed in a dedicated DVD drive in the navigation computer. Navigation computer is located in the cargo area behind left trim panel.

Warnings and Cautions

> *WARNING—*
> • *X3 vehicles are equipped with front door airbags. Rear door airbags are optional. See airbag warnings and cautions in* **721 Airbag System**.

> *CAUTION—*
> • *Before beginning work on the radio or sound system, verify that the radio is an original equipment BMW radio and that the wiring harness is not modified.*
> • *Do not disconnect power from the navigation computer while the LED on the computer remains lit. The LED switches OFF approx. 1 minute after powering unit OFF.*
> • *Refer servicing of aftermarket sound equipment to an authorized agent of the equipment manufacturer.*
> • *When handling electronic equipment (monitors, control modules, relays), use anti-static tools and techniques to prevent static discharge damage. See* **600 Electrical System– General**.
> • *To avoid damaging plastic interior trim, use a plastic prying tool or a screwdriver with the tip wrapped with masking tape.*

SOUND SYSTEM

Radio service mode

BMW Business CD

- With ignition switch in ACCESSORY position, switch on radio: Within 8 seconds of turning on radio. Press and hold "m" button for more than 8 seconds until serial number displays. Switch off radio to exit service mode.

CID Radio

- With ignition switch in ACCESSORY position, switch on radio: Within 8 seconds of turning on radio. Press and hold "SEL" button for more than 8 seconds until serial number displays. Switch off radio to exit service mode.

- Test functions include:
  - Radio serial number.
  - Radio production date.
  - DSP recognition.
  - Road speed dependent volume control.
  - Station signal strength.
  - Area use control (US, EC, Canada).
  - Audio frequency (manual or OFF).

Radio, removing and installing

- Remove center dash air vents. See **513 Interior Trim**.

- Remove IHKA control panel. See **640 Heating and Air Conditioning**.

◄ Remove fasteners (**A**) to pull radio (**B**) from dashboard and disconnect electrical harness connectors and antenna lead.

- Installation is reverse of removal. Making sure that guide pin (**C**) is seated correctly.

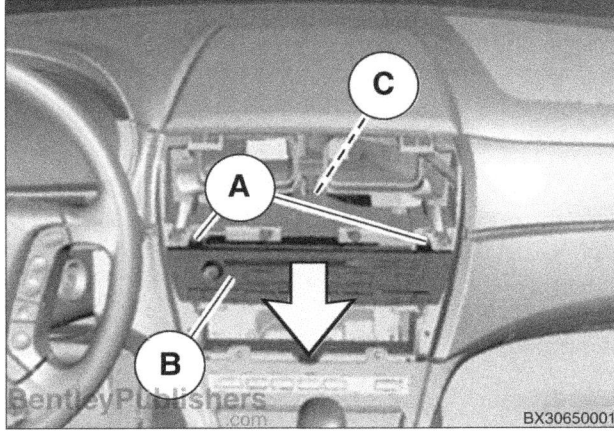

BX30650001

650

CD changer, removing and installing

The optional audio CD changer is located in center console.

- Remove CD magazine.

- Remove center console. See **513 interior trim.**

◄ Remove CD changer mounting screws (**A**).

- Slide out CD changer (**B**) and turn over. Disconnect electrical connectors.

- Installation is reverse of removal.

BX30650003

Amplifier, removing and installing

HiFi amplifier shown, Top Hifi amplifier removing and installing is similar. The sound system amplifier is behind the left rear trim panel in cargo area.

– Remove cargo compartment left side trim panel. See **513 Interior Trim**.

◄ Working at amplifier:
  • Disconnect amplifier electrical connector (**A**).
  • Remove amplifier mounting fasteners (**arrows**) and lift out amplifier.
  • Separate amplifier from bracket.

– Installation is reverse of removal.

SPEAKERS

Door speakers, removing and installing

The tweeters and mid-range speakers in the front and rear doors are mounted in a similar manner. The procedure below illustrates front door speaker replacement. Rear door is similar.

Tweeter speaker

– Remove door trim panel. See **411 Doors**.

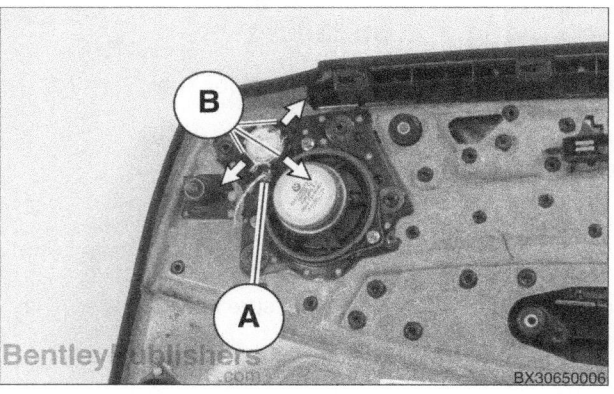

◄ Working at door speaker:
  • Detach speaker electrical connector (**A**).
  • Un-clip tweeter speaker from clips (**B**) in direction of **arrows**. Lift off speaker.

– Installation is reverse of removal.

Mid-range speaker

– Remove door trim panel. See **411 Doors**.

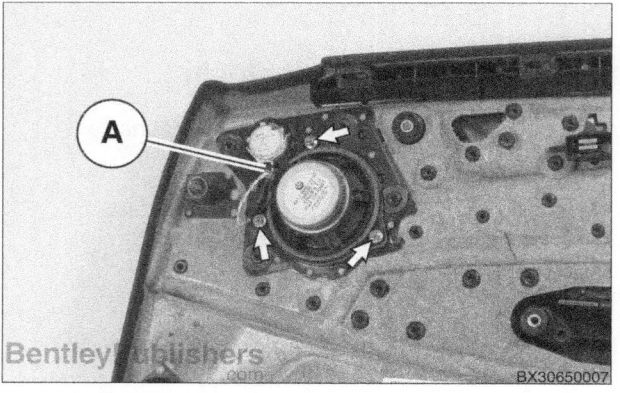

◄ Working at door speaker:
  • Detach speaker electrical connector (**A**).
  • Remove speaker mounting nuts (**arrows**). Lift off speaker.

– Installation is reverse of removal.

Subwoofers

Subwoofers are located under front seats.

− Remove front seat. See **520 Seats.**

− Remove b-pillar trim. See **513 Interior Trim**.

◀ Fold back carpet (**A**) in direction of arrow.

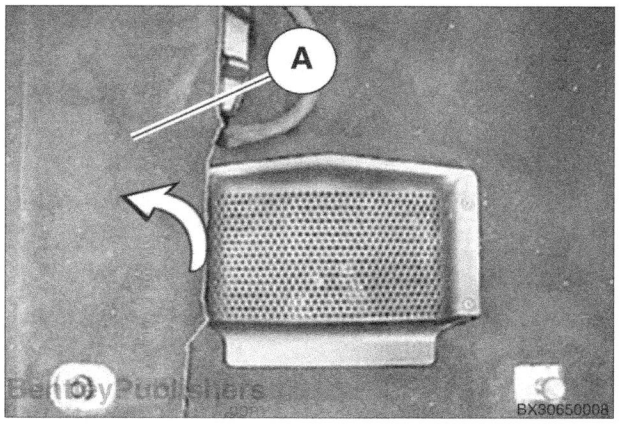

◀ Remove screws (**A**) and remove subwoofer trim (**B**).

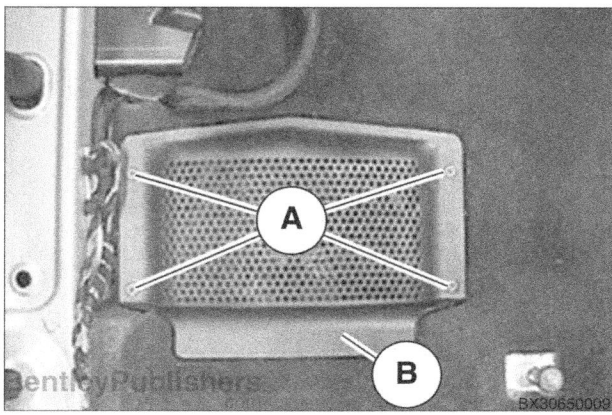

◀ fold back carpet (**A**) in direction of **arrow** from under heater duct (**B**) feeding out wiring harness (**C**) at same time.

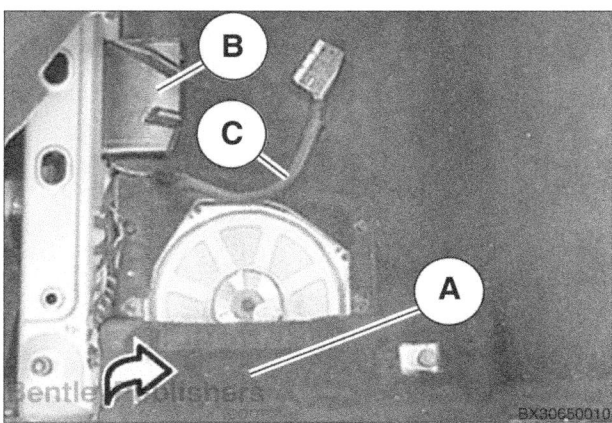

650

Diversity antenna amplifier components

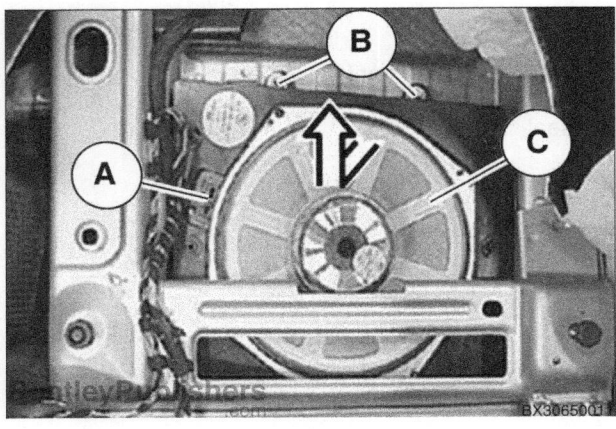

◄ Disconnect electrical connection (**A**).

– Remove fasteners (**B**) and lift out subwoofer (**C**) from floor cavity.

– Installation is reverse of removal.

ANTENNA

The antennas used for radio and remote entry system are integrated with the rear window and the side rear windows. GPS navigation antenna is located in shark fin on roof. GPS antenna replacement requires delicate removal of the antenna housing which is glued to the roof. See **ECL Electrical Component Locations**.

Diversity antenna amplifier components

1. Rear window heating elements with built in FM antenna.
2. Input terminal 30, FZV output.
3. Input/output: coaxial cable.
4. Input: FM 4 aerial, FZV input, AM aerial.
5. Input: FM aerial 1- 3.
6. Aerial amplifier with diversity antenna.

Diversity antenna, removing and installing

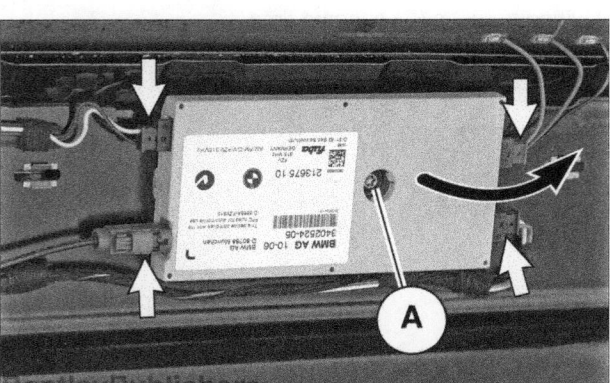

◄ Disconnect electrical connections (**arrows**).

– Remove fastener (**A**) and lift antenna off of tailgate in direction of arrow.

– Installation is reverse of removal.

TELEPHONE (TCU)

Telematic control unit (TCU) is an option on X3 models. The phone system is integrated into the vehicle electrical system via K-bus. This allows the sharing of functions between the telephone and other vehicle features, including:

• Telephone numbers displayed on CID.

• Telephone control via CID.

• Telephone control via MFL steering wheel.

• Hand-free telephone operation via bluetooth: Sound system mutes automatically and telephone volume increases automatically.

• Emergency and break down call button.

• GPS receiver for location

Telematic control unit (TCU), removing and installing

— Disconnect negative (–) cable from battery.

> **WARNING—**
> • *Prior to disconnecting the battery, read the battery disconnection cautions given in* **001 Warnings and Cautions**.

— Remove driver's side cargo area trim. TCU is located in the body cavity below the DVD navigation system.

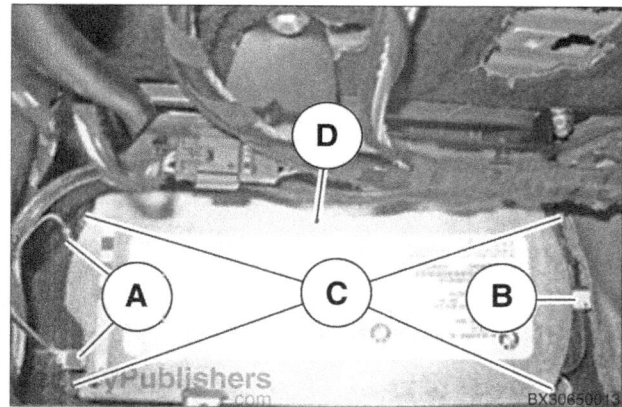

◄ Disconnect antenna plugs (**A**) and electrical connection (**B**).

— Remove fasteners (**C**) and lift out TCU (**D**) to remove.

— Installation is reverse of removal.

— Code new TCU using DISplus, MoDiC, GT1 or equivalent.

650

Bluetooth antenna, removing and installing

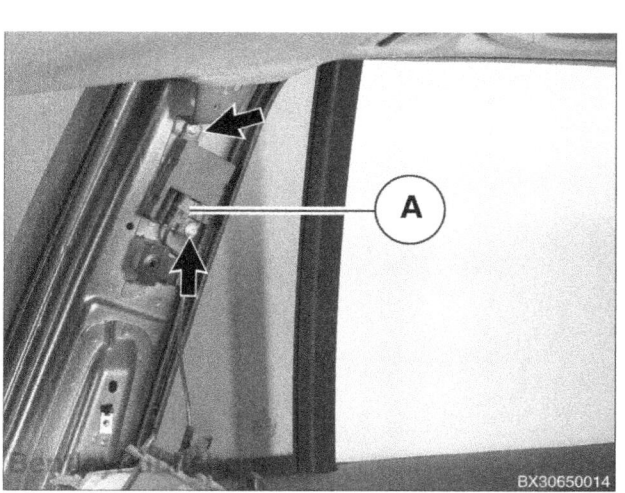

— Remove driver's side c-pillar trim. See **513 interior Trim**.

◄ Disconnect electrical connection (**A**) and remove fasteners (**arrows**) lift off bluetooth antenna.

— Installation is reverse of removal.

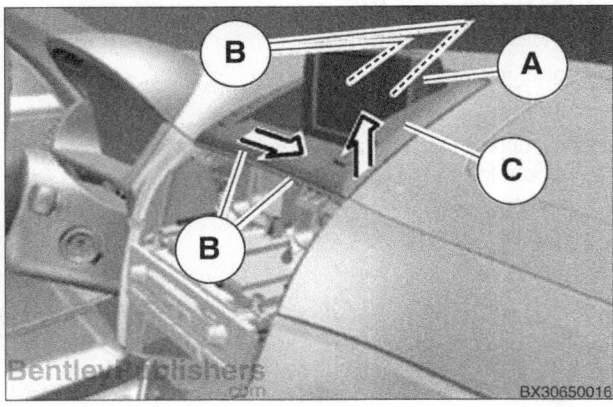

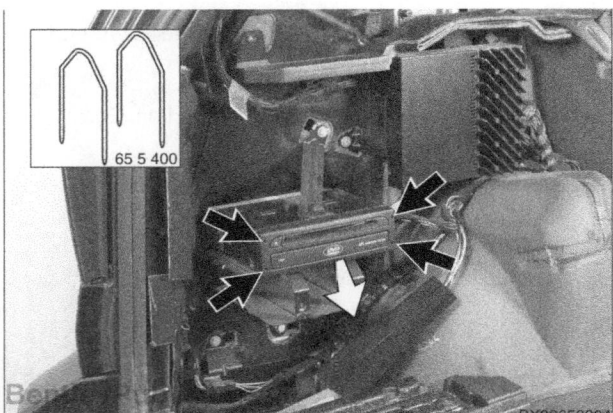

CENTRAL INFORMATION DISPLAY (CID)

Central information display, removing and installing

— Remove center dashboard fresh air grill. See **513 Interior Trim.**

— Remove IHKA control panel. See **640 Heating and Air Conditioning**.

◀ With display (**A**) in the up position:

— Remove screws (**B**) holding display.

— Lift out display (**C**) toward passenger side and disconnect electrical connectors.

— Installation is reverse of removal making sure that wiring harness is routed correctly.

Navigation DVD computer, removing and installing

The navigation DVD reader is behind the left cargo compartment trim panel. See **513 Interior Trim.**

NOTE —

 • *Cargo area trim is completely removed for clarity.*

— Remove cargo compartment left side trim panel.

◀ Using special tool 65 5 400 or equivalent, remove DVD computer by inserting tool in holes (**arrows**) to release from holder.

— Slide out DVD computer and turn over. Disconnect electrical connectors.

— Installation is reverse of removal.

720 Seat Belts

GENERAL

This section covers mechanical repairs to seat belts and seat belt tensioner components. Airbag system electronics integrate seat belt operations and airbag deployment. Airbag repair information is covered in **721 Airbag System**.

See also:

• **520 Seats**

• **513 Interior Trim**

The front seat belt locks are equipped with pyrotechnic (explosive charge) automatic tensioners. These tensioners are designed to automatically retract and tension the seat belt by 55 mm (approximately 2 inches) in case of an accident.

Pyrotechnic tensioners are controlled by the Multiple Restraint System (MRS) control module. MRS electronics integrate seat belt operation and airbag deployment. Additional MRS information is in **721 Airbag System**.

Child safety seat installation anchors

 Three tether points behind rear seat, under plastic covers (**arrow**), in cargo compartment floor.

NOTE—

• *For information on proper installation of child safety seats, child safety seat recalls, or for location of child safety seat inspection station in your area, visit the National Highway Traffic Safety Administration (NHTSA) web site at* **www.nhtsa.dot.gov**.

720

Troubleshooting

The seat belt reel should lock when driving quickly through curves, during severe braking or in case of a collision. The automatic reel does not require any servicing and should never be opened.

NOTE—

• *Rear bench seat belt strap may not retract fully due to increased friction between strap and seat cover. A small remaining loop in belt strap when fully retracted is acceptable.*

Troubleshooting procedures are presented in **Table a**.

Table a. Seat belt troubleshooting

Problem	Probable cause	Repairs
Damage to seat belt.	Accident in which bumper impact absorbers were permanently deformed.	Replace complete automatic seat belt. Also check and replace, if necessary, seat belt mounting on car body and seat belt mounting on seat runner.
Belt creased, unraveled, pinched, cut or melted. Belt buckle or belt lock plastic casing worn, damaged or missing.	Seat belts aged or worn.	Replace complete automatic seat belt.
Seat belt buckle not ejected with spring pressure when red button on seat belt lock pressed.	Seat belt lock mechanism worn or damaged.	Replace seat belt lock.
Seat belt automatic reel does not lock when pulled out suddenly.	Automatic reel defective.	Replace reel assembly.
Seat belt automatic reel jams when pulled out.	Automatic reel loose. Return spring broken inside reel.	Tighten reel mounting bolt. Replace reel assembly.
Seat belt does not retract automatically (see note above).	Automatic reel loose. Return spring broken inside reel.	Tighten reel mounting bolt. Replace reel assembly.
Automatic belt squeaks when fastened or unfastened.	Excessive friction in belt guides Automatic reel loose. Return spring broken inside reel.	Replace reel assembly. Tighten reel mounting bolt. Replace reel assembly.
Seat belt pyrotechnic tensioner triggered.	Accident triggered pyrotechnic deployment.	Replace complete automatic seat belt. Also check retaining bracket of belt tensioner for twist.

Warnings

> **WARNING—**
> - *For maximum protection from injury, replace seat belts as a set (including all hardware) if they are subject to occupant loading in a collision.*
> - *Do not modify or repair seat belts. Do not change or modify seat belt mounting points.*
> - *Do not bleach or dye seat belt webbing. Webbing that is severely faded or redyed does not meet the strength requirements of a collision. Replace it.*
> - *Clean belts with a luke-warm soap solution only.*
> - *Periodically inspect seat belts for webbing defects such as cuts or pulled threads.*
> - *Immediately after replacing a damaged or worn seat belt, destroy the old belt to prevent it from being used again.*
> - *Pyrotechnic seat belt tensioners are powerful devices. Handle with extreme care. Incorrect handling can trigger the tensioner and cause injury.*
> - *BMW recommends that all repair or replacement work on pyrotechnic devices be carried out by a qualified BMW technician.*
> - *Be sure to disconnect the battery and wait 1 minute before attempting to work on pyrotechnic devices.*
> - *Pyrotechnic devices cannot be repaired. Always replace them.*
> - *Do not treat pyrotechnic components with cleaning agents or grease.*
> - *Do not expose pyrotechnic components to temperatures above 167°F (75°C).*
> - *Pyrotechnic components can only be tested electrically when installed using a BMW diagnostic scan tool.*
> - *Do not fire a pyrotechnic gas generator prior to disposal. It must be fired by a special disposal company or shipped back to BMW in the packaging of the new component.*
> - *During body straightening and welding with an electric arc welder, disconnect the battery and the connection to the pyrotechnic gas generators.*

720

FRONT SEAT BELTS

Front seat belt assembly

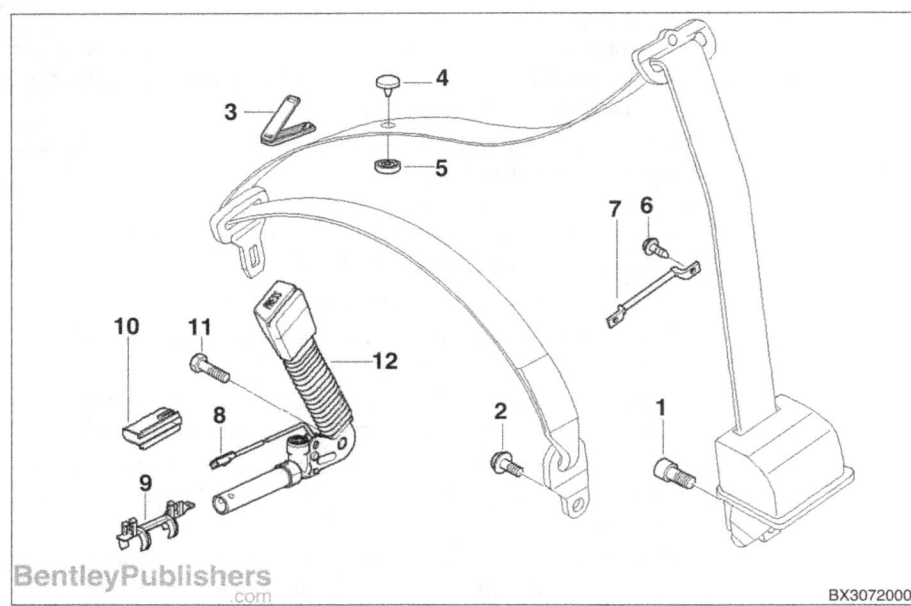

1. Seat belt reel mounting bolt
2. Seat belt anchor mounting bolt
3. Clamping
4. Seat belt stop button, top
5. Seat belt stop button, bottom
6. Fastener
7. Belt guide
8. Wire, seat belt tensioner plug
9. Tensioner clip
10. Covering cap
11. Tensioner bolt
12. Tensioner / lock assembly

Front seat belt tensioner (lock), removing and installing

> **WARNING—**
> • The seat belt tensioner is a pyrotechnic device. Use care when working on or near MRS components. See **712 Airbag System**.

— Disconnect negative (–) battery cable.

> **CAUTION—**
> • Prior to disconnecting the battery, read the battery disconnection cautions given in **001 Warnings and Cautions**.

— Remove front seat. See **520 Seats**.

◄ Working at side of seat remove, pyrotechnic belt tensioner:
  • Detach tensioner harness connector from seat rail by cutting wire tie (**A**).
  • Detach harness connection (**B**).
  • Remove tensioner mounting bolt (**C**).

— When reinstalling:
  • Position hole in plate over locating tab (**arrow**) on seat frame.
  • Replace cut wire ties and reconnect all harness connectors.

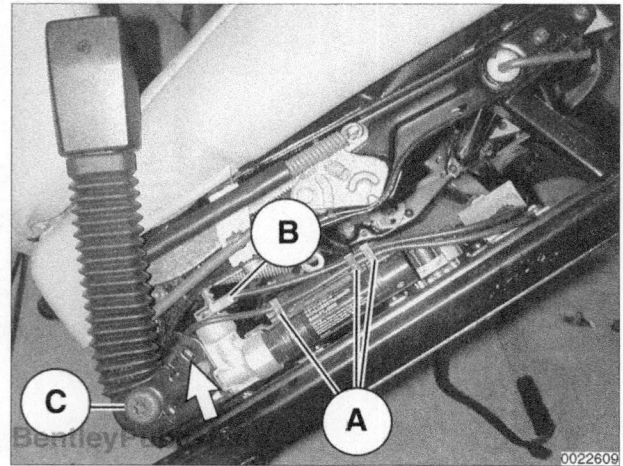

Tightening torques	
Front seat to floor (M10)	45 Nm (33 ft-lb)
Belt tensioner to mounting bracket (replace fasteners)	45 Nm (33 ft-lb)
Tensioner mounting bracket to seat (replace fasteners)	24 Nm (18 ft-lb)

Front seat belt reel, removing and installing

– Detach negative (–) battery cable.

> **CAUTION—**
> • *Prior to disconnecting the battery, read the battery disconnection cautions given in* **001 Warnings and Cautions.**

– Remove B-pillar trim. See **513 Interior trim**

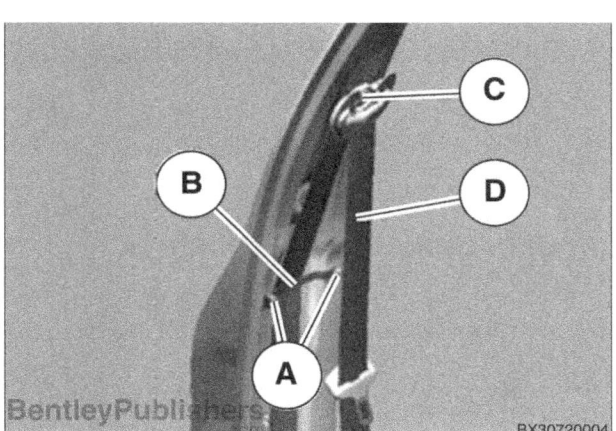

◄ Working at seat base, remove bolt (**A**)

– Installation is reverse of removal making sure to align tab of seat belt with retaining lugs on seat base.

◄ Remove mounting bolts (**A**) for belt guide (**B**).

– Remove upper seat belt anchor bolt (**C**) and place belt (**D**) on floor.

> **NOTE—**
> • *If removing seat belt height adjuster, remove two mounting screws simultaneously to prevent height adjuster from tilting.*

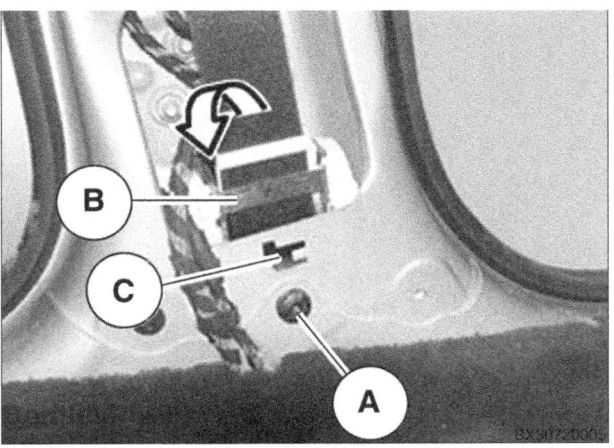

◄ Remove seat belt reel mounting bolt (**A**).

– Lift out reel (**B**).

– Installation is reverse of removal:
  • When installing automatic reel housing to B-pillar, slide tab into locating slot (**C**).

Tightening torques	
Height adjuster to body (replace fasteners)	22 Nm (18 ft-lb)
Seat belt reel to B-pillar bottom (replace fasteners)	31 Nm (23 ft-lb)
Seat belt to height adjuster (replace fasteners)	31 Nm (23 ft-lb)
Seat belt to seat (replace fasteners)	45 Nm (33 ft-lb)

720

REAR SEAT BELTS

Rear seat belt assembly

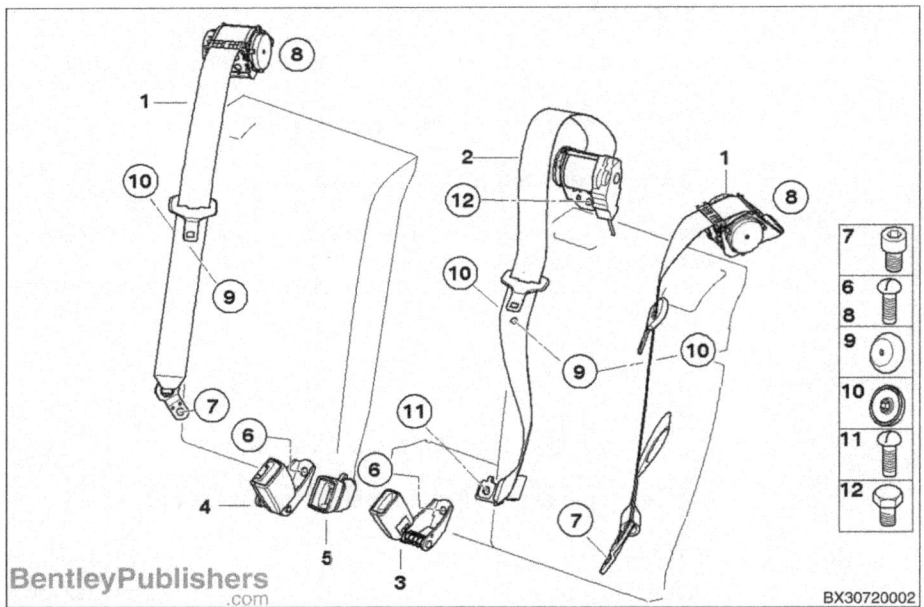

1. Outer rear belts
2. Center belt
3. Left belt lock
4. Right belt lock
5. Center belt lock
6. Belt lock bolts
7. Outer rear belt mounting bolts
8. Mounting bolts for seat belt retractor
9. Seat belt stop button, top
10. Seat belt stop button, bottom
11. Center seat belt lower mounting bolt
12. Center seat belt mounting bolt for retractor.

Rear left/right seat belts, removing and installing

— Remove rear seat side bolster and seat bottom. See **520 Seats**.

— Fold down rear seat.

◁ Remove upper cover (**A**) from seat belt reel by levering it off of base.

— Remove fasteners (**arrows**).

◁ Working between seat belt reel and upper trim (**arrow**), remove fastener for seat belt reel cover.

— Remove seat belt reel inner cover. If necessary, remove upper plastic trim (**A**) and lower carpeted trim (**B**). See **513 Interior Trim**.

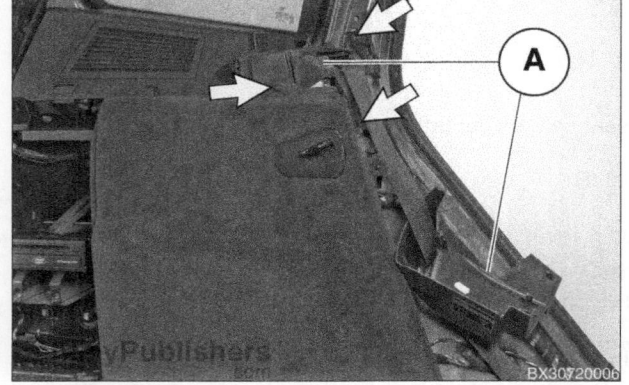

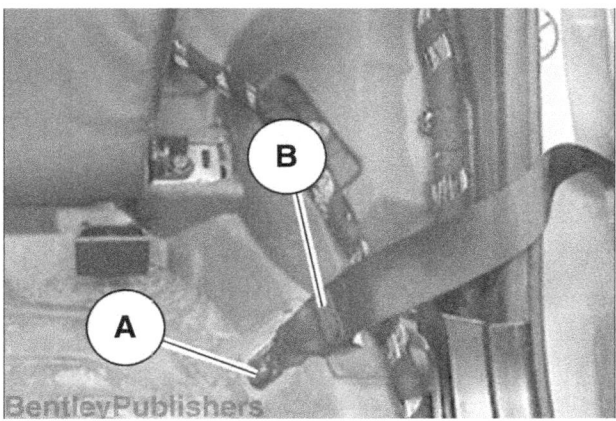

◀ Remove mounting bolt (**arrow**) for seat belt reel.

◀ Remove fastener (**A**) and remove seat belt (**B**) from vehicle.

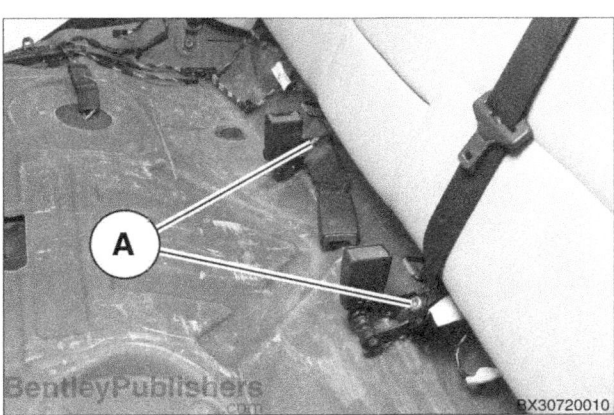

Rear seat belt locks, removing and installing

◀ Remove mounting bolts (**A**) for belt locks, as applicable. Remove belt lock.

– Install in reverse order of removal, noting the following:
  • Be sure that locating tabs for belt reel and locks are properly positioned.

Tightening torques	
Belt lock to body (replace fasteners)	31 Nm (23 ft-lb)
Seat belt end to body (replace fasteners)	31 Nm (23 ft-lb)
Seat belt reel to rear body side panel (replace fasteners)	35 Nm (26 ft-lb)

720

Rear center seat belt, removing and installing

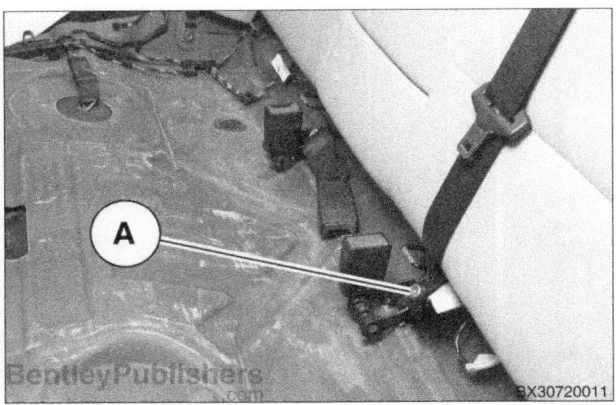

Rear center seat belt, removing and installing

– Remove rear seat bottom. See **520 Seats.**

◀ Remove center shoulder belt mounting bolt (**A**).

– Remove seat backrest from vehicle, See **520 Seats.**

– Remove shoulder belt guide trim at top of seat backrest. Feed belt out through slot in trim.

– Remove backrest upholstery (covering) to access shoulder belt reel.

◀ Once upholstery is removed, remove fastener (**A**) for center seat belt reel (**B**).

– Remove Bowden cable from backrest brackets and unhook from backrest release latch. Remove center seat belt reel.

– Installation is reverse of removal.

Tightening torques	
Rear seat belt reel to rear seat backrest (replace fasteners)	35 Nm (26 ft-lb)
Upper belt to body	31 Nm (23 ft-lb)

721 Airbag System

GENERAL

This repair group covers airbag components and replacement. Airbag system diagnostics, component testing, and airbag system repair should be carried out by a trained service technician using a BMW diagnostic scan tool.

Individual airbag system components can only be tested electronically when installed in the car.

The airbag system (including pyrotechnic seat belt tensioners) is sometimes referred to as the Multiple Restraint System (MRS) in BMW literature.

See also:

- **121 Battery, Starter, Alternator** for battery safety terminal information
- **513 Interior Trim**
- **411 Doors**
- **520 Seats**
- **720 Seat Belts** for front seat belt tensioner (lock) replacement
- **ECL Electrical Component Locations**

Multiple restraint system (MRS)

MRS4RD detects accidents using multiple sensors to selectively activate restraint systems based on crash severity. MRS4RD control unit is centrally located on the transmission tunnel inside the vehicle under the center console trim. Inside of the control unit are x-axis and y-axis acceleration sensors to detect impacts from any direction, front, rear, left and right. MRS4RD also uses front impact sensors mounted on the front of each subframe. B-pillar satellite sensors and door compression sensors provide additional information about side and rear impacts. Communication with MRS4RD is via K-bus.

721

Crash signal

When a crash occurs, MRS4RD sends a signal along the K-bus alerting vehicle systems. Based on severity of the crash, MRS4RD will:

- Shut down fuel pump
- Switch off alternator, partial battery defeat
- Unlock central locking
- Switch on hazard warning flashers
- Make emergency call if equipped w/Telematics.

MRS4RD includes the following restraint components:

- Driver and passenger front two-stage airbags
- Seat occupancy classifier (OC3)
- Side impact airbags for driver and front passenger
- Side impact airbags for rear passengers (optional)
- Head airbags for driver and front passenger
- Battery safety terminal (BST)
- Front pyrotechnic seat belt tensioners
- Fuel pump cut off feature when airbags are deployed
- Satellite crash sensors in B-pillar
- Door compression sensors
- Front impact sensors
- Belt buckle switch
- Back up power supply capacitor

MRS4RD sensor components

1. MRS4RD control unit
2. Front impact sensors
3. Door pressure sensors
4. B-pillar pressure sensors

BX30721001

Curtain airbag (head airbag)

◄ X3 vehicles use a curtain airbag for head protection. This differs from other BMW models. Curtain airbag extends from A-pillar to C-pillar covering entire side window area. Combined with side impact airbags in doors it provides enhanced protection to occupants during a side impact collision.

A-pillar   C-pillar

Curtain airbag

BX30721004

Two-stage airbags

The front airbags use smart or two-stage airbag technology. This airbag deployment strategy ensures that the force of airbag inflation is not greater than necessary to provide protection. The airbags are designed to provide soft deployment if the acceleration sensor detects a low-speed impact, and hard deployment in a higher speed impact.

Stage one of the airbag is designed to ignite first during an impact. Stage two ignites, if necessary, after a timed period, as programmed in the MRS4RD control module.

Seat occupancy detector (OC3)

◀ Passenger side airbag deployment by MRS4RD is based on a signal via K-bus from the seat occupancy classifier (OC3). OC3 sensor mat is integrated in to the passenger side seat cushion. Instead of working just as a weight sensor to turn off the passenger side airbag, OC3 analyzes signals from individual sensors mapping pressure distribution on seat cushion allowing it to identify differences between a person or childseat. When a childseat is present MRS4RD will deactivate passenger side airbag. Passenger airbag "off" light will then illuminate. Light should never be illuminated with a passenger on seat. Otherwise have them move to the rear seat for safety.

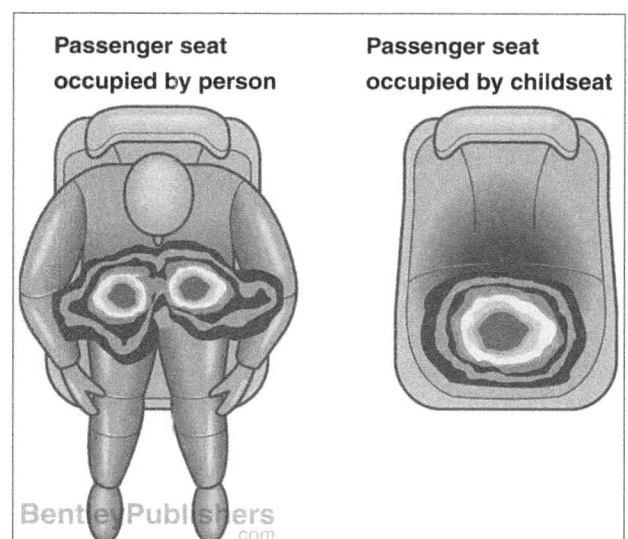

Passenger seat occupied by person

Passenger seat occupied by childseat

NOTE —

* *Passenger airbag "off" light is illuminated when seat is unoccupied.*
* *If the OC3 mat is defective, it must be replaced with the seat bottom as one unit.*

Airbag warning light

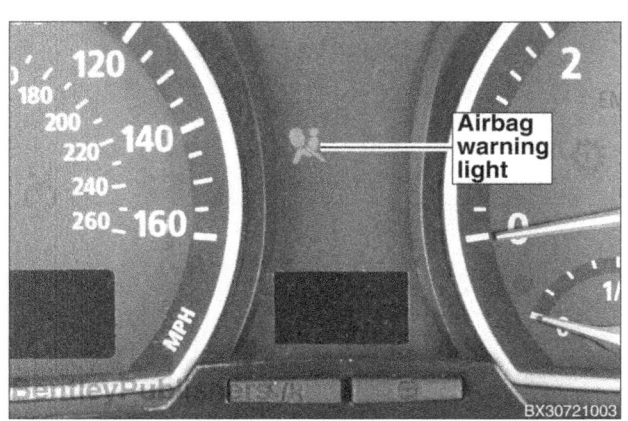

Airbag warning light

◀ The airbag warning light in instrument cluster displays the status of the airbag system when the ignition key is in ACCESORY or ON positions.

* System normal: Warning light illuminates briefly, then goes out.
* System malfunction: Warning light fails to illuminate.
* System malfunction: Warning light illuminates briefly, goes out and illuminates again.

Pre-drive check

MRS4RD performs a pre-drive check as soon as the ignition is turned on. Airbag warning light illuminates for 3-5 seconds while pre-drive check is in progress. During this time all components of the MRS system are checked for functionality. As long as ignition is turned on, MRS5RD will continue to monitor MRS system for faults. System fault codes are stored in non-volatile memory.

NOTE —

* *Individual airbag system components can only be tested electronically when installed in the car. Use BMW diagnostic scan tool for diagnostic work.*

721

Warnings

> **WARNING —**
> - *The airbags and other pyrotechnic devices (seat belt tensioners, active headrests) are inflated by an explosive device. Handled improperly or without adequate safeguards, it can be very dangerous. Observe precautions when working at or near airbags and MRS pyrotechnic devices.*
> - *Serious injury may result if system service is attempted by persons unfamiliar with the BMW airbag system and its approved service procedures.*
> - *Special test equipment is required to retrieve airbag fault codes, diagnose system faults and switch the airbag warning light OFF. The warning light remains ON until problems are corrected and fault memory cleared.*
> - *If the airbag warning light is ON, there is a risk that airbags are not triggered in case of an accident. Be sure to have the system inspected and repaired immediately.*
> - *Disconnect the battery and cover the negative (–) battery terminal with an insulator before starting diagnostic, troubleshooting or service work associated with the airbags, and before doing any welding on the car.*
> - *After disconnecting the battery, wait 1 minute before beginning work on airbag components.*
> - *If an airbag is activated due to an accident, BMW specifies that airbag components be replaced. For more information on post-collision airbag service, see an authorized BMW dealer.*
> - *Do not fire an airbag unit prior to disposal. It must be fired by a special disposal company or shipped back to BMW in the packaging of the new components.*
> - *Wear gloves and avoid skin contact when removing a fired airbag unit. In case of skin contact, wash with water.*
> - *Do not allow airbag system components to come in contact with cleaning solutions or grease. Do not subject airbag components to temperatures above 75°C (167°F). When reconnecting the battery, make sure no person is inside the vehicle.*
> - *Place a removed airbag unit with the padded side facing upward. Do not leave an airbag unit unattended.*
> - *If the airbag unit or airbag control module is dropped from a height of ½ meter (1½ feet) or more, do not reuse.*

AIRBAG SYSTEM

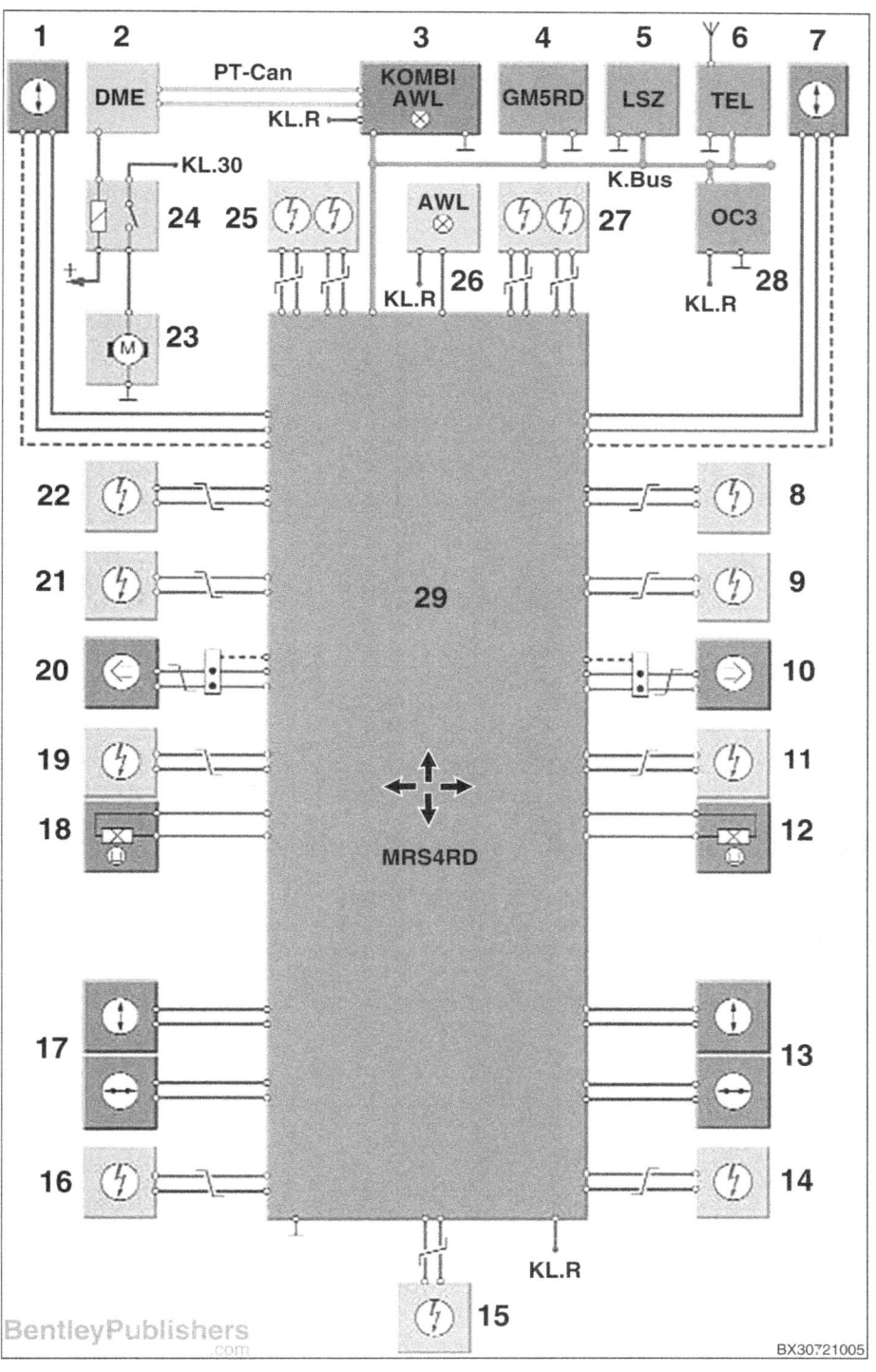

MRS4RD diagram

1. Left front impact sensor
2. Digital motor electronics (DME)
3. Instrument cluster
4. General module (GM5RD)
5. Light switch module (LSZ)
6. Telemetrics unit (TCU)
7. Right front impact sensor
8. Right curtain airbag
9. Side impact airbag
10. Right door compression sensor
11. Right seat belt tensioner
12. Right seat belt switch
13. Right B-pillar satellite sensor
14. Right rear side airbag (optional)
15. Battery safety terminal (BST)
16. Left rear side airbag (optional)
17. Left B-pillar satellite sensor
18. Left seat belt switch
19. Left seat belt tensioner
20. Left door compression sensor
21. Left front side airbag
22. Left front curtain airbag
23. Electric fuel pump
24. Fuel pump relay
25. Driver airbag
26. Airbag warning lamp (AWL
27. Passenger airbag
28. Seat occupancy detector (OC3)
29. MRS4RD control unit

721

AIRBAG ELECTRONICS

Before working on any airbag electronics:

— Disconnect negative (–) cable from battery and cover negative terminal with insulating material.

> **CAUTION—**
> • *Prior to disconnecting the battery, read the battery disconnection cautions given in* **001 Warnings and Cautions**.

Airbag control module, removing and installing

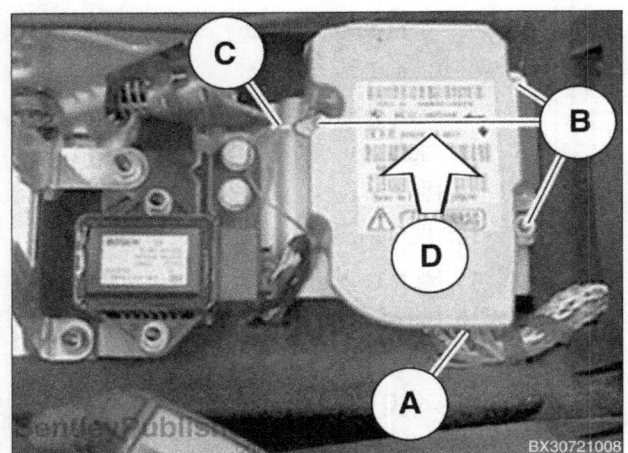

— Remove center console between front seats. See **513 Interior Trim**.

◀ Disconnect electrical harness connector (**A**). Remove airbag control module mounting nuts (**B**) and remove control module (**D**) indirection of arrow.

— Installation is reverse of removal.
- Make sure ground (**C**) is reconnected.

Tightening torque	
Airbag control module to floor	8 Nm (71 in-lb)

Side impact crash sensor, removing and installing

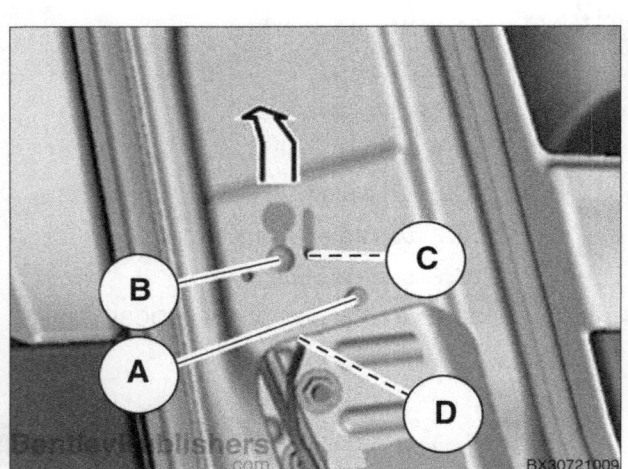

— Remove B-pillar trim. See **513 Interior Trim** and **520 Seats**.

◀ Remove sensor mounting screws (**A**) and (**B**) Remove sensor (**C**) from inside of B-pillar and remove electrical harness connector from crash sensor. Note mounting direction of sensor before removing.

— Installation is reverse of removal.
- Make sure guide pin on sensor is seated in sheet metal of B-pillar correctly.

Tightening torque	
Side impact sensor to B-pillar	8 Nm (71 in-lb)

Door compression sensor, removing and installing

— Remove door trim panel. See **411 Doors**.

— Remove vapor barrier. See **512 Door Windows**.

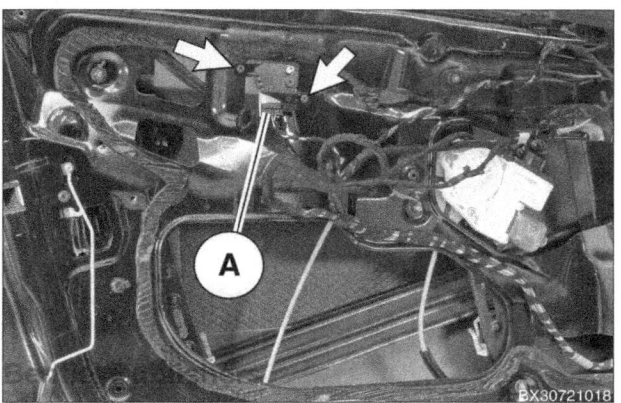

◄ Disconnect electrical connection (**A**) and remove fasteners (**arrows**) to remove compression sensor.

• Installation is reverse of removal.

Tightening torque	
Compression sensor to door shell	4.6 Nm (41 in-lb)

AIRBAGS

Before working on any airbag modules, disconnect negative (–) cable from battery and cover negative terminal with insulating material.

> *WARNING* —
> • *After disconnecting the battery, wait 1 minute before beginning work on airbag components.*

> *CAUTION*—
> • *Prior to disconnecting the battery, read the battery disconnection cautions given in* **001 Warnings and Cautions**.

Driver airbag, removing and installing

Vehicles covered by this manual are equipped with either a multifunction steering wheel, or a sport steering wheel. Follow applicable procedure below to remove airbag.

With multifunction (MFL) steering wheel 2004 - 2007 (pre-LCI) vehicles

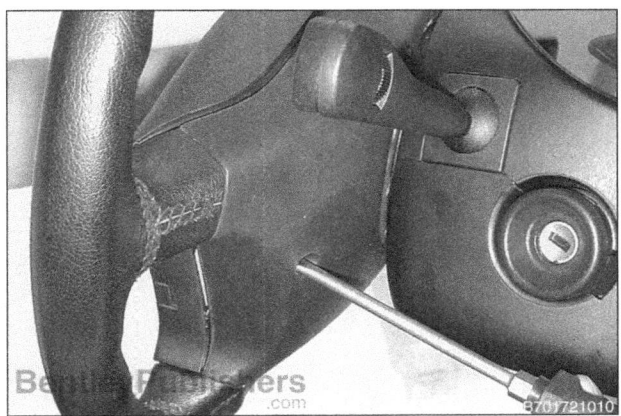

◄ Working behind steering wheel, completely loosen Torx screws (T30) while holding airbag in place.

• Support airbag unit to prevent it from falling out.

721

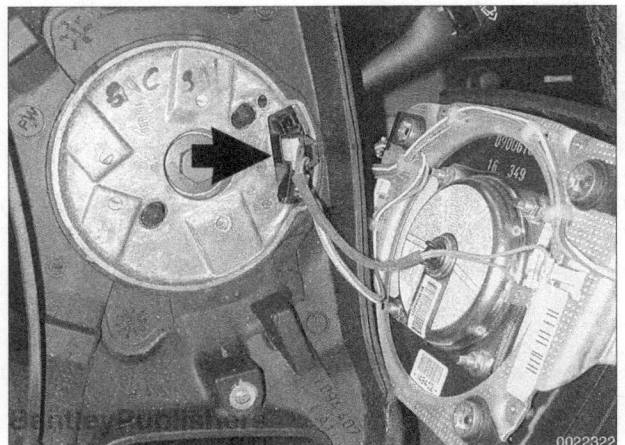

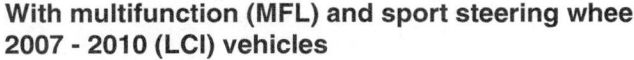
Carefully lift airbag unit off steering wheel and disconnect harness connectors (**arrow**) from rear of airbag unit.

> **CAUTION—**
> • Do not pinch airbag harness in center of steering wheel when removing or installing airbag.

With multifunction (MFL) and sport steering wheel 2007 - 2010 (LCI) vehicles

NOTE—
• Airbag removal on LCI MFL steering wheel is similar to sport steering wheel for all models.

Insert Torx driver through opening (**arrow**) in rear of steering wheel.

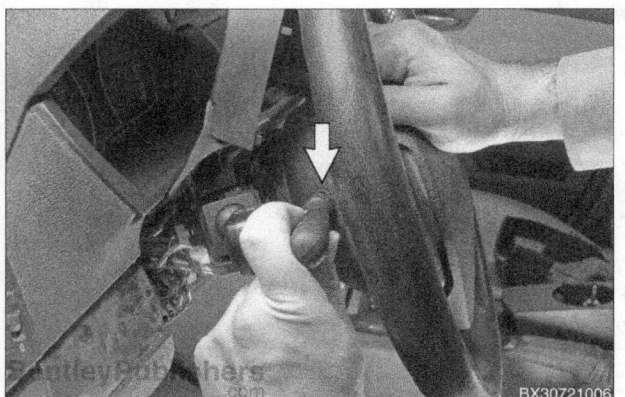

Push against lock spring in direction of **arrow** and lift airbag slightly to release airbag lock.

— Repeat procedure on other side of steering wheel to remove airbag unit.

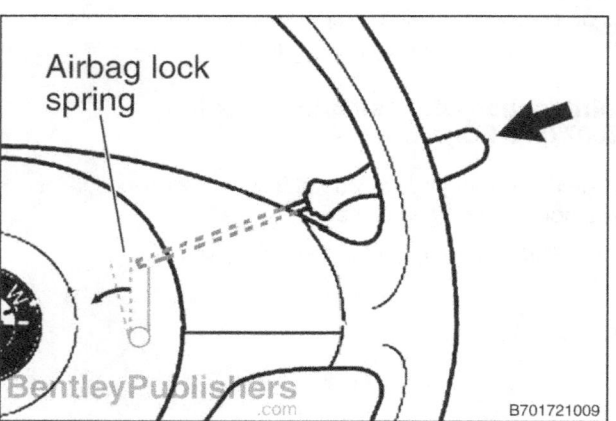

Airbag lock spring

Gently release electrical harness connector (**arrow**) using screwdriver as shown.

> **WARNING—**
> * Store the removed airbag unit with the horn pad facing up. If stored facing down, accidental deployment could propel it violently into the air, causing injury.
> * Once an airbag is removed, do not drive the car.
> * Do not connect the battery with the airbag disconnected. A fault code is stored and the airbag warning light is illuminated.

Continued for all vehicles

– Installation is reverse of removal.

   • MFL steering wheel: Torque airbag using specification listed below.

   • Sport steering wheel: Press airbag unit mounting pins into spring locks in steering wheel until they snap in firmly.

Tightening torque	
Airbag to steering wheel (MFL)	8 Nm (71 in-lb)

> **WARNING—**
> * Once airbag unit is installed and all other service procedures are completed, start engine and check that airbag warning light goes out. If warning light stays on, the airbag system will not function as designed. Further system diagnosis is required.

Passenger airbag, removing and installing

– Disconnect negative (–) cable from battery and cover negative terminal with insulating material.

> **WARNING—**
> * After disconnecting the battery, wait 1 minute before beginning work on airbag components.

> **CAUTION—**
> * Prior to disconnecting the battery, read the battery disconnection cautions given in **001 Warnings and Cautions**.

– Remove glove box and lower fuse holder. See **513 Interior Trim**.

 Working inside glove box opening, disconnect airbag electrical connection (**arrows**).

721

Door mounted side impact airbag, removing and installing

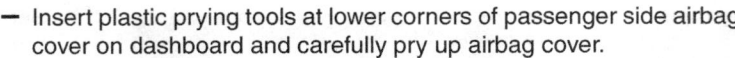

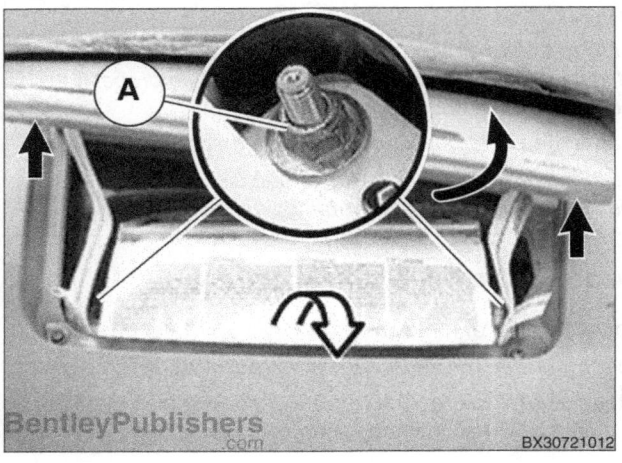

BX30721012

– Insert plastic prying tools at lower corners of passenger side airbag cover on dashboard and carefully pry up airbag cover.

• Cover is tethered to dashboard with straps.

◀ Remove nuts (**A**) and lift airbag module and wring out of dash.

> **WARNING**—
> • Store the removed airbag unit with the soft pad facing up. If stored facing down, accidental deployment could propel it violently into the air, causing injury.

– Installation is reverse of removal. Make sure wiring harness is not pinched when installing airbag unit in dashboard.

Tightening torques	
Passenger airbag to instrument panel carrier (M6)	6 Nm (53 in-lb)

Door mounted side impact airbag, removing and installing

Front and rear door panel mounted airbag removing and installing is similar.

– Disconnect negative (–) cable from battery and cover negative terminal with insulating material.

> **WARNING**—
> • After disconnecting the battery, wait 1 minute before beginning work on airbag components.

> **CAUTION**—
> • Prior to disconnecting the battery, read the battery disconnection cautions given in **001 Warnings and Cautions**.

– Remove inside door panel. See **411 Doors**.

◀ Remove airbag mounting bolts (**arrows**) and lift airbag module out of door panel.

> **CAUTION**—
> • When removing and installing the airbag unit, pay attention to the routing of the electrical harness to avoid kinks or breaks in the wire.

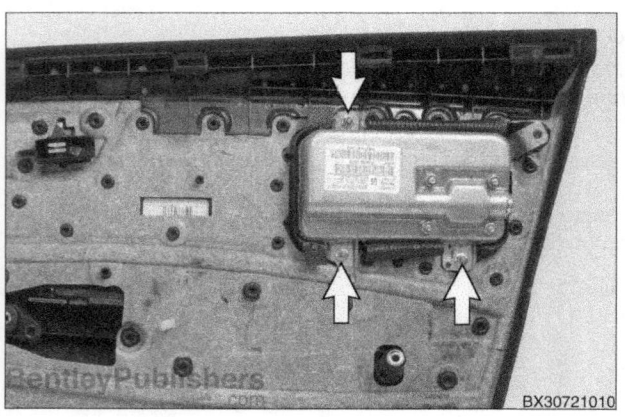

BX30721010

– Installation is reverse of removal.

• Route electrical harnesses as they were before.

• Use new wire ties as necessary.

• Use new self-locking mounting bolts.

Tightening torque	
Side impact airbag to door panel	8.5 Nm (75 in-lb)

Curtain airbag, removing and installing

– Before starting work on the head protection airbag, disconnect negative (–) cable from battery.

> **CAUTION—**
> • Prior to disconnecting the battery, read the battery disconnection cautions given in **001 Warnings and Cautions**.

– Curtain airbag components include:
  • Gas generator
  • Head protection airbag

Replacement of head protection airbag is an extensive operation, including removal of the following:
  • Complete headliner
  • Windshield pillar (A-pillar) trim
  • Front door pillar (B-pillar) trim
  • Rear door pillar (C-pillar) trim
  • Cargo area pillar (D-pillar) trim

◄ Working above the B-pilar area, unlock and disconnect electrical connection (**A**) from curtain air bag gas generator (**B**).

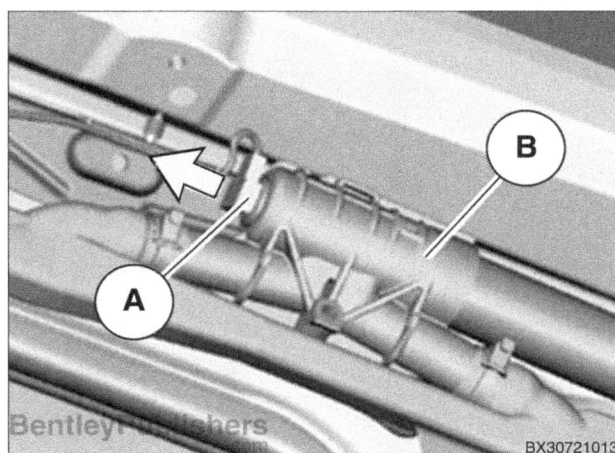

BX30721013

◄ Remove bolt (**A**) located on A-pillar. Bolt is held in place using a lock washer.

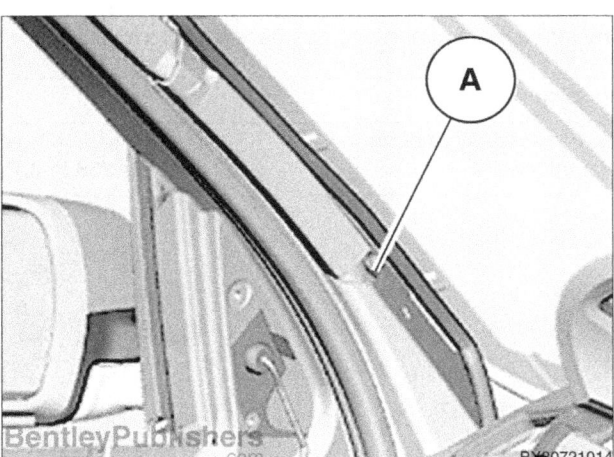

BX30721014

Curtain airbag, removing and installing

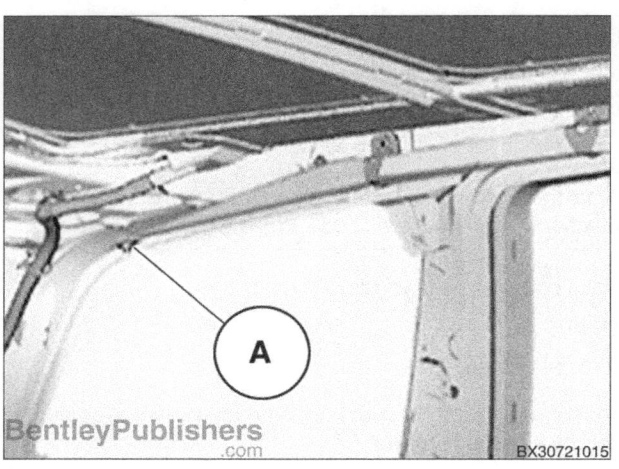

◄ Remove bolt (**A**) located on D-pillar. Bolt is held in place using a lock washer.

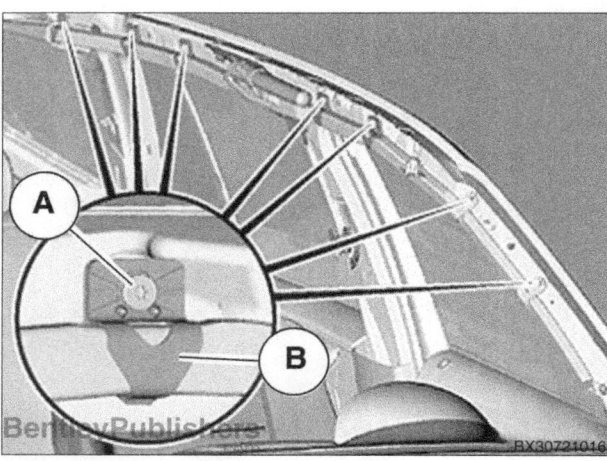

◄ Remove fasteners (**A**) from curtain airbag retaining clips (**B**).

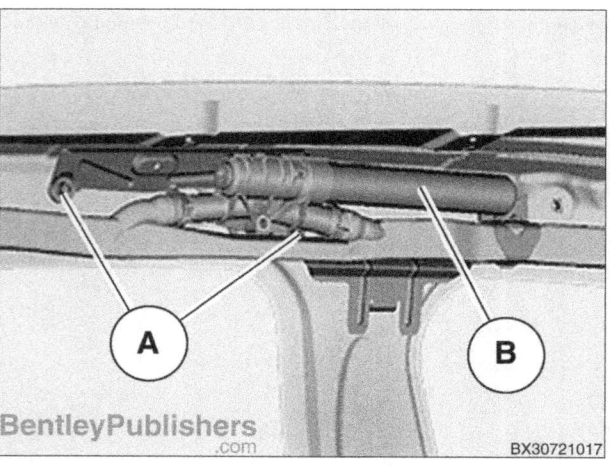

◄ Working at B-pilar, remove fasteners (**A**) gas generator (**B**) and remove complete curtain airbag and gas generator from vehicle.

Tightening torques	
Curtain airbag assembly to body (M6, replace fasteners)	6.5 Nm (58 in-lb)

ECL Electrical Component Locations

GENERAL

This repair group covers electrical component location information. Fuse locations and ground points are also covered.

Electrical equipment and accessories included vary with model and model year. Confirm component identification whenever you begin work on the electrical system.

See also:

• **130 Fuel Injection** for engine management components

• **520 Seats** for seat control and seat heating components

• **540 Sunroof** for retractable sun roof components

• **600 Electrical System–General** for bus systems

• **640 Air-conditioning and Heating** for climate control system components

• **650 Radio** for communication equipment components

• **ELE Electrical Wiring Diagrams** for electrical schematics

ECL

BMW acronyms

BMW uses many abbreviations and acronyms in the technical literature, service bulletins, wiring diagrams and parts bulletins it distributes. See **Table a** for common BMW and industry acronyms.

Table a. Common BMW acronyms	
Acronym	**Component or system**
A/C	air-conditioning
ABS	antilock brakes
AHL	adaptive headlights
AUC	automatic air recirculation control
BSD	bit serial data interface
BST	battery safety terminal
CA	comfort access
CAN	controller area network (bus)
CAS	car access system (module)
CDC	CD changer
CID	central information display
DISA	variable intake manifold system
DME	digital motor electronics
DM-TL	diagnosis module - tank leakage
DSC	dynamic stability control
DWA	antitheft alarm
DXC	dynamic X Drive control
ECM	engine control module
ECT	engine coolant temperature (sensor)
EDK	electronic throttle
EGS	electronic transmission control
EVAP	fuel tank evaporative control system
EWS	electronic immobilizer
FH	power windows
GM	general module
GPS	global positioning system
HPS	head protection airbag
IAT	intake air temperature (sensor)
IHKA	automatic heating and air-conditioning system
ITS	inflatable tubular structure (head protection airbag)
K-CAN	body CAN
KL R	battery positive, ignition on accessories
KL 15	battery positive, ignition switch on RUN
KL 30	battery positive (B+), power
KL 31	battery / chassis ground
KL 50	ignition start position, power
KOMBI	instrument cluster

Table a. Common BMW acronyms	
Acronym	**Component or system**
LCM	light control module
LDP	fuel tank leak diagnosis pump
LED	light emitting diode
LEV	low emissions vehicle
LIN	local interconnect network (bus)
LSZ	light switch cluster
MDS	multi drive sunroof control unit
MIL	malfunction indicator light
MRS	multiple restraint system (airbags)
NAV	navigation system
NG	tilt sensor
NLEV	national low emissions vehicle
NTC	negative temperature coefficient (resistor)
OBD II	second generation on-board diagnostics
PDC	park distance control
PT-CAN	powertrain CAN
PWG	accelerator pedal module
RAM	random access memory
RPA	tire pressure control system (early)
RDC	tire pressure control system (late)
RLS	rain light sensor
RXD	receive data line
SDARS	satellite radio receiver
SIA	service interval indicator
SRS	supplemental restraint system (airbags)
SULEV	super ultra low emissions vehicle
SZM	center console switch center
TCM	automatic transmission control module
TCU	telematics control module
TDC	top dead center
TI	injection signal
TLEV	transitional low emissions vehicle
TPM	tire pressure monitoring
TXD	transmit data line
USIS	ultrasonic car alarm
ULEV	ultra low emissions vehicle
VANOS	variable camshaft timing
VTG	Transfer case electroncs (xDrive)
VVT	Valvetronic

Warnings and Cautions

> **WARNING** —
> - *The battery safety terminal, pyrotechnic seat belt tensioners and airbags utilize explosive devices. Handle with extreme care. See warnings and cautions in* **121 Battery, Alternator, Starter, 720 Seat Belts,** *and* **721 Airbag System.**

> **CAUTION** —
> - *Prior to disconnecting the battery, read the battery disconnection precautions in* **001 Warnings and Cautions.**
> - *Relay and fuse positions vary from car to car. If questions arise, an authorized BMW dealer is the best source for the most accurate and up-to-date information.*
> - *A good way to verify a relay position is to compare the wiring colors at the relay socket to the colors indicated on the wiring diagrams in* **ELE Electrical Wiring Diagrams.**
> - *Switch the ignition OFF and remove the negative (-) battery cable before removing any electrical components. Connect and disconnect ignition system wires, multiple connectors, and ignition test equipment leads while the ignition is switched OFF.*
> - *Use a digital multimeter for electrical tests.*

FUSE LOCATIONS AND RATINGS

For a description of the power supply system, see **600 Electrical System–General**.

Fuses and fusible links in X3 vehicles are located as follows:

1. **A41** Main power distribution panel (**F1 - F71**). Located above glove box.
   - High-amp fuses for DME and ignition/starter switch (**F102 - F107**) are located on rear side of **A41**.

2. **Electronics box (E-box) fuses**. Located inside of E-box.
   - **M54 engine:** F01 - F05
   - **N52 engine:** F01- F09

3. **A400** Cargo compartment fuse box (**F108 - F109**). Located ahead of battery under cargo compartment floor panel.

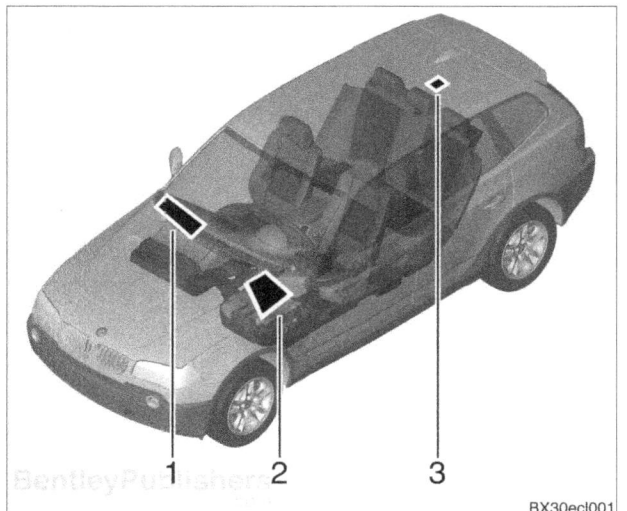

1   2   3

BX30ecl001

ECL

Main power distribution panel (A41)

The main power distribution panel (A41) is underneath right side of the dashboard, behind the glove compartment. Fuses **F1** through **F71** are located on the front of the main power distribution panel.

 Open glove compartment. Twist plastic retainers (**arrows**) 90° to remove fuse cover. Cover lists fuse applications and ratings.

Fuse applications and ratings vary by year. Fuse applications for each model year are shown in **Table c**.

NOTE—

- *When the fuse box is up in locked position, the plastic tabs should point toward each other. When unlocked, they point to the back of the car.*
- *No vehicle is equipped with every one of the components or fuses in the fuse tables.*
- *A small built in flashlight (**A**) is in the glove compartment next to the fuse box.*
- *A red plastic fuse puller (**B**) is in the center of the fuse box.*
- *The sheet of paper with the fuse assignments, below the fuses, can be slid out for reference.*
- *Vertical fuses are active. Horizontal fuses are spares.*

Main power distribution panel (A41)

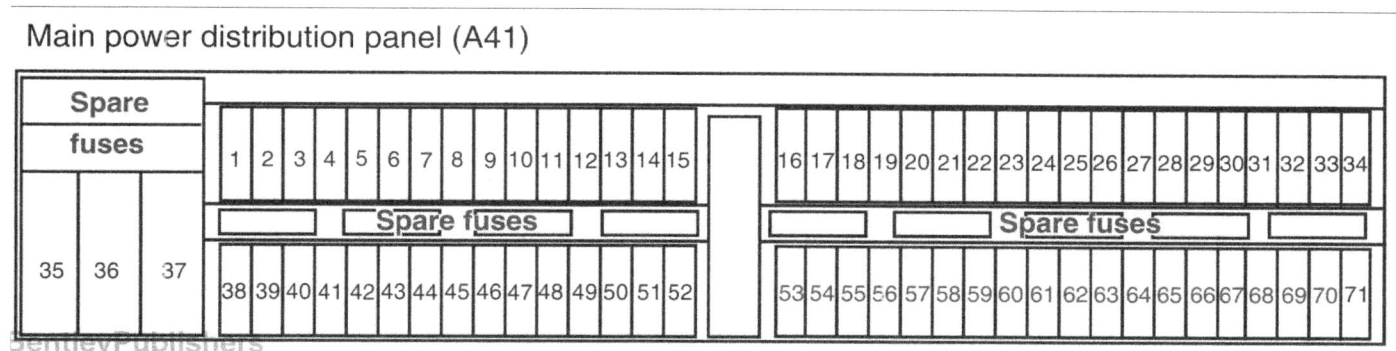

BX30ecl004

Fuse	Rating in amps	Protected circuits
F1		not used
F2		not used
F3		not used
F4		not used
F5	5	Horn relay
F6	5	Make-up mirror light
F7	5	Central information display (CID), navigation, radio, telephone,
F8		not used
F9	5	Clutch switch, Light switch cluster (to 09/2006) Light module (from 09/2006)
F10	5	Instrument cluster
F11	5	Airbag, multiple restraint system (MRS), side airbag
F12	7.5	Dynamic stability control (DSC), electric seat heating, thermostat
F13		not used
F14	5	Electric vehicle imobilizer (EWS)
F15	5	Rain sensor, rear wiper
F16		not used
F17		not used
F18		not used
F19		not used
F20		not used
F21	7.5	Engine electronics
F22	5	Engine electronics
F23	5	Adaptive headlight control
F24	5	Electrochromic rear view mirror, park distance control

Table b. Main power distribution panel (A41) fuses

Fuse	Rating in amps	Protected circuits
F25	5	Heated washer nozzles, outside mirror
F26	5	Cigar lighter, transfer gear
F27	10	Engine electronics, reversing light
F28	5	Heating / air conditioning, rear window defroster
F29	5	Engine electronics / DME
F30	7.5	Engine electronics / OBD II, oil level sensor
F31	5	Side mirror
F32	5	Light switch cluster (to 09/2006) Light module (from 09/2006)
F33	5	Dynamic stability control (DSC)
F34	5	Fuel pump control (EKPS), Instrument cluster
F35	40	Dynamic stability control (DSC)
F36	50	Secondary air pump
F37	60	Electric fan
F38	15	Fog light
F39	5	Telephone
F40	5	Gear indicator lighting, steering angle sensor (DSC)
F41	30	Amplifier, radio
F42	10	Central information display (CID), CD changer, navigation, TV
F43	5	Instrument cluster, on-board diagnostics (OBD II)
F44	20	Trailer socket
F45	20	Rear wiper
F46	20	Panoramic sunroof
F47	20	Cigar lighter, cargo compartment charging socket
F48	30	Central locking system, power window

ECL

Main power distribution panel (A41)

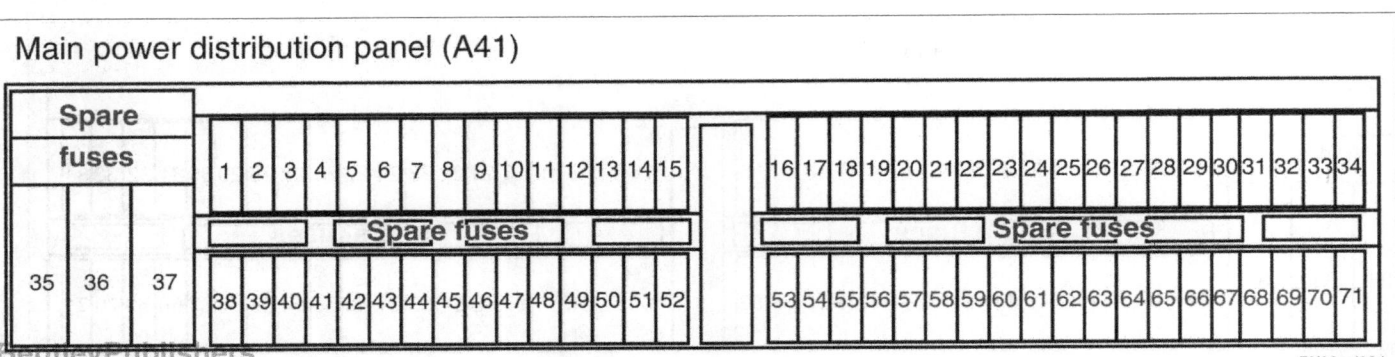

Table b. Main power distribution panel (A41) fuses

Fuse	Rating in amps	Protected circuits
F49	5	Antitheft alarm system, central locking system, interior lights, power window, wiper-washer control
F50	40	Blower motor
F51	30	Headlight washer system
F52	30	Central locking system, heated washer nozzles, interior lights, wiper-washer control
F53	25	Dynamic stability control (DSC)
F54	20	Fuel pump control (EKPS)
F55	15	Horn relay
F56	5	to 03/2007 Transmission control
	7.5	from 03/2007 Preparations, rear seat entertainment
F57	7.5	Mirror with fold-in function, power window
F58	7.5	to 03/2007 Adaptive headlight
	10	from 03/2007 Lumbar support

Table b. Main power distribution panel (A41) fuses

Fuse	Rating in amps	Protected circuits
F59	10	Wiper-washer control
F60	30	Central locking system,
F61	25	Seat heating
F62	7.5	Auxiliary water pump, heating / air-conditioning, water valve
F63	7.5	Air-conditioning compressor
F64		not used
F65	30	Driver's seat adjustment (to 03/2007) Driver's seat memory (from 03/2007)
F66	10	Steering wheel heating
F67	5	Alarm horn / siren, antitheft alarm system, electrochromic mirror, electronic vehicle imobilizer (EWS), interior movement detector
F68	30	Rear window defroster
F69	5	Servotronic, Tire pressure control (RDC)
F70	30	Passenger's seat adjustment, passenger's lumbar support switch
F71	30	Rear window lift

High amperage fuses above panel A41

Additional high amperage fuses are found on top of the main power distribution fuse panel (A41).

◄ To access high amperage fuse panel, lower main power distribution fuse panel fully.

– Slide harness connector block off top of panel (**curved arrow**).

– Detach access panel by squeezing retaining clips to release. (**arrows**).

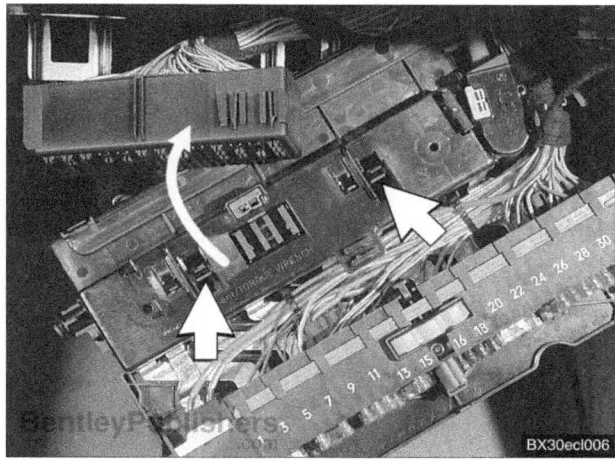

◄ Fuse numbers **F101 - F107** are located on top of main power distribution panel (A41). See **Table d**.

Table c. High amperage fuses (above panel A41)		
Fuse	**Rating in amps**	**Protected circuits**
F101	not used	
F102	80	**M54 engine:** • B+ terminal • DME mail relay • Engine control module • Fuse 5 E-box fuse pack • Transmission control module (TCM) **N52 engine:** • Integrated supply module (IVM)
F103	not used	
F104	not used	
F105	50	Ignition switch
F106	50	Light switch cluster (M54 engine) Light module (N52 engine) Ignition switch
F107	50	Light switch cluster (M54 engine) Light module (N52 engine) Trailer module

E-box engine electronics fuses

M54 engine (2004 - 2006)

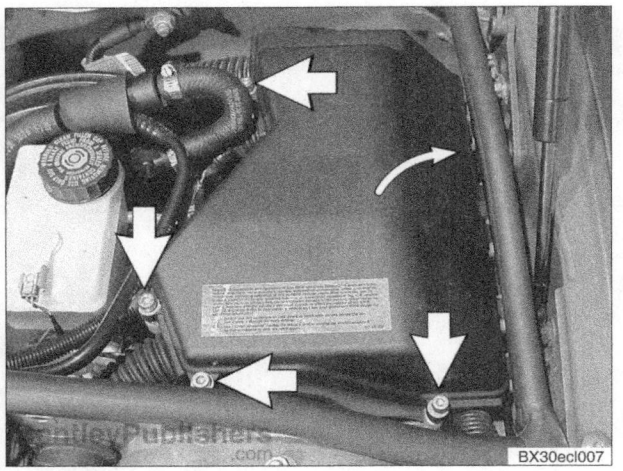

◄ Working in right rear engine compartment:
- Remove fasteners (**arrows**).
- Tilt E-box cover up towards fender and remove from clips.

◄ F01 - F05 are located in fuse carrier A8680.

– To replace fuses F01 - F05 unclip fuse carrier from connector.

◄ Carefully pry open A8680 cover. Fuse ratings are in **Table e**.

Table d. M54 engine electronics fuses (A8680)		
Fuse	**Rating in amps**	**Protected circuits**
F01	30	Ignition coils (T6151 - T6156)
F02	30	Vanos solenoid valves (Y6275 - Y6276)) Characteristic map thermostat (B6279) DISA valve (Y6176) Fuel tank vent valve (Y6120) Idle actuator (Y6130)
F03	20	Reverse light relay (K6325) Secondary air pump relay (K6304a) Steering angle sensor (A68) Fuel tank leakage diagnostic module (DMTL) (M119a) Mass air flow sensor (B6207a) Secondary air mini mass air flow sensor (B6206) Dynamic stabilty control (DSC) (A65a) Crankshaft sensor (B6203) Fuel pump relay (K6301) DSC sensor (B75) Camshaft sensors (B6214 - B6224) Exhaust flap (Y198) E-box fan (M6506) A/C compressor relay (K19)
F04	30	Oxygen sensors (B62101 - B62202) Transmission control module (A7000a)
F05	30	Fuel injector relay (K6327)

ECL

E-box engine electronics fuses

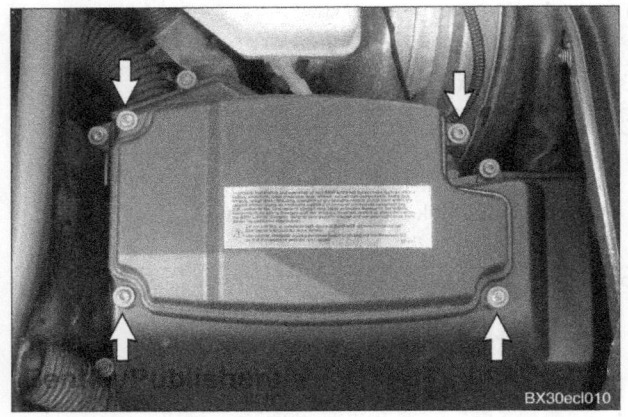

BX30ecl010

N52 engine (2007 - 2010)

◄ Working in right rear engine compartment:
- Remove fasteners (**arrows**).
- Lift cover off E-box lid.

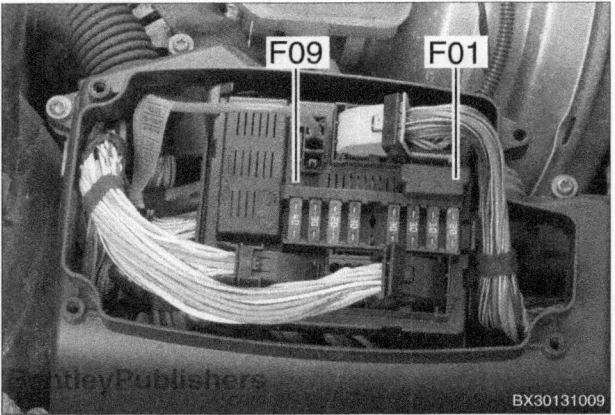

F09   F01

BentleyPublishers

BX30131009

◄ F01 - F09 are located on integrated voltage supply module (IVM) (A6009). IVM fuse ratings are in **Table e**.

Fuse	Rating in amps	Protected circuits
Table e. N52 engine integrated voltage supply module (IVM) (A6009) fuses		
F01	20	Crankshaft sensor (B6203a) Intake camshaft sensor (B6214a) Exhaust camshaft sensor B6224a) Vanos solenoid valve, intake (Y6275) Vanos solenoid valve, exhaust (Y6276) DISA controller 1 (Y6540) DISA controller 2 (Y6541) Heated air mass meter (B6207b) Characteristic map thermostat (Y6279) Electric coolant pump (M6035) Oil condition sensor (B62540a) Fuel tank vent valve (Y6120)
F02	10	Exhaust flap (Y198) Relay for A/C compressor (K19) DMTL pump (M119a), Power distribution (A41) Dynamic stability control (A65a) DSC sensor (B75) Steering angle sensor (A68) E-box fan (M6506)
F03	30	Relay, variable valve timing gear
F04	20	Crankshaft breather heating (E65390) Oxygen sensors
F05	-	not used
F06	30	Ignition coils (T6151 - T6156)
F07	20	Fuel injectors (Y6101 - Y6106)
F08	30	Electric coolant pump (M6035)
F09	40	Electronic control unit (ECU)

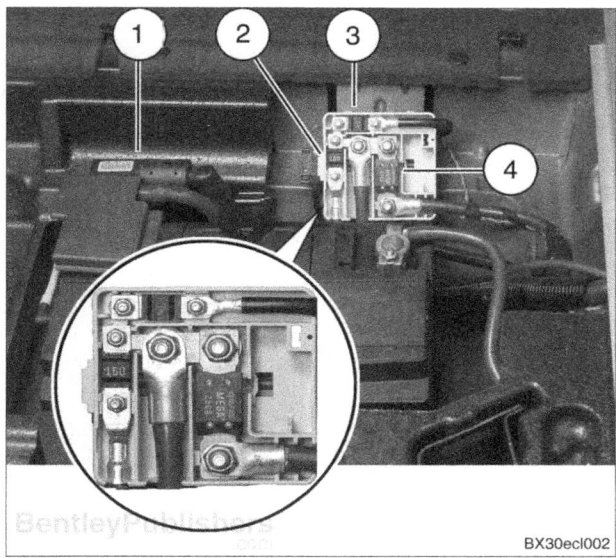

BX30ecl002

Cargo compartment fuse box (A400)

◁ Cargo compartment fuse box (A400) is installed under cargo compartment floor panel in front of vehicle battery.

1. **G19a** Battery safety terminal (BST):
   - Battery safety terminal is incorporated in the main power line (B+) to starter/alternator.
2. **F203** N52 engine only:
   - Provides power to integrated supply module (IVM) for valvetronic relay circuit.
3. **F109** Transfer case control module (A70006) power:
   - Fuses, **F80** and **F81** may be installed in an additional fuse holder (A48), dividing this circuit in vehicles equipped with Hi-Fi sound option.
   - **F80**: Hi-Fi amplifier.
   - **F81**: Transfer case control module (A70006).
4. **F108** power line (B+) to main power distribution panel (A41).

Fuse ratings for high amperage fuses are in **Table f**.

	Table f. Fuses (high amperage) in cargo compartment fuse box (A400)	
Fuse	**Rating in amps**	**Protected circuits**
F108	250	Main power distribution panel (A41)
F109	40	Transfer case control module (A70006)
F109	60	Hi-Fi sound option only: • **F80** (30A) Hi-Fi amplifier • **F81** (40A) Transfer case control module
F203	100	N52 engine only: • Integrated supply module (IVM)

RELAY POSITIONS

Main relay panel

◁ Main relay panel is located under right side of dashboard above main power distribution panel (A41). To access main relay panel remove glove compartment. See **513 Interior trim**.

1. Headlight washer (K6)
2. Secondary air pump (K6304) (M54 engine)
3. Fuel pump relay (K6301) (M54 engine)
4. A/C compressor relay
5. Foglight relay (K47)
6. Horn relay (K2)
7. General module (A1)

NOTE—

- *Main power distribution panel (A41) and dash are shown removed for clarity.*
- *Not all vehicles will be equipped with all relays listed.*

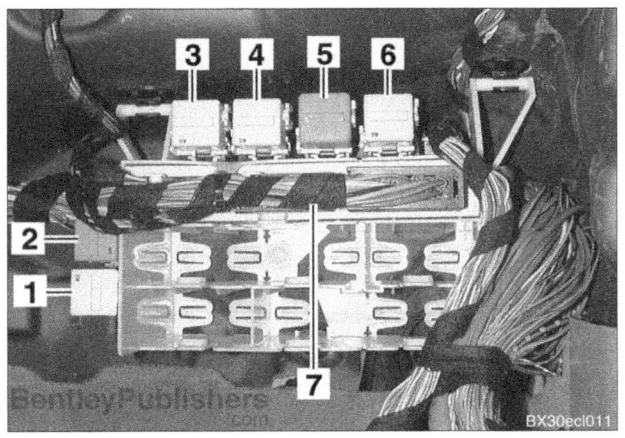

BX30ecl011

ECL

Electronics box (E-box) relays

M54 engine

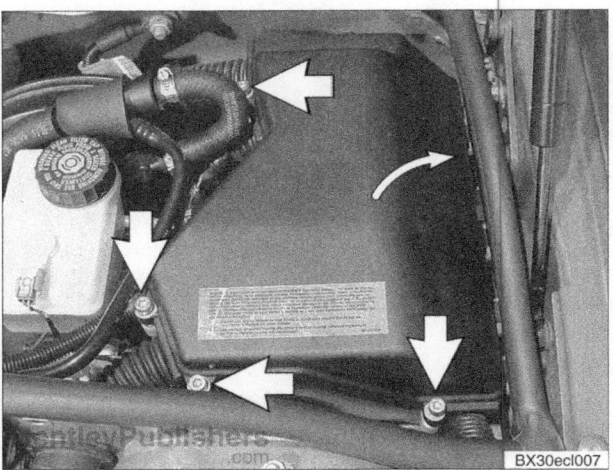

◄ Working in right rear engine compartment:

- Remove fasteners (**arrows**). Tilt E-box cover up towards fender and remove from clips.

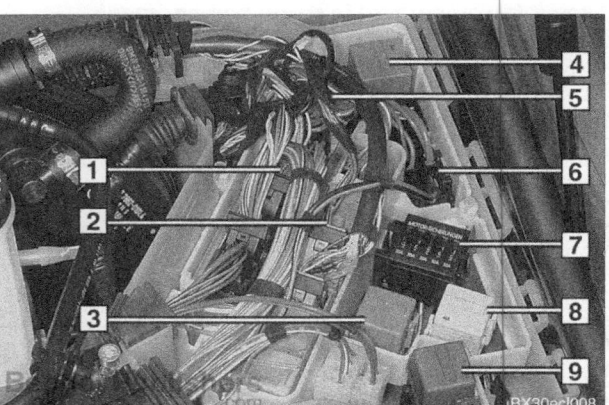

◄ M54 engine electronics (E-box) relays:

1. Engine control module (ECM).
2. Automatic transmission control module (K6300).
3. DME main relay (K6300).
4. Windshield washer double relay (K11).
5. E-box temperature sensor.
6. B+ connector.
7. Engine electronics fuse holder.
8. Fuel injector relay (K6327).
9. Back-up light relay (K6325) (automatic transmission only).

N52 engine

The Integrated Voltage Supply Module (IVM) (A6009) contains integral relays and replaceable fuses. The relays contained within the IVM are non-replaceable. If a faulty relay is suspected the complete IVM must be replaced. The following relays are contained as part of the IVM:

- DME main relay
- Variable valve timing relay
- Fuel injector relay
- Reversing light relay

◀ Working in right rear engine compartment:

- Remove fasteners (**arrows**), lift cover off E-box lid.

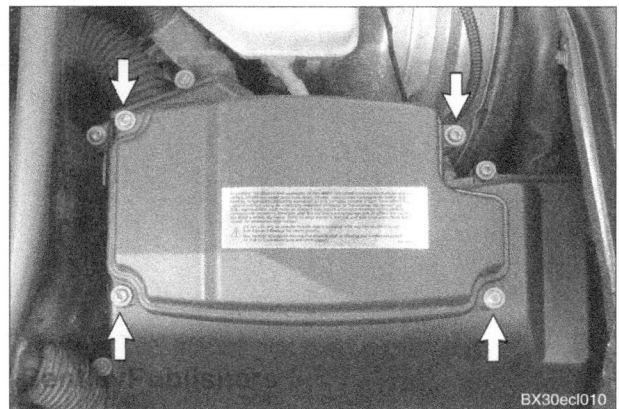

◀ Remove E-box cover:

- Remove electrical connections from integrated voltage module (IVM).
- Release clip (**A**) and remove IVM from E-box cover.
- Remove fasteners (**arrows**), Tilt E-box cover up towards fender.
- Feed wiring harnesses out of E-box cover while removing.

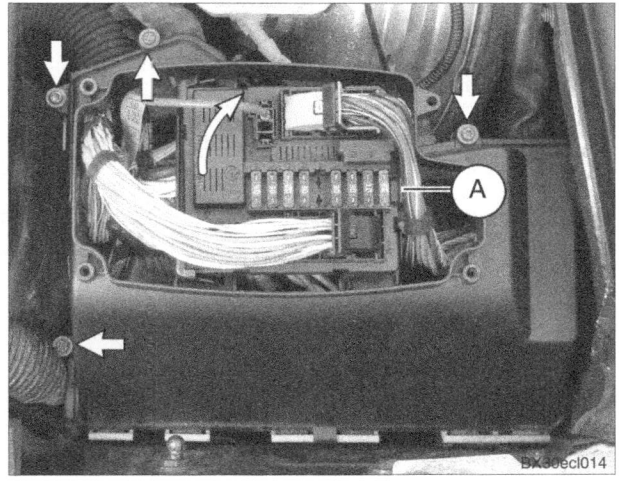

◀ N52 engine electronics (E-box) relay:

1. Windshield washer double relay (K11).

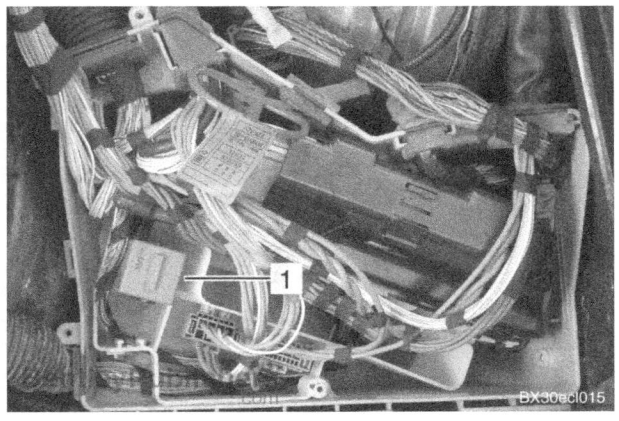

ELECTRICAL COMPONENT LOCATIONS

Electrical components table

Table g is a cross-referenced listing of electrical components in X3 vehicles.

- **Column 1**: Components alphabetized by names in current usage
- **Column 2**: BMW alphanumeric code
- **Column 3**: Location in vehicle
- **Column 4**: Figure number in this repair group, if illustrated

Photos in this repair group illustrate a 2007 X3 unless indicated otherwise.

Table g. X3 Component locations

Component	Code	Location	Fig #
12v socket, center console	E28	Center console front	
12v socket, rear	E30	Center console rear	
12v socket, cargo compartment	A840	Right side cargo compartment	
12v socket relay	k31	Main relay panel behind glove box	
A/C and heating control panel (module)	A11a	Center dashboard	
A/C and heating electrical components		*see* **640 Heating and Air-conditioning** *see also* Heater	
A/C compressor control valve	Y2a	Right side of engine	
A/C compressor control relay	K19	Main relay panel behind glove box	
ABS		*see also* DSC entries	
ABS / DSC control module	A65a	Left rear engine compartment	
ABS wheel speed sensor	B1, B2 B3, B4	Wheel hub, left front, right front, left rear, or right rear wheel *see also* **340 Brakes**	19
Accelerator pedal module	R10	Underneath accelerator pedal	26
Airbag		*see also* MRS	
Airbag contact spring, driver side	I01086	Underneath steering wheel in steering column	
Airbag control module	A12	Between front seats, under center console	30
Airbag sensors, front, left, right	S71, S72	Engine compartment inner fender, left, right	
Airbag sensors, B-pillar satellite, left, right	A157, A158	Bottom of B-pillar left, right	
Airbag door pressure sensors, front door, left, right	A162, A163	Front door left, front door right	
Airbag, driver	G5	In steering wheel under horn button	
Airbag, head protection, left, right	G37, G38	Top of D-pillar, left, right	
Airbag, passenger	G6	Under right end of dashboard	
Airbag, side front, driver, passenger	G14b, G15b	Underside of front door trim panel, left, right	
Airbag, side rear, driver, passenger	G20a, G21a	Underside of front door trim panel, left, right	
Air quality sensor (AUC)	B414	Engine compartment, center, front, under air intake cowl	1, 10
Alarm		*see* Anti-theft	
Adaptive headlight control module	A214	Behind glove compartment, on main power distribution panel (A41)	

Table g. X3 Component locations

Component	Code	Location	Fig #
Alternator (generator)	G6524	Left front of engine	
Amplifier	A18	Left side cargo compartment behind trim	
Antenna		*see* **650 Radio** *see also* Tire pressure control	
Antenna diversity module	A421	Center cargo compartment lid	
Anti-theft siren with tilt sensor (DWA)	H16025	Right side, within fresh air plenum	
AUC sensor		*see* Automatic air recirculation (AUC) sensor	
Audio system components		*see* **650 Radio**	
Audio-visual socket	A18807	Center console, rear	
Automatic air recirculation (AUC) sensor	B414	Electric cooling fan shroud, top	
Automatic transmission control module (TCM)	A7000a	M54 engine: E-box, left rear engine compartment N52 engine: Integrated in rear of transmission housing	
B+ jump start terminal	G6430	Right rear engine compartment	
B+ power	A2076	Left rear engine compartment in electronics box (E-box)	
Back-up light switch	S8511	Manual transmission: Right rear transmission housing	17
Battery	G1	Right side cargo compartment, under trim	
Battery safety terminal (BST)	G19a	Positive battery terminal, in cargo compartment	
Blower	M30	Within fresh air plenum	
Blower output stage	N2	On blower under right side dashboard	
Brake fluid level switch	B18a	Brake fluid reservoir, left rear engine compartment	1, 10
Brake light switch	S29	Above brake pedal	26
Brake pad wear sensor	B16a B17a	Brake caliper, left front, right rear	19
Camshaft sensor, intake, exhaust	B6214, B6224	Front of cylinder head (N52 engine) Front of cylinder head left side, right side (M54 engine)	2, 3, 11
CD changer		Center console	
Center brake light	H34a	Center rear spoiler	
Center console switch center	A169	Center dashboard	
Central information display	A165a	Center dashboard	
Characteristic map thermostat	Y6279	Right front lower engine block	
Classification resistor	R8554	*see* xDrive classification resistor	18
Clutch switch	S805a	Above clutch pedal	
Compensator	N27a	Behind left side trim panel, cargo compartment	34
Crankshaft breather heating	E65390	Left side cylinder head	13
Crankshaft sensor	B6203a	Left rear of engine block near bell housing	5
DISA controllers		*see* Variable intake manifold (DISA) controllers	
DLC		*see* OBD II socket	
DME main relay (M54 engine)	K6300	In electronics box (E-box)	
DME main relay (N52 engine)		*see* Integrated supply module (IVM)	
Door locks, driver door, passenger door	S47 S49	Rear of door in door cavity, left, right	
Door locks, right rear, left rear	M14 M15	Rear lower edge of door inside door cavity, right, left,	
Door door module	A23a	Driver door arm rest	

ECL

Table g. X3 Component locations

Component	Code	Location	Fig #
Driver seat control module	A21	Integrated in driver seat switch panel	
DSC		*see also* ABS	
DSC acceleration sensor	B75	Under center console, bolted to floor	30
DSC control module		*see* ABS / DSC control module	
DSC hydraulic unit		On DSC control module	
DSC steering angle sensor	A68	Bottom of upper steering column, under dash	
DSC switch		*see* Center console switch center	
Dynamic stability control		*see* ABS / DSC *see also* DSC	
EAC sensor		*see* Environmental air catalyst (EAC) sensor	
E-box		Left rear engine compartment under cover	1, 10
E-box fan	M6506	Base of E-box	
Eccentric shaft sensor (N52 engine)	B60213	Top front of cylinder head cover	
ECM		*see* Engine control module (ECM)	
Electronic vehicle immobilizer (EWS)	A836	Underneath left side dashboard, driver's footwell	26
Electronics box		*see* E-box	
Engine control module (ECM) M54, N52	A6000	Left rear engine compartment in electronics box (E-box)	
Engine control module relay		*see* DME main relay	
Engine coolant level switch	S63b	Bottom of coolant reservoir, left front engine compartment	
Engine coolant pump, electric (N52 engine)	M6035	Right front lower engine block	12
Engine coolant temperature (ECT) sensor	B6236a B6236	Right front engine compartment on thermostat housing	2, 7 10, 12
Engine coolant temperature sensor, radiator outlet (M54 engine)	B604	Lower radiator hose, right front engine compartment	
Engine coolant thermostat	B6279	Lower radiator hose, right front engine compartment	
Engine cooling fan	M9	Between radiator and engine	
Engine electronics fuse carriers		*see* **Fuse Locations and Ratings** in this repair group *see also* **E-box engine electronics fuse carriers** in this repair group *see also* **130 Fuel Injection**	
Engine hood contact switch	S19a	Right rear engine compartment behind plenum bulkhead	1, 10
Evaporative emissions valve	Y6120	Underneath intake manifold	14
Exhaust camshaft sensor		*see* Camshaft sensor	
Exhaust flap solenoid valve	Y198	Left cargo compartment behind trim	33
Final stage unit		*see* Blower final stage	
Foglight switch		On dashboard, left of steering column	
Fuel filler flap lock motor	M16	Right side cargo compartment behind trim	35
Fuel injector relay (M54 engine)	K6327	Left rear engine compartment in electronics box (E-box) *See* **130 Fuel Injection**	
Fuel injectors	Y6101 - Y6106	Intake manifold	
Fuel level sensor right side, left side		Inside fuel tank, right side, left side	
Fuel pump	M2	Inside fuel tank, right side	

Table g. X3 Component locations

Component	Code	Location	Fig #
Fuel pump control module (EKPS) N52 engine	A13663	Right C-pillar behind rear seat side bolster	31
Fuel pump relay M54 engine	K96	Power distribution relay panel, underneath right side dashboard, behind glove compartment	
Fuel tank flap emergency release cable		Cargo compartment, behind right trim	
Fuel tank leakage diagnostic module	M119a	Underneath vehicle, behind left rear wheel housing	
Fuse carrier, engine electronics		*see* **E-box engine electronics fuse carriers** in this repair group	
Fuses		*see* **Fuse Locations and Ratings** in this repair group	
General module	A1	Behind glove compartment	24
Generator		*see* Alternator (generator)	
GPS		*see* Audio system controller / car communications computer (CCC/M-ASK) *see also* Navigation	
Grounds		*see* **Grounds** in this repair group	
Hand-free microphone	H65	Dome light unit	
Hazard warning switch	S18	Upper center dash	
Headlight aim control motor, right, left	M80 M81	Rear of headlight assembly, right, left	
Headlight washer pump	M7	Washer fluid reservoir, behind right engine compartment	
Headlight washer relay	K6	Power distribution relay panel, underneath right side dashboard, behind glove compartment	
Heated oxygen sensor		*see* Oxygen sensor	
Heated washer nozzles, left, right		*see* Windshield washer nozzle heater, left, right	
Heater valve	Y4a	Left rear engine compartment	
Heating		*see* Air-conditioning and heating	
High amperage fuses	A400	Forward of battery, cargo compartment	
Hood contact switch	S19a	Engine compartment, passenger's side, near strut tower,	
Horn relay	K2	Power distribution relay panel, underneath right side dashboard, behind glove compartment	
Horn switch	S4a	Steering wheel	
Horns	H2a H3a	Behind front bumper, left, right	
Hot-film mass air flow sensor		*see* Mass air flow sensor	
Ignition coil suppression capacitor (N52 engine)	I01046	Top of cylinder head cover in ignition coil harness	
Ignition coils	T6151 - T6156	Top of cylinder head cover above spark plugs	10
Ignition switch	S2	Right of steering column	
IHKA		*see* **640 Air-conditioning and Heating**	
Instrument cluster module	A2a	Dashboard	
Intake camshaft sensor		*see* Camshaft sensor	
Intake pressure sensor (N52 engine)	B6239	Left rear cylinder head, on cylinder head cover	13
Intake resonance valve		*see* Variable intake manifold (DISA) controllers	
Integrated supply module (IVM)	A6009	*see* E-box	1, 10

ECL

Electrical components table

Table g. X3 Component locations

Component	Code	Location	Fig #
Interior movement sensor (ultrasonic detector)	A121b	Dome light unit	
Jump start terminal	G6430	Engine compartment, passenger's side, near strut tower, inside cover	1, 10
Knock sensors	B62400	Left side engine block	7
Level sensor		*see* Ride height sensor, front, rear	
Light module	A3a	Behind left side dash panel	
Light sensor		*see* Rain / light sensor	
Light switch	S8	Left of steering column	
Light switch cluster	A3	Left of steering column	
Main power distribution panel	A41	Behind glove compartment	23
Mass air flow sensor	B6207b	Air intake duct between air filter housing and throttle housing *see also* Secondary air injection intake mass air flow sensor	1, 10
Mirror module, electrochromic (inside)	A22	Top center of windshield	
Mirror, outside, left, right	Y5 Y6	Driver door, passenger door	
MRS		*see* Airbag entries	
Multifunction steering wheel (switches)	A105	On steering wheel	
Multiple restraint system		*see* Airbag entries	
Navigation module	A112a	Left side cargo compartment behind trim panel	
Neutral safety switch	Y19	Under selector lever bezel, center console	29
O_2 sensor		*see* Oxygen sensor	
OBD II socket	X19527	Edge of driver door post	
Oil condition sensor	B62540	Engine rear, transmission bell housing	15, 16
Oil pressure switch	B6231	Left front of cylinder head	10
Outside temperature sensor	B21a	In front of left wheel housing liner behind front bumper	
Oxygen sensor	B62101a B62102a B62201a B62202a	In exhaust pipes before and after catalytic converters	
Oxygen sensor connectors (post-catalyst) M54 engine	X62102 X62202	Above intake manifold	
Oxygen sensor connectors (pre-catalyst) M54 engine	X62101 X62201	Above exhaust manifold	9
Oxygen sensor connectors (post-catalyst) N52 engine	X62102 X62202	Underneath transmission bell housing	
Oxygen sensor connectors (pre-catalyst) N52 engine	X62101 X62201	Above intake manifold	10
Park / neutral position switch		*see* Neutral safety switch	
Park distance control (PDC) module	A81	Left side cargo compartment, under floor panel	36
Park distance control sensor, rear	B34a - B37a	Rear bumper	
Park distance control sensors, front	B30a - B33a	Front bumper	
Park distance control signal	H10	Panel under left side of dash	
Parking brake warning switch	S31	Base of parking brake handle, under center console	30

Table g. X3 Component locations

Component	Code	Location	Fig #
PDC		*see* Park distance control (PDC) entries	
Power steering		*see* Steering	
Radiator outlet coolant temperature sensor		*see* Engine coolant temperature sensor, radiator outlet	
Radio	N9	Center dashboard *see also* **650 Radio**	
Rain / light sensor	B57b	Top center of windshield	
RDC		*see* Tire pressure control (RDC) entries	
Rear window defroster	E9	Rear window	
Rear window defroster relay	K13	Right cargo compartment, behind trim panel	35
Rear lid lock motor	M17a	Center rear bottom cargo compartment	
Rear lid release button	E9016	Incorporated in rear lid release handle	
Rear window washer pump	M95	Washer fluid reservoir, right side engine compartment	
Resonance valve		*see* Variable intake manifold (DISA) controllers	
Ride height sensor, front, rear	B42a B64	Right front, right rear suspension	20, 21
Seat belt pyrotechnic tensioner, driver seat belt, passenger seat belt	G12 G13	Seat belt buckle, driver seat belt, passenger seat belt	
Seat control, seat heater components		*see* **520 Seats**	
Secondary air injection intake mass air flow sensor	B6206	Right front engine compartment in secondary air intake hose	
Secondary air injection pump, (M54 engine)	M63	Right front engine compartment	
Secondary air injection pump relay (M54 engine)	K6304	Power distribution relay panel, underneath right side dashboard, behind glove compartment	
Servotronic control module	A17	Behind glove compartment, on main power distribution panel (A41)	
Servotronic valve	B15a	Power steering rack	
Selector lever position switch	S227	Integrated in shifter console	
Solar sensor	B66	Front center of dashboard	
Speakers		*see* **650 Radio**	
Speed (rpm) sensor		*see* Crankshaft sensor	
SRS		*see* Airbag entries	
Starter	M6510	Left side of engine under intake manifold	5
Steering angle sensor	A68	Bottom of upper steering column, under dash	26
Stepper motor		*see* **640 Heating and Air-conditioning**	
Steptronic switch	S224a	Under selector lever bezel, center console	
Sunroof control module	A33b	Above center dome light unit	
Sunroof motors	M14105	Above center of windshield, behind dome light unit	
Sunroof switch	S38b	Center dome light unit	
Sunroof shade motor	M14104	Above headliner at rear of cargo compartment	
Supplemental restraint system		*see* Airbag entries	
Suspension level sensor		*see* Ride height sensor, front, rear	
Tailgate lock motor	M17a	Tailgate lock	
Tailgate release button	E9016	Center tailgate	
TCM		*see* Automatic transmission control module (TCM)	

ECL

Electrical components table

Table g. X3 Component locations

Component	Code	Location	Fig #
Telephone		*see* **650 Radio**	
Telematics control module (TCU)	U400a	Left side cargo compartment, behind trim panel *see also* **650 Radio**	
Temperature sensor, outside	B21a	In front of left wheel liner, behind bumper	
Thermostat, coolant (M54 engine)	Y6279	Front of engine above coolant pump housing	
Thermostat, coolant (N52 engine)	Y6279	Right front lower engine compartment, mounted on coolant pump housing	
Throttle valve	Y6390	Underneath intake manifold	14
Tire pressure control (RDC) control module	A85a	Power distribution relay panel, underneath right side dashboard, behind glove compartment	
Tire pressure control (RDC) switch	A169	Center console switch center	
Tire pressure control (RDC) transmitter	B43a - B47a	Left front, right front, left rear, right rear fender housing	19
Tire pressure control (RDC) wheel electronics	B43b - B47b	Inside each wheel	
Trailer module	A6	Left side trunk below cargo floor panel	
Transfer case control module (VGSG)	A70006	Left side trunk below cargo floor panel	36
Transmission		*see* Automatic transmission	
Turn signal / high beam switch	S7	Steering column stalk switch	
Tweeter		*see* **650 Radio**	
Ultrasonic detector		*see* Interior movement sensor (ultrasonic detector)	
Valvetronic drive motor (N52 engine)	M6352	Top center of cylinder head cover	10
Valvetronic relay (N52 engine)	K6319	*see* Integrated supply module (IVM)	
Vanity mirror switch, left, right	S77 S78	Sun visor, left, right	
VANOS solenoid, intake, exhaust	Y6275, Y6276	Front of cylinder head	2, 10, 11
Variable intake manifold (DISA) controllers	Y6540 Y6541	Intake manifold	8, 13
Video module	A197	Left side cargo compartment behind trim	
Voice control system	U6a	Behind left side trim panel, cargo compartment	
VTG actuator		*see* xDrive clutch (VTG) actuator	
Washer fluid level switch	S136a	Washer fluid reservoir	
Washer pumps	M4 M7 M95	Washer fluid reservoir	1, 10
Wheel speed sensor		*see* ABS wheel speed sensor *see also* **340 Brakes**	
Window regulator motors, left front, right front	M21 M23	Center of front door inside door cavity, left, right	
Window regulator motors, left rear, right rear	M20a M22a	Center of rear door inside door cavity, left, right	
Window switch, driver		*see* Driver door module	
Window switch, passenger	S127	Passenger door armrest	
Window switches, left rear, right rear	S41a S42a	Rear door armrests, left, right	

Table g. X3 Component locations

Component	Code	Location	Fig #
Windshield washer nozzle heater, left, right	E51a E52a	Base of engine compartment hood	
Windshield washer pump	M4	Washer fluid reservoir	
Wiper and washer control module, rear	A36	Integrated in rear wiper motor, rear lid, behind trim	
Wiper motor, windshield	M3a	Underneath plenum chamber cover, left rear engine compartment	
Wiper relay	K11	E-box, left rear engine compartment	
X connector		*see* **Harness connectors, wire splices (X connectors)** in this repair group.	
X ground		*see* **Grounds** in this repair group	
xDrive classification resistor	R8554	Rear of transfer case	
xDrive clutch (VTG) actuator	M8533	On transfer case. See **270 Transfer Case**.	18
xDrive control module		*see* Transfer case control module (VGSG)	

ECL

Harness connectors, wire splices (X connectors)

Harness connectors, wire splices (X connectors)

BMW electrical components connect to the electrical harness via X connectors. Most connectors bear the same numerical designation as the component they attach to. For example, the connector for Y6279 (coolant thermostat) is designated X6279.

Table c lists harness connectors and wire splices not attached directly to components and gives brief location information for each connector. This can be a helpful resource when using the wiring diagrams.

Table h. E83 X connectors		
Code	**Location**	**Fig #**
X01003	Inside steering wheel, under horn button	
X04545	Center console storage compartment, driver's side	
X0580	Rear door, right, between power window switch and door connector, rear right	
X10116	Under glovebox, behind fuse panel, under plastic cover	23
X10148	Under glovebox, behind fuse panel, under plastic cover (to 09/2005) Center console, driver's side, under plastic cover (from 09/2005)	23
X10170	Inside steering wheel, attached to director indicator and high beam headlight switch	
X10185	Center console, wire cluster, passenger's side	
X10189	Under glovebox, behind fuse panel, under plastic cover	23
X1019	Center console, passenger's side	
X10466	Center console, wire cluster, passenger's side	
X1073	Cargo compartment, under floor cover, center	
X10861	Passenger's door, inside, right of speaker	
X1101	Center console, inside cover, driver's side	
X1121	Center console, inside cover, driver's side	
X11212	Center console, inside cover, driver's side	
X1123	Driver's footwell, above brake pedal	
X11409	Cargo compartment, under floor cover, center	
X1149	Center console, wire cluster, central	
X11416	Cargo compartment, left trim panel, right of A18 amplifier	
X1215	Center console, wire cluster, driver's side	
X1218	Center console, inside cover, driver's side	
X1232	Center console, wire cluster, driver's side	
X1234	Center console, driver's side	
X1265	Cargo compartment lid, right side, above rear taillight, right	
X1266	Cargo compartment lid, left side, above rear taillight, left	
X1272	Center console, wire cluster, passenger's side	
X1276	Cargo compartment, right trim panel, on floor beside railing	
X13033	Center console, wire cluster, passenger's side	
X13250	Rear seat side bolster, driver's side, between seat belt and rear door	
X13394	Passenger's side fender well, behind strut	
X13395	Driver's side fender well, behind strut	19
X13713	Wheel well, driver's side, above axle, central wheel well, on Servotronic valve	
X13755	Driver's door, centered inside door, near armrest	
X13843	Dashboard, centered	

Table h. E83 X connectors		
Code	**Location**	**Fig #**
X14087	A-pillar, passenger's side, base	
X14247	Center console, wire cluster, passenger's side	
X14248	Driver's door, centered inside door, above front compartment	
X14277	Between general module and plug connectors for driver's and passenger's door	
X1520	Passenger's door, inside, right of speaker	
X163	Engine compartment, front, left side of refrigerant compressor	
X1658	Driver's footwell, above accelerator	
X1736	Center console, wire cluster, central	
X181	Under glovebox, behind fuse panel, under plastic cover (to 09/2005) Center console, driver's side, under plastic cover (from 09/2005)	23
X18122	Above sun visor, passenger's side	
X18145	Driver's side fender well, behind strut	
X18146	Rear wheel, passenger's side fender well, right side	
X18241	Center console, driver's side, under plastic cover	
X183	Under glovebox, behind fuse panel, under plastic cover	23
X18722	Center console, inside center, below CD drive and radio buttons	
X18786	Center console, inside center, right side, above cigar lighter	
X18802	Dashboard, center, central information display (CID)	
X18826	Center console, passenger's side, above ground	27
X18827	Center console, passenger's side, above ground	27
X18835	Passenger's seat, right side bolster (N52 engine)	
X18836	Passenger's seat, right side bolster (M54 engine)	
X18840	Driver's seat adjustment, left side of seat base	
X18841	Passenger's seat adjustment, right side of seat base	
X1893	Driver's footwell, above brake pedal	
X1894	Driver's footwell, above brake pedal	
X19527	Driver's footwell, left footrest	
X205	Center console, inside cover, driver's side	
X218	Center console, passenger's side, left of ground	27
X219	Under glovebox, behind fuse panel, under plastic cover	23
X229	Above sun visor, passenger's side	
X256	Passenger's door, between hinges, plug connector	
X257	Driver's door, between hinges, plug connector	
X273	Rear door, driver's side, between hinges, plug connector	
X274	Rear door, passenger's side, between hinges, plug connector	
X275	Passenger's seat. underside	
X279	Driver's seat. underside	
X2795	Cargo compartment, left trim panel, wire cluster on U400a Telephone transceiver	
X313	Center console, inside cover, driver's side	
X314	Center console, wire cluster, driver's side	
X322	Center console, inside center, below CD drive and radio buttons	
X3601	Above sun visor, passenger's side	
X3678	Above sun visor, passenger's side	
X376	Rear wheel, driver's side fender well, left side	

ECL

Harness connectors, wire splices (X connectors)

Code	Location	Fig #
Table h. E83 X connectors		
X377	Rear wheel, passenger's side fender well, right side	
X428	Under glovebox, behind fuse panel, under plastic cover	23
X461	Cargo compartment lid, right side, right of rear taillight	
X465	Cargo compartment, right trim panel, left, towards rear seatbelt	
X473	Above sun visor, passenger's side	
X595	Cargo compartment, under floor cover, center	
X6011	Engine compartment, driver's side near windshield wiper, in engine electronics box (E-box)	
X6021	Engine compartment, driver's side near windshield wiper, in engine electronics box (E-box)	
X6038	Engine compartment, driver's side near windshield wiper, in engine electronics box (E-box) (N52 engine)	
X60531	Engine compartment, driver's side near windshield wiper, in engine electronics box (E-box)	
X60541	Engine compartment, driver's side near windshield wiper, in engine electronics box (E-box)	
X60554	Engine compartment, driver's side near windshield wiper, in engine electronics box (E-box)	
X60555	Engine compartment, driver's side near windshield wiper, in engine electronics box (E-box)	
X623	Driver's side-view mirror	
X624	Passenger's side-view mirror	
X630	Rear bumper, left of center, right of tailpipes	
X6356	Engine compartment, driver's side near windshield wiper, in engine electronics box (E-box) (N52 engine)	
X6357	Engine compartment, driver's side near windshield wiper, in engine electronics box (E-box) (N52 engine)	
X6358	Engine compartment, driver's side near windshield wiper, in engine electronics box (E-box) (N52 engine)	
X6402	Cargo compartment, right trim panel, left, towards rear seatbelt, on floor near trunk lid	
X6410	Engine compartment, driver's side near windshield wiper, in engine electronics box (E-box) (N52 engine)	
X6419	Driver's door, centered inside door,	
X6458	Engine compartment, driver's side near windshield wiper, in engine electronics box (E-box)	
X6460	Engine compartment, driver's side near windshield wiper, in engine electronics box (E-box) (N52 engine)	
X6476	Cargo compartment, under floor cover, center	
X6831	Engine compartment, driver's side near windshield wiper, in engine electronics box (E-box)	
X6866	On automatic transmission	
X6960	Engine compartment, driver's side near windshield wiper, in engine electronics box (E-box) (N52 engine)	
X6961	Engine compartment, driver's side near windshield wiper, in engine electronics box (E-box) (N52 engine)	
X6962	Engine compartment, driver's side near windshield wiper, in engine electronics box (E-box)	
X6964	Engine compartment, driver's side near windshield wiper, in engine electronics box (E-box)	
X6965	Engine compartment, driver's side near windshield wiper, in engine electronics box (E-box)	
X6969	Engine compartment, driver's side near windshield wiper, in engine electronics box (E-box)	
X6970	Engine compartment, M54 engine, on top, centered	
X6970	Engine compartment, N52 engine, on top, centered	
X8090	On automatic transmission	
X8091	On automatic transmission	
X834	Rear door, driver's side, centered, left of speaker	
X835	Rear door, passenger's side, centered, right of speaker	
X849	Driver's door, centered inside door, near front of armrest	
X878	Above sun visor, passenger's side	
X891	Passenger's door, inside, center	
X942	Driver's door, harness connector, between X849 and components, centered	
X9438	Cargo compartment, under floor cover, center	

GROUNDS

Ground distribution

Main grounds are distributed throughout the vehicle body. Many are found under the interior carpets or behind trim panels. Several components grounds are often ganged. Ground positions vary among models. Lugs and connectors attached to ground are susceptible to damage and corrosion. Clean or renew as necessary.

Most ground positions are illustrated in photos in this repair group. See figure and page references in **Table i**.

Table i. Ground locations

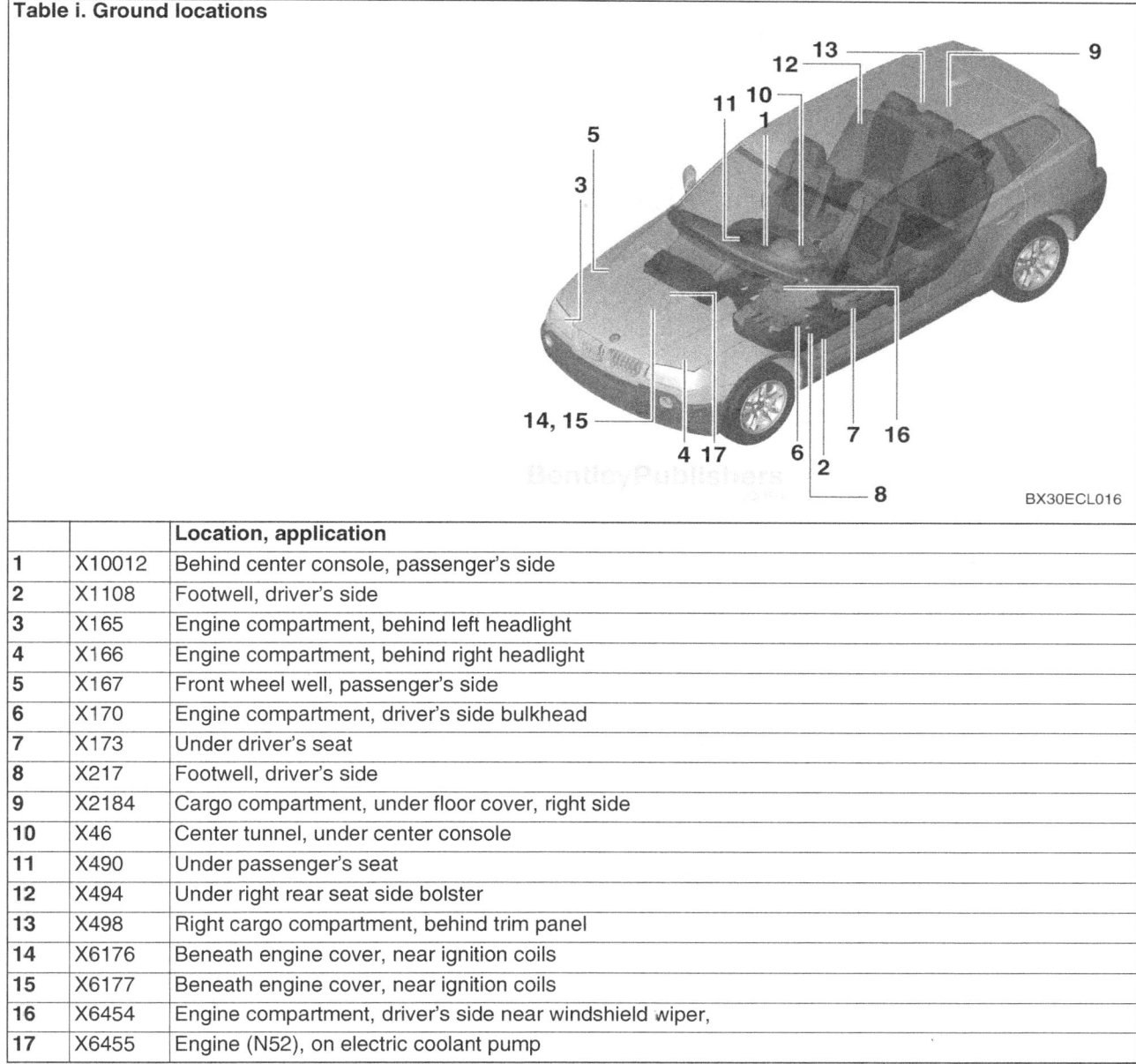

BX30ECL016

		Location, application
1	X10012	Behind center console, passenger's side
2	X1108	Footwell, driver's side
3	X165	Engine compartment, behind left headlight
4	X166	Engine compartment, behind right headlight
5	X167	Front wheel well, passenger's side
6	X170	Engine compartment, driver's side bulkhead
7	X173	Under driver's seat
8	X217	Footwell, driver's side
9	X2184	Cargo compartment, under floor cover, right side
10	X46	Center tunnel, under center console
11	X490	Under passenger's seat
12	X494	Under right rear seat side bolster
13	X498	Right cargo compartment, behind trim panel
14	X6176	Beneath engine cover, near ignition coils
15	X6177	Beneath engine cover, near ignition coils
16	X6454	Engine compartment, driver's side near windshield wiper,
17	X6455	Engine (N52), on electric coolant pump

Electrical components

COMPONENT LOCATION PHOTOS

Electrical components

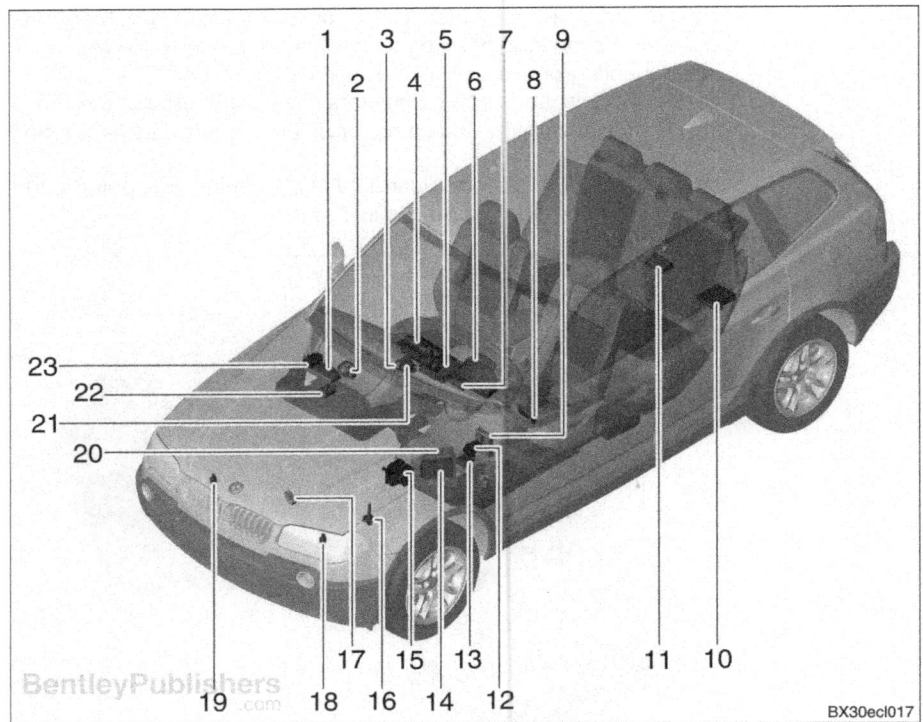

BX30ecl017

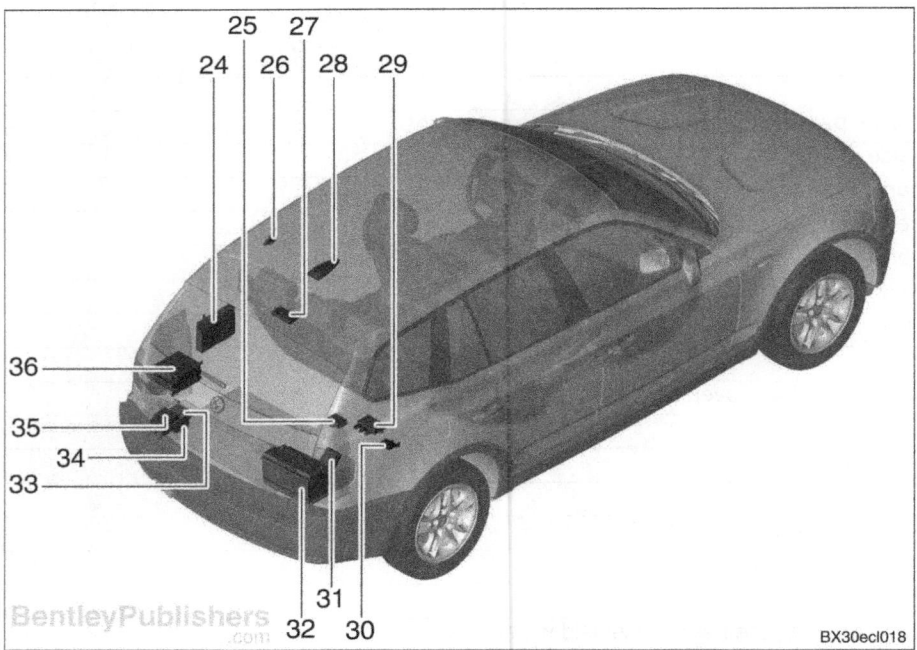

BX30ecl018

1. Power distribution (A41)
2. Horn relay (K2)
3. Solar sensor (B66)
4. Central information display (CID) (A196)
5. Radio
6. Instrument cluster module (A2a)
7. Not applicable
8. Outside mirror, left (Y5)
9. Transmission control (A7000)
10. Not applicable
11. Control module, transfer case (A70006)
12. Electronic immobilizer (EWS) (A836)
13. Integrated supply module (IVM) (A6009)
14. Engine control module (DME) A6000
15. Dynamic stability control (DSC) (A65a)
16. Outside temperature sensor (B21a)
17. Automatic air recirculation sensor (AUC) (B414)
18. Front crash sensor (S71)
19. Front crash sensor (S72)
20. Fuse carrier, engine electronics (E-box) (A8680)
21. Hazard warning/central locking switch (S18)
22. Adaptive headlight (A214)
23. Tire pressure control (RDC) (A85a)
24. Amplifier (A18)
25. Trailer module (A6)
26. Bluetooth antenna (U6a)
27. Antenna amplifier with diversity module (A421)
28. Roof-mounted shark fin, with aerial for telephone, nav and SDARS
29. Park distance control (PDC) (A81)
30. Tilt sensor (B28)
31. Luggage compartment fuse holder (A400)
32. Vehicle Battery
33. Telematics control unit (TCU)
34. Compensator (N27a)
35. Satellite radio receiver (SDARS)
36. Navigation DVD computer (A112a)

Engine compartment components (M54 engine)

Fig 1   Engine compartment

NOTE —
• *3 series (E46) M54 engine compartment shown.*

1. Hood contact switch
2. B+ jumper connector
3. DSC control module/hydraulic unit
4. Secondary air pump
5. Interior microfilter housing
6. Resonance valve, intake manifold (changeover valve)
7. Mass air flow sensor
8. Brake fluid level sensor
9. Ground X6454
10. Electronics box (E-box)
11. Air quality sensor (AUC) (for automatic recirculation control)
12. Intake camshaft VANOS solenoid
13. Engine cooling fan (electric)

ECL

Engine compartment components (M54 engine)

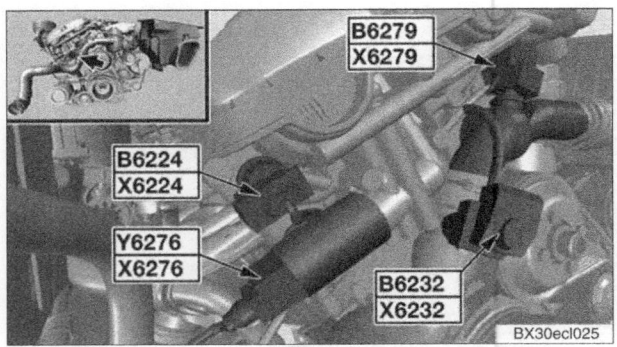

Fig 2   Front of cylinder head

◀ Above crankshaft vibration damper:
- **B6224** Exhaust camshaft sensor
- **B6232** Engine coolant temperature (ECT) sensor
- **B6279** Coolant thermostat
- **X6224** Connector
- **X6232** Connector
- **X6276** Connector
- **X6279** Connector
- **Y6276** Exhaust VANOS solenoid

Fig 3   Left front of cylinder head

◀ Above crankshaft vibration damper:
- **B6214** Intake camshaft sensor
- **X6275** Connector
- **Y6275** Intake VANOS solenoid

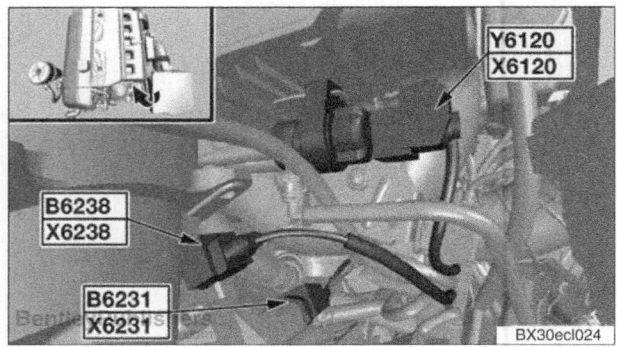

Fig 4   Left front of engine

◀ Behind and below oil filter housing:
- **B6231** Oil pressure switch
- **B6238** Oil temperature sensor
- **X6120** Connector
- **X6231** Connector
- **X6238** Connector
- **Y6120** Fuel tank evaporative emissions control valve

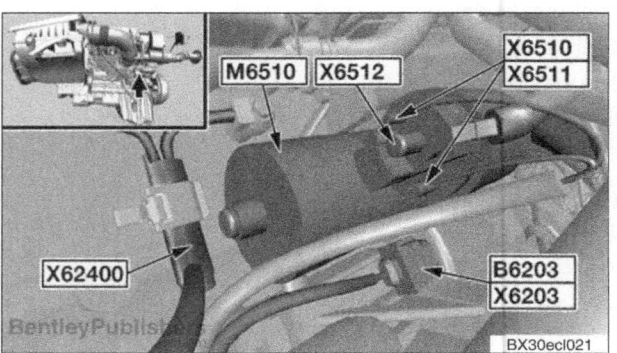

Fig 5   Left rear engine

◀ At transmission bellhousing, underneath intake manifold:
- **B6203** Crankshaft sensor
- **M6510** Starter
- **X6203** Connector
- **X6510 - X6512** Starter connectors
- **X62400** Knock sensor connector

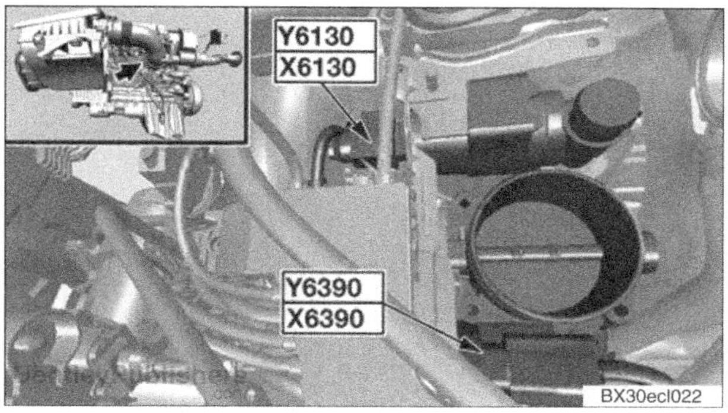

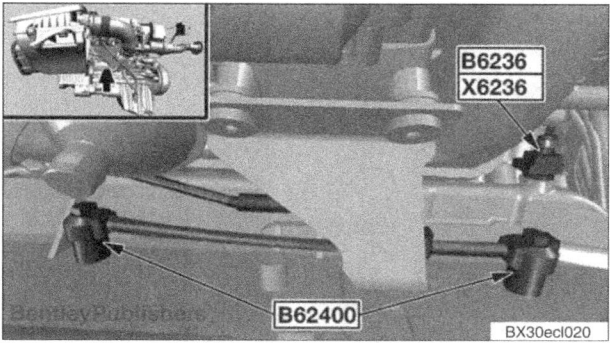

Fig 6   Left side engine

◁ Underneath intake manifold:
- **X6130** Connector
- **X6390** Connector
- **Y6130** Idle speed control valve
- **Y6390** Throttle valve

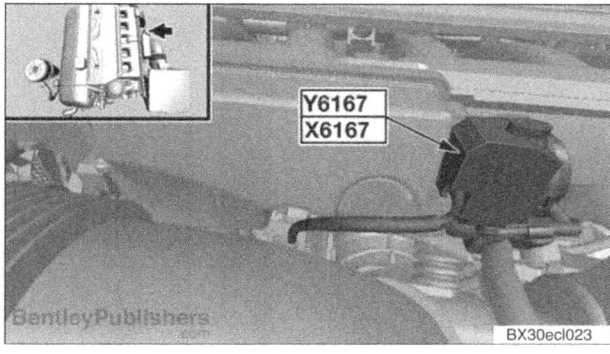

Fig 7   Left side engine

◁ Underneath intake manifold:
- **B6236** Engine coolant temperature (ECT) sensor
- **B62400** Knock sensors
- **X6236** Connector

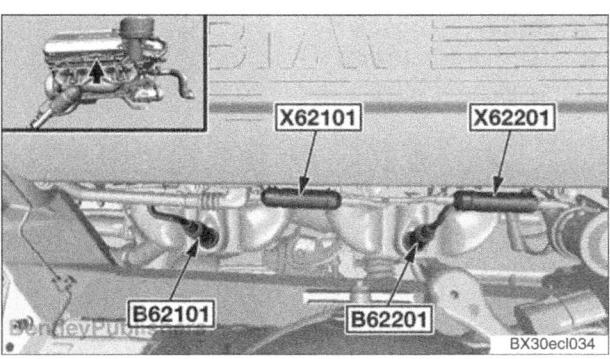

Fig 8   Left side engine

◁ On intake manifold:
- **X6167** Connector
- **Y6167** Variable intake manifold (DISA) solenoid

Fig 9   Right side engine

◁ Exhaust manifold:
- **B62202** Oxygen sensor, pre-catalyst, bank 1
- **B62101** Oxygen sensor, pre-catalyst, bank 2
- **X62201** Oxygen sensor connector, pre-catalyst, bank 1
- **X62101** Oxygen sensor connector, pre-catalyst, bank 2

ECL

Engine compartment components (N52 engine)

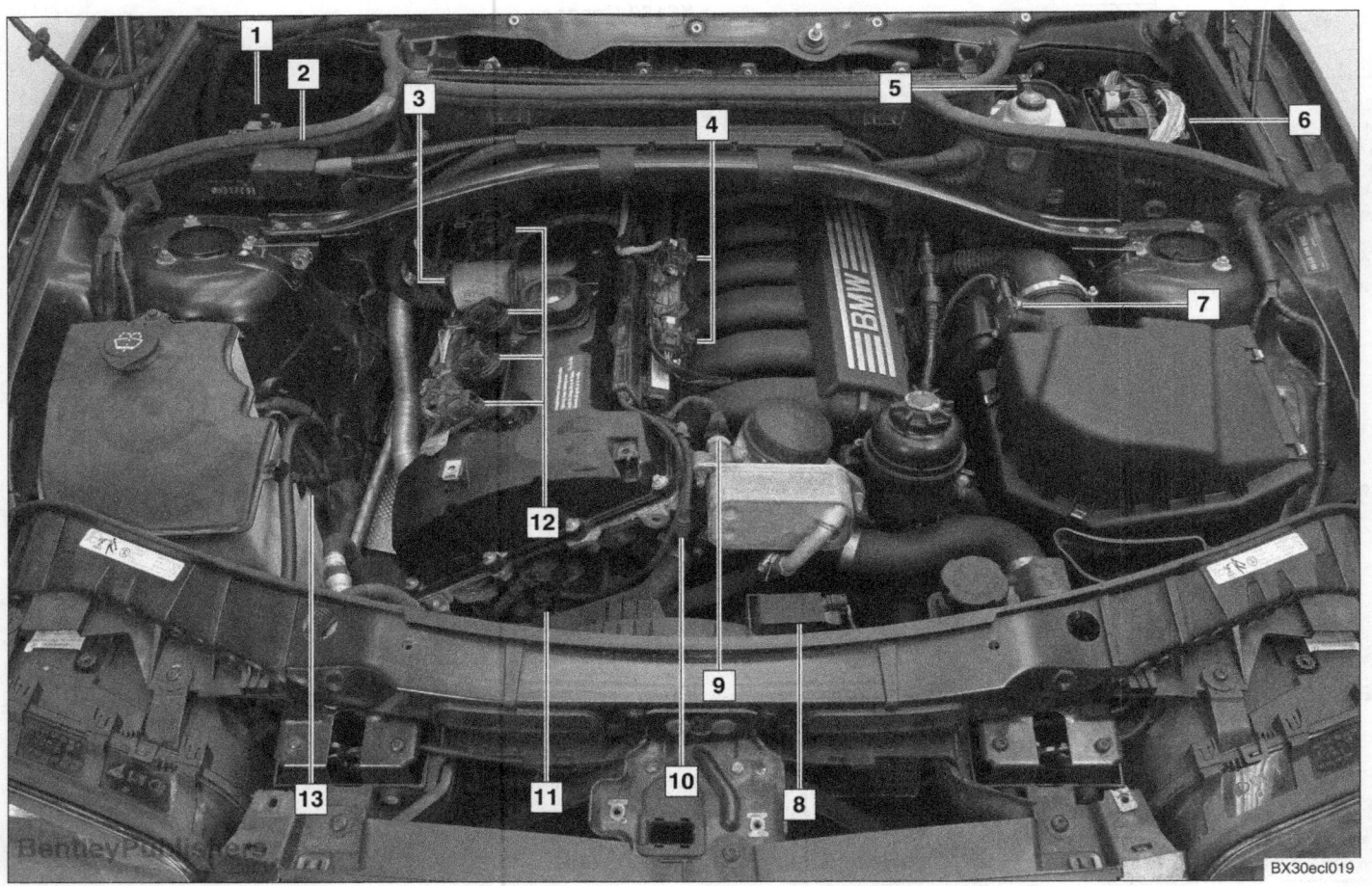

BX30ecl019

Fig 10   Engine compartment, covers removed

1. Engine hood contact switch (S19a)
2. Jump start terminal (G6430)
3. Valvetronic motor (M6352)
4. O2 sensor connectors (precatalyst) (X62101, X62201)
5. Brake fluid level sensor (B18a)
6. E-box and IVM (A6009)
7. Mass airflow sensor (MAF), (B6207b)
8. Air quality sensor (AUC), (B414)
9. Oil pressure switch (B6231)
10. Coolant temp sensor (ECT), (B6236a)
11. VANOS solenoids (Y6275, Y6276)
12. Ignition coils (T6151-T6156)
13. Washer pumps, heated washer nozzle, left, right (M4, M7, M95, E51a, E52a)

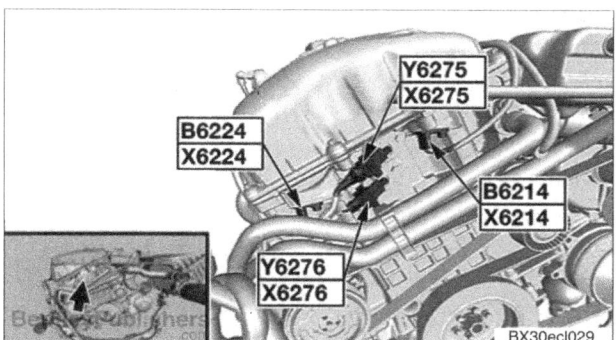

Fig 11   Front of cylinder head

◄ Top of timing chain housing:
- **B6214** Intake camshaft sensor
- **B6224** Exhaust camshaft sensor
- **X6214** Connector
- **X6224** Connector
- **X6275** Connector
- **X6276** Connector
- **Y6275** Intake VANOS solenoid
- **Y6276** Exhaust VANOS solenoid

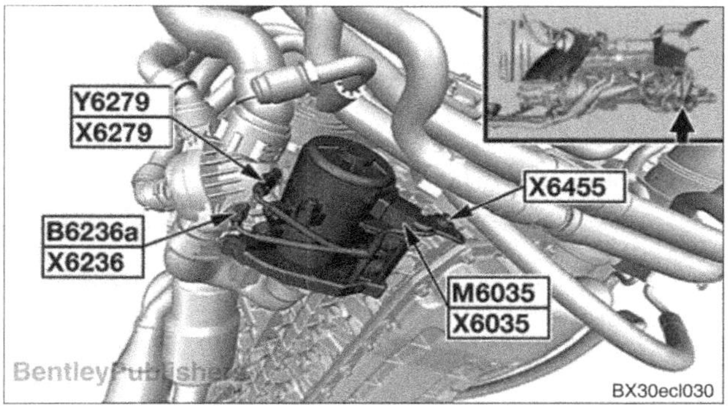

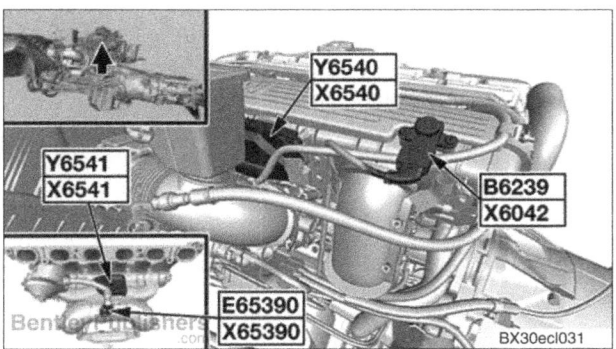

Fig 12   Right front engine compartment

◄ Bolted to lower front right of engine:
- **B6236a** Engine coolant temperature (ECT) sensor
- **M6035** Electric engine coolant pump
- **X6035** Connector
- **X6236** Connector
- **X6279** Connector
- **X6455** Ground
  Electric coolant pump
- **Y6279** Characteristic map thermostat

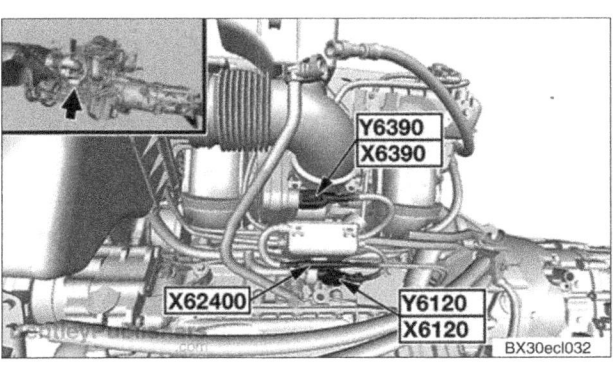

Fig 13   Left side cylinder head

◄ Top of intake manifold:
- **B6239** Intake pressure sensor
- **E65390** Crankcase breather heater
- **X6042** Connector
- **X6540** Connector
- **X6541** Connector
- **X65390** Connector
- **Y6540** Variable intake manifold (DISA) controller 1
- **Y6541** Variable intake manifold (DISA) controller 2

Fig 14   Left side cylinder head

◄ Underneath intake manifold:
- **X6120** Connector
- **X6390** Connector
- **X62400** Knock sensor connector
- **Y6120** Evaporative emissions valve
- **Y6390** Throttle valve

ECL

Components underneath vehicle

Fig 15　Underneath vehicle (M54 engine)

◄ Engine rear, transmission bell housing:
- **B62540** Oil condition sensor
- **X62540** Connector

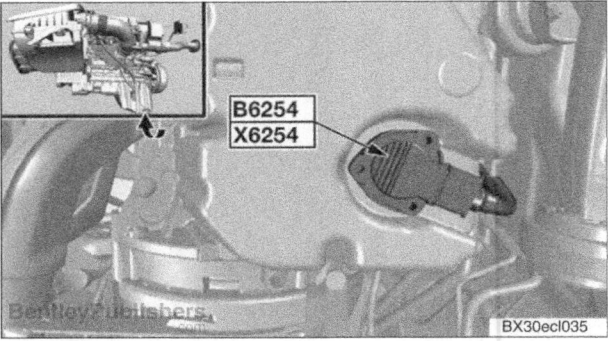

Fig 16　Underneath vehicle (N52 engine)

◄ Engine rear, transmission bell housing:
- **B62540** Oil condition sensor
- **X62540** Connector
- **X62102** Oxygen sensor connector, post-catalyst, bank 1
- **X62202** Oxygen sensor connector, post-catalyst, bank 2

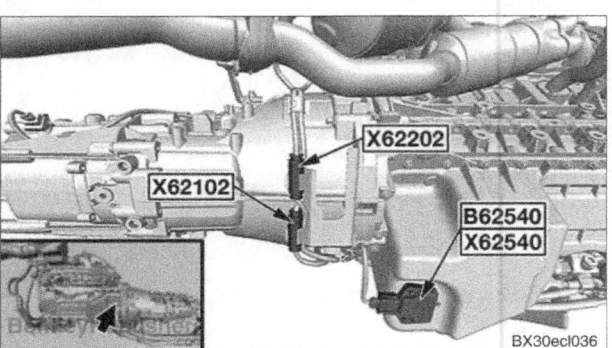

Fig 17　Manual transmission

◄ Right rear manual transmission housing (**arrow**):
- **S8511** Back-up light switch
- **X8511** Connector

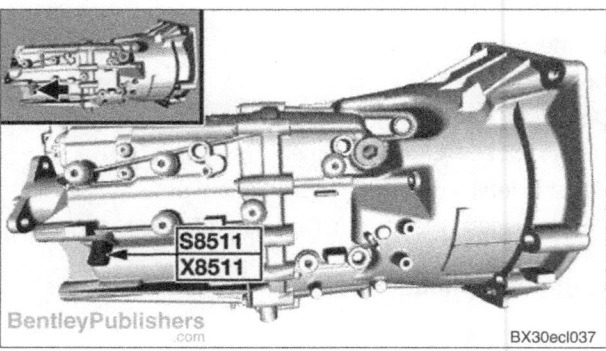

Fig 18　Transfer case

◄ Left side of transfer case housing (**arrow**):
- **M8533** X-drive (VTG) actuator motor
- **R8554** Classification resistor
- **X8533** Connector
- **X4019** Connector

Fig 19   Left front wheel

BX30ecl039

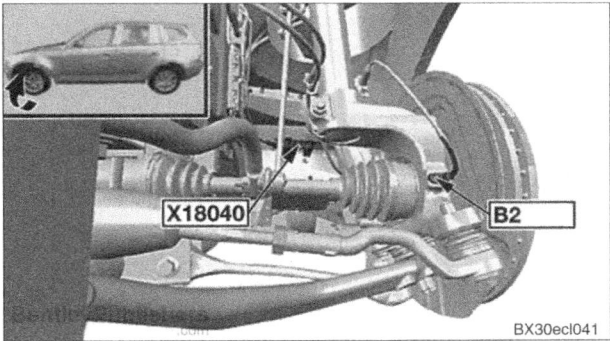

BX30ecl040

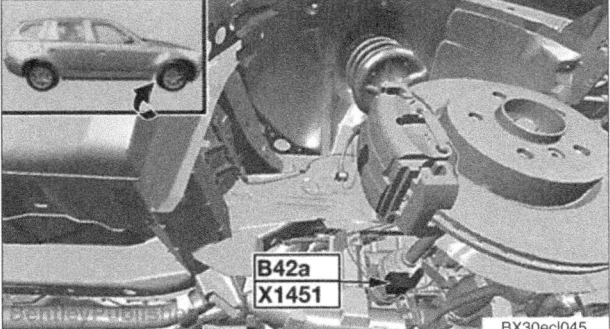

BX30ecl041

◅ Wheel housing liner removed:

- **B43a** Left front tire pressure control (RDC) transmitter
  Additional transmitters at similar position for other wheels
- **B46a** Tire pressure control (RDC) antenna
- **X18040** Connector
- **X18036** Connector
- **B16a** Brake wear sensor, front left
  Additional brake wear sensor at right rear wheel
- **X13395** Connector
- **X18145** Connector
- **B2** Wheel speed sensor, front left wheel
  Additional wheel speed sensors at similar position for other wheels

Fig 20   Front right suspension

◅ Right side front suspension (**arrow**):

- **B42a** Front ride height sensor
- **X1451** Connector

BX30ecl045

ECL

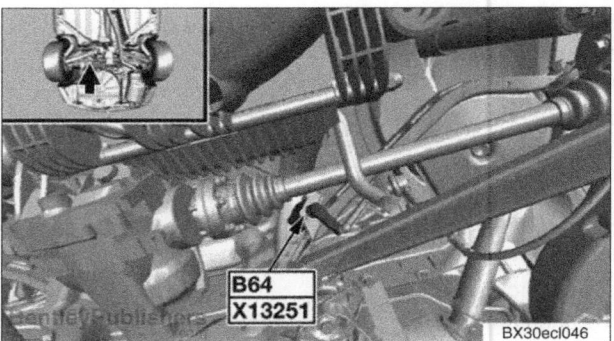

Fig 21   Rear right suspension

◁ Right side rear suspension arm (**arrow**):
 • **B64** Rear ride height sensor
 • **X13251** Connector

Fig 22   Steering

◁ Power steering rack:
 • **B15a** Servotronic valve
 • **X13713** Connector

Main power distribution panel (A41)

Fig 23   Main power distribution fuse panel (A41)

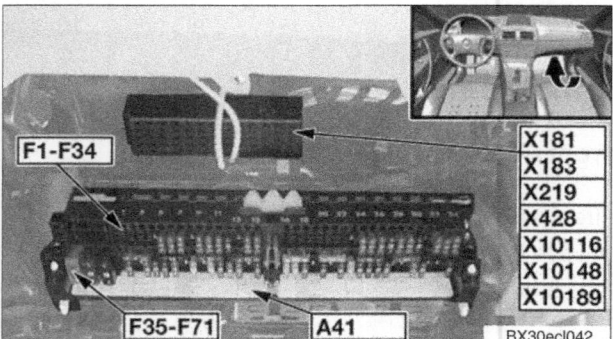

◁ Behind glove compartment (glove compartment removed):
 • **A41** Main power distribution panel
 • **Fuse F01 to F71**
 • **X181, X183, X219, X428, X10116, X10148, X10189**
   Connectors located under cover on main power distribution panel

Fig 24   Main power distribution panel (A41)
control modules

◁ Behind glove compartment (glove compartment removed):
 • **General Module (A1)**
 • **X254** Connector, 26-pin
 • **X253** Connector, 54-pin
 • **X332** Connector, 15-pin

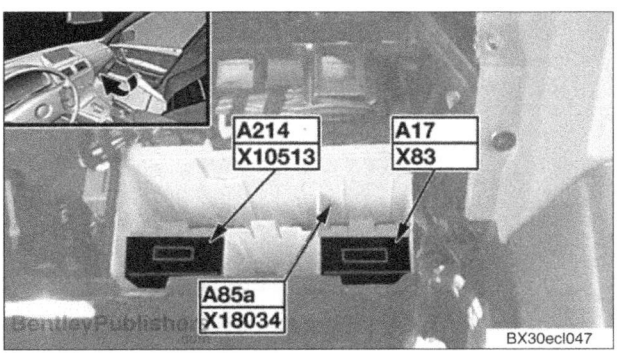

BX30ecl047

Fig 25 Main power distribution panel (A41) control modules

 The following modules may also be installed in main power distribution panel depending on vehicle equipment:

- **A17** Servotronic control module
- **X83** Connector, Servotronic control module
- **A214** Adaptive headlight control module
- **X10513** Connector, adaptive headlight control module
- **A85a** Tire pressure monitoring system (RDC) control module (not shown)
- **X18034** Conector, RDC control module (not shown)

Components in passenger compartment

Fig 26 Left side dashboard

 Underneath dashboard (**arrow**):

- **A836** Electronic vehicle immobilizer (EWS)
- **X1659** EWS control module connector
- **A68** Steering angle sensor
- **X1658** Steering angle sensor connector
- **S29** Brake light switch
- **X1658** Brake light switch connector
- **R10** Accelerator pedal module (PWG)
- **X11400** PWG connector
- **X1108** Ground
  See **Ground applications** in this repair group.
- **X1893, X10062, X1123, X1894**
  Splice connectors

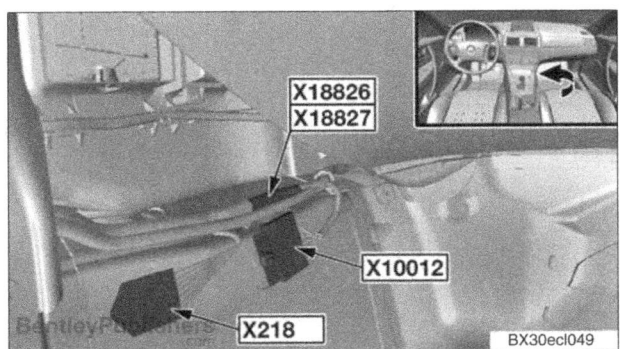

BX30ecl048

Fig 27 Right footwell

 Underneath carpet (**arrow**):

- **X218** Ground
  See **Ground applications** in this repair group.
- **X18826** Splice in harness
- **X18827** Splice in harness
- **X10012** Ground
  See **Ground applications** in this repair group.

BX30ecl049

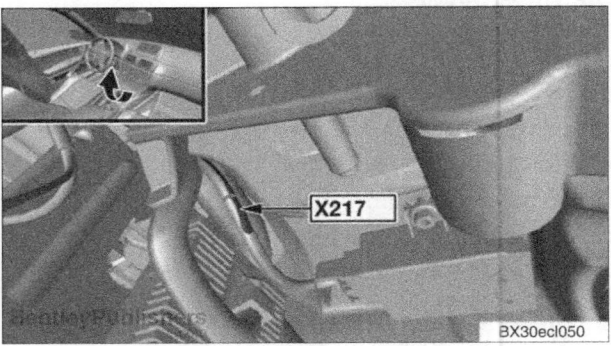

BX30ecl050

Fig 28 Underneath dashboard

◄ Underneath left side dashboard, driver's footwell (**arrow**):
- **X217** Splice in harness

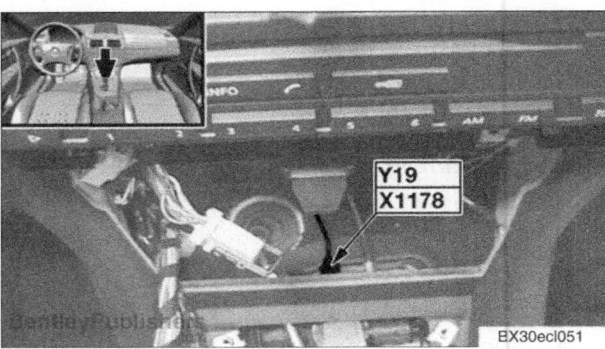

BX30ecl051

Fig 29 Center console (below radio functions)

◄ Beside cigar lighter:
- **Y19** Neutral safety switch
- **X1178** Adapter

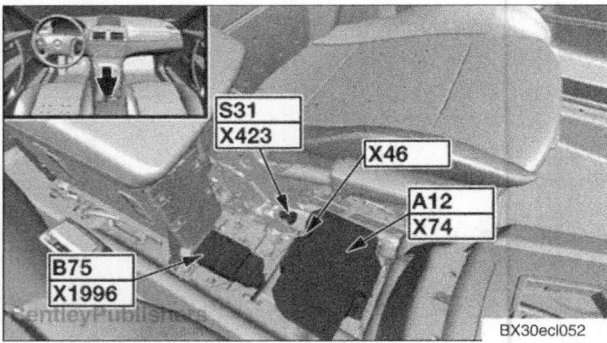

BX30ecl052

Fig 30 On center tunnel

◄ Underneath center console:
- **A12** Multiple restraint system control unit (MRS)
- **X74** Connector, 75-pin
- **B75** Dynamic stability control sensor (DSC)
- **X1996** Connector, 4-pin
- **S31** Parking brake warning switch
- **X423** Connector
- **X46** Ground
  See **Ground applications** in this repair group.

Fig 31 Right C-pillar

◄ Behind rear seat side bolster (**arrow**):
- **A13663** Fuel pump control module (EKPS)
- **X13663** Connector
- **X18203** Connector

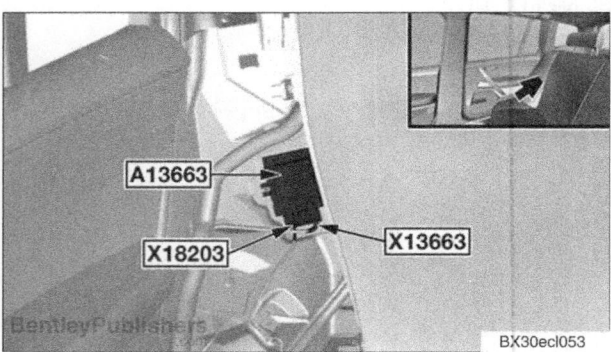

BX30ecl053

Components in cargo compartment

Fig 32   Cargo compartment lid

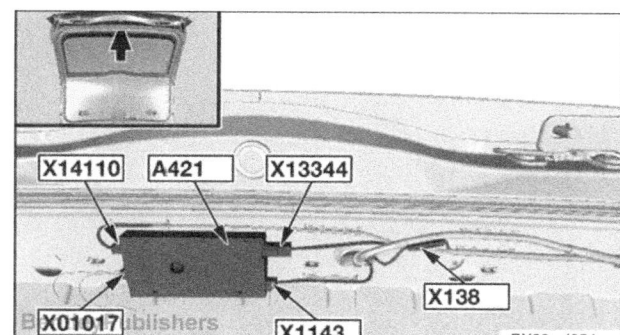

◀ Center cargo compartment lid (**arrow**):
- **A421** Antenna diversity module
- **X01017** Connector
- **X1143** Connector
- **X13344** Connector
- **X138** Connector
- **X14110** Connector

Fig 33   cargo compartment, left side

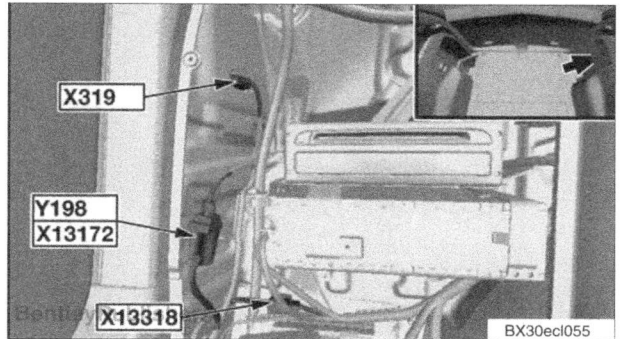

◀ Behind trim panel (**arrow**):
- **Y198** Exhaust flap
- **X13172** Connector
- **X13318** Connector
- **X319** Connector

Fig 34   Cargo compartment, left side

◀ Behind trim panel (**arrow**):
- **N27a** Compensator
- **U6a** Voice control system
- **X10390** Connector
- **X13323** Connector
- **X13337** Connector
- **X13546** Connector

Fig 35   Cargo compartment, right side

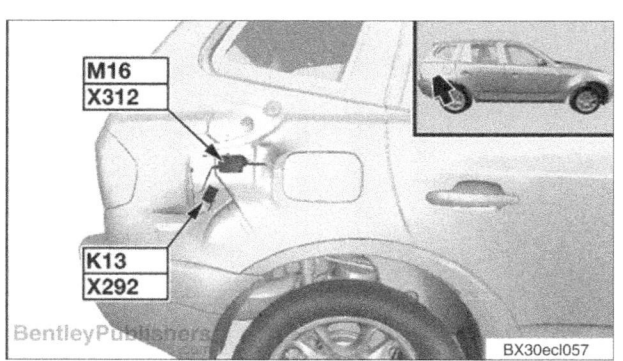

◀ Behind trim panel, right (**arrow**):
- **M16** Fuel filler flap lock motor
- **X312** Connector
- **K13** Rear window defroster relay
- **X292** Connector

Components in cargo compartment

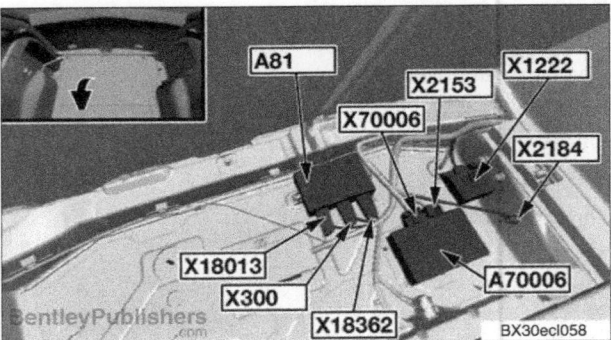

Fig 36   Cargo compartment floor

Underneath cargo compartment floor (**arrow**):

- **A70006** Transfer box, control module
- **X70006** Connector
- **X2153** Connector
- **A81** Park distance control (PDC)
- **X18013** Connector
- **X18362** Connector
- **X300** Connector
- **X1222** Connector
- **X2184** Connector

ELE Electrical Wiring Diagrams

ELECTRICAL COMPONENT LOCATIONS (relay and fuse positions, ground locations) see **Repair Group ECL**

GENERAL

This section contains selected electrical wiring diagrams for E83 models. A detailed index of the diagrams and electrical component is listed in the opening pages.

Schematic conventions

The schematics (wiring diagrams) divide the vehicle electrical system into individual circuits. Interacting electrical components are shown on one schematic.

Electrical components are represented in such a way that their general layout and function are self-explanatory. They are usually arranged in the diagrams so that the current path can be followed from positive at the top to negative at the bottom.

- If a schematic spans several pages, this fact is clearly indicated at the top of each page.

- A component (or connector) which is completely represented in the schematic is shown as a solid box.

- A component (or connector) which has other connectors in addition to the ones shown in the schematic is shown with a dashed line.

- Switches and relays are always shown in rest position (generally OFF).

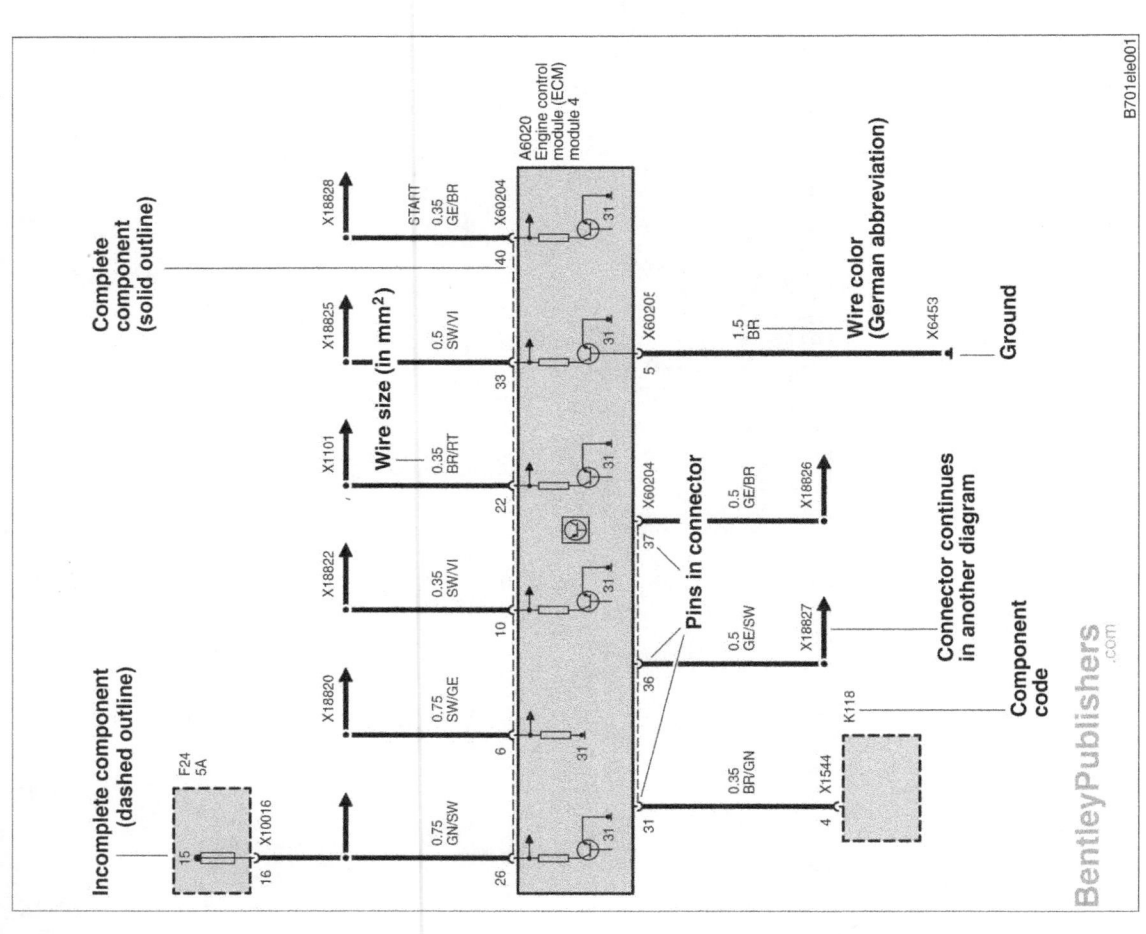

B701ele001

BentleyPublishers.com

Symbols

▽ The schematics utilize simplified electrical symbols.

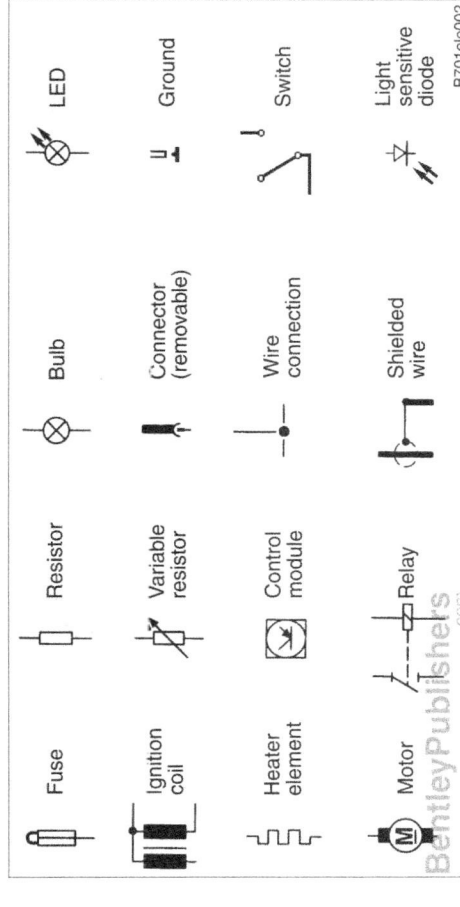

Fuse	Resistor	Bulb	LED
Ignition coil	Variable resistor	Connector (removable)	Ground
Heater element	Control module	Wire connection	Switch
Motor	Relay	Shielded wire	Light sensitive diode

B701ele002

BentleyPublishers.com

▽ Wire insulation colors in this section are given with German color abbreviations.

Wire sizes follow the DIN (European) convention.

Example: 0.5 wire is $\frac{1}{2}$ mm^2 in cross-section area. This corresponds to approx. SAE 16 gauge wire.

BMW identifies many electrical circuits with unique designations which follow the DIN standard. Also, BMW designates electrical components, junctions and grounds with a unique alphanumeric designation, most of which also follow the DIN standard.

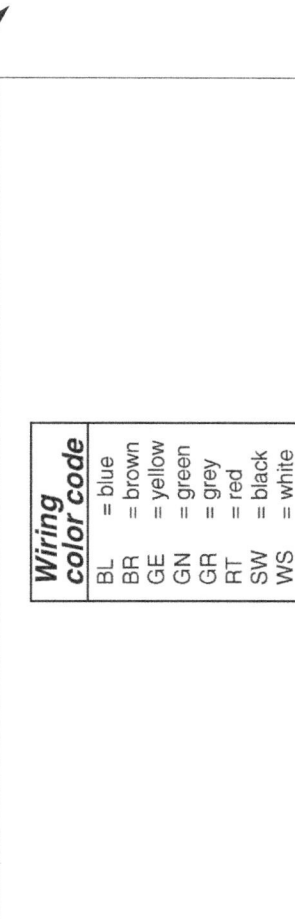

Wiring color code

BL	= blue
BR	= brown
GE	= yellow
GN	= green
GR	= grey
RT	= red
SW	= black
WS	= white
VI	= violet

B701ele003

BentleyPublishers.com

Fuse F01
M54 engine

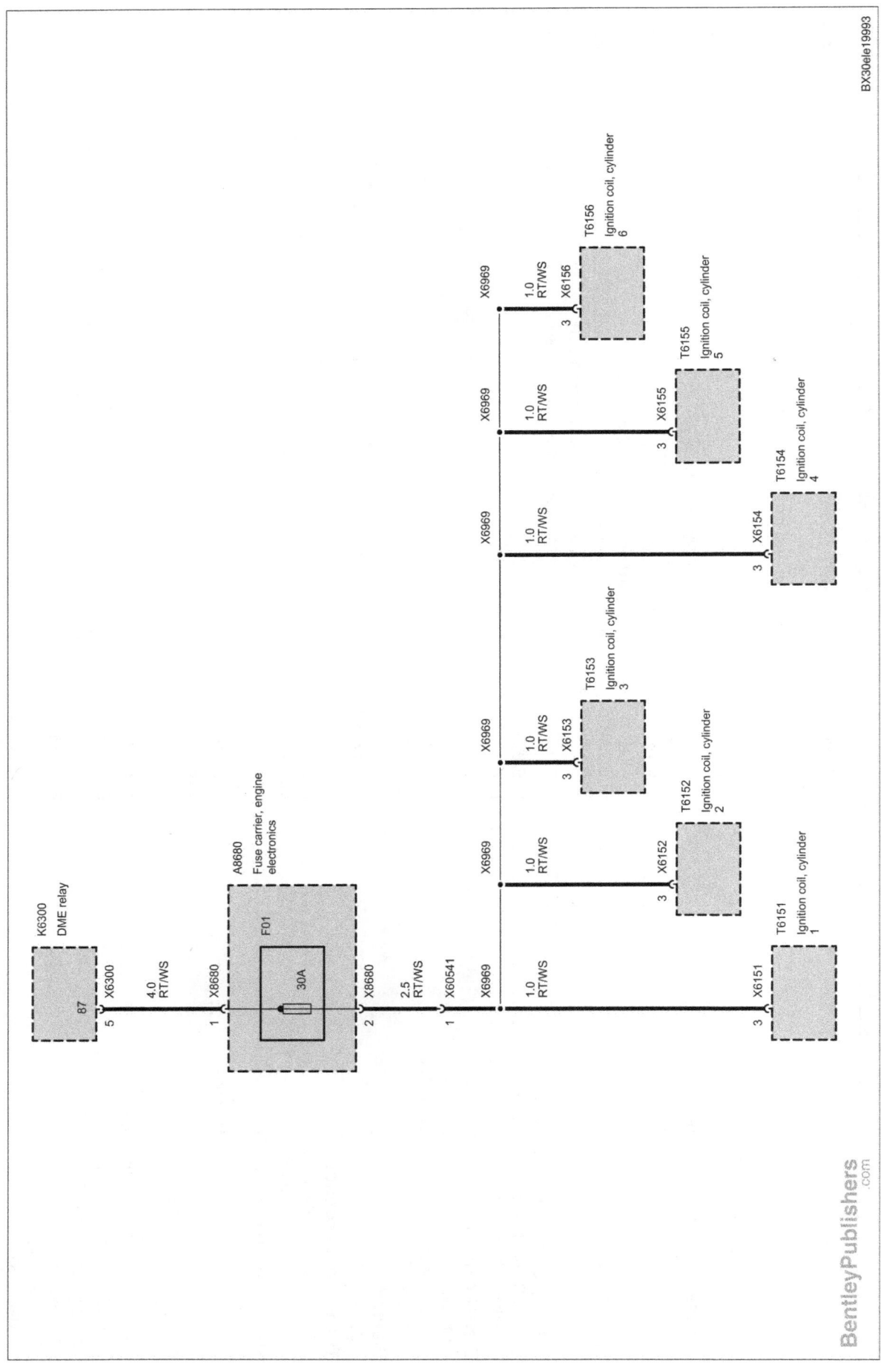

Fuse F02
M54 engine

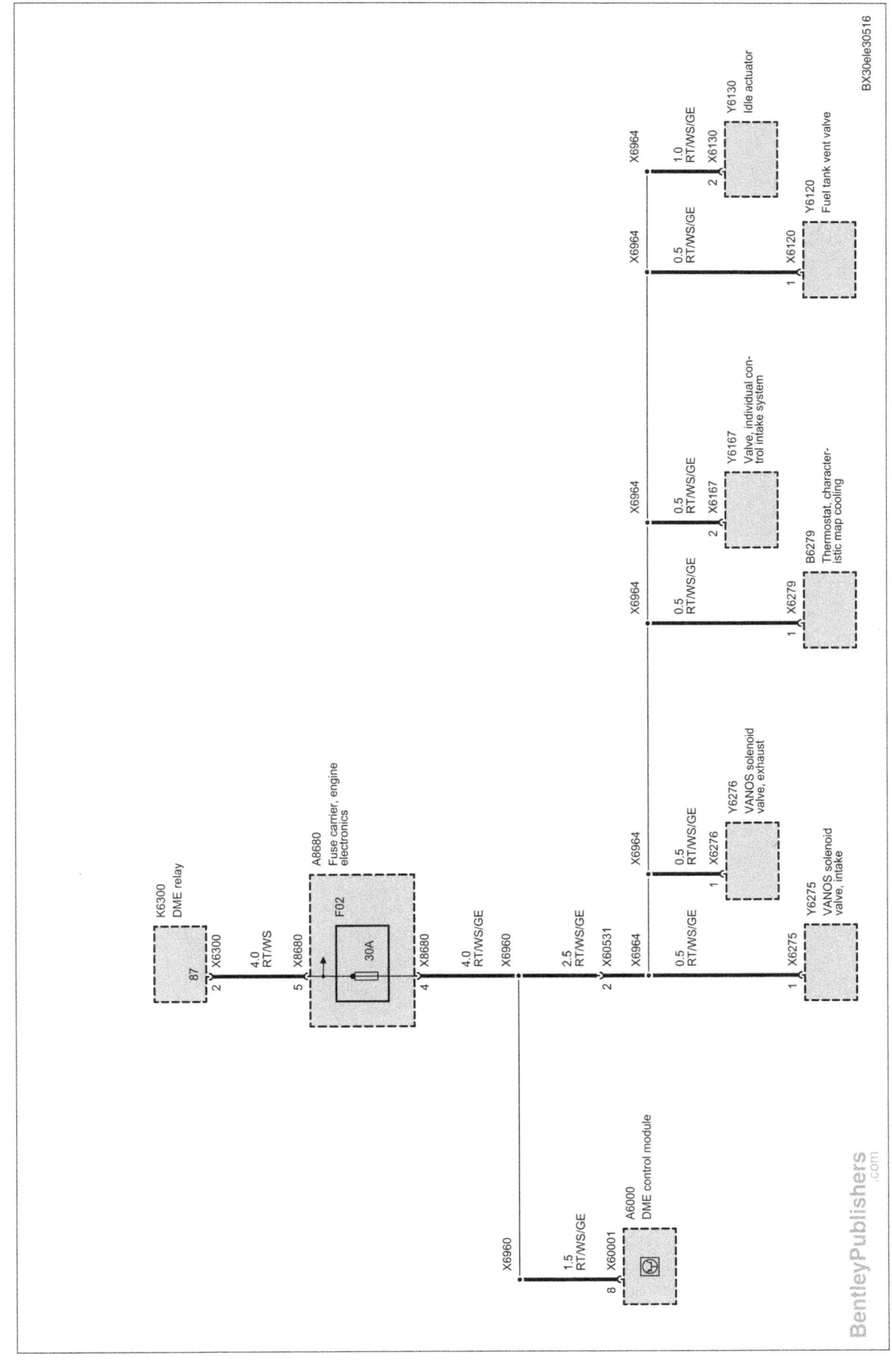

BX30ele30516

BentleyPublishers
.com

Fuse F03
M54 engine
(to 09 / 2005)

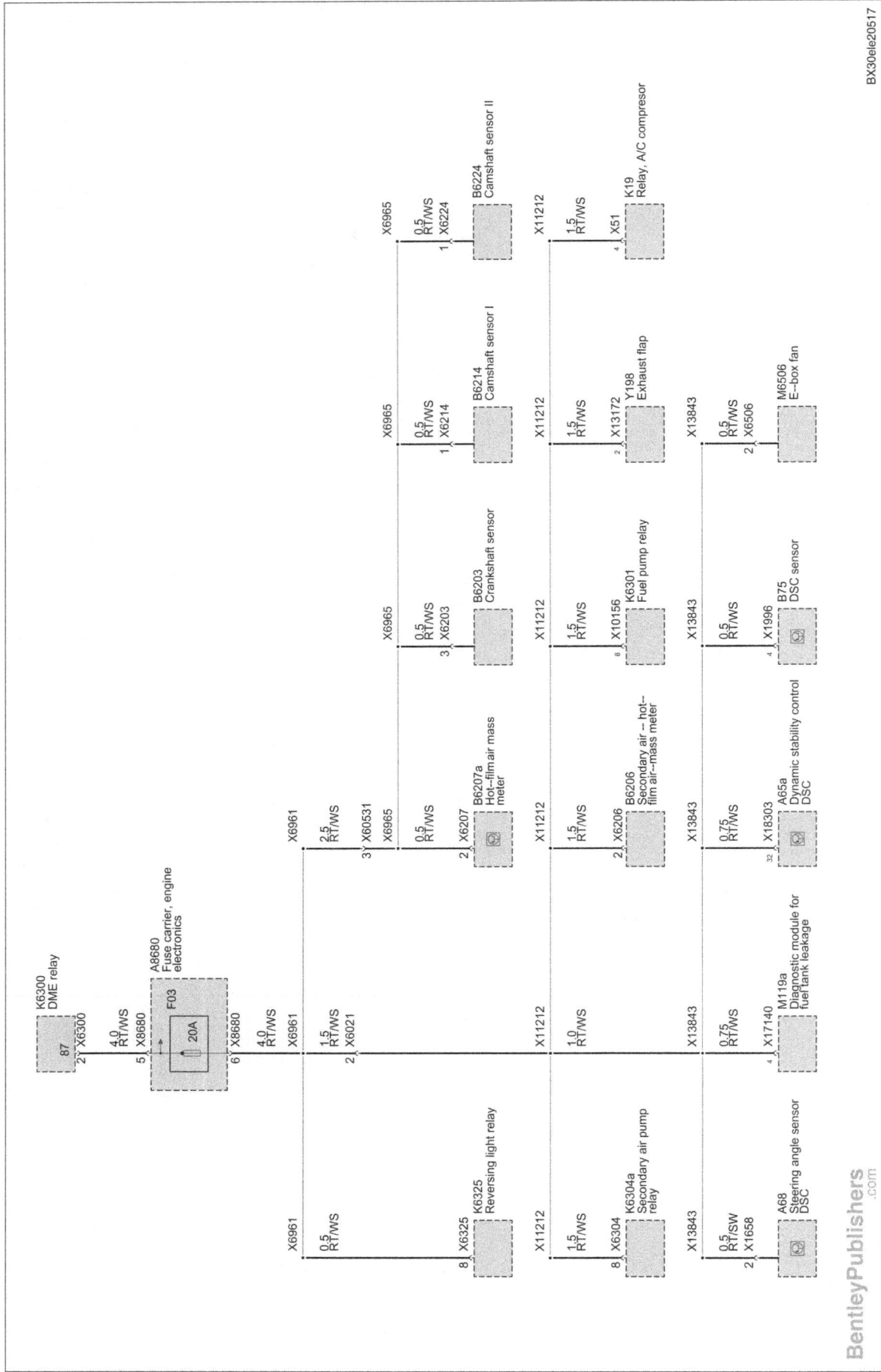

BX30ele20517

Fuse F03
M54 engine
(from 09 / 2005)

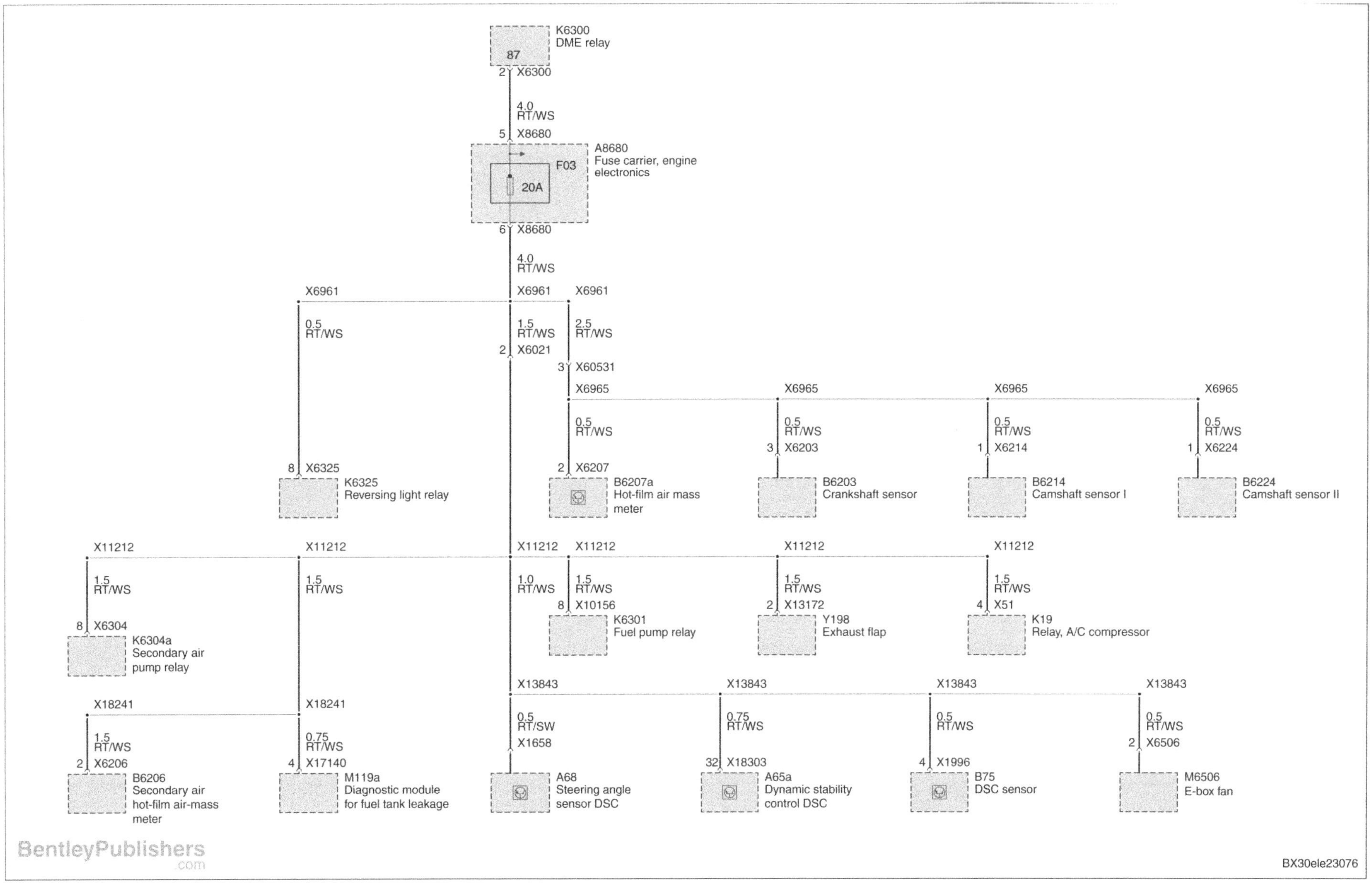

K6300 DME relay

A8680 Fuse carrier, engine electronics

F03 20A

K6325 Reversing light relay

K6304a Secondary air pump relay

B6206 Secondary air hot-film air-mass meter

M119a Diagnostic module for fuel tank leakage

B207a Hot-film air mass meter

K6301 Fuel pump relay

B6203 Crankshaft sensor

B6214 Camshaft sensor I

B6224 Camshaft sensor II

Y198 Exhaust flap

K19 Relay, A/C compressor

A65a Dynamic stability control DSC

A68 Steering angle sensor DSC

B75 DSC sensor

M6506 E-box fan

Electrical Wiring Diagrams   ELE-11

BX30ele23076

Fuse F04
M54 engine

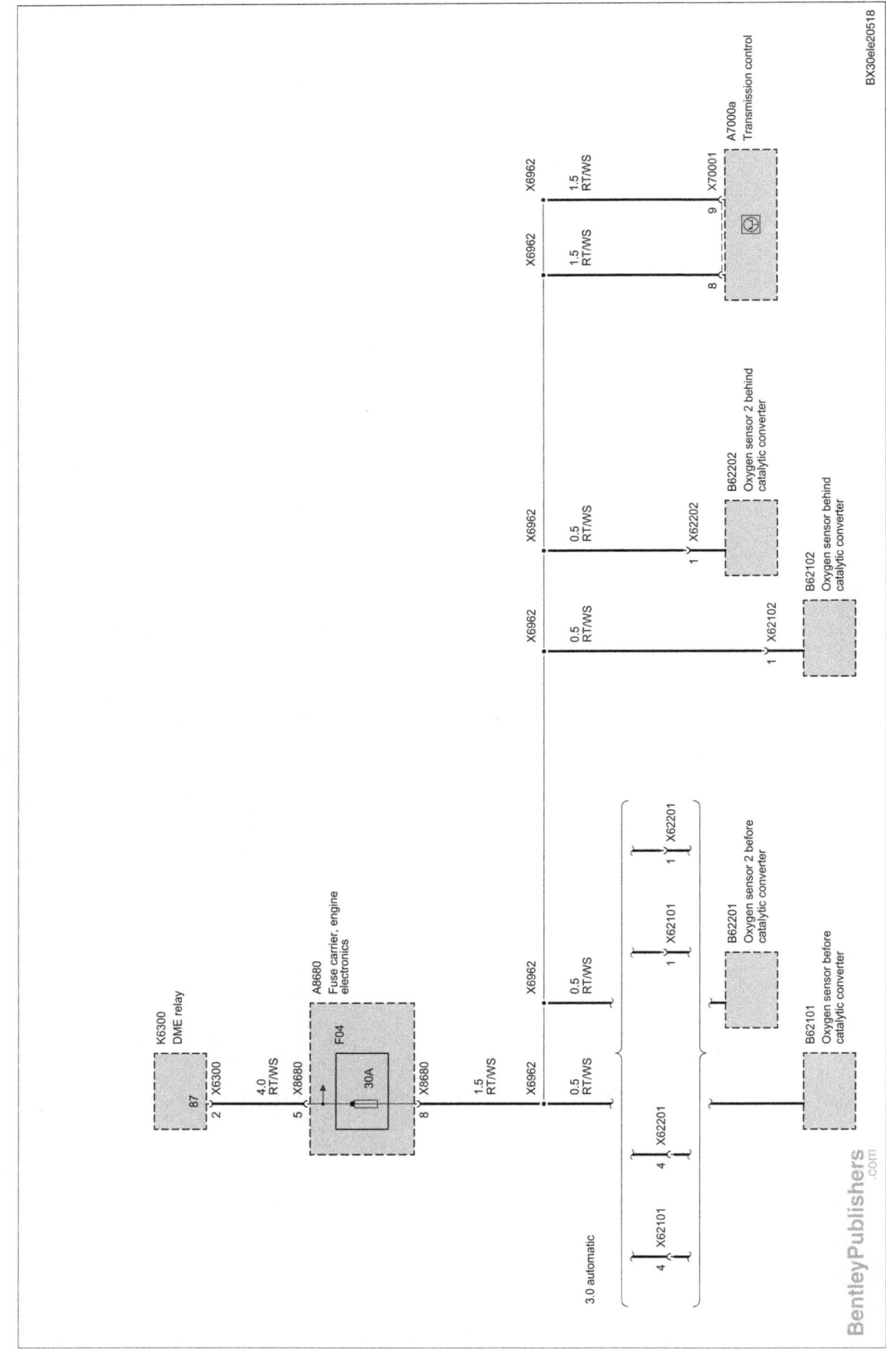

BX30ele20518

Fuse F04
N52 engine

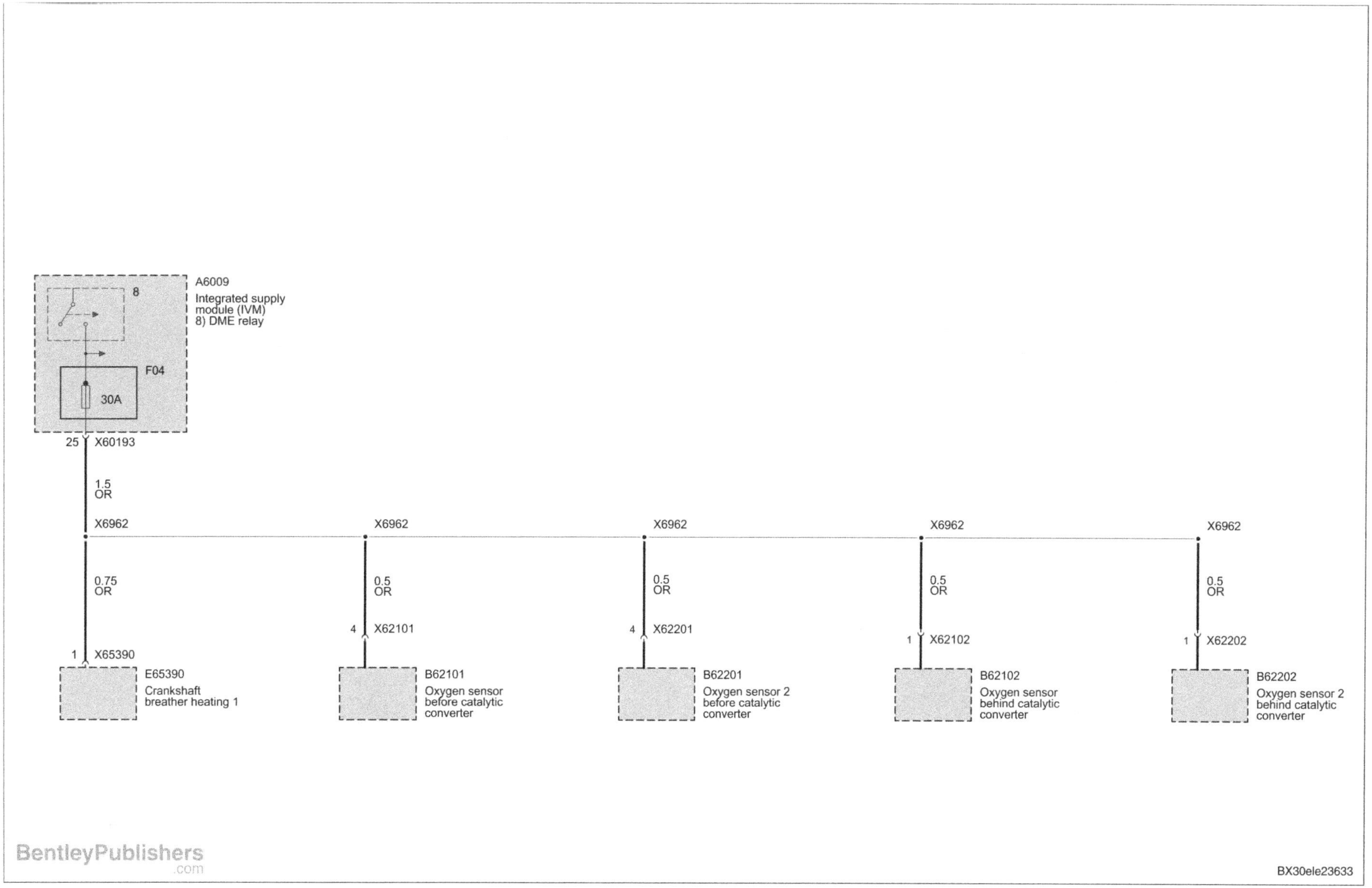

BX30ele23633

B62202
Oxygen sensor 2
behind catalytic
converter

X6962

0.5
OR

X62202

1

B62102
Oxygen sensor
behind catalytic
converter

X6962

0.5
OR

X62102

1

B62201
Oxygen sensor 2
before catalytic
converter

X6962

0.5
OR

X62201

4

B62101
Oxygen sensor
before catalytic
converter

X6962

0.5
OR

X62101

4

A6009
Integrated supply
module (IVM)
8) DME relay

8

F04

30A

25 X60193

1.5
OR

X6962

0.75
OR

X65390

1

E65390
Crankshaft
breather heating 1

BentleyPublishers
.com

**Fuse F08
N52 engine**

**Fuse F05
M54 engine**

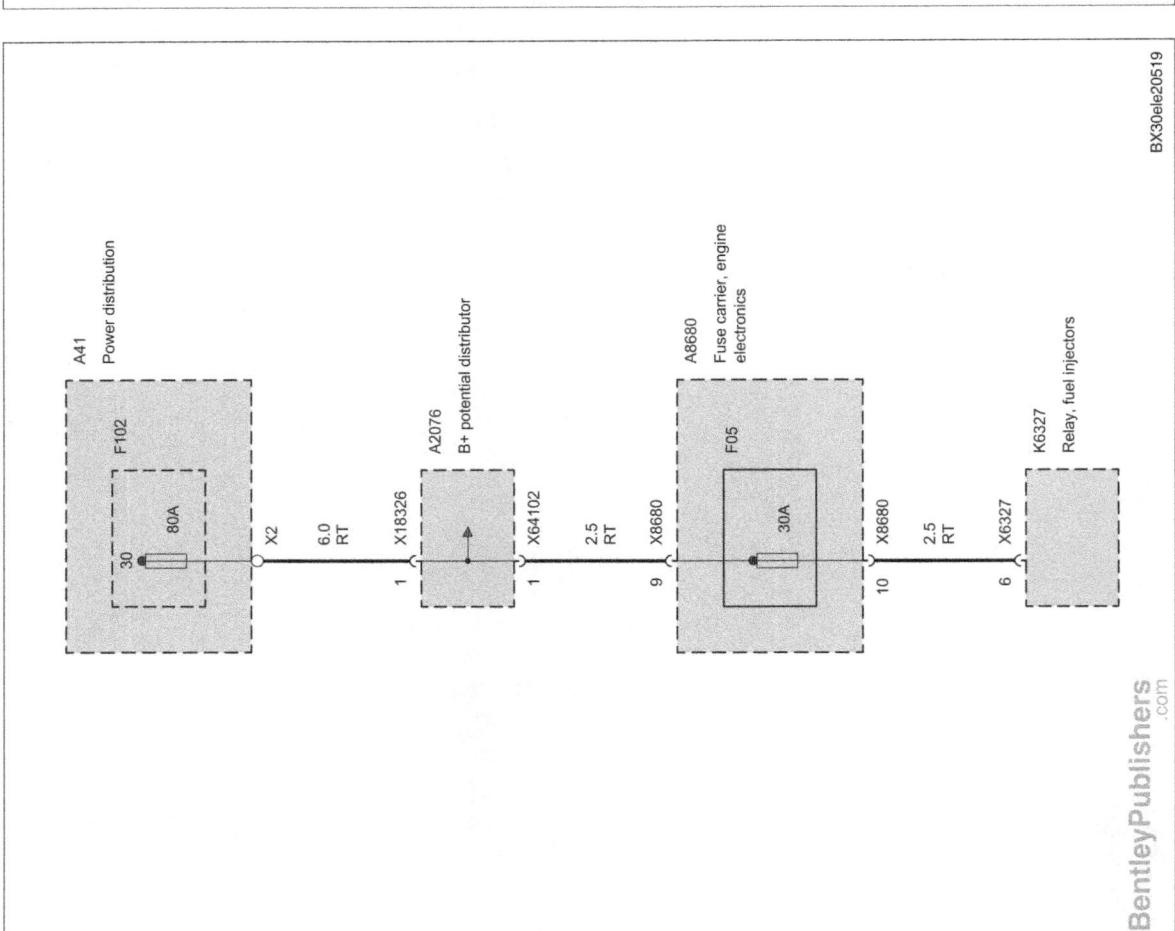

BX30ele25137

BX30ele20519

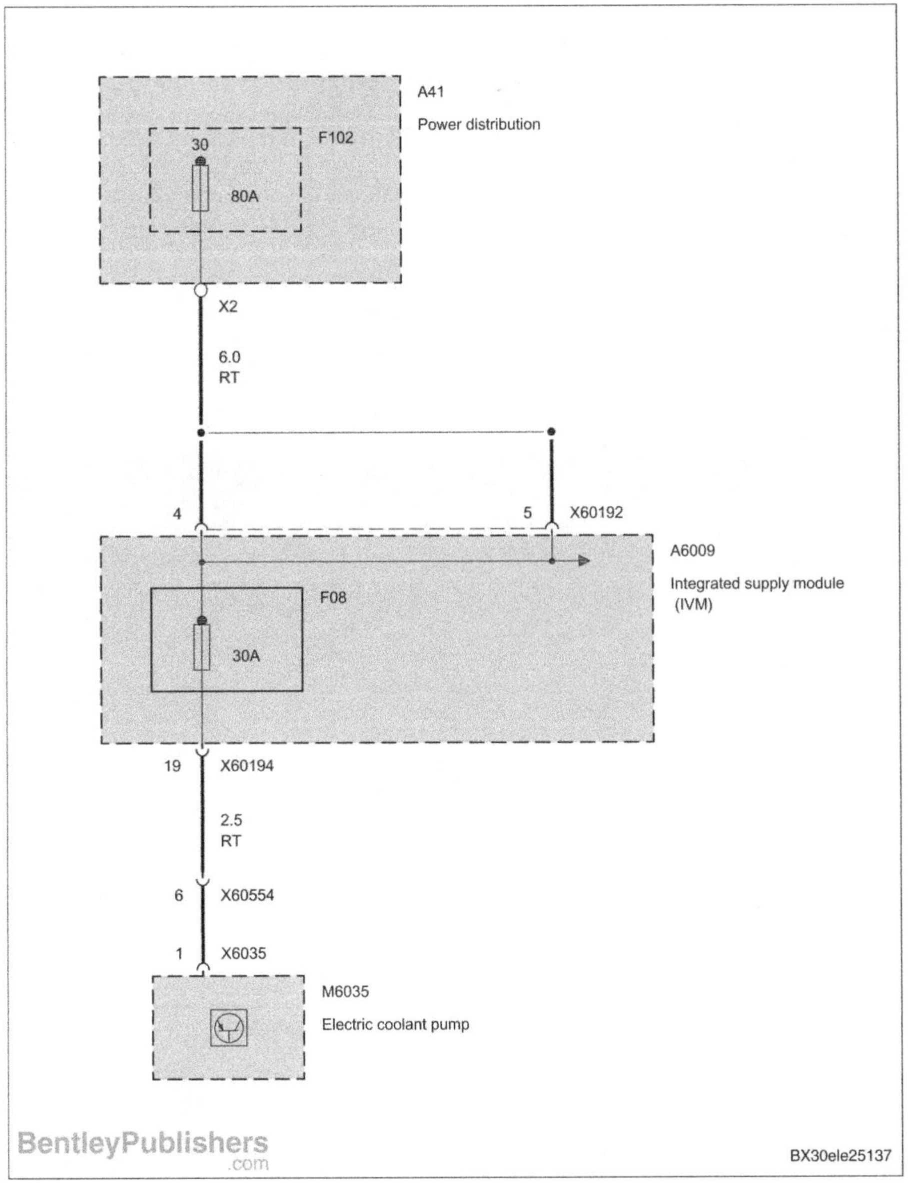

Fuse F6

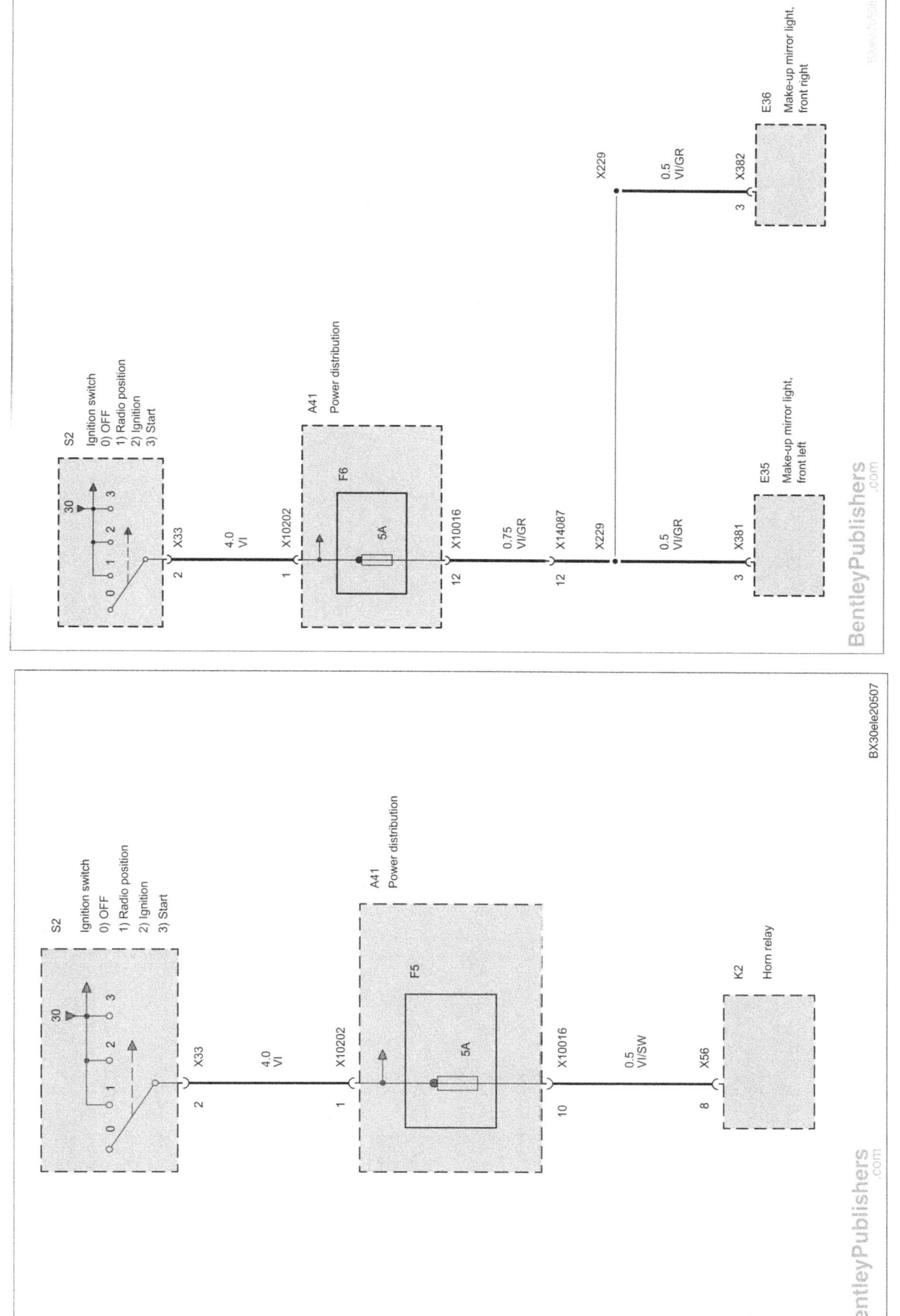

Fuse F5

BX30ele20507

Fuse F6 diagram labels:

S2 — Ignition switch
0) OFF
1) Radio position
2) Ignition
3) Start

A41 — Power distribution
F6
5A

E35 — Make-up mirror light, front left

E36 — Make-up mirror light, front right

X33 4.0 VI X10202 X10016 0.75 VI/GR X14087 X229 0.5 VI/GR X381
2 1 12 12 3

X229 0.5 VI/GR X382
3

Fuse F5 diagram labels:

S2 — Ignition switch
0) OFF
1) Radio position
2) Ignition
3) Start

A41 — Power distribution
F5
5A

K2 — Horn relay

X33 4.0 VI X10202 X10016 0.5 VI/SW X56
2 1 10 8

BentleyPublishers.com

Fuse F7
(to 09 / 2005)

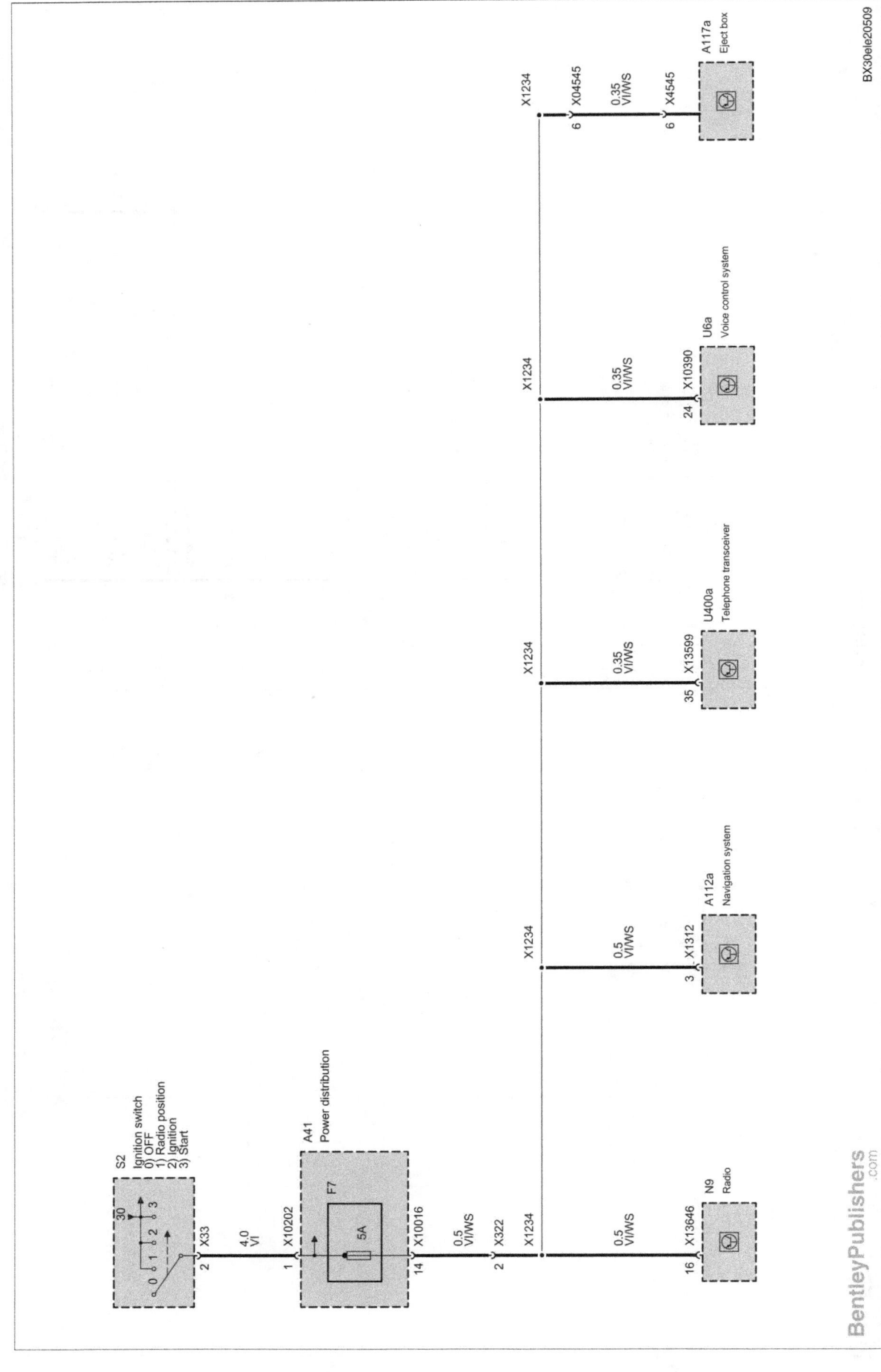

**Fuse F7
(from 09 / 2005)**

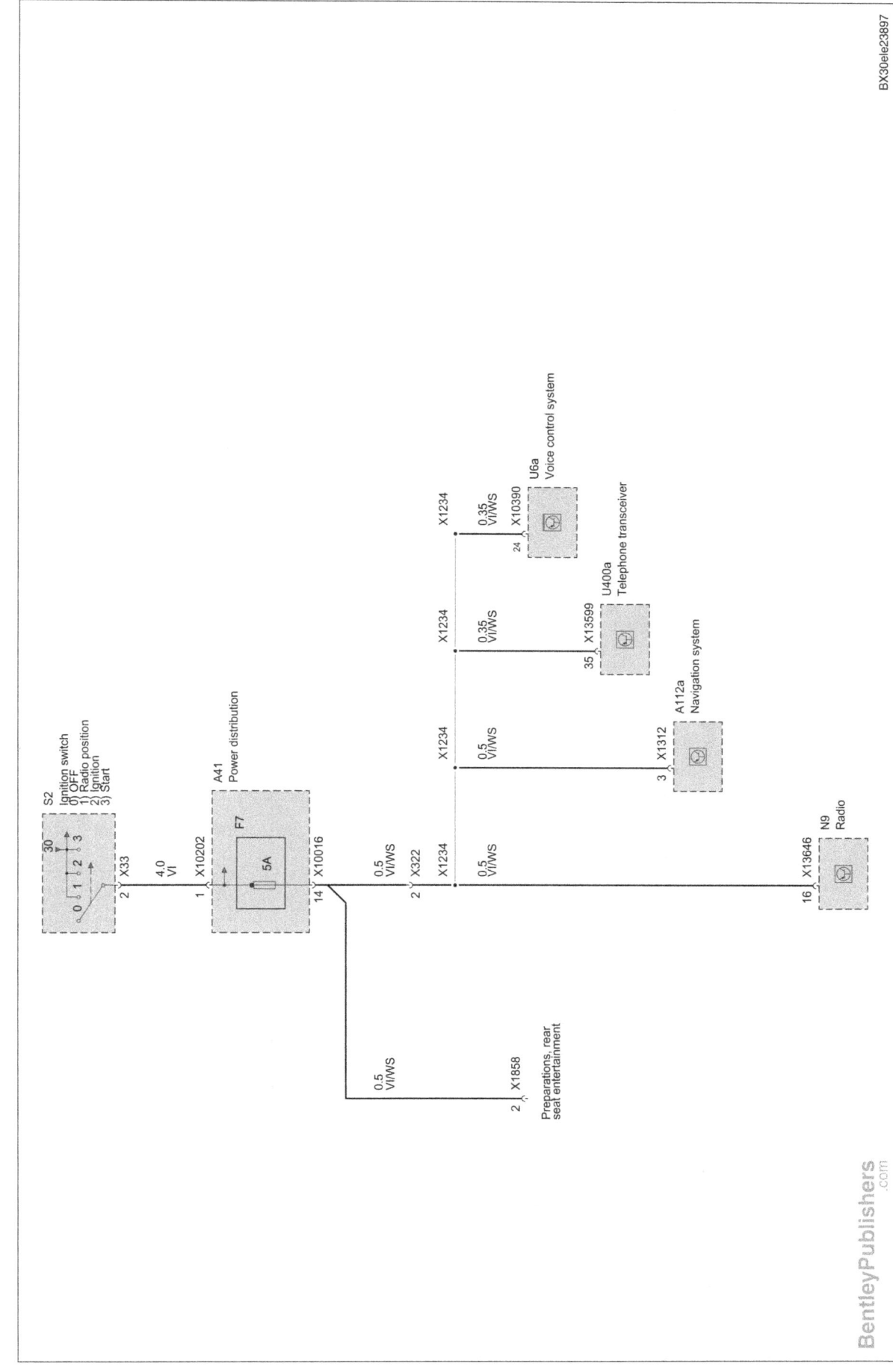

BX30ele23887

Fuse F9

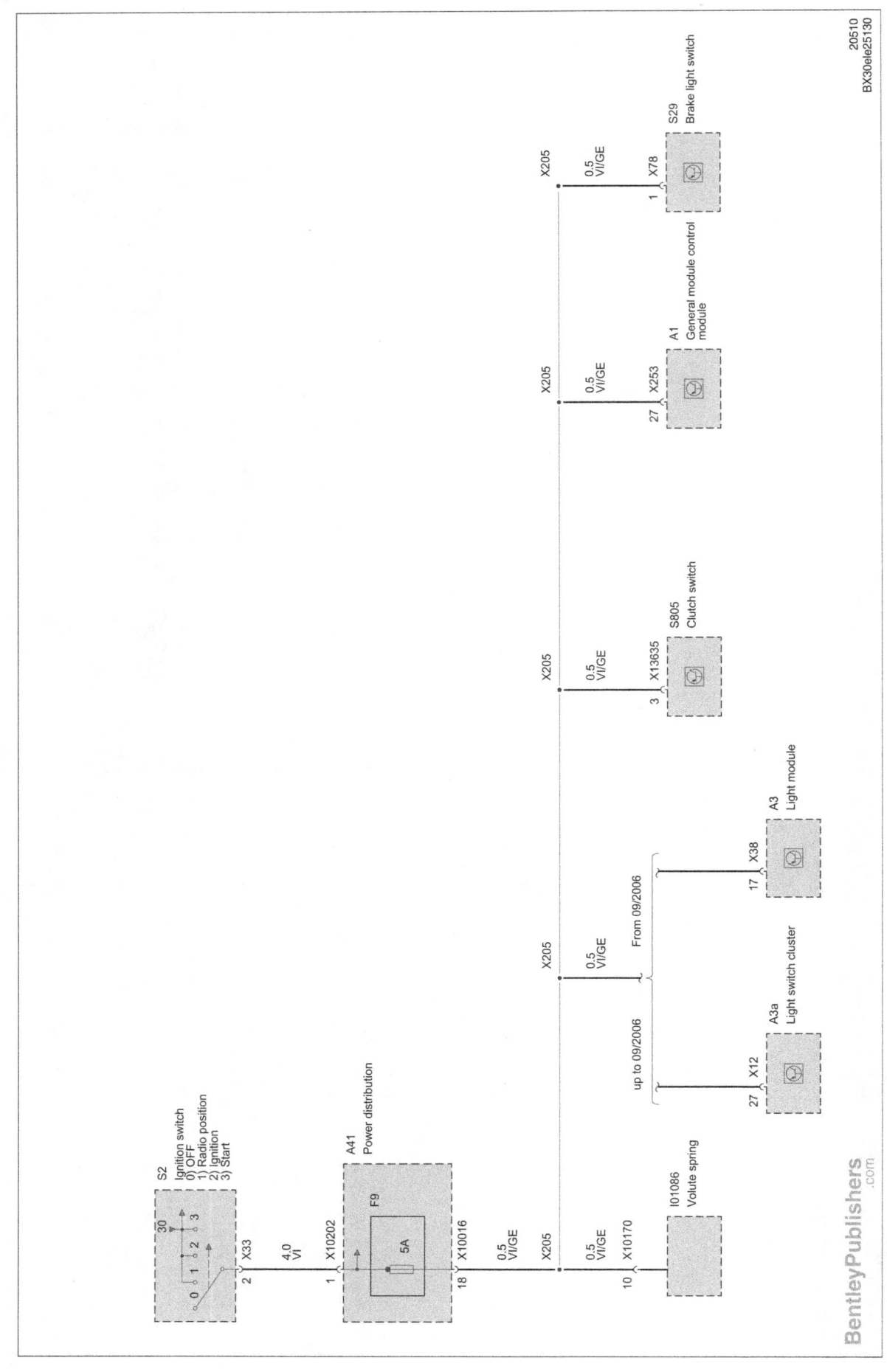

20510
BX30ele25130

Fuse F10

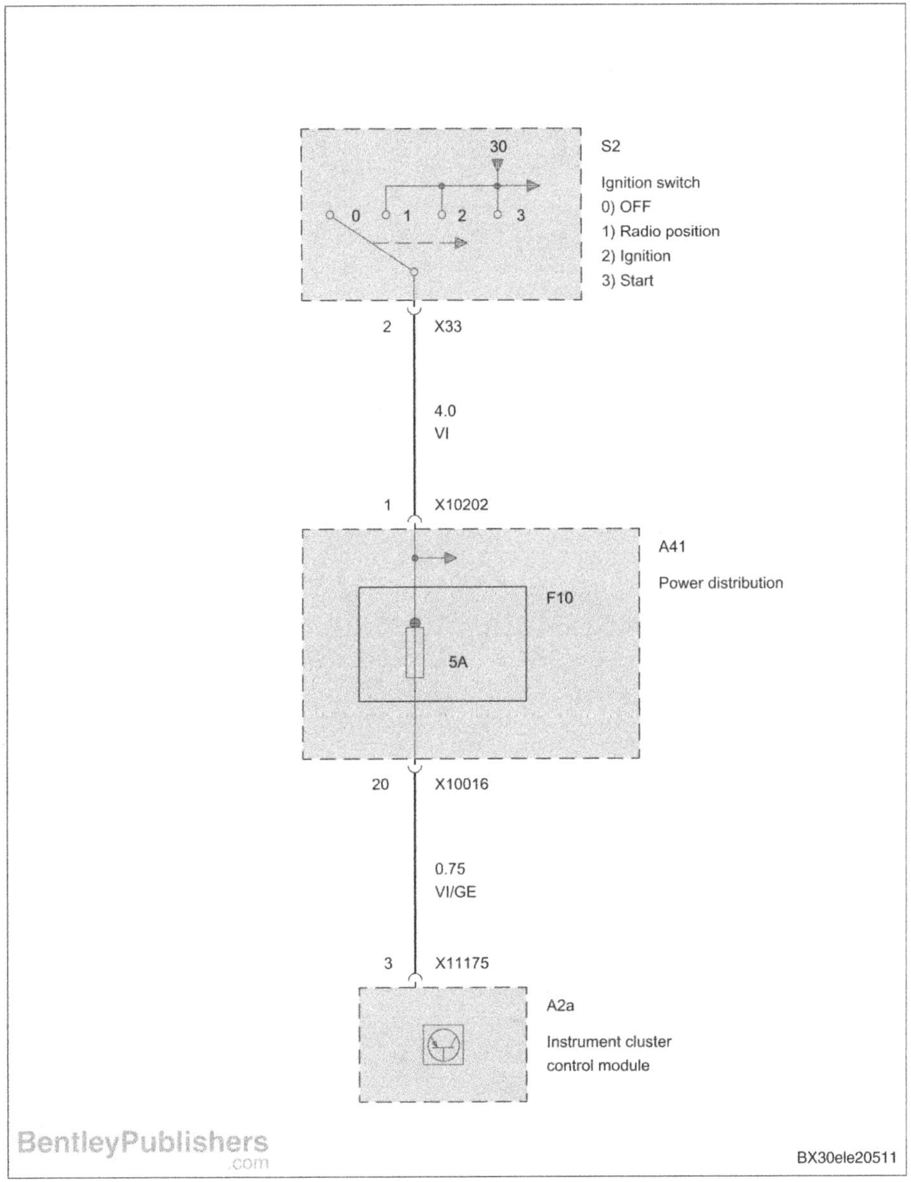

S2

Ignition switch
0) OFF
1) Radio position
2) Ignition
3) Start

30
3
2
1
0

X33

2

4.0
VI

X10202

1

A41

Power distribution

F10

5A

X10016

20

0.75
VI/GE

X11175

3

A2a

Instrument cluster
control module

BX30ele20511

BX30ele20512

Fuse F11

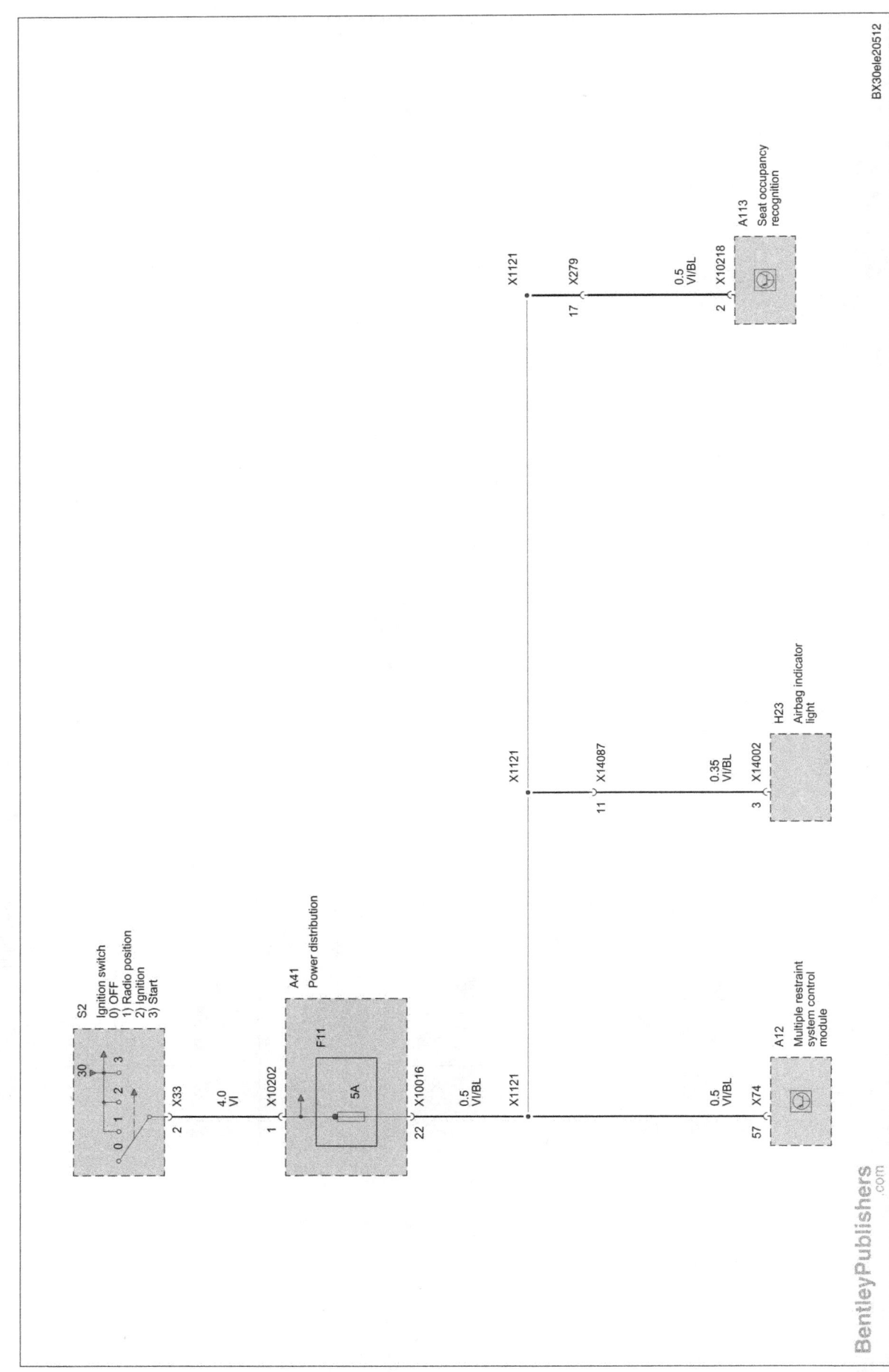

S2
Ignition switch
0) OFF
1) Radio position
2) Ignition
3) Start

A41
Power distribution

F11
5A

A113
Seat occupancy recognition

H23
Airbag indicator light

A12
Multiple restraint system control module

Fuse F14

Fuse F12

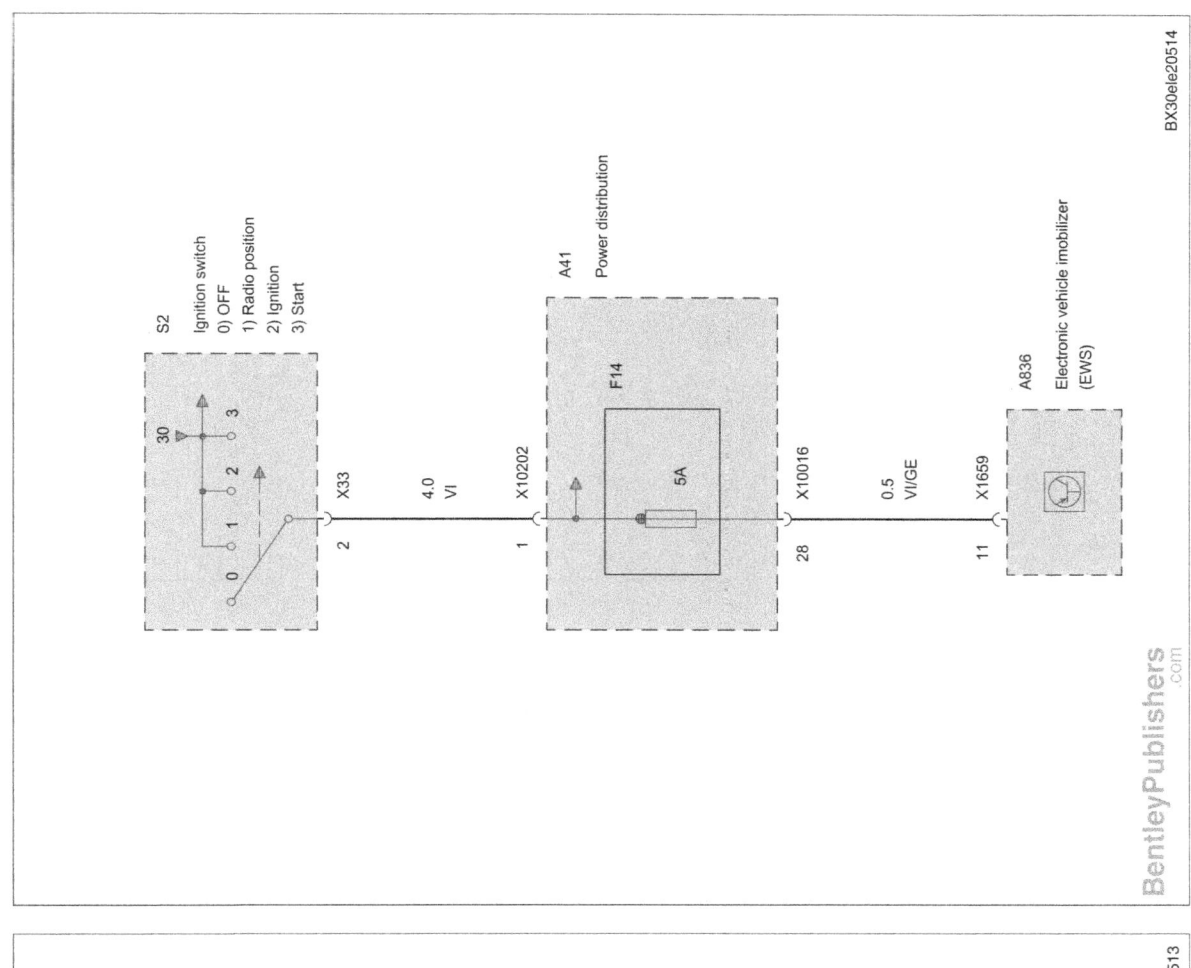

BX30ele20514

BX30ele20513

F14 diagram (top):

S2
Ignition switch
0) OFF
1) Radio position
2) Ignition
3) Start

30

A41
Power distribution

F14

5A

A836
Electronic vehicle imobilizer
(EWS)

X33
2

4.0
VI

X10202
1

X10016
28

0.5
VI/GE

X1659
11

F12 diagram (bottom):

S2
Ignition switch
0) OFF
1) Radio position
2) Ignition
3) Start

30

A41
Power distribution

F12

7.5A

A169
Center console switch
center

X33
2

4.0
VI

X10202
1

X10016
24

0.75
VI/BL

X1869
23

Fuse F21

Fuse F15

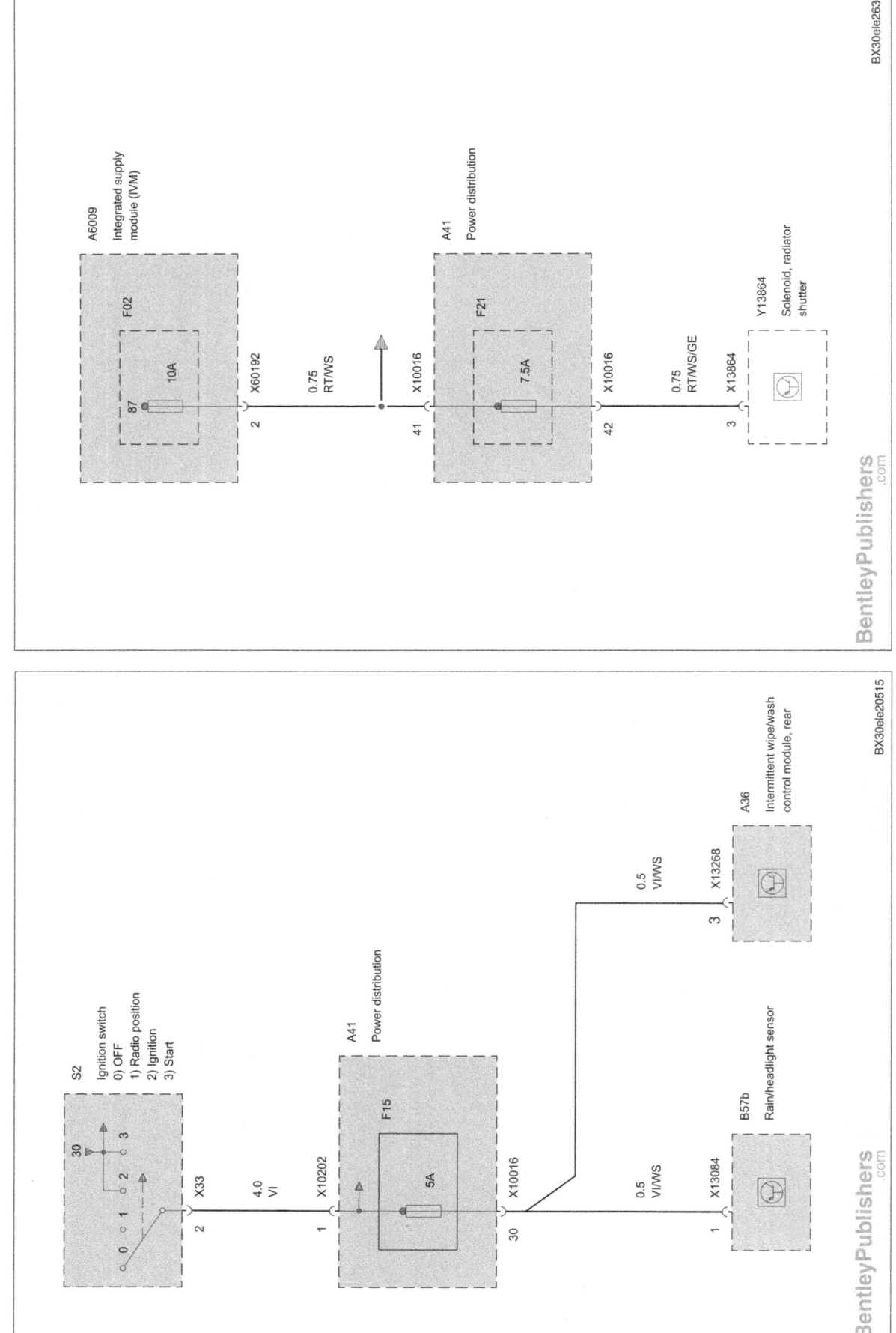

A6009
Integrated supply
module (IVM)

F02

10A

87

X60192

2

0.75
RT/WS

X10016

41

A41
Power distribution

F21

7.5A

X10016

42

0.75
RT/WS/GE

X13864

3

Y13864
Solenoid, radiator
shutter

S2
Ignition switch
0) OFF
1) Radio position
2) Ignition
3) Start

30

3

2

1

0

X33

2

4.0
VI

X10202

1

A41
Power distribution

F15

5A

X10016

30

0.5
VI/WS

X13084

1

B57b
Rain/headlight sensor

0.5
VI/WS

X13268

3

A36
Intermittent wipe/wash
control module, rear

BX30ele26368

BX30ele20515

Fuse F23

Fuse F22

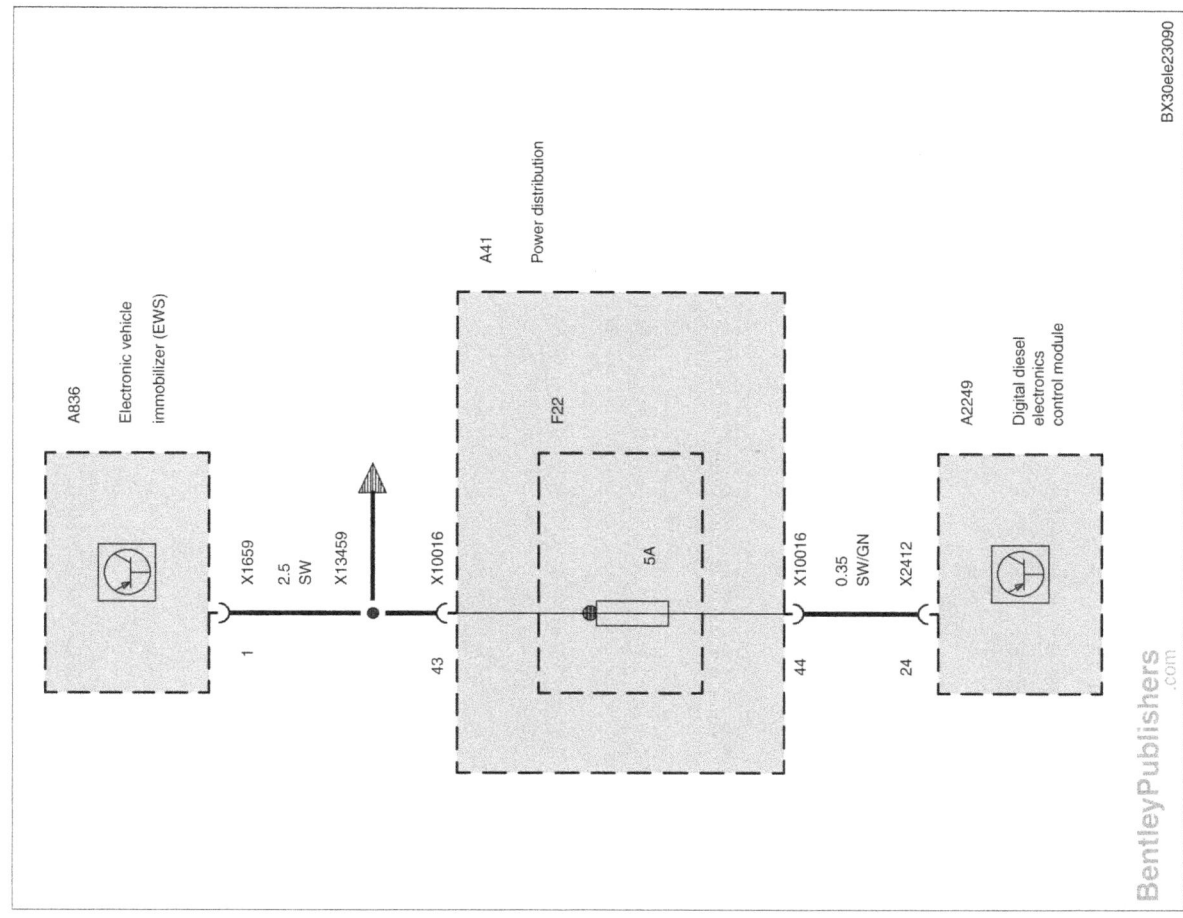

BX30ele20495

BX30ele23090

Fuse F25
(to 06 / 2004)

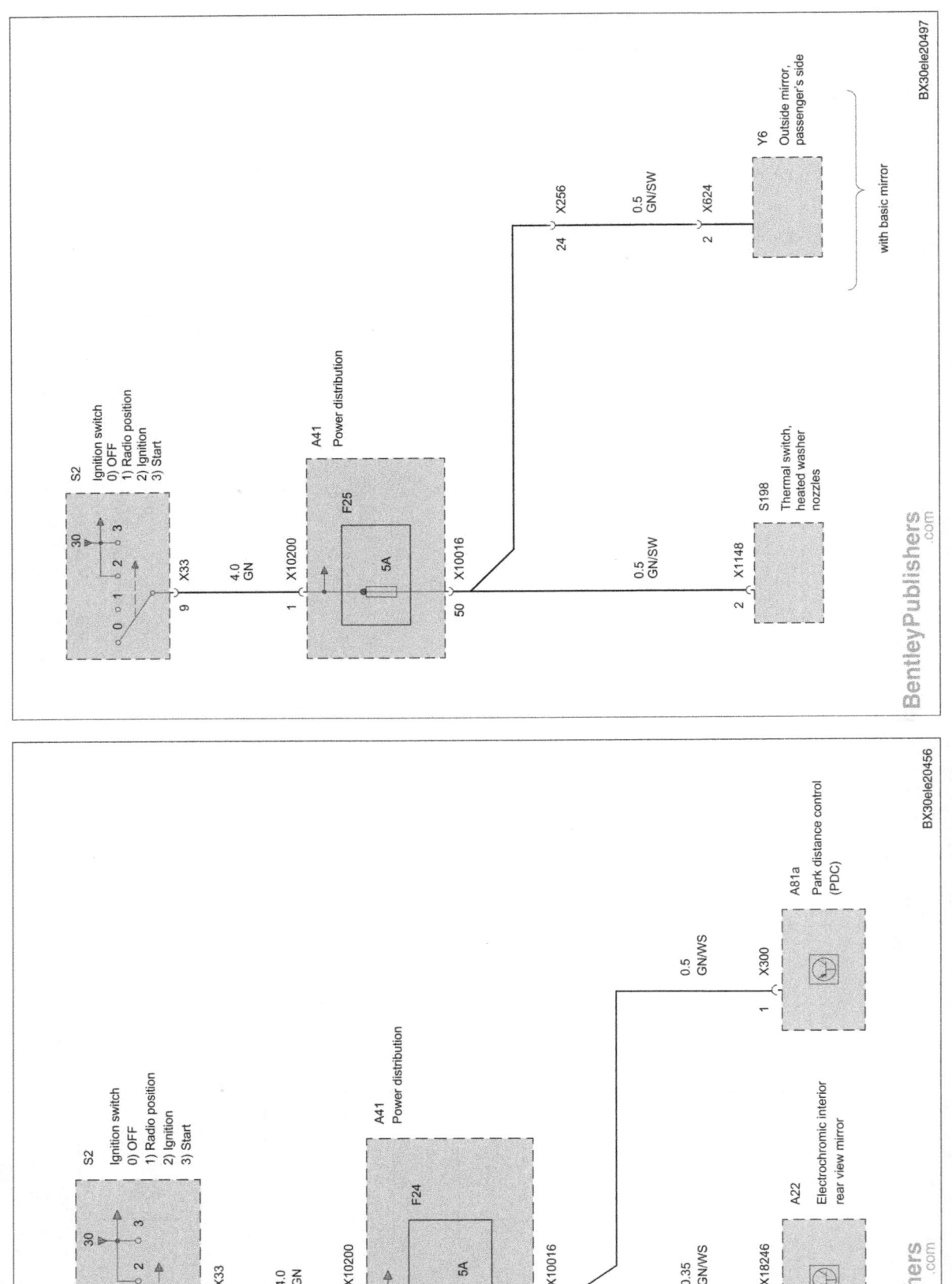

Fuse F24

Fuse F26

**Fuse F25
(from 06 / 2004)**

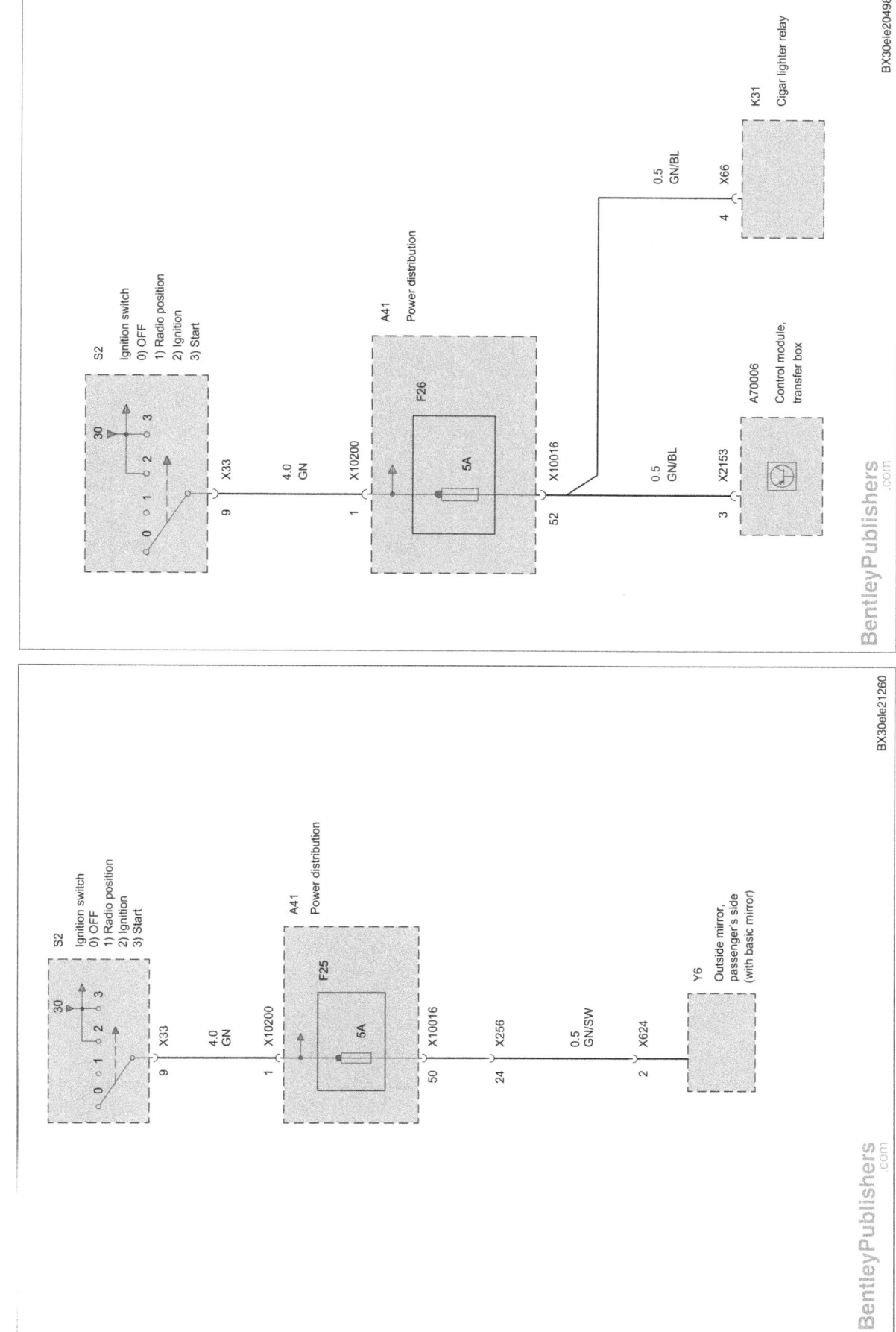

BX30ele20498

BX30ele21260

**Fuse F27
(to 09 / 2007)**

**Fuse F27
(from 09 / 2007)**

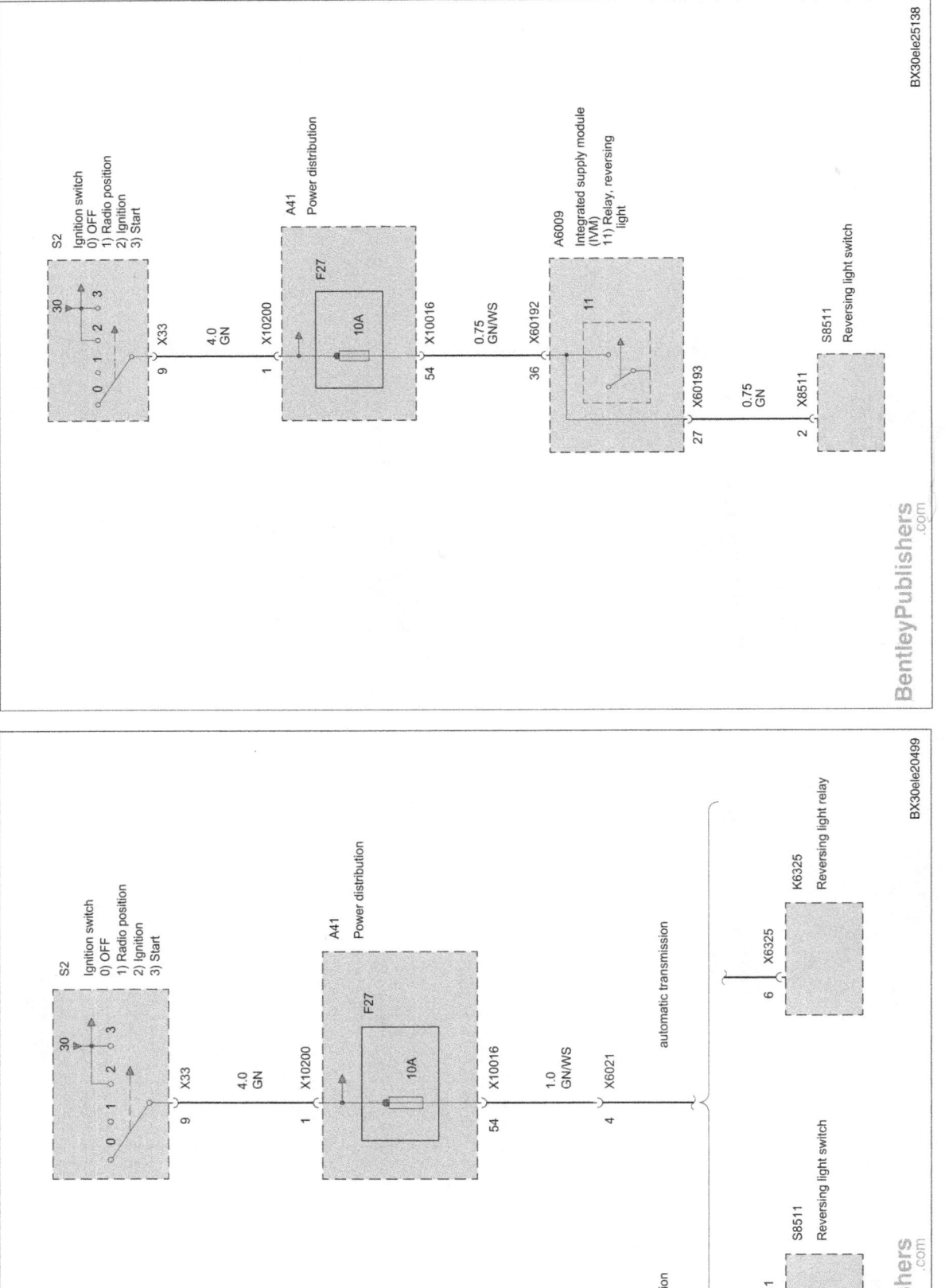

BX30ele25138

BX30ele20499

Fuse F29
M54 engine

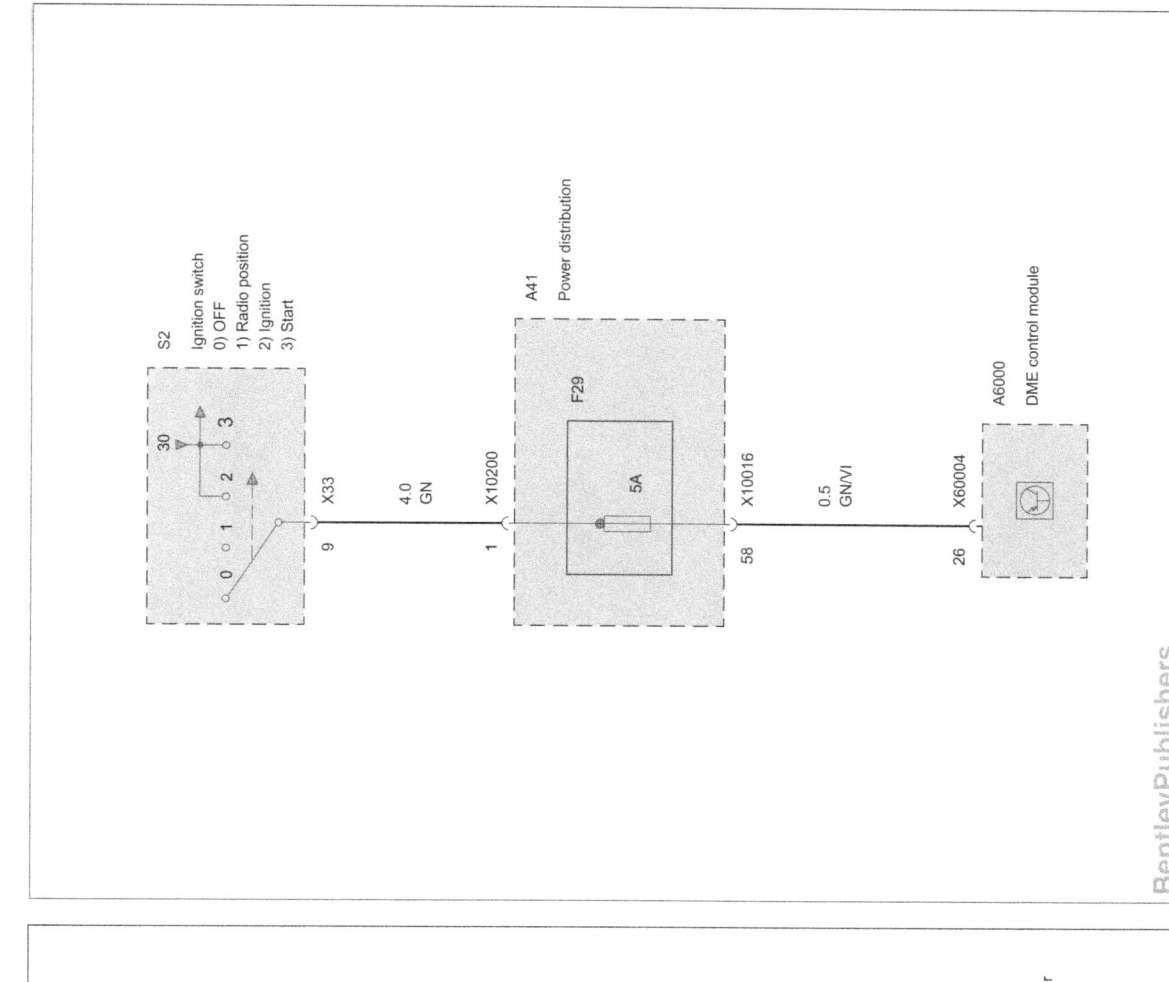

BX30ele20501

Fuse F28

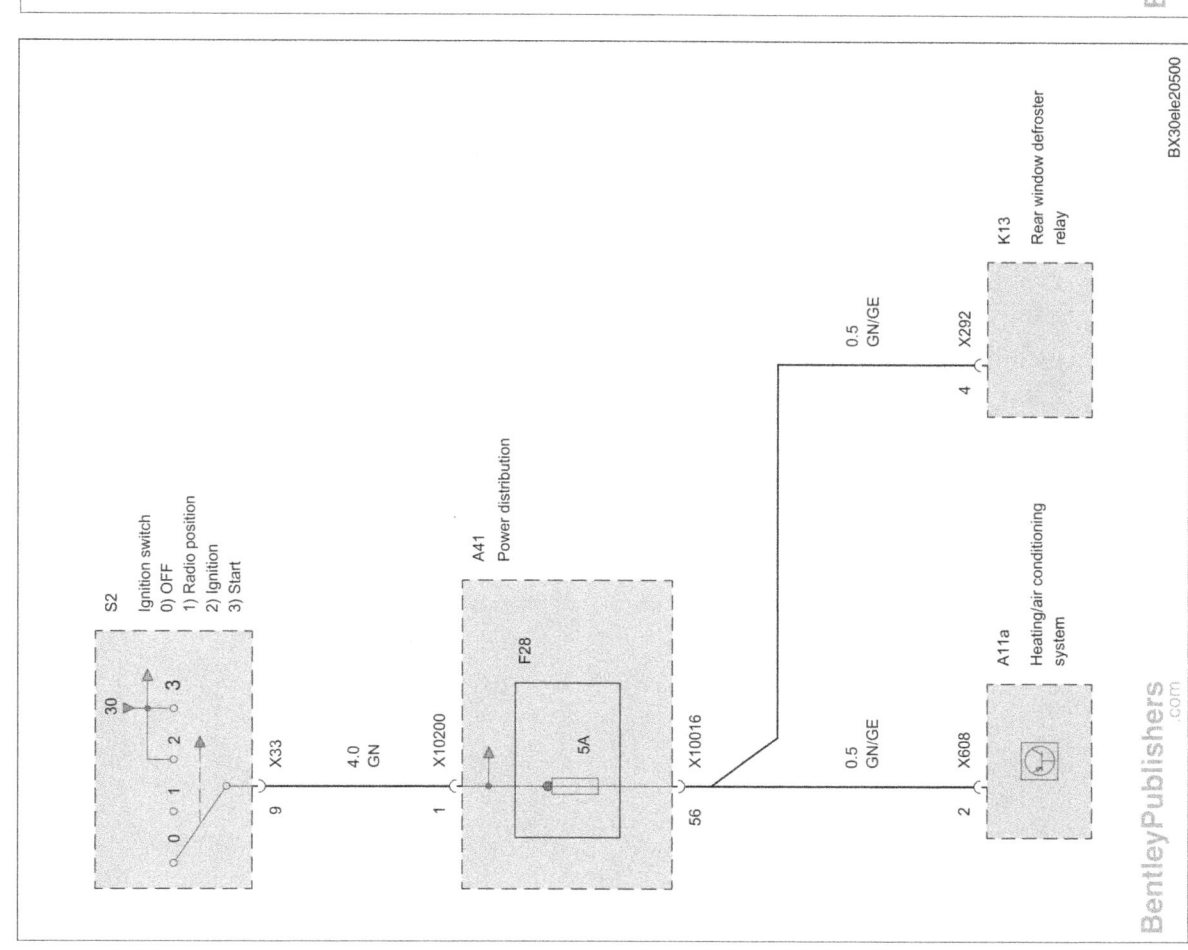

BX30ele20500

Fuse F31

**Fuse F30
M54 engine**

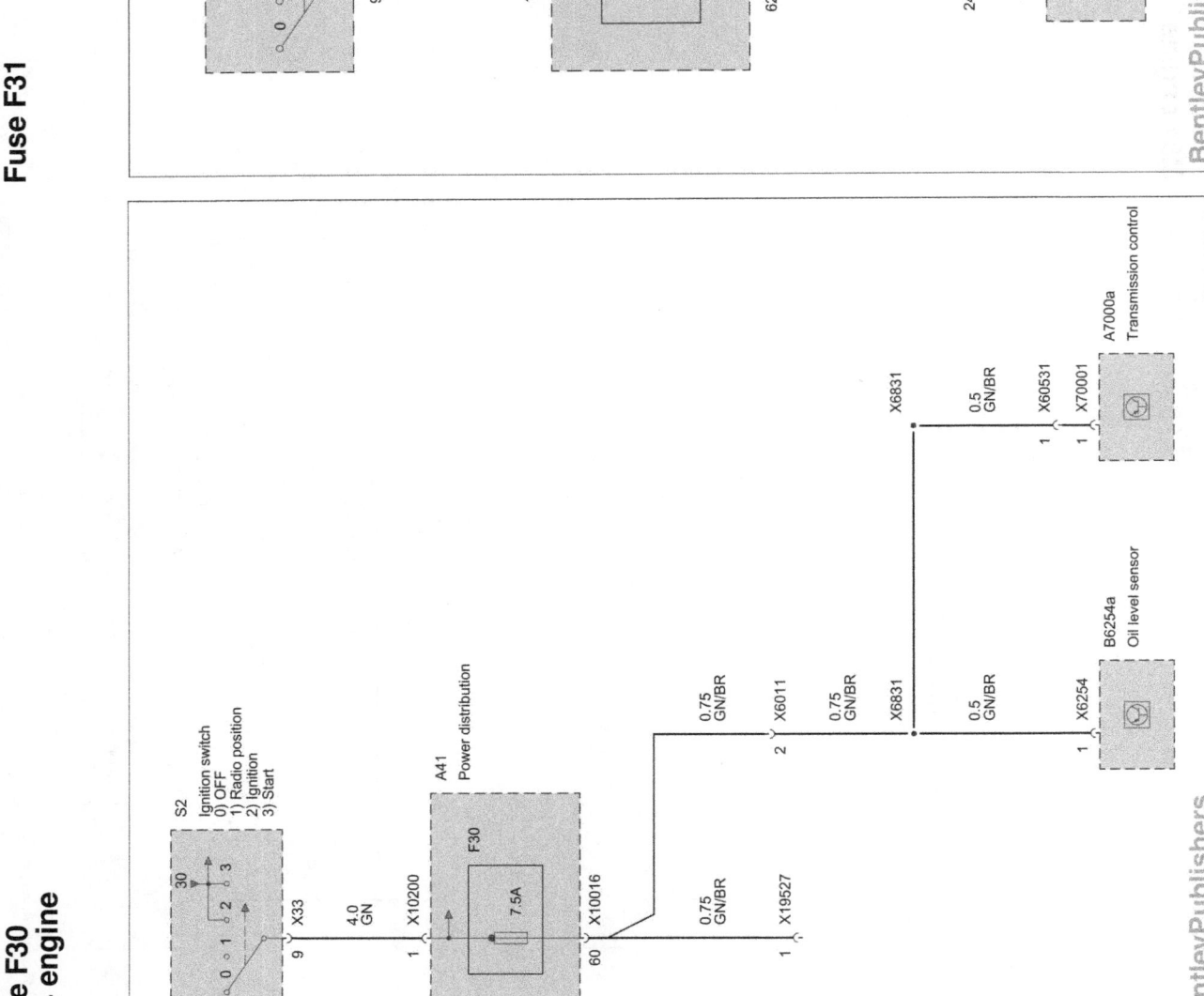

**Fuse F32
(from 09 / 2006)**

**Fuse F32
(to 09 / 2006)**

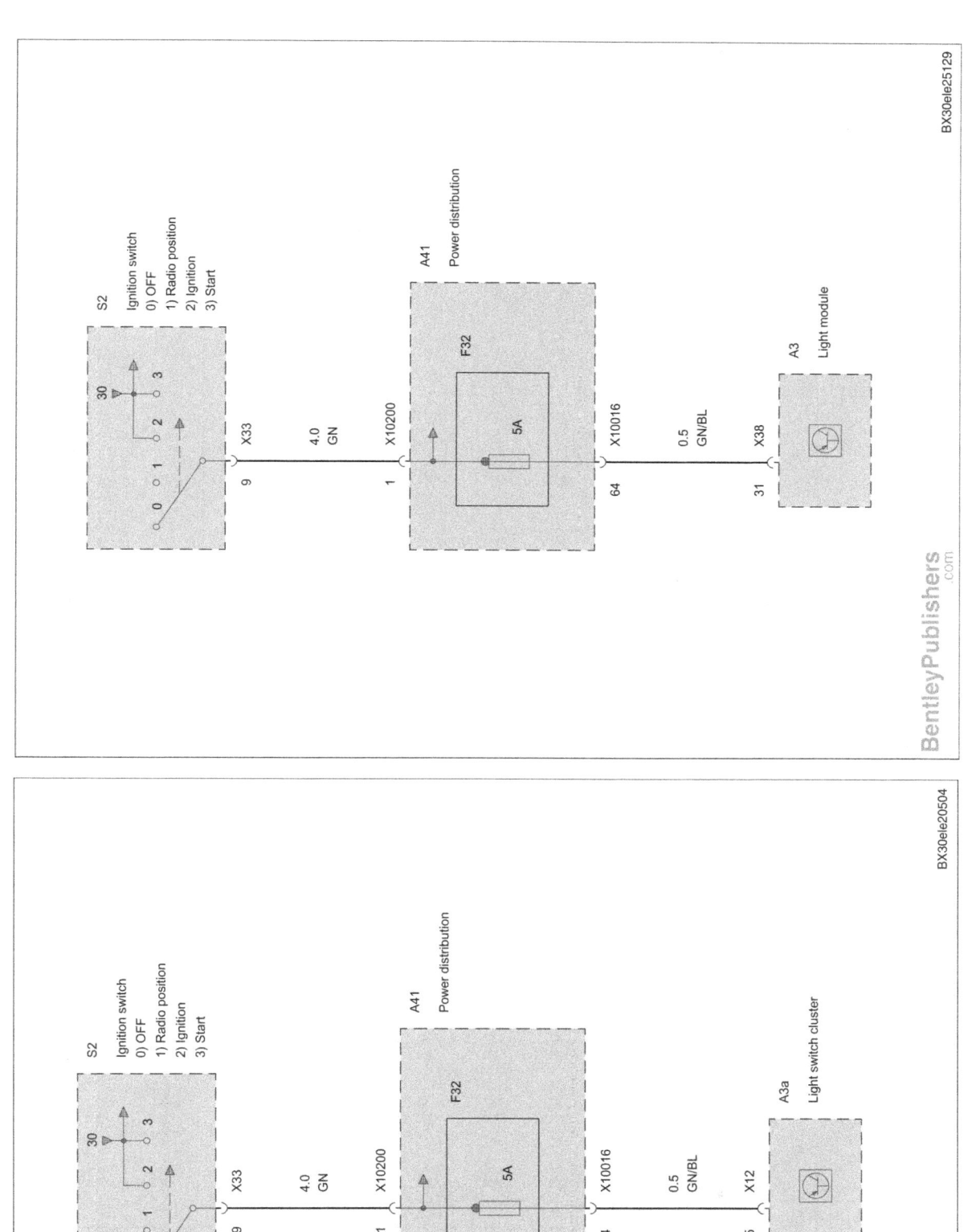

BX30ele25129

BX30ele20504

Fuse F34

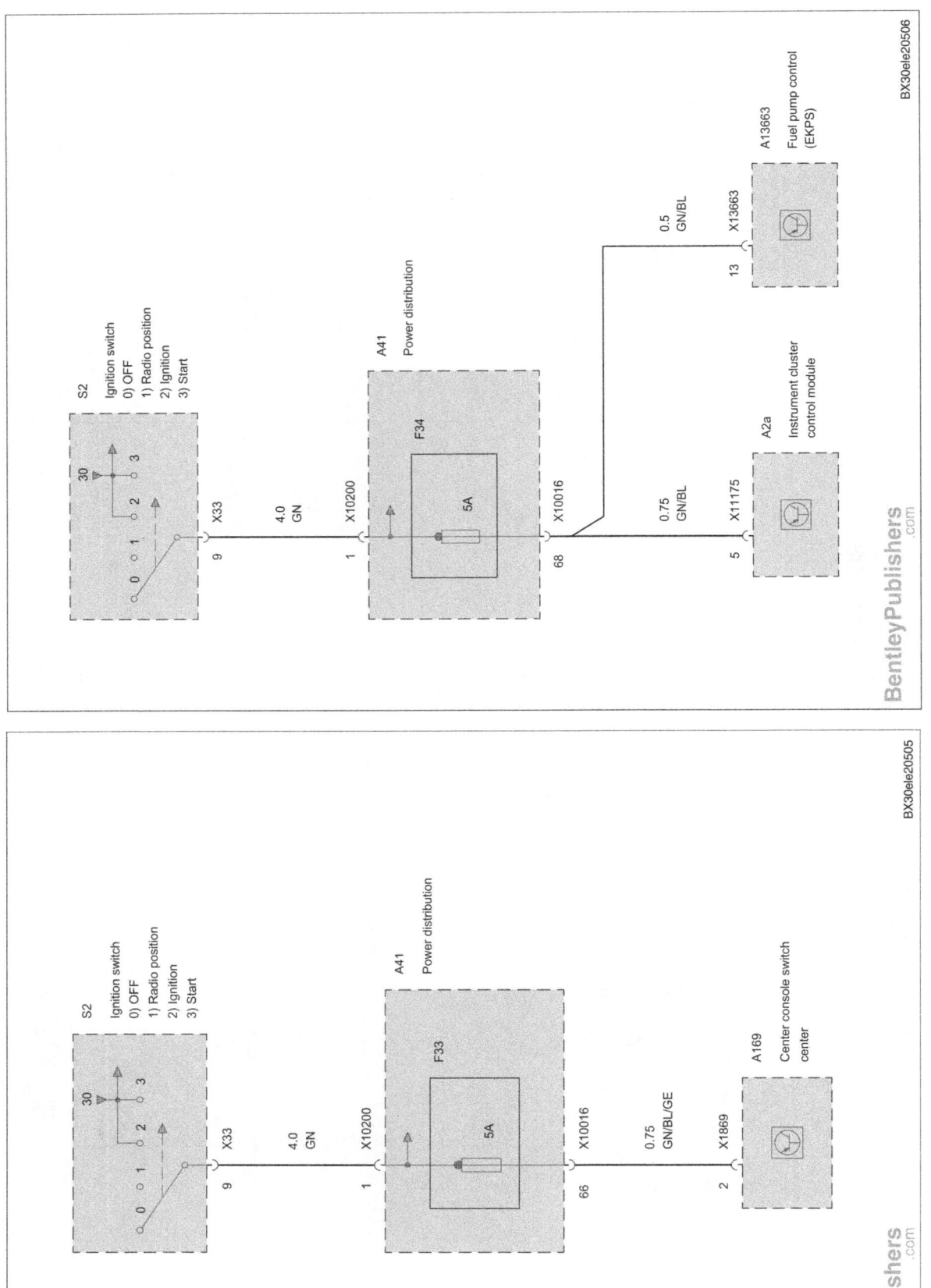

BX30ele20506

BX30ele20505

Fuse F33

Fuse F36

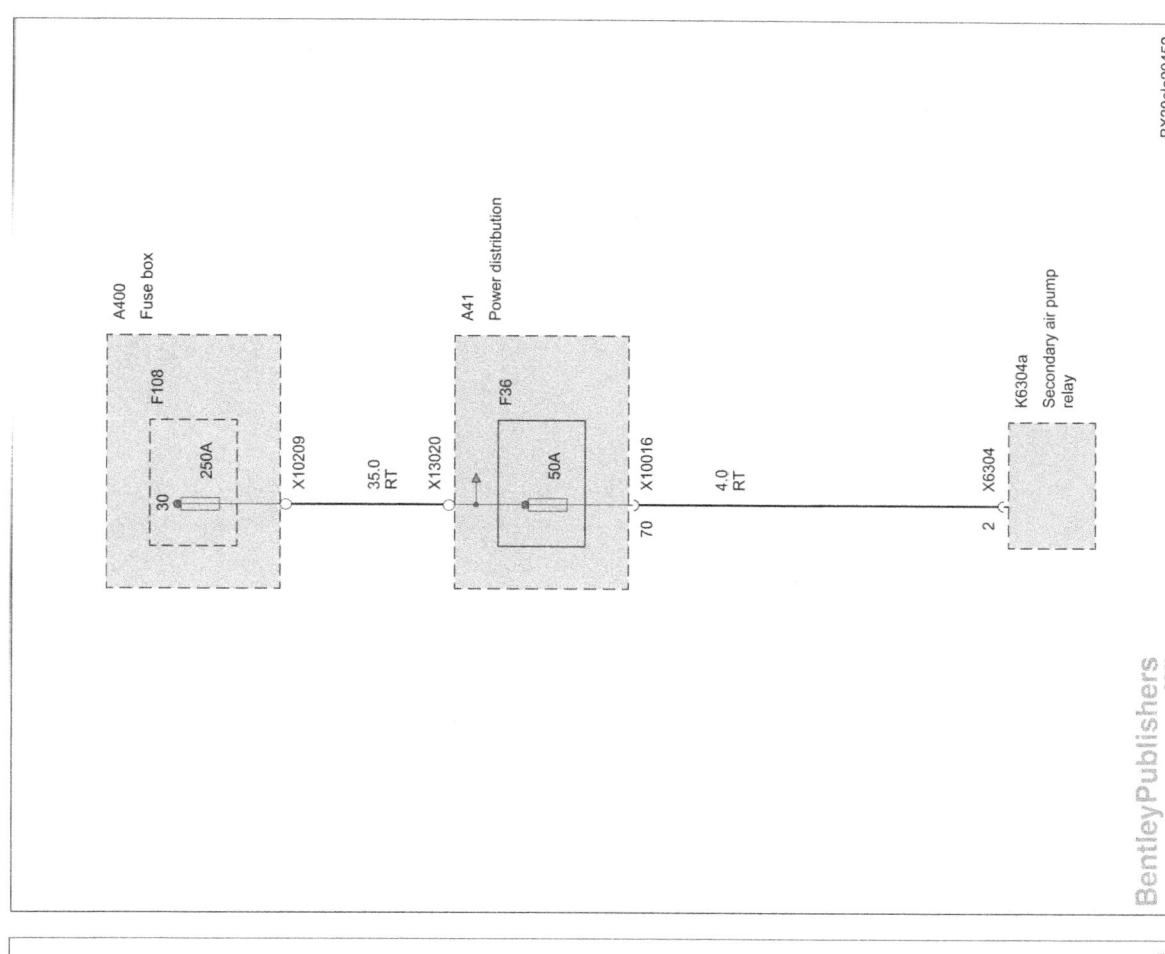

Fuse F35

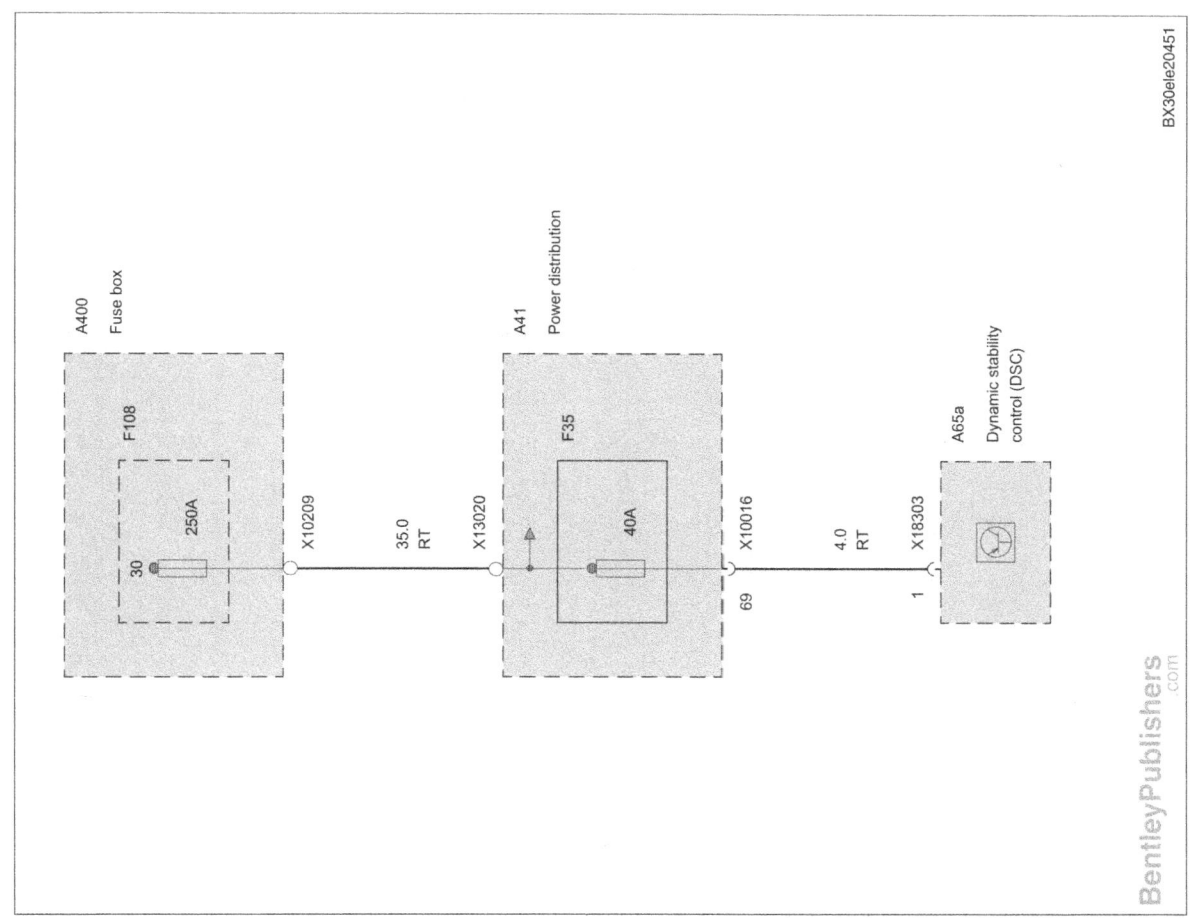

Fuse F38

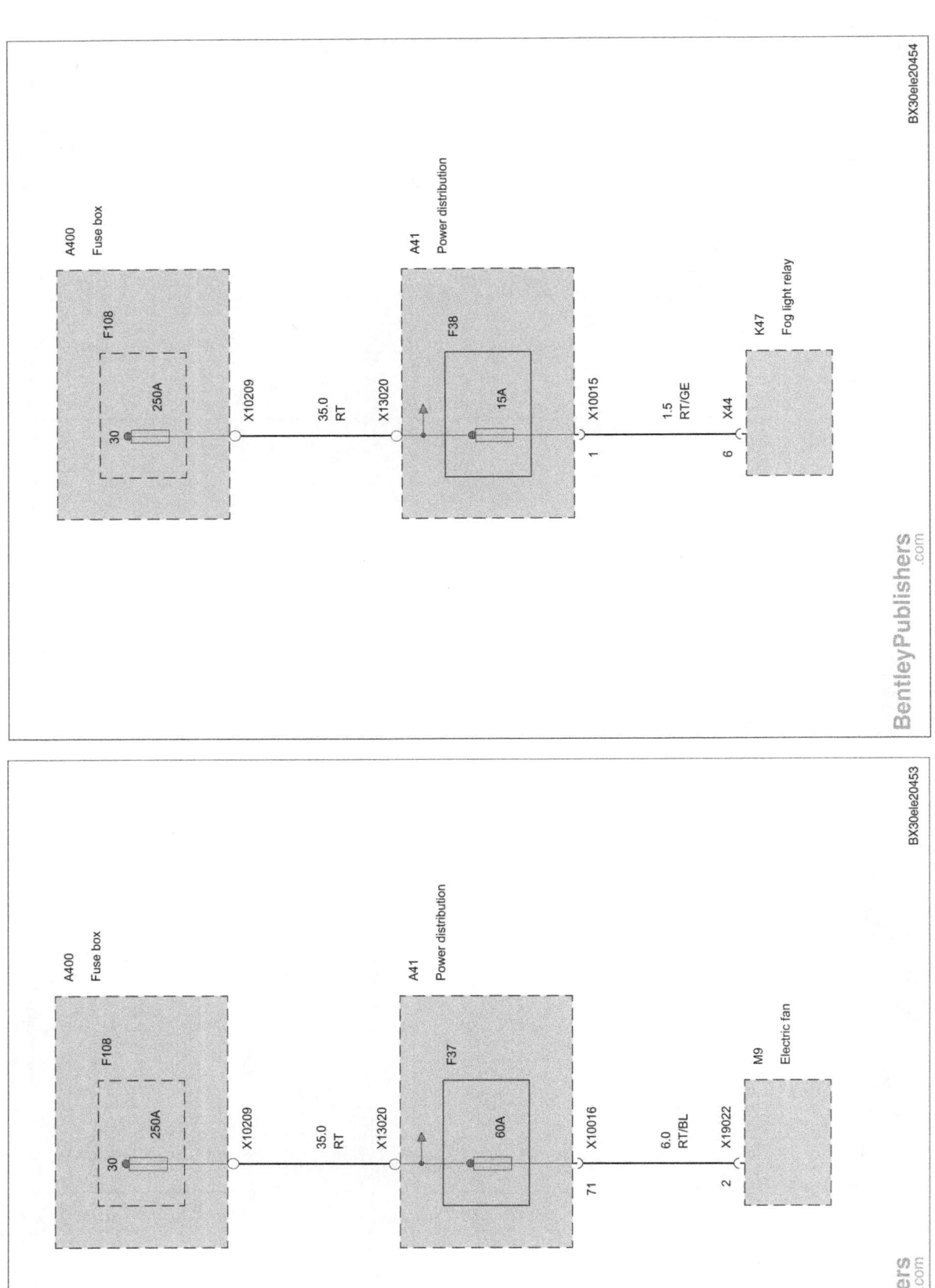

Fuse F37

Fuse F39

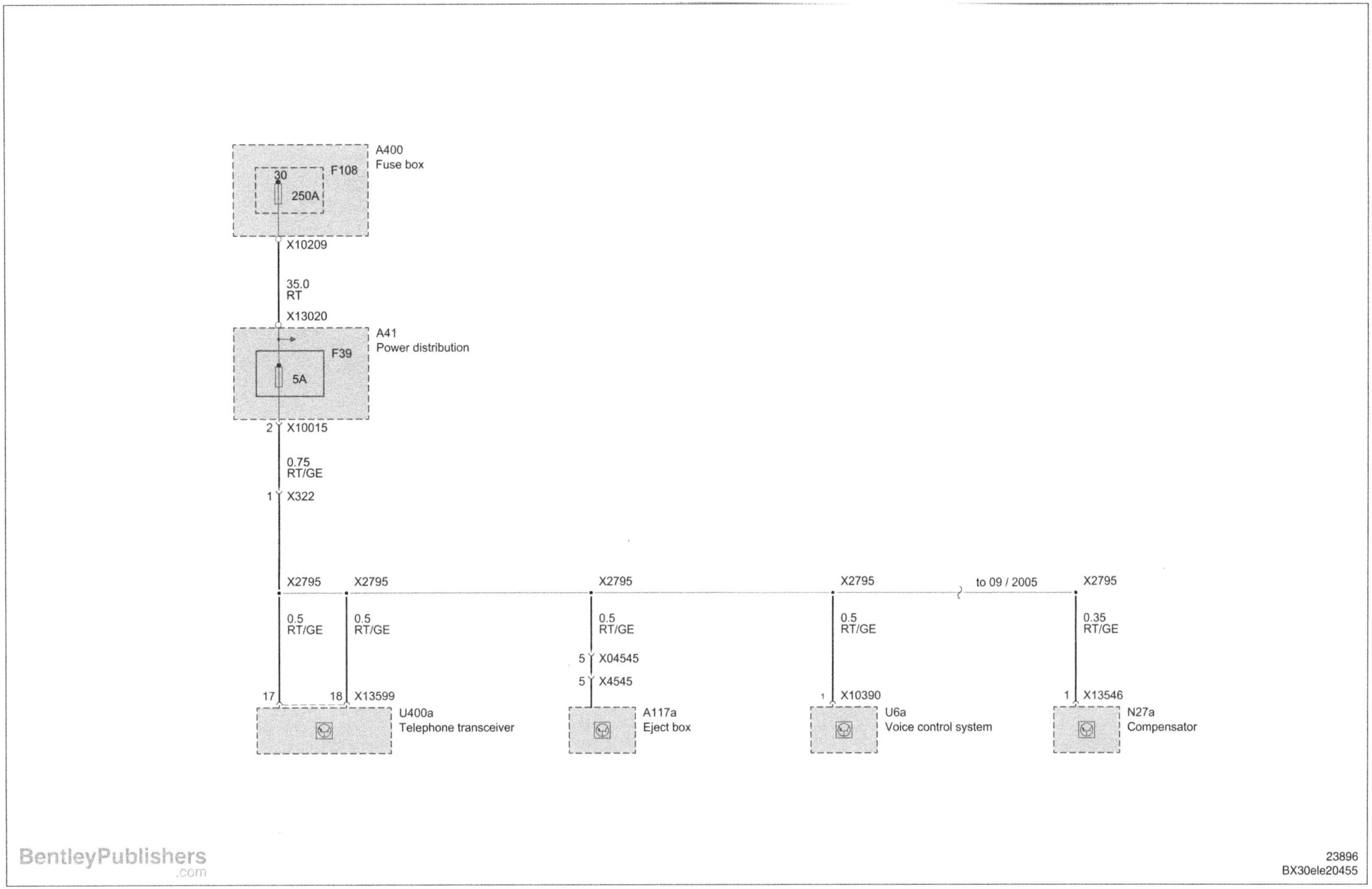

A400
Fuse box

F108

30 250A

X10209

35.0
RT

X13020

A41
Power distribution

F39

5A

2 X10015

0.75
RT/GE

1 X322

X2795

0.5
RT/GE

X2795

0.5
RT/GE

17

18 X13599

U400a
Telephone transceiver

X2795

0.5
RT/GE

5 X04545

5 X4545

A117a
Eject box

X2795

0.5
RT/GE

1 X10390

U6a
Voice control system

to 09 / 2005

X2795

0.35
RT/GE

1 X13546

N27a
Compensator

Fuse F41

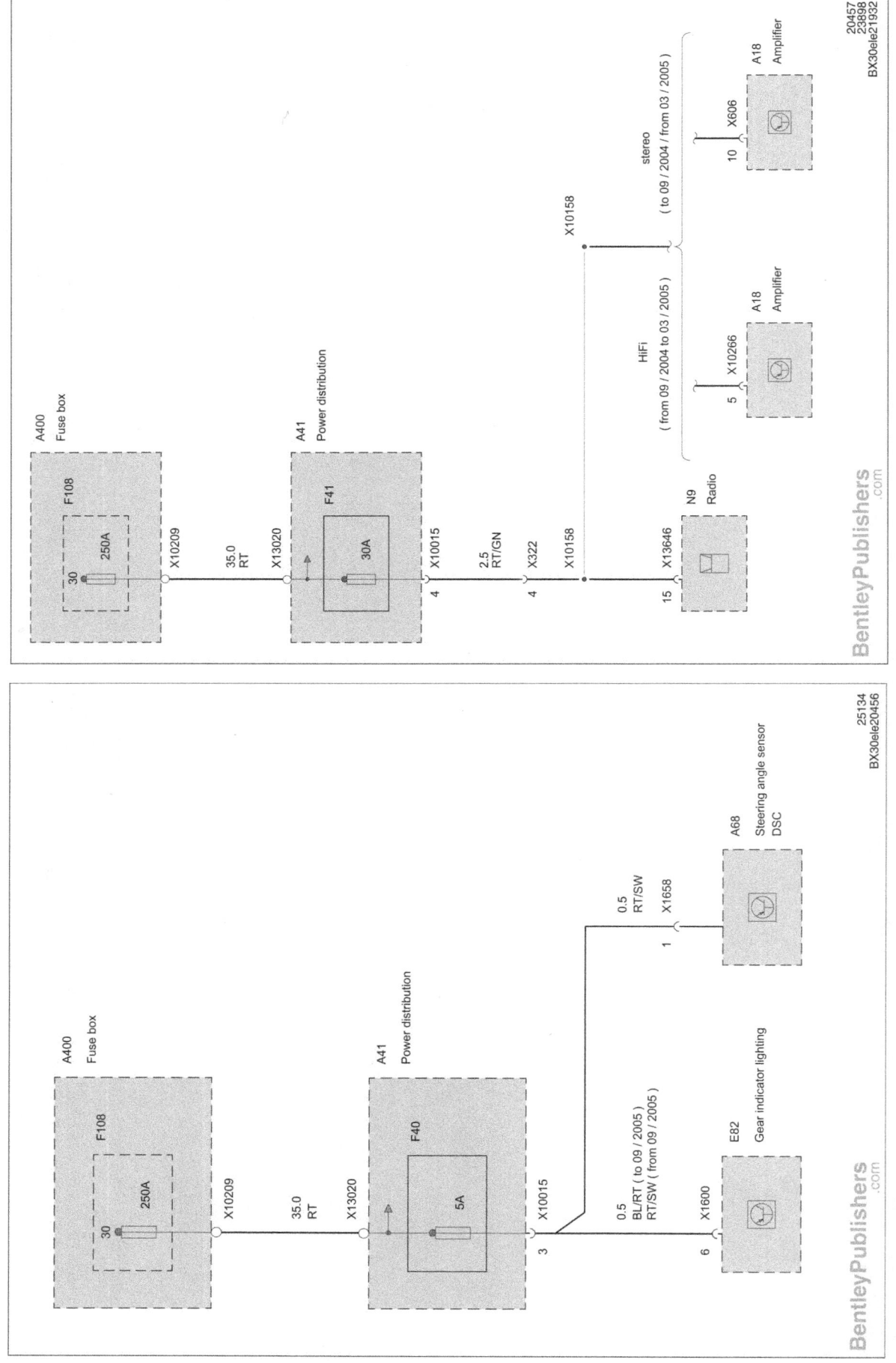

Fuse F40

Fuse F42

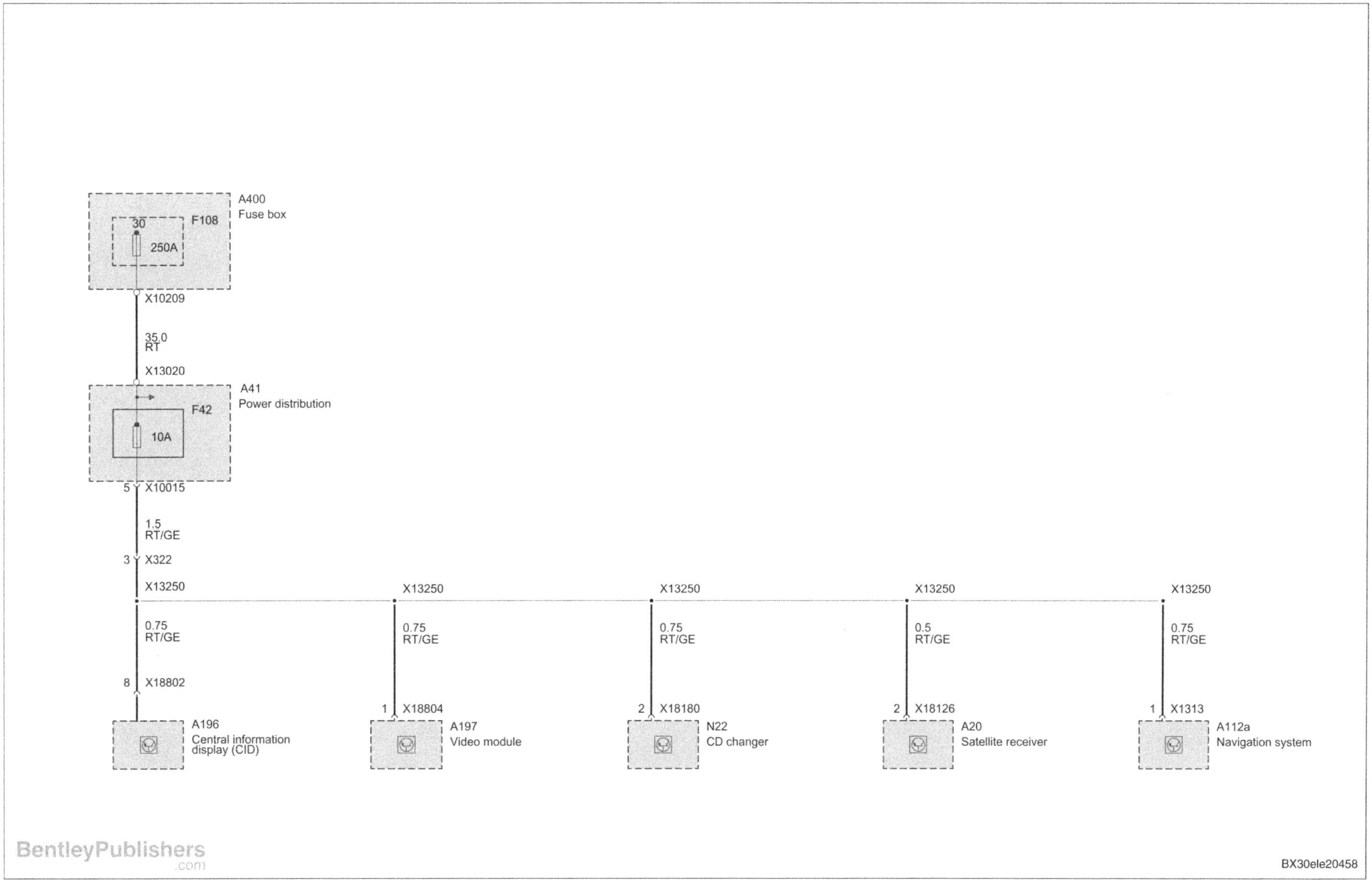

A400
Fuse box
F108
30
250A
X10209
35.0
RT
X13020
A41
Power distribution
F42
10A
5 X10015
1.5
RT/GE
3 X322
X13250
X13250
X13250
X13250
X13250
0.75
RT/GE
0.75
RT/GE
0.75
RT/GE
0.5
RT/GE
0.75
RT/GE
8 X18802
1 X18804
2 X18180
2 X18126
1 X1313
A196
Central information display (CID)
A197
Video module
N22
CD changer
A20
Satellite receiver
A112a
Navigation system
BentleyPublishers.com
BX30ele20458

**Fuse F43
(from 03 / 2007)**

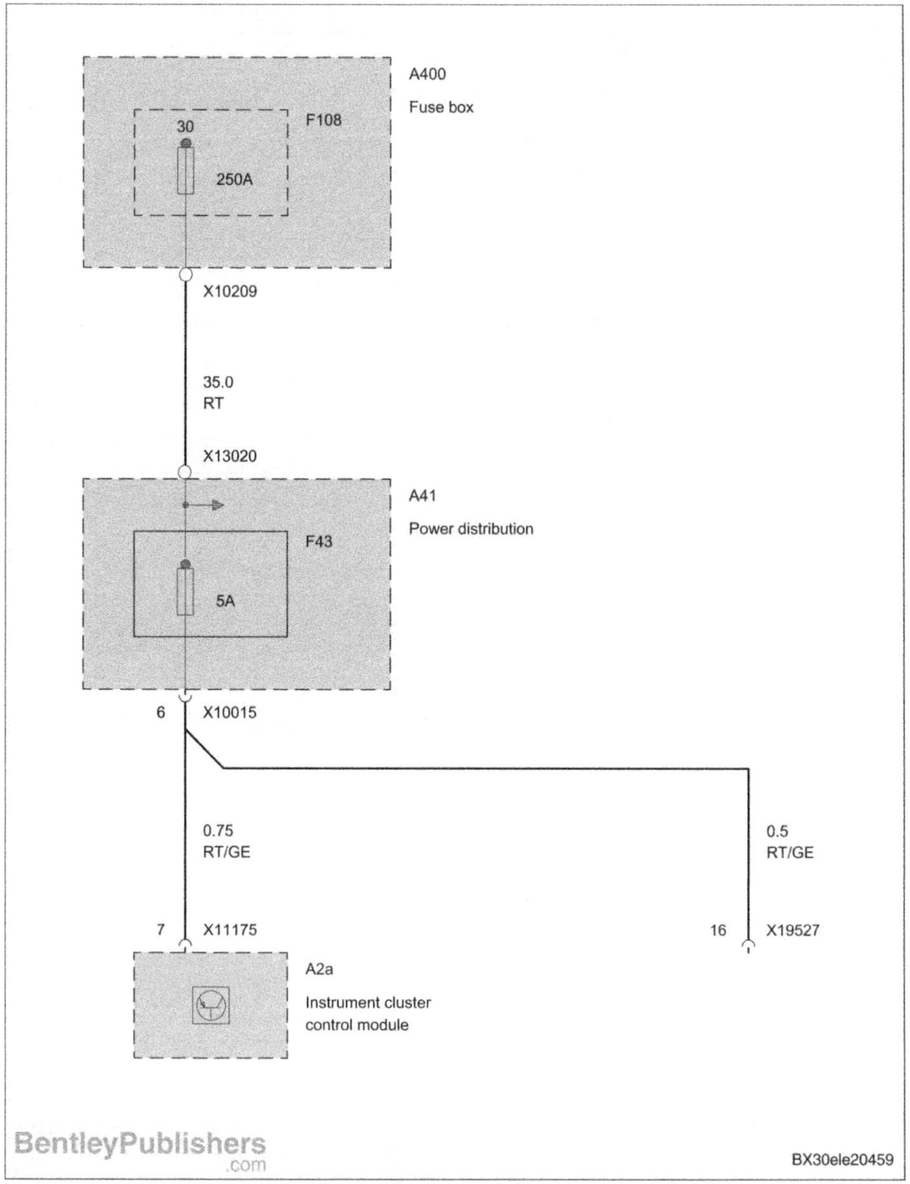

A400
Fuse box

F108

250A

30

X10209

35.0
RT

X13020

A41
Power distribution

F43

5A

X10015

6

0.75
RT/GE

X11175

7

A2a
Instrument cluster
control module

I01227

Terminating
resistor TXD

0.35
RT/GE

X19527

16

BX30ele26362

**Fuse F43
(to 03 / 2007)**

A400
Fuse box

F108

250A

30

X10209

35.0
RT

X13020

A41
Power distribution

F43

5A

X10015

6

0.75
RT/GE

X11175

7

A2a
Instrument cluster
control module

0.5
RT/GE

X19527

16

BX30ele20459

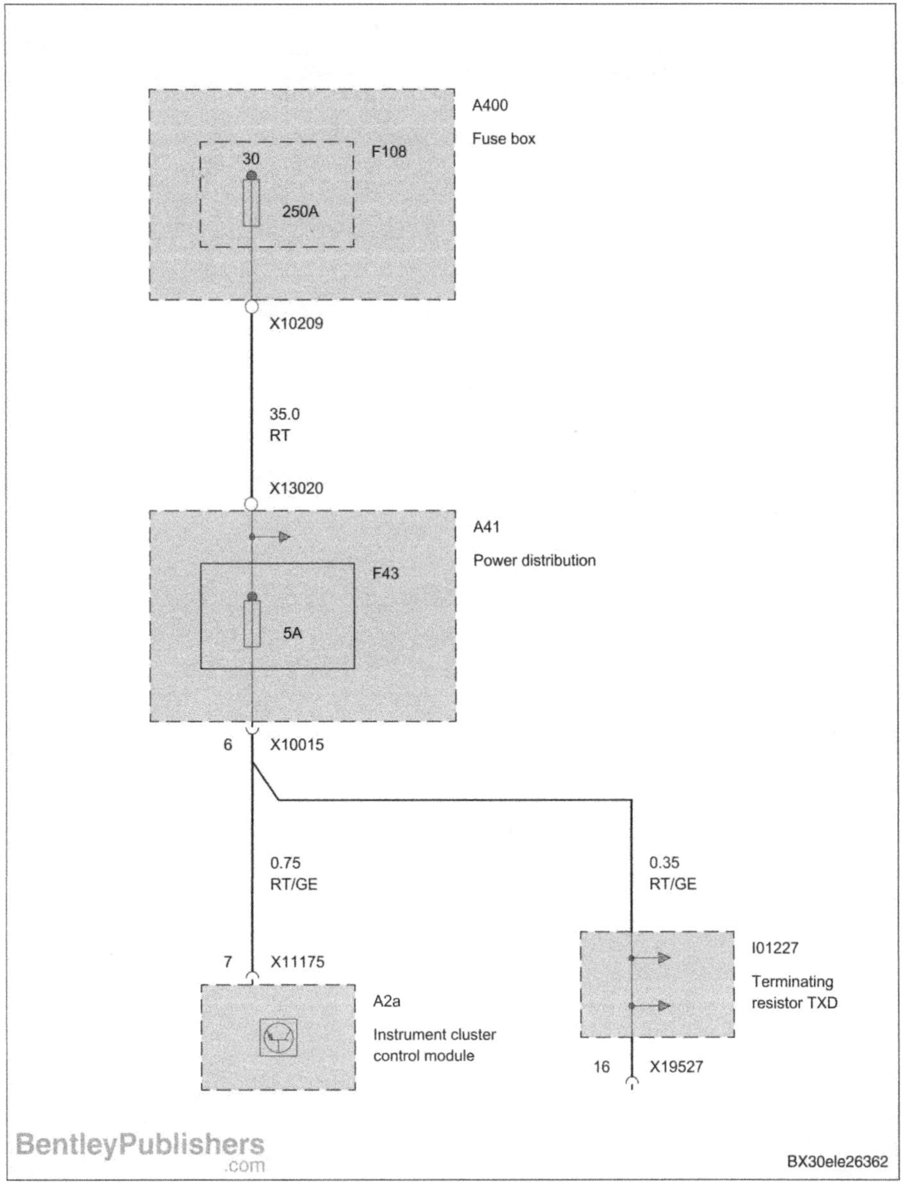

Fuse F45

Fuse F44

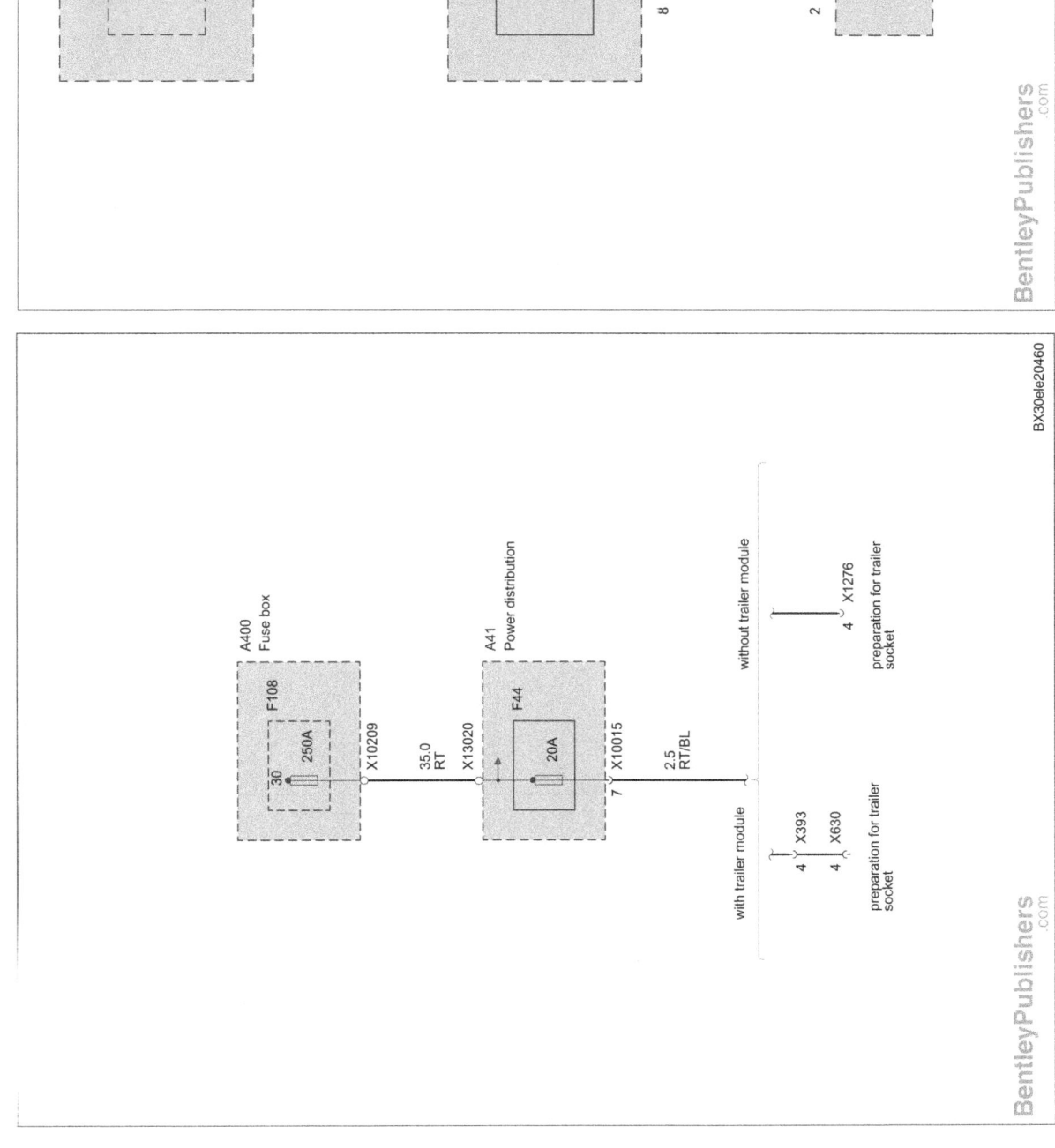

Fuse F47

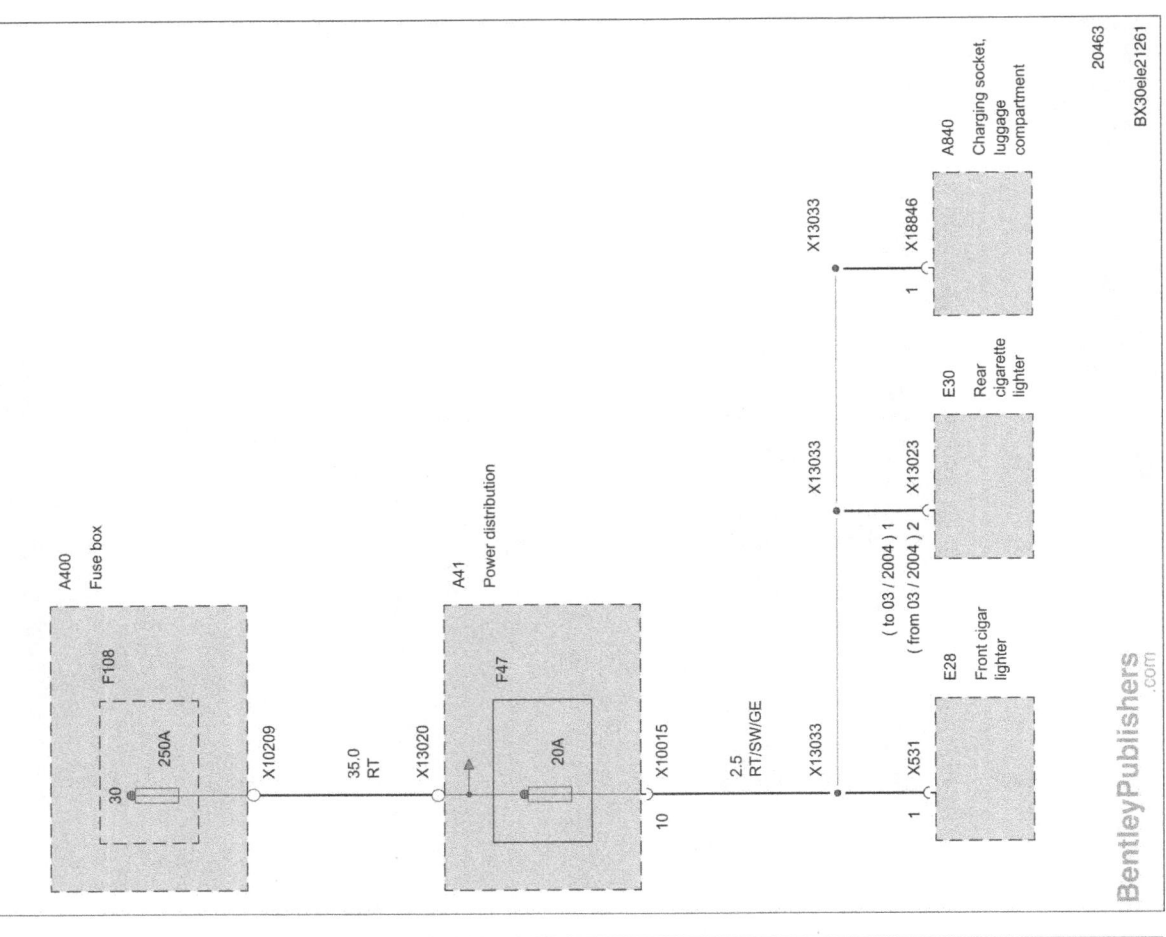

A400 Fuse box
F108
30 250A
X10209
35.0 RT
X13020

A41 Power distribution
F47
20A
10
X10015
2.5 RT/SW/GE
X13033

X13033
X13033

(to 03 / 2004) 1
(from 03 / 2004) 2

1 X531
E28 Front cigar lighter

X13023
E30 Rear cigarette lighter

1 X18846
A840 Charging socket, luggage compartment

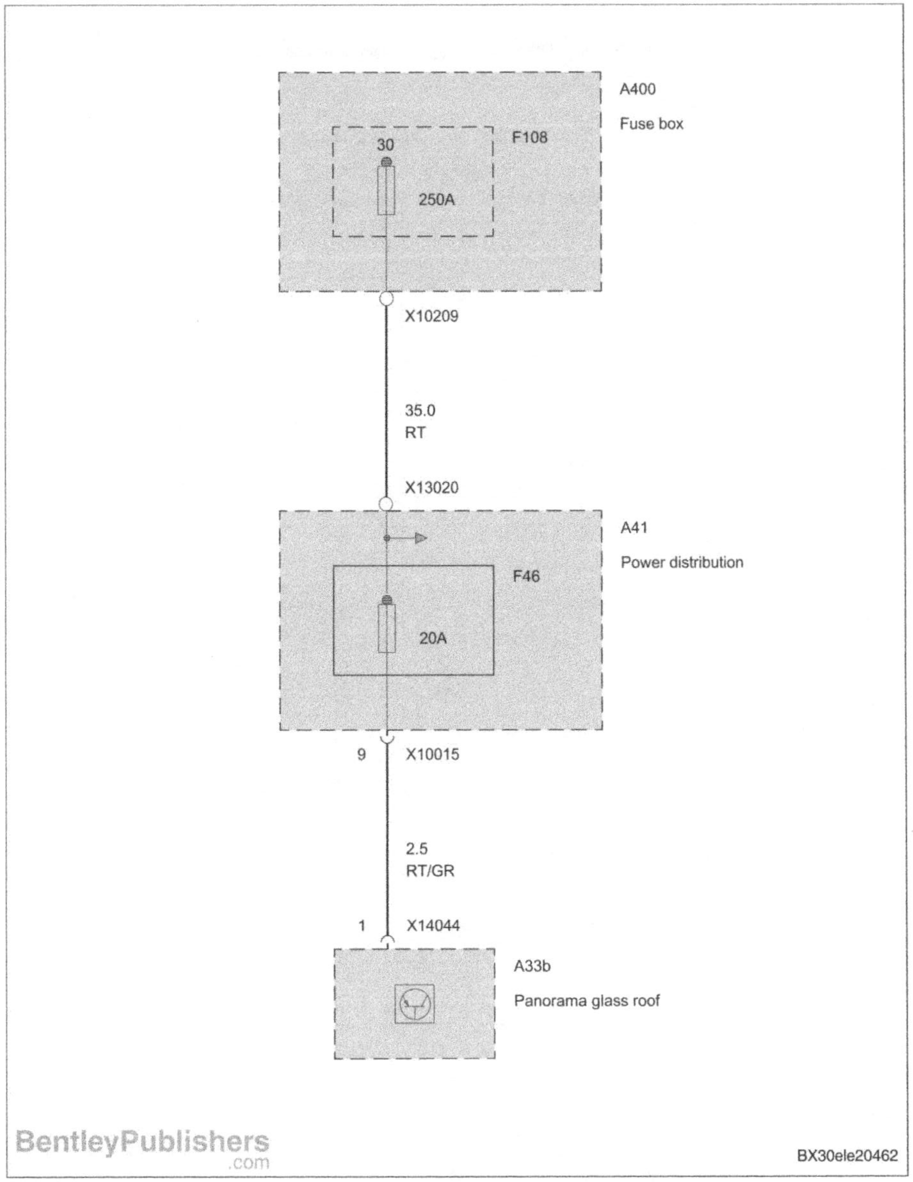

20463
BX30ele21261

BentleyPublishers.com

Fuse F46

A400 Fuse box
F108
30 250A
X10209
35.0 RT
X13020

A41 Power distribution
F46
20A
9
X10015
2.5 RT/GR
X14044

1
A33b Panorama glass roof

BX30ele20462

BentleyPublishers.com

Fuse F49

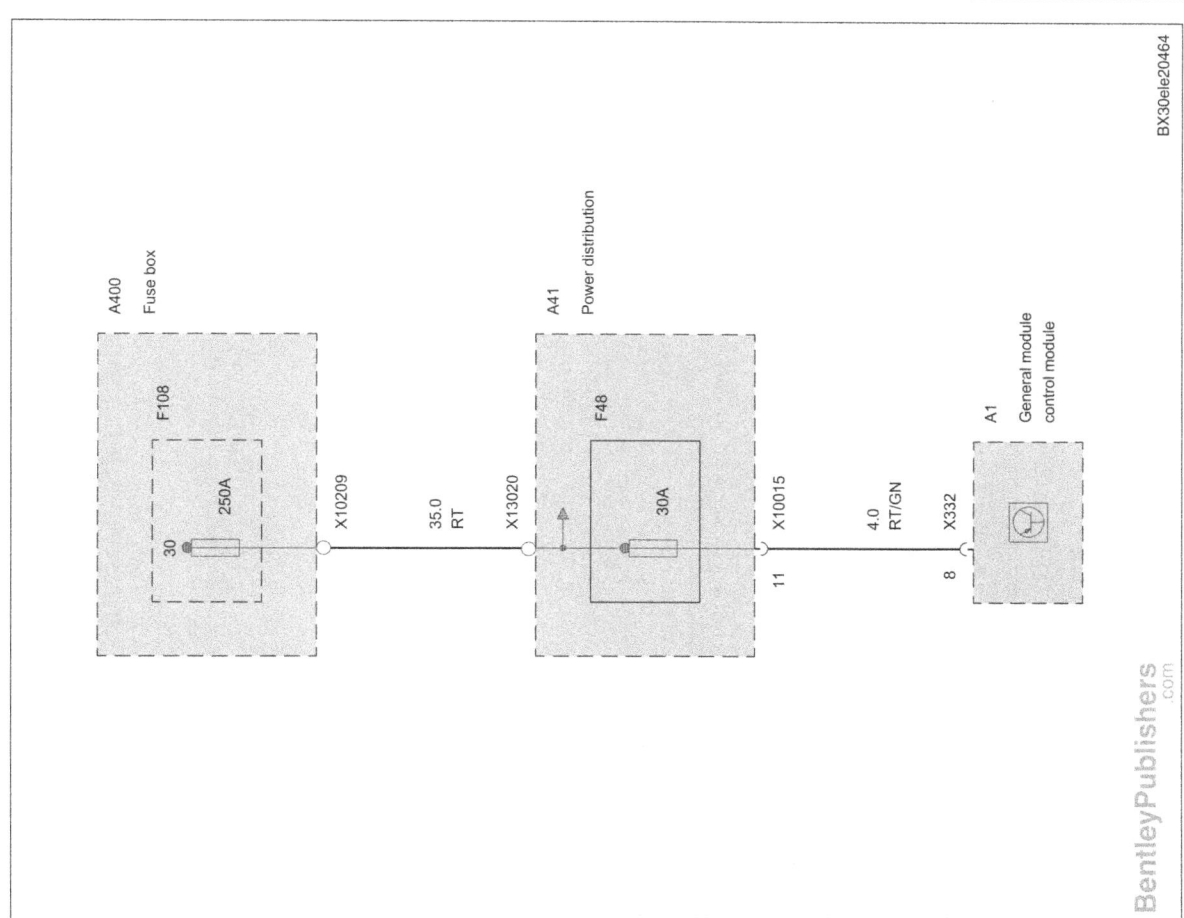

BX30ele20465

A400
Fuse box

F108

30   250A

X10209

35.0
RT

X13020

A41
Power distribution

F49

5A

X10015

12

A421
Antenna diversity
1) With remote
control receiver

0.5
RT/VI

X322

7

1

X1143

0.5
RT/VI

A1
General module
control module

47   X253

BentleyPublishers
.com

Fuse F48

BX30ele20464

A400
Fuse box

F108

30   250A

X10209

35.0
RT

X13020

A41
Power distribution

F48

30A

X10015

11

4.0
RT/GN

X332

8

A1
General module
control module

BentleyPublishers
.com

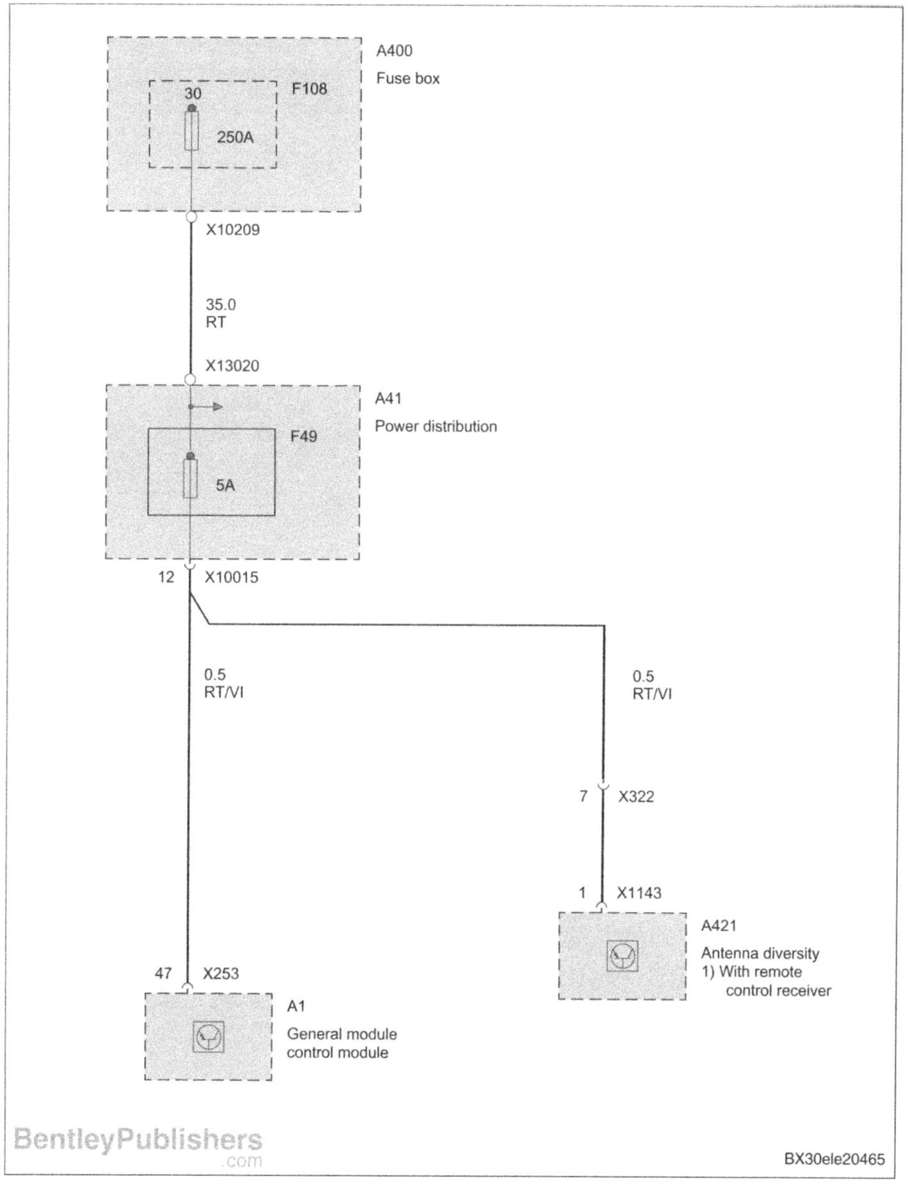

Fuse F51

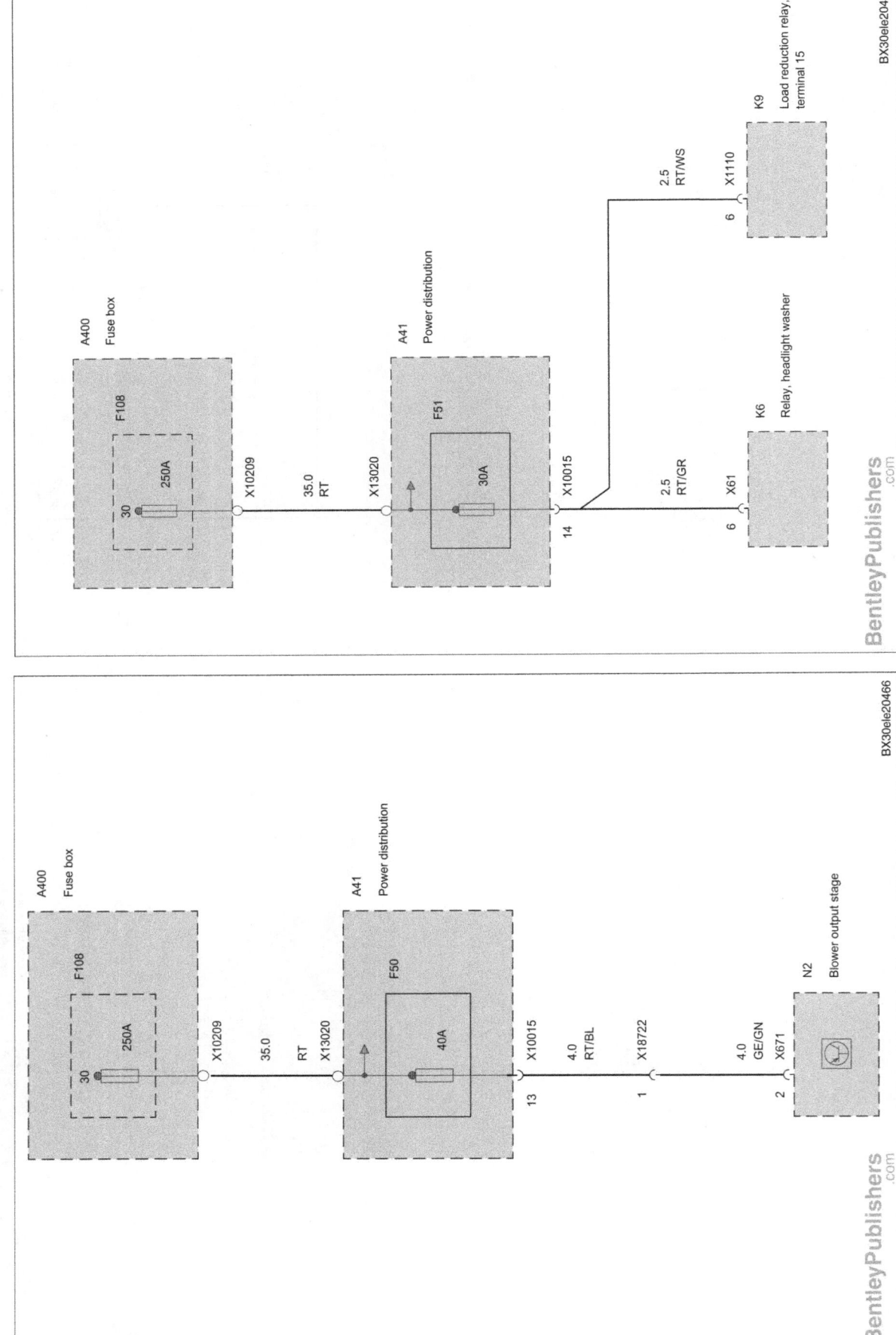

Fuse F50

Fuse F53

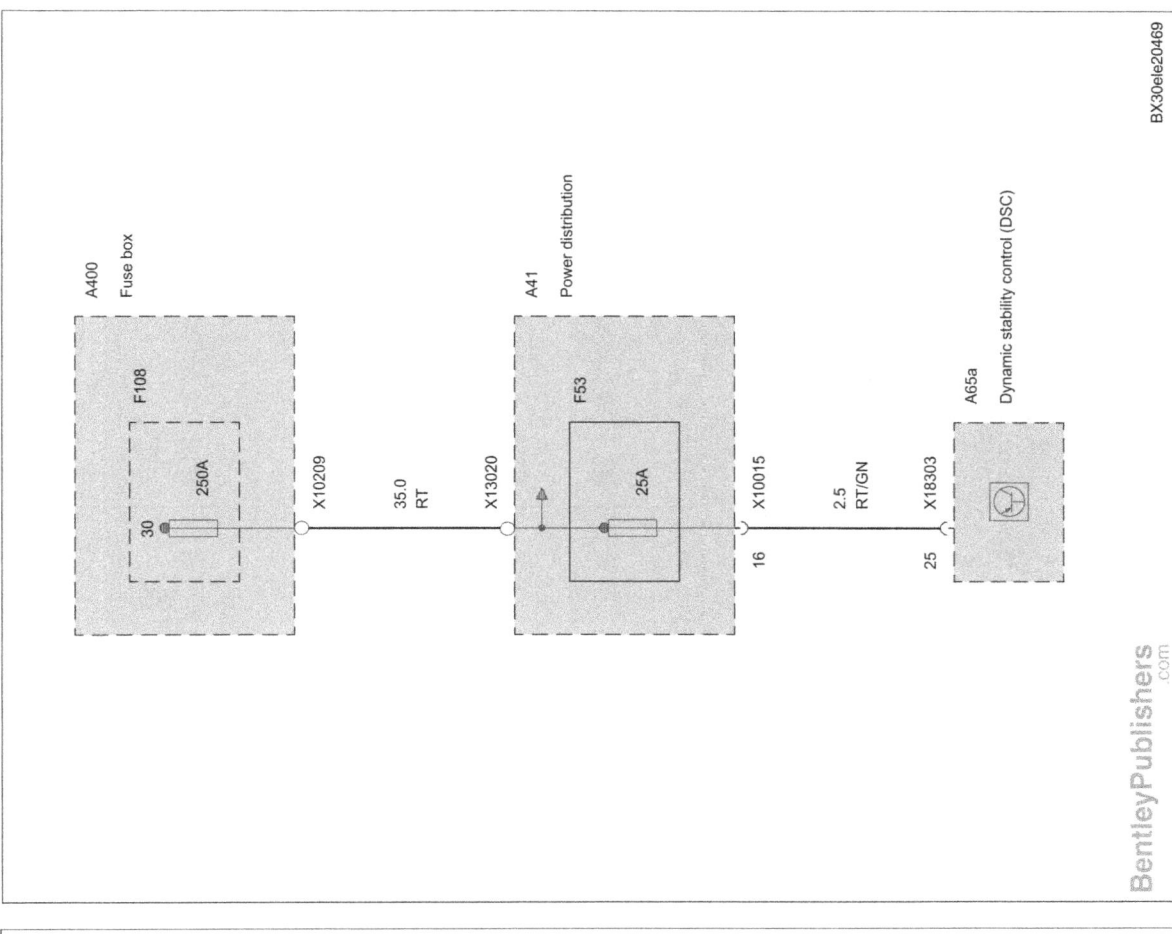

Fuse F52

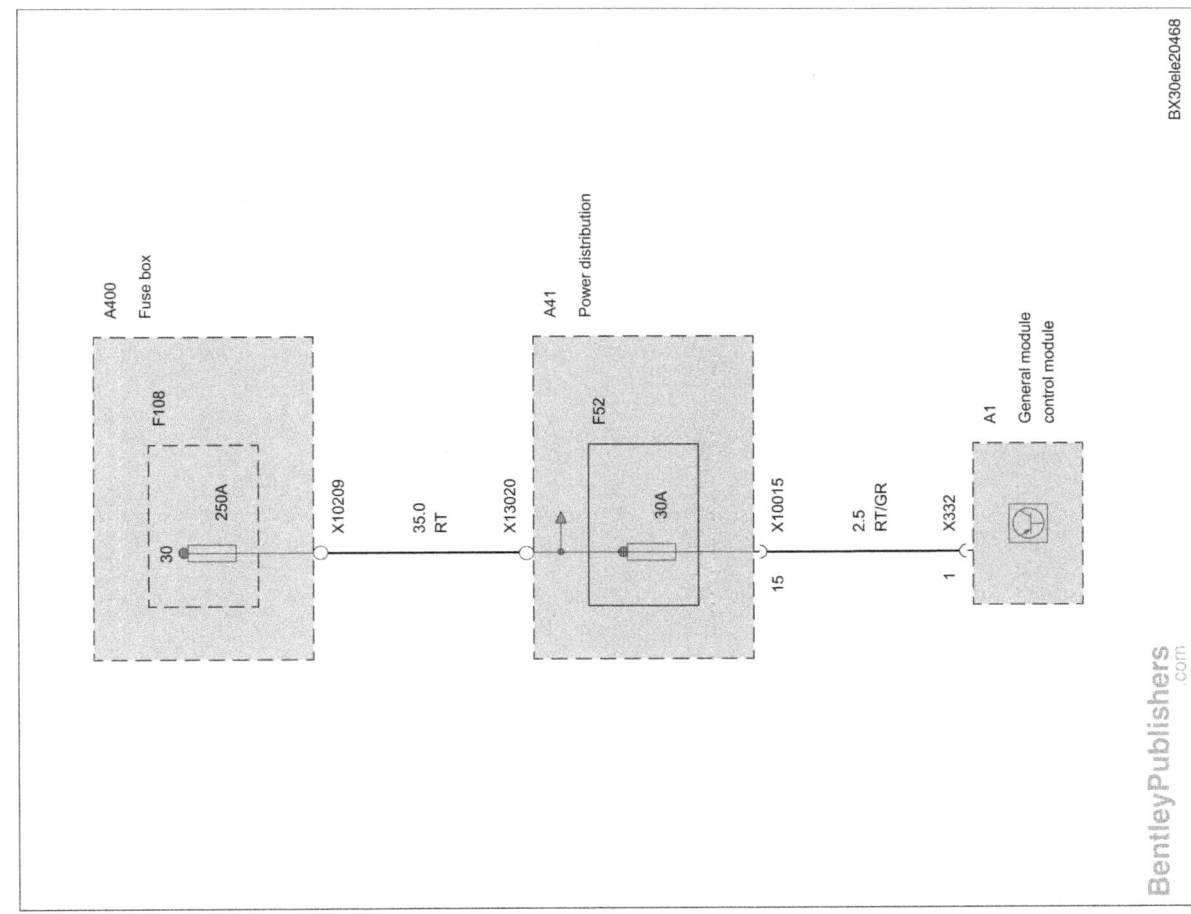

Fuse F55

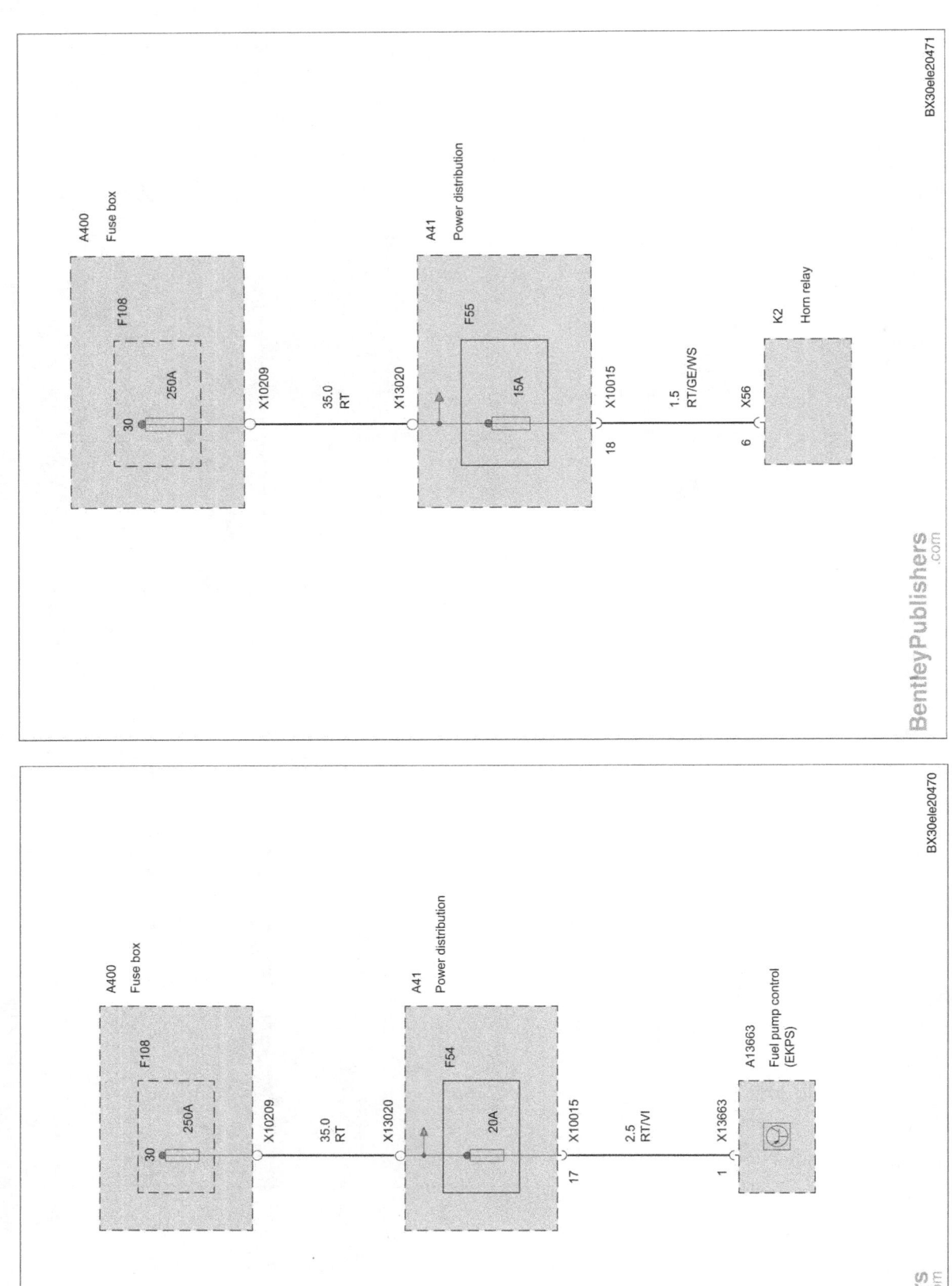

A400
Fuse box

F108

30   250A

X10209

35.0
RT

X13020

A41
Power distribution

F55

15A

X10015

18

1.5
RT/GE/WS

K2
Horn relay

X56

6

BX30ele20471

Fuse F54

A400
Fuse box

F108

30   250A

X10209

35.0
RT

X13020

A41
Power distribution

F54

20A

X10015

17

2.5
RT/VI

A13663
Fuel pump control
(EKPS)

X13663

1

BX30ele20470

**Fuse F56
(from 03 / 2007)**

A400
Fuse box

F108

30

250A

X10209

35.0
RT

X13020

A41
Power distribution

F56

7.5A

X10015

19

0.75
RT/GE

X1858

3

preparations, rear
seat entertainment

BX30ele25645

Electrical Wiring Diagrams   ELE-43

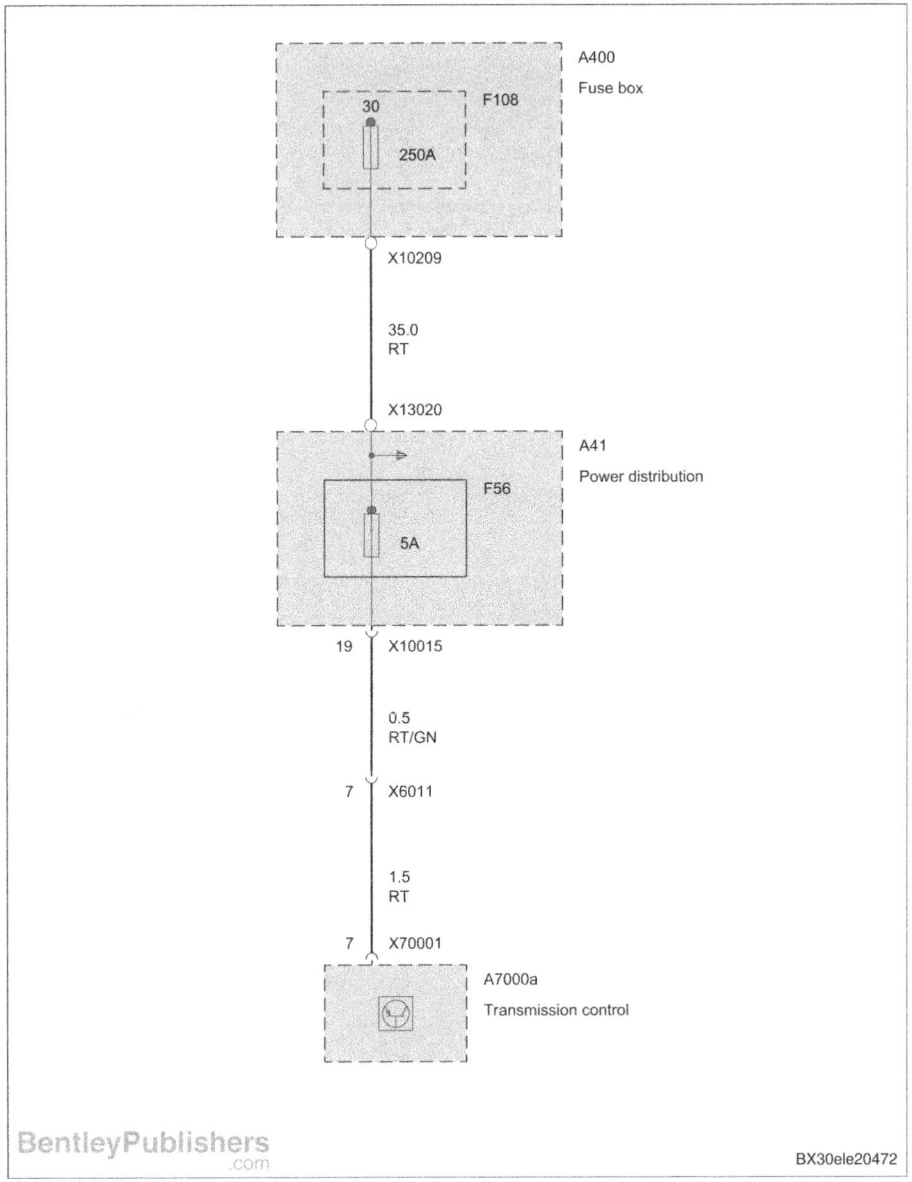

**Fuse F56
(to 03 / 2007)**

A400
Fuse box

F108

30

250A

X10209

35.0
RT

X13020

A41
Power distribution

F56

5A

X10015

19

0.5
RT/GN

X6011

7

1.5
RT

X70001

7

A7000a
Transmission control

BX30ele20472

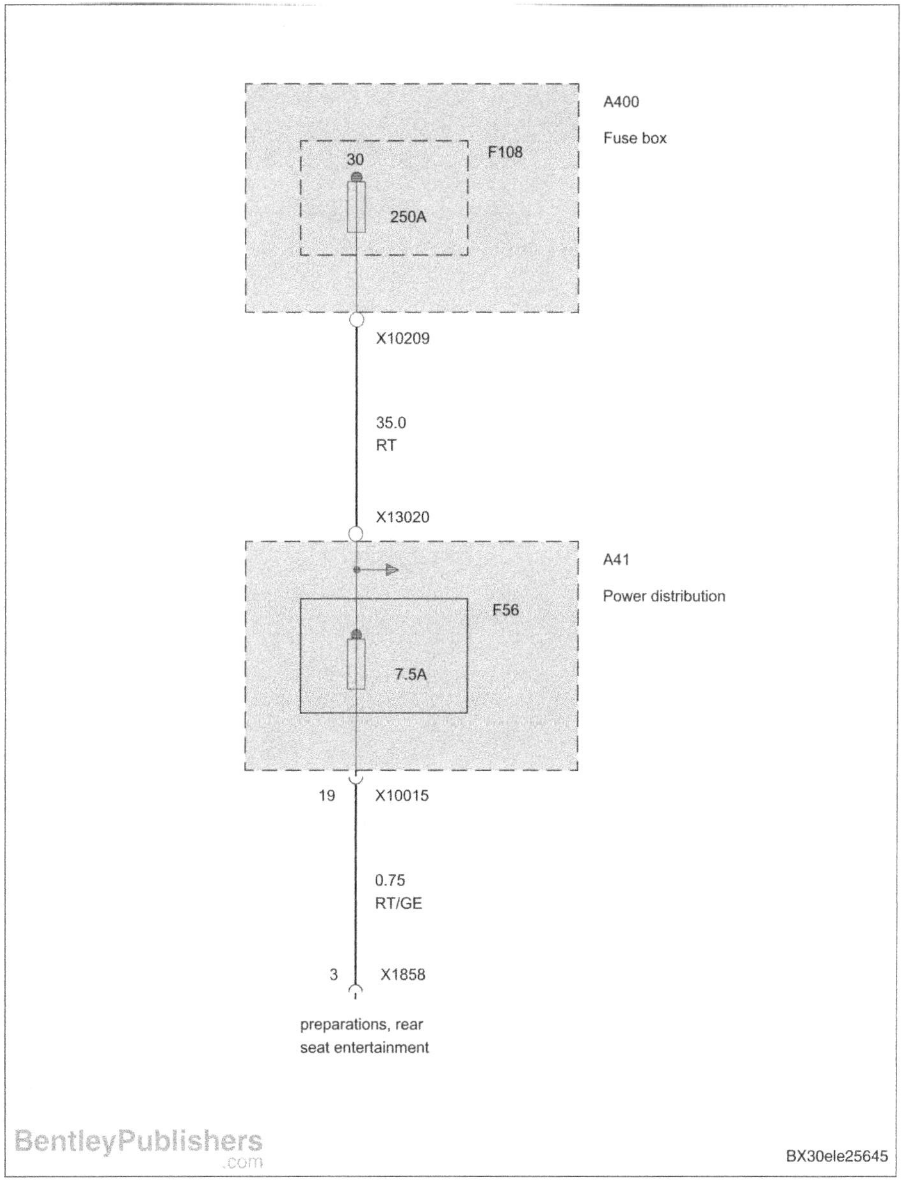

Fuse F57
(without seat memory or folding mirrors)

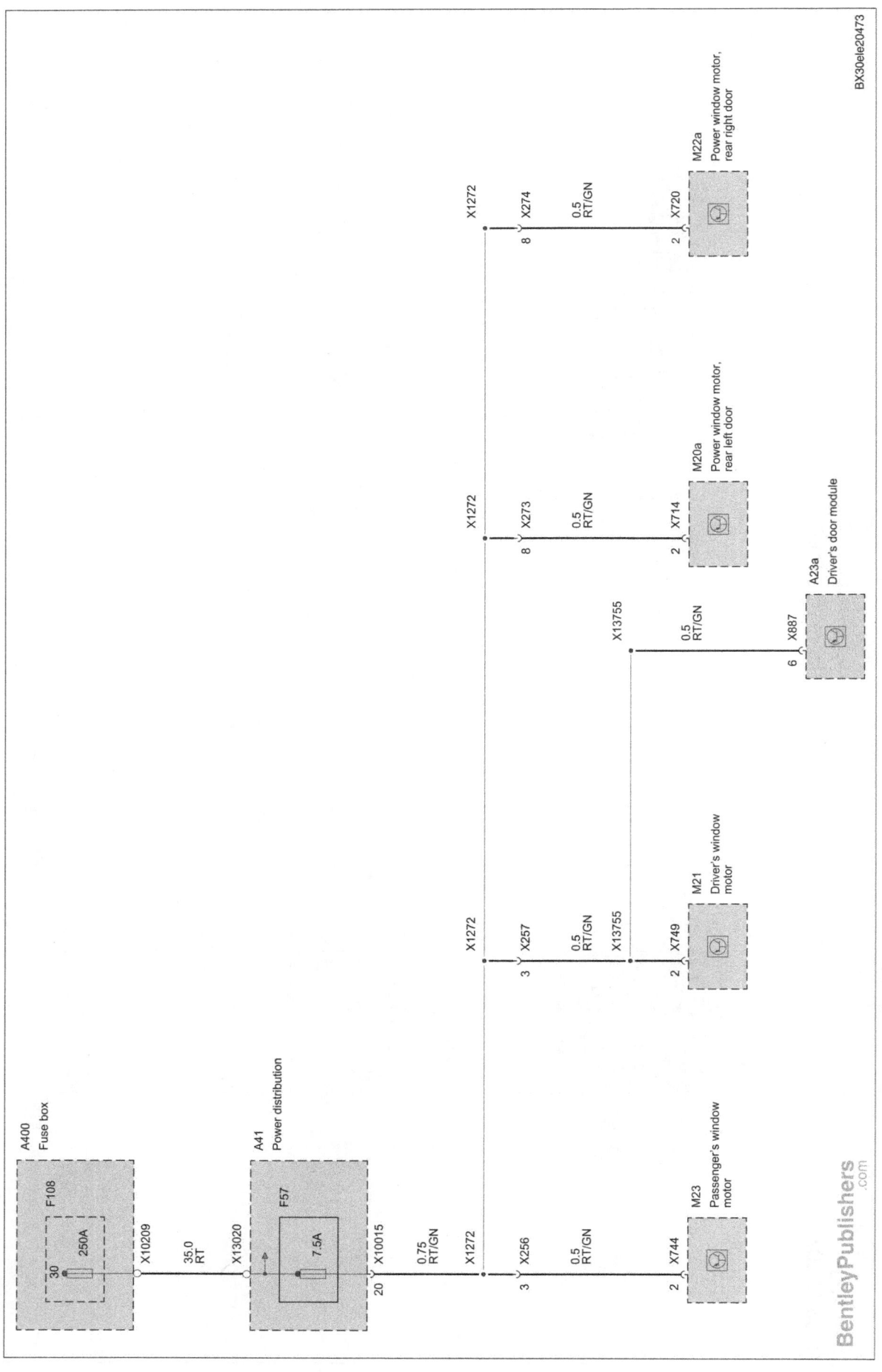

BX30ele20473

Fuse F57
(with seat memory and folding mirrors)

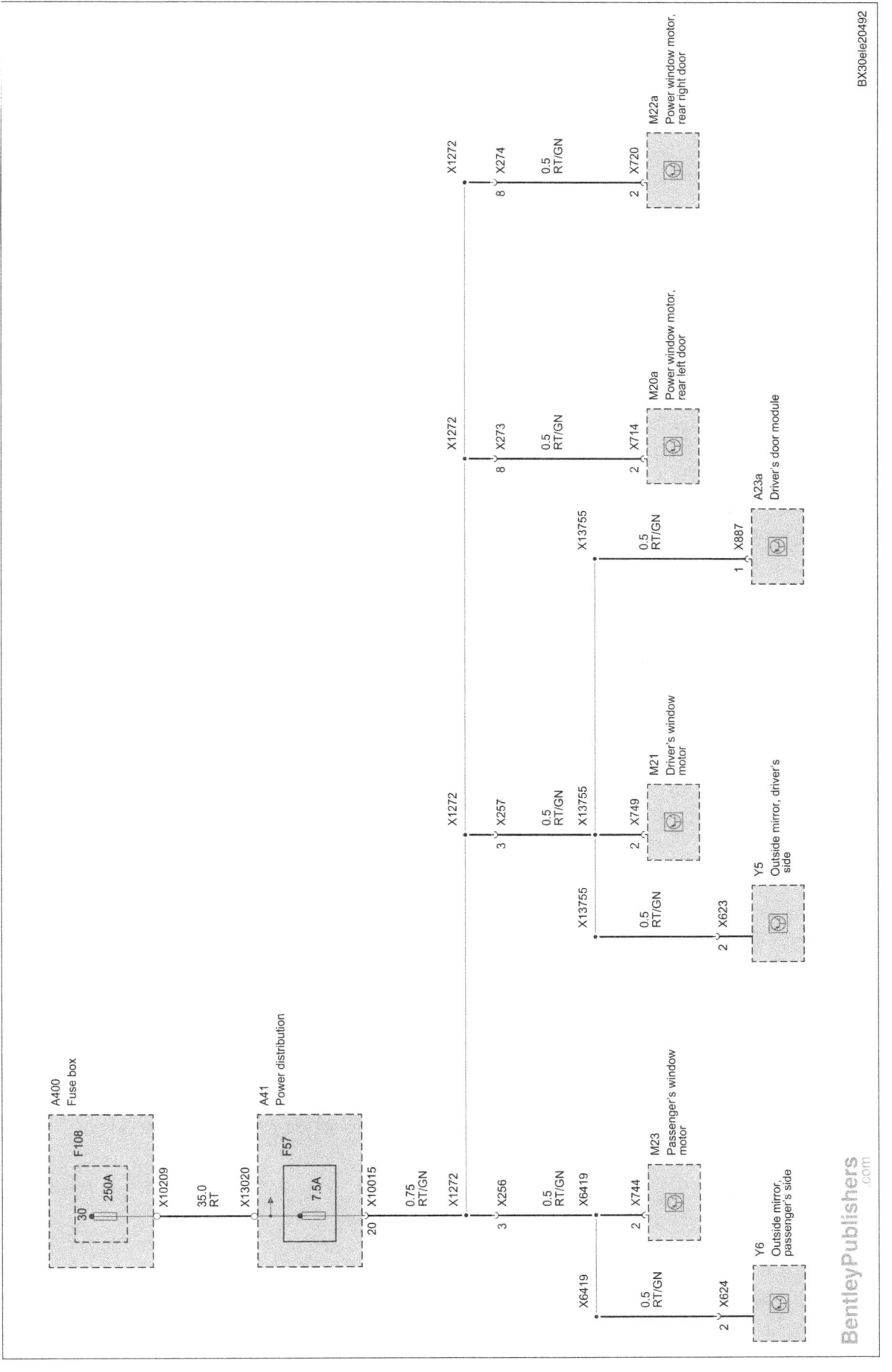

BX30ele20492

**Fuse F58
(from 03 / 2007)**

**Fuse F58
(to 03 / 2007)**

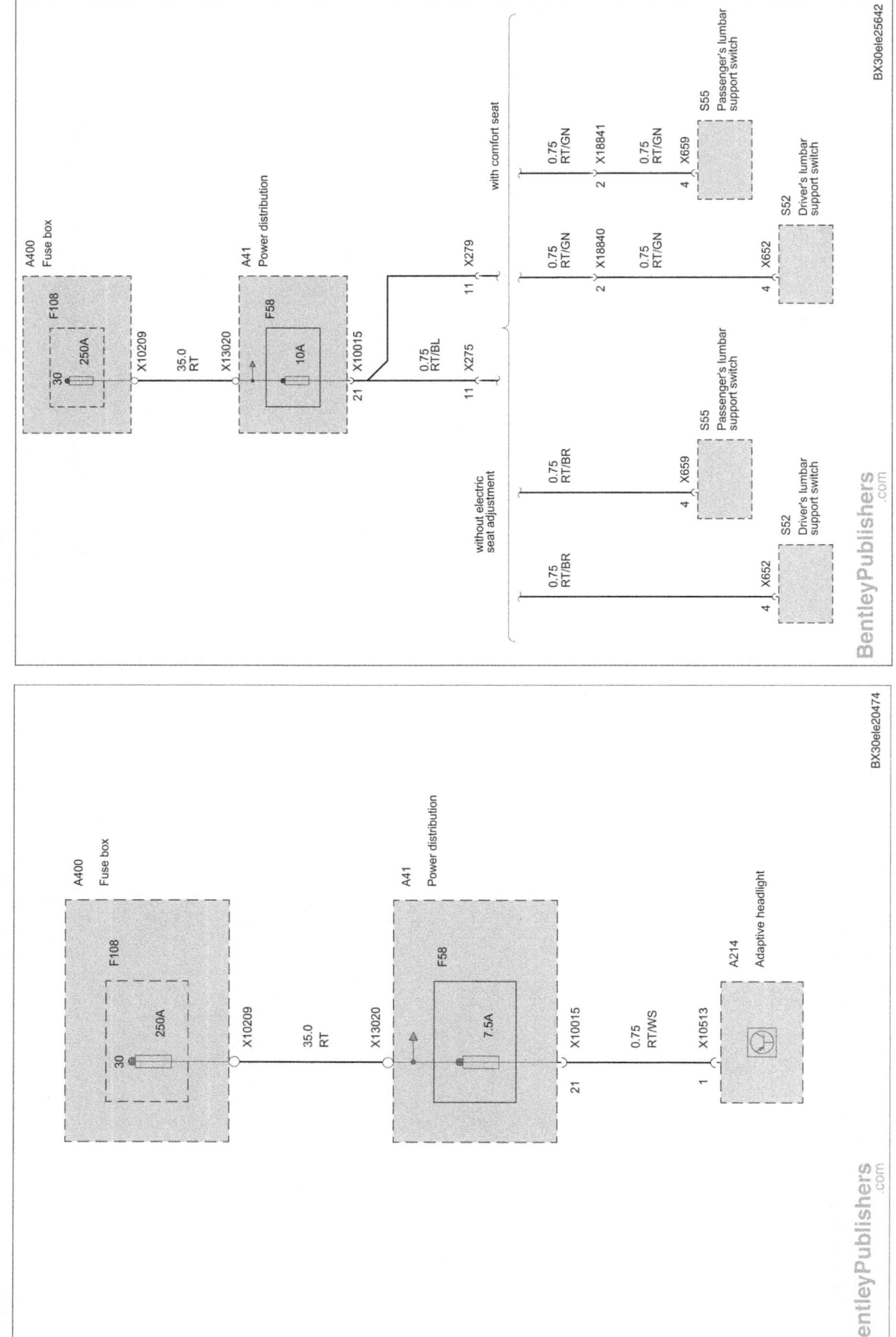

BX30ele25642

BX30ele20474

Fuse F60

Fuse F59

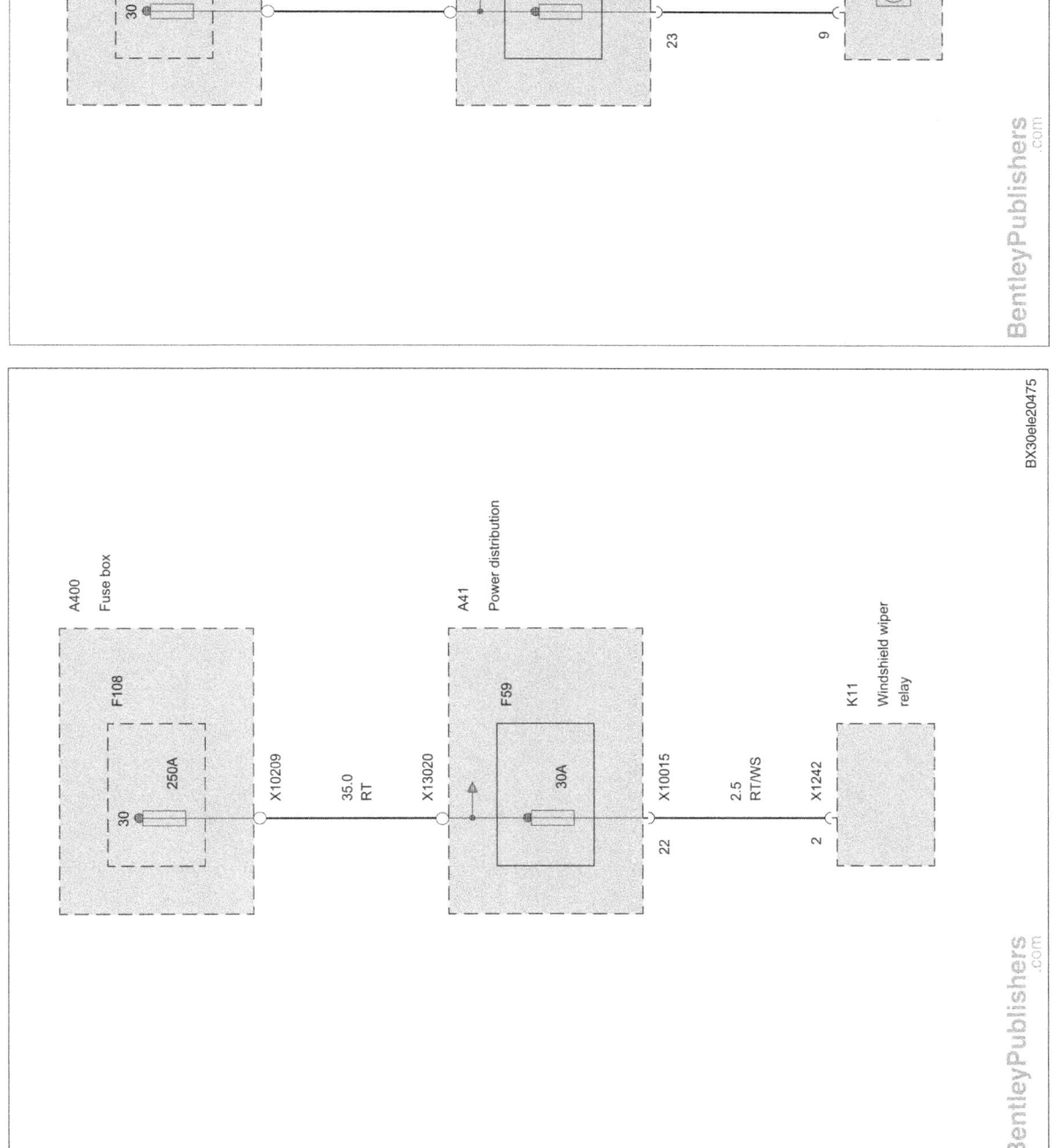

BX30ele20492

BX30ele20475

Fuse F62

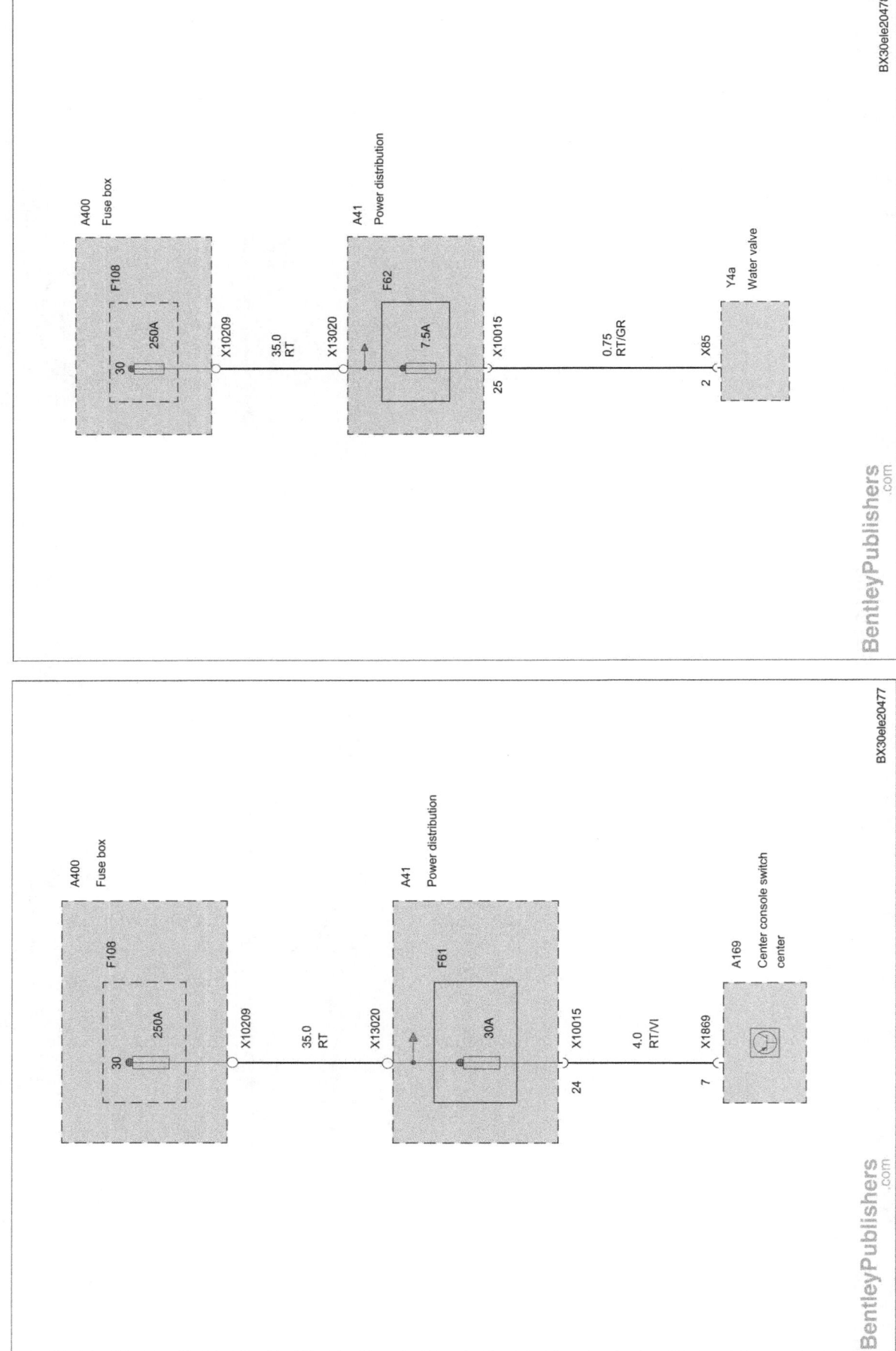

Fuse F61

BX30ele20478

BX30ele20477

**Fuse F65
(to 03 / 2007)**

Fuse F63

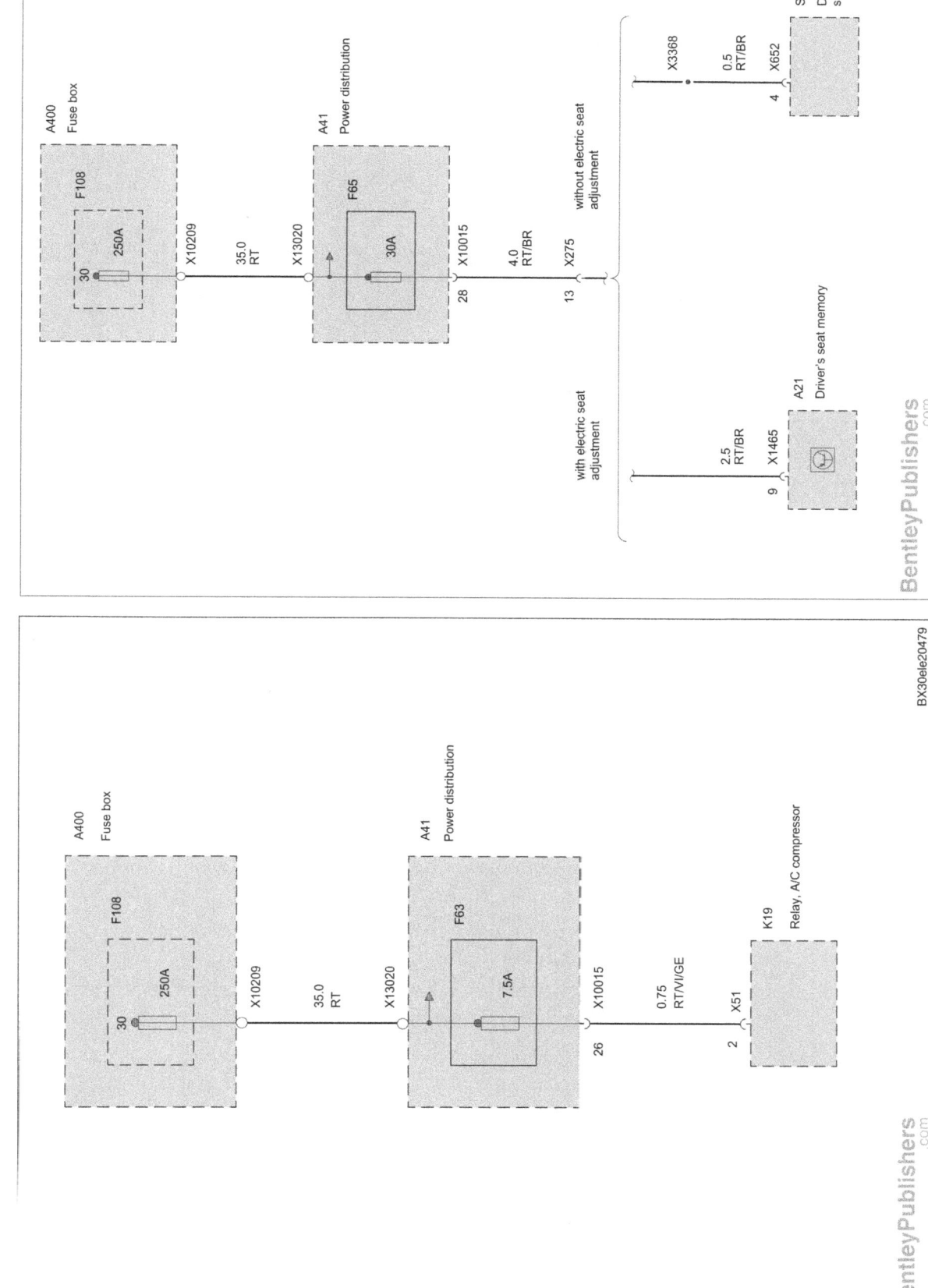

BX30ele20480

A400
Fuse box

F108

30   250A

X10209

35.0
RT

X13020

A41
Power distribution

F65

30A

X10015

28

4.0
RT/BR

X275

13

with electric seat
adjustment

without electric seat
adjustment

2.5
RT/BR   X1465

9

A21
Driver's seat memory

X3368

0.5
RT/BR   X652

4

S52
Driver's lumbar
support switch

BX30ele20479

A400
Fuse box

F108

30   250A

X10209

35.0
RT

X13020

A41
Power distribution

F63

7.5A

X10015

26

0.75
RT/VI/GE   X51

2

K19
Relay, A/C compressor

Fuse F66

Fuse F65
(from 03 / 2007)

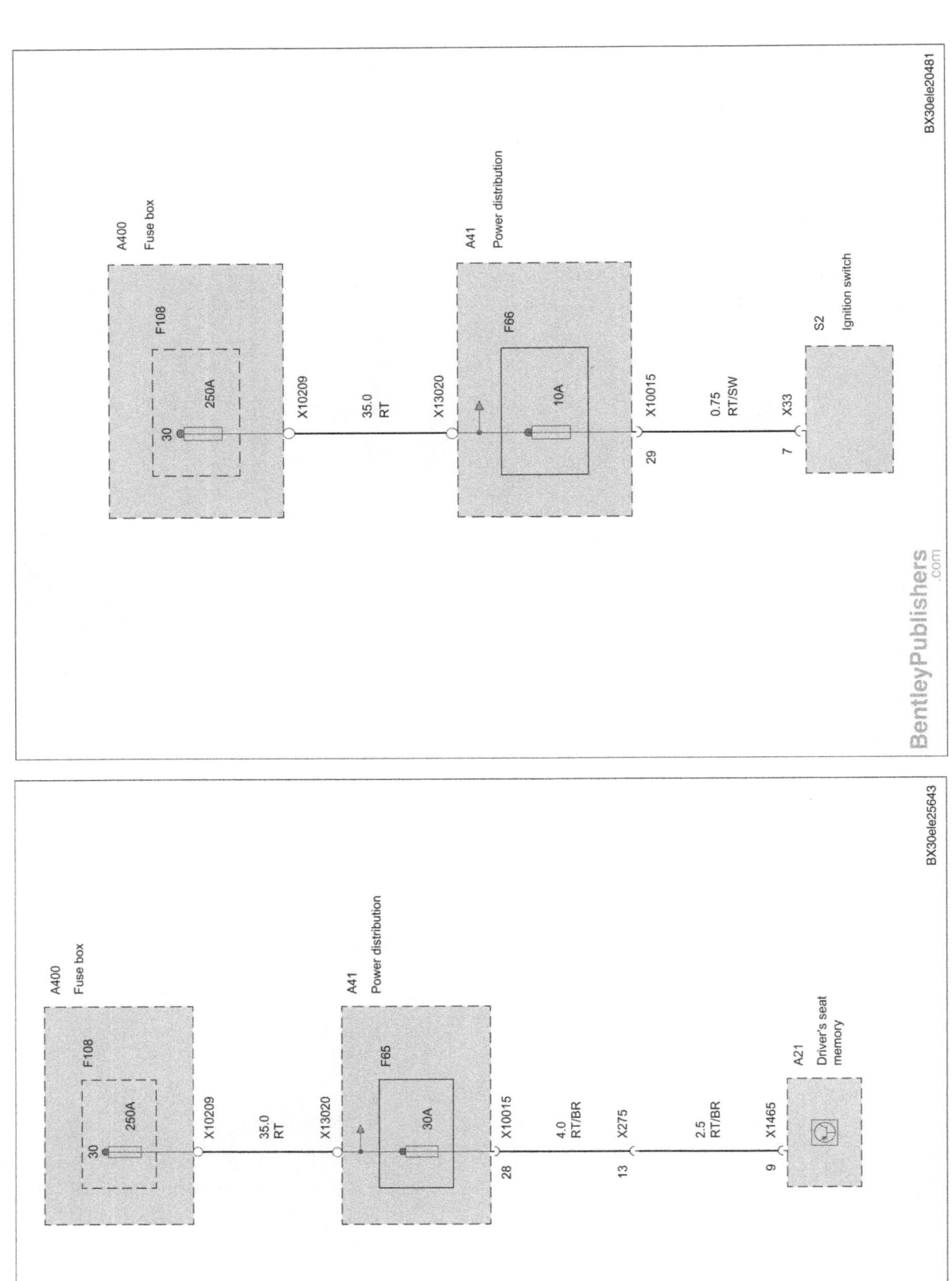

BX30ele20481

BX30ele25643

**Fuse F67
(to 09 / 2006)**

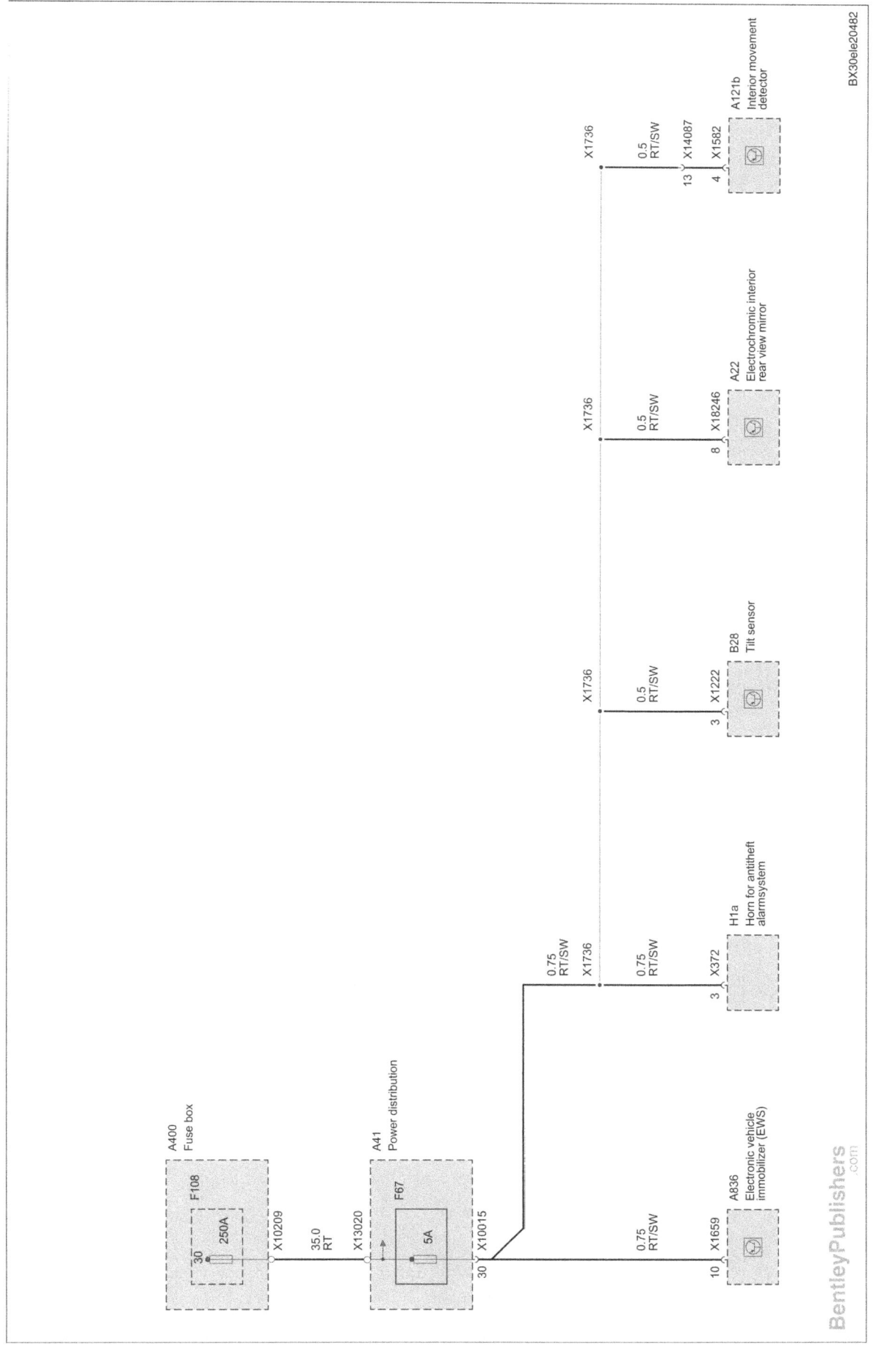

BX30ele20482

BentleyPublishers
.com

**Fuse F67
(from 09 / 2006)**

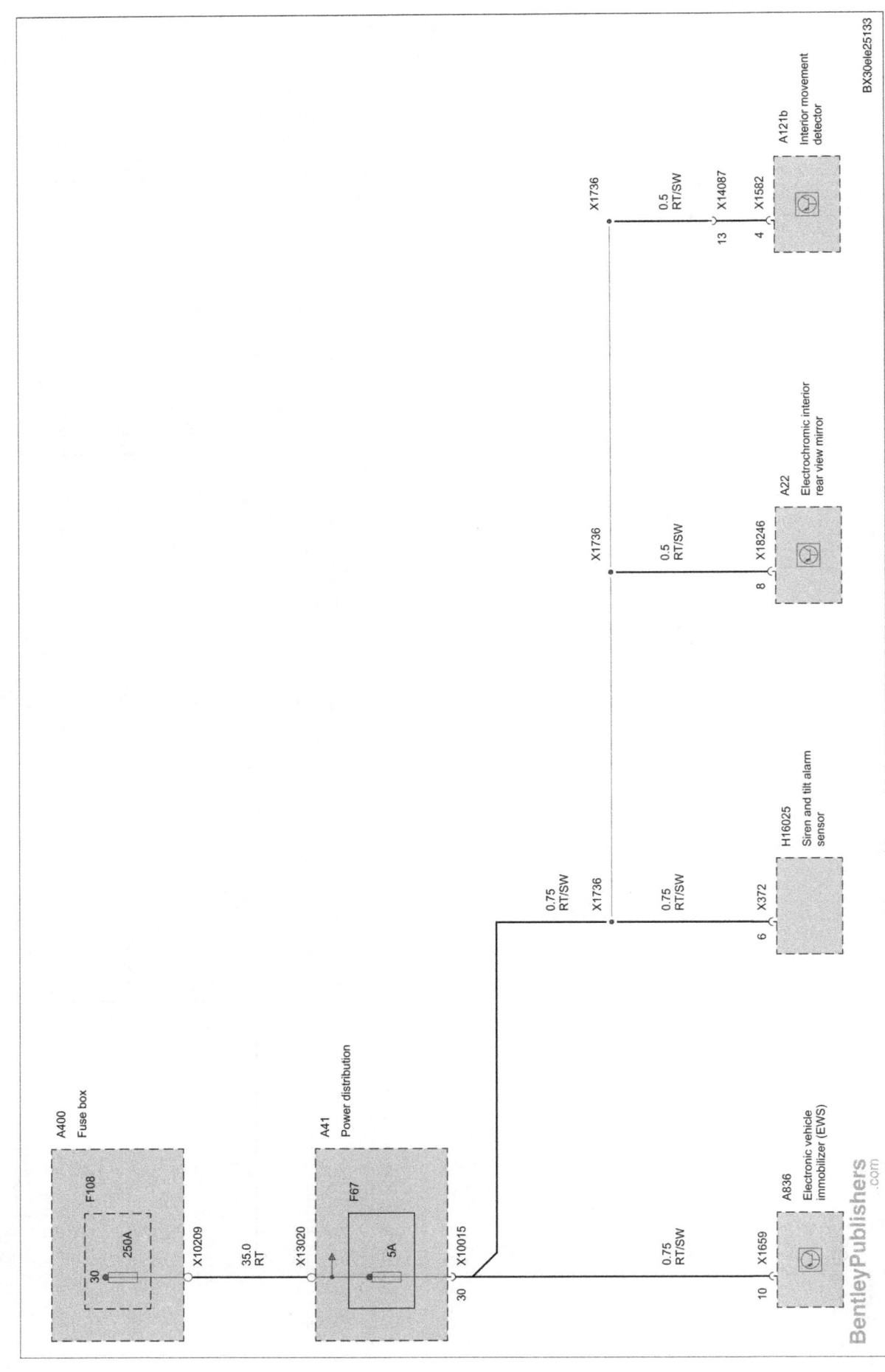

BX30ele25133

Fuse F69

Fuse F68

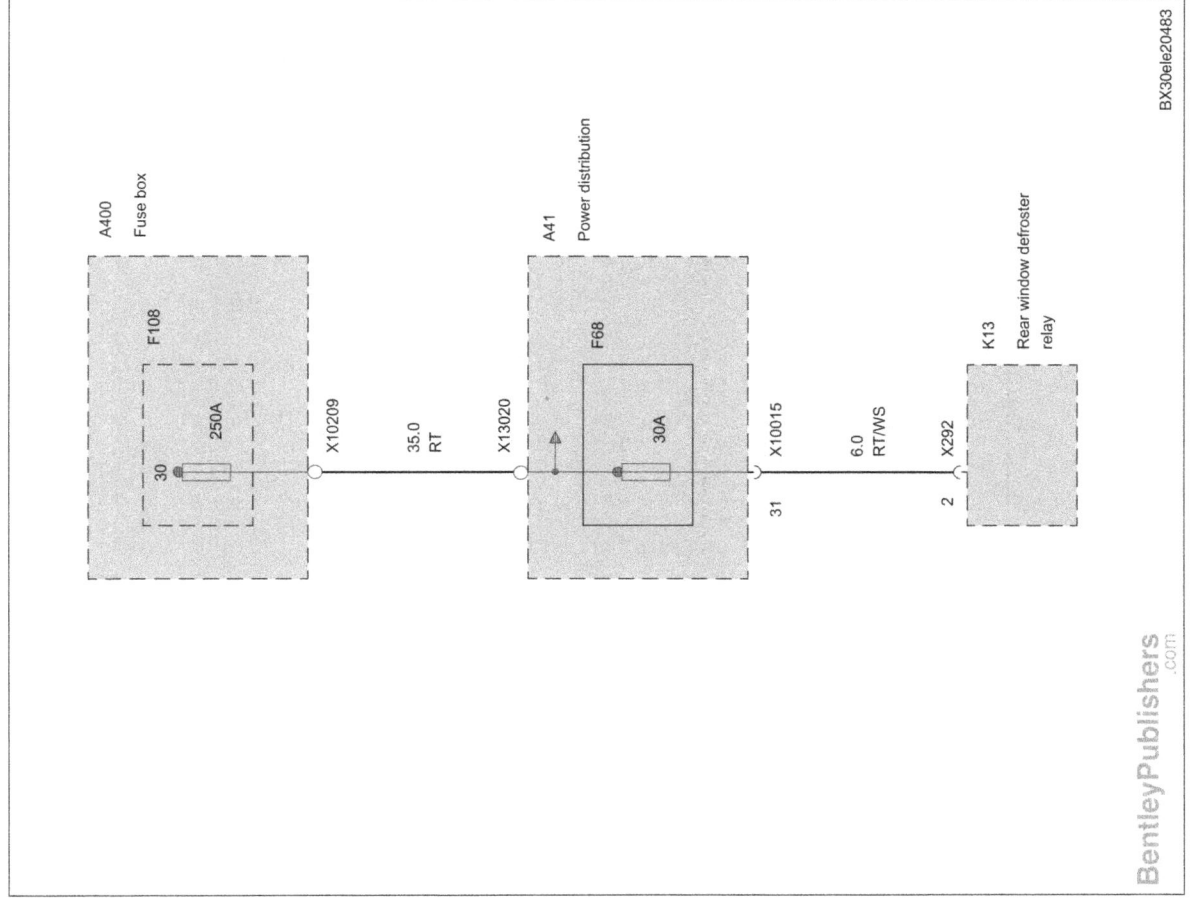

BX30ele20483

Fuse F71

Fuse F70

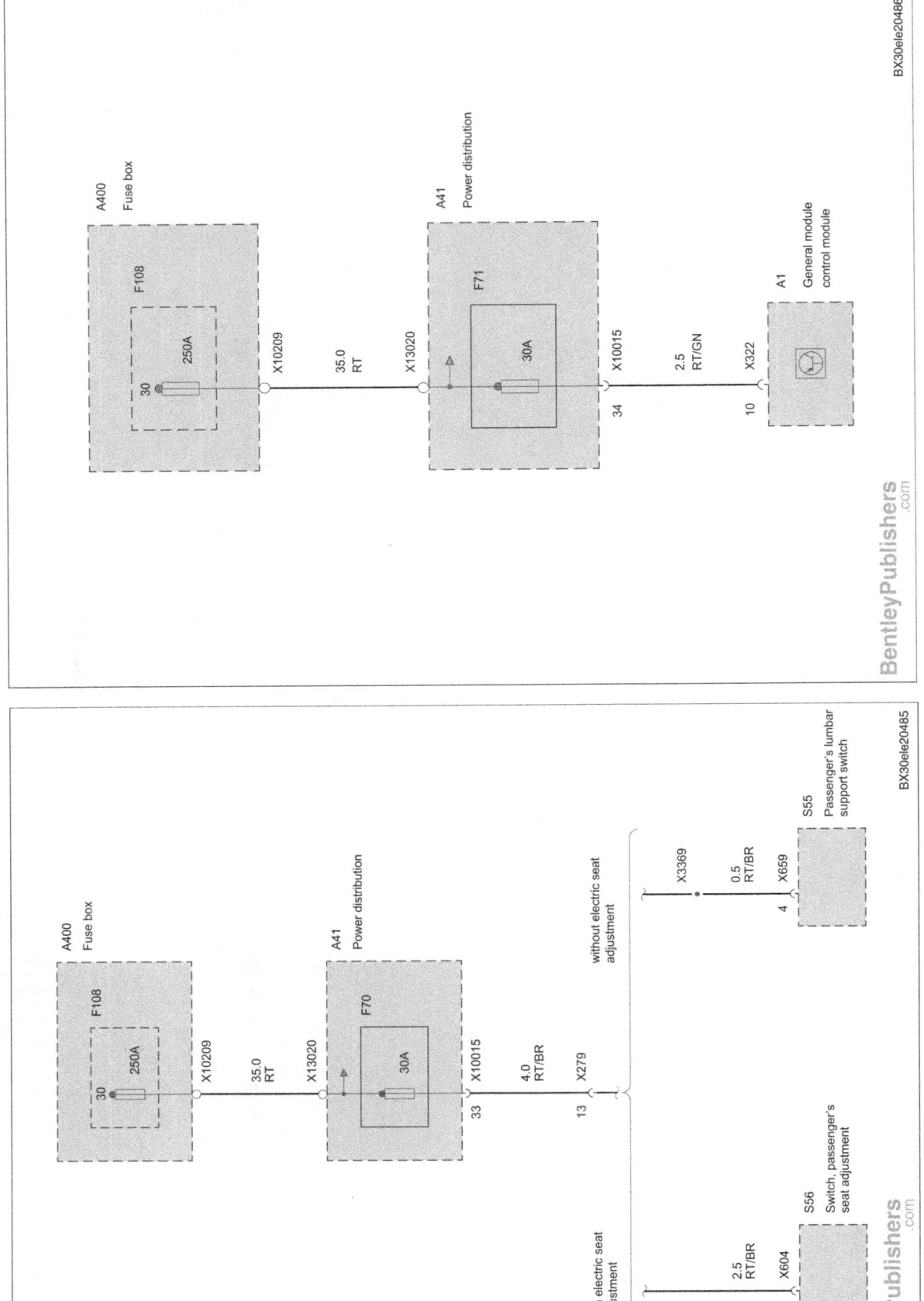

BX30ele20486

BX30ele20485

Fuse F81

Fuse F80
(w / Top Hifi)

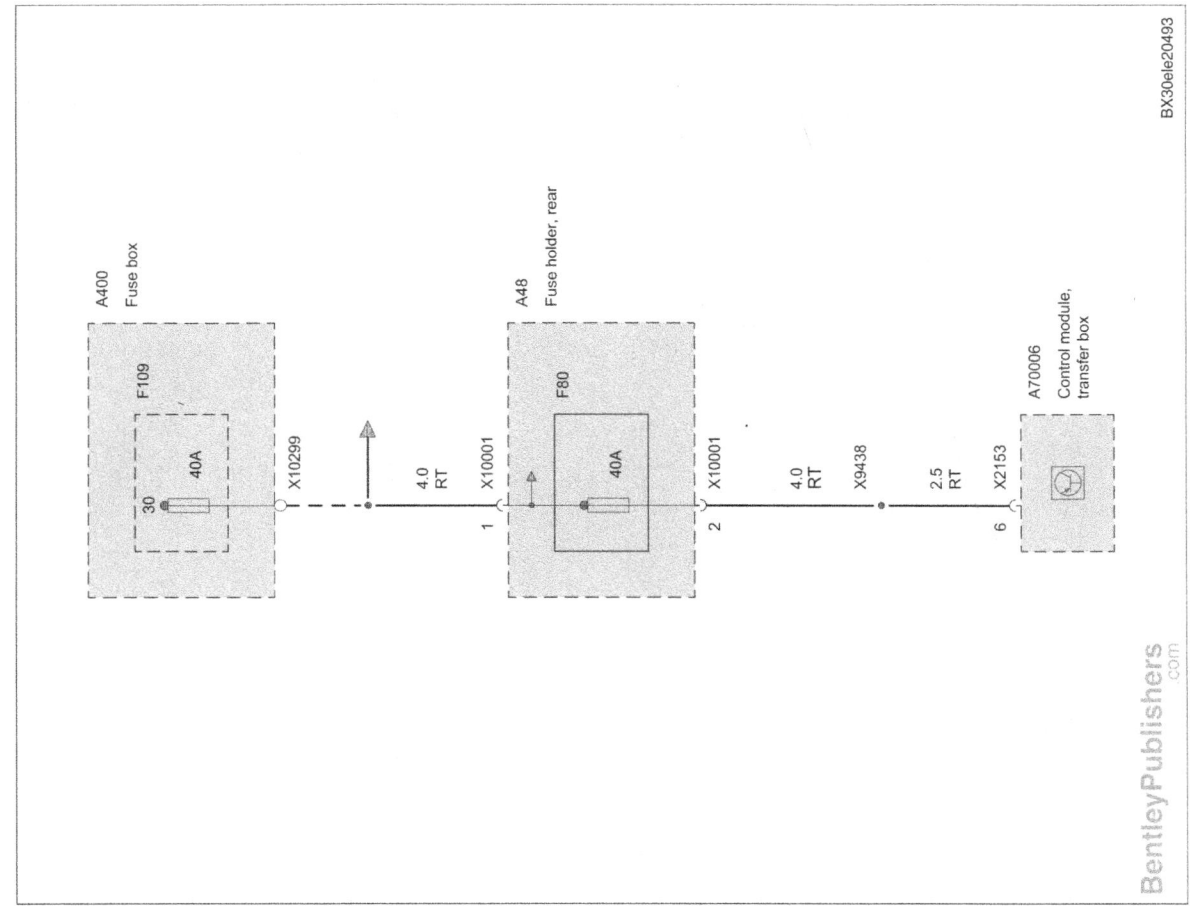

BX30ele20494

BX30ele20493

Top diagram (Fuse F81):

A400 Fuse box
F109
30
40A
X10299
4.0 RT
1 X10002
A49 Fuse holder, rear
F81
30A
2 X10002
4.0 RT
1 X11109
4.0 RT/GN
X11416
2.5 RT/GN
5 X10266
A18 Amplifier

Bottom diagram (Fuse F80):

A400 Fuse box
F109
30
40A
X10299
4.0 RT
1 X10001
A48 Fuse holder, rear
F80
40A
2 X10001
4.0 RT
X9438
2.5 RT
6 X2153
A70006 Control module, transfer box

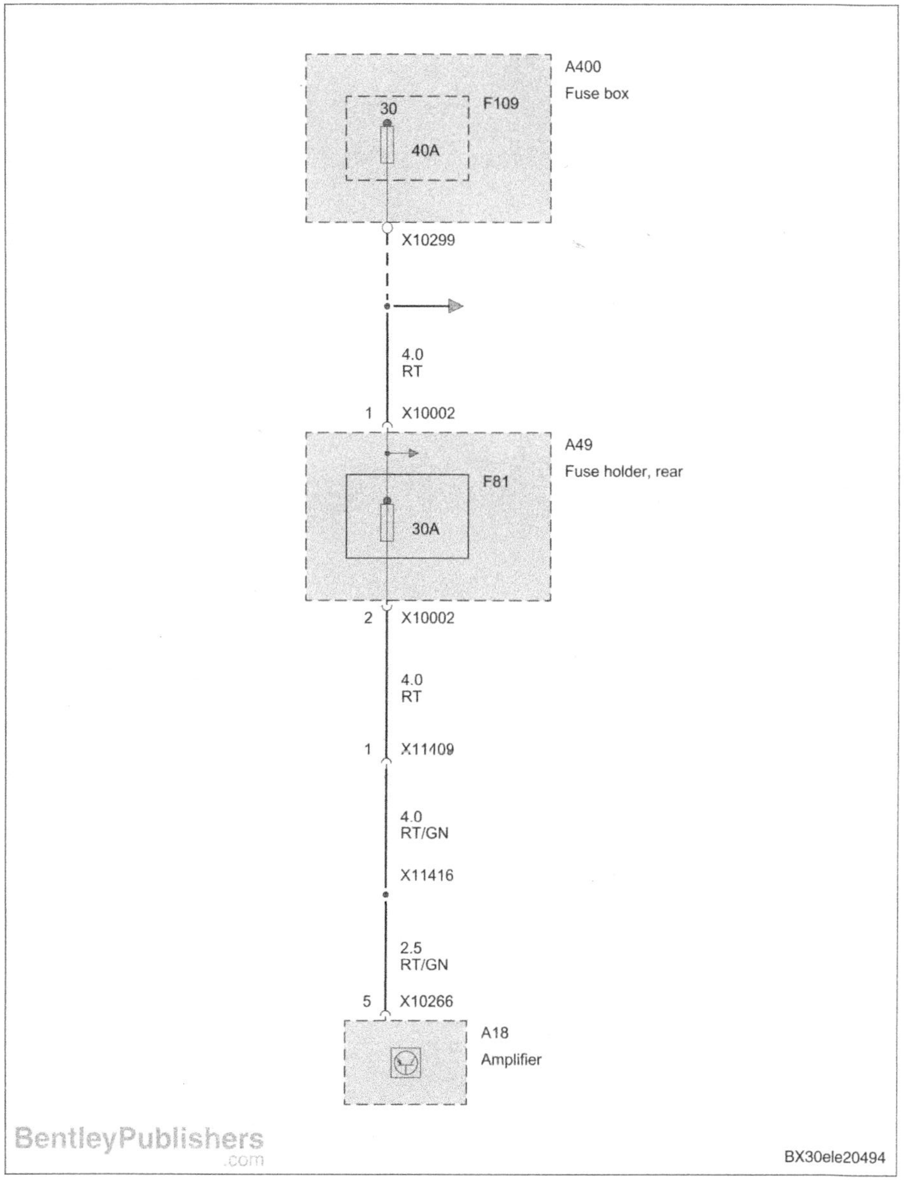

Fuses F102
N52 engine

Fuse 102
M54 engine

BX30ele25135

BX30ele20487

BentleyPublishers.com

BentleyPublishers.com

Fuse F106
(to 09 / 2006)

A400
Fuse box

F108

250A

30

X10209

35.0
RT

X13020

A41
Power distribution

F106

50A

X3

4.0
RT/GN

X12

A3a
Light switch cluster

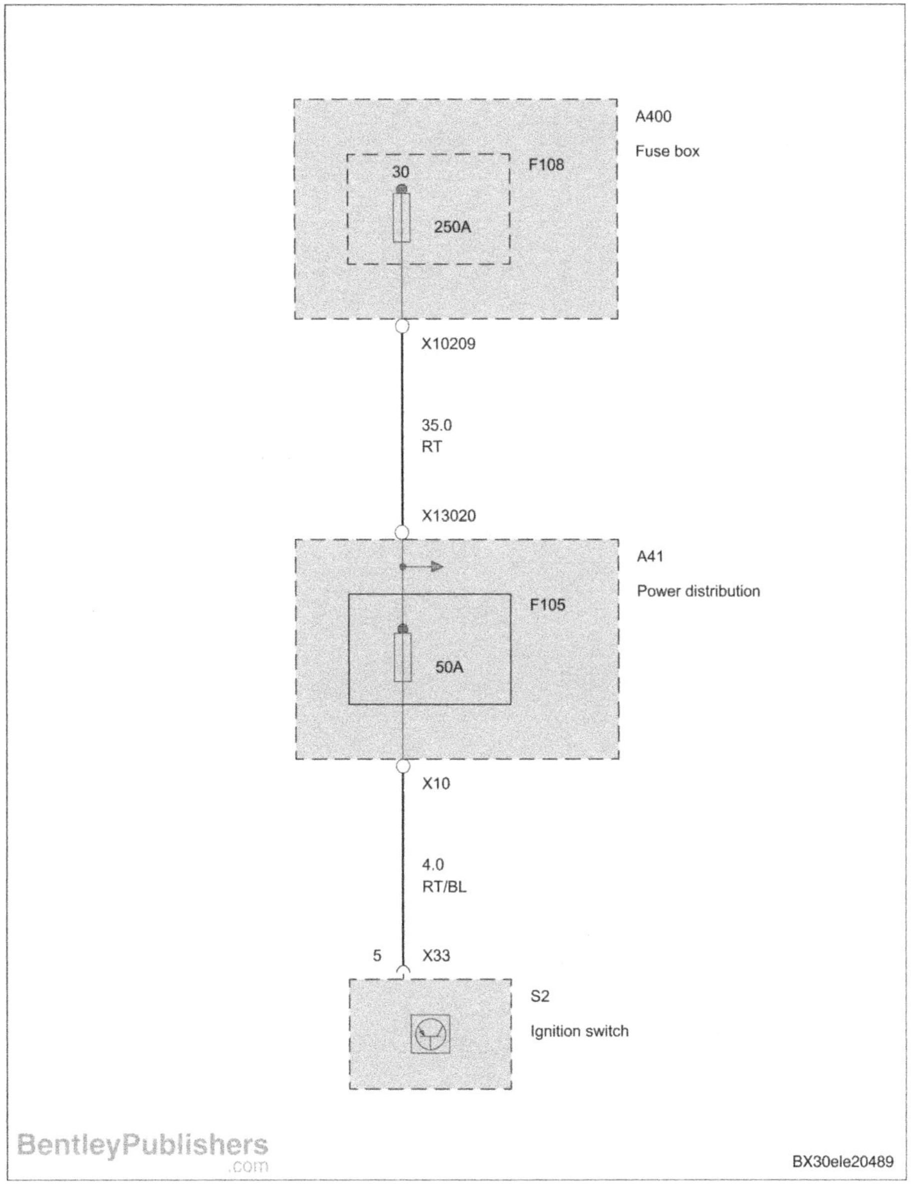

6

4.0
RT/GN

X33

6

S2
Ignition switch

BX30ele20490

Fuse F105

A400
Fuse box

F108

250A

30

X10209

35.0
RT

X13020

A41
Power distribution

F105

50A

X10

4.0
RT/BL

X33

5

S2
Ignition switch

BX30ele20489

Electrical Wiring Diagrams   ELE-57

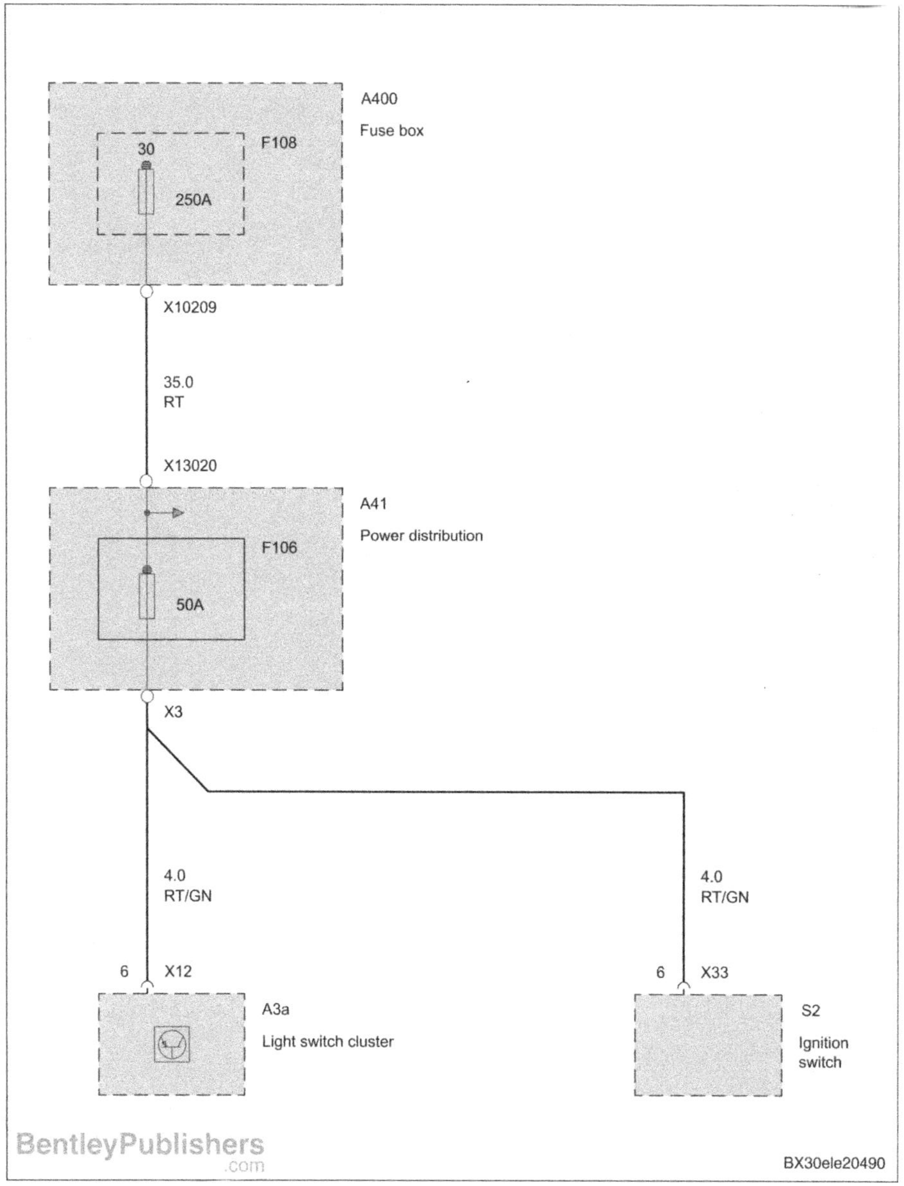

**Fuse F106
Supply terminal 15**

**Fuse F106
(from 09 / 2006)**

BX30ele20449

BX30ele25127

Fuse 107

Fuse F106
Supply terminal R

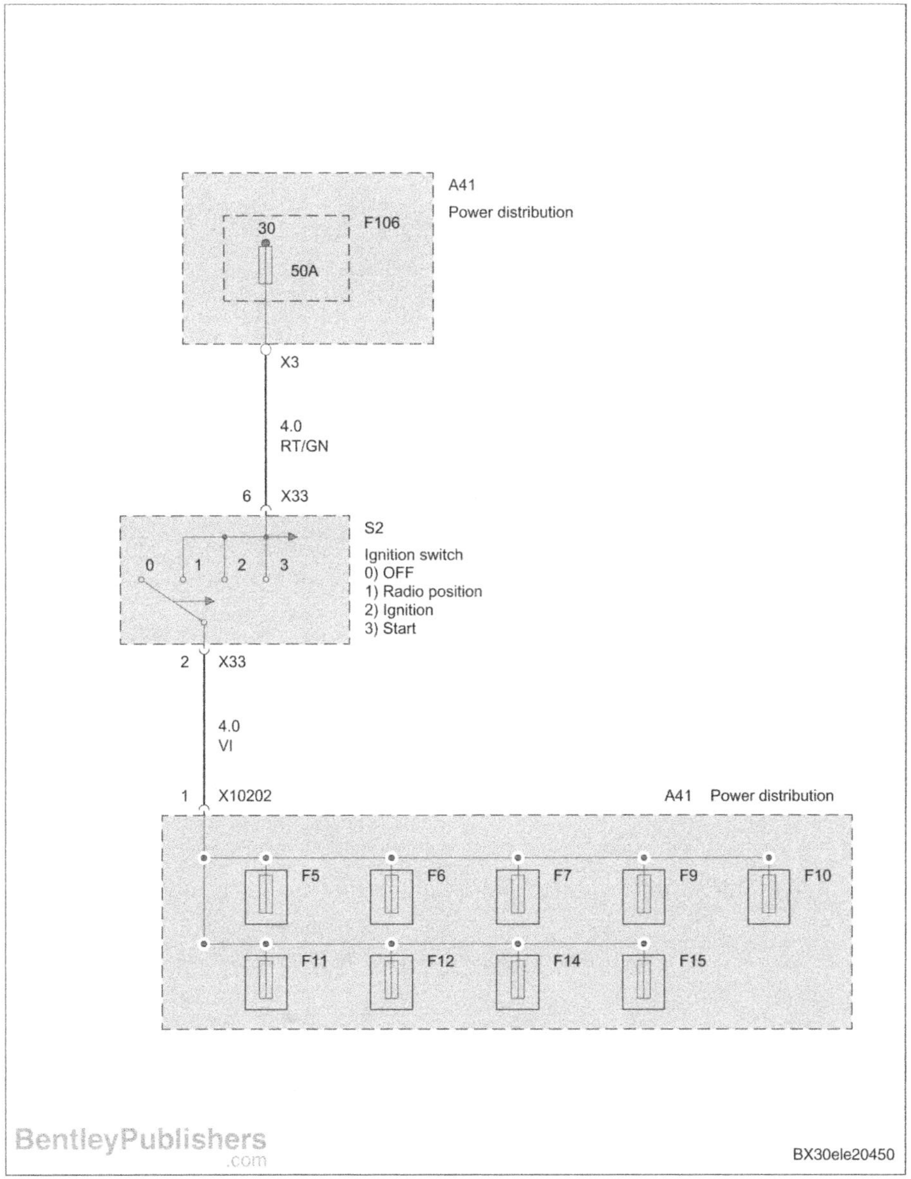

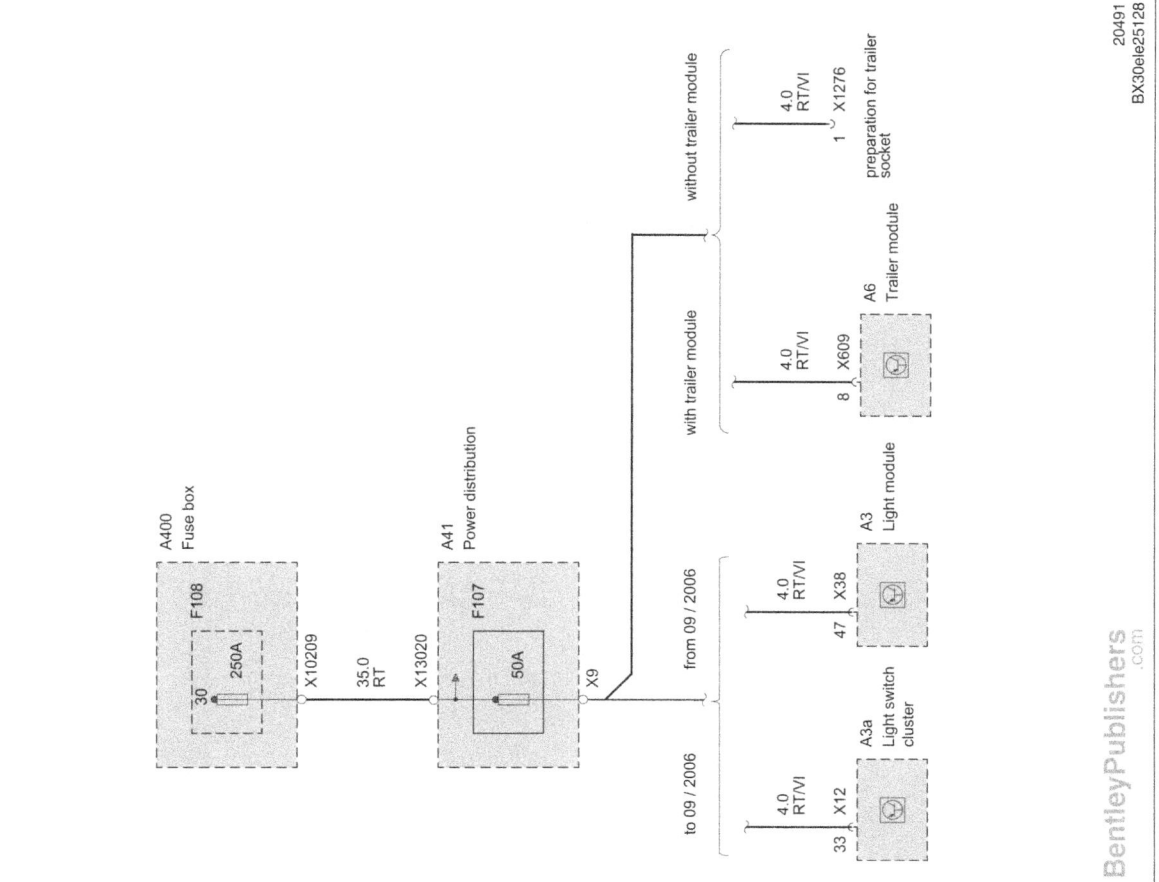

20491
BX30ele25128

BX30ele20450

A400 Fuse box
F108
250A
30
X10209

35.0
RT

X13020

A41 Power distribution
F107
50A
X9

to 09 / 2006
from 09 / 2006
with trailer module
without trailer module

33 X12
4.0
RT/VI
A3a Light switch cluster

47 X38
4.0
RT/VI
A3 Light module

8 X609
4.0
RT/VI
A6 Trailer module

1 X1276
4.0
RT/VI
preparation for trailer socket

A41 Power distribution
F106
50A
30
X3

4.0
RT/GN

X33
6

S2 Ignition switch
0) OFF
1) Radio position
2) Ignition
3) Start
3
2
1
0

X33
2

4.0
VI

X10202
1

A41 Power distribution
F10
F9 F15
F7 F14
F6 F12
F5 F11

Fuses F108, F109
M54 engine with Top HiFi

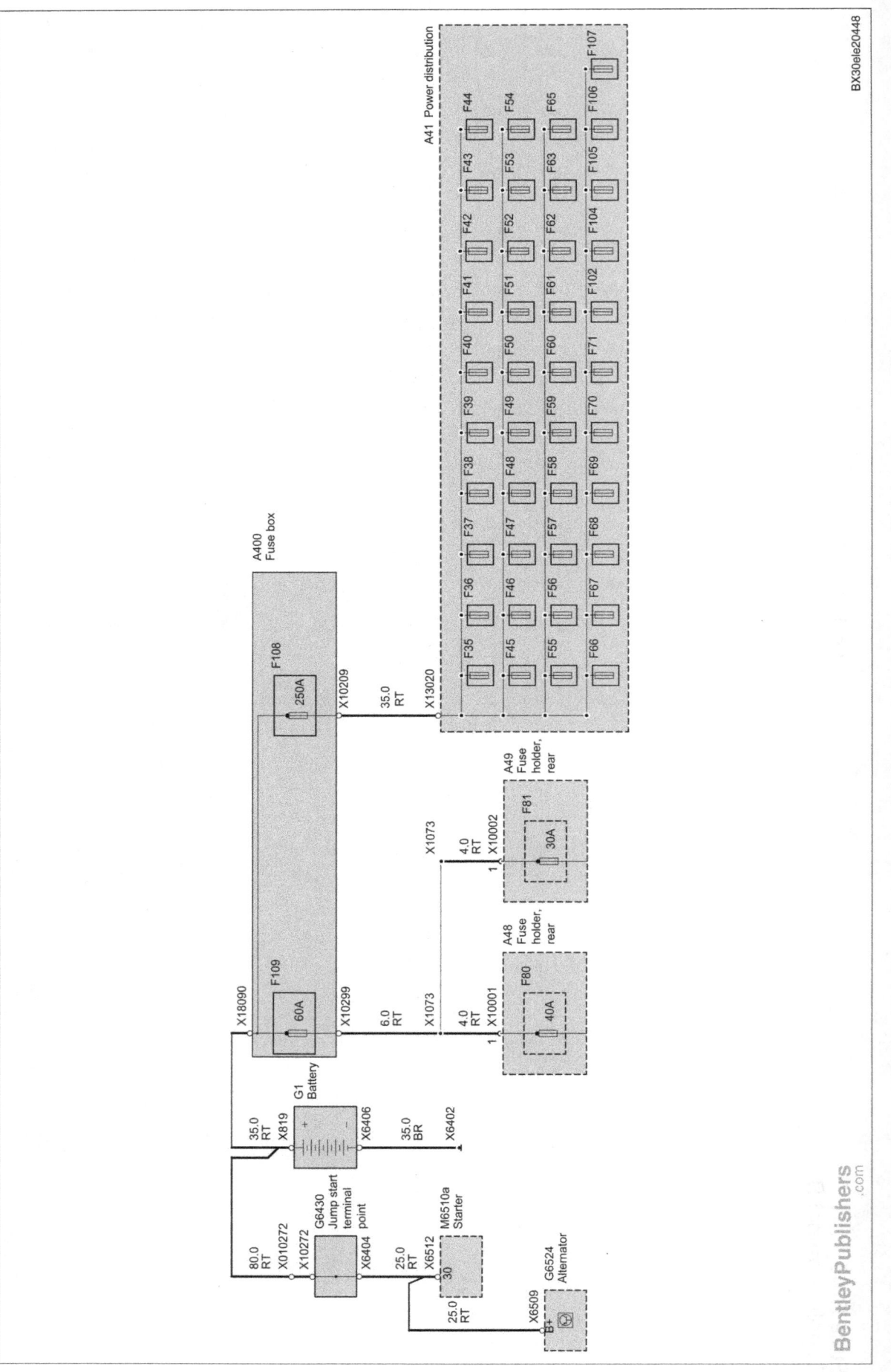

BX30ele20448

Fuses F108, F109
M54 engine without Top HiFi

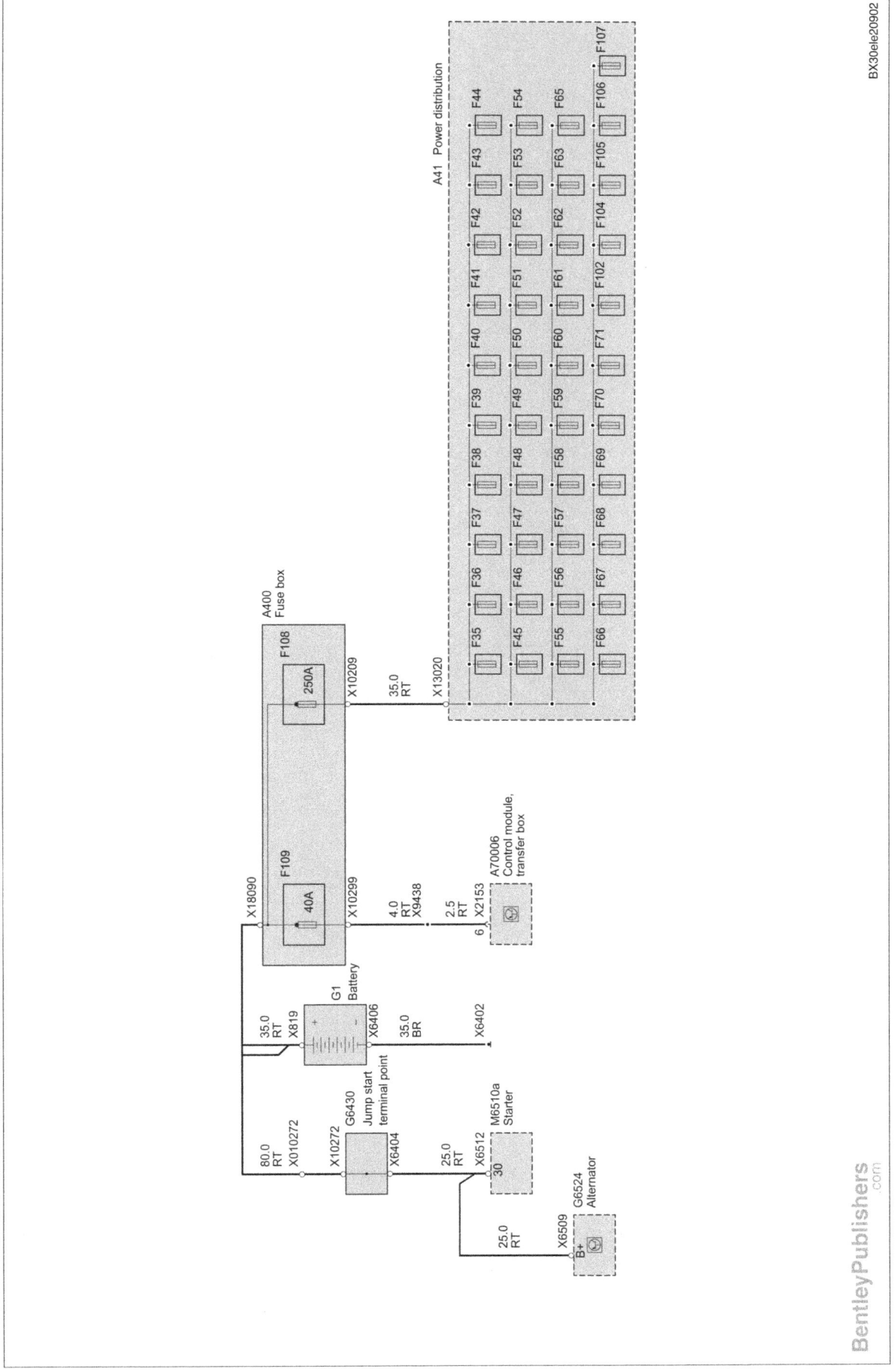

Electrical Wiring Diagrams ELE-61

BX30ele20902

Fuses F108 and 109
N52 engine with Top HiFi
page 1 of 2

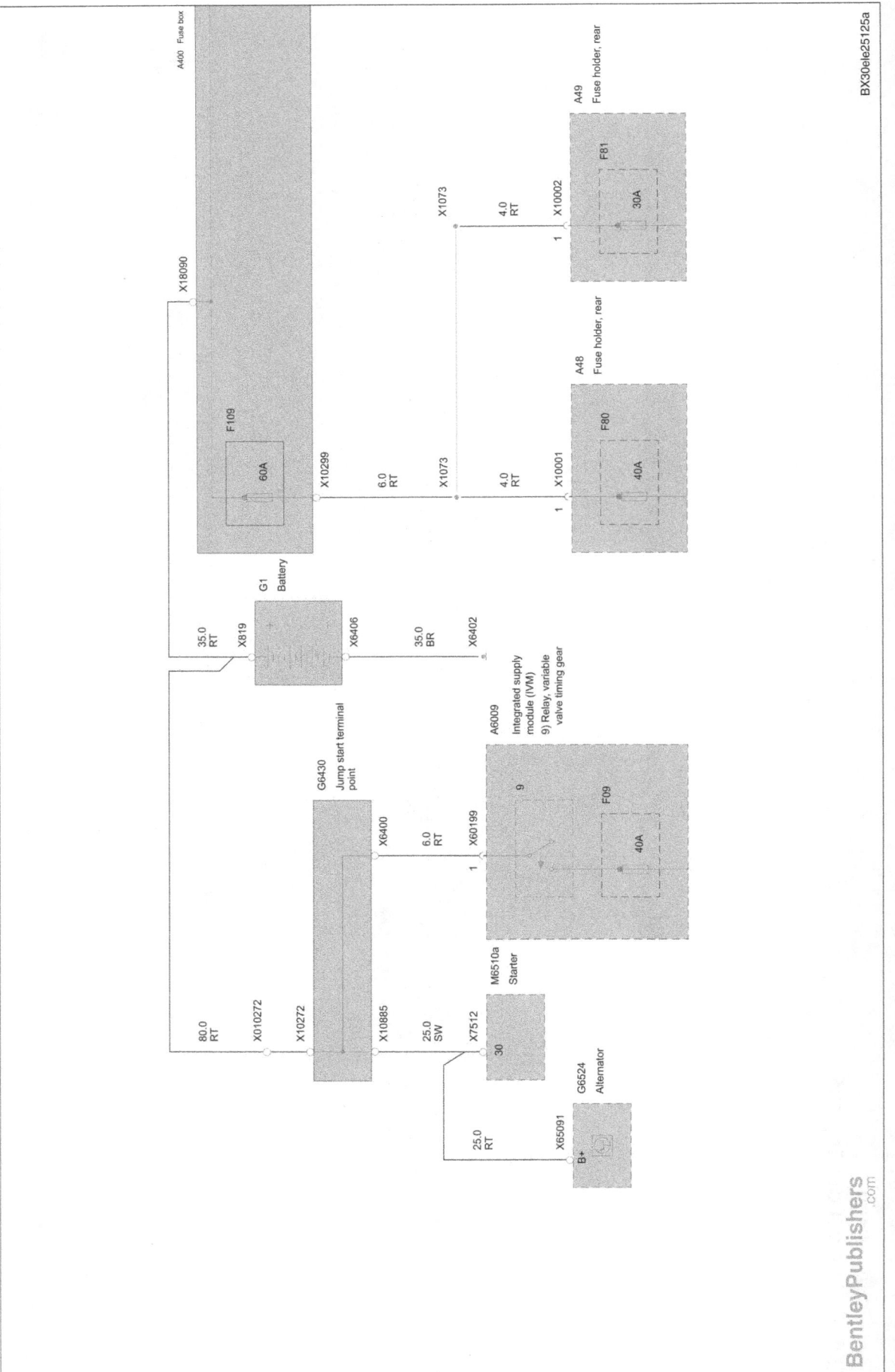

Fuses F108 and F109
N52 engine with Top HiFi
page 2 of 2

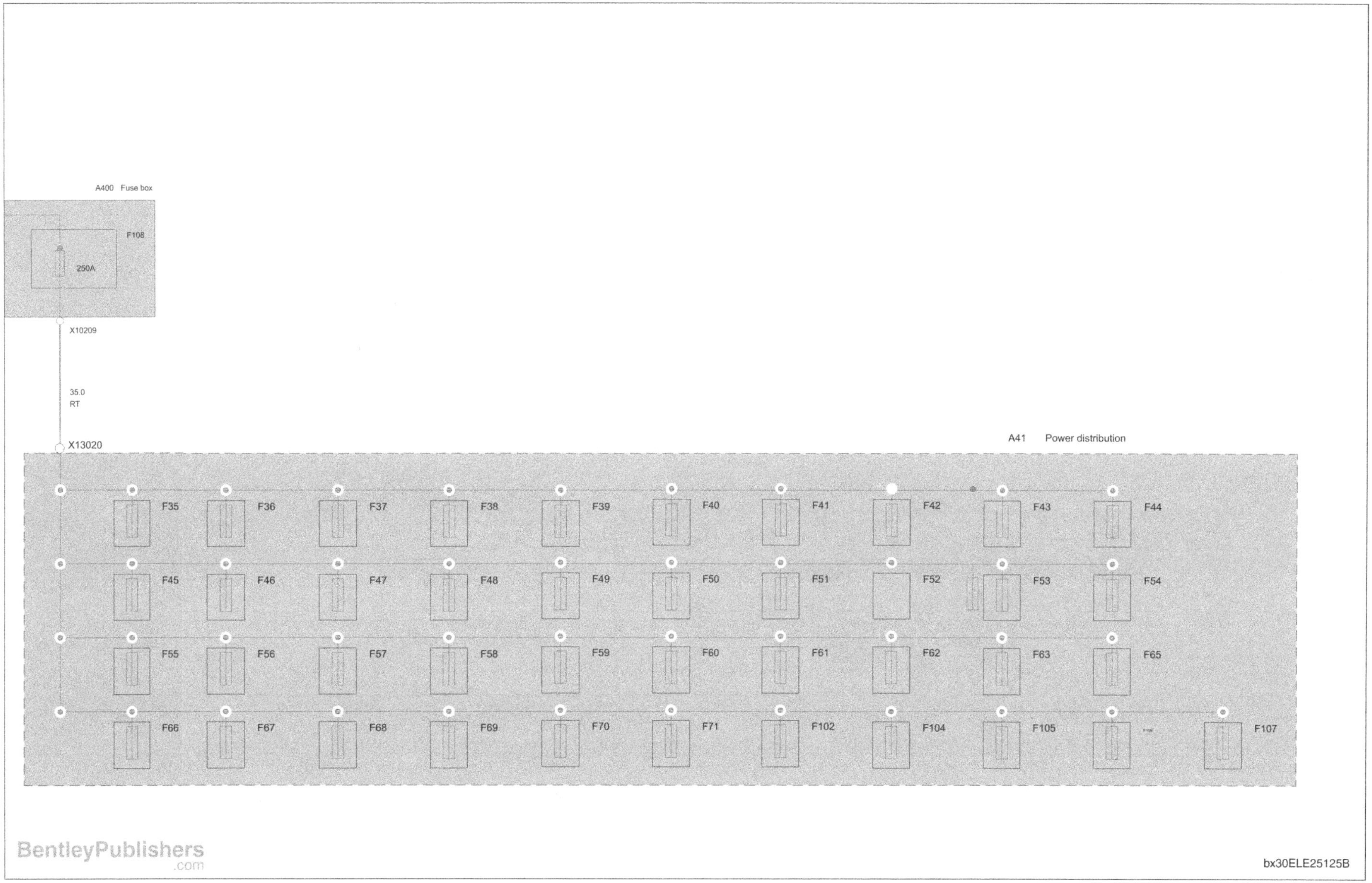

A400 Fuse box

F108

250A

X10209

35.0
RT

X13020

A41 Power distribution

F44 F43 F42 F41 F40 F39 F38 F37 F36 F35

F54 F53 F52 F51 F50 F49 F48 F47 F46 F45

F65 F63 F62 F61 F60 F59 F58 F57 F56 F55

F107 F105 F104 F102 F71 F70 F69 F68 F67 F66

**Fuses F108 and F109
N52 engine without Top HiFi
page 1of 2**

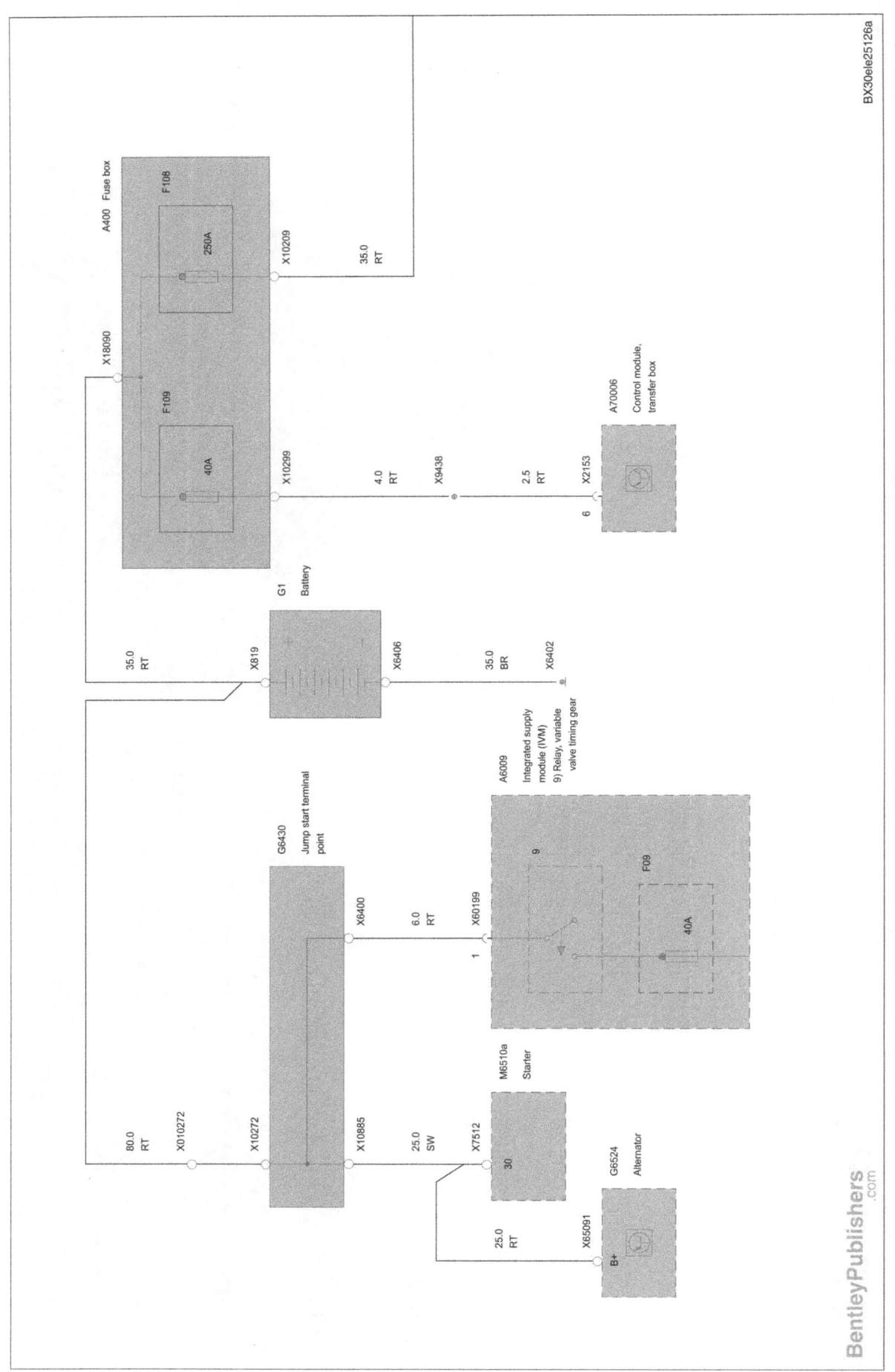

BX30ele25126a

Fuses F108 and F109
N52 engine without Top HiFi
page 2 of 2

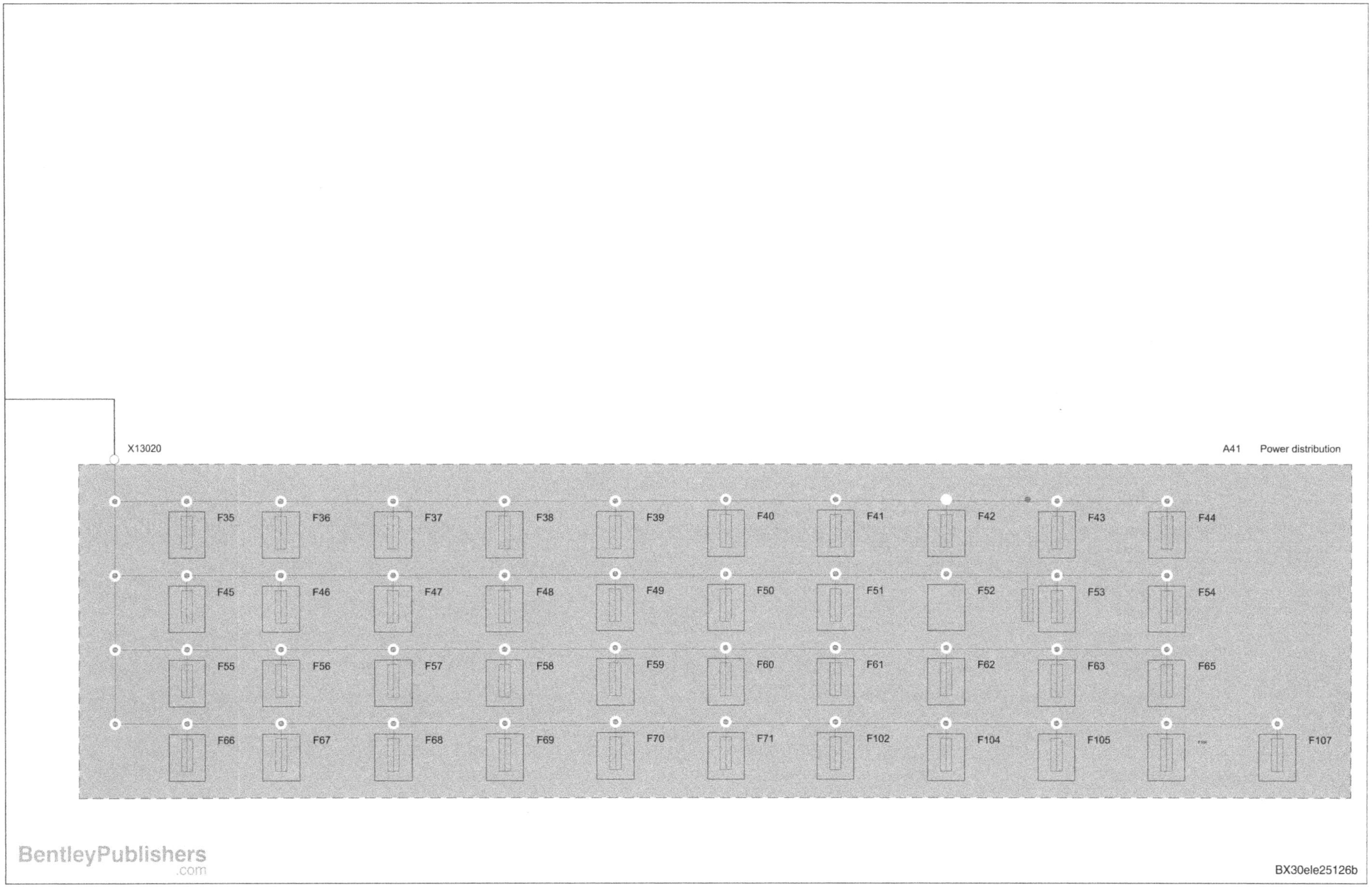

A41   Power distribution

F107

F44   F43   F42   F41   F40   F39   F38   F37   F36   F35

F54   F53   F52   F51   F50   F49   F48   F47   F46   F45

F65   F63   F62   F61   F60   F59   F58   F57   F56   F55

F105   F104   F102   F71   F70   F69   F68   F67   F66

X13020

Electrical Wiring Diagrams   ELE-65

BX30ele25126b

Alternator (BSD)
N52 engine

Alternator (BSD)
M54 engine

BX30ele25246

BX30ele18107

Brake light switch
M54 engine

Pedal position sensor (PWG)
M54 engine

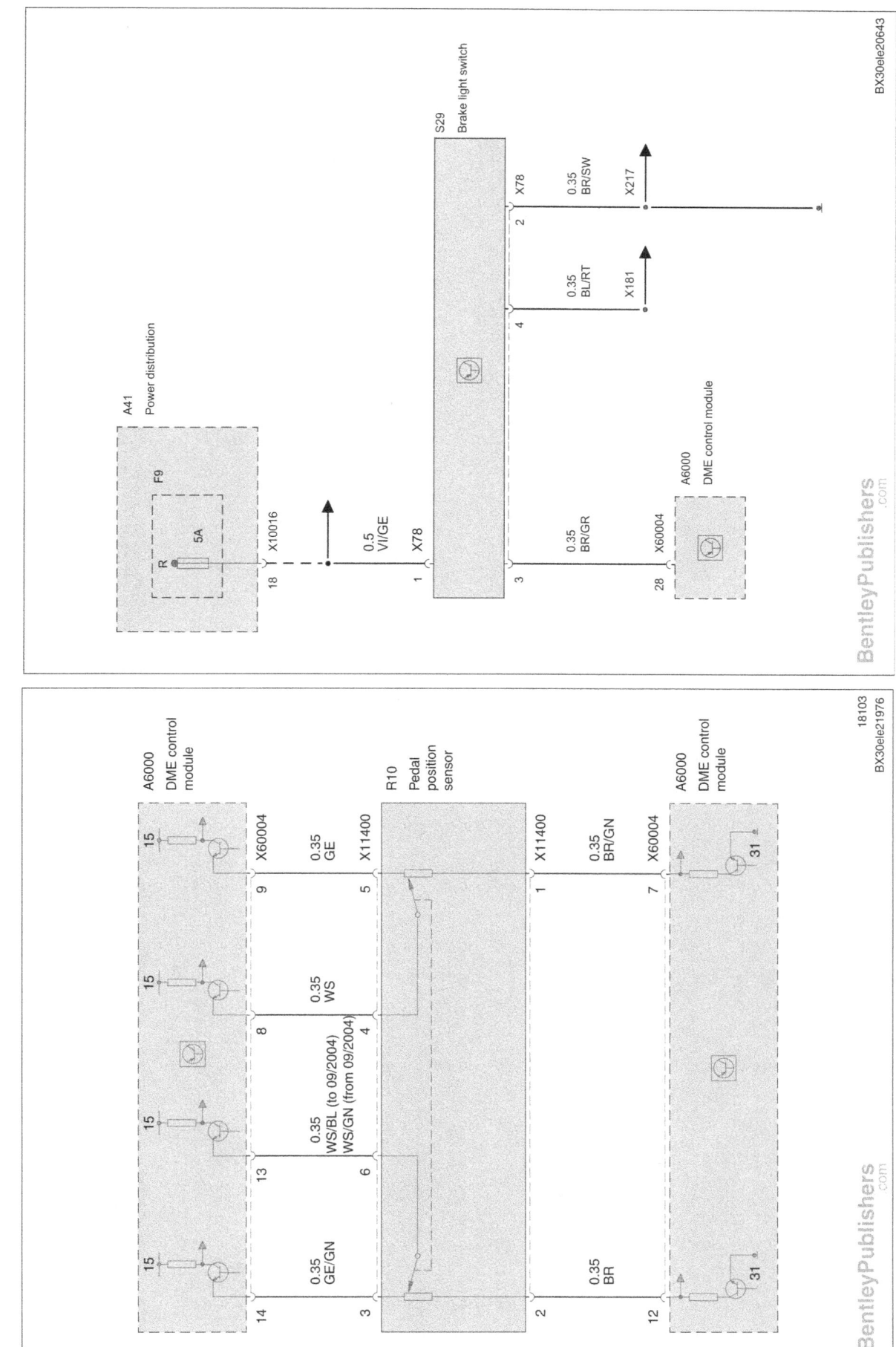

Accelerator pedal module, brake light switch
Clutch switch module
N52 engine

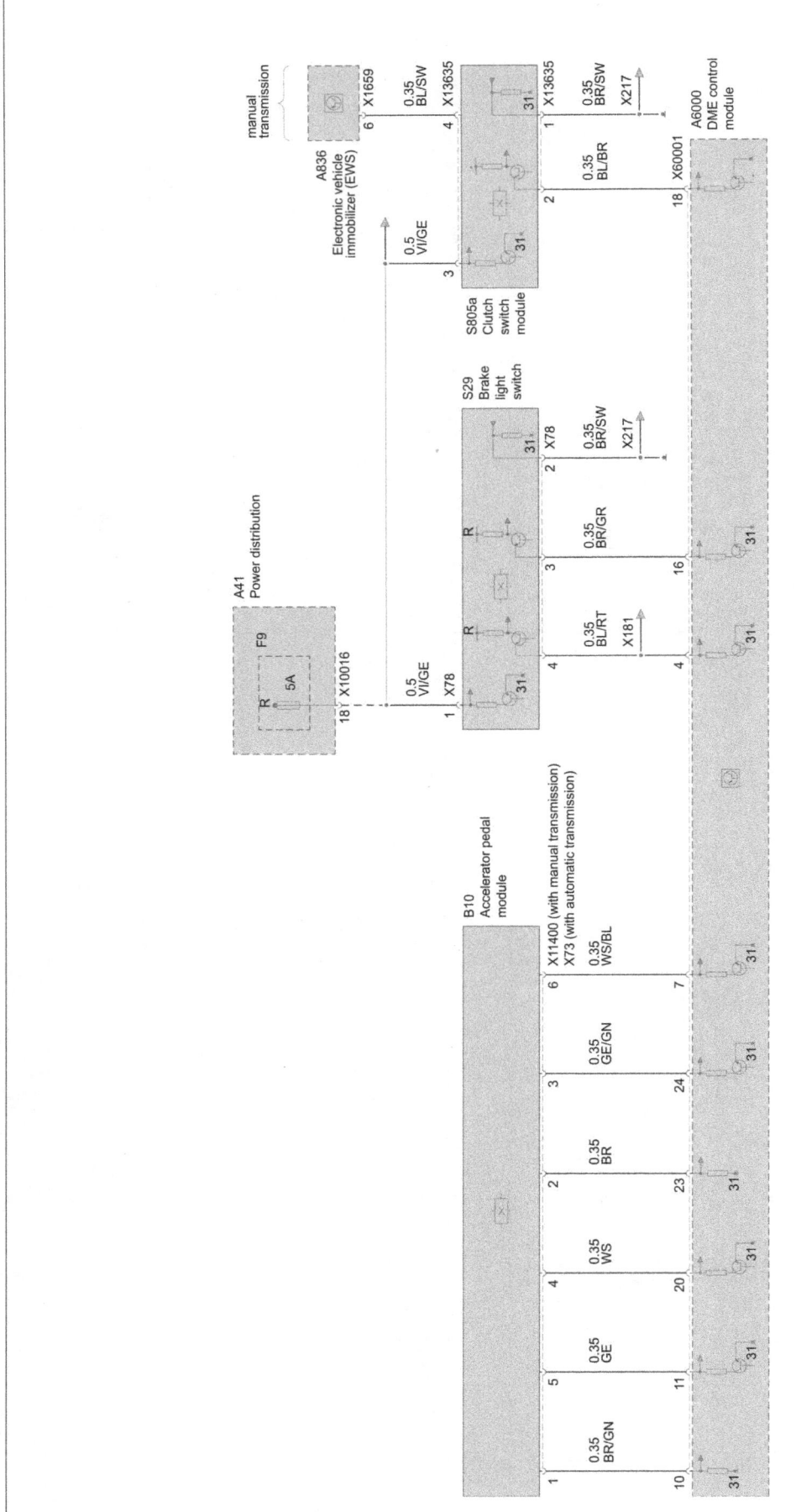

**Air supply, DISA changeover valve
M54 engine**

**Air supply, electric throttle valve (EDK)
M54 engine
(from 09 / 2004)**

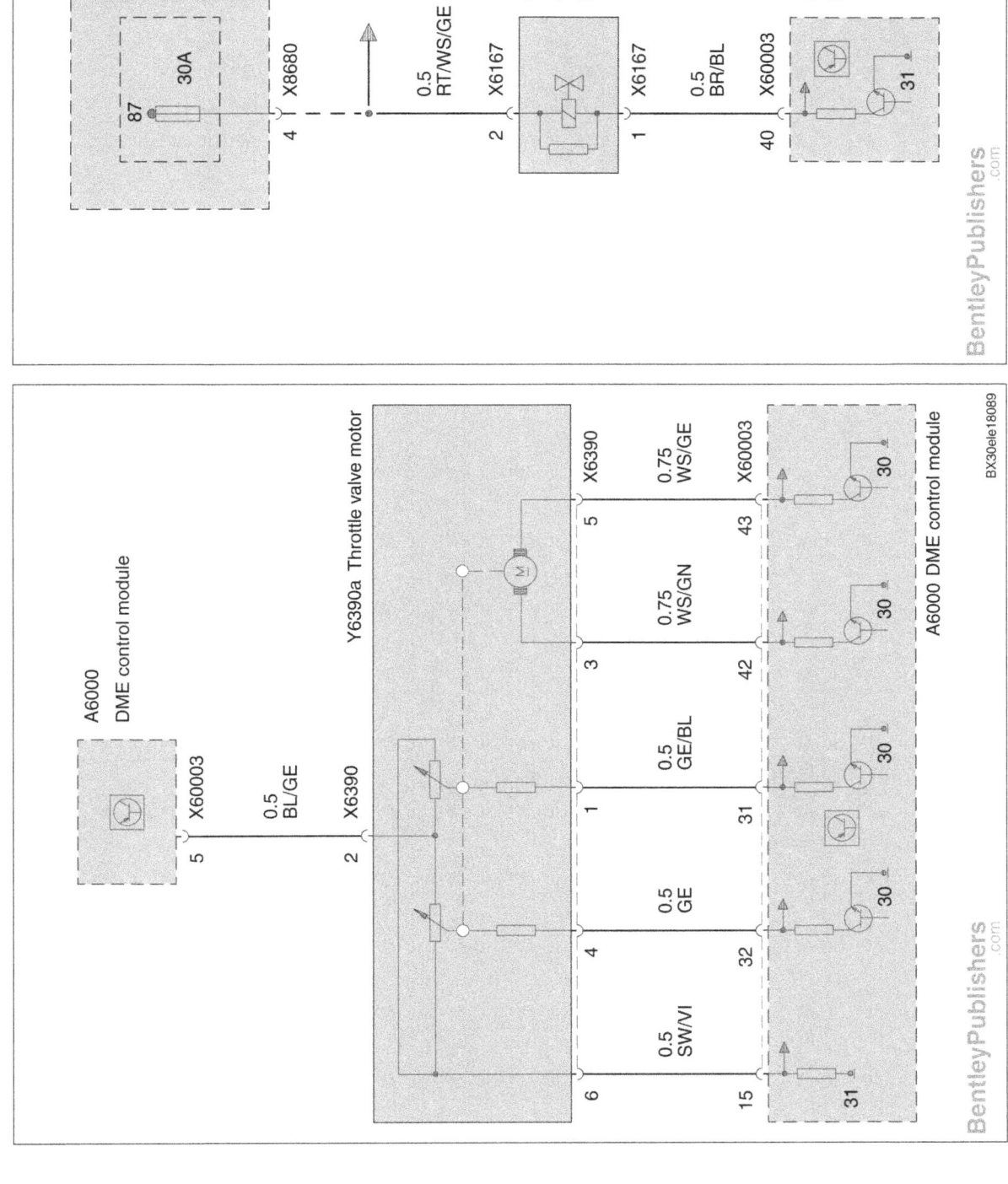

BX30ele18097

BX30ele18089

BentleyPublishers
.com

BentleyPublishers
.com

Hot-film mass air meter
M54 engine

Idle speed control valve (ISC)
M54 engine

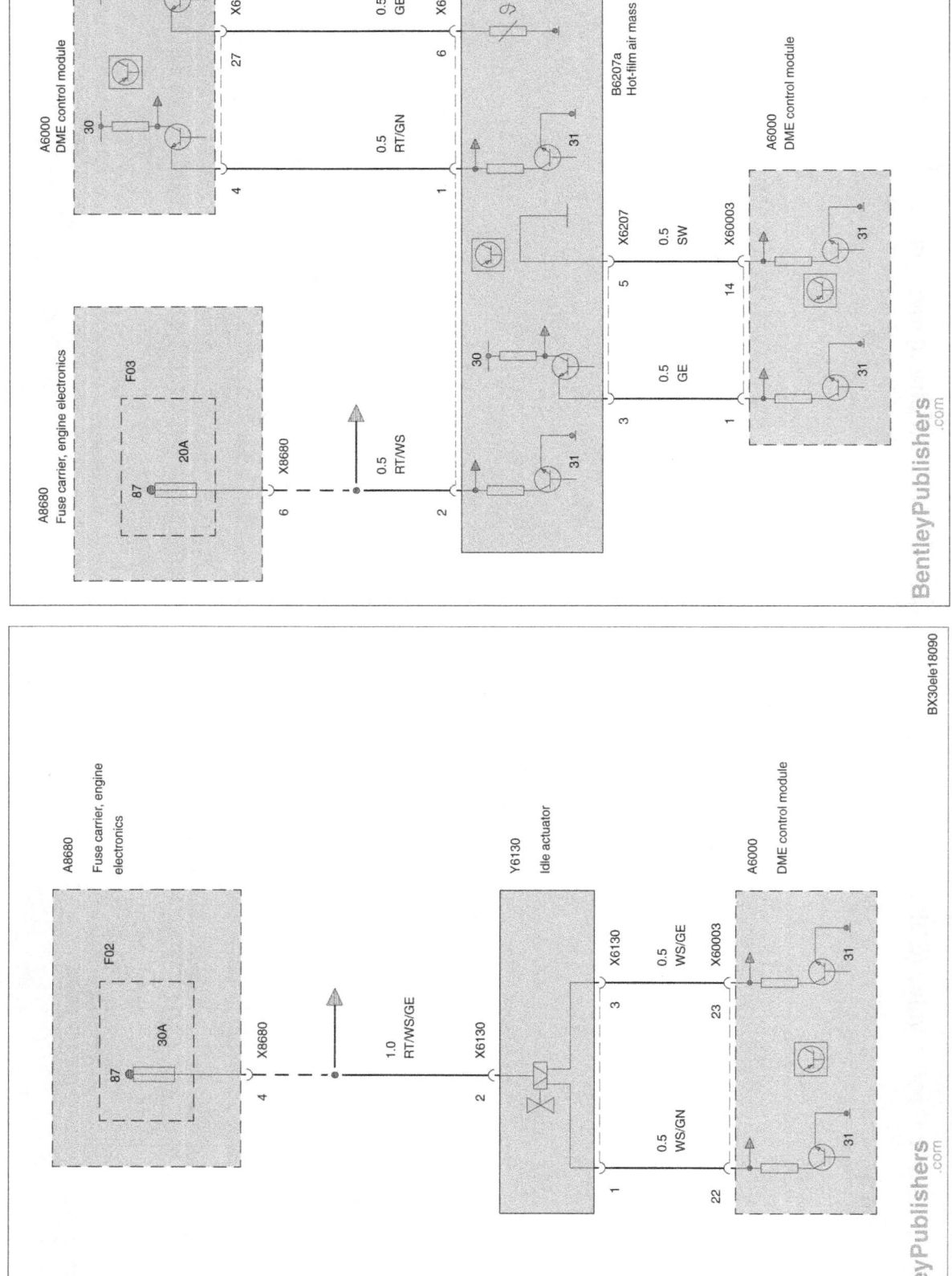

BX30ele18088

BX30ele18090

Air supply, DISA, mass air flow sensor
Electric throttle valve actuator
N52 engine (1 of 2)

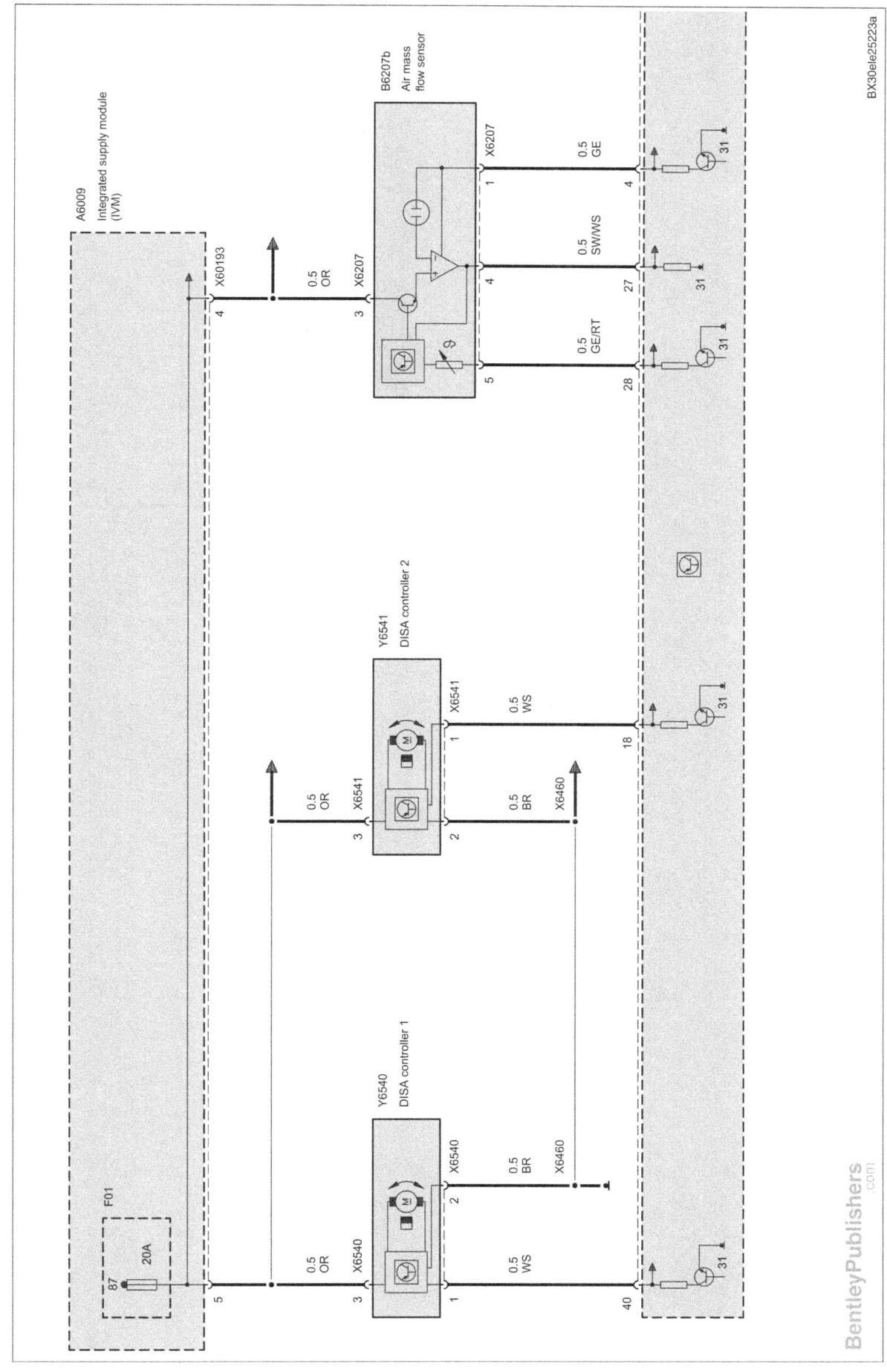

BX30ele25223a

BentleyPublishers
.com

Air supply, DISA, mass air flow sensor
Electric throttle valve actuator
N52 engine (2 of 2)

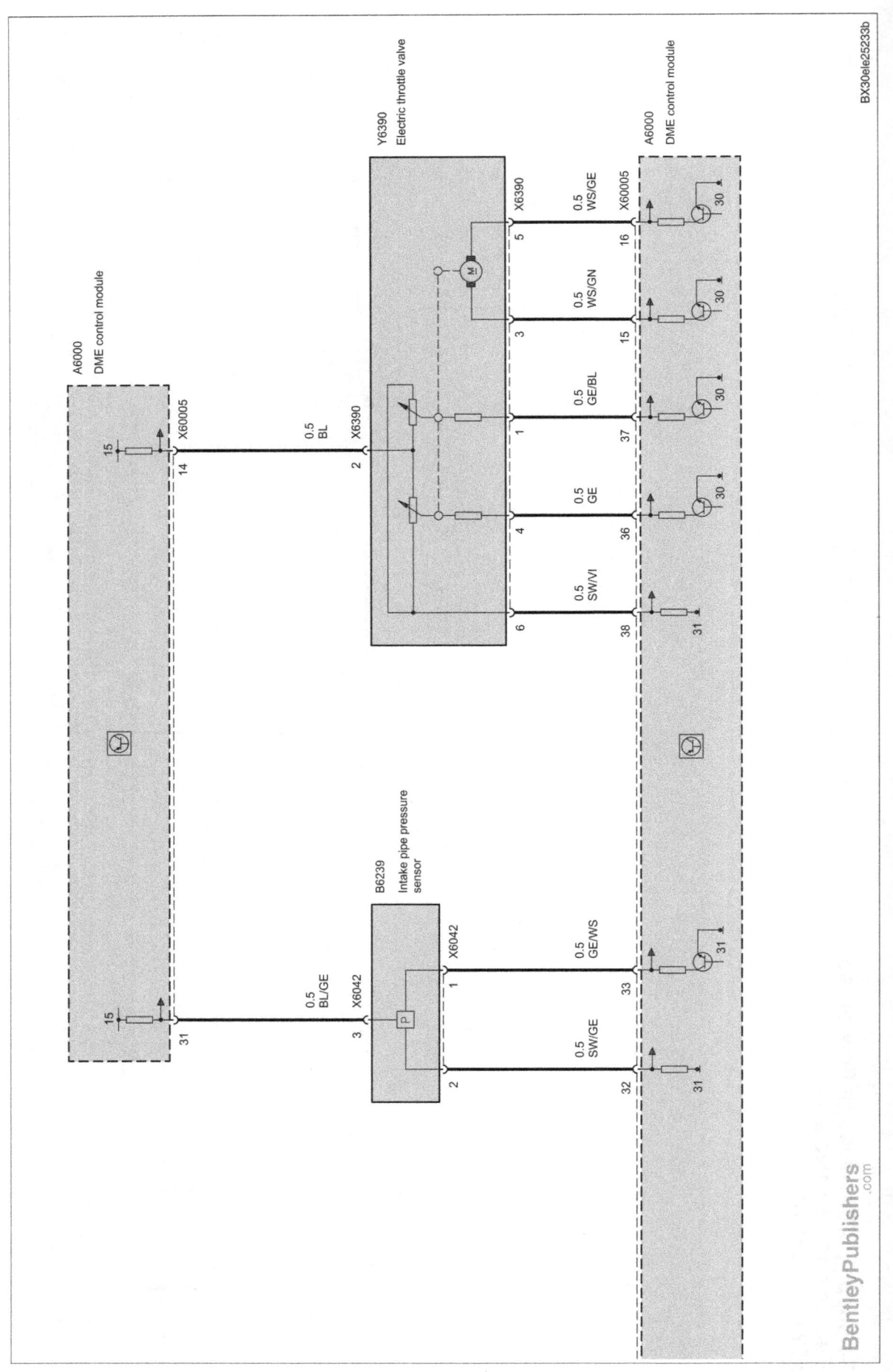

BX30ele25233b

Camshaft Position Sensors
M54 engine

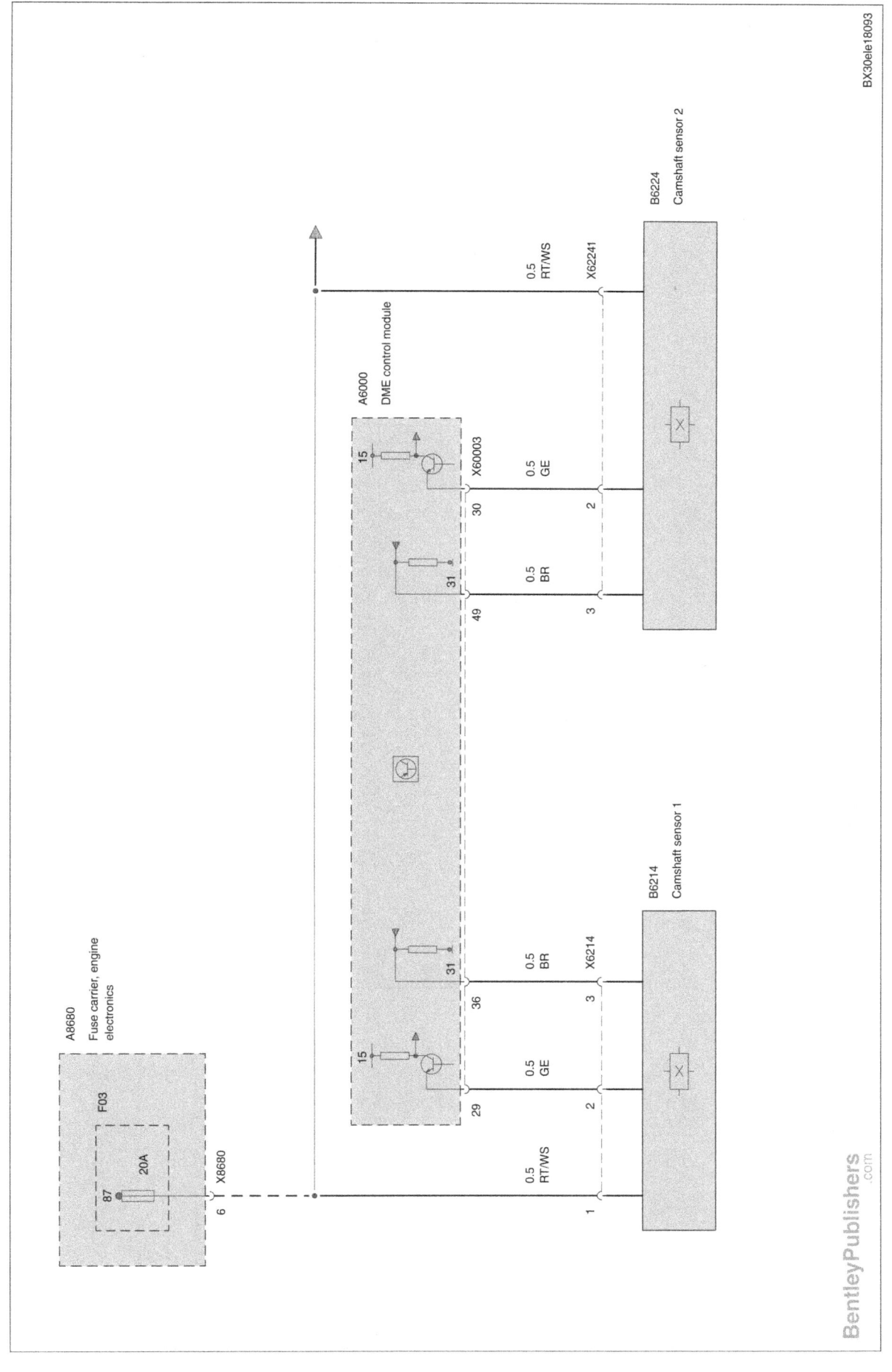

BX30ele18093

BentleyPublishers
.com

Valve gear (Camshaft sensors, VANOS solenoids, Eccentric shaft sensor, Relay, Actuator varible valve timing gear) N52 engine (1 of 2)

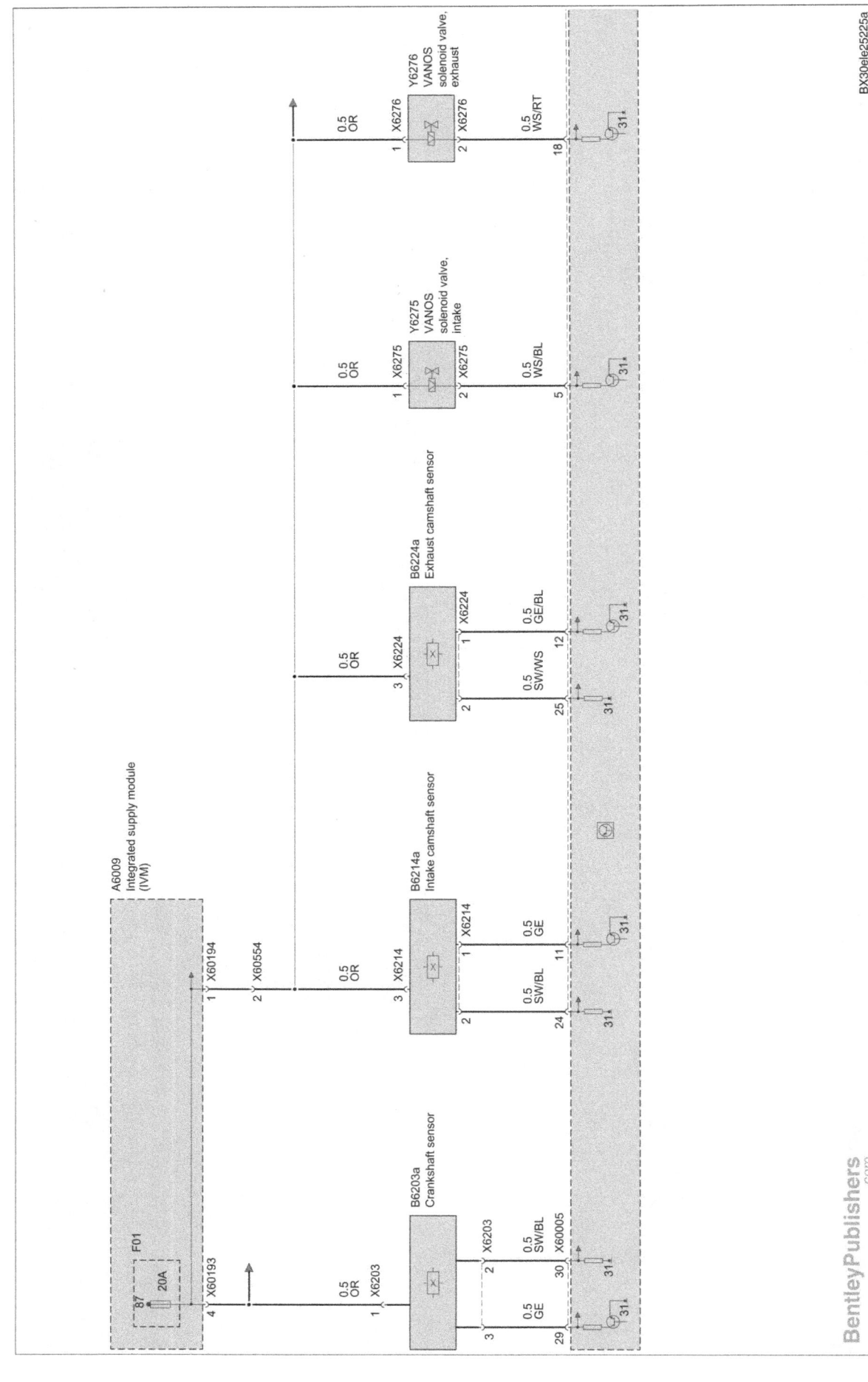

BX30ele25225a

Valve gear (Camshaft sensors, VANOS solenoids, Eccentric shaft sensor, Relay, Actuator varible valve timing gear) N52 engine (2 of 2)

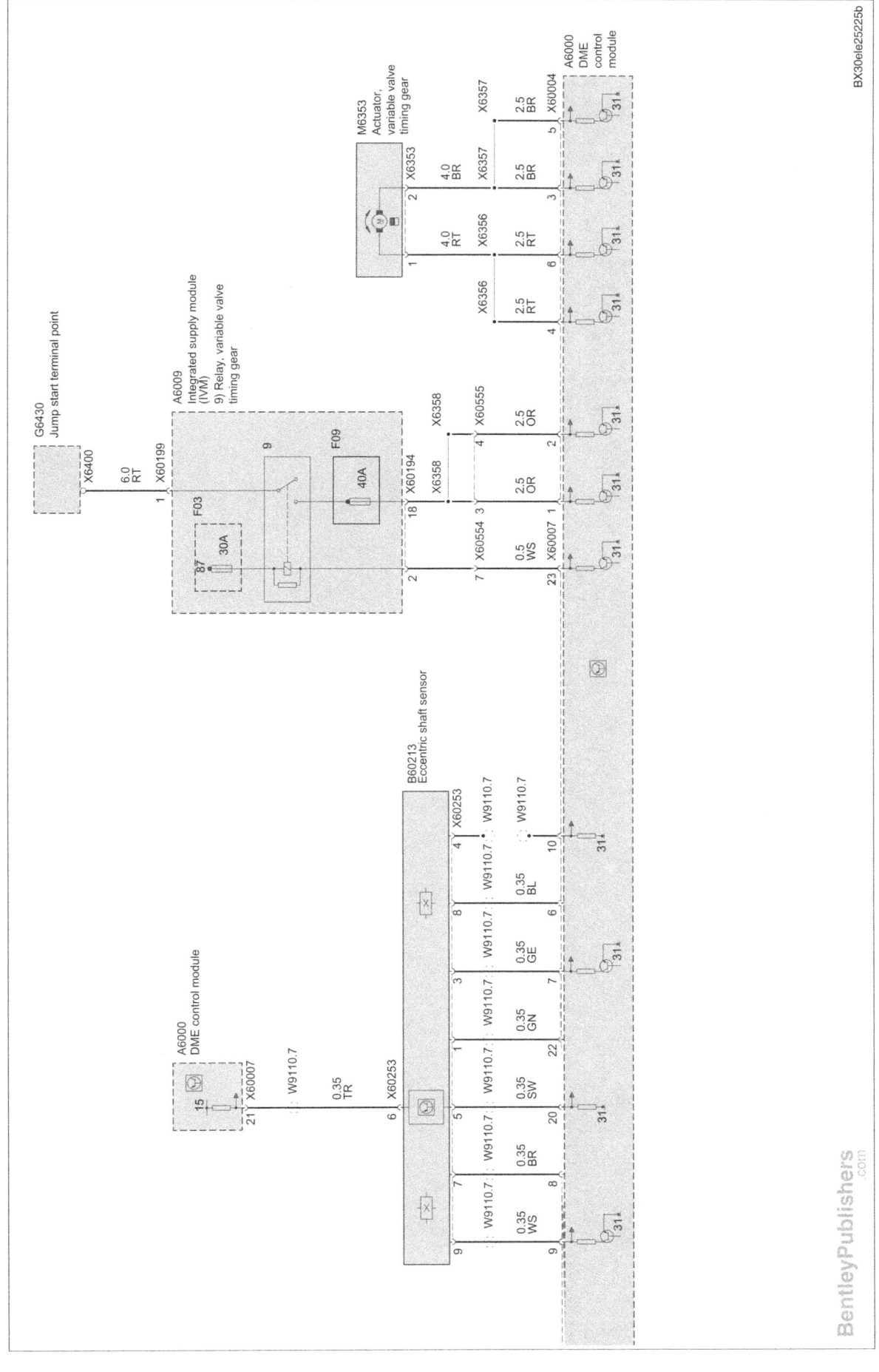

BX30ele25225b

Clutch switch
(M54 engine)

VANOS solenoid valves
M54 engine

A836 — Electronic vehicle immobilizer (EWS)

A41 — Power distribution
F9 — 5A — R

A6000 — DME control module

S805 — Clutch switch

BX30ele23146

X1659 — 6

0.35 BL/SW — X13635 — 4

X10016 — 18

0.5 VI/GE — 3

X60004 — 15 — 23

0.35 BL/BR — X13635 — 2 — 1 — 0.35 BR/SW — X217

A8680 — Fuse carrier, engine electronics
F02 — 30A — 87

X8680 — 4

0.5 RT/WS/GE

0.5 RT/WS — X6276 — 1

Y6276 — VANOS solenoid valve, exhaust

X6276 — 2 — 0.5 GN/VI — X60003 — 9 — 31

Y6275 — VANOS solenoid valve, intake

X6275 — 1 — 2 — X6275 — 0.5 GN/BL — X60003 — 10 — 31

A6000 — DME control module

BX30ele18091

Diagnostic module for Fuel tank leakage (M54 engine)

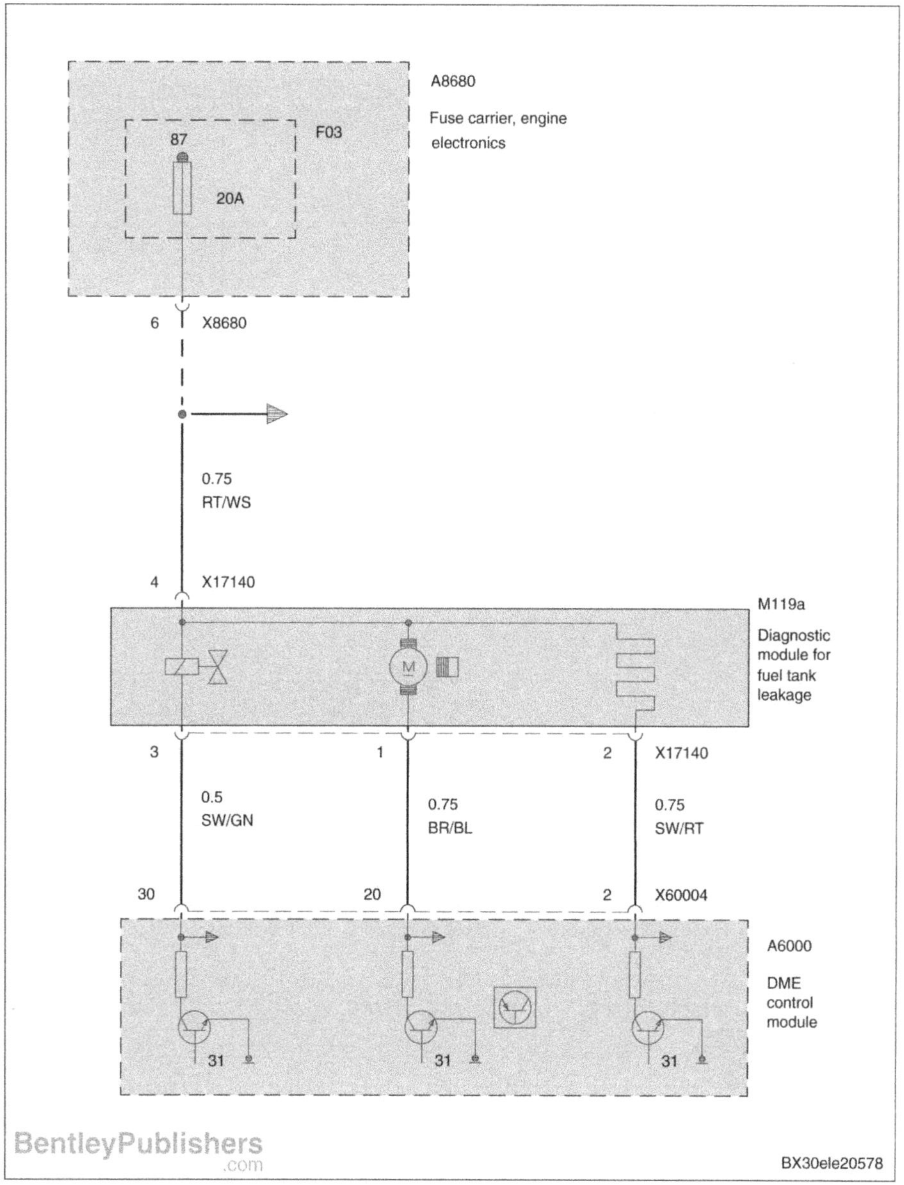

A8680 Fuse carrier, engine electronics

F03

20A

87

X8680

6

0.75 RT/WS

X17140

4

M119a Diagnostic module for fuel tank leakage

M

2

X17140

0.75 SW/RT

X60004

2

1

0.75 BR/BL

20

3

0.5 SW/GN

30

A6000 DME control module

31

31

31

BX30ele20578

Crankshaft position sensor (M54 engine)

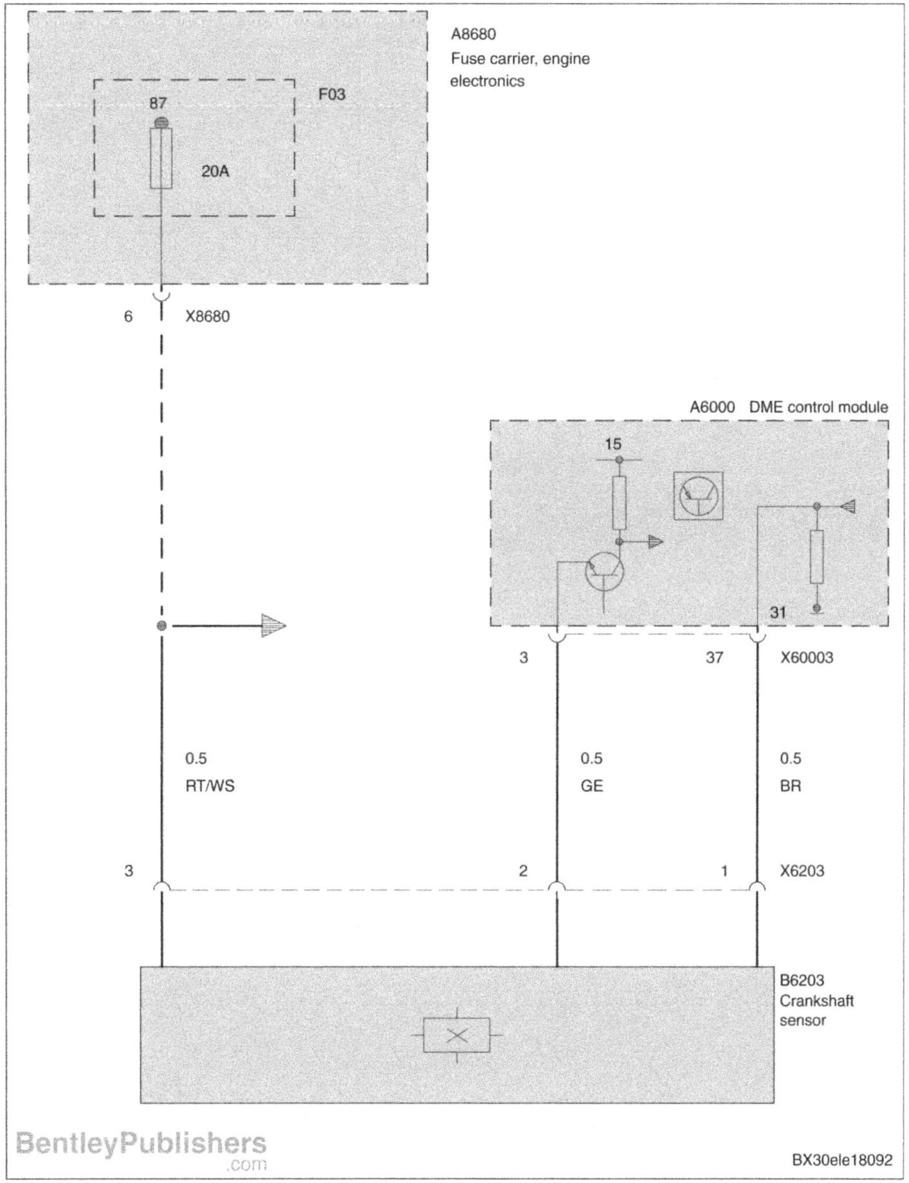

A8680 Fuse carrier, engine electronics

F03

20A

87

X8680

6

0.5 RT/WS

3

A6000 DME control module

31

X60003

37

0.5 BR

X6203

1

15

3

0.5 GE

2

B6203 Crankshaft sensor

X

BX30ele18092

**E-Box fan
(M54 engine)**

**Diagnostic module for Fuel tank leakage
(N52 engine)**

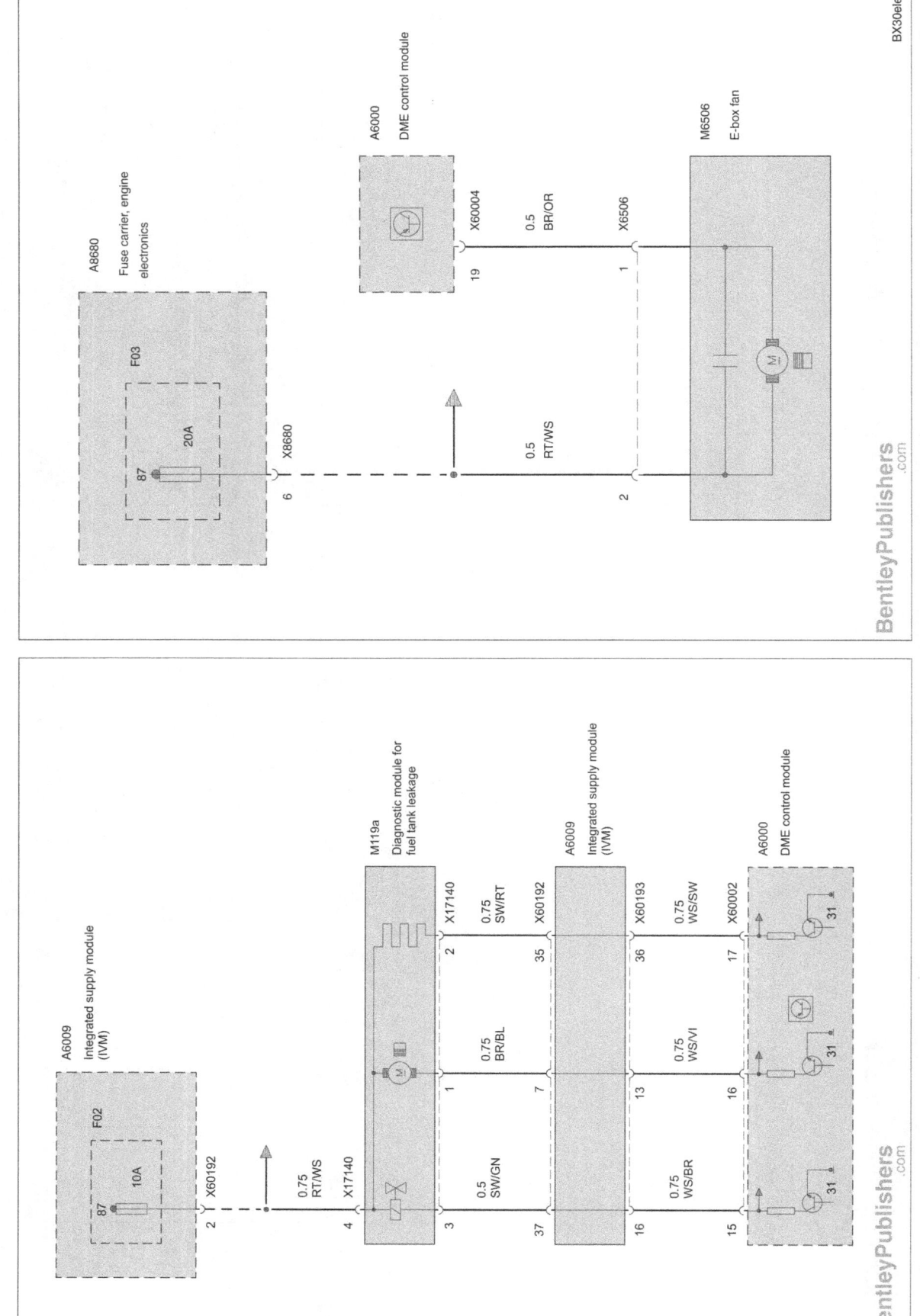

BX30ele20584

**Electronic vehicle immobilizer (EWS)
power supply**

**E-Box fan
(N52 engine)**

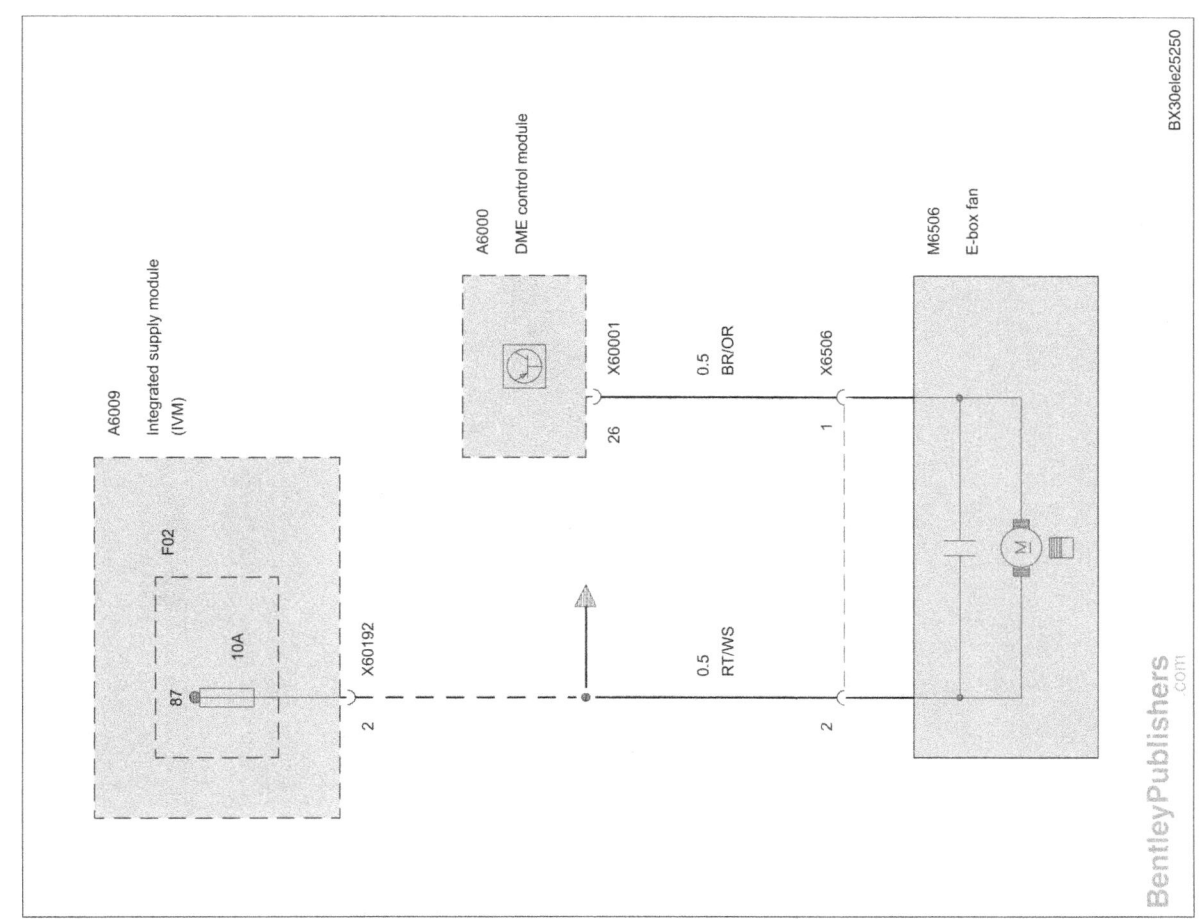

BX30ele20625

BX30ele25250

Electronic vehicle immobilizer interface signals (EWS)

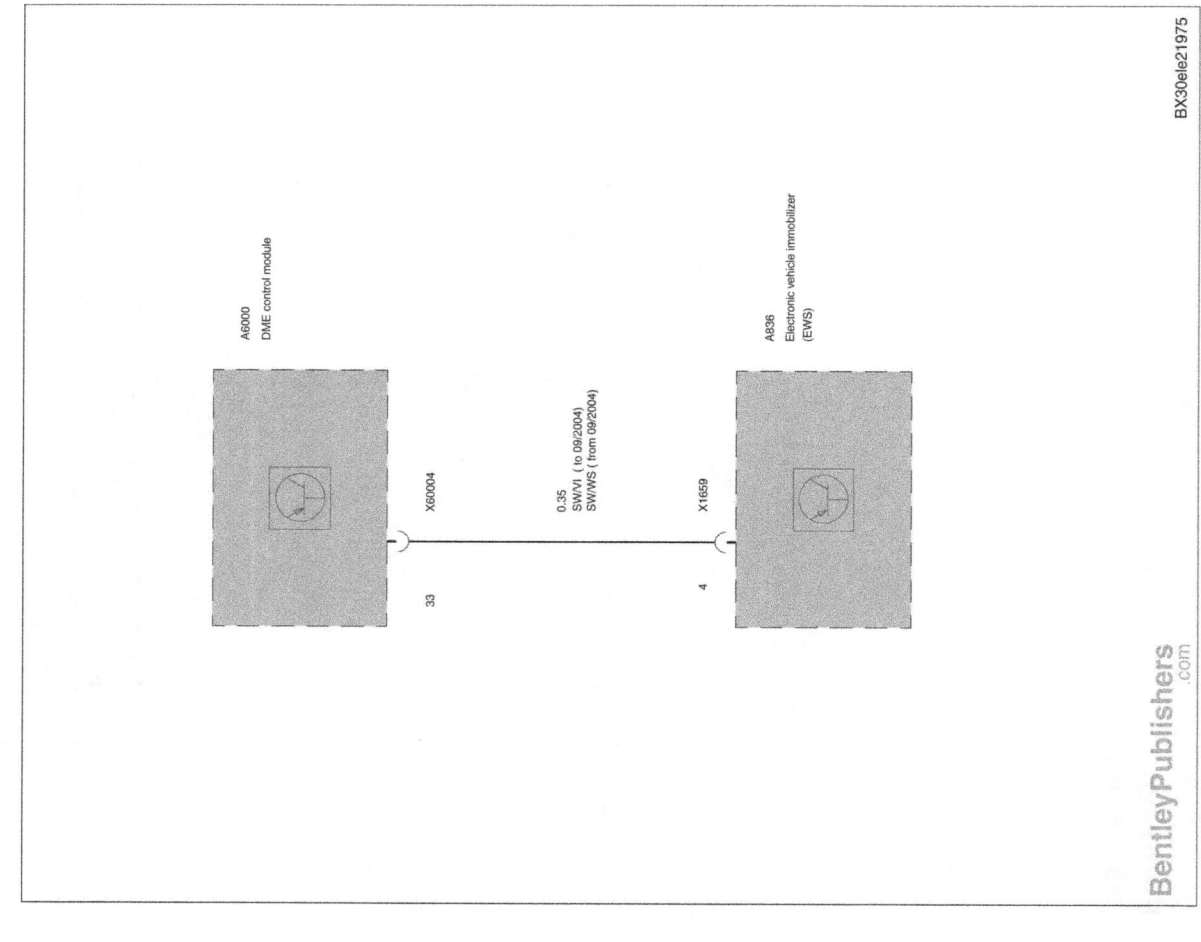

A6000
DME control module

X60004

0.35
SW/VI (to 09/2004)
SW/WS (from 09/2004)

X1659

A836
Electronic vehicle immobilizer
(EWS)

33

4

BX30ele21975

Electronic vehicle immobilizer (EWS)
M54 engine

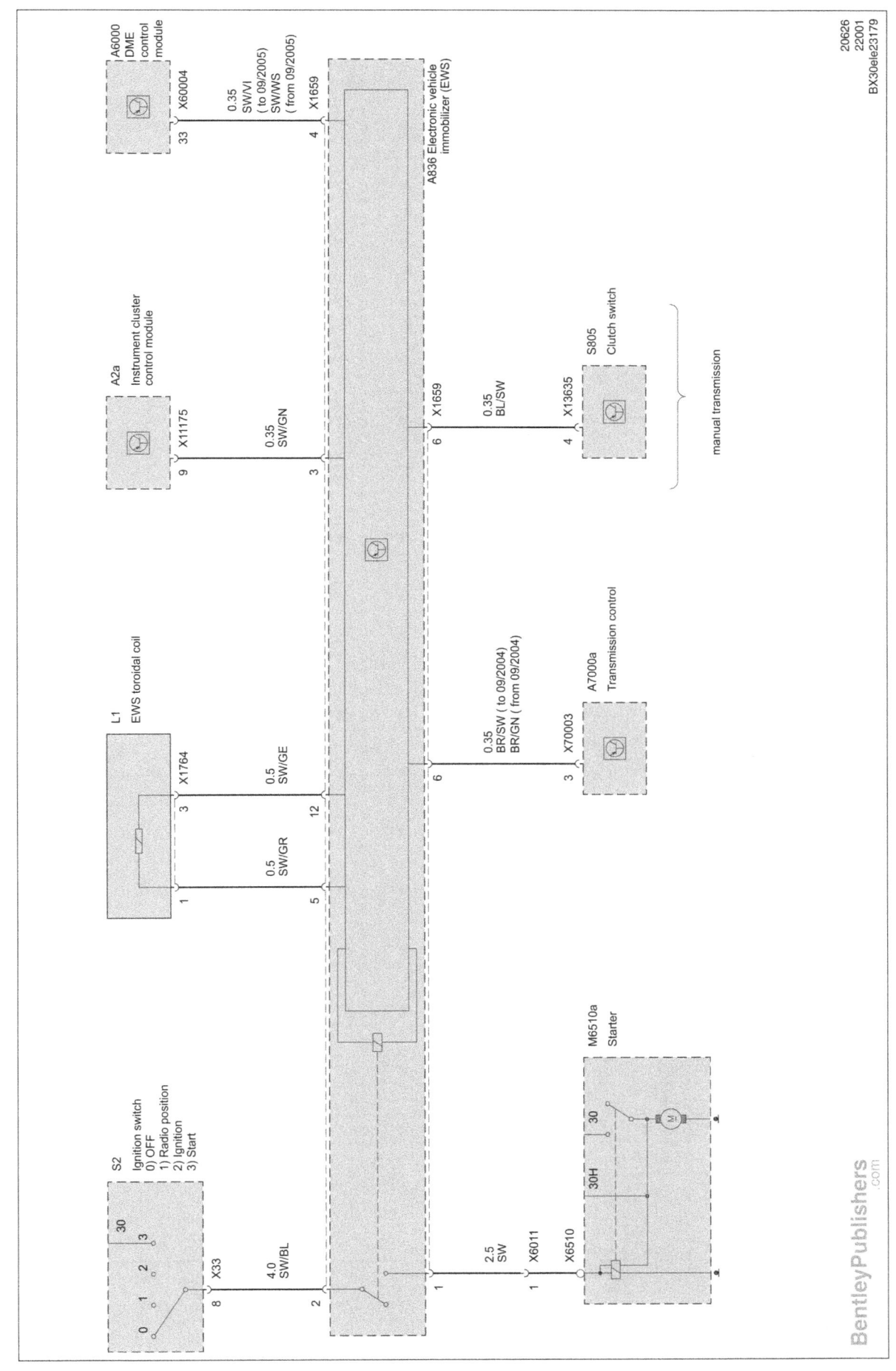

20626
22001
BX30ele23179

Electronic vehicle immobilizer (EWS)
N52 engine

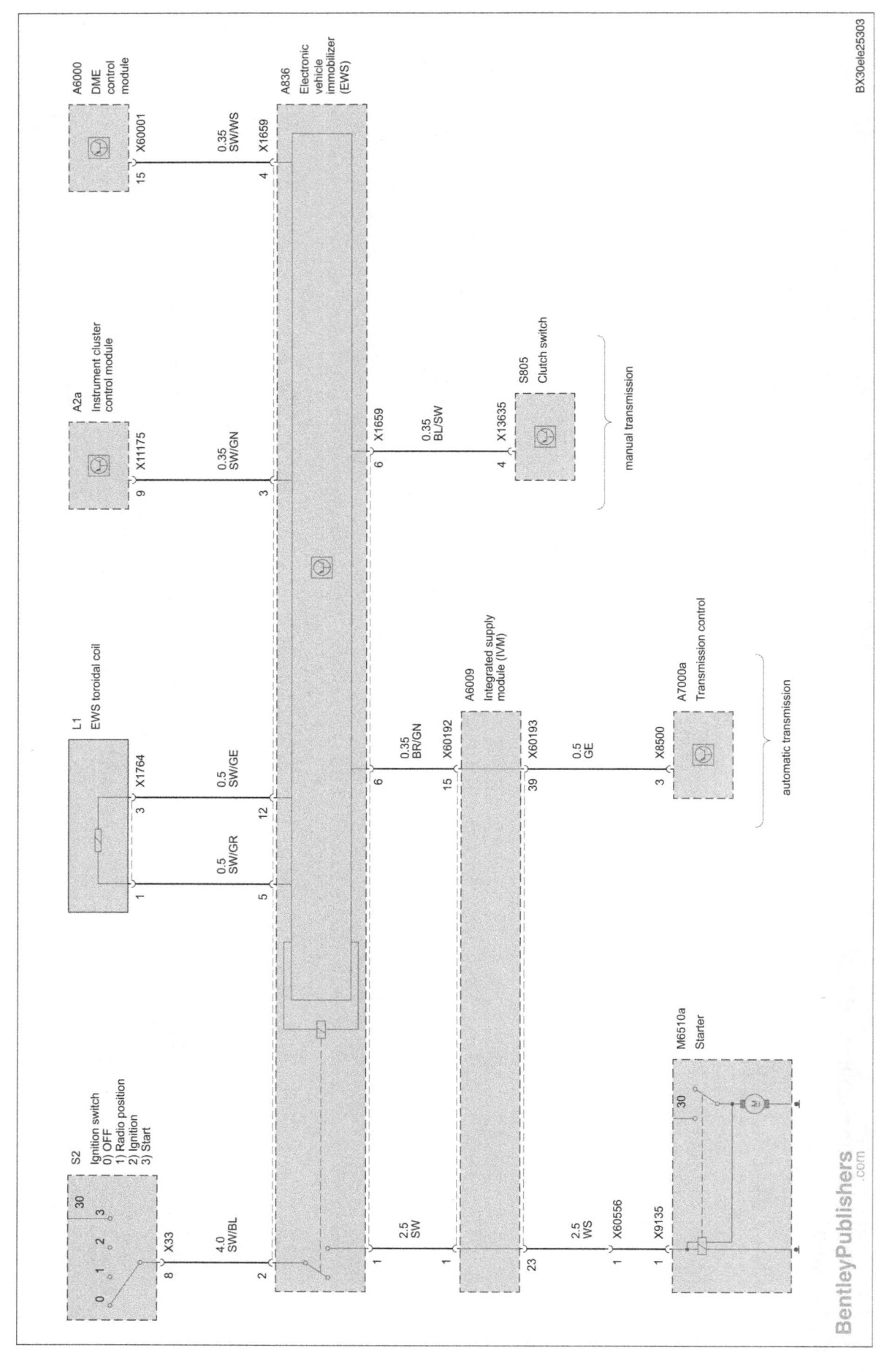

BX30ele25303

Electronic vehicle immobilizer interface signals (EWS)
N52 engine
(to 03 / 2007)

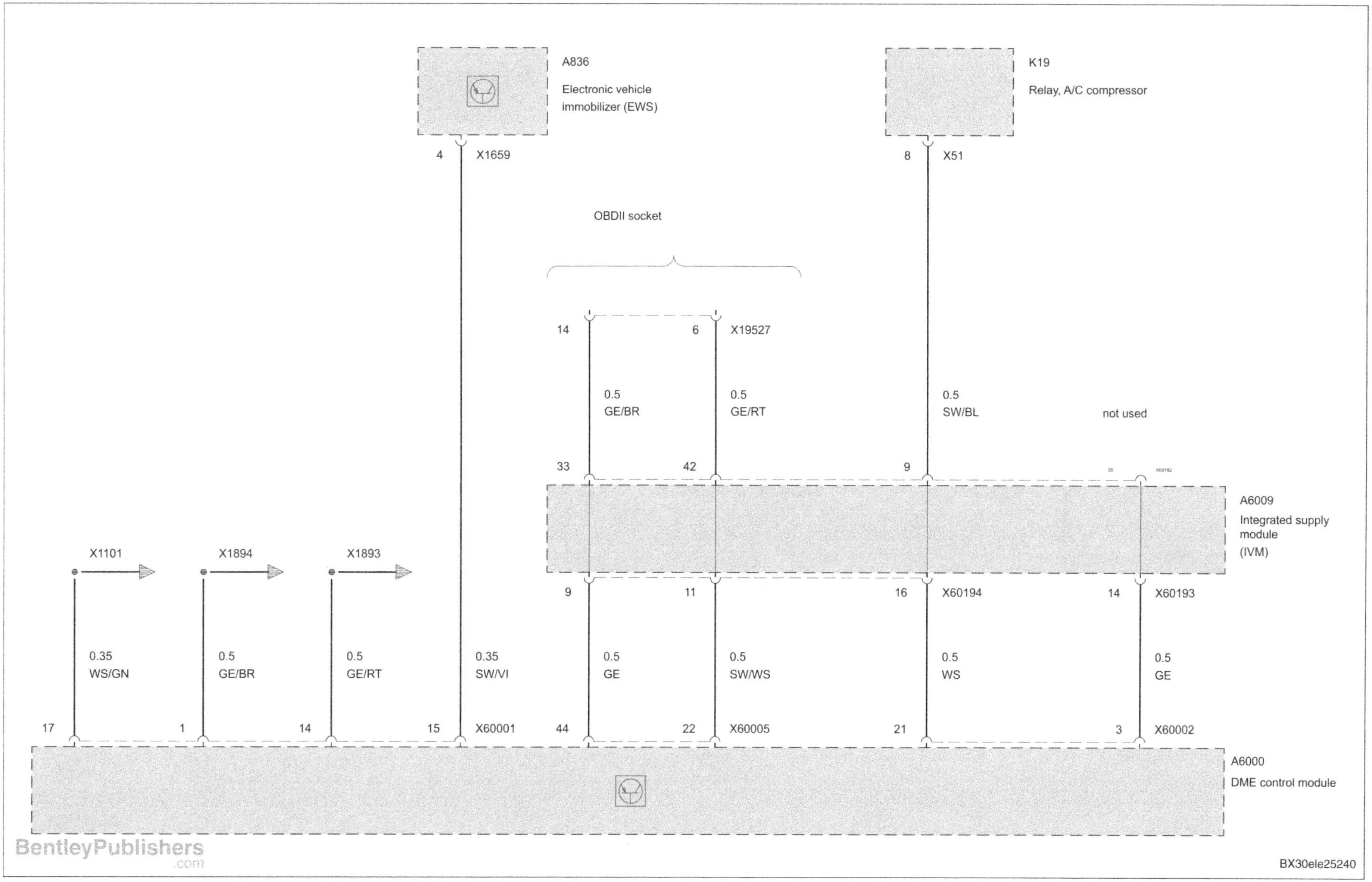

K19
Relay, A/C compressor

A836
Electronic vehicle immobilizer (EWS)

A6009
Integrated supply module (IVM)

A6000
DME control module

OBDII socket

not used

X51 — 8

X1659 — 4

X19527 — 6 — 0.5 GE/RT
14 — 0.5 GE/BR

0.5 SW/BL — 9

0.35 SW/VI — X60001

42 — X60193 — 14 — 0.5 GE
33 — 9

X60194 — 16 — 0.5 WS
11 — X60005 — 0.5 SW/WS
9

0.5 GE — X60002 — 3
21
22
44
15

X1893 — 0.5 GE/RT — 14
X1894 — 0.5 GE/BR — 1
X1101 — 0.35 WS/GN — 17

BX30ele25240

Electronic vehicle immobilizer interface signals (EWS)
N52 engine
(from 03 / 2007)

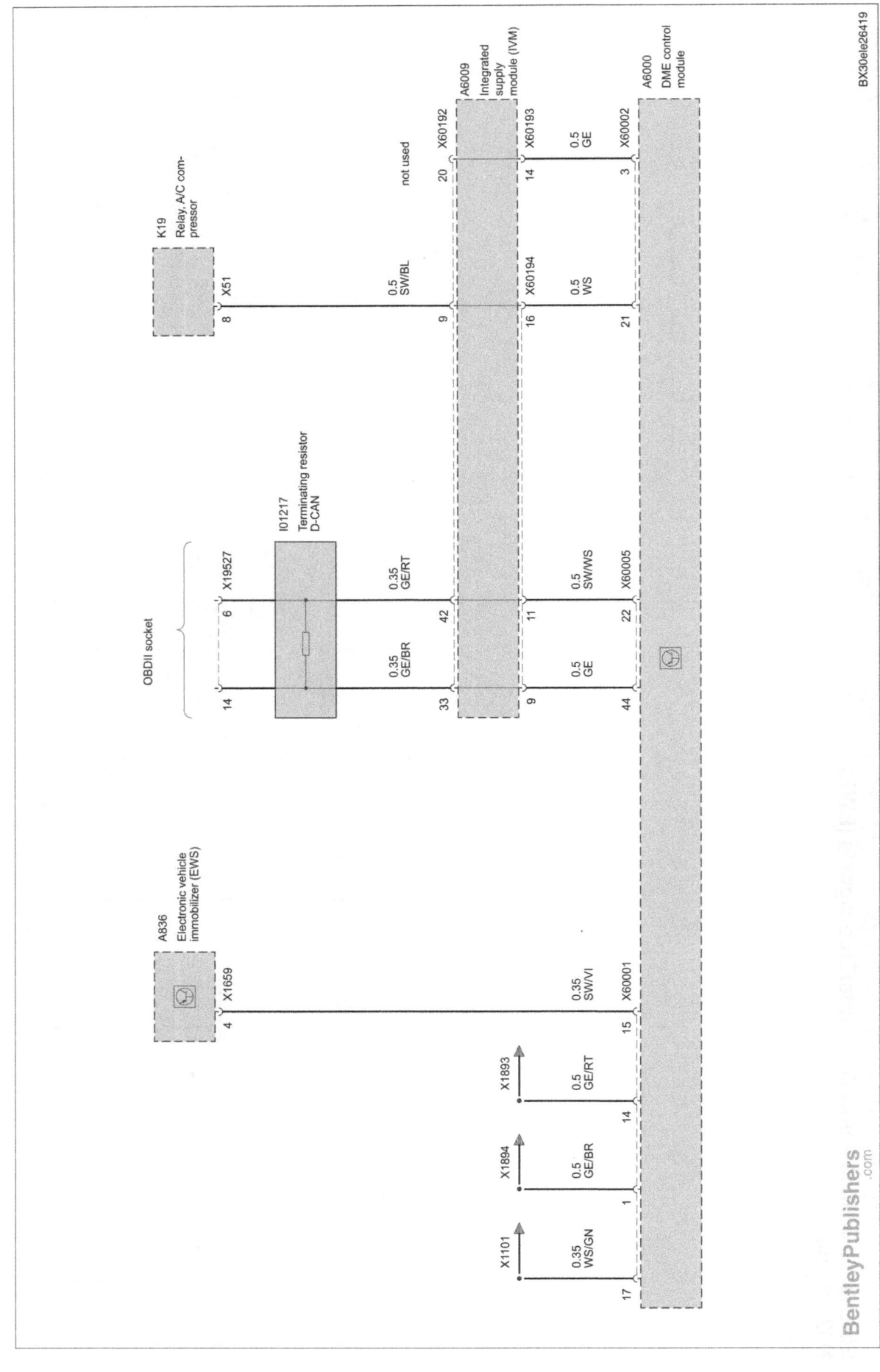

BX30ele26419

DME control module
voltage supply
M54 engine

A8680
Fuse carrier, engine
electronics

F02

30A

87

4 X8680

1.5
RT/WS/GE

A41
Power distribution

F29

5A

15

58 X10016

0.5
GN/VI

F102

80A

30

X2

6.0
RT

A2076
B+ potential distributor

30

1 X18326

1 X64101

1.5
RT

X60001

X19527

9 X60004

0.35
SW

7

0.5
WS/VI

32

X1894

0.5
GE/BR

37

X1893

0.5
GE/RT

36

26

31

31

X60005

31

5

2.5
BR

X60541

X6454

2

X60001

31

6

1.5
BR

X6458

31

5

1.5
BR

X6458

7

31

8

31

31

4

1.5
BR/OR

manual transmission

X6454

automatic transmission

X6459

A6000
DME control module

17

X6454

BentleyPublishers.com

Electrical Wiring Diagrams ELE-85

BX30ele20570

DME control module
voltage supply
N52 engine

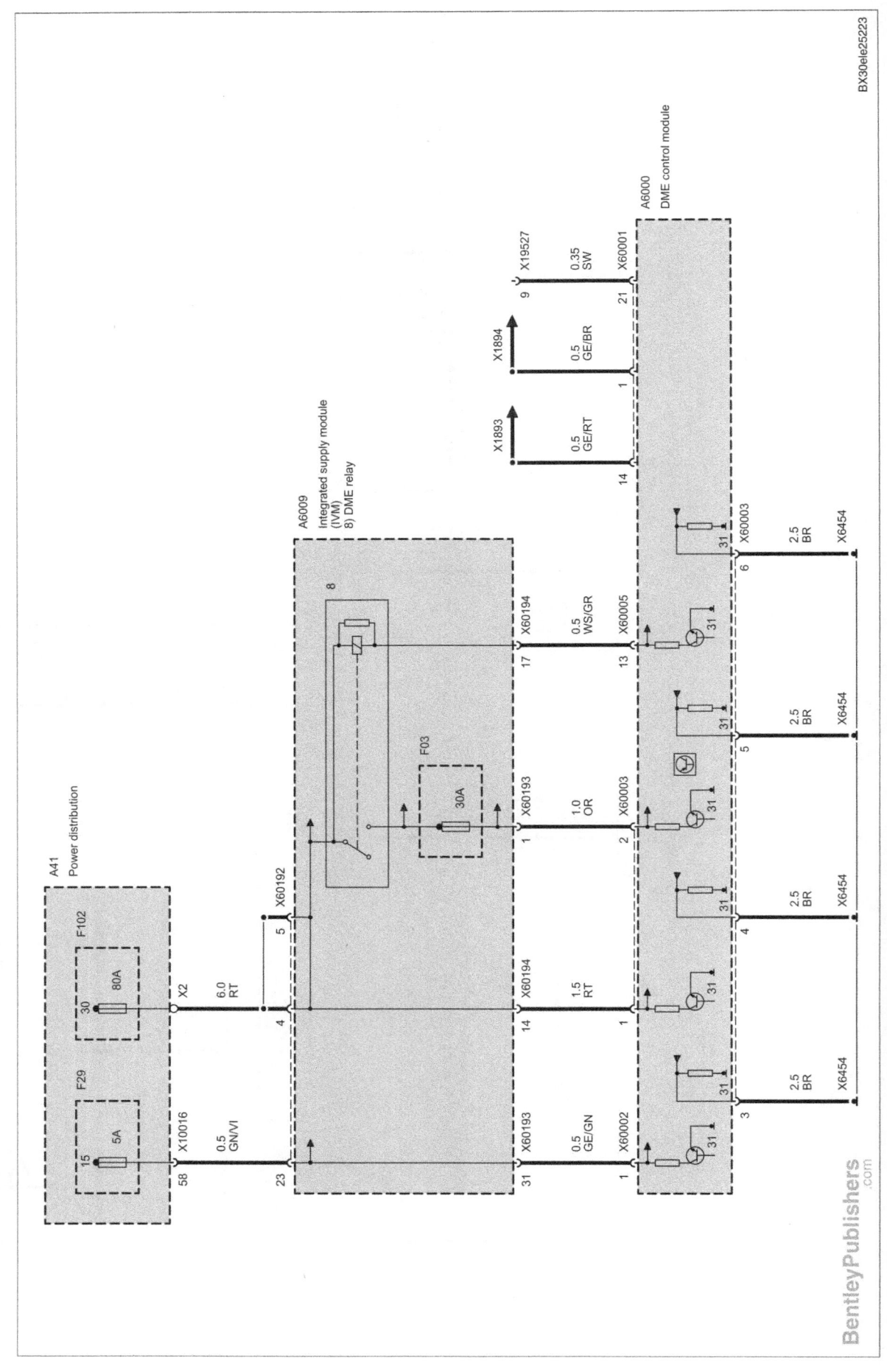

BX30ele25223

Exhaust flap
N52 engine

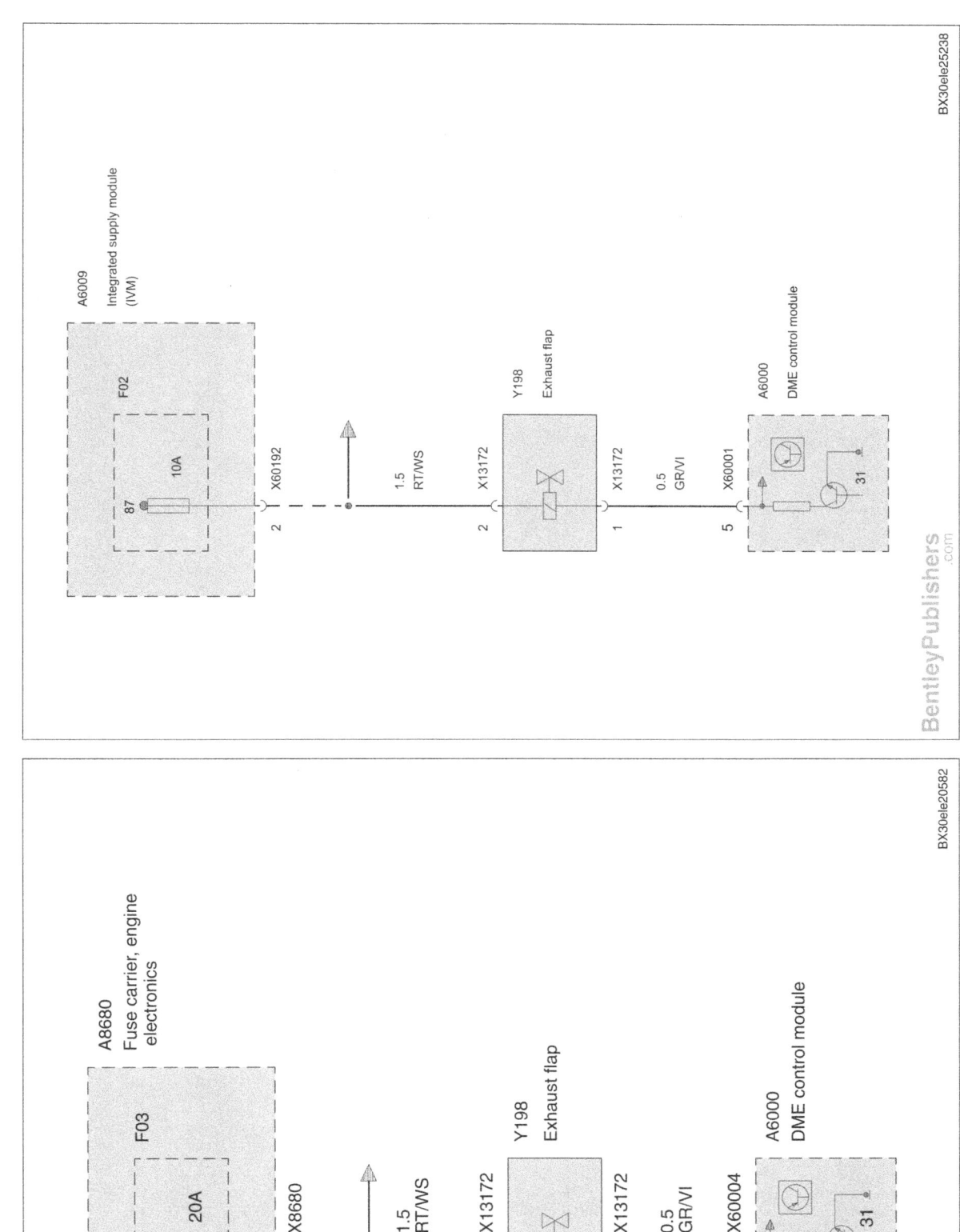

Exhaust flap
M54 engine

BX30ele25238

BX30ele20582

BentleyPublishers
.com

BentleyPublishers
.com

Fuel injectors
M54 engine

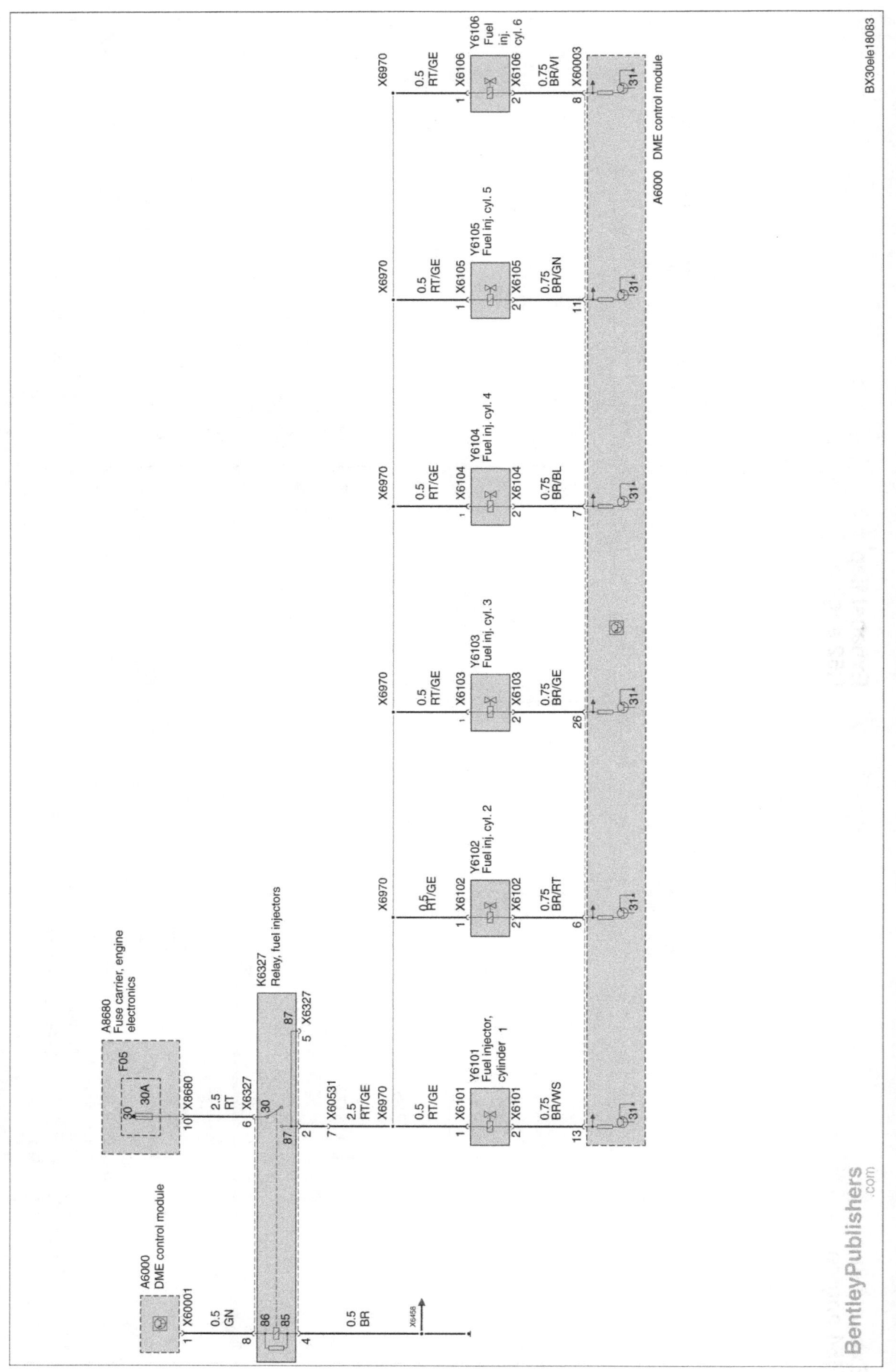

Fuel injectors
N52 engine

BX30ele25231

A41
Power distribution

F102

80A
30

X2

6.0
RT

F29

5A
15

58 X10016

0.5
GN/VI

A6009
Integrated supply module
(IVM)
10) Relay, fuel injectors

X60192

5

4

23

10

F07

20A

20 X60194

1 Y X60554

3 X60193

2.5
OR

Y6101
Fuel injector, cylinder 1

X6970

0.5
OR

1 X6101

X6101

0.75
WS

31

1

1.0
BR

X6454

Y6102
Fuel injector, cylinder 2

X6970

0.5
OR

1 X6102

X6102

0.75
WS/GN

31

2

Y6103
Fuel injector, cylinder 3

X6970

0.5
OR

1 X6103

X6103

0.75
WS/GE

31

3

Y6104
Fuel injector, cylinder 4

X6970

0.5
OR

1 X6104

X6104

0.75
WS/BR

31

14

Y6105
Fuel injector, cylinder 5

X6970

0.5
OR

1 X6105

X6105

0.75
WS/VI

15

Y6106
Fuel inj.
cyl. 6

X6970

0.5
OR

1 X6106

X6106

0.75
WS/SW

16 X60007

A6000 DME control module

**Electrically controlled fuel pump
M54 engine**

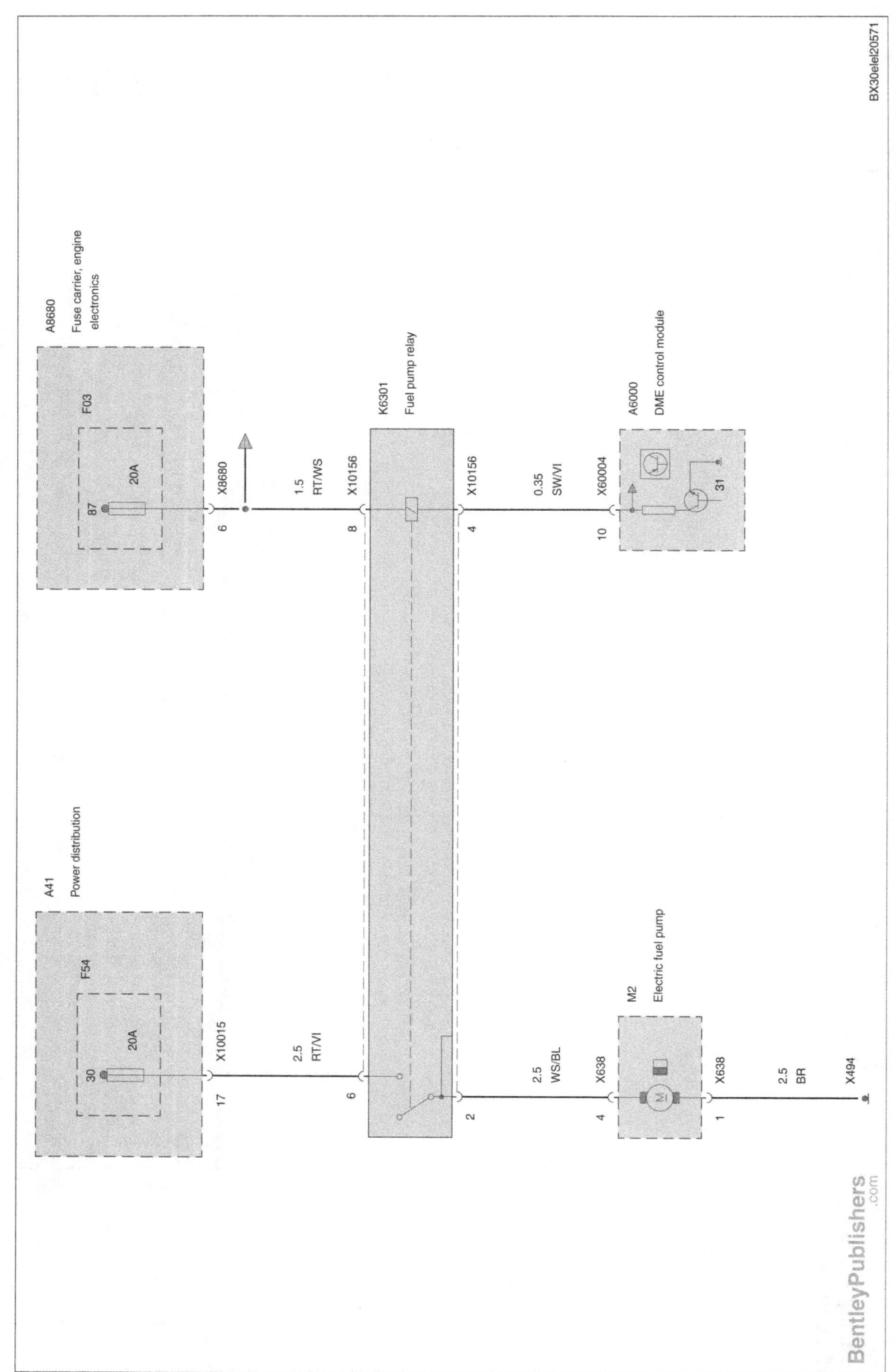

BX30ele20571

Electronically controlled fuel pump (EKPS)
N52 engine

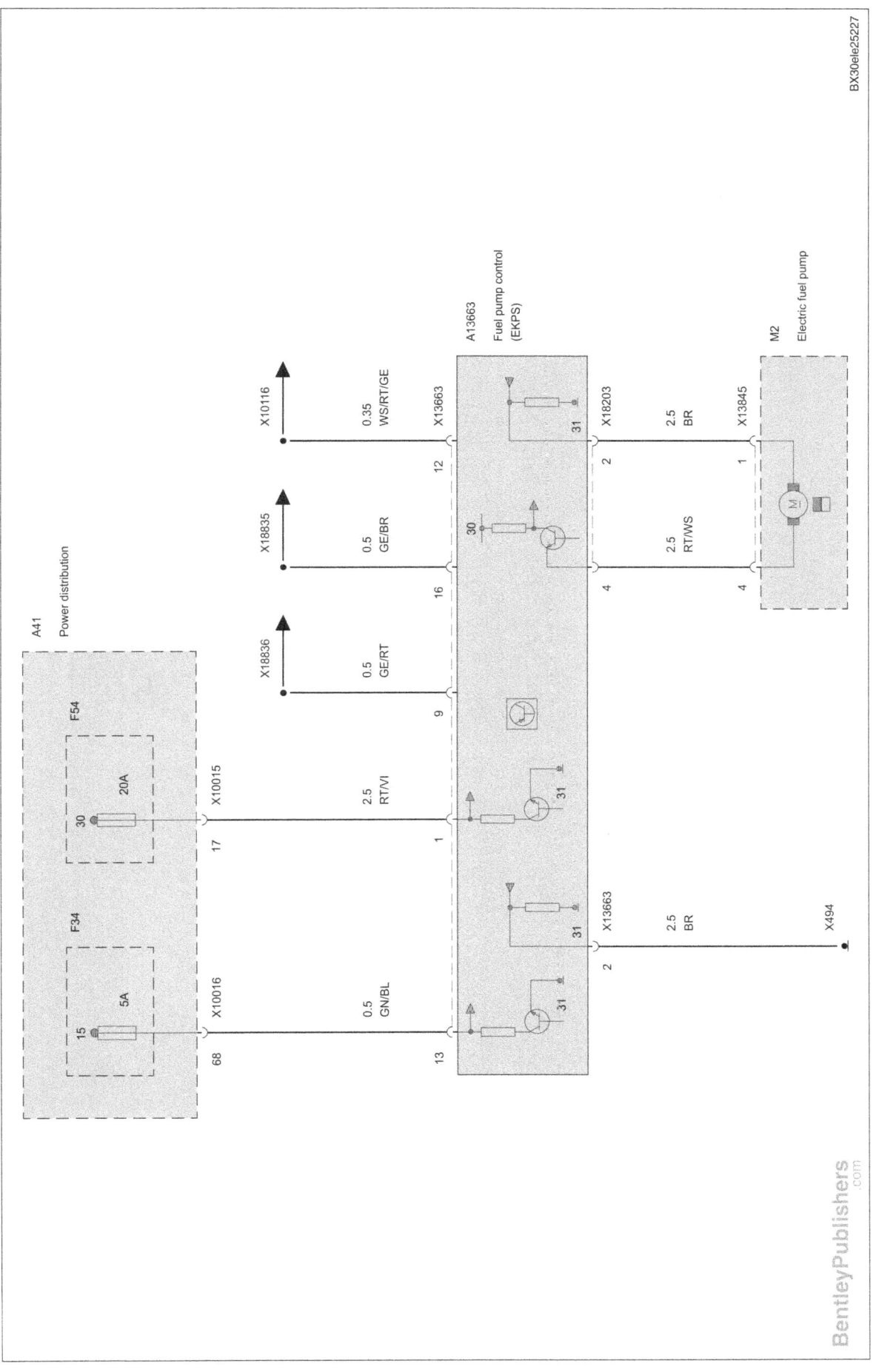

BX30ele25227

**Fuel tanke vent valve
N52 engine**

**Fuel tank vent valve
M54 engine**

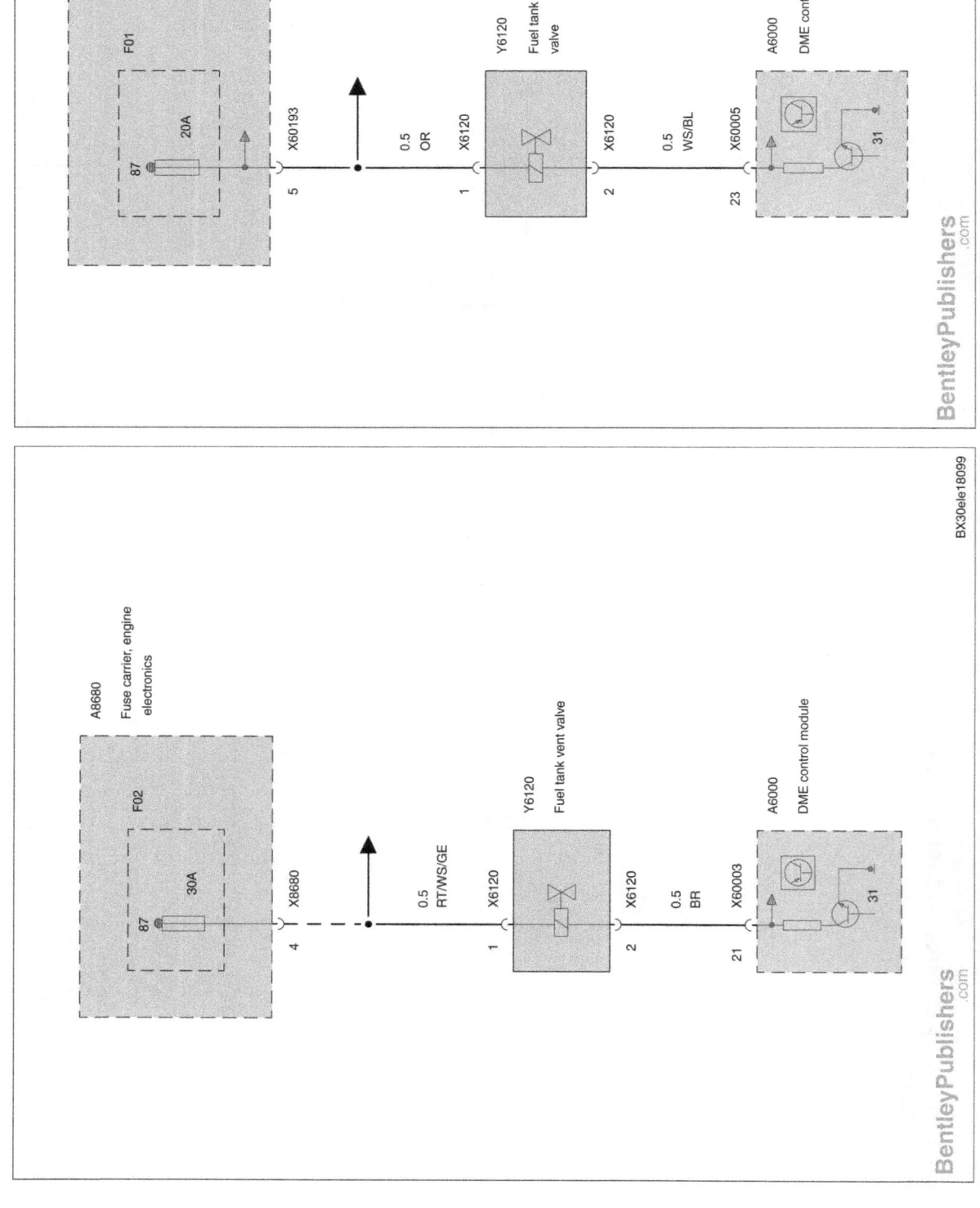

A6009
Integrated supply module (IVM)

F01

20A

87

X60193

5

0.5
OR

X6120

1

Y6120
Fuel tank vent valve

X6120

2

0.5
WS/BL

X60005

23

A6000
DME control module

31

BX30ele23711

A8680
Fuse carrier, engine electronics

F02

30A

87

X8680

4

0.5
RT/WS/GE

X6120

1

Y6120
Fuel tank vent valve

X6120

2

0.5
BR

X60003

21

A6000
DME control module

31

BX30ele18099

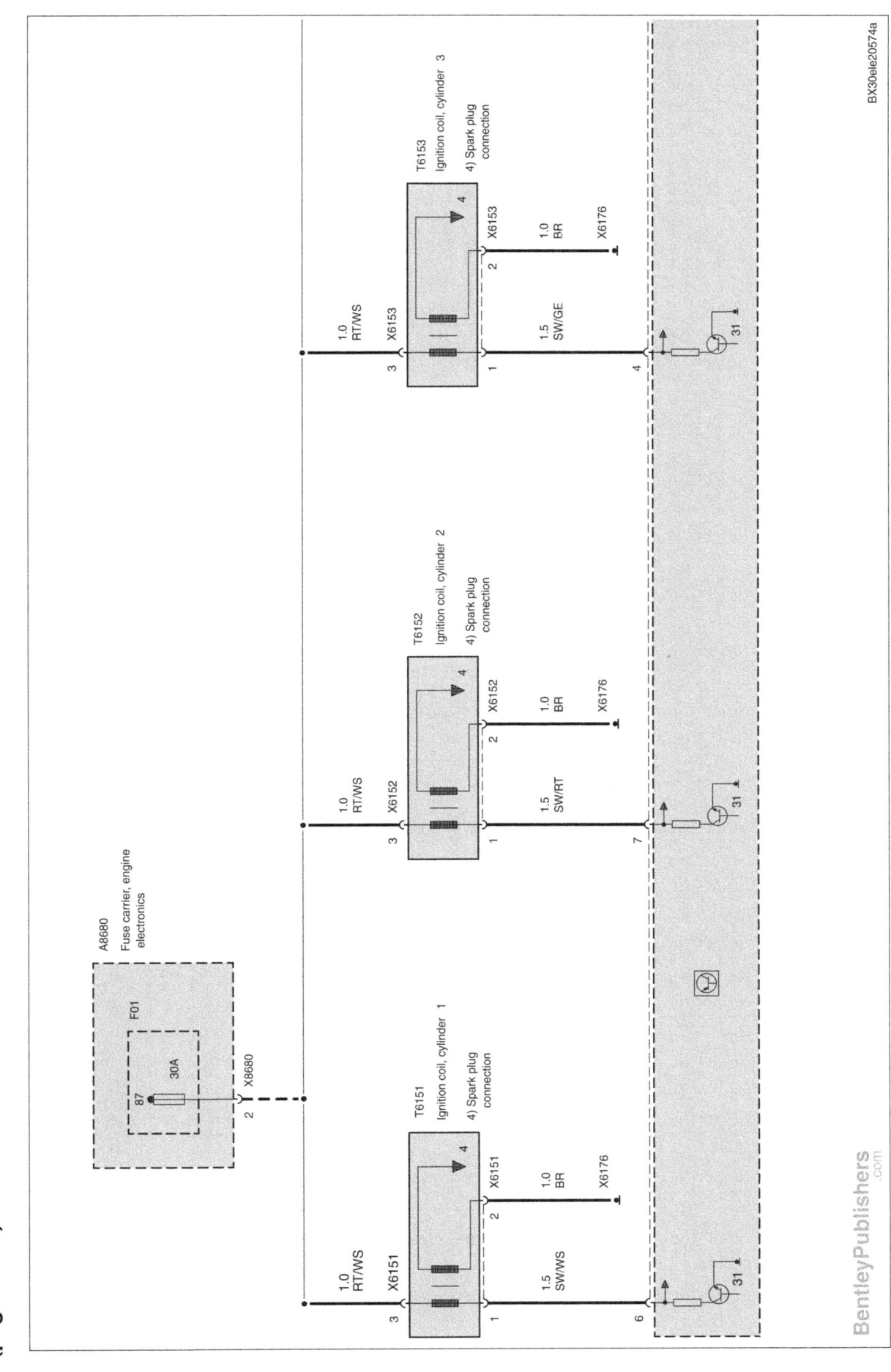

Electrical Wiring Diagrams ELE-94

Ignition coils
M54 engine
(page 2 of 2)

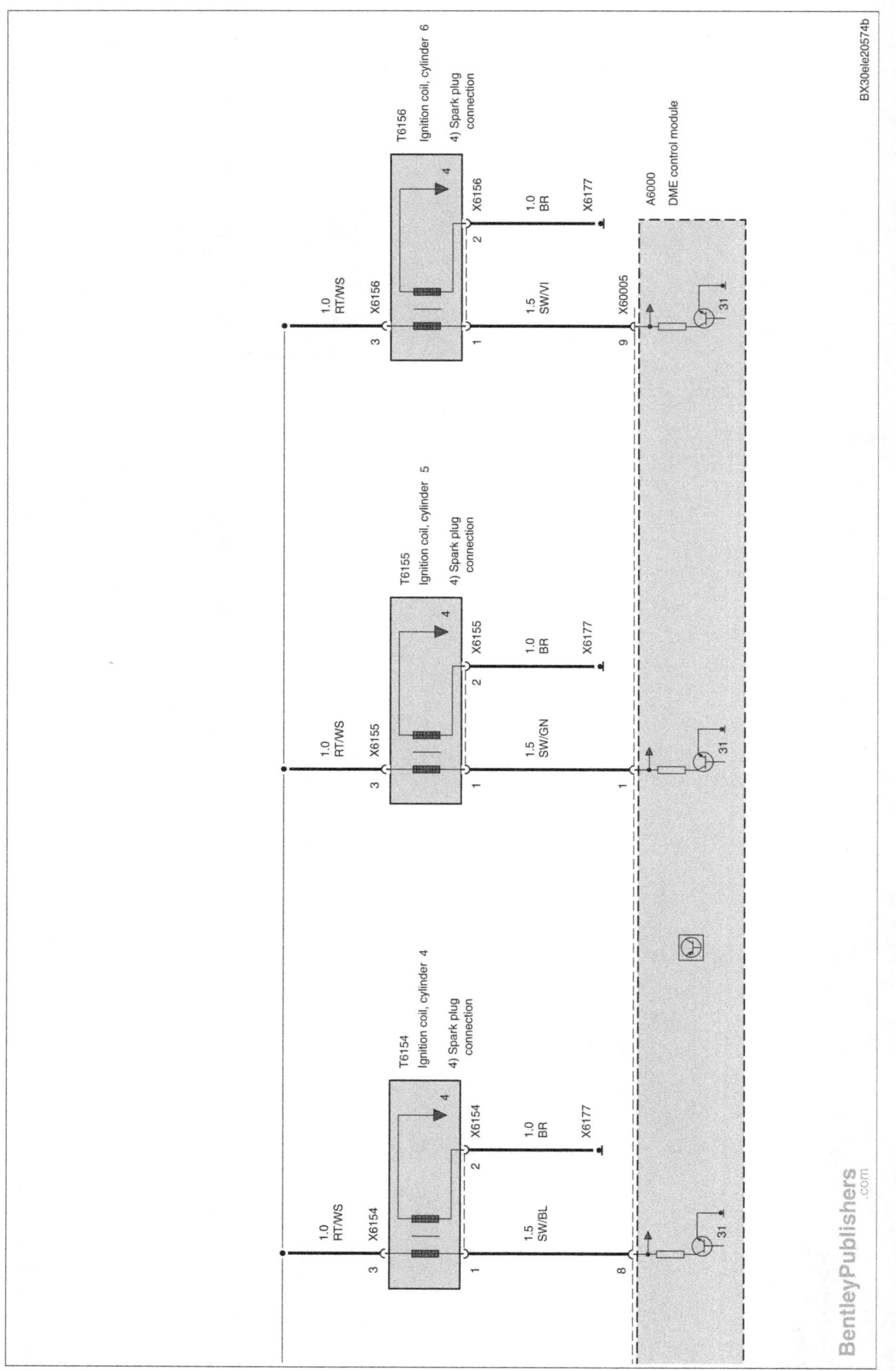

BX30ele20574b

**Ignition coils
N52 engine
(page 1 of 2)**

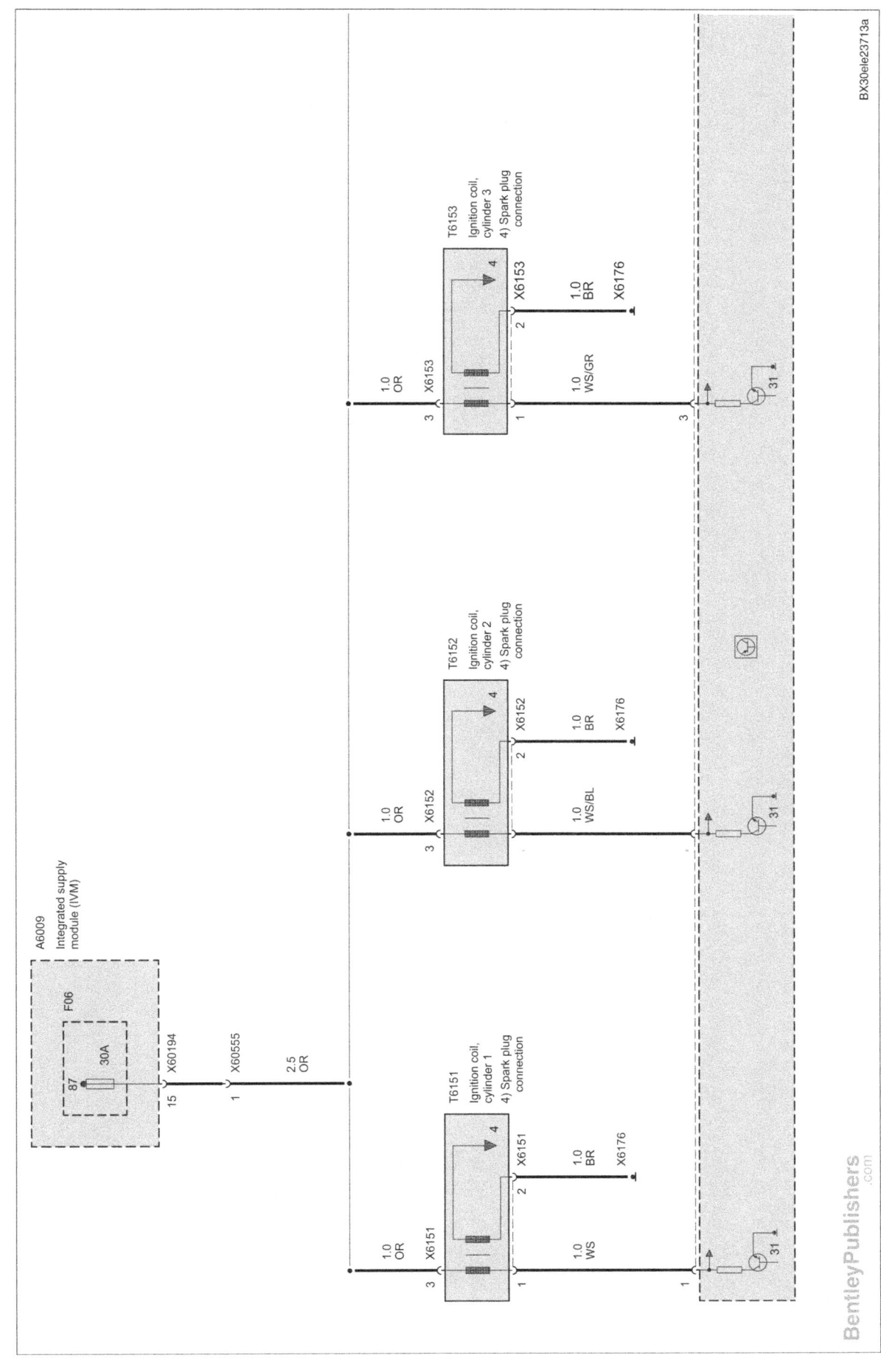

BX30ele2713a

Ignition coils
N52 engine
(page 2 of 2)

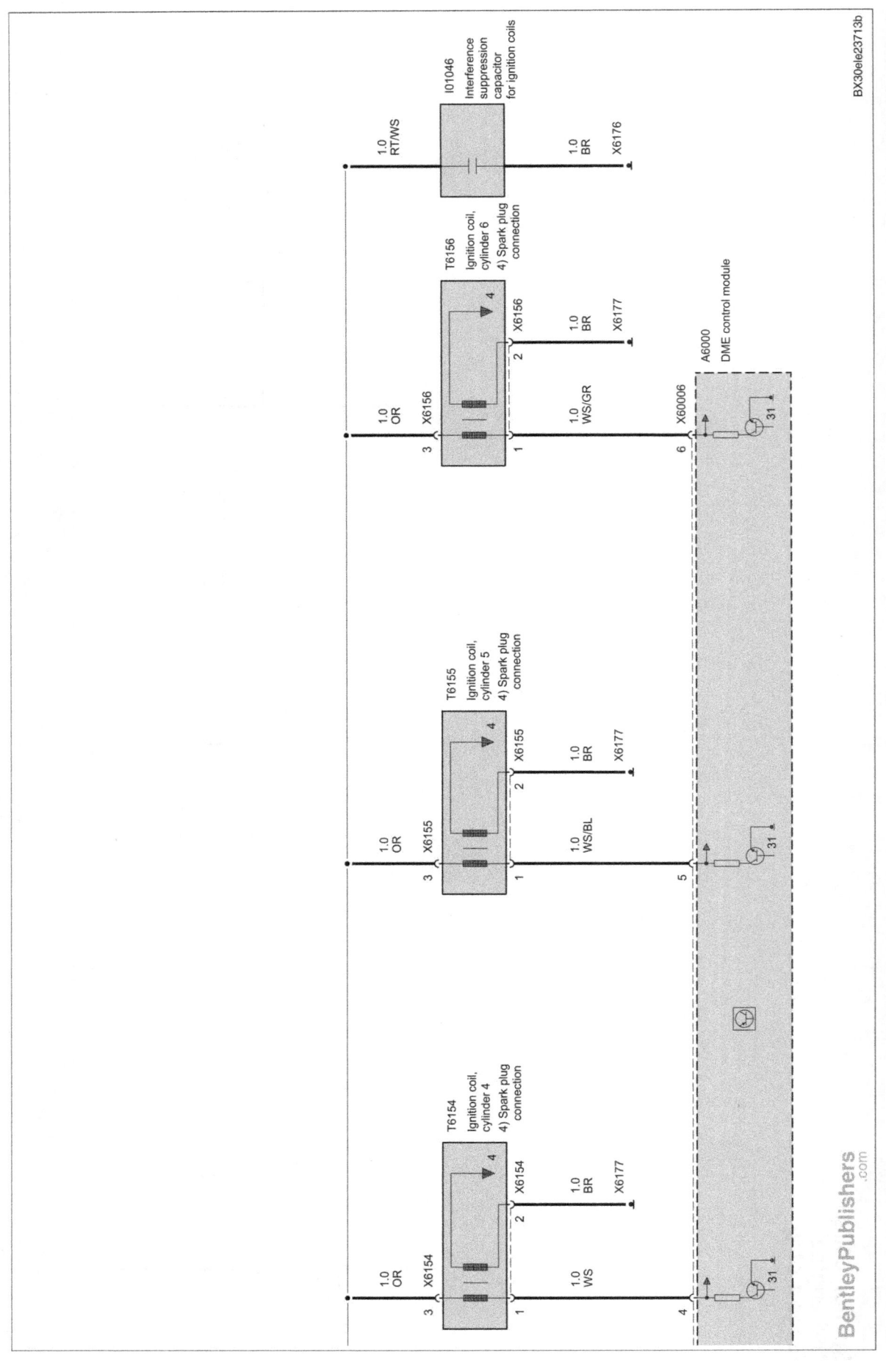

BX30ele23713b

**Double knock sensors
N52 engine**

**Double knock sensors
M54 engine**

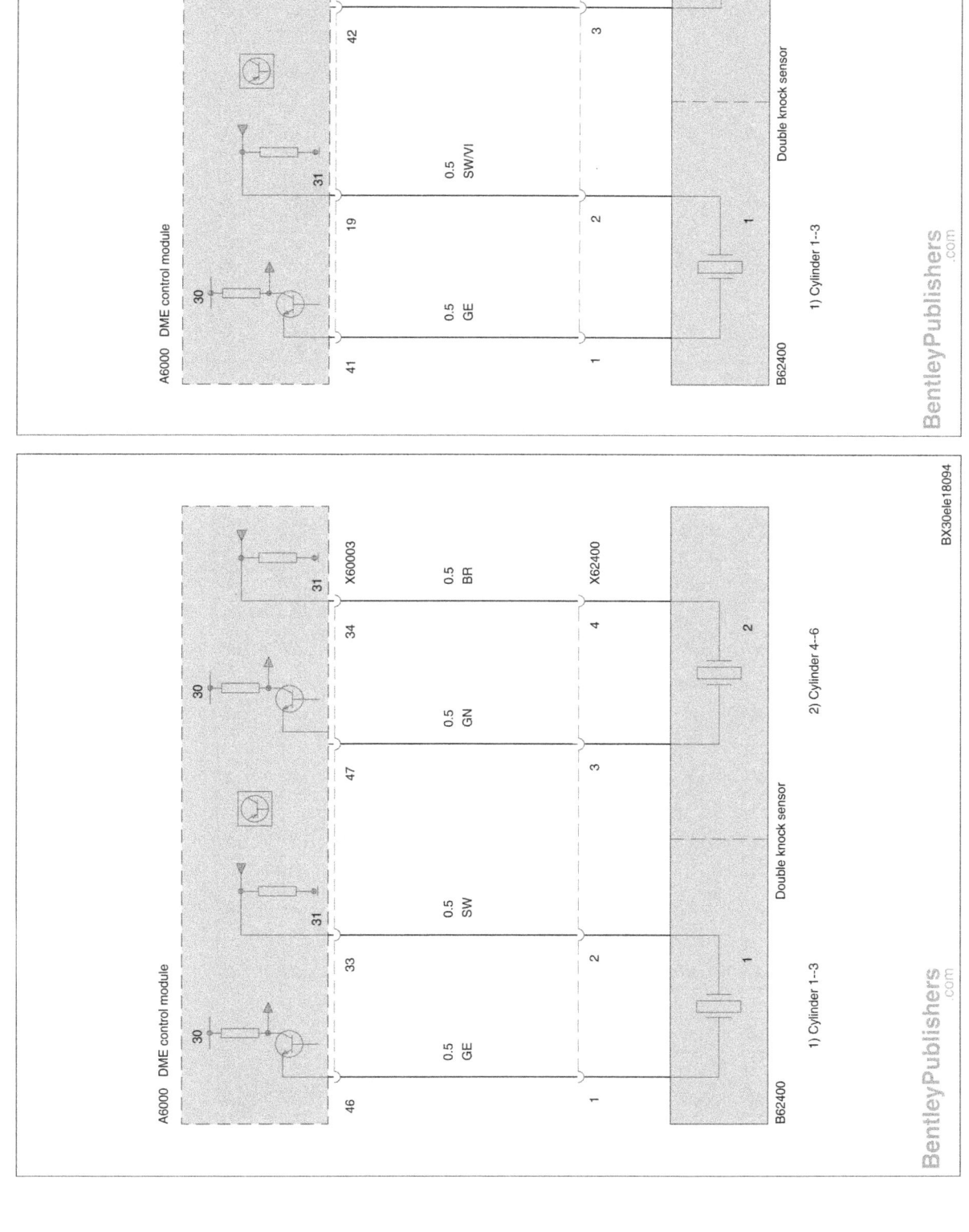

OBD II connector
N52 engine (to 03 / 2007)

OBD II connector
M54 engine

BX30ele25193

BX30ele21955

OBD II connector
N52 engine
(from 03 / 2007)

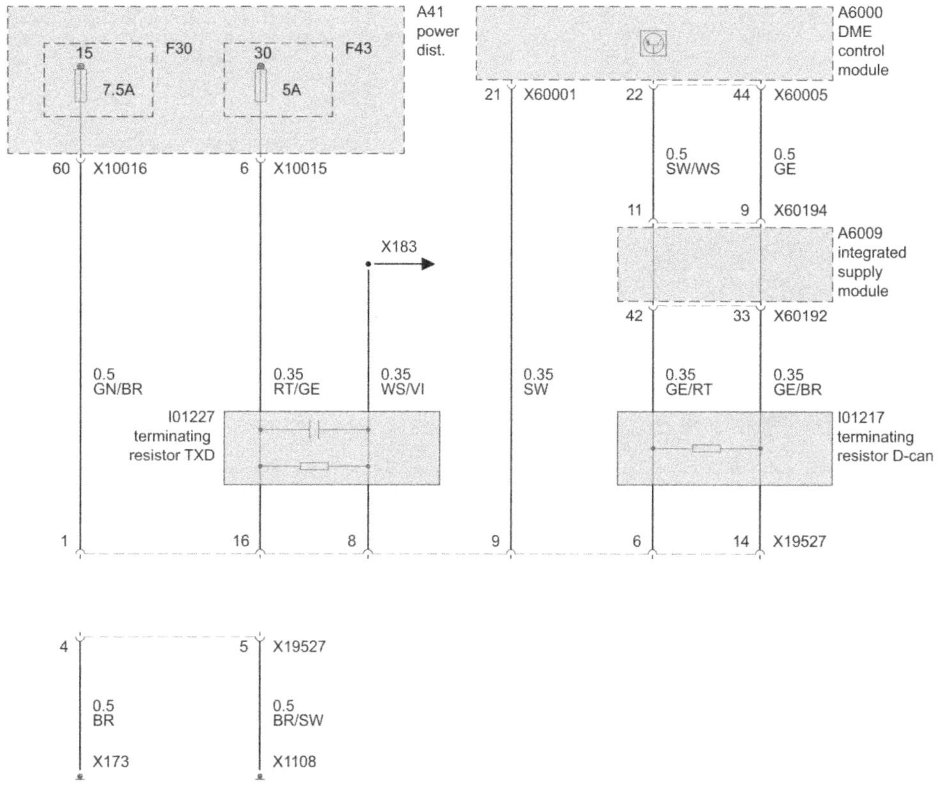

A6000
DME
control
module

X60005

44   0.5
     GE

22   0.5
     SW/WS

X60001

21   0.35
     SW

A6009
integrated
supply
module

X60194

9

11

X60192

33   0.35
     GE/BR

42   0.35
     GE/RT

I01217
terminating
resistor D-can

X19527

14

6

9

A41
power
dist.

F43

30   5A

X10015

6

F30

15   7.5A

X10016

60   0.5
     GN/BR

X183

0.35
WS/VI

8

0.35
RT/GE

I01227
terminating
resistor TXD

16

1

X19527

5   0.5
    BR/SW

X1108

X173

4   0.5
    BR

**Oxygen sensors
before catalytic converters
M54 engine**

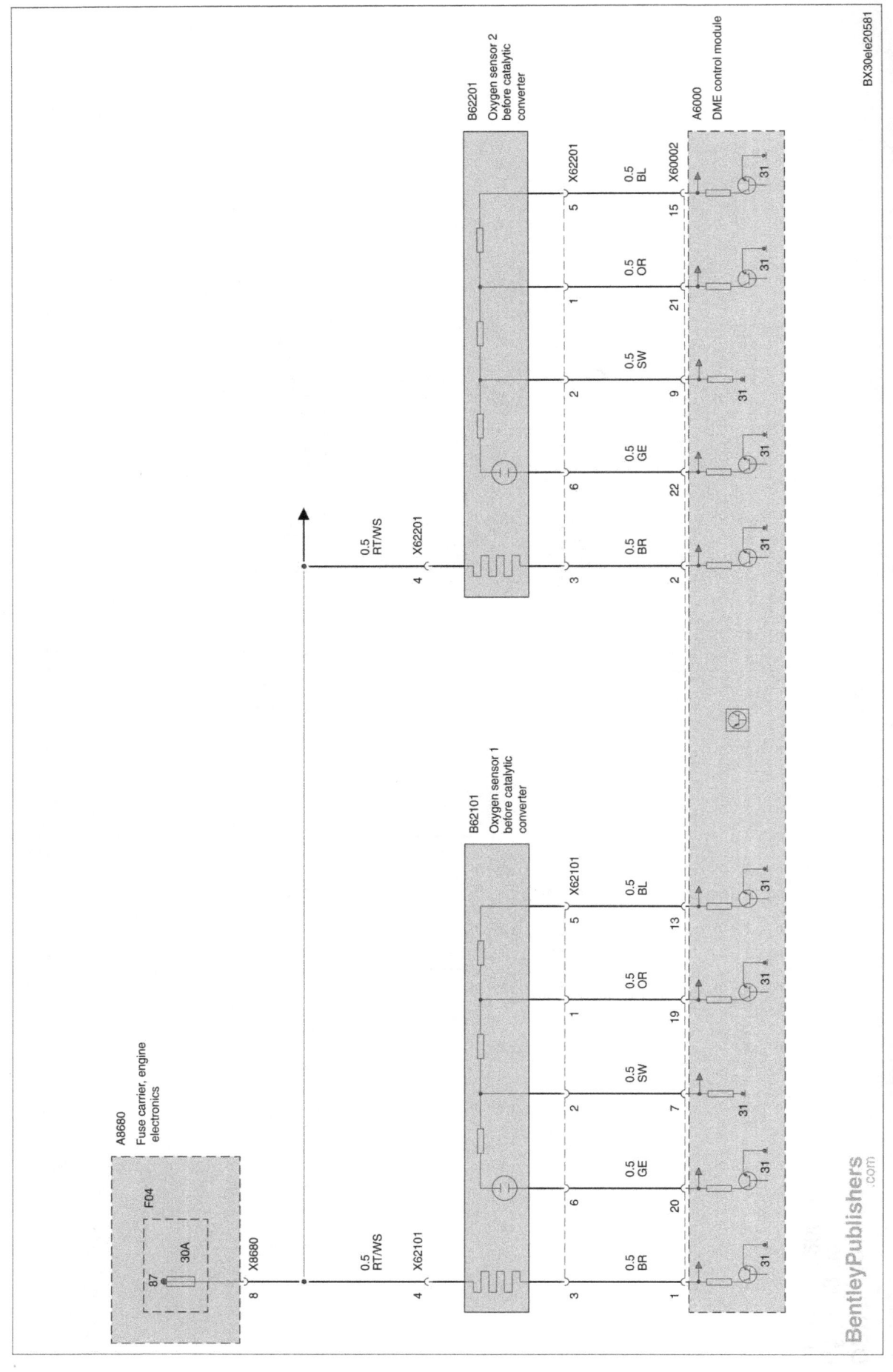

BX30ele20581

**Oxygen sensors
after catalytic converters
M54 engine**

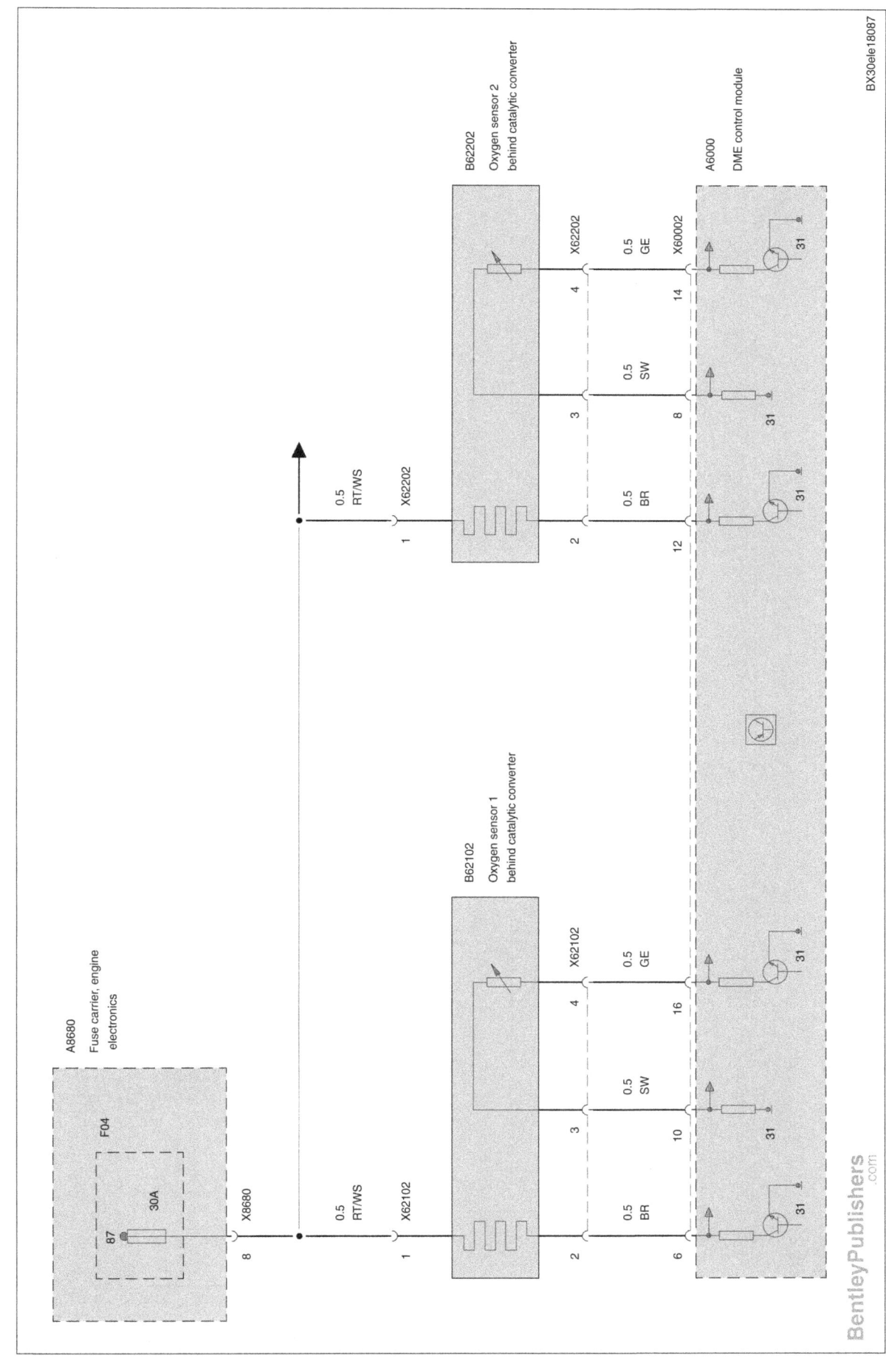

Electrical Wiring Diagrams ELE-101

BX30ele18087

**Oxygen sensors
N52 engine
(page 1 of 2)**

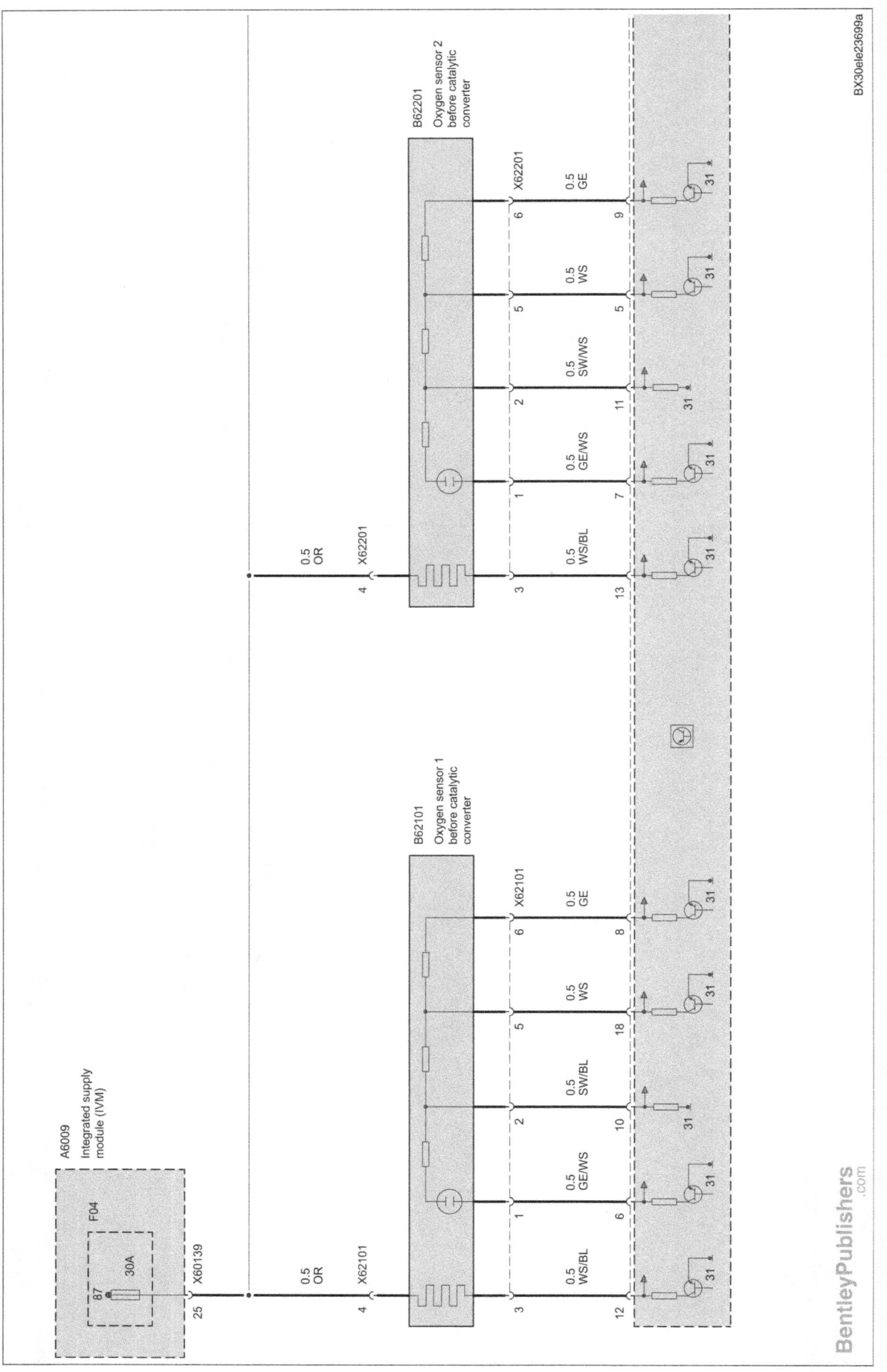

BX30ele23699a

Oxygen sensors
N52 engine
(page 2 of 2)

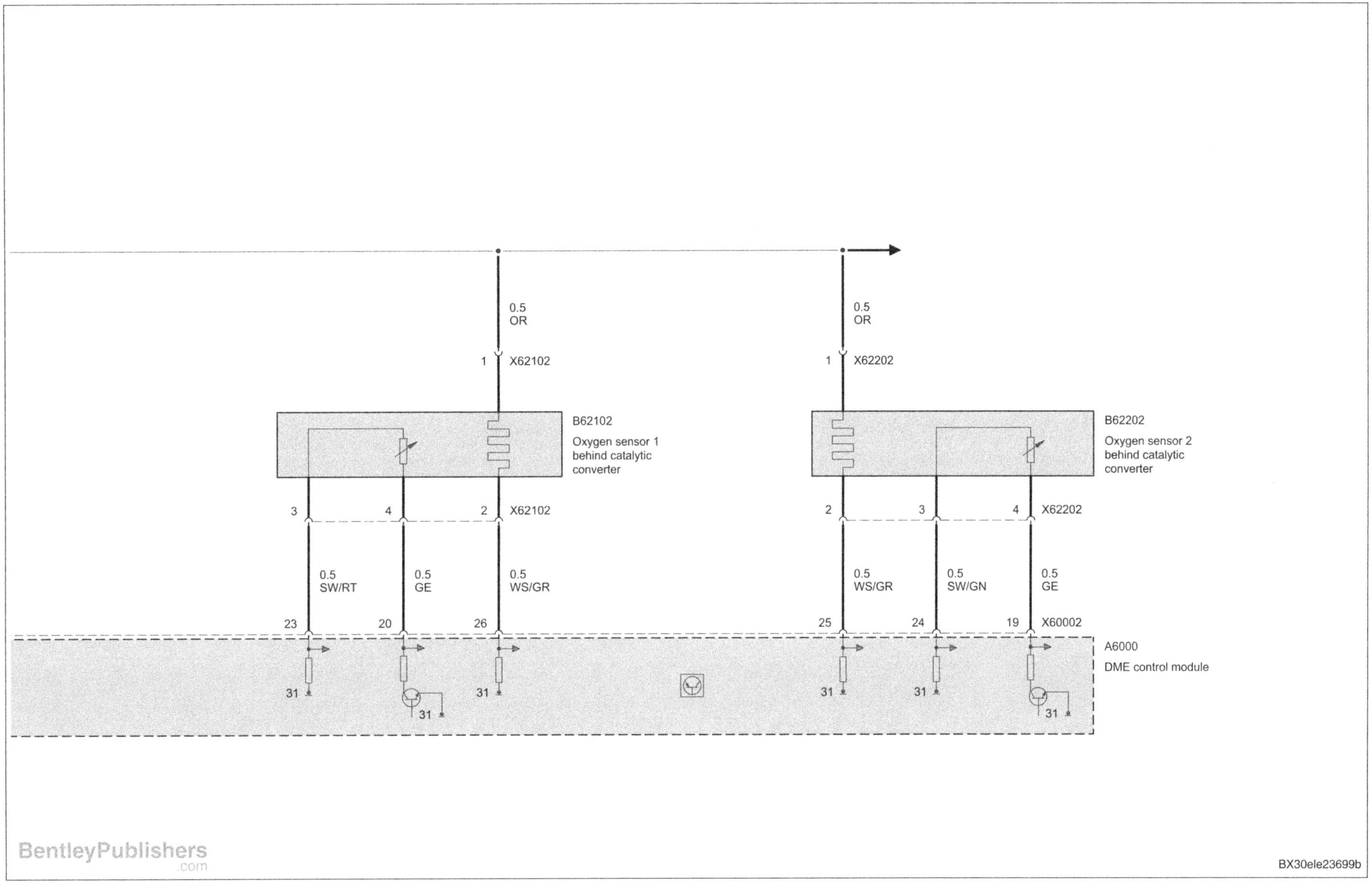

B62202
Oxygen sensor 2
behind catalytic
converter

A6000
DME control module

X62202

0.5
OR

X62202

0.5
GE

X60002

1

4

19

31

0.5
SW/GN

3

24

31

0.5
WS/GR

2

25

31

B62102
Oxygen sensor 1
behind catalytic
converter

X62102

0.5
OR

X62102

0.5
WS/GR

1

2

26

31

0.5
GE

4

20

31

0.5
SW/RT

3

23

31

Electrical Wiring Diagrams   ELE-103

BX30ele23699b

**Secondary air system
M54 engine**

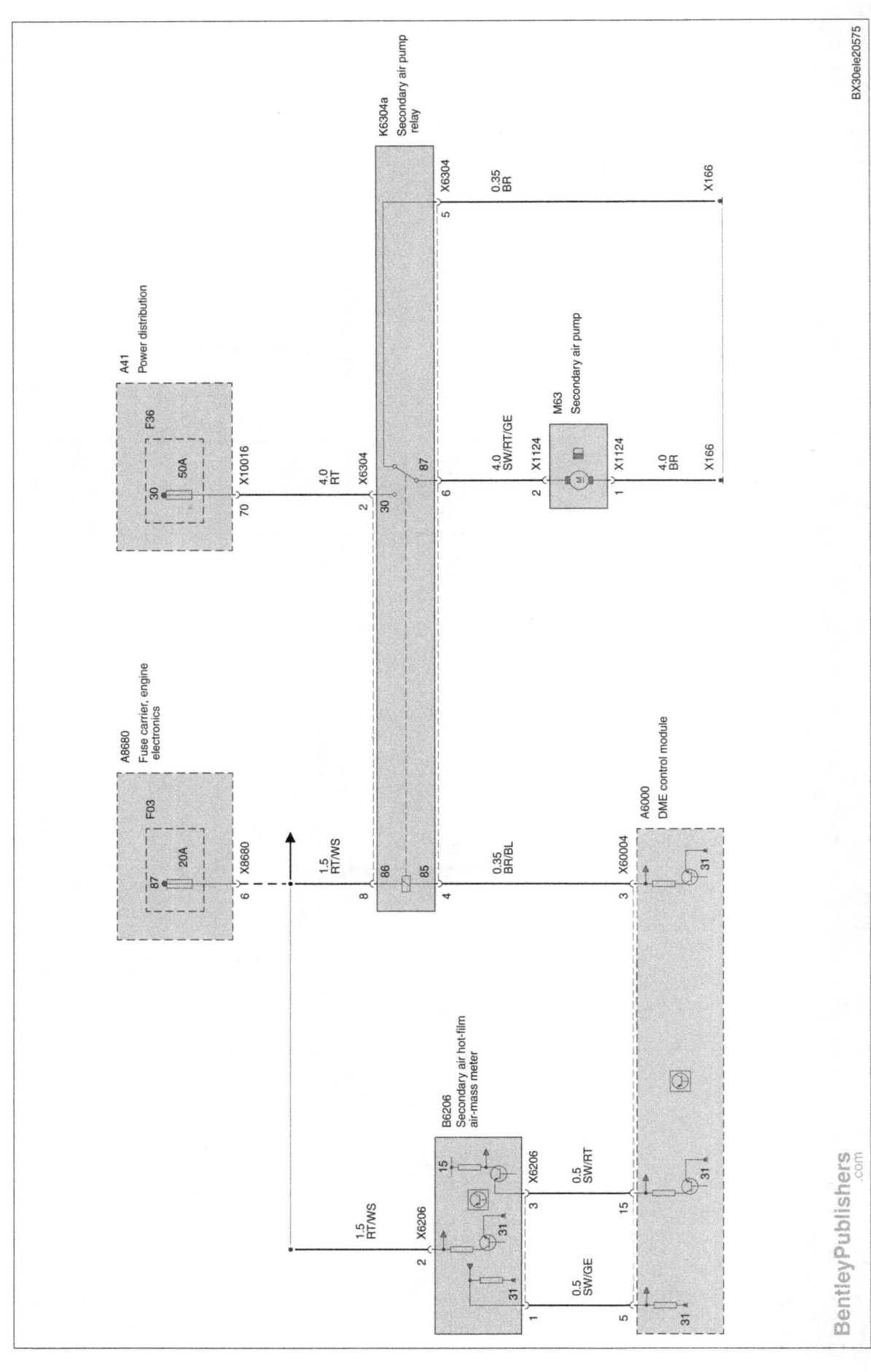

BX30ele20575

**Vehicle speed control
(to 09 / 2006)**

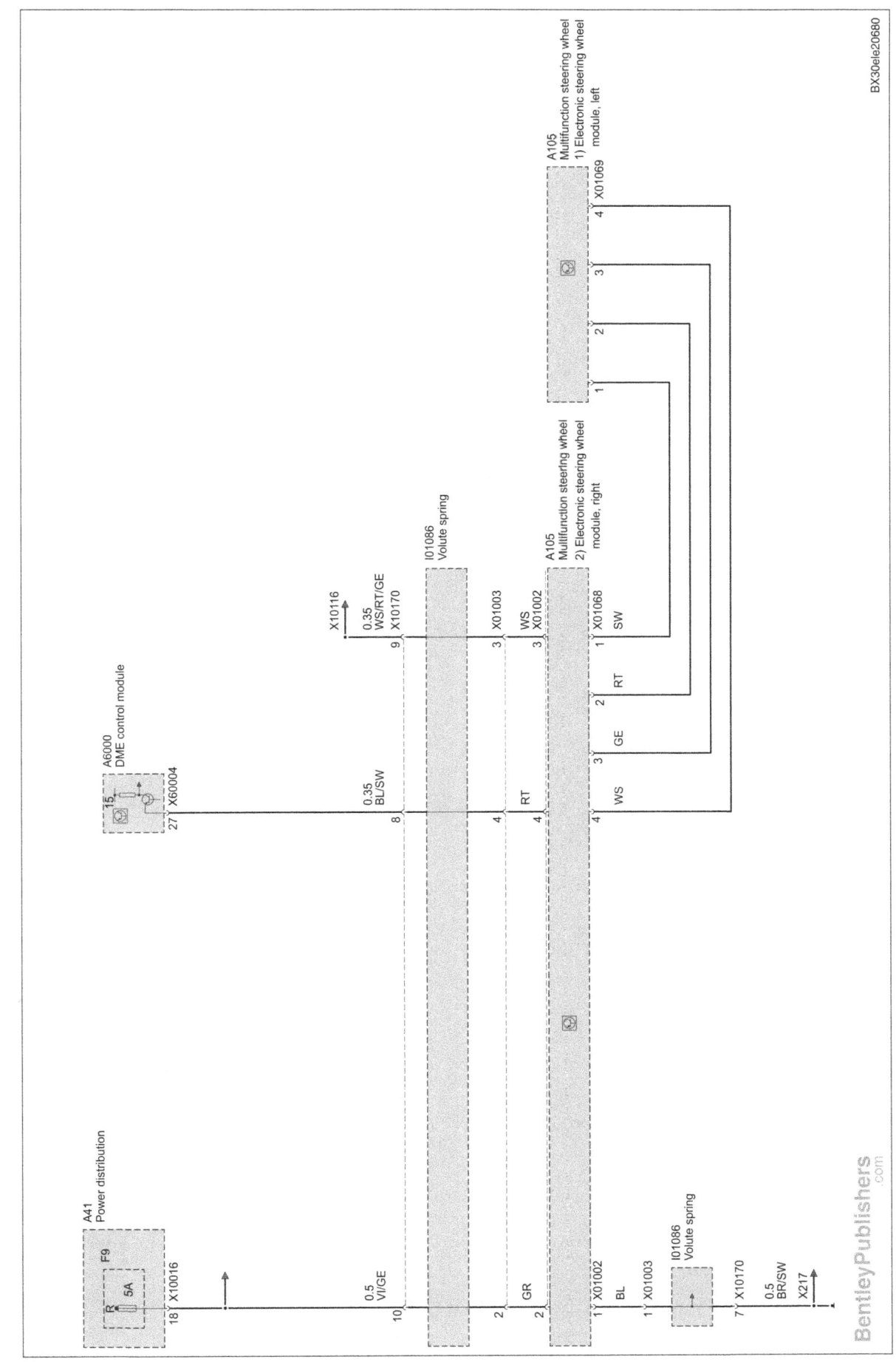

BX30ele20680

**Vehicle speed control
(from 09 / 2006)**

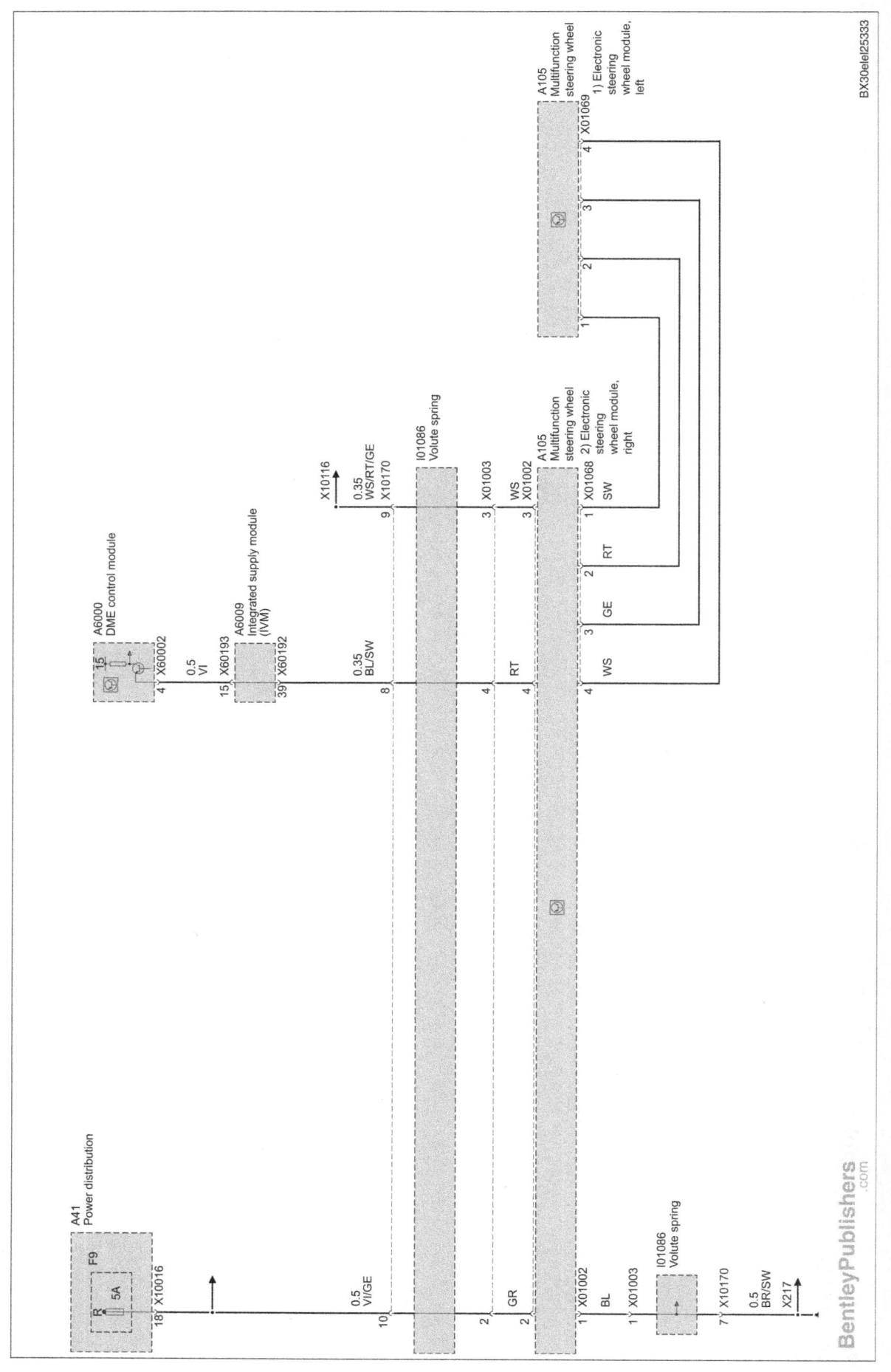

BX30elel25333

**Thermostat, characteristic map cooling
M54 engine**

**Engine coolant temperature sensor
M54 engine**

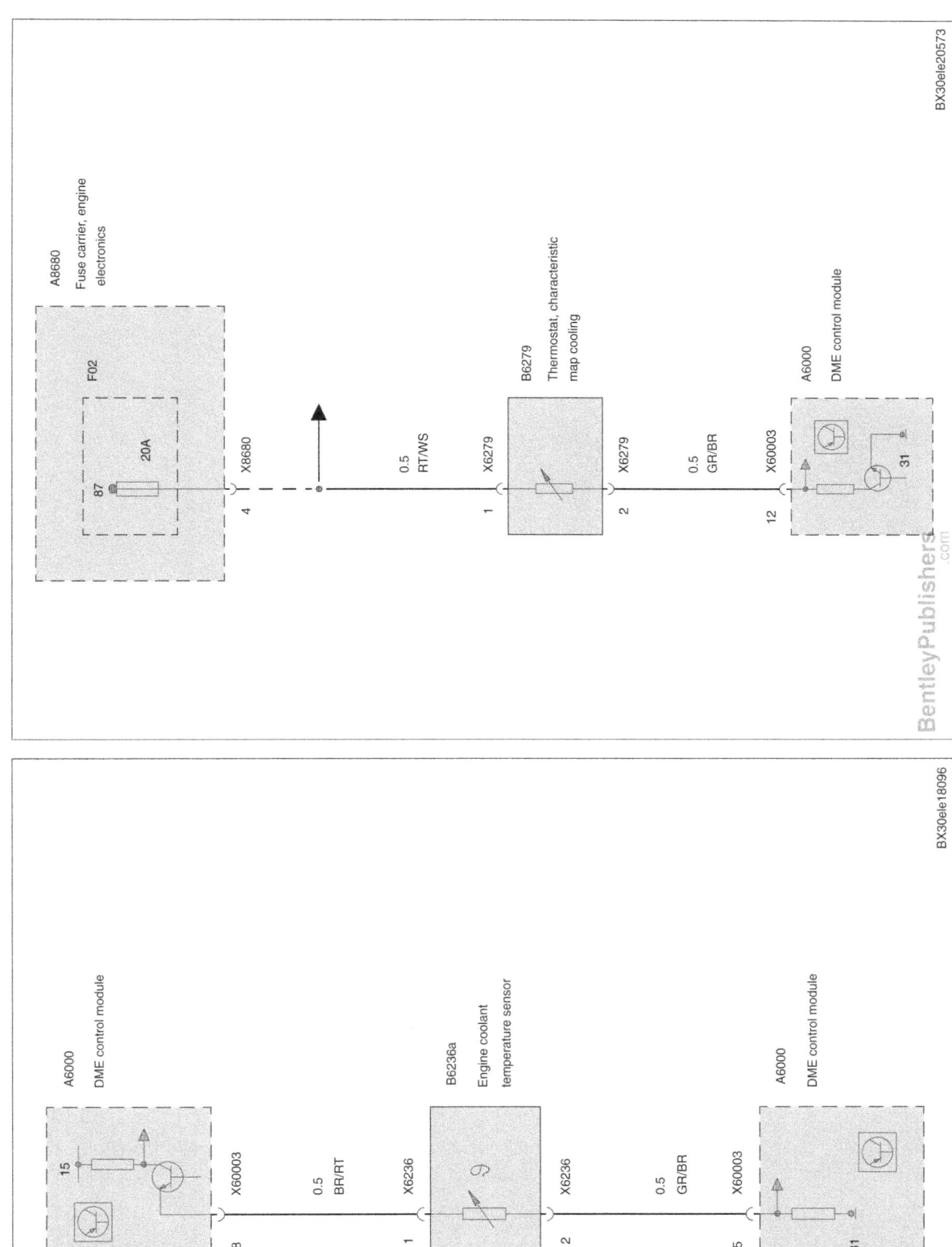

BX30ele20573

BX30ele18096

A8680
Fuse carrier, engine
electronics

F02

20A

87

X8680

4

0.5
RT/WS

X6279

1

B6279
Thermostat, characteristic
map cooling

X6279

2

0.5
GR/BR

X60003

12

A6000
DME control module

31

A6000
DME control module

15

X60003

28

0.5
BR/RT

X6236

1

B6236a
Engine coolant
temperature sensor

X6236

2

0.5
GR/BR

X60003

35

A6000
DME control module

31

BentleyPublishers
.com

BentleyPublishers
.com

Temperature sensor at radiator outlet
M54 engine

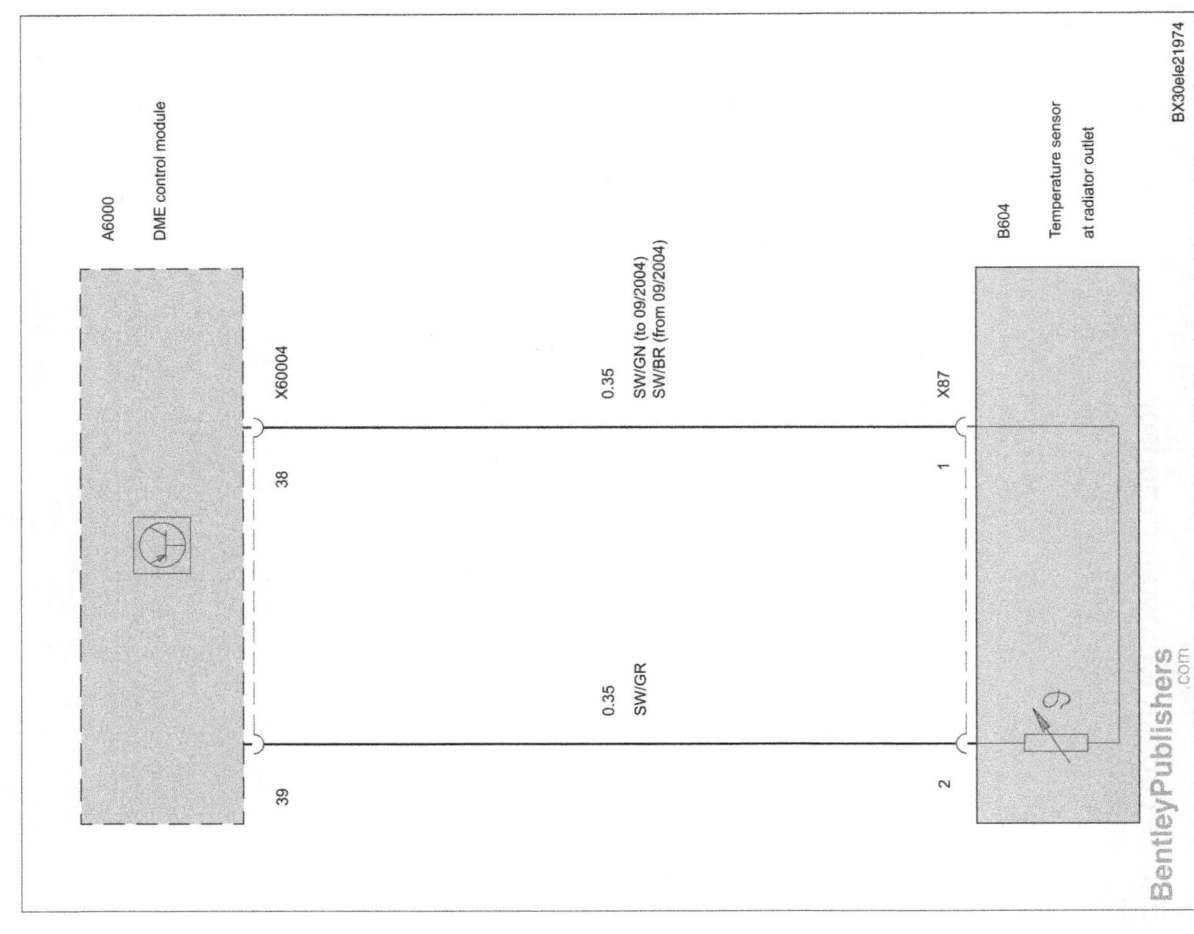

A6000

DME control module

X60004

38

0.35

SW/GN (to 09/2004)
SW/BR (from 09/2004)

0.35

SW/GR

39

B604

Temperature sensor
at radiator outlet

X87

1

2

BentleyPublishers
.com

BX30ele21974

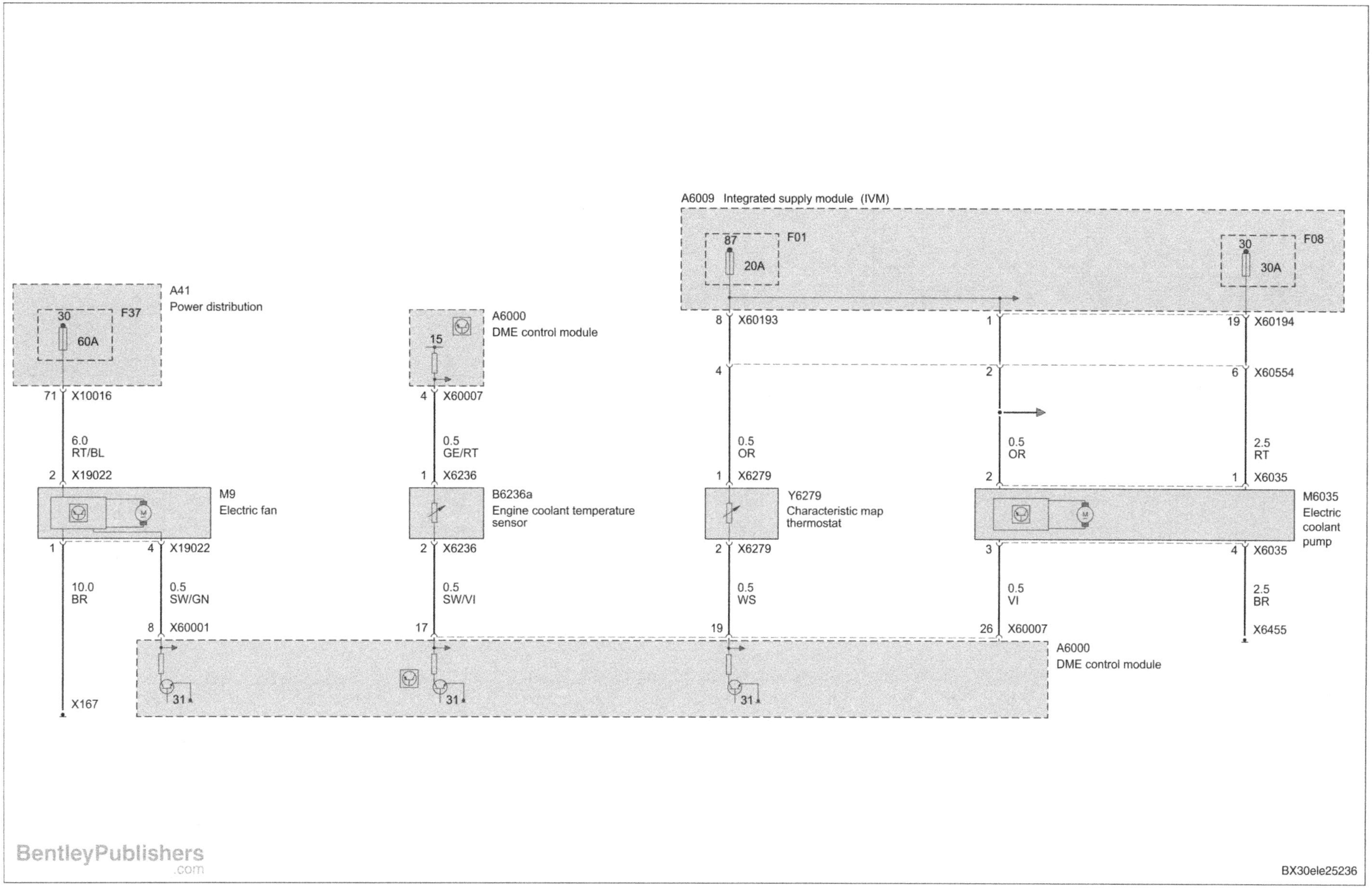

Cooling system
N52 engine (to 09/2007)

Electrical Wiring Diagrams   ELE-109

BX30ele25236

F08

30A
30
19 X60194
6   X60554

2.5
RT
1   X6035

M6035
Electric
coolant
pump

4   X6035
2.5
BR
X6455

A6009   Integrated supply module (IVM)

F01
20A
87
8   X60193
4

0.5
OR
1   X6279

Y6279
Characteristic map
thermostat

2   X6279
0.5
WS
19

31

A6000   DME control module

1
2
2   0.5 OR
3   0.5 VI X60007
26

A6000   DME control module

A6000
DME control module

15 X60007
4   0.5 GE/RT
1   X6236

B6236a
Engine coolant temperature
sensor

2   X6236
0.5
SW/VI
17

31

A41
Power distribution

F37
60A
30
71 X10016
2

6.0
RT/BL
X19022

M9
Electric fan

4   X19022
0.5
SW/GN
8   X60001

31

1
10.0
BR
X167

31

BentleyPublishers
.com

Cooling system
N52 engine (from 09/2007)

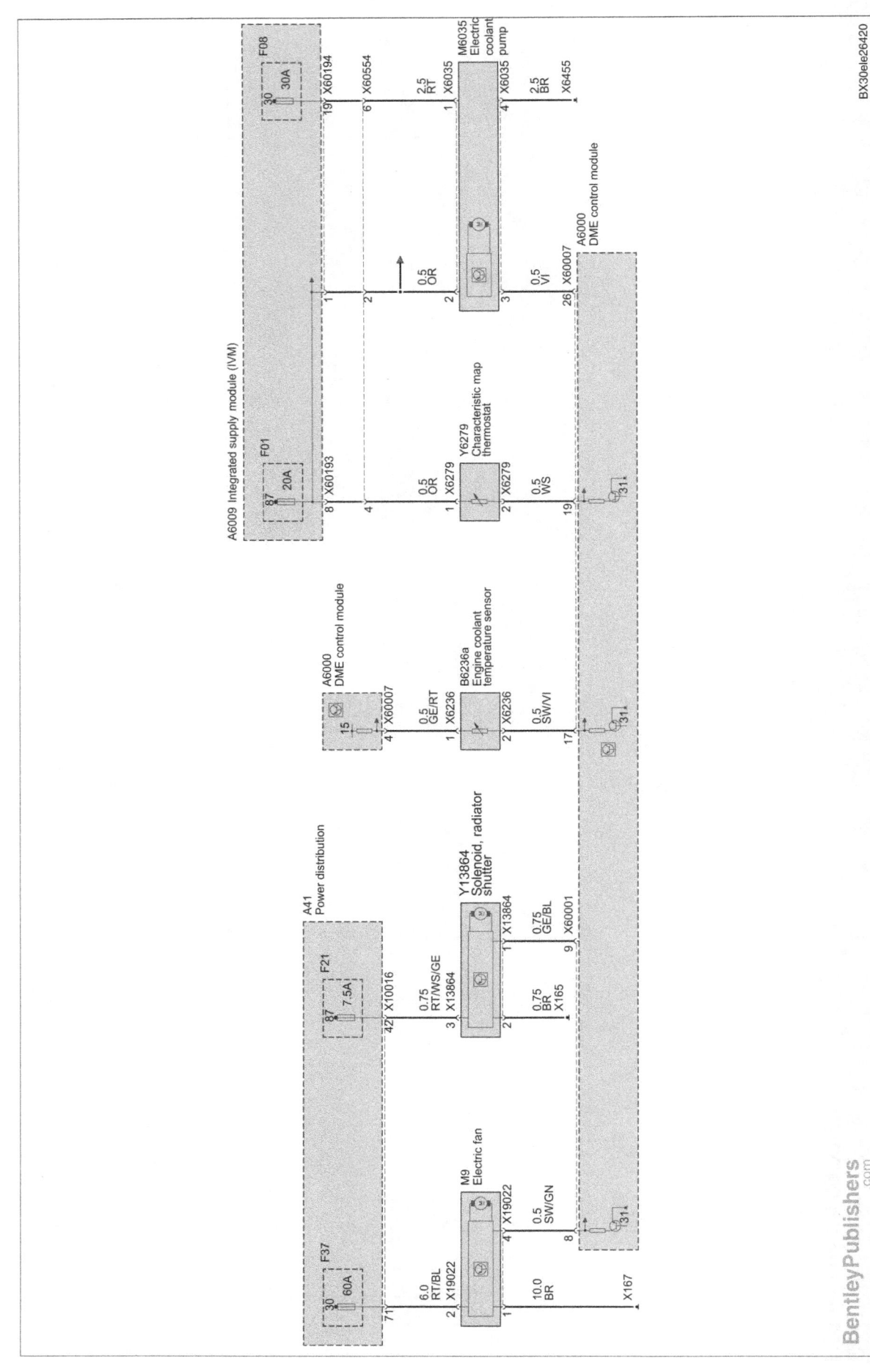

BX30ele26420

**Engine oil supply
M54 engine**

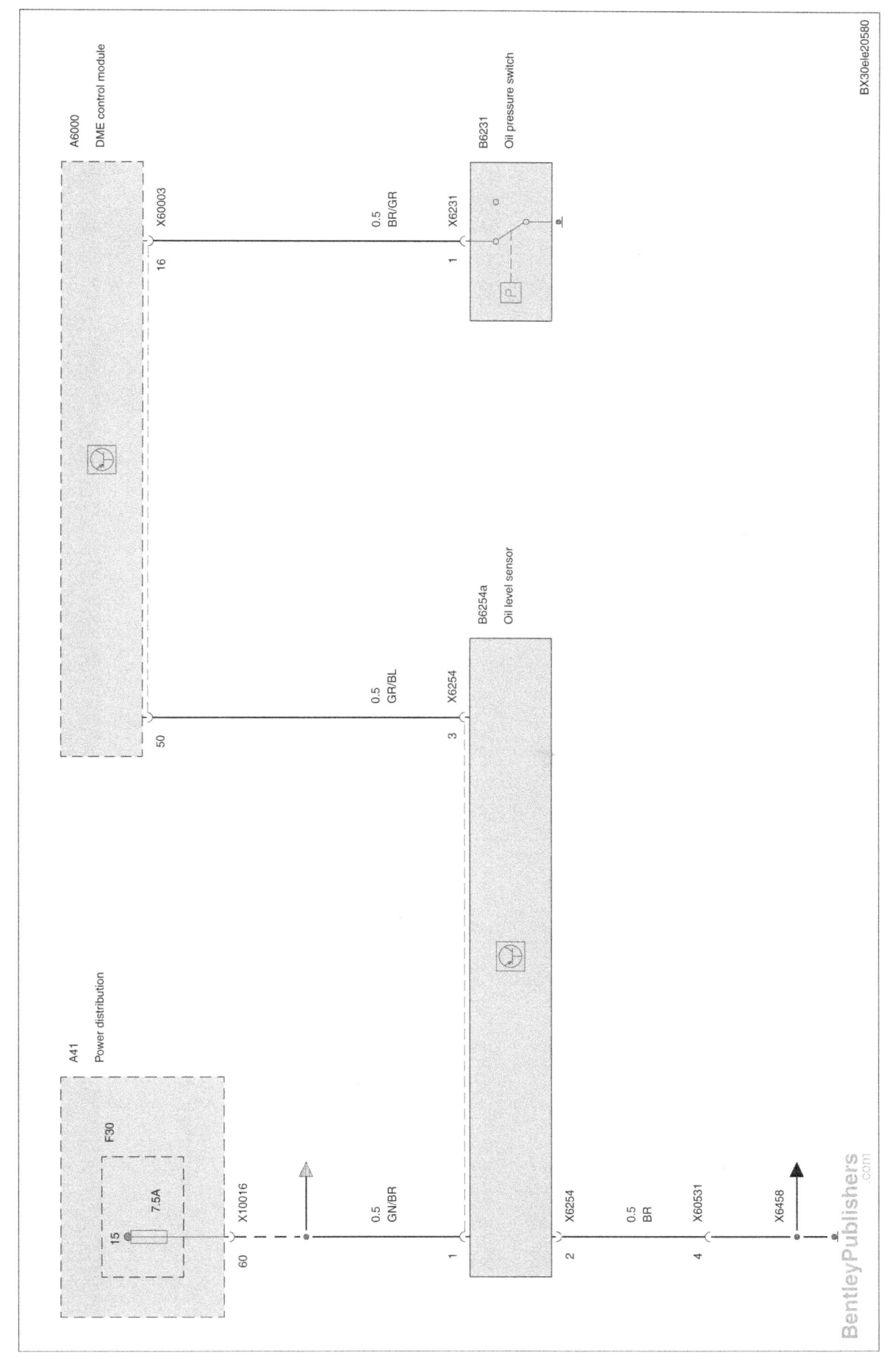

A6000 — DME control module

B6231 — Oil pressure switch

B6254a — Oil level sensor

A41 — Power distribution

F30

7.5A

X60003
16
0.5 BR/GR
X6231
1
P

50
0.5 GR/BL
X6254
3

X10016
60
0.5 GN/BR

X6254
1
2
0.5 BR
X60531
4
X6458

15

BX30ele20580

BentleyPublishers.com

Engine oil supply
N52 engine

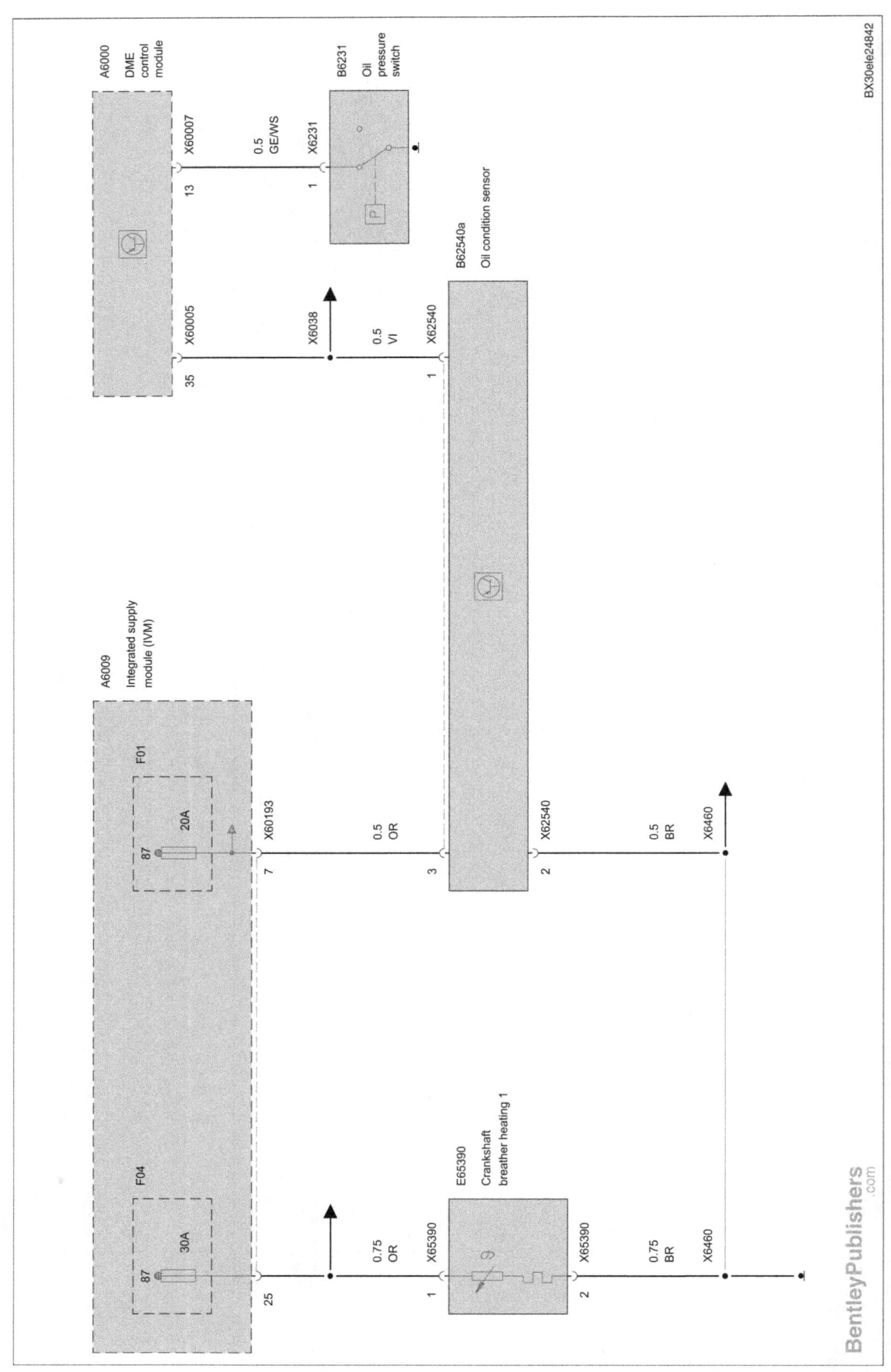

BX30ele24842

Tire defect indicator (RPA)

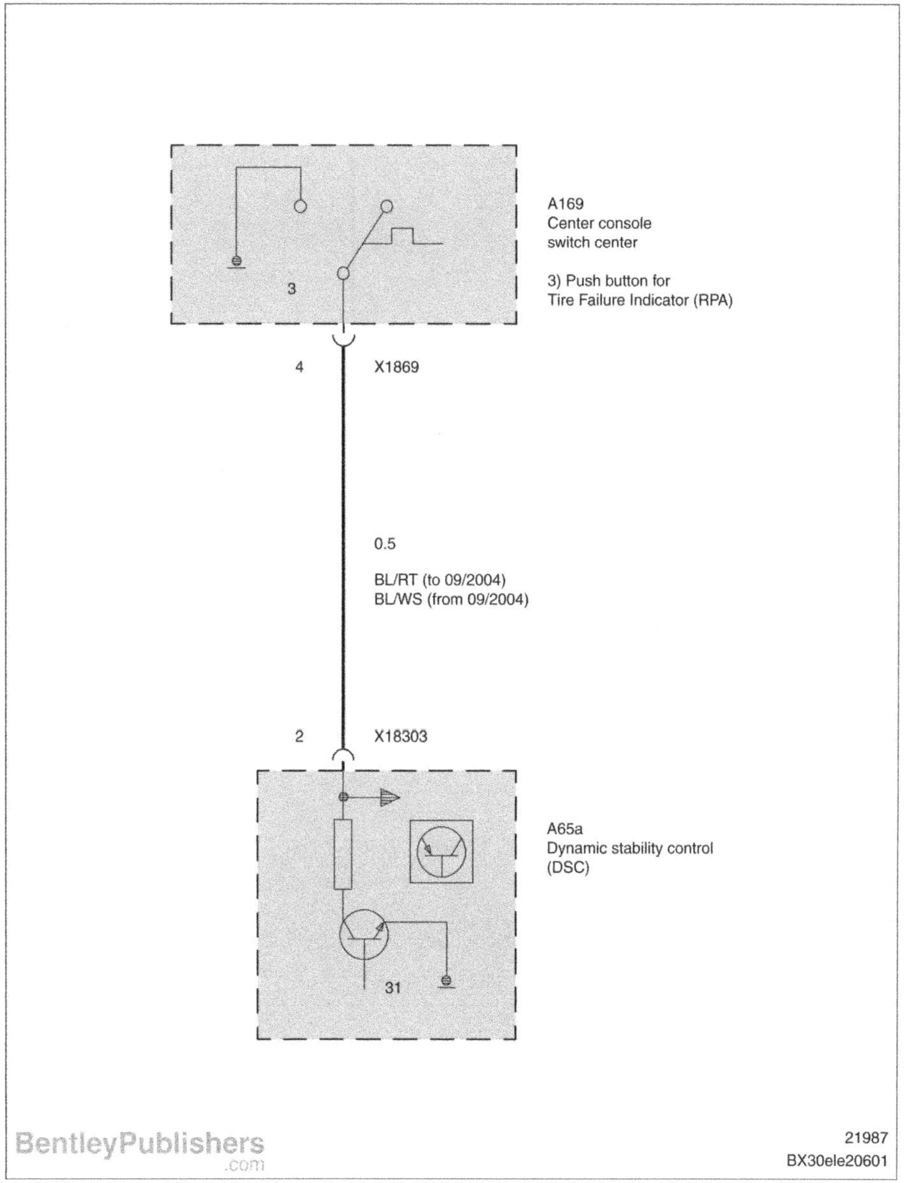

A169
Center console
switch center

3) Push button for
Tire Failure Indicator (RPA)

X1869

3

4

0.5

BL/RT (to 09/2004)
BL/WS (from 09/2004)

X18303

2

A65a
Dynamic stability control
(DSC)

31

21987
BX30ele20601

**Engine oil temp sensor
M54 engine**

A6000
DME control module

15

X60003

44

0.5
RT/BL

X6238

1

B6238a
Oil temperature sensor

2

X6238

0.5
GR/BR

X60003

45

A6000
DME control module

31

BX30ele18098

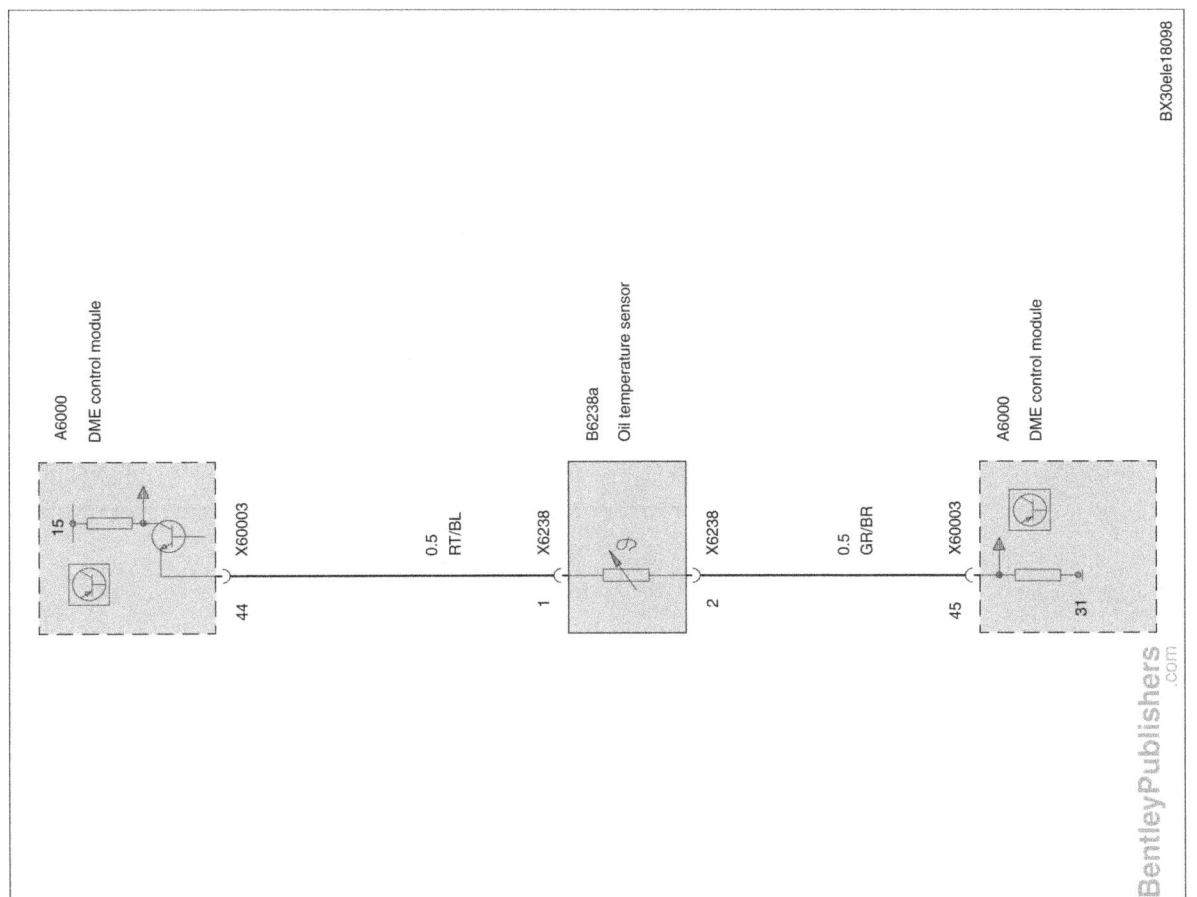

CAN bus - outputs
M54 engine
page 1 of 2

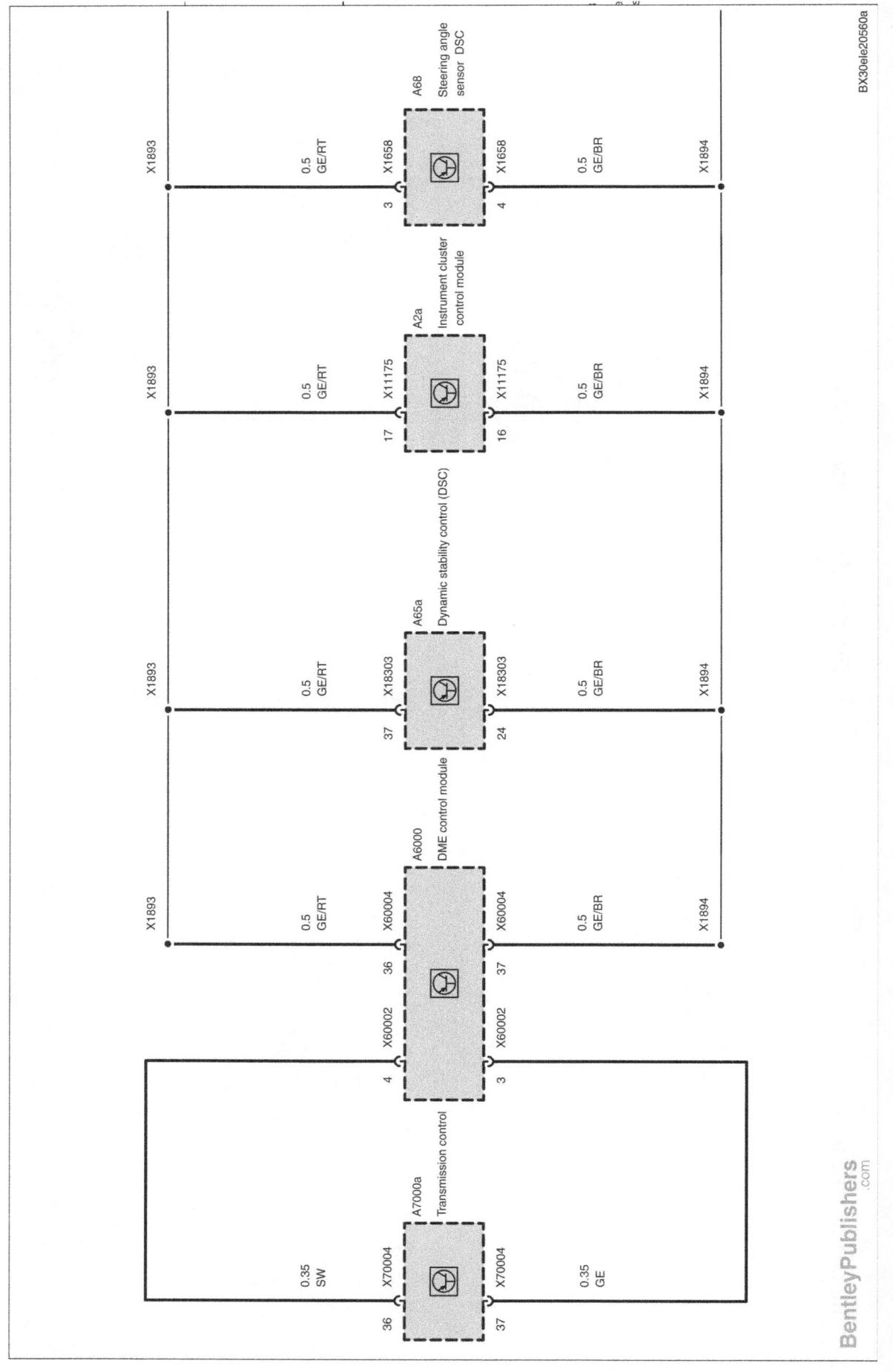

BX30ele20560a

Electrical Wiring Diagrams   ELE-115

A70006
Control module,
transfer box

X18827

0.5
GE/RT

X2153

4

1

X2153

0.5
GE/BR

X18826

A17
Servotronic

X18827

0.5
GE/RT

X83

5

6

X83

0.5
GE/BR

X18826

B75
DSC sensor

X18827

0.5
GE/RT

X1996

3

2

X1996

0.5
GE/BR

X18826

A214
Adaptive headlight

X1893
X18827

0.5
GE/RT

X10513

13

14

X10513

0.5
GE/BR

X18826
X1894

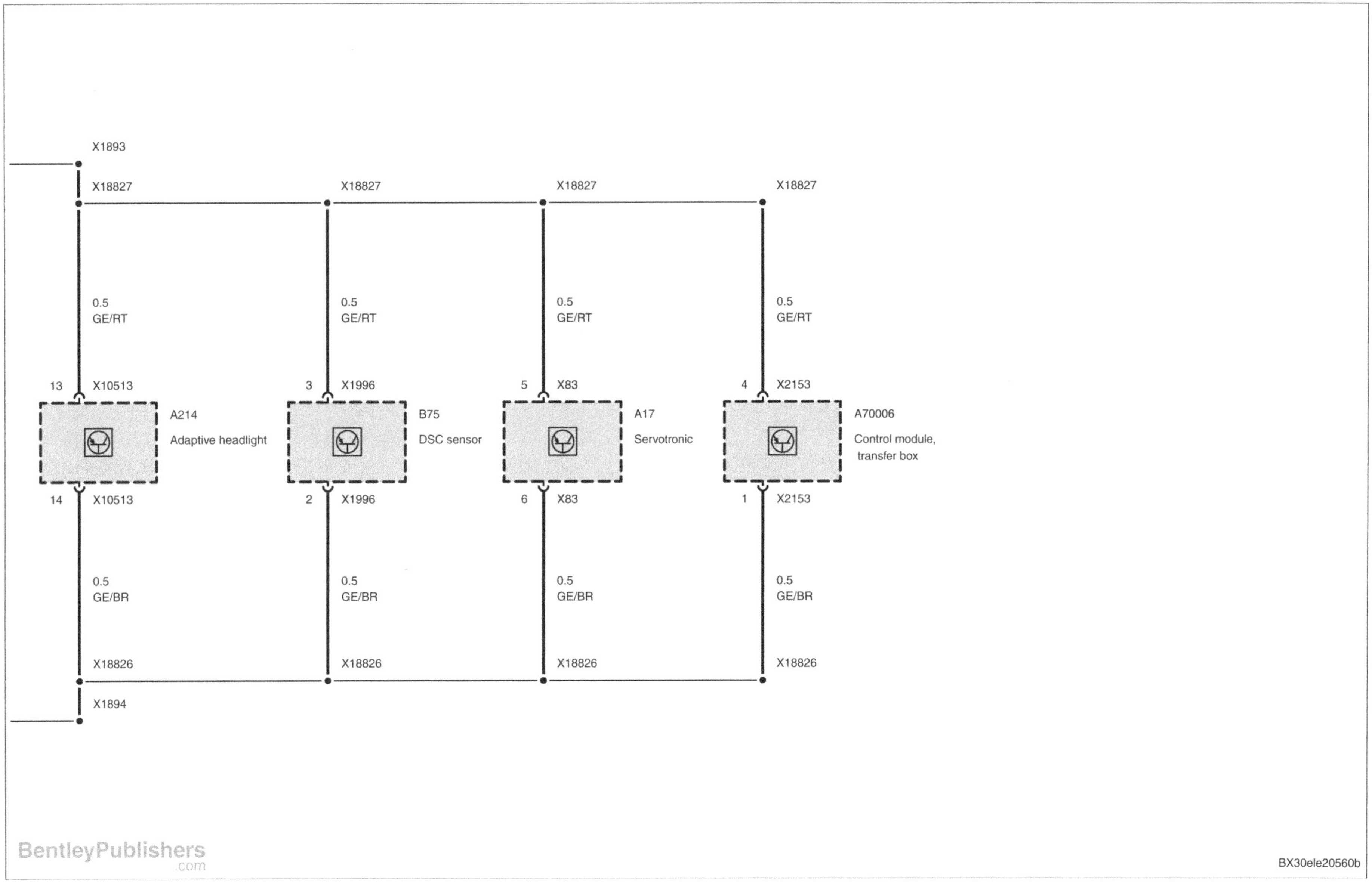

CAN bus - outputs
N52 engine
page 1 of 2

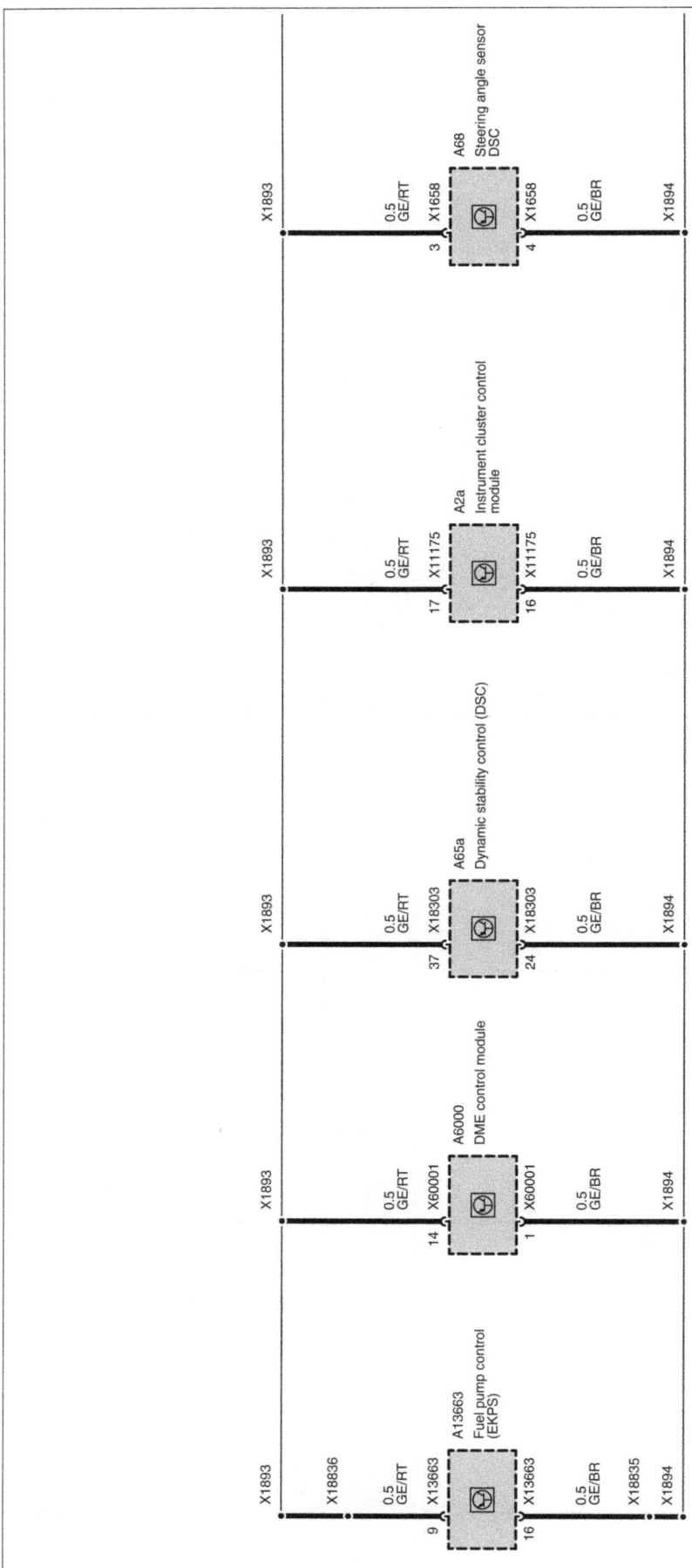

BX30ele25173a

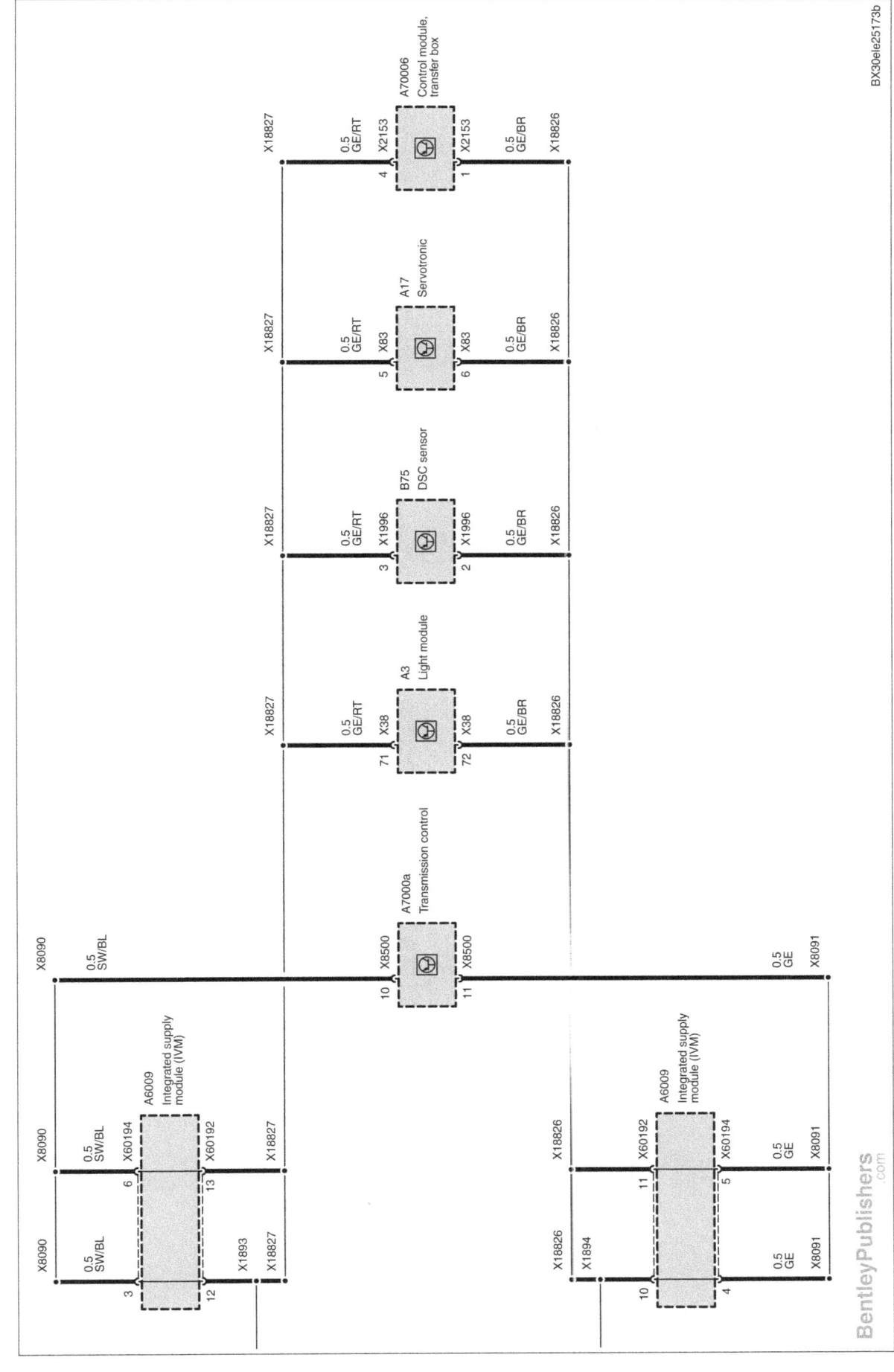

BX30ele25173b

Central locking system
general

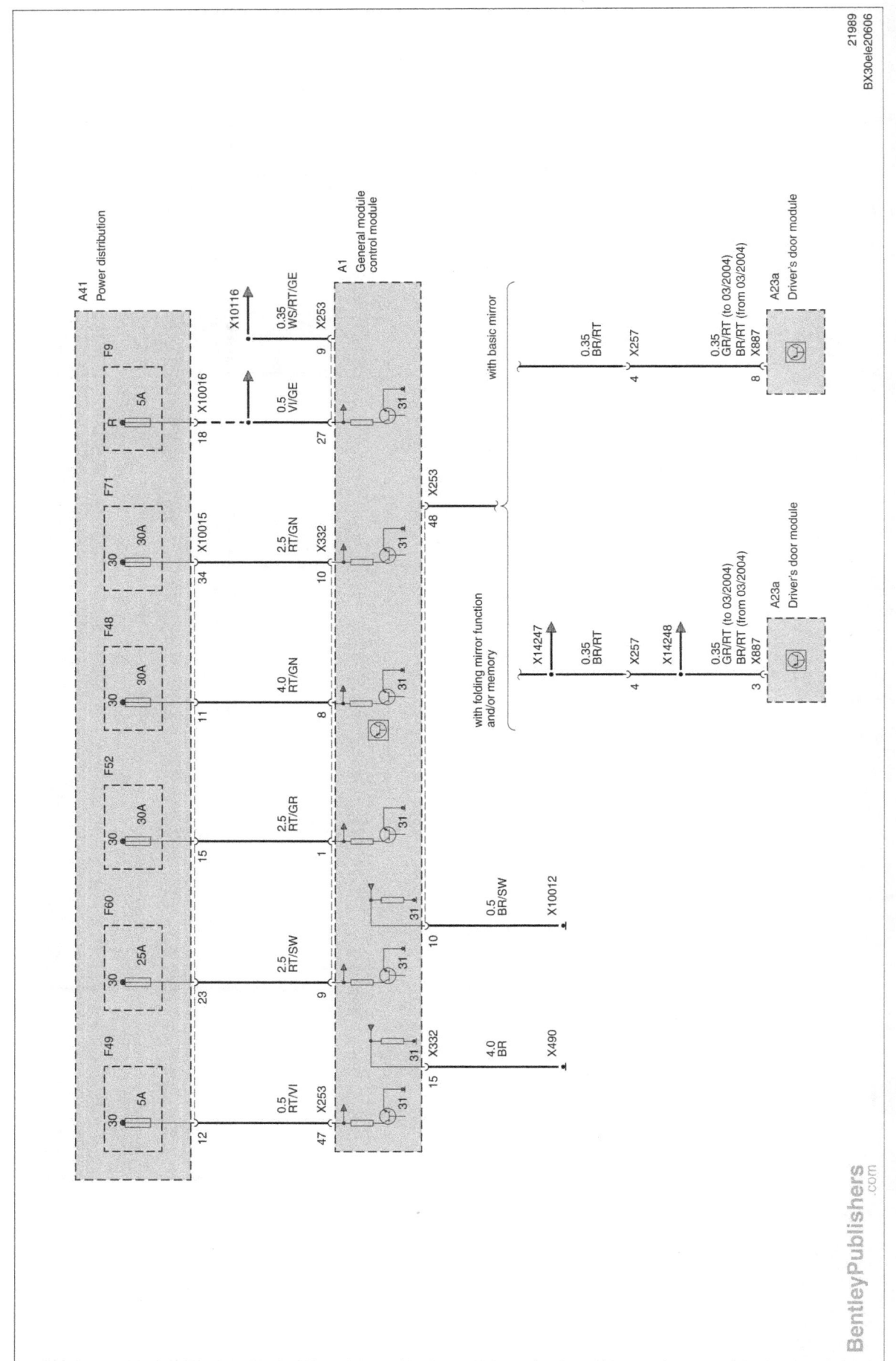

21989
BX30ele20606

Central locking system
drives
page 1 of 2

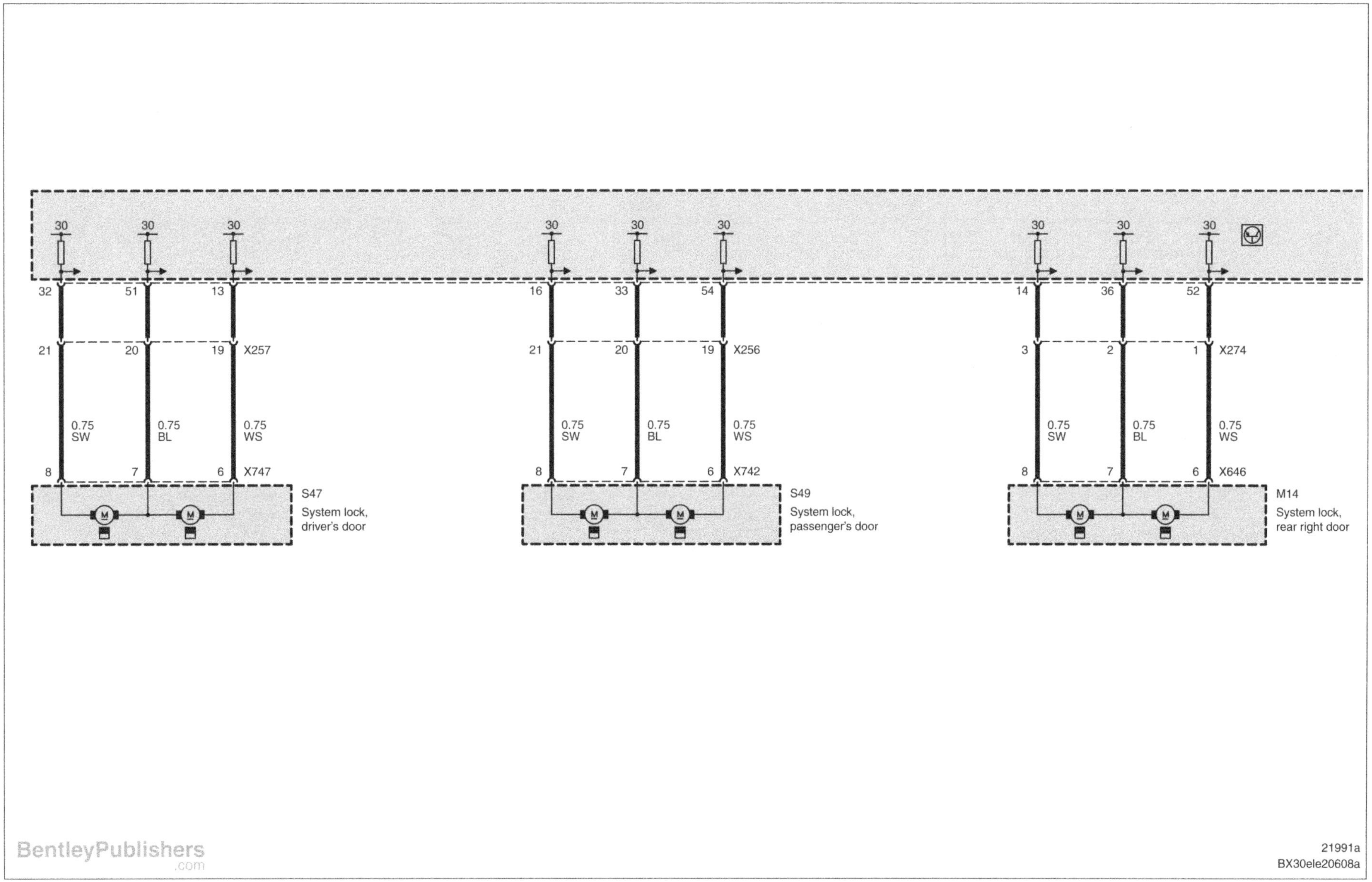

30 52 X274 1 0.75 WS 6 X646

30 36 2 0.75 BL 7

30 14 3 0.75 SW 8

M14
System lock,
rear right door

30 54 X256 19 0.75 WS 6 X742

30 33 20 0.75 BL 7

30 16 21 0.75 SW 8

S49
System lock,
passenger's door

30 13 X257 19 0.75 WS 6 X747

30 51 20 0.75 BL 7

30 32 21 0.75 SW 8

S47
System lock,
driver's door

21991a
BX30ele20608a

**Central locking system
drives
page 2 of 2**

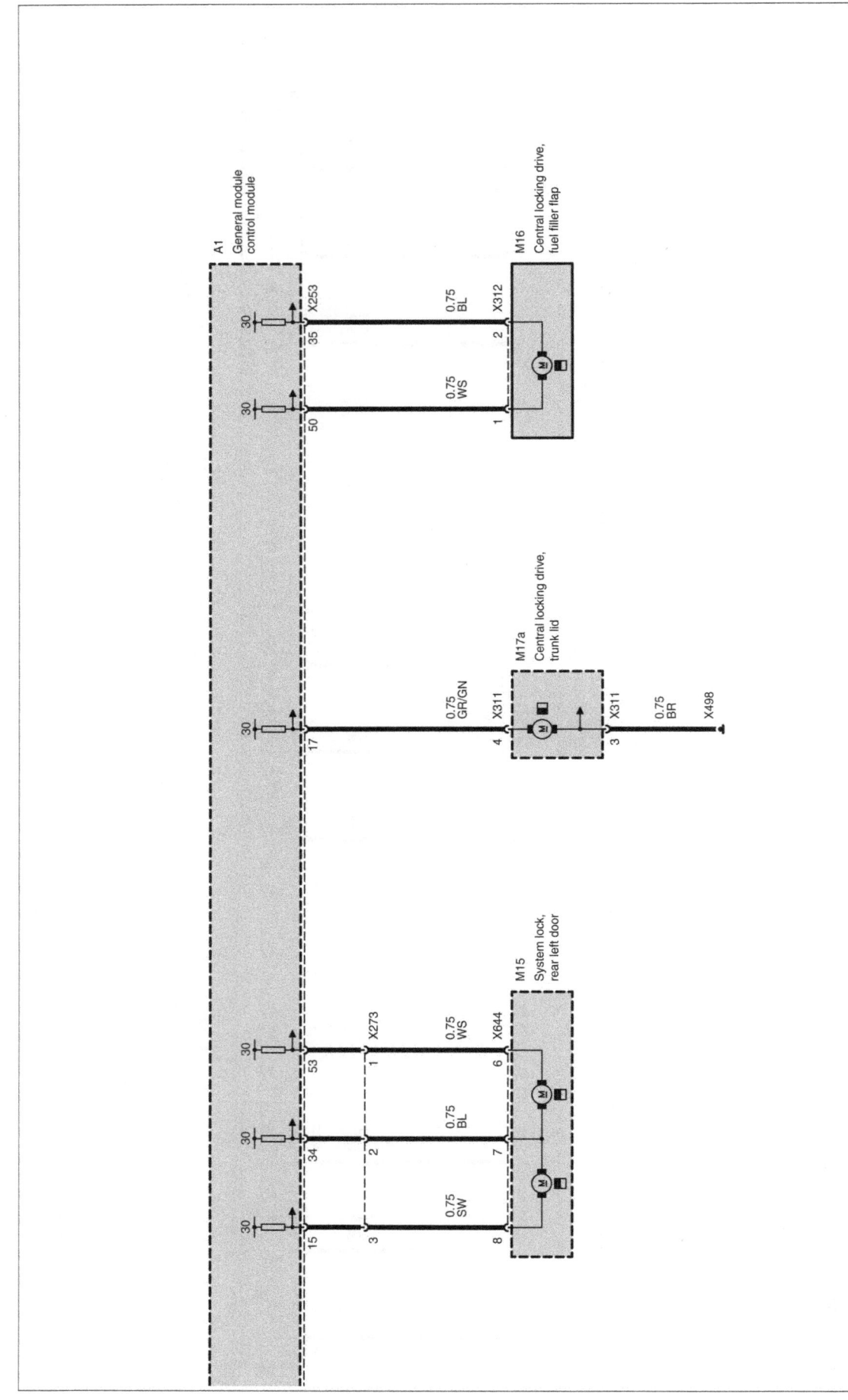

21991b
BX30ele20608b

Central locking system
inputs
page 1 of 2

30   23

0.35
BR/WS (up to 09/2004)
GE/GN (as of 09/2004)

X274

6

0.35
BR/GR

2   X646

M14
System lock, rear right door
1) Door contact
switch

1

3   X646

0.35
BR

X835

---

30   24

X273

6

0.35
BR/GR

2   X644

M15
System lock, rear left door
1) Door contact
switch

1

3   X644

0.35
BR

X834

---

30   25

16   X256

0.5
BR/GR/GE (up to 09/2004)
VI/SW (as of 09/2004)

2   X742

S49
System lock, passenger's door
1) Door contact

1

3   X742

0.75
BR

X891

---

30   26

16   X257

0.5
BR/GR/GE

2   X747

S47
System lock, driver's door
1) Door contact

1

31   20

17

0.5
WS/SW

5

X

3   X747

0.75
BR

X849

31   22

18

4

X

0.5
BL/RT (up to 09/2004)
BR/GE (as of 09/2004)

**Central locking system
inputs
page 2 of 2**

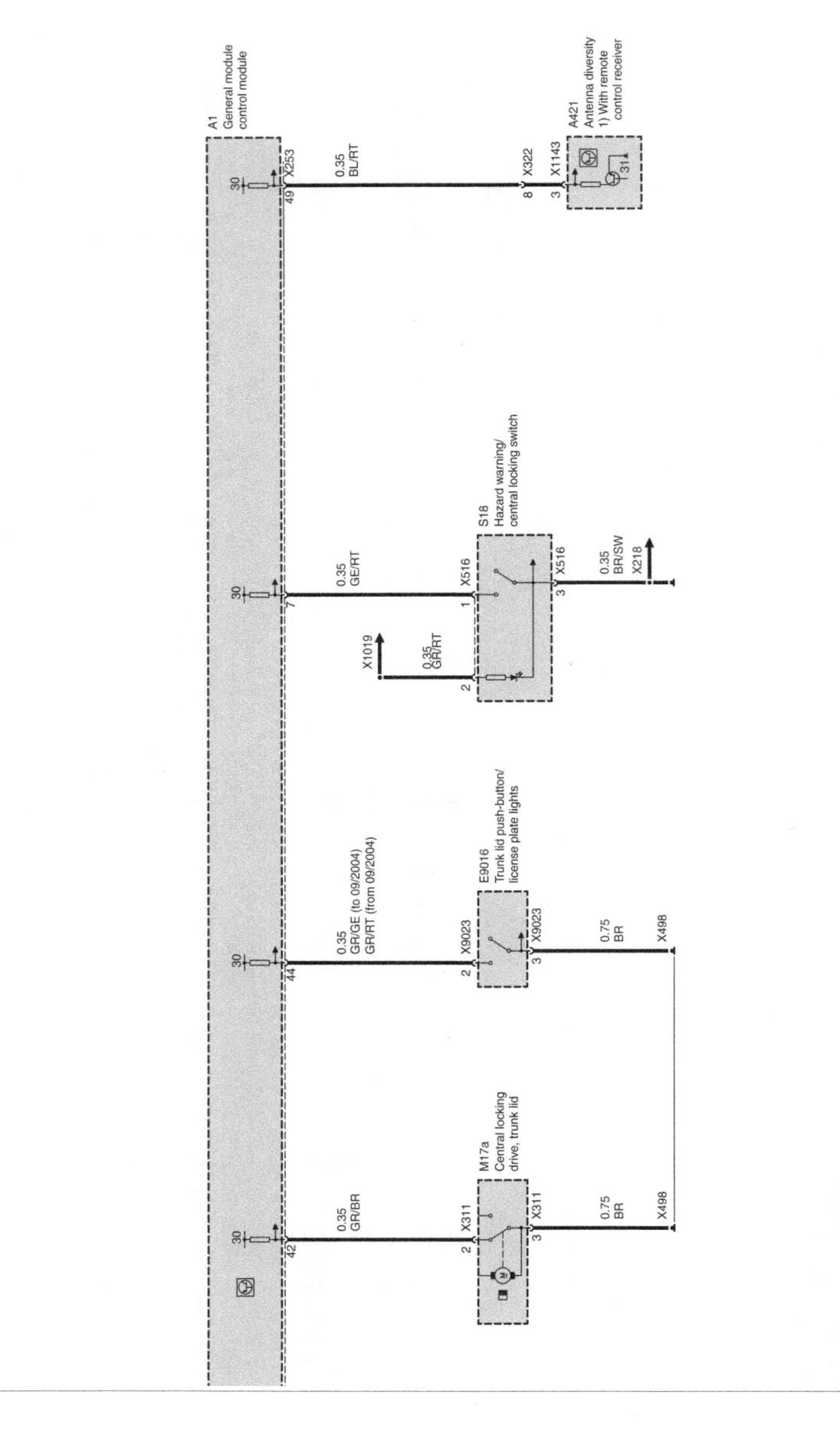

221990b
BX30ele20607b

**Blower motor,
final stage (series resistor)**

**Heating and air-conditioning control unit,
power supply**

BX30ele20659

BX30ele20658

BentleyPublishers
.com

BentleyPublishers
.com

Compressor control
M54 engine

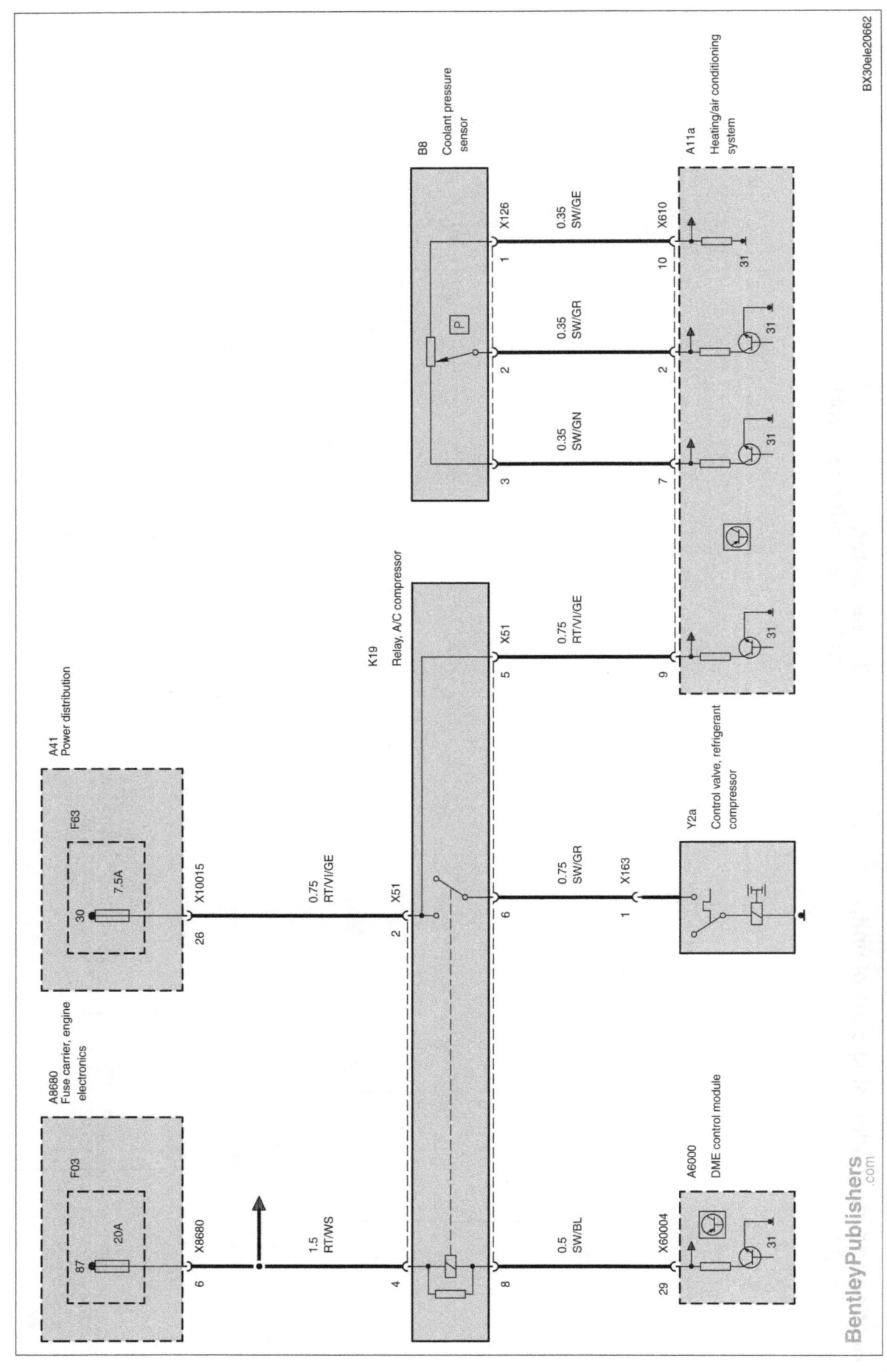

BX30ele20662

**Compressor control
N52 engine**

Electrical Wiring Diagrams ELE-125

A6009
Integrated supply
module (IVM)

A41
Power distribution

B8
Coolant pressure sensor

F02

F63

10A

7.5A

87

30

X60192

X10015

0.75
RT/VI/GE

X51

2

26

2

1.5 (up to 09/2007)
0.75 (as of 09/2007)
RT/WS

K19
Relay, A/C compressor

X51

0.75
RT/VI/GE

5

X126

1

0.35
SW/GE

X610

10

31

4

8

0.5
SW/BL

9

0.75
SW/GR

X60192

34

2

0.35
SW/GR

2

31

A6009
Integrated supply module (IVM)

A11a
Heating/air conditioning
system

3

0.35
SW/GN

7

31

9

31

A6000
DME control module

16

0.5
WS

21

X60002

31

X60194

10

0.5
WS

3

X60554

0.75
WS

1

X8099

Y2a
Control valve,
refrigerant compressor

BentleyPublishers
.com

26496
BX30ele25329

**Heating and air conditioning (IHKA)
page 1 of 3**

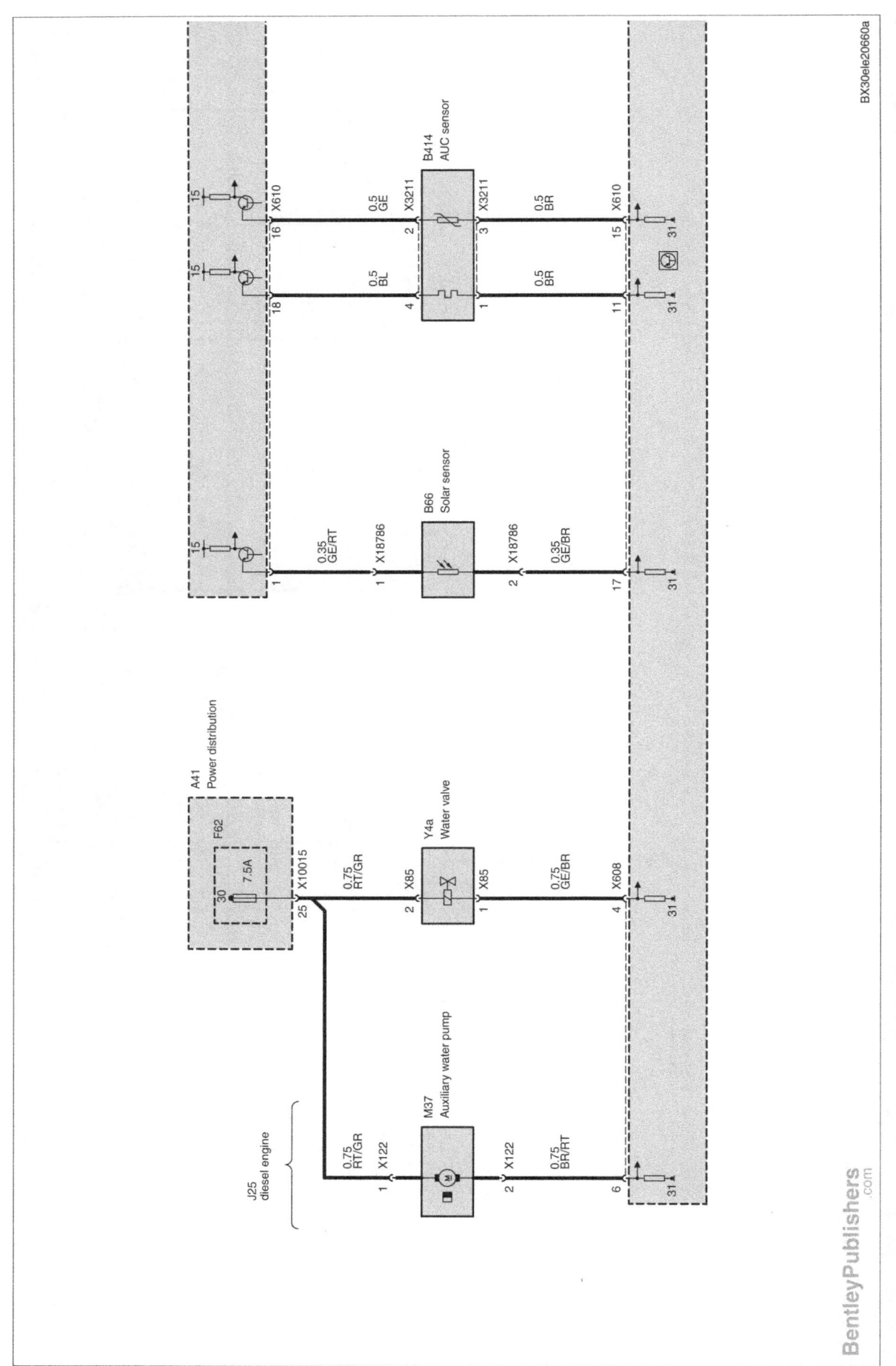

BX30ele20660a

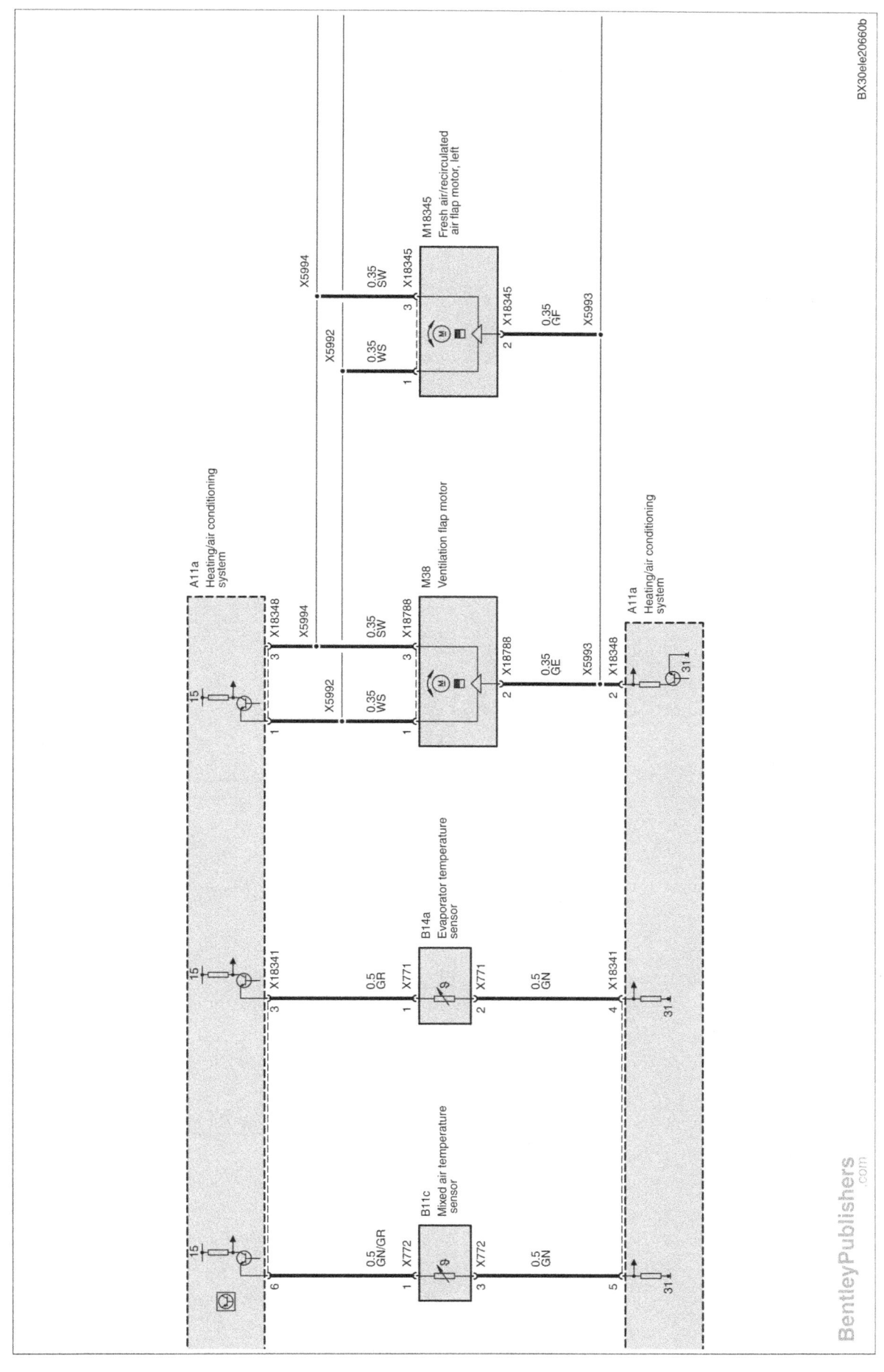

BX30ele20660b

**Heating and air conditioning (IHKA)
page 3 of 3**

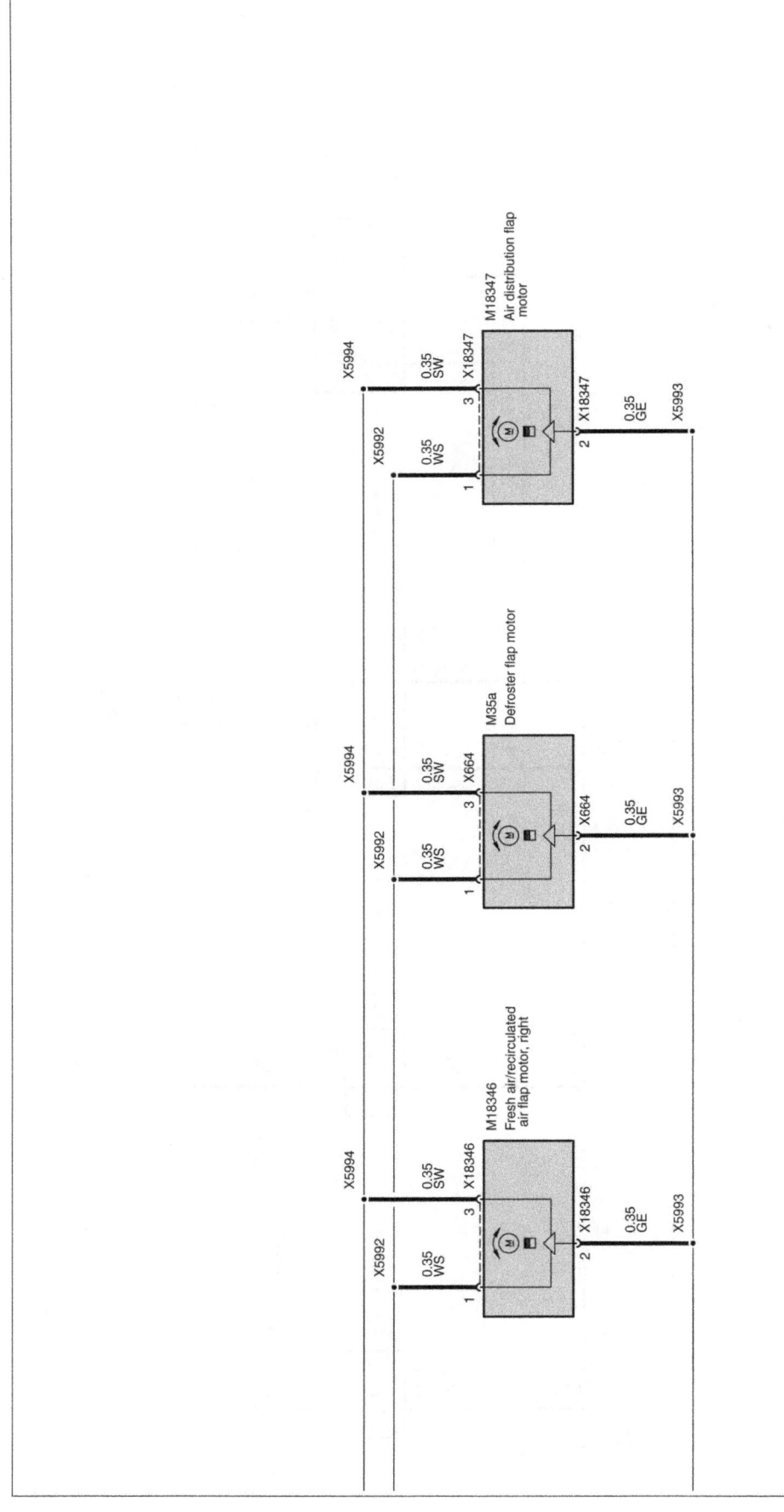

BX30ele20660c

Rear window defogger

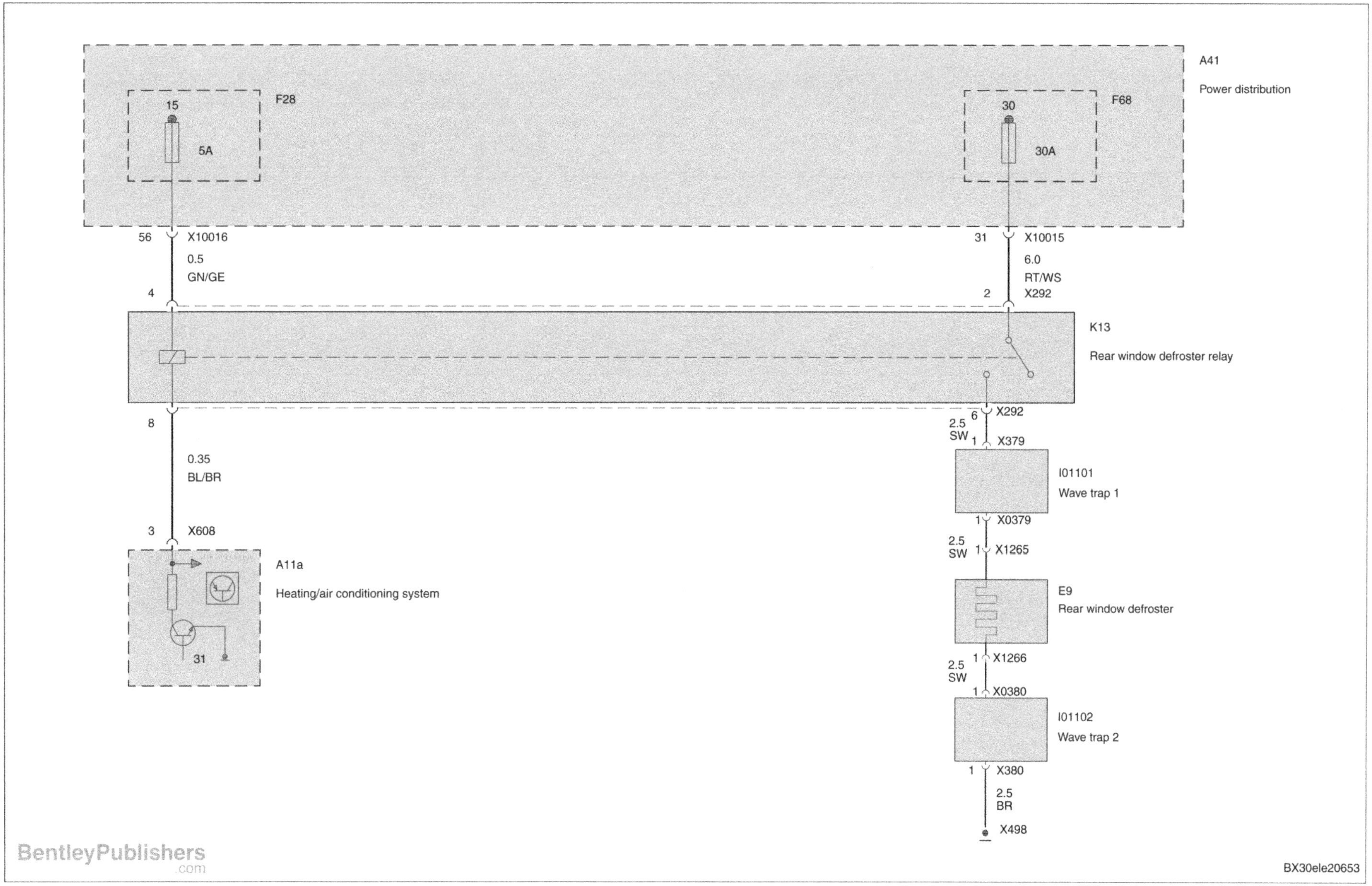

A41
Power distribution
F28
15
5A
F68
30
30A
56
X10016
0.5
GN/GE
31
X10015
6.0
RT/WS
X292
4
2
K13
Rear window defroster relay
8
6
X292
0.35
BL/BR
2.5
SW
1
X379
I01101
Wave trap 1
1
X0379
2.5
SW
1
X1265
E9
Rear window defroster
1
X1266
2.5
SW
1
X0380
I01102
Wave trap 2
1
X380
2.5
BR
X498
3
X608
A11a
Heating/air conditioning system
31
BentleyPublishers
.com
BX30ele20653

**Instrument cluster, inputs
(to 09/2004)
page 1 of 3**

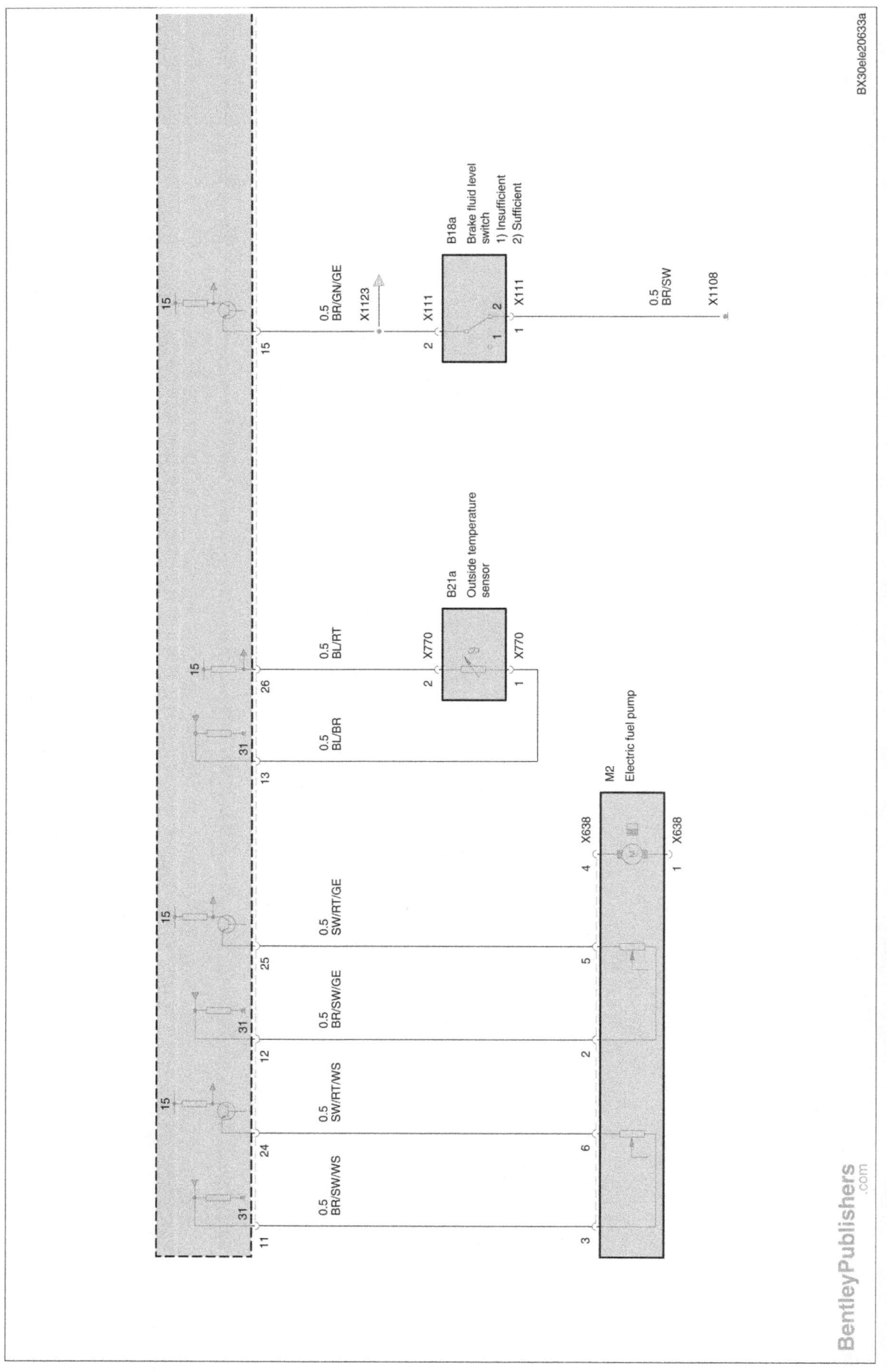

BX30ele20633a

**Instrument cluster, inputs
(to 09/2004)
page 2 of 3**

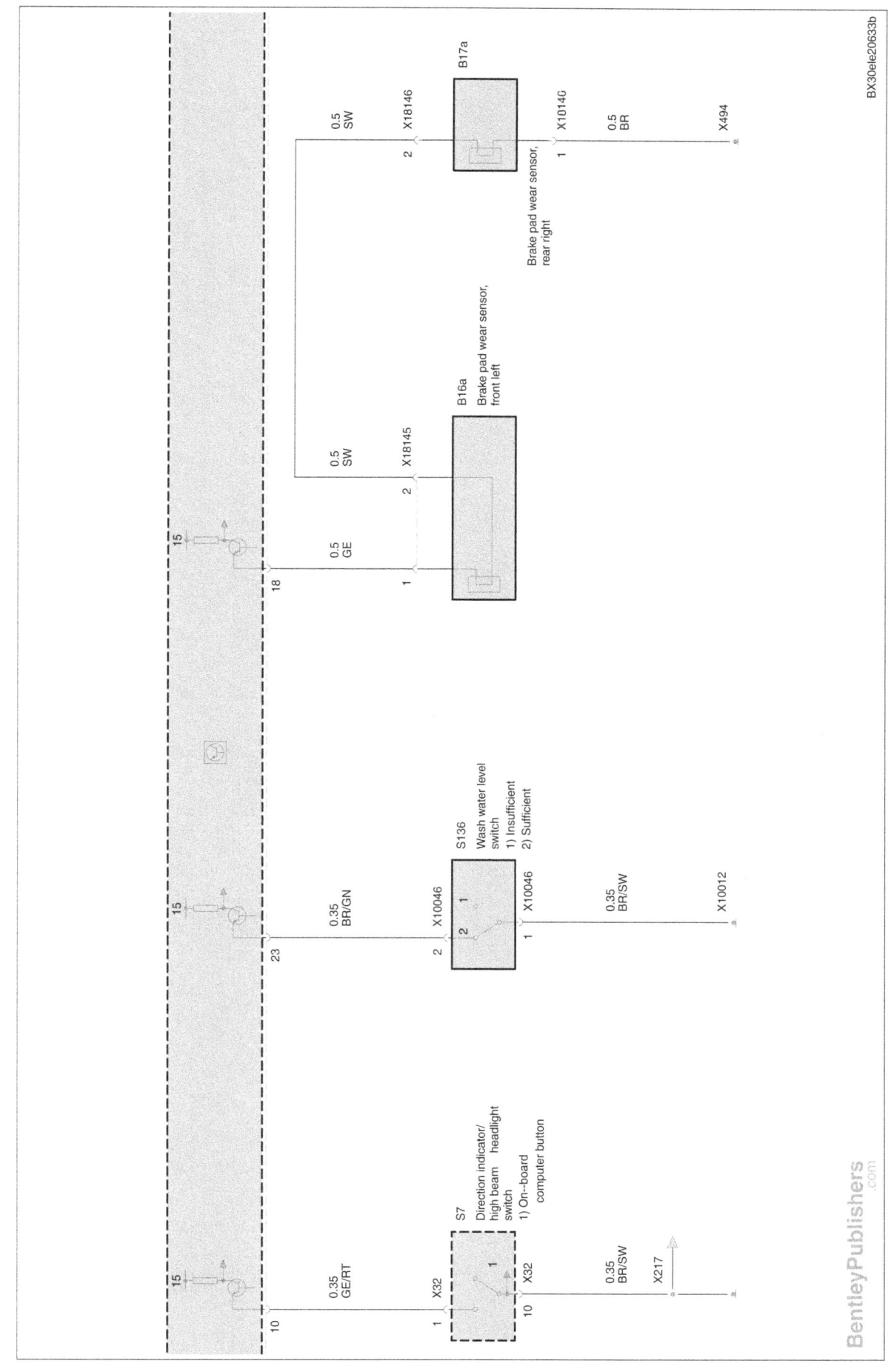

BX30ele20633b

**Instrument cluster, inputs
(to 09/2004)
page 3 of 3**

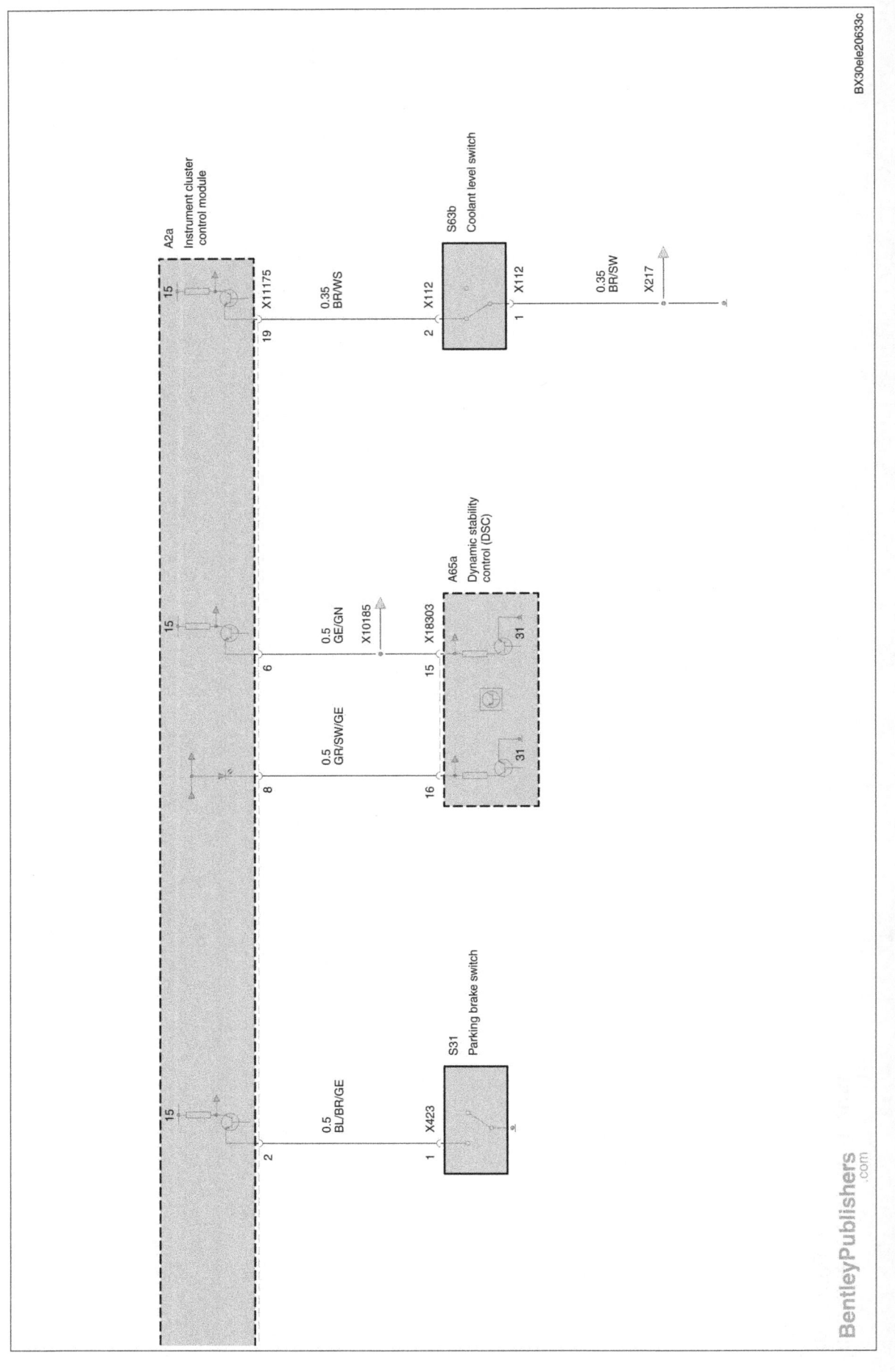

BX30ele20633c

Instrument cluster, inputs
(from 09/2004)
page 1 of 3

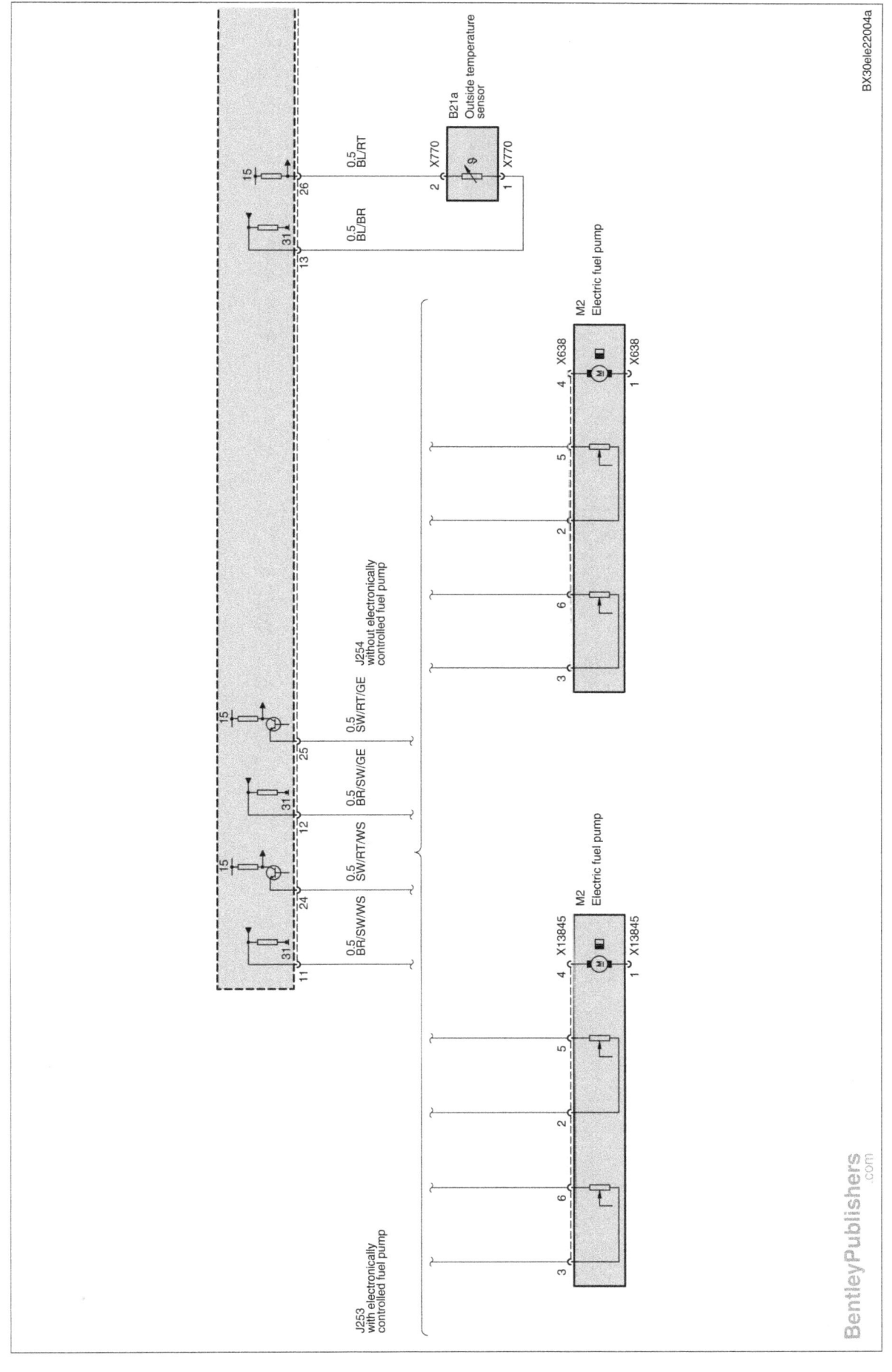

Electrical Wiring Diagrams   ELE-133

BX30ele22004a

**Instrument cluster, inputs
(from 09/2004)
page 2 of 3**

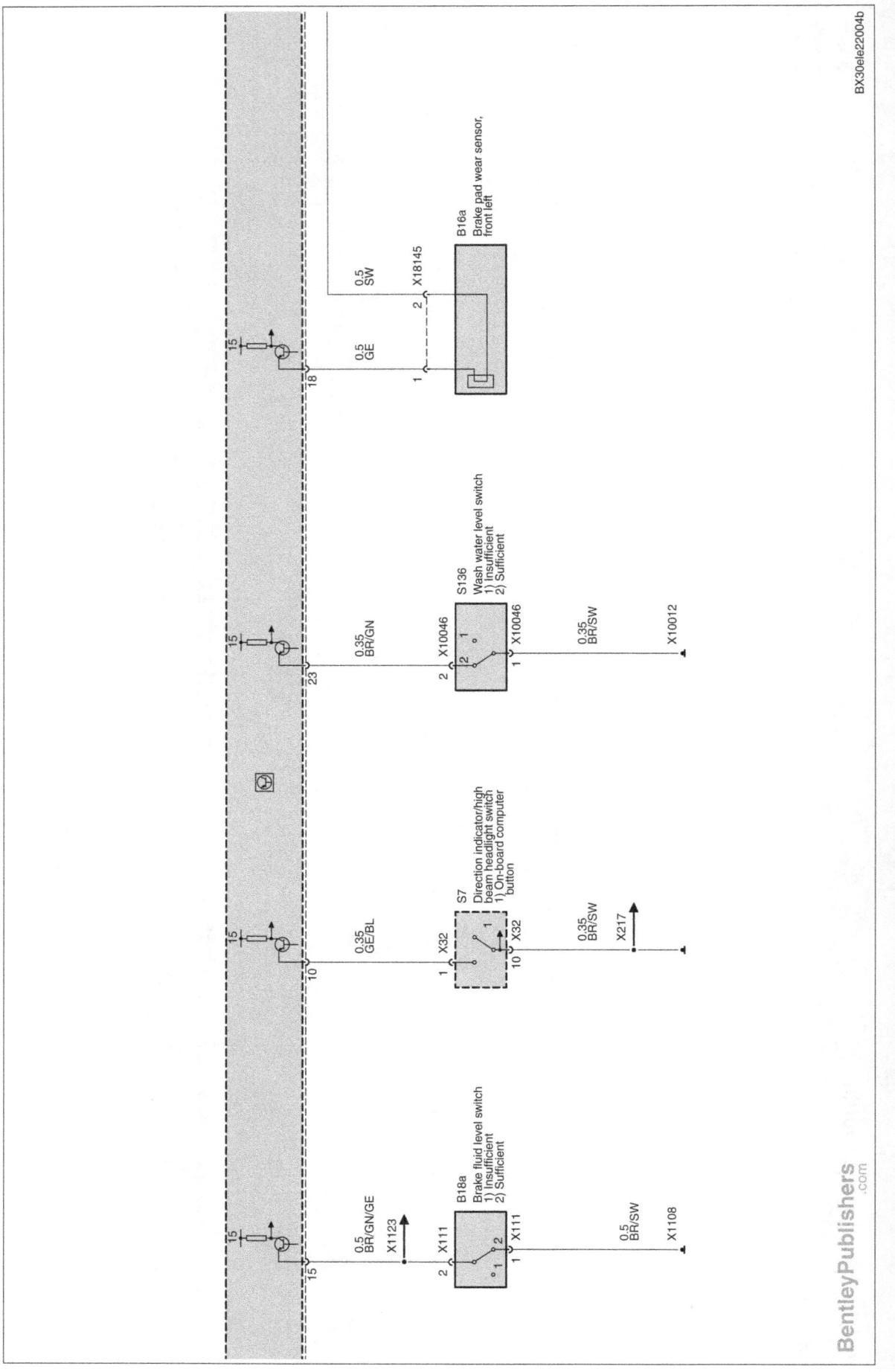

BX30ele22004b

A2a
Instrument cluster
control module

S63b
Coolant level switch

A65a
Dynamic stability control
(DSC)

S31
Parking brake switch

B17a
Brake pad wear sensor,
rear right

15

X11175
19
0.35
BR/WS
2   X112
1   X112
0.35
BR/SW
X217

15
6
0.5
GE/GN
X10185
X18303
15
31

8
0.5
GR/SW/GE
16
31

15
2
0.5
BL/BR/GE
1   X423

0.5
SW
2   X18146
X18146   1
0.5
BR
X494

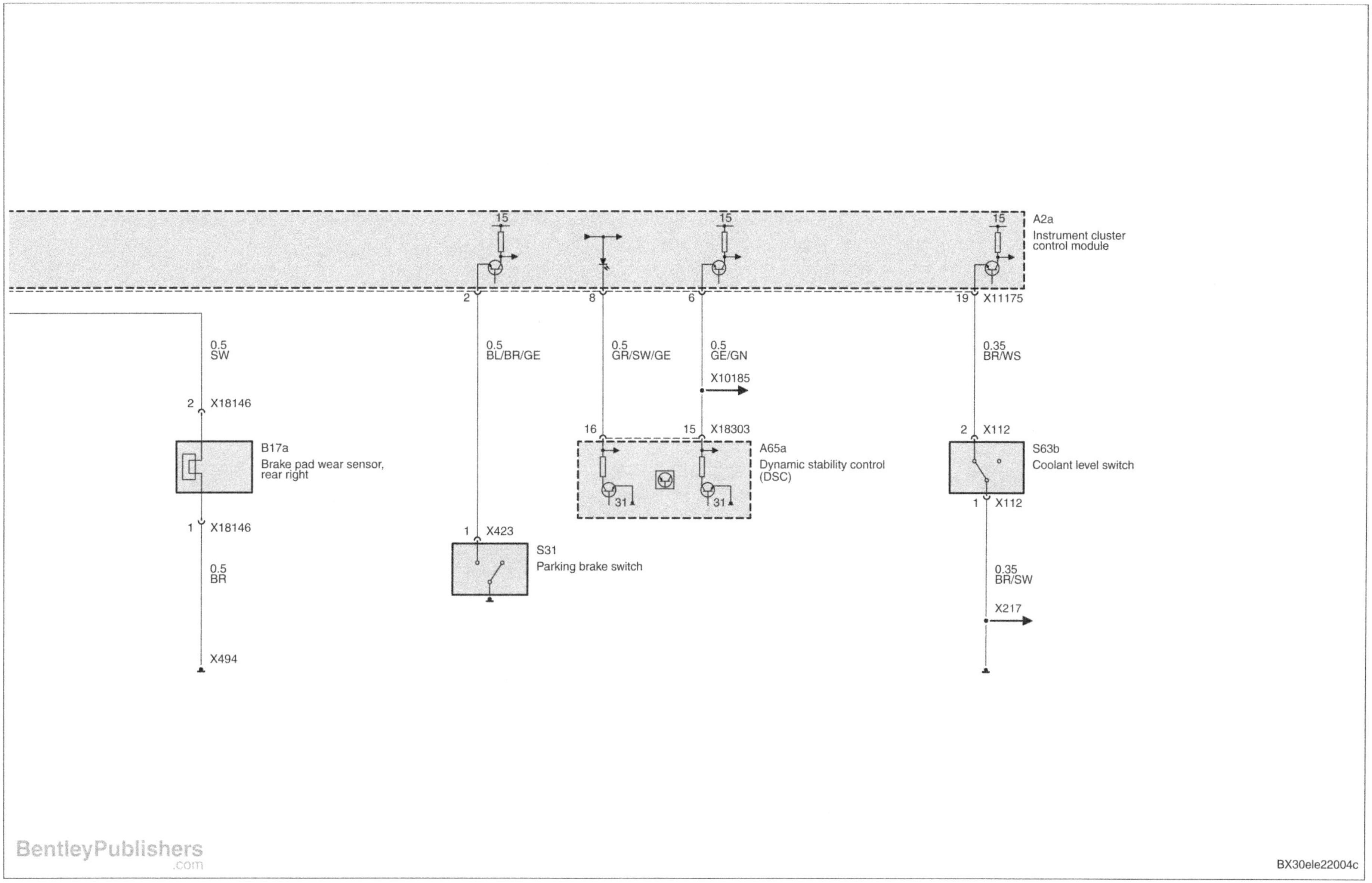

Instrument cluster, supply

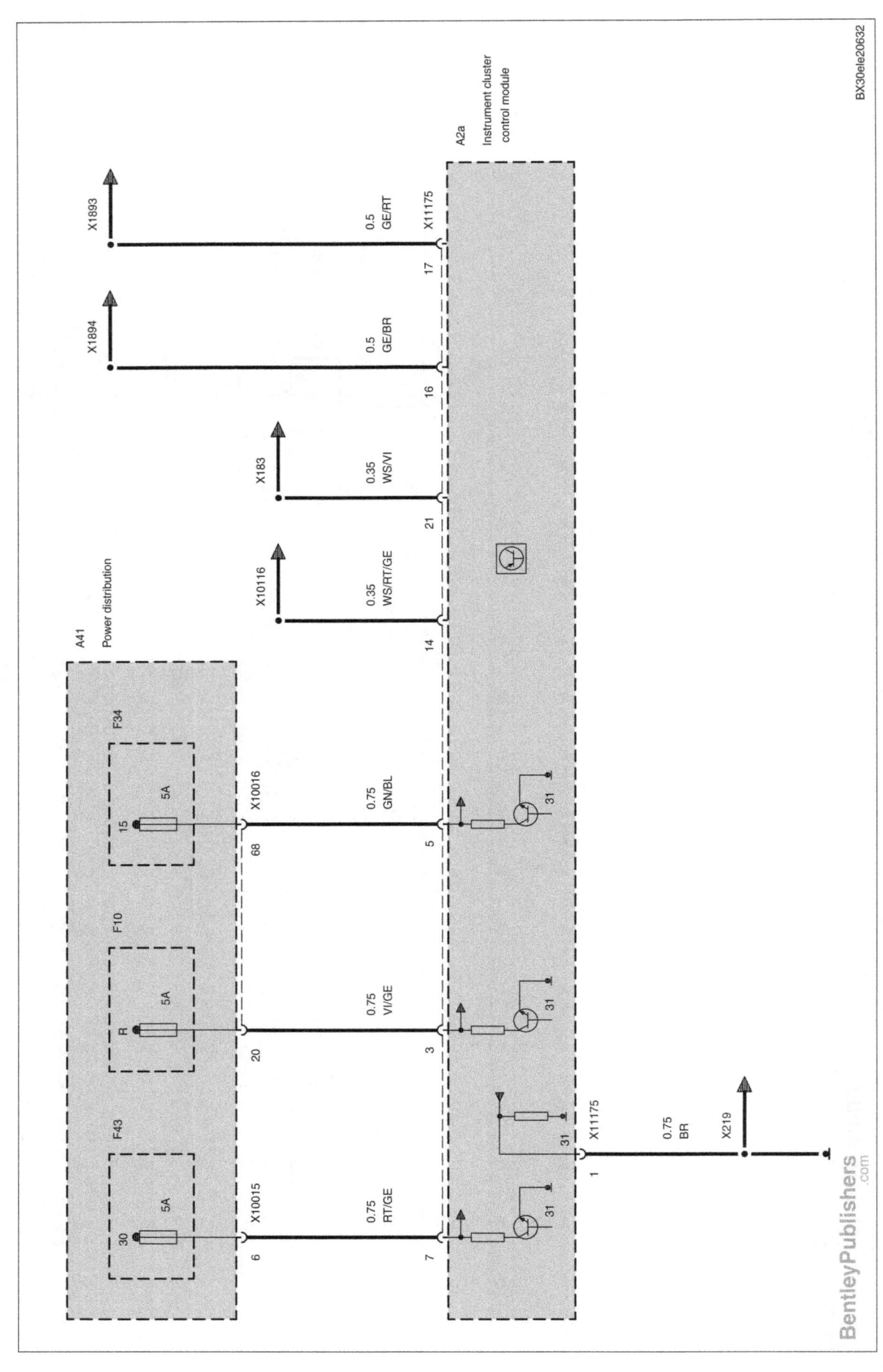

BX30ele20632

Instrument cluster, interface signals

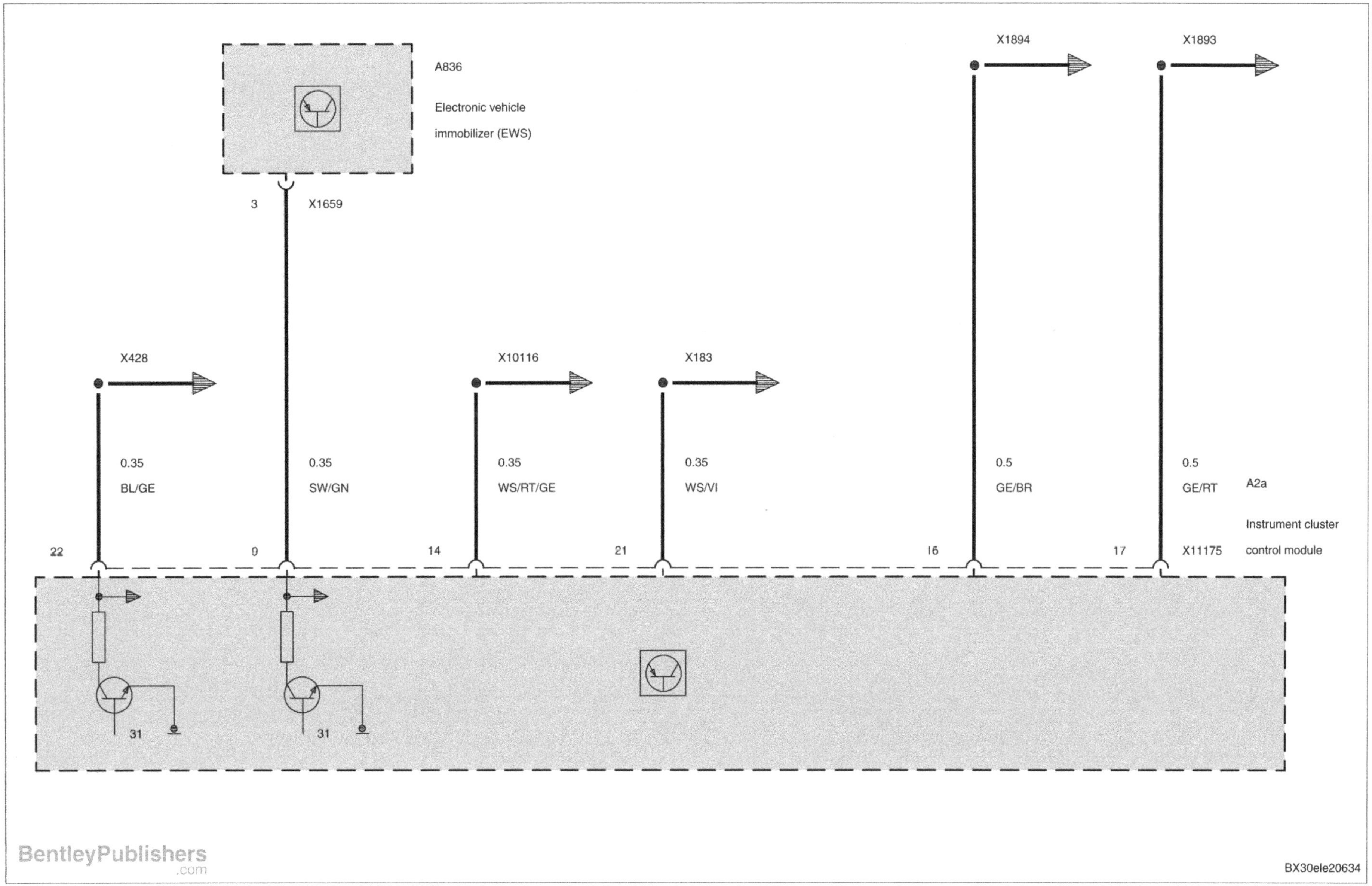

A836
Electronic vehicle
immobilizer (EWS)

X1659

3

0.35
SW/GN

0

22

0.35
BL/GE

X428

31

31

14

0.35
WS/RT/GE

X10116

21

0.35
WS/VI

X183

I6

0.5
GE/BR

X1894

17

0.5
GE/RT

X11175

A2a
Instrument cluster
control module

X1893

Electrical Wiring Diagrams   ELE-137

BX30ele20634

Adaptive headlights
(to 09/2006)

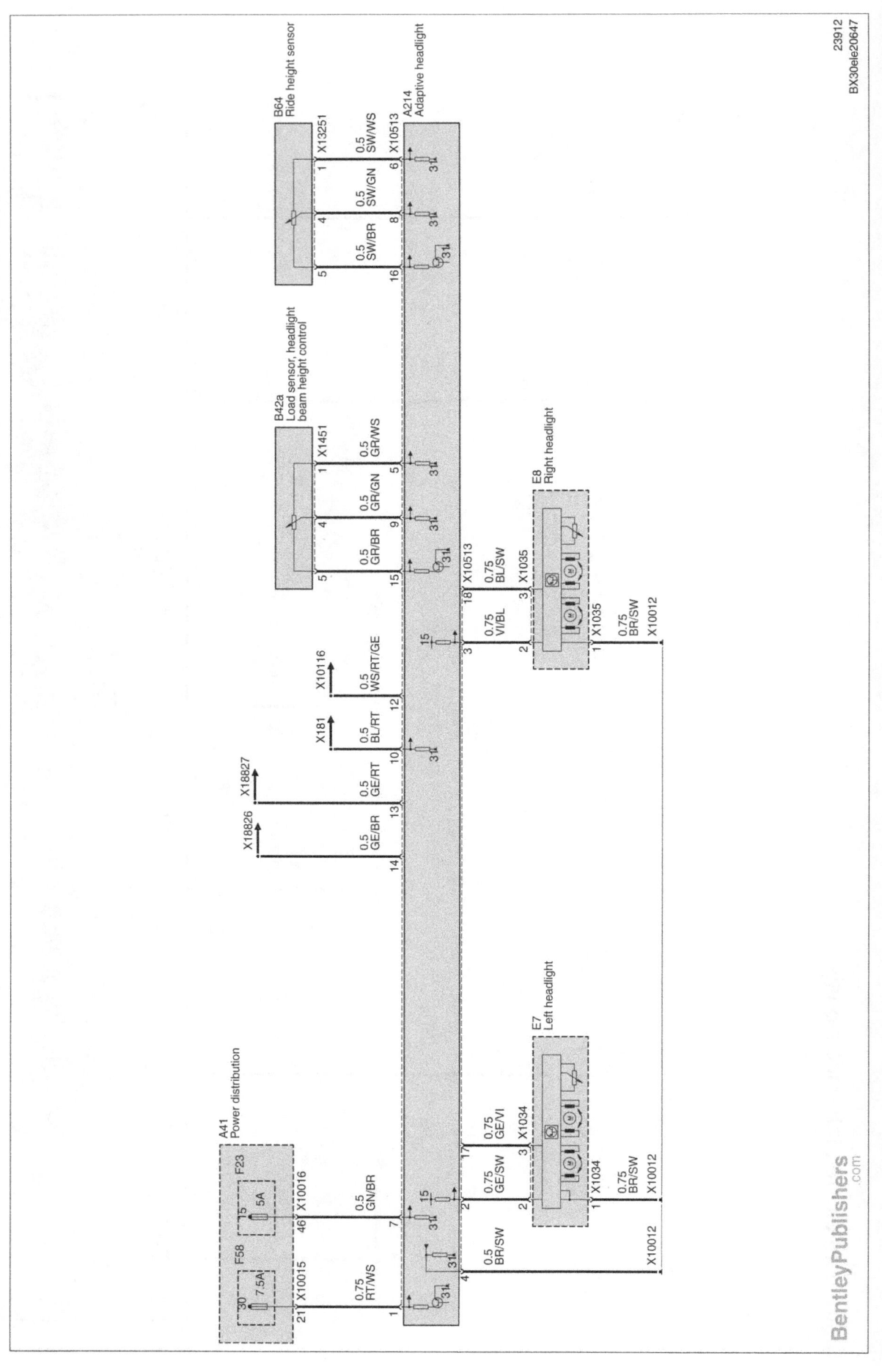

23912
BX30ele20647

**Adaptive headlights
(from 09/2006)**

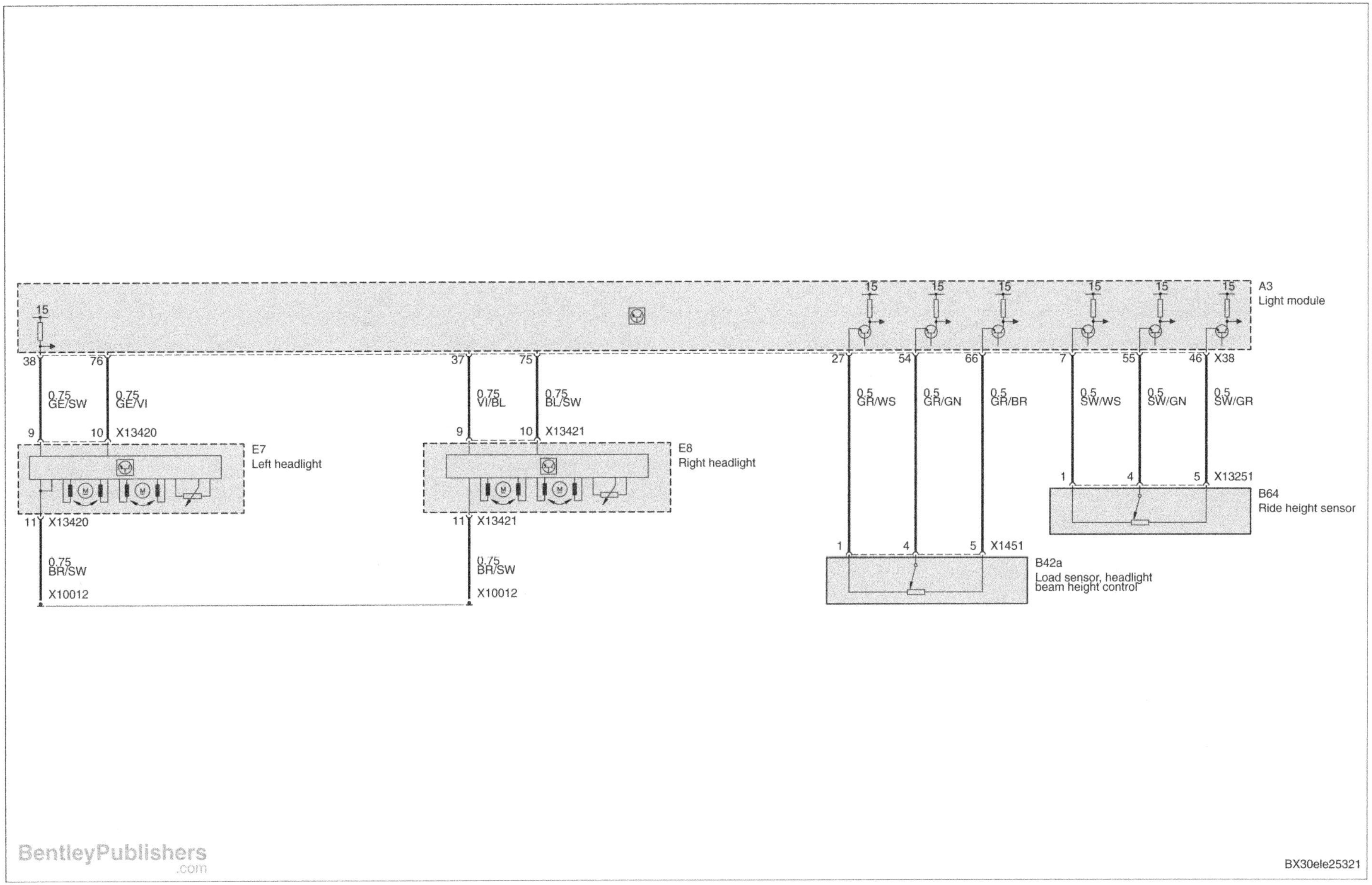

A3
Light module

B64
Ride height sensor

B42a
Load sensor, headlight
beam height control

E8
Right headlight

E7
Left headlight

X38

46 X38 0.5 SW/GR X13251 5

55 0.5 SW/GN 4

7 0.5 SW/WS 1

66 0.5 GR/BR X1451 5

54 0.5 GR/GN 4

27 0.5 GR/WS 1

75 0.75 BL/SW X13421 10

37 0.75 VI/BL 9

11 0.75 BR/SW X10012 X13421

76 0.75 GE/VI X13420 10

38 0.75 GE/SW 9

11 0.75 BR/SW X10012 X13420

15

Electrical Wiring Diagrams ELE-139

BX30ele25321

Electrical Wiring Diagrams ELE-140

Headlights,
vertical aim control
(to 09/2006)

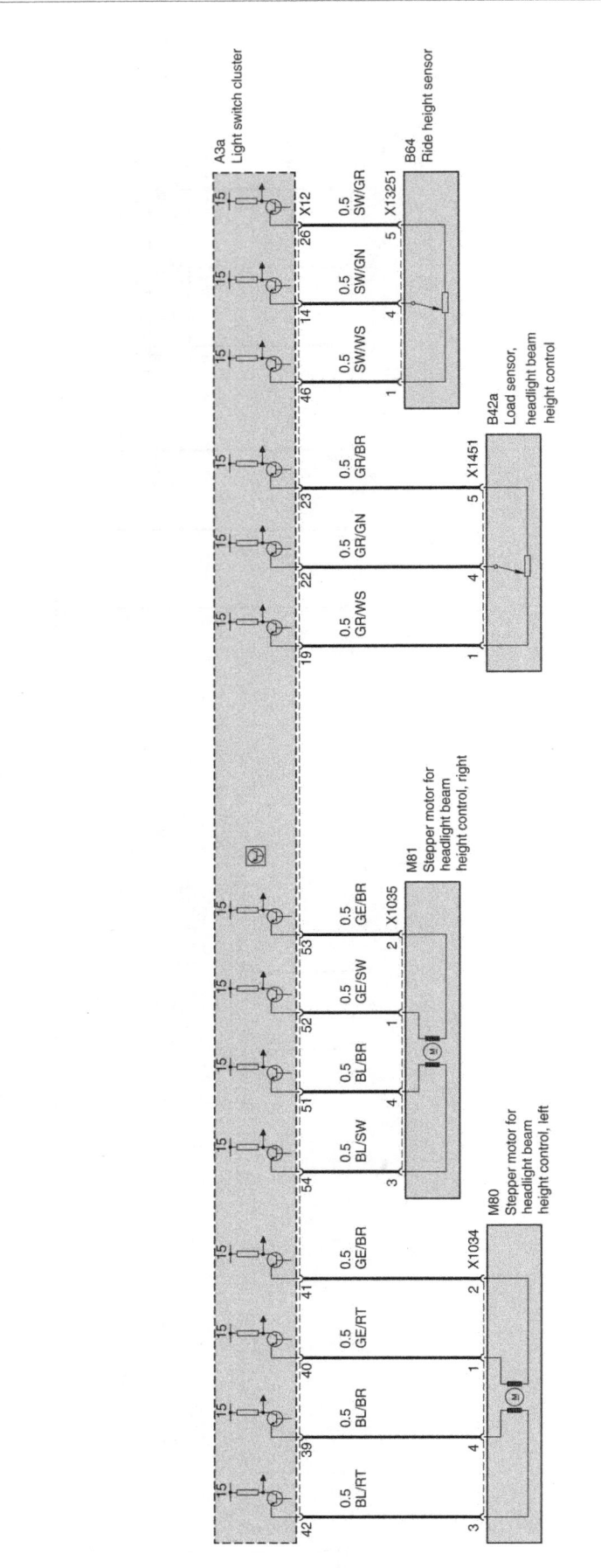

BX30ele20648

BentleyPublishers
.com

**Headlights,
vertical aim control
(from 09/2006)**

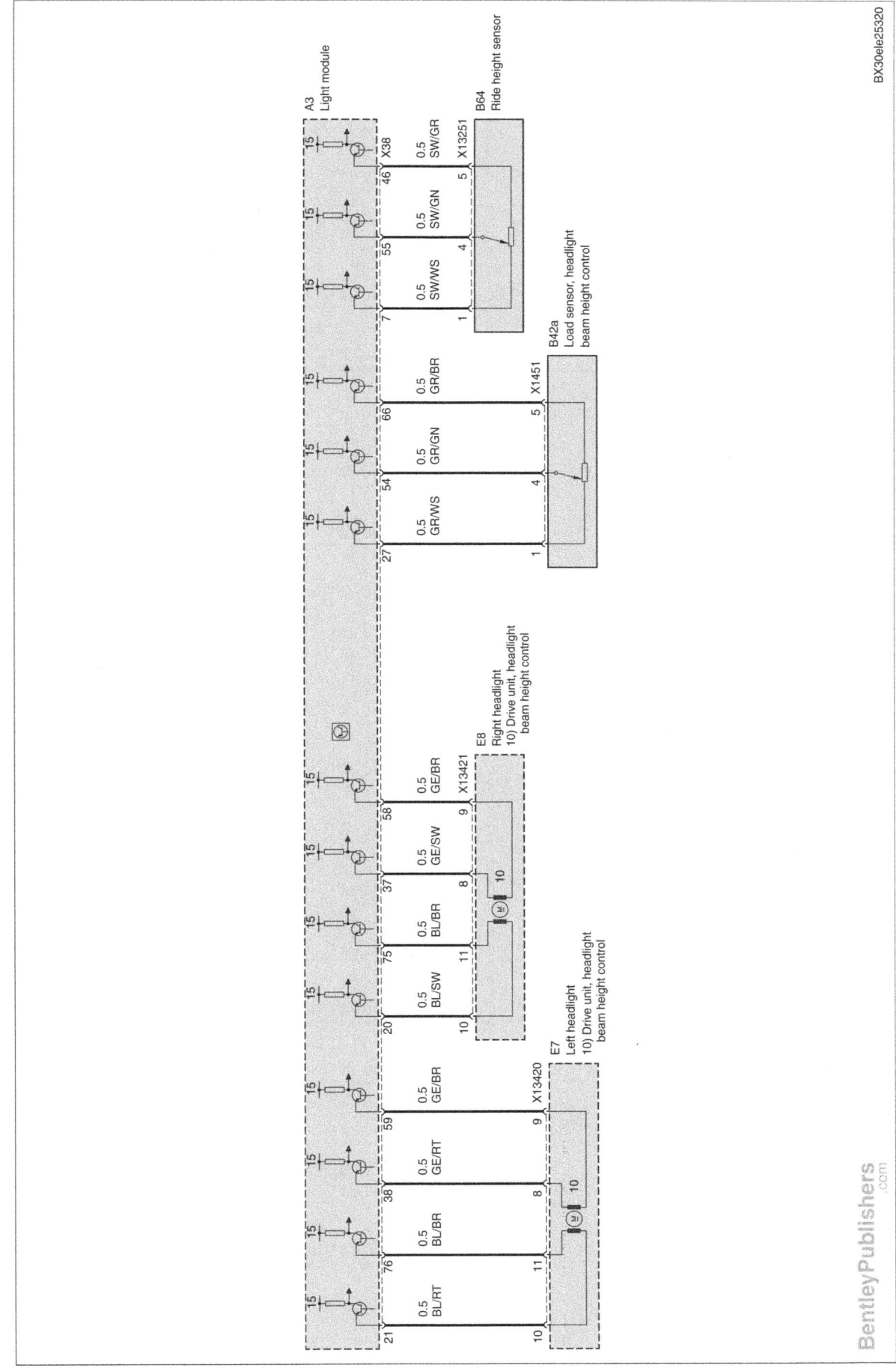

BX30ele25320

Back-up lights
M54 engine

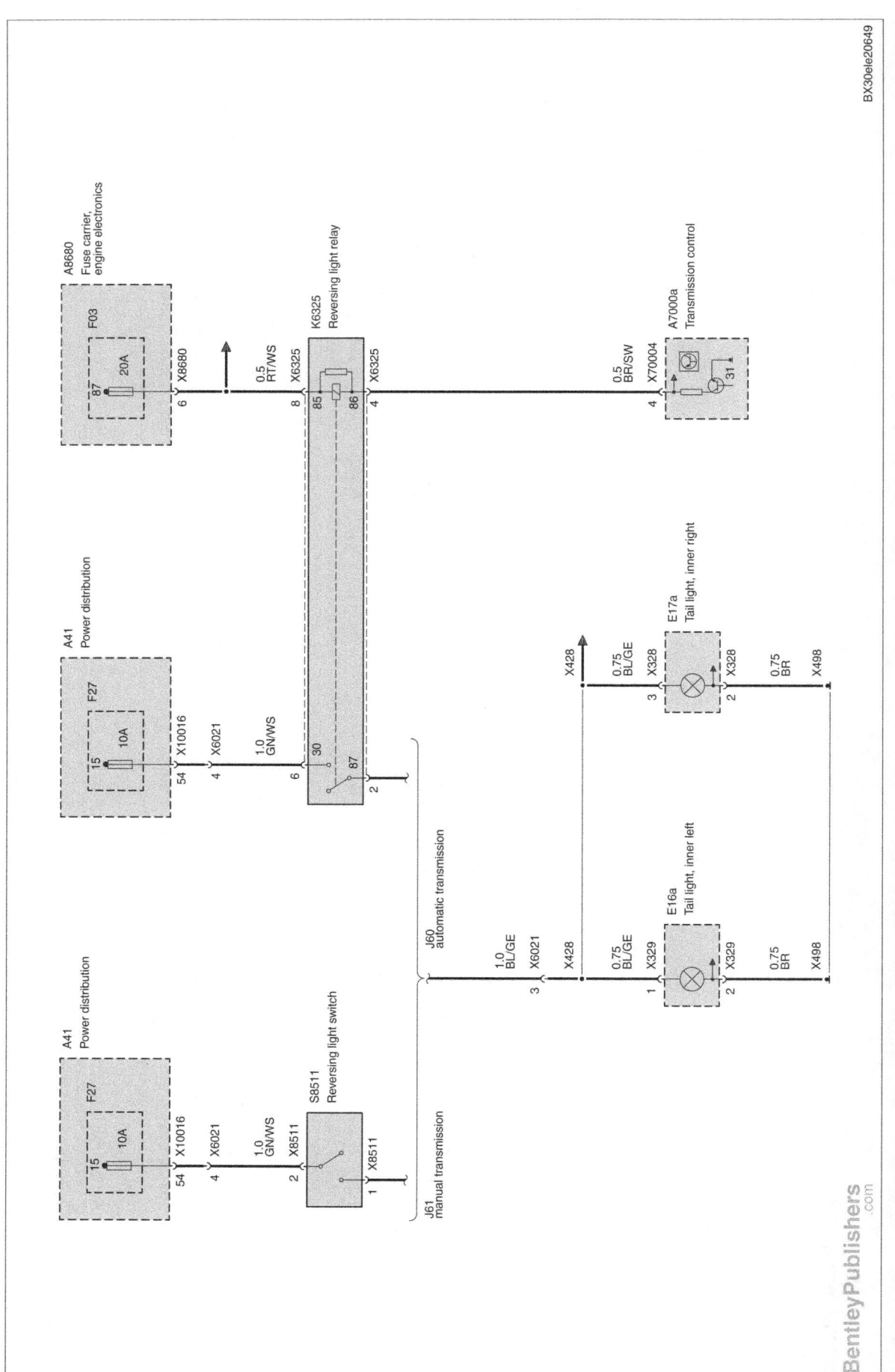

Back-up lights
N52 engine

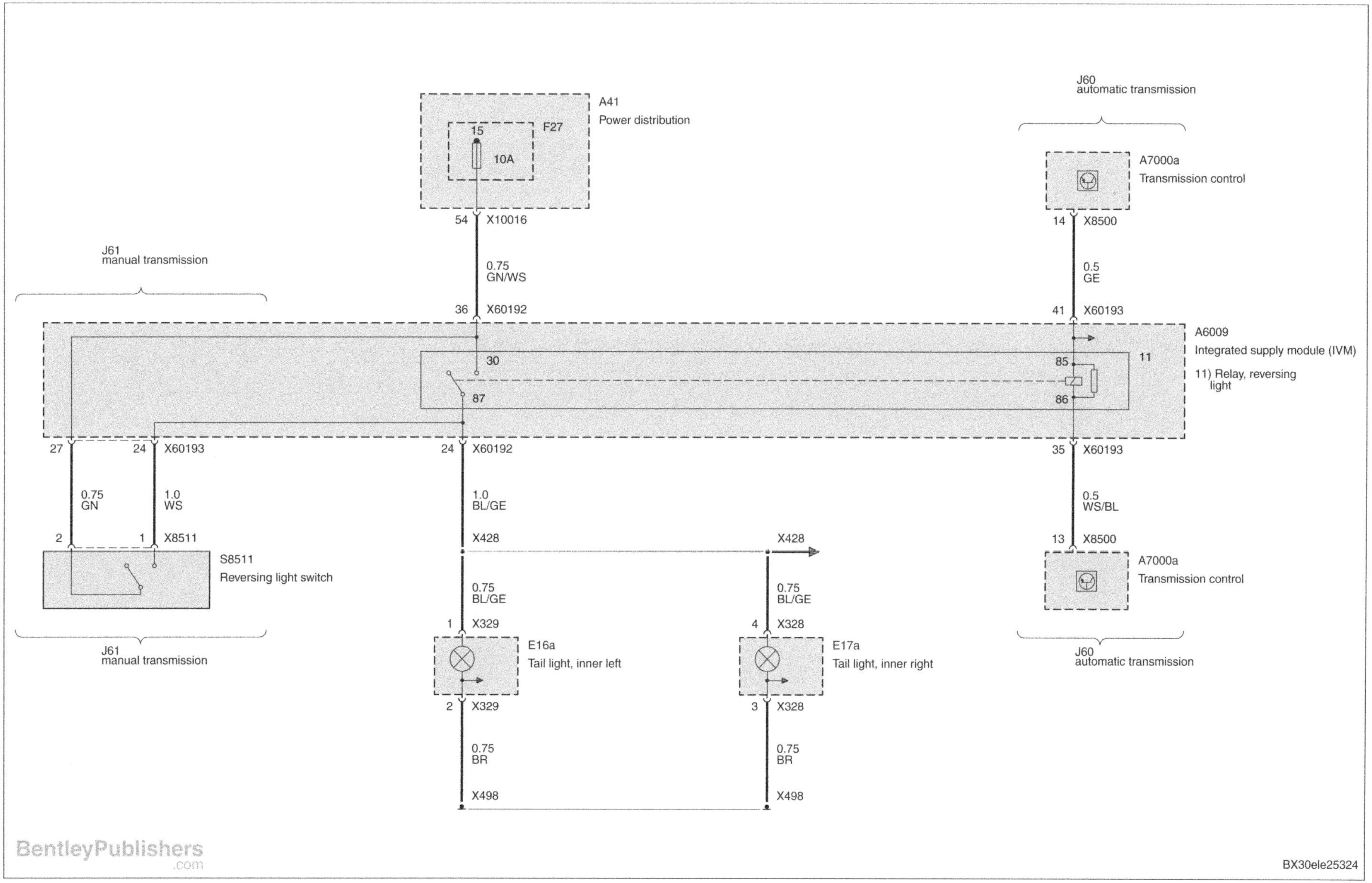

A7000a
Transmission control
J60 automatic transmission

A6009
Integrated supply module (IVM)
11) Relay, reversing light

A7000a
Transmission control
J60 automatic transmission

A41
Power distribution
F27
15 10A

E17a
Tail light, inner right

E16a
Tail light, inner left

S8511
Reversing light switch

J61 manual transmission

J61 manual transmission

14 X8500
0.5 GE
41 X60193

11

85 86
35 X60193
0.5 WS/BL
13 X8500

X428
0.75 BL/GE
4 X328
3 X328
0.75 BR
X498

15
X10016
0.75 GN/WS
54 36 X60192
30
87
24 X60192
1.0 BL/GE
X428
0.75 BL/GE
1 X329
2 X329
0.75 BR
X498

24 X60193
1.0 WS
X8511 1
2
0.75 GN
27

BX30ele25324

Brake lights

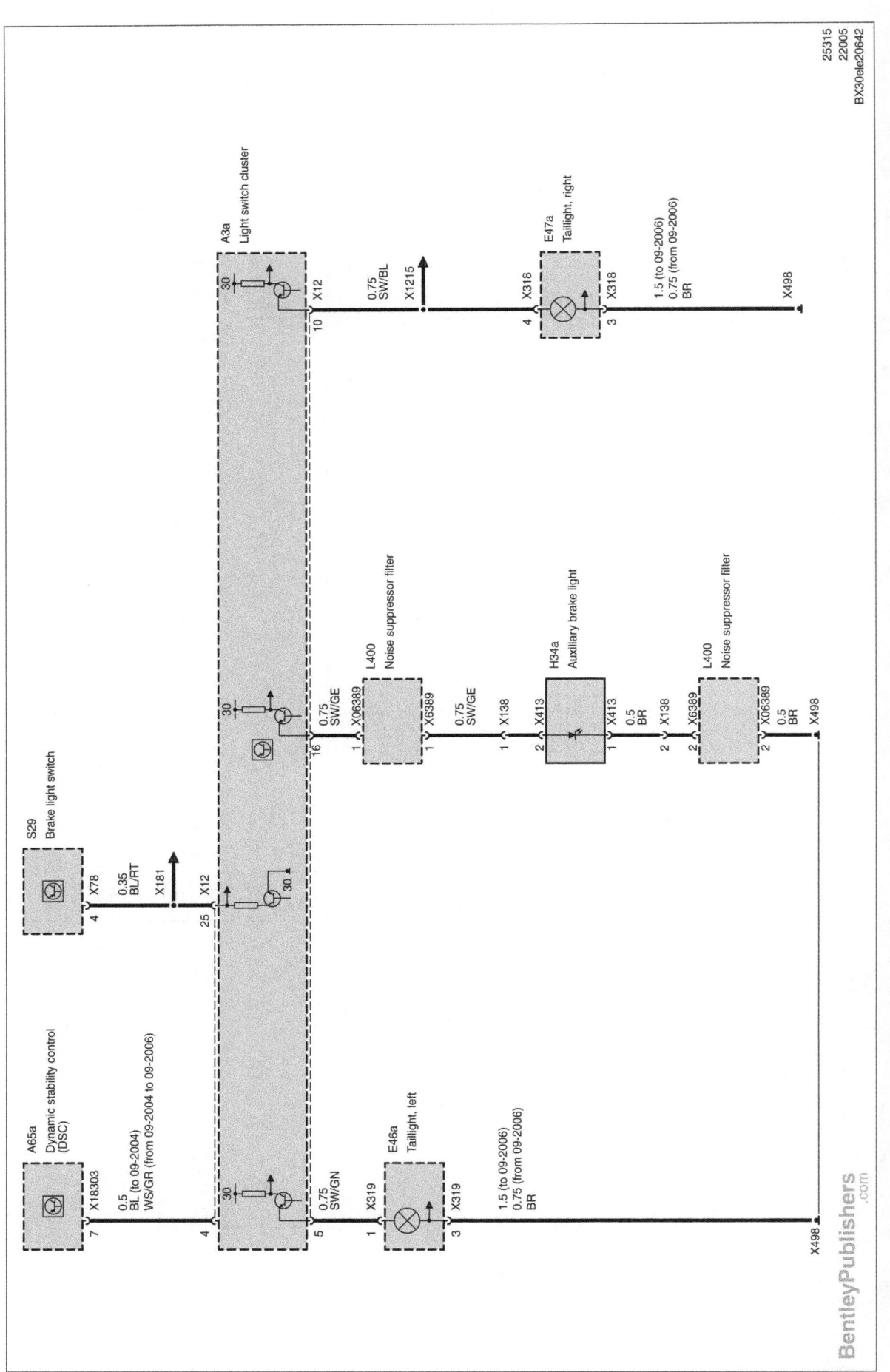

Fog lights, front and rear (from 09/2006)

Fog lights, front and rear (to 09/2006)

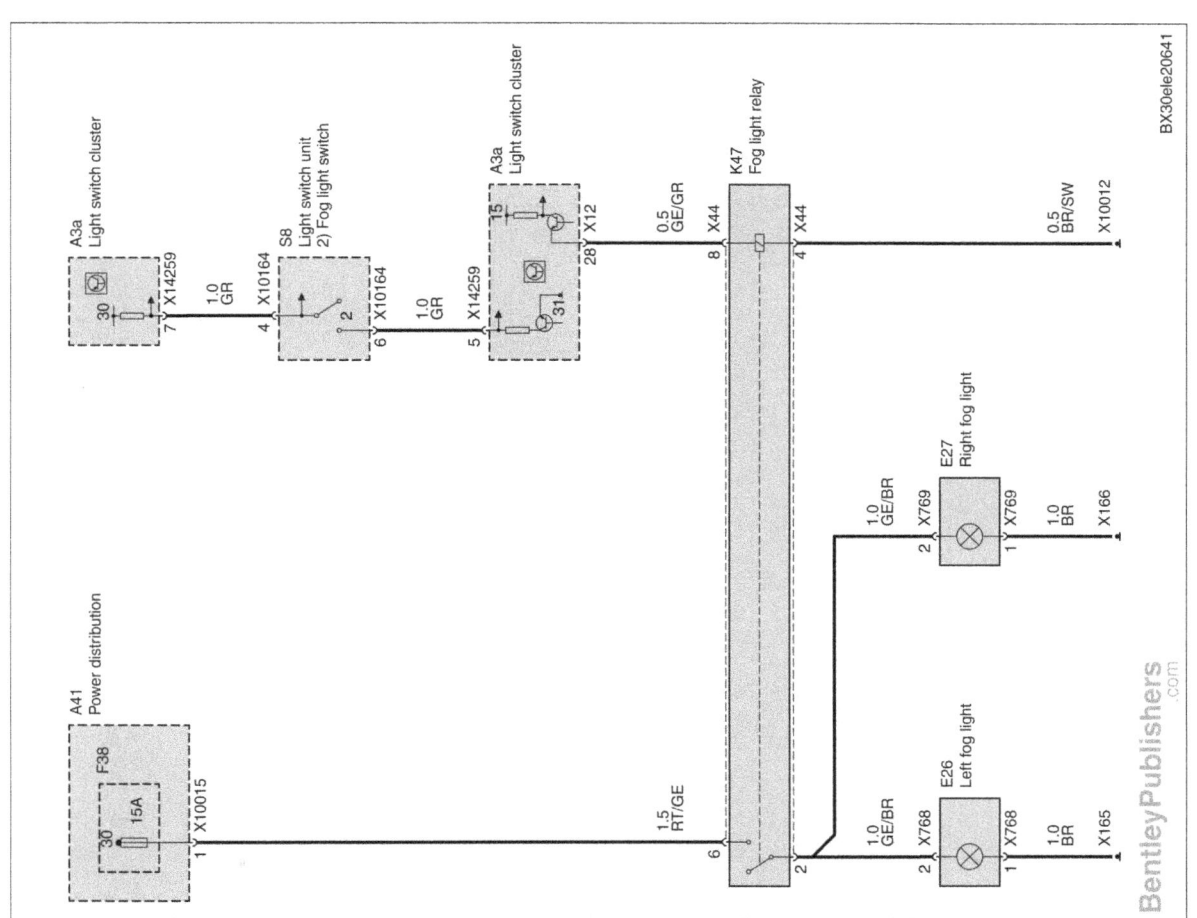

BX30ele25313

BX30ele20641

Electrical Wiring Diagrams   ELE-145

**Headlights, with xenon lights
(to 09/2006)**

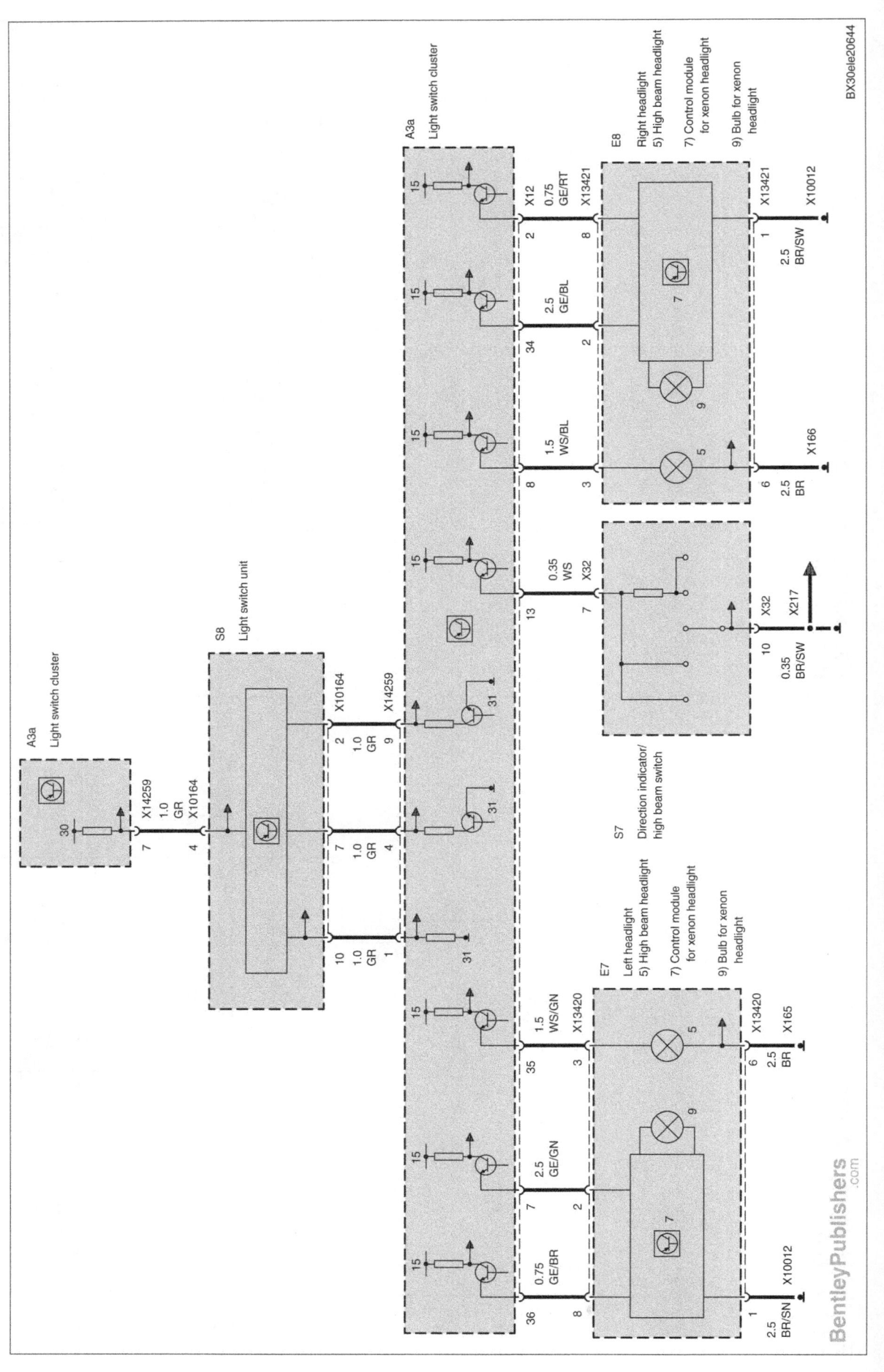

BX30ele20644

**Headlights, with xenon lights
(from 09/2006)**

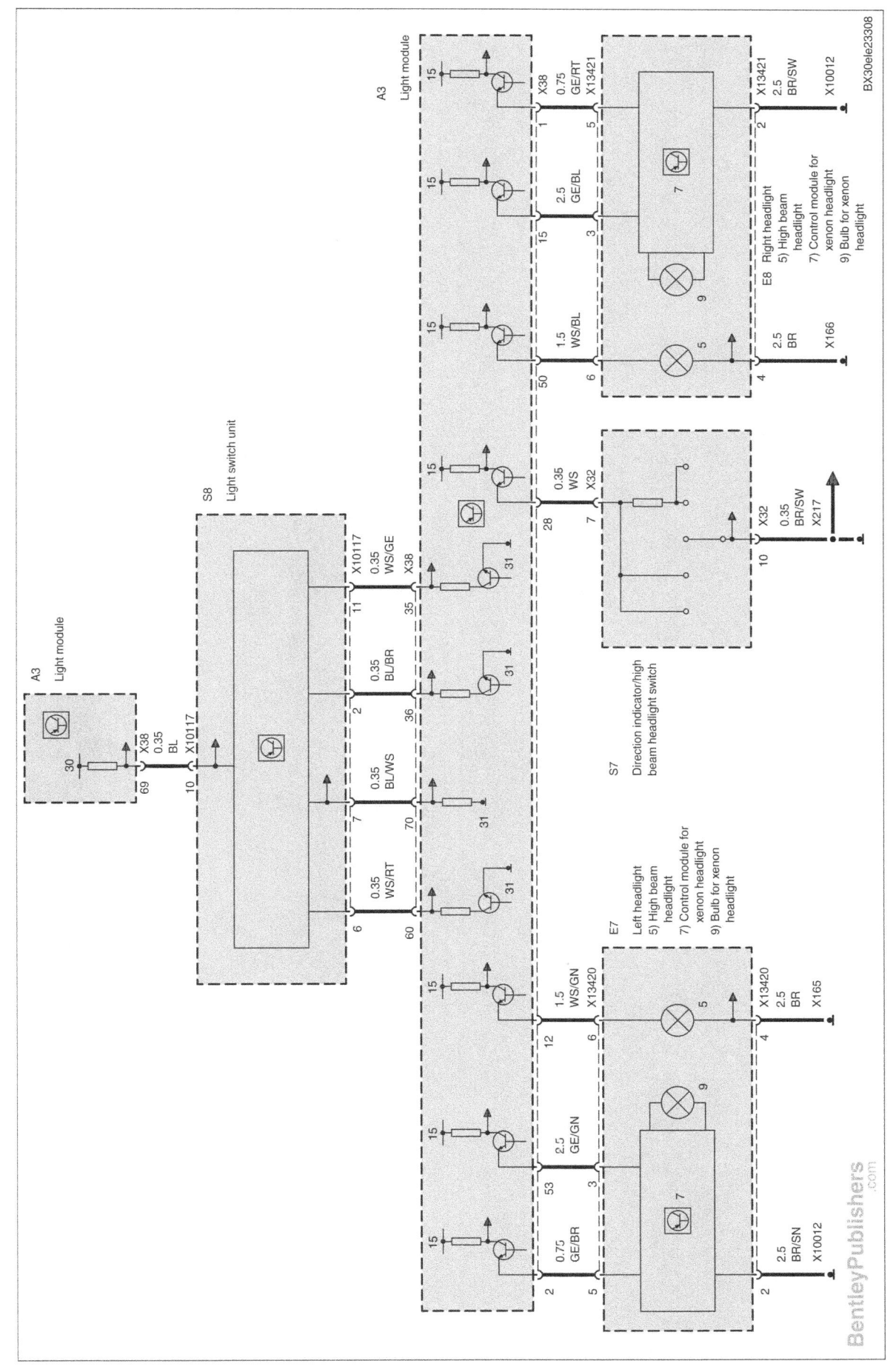

Electrical Wiring Diagrams ELE-147

BX30ele23308

**Headlights, without xenon lights
(to 09/2006)**

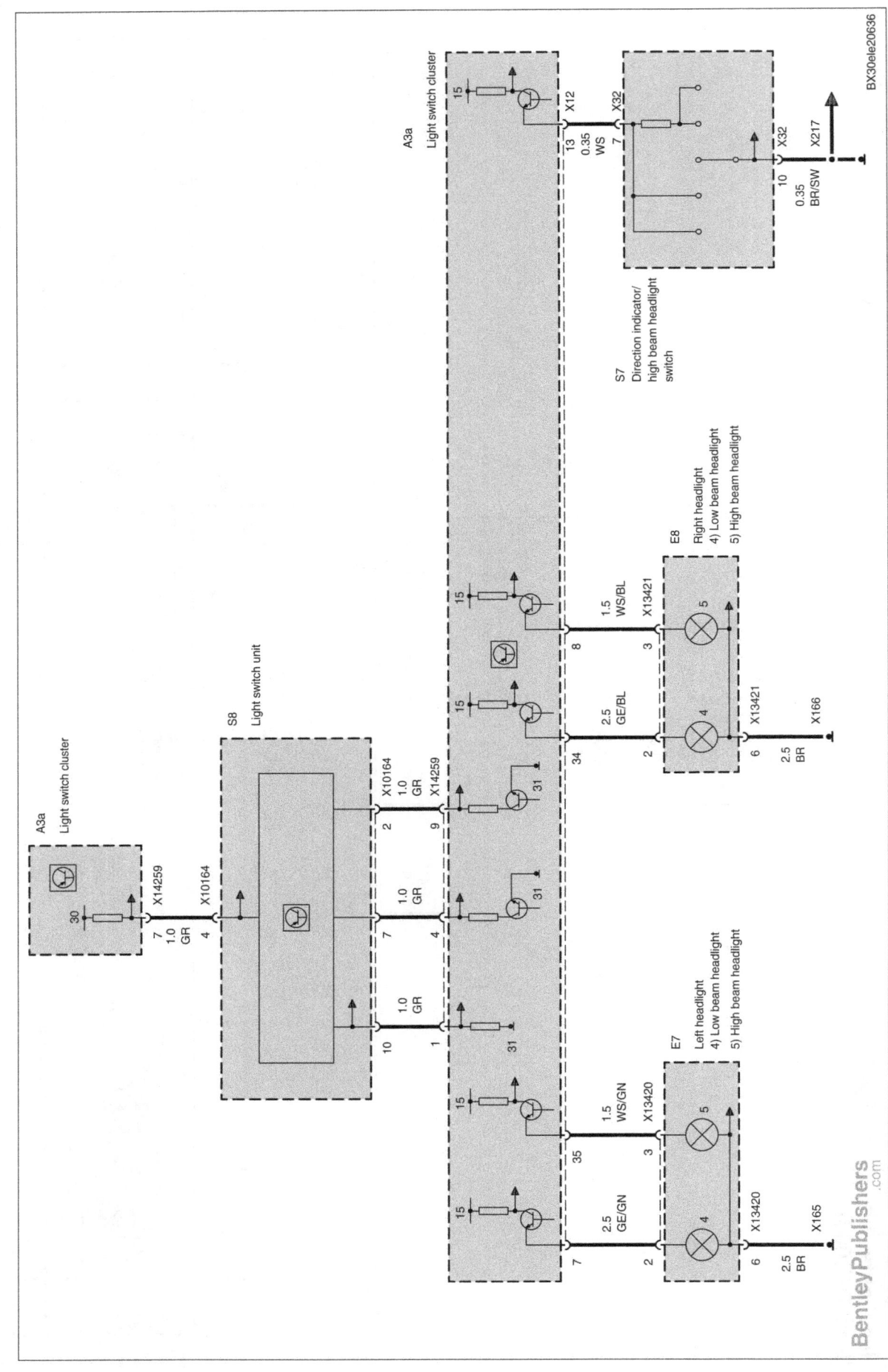

BX30ele20636

**Headlights, without xenon lights
(from 09/2006)**

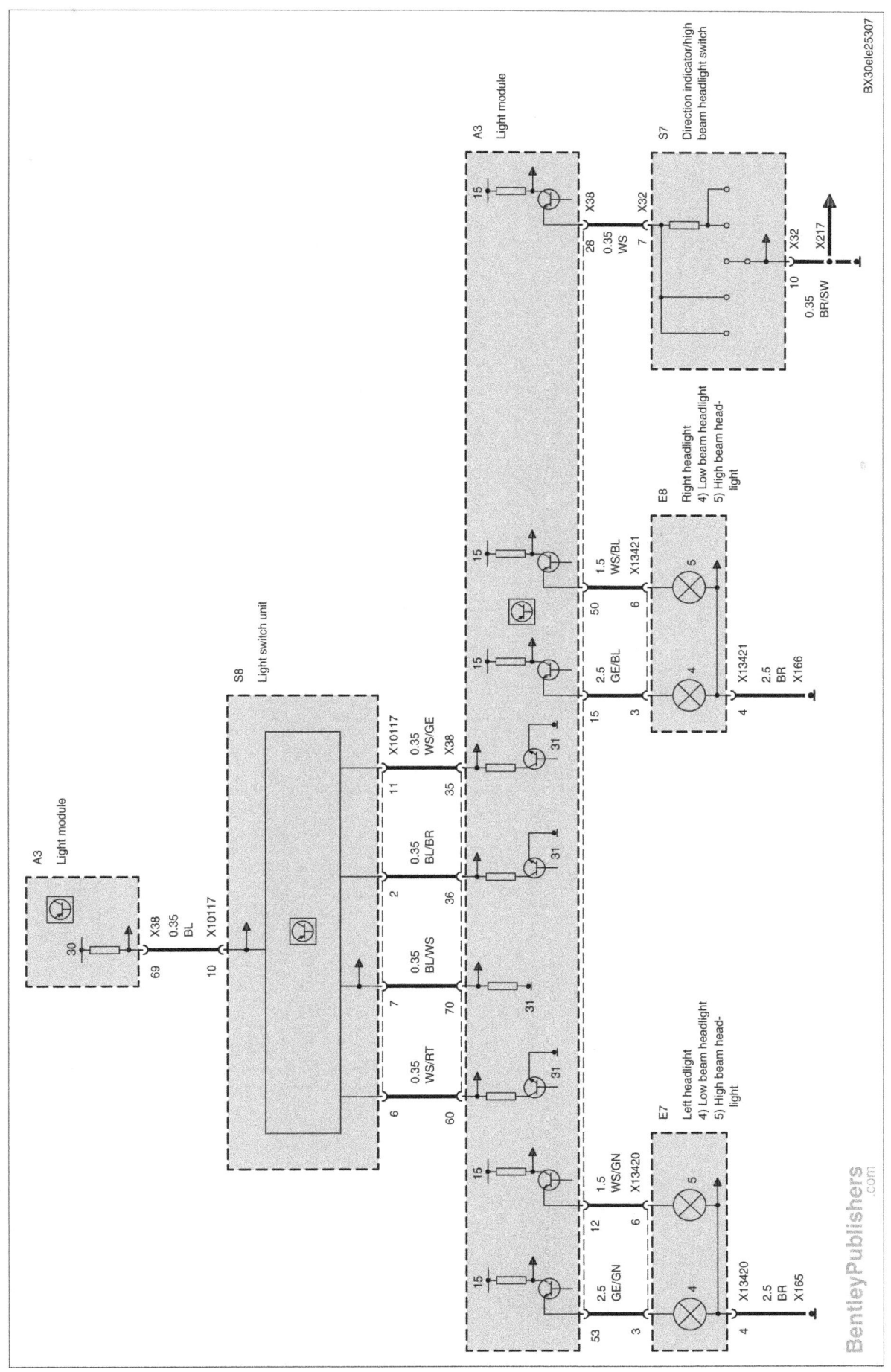

Electrical Wiring Diagrams   ELE-149

BX30ele25307

**Interior lights
(to 09/2007)
page 1 of 2**

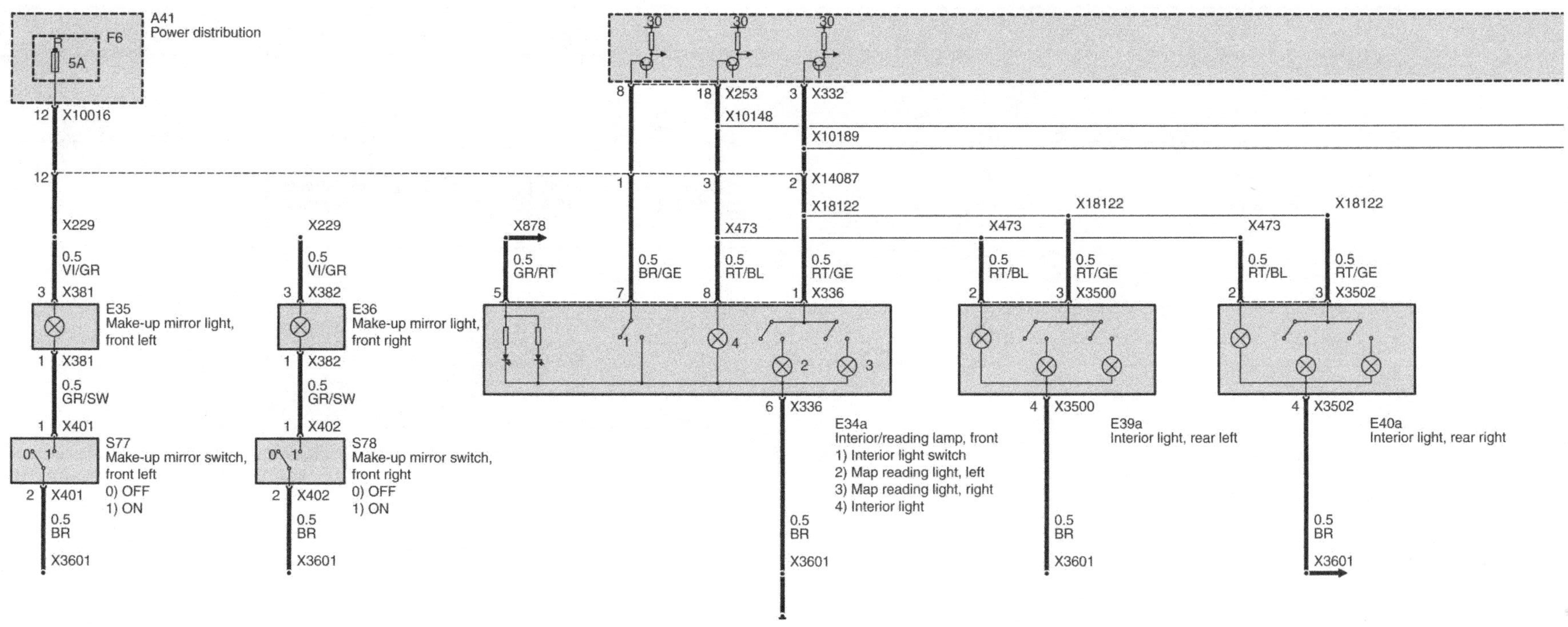

A41
Power distribution

F6

5A

X10016

12

12

X229
0.5
VI/GR
X381

E35
Make-up mirror light,
front left

3

X381
0.5
GR/SW
X401

1

S77
Make-up mirror switch,
front left
0) OFF
1) ON

0 1

2 X401
0.5
BR
X3601

X229
0.5
VI/GR
X382

E36
Make-up mirror light,
front right

3

X382
0.5
GR/SW
X402

1

S78
Make-up mirror switch,
front right
0) OFF
1) ON

0 1

2 X402
0.5
BR
X3601

30

X332
3

X10189

X14087
2

X18122

0.5
RT/GE
X336
1

30

X253
18

X10148

X473
3

0.5
RT/BL
X473
8

30

X878
0.5
GR/RT

8

1

0.5
BR/GE

7 1

5

E34a
Interior/reading lamp, front
1) Interior light switch
2) Map reading light, left
3) Map reading light, right
4) Interior light

3

2

4

6 X336
0.5
BR
X3601

X18122
X473

0.5
RT/GE
X3500
3

0.5
RT/BL
2

E39a
Interior light, rear left

4 X3500
0.5
BR
X3601

X18122
X473

0.5
RT/GE
X3502
3

0.5
RT/BL
2

E40a
Interior light, rear right

4 X3502
0.5
BR
X3601

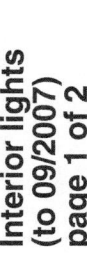

BX30ele25321

A1
General module control module

30 23 X253 0.35 BR/WS X274 6 0.35 BR/GR X646 X646 2 1 3 M14 System lock, rear right door 1) Door contact switch 0.35 BR X835

30 24 0.35 BR/GR X273 6 X644 X644 2 1 3 M15 System lock, rear left door 1) Door contact switch 0.35 BR X834

30 26 X257 16 0.5 BR/GR/GE X747 X747 2 1 3 S47 System lock, driver's door 1) Door contact 0.75 BR X849

30 25 X256 16 0.5 BR/GR/GE X742 X742 2 1 3 S49 System lock, passenger's door 1) Door contact 0.75 BR X891

X10148 0.5 RT/BL X745 X745 2 1 E62a Passenger's side footwell light 0.5 BR X219

X10148 0.5 RT/BL X748 X748 2 1 E61a Driver's side footwell light 0.5 BR X173

X10189 0.5 RT/GE X18336 1 E42a Glove compartment light 1) Glove compartment, closed 2) Glove compartment, open 2 X18336 4 0.5 BR X219

X10189 0.5 RT/GE X712 1 E33 Luggage compartment light, trunk lid/tailgate 3 X712 0.5 WS/BR X465

X10189 0.5 RT/GE X3026 1 E401 Interior lights, left D-pillar 3 X3026 0.5 WS/BR X465

M17a Central locking drive, trunk lid 1) Trunk lid closed 2) Trunk lid open 0.5 WS/BR X311 1 2 X311 3 0.75 BR X498

X10189 0.5 RT/GE X3025 1 E400 Interior lights, right D-pillar 3 X3025 0.5 WS/BR X465

BX30ele20652b

Electrical Wiring Diagrams ELE-151

**Interior lights
(from 09/2007)
page 1 of 3**

A41 Power distribution

F6
5A
X10016

E33 Luggage compartment light, trunk lid/tailgate
X712
X10189
0.5 RT/GE
WS/BR
X465

E401 Interior lights, left D-pillar
X3026
X10189
0.5 RT/GE
0.5 WS/BR
X465
X311
WS/BR

M17a Central locking drive, trunk lid
1) Trunk lid closed
2) Trunk lid open
X311
0.75 BR
X498

E400 Interior lights, right D-pillar
X3025
X10189
0.5 RT/GE
0.5 WS/BR
X465

E40a Interior light, rear right
X3502
X18122
0.5 RT/GE
X473
0.5 RT/BL
0.5 BR
X3601

E39a Interior light, rear left
X3500
X18122
0.5 RT/GE
X473
0.5 RT/BL
0.5 BR
X3601

E34a Interior/reading lamp, front
1) Interior light switch
2) Map reading light, left
3) Map reading light, right
4) Interior light
X332
X253
X10148
X10189
X14087
X18122
X336
0.5 RT/GE
X473
0.5 RT/BL
0.5 BR/GE
X336
0.5 BR
X3601
X878
0.5 GR/RT
30
30
30
18
8
2
3

E36 Make-up mirror light, front right
X229
X382
0.5 VI/GR
X382
0.5 GR/SW
X402

S78 Make-up mirror switch, front right
0) OFF
1) ON
X402
0.5 BR
X3601

E35 Make-up mirror light, front left
X229
X381
0.5 VI/GR
X381
0.5 GR/SW
X401

S77 Make-up mirror switch, front left
0) OFF
1) ON
X401
0.5 BR
X3601

12
12

BX30ele26492a

E42a Glove compartment light
1) Glove compartment closed
2) Glove compartment open

E61a Driver's side footwell light

E62a Passenger's side footwell light

E63 Rear left footwell light

E64 Rear right footwell light

E88 Exit light, driver's door

E89 Exit light, passenger's door

E90a Exit light, rear left door

E91a Exit light, rear right door

**Interior lights
(from 09/2007)
page 3 of 3**

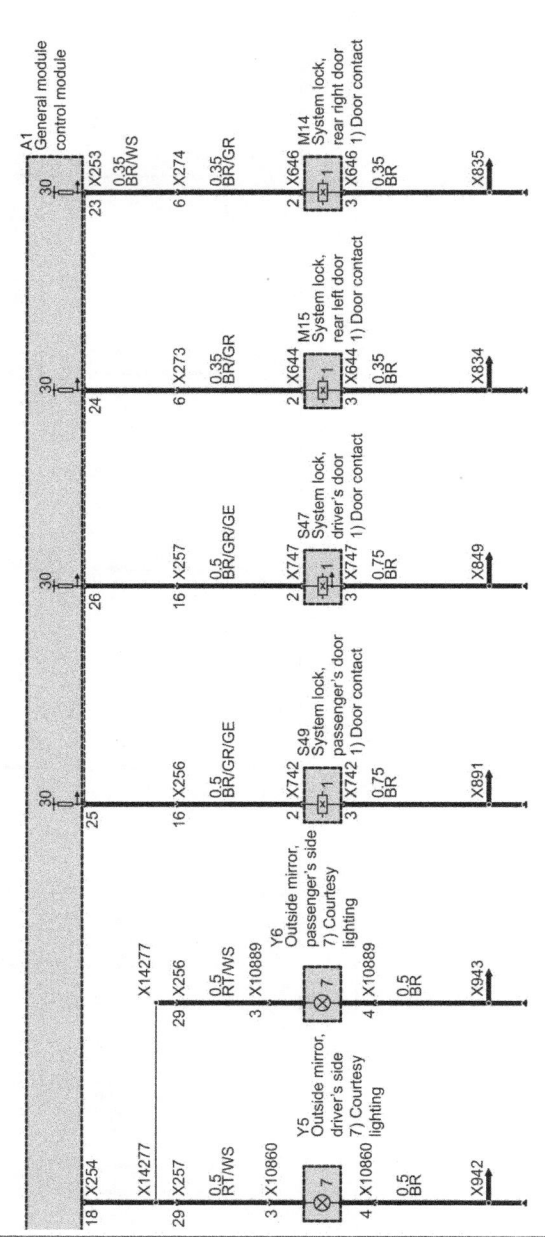

BX30ele26492c

**Electrochromic mirror
to 09/2005**

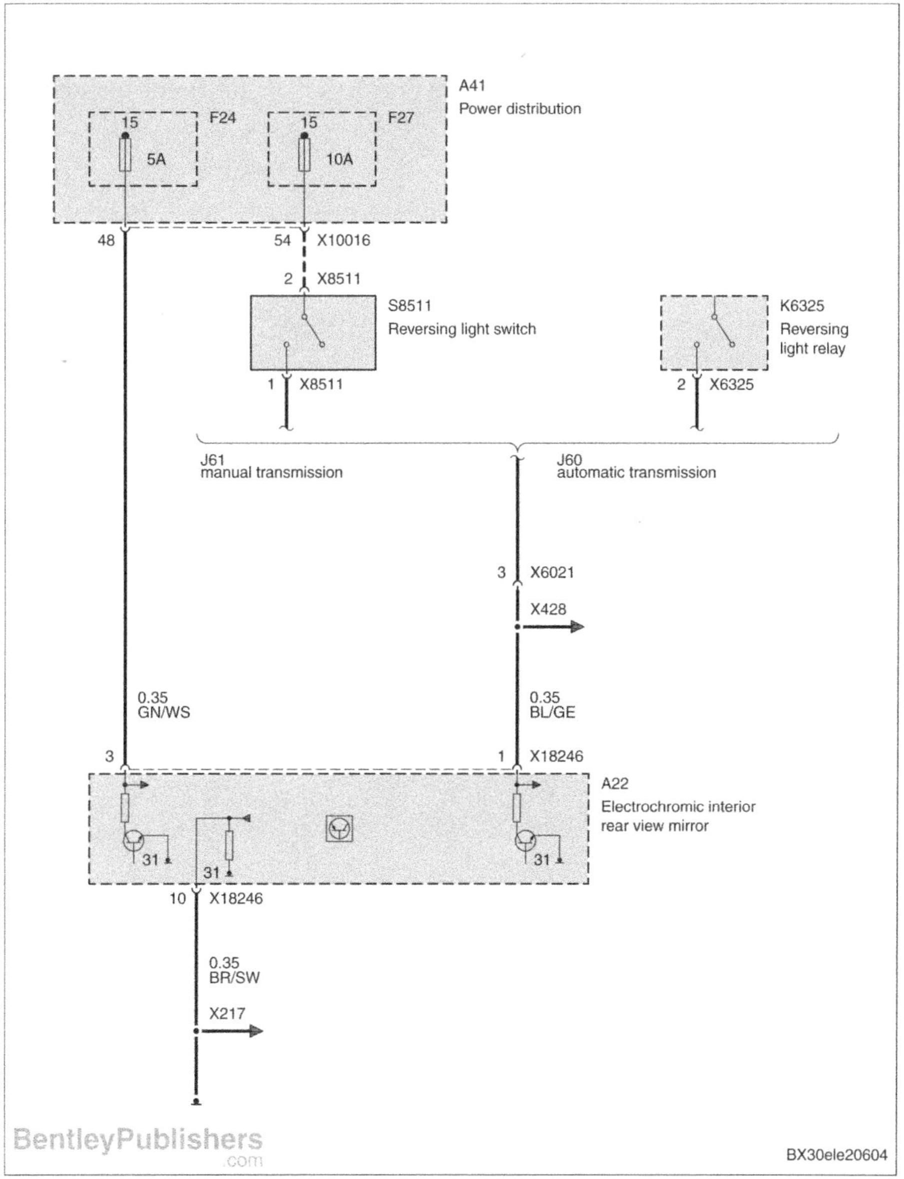

**Automatic driving lights,
rain sensor**

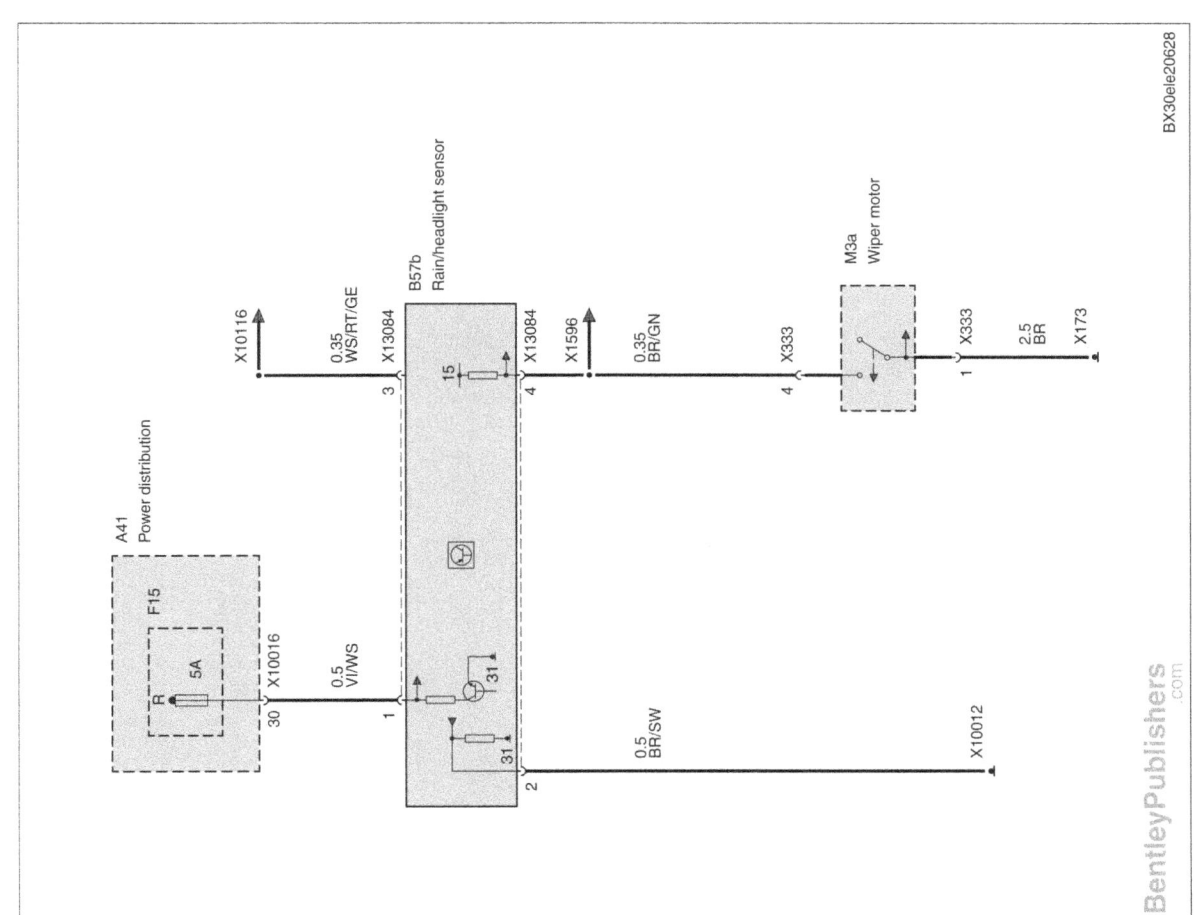

BX30ele20604

BX30ele20628

Side light, parking light
(to 09/2006)
page 1 of 2

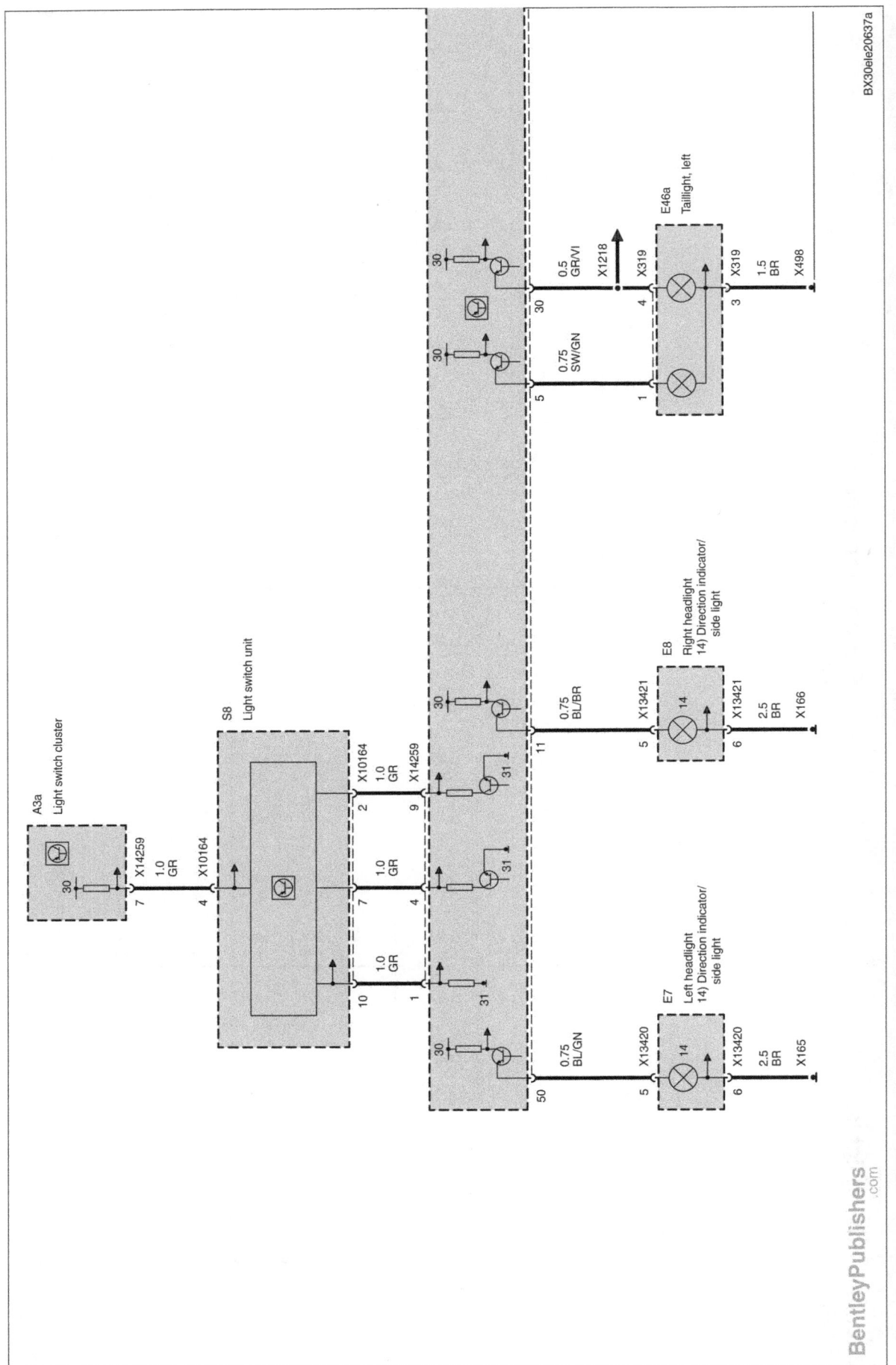

BX30ele20637a

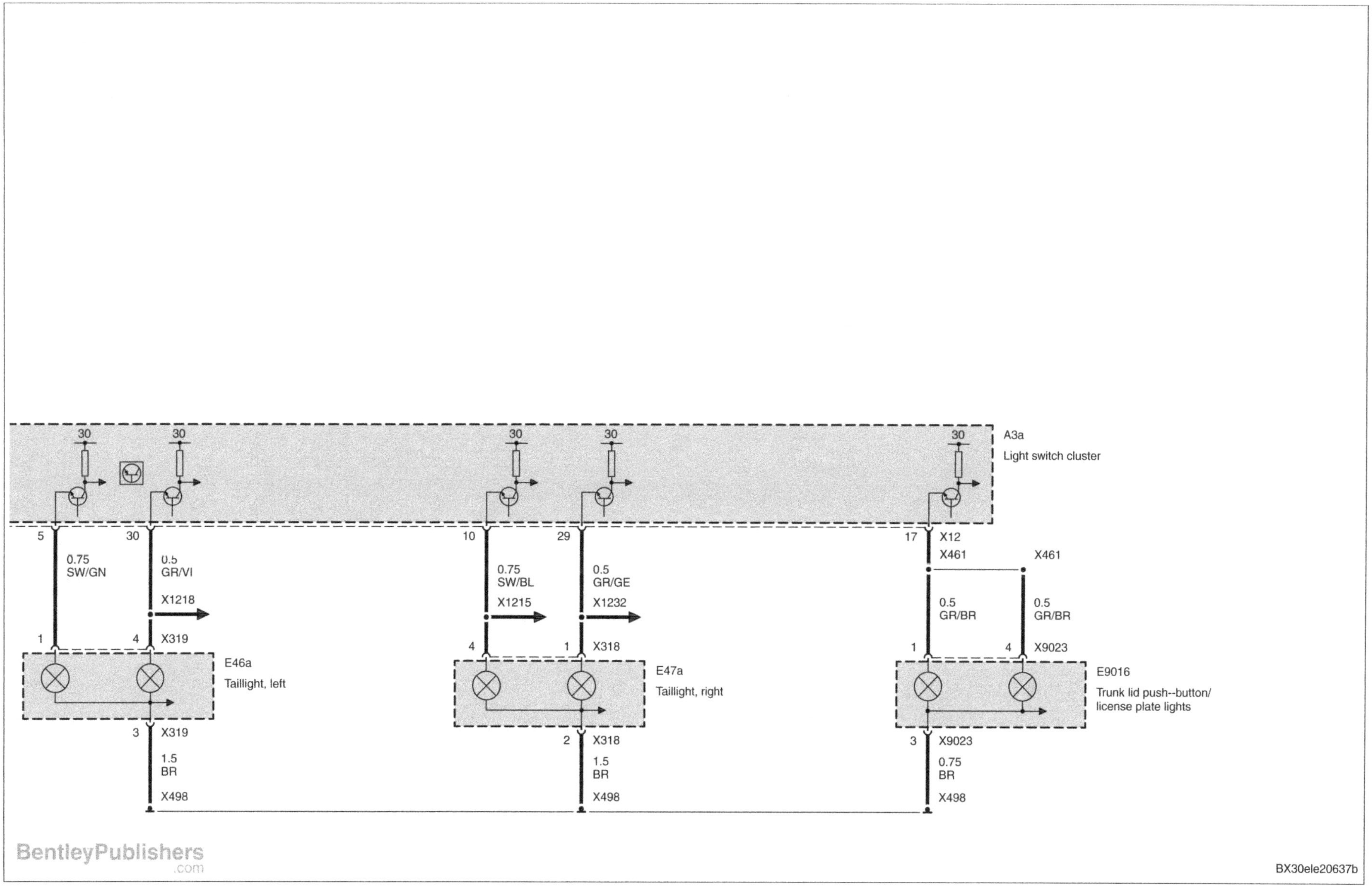

Side light, parking light
(to 09/2006)
page 2 of 2

A3a
Light switch cluster

E9016
Trunk lid push–button/
license plate lights

30

30

X461

17
X12
X461

0.5
GR/BR
X461

0.5
GR/BR
X9023

4

X9023

0.5
GR/BR

1

3
X9023

0.75
BR
X498

E47a
Taillight, right

30

30

29

0.5
GR/GE
X1232

X318

1
X318

10

0.75
SW/BL
X1215

4

2
X318

1.5
BR
X498

E46a
Taillight, left

30

30

30

0.5
GR/VI
X1218

X319

4
X319

5

0.75
SW/GN

1

3
X319

1.5
BR
X498

**Side light, parking light
(from 09/2006)
page 1 of 2**

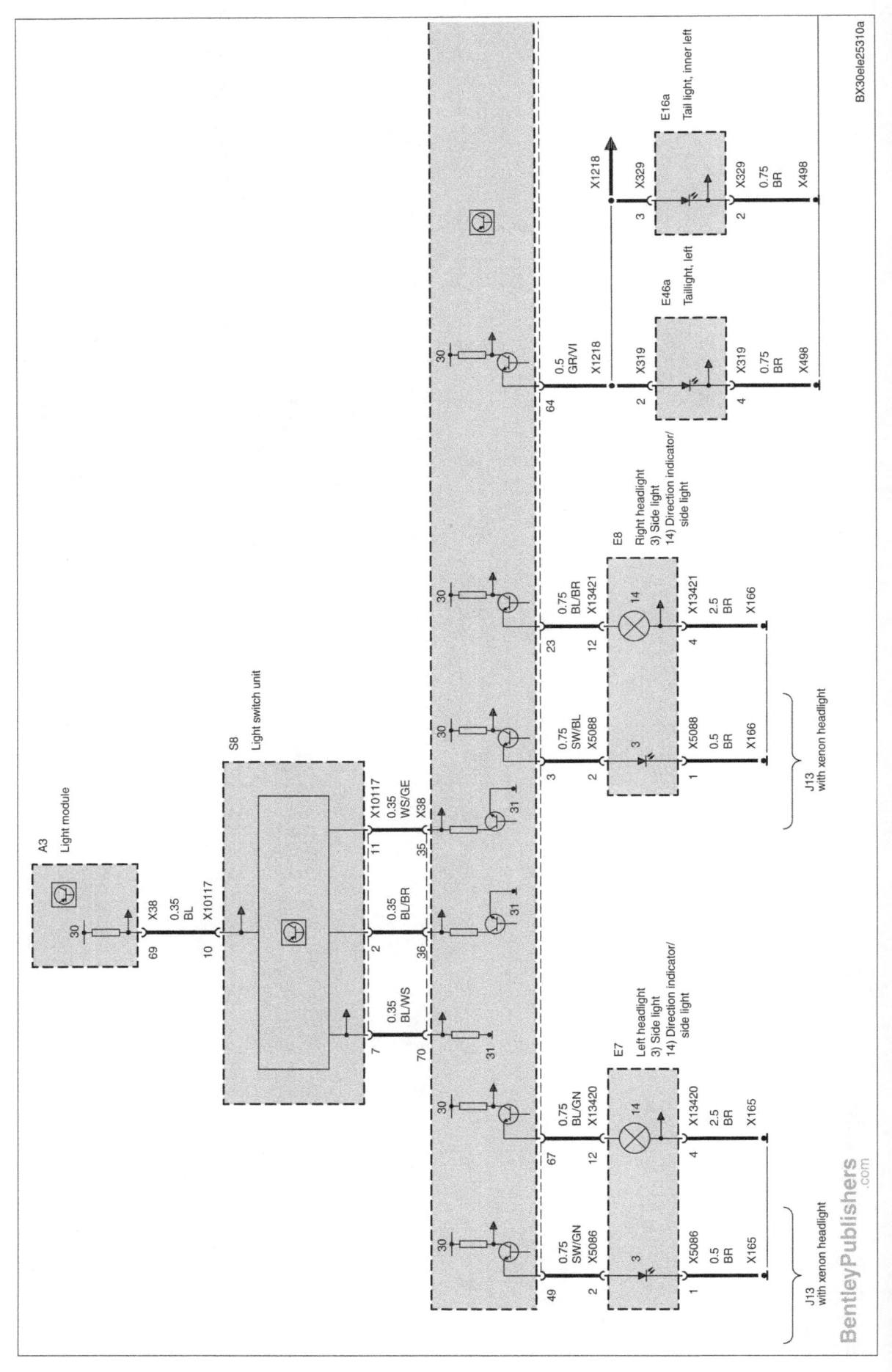

BX30ele25310a

**Side light, parking light
(from 09/2006)
page 2 of 2**

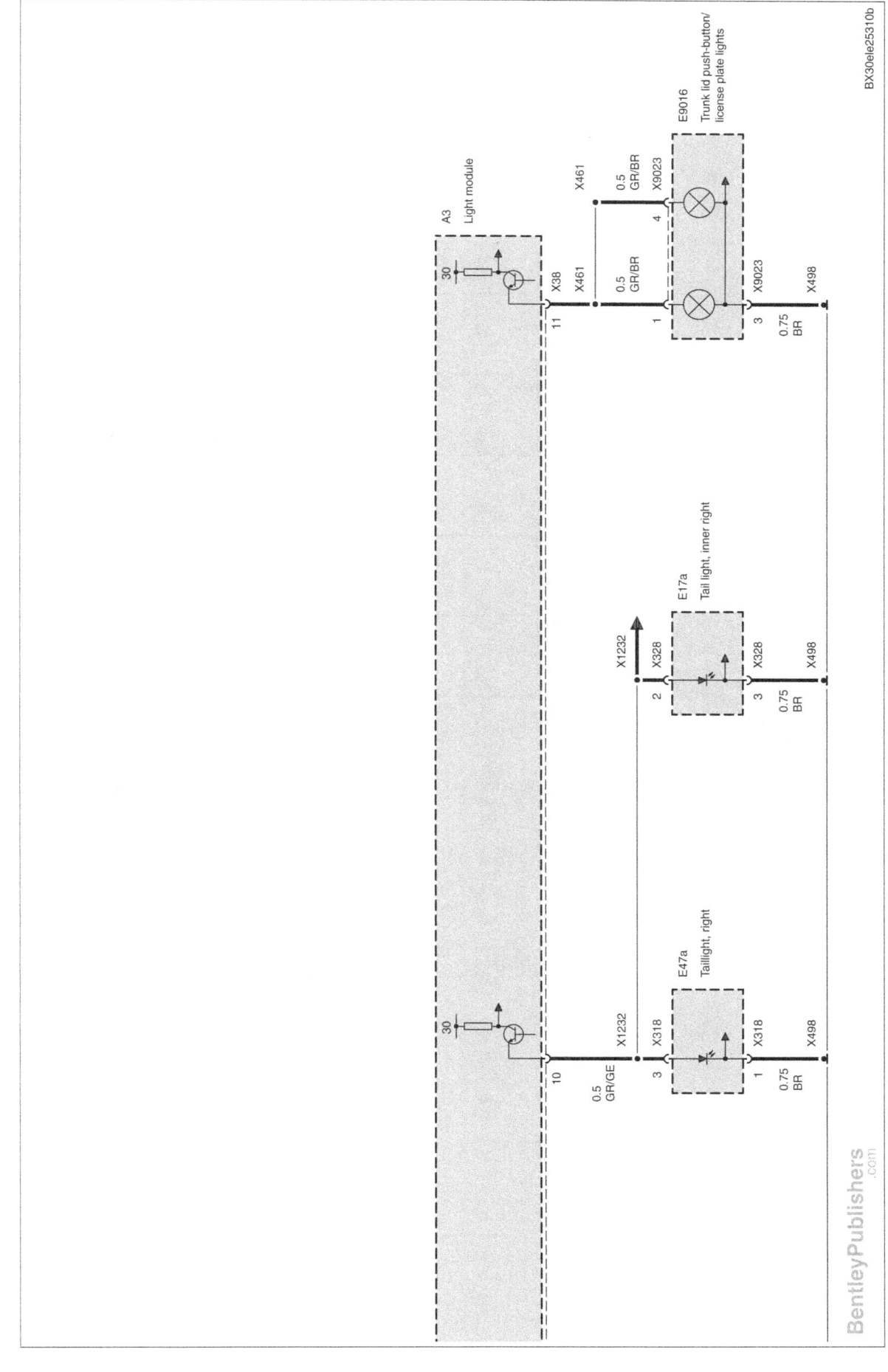

Trailer lighting
(to 09/2006)

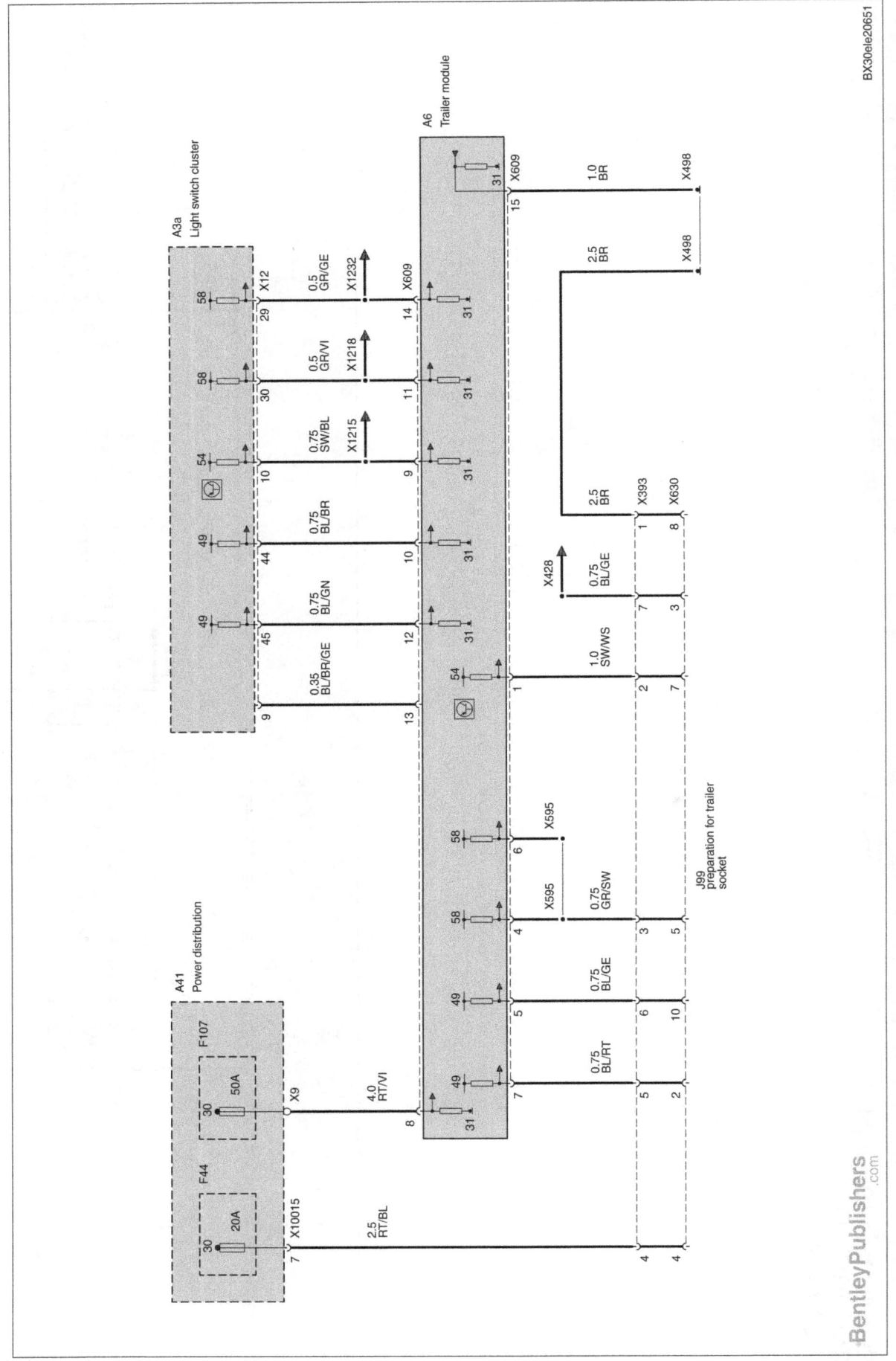

BX30ele20651

**Trailer lighting
(from 09/2006)**

Electrical Wiring Diagrams ELE-161

**Turn signal indicator
page 1 of 2**

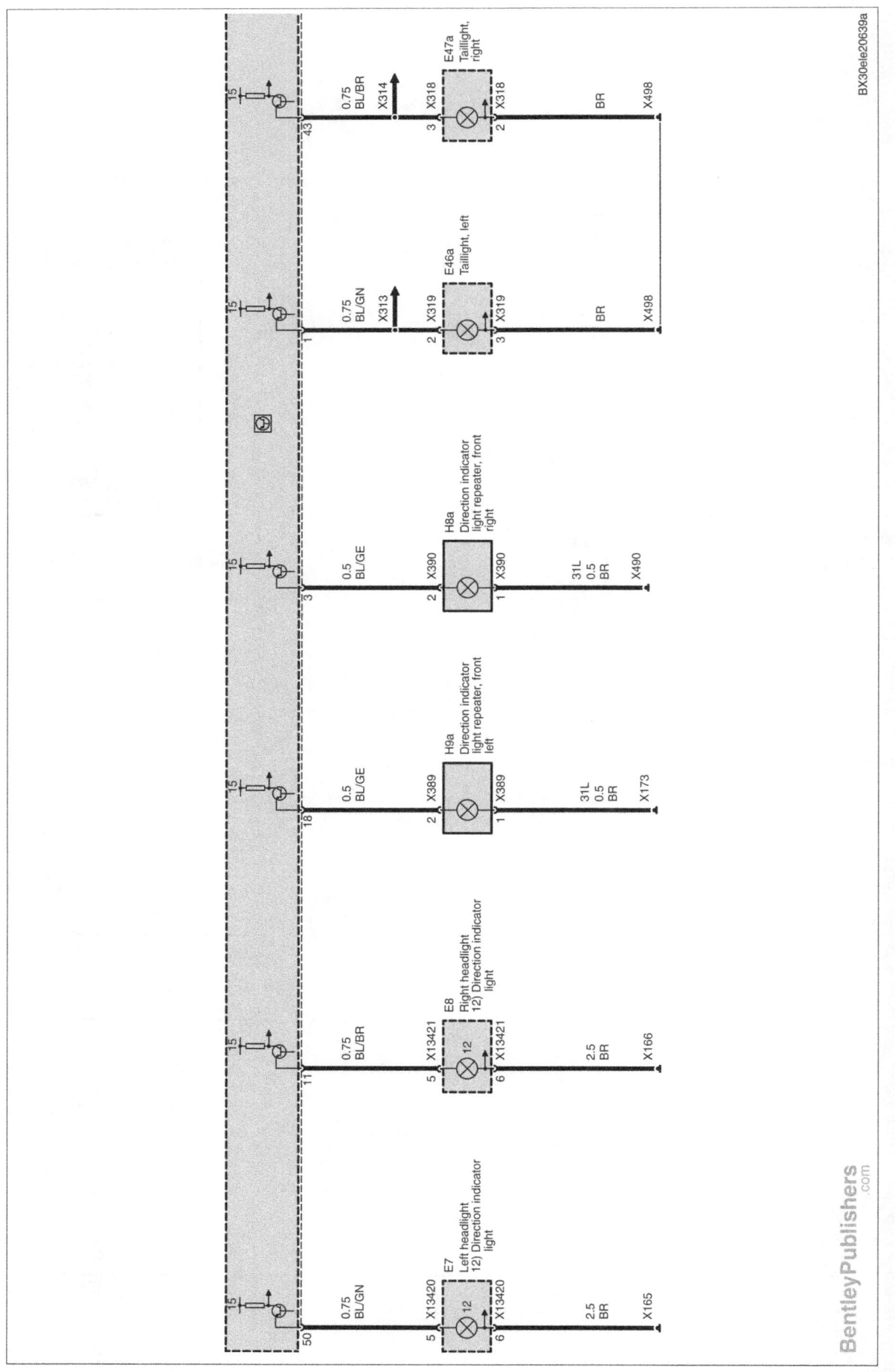

BX30ele20639a

Turn signal indicator
page 2 of 2

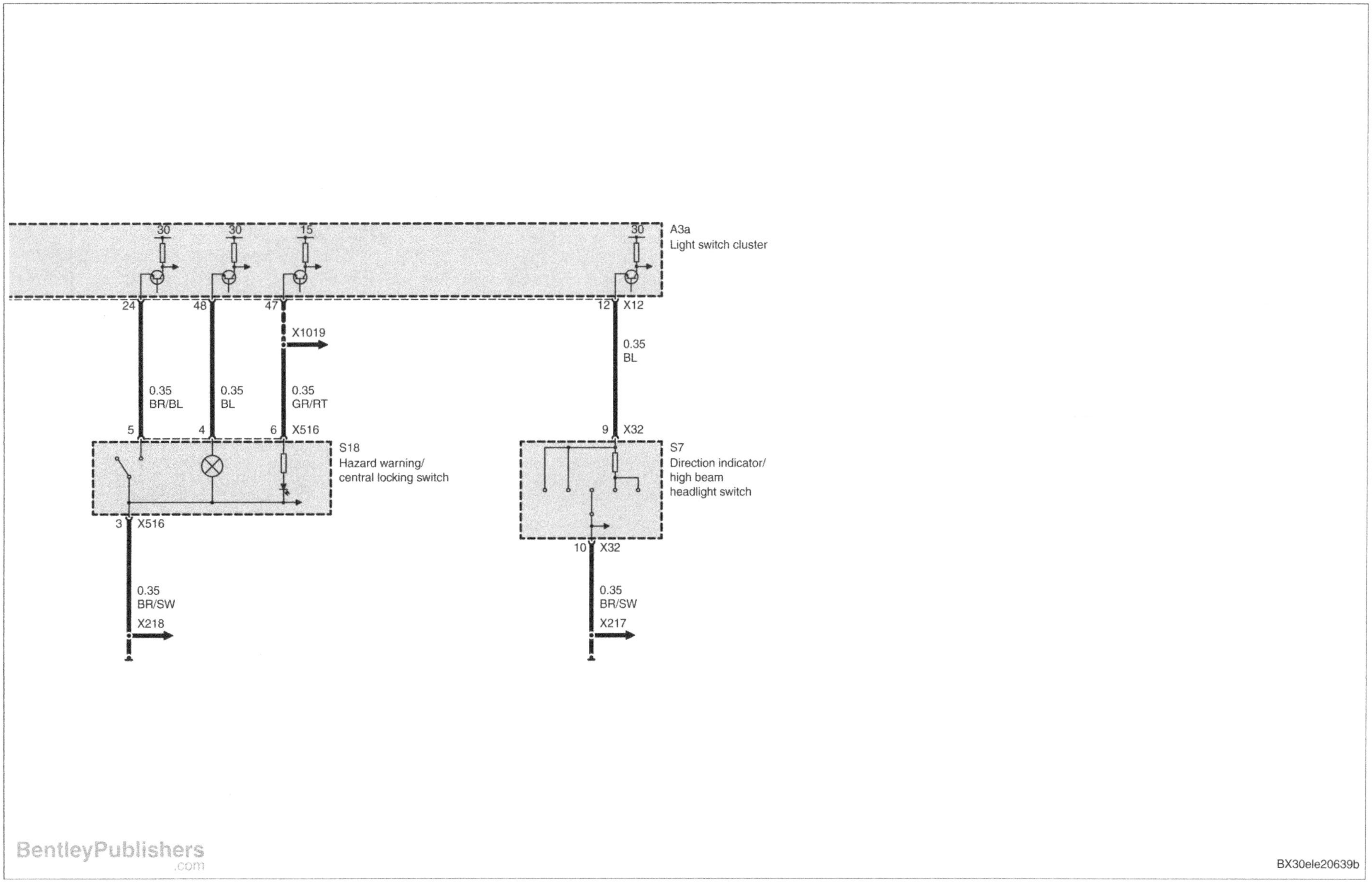

A3a
Light switch cluster
30
30
15
30
24
48
47
12
X12
X1019
0.35
BL
0.35
BR/BL
0.35
BL
0.35
GR/RT
5
4
6
X516
9
X32
S18
Hazard warning/
central locking switch
S7
Direction indicator/
high beam
headlight switch
3
X516
10
X32
0.35
BR/SW
X218
0.35
BR/SW
X217
BentleyPublishers
.com
BX30ele20639b

**Electrochromic mirror
from 09/2005**

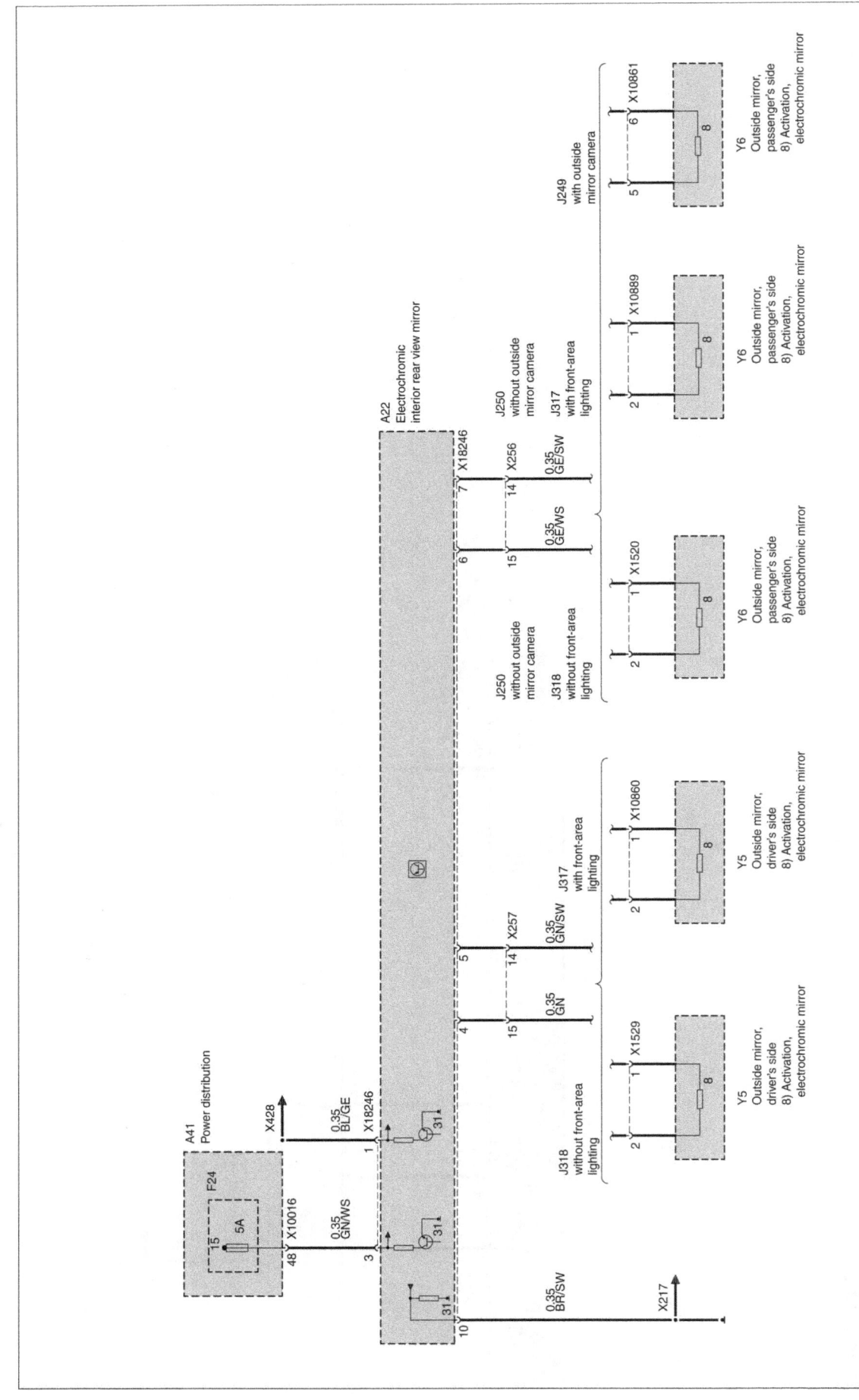

BX30ele23173

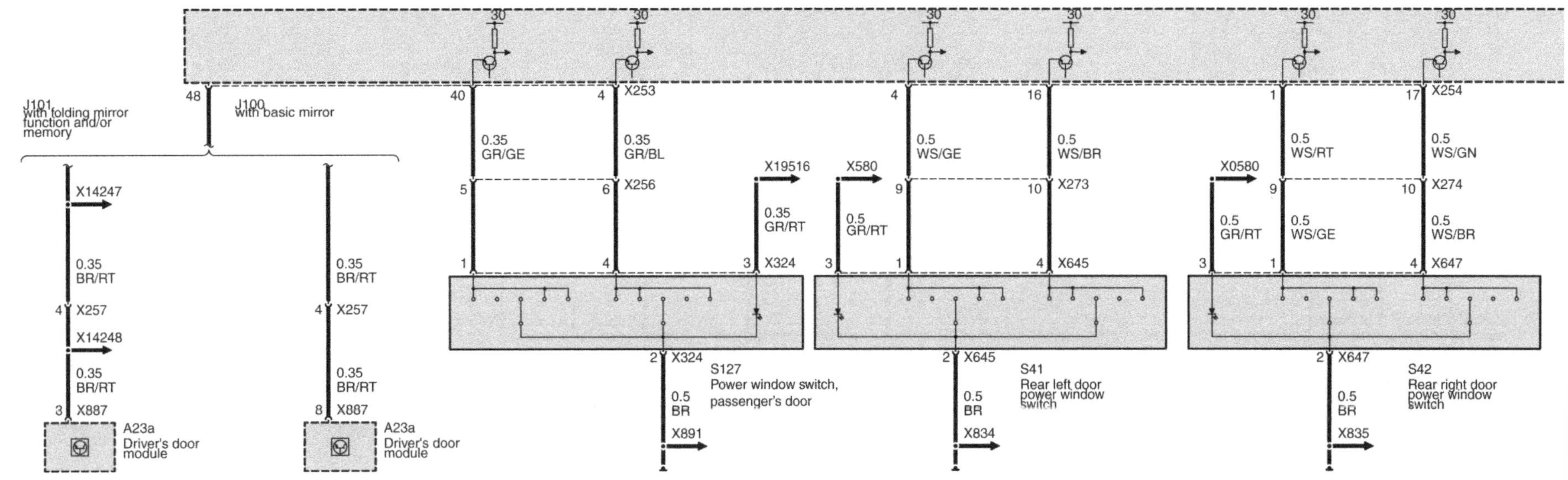

Electrical Wiring Diagrams   ELE-165

S42
Rear right door
power window
switch

S41
Rear left door
power window
switch

S127
Power window switch,
passenger's door

J101
with folding mirror
function and/or
memory

J100
with basic mirror

A23a
Driver's door
module

A23a
Driver's door
module

BX30ele26484a

**Power window
page 2 of 2**

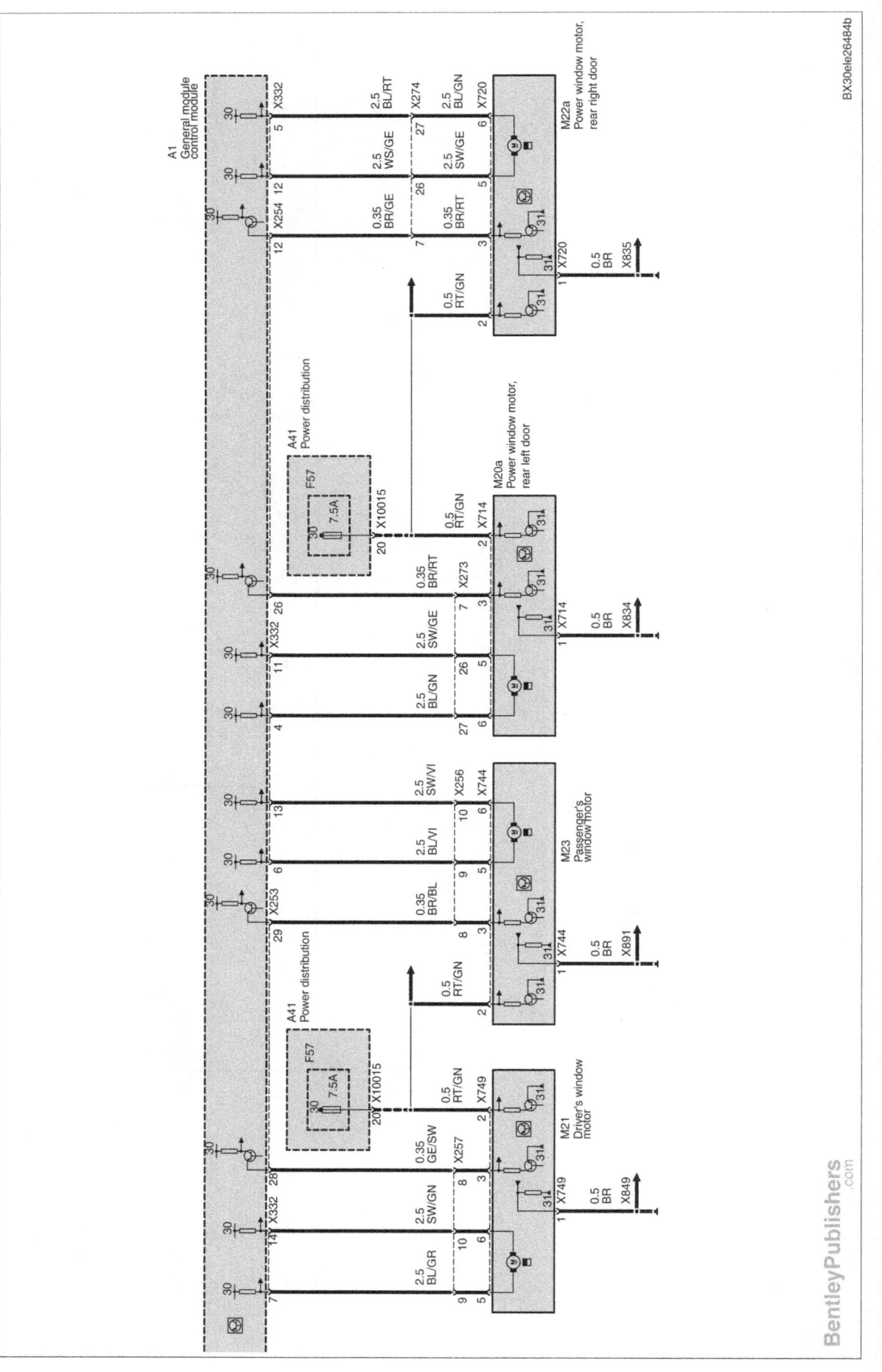

BX30ele26484b

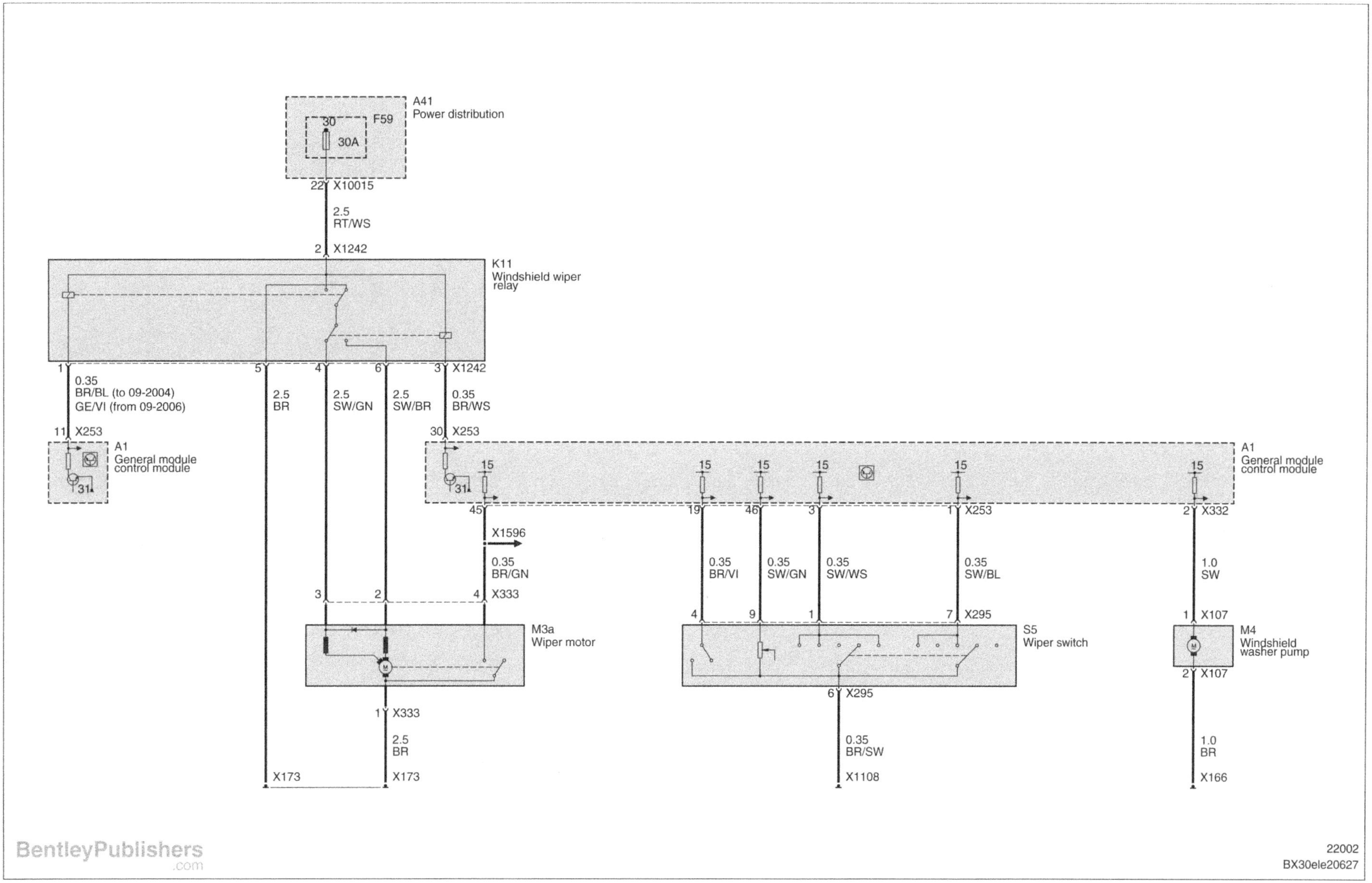

Wiper-washer control

Electrical Wiring Diagrams ELE-167

A41 Power distribution

F59 30A

K11 Windshield wiper relay

A1 General module control module

A1 General module control module

M4 Windshield washer pump

S5 Wiper switch

M3a Wiper motor

22002
BX30ele20627

**Dynamic stability control (DSC)
sensor system
page 1 of 2**

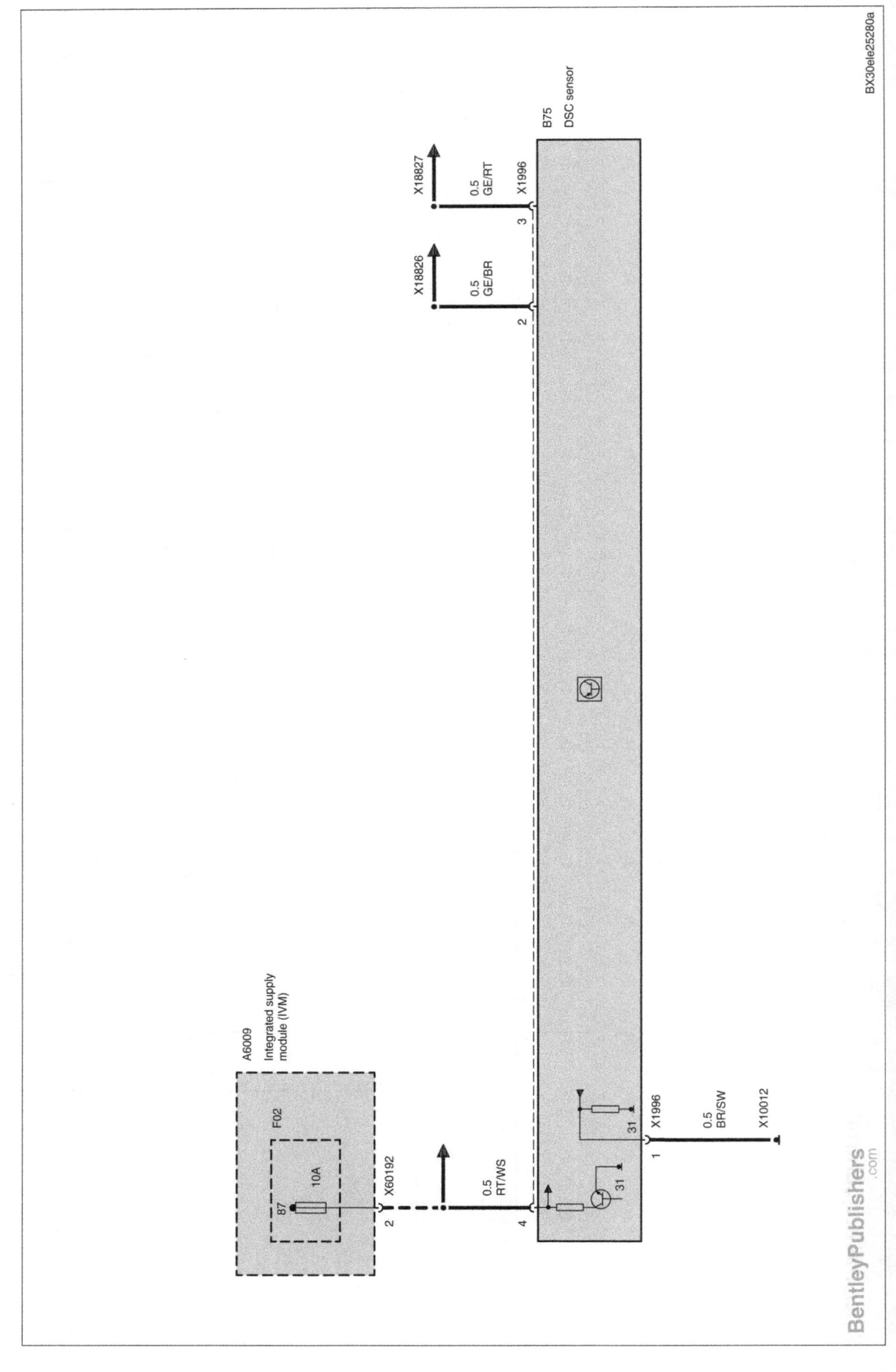

BX30ele25280a

Dynamic stability control (DSC)
sensor system
page 2 of 2

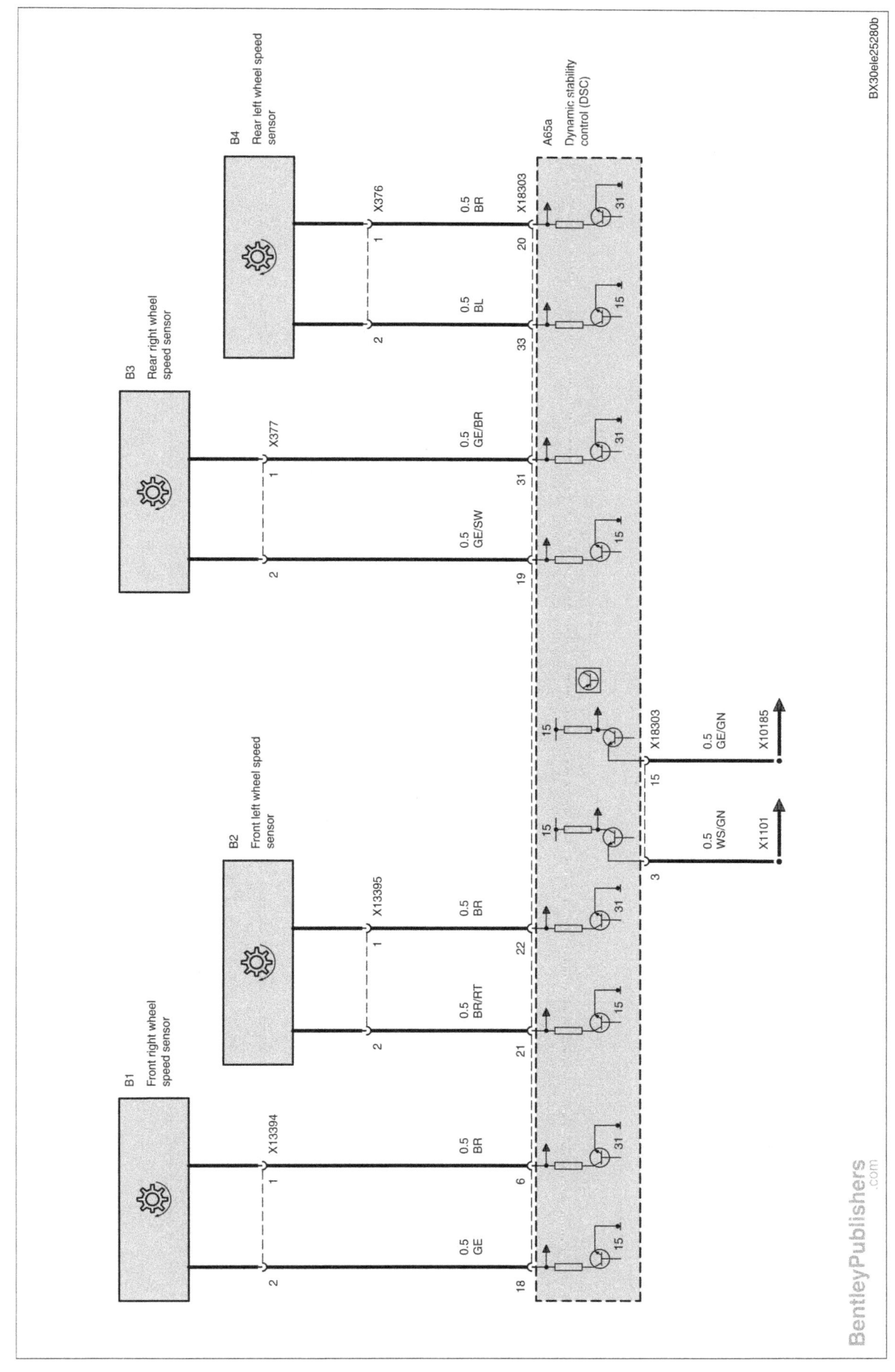

Electrical Wiring Diagrams   ELE-169

BX30ele25280b

BentleyPublishers
.com

Dynamic stability control (DSC) supply

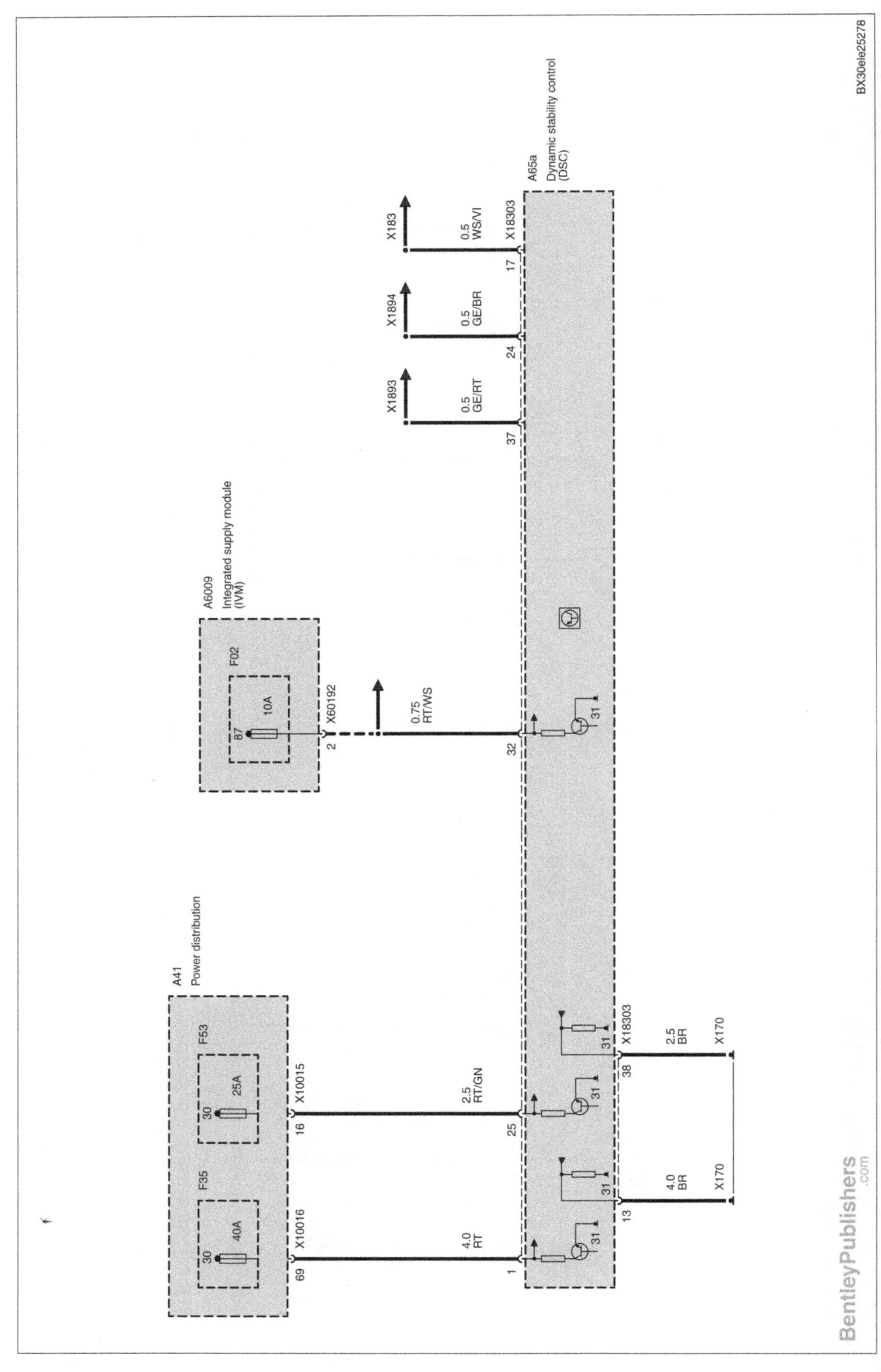

Dynamic stability control (DSC) unit

Dynamic stability control (DSC) switch functions

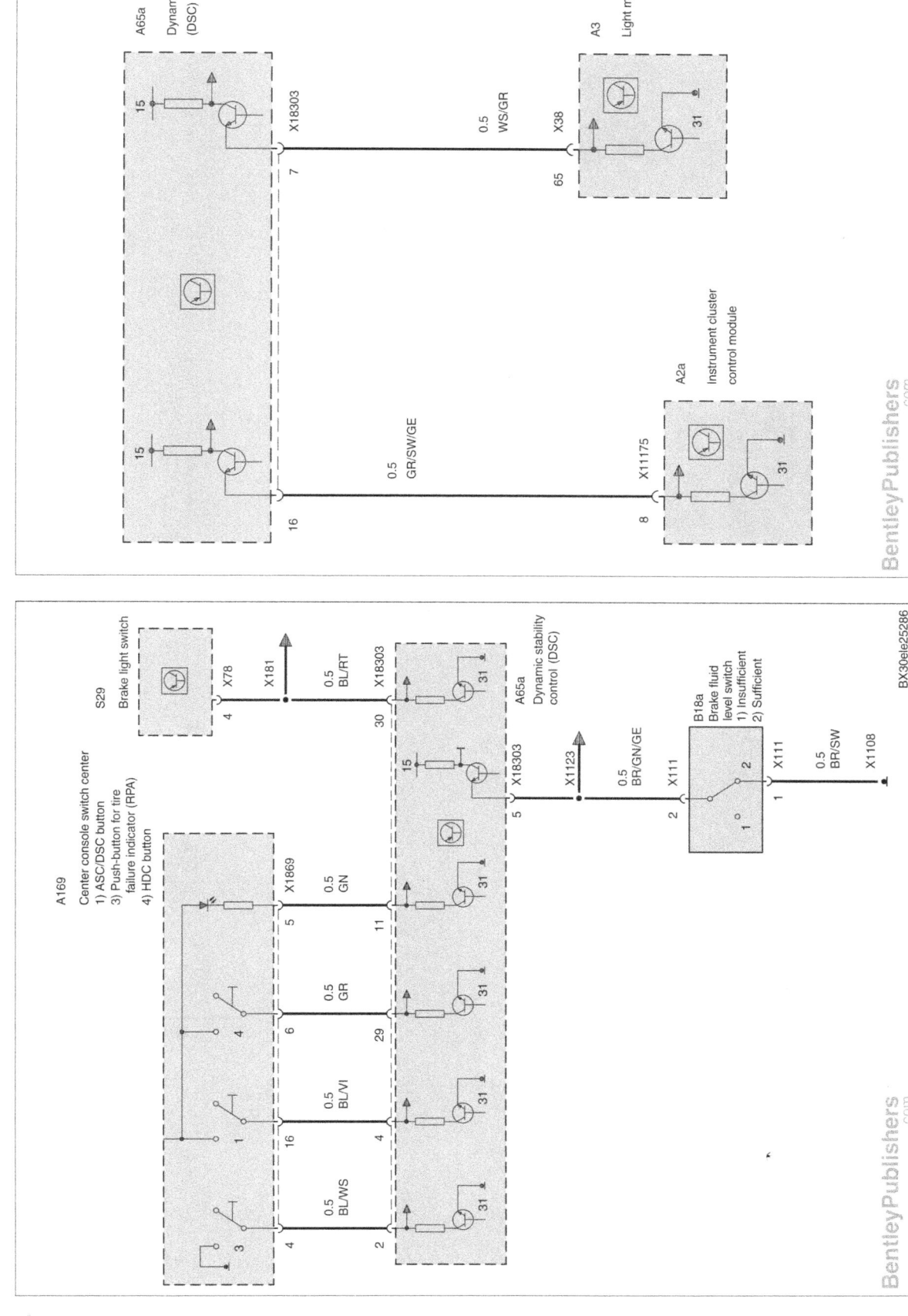

BX30ele25284

BX30ele25286

BentleyPublishers.com

Servotronic

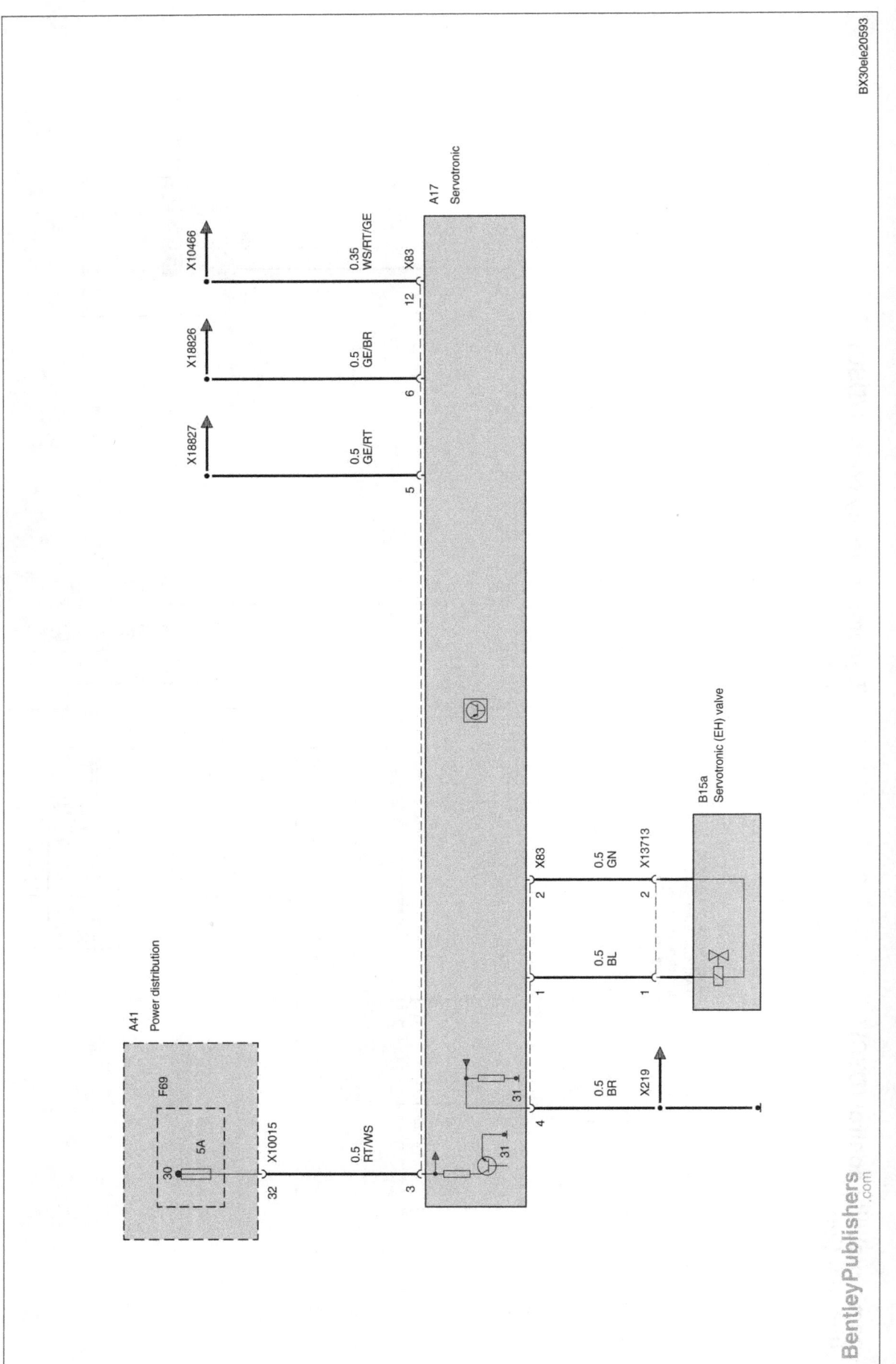

BX30ele20593

Tire pressure control (RDC)
page 1 of 2

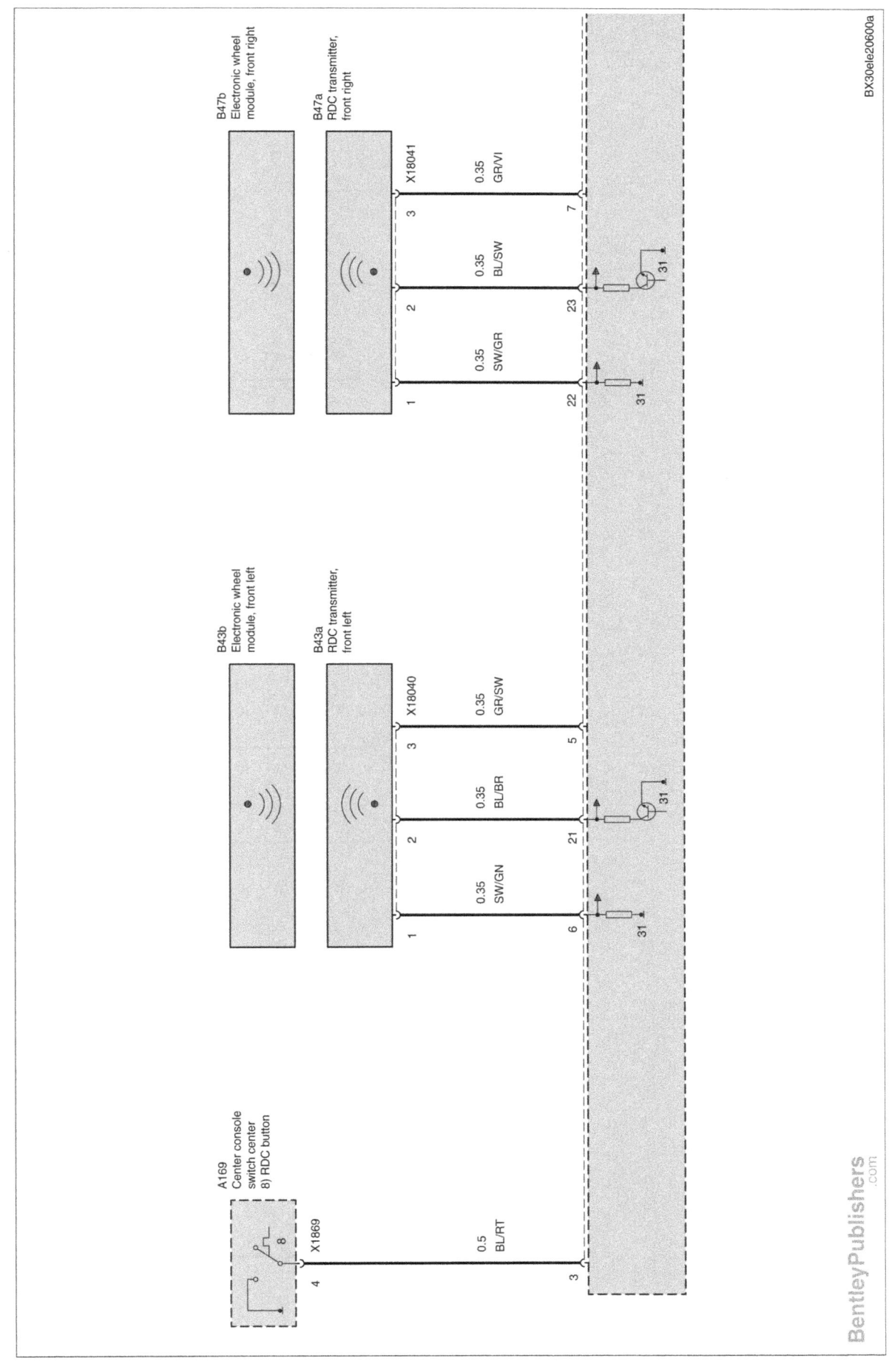

BX30ele20600a

B47b
Electronic wheel
module, front right

B47a
RDC transmitter,
front right

X18041

3   0.35
    GR/VI
    7

2   0.35
    BL/SW
    23
    31

1   0.35
    SW/GR
    22
    31

B43b
Electronic wheel
module, front left

B43a
RDC transmitter,
front left

X18040

3   0.35
    GR/SW
    5

2   0.35
    BL/BR
    21
    31

1   0.35
    SW/GN
    6
    31

A169
Center console
switch center
8) RDC button

8

X1869

4   0.5
    BL/RT
    3

**Tire pressure control (RDC)
page 2 of 2**

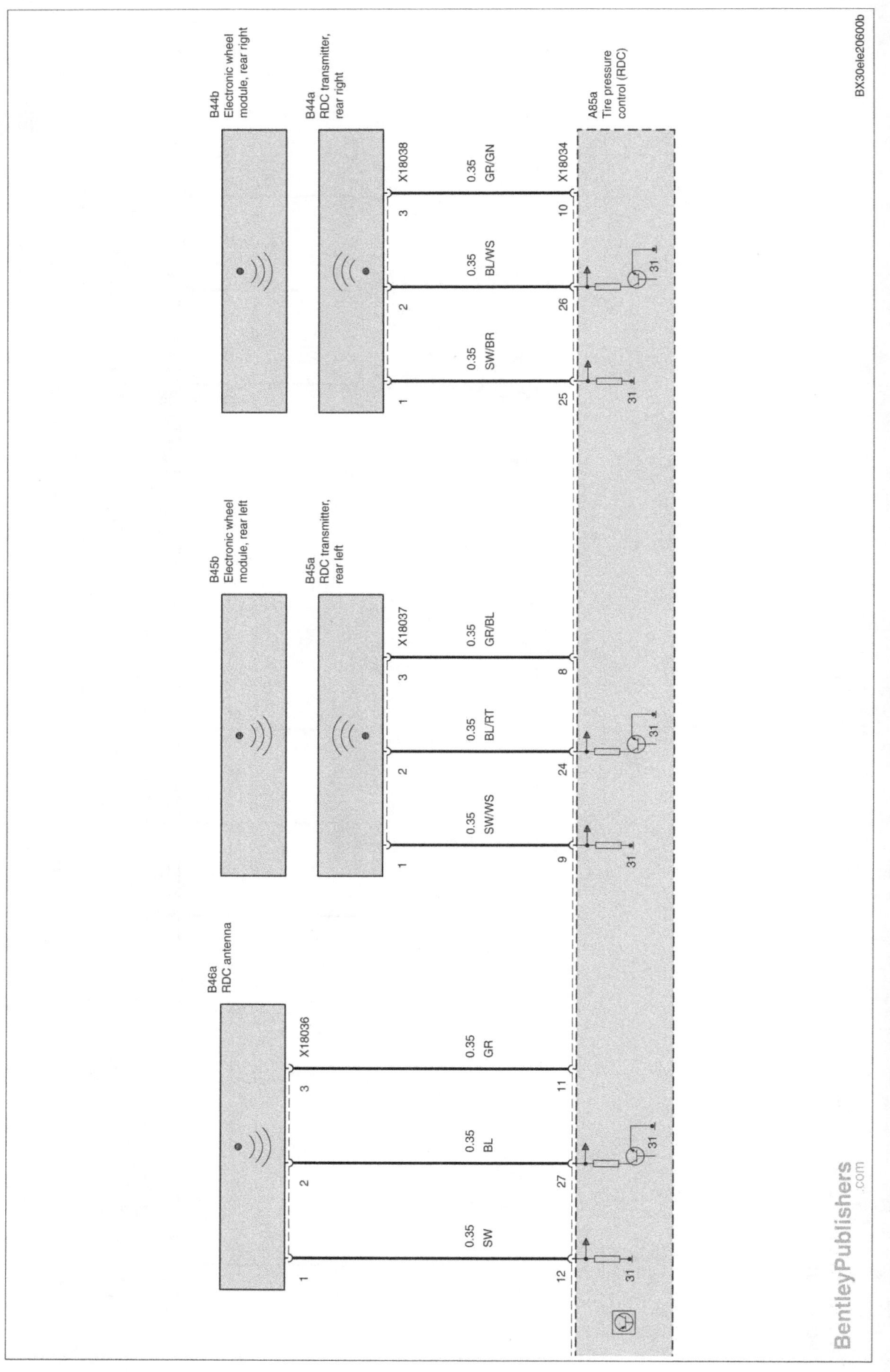

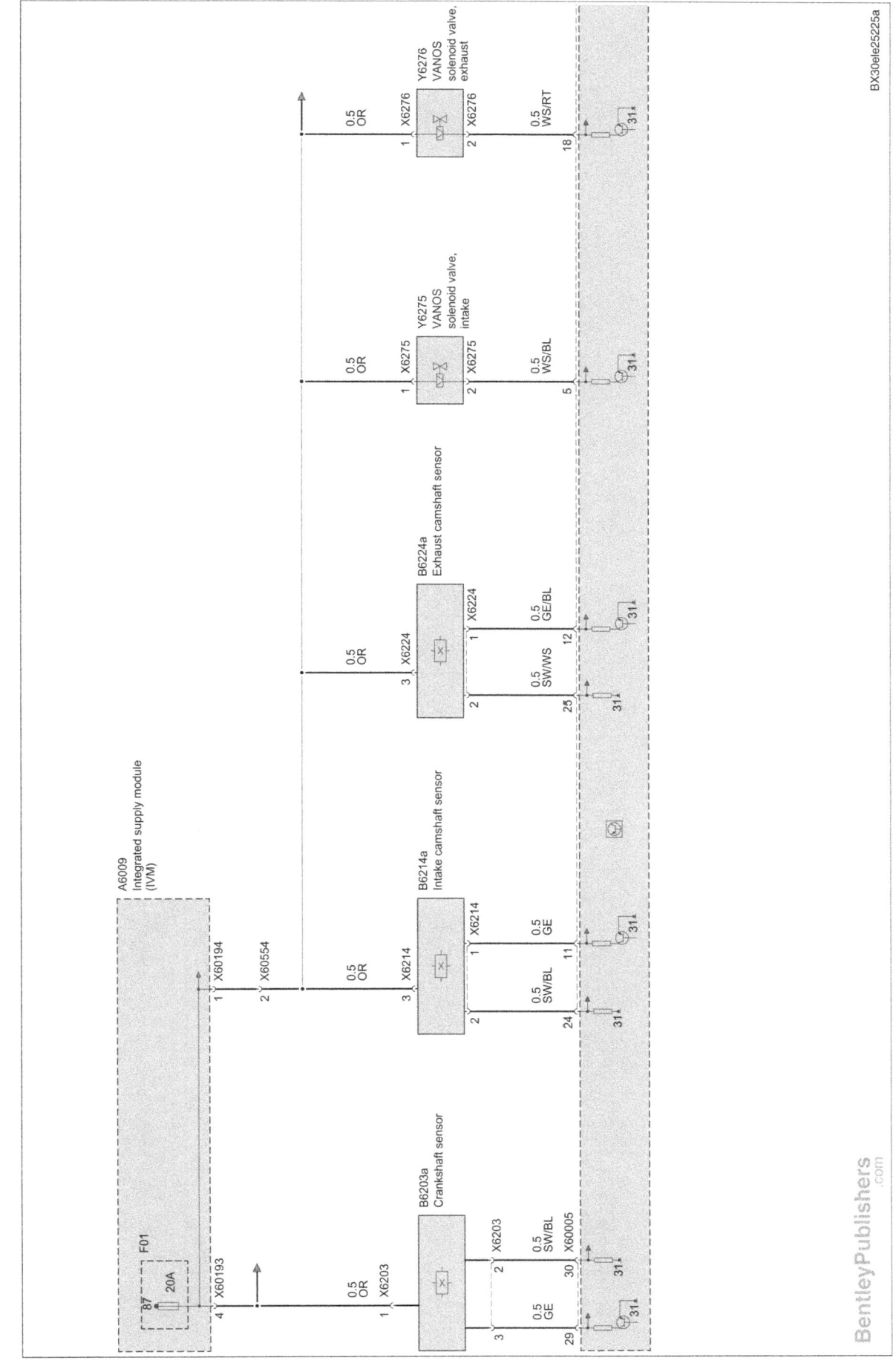

BX30ele2525a

Valve gear (VANOS)
page 2 of 2

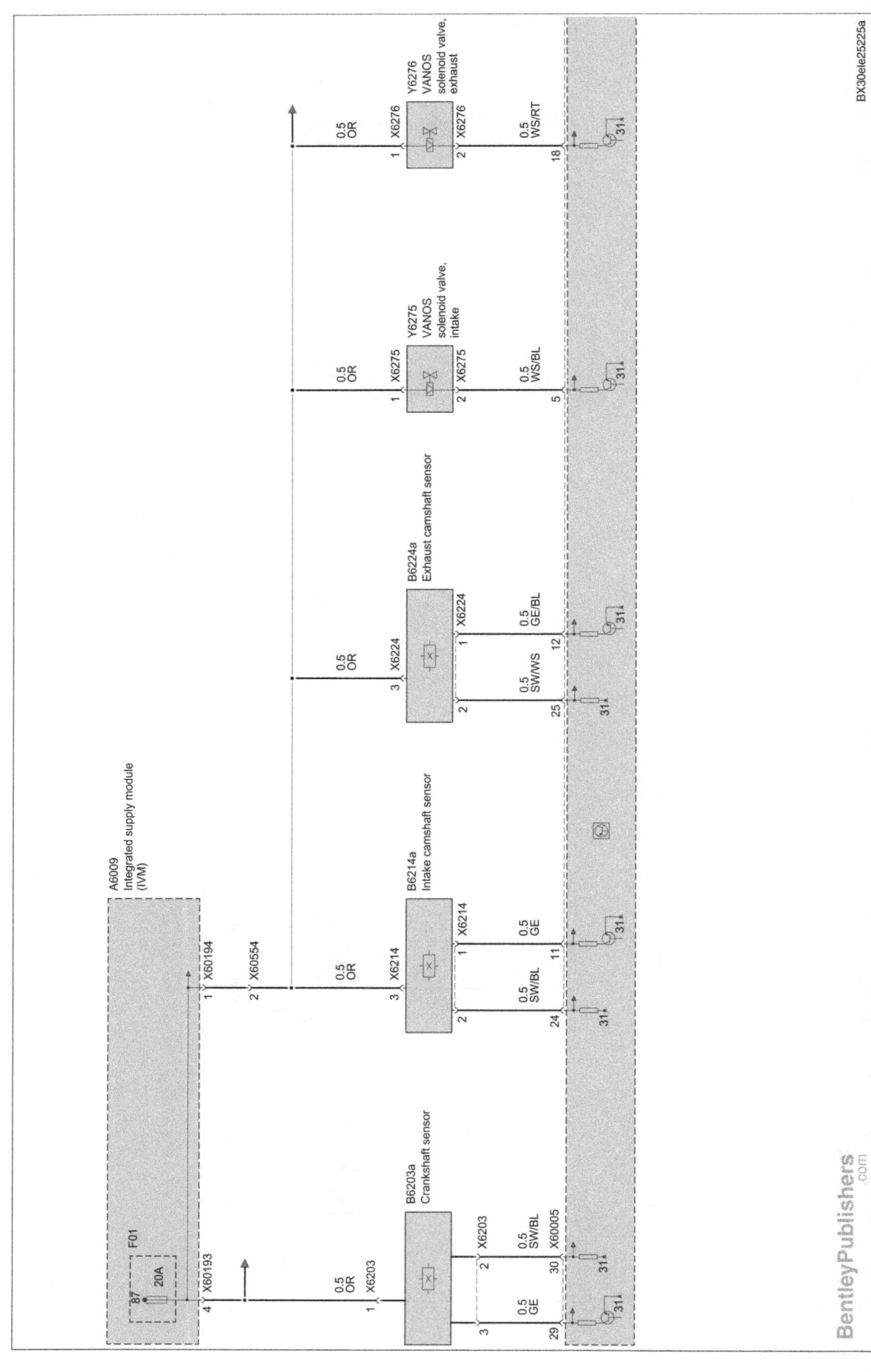

BX30ele25225a

VTG transmission control (transfer case)

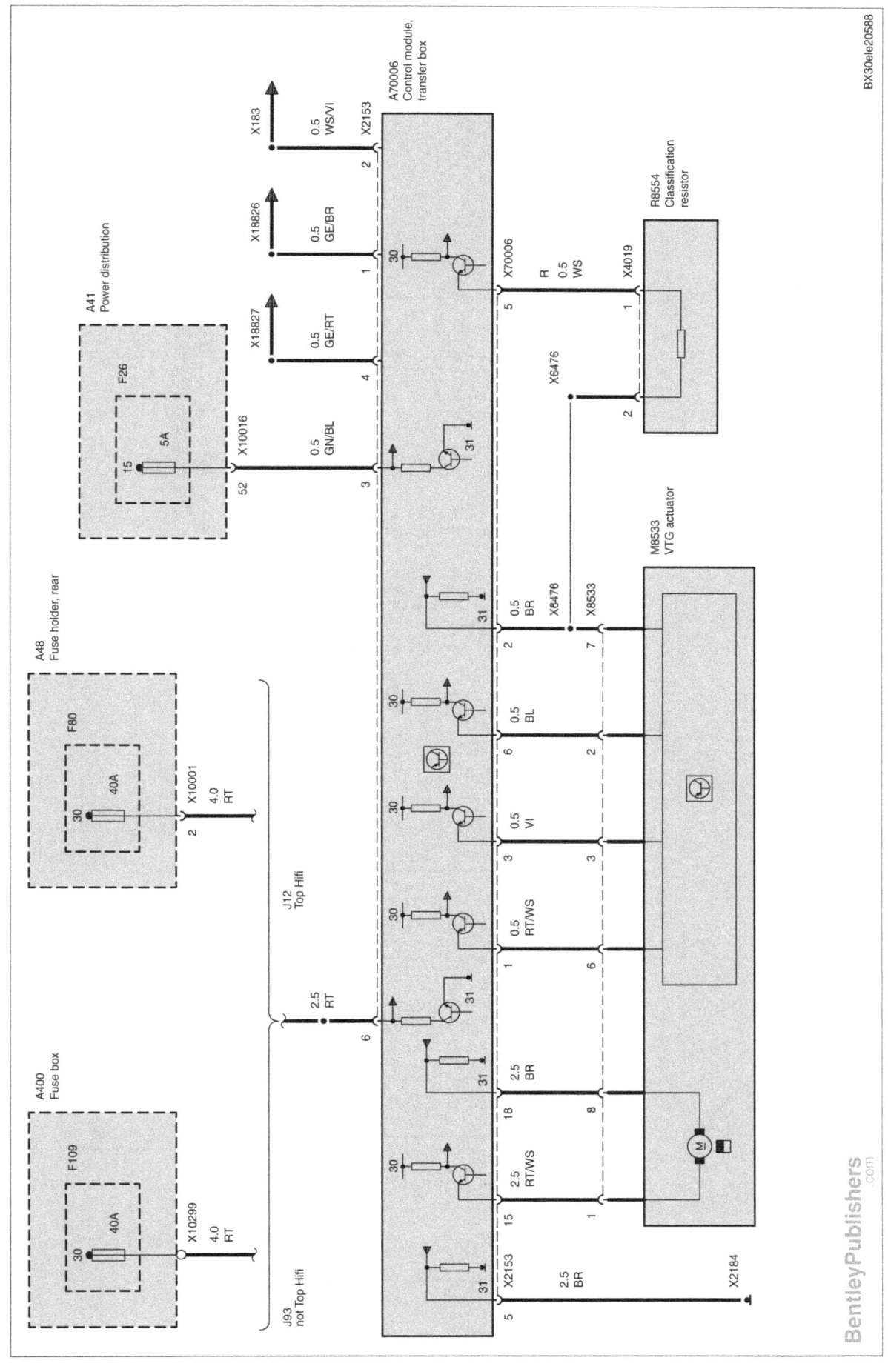

BX30ele20588

Steptronic switch

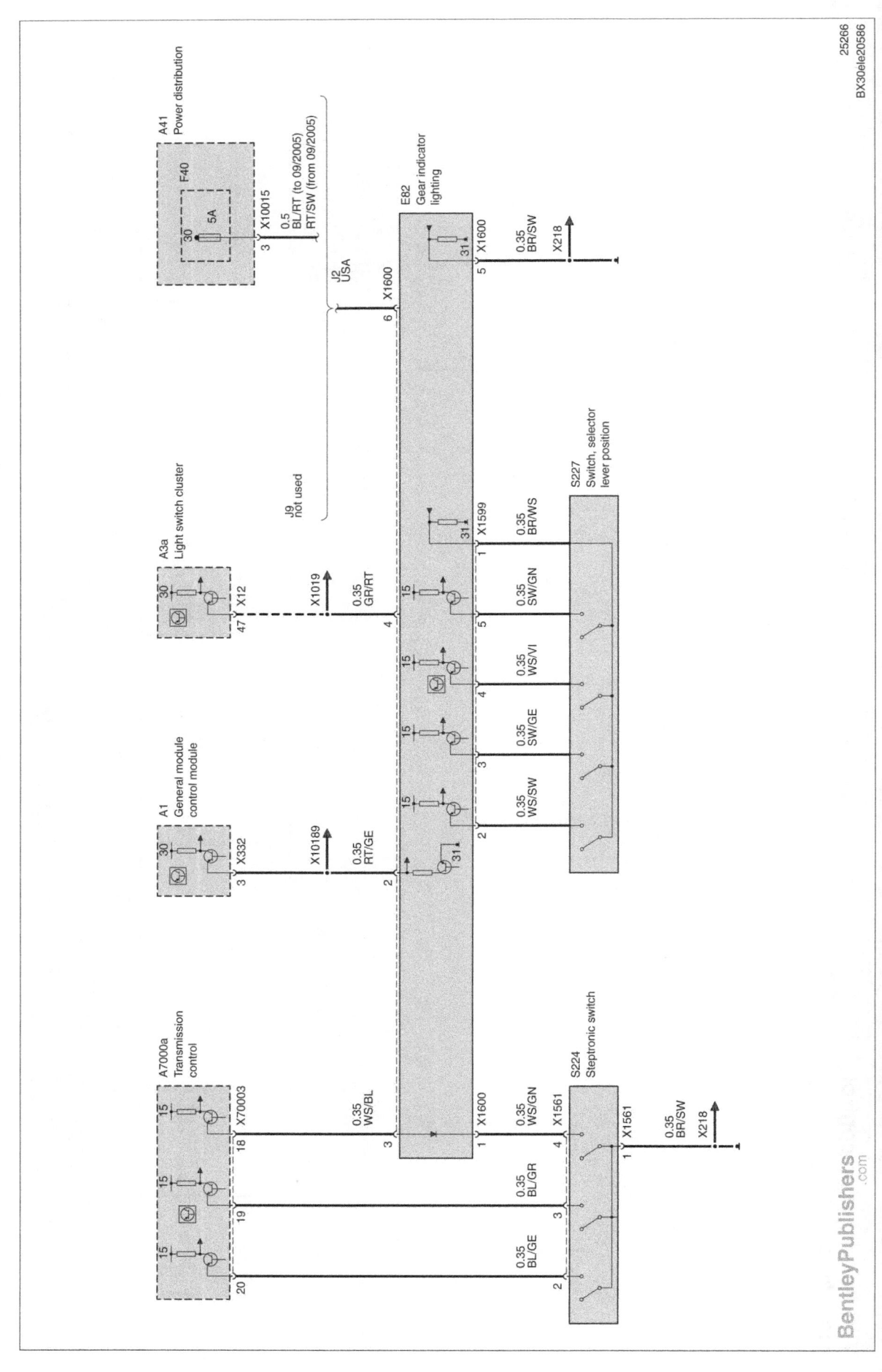

25266
BX30ele20586

BentleyPublishers
.com

**Transmission control unit
(A5S390R)**

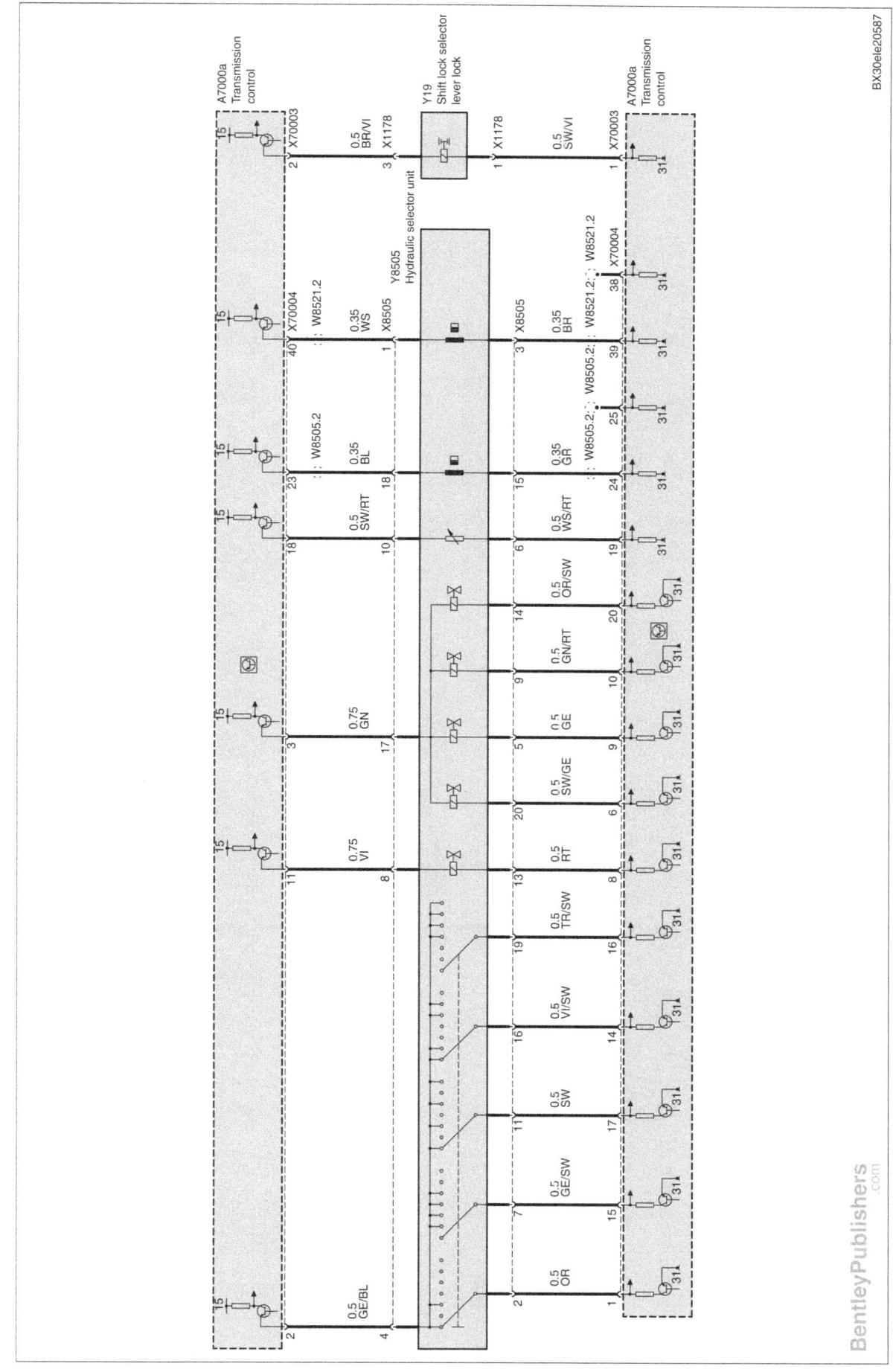

BX30ele20587

Voltage supply, transmission control

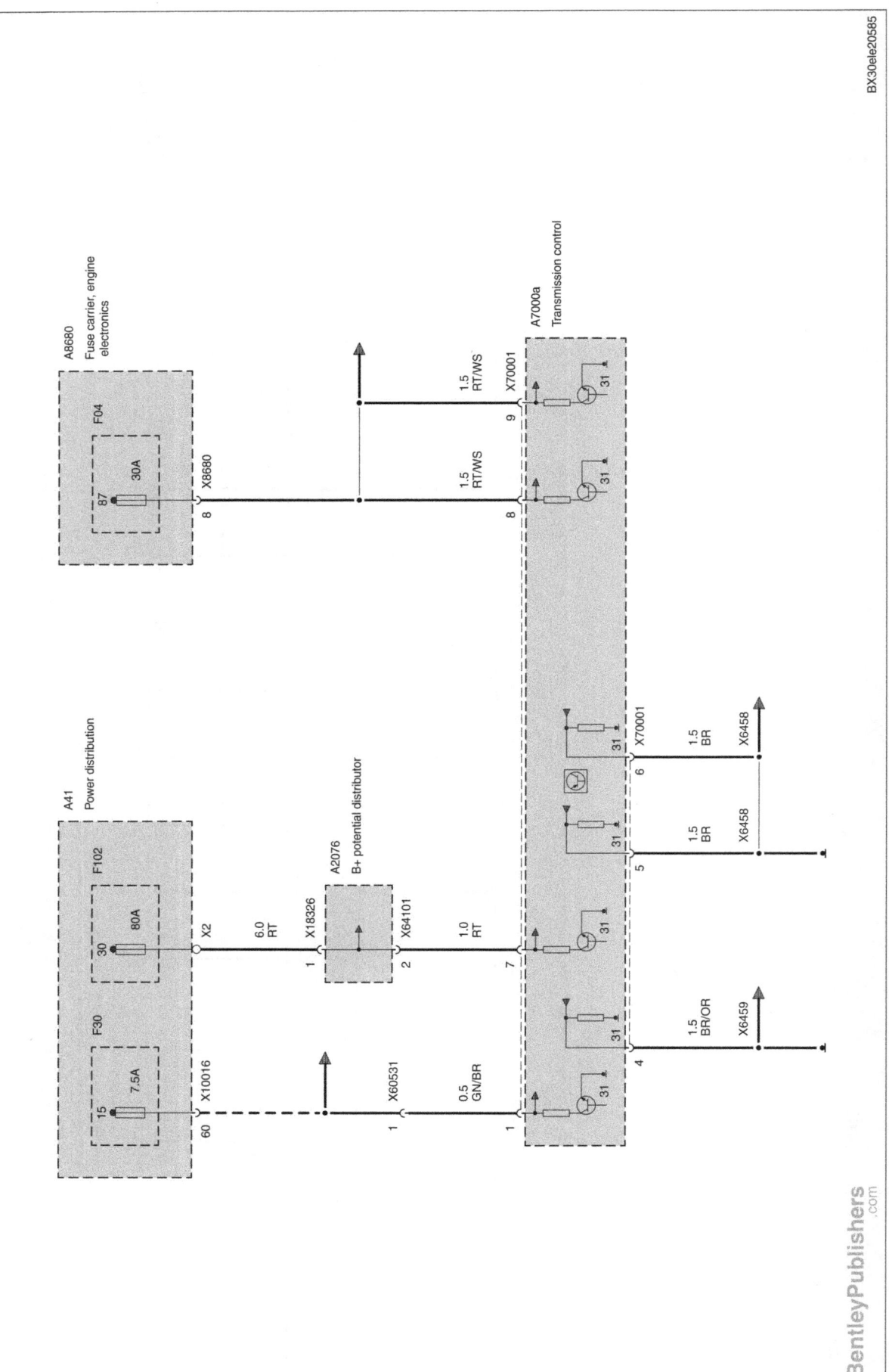

Shift lock selector lever lock

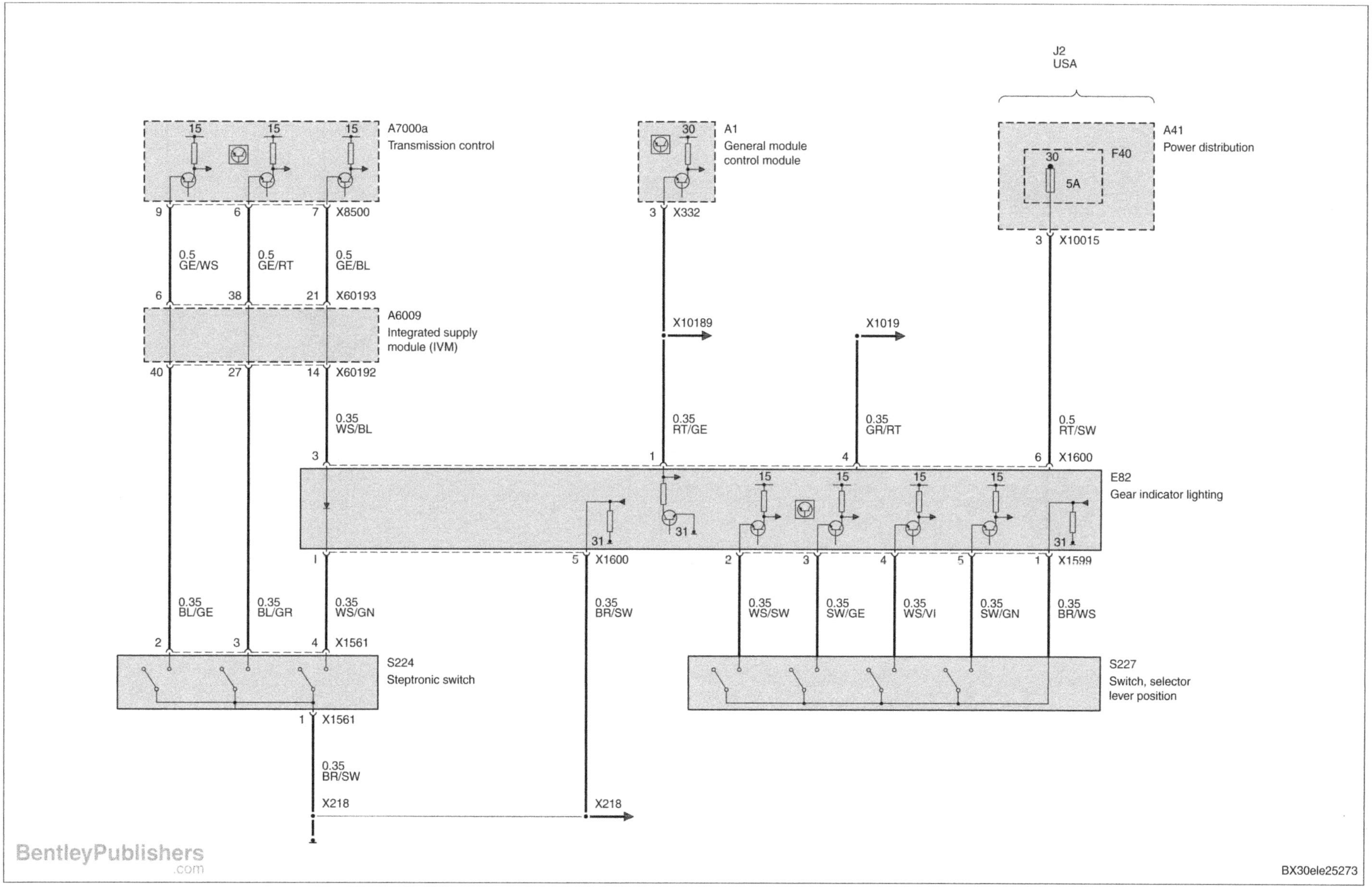

BX30ele25273

BentleyPublishers
.com

**Steptronic switch
(GA6L45R)**

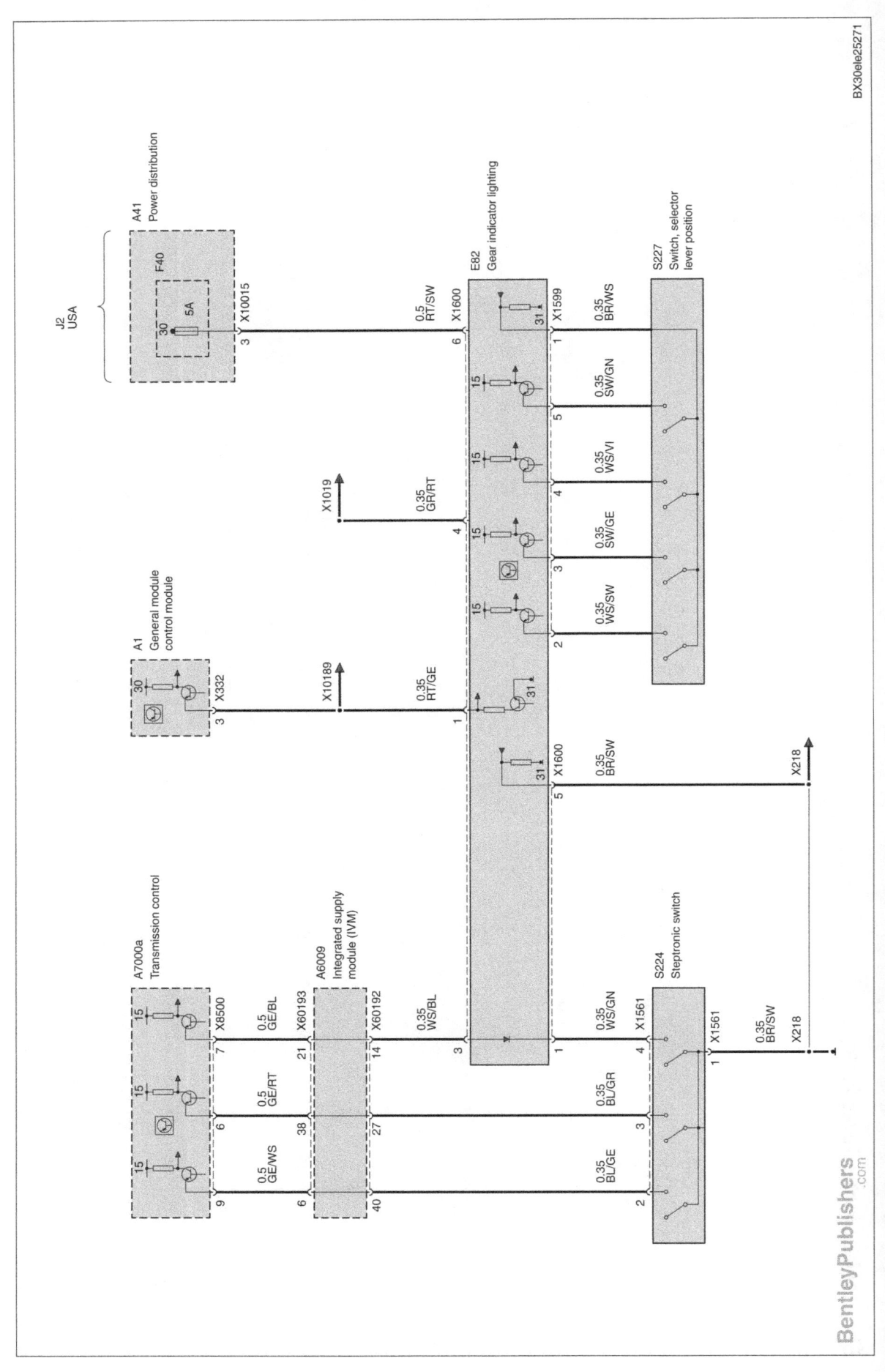

BX30ele25271

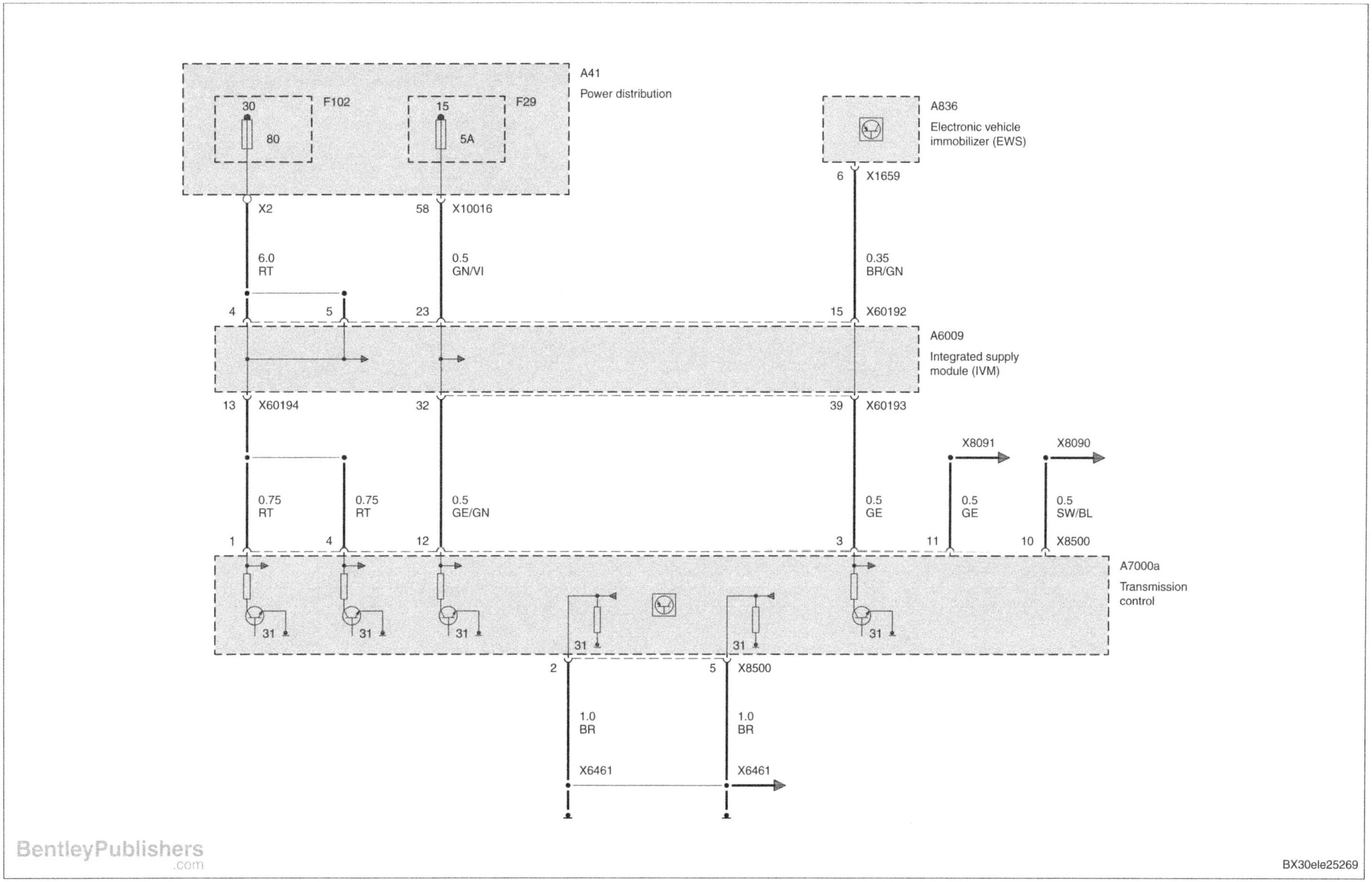

Supply, mechatronics

BX30ele25269

Electronically controlled fuel pump

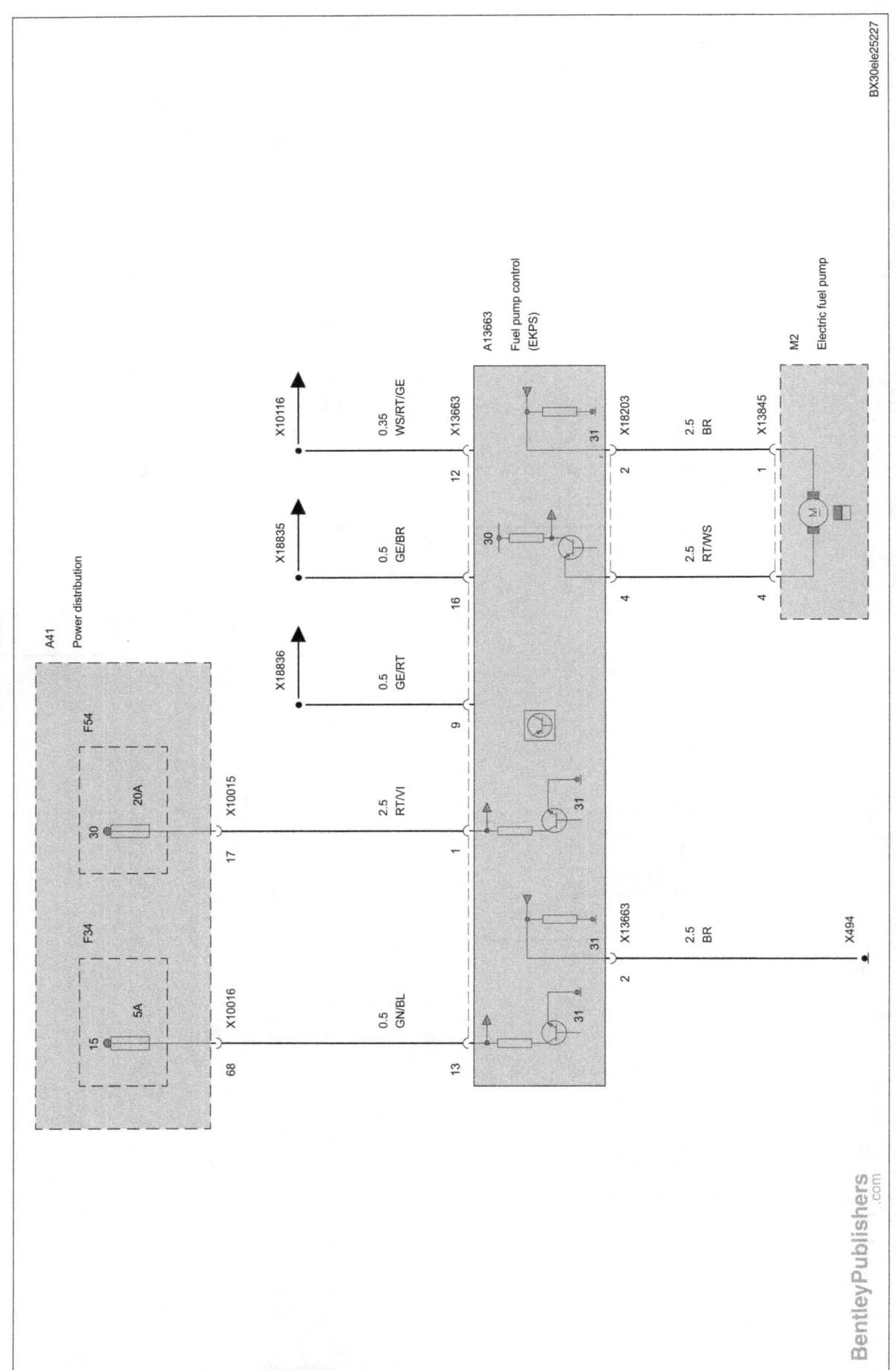

BX30ele25227

Starter
M54 engine

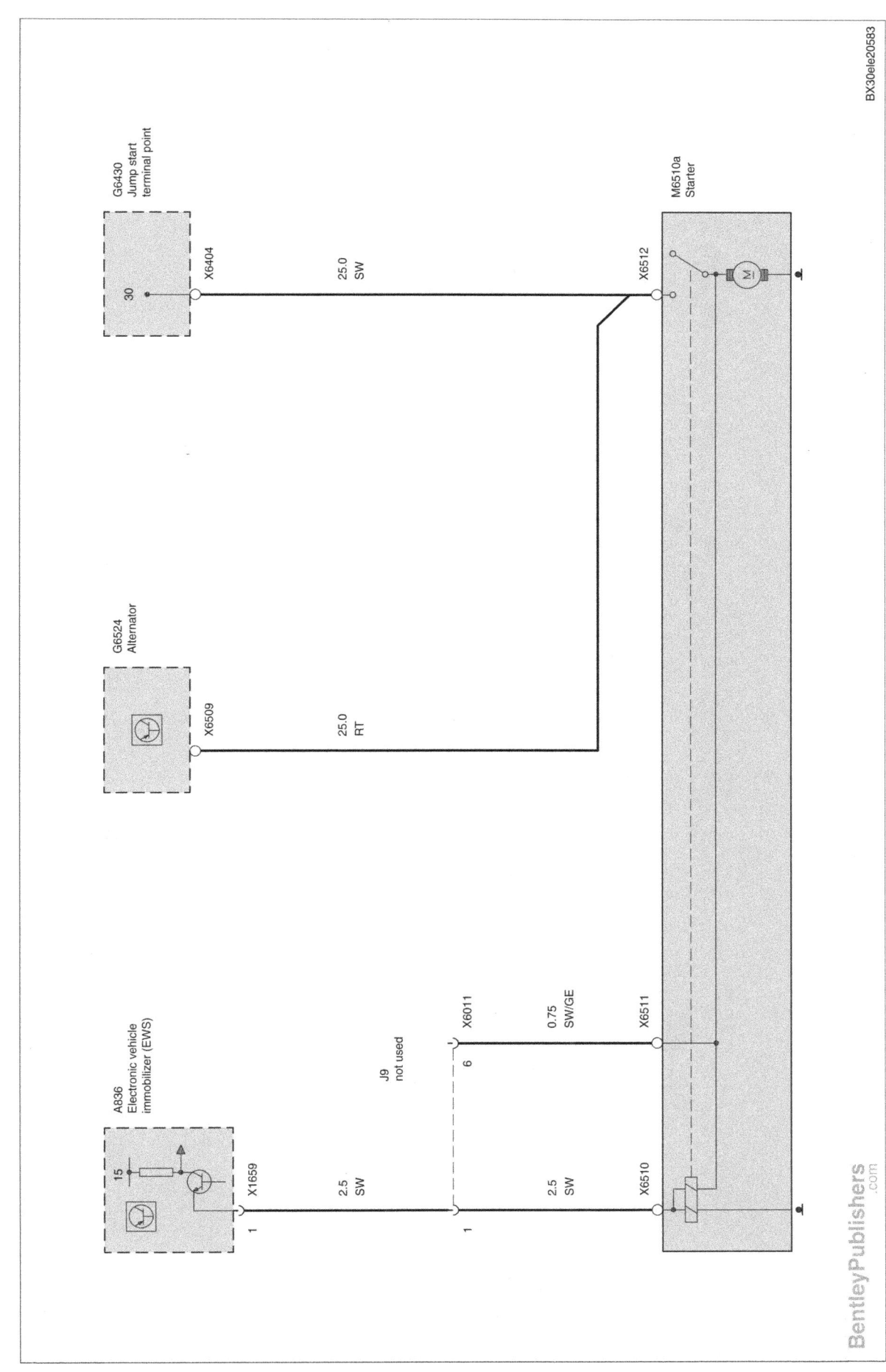

BX30ele20583

G6430
Jump start
terminal point

X6404

30

25.0
SW

M6510a
Starter

X6512

G6524
Alternator

X6509

25.0
RT

X6511

A836
Electronic vehicle
immobilizer (EWS)

X6011

0.75
SW/GE

J9
not used

6

15

X1659

2.5
SW

1

2.5
SW

1

X6510

Starter
N52 engine

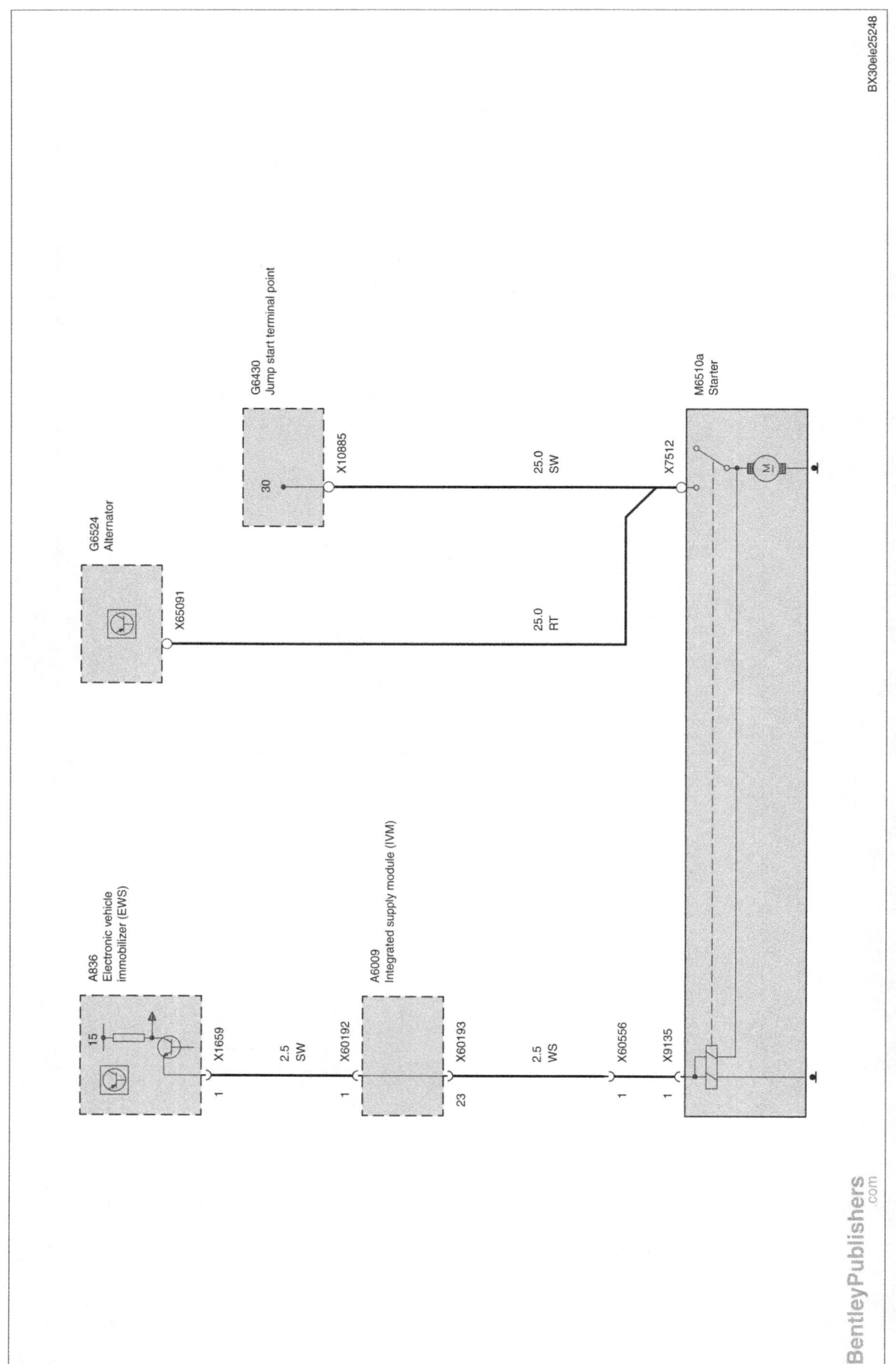

G6430
Jump start terminal point

G6524
Alternator

A836
Electronic vehicle
immobilizer (EWS)

A6009
Integrated supply module (IVM)

M6510a
Starter

X10885

X65091

X7512

30

25.0
SW

25.0
RT

15

X1659   X60192   X60193   X60556   X9135

2.5
SW

2.5
WS

1   1   23   1   1

BX30ele25248

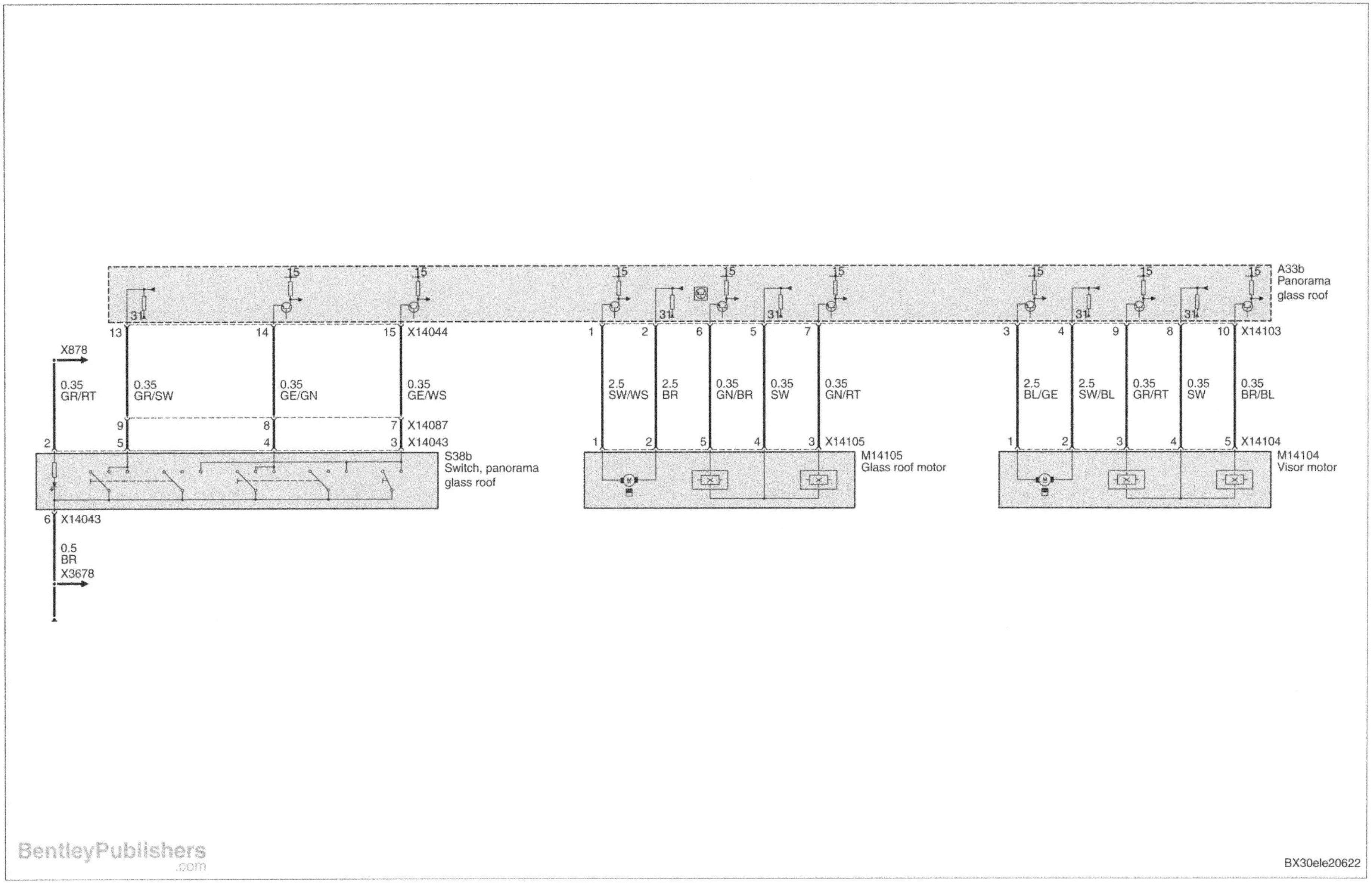

A33b
Panorama
glass roof

M14104
Visor motor

15 X14103 0.35 BR/BL X14104
10 5

31 0.35 SW
8 4

15 0.35 GR/RT
9 3

31 2.5 SW/BL
4 2

15 2.5 BL/GE
3 1

M14105
Glass roof motor

15 0.35 GN/RT X14105
7 3

31 0.35 SW
5 4

15 0.35 GN/BR
6 5

31 2.5 BR
2 2

15 2.5 SW/WS
1 1

S38b
Switch, panorama
glass roof

15 X14044 0.35 GE/WS X14087 X14043
15 7 3

15 0.35 GE/GN 8 4

31 0.35 GR/SW 9 5
13

X878 0.35 GR/RT
2

X14043 0.5 BR X3678
6

**Fuse supply, terminal 30
M54 engine**

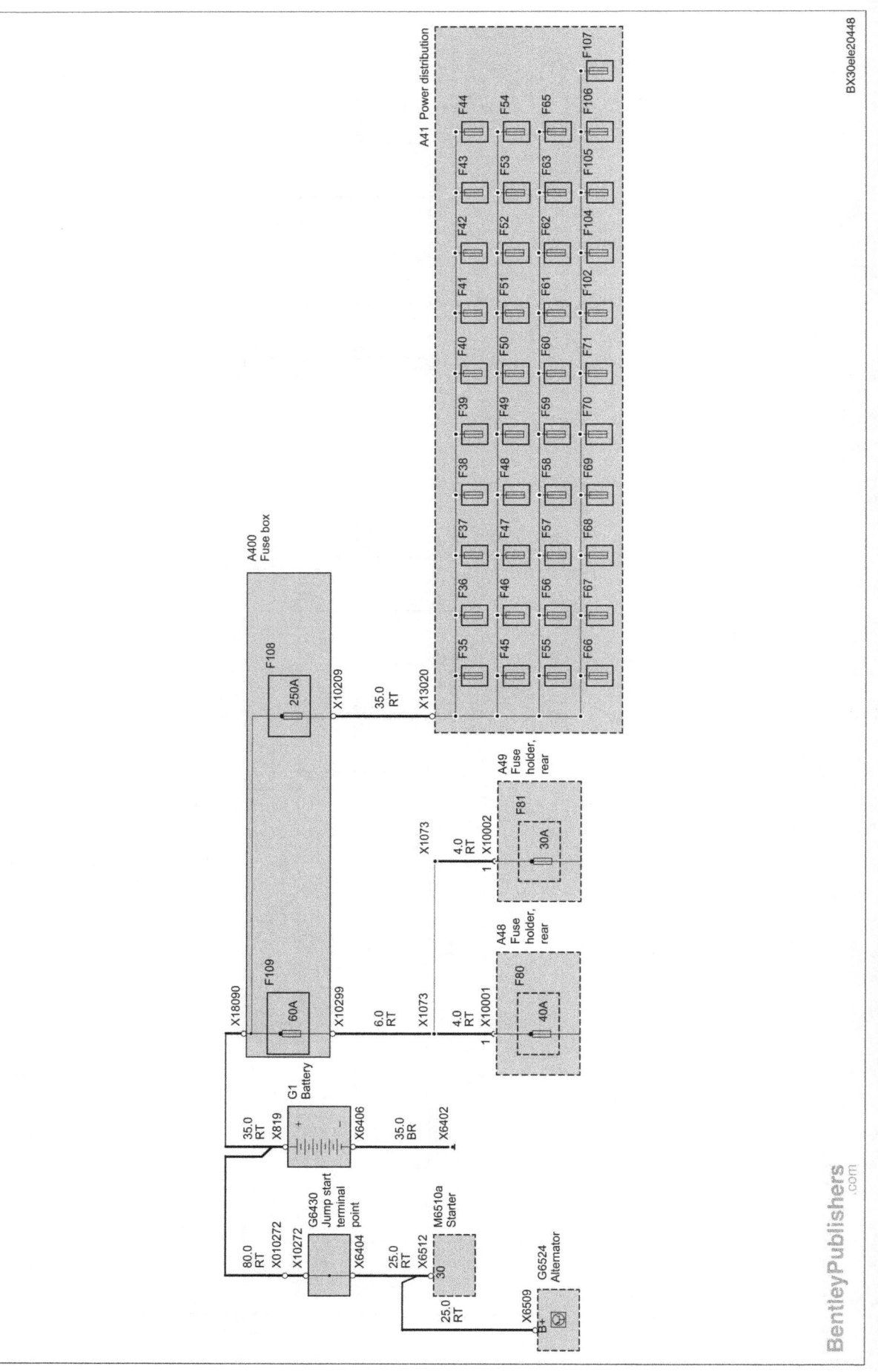

BX30ele20448

Fuse supply, terminal 30
N52 engine
page 1 of 2

80.0
RT
X010272
X10272
G6430
Jump start terminal point
X10885
X6400
25.0
SW
6.0
RT
25.0
RT
X7512
30
M6510a
Starter
1
X60199
X65091
B+
G6524
Alternator
9
F09
40A
A6009
Integrated supply module (IVM)
9) Relay, variable valve timing gear
35.0
RT
X819
G1
Battery
X6406
35.0
BR
X6402
X18090
A400 Fuse box
F109
60A
X10299
6.0
RT
X1073
X1073
4.0
RT
4.0
RT
1
X10001
1
X10002
A48
Fuse holder, rear
F80
40A
A49
Fuse holder, rear
F81
30A

BX30ele25125a

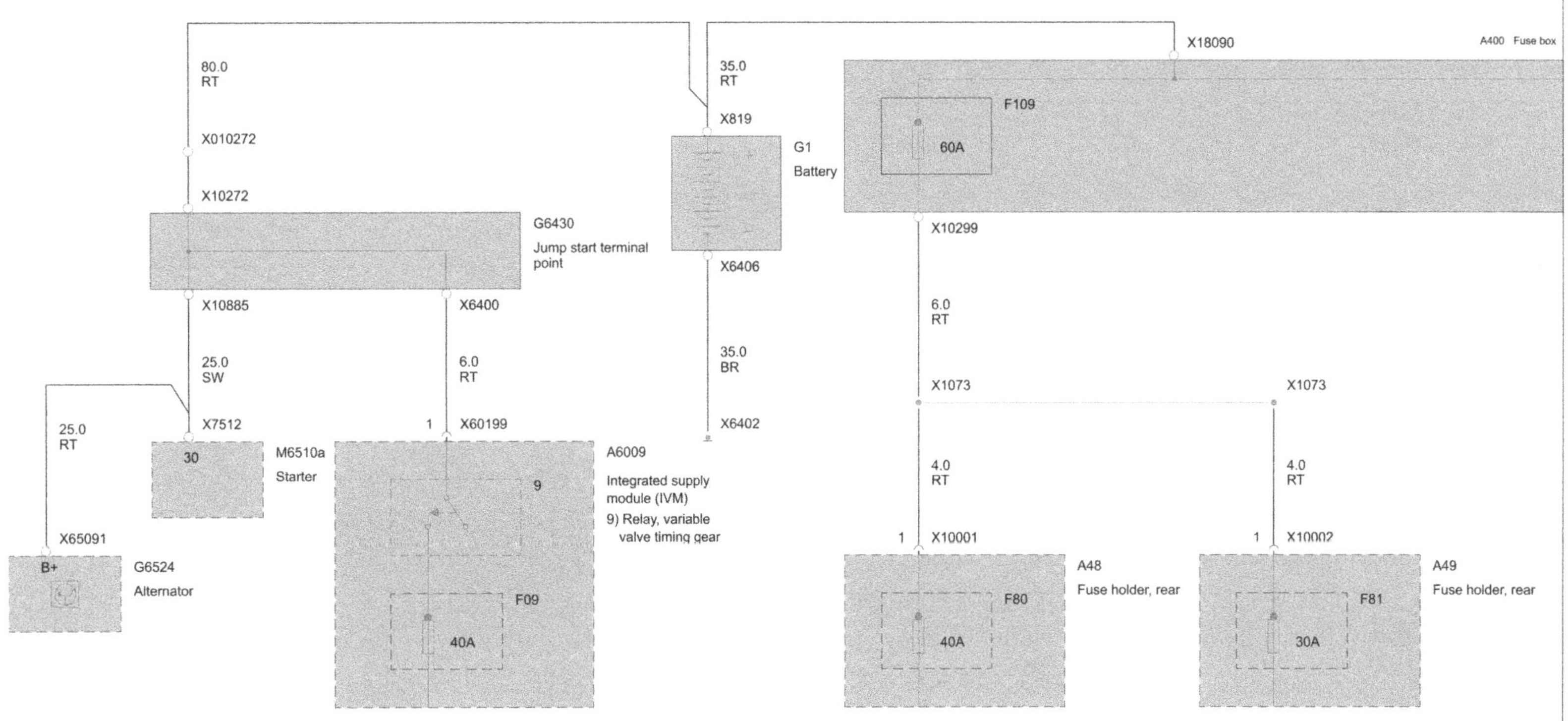

Fuse supply, terminal 30
N52 engine
page 2 of 2

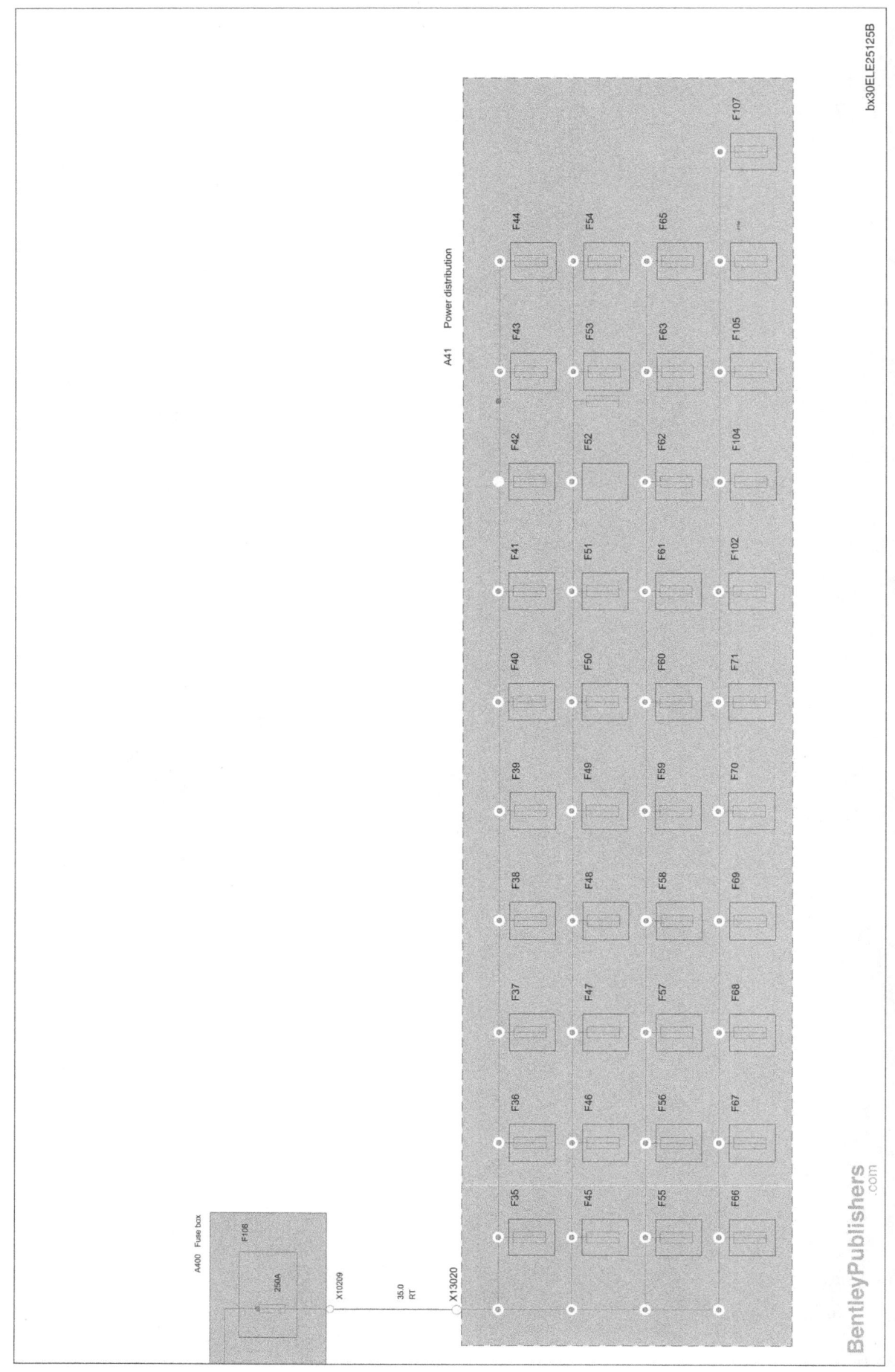

A41   Power distribution

A400   Fuse box

F108

250A

X10209

35.0
RT

X13020

F35 F36 F37 F38 F39 F40 F41 F42 F43 F44

F45 F46 F47 F48 F49 F50 F51 F52 F53 F54

F55 F56 F57 F58 F59 F60 F61 F62 F63 F65

F66 F67 F68 F69 F70 F71 F102 F104 F105

F107

Electrical Wiring Diagrams   ELE-191

BX30ele26484a

30   X254

0.5
WS/GN
X274

0.5
WS/BR
X647

17   10   4

S42
Rear right door
power window
switch

2 X647

0.5
BR
X835

30

0.5
WS/RT
X580

0.5
WS/GE

1   9   1

X0580

0.5
GR/RT

3

30   X253

0.35
GR/BL
X256

4   6   4

0.5
GR/RT
X19516

0.35
GR/RT
X324

3

S127
Power window switch,
passenger's door

2 X324

0.5
BR
X891

30

0.35
GR/GE

40   5   1

30   X254

0.5
WS/BR
X273

0.5
X645

16   10   4

S41
Rear left door
power window
switch

2 X645

0.5
BR
X834

30

0.5
WS/GE

4   9   1

X580

0.5
GR/RT

3

0.35
BR/RT
X257

0.35
BR/RT
X887

4   8

A23a
Driver's door
module

J101
with folding mirror
function and/or
memory

J100
with basic mirror

48

X14247

0.35
BR/RT
X257

X14248

0.35
BR/RT
X887

4   3

A23a
Driver's door
module

**Power window
page 2 of 2**

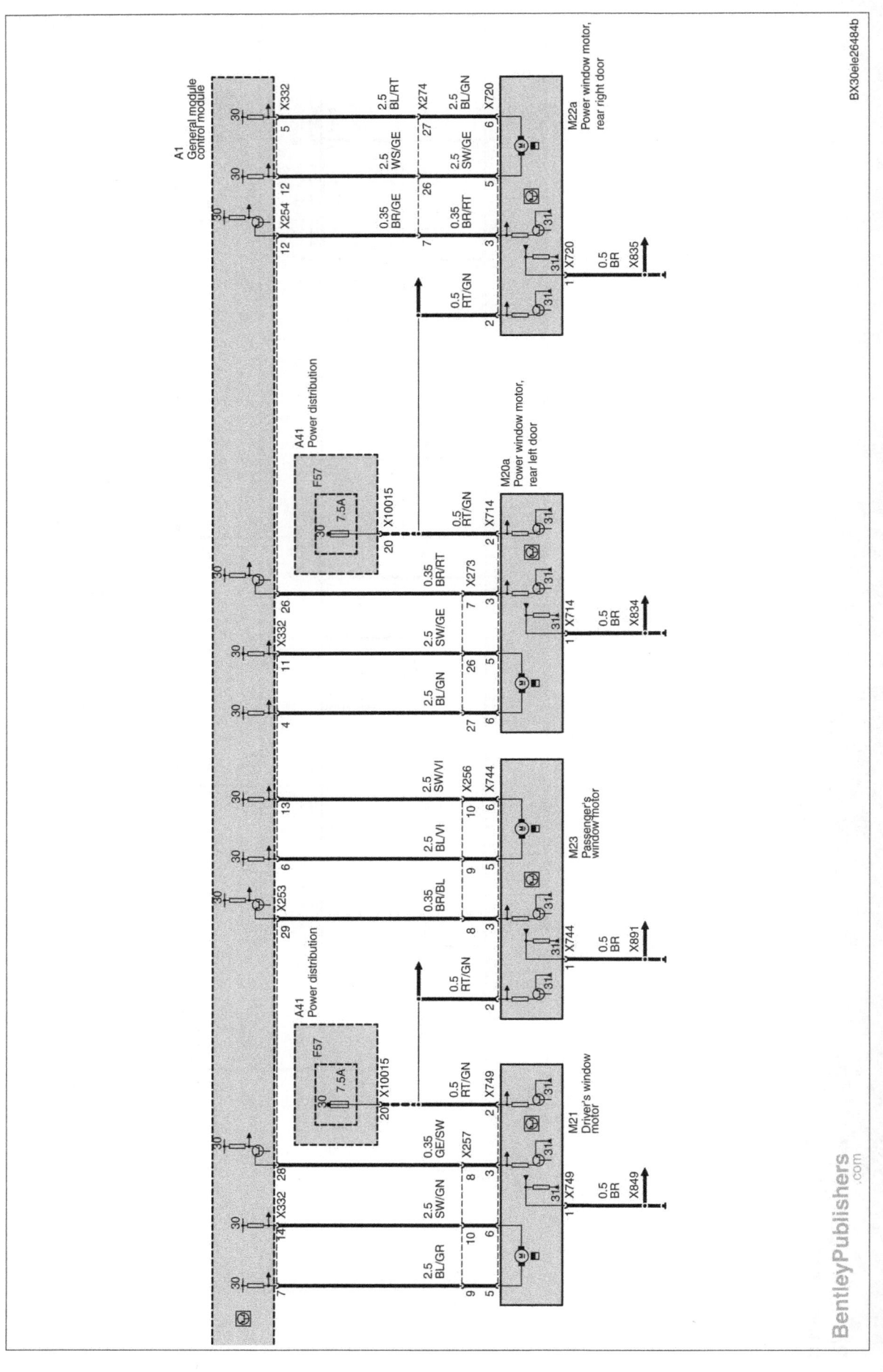

BX30ele26484b

**Driver's seat adjustment
with Comfort seat
page 1 of 2**

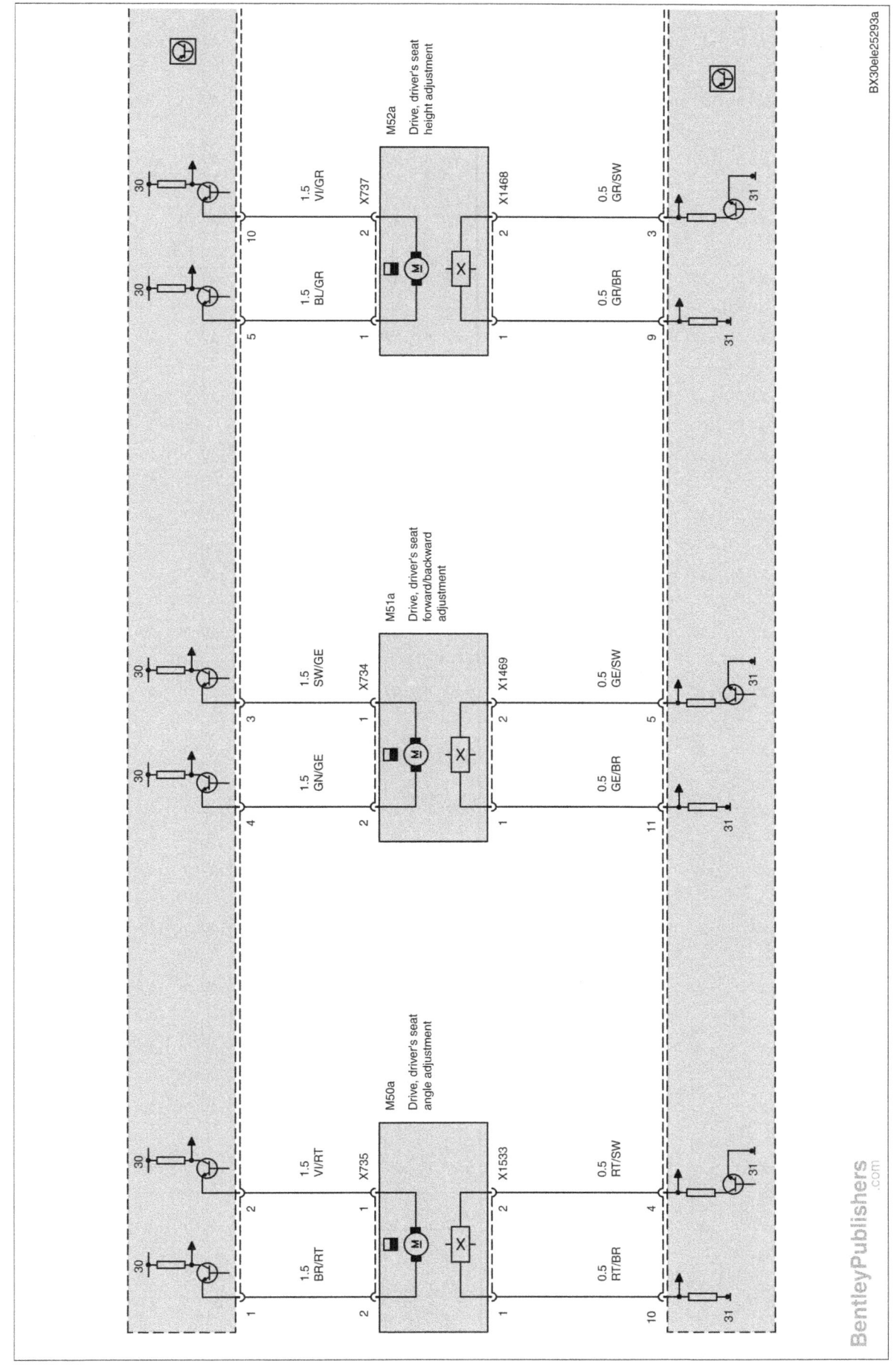

Electrical Wiring Diagrams   ELE-193

BX30ele25293a

BentleyPublishers
.com

Electrical Wiring Diagrams ELE-194

**Driver's seat adjustment
with Comfort seat
page 2 of 2**

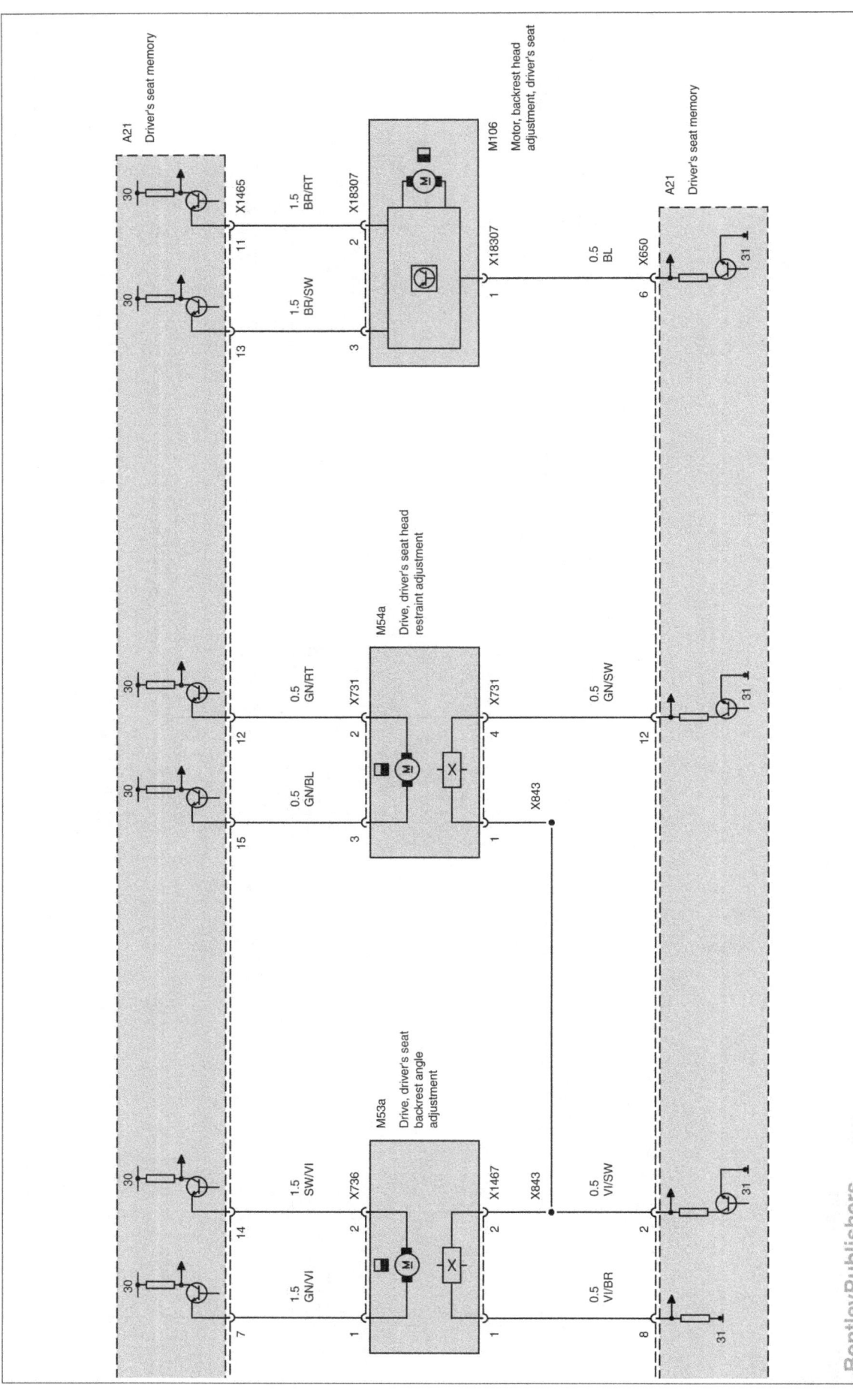

BX30ele25293b

BentleyPublishers
.com

**Driver's seat adjustment
without Comfort seat**

Electrical Wiring Diagrams   ELE-195

BX30ele18140

**Passenger's seat adjustment
with Comfort seat**

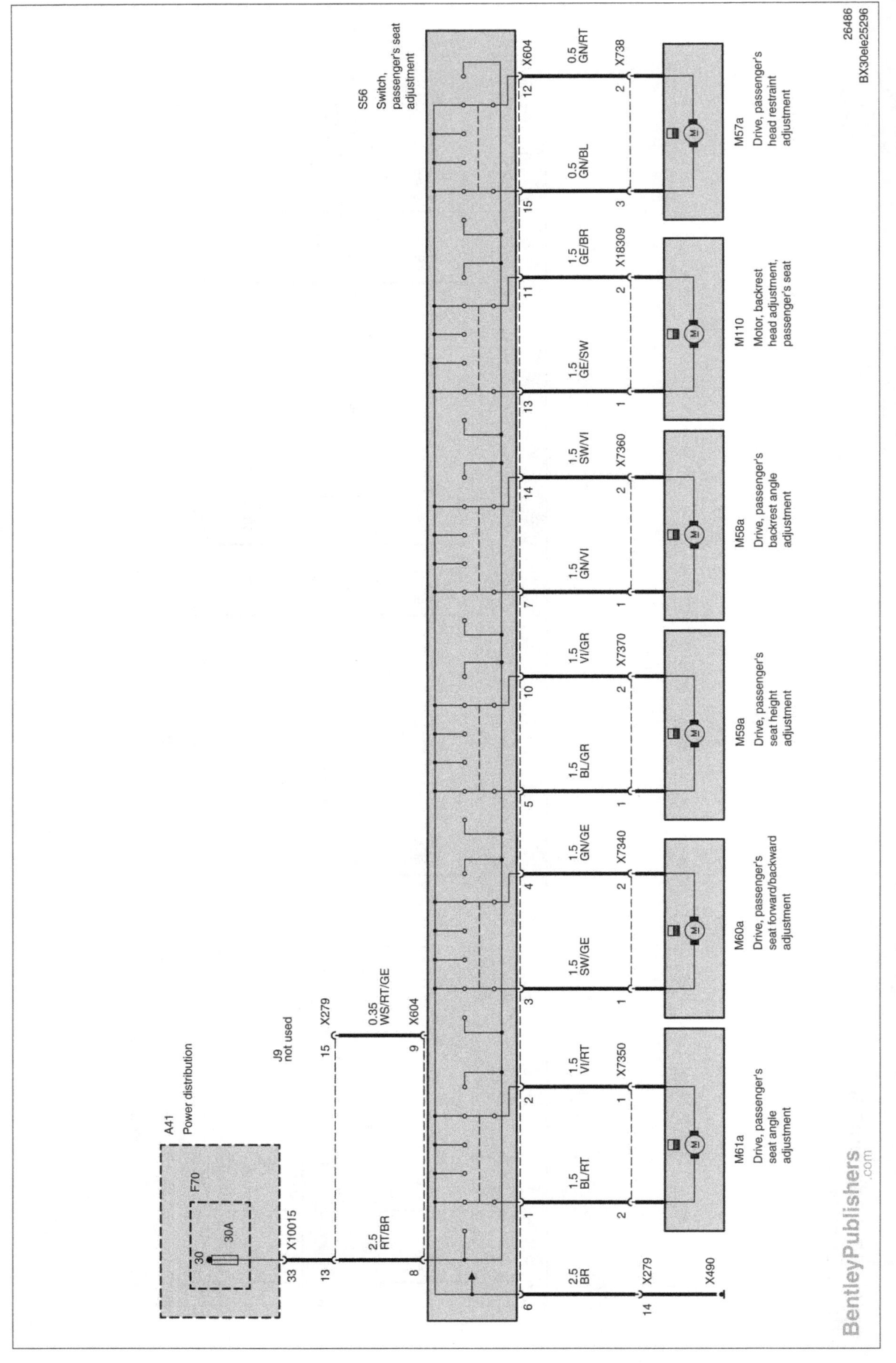

26486
BX30ele25296

**Passenger's seat adjustment
without Comfort seat**

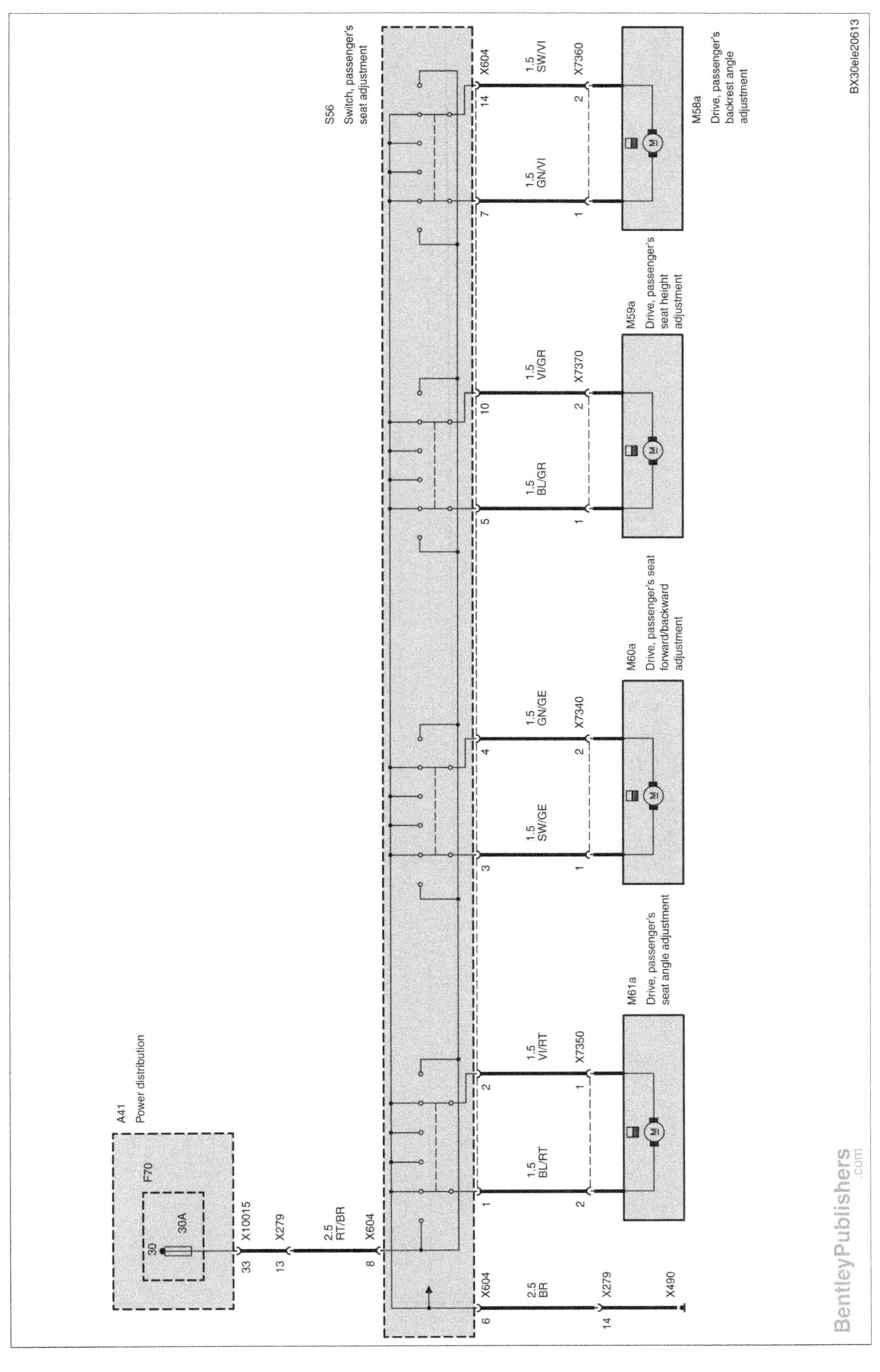

BX30ele20613

BentleyPublishers
.com

Seat heating, passenger's side

Seat heating, driver's side

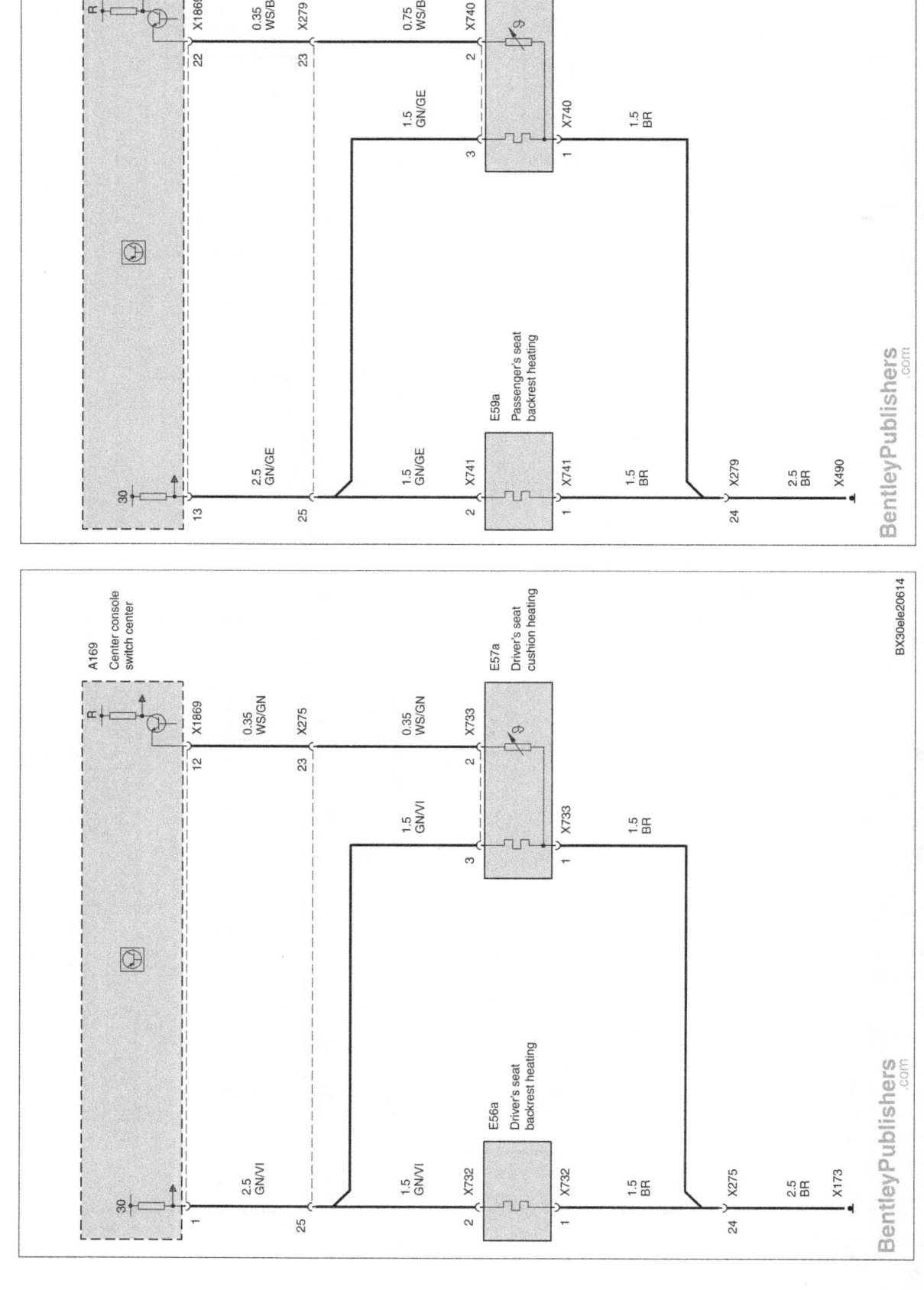

BX30ele20615

BX30ele20614

Seat heating, rear

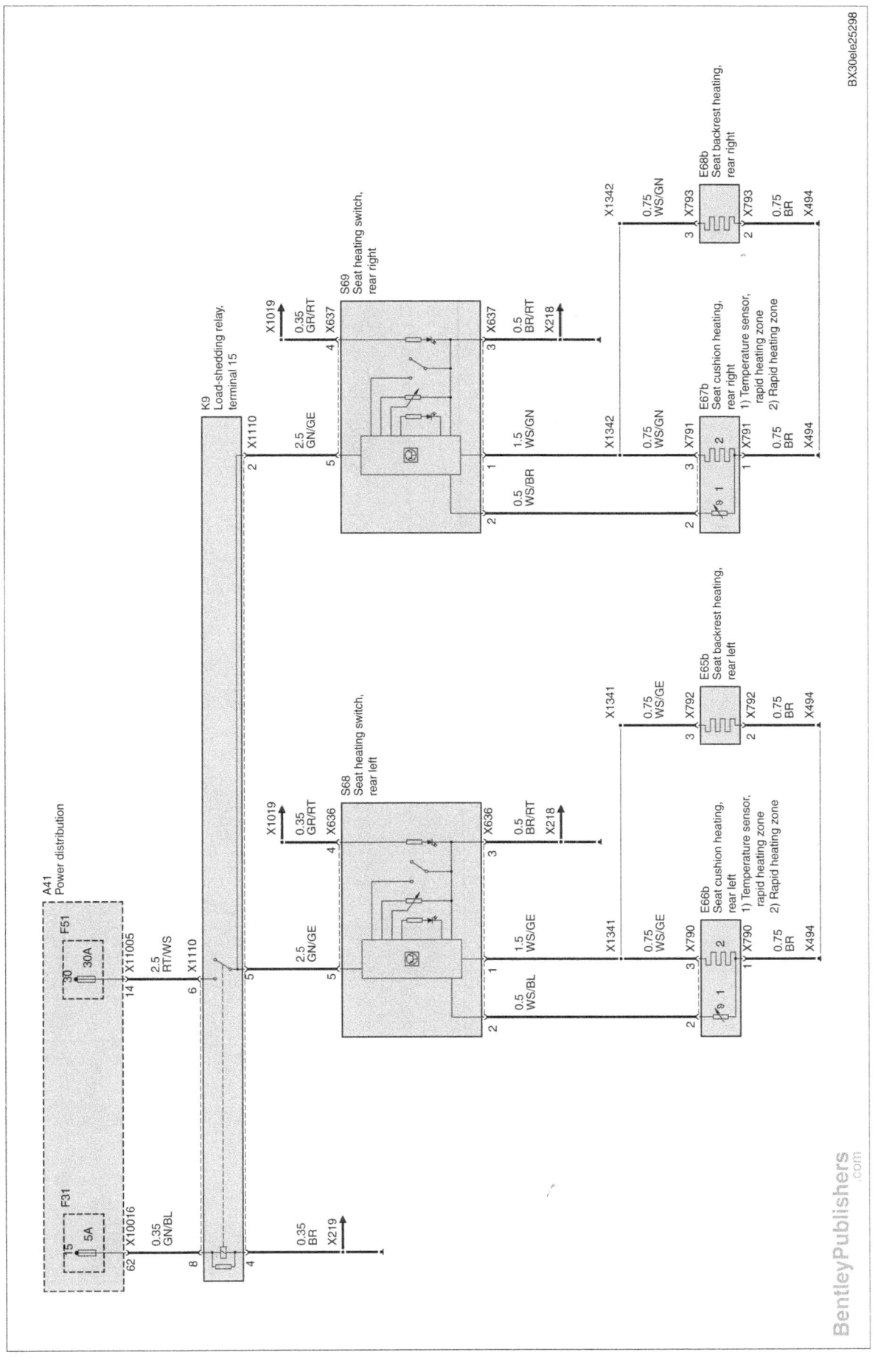

BX30ele25298

BentleyPublishers
.com

Supply, driver's seat adjustment without Comfort seat from 03/2007

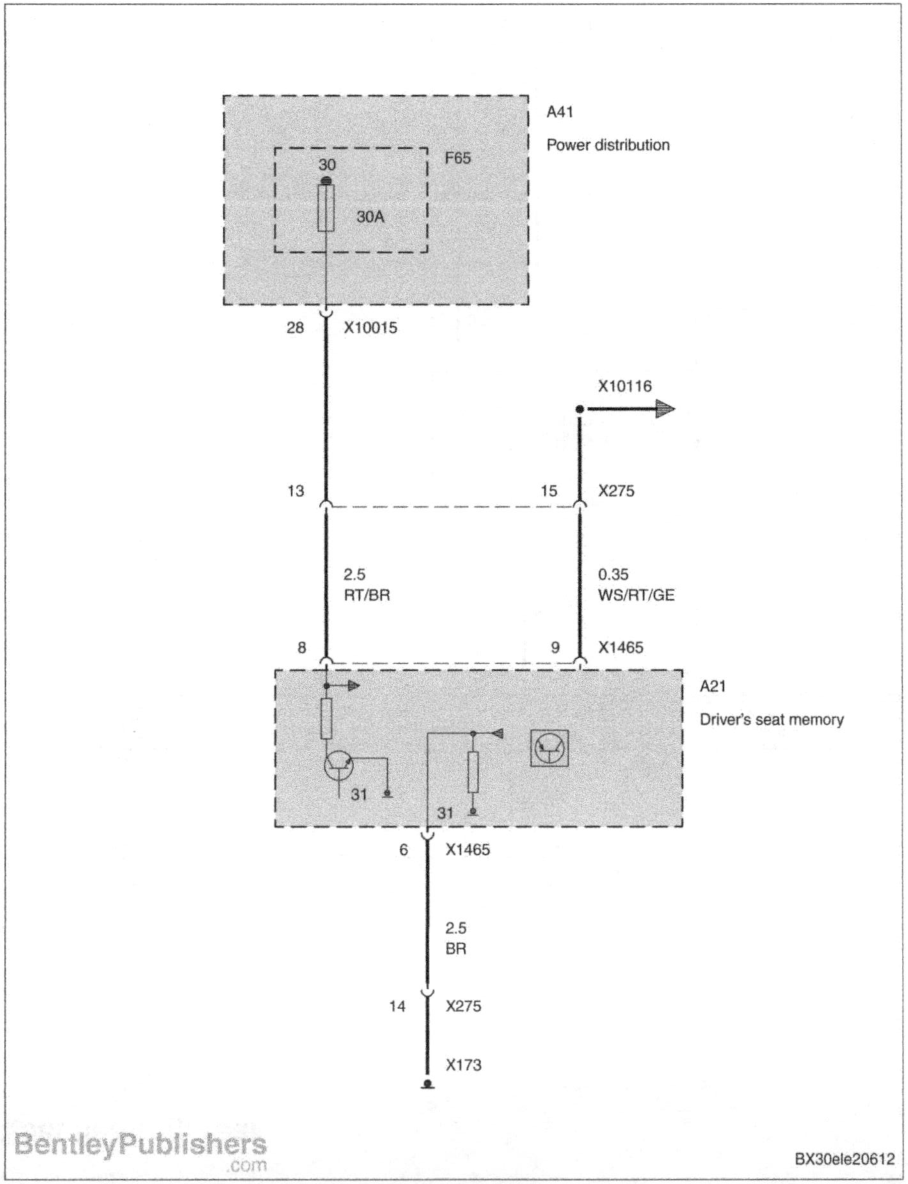
A41
Power distribution
F65
30
30A
28
X10015
X10116
13
15
X275
2.5
RT/BR
0.35
WS/RT/GE
8
9
X1465
A21
Driver's seat memory
31
31
6
X1465
2.5
BR
14
X275
X173
BentleyPublishers.com
BX30ele20612

Supply, driver's seat adjustment with Comfort seat from 03/2007

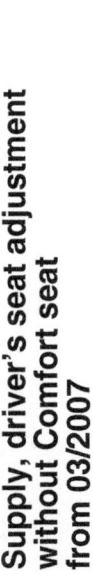

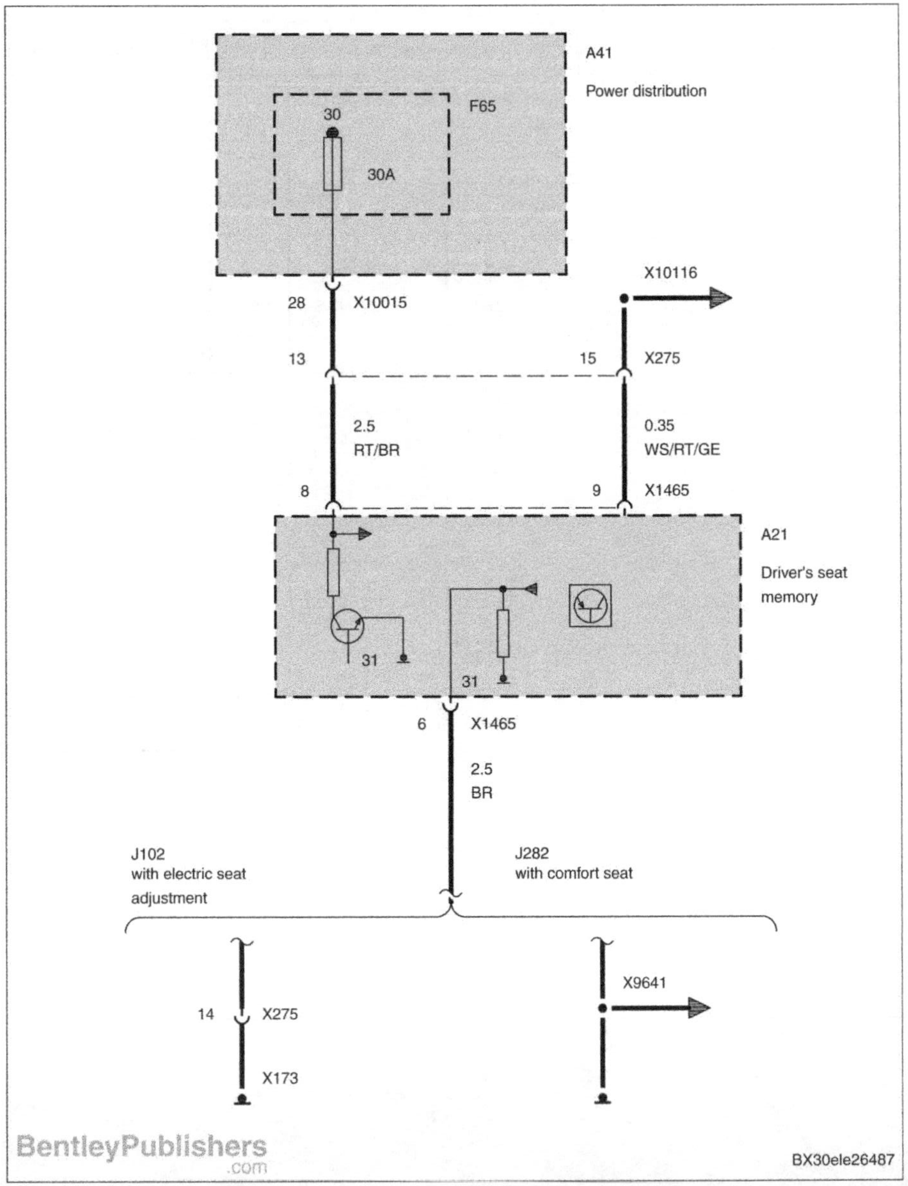
A41
Power distribution
F65
30
30A
X10116
28
X10015
13
15
X275
2.5
RT/BR
0.35
WS/RT/GE
8
9
X1465
A21
Driver's seat memory
31
31
6
X1465
2.5
BR
J102
with electric seat adjustment
J282
with comfort seat
X9641
14
X275
X173
BentleyPublishers.com
BX30ele26487

**Electric outside mirror,
with seat memory or mirror fold-in function**

Electrical Wiring Diagrams   ELE-201

21988
BX30ele20603

A41
Power distribution

F57

7.5A

30

X10015

20

0.5
RT/GN

A23a
Driver's door module

X887

3

X14248

X14248

0.35
GR/RT (to 09-2004)
BR/RT (from 09-2004)

X623

1

Y5
Outside mirror,
driver's side

31

2

31

X623

0.5
BR

X849

3

X257

4

X14247

X256

4

0.35
BR/RT

1

Y6
Outside mirror,
passenger's side

X624

2

31

31

X624

3

0.5
BR

X891

0.5
RT/GN

BentleyPublishers
.com

Electric outside mirror,
without seat memory or mirror fold-in function

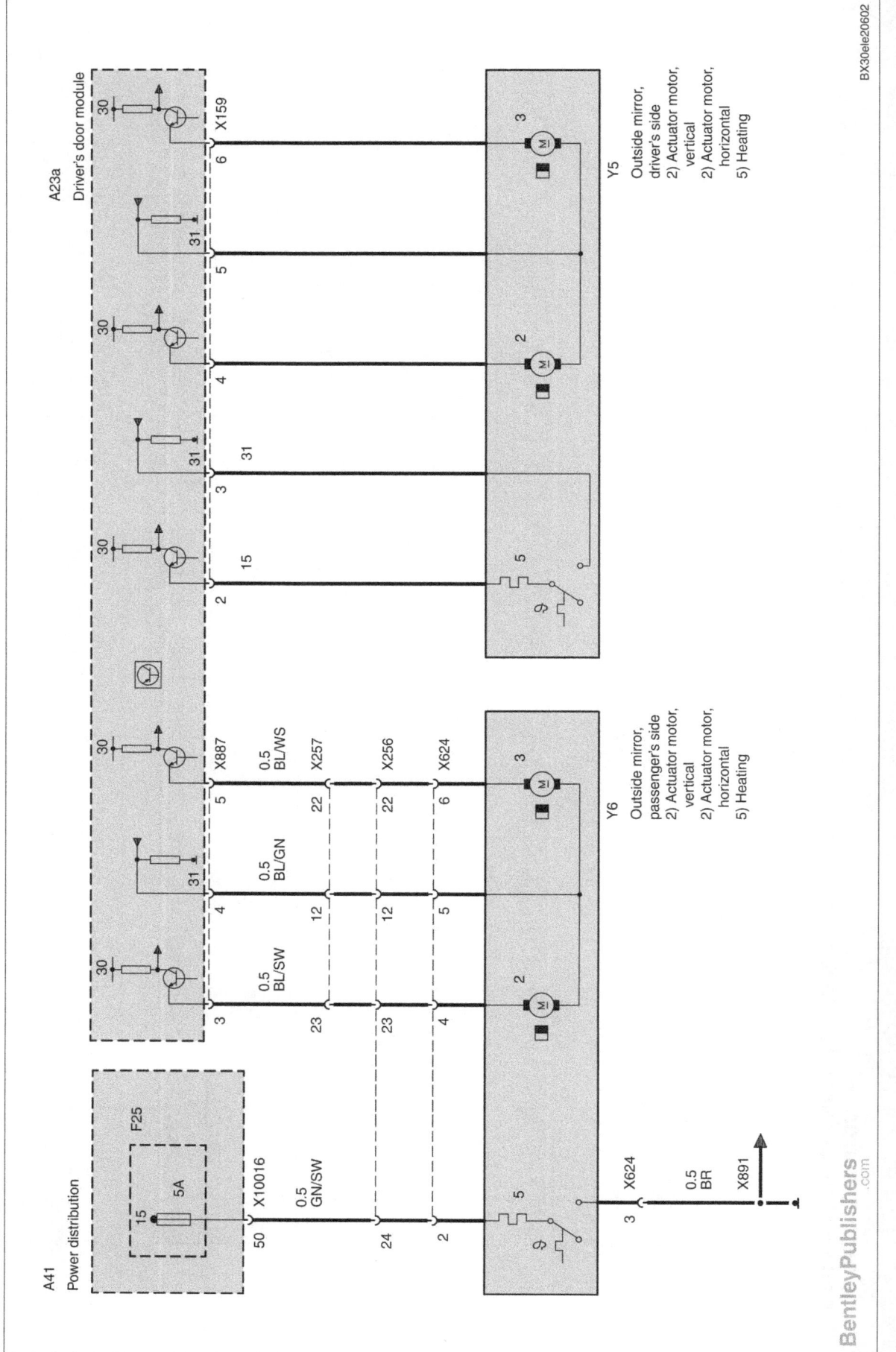

BX30ele20602

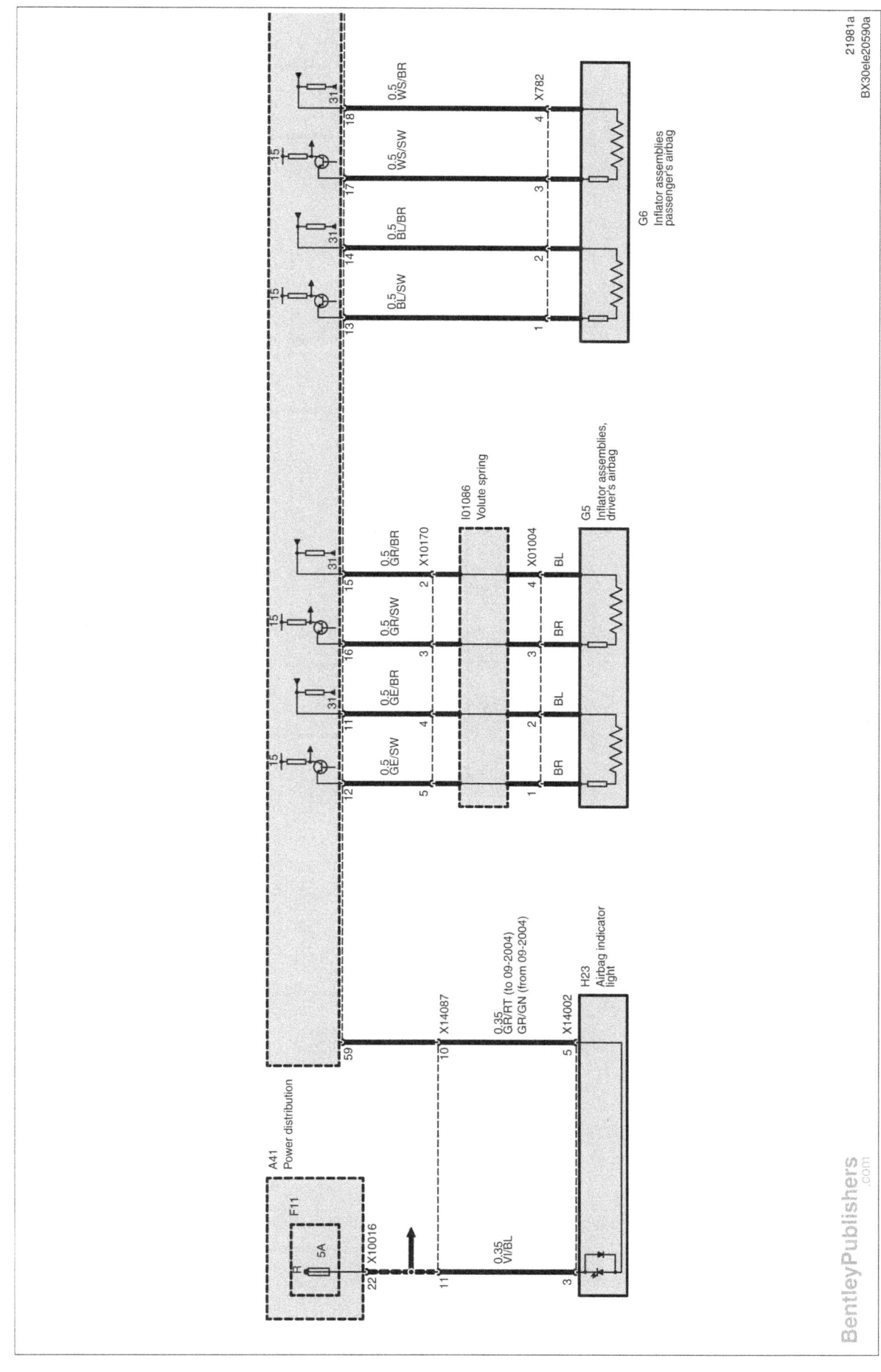

Electrical Wiring Diagrams   ELE-203

21981a
BX30ele20590a

**Airbag triggering circuits
to 09/2007
page 2 of 3**

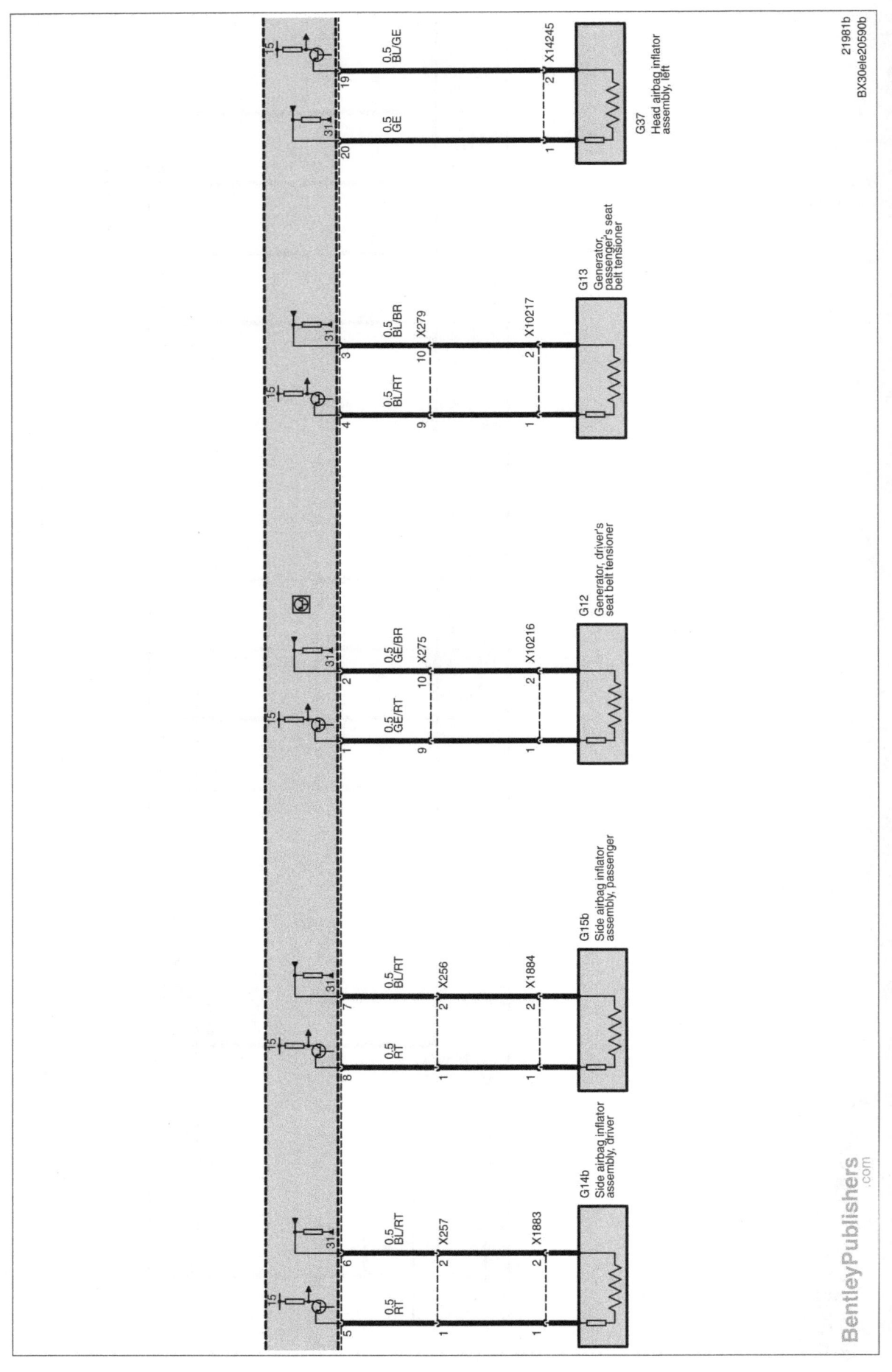

21981b
BX30ele20590b

**Airbag triggering circuits
to 09/2007
page 3 of 3**

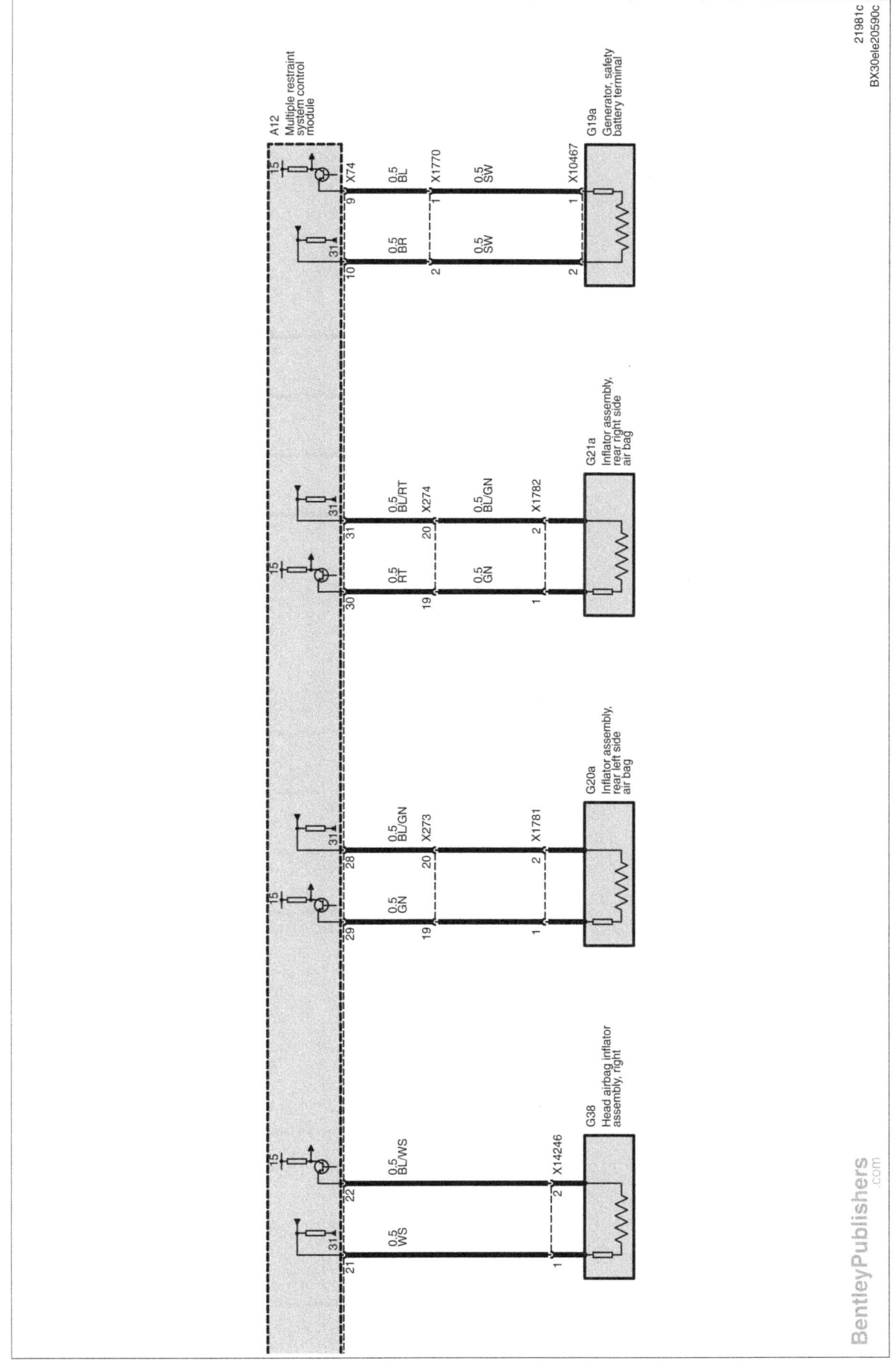

21981c
BX30ele20590c

A12
Multiple restraint
system control
module

9 X74
0.5
BL
X1770
0.5
SW
X10467

10
0.5
BR
2
0.5
SW
2

G19a
Generator, safety
battery terminal

31
0.5
BL/RT
X274
20
0.5
BL/GN
X1782
2

30
0.5
RT
19
0.5
GN
X1
1

G21a
Inflator assembly,
rear right side
air bag

28
0.5
BL/GN
X273
20
X1781
2

29
0.5
GN
19
1

G20a
Inflator assembly,
rear left side
air bag

22
0.5
BL/WS
X14246
2

21
0.5
WS
1

G38
Head airbag inflator
assembly, right

**Airbag triggering circuits
from 09/2007
page 1 of 3**

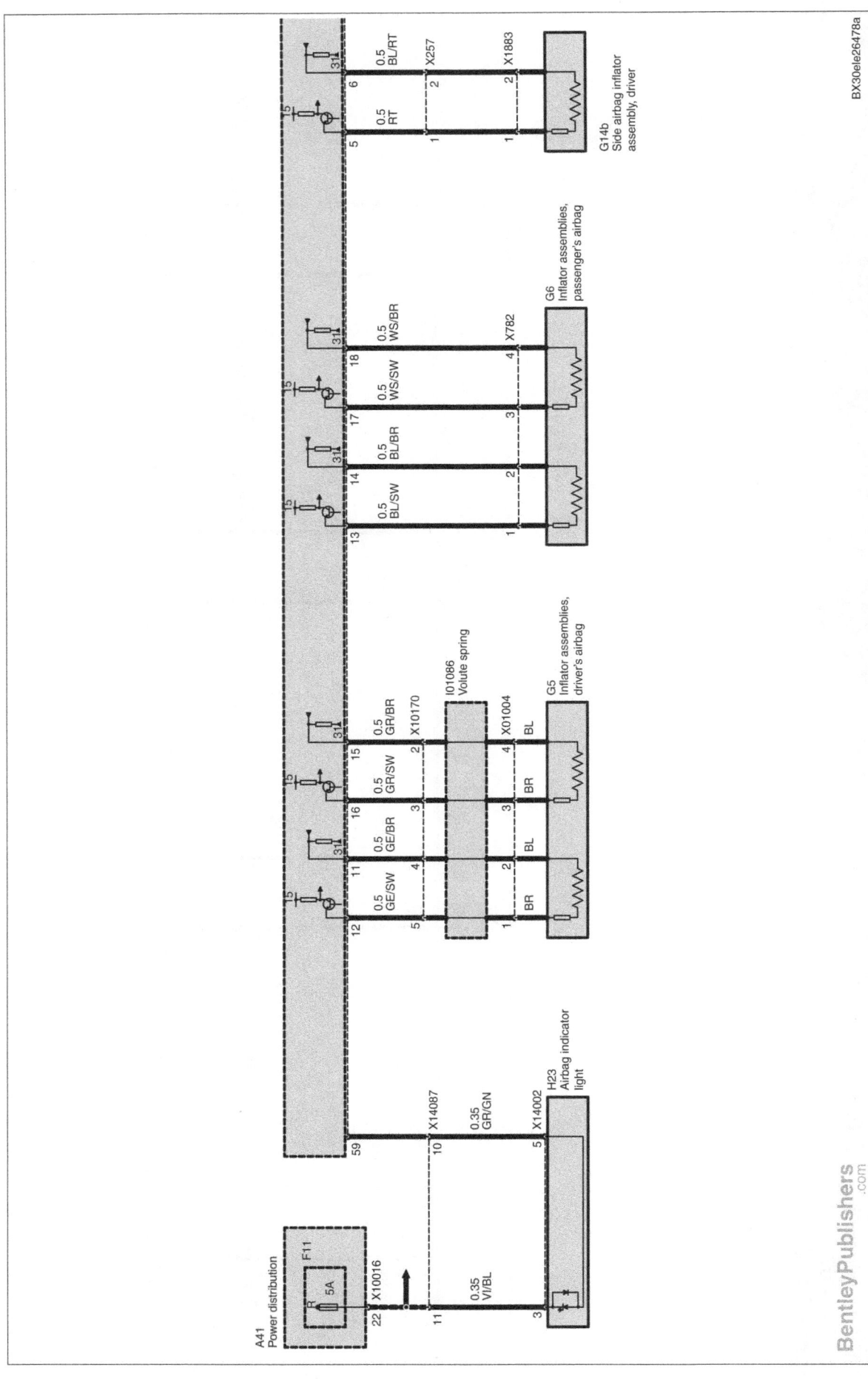

BX30ele26478a

15

22
0.5
BL/WS

31
21
0.5
WS

X14246

G38
Head airbag inflator
assembly, right

15

19
0.5
BL/GE

31
20
0.5
GE

X14245

G37
Head airbag inflator
assembly, left

31
3
0.5
BL/BR
X279
10

X10217

15
4
0.5
BL/RT
9
1

G13
Generator,
passenger's seat
belt tensioner

31
2
0.5
GE/BR
X275
10

X10216

15
1
0.5
GE/RT
9
1

G12
Generator,
driver's seat
belt tensioner

31
7
0.5
BL/RT
X256
2

X1884

15
8
0.5
RT
1
1

G15b
Side airbag inflator
assembly, passenger

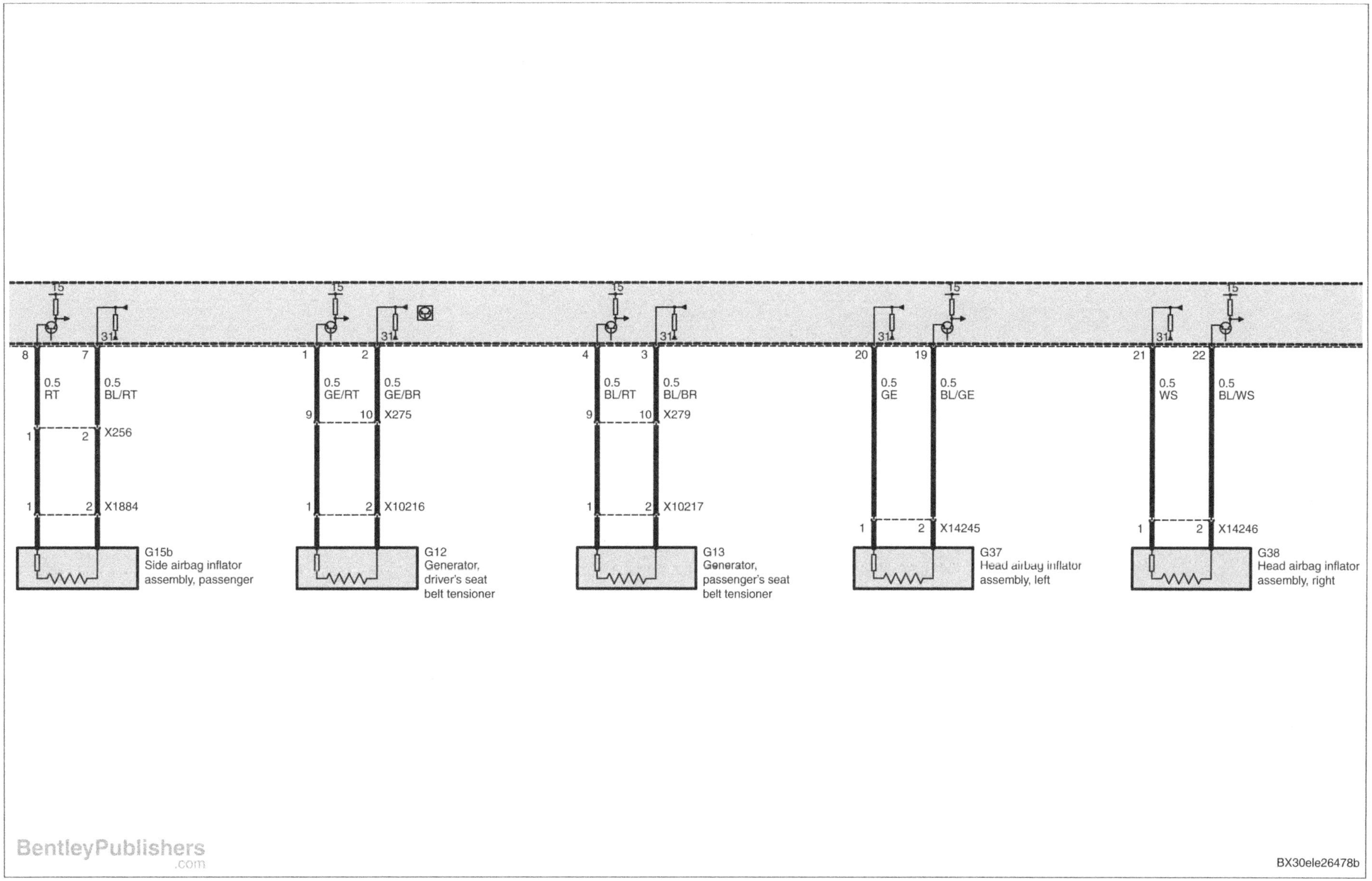

**Airbag triggering circuits
from 09/2007
page 3 of 3**

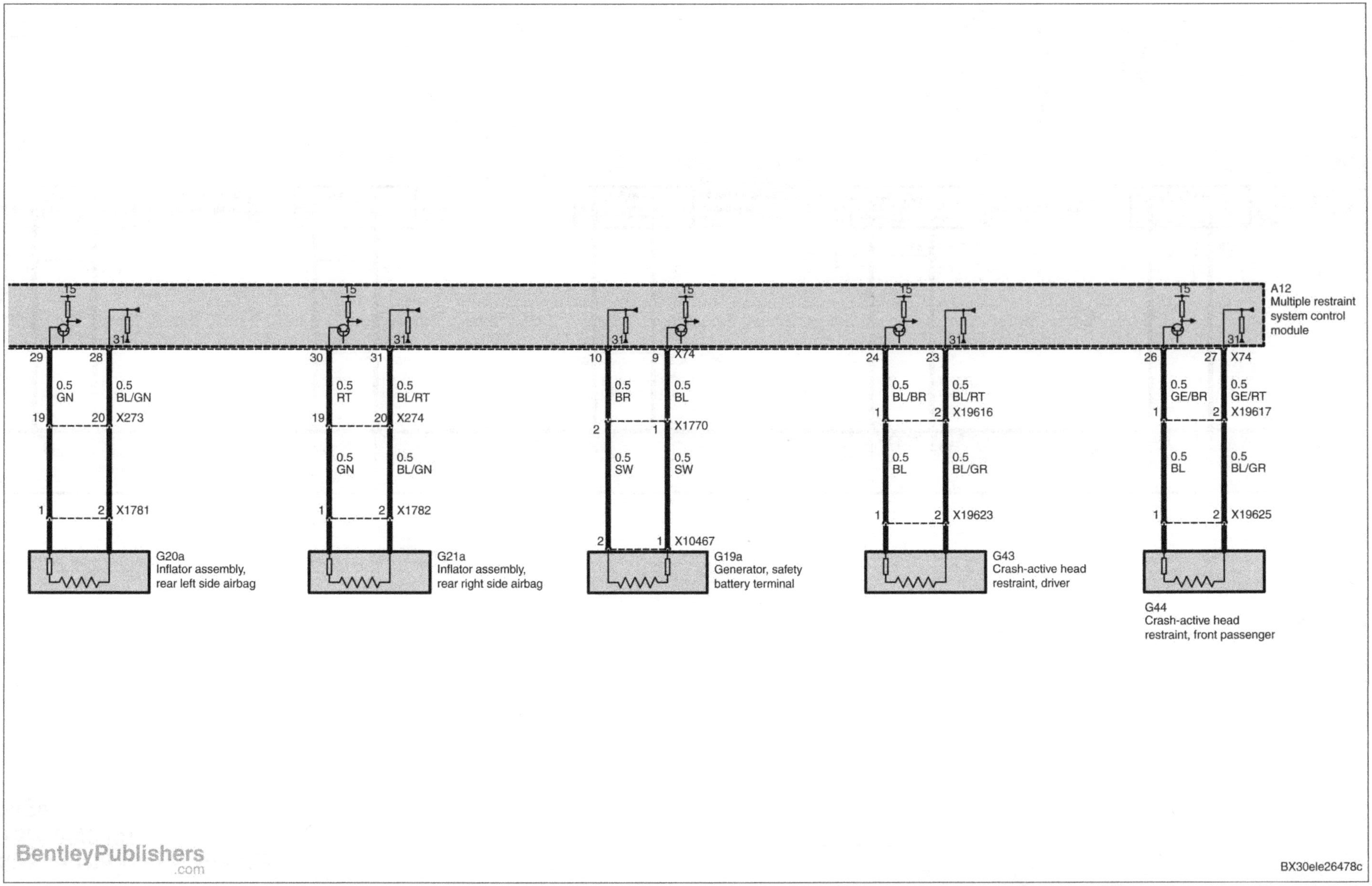

A12
Multiple restraint
system control
module

X74

31 X74

27 0.5 GE/RT X19617 2 0.5 BL/GR X19625 2

G44
Crash-active head
restraint, front passenger

26 0.5 GE/BR 1 0.5 BL 1

X74

31 23 0.5 BL/RT X19616 2 0.5 BL/GR X19623 2

G43
Crash-active head
restraint, driver

24 0.5 BL/BR 1 0.5 BL 1

X74

9 0.5 BL X1770 1 0.5 SW X10467 1

G19a
Generator, safety
battery terminal

31 10 0.5 BR 2 0.5 SW 2

31 31 0.5 BL/RT X274 20 0.5 BL/GN X1782 2

G21a
Inflator assembly,
rear right side airbag

30 0.5 RT 19 0.5 GN 1

31 28 0.5 BL/GN X273 20 X1781 2

G20a
Inflator assembly,
rear left side airbag

29 0.5 GN 19 1

BX30ele26478c

Integrated supply module (IVM)
page 1 of 4

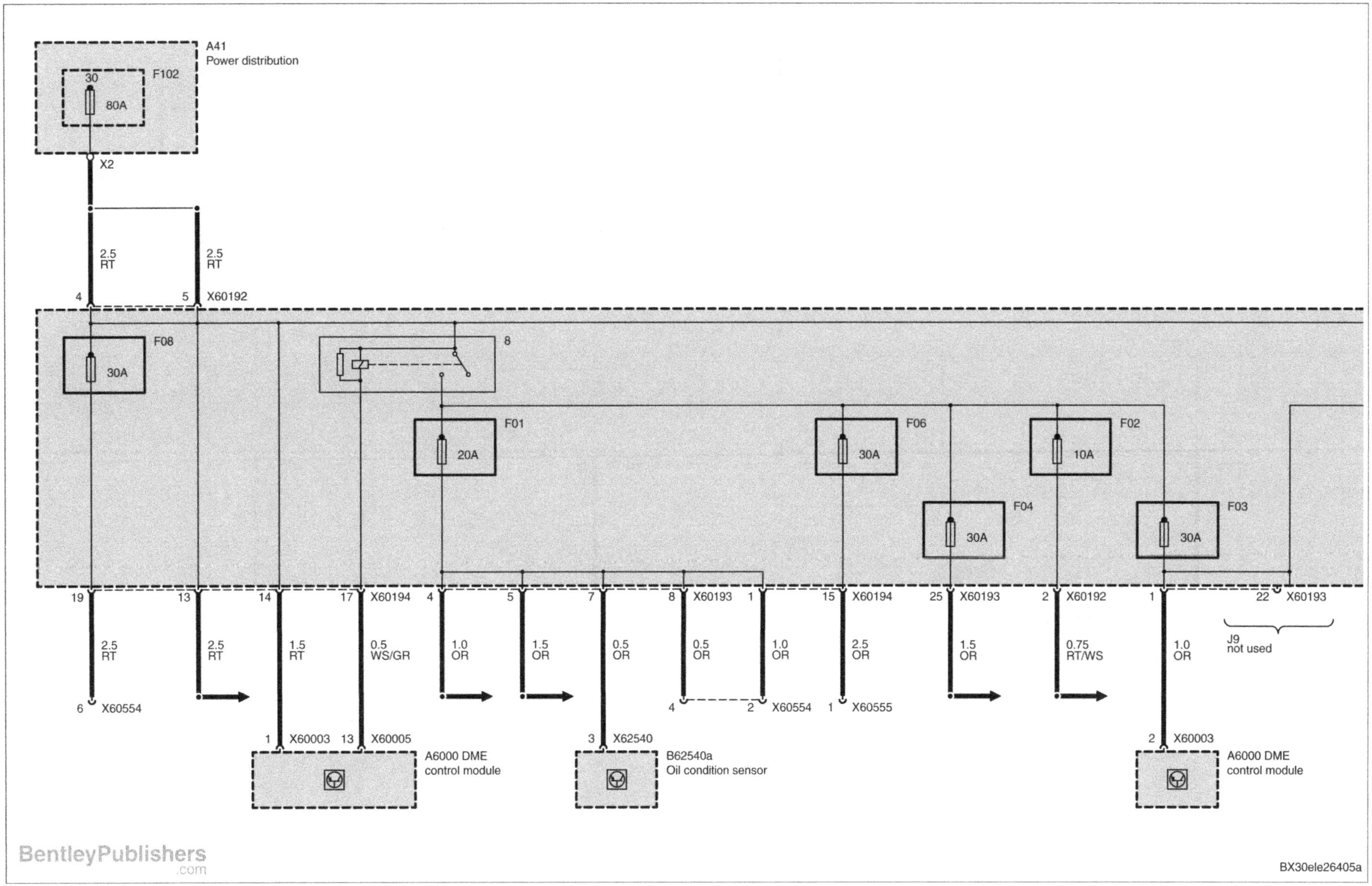

BX30ele26405a

BentleyPublishers
.com

**Integrated supply module (IVM)
page 2 of 4**

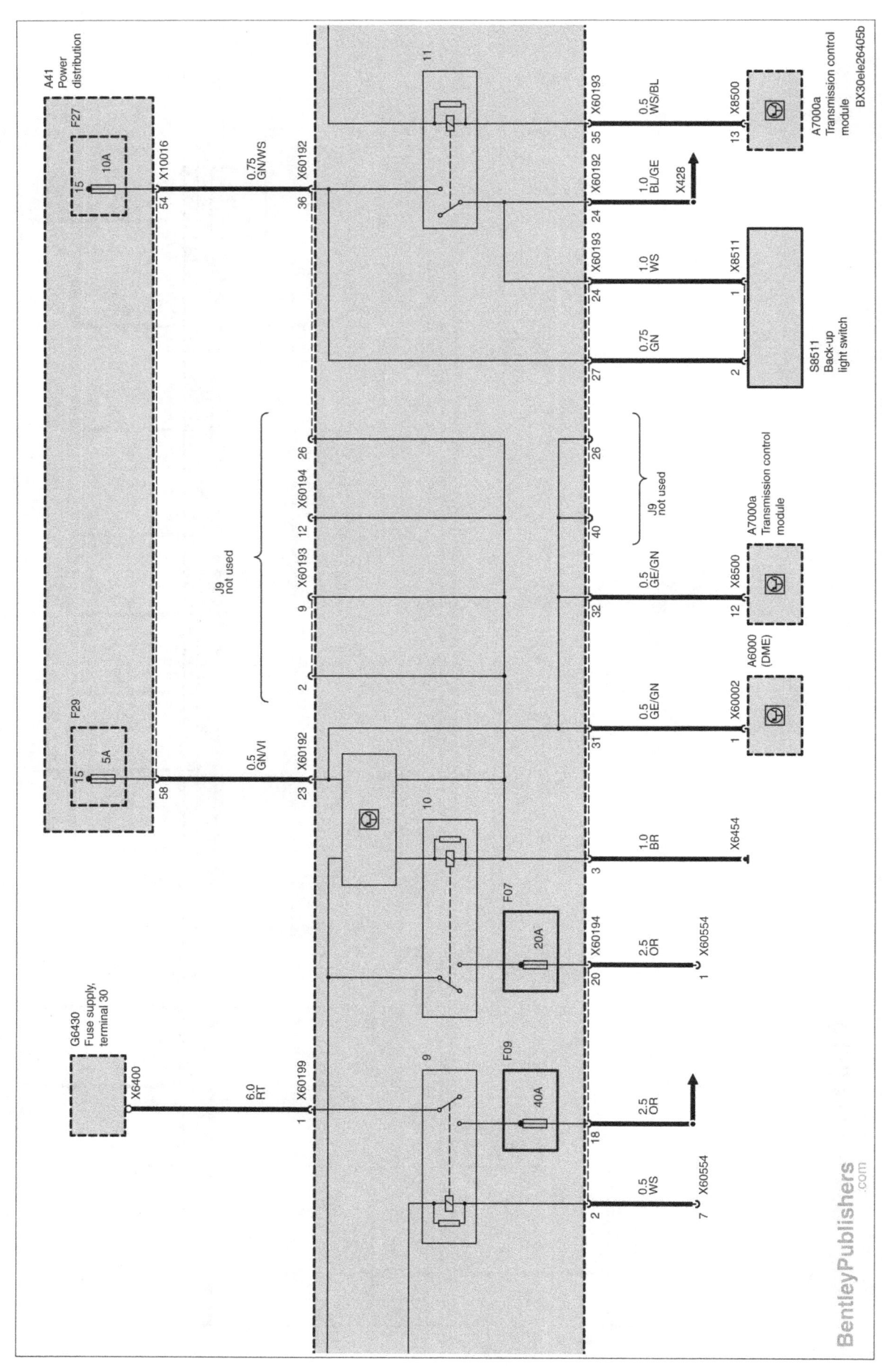

BX30ele26405b

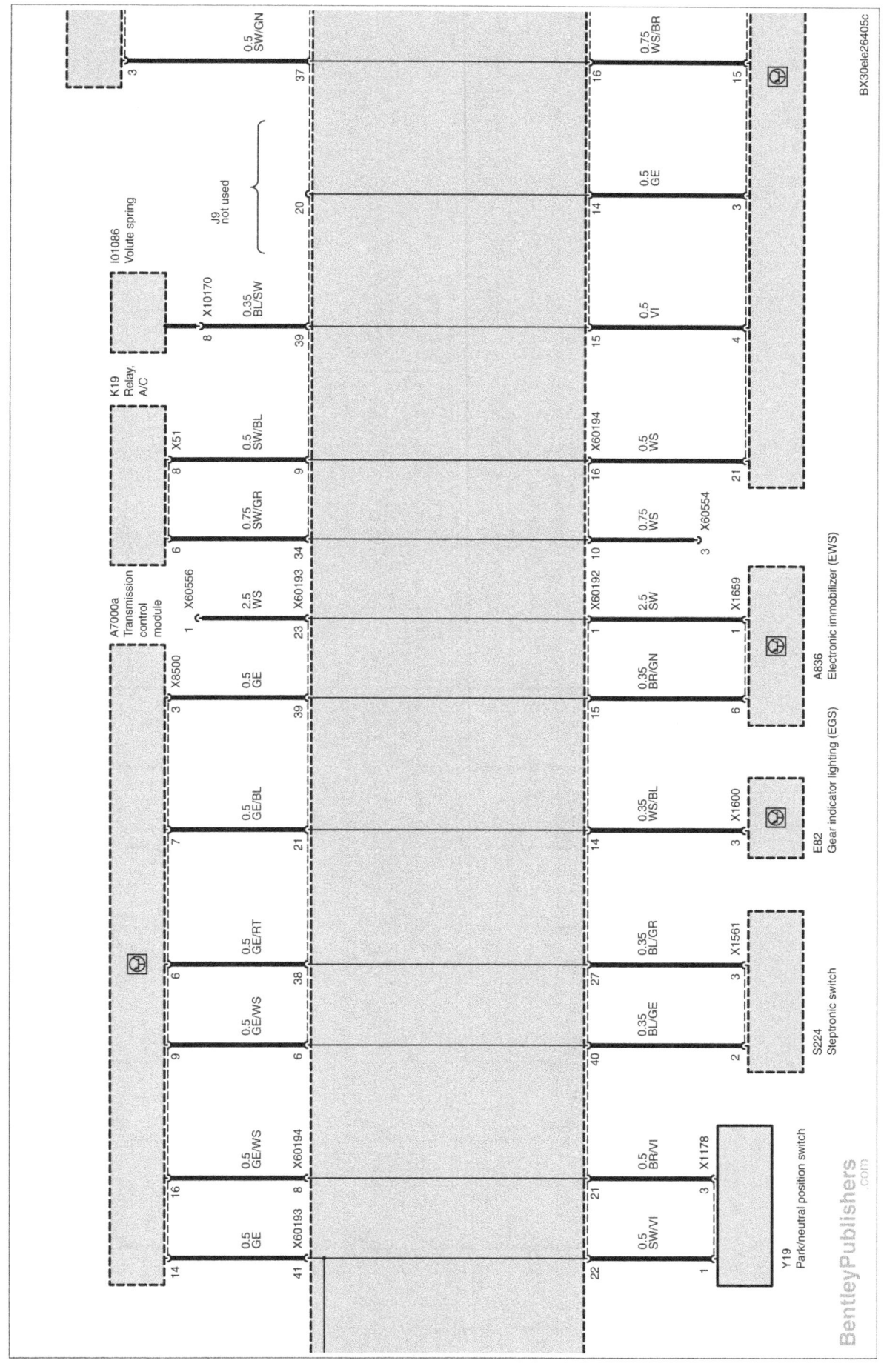

BX30ele26405c

**Integrated supply module (IVM)
page 4 of 4**

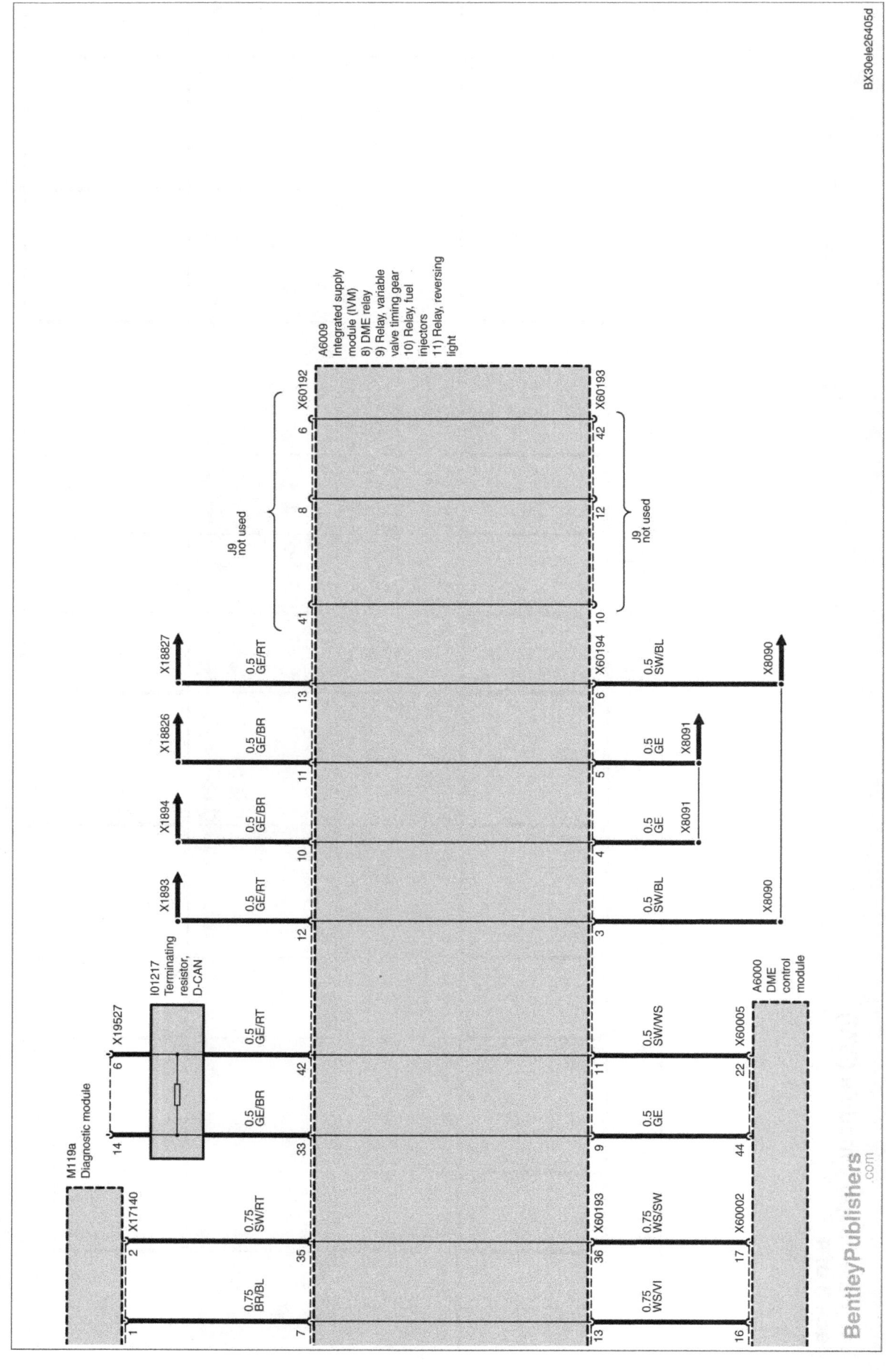

BX30ele26405d

OBD On-Board Diagnostics

GENERAL

This chapter outlines the fundamentals and equipment requirements of On-Board Diagnostics II (OBD II) standards as they apply to BMW vehicles. Also covered here is a listing of BMW and OBD II diagnostic trouble codes (DTCs).

ON-BOARD DIAGNOSTICS (OBD II)

OBD II standards were developed by the SAE (Society of Automotive Engineers) and CARB (California Air Resources Board). OBD II is the second generation of on-board self-diagnostic equipment requirements. These standards were originally mandated for California vehicles. Since 1996 they have been applied to all passenger vehicles sold in the United States.

On-board diagnostic capabilities are incorporated into the hardware and software of the engine control module (ECM) to monitor virtually every component that can affect vehicle emissions. The OBD II system works to ensure that emissions remain as clean as possible over the life of the vehicle.

Each emission-influencing component is checked by a diagnostic routine (called a monitor) to verify that it is functioning properly. If a problem or malfunction is detected, the diagnostic executive built into the OBD II system illuminates a malfunction indicator light (MIL) on the instrument panel.

The OBD II system also stores diagnostic trouble codes (DTCs) about the detected malfunction in the ECM so that a repair technician can accurately find and fix the problem. Specialized OBD II scan tool equipment is needed to access the fault memory and OBD II data.

OBD

The extra hardware needed to operate the OBD II system consists mainly of the following:

- Additional oxygen sensors downstream of the catalytic converters
- Fuel tank pressure sensor and device to pressurize fuel storage system
- Several engine and performance monitoring devices
- Standardized 16-pin OBD II connector under the dashboard
- Upgraded components for the federally required reliability mandate

Malfunction indicator light (MIL)

OBD II software cause the malfunction indicator light (MIL) to illuminate when emission levels exceed 1.5 times Federal standards.

 For X3 vehicles covered by this manual, two MIL symbols are used.

MIL illuminates under the following conditions:

- Engine management system fault detected for **two** consecutive OBD II drive cycles. See **Drive cycle** in this repair group.
- Catalyst damaging fault detected.
- Component malfunction causes emissions to exceed 1.5 times OBD II standards.
- Manufacturer-defined specifications exceeded.
- Implausible input signal.
- Misfire faults.
- Leak in evaporative system.
- Oxygen sensors observe no purge flow from purge valve / evaporative system.
- ECM fails to enter closed-loop operation within specified time.
- ECM or automatic transmission control module (TCM) in "limp home" mode.
- Ignition key ON before cranking (bulb check function).

OBD II fault memory (including the MIL) can only be reset using a special scan tool. Removing the connector from the ECM or disconnecting the battery does not erase the fault memory.

Additional MIL information:

- A fault code is stored within the ECM upon the first occurrence of a fault in the system being checked.
- Two **complete** consecutive drive cycles with the fault present illuminate the MIL. The exception to the two-fault requirement is a catalyst-damaging fault, which illuminates the MIL immediately.
- If the second drive cycle was not complete and the fault was not checked, the ECM counts the third drive cycle as the next consecutive drive cycle. The MIL illuminates if the system is checked and the fault is still present.
- Once the MIL is illuminated, it remains illuminated until the vehicle completes three consecutive drive cycles without detecting a fault.

A generic scan tool connected to the OBD II plug can display diagnostic trouble codes (DTCs), along with the conditions associated with the illumination of the MIL. Using a more advanced or BMW-dedicated scan tool, additional proprietary information is normally available.

Scan tool and scan tool display

 The complexity of the OBD II system requires that all diagnostics begin by connecting a scan tool to the 16-pin OBD II plug inside the vehicle (**arrow**).

OBD II standards require that the 16-pin OBD II plug be located within three (3) feet of the driver and not require any tools to access.

Professional diagnostic scan tools available at the time of this printing include the BMW factory tools (ISTA) and a small number of aftermarket BMW-specific tools, such as the Autologic scan tool shown here. See **020 Maintenance**.

In addition to the professional line of scan tools, inexpensive generic OBD II scan tool software programs and handheld units are readily available. Though limited, they are nonetheless powerful diagnostic tools. These tools read live data streams and freeze frame data as well as a host of other valuable diagnostic data.

Diagnostic monitors

Diagnostic monitors run tests and checks on specific emission control systems, components, and functions.

A complete drive cycle is required for the tests to be valid. See **Drive cycle** in this repair group. The diagnostic monitor signals the ECM of the loss or impairment of the signal or component and determines if a signal or sensor is faulty based on 3 conditions:

• Signal or component shorted to ground

• Signal or component shorted to B+

• Signal or component missing (open circuit)

The OBD II system monitors all emission control systems that are installed. Emission control systems vary by vehicle model and year. For example, a vehicle may not be equipped with secondary air injection, so no secondary air readiness code would be present.

OBD II software monitors the following:

• Oxygen sensors

• Catalysts

• Engine misfire

• Fuel tank evaporative control system

• Secondary air injection

• Fuel system

OBD

Oxygen sensor monitoring. When driving conditions allow, response rate and switching time of each oxygen sensor is monitored. The oxygen sensor heater function is also monitored. The OBD II system differentiates between precatalyst and post-catalyst oxygen sensors and reads each one individually. In order for the oxygen sensor to be effectively monitored, the system must be in closed loop operation.

Catalyst monitoring. This strategy monitors the two heated oxygen sensors per bank of cylinders. It compares the oxygen content going into the catalytic converter to the oxygen leaving the converter.

The diagnostic executive knows that most of the oxygen should be used up during the oxidation phase. If it sees higher than programmed values, a fault is set and the MIL illuminates.

Misfire detection. This strategy monitors crankshaft speed fluctuations and determines if an engine misfire occurs by monitoring variations in speed between each crankshaft sensor trigger point. This strategy is so finely tuned that it can determine the severity of the misfire.

The system determines if a misfire is occurring, as well as other pertinent misfire information such as:

• Specific cylinder(s)

• Severity of the misfire event

• Emissions relevant or catalyst damaging

Misfire detection is an on-going monitoring process that is only disabled under certain limited conditions.

Secondary air injection monitoring (M54 engine only). Secondary air injection is used to reduce HC and CO emissions during engine warm up. Immediately following a cold engine start (-10° to 40°C), fresh air (and therefore oxygen) is pumped directly into the exhaust manifold. By injecting additional oxygen into the exhaust manifold, catalyst warm-up time is reduced.

Secondary air system components are:

• Electric air injection pump

• Electric pump relay

• Non-return valve

• Vacuum / vent valve

• Mini air mass meter (M54 with 3.0 and automatic transmission)

The secondary air system is monitored via the use of the pre-catalyst oxygen sensors and a mini air mass meter (where applicable). The oxygen sensors monitor exhaust gas for a lean condition once the air pump is active and air is injected into the system. If the oxygen sensor signal does not change, a fault is set and the faulty bank(s) identified. If after completing the next cold start a fault is again present, the MIL illuminates.

On 3.0 liter models with automatic transmission, the mini air mass meter monitors the air supplied by the secondary air pump when commanded on. If the mini air mass meter detects no air mass or insufficient air mass, a fault is stored in the ECM and the malfunction indicator light (MIL) is activated.

Fuel system monitoring. This monitor looks at the fuel delivery needed (long / short term fuel trim) for proper engine operation based on programmed data. If too much or not enough fuel is delivered over a predetermined time, a DTC is set and the MIL is turned on. Fuel trim refers to adjustments to base fuel schedule. Long-term fuel trim refers to gradual adjustments to the fuel calibration adjustment as compared to short term fuel trim. Long term fuel trim adjustments compensate for gradual changes that occur over time. Fuel system monitoring monitors the calculated injection time (ti) in relation to engine speed, load, and precatalytic converter oxygen sensor(s) signals. Using this data, the system optimizes fuel delivery for all engine operating conditions.

Evaporative system monitoring. This monitor checks the fuel storage system and related fuel lines for leaks. It can detect very small leaks anywhere in the system. A leak detection unit (DMTL) is used to pressurize the EVAP system on a continuous basis (as the drive cycle allows) and to check system integrity.

Drive cycle

The OBD II drive cycle is an important concept in understanding OBD II requirements. The purpose of the drive cycle is to run all of the emission-related on-board diagnostics over a broad range of driving conditions. A drive cycle is considered complete when all of the diagnostic monitors have run their tests without interruption. For a drive cycle to be initiated, the vehicle must be started cold and brought up to 160°F and at least 40°F above its original starting temperature.

Readiness codes

Inspection/maintenance (I/M) readiness codes are mandated as part of OBD II. The readiness code is stored after complete diagnostic monitoring of specified components and systems is carried out. The readiness code function was designed to prevent manipulating an I/M emission test procedure by clearing faults codes or disconnecting the ECM or battery.

Readiness codes indicate whether the OBD II system is actually ready to monitor the various emission control systems on the vehicle. The vehicle must complete a drive cycle to set readiness codes. The code is binary: 0 for ready, 1 for not ready.

 The parameters which are monitored for readiness are:

1. Catalyst efficiency
2. Catalyst heating
3. Fuel tank evaporative control
4. Secondary air injection
5. A/C refrigerant
6. Oxygen sensors
7. Oxygen sensor heaters
8. Exhaust gas recirculation

When all zeros are displayed, the system has established readiness. Readiness codes can be displayed using BMW and aftermarket scan tools. Readiness codes are set to 1 (not ready) in the following cases: The battery or ECM is disconnected, DTCs are erased after completion of repairs and a drive cycle is not completed.

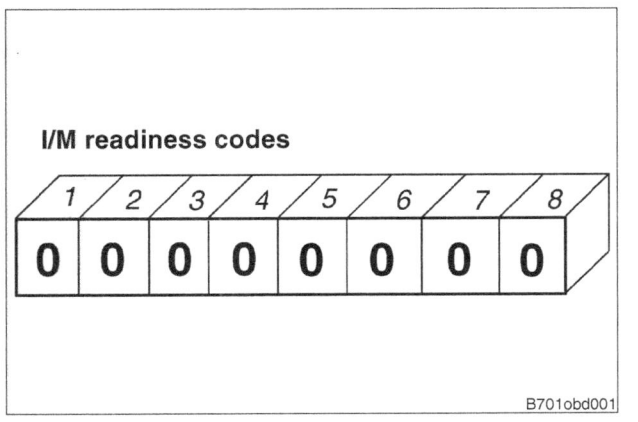

I/M readiness codes

1	2	3	4	5	6	7	8
0	0	0	0	0	0	0	0

B701obd001

OBD

Diagnostic trouble codes (DTCs)

SAE standard J2012 mandates a 5-digit diagnostic trouble code (DTC) standard. Each digit represents a specific value. Emission related DTCs start with the letter P for power train. When the MIL illuminates it indicates that a DTC has been stored:

- DTCs are stored as soon as they occur, whether or not the MIL illuminates.
- DTCs store and display a time stamp.
- DTCs record the current fault status: Present, not currently present, or intermittent.

DTC digit interpretation	
1st digit P B C	 powertrain body chassis
2nd digit 0 1	 SAE BMW specific
3rd digit 0 1 2 3 4 5 6 7	 total system air / fuel induction fuel injection ignition system or misfire auxiliary emission control vehicle speed & idle control ECM inputs / outputs transmission
4th - 5th digits	individual circuits or components

DTC example: P 0 3 0 6

- **P:** A powertrain problem
- **0:** SAE sanctioned ('generic')
- **3:** Related to an ignition system / misfire
- **06** Misfire detected at cylinder #6

DTCs provide a freeze frame or snap-shot of a vehicle performance or emissions fault at the moment that the fault first occurs. This information is accessible through generic scan tools.

Freeze frame data contains, but isn't limited to, the following information:

- Engine load (calculated)
- Engine rpm
- Short and long-term fuel trim
- Vehicle speed
- Coolant temperature
- Intake manifold pressure
- Open / closed loop operation
- Fuel pressure (if available)

Table a. M54 engine
Diagnostic trouble codes (DTCs)

PCode	BMW-FC	PCode text
P0012	10426	'A' Camshaft Position Timing Over-Retarded (Bank 1)
P0015	10428	'B' Camshaft Position Timing Over-Retarded (Bank 1)
P0030	10660	HO2S Heater Control Circuit (Bank 1 Sensor 1)
P0031	10660	HO2S Heater Control Circuit Low (Bank 1 Sensor 1)
P0032	10660	HO2S Heater Control Circuit High (Bank 1 Sensor 1)
P0036	10006	HO2S Heater Control Circuit (Bank 1 Sensor 2)
P0037	10006	HO2S Heater Control Circuit Low (Bank 1 Sensor 2)
P0038	10006	HO2S Heater Control Circuit High (Bank 1 Sensor 2)
P0040	10602	O2 Sensor Signals Swapped Bank 1 Sensor 1 / Bank 2 Sensor 1
P0041	10603	O2 Sensor Signals Swapped Bank 1 Sensor 2 / Bank 2 Sensor 2
P0050	10661	HO2S Heater Control Circuit (Bank 2 Sensor 1)
P0051	10661	HO2S Heater Control Circuit Low (Bank 2 Sensor 1)
P0052	10661	HO2S Heater Control Circuit High (Bank 2 Sensor 1)
P0056	10007	HO2S Heater Control Circuit (Bank 2 Sensor 2)
P0057	10007	HO2S Heater Control Circuit Low (Bank 2 Sensor 2)
P0058	10007	HO2S Heater Control Circuit High (Bank 2 Sensor 2)
P0101	10461	Mass or Volume Air Flow Circuit Range/Performance
P0102	10115	Mass or Volume Air Flow Circuit Low Input
P0103	10115	Mass or Volume Air Flow Circuit High Input
P0112	10124	Intake Air Temperature Sensor 1 Circuit Low
P0113	10124	Intake Air Temperature Sensor 1 Circuit High
P0117	10123	Engine Coolant Temperature Circuit Low
P0118	10123	Engine Coolant Temperature Circuit High
P0121	10036	Throttle/Pedal Position Sensor/Switch 'A' Circuit Range/Performance
P0121	10118	Throttle/Pedal Position Sensor/Switch 'A' Circuit Range/Performance
P0122	10118	Throttle/Pedal Position Sensor/Switch 'A' Circuit Low
P0123	10118	Throttle/Pedal Position Sensor/Switch 'A' Circuit High
P0125	10206	Insufficient Coolant Temperature for Closed Loop Fuel Control
P0128	10139	Coolant Thermostat (Coolant Temperature Below Thermostat Regulating Temperature)
P0131	10470	O2 Sensor Circuit Low Voltage (Bank 1 Sensor 1)
P0132	10470	O2 Sensor Circuit High Voltage (Bank 1 Sensor 1)
P0133	10594	O2 Sensor Circuit Slow Response (Bank 1 Sensor 1)
P0135	10394	O2 Sensor Heater Circuit (Bank 1 Sensor 1)
P0135	10435	O2 Sensor Heater Circuit (Bank 1 Sensor 1)
P0137	10654	O2 Sensor Circuit Low Voltage (Bank 1 Sensor 2)
P0138	10012	O2 Sensor Circuit High Voltage (Bank 1 Sensor 2)
P0140	10655	O2 Sensor Circuit No Activity Detected (Bank 1 Sensor 2)
P0141	10396	O2 Sensor Heater Circuit (Bank 1 Sensor 2)
P0151	10471	O2 Sensor Circuit Low Voltage (Bank 2 Sensor 1)

Diagnostic trouble codes (DTCs)

Table a. M54 engine
Diagnostic trouble codes (DTCs)

PCode	BMW-FC	PCode text
P0152	10471	O2 Sensor Circuit High Voltage (Bank 2 Sensor 1)
P0153	10595	O2 Sensor Circuit Slow Response (Bank 2 Sensor 1)
P0155	10395	O2 Sensor Heater Circuit (Bank 2 Sensor 1)
P0155	10436	O2 Sensor Heater Circuit (Bank 2 Sensor 1)
P0157	10656	O2 Sensor Circuit Low Voltage (Bank 2 Sensor 2)
P0158	10020	O2 Sensor Circuit High Voltage (Bank 2 Sensor 2)
P0160	10657	O2 Sensor Circuit No Activity Detected (Bank 2 Sensor 2)
P0161	10397	O2 Sensor Heater Circuit (Bank 2 Sensor 2)
P0171	10370	System Too Lean (Bank 1)
P0172	10370	System Too Rich (Bank 1)
P0174	10371	System Too Lean (Bank 2)
P0175	10371	System Too Rich (Bank 2)
P0197	10258	Engine Oil Temperature Sensor Low
P0198	10258	Engine Oil Temperature Sensor High
P0201	10150	Injector Circuit/Open - Cylinder 1
P0202	10154	Injector Circuit/Open - Cylinder 2
P0203	10152	Injector Circuit/Open - Cylinder 3
P0204	10155	Injector Circuit/Open - Cylinder 4
P0205	10151	Injector Circuit/Open - Cylinder 5
P0206	10153	Injector Circuit/Open - Cylinder 6
P0221	10037	Throttle/Pedal Position Sensor/Switch 'B' Circuit Range/Performance
P0221	10119	Throttle/Pedal Position Sensor/Switch 'B' Circuit Range/Performance
P0222	10119	Throttle/Pedal Position Sensor/Switch 'B' Circuit Low
P0223	10119	Throttle/Pedal Position Sensor/Switch 'B' Circuit High
P0261	10150	Cylinder 1 Injector Circuit Low
P0262	10150	Cylinder 1 Injector Circuit High
P0264	10154	Cylinder 2 Injector Circuit Low
P0265	10154	Cylinder 2 Injector Circuit High
P0267	10152	Cylinder 3 Injector Circuit Low
P0268	10152	Cylinder 3 Injector Circuit High
P0270	10155	Cylinder 4 Injector Circuit Low
P0271	10155	Cylinder 4 Injector Circuit High
P0273	10151	Cylinder 5 Injector Circuit Low
P0274	10151	Cylinder 5 Injector Circuit High
P0276	10153	Cylinder 6 Injector Circuit Low
P0277	10153	Cylinder 6 Injector Circuit High
P0300	10062	Random/Multiple Cylinder Misfire Detected
P0301	10050	Cylinder 1 Misfire Detected
P0302	10054	Cylinder 2 Misfire Detected

Table a. M54 engine
Diagnostic trouble codes (DTCs)

PCode	BMW-FC	PCode text
P0303	10052	Cylinder 3 Misfire Detected
P0304	10055	Cylinder 4 Misfire Detected
P0305	10051	Cylinder 5 Misfire Detected
P0306	10053	Cylinder 6 Misfire Detected
P0313	10386	Misfire Detected with Low Fuel
P0316	10062	Engine Misfire Detected on Startup (First 1000 Revolutions)
P0328	10210	Knock Sensor 1 Circuit High (Bank 1 or Single Sensor)
P0335	10389	Crankshaft Position Sensor 'A' Circuit
P0363	10062	Misfire Detected - Fueling Disabled
P0370	100C8	Timing Reference High Resolution Signal 'A'
P0411	10081	Secondary Air Injection System Incorrect Flow Detected
P0412	10085	Secondary Air Injection System Switching Valve A Circuit
P0413	10085	Secondary Air Injection System Switching Valve A Circuit Open
P0414	10085	Secondary Air Injection System Switching Valve A Circuit Shorted
P0420	10040	Catalyst System Efficiency Below Threshold (Bank 1)
P0430	10045	Catalyst System Efficiency Below Threshold (Bank 2)
P0440	10093	Evaporative Emission System
P0442	10188	Evaporative Emission System Leak Detected (small leak)
P0443	10093	Evaporative Emission System Purge Control Valve Circuit
P0444	10093	Evaporative Emission System Purge Control Valve Circuit Open
P0445	10093	Evaporative Emission System Purge Control Valve Circuit Shorted
P0455	10188	Evaporative Emission System Leak Detected (large leak)
P0500	10120	Vehicle Speed Sensor 'A'
P0505	10241	Idle Air Control System
P0604	10105	Internal Control Module Random Access Memory (RAM) Error
P0700	10650	Transmission Control System (MIL Request)
P1111	10125	Engine Coolant Temperature Sensor Radiator Outlet Low Input
P1112	10125	Engine Coolant Temperature Sensor Radiator Outlet High Input
P1120	10247	Pedal Position Sensor Circuit
P1121	10248	Pedal Position Sensor 1 Range/Performance Problem
P1122	10231	Pedal Position Sensor 1 Low Input
P1123	10231	Pedal Position Sensor 1 High Input
P1222	10232	Pedal Position Sensor 2 Low Input
P1223	10232	Pedal Position Sensor 2 High Input
P1247	10461	Barometric Pressure Plausibility
P1315	10086	Camshaft Position Sensor 'A' Circuit Signal Duration after Initialization (Bank 1)
P1316	10086	Camshaft Position Sensor 'A' Signal Duration during Initialization (Bank 1)
P1318	10087	Camshaft Position Sensor 'B' Circuit Signal Duration after Initialization (Bank 1)
P1319	10087	Camshaft Position Sensor 'B' Signal Duration during Initialization (Bank 1)

OBD

Diagnostic trouble codes (DTCs)

Table a. M54 engine
             Diagnostic trouble codes (DTCs)

PCode	BMW-FC	PCode text
P1326	10422	'A' Camshaft Position Timing Reference Position out of Range (Bank 1)
P1328	10211	Knock Sensor 2 Circuit High Input (Bank 1)
P1331	10424	'B' Camshaft Position Timing Reference Position out of Range (Bank 1)
P1338	10088	Camshaft Position Sensor 'A' Faulty Phase Position (Bank 1)
P1339	10092	Camshaft Position Sensor 'B' Faulty Phase Position (Bank 1)
P1342	10050	Misfire During Start Cylinder 1
P1343	10050	Misfire Cylinder 1 with Fuel Cut-Off
P1344	10054	Misfire During Start Cylinder 2
P1345	10054	Misfire Cylinder 2 with Fuel Cut-Off
P1346	10052	Misfire During Start Cylinder 3
P1347	10052	Misfire Cylinder 3 with Fuel Cut-Off
P1348	10055	Misfire During Start Cylinder 4
P1349	10055	Misfire Cylinder 4 with Fuel Cut-Off
P1350	10051	Misfire during Start Cylinder 5
P1351	10051	Misfire Cylinder 5 with Fuel Cut-Off
P1352	10053	Misfire during Start Cylinder 6
P1353	10053	Misfire Cylinder 6 with Fuel Cut-Off
P1411	10081	Secondary Air Pump No Activity Detected
P1412	10081	Secondary Air Pump/Secondary Air Valve Large Leak
P1413	10084	Secondary Air Injection Pump Relay Control Circuit Signal Low
P1414	10084	Secondary Air Injection Pump Relay Control Circuit Signal High
P1416	10082	Secondary Air Injection Valve Stuck Off
P1418	10081	Secondary Air Injection Valve/Secondary Air Hose Clamped
P1419	10096	Secondary Air Mass Flow Sensor Circuit
P1429	10201	Diagnostic Module Tank Leakage (DM-TL) Heater
P1430	10201	Diagnostic Module Tank Leakage (DM-TL) Heater Low
P1431	10201	Diagnostic Module Tank Leakage (DM-TL) Heater High
P1434	10189	Diagnostic Module Tank Leakage (DM-TL)
P1444	10186	Diagnostic Module Tank Leakage (DM-TL) Pump Control Open Circuit
P1445	10186	Diagnostic Module Tank Leakage (DM-TL) Pump Control Circuit Signal Low
P1446	10186	Diagnostic Module Tank Leakage (DM-TL) Pump Control Circuit Signal High
P1447	10189	Diagnostic Module Tank Leakage (DM-TL) Pump Current Too High during Switching Solenoid Test
P1448	10189	Diagnostic Module Tank Leakage (DM-TL) Pump Current Too Low
P1449	10189	Diagnostic Module Tank Leakage (DM-TL) Pump Current Too High
P1450	10002	Diagnostic Module Tank Leakage (DM-TL) Switching Solenoid Control Open Circuit
P1451	10002	Diagnostic Module Tank Leakage (DM-TL) Switching Solenoid Control Circuit Signal Low
P1452	10002	Diagnostic Module Tank Leakage (DM-TL) Switching Solenoid Control Circuit Signal High
P1453	10084	Secondary Air Injection Pump Relay Control Circuit Electrical
P1502	10198	Idle-Speed Control Valve Closing Solenoid Control Circuit Signal High

PCode	BMW-FC	PCode text
		Table a. M54 engine **Diagnostic trouble codes (DTCs)**
P1503	10198	Idle-Speed Control Valve Closing Solenoid Control Circuit Signal Low
P1504	10198	Idle-Speed Control Valve Closing Solenoid Control Open Circuit
P1506	10199	Idle-Speed Control Valve Opening Solenoid Control Circuit Signal High
P1507	10199	Idle-Speed Control Valve Opening Solenoid Control Circuit Signal Low
P1508	10199	Idle-Speed Control Valve Opening Solenoid Control Open Circuit
P1510	10461	Idle-Speed Control Valve Stuck
P1511	10270	DISA (Differentiated Intake Manifold) Control Circuit Electrical
P1512	10270	DISA (Differentiated Intake Manifold) Control Circuit Signal Low
P1513	10270	DISA (Differentiated Intake Manifold) Control Circuit Signal High
P1525	10165	'A' Camshaft Position Actuator Control Open Circuit (Bank 1)
P1531	10173	'B' Camshaft Position Actuator Control Open Circuit (Bank 1)
P16A9	10404	Control Module Self-Test, Speed Monitoring Reset
P1611	10220	Serial Communication Link Transmission Control Module
P1618	10103	Control Module Self-Test, AD-Converter Monitoring
P1619	10140	Map Cooling Thermostat Control Circuit Signal Low
P1620	10140	Map Cooling Thermostat Control Circuit Signal High
P1622	10140	Map Cooling Thermostat Control Circuit Electrical
P1624	10048	Pedal Position Sensor Potentiometer Supply Channel 1 Electrical (M52: Coolant Thermostat (Coolant Temperature Below Thermostat Regulating Temperature))
P1625	10049	Pedal Position Sensor Potentiometer Supply Channel 2 Electrical
P1632	10134	Throttle Valve Adaptation Conditions Not Met
P1633	10134	Throttle Valve Adaptation Limp-Home Position Unknown
P1634	10134	Throttle Valve Adaptation Spring Test Failed
P1634	10145	Throttle Valve Adaptation Spring Test Failed
P1635	10134	Throttle Valve Adaptation Lower Mechanical Stop not Adapted
P1635	10419	Throttle Valve Adaptation Lower Mechanical Stop not Adapted
P1636	10132	Throttle Valve Control Circuit
P1637	10066	Throttle Valve Position Control, Control Deviation
P1638	10064	Throttle Valve Position Control Throttle Stuck Temporarily
P1639	10065	Throttle Valve Position Control Throttle Stuck Permanently
P1675	10149	Throttle Valve Actuator Start Test Re-Adaptation Required
P1694	10145	Throttle Valve Actuator Start Test Spring Test and Limp-Home Position Failed
P16A0	10288	Internal Control Module Memory Checksum Error in Boot Software
P16A1	10288	Internal Control Module Memory Checksum Error in Application Software
P16A2	10288	Internal Control Module Memory Checksum Error in Data
P16A3	10345	Internal Control Module Non-Volatile Memory (NVMY) Error
P16A4	10346	Timeout Control Module Knock Sensor SPI-Bus
P16A5	10347	Timeout Control Module Multiple Output Stage SPI-Bus
P16A6	10401	Control Module Self-Test, Cruise Control Monitoring

OBD

Diagnostic trouble codes (DTCs)

PCode	BMW-FC	PCode text
Table a. M54 engine		
Diagnostic trouble codes (DTCs)		
P16A7	10402	Control Module Self-Test, Hot Film Air Mass Meter Monitoring
P16A8	10402	Control Module Self-Test, Throttle Position Monitoring
P16B0	10405	Control Module Self-Test, Pedal Position Sensor Monitoring
P16B1	10410	Control Module Self-Test, Idle Air Control System Integrated Component Plausibility
P16B2	10410	Control Module Self-Test, Idle Air Control System PD-Component Plausibility
P16B3	10411	Control Module Self-Test, MSR (Engine-Drag-Torque Control) Monitoring
P16B4	10411	Control Module Self-Test, DCC (Distance Cruise Control) Monitoring
P16B5	10411	Control Module Self-Test, AMT (Automatic Manual Transmission) Monitoring
P16B6	10411	Control Module Self-Test, ETC Monitoring
P16B7	10412	Control Module Self-Test, Clutch Torque Monitoring Maximum Value Plausibility
P16B8	10412	Control Module Self-Test, Clutch Torque Monitoring Minimum Value Plausibility
P16B9	10412	Control Module Self-Test, Torque Loss Monitoring
P16C0	10412	Control Module Self-Test, Driving Dynamics Control Switch Monitoring
P16C1	10413	Control Module Self-Test, Torque Monitoring Current Indicated Value Plausibility
P16C2	10417	Control Module Self-Test, Speed Limitation Monitoring
P16C3	10418	Control Module Self-Test, Speed Limitation Reset
P2088	10165	'A' Camshaft Position Actuator Control Circuit Low (Bank 1)
P2089	10165	'A' Camshaft Position Actuator Control Circuit High (Bank 1)
P2090	10173	'B' Camshaft Position Actuator Control Circuit Low (Bank 1)
P2091	10173	'B' Camshaft Position Actuator Control Circuit High (Bank 1)
P2096	10482	Post Catalyst Fuel Trim System Too Lean (Bank 1)
P2097	10482	Post Catalyst Fuel Trim System Too Rich (Bank 1)
P2098	10483	Post Catalyst Fuel Trim System Too Lean (Bank 2)
P2099	10483	Post Catalyst Fuel Trim System Too Rich (Bank 2)
P2195	10630	O2 Sensor Signal Stuck Lean (Bank 1 Sensor 1)
P2196	10632	O2 Sensor Signal Stuck Rich (Bank 1 Sensor 1)
P2197	10631	O2 Sensor Signal Stuck Lean (Bank 2 Sensor 1)
P2198	10633	O2 Sensor Signal Stuck Rich (Bank 2 Sensor 1)
P2228	10164	Barometric Pressure Circuit Low
P2229	10164	Barometric Pressure Circuit High
P2231	10592	O2 Sensor Signal Circuit Shorted to Heater Circuit (Bank 1 Sensor 1)
P2234	10593	O2 Sensor Signal Circuit Shorted to Heater Circuit (Bank 2 Sensor 1)
P2237	10611	O2 Sensor Positive Current Control Circuit/Open (Bank 1 Sensor 1)
P2240	10612	O2 Sensor Positive Current Control Circuit/Open (Bank 2 Sensor 1)
P2243	10611	O2 Sensor Reference Voltage Circuit/Open (Bank 1 Sensor 1)
P2247	10612	O2 Sensor Reference Voltage Circuit/Open (Bank 2 Sensor 1)
P2251	10611	O2 Sensor Negative Current Control Circuit/Open (Bank 1 Sensor 1)
P2254	10612	O2 Sensor Negative Current Control Circuit/Open (Bank 2 Sensor 1)
P2270	10437	O2 Sensor Signal Stuck Lean (Bank 1 Sensor 2)

Table a. M54 engine
     Diagnostic trouble codes (DTCs)

PCode	BMW-FC	PCode text
P2271	10437	O2 Sensor Signal Stuck Rich (Bank 1 Sensor 2)
P2272	10438	O2 Sensor Signal Stuck Lean (Bank 2 Sensor 2)
P2273	10438	O2 Sensor Signal Stuck Rich (Bank 2 Sensor 2)
P2297	10433	O2 Sensor Out of Range During Deceleration (Bank 1 Sensor 1)
P2298	10434	O2 Sensor Out of Range During Deceleration (Bank 2 Sensor 1)
P2414	10598	O2 Sensor Exhaust Sample Error (Bank 1 Sensor 1)
P2415	10599	O2 Sensor Exhaust Sample Error (Bank 2 Sensor 1)
P2626	10611	O2 Sensor Pumping Current Trim Circuit/Open (Bank 1 Sensor 1)
P2629	10612	O2 Sensor Pumping Current Trim Circuit/Open (Bank 2 Sensor 1)
P3010	10486	O2 Sensor Low Input after Cold Start (Bank 1 Sensor 2)
P3011	10487	O2 Sensor Low Input after Cold Start (Bank 2 Sensor 2)
P3014	10470	O2 Sensor WRAF-IC Supply Voltage Too Low (Bank 1 Sensor 1)
P3015	10471	O2 Sensor IC Supply Voltage Too Low (Bank 2 Sensor 1)
P3022	10495	O2 Sensor Disturbed SPI Communication to WRAF-IC (Bank 1 Sensor 1)
P3023	10496	O2 Sensor Disturbed SPI Communication to WRAF-IC (Bank 2 Sensor 1)
P3024	10495	O2 Sensor Initialization Error WRAF-IC (Bank 1 Sensor 1)
P3025	10496	O2 Sensor Initialization Error WRAF-IC (Bank 2 Sensor 1)
P3026	10435	O2 Sensor Operating Temperature not Reached (Bank 1 Sensor 1)
P3027	10436	O2 Sensor Operating Temperature not Reached (Bank 2 Sensor 1)
P3034	10433	O2 Sensor Characteristic Curve Gradient Too Low (Bank 1 Sensor 1)
P3035	10434	O2 Sensor Characteristic Curve Gradient Too Low (Bank 2 Sensor 1)
P3198	10205	Engine Coolant Temperature Gradient Too High
P3199	10207	Engine Coolant Temperature Signal Stuck
P3238	10289	Control Module Monitoring TPU Chip Defective

Table b. N52 engine
Diagnostic trouble codes (DTCs)

P-code	BMW FC	Definition
P00B2	2EEC	Radiator Coolant Temperature Sensor Circuit Range / Performance
P00B3	2EEA	Radiator Coolant Temperature Sensor Circuit Low
P00B4	2EEA	Radiator Coolant Temperature Sensor Circuit High
P0010	2A80	'A' Camshaft Position Actuator Circuit Open (Bank 1)
P0011		'A' Camshaft Position Timing Over-Advanced or System Performance (Bank 1)
P0012	2A82	'A' Camshaft Position Timing Over-Retarded (Bank 1)
P0013	2A85	'B' Camshaft Position Actuator Circuit Open (Bank 1)
P0014		'B' Camshaft Position Timing Over-Advanced or System Performance (Bank 1)
P0015	2A87	'B' Camshaft Position Timing Over-Retarded (Bank 1)
P0016	2AA4	Camshaft Position Sensor Correlation) Bank 1 Sensor 'A')
P0017	2AA5	Camshaft Position Sensor Correlation) Bank 1 Sensor 'B')
P0030	2C9C	HO2S Heater Control Circuit (Bank 1 Sensor 1)
P0031	2C9C	HO2S Heater Control Circuit Low (Bank 1 Sensor 1)
P0032	2C9C	HO2S Heater Control Circuit High (Bank 1 Sensor 1)
P0036	2C9E	HO2S Heater Control Circuit (Bank 1 Sensor 2)
P0037	2C9E	HO2S Heater Control Circuit Low (Bank 1 Sensor 2)
P0038	2C9E	HO2S Heater Control Circuit High (Bank 1 Sensor 2)
P0040	2C24	HO2S Signals Swapped Bank 1 Sensor 1 / Bank 2 Sensor 1
P0041	2C64	HO2S Signals Swapped Bank 1 Sensor 2/ Bank 2 Sensor 2
P0050	2C9D	HO2S Heater Control Circuit (Bank 2 Sensor 1)
P0051	2C9D	HO2S Heater Control Circuit Low (Bank 2 Sensor 1)
P0052	2C9D	HO2S Heater Control Circuit High (Bank 2 Sensor 1)
P0053	2CA6	HO2S Heater Resistance (Bank 1 Sensor 1)
P0056	2C9F	HO2S Heater Control Circuit (Bank 2 Sensor 2)
P0057	2C9F	HO2S Heater Control Circuit Low (Bank 2 Sensor 2)
P0058	2C9F	HO2S Heater Control Circuit High (Bank 2 Sensor 2)
P0059	2CA7	HO2S Heater Resistance (Bank 2 Sensor 1)
P0070	2F9A	Ambient Air Temperature Sensor Circuit
P0071	2F99	Ambient Air Temperature Sensor Circuit Range / Performance
P0072	2F9A	Ambient Air Temperature Sensor Circuit Low
P0073	2F9A	Ambient Air Temperature Sensor Circuit High
P0090	2FBC	Fuel Pressure Regulator 1 Control Circuit Open
p0091	2FBC	Fuel Pressure Regulator 1 Control Circuit Low
P0092	2FBC	Fuel Pressure Regulator 1 Control Circuit High
P0A14	2FAB	Engine Mount 'A' Control Circuit Open
P0A15	2FAB	Engine Mount 'A' Control Circuit Low
P0A16	2FAB	Engine Mount 'A' Control Circuit High
P0A3B	2E97	Generator Over Temperature
P0A3B	2ECF	Generator Over Temperature

Table b. N52 engine		
Diagnostic trouble codes (DTCs) (continued)		
P-code	**BMW FC**	**Definition**
P0100	2D16	Mass Air Flow or Volume 'A' Circuit
P0101	2D15	Mass or Volume Air Flow Circuit Range/Performance
P0102		Mass or Volume Air Flow Circuit Low Input
P0103		Mass or Volume Air Flow Circuit High Input
P0107		Manifold Absolute Pressure/Barometric Pressure Circuit Low Input
P0108		Manifold Absolute Pressure/Barometric Pressure Circuit High Input
P0111	2F09	Intake Temperature Sensor Bank 1 Temperature Range / Performance
P0112	2F08	Intake Air Temperature Sensor 1 Circuit Low
P0113	2F08	Intake Air Temperature Sensor 1 Circuit High
P0117	2EE0	Engine Coolant Temperature Circuit Low
P0118	2EE0	Engine Coolant Temperature Circuit High
P0121	2CF6	Throttle/Pedal Position Sensor/Switch 'A' Circuit Range/Performance
P0122	2CF9	Throttle/Pedal Position Sensor/Switch 'A' Circuit Low
P0123	2CF9	Throttle/Pedal Position Sensor/Switch 'A' Circuit High
P0125		Insufficient Coolant Temperature for Closed Loop Fuel Control
P0128	2EF4	Coolant Thermostat (Coolant Temperature Below Thermostat Regulating Temperature)
P0131	2C3F	O2 Sensor Circuit Low Voltage (Bank 1 Sensor 1)
P0132	2C3F	O2 Sensor Circuit High Voltage (Bank 1 Sensor 1)
P0133	2C39	O2 Sensor Circuit Slow Response (Bank 1 Sensor 1)
P0134		O2 Sensor Circuit No Activity Detected (Bank 1 Sensor 1)
P0135	2CA6	O2 Sensor Heater Circuit (Bank 1 Sensor 1)
P0137	2C75	O2 Sensor Circuit Low Voltage (Bank 1 Sensor 2)
P0138	2C73	O2 Sensor Circuit High Voltage (Bank 1 Sensor 2)
P0139	2C7B	O2 Sensor Circuit Slow Response (Bank 1 Sensor 2)
P0139		O2 Sensor Circuit Slow Response (Bank 1 Sensor 2)
P0140	2C77	O2 Sensor Circuit No Activity Detected (Bank 1 Sensor 2)
P0141	2CA8	O2 Sensor Heater Circuit (Bank 1 Sensor 2)
P0151	2C40	O2 Sensor Circuit Low Voltage (Bank 2 Sensor 1)
P0152	2C40	O2 Sensor Circuit High Voltage (Bank 2 Sensor 1)
P0153	2C3A	O2 Sensor Circuit Slow Response (Bank 2 Sensor 1)
P0154		O2 Sensor Circuit No Activity Detected (Bank 2 Sensor 1)
P0155	2CA7	O2 Sensor Heater Circuit (Bank 2 Sensor 1)
P0157	2C76	O2 Sensor Circuit Low Voltage (Bank 2 Sensor 2)
P0158	2C74	O2 Sensor Circuit High Voltage (Bank 2 Sensor 2)
P0159	2C7E	O2 Sensor Circuit Slow Response (Bank 2 Sensor 2)
P0159	2C7C	O2 Sensor Circuit Slow Response (Bank 2 Sensor 2)
P0160	2C78	O2 Sensor Circuit No Activity Detected (Bank 2 Sensor 2)
P0161	2CA9	O2 Sensor Heater Circuit (Bank 2 Sensor 2)
P0171	29E0	System Too Lean (Bank 1)

OBD

Diagnostic trouble codes (DTCs)

Table b. N52 engine
Diagnostic trouble codes (DTCs) (continued)

P-code	BMW FC	Definition
P0171	2A2B	System Too Lean (Bank 1)
P0172	29E0	System Too Rich (Bank 1)
P0172	2A2B	System Too Rich (Bank 1)
P0174	29E1	System Too Lean (Bank 2)
P0174	2A2C	System Too Lean (Bank 2)
P0175	29E1	System Too Rich (Bank 2)
P0175	2A2C	System Too Rich (Bank 2)
P0190	29E2	Fuel Rail Pressure Sensor 'A' Circuit
P0192	29E2	Fuel Rail Pressure Sensor 'A' Circuit Low
P0197		Engine Oil Temperature Sensor Low
P0198		Engine Oil Temperature Sensor High
P02AA	3074	Cylinder 5 Fuel Trim at Maximum Limit
P02AB	3074	Cylinder 5 Fuel Trim at Minimum Limit
P02AE	3075	Cylinder 6 Fuel Trim at Maximum Limit
P02AF	3075	Cylinder 6 Fuel Trim at Minimum Limit
P02A2	3072	Cylinder 3 Fuel Trim at Maximum Limit
P02A3	3072	Cylinder 3 Fuel Trim at Minimum Limit
P02A6	3073	Cylinder 4 Fuel Trim at Maximum Limit
P02A7	3073	Cylinder 4 Fuel Trim at Minimum Limit
P0201	2E30	Injector Circuit/Open - Cylinder 1
P0202	2E31	Injector Circuit/Open - Cylinder 2
P0203	2E32	Injector Circuit/Open - Cylinder 3
P0204	2E33	Injector Circuit/Open - Cylinder 4
P0205	2E34	Injector Circuit/Open - Cylinder 5
P0206	2E35	Injector Circuit/Open - Cylinder 6
P0221	2CF7	Throttle/Pedal Position Sensor/Switch 'B' Circuit Range/Performance
P0222	2CFA	Throttle/Pedal Position Sensor/Switch 'B' Circuit Low
P0223	2CFA	Throttle/Pedal Position Sensor/Switch 'B' Circuit High
P0261	2E30	Cylinder 1 Injector Circuit Low
P0262	2E30	Cylinder 1 Injector Circuit High
P0264	2E31	Cylinder 2 Injector Circuit Low
P0265	2E31	Cylinder 2 Injector Circuit High
P0266	2E32	Cylinder 3 Injector Circuit High
P0267	2E32	Cylinder 3 Injector Circuit Low
P0268	2E32	Cylinder 3 Injector Circuit High
P0270	2E33	Cylinder 4 Injector Circuit Low
P0271	2E33	Cylinder 4 Injector Circuit High
P0273	2E34	Cylinder 5 Injector Circuit Low
P0274	2E34	Cylinder 5 Injector Circuit High

Table b. N52 engine
Diagnostic trouble codes (DTCs) (continued)

P-code	BMW FC	Definition
P0276	2E35	Cylinder 6 Injector Circuit Low
P0277	2E35	Cylinder 6 Injector Circuit High
P029A	3070	Cylinder 1 Fuel Trim at Maximum Limit
P029B	3070	Cylinder 1 Fuel Trim at Minimum Limit
P029E	3071	Cylinder 2 Fuel Trim at Maximum Limit
P029F	3071	Cylinder 2 Fuel Trim at Minimum Limit
P0300	29CC	Cylinder Misfire, Several Cylinders
P0301	29CD	Cylinder 1 Misfire Detected
P0302	29CE	Cylinder 2 Misfire Detected
P0303	29CF	Cylinder 3 Misfire Detected
P0304	29D0	Cylinder 4 Misfire Detected
P0305	29D1	Cylinder 5 Misfire Detected
P0306	29D2	Cylinder 6 Misfire Detected
P0313	29D9	Misfire Detected with Low Fuel
P0326	2E68	Knock Sensor 1 Circuit Range / Performance (Bank 1 or Single Sensor)
P0326	2CA6	Knock Sensor 1 Circuit Range / Performance (Bank 1 or Single Sensor)
P0327	2E68	Knock Sensor 1 Circuit Low (Bank 1 or Single Sensor)
P0328	2E68	Knock Sensor 1 Circuit High (Bank 1 or Single Sensor)
P0332		Knock Sensor 2 Circuit Low (Bank 2)
P0335	2A94	Crankshaft Position Sensor 'A' Circuit
P0339		Crankshaft Position Sensor 'A' Circuit Intermittent
P0340	2AA0	Camshaft Position Sensor 'A' Circuit (Bank 1 or Single Sensor)
P0341	2A9A	Camshaft Position Sensor 'A' Performance (Bank 1)
P0344	2A9E	Camshaft Position Sensor 'A' Circuit Intermittent (Bank 1 or Single Sensor)
P0351	2E24	Ignition Coil 'A' Primary / Secondary Circuit
P0352	2E25	Ignition Coil 'B' Primary / Secondary Circuit
P0353	2E26	Ignition Coil 'C' Primary / Secondary Circuit
P0354	2E27	Ignition Coil 'D' Primary / Secondary Circuit
P0355	2E28	Ignition Coil 'E' Primary / Secondary Circuit
P0356	2E29	Ignition Coil 'F' Primary / Secondary Circuit
P0365	2AA1	Camshaft Position Sensor 'B' Circuit (Bank 1)
P0366	2A9B	Camshaft Position Sensor 'B' Performance (Bank 1)
P0369	2A9F	Camshaft Position Sensor 'B' Circuit Intermittent (Bank 1)
P0370	29DB	Smooth Running Segment Timing
P0370	2A96	Timing Reference High Signal 'A' Resolution
P0370	2A97	Timing Reference High Signal 'A' Resolution
P0373	2A95	Timing Reference High Signal 'A' Resolution Erratic
P0413		Secondary Air Injection System Switching Valve A Circuit Open
P0414		Secondary Air Injection System Switching Valve A Circuit Shorted

OBD

Table b. N52 engine
Diagnostic trouble codes (DTCs) (continued)

P-code	BMW FC	Definition
P0420	29F4	Catalyst System Efficiency Below Threshold (Bank 1)
P0420	29F6	Catalyst System Efficiency Below Threshold (Bank 1)
P0430	29F5	Catalyst System Efficiency Below Threshold (Bank 2)
P0440	2A1A	Evaporative Emission System Incorrect Flow
P0441	2A1A	Evaporative Emission System Incorrect Purge Flow
P0442	2A15	Evaporative Emission System Leak Detected (small leak)
P0443		Evaporative Emission System Purge Control Valve Circuit
P0444	2A19	Evaporative Emission System Purge Control Valve Circuit Open
	2A1A	Fuel Tank Venting Function Fault
P0445		Evaporative Emission System Purge Control Valve Circuit Shorted
P0455		Evaporative Emission System Leak Detected (large leak)
P0456	2A16	Evaporative Emission System Leak Detected (very small leak)
P0457	2A1B	Evaporative Emission System Leak Detected (Fuel Filler Cap Loose)
P0458	2A19	Evaporative Emission System Purge Control Valve Circuit Low
P0459	2A19	Evaporative Emission System Purge Control Valve Circuit High
P0461	2A1C	Fuel Level Sensor A Performance
P0462	2DE2	Fuel Level Sensor 'A' Circuit Low
P0463	2DE2	Fuel Level Sensor 'A' Circuit High
P0475	2F6C	Exhaust Pressure Control Valve
P0476	2F6C	Exhaust Pressure Control Valve Low
P0477	2F6C	Exhaust Pressure Control Valve Low
P0478	2F6C	Exhaust Pressure Control Valve High
P0480	2EFE	Fan 1 Control Circuit
P0491	2A00	Secondary Air Injection System Insufficient Flow (Bank 1)
P0492	2A00	Secondary Air Injection System Insufficient Flow (Bank 2)
P0500	2F4E	Vehicle Speed Sensor 'A'
P0503	2F4F	Vehicle Speed Sensor 'A' Intermittent / Erratic
P0505		Idle Air Control System
P0506	2ADF	Idle Air Control System Lower Than Expected
P0507	2ADF	Idle Air Control System Higher Than Expected
P0512	2F58	Starter Request Circuit
P0520	2F7B	Engine Oil Pressure Switch Circuit
P0521	30C6	Engine Oil Pressure Switch Range / Performance
P0522	30C3	Engine Oil Pressure Switch Open
P0523	30C3	Engine Oil Pressure Switch High
P0524	30C5	Engine Oil Pressure Too Low
P053A	2AE4	Positive Crankcase Ventilation Heater Circuit Open
P053B	2AE4	Positive Crankcase Ventilation Heater Circuit Low
P053C	2AE$	Positive Crankcase Ventilation Heater Circuit High

P-code	BMW FC	Definition
		Table b. N52 engine **Diagnostic trouble codes (DTCs) (continued)**
P0545	2C87	Exhaust Gas Temperature Sensor Circuit Low (Bank1 Sensor 1)
P0546	2C87	Exhaust Gas Temperature Sensor Circuit High (Bank1 Sensor 1)
P0571	2F63	Brake Switch 'A' Circuit
P0597	2EF5	Thermostat Heater Control Circuit / Open
P0598	2EF5	Thermostat Heater Control Circuit Low
P0599	2EF5	Thermostat Heater Control Circuit High
P060C	2D67	Internal Control Module Internal Processor fault
P0600		Serial Communication Link
P0604	2AB2	Internal Control Module Random Access Memory (RAM) Error
P0605	2D67	Internal Control Module ROM
P0606	2D67	ECM Processor
P062F	2FA3	Internal Control Module EEPROM Error
P0620	2ECD	Generator Control Circuit
P0620	2E97	Generator Control Circuit
P0645	2F12	A/C Clutch Relay Control Circuit
P0646	2F12	A/C Clutch Relay Control Circuit Low
P0647	2F12	A/C Clutch Relay Control Circuit High
P0668	2F85	ECM / TCM Internal Temperature Sensor Circuit Low
P0669	2F85	ECM / TCM Internal Temperature Sensor Circuit High
P0686	2ACB	ECM Power Relay Control Circuit Low
P0687	2ACB	ECM Power Relay Control Circuit High
P0691	2EFE	Fan 1 Control Circuit Low
P0692	2EFE	Fan 1 Control Circuit High
P0700	2AD0	Transmission Control System MIL Request
P0703	2F64	Brake Switch 'B' Circuit
P0831	2F67	Clutch Pedal Switch 'A' Circuit Low
P0832	2F67	Clutch Pedal Switch 'A' Circuit High
P101A	2A39	VVT Self Learning Function Stops Not Learned
P101A	2A46	VVT Self Learning Function Stops Not Learned
P102C	2A34	VVT Eccentric Shaft Sensor Diagnostic Error
P103A	2A45	VVT System Temperature Too High
P104E	2F0A	Turbocharger Intake Air Temperature Sensor 1 Circuit High or Open
P104F	2F0A	Turbocharger Intake Air Temperature Sensor 1 Circuit Input Low
P105A	2A77	Internal Control Module Fault VVT Current Too High
P105B	2A77	Internal Control Module Fault VVT Current Too Low
P107A	2A43	VVT Overload Protection Current Too High (Bank 1)
P107B	2A43	VVT Overload Protection (Bank 1)
P107C	2A43	VVT Overload Protection Current Too High (Bank 1)
	2A44	Valvetronic Power Limitation

OBD

Table b. N52 engine
Diagnostic trouble codes (DTCs) (continued)

P-code	BMW FC	Definition
P1004	2A35	VVT Guiding Sensor Solenoid Loss (Bank 1)
P1006	2A31	VVT Eccentric Shaft Sensor Parity Error (Bank 1)
P1012	2A36	VVT Guiding Sensor Solenoid Loss (Bank 1)
P1014	2A32	VVT Eccentric Shaft Sensor Parity Error (Bank 1)
P1017	2A37	VVT Guiding Sensor Plausibility (Bank 1)
P1019	2A30	VVT Eccentric Shaft Sensor Circuit Low
P102B	2A33	VVT Guiding Sensor Diagnostic Error (Bank 1)
P102C	2A34	VVT Reference Sensor Diagnostic Error (Bank 1)
P1020	2A30	VVT Eccentric Shaft Sensor Circuit High
P1023	2A39	VVT Self Learning Function Faulty Adjustment Range (Bank 1)
P1024	2A39	VVT Self Learning Function Faulty Lower Learning Range (Bank 1)
P1030	2A38	VVT Control Motor Position Control Deviation (Bank1)
P1041	2A3A	Internal VVT Module EEPROM Error
P1047	2A3D	VVT Control Circuit High (Bank 1)
P1048	2A3D	VVT Control Circuit Low (Bank 1)
P1049	2A3D	VVT Control Circuit Short (Bank 1)
P1055	2A3F	VVT Control Circuit High (Bank 1)
P1056	2A3F	VVT Control Circuit High (Bank 1)
P1057	2A3C	VVT Motor Supply Voltage (Bank 1)
P1062	2A44	VVT Limp Home Request Full Stroke Position Reached (Bank 1)
P1064	2A42	VVT Value Comparison Starting / Parking Position Plausibility
P1075	2A41	VVT Overload Protection (Bank 1)
P1076	2A40	VVT Overload Protection ECM temperature (Bank 1)
P1078	2A3E	VVT Overload Protection Current Too High (Bank 1)
P1083		Fuel Control Limit Mixture Too Lean (Bank 1 Sensor 1)
P1084		Fuel Control Limit Mixture Too Rich (Bank 1 Sensor 1)
P1085		Fuel Control Limit Mixture Too Lean (Bank 2 Sensor 1)
P1086		Fuel Control Limit Mixture Too Rich (Bank 2 Sensor 1)
P1087		O2 Sensor Circuit Slow Response in Lean Control Range (Bank 1 Sensor 1)
P1088		O2 Sensor Circuit Slow Response in Rich Control Range (Bank 1 Sensor 1)
P1089		O2 Sensor Circuit Slow Response in Lean Control Range (Bank 1 Sensor 2)
P1090		Pre Catalyst Fuel Trim System Too Lean (Bank 1)
P1091		Pre Catalyst Fuel Trim System Too Lean (Bank 2)
P1092		Pre Catalyst Fuel Trim System Too Rich (Bank 1)
P1093		Pre Catalyst Fuel Trim System Too Rich (Bank 2)
P1094		O2 Sensor Circuit Slow Response in Rich Control Range (Bank 2 Sensor 1)
P110D	2D07	Throttle Position Sensor 'A' and 'B' Range / Performance
P110D	2D61	Throttle Position Sensor 'A' and 'B' Range / Performance
P1104	2D29	Differential Pressure Sensor Intake Manifold Pressure Too Low Bank 1

Table b. N52 engine
Diagnostic trouble codes (DTCs) (continued)

P-code	BMW FC	Definition
P1105	2D29	Differential Pressure Sensor Intake Manifold Pressure Too High Bank 1
P111E	2F09	Intake Temperature Sensor Bank 1 Maximum Temperature Implausible
P111F	2F09	Intake Temperature Sensor Bank 1 Temperature Implausible
P1111		Engine Coolant Temperature Sensor Radiator Outlet Low Input
P1112		Engine Coolant Temperature Sensor Radiator Outlet High Input
P112C	2C3D	O2 Sensor Negative Current or Positive Current Control Circuit Open (Bank 1 Sensor 1)
P112D	2C3E	O2 Sensor Negative Current or Positive Current Control Circuit Open (Bank 2 Sensor 1)
P112F	2D2E	Manifold Absolute Pressure to Throttle Angle - Too High
P1120		Pedal Position Sensor Circuit
P1121		Pedal Position Sensor 1 Range/Performance Problem
P1122		Pedal Position Sensor 1 Low Input
P1123		Pedal Position Sensor 1 High Input
P1124	2D2A	Differential Pressure Sensor Intake Manifold Pressure Offset Bank 1
P1130	2C6D	O2 Sensor Circuit Dynamic Test (Bank 1 Sensor 2)
P1131	2C6E	O2 Sensor Circuit Dynamic Test (Bank 2 Sensor 2)
P1134		O2 Sensor Heater Circuit Signal Intermittent (Bank 1 Sensor 1)
P1135		O2 Sensor Heater Circuit Low Voltage (Bank 1 Sensor 1)
P1136		O2 Sensor Heater Circuit High Voltage (Bank 1 Sensor 1)
P1137		O2 Sensor Heater Circuit Signal Intermittent (Bank 1 Sensor 2)
P1138		O2 Sensor Heater Circuit Low Voltage (Bank 1 Sensor 2)
P1139		O2 Sensor Heater Circuit High Voltage (Bank 1 Sensor 2)
P114A	2C7E	Post Catalyst Fuel Trim Too Rich Bank 1
P114B	2C7E	Post Catalyst Fuel Trim Too Lean Bank 1
P114C	2C7F	Post Catalyst Fuel Trim Too Rich Bank 2
P114D	2C7F	Post Catalyst Fuel Trim Too Lean Bank 2
P114F	2D16	Air Mass Flow Sensor Defective
P1143		O2 Sensor Activity Check Signal Too High (Bank 1 Sensor 2)
P1144		O2 Sensor Activity Check Signal Too Low (Bank 1 Sensor 2)
P1149		O2 Sensor Activity Check Signal Too High (Bank 2 Sensor 2)
P115A	2D15	Mass or Volume Air Flow 'A' Maximum Exceeded
P115E	2F0C	Turbocharger Intake Air Temperature Sensor 1 Gradient Implausible
P1150		O2 Sensor Activity Check Signal Too Low (Bank 2 Sensor 2)
P1151		O2 Sensor Heater Circuit Signal Intermittent (Bank 2 Sensor 1)
P1152		O2 Sensor Heater Circuit Low Voltage (Bank 2 Sensor 1)
P1153		O2 Sensor Heater Circuit High Voltage (Bank 2 Sensor 1)
P1155		O2 Sensor Heater Circuit Signal Intermittent (Bank 2 Sensor 2)
P1156		O2 Sensor Heater Circuit Low Voltage (Bank 2 Sensor 2)
P1157		O2 Sensor Heater Circuit High Voltage (Bank 2 Sensor 2)
P116C	2D0F	Air Mass Flow Sensor Signal Range

OBD

Table b. N52 engine
  Diagnostic trouble codes (DTCs) (continued)

P-code	BMW FC	Definition
P116E	2D0F	Air Mass Flow Sensor Signal Electrical
P1171		Ambient Pressure Sensor Variant Recognition Value in Boot Range Implausible
P1172		Ambient Pressure Sensor Variant Recognition Error Value Stored in Boot Range
P1173		Ambient Pressure Sensor Variant Recognition Learning Failed
P119A	2D33	Manifold Absolute Pressure Sensor High (Bank 1)
P119B	2D33	Manifold Absolute Pressure Sensor Low (Bank 1)
P119D	2E74	Fuel Trim, Injector Aging Long Term Adaptation Too High (Bank 1)
P119E	2E75	Fuel Trim, Injector Aging Long Term Adaptation Too High (Bank 2)
P1190		Pre Catalyst Fuel Trim System (Bank 1)
P1191		Pre Catalyst Fuel Trim System (Bank 2)
P1192		Post Catalyst Fuel Trim System (Bank 1)
P1193		Post Catalyst Fuel Trim System (Bank 2)
P1197	2D28	Differential Pressure Sensor Intake Manifold High Input Bank 1
P1198	2D28	Differential Pressure Sensor Intake Manifold Low Input Bank 1
P121C	2AF0	NOx Sensor Heater Control Circuit Shorted (Bank 1)
P121E	2AF2	NOx Sensor Heater Control Circuit Open (Bank 1)
P121F	2AF2	NOx Sensor Circuit Shorted (Bank 1)
P1214	2AAE	Fuel Pump Speed Too High
P1215	2AAE	Fuel Pump Speed Too Low
P1216	2AAE	Fuel Pump Emergency Operation
P1217	2AAE	Fuel Pump Over temperature Condition
P122E	2AF6	NOx Sensor Binary Oxygen Sensor Signal Control Circuit Open (Bank 1)
P122F	2AF6	NOx Sensor Binary Oxygen Sensor Signal Control Circuit Shorted (Bank 1)
P1222		Pedal Position Sensor 2 Low Input
P1223		Pedal Position Sensor 2 High Input
P1230	2F94	Fuel Pump Relay Circuit
P1234	2F94	Fuel Pump Relay Circuit Low
P1236	2F94	Fuel Pump Relay Circuit High
P1244	2AAD	Fuel Pump Emergency Cut Off
P126F	30E2	NOx Sensor Linear Oxygen Sensor Signal Too Rich During Deceleration Test (Bank 1)
P127A	30E2	NOx Sensor Signal Too Low During Deceleration Test (Bank 1)
P127B	30E2	NOx Sensor Signal Too High During Deceleration Test (Bank 1)
P129B	2D2B	Manifold Absolute Pressure Sensor Diagnosis Performance
P1298	2EAF	Serial Communication NOx Sensor (Bank 1)
P1299	2EAF	Serial Communication NOx Sensor (Bank 2)
P130A	2AA3	Camshaft Position Sensor 'B' Segment Timing Error (Bank 1)
P1300	2AA2	Camshaft Position Sensor 'A' Segment Timing Error (Bank 1)
P1301	2E18	Ignition Monitoring Cylinder 1 Spark Duration Too Short
P1302	2E19	Ignition Monitoring Cylinder 2 Spark Duration Too Short

P-code	BMW FC	Definition
Table b. N52 engine		
Diagnostic trouble codes (DTCs) (continued)		
P1303	2E1A	Ignition Monitoring Cylinder 3 Spark Duration Too Short
P1304	2E1B	Ignition Monitoring Cylinder 3 Spark Duration Too Short
P1305	2E1C	Ignition Monitoring Cylinder 5 Spark Duration Too Short
P1306	2E1D	Ignition Monitoring Cylinder 6 Spark Duration Too Short
P1314		Fuel Mixture Deviation Detected with Low Fuel
P1327	2E69	Knock Sensor 2 Circuit Low (Bank 1 or Single Sensor)
P1328	2E69	Knock Sensor 2 Circuit Range / Performance (Bank 1 or Single Sensor)
P1342		Misfire During Start Cylinder 1
P1343		Misfire Cylinder 1 with Fuel Cut-Off
P1344		Misfire During Start Cylinder 2
P1345		Misfire Cylinder 2 with Fuel Cut-Off
P1346		Misfire During Start Cylinder 3
P1347		Misfire Cylinder 3 with Fuel Cut-Off
P1348		Misfire During Start Cylinder 4
P1349		Misfire Cylinder 4 with Fuel Cut-Off
P135B	2E69	Knock Sensor 2 Circuit Range / Performance (Bank 1 or Single Sensor)
P1350		Misfire during Start Cylinder 5
P1351		Misfire Cylinder 5 with Fuel Cut-Off
P1352		Misfire during Start Cylinder 6
P1353		Misfire Cylinder 6 with Fuel Cut-Off
P1383	2E77	Ignition Monitoring Malfunction
P1396	29DA	Crankshaft Position Sensor Segment Timing Plausibility
P140A	2A00	Secondary Air Injection System Flow Bank 1 and Bank 2
P140E	29DC	Cylinder Injection Cut Off, Fuel Level Too Low
P14C0	2EFF	Fan Mechanical Hardware Defect
P14C1	2F0F	Radiator Shutter Mechanical hardware Defect
P14C2	2AAB	DISA (Differentiated Intake Manifold) Actuator 1 Fault
P14C3	2AAC	DISA (Differentiated Intake Manifold) Actuator 2 Fault
P14C4	2F11	Upper Radiator Shutter Mechanical fault
P14C5	2F11	Upper Radiator Shutter Electrical fault
P14C6	2F10	Lower Radiator Shutter Electrical fault
P140E	29DC	Cylinder Injection Cut Off, Fuel Level Too Low
P1413	2A03	Secondary Air Injection Pump Relay Control Circuit Signal Low
P1414	2A03	Secondary Air Injection Pump Relay Control Circuit Signal High
P1407	2DE2	Fuel Level Signal 1
P1408	2DE1	Fuel Level Signal 2
P1415	2D06	Mass or Volume Air Flow Too Low
P1417	2D06	Throttle Control Incorrect Air Supply
P1417	2D09	Throttle Control Incorrect Air Supply

OBD

Table b. N52 engine
   Diagnostic trouble codes (DTCs) (continued)

P-code	BMW FC	Definition
P142A	2AE4	Crankcase Ventilation Heater Relay Circuit Input High
P142B	2AE4	Crankcase Ventilation Heater Relay Circuit Input Low
P142C	2AE4	Crankcase Ventilation Heater Relay Circuit Input Open
P142E	29DC	Cylinder Injection Cut Off, Pressure Too Low (High Pressure Fuel System)
P142F	29DC	Cylinder Injection Cut Off, Pressure Too Low (Low Pressure Fuel System)
P1424	2D06	Mass or Volume Air Flow Too High
P1429	2A18	DMTL Heater
P143B	2AD9	Direct Ozone Reduction Catalyst Temperature Sensor Wrong Code
P143C	2AD8	Direct Ozone Reduction Catalyst Temperature / Radiator Temperature Correlation
P143E	2AD8	Direct Ozone Reduction Catalyst Temperature Sensor Gradient Too Low
P1430	2A18	DMTL Heater Circuit Low
P1431	2A18	DMTL Heater Circuit High
P1434	2A17	DMTL Tank Leakage
P1444		Diagnostic Module Tank Leakage (DMTL) Pump Control Open Circuit
P1445		Diagnostic Module Tank Leakage (DMTL) Pump Control Circuit Signal Low
P1446		Diagnostic Module Tank Leakage (DMTL) Pump Control Circuit Signal High
P1447	2A17	Diagnostic Module Tank Leakage (DMTL) Pump Current Too High during Switching Solenoid Test
P1448	2A17	Diagnostic Module Tank Leakage (DMTL) Pump Current Too Low
P1449	2A17	Diagnostic Module Tank Leakage (DMTL) Pump Current Too High
P1451		Diagnostic Module Tank Leakage (DMTL) Switching Solenoid Control Circuit Signal Low
P1452		Diagnostic Module Tank Leakage (DMTL) Switching Solenoid Control Circuit Signal High
P1453	2A03	Secondary Air Injection Pump Relay Control Circuit Fault
P15AA	30FC	Turbocharger Leak in System
P15A1	30C4	Engine Oil Pressure Mechanical Valve Stuck in De-energized Position
P15A2	30C4	Engine Oil Pressure Mechanical Valve Stuck in Fully Energized Position
P15A3	30C5	Engine Oil Pressure Too High
P15A6	30C6	Engine Oil Pressure Too High Before Start
P15A7	30C6	Engine Oil Pressure Too Low Before Start
P15A9	2FC7	Energy Saving Mode - Transportation Mode
P15B0	2DC3	Terminal 15 Sense Circuit Input High
P15B1	2DC3	Terminal 15 Sense Circuit Input Low
P15B2	2DC3	Terminal 15 Sense Circuit CAS Error
P15B3	2DC3	Terminal 15 Sense Circuit Range / Performance
P150A	2E8B	Battery Sensor Extended Communication Circuit
P150B	2E8B	Battery Sensor Serial Data Interface
P150C	2E8B	Battery Sensor Firmware Implausible
P150D	2E8B	Battery Sensor Temperature Error
P150E	2E8C	Battery Sensor Voltage Error
P150F	28EC	Battery Sensor Current Error

Table b. N52 engine
Diagnostic trouble codes (DTCs) (continued)

P-code	BMW FC	Definition
P1500		Idle-Speed Control Valve Stuck Open
P1501		Idle-Speed Control Valve Stuck Closed
P1502		Idle-Speed Control Valve Closing Solenoid Control Circuit Signal High
P1503		Idle-Speed Control Valve Closing Solenoid Control Circuit Signal Low
P1504		Idle-Speed Control Valve Closing Solenoid Control Open Circuit
P1506		Idle-Speed Control Valve Opening Solenoid Control Circuit Signal High
P1507		Idle-Speed Control Valve Opening Solenoid Control Circuit Signal Low
P1508		Idle-Speed Control Valve Opening Solenoid Control Open Circuit
P151A	2E8D	Battery Sensor Terminal 15 / 30 Wakeup Circuit
P151B	2E8D	Battery Sensor Wakeup Circuit
P151C	2E8D	Battery Sensor System Error
P1511	2AA8	DISA (Differentiated Intake Manifold) Control Circuit
P1511	2AA9	DISA (Differentiated Intake Manifold) Control Circuit
	2AAA	Variable Intake System Plausibility
P1512	2AA8	DISA (Differentiated Intake Manifold) Control Circuit Signal Low
P1512	2AA9	DISA (Differentiated Intake Manifold) Control Circuit Signal Low
P1513	2AA8	DISA (Differentiated Intake Manifold) Control Circuit Signal High
P1513	2AA9	DISA (Differentiated Intake Manifold) Control Circuit Signal High
P1515	2F80	Engine OFF Timer Plausibility
P1521	2E9F	Engine Oil Quality Sensor Temperature Communication Error
P1523		'A' Camshaft Position Actuator Signal Low (Bank 1)
P1524		'A' Camshaft Position Actuator Control Circuit Signal High (Bank 1)
P1525		'A' Camshaft Position Actuator Control Open Circuit (Bank 1)
P1529		'B' Camshaft Position Actuator Control Circuit Signal Low (Bank 1)
P1530		'B' Camshaft Position Actuator Control Circuit Signal High (Bank 1)
P1531		'B' Camshaft Position Actuator Control Open Circuit (Bank 1)
P1540	2AC6	Driving Dynamics Switch Input High
P1541	2AC6	Driving Dynamics Switch Input Low
P155A	2DB7	Multifunction Steering Wheel Toggle-Bit Fault
P1551	2F80	Engine OFF Timer Time-out
P1553	2A99	Engine Position System 'B' Performance (Bank 1)
P1554	2A98	Engine Position System 'A' Performance (Bank 1)
P1561	2AE0	Cold Start Idle RPM Lower Than Expected
P1562	2AE0	Cold Start Idle RPM Higher Than Expected
P1563	2DB6	Multifunction Steering Wheel Rocker Switch Defective
P1565	2DB5	Multifunction Steering Wheel Rocker Switch + / - Pressed Simultaneously
P1567	2DB7	Multifunction Steering Wheel Toggle Bit Error
	2DBE	Adaptive Cruise Control Blocked for Driving Cycle
	2DC0	No Message From LDM

OBD

P-code	BMW FC	Definition
	2DC3	Monitoring Terminal 15
P1576	2DB5	Multifunction Steering Wheel Interface Error
P1582	30C2	Oil Pump Circuit High
P1583	30C2	Oil Pump Circuit Low
P1584	30C2	Oil Pump Circuit Open
P1586	2E9F	Engine Oil Quality Sensor Temperature Measurement
P1587	2E9F	Engine Oil Quality Sensor Temperature Level Measurement
P1588	2E9F	Engine Oil Quality Sensor Temperature Permeability Measurement
P16A0	2AB3	Internal Control Module Checksum Fault
P16A1	2AB3	Internal Control Module Application Software Checksum Fault
P16A2	2AB3	Internal Control Module Checksum Fault in Data
P16A3	2AB4	Internal Control Module Checksum Fault in Non-Volatile Memory
P16A4	2AB5	Time-out Control Module Knock Sensor SPI-Bus
P16A5	2AB6	Time-out Control Module Multiple Output Stage SPI-Bus
P16A6	2D50	Control Module Self test / Cruise Control Monitoring
P16A7	2D51	Control Module Self Test Hot Film Air Mass Meter Monitoring
P16A8	2D51	Control Module Self Test Throttle Position Monitoring
P16A9	2D52	Control Module Self Test Speed Monitoring Reset
P16B1	2D56	Control Module Self Test Idle Air Control System Plausibility
P16B2	2D56	Control Module Self Test Idle Air Control System Component Plausibility
P16B3	2D57	Control Module Self Test Engine Drag Torque
P16B4	2D50	Control Module Self Test Dynamic Cruise Control Monitoring
P16B5	2D57	Control Module Self Test Automatic Manual Transmission
P16B6	2D57	Control Module Self Test ETC Monitoring
P16B7	2D58	Control Module Self Test Clutch Torque Monitoring Maximum value Plausibility
P16B8	2D58	Control Module Self Test Clutch Torque Monitoring
P16B9	2D58	Control Module Self Test Torque Loss Monitoring
P16C0	2D58	Control Module Self Test Driving Dynamics Control Switch Monitoring
	2D5A	Monitoring Engine Torque Limiting
P16C1	2D59	Control Module Self Test Torque Monitoring Current Indicated value Plausibility
P16C2	2D53	Control Module Self Test Speed Limitation Monitoring
P16C3	2D54	Control Module Self Test Speed Limitation Reset
P16C5	2AAC	DME Main Relay Switching Delay
P16C6	2E7C	CAN Time-out Bit Serial Data Interface
P16C8	2DE0	Serial Communication Link EKP (Electronic Fuel Pump)
P164C	2D1D	Pedal Position Sensor Potentiometer Supply Channel 1 Electrical
P16B0	2D55	Control Module Self Test Pedal Position Monitoring
P160A	2DEC	Powermanagement Exhaustive Discharge
P160B	2DEC	Powermanagement Defective

Table b. N52 engine
Diagnostic trouble codes (DTCs) (continued)

P-code	BMW FC	Definition
Table b. N52 engine		
Diagnostic trouble codes (DTCs) (continued)		
P160C	2DEB	Powermanagement Overvoltage
P160D	2DEB	Powermanagement Undervolatge
P160E	2DEB	Powermanagement Operation Without Battery
P160F	2DED	Powermanagement No Load Current Error
P165F	2CA6	Internal Control Module Measurement Error O2 Sensor Heating (Bank 1 Sensor 1)
P1602		Control Module Self-Test, Control Module Defective
P1603		Control Module Self-Test, Torque Monitoring
P1604		Control Module Self-Test, Speed Monitoring
P1611	2DC8	Serial Communication Link TCM
P1612	2DD0	Serial Communication Link Instrument Panel
P1613	2DCC	Serial Communication Link ASC
P1613	2DCD	Serial Communication Link ASC
P1613	2DCE	Serial Communication Link ASC
P1618	2D5C	Control Module Self Test AD-Converter Monitoring
P1619		Map Cooling Thermostat Control Circuit Signal Low
P1620		Map Cooling Thermostat Control Circuit Signal High
P1624	2D1D	Pedal Position Sensor Potentiometer Supply Channel 1 Electrical (M52: Coolant Thermostat (Coolant Temperature Below Thermostat Regulating Temperature))
P1625	2D1E	Pedal Position Sensor Potentiometer Supply Channel 2 Electrical
P1632	2CFB	Throttle Valve Adaptation Conditions Not Met
P1633	2CFB	Throttle Valve Adaptation Limp-Home Position Unknown
P1634		Throttle Valve Adaptation Spring Test Failed
P1634	2CFC	Throttle Valve Adaptation Spring Test Failed
P1635	2CFE	Throttle Valve Adaptation Lower Mechanical Stop not Adapted
P1636	2CEF	Throttle Valve Control Circuit
P1637	2CEE	Throttle Valve Position Control, Control Deviation
P1638	2CEC	Throttle Valve Position Control Throttle Stuck Temporarily
P1639	2CED	Throttle Valve Position Control Throttle Stuck Permanently
P164E	2D0C	Throttle Deicing Stuck in Closed Direction
P164F	2D0C	Throttle Deicing Stuck in Open Direction
P1644	2CFB	Throttle Valve Adaptation Relearning Lower Mechanical Stop
P166A	2D50	Control Module Self Test, Hot Film Air Mass Meter Monitoring
P166B	2DC0	Longitudinal Dynamics Module Torque Request Inspite of Brake Signal
P166C	2DC0	Longitudinal Dynamics Module Request Implausible
P166F	2CA7	Internal Control Module Measurement Error O2 Sensor Heating (Bank 2 Sensor 1)
P166F	2CAB	Internal Control Module Measurement Error O2 Sensor Heating (Bank 2 Sensor 1)
P1660	2F4A	EWS Telegram Error
P1661	2F4A	Time-out EWS Telegram
P165A	2F4A	EWS Interface to ECM Error

OBD

Diagnostic trouble codes (DTCs)

Table b. N52 engine
Diagnostic trouble codes (DTCs) (continued)

P-code	BMW FC	Definition
P165B	2F4A	EWS Interface to ECM Checksum Error
P165C	2F4B	EWS Data, No Available Storage Possible
P165D	2F4B	EWS Data, Faulty Release Code
P165E	2F4B	EWS Data Checksum Error
P1667	2F49	EWS Start Value not yet Programmed
P1668	2F4B	EWS Start Value Destroyed
P167C	2D08	Throttle Heating Relay Circuit Input Low
P167D	2D08	Throttle Heating Relay Circuit
P1675	2CFD	Throttle Valve Actuator Start Test Re-Adaptation Required
P169A	2CFC	Throttle Valve Actuator Start Test Failed Limp Home Position
P1694	2CFB	Throttle Valve Actuator Start Test Spring Test and Limp-Home Position Failed
P1794	2DD3	TCM Checksum Error
P2067	2DE1	Fuel Level Sensor 'B' Circuit Low
P2068	2DE1	Fuel Level Sensor 'B' Circuit High
P2088	2A80	'A' Camshaft Position Actuator Control Circuit Low (Bank 1)
P2089	2A80	'A' Camshaft Position Actuator Control Circuit High (Bank 1)
P2090	2A85	'B' Camshaft Position Actuator Control Circuit Low (Bank 1)
P2091	2A85	'B' Camshaft Position Actuator Control Circuit High (Bank 1)
P2096	2C31	Post Catalyst Fuel Trim System Too Lean (Bank 1)
P2097	2C31	Post Catalyst Fuel Trim System Too Rich (Bank 1)
P2098	2C32	Post Catalyst Fuel Trim System Too Lean (Bank 2)
P2099	2C32	Post Catalyst Fuel Trim System Too Rich (Bank 2)
P213F	2AAD	Fuel Pump System Fault Engine Shut Down
P2120	2D1F	Throttle / Pedal Position Sensor 'D' Circuit
P2122	2D1B	Throttle Pedal Position Sensor 'D' Circuit Low
P2123	2D1B	Throttle Pedal Position Sensor 'D' Circuit High
P2127	2D1C	Throttle Pedal Position Sensor 'E' Circuit Low
P2128	2D1C	Throttle Pedal Position Sensor 'E' Circuit High
P213F	2AAD	Fuel Pump Emergency Cut Off
P2138	2D20	Throttle / Pedal Position Sensor 'D' 'E' Voltage Correlation
P2183	2EEC	Engine Coolant Temperature Sensor 2 Circuit Range / Performance
P2184	2EEA	Engine Coolant Temperate Sensor 2 Circuit Low
P2185	2EEA	Engine Coolant Temperate Sensor 2 Circuit High
P2187	29E0	System Too Lean at Idle (Bank 1)
P2188	29E0	System Too Rich at Idle (Bank 1)
P2189	29E1	System Too Lean at Idle (Bank 2)
P2190	29E1	System Too Rich at Idle (Bank 2)
P2191	29E5	System Too Lean, Higher Load (Bank 1)
P2192	29E5	System Too Rich, Higher Load (Bank 1)

Table b. N52 engine
   Diagnostic trouble codes (DTCs) (continued)

P-code	BMW FC	Definition
P2193	2E96	System Too Lean, Higher Load (Bank 2)
P2194	2E96	System Too Rich, Higher Load (Bank 2)
P2195	2C27	O2 Sensor Signal Stuck Lean (Bank 1 Sensor 1)
P2196	2C27	O2 Sensor Signal Stuck Rich (Bank 1 Sensor 1)
P2196	2C2B	O2 Sensor Signal Stuck Rich (Bank 1 Sensor 1)
P2196	2C2C	O2 Sensor Signal Stuck Rich (Bank 1 Sensor 1)
P2197	2C28	O2 Sensor Signal Stuck Lean (Bank 2 Sensor 1)
P2198	2C2C	O2 Sensor Signal Stuck Rich (Bank 2 Sensor 1)
P2200	2AF4	NOx Sensor Circuit (Bank 1)
P2205	2AF0	NOx Sensor Heater Control Circuit Open (Bank 1)
P2228	2F76	Barometric Pressure Circuit Low
P2229	2F76	Barometric Pressure Circuit High
P2243	2C3D	O2 Sensor reference Voltage Circuit Open (Bank 1 Sensor 1)
P2247	2C3E	O2 Sensor Reference Voltage Circuit Open (Bank 2 Sensor 1)
P2270	2C6B	O2 Sensor Signal Stuck Lean (Bank 1 Sensor 2)
P2271	2C6B	O2 Sensor Signal Stuck Lean (Bank 1 Sensor 2)
P2272	2C6C	O2 Sensor Signal Stuck Lean (Bank 2 Sensor 2)
P2273	2C6C	O2 Sensor Signal Stuck Lean (Bank 2 Sensor 2)
P2297	2C2D	O2 Sensor Signal Out Of Range During Decel (Bank 1 Sensor 1)
P2298	2C2E	O2 Sensor Signal Out Of Range During Decel (Bank 2 Sensor 1)
P2299	2F8F	Brake Pedal Position / Accelerator Pedal Position Incompatible
P2301	30A0	Ignition Coil Primary 'A' Circuit High
P2304	30A1	Ignition Coil Primary 'B' Circuit High
P2307	30A2	Ignition Coil Primary 'C' Circuit High
P2310	30A3	Ignition Coil Primary 'D' Circuit High
P2313	30A4	Ignition Coil Primary 'E' Circuit High
P2316	30A5	Ignition Coil Primary 'F' Circuit High
P240A	2A18	DMTL Pump Heater Circuit Open
P240B	2A18	DMTL Pump Heater Circuit Low
P240C	2A18	DMTL Pump Heater Circuit High
P2400	2A13	DMTL Activation Control Circuit Open
P2401	2A13	DMTL Activation Control Circuit Low
P2402	2A13	DMTL Activation Control Circuit High
P2414	2C3B	O2 Sensor Oxygen Sample Error (Bank 1 Sensor 1)
P2415	2C3C	O2 Sensor Oxygen Sample Error (Bank 2 Sensor 1)
P2418	2A12	DMTL Solenoid Control Circuit Open
P2419	2A12	DMTL Solenoid Control Circuit Low
P2420	2A12	Evaporative Emission System Switching Valve Control Circuit High
P250A	2F9E	Engine Oil Level Sensor Circuit

OBD

Table b. N52 engine
Diagnostic trouble codes (DTCs) (continued)

P-code	BMW FC	Definition
P250B	2F9E	Engine Oil Level Sensor Range / Performance
P250F	2F9E	Engine Oil Level Too Low
P252A	2EA1	Engine Oil Quality Sensor Circuit
P2420	2A12	DMTL Solenoid Control Circuit High
P2541	29F3	Low Pressure Fuel System Sensor Circuit Low
P2542	29F3	Low Pressure Fuel System Sensor Circuit High
P2568	2ADA	Direct Ozone Reduction Catalyst Temperature Sensor Performance
P2569	2ADA	Direct Ozone Reduction Catalyst Temperature Sensor Circuit Low
P2570	2ADA	Direct Ozone Reduction Catalyst Temperature Sensor Circuit High
P2626	2C3D	O2 Sensor Pumping Current Circuit Open (Bank 1 Sensor 1)
P2629	2C3E	O2 Sensor Pumping Current Circuit Open (Bank 2 Sensor 1)
P300A	2F0D	Controlled Air Guiding Circuit High
P300B	2F0D	Controlled Air Guiding Circuit Low
P300C	2F0D	Controlled Air Guiding Circuit
P3003	29F2	Fuel Rail Pressure Flow Rate Controlled, Pressure Too High
P3004	29F2	Fuel Rail Pressure Flow Rate Controlled, Maximum Pressure Exceeded
P3022	2C41	O2 Sensor Disturbed SPI WRAF-IC (Bank 1 Sensor 1)
P3023	2C42	O2 Sensor Disturbed SPI WRAF-IC (Bank 2 Sensor 1)
P3024	2C41	O2 Sensor Initialization Error WRAF-IC (Bank 1 Sensor 1)
P3025	2C42	O2 Sensor Initialization Error WRAF-IC (Bank 1 Sensor 1)
P3026	2CAA	O2 Sensor Operating Temperature Not Reached (Bank 1 Sensor 1)
P3027	2CAA	O2 Sensor Operating Temperature Not Reached (Bank 2 Sensor 1)
P3041		O2 Sensor Lean and Rich Voltage Thresholds not Reached (Bank 2 Sensor 2)
P3090	29F2	Fuel Rail Pressure Flow Rate Controlled, Fallen Below Minimum Pressure
P3094	2A2D	Fuel Low Pressure System Pressure Too High
P3095	2A2D	Fuel Low Pressure System Pressure Maximum Pressure Exceeded
P3096	2A2D	Fuel Low Pressure System Pressure Minimum Pressure Fallen Below
P310B	2E30	Cylinder 1 High Pressure Injector Low Side / High Side Electrical
P310E	2E31	Cylinder 2 High Pressure Injector Low Side / High Side Electrical
P3101	30AC	Cylinder 1 High Pressure Injector Low Side Circuit Low
P3102	30AC	Cylinder 1 High Pressure Injector Low Side Circuit High
P3105	30AD	Cylinder 2 High Pressure Injector Low Side Circuit Low
P3106	30AD	Cylinder 2 High Pressure Injector Low Side Circuit high
P3109	30AE	Cylinder 3 High Pressure Injector Low Side Circuit Low
P311B	2E32	Cylinder 3 High Pressure Injector Low Side / High Side Electrical
P311E	2E33	Cylinder 4 High Pressure Injector Low Side / High Side Electrical
P3110	30AE	Cylinder 3 High Pressure Injector Low Side Circuit High
P3113	30AF	Cylinder 4 High Pressure Injector Low Side Circuit Low
P3114	30AF	Cylinder 4 High Pressure Injector Low Side Circuit High

Table b. N52 engine
    Diagnostic trouble codes (DTCs) (continued)

P-code	BMW FC	Definition
P3117	30B0	Cylinder 5 High Pressure Injector Low Side Circuit Low
P3118	30B0	Cylinder 5 High Pressure Injector Low Side Circuit High
P312B	2E34	Cylinder 5 High Pressure Injector Low Side / High Side Electrical
P312E	2E35	Cylinder 6 High Pressure Injector Low Side / High Side Electrical
P3121	30B1	Cylinder 6 High Pressure Injector Low Side Circuit Low
P3122	30B1	Cylinder 6 High Pressure Injector Low Side Circuit High
P3149	30AC	Cylinder 1 High Pressure Injector High Side Circuit Low
P3150	30AC	Cylinder 1 High Pressure Injector High Side Circuit High
P3152	30AC	Cylinder 2 High Pressure Injector High Side Circuit Low
P3153	30AD	Cylinder 2 High Pressure Injector High Side Circuit High
P3155	30AD	Cylinder 3 High Pressure Injector High Side Circuit Low
P3156	30AE	Cylinder 3 High Pressure Injector High Side Circuit High
P3158	30AF	Cylinder 4 High Pressure Injector High Side Circuit Low
P3159	30AF	Cylinder 4 High Pressure Injector High Side Circuit High
P316A	2EE6	Engine Coolant Temperature Signal Stuck High
P3161	30B0	Cylinder 5 High Pressure Injector High Side Circuit Low
P3162	30B0	Cylinder 5 High Pressure Injector High Side Circuit High
P3164	30B1	Cylinder 6 High Pressure Injector High Side Circuit Low
P3165	30B1	Cylinder 6 High Pressure Injector High Side Circuit High
	2FBF	Fuel Supply Pressure Low During Release of Injection
	2FC0	Fuel Rail Pressure Management Range
P319A	2FBD	Fuel Pressure Control Minimum Characteristic Curve Operation 1 Out of Range
P3194	2FBD	Fuel Pressure Control Basic Characteristic Curve Operation 1 Out of Range
P3196	2EEC	Radiator Coolant Temperature Sensor High
P3197	2EEB	Radiator Coolant Temperature Gradient Too High
P3198	2EE3	Engine Coolant Temperature Gradient Too High
P3199	2EE2	Engine Coolant Temperature Signal Stuck
P3202	CD87	Powertrain CAN Chip Cut-Off
P3205	CD8B	Local CAN Chip Cut-Off
P321E	2F77	Ambient Pressure Sensor Maximum Pressure Implausible
P321F	2F77	Ambient Pressure Sensor Minimum Pressure Implausible
P3213	2DD3	CAN Message Monitoring ETC Alive Check
P3223	2E97	Generator Mechanical
P2332	2ED1	Generator Mechanical
P3226	27F1	E-box Control Fan High Input
P3227	27F1	E-box Control Fan Low Input
P3228	27F1	E-box Control Fan Open Circuit
P323F	2D60	Control Module Monitoring Fuel Volume, Air Mass Injected Fuel Volume Correlation
P3235	2FA4	Control Module Monitoring Version Coding Plausibility

OBD

Table b. N52 engine
Diagnostic trouble codes (DTCs) (continued)

P-code	BMW FC	Definition
P3238		Control Module Monitoring TPU Chip Defective
P324A	2E97	Generator Type Implausible
P324A	2ED3	Generator Type Implausible
P324C	2ED0	Generator Over Temperature Calculated
P324E	2ED2	Generator Regulator Type Implausible
P325A	2ECE	Generator Electrical Error Calculated
P3255	2E96	Generator Voltage In Starting Above Threshold
P3256	2DD2	CAN Time-out Steering Angle Sensor
P3259	2D60	Control Module Monitoring Fuel Volume, Lambda Implausible to Operating Mode
P3283	29F1	Fuel Pressure Control Adaptive Fuel Volume Out of Range (Bank 1)
P3284	29F1	Fuel Pressure Control Adaptive Fuel Volume Implausible (Bank 1)

WARNING

Your common sense, good judgement and general alertness are crucial to safe and successful service work. Before attempting any work on your BMW, be sure to read **001 Warnings and Cautions** *and the copyright page at the front of the manual. Review these warnings and cautions each time you prepare to work on your car. Please also read any warnings and cautions that accompany the procedures in the manual.*

WARNING

Your common sense, good judgement and general alertness are crucial to safe and successful service work. Before attempting any work on your BMW, be sure to read 001 Warnings and Cautions and the copyright page at the front of the manual. Review these warnings and cautions each time you prepare to work on your car. Please also read any warnings and cautions that accompany the procedures in the manual.

10 INDEX

Selected Books and Repair Information From Bentley Publishers

Motorsports

Alex Zanardi: My Sweetest Victory *Alex Zanardi and Gianluca Gasparini*
ISBN 978-0-8376-1249-2

The Unfair Advantage
Mark Donohue and Paul van Valkenburgh
ISBN 978-0-8376-0069-7

Equations of Motion - Adventure, Risk and Innovation *William F. Milliken*
ISBN 978-0-8376-1570-7

Engineering

The Hack Mechanic Guide to European Automotive Electrical Systems
Rob Siegel ISBN 978-0-8376-1751-0

**Mechanical Ignition Handbook
The Hack Mechanic Guide to Vintage Ignition Systems** *Rob Siegel*
ISBN 978-0-8376-1767-1

Bosch Automotive Handbook *Robert Bosch GmbH* ISBN 978-0-8376-1732-9

Bosch Fuel Injection and Engine Management *Charles O. Probst, SAE*
ISBN 978-0-8376-0300-1

Maximum Boost: Designing, Testing, and Installing Turbocharger Systems
Corky Bell ISBN 978-0-8376-0160-1

Supercharged! Design, Testing and Installation of Supercharger Systems
Corky Bell ISBN 978-0-8376-0168-7

Physics for Gearheads
Randy Beikmann ISBN 978-0-8376-1615-5

Audi

Audi A4 Service Manual: 2002-2008, 1.8L Turbo, 2.0L Turbo, 3.0L, 3.2L
Bentley Publishers ISBN 978-0-8376-1574-5

Audi A4 Service Manual: 1996-2001, 1.8L Turbo, 2.8L *Bentley Publishers*
ISBN 978-0-8376-1675-9

Audi TT Service Manual: 2000-2006, 1.8L turbo, 3.2 L *Bentley Publishers*
ISBN 978-0-8376-1625-4

Audi A6 (C5 platform) Service Manual: 1998-2004 *Bentley Publishers*
ISBN 978-0-8376-1670-4

BMW

Memoirs of a Hack Mechanic
Rob Siegel ISBN 978-0-8376-1720-6

BMW 3 Series (F30, F31, F34) Service Manual: 2012-2015 *Bentley Publishers*
ISBN 978-0-8376-1752-7

BMW X3 (E83) Service Manual: 2004-2010 *Bentley Publishers*
ISBN 978-0-8376-1731-2

BMW X5 (53) Service Manual: 2000-2006 *Bentley Publishers*
ISBN 978-0-8376-1643-8

BMW 3 Series (E90, E91, E92, E93) Service Manual: 2006-2011
Bentley Publishers ISBN 978-0-8376-1723-7

BMW 3 Series (E46) Service Manual: 1999-2005 *Bentley Publishers*
ISBN 978-0-8376-1657-5

BMW 4 Series (F32, F33, F36) Service Manual: 2014-2016 *Bentley Publishers*
ISBN 978-0-8376-1765-7

BMW Z3 (E36/7) Service Manual: 1996-2002 *Bentley Publishers*
ISBN 978-0-8376-1617-9

BMW 5 Series (E60, E61) Service Manual: 2004-2010 *Bentley Publishers*
ISBN 978-0-8376-1689-6

BMW 5 Series (E39) Service Manual: 1997-2003 *Bentley Publishers*
ISBN 978-0-8376-1672-8

Corvette

Corvette: America's Star-Spangled Sports Car *Karl Ludvigsen*
ISBN 978-0-8376-1659-9

Corvette by the Numbers: The Essential Corvette Parts Reference 1955-1982 *Alan Covin*
ISBN 978-0-8376-0228-2

Zora Arkus-Duntov: The Legend Behind Corvette *Jerry Burton*
ISBN 978-08376-0858-7

Porsche

Porsche 911 (996) Service Manual: 1999-2005 *Bentley Publishers*
ISBN 978-0-8376-1710-7

Porsche 911 (993) Service Manual: 1995-1998 *Bentley Publishers*
ISBN 978-0-8376-1719-0

Porsche Boxster Service Manual: 1997-2004 *Bentley Publishers*
ISBN 978-0-8376-1645-2

Porsche 911 Carrera Service Manual: 1984-1989 *Bentley Publishers*
ISBN 978-0-8376-1696-4

Porsche 911 SC Service Manual: 1978-1983 *Bentley Publishers*
ISBN 978-0-8376-1705-3

Porsche: Excellence Was Expected
Karl Ludvigsen
ISBN 978-0-8376-0235-6

Porsche — Origin of the Species
Karl Ludvigsen
ISBN 978-0-8376-1331-4

Volkswagen

Volkswagen Rabbit, GTI Service Manual: 2006-2009 *Bentley Publishers*
ISBN 978-0-8376-1664-3

Volkswagen Jetta Service Manual: 2005-2010 *Bentley Publishers*
ISBN 978-0-8376-1616-2

Volkswagen Jetta, Golf, GTI Service Manual: 1999-2005 *Bentley Publishers*
ISBN 978-0-8376-1678-0

Volkswagen Jetta, Golf, GTI: 1993-1999, Cabrio: 1995-2002 Service Manual *Bentley Publishers*
ISBN 978-0-8376-1660-5

Volkswagen GTI, Golf, Jetta Service Manual: 1985-1992 *Bentley Publishers*
ISBN 978-0-8376-1637-7

Volkswagen Corrado Repair Manual: 1990-1994 *Bentley Publishers*
ISBN 978-0-8376-1699-5

Volkswagen Passat, Passat Wagon Service Manual: 1998-2005
Bentley Publishers
ISBN 978-0-8376-1669-8

MINI Repair Manuals

MINI Cooper Service Manual: 2007-2013 *Bentley Publishers*
ISBN 978-0-8376-1730-5

MINI Cooper Service Manual: 2002-2006 *Bentley Publishers*
ISBN 978-0-8376-1639-1

Mercedes-Benz

Mercedes-Benz C-Class (W202) Service Manual 1994-2000
Bentley Publishers
ISBN 978-0-8376-1692-6

Mercedes Benz E-Class (W124) Owner's Bible: 1986-1995
Bentley Publishers
ISBN 978-0-8376-0230-1

Mercedes-Benz Technical Companion
Staff of The Star and members of Mercedes-Benz Club of America
ISBN 978-0-8376-1033-7

B BentleyPublishers®
Automotive Reference

Bentley Publishers has published service manuals and automobile books since 1950. For more information, please contact Bentley Publishers at 1734 Massachusetts Avenue, Cambridge, MA 02138 USA, or visit our web site at
BentleyPublishers.com